# BANKRUPTCY

SEVENTH EDITION

*by*

## WILLIAM D. WARREN
University of California, Los Angeles

## DANIEL J. BUSSEL
University of California, Los Angeles

New York, New York
**FOUNDATION PRESS**

This publication was created to provide you with accurate and authoritative information concerning the subject matter covered; however, this publication was not necessarily prepared by persons licensed to practice law in a particular jurisdiction. The publisher is not engaged in rendering legal or other professional advice and this publication is not a substitute for the advice of an attorney. If you require legal or other expert advice, you should seek the services of a competent attorney or other professional.

Nothing contained herein is intended or written to be used for the purposes of 1) avoiding penalties imposed under the federal Internal Revenue Code, or 2) promoting, marketing or recommending to another party any transaction or matter addressed herein.

© 1985, 1989, 1993, 1995, 1999, 2002 FOUNDATION PRESS
© 2006 By FOUNDATION PRESS
        395 Hudson Street
        New York, NY 10014
        Phone Toll Free 1–877–888–1330
        Fax (212) 367–6799
        foundation–press.com
Printed in the United States of America

**ISBN–13:** 978–1–59941–066–1
**ISBN–10:** 1–59941–066–4

*TEXT IS PRINTED ON 10% POST CONSUMER RECYCLED PAPER*

# PREFACE TO THE SEVENTH EDITION

The "Bankruptcy Abuse Prevention and Consumer Protection Act of 2005" (the "2005 Act"), seven years in gestation, is the most fundamental rewriting of the Nation's bankruptcy laws in 26 years. The amendments relating to consumer bankruptcy are wholesale and dramatic. They appear to make bankruptcy relief as unpleasant as possible for all consumer debtors, whether they seek relief under Chapter 7 or Chapter 13, and deny access to Chapter 7 altogether for some. On the business bankruptcy side, the changes individually appear incremental, but their cumulative effect, combined with past reform efforts, seems likely to make marginal reorganizations significantly more difficult to accomplish, and may feed the recent trend favoring sales and so-called "liquidating Chapter 11" cases over traditional Chapter 11 restructurings.

So it seems. Over the years, the bankruptcy system has proved remarkably resistant to reform emanating from Congress, and the Supreme Court too, that is perceived to be ham-handed, impractical, dysfunctional or distasteful by the lawyers, judges and parties that spend their daily lives working in the system. The bankruptcy advance sheets over the next several years will provide a fascinating study of "law in action" as these actors react to what Congress has wrought.

This Seventh Edition then is a bridge between bankruptcy law as developed and understood under the 1978 Code over the past 26 years, and bankruptcy law as it will come to be developed and understood under the 2005 Act. In this respect, this Seventh Edition is perhaps more like the First Edition, which of necessity relied on its authors' speculations as to the direction of bankruptcy law under the then-new 1978 Code, than the Sixth Edition which had the luxury of a well-developed body of caselaw and commentary to explicate the purposes, functioning and limitations of the 1978 Code.

As with past editions, this Seventh Edition provides the materials necessary for a 4-unit in-depth business bankruptcy course, a 4-unit overview of both business and consumer bankruptcy law, or a 3-unit in-depth consumer bankruptcy course.

We continue to be indebted to our friend Professor Robert L. Jordan for his thorough and insightful analysis which permeated earlier editions and which in many instances remains reflected in the current edition. Our "bankruptcy" colleagues on this law faculty, Kenneth Klee and Lynn LoPucki are an invaluable resource and make UCLA School of Law the very best place to do academic work in this field. Aluyah Imoisili, UCLA School of Law Class of 2006, provided excellent research and editing assistance. Our staff assistant, Tal Grietzer, prepared a camera-ready manuscript of these materials through the miracle of modern desk-top publishing. His efforts, skill and care made timely publication of this Seventh Edition possible.

W.D.W.
D.J.B.

Los Angeles, California
November 2005

# ACKNOWLEDGMENTS

We gratefully acknowledge the permission extended to reprint excerpts from the following works:

Walter Blum & Stanley Kaplan, *The Absolute Priority Doctrine in Corporate Reorganizations*, 41 U. Chi.L.Rev. 651, 656-657 (1974). Reprinted by permission of the authors and the University of Chicago Law Review.

Richard Broude, *Cramdown and Chapter 11 of the Bankruptcy Code: The Settlement Imperative*, 39 Bus.Law. 441, 448-449 (1984). Copyright © 1984 by the American Bar Association. All rights reserved. Reprinted by permission of the American Bar Association and its Section of Corporation, Banking and Business Law.

Daniel J. Bussel, *Power, Authority, and Precedent in Interpreting the Bankruptcy Code*, 41 UCLA L.Rev. 1063, 1071-1075, 1094 (1994). Originally published in 41 UCLA Law Review 1063. Copyright © 1994, The Regents of the University of California. All rights reserved.

Daniel J. Bussel & Edward A. Friedler, *The Limits on Assuming and Assigning Executory Contracts*, 74 Am. Bankr. L.J. 321 (2000). Reprinted by permission of the authors and the American Bankruptcy Law Journal.

*Collier on Bankruptcy*, ¶1129.06 [1][c] (15th ed. rev. 2000). Reprinted with the permission of Matthew Bender & Company, Inc., a member of the LexisNexis Group.

Vern Countryman, *Executory Contracts in Bankruptcy: Part I*, 57 Minn.L.Rev. 439, 460 (1973). Reprinted by permission of the Minnesota Law Review.

Chaim J. Fortgang & Lawrence P. King, *The 1978 Bankruptcy Code: Some Wrong Policy Decisions*, 56 N.Y.U.L.Rev. 1148, 1165-1166 (1981). Reprinted by permission of the authors and the New York University Law Review.

Delmar Karlen, *Exemptions From Execution*, 22 Bus.Law. 1167, 1169 (1967). Copyright © 1967 by the American Bar Association. All rights reserved. Reprinted by permission of the American Bar Association and its Section of Corporation, Banking and Business Law.

Kenneth N. Klee, *Cram Down II*, 64 Am. Bankr. L.J. 229, 244 (1990). Reprinted by permission of the author and the American Bankruptcy Law Journal.

Kenneth N. Klee, *Restructuring Individual Debts*, 71 Am.Bankr. L.J. 431, 445-446 (1997). Reprinted by permission of the author and the American Bankruptcy Law Journal.

Louis E. Levinthal, *The Early History of Bankruptcy Law*, 66 U.Pa.L. Rev. 223, 224-225 (1918). Copyright © 1918 by the University of Pennsylvania Law Review. Reprinted by permission of the University of Pennsylvania Law Review.

Lynn M. LoPucki, *The Death of Liability*, 106 Yale L.J. 32-34 (1996). Reprinted by permission of the author and The Yale Law Journal Company and Fred B. Rothman & Company from The Yale Law Journal Vol. 106, pages 32-34.

Lynn M. LoPucki, *The Debtor in Full Control—Systems Failure Under Chapter 11 of the Bankruptcy Code?* 57 Am.Bankr. L.J. 99, 114 (1983). Reprinted by permission of the author and the American Bankruptcy Law Journal.

Lynn M. LoPucki & William C. Whitford, *Bargaining Over Equity's Share in the Bankruptcy Reorganization of Large, Publicly Held Companies*, 139 U.Pa.L.Rev. 125, 149, 194-195 (1990). Copyright © 1990 by the University of Pennsylvania Law Review. Reprinted by permission of the authors and the University of Pennsylvania Law Review.

Charles Jordan Tabb, *The Law of Bankruptcy* 431 (Foundation Press 1997). Reprinted by permission of the author and the Foundation Press.

Jay L. Westbrook, *A Functional Analysis of Executory Contracts*, 74 Minn.L.Rev. 227, 243 (1989). Reprinted by permission of the author and the Minnesota Law Review.

National Bankruptcy Conference, *Reforming the Bankruptcy Code* 124 (Rev.ed. 1997). Reprinted by permission of the National Bankruptcy Conference.

# SUMMARY OF CONTENTS

# TABLE OF CONTENTS

# Chapter 3.   Claims        83

## Chapter 4.   Discharge                                      153

# Chapter 7.    The Avoiding Powers of the Trustee    349

## Chapter 10.  Reorganization in Chapter 11: Operating the Debtor and Proposing a Plan  589

## Chapter 11.  Reorganization in Chapter 11: Confirming the Plan

# Chapter 12. The Bankruptcy Courts 817

# TABLE OF CASES

Principal cases are in **bold** type. Non-principal cases are in roman type. References are to Pages.

# CHAPTER 1

# INTRODUCTION TO BANKRUPTCY

## A. CONSENSUAL AND JUDICIAL LIENS

### 1. INTRODUCTION

Bankruptcy Law is federal law. The applicable statute is the Bankruptcy Reform Act of 1978, codified in Title 11 of the United States Code, which replaced the Bankruptcy Act of 1898 as subsequently amended. We will refer to the 1978 Act as the Bankruptcy Code, and to the previous law as the Bankruptcy Act. The Bankruptcy Code is supplemented by various provisions in Title 18 of the United States Code relating to bankruptcy crimes and in Title 28 of the United States Code relating to bankruptcy courts, jurisdiction in bankruptcy, bankruptcy procedure and administration. Bankruptcy procedure is also governed by Bankruptcy Rules promulgated under the authority of the Supreme Court of the United States.

Although bankruptcy is federal law, the rights in bankruptcy of debtors and creditors are governed in large part by rights under applicable state law. *Butner v. United States*, 440 U.S. 48 (1979). In order to understand the rights of the creditor in bankruptcy it is essential to understand the various rights and remedies created by state law regarding the collection of a debt from a debtor in default. If the debtor does not voluntarily pay the debt the creditor normally obtains payment by first obtaining an interest, generically referred to as a lien, in the debtor's property. A creditor who has a lien may have the liened property sold and the proceeds of sale applied to payment of the debt. Liens are obtained in three ways: by voluntary grant by the debtor; by judicial action taken by the creditor; or by statute because of the status of the particular creditor. Liens in these three categories are usually referred to respectively as consensual liens, judicial liens and statutory liens.

Consensual liens usually arise at the inception of a credit transaction. They are defined in the Bankruptcy Code as security interests in § 101(51) and may relate to both personal and real property. Article 9 of the Uniform Commercial Code, in effect in all of the states, governs the creation and enforcement of security interests in most forms of personal property. Thus, the law of personal property security interests is substantially uniform throughout the United States. Security interests in real property, arising under mortgages or deeds of trust granted by the debtor, are governed by the real property law of the jurisdiction in which the real property is located. This law varies substantially from state to state.

Judicial liens, defined in § 101(36), are created in the litigation process in which the creditor seeks a money judgment on the debt. They may arise either before or after judgment. After a money judgment has been given by the court the creditor, under the law of all of the states, is entitled to seizure of the debtor's property to pay the debt, subject to certain exemptions which allow the debtor to protect some property from the reach of creditors. Sometimes the seizure is a physical taking of the property. In other cases the seizure is symbolic and occurs by the public filing of a document. In either case the seizure results in the transfer from the debtor to the creditor of an interest in the seized property, and that interest is called a judicial lien. The lien gives to the creditor a secured status akin to that of a creditor holding a security interest. Some creditors may be able to acquire secured status at the inception of the judicial action if the applicable law provides for prejudgment seizure. Prejudgment judicial liens are severely limited in most states, and the grounds for obtaining them vary widely among the various jurisdictions.

Statutory liens, defined in § 101(53), are not consensual and do not depend upon judicial action by the creditor. Rather, they are status liens. Certain creditors, favored by the state, are given the rights of secured creditors even though they did not bargain for security. There are many examples of statutory liens. Among the most common are those that arise in favor of creditors who have performed some service or otherwise gave value which resulted in improvement or other benefit to the property to which the lien applies. Illustrations are the mechanic's and materialman's real property lien in favor of unpaid suppliers of services and goods used to improve the property, and the warehouseman's lien which allows an unpaid storer of goods to retain possession of the goods until the storage charges are paid. A more modern statutory lien that has become pervasive is the tax lien that allows the state or federal government to obtain a lien in all of the property of the taxpayer to secure assessed taxes.

Liens are of paramount importance in bankruptcy. The creditor whose debt is secured by a lien in the debtor's property has absolute priority with respect to that property over other creditors who have no lien or a lien with lower priority. Usually bankrupts are insolvent, i.e., the value of their assets is less than their debts, and, particularly in the case of business debtors, the debtor's property is normally encumbered. The result in many of these cases is that the bulk of the bankrupt's assets is applied to the payment of secured debts. Much of bankruptcy law is concerned with striking an equitable balance between the rights of secured and unsecured creditors to the debtor's assets. Toward this end bankruptcy law allows some liens that are valid outside bankruptcy to be invalidated in the bankruptcy proceedings, thus demoting the lienholder from the status of secured creditor to that of unsecured creditor. Sometimes bankruptcy law recognizes the validity of a lien but the rights of the lienholder are restricted in some fashion in order to enhance the rights of unsecured creditors.

We summarize below the most essential aspects of state law regarding the creation and enforcement of security interests and judicial liens. Statutory liens are discussed in Chapter 7.

## 2. CONSENSUAL LIENS

### a. Security Interests in Personal Property

#### (i)  *Types of Security Devices*

Security interests in personal property can be created in a variety of ways. The earliest and simplest method was the common law pledge, which remained the only form of chattel security until early in the nineteenth century. In a pledge the creditor takes possession of the collateral as security for payment of the debt. A pledge can apply not only to tangible property but also to reified intangibles such as negotiable instruments, investment securities and documents of title. The two most important nonpossessory security interests in personal property—the chattel mortgage and the conditional sale—were developed in the nineteenth century as alternatives to the pledge for situations where it was not convenient or practical for the creditor to remain in possession of the collateral.

The chattel mortgage, validated by statutory law, was modeled on the real property mortgage. The mortgagor, who retained possession of the collateral, conveyed it to the mortgagee as security for payment of the debt owed to the mortgagee. The validating law required, however, that the mortgage be recorded in the public records in order to be valid against third parties.

Under a conditional sale the seller delivered goods to the buyer under a contract of sale that provided that title to the goods remained in the seller until the buyer paid the purchase price. If the price was paid, the sale became absolute by passage of title from the seller to the buyer. If the buyer failed to pay according to the sales contract, the sale was not consummated and the seller could retake the goods to which the seller still had title. The conditional sale device was originally validated by judicial authority but in many states it was later regulated by statute. Although the conditional sale was functionally a security device similar to the chattel mortgage, the conditional seller was treated as owner of the goods rather than as a lienholder.

There were a variety of other security devices based either on assignment of rights by the debtor or retention of title by the creditor under which a creditor could get a nonpossessory security interest in collateral. Before the adoption of the Uniform Commercial Code, each security device was governed by a separate body of law. The result was law that was not only complex but also uncertain because it was often unclear what law governed a given transaction. Article 9 of the Uniform Commercial Code greatly simplified the law by adopting a functional approach to secured transactions. UCC § 9-109(a)(1) states that Article 9 applies to "a transaction, regardless of its form, that creates a security interest in personal property * * *." Thus, all of the pre-Code security devices are simply Article 9 security interests and are governed by a single law.

### (ii) Creation of the Security Interest

Security interest is defined in UCC § 1-201(b)(35) to mean "an interest in personal property * * * which secures payment or performance of an obligation." This definition is broader than the bankruptcy definition of security interest in § 101. The UCC definition includes nonconsensual as well as consensual liens. The Bankruptcy Code definition is limited to consensual liens. Under the UCC security interests in goods can arise under either Article 2, which governs sales, or Article 9, which governs secured transactions. Article 9 security interests are those created "by contract" (UCC § 9-109(a)(1)) and thus are included in the Bankruptcy Code definition. Article 2 security interests are nonconsensual and can arise in favor of either the seller or the buyer.

How do Article 9 security interests arise? UCC § 9-203(a) uses the word "attach" to describe when the security interest is created. A security interest attaches upon the occurrence of three events: (1) value has been given; (2) the debtor has rights in the collateral; and (3) either the debtor has authenticated a security agreement describing the collateral, or the debtor has agreed to the security interest and the collateral is in the possession of the secured party pursuant to that agreement. The three events can occur in any order. For example, suppose a bank and a prospective borrower sign a security agreement under which the bank will make future loans to be secured by "all of the borrower's business equipment whether then owned or subsequently acquired." If the bank makes a loan pursuant to the agreement, a security interest in all of the business equipment owned by the borrower at that time will attach at the time the loan is made. The giving of value (the loan) was the last of the three events to occur. If the borrower subsequently acquires additional business equipment, a security interest in that equipment will attach at the time it is acquired. In this case the obtaining of rights in the collateral by the debtor was the last of the three events to occur. The effect of UCC § 9-203 is to greatly simplify the creation of security interests. It also makes it possible for a lender, by virtue of one security agreement, to secure any loan that it might make in the future by a security interest in any personal property that the debtor owns or may own in the future.

If an Article 9 security interest attaches to the collateral, it continues in the collateral notwithstanding sale or other transfer of the collateral to a third party unless transfer free of the security interest was authorized by the secured party. UCC § 9-315(a)(1). In addition to retaining the security interest in the transferred collateral, the secured party, by virtue of this section, also gets a security interest in identifiable proceeds of the transfer, whether or not the transfer was authorized. Thus, if the debtor sells the collateral for money or exchanges it for other property, the secured party has a security interest in the money or other property received by the debtor. If any proceeds are used to acquire property, the security interest attaches to this property as well. This proceeds rule is very important in cases in which the collateral is property such as inventory or accounts receivable, which by its nature will be disposed of for cash or other property when it is sold or collected by the debtor in the ordinary course of business.

### (iii) Perfection and Priorities

Attachment of the security interest means that the lien of the secured party may be enforced against the debtor. But "perfection" of the security interest normally determines whether the security interest will be effective against third parties. Suppose the debtor, after granting a security interest in collateral to Creditor #1, either sells the collateral to Buyer or grants a security interest in the collateral to Creditor #2. In most cases Creditor #1 can have priority over Buyer or Creditor #2 only if the security interest of Creditor #1 was perfected. By requiring perfection the law accommodates the interests of the secured party and creditors of the debtor or other third parties who deal with the collateral. Since these third parties may not know that the debtor's assets are burdened with a security interest, it may be unfair for the secured party to assert rights against them based on the security interest unless some public notice of the security interest has been given. To protect the interests of these third parties the secured party is not allowed, in most cases, to assert the security interest against these third parties unless the security interest is perfected. UCC § 9-308(a), which defines perfection, states that "a security interest is perfected if it has attached and all of the applicable requirements for perfection * * * have been satisfied." The "applicable requirements" refer to some action by the secured party that gives notice of the security interest, usually possession of the collateral by the secured party or filing in a designated public office of a notice of the secured transaction.

With respect to some kinds of collateral, possession is a common method of perfection; for example, pledges of negotiable instruments or securities. On the other hand, possession cannot be used as a method of perfection if the nature of the collateral does not permit it. This is usually true in the case of intangible property. A common example is the account receivable that is defined in UCC § 9-102(a)(2) as meaning a right to payment for certain specified monetary obligations. In cases in which perfection by possession is not possible, perfection by filing may be necessary. With respect to most types of personal property, possession and filing represent alternative methods of perfection, but perfection by filing is far more common.

The great majority of all secured transactions in personal property represent the financing of the purchase price of "consumer goods," defined in UCC § 9-102(a)(23) as goods "used or bought for use primarily for personal, family or household purposes." The secured party, who may be the seller of the goods or a financial institution that lends the purchase price to the buyer, is secured by a security interest in the goods purchased. With respect to these purchase money security interests in consumer goods, no filing under the UCC is necessary to perfect the security interest. Rather, the security interest is automatically perfected when it attaches. A special rule, however, applies to motor vehicles that are required to be registered under state law. Perfection requires notice of the security interest even in the case of purchase money consumer transactions. Motor vehicles are registered under certificate of title laws that require security interests in the vehicle to be noted on the certificate of title. Perfection under the UCC is accomplished by compliance with the certificate of title law.

Perfection by filing under the UCC may be accomplished by filing of the security agreement between the secured party and the debtor. This carries forward the practice under the pre-Code chattel mortgage statutes that required filing of the mortgage. But this method is not typical. The normal practice is to file a document or other record known as a financing statement, which is described in UCC § 9-502(a). This document provides very little information. It need only disclose the names of the debtor and the secured party and indicate the collateral involved in the transaction. For example, the financing statement might indicate that the collateral is "business equipment." One cannot, by looking at the financing statement, identify the particular items of business equipment involved, the nature or amount of the debt secured or any other details of the transaction. Thus, the UCC adopts the principle of "notice filing," that is, that the secured party need only give notice that the secured party has, or may obtain in the future, a security interest in the indicated collateral. The burden is on the third party to determine the facts concerning the transaction.

Filing of the financing statement may either precede or follow the attachment of the security interest. In loan transactions it is common for the lender to file before the loan is made. By filing before the transaction is made the lender can be sure that the security interest will be perfected at the same time that it attaches. UCC § 9-308(a) provides that a security interest is perfected when it has attached and the steps required for perfection—in this case filing—have been taken. If the financing statement is filed after attachment, the security interest will become perfected at the time of filing.

If the filing of a financing statement results in perfection of a security interest in collateral, the perfection will automatically carry over for at least 20 days to identifiable proceeds if the collateral is sold or otherwise disposed of by the debtor. In most cases this perfection will continue after the 20–day period without any further act of the secured party. In some cases, however, the secured party must either take possession of the proceeds or file a financing statement with respect to the proceeds in order to obtain perfection after the 20–day period. The perfection rules for proceeds are stated in UCC § 9-315.

Unperfected security interests, although enforceable against the debtor, are given very little protection against the claims of third parties who subsequently acquire property interests in the collateral. UCC § 9-

317(a). If a creditor of the debtor acquires a judicial lien in the collateral the judicial lien has priority over the unperfected security interest. Moreover, as we shall see later, an unperfected security interest may be avoided in bankruptcy. An unperfected security interest is also subordinated to the title of most third parties who buy the collateral from the debtor. The only exception is that some buyers who buy with knowledge of the security interest take subject to it.

Suppose Debtor granted competing security interests in the same collateral to secure debts owed to two different creditors. Assume that each creditor perfected by filing a financing statement. There are a number of ways in which the priority between the two creditors might be determined. For example, the rule might be that the first security interest to attach has priority, or the first security interest to be perfected might be given priority. The UCC rejects both these solutions by adopting a rule that gives priority to the creditor who first files a financing statement. UCC § 9-322(a). The effects of this rule are far-reaching and surprising. Suppose, in our example, Creditor #1 and Debtor signed a security agreement in which Debtor granted a security interest in the collateral to secure any loans that Creditor #1 might make to Debtor in the future. Creditor #1 then filed a financing statement relating to the collateral. Later, but before any loan was made by Creditor #1, Debtor borrowed from Creditor #2 on the security of the same collateral. Creditor #2 filed. At that point Creditor #2 had a perfected security interest in the collateral. Creditor #1 had no security interest, perfected or unperfected, in the collateral because Creditor #1 had not yet made any loan to Debtor. If Creditor #1 then lends money to Debtor, Creditor #1 will at that time take a perfected security interest in the collateral. Because Creditor #1 was the first to file a financing statement, the security interest of Creditor #1 will have priority even though it attached and was perfected after the security interest of Creditor #2 attached and was perfected. This result follows even if Creditor #1 made the loan to Debtor with knowledge of the transaction between Debtor and Creditor #2. There are some exceptions to this rule.

### (iv) Default

If a debtor in default refuses or is unable to pay, an unsecured creditor can collect the debt only by bringing an action against the debtor and obtaining judgment. The action may be costly and there may be a substantial delay before judgment can be obtained. The secured creditor need not get judgment against the debtor in order to collect the debt and in many cases can obtain payment with either no judicial intervention or after a summary court procedure. UCC § 9-609 states that on the debtor's default the secured party has the right to take possession of the collateral. The secured party can seize the collateral without judicial intervention if the seizure can be accomplished "without breach of the peace." The quoted phrase has been given a very broad interpretation by the courts to exclude seizure in any case in which there is any resistance, verbal as well as physical, or in which the seizure involves a nonconsensual entry on property of the debtor or other person. As a practical matter, self-help seizure is restricted to cases in which the debtor voluntarily gives up possession or in which the collateral is property, such as an automobile, that can be found in some public place while the debtor or other custodian is not present.

If self-help is not possible, the secured party can obtain possession by judicial process in a summary proceeding. State law normally provides a provisional remedy under which the secured party can get immediate possession of the collateral by a judicial seizure. There must be a noticed hearing in which the secured party must establish, usually by affidavit, the probable validity of its claim, but the only litigable issue is whether the debtor is in default. The law normally provides for the posting of a surety bond or other undertaking by the plaintiff to protect the debtor in case of a wrongful seizure. Thus, a secured creditor can normally get possession of the collateral either by self-help or after a quick summary proceeding.

A secured party in possession of the collateral after default is entitled by UCC § 9-610 to "sell, lease, license or otherwise dispose of" the collateral. Normally the collateral is sold in either a public or private sale after notice to the debtor, UCC § 9-611. The proceeds of the sale are applied to the expenses of retaking and sale and satisfaction of the debt, UCC § 9-615. If the proceeds of sale are not sufficient to satisfy the debt, the secured party can usually sue for any deficiency, UCC § 9-615(d).

### b.   Security Interests in Real Property

The sources of real property security law differ greatly from those of personal property security law. As we have seen, personal property security law is virtually uniform throughout the nation; moreover, it is conveniently available in Article 9 of the UCC. In contrast, the principles of real property security law are found in a complex mosaic of case and statutory law unique to each state. Hence, the description below is only an approximate generalization from the great body of diverse doctrine in this area. The publication in 1997 of the *Restatement (Third) of Property, Mortgages* offers a welcome synthesis of this body of law.

#### (i)   Introduction

Like the pledge of personal property, the early mortgage of real property involved the creditor's taking possession of the property. The mortgagor (debtor) deeded the property to the mortgagee (creditor) on condition subsequent that if the mortgagor paid the debt by a given day, called the "law day," the mortgagee would reconvey the land to the mortgagor. Under the deed, the mortgagee was entitled to possession and to the crops and rents from the land. In time, the practice developed of leaving the mortgagor in possession with a right in the mortgagee to take possession and obtain payment from the rents and profits upon default.

A mortgagor who failed to repay the debt on the law day lost all interest in the land. Time was of the essence. However, equity intervened to allow mortgagors to redeem their property by paying the debt after the law day. To the present day the debtor's interest under a mortgage is described as the "equity of redemption." Since the intervention of the courts of equity in giving the mortgagor the right to redeem made the mortgagee's rights uncertain, the procedure developed in equity of allowing the mortgagee to request that the court order the mortgagor to redeem by a certain date and, if the mortgagor failed to do so, to foreclose the mortgagor of the right to redeem. The term "foreclosure" has come to mean any method of realizing on the mortgagee's security interest. Since no sale was required in this earliest procedure, and the potential for forfeiture was present, this type of foreclosure, called "strict foreclosure," is prohibited in most states. Foreclosure today requires that the mortgaged land be sold at public sale with any surplus over the mortgagee's debt returned to the mortgagor. Some states by statute allow the mortgagor to redeem for a period after the foreclosure sale from the purchaser at that sale.

### (ii) Types of Security Devices

Three types of real property security devices are prevalent in the United States: the mortgage, the deed of trust, and the installment sale contract. For convenience, we will refer throughout this book to the mortgage as the generic security device in real property transactions.

Mortgage. The early mortgage conveyed title to the mortgagee with a right to take possession. Although some states still purport to retain the "title" theory of mortgages, most states have adopted the "lien" theory that views a mortgage transaction as one granting the mortgagee merely a security interest in the land. These jurisdictions have done by case law what UCC § 9-202 has done in personal property secured transactions: whether title is nominally in the mortgagee or not is immaterial; if the transaction is for security, the creditor's only interest is a security interest. Differences between the title and lien theories have been eroded. The modern mortgage is a contract, usually written by the mortgagee, and the law of mortgages today largely concerns the question of the extent to which courts will enforce against mortgagors the terms of the mortgage. These decisions are more influenced by present day views on contracts of adhesion and debtor protection than by conceptual distinctions based on the location of legal title.

Deed of Trust. In this transaction the trustor (debtor) conveys legal title to a trustee in trust for the benefit of the beneficiary (creditor). The probable reason for the growth of the deed of trust was the desire of creditors to avoid the time-consuming requirement of judicial foreclosure and to supplant it by foreclosure by exercise of a private power of sale. An early view was that a mortgage could not contain a power of sale for the power had to be vested in a third party as trustee. Hence, the deed of trust was devised to allow the trustee to sell the property on default by the trustor. Today, there has been a general assimilation of the deed of trust and the mortgage. Although one device may be more popular in some jurisdictions than in others, the rights of the parties vary only marginally under either. A mortgage may contain an enforceable power of sale and, although the trustee under a deed of trust holds legal title, the rights of the trustor and beneficiary are quite similar to those of the mortgagor and mortgagee in a lien state.

Installment Sale Contract. Here the seller sells land to the buyer on the condition that title will pass to the buyer only when the buyer has completed the installment payments called for by the contract. In its early usage, the device was advantageous to sellers because default by the buyer resulted in forfeiture of all payments the buyer had made and terminated the buyer's right to possession. Thus, the land contract gave sellers what amounted to strict foreclosure of the buyer's interest: the debtor's interest was cut off without a foreclosure sale. However, the 20th century saw a remarkable case law development that relieved the debtor from forfeiture in defaults on installment contracts and went far toward assimilating the land contract with the mortgage and deed of trust. *Restatement (Third) of Property, Mortgages* § 3.4 (1997) makes the assimilation complete. Nonetheless, in some states the assimilation has not been complete, and the installment contract remains a special security device of limited usefulness to both sellers and buyers. Sellers may have no expedited method to cut off the buyer's interests akin to foreclosure by exercise of private power of sale. Buyers may have no absolute right to compel a sale to prevent forfeiture of their interests.

### (iii) Creation of Security Interest

A security interest in personal property may arise under UCC § 1-201(b)(35) only when there is an obligation to be secured. Similarly, there can be no enforceable real property mortgage if there is no underlying obligation. Hence, in some jurisdictions a gift of a mortgage and note to a donee does not create a right in the donee to enforce the note and mortgage. The *Restatement (Third) of Property, Mortgages* § 1.2 (1997) takes a contrary view. However, a mortgage may be enforceable even though the debtor is not personally liable. This may occur when the mortgagor has been discharged in bankruptcy, when personal liability is barred by anti-deficiency statutes, or when the parties contractually agree to limit liability to the value of the collateral. This latter "nonrecourse" transaction is of growing importance in commercial financing.

Under the UCC, if a transaction results in the creation of a security interest under § 1-201(b)(35), the provisions of Article 9 apply whatever the form of the transaction. At an early date a parallel doctrine had emerged in real property law to the effect that if rights in land were conveyed to secure a debt, the law of mortgages applied to protect the debtor however the transaction was disguised. One of the earliest examples of this rule was the "deed absolute" transaction. If the grantor conveys land to the grantee by an unconditional deed with an oral agreement that if the grantor pays a debt owed to the grantee by a given date the grantee will reconvey, the court will allow proof of the oral agreement and will allow the grantor either to redeem or compel foreclosure by sale. A familiar modern example of a disguised secured transaction is a sale and lease-back. Seller sells land to Buyer for $100,000. Buyer leases the land back to Seller for a rental of $12,000 per year. Seller agrees to repurchase the land in five years for $100,000. Courts see this transaction as a disguised loan transaction and apply mortgage principles to it. Sales with options to repurchase that are the functional equivalent of obligations to repurchase are treated in the same way.

Once a transaction is recognized as being one for security, courts will not enforce terms of a security agreement that give up the debtor's basic rights as a mortgagor, that is, the rights to redemption or foreclosure. For instance, if the parties agree at the time of the credit extension that in order to avoid the expense of foreclosure the mortgagor will place a deed to the land in escrow to be delivered to the mortgagee upon default by the mortgagor, the court will consider this an invalid attempt to waive fundamental rights of a mortgagor. On the other hand, an agreement to waive the mortgagor's rights in foreclosure is enforceable if entered into after the mortgagor is already in default.

### (iv) Perfection and Priorities

The mortgagee perfects rights against third-party claimants by recording the mortgage document in the records of the county in which the land is located. But a mortgagee has priority over third parties who know of the mortgage when they acquire their interests even if the mortgage is not recorded. Moreover, unlike the UCC rule under § 9-317, the majority view is that although a good faith purchaser of real property without knowledge of the mortgage takes free of an unrecorded mortgage, a judicial lien creditor whether with or without knowledge does not. Later we will see this distinction between real property security law and personal property security law acknowledged in § 544(a) which grants the trustee in bankruptcy power to avoid unperfected security interests in both real and personal property.

A major problem in real property law is the priority of the mortgagee's future advances against intervening secured interests. Of growing popularity are "open end" mortgages in which the mortgagee has the option but not the obligation to advance additional funds to the mortgagor upon request. Another common use of future advances is the construction mortgage in which funds are advanced by the mortgagee as progress payments conditional on a structure's reaching prescribed stages of completion. The prevailing priority rule distinguishes between future advances made pursuant to commitment and those that are made at the option of the mortgagee, the so-called "optional-obligatory" distinction. Advances made pursuant to commitment take their priority from the date of the commitment. Optional advances relate back to the date of the mortgage only if made by the mortgagee without knowledge of an intervening security interest. Hence, unlike a junior secured party subject to the UCC rule of § 9-322(a), a second mortgagee can be sure that no optional future advance by the first mortgagee will have priority over the second mortgage by notifying the first mortgagee of the second mortgagee's interest.

### (v)  Rents

In lending on commercial property, mortgagees not only want a security interest in the land but also in the rents arising from leases made by the mortgagor. If the mortgagor is in default, it may be of great importance for the mortgagee to be able to collect the rentals until the property is sold by foreclosure. Commonly, the mortgage will expressly grant the mortgagee rights in the rentals. Real property rents are rights to the payment of money and, as such, have much in common with accounts receivable. A seller who sells goods on credit may assign the buyer's debt, described as an account by UCC § 9-102(a)(2), to a creditor as security for a loan. As we have seen, under Article 9 of the UCC, the creditor may take a perfected security interest in the account as soon as the buyer owes the debt, and the priority of the creditor's interest dates from the time of filing a financing statement. The UCC does not apply to real property rentals (UCC § 9-109(d)(11)).

### (vi)  Foreclosure

When a debtor is in default under a personal property security agreement, UCC § 9-601(c) provides that the secured party's remedies are cumulative, that is, the secured party may sue to obtain a personal judgment against the debtor, may proceed to foreclose on the collateral, or may do both at the same time. If the secured party forecloses on the collateral, the debtor is liable for any deficiency remaining after the sale. In some states the real property mortgagee's remedies are also cumulative. In others the mortgagee has the option either of suing on the debt or foreclosing on the collateral, but must elect one or the other and cannot do both. In some of the Western states, including California, the mortgagee's only action is to foreclose on the collateral and to ask for a deficiency judgment in that action. This rule is called the "one-action rule."

The traditional method of foreclosing a real property mortgage is the often long and costly process of judicial foreclosure. The mortgagee sues to foreclose; the mortgagor and junior lienholders must be joined; after a hearing the court orders a sale; public sale by a judicial officer follows the requisite statutory notice; the proceeds of the sale are applied to pay the mortgage debt; any surplus goes first to junior lienholders and then to the mortgagor; any deficiency is assessed as a personal judgment against the mortgagor. Frequently, the property is sold to the mortgagee who is entitled to make a "credit bid" at the sale, that is, the amount of the mortgage debt may be credited against the price of the land at the sale.

The protection afforded the mortgagor to ensure that the land will bring a fair price is based on formal compliance with the requirements of the statute. If the sale is regularly conducted with respect to notice and other formal statutory requirements, courts are very unlikely to allow the sale to be challenged as not fetching a high enough price. In contrast, Article 9 of the UCC imposes a general duty on a secured party to sell collateral in a "commercially reasonable" manner. In some instances this may entail selling the property in the manner that a dealer in that kind of property would utilize. The more flexible, result-oriented UCC rules on fore-closure sales were a deliberate reaction to the formalistic approach to fore-closure of real property law.

In about half the states, mortgagees may foreclose by exercise of the power of sale contained in the mortgage. Here, the mortgagee gives notice of default to the mortgagor who usually has a statutory right to cure the default within a few weeks. If the default is not cured, notice of sale is given, and the land is sold at public sale by the mortgagee or, in the case of a deed of trust, by the trustee. The mortgagor has no automatic right to a presale hearing. The mortgagor may contest the existence of default by moving to enjoin the sale. Power of sale foreclosure is much faster and cheaper than judicial foreclosure, and in those states in which it is permit-ted it has become the most commonly used method of foreclosure. Its ma-jor shortcoming is that it cannot resolve disputes between competing in-terests in the manner that a court decree does in a judicial foreclosure. Unlike non-judicial foreclosure sales under the UCC, the price of proceed-ing by non-judicial sale against real estate under a private power of sale is usually that the mortgagee forfeits any right to a deficiency judgment.

In a number of states, the mortgagor may redeem from the foreclosure sale by acting within a statutory period that runs from three months in some states to two years in others. In some of these states a junior lien-holder can also redeem. The chilling effect that the potential for postsale redemption poses for foreclosure sales has led many other states to pro-vide for no postsale redemption. The Great Depression spawned a number of statutes limiting or prohibiting deficiency judgments. These debtor pro-tection statutes have by and large remained in force despite their question-able relevance to contemporary conditions.

### 3. JUDICIAL LIENS

#### a. Judgment and Execution Liens

A money judgment against a defendant can be collected by a levy (sei-zure) on property of the defendant and a subsequent sale of that property. Levy and sale are done pursuant to a writ of execution which is usually issued by the clerk of the court upon application of the judgment creditor. The writ orders the levying officer (sheriff, marshal or similar officer) to enforce the judgment by levying on property of the debtor. The property to be levied on is usually identified in instructions to the levying officer signed by the judgment creditor or the creditor's attorney. In this process of judgment and execution of judgment, two types of judicial lien can re-sult. One is a specific lien, called an execution lien, which attaches to the property on which levy is made under the writ of execution. The other is a general lien, called a judgment lien which arises as a result of the judg-ment itself. It applies to all of the property of the debtor to which a judg-ment lien can apply. Both liens can arise only after a judgment has been obtained but the execution lien can arise only if a writ of execution also has been obtained.

### (i)   Judgment Liens

Judgment liens are recognized in a large majority of the states. Historically they applied only to real property, and that continues to be the rule in all but a few jurisdictions. The kinds of interests in real property to which a judgment lien attaches may vary in different jurisdictions. The procedure for obtaining the lien may also vary, but generally the lien attaches to all real property of the judgment debtor in the county in which the judgment is docketed or in which the judgment or an abstract is recorded in the land records. In most states, the lien attaches not only to property of the debtor existing at the time the judgment was docketed or recorded but to after-acquired property as well. Typically, duration of the judgment lien is equal to the life of the judgment, a relatively long period. Ten years or more from the entry of the judgment is common. In most states the lien can be extended beyond the original period by a renewal of the judgment. One of the advantages of a judgment lien is its generality. It allows the judgment creditor to obtain the security of a lien in the debtor's property even though that property has not yet been identified by the creditor.

In a few states the judgment lien attaches to personal property as well as real property. One of the most innovative and sophisticated statutes providing for a judgment lien in personal property is that of California, which became effective in 1983. Cal. Civ. Proc. Code §§ 697.510 to 697.670. It allows a money judgment creditor to obtain a judgment lien in personal property by filing a notice of lien in the office of the Secretary of State. The lien applies only to specified business property: accounts receivable, chattel paper, equipment, farm products, inventory, and negotiable documents of title. These terms are defined in the same way as the comparable terms were defined in the original draft of Article 9. The lien attaches only to property in which an Article 9 security interest could be perfected by filing a financing statement with the Secretary of State. In effect, the statute gives to the judgment creditor the functional equivalent of an Article 9 security interest in the property affected. The filing of the notice of lien is the equivalent of perfection under the UCC. The lien applies both to property owned by the judgment debtor at the time of filing the notice of lien and to property acquired thereafter. In most respects the judgment lien is treated like an Article 9 security interest. As under the UCC, the lien attaches to identifiable cash proceeds of the sale of any property subject to the lien. Noncash proceeds are, in effect, treated as after-acquired property. If noncash proceeds do not fall within one of the enumerated classes of property to which the lien applies, the judgment lien does not attach. The judgment lien continues in property that is disposed of by the judgment debtor, but third parties who would have taken free of a perfected Article 9 security interest in the same property also take free of the judgment lien. Priorities among conflicting judgment liens are governed by a first-to-file rule similar to that governing Article 9 security interests. There is also a first-to-file rule governing conflicts between judgment liens and Article 9 security interests subject to certain exceptions.

### (ii)  Execution Liens

The method of carrying out levy pursuant to a writ of execution may vary from state to state, and it also varies depending upon the type of property involved. With respect to real property, we have seen that the judgment creditor, by virtue of the judgment, usually can obtain a judgment lien in real property of the debtor. In some states the creditor with a judgment lien can obtain sale of the liened property by judicial foreclosure in proceedings similar to foreclosure of a mortgage. In other states the judgment lienholder obtains sale by levying on the property pursuant to a writ of execution. Levy on real property usually requires the recording by the levying officer in the land records of the writ of execution or a notice of levy. An execution lien arises in the real property when the recording occurs. With respect to tangible personal property in the possession of the debtor, levy usually is done by physical seizure. The levying officer either takes custody by removing the property to a place of safekeeping or, if the property is not portable, by installing a keeper who maintains custody. In some states levy on property that cannot be conveniently moved is done by serving a notice of levy on the debtor or by some public filing. With respect to intangible property that represents an obligation owed to the debtor, such as wages, deposit accounts, accounts receivable and general intangibles, levy is normally done by garnishment. A copy of the writ of execution or a notice of levy is served on the person owing the debt to the judgment debtor. The effect of garnishment is to require the garnishee to make payment of the obligation to the levying officer. A similar procedure is often provided for in the case of levy on tangible property of the debtor which is in the hands of a third party under some claim of right as in the case of a lease or pledge. Within these general categories, the law of the jurisdiction may provide special methods of levy for particular types of property.

Levy on personal property pursuant to a writ of execution gives rise to an execution lien in favor of the judgment creditor, but the time that the lien arises may vary in different jurisdictions. Some states follow the common law rule that delivery of the writ of execution to the levying officer gives rise to an execution lien in the personal property of the debtor covered by the writ. However, this lien is inchoate. If no valid levy is made, either because the levying officer cannot find property of the debtor or because the writ of execution expired before levy was made, the lien lapses. If a valid levy is made, the inchoate lien becomes perfected and dates from the date of delivery of the writ of execution. In other states the rule is that the execution lien arises at the time the levy is made. In some cases the validity of a lien in bankruptcy depends upon the time that the lienholder obtained the lien. For example, a judicial lien obtained within 90 days of bankruptcy while the debtor was insolvent can usually be avoided by the trustee in bankruptcy while a lien obtained more than 90 days before bankruptcy may be indefeasible. Sometimes a creditor has more than one judicial lien in the same property. For example, suppose a judgment creditor obtained a judgment lien in real property of the debtor and later the creditor obtained an execution lien by levying on that real property. The normal result in this case is that the effective date of the execution lien relates back to the date of the earlier judgment lien.

### b.    Attachment Liens

We have seen that upon default by the debtor a secured creditor may normally get payment by selling the collateral. In most cases little or no judicial intervention is required for the secured creditor to assert rights to the collateral. The creditor's remedy is fast and inexpensive. Consider the rights of an unsecured creditor against a debtor in default. The only remedy of the creditor is to bring an action on the debt. When judgment is eventually recovered it may be satisfied by seizure and sale of property of the debtor, but judgment may be delayed for a long period during which the creditor is subject to substantial risks. An improvident debtor may dissipate assets before judgment can be obtained. A dishonest debtor may conceal property or remove it from the jurisdiction or may dispose of it in order to defraud creditors. An unsecured creditor may obtain protection against these risks by obtaining prejudgment seizure of the debtor's assets. This prejudgment seizure is known as attachment. Do not confuse this term with the same term that is used in the UCC to describe the creation of an Article 9 security interest.

Prejudgment attachment is generally available as a provisional remedy in conjunction with the commencement of the action on the debt. The grounds for obtaining the remedy vary widely from state to state. Attachment may not be available in all kinds of actions. For example, in some states the remedy is restricted to contract claims in which the amount of the claim is readily ascertainable. In most states attachment is allowed only in cases in which the defendant is not resident in the state or in which the defendant is avoiding service of process or in which there is basis for believing that the defendant will conceal assets, remove assets from the state or convey them in fraud of creditors. In some states attachment can be obtained if the action is based on a debt fraudulently contracted by the debtor. In a minority of states attachment is available with respect to certain kinds of claims even in the case of resident defendants and even in the absence of grounds for believing that the defendant will conceal or fraudulently dispose of assets.

Attachment involves a levy on the property of the defendant that is similar to a levy under a writ of execution, although in some cases physical seizure, which is the norm with respect to execution on chattels, is replaced by levy by filing with respect to some kinds of property. An attachment lien arises at the time the levy is made. Attachment is a very drastic remedy since it may allow the debtor to be deprived of the use of property and since it always burdens that property with a lien that may prevent the debtor from freely disposing of the property. The debtor can normally prevent attachment by posting a surety bond, but this requirement may in some cases be just as onerous as attachment itself. Since the remedy is given before a judgment on the claim has been made, serious constitutional issues of taking without due process of law are involved. Because of constitutional law considerations the remedy of attachment has been substantially limited in recent years. The remedy is not normally available unless there has been a judicial determination of the probable validity of the creditor's claim. That determination, however, is normally made in a summary proceeding and can, in some cases, be made ex parte so long as the debtor is given opportunity to promptly challenge the attachment.

## B. EARLY BANKRUPTCY LAW

The law of bankruptcy can be traced to the law of various Italian city states of the fourteenth century, which in turn was based on Roman origins. Some of the principles of the Italian law and the law of other Continental countries eventually found their way into the English law and thus into the law of the United States. The concept of bankruptcy viewed historically and comparatively has been described as follows:

> All bankruptcy law, however, no matter when or where devised and enacted, has at least two general objects in view. It aims, first, to secure an equitable division of the insolvent debtor's property among all his creditors, and, in the second place, to prevent on the part of the insolvent debtor conduct detrimental to the interests of his creditors. In other words, bankruptcy law seeks to protect the creditors, first, from one another and, secondly, from their debtor. A third object, the protection of the honest debtor from his creditors, by means of the discharge, is sought to be attained in some of the systems of bankruptcy, but this is by no means a fundamental feature of the law.
>
> * * *
>
> The laws that have for their object the protection of the creditors from one another seek to prevent any one of the creditors from obtaining more than his proportionate share of the debtor's assets. A special process of collective execution is devised, a process directed against all of the property of the debtor, resorted to for the common benefit and at the common expense of all the creditors.

Louis E. Levinthal, *The Early History of Bankruptcy Law*, 66 U.Pa.L.Rev. 223, 225 (1918).

The most important early English bankruptcy law was the Statute of Bankrupts, 13 Elizabeth, c. 7 (1570). It was directed against fraudulent debtors and was punitive in nature. It applied only to debtors who were merchants and it provided that a debtor who committed an act of bankruptcy "shall be reputed, deemed and taken for a bankrupt." There were various acts of bankruptcy including the debtor's departure from the realm, the debtor's taking refuge in the debtor's house, taking sanctuary and various other acts if the debtor's purpose was to avoid process with the intent of defrauding or hindering creditors. Upon complaint, the Lord Chancellor could appoint a commission of "wise, honest and discreet" persons who were authorized to seize the property of the bankrupt and sell it for the payment, pro rata, of the debts of the bankrupt. The bankrupt remained liable to the extent that creditors were not paid in full. The bankrupt could be imprisoned by the commissioners and, by virtue of a later statute, could be subjected to pillory and the loss of an ear as well. Louis E. Levinthal, *The Early History of English Bankruptcy*, 67 U.Pa.L.Rev. 1, 16–18 (1919). Thus, early English bankruptcy law was designed to protect creditors and to punish debtors who were avoiding the payment of just debts. The Statute of Bankrupts was amended or supplemented by numerous statutes over the years. It was not until the early eighteenth century with the Statutes of 4 Anne, c. 17 (1705), and 10 Anne, c. 15 (1711), that the law allowed discharge of the bankrupt of the debts owing at the time of bankruptcy. Levinthal, *supra* at 18-19.

The Statute of Bankrupts was the bankruptcy law during the colonial period in America. The first federal bankruptcy law, the Bankruptcy Act of 1800, followed closely the Statute of Bankrupts. Other bankruptcy laws were enacted in 1841 and 1867 as emergency legislation in the wake of financial panics. Each of these three laws was repealed shortly after enactment. Agrarian populists opposed federal bankruptcy laws, which they saw as instruments of oppression that allowed bankers to take their land. Financial interests favored these laws as giving them a way to share equally in the assets of insolvent debtors. David A. Skeel, Jr., *Debt's Dominion: A History of Bankruptcy Law in America* 3 (2001). The notion of allowing a debtor to voluntarily choose bankruptcy as a means of finding relief from creditors did not become a part of English bankruptcy law until well into the nineteenth century. Voluntary bankruptcy did not become a part of the American law until the Bankruptcy Act of 1841.

Not until the Bankruptcy Act of 1898 did America have a permanent bankruptcy statute, and this act, as amended on numerous occasions, was the bankruptcy law of the United States until 1979 when the present Bankruptcy Code became effective. The Bankruptcy Act was our first modern bankruptcy statute, and is, in large part, the basis of the Bankruptcy Code. However, during the 19th century, development of the law of corporate reorganization occurred largely outside the Bankruptcy Act by use of equity receiverships principally in cases involving insolvent railroads. Equity receivership law was reformed and codified as part of the Bankruptcy Act during the Great Depression of the 1930s and then reformed again and recodified as modern Chapter 11 in the Bankruptcy Code.

## C. OVERVIEW OF BANKRUPTCY

### 1. INTRODUCTION

We have seen that under the early law bankruptcy was exclusively a creditor's remedy. In modern times bankruptcy is still an important, though little used, creditor's remedy. Some creditors who would receive little or nothing in payment of their claims outside bankruptcy may be able to obtain substantial payment by forcing the debtor into involuntary bankruptcy under § 303. But bankruptcy today is most important as a debtor's remedy, and the overwhelming majority of bankruptcies occur by voluntary act of debtors who are seeking relief from the demands of their creditors.

Outside of bankruptcy, there is often little relief for a debtor who is unable to pay creditors. Creditors with security interests may seize and sell collateral. Other creditors may have obtained, or are threatening to obtain, judicial liens in the debtor's property. Although state law may allow the debtor to protect exempt property from execution or attachment, that law may not apply to some property that the debtor vitally needs. Most debtors that are not natural persons cannot protect any property from creditors under nonbankruptcy law. For debtors beset by creditors, bankruptcy can provide instant and dramatic relief. The paragraphs that follow provide a brief description of the principal characteristics of bankruptcy proceedings. Because involuntary bankruptcy is relatively uncommon, we will deal only with voluntary bankruptcy.

The United States is divided into 91 judicial districts. In each district there is a bankruptcy court with one or more bankruptcy judges. There are also United States Trustees, each of whom is assigned to one or more of the judicial districts. They are officials of the United States Department of Justice, whose function it is to supervise the administration of bankruptcy cases. The duties of the United States Trustee are stated in 28 U.S.C. § 586. Two judicial districts, those for Alabama and North Carolina, were allowed to remain out of the U.S. Trustee system until the earlier of October 1, 2002, or the date the district elects to be included. *Collier on Bankruptcy* ¶ 6.33[1] (15th ed. rev. 2004). In these jurisdictions, a Bankruptcy Administrator is given roughly the same responsibilities as the United States Trustee.

### 2. TYPES OF BANKRUPTCY

The debtor can choose two types of bankruptcy. The first, and most simple type, is a bankruptcy liquidation under Chapter 7 of the Bankruptcy Code. In a liquidation bankruptcy all of the property of the debtor owned at the date of bankruptcy becomes part of the bankruptcy estate. § 541. A debtor who is an individual is entitled to exempt certain property from the bankruptcy estate. The exempt property is released to the debtor.

The property that may be exempted is in most cases determined by the law of the state of the debtor's domicile and consists of property that is exempt from judicial liens in that state. In some cases the debtor has the option of electing to exempt property listed in § 522(d). The trustee in bankruptcy must also dispose of property in which a lienholder or other person such as a co-owner has a property interest. In some cases the property is released by the trustee. In other cases the property is sold by the trustee and the property interest of the lienholder or other person is satisfied from the proceeds of sale. Any remaining property of the estate is sold by the trustee in bankruptcy and the proceeds are applied to payment of the debts of the debtor and the expenses of the bankruptcy proceedings. A debtor who is an individual normally will be discharged of personal liability on all or most prebankruptcy debts. The ability of an individual to obtain a discharge of prebankruptcy debts is one of the most important characteristics of modern bankruptcy law. The overextended debtor can get a "fresh start" by having personal liability on prebankruptcy debts wiped out while being allowed to retain all exempt property. Liquidating debtors other than individuals, such as corporations and partnerships, have no need for a fresh start. After distributing all its assets to creditors, an insolvent organization can simply be dissolved. Thus, in Chapter 7, only an individual can be discharged. § 727(a)(1). Since 2005, access to Chapter 7 for an individual whose income prior to the bankruptcy exceeded State medians, has been limited by a "means test" that is designed to require individuals who are deemed to have sufficient future income to obtain relief in Chapter 13 rather than Chapter 7.

The second type of bankruptcy is usually referred to as reorganization or rehabilitation bankruptcy and is governed by Chapter 11, Chapter 12, or Chapter 13 of the Bankruptcy Code. Chapter 13 can be used only by a debtor who is "an individual with regular income that owes, on the date of the filing of the petition, noncontingent, liquidated, unsecured debts of less than $307,675 and noncontingent, liquidated, secured debts of less than $922,975 * * *." § 109(e). The great advantage of Chapter 13 is that the debtor can get the benefit of discharge without losing nonexempt property. The debtor is required to formulate a plan under which the debtor proposes to pay, in whole or in part, some or all prebankruptcy debts over a period of time which is usually five years. Creditors are paid in accordance with the plan normally from postbankruptcy earnings although the plan could provide for a liquidation of some assets. The plan need not be approved by creditors. If the plan is confirmed by the bankruptcy court, creditors are bound by its terms. § 1327(a). But a plan cannot be confirmed over the objection of a creditor unless certain requirements are met. If the plan does not propose payment in full of unsecured claims, the plan must provide for the payment of all of the debtor's "projected disposable income" for the period of the plan. § 1325(b)(1). In most cases, disposable income means total income received by the debtor less the amount reasonably necessary for the maintenance or support of the debtor and the debtor's dependents. § 1325(b)(2). But for debtors whose incomes exceed state family medians, this amount is limited by certain standards that rely on statistical medians published by the Internal Revenue Service and the Bureau of the Census. § 1325(b)(3). When all payments are completed, the debtor is entitled to a discharge of those debts (with some exceptions) that are provided for in the plan. § 1328(a). Under some circumstances the debtor can obtain a discharge even if payments under the plan have not been completed if the failure to complete the plan is not the fault of the debtor. § 1328(b).

Chapter 11 may be used by both individuals and organizations, but it is designed primarily for business organizations. It resembles Chapter 13 in that the debtor is normally allowed to retain its assets and to continue operation of its business as a debtor in possession. The debtor in possession proposes a plan of reorganization under which creditors will be paid, sometimes over a period of time, from assets of the estate or postconfirmation earnings of the debtor. Unlike Chapter 13, confirmation of a plan in Chapter 11 is considered only after it has been voted on by the various classes of creditors and stockholder interests of the debtor. Acceptance by a class is accomplished by a vote of members of the class in specified majorities. Under some circumstances, a plan can be confirmed even though not all classes accept the plan. Other plans that fail to meet certain statutory requirements cannot be confirmed even if all classes accept the plan. Upon confirmation of the plan, the debtor, whether an individual or an organization, is normally given a discharge of all preconfirmation debts. In return, creditors and stockholder interests have rights that are given to them by the plan. There are various provisions in Chapter 11 designed to protect the interests of creditors and stockholder interests who did not accept the plan.

Chapter 12 was added to the Bankruptcy Code in 1986 to provide for the rehabilitation of "family farmers" defined in § 101(18). Chapter 12 is similar to Chapter 13, but it incorporates some elements of Chapter 11. It is specifically designed to make it easier for family farmers who are threatened with loss of their farms to restructure their debts in bankruptcy while continuing to operate their farms.

Chapter 9 of the Bankruptcy Code, which governs the bankruptcy of municipalities, is not discussed in this book.

### 3. Eligibility for Bankruptcy

Under § 301 a voluntary case can be commenced by any "entity that may be a debtor." Section 101(15) defines entity to include "person, estate, trust, [and] governmental unit." It apparently can "include" others because "includes" is not limiting (§ 102(3)), but we are given no guidance as to what those others might be. But not all entities can qualify as debtors. Only a person or a municipality may be a debtor. §§ 101(13), 109(a). "Person" is defined in § 101(41) to include individuals, partnerships and corporations, but not governmental units. "Corporation" is defined in § 101(9) to include some entities that aren't corporations such as joint stock companies, unincorporated associations and business trusts. The effect of this mystifying series of definitions within definitions is that an applicant for voluntary bankruptcy qualifies if either a person or a municipality. The definitions exclude governmental units, other than municipalities, and estates and trusts, unless the trust is a business trust. Thus, the City of New York, but not the State of New York or the United States of America, can go into bankruptcy. Estates and trusts, whose affairs are governed by state courts exercising traditional equity powers, are left to those courts. A business trust, which is undefined in the Bankruptcy Code, qualifies as a "debtor" because it is included in the definition of "corporation" and thus is also included in the definition of "person." Section 109(b) and (d) further limit the persons eligible for bankruptcy. Insurance companies, banks and similar financial institutions may not be debtors. These institutions are regulated by other statutes that provide for insolvency proceedings. Railroads may be debtors under Chapter 11 (§ 109(d)) but not under Chapter 7 (§ 109 (b)(1)). Brokerages, on the other hand, may not reorganize under Chapter 11, but may liquidate under special provisions in Chapter 7. §§ 741 et seq.

Most debtors who file in bankruptcy are insolvent, but insolvency, which is defined in § 101(32), is not necessary. For individuals, access to Chapter 7 bankruptcy may be limited by the "means test" described in Chapter 9 of these materials.

## 4.  THE PETITION IN BANKRUPTCY AND THE AUTOMATIC STAY

Voluntary bankruptcy, or a "voluntary case" as it is called in the Bankruptcy Code, is commenced by the debtor's filing a petition in bankruptcy in the bankruptcy court. § 301. In addition to the petition, the debtor must file various statements and schedules of information including a statement of assets and liabilities with descriptions of each and a list of creditors identified by name and address.

The filing of the petition in bankruptcy results in an automatic stay against a variety of acts that might otherwise be taken against the debtor or with respect to property of the bankruptcy estate. § 362. The automatic stay bars: the commencement or continuation of judicial proceedings against the debtor to recover a prebankruptcy claim; the enforcement of any prebankruptcy judgment against the debtor or against property of the estate; any act to obtain possession of property of the estate or property held by the estate; and any act to create, perfect or enforce any lien against property of the estate. The stay even applies to informal acts to collect a prebankruptcy debt such as dunning letters, telephone calls and the like. There are some exceptions to the very broad scope of the stay, but the stay effectively insulates the debtor from any kind of action to collect prebankruptcy debts. A creditor can get relief from the stay in some cases, but the effect of the stay is to require all collection action to be made through the bankruptcy court. The importance of the automatic stay cannot be over-emphasized. Frequently the primary purpose of the filing of a bankruptcy petition is to obtain the benefit of the stay.

## 5. THE TRUSTEE IN BANKRUPTCY

In a Chapter 7 bankruptcy, the bankruptcy estate is administered by a trustee in bankruptcy who can be either an individual or a corporation. § 321. The duties of the trustee are listed in § 704. The principal role of the trustee is to collect the property of the estate, sell it, and use the proceeds to pay expenses and creditor claims. Collecting the property of the estate sometimes requires the trustee to recover property that was transferred by the debtor prior to bankruptcy in transactions that are avoidable in bankruptcy. The trustee's "avoiding powers" are among the most important aspects of bankruptcy. In asserting these powers the trustee acts primarily for the benefit of unsecured creditors. The trustee also has wide powers of investigation of the financial affairs of the debtor and may oppose discharge of the debtor if the circumstances warrant. The trustee may also examine the validity of claims of creditors and may oppose improper claims. The trustee, who must be a disinterested person, is a fiduciary although the Bankruptcy Code does not specify the nature of the fiduciary relationship. The trustee's duties, particularly those of collecting, holding and disposing of property of the estate, are exercised on behalf of creditors generally, but often the trustee must oppose some creditors to benefit others. Basically the job of the trustee is to maximize the assets available for payment to general unsecured creditors.

Promptly after a Chapter 7 case is commenced, an interim trustee in bankruptcy is appointed by the United States Trustee. In each district there is a panel of persons who are qualified to serve as trustees. The interim trustee is appointed from this panel. § 701. In most cases involving consumer debtors, the interim trustee becomes the permanent trustee, and in such cases is referred to as the panel trustee.

In Chapter 7 cases, § 326(a) states the maximum compensation that can be paid to the trustee in bankruptcy based on "all moneys" disbursed by the trustee after liquidating assets of the estate. The maximum fee schedule is: 25 percent on the first $5,000; 10 percent on any amount in excess of $5,000 but not in excess of $50,000; 5 percent on any amount in excess of $50,000 but not in excess of $1 million; and reasonable compensation not to exceed 3 percent of any amount in excess of $1 million. In "no-asset" cases the trustee is entitled to $60. The United States Trustee will serve as trustee in cases in which nobody is willing to serve as interim trustee.

The trustee in bankruptcy, with the court's approval, may employ professional persons such as attorneys and accountants to represent or assist the trustee in carrying out the trustee's duties, and may agree to pay reasonable compensation. §§ 327, 328. The court may also allow the trustee to personally perform the duties of attorney or accountant and to be paid for professional services rendered. § 327(d). Whether compensation is reasonable is to be judged by a variety of factors, § 330(a), including the cost of comparable services in nonbankruptcy cases. Since a large part of the work in administering the bankruptcy estate is done by professionals, the relatively generous payments for professional services allow the trustee's duties to be performed in spite of relatively low trustee's fees. Payments to the trustee and to professionals are administrative expenses that are paid from assets of the estate before payments to any unsecured creditors.

There is a trustee in bankruptcy in a case under Chapter 12 or Chapter 13, but the trustee's duties are somewhat different. The only property of the bankruptcy estate that normally comes into the hands of the trustee is the earnings of the debtor that are the source of the payments under the plan. The primary duty of the trustee is to disburse to creditors payments due under the plan. The trustee is either appointed by the bankruptcy court to serve in the particular case or is a "standing trustee" appointed by the court to act generally in Chapter 12 or Chapter 13 cases filed in the district. Normally, there is no trustee in bankruptcy in a Chapter 11 case. Rather, the debtor continues in possession of its property as a "debtor in possession" that exercises the powers of a trustee in bankruptcy. A trustee in bankruptcy is appointed in a Chapter 11 case only in unusual cases, such as those involving fraud or gross mismanagement by the debtor.

### 6. MEETING OF CREDITORS

A meeting of creditors, after notice to the debtor and the creditors, must be convened by the United States Trustee within a reasonable time after the filing of the petition in bankruptcy. § 341. The debtor is required to attend. § 343. One of the purposes of the meeting is to allow the creditors to examine the debtor under oath. The principal purposes of the examination are to determine the accuracy of the debtor's statement of assets, whether avoidable transfers of property have occurred, and whether there are any grounds for objecting to the discharge of the debtor. Because the examination may disclose facts that may bear on matters that may subsequently be presented to the bankruptcy court for judicial determination, the bankruptcy judge may not attend the meeting. § 341(c). The presiding officer at the meeting is the United States Trustee.

In a Chapter 7 bankruptcy, the other principal purpose of the meeting of creditors is to elect a permanent trustee in bankruptcy. § 702(b). Election is by the creditors, and voting is done on the basis of the amount of the claims. Not all claims qualify a creditor to vote. Creditors whose claims are secured or that are entitled to priority of payment over general creditors cannot vote on the basis of those claims. Furthermore, claims must be allowable, undisputed, liquidated and fixed. Conflicts of interest are also disqualifying; relatives or affiliates of the debtor as well as creditors with interests materially adverse to those of general creditors can't vote. Election of a trustee is permissible only if creditors holding at least 20% in amount of eligible claims request election. Election requires a majority of the claims voted, and at least 20% of the eligible claims must be voted. The 20% requirement is designed to prevent the election of a trustee in cases in which there is little creditor interest in election. Under previous law it sometimes happened that a trustee was elected by one creditor whose sole purpose was to provide fees for lawyers who would act as counsel for the trustee. If no trustee is elected, the interim trustee serves as trustee. In many Chapter 7 cases the debtor's schedule of assets will indicate that there are no substantial assets available for distribution to creditors. In many of these cases there is no incentive for creditors to file claims or to attend the meeting of creditors. The clerk will notify creditors when no bankruptcy dividend is likely.

## 7. CLAIMS IN BANKRUPTCY

A claim is the basis for a distribution from the bankruptcy estate. A "proof of claim," which is a written statement setting forth a creditor's claim, is normally filed by the creditor. § 501 and Bankruptcy Rule 3001. Creditor is defined by § 101(10) to mean an entity (which in turn is defined in § 101(15)) holding a claim that arose before the filing of the petition in a voluntary case. Thus, rights against the debtor that arise after bankruptcy are not treated as claims in bankruptcy. There are a few exceptions to this statement.

A claim can be paid only if it is "allowed." Allowance of a claim means simply that it has been recognized by the court as valid in the amount claimed. If there is a dispute concerning a claim, the court must determine whether the claim should be allowed. Section 502 contains detailed provisions governing allowance and disallowance.

Claims are classified as either secured or unsecured. Suppose the debtor owes Bank $20,000 and the debt is secured by a security interest in collateral of the debtor on which there are no other liens. The collateral, because it was owned by the debtor, is part of the bankruptcy estate. § 541(a)(1). If Bank's security interest is valid in bankruptcy, Bank has a secured claim to the extent its claim is covered by value of the collateral. To the extent the claim exceeds the value of the collateral, Bank has an unsecured claim. § 506(a)(1). For example, if the collateral has a value of $30,000, Bank is oversecured and has a secured claim of $20,000; if the collateral has a value of $15,000, Bank is undersecured, and it has a secured claim of $15,000 and an unsecured claim of $5,000. The value of the collateral is determined by the bankruptcy court.

## 8. DISTRIBUTION OF ASSETS TO UNSECURED CREDITORS

After all priority claims have been paid in their order of priority, distribution is made pursuant to § 726 to the remaining creditors. With some exceptions, these claims are paid on a pro rata basis to the extent of the property available. First to be paid are the ten priority claims set out in § 507(a) in the order of priority prescribed in that provision. The first priority is domestic support obligations, defined in § 101(14A). Second priority is administrative expenses described in § 503. Other priority claims are ranked in an ever-growing list of additional categories by § 507(a)(3)-(10). The most important are certain claims of employees of the debtor that have a fourth and fifth priority and taxes with an eighth priority.

The § 507 priorities also apply to cases under Chapters 11, 12 and 13. Under Chapters 12 and 13, the plan must provide for payment in full of all priority claims, but deferred payment can be made, with interest, over the period of the plan. A Chapter 11 plan must provide for payment in full of all priority claims. Some priority claims must be paid in cash on the effective date of the plan and some can be paid, with interest, over time.

## 9. DISCHARGE

In a Chapter 7 bankruptcy, a debtor who is an individual will normally receive a discharge from pre-bankruptcy debts. § 727(b). For individuals, the primary purpose of filing a petition in Chapter 7 is to obtain this discharge. In some cases, however, the debtor is not entitled to a discharge. The various grounds for denying a discharge to a debtor in Chapter 7 are set forth in § 727(a). A debtor is not entitled to a discharge if the debtor has received a discharge under Chapter 7 in a case commenced within six years of the time the current case was commenced. The other grounds stated for denying discharge refer to misconduct by the debtor. This reflects the fact that bankruptcy is an equitable proceeding and that a debtor guilty of certain inequitable conduct should not enjoy the benefit of a discharge. Even in cases in which the debtor is entitled to discharge, not all debts are dischargeable. Discharge is a benefit to the debtor and a concomitant loss to the creditor. While a debtor is generally entitled to a discharge of prepetition debts, in some cases the creditor may have equities that are greater than those of the debtor. In those cases, the law provides that a debt of that creditor is nondischargeable. In effect, that creditor can participate in the distribution of the debtor's property, but, to the extent the creditor's debt has not been satisfied, the creditor will have a claim against the debtor that survives bankruptcy. Debts that are excepted from a Chapter 7 discharge are described in § 523(a). Chapters 11, 12 and 13 have their own discharge provisions. Corporations and partnerships may be discharged in Chapter 11 and Chapter 12, but not in Chapter 7. The Chapter 11 discharge for non-individual debtors is extremely broad and is not subject to the special exceptions to dischargeability applicable under § 523(a).

# CHAPTER 2

# THE BANKRUPTCY ESTATE

## A. INTRODUCTION

Commencing a bankruptcy case creates a bankruptcy estate. Section 541, which defines the estate, applies both to Chapter 7 liquidations and to reorganizations and rehabilitations under Chapters 11, 12 and 13. With respect to cases under Chapters 12 and 13, however, the bankruptcy estate is augmented by earnings and other property acquired by the debtor after commencement of the case but before it is closed. §§ 1207, 1306. The special treatment of property of the estate in Chapter 13 is considered later in the book.

Section 541(a)(1), the basic provision, states that the estate is comprised of "all legal or equitable interests of the debtor in property as of the commencement of the case." There are a number of reasons why it is important to define the bankruptcy estate. First, the estate constitutes the pool of assets available to satisfy creditors' claims. Exclusions from the estate limit general creditors' right to share in the excluded assets. In the case of an individual who has filed in Chapter 7, an important corollary to § 541(a)(1) is that, as a general rule, property that is obtained after the start of bankruptcy is not property of the estate and thus is not available for the enforced payment of prebankruptcy claims. For an individual, the primary purpose of Chapter 7 bankruptcy is to insulate after-acquired property from the collection of prebankruptcy debts. This time-honored purpose of the bankruptcy law is referred to as the "fresh start" principle. It was articulated by the Supreme Court in *Local Loan Co. v. Hunt*, 292 U.S. 234, 244 (1934) as follows:

> One [of] the primary purposes of the bankruptcy act is to "relieve the honest debtor from the weight of oppressive indebtedness and permit him to start afresh free from the obligations and responsibilities consequent upon business misfortunes." *Williams v. U.S. Fidelity & Guaranty Co.*, 236 U.S. 549, 554–555. This purpose of the act has been again and again emphasized by the courts as being of public as well as private interest, in that it gives to the honest but unfortunate debtor who surrenders for distribution the property which he owns *at the time of bankruptcy*, a new opportunity in life and a clear field for future effort, unhampered by the pressure and discouragement of preexisting debt.

Second, the definition of property of the estate is also important with respect to the automatic stay of § 362. In the case of an individual who files in bankruptcy, property of the estate includes all property that the debtor owned at the time of filing, but some or all of that property may lose its status as property of the estate when it is claimed by the debtor as exempt property under § 522 or when it is "abandoned" or released to the debtor under § 554. If the debtor receives property under § 522 or § 554, the property becomes property of the debtor. During the bankruptcy case, § 362 prevents third parties from taking any action to recover property of the estate without obtaining prior permission of the bankruptcy court, and with respect to prebankruptcy debts, the same protection is given to property of the debtor as well. For example, with respect to property that is subject to a security interest or other lien, § 362(a)(4) applies to property of the estate and § 362(a)(5) applies to property of the debtor.

Sometimes property of the estate is not in the possession of the debtor at the time of bankruptcy, but rather is in the hands of a third party such as a creditor. In that case § 542(a) allows the trustee in bankruptcy to recover possession of that property for the benefit of the estate if the trustee can "use, sell or lease" the property under § 363(b)(1) or (c)(1). Under § 542(a), the trustee may also recover property of the estate for the benefit of the debtor if the property may be claimed by the debtor as exempt property under § 522.

To a limited extent, property of the estate can also include some property of the debtor transferred before the start of bankruptcy and some property that was acquired by the debtor after the start of bankruptcy. This property is described in § 541(a)(3)—(7).

## B. DIVIDED PROPERTY INTERESTS AND POSSESSION AT TIME OF BANKRUPTCY

Section § 541(a)(1) gives the bankruptcy estate whatever beneficial rights in property the debtor had at the time bankruptcy was initiated. Section 541(a)(1) refers to "legal or equitable interests of the debtor in property." The usual metaphor for this legal principle is that the bankruptcy trustee "steps into the shoes" of the debtor. For example, if the debtor was the lessee of Blackacre the leasehold becomes part of the bankruptcy estate, but title to Blackacre does not. Suppose that at the time of initiation of bankruptcy the debtor possessed a chattel owned by X but had no proprietary interests in it. The debtor's possession might arise because X delivered the chattel for temporary safekeeping, or the debtor's possession might be wrongful as in the case of theft or conversion. In neither case does the chattel become part of the bankruptcy estate. In the latter case possession was wrongful. In the former case possession was lawful but it was not held by the debtor pursuant to a property right in the chattel. But even though the chattel does not become property of the estate, the debtor's possession has bankruptcy significance. Although the chattel remains the property of X, it falls under the jurisdiction of the bankruptcy court. Section 362(a)(3) automatically stays acts to obtain property *of* the estate but it also applies to acts to obtain property *from* the estate. Thus, X cannot lawfully take possession of the chattel unless it is voluntarily surrendered or unless X obtains relief from the automatic stay. § 362(d).

In some cases both the debtor and some other person each have a property interest in the same personal or real property. A very common example is with respect to property owned by one person subject to a security interest or other lien held by another. In the typical case, the lien is in property to which the bankruptcy debtor holds the legal title. But sometimes the property is owned by somebody else, and the bankruptcy debtor is the lienholder. In the latter case only the lien becomes part of the bankruptcy estate. The trustee in bankruptcy can assert rights as a secured creditor under the applicable nonbankruptcy law with respect to the lien and the debt secured by the lien. The analysis is more complex if the bankruptcy debtor is the owner of the property rather than the lienholder. In the typical case the bankruptcy debtor is in default on the debt that is secured by the lien and, under the applicable nonbankruptcy law, the lienholder has the right to take possession of the collateral, to sell it, and to apply the proceeds of sale to payment of the debt. Under the applicable nonbankruptcy law, after the creditor takes possession upon default, the debtor may have no right to the collateral other than the right to redeem it by paying the debt owed to the creditor and the right to any surplus proceeds upon sale. Under § 541(a)(1), does the collateral in possession of the creditor become property of the estate or does the estate acquire only the debtor's "legal or equitable interests" in the property, i.e. the right under the nonbankruptcy law to recover the collateral by paying the debt? That is the issue decided in *Whiting Pools*, the case that follows.

## United States v. Whiting Pools, Inc.

Supreme Court of the United States, 1983.
462 U.S. 198.

■ Justice BLACKMUN delivered the opinion of the Court.

Promptly after the Internal Revenue Service (IRS or Service) seized respondent's property to satisfy a tax lien, respondent filed a petition for reorganization under the Bankruptcy Reform Act of 1978, hereinafter referred to as the "Bankruptcy Code." The issue before us is whether § 542(a) of that Code authorized the Bankruptcy Court to subject the IRS to a turnover order with respect to the seized property.

### I

Respondent Whiting Pools, Inc., a corporation, sells, installs, and services swimming pools and related equipment and supplies. As of January 1981, Whiting owed approximately $92,000 in Federal Insurance Contribution Act taxes and federal taxes withheld from its employees, but had failed to respond to assessments and demands for payment by the IRS. As a consequence, a tax lien in that amount attached to all of Whiting's property.[1]

On January 14, 1981, the Service seized Whiting's tangible personal property—equipment, vehicles, inventory, and office supplies—pursuant to the levy and distraint provision of the Internal Revenue Code of 1954.[2] According to uncontroverted findings, the estimated liquidation value of the property seized was, at most, $35,000, but its estimated going-concern value in Whiting's hands was $162,876. The very next day, January 15, Whiting filed a petition for reorganization, under the Bankruptcy Code's Chapter 11 in the United States Bankruptcy Court for the Western District of New York. Whiting was continued as debtor-in-possession.[3]

The United States, intending to proceed with a tax sale of the property,[4] moved in the Bankruptcy Court for a declaration that the automatic stay provision of the Bankruptcy Code, § 362(a), is inapplicable to the IRS or, in the alternative, for relief from the stay. Whiting counterclaimed for an order requiring the Service to turn the seized property over to the bankruptcy estate pursuant to § 542(a) of the Bankruptcy Code. Whiting intended to use the property in its reorganized business.

The Bankruptcy Court determined that the IRS was bound by the automatic stay provision. Because it found that the seized property was essential to Whiting's reorganization effort, it refused to lift the stay. * * * [T]he court directed the IRS to turn the property over to Whiting on the

---

[1] Section 6321 of the Internal Revenue Code of 1954 provides: "If any person liable to pay any tax neglects or refuses to pay the same after demand, the amount * * * shall be a lien in favor of the United States upon all property and rights to property, whether real or personal, belonging to such person."

[2] Section 6331 of that Code provides:

"(a) Authority of Secretary

"If any person liable to pay any tax neglects or refuses to pay the same within 10 days after notice and demand, it shall be lawful for the Secretary to collect such tax (and such further sum as shall be sufficient to cover the expenses of the levy) by levy upon all property and rights to property * * * belonging to such person or on which there is a lien provided in this chapter for the payment of such tax * * *.

"(b) Seizure and sale of property

"The term 'levy' as used in this title includes the power of distraint and seizure by any means * * *. In any case in which the Secretary may levy upon property or rights to property, he may seize and sell such property or rights to property (whether real or personal, tangible or intangible)."

[3] With certain exceptions not relevant here, a debtor-in-possession, such as Whiting, performs the same functions as a trustee in a reorganization. § 1107(a).

[4] Section 6335, as amended, of the 1954 Code provides for the sale of seized property after notice. The taxpayer is entitled to any surplus of the proceeds of the sale. § 6342(b).

condition that Whiting provide the Service with specified protection for its interests. * * *

The United States District Court reversed, holding that a turnover order against the Service was not authorized by either § 542(a) or § 543(b)(1). The United States Court of Appeals for the Second Circuit, in turn, reversed the District Court. It held that a turnover order could issue against the Service under § 542(a), and it remanded the case for reconsideration of the adequacy of the Bankruptcy Court's protection conditions. The Court of Appeals acknowledged that its ruling was contrary to that reached by the United States Court of Appeals for the Fourth Circuit and noted confusion on the issue among bankruptcy and district courts. * * * We granted certiorari to resolve this conflict in an important area of the law under the new Bankruptcy Code. * * *

## II

By virtue of its tax lien, the Service holds a secured interest in Whiting's property. We first examine whether § 542(a) of the Bankruptcy Code generally authorizes the turnover of a debtor's property seized by a secured creditor prior to the commencement of reorganization proceedings. Section 542(a) requires an entity in possession of "property that the trustee may use, sell, or lease under § 363" to deliver that property to the trustee. Subsections (b) and (c) of § 363 authorize the trustee to use, sell, or lease any "property of the estate," subject to certain conditions for the protection of creditors with an interest in the property. Section 541(a)(1) defines the "estate" as "comprised of all the following property, wherever located: (1) * * * all legal or equitable interests of the debtor in property as of the commencement of the case." Although these statutes could be read to limit the estate to those "interests of the debtor in property" at the time of the filing of the petition, we view them as a definition of what is included in the estate, rather than as a limitation.

In proceedings under the reorganization provisions of the Bankruptcy Code, a troubled enterprise may be restructured to enable it to operate successfully in the future. Until the business can be reorganized pursuant to a plan under [Chapter 11], the trustee or debtor-in-possession is authorized to manage the property of the estate and to continue the operation of the business. See § 1108. By permitting reorganization, Congress anticipated that the business would continue to provide jobs, to satisfy creditors' claims, and to produce a return for its owners. * * * Congress presumed that the assets of the debtor would be more valuable if used in a rehabilitated business than if "sold for scrap." * * * The reorganization effort would have small chance of success, however, if property essential to running the business were excluded from the estate. * * * Thus, to facilitate the rehabilitation of the debtor's business, all the debtor's property must be included in the reorganization estate.

This authorization extends even to property of the estate in which a creditor has a secured interest. § 363(b) and (c) * * *. Although Congress might have safeguarded the interests of secured creditors outright by excluding from the estate any property subject to a secured interest, it chose instead to include such property in the estate and to provide secured creditors with "adequate protection" for their interests. § 363(e) * * *. At the secured creditor's insistence, the bankruptcy court must place such limits or conditions on the trustee's power to sell, use, or lease property as are necessary to protect the creditor. The creditor with a secured interest in property included in the estate must look to this provision for protection, rather than to the nonbankruptcy remedy of possession.

Both the congressional goal of encouraging reorganizations and Congress' choice of methods to protect secured creditors suggest that Congress intended a broad range of property to be included in the estate.

The statutory language reflects this view of the scope of the estate. As noted above, § 541(a) provides that the "estate is comprised of all the following property, wherever located: * * * all legal or equitable interests of the debtor in property as of the commencement of the case." § 541(a)(1).[8] The House and Senate Reports on the Bankruptcy Code indicate that § 541(a)(1)'s scope is broad.[9] Most important, in the context of this case, § 541(a)(1) is intended to include in the estate any property made available to the estate by other provisions of the Bankruptcy Code. * * * Several of these provisions bring into the estate property in which the debtor did not have a possessory interest at the time the bankruptcy proceedings commenced.[10]

---

[8] Section 541(a)(1) speaks in terms of the debtor's "interests * * * in property," rather than property in which the debtor has an interest, but this choice of language was not meant to limit the expansive scope of the section. The legislative history indicates that Congress intended to exclude from the estate property of others in which the debtor had some minor interest such as a lien or bare legal title. * * * cf. § 541(d) (property in which debtor holds legal but not equitable title, such as a mortgage in which debtor retained legal title to service or to supervise servicing of mortgage, becomes part of estate only to extent of legal title); 124 Cong.Rec. 33999 (1978) (remarks of Sen. De-Concini) (§ 541(d) "reiterates the general principle that where the debtor holds bare legal title without any equitable interest, * * * the estate acquires bare legal title without any equitable interest in the property"). Similar statements to the effect that § 541(a)(1) does not expand the rights of the debtor in the hands of the estate were made in the context of describing the principle that the estate succeeds to no more or greater causes of action against third parties than those held by the debtor. * * * These statements do not limit the ability of a trustee to regain possession of property in which the debtor had equitable as well as legal title.

[9] "The scope of this paragraph [§ 541(a)(1)] is broad. It includes all kinds of property, including tangible or intangible property, causes of action (see Bankruptcy Act § 70a(6)), and all other forms of property currently specified in section 70a of the Bankruptcy Act." H.R.Rep. No. 95–595, p. 367 (1977); S.Rep. No. 95–989, p. 82 (1978).

[10] See, e.g., §§ 543, 547, and 548. These sections permit the trustee to demand the turnover of property that is in the possession of others if that possession is due to a

Section 542(a) is such a provision. It requires an entity (other than a custodian) holding any property of the debtor that the trustee can use under § 363 to turn that property over to the trustee.[11] Given the broad scope of the reorganization estate, property of the debtor repossessed by a secured creditor falls within this rule, and therefore may be drawn into the estate. While there are explicit limitations on the reach of § 542(a),[12] none requires that the debtor hold a possessory interest in the property at the commencement of the reorganization proceedings.

As does all bankruptcy law, § 542(a) modifies the procedural rights available to creditors to protect and satisfy their liens.[14] * * * In effect, § 542(a) grants to the estate a possessory interest in certain property of the debtor that was not held by the debtor at the commencement of reorganization proceedings.[15] The Bankruptcy Code provides secured creditors various rights, including the right to adequate protection, and these rights replace the protection afforded by possession.

---

custodial arrangement, § 543, to a preferential transfer, § 547, or to a fraudulent transfer, § 548. * * *

[11] The House Report expressly includes property of the debtor recovered under § 542(a) in the estate: the estate includes "property recovered by the trustee under section 542 * * *, if the property recovered was merely out of the possession of the debtor, yet remained 'property of the debtor.' " H.R.Rep. No. 95–595, p. 367 (1977) * * *.

[12] Section 542 provides that the property be usable under § 363, and that turnover is not required in three situations: when the property is of inconsequential value or benefit to the estate, § 542(a), when the holder of the property has transferred it in good faith without knowledge of the petition, § 542(c), or when the transfer of the property is automatic to pay a life insurance premium, § 542(d).

[14] One of the procedural rights the law of secured transactions grants a secured creditor to enforce its lien is the right to take possession of the secured property upon the debtor's default. Uniform Commercial Code § 9-503. A creditor's possessory interest resulting from the exercise of this right is subject to certain restrictions on the creditor's use of the property. See § 9-504. Here, we address the abrogation of the Service's possessory interest obtained pursuant to its tax lien, a secured interest. We do not decide whether any property of the debtor in which a third party holds a possessory interest independent of a creditor's remedies is subject to turnover under § 542(a). For example, if property is pledged to the secured creditor so that the creditor has possession prior to any default, 542(a) may not require turnover. See 4 L. King, Collier on Bankruptcy § 541.08[9], p. 541–53 (15th ed.1982).

[15] Indeed, if this were not the effect, § 542(a) would be largely superfluous in light of § 541(a)(1). Interests in the seized property that could have been exercised by the debtor—in this case, the rights to notice and the surplus from a tax sale, see n. 4, supra—are already part of the estate by virtue of § 541(a)(1). No coercive power is needed for this inclusion. The fact that § 542(a) grants the trustee greater rights than those held by the debtor prior to the filing of the petition is consistent with other provisions of the Bankruptcy Code that address the scope of the estate. See, e.g., § 544 (trustee has rights of lien creditor); § 545 (trustee has power to avoid statutory liens); § 549 (trustee has power to avoid certain post-petition transactions).

This interpretation of § 542(a) is supported by the section's legislative history. Although the legislative reports are silent on the precise issue before us, the House and Senate hearings from which § 542(a) emerged provide guidance. Several witnesses at those hearings noted, without contradiction, the need for a provision authorizing the turnover of property of the debtor in the possession of secured creditors. Section 542(a) first appeared in the proposed legislation shortly after these hearings. * * * The section remained unchanged through subsequent versions of the legislation.

Moreover, this interpretation of § 542 in the reorganization context is consistent with judicial precedent predating the Bankruptcy Code. Under Chapter X, the reorganization chapter of the Bankruptcy Act of 1898, * * * the bankruptcy court could order the turnover of collateral in the hands of a secured creditor. * * * Nothing in the legislative history evinces a congressional intent to depart from that practice. Any other interpretation of § 542(a) would deprive the bankruptcy estate of the assets and property essential to its rehabilitation effort and thereby would frustrate the congressional purpose behind the reorganization provisions.[17]

We conclude that the reorganization estate includes property of the debtor that has been seized by a creditor prior to the filing of a petition for reorganization.

### III

We see no reason why a different result should obtain when the IRS is the creditor. The Service is bound by § 542(a) to the same extent as any other secured creditor. * * *

Of course, if a tax levy or seizure transfers to the IRS ownership of the property seized, § 542(a) may not apply. The enforcement provisions of the Internal Revenue Code of 1954 do grant to the Service powers to enforce its tax liens that are greater than those possessed by private secured creditors under state law. * * * But those provisions do not transfer ownership of the property to the IRS.

The Service's interest in seized property is its lien on that property. The Internal Revenue Code's levy and seizure provisions are special procedural devices available to the IRS to protect and satisfy its liens, * * * and are analogous to the remedies available to private secured creditors. See Uniform Commercial Code § 9-503, n. 14, supra. They are provisional remedies that do not determine the Service's rights to the seized property, but merely bring the property into the Service's legal custody. * * * The IRS is obligated to return to the debtor any surplus from a sale. 26 U.S.C. § 6342(b). Ownership of the property is transferred only when the prop-

---

[17] Section 542(a) also governs turnovers in liquidation and individual adjustment of debt proceedings under Chapters 7 and 13 of the Bankruptcy Code * * *. See § 103(a). Our analysis in this case depends in part on the reorganization context in which the turnover order is sought. We express no view on the issue whether § 542(a) has the same broad effect in liquidation or adjustment of debt proceedings.

erty is sold to a bona fide purchaser at a tax sale. * * * In fact, the tax sale provision itself refers to the debtor as the owner of the property after the seizure but prior to the sale. Until such a sale takes place, the property remains the debtor's and thus is subject to the turnover requirement of § 542(a).

**IV**

When property seized prior to the filing of a petition is drawn into the Chapter 11 reorganization estate, the Service's tax lien is not dissolved; nor is its status as a secured creditor destroyed. The IRS, under § 363(e), remains entitled to adequate protection for its interests, to other rights enjoyed by secured creditors, and to the specific privileges accorded tax collectors. Section 542(a) simply requires the Service to seek protection of its interest according to the congressionally established bankruptcy procedures, rather than by withholding the seized property from the debtor's efforts to reorganize.

The judgment of the Court of Appeals is affirmed.

## NOTES

**1.** In 1984 the phrase "and by whomever held" was added at the end of the introductory paragraph of § 541(a). This makes explicit the point made by Justice Blackmun in *Whiting Pools* that property of the estate includes property of the debtor lawfully held by a third party under claim of right. The majority view continues to follow *Whiting Pools* in allowing debtors to compel a secured creditor to return repossessed property provided the creditor's interest in the collateral is adequately protected and the debtor has more than a minor interest in the property. For the meaning of the phrase "more than a minor interest," *see*, e.g., *In re Chiodo*, 250 B.R. 407 (Bankr.M.D.Fla.2000).

**2.** Thomas E. Plank, *The Outer Boundaries of the Bankruptcy Estate*, 47 Emory L. J. 1193 (1998), views *Whiting Pools* as a fundamental misreading of § 541(a)(1). In a detailed analysis, Professor Plank agrees with the government's position that under the statute Whiting Pools had no interest in the property after seizure by the IRS other than a right to notice of sale, a right of redemption and a right to any surplus proceeds. Under this argument, only these rights became property of the estate, and since these rights do not include the right to possession, a trustee in bankruptcy is not entitled to turnover under § 542(a). This interpretation finds support in the language of § 541(a)(1), and *In re Lewis*, 137 F.3d 1280 (11th Cir. 1998), takes this view. What is the basis of the Court's rejection of this view? The conflicting views are discussed in Stephen J. Ware, *Security Interests, Repossessed Collateral, and Turnover of Property to the Bankruptcy Estate*, 2 Utah L. Rev. 775 (2002).

**3.** In *Whiting Pools* the debtor in possession alleged that the property to which the turnover order applied was necessary for the reorganization of the debtor under Chapter 11. In footnote 17 the Court reserved judgment on whether § 542(a) applied to the same extent in a Chapter 7 liquidation case as it did in Chapter 11 reorganizations. There is no basis in the statute for limiting § 542(a) to Chapter 11. That section authorizes turnover orders against third parties in possession in cases in which the trustee may "use, sell or lease" the property recovered. The function of a trustee in Chapter 7 is to gather the property of the estate, liquidate it and distribute the proceeds to creditors. Pursuant to this function, § 542(a) allows a trustee to recover property of the estate in possession of others and sell it, so long as the trustee has the power under § 363 to sell the property recovered. Thus, a Chapter 7 trustee may sell free of the lien of a UCC Article 9 secured party who has repossessed collateral that is property of the estate under § 363(f)(3), if the debtor has an equity in the property (the value of the collateral exceeds the amount of the debt) and the creditor's security interest is adequately protected under § 363(e). Adequate protection may consist of giving the secured party a lien on the proceeds of the sale to the extent of the debt owed. If the debtor does not have an equity in the collateral held by the secured party, there is no point to the trustee's recovering the property and selling it because there is no benefit to the estate. A Chapter 7 trustee normally abandons property that has no value to the estate, § 554, and the secured party is allowed to proceed against the abandoned property under state law in satisfaction of its claim. This analysis should also resolve the question left open in footnote 14 on whether § 542(a) allows turnover if the property of the estate is in possession of a creditor under a pledge agreement that allows the pledgee to retain possession of the property until the debt is paid. *In re Gerwer*, 898 F.2d 730 (9th Cir.1990), responds to both footnotes 14 and 17 of *Whiting Pools*. It held that a Chapter 7 trustee can employ § 542(a) to obtain possession of collateral held by a pledgee. It rejected the contrary opinion expressed in *Collier on Bankruptcy* cited in footnote 14 of *Whiting Pools*. Later in the course, we will consider the impact of the automatic stay under § 362 in cases in which creditors hold property of the estate.

## C. CONTINGENT RIGHTS TO PAYMENT

### In re Ryerson
United States Court of Appeals, Ninth Circuit, 1984.
739 F.2d 1423.

■ CANBY, Circuit Judge:

Ryerson appeals from a decision of by the Bankruptcy Appellate Panel. The panel determined that money to which Ryerson became entitled upon the termination of his employment, some eight months following the filing of his petition in bankruptcy, should be included with the bankruptcy estate.

On January 12, 1977, Ryerson entered into an Appointment Agreement with the Farmers Insurance Company of Arizona appointing him to the position of District Manager for District 25. The Agreement provided that in the event of cancellation or other termination of the appointment "the Companies may at their option elect to pay 'contract value,' as hereinafter defined, to the District Manager." "Contract value" was defined as the service commission overwrite paid to the District Manager during the six months immediately preceding termination times a factor determined by the number of years of service as District Manager. Nothing was payable until the District Manager had served one full year. The Agreement further provided that as a condition precedent to the District Manager's right to receive "contract value" he must be in good standing with the Companies on the date of his termination and that he not have been guilty of certain specified forms of misconduct. Termination occurred upon the death of the District Manager, and the contract could be cancelled by either party without cause upon 30 days written notice.

Ryerson filed a chapter 7 bankruptcy proceeding on February 10, 1981. His appointment as District Manager for the Farmers Insurance Group terminated on November 1, 1981. The "contract value" on the date of termination was determined to be $18,588, which has not yet been paid to the debtor. Ryerson sought a declaratory judgment from the bankruptcy court declaring that this sum was not property of the bankruptcy estate.

The old Bankruptcy Act provided that all "rights of action arising upon contracts" passed to the trustee in bankruptcy. The current Bankruptcy Code defines the bankrupt estate as consisting of "all legal or equitable interests of the debtor in property as of the commencement of the case." § 541(a)(1). Among the debtor's legal interests that become a part of the bankruptcy estate under the Code are his choses in action and claims against third parties as of the commencement of the case. * * * These choses in action and claims clearly include rights of action based upon contract. * * *

Under the Appointment Agreement, the contract has value upon termination or cancellation after the District Manager completes one year of service in that position. At the time this case was commenced, Ryerson had served four full years as District Manager. He therefore had accumulated value to which he was entitled upon termination or cancellation of his Appointment Agreement. The debtor nevertheless argues that at the time of the filing of the bankruptcy petition his appointment had not yet been terminated or cancelled and that therefore he had no claim to the "contract value." He asserts that an unvested, contingent interest is not includable within the bankruptcy estate if it cannot be transferred by the debtor or levied upon or otherwise reached by the debtor's creditors. Under the Act, a contingent interest in personal property passed to the trustee only if it was capable of being assigned or was subject to execution, seizure, or sequestration. * * * However, the requirement that the debtor must be able to transfer the interest or that his creditors by some means must be able to reach it has been eliminated under the Code. * * * By including all legal interests without exception, Congress indicated its intention to include all legally recognizable interests although they may be contingent and not subject to possession until some future time. * * * We therefore conclude that Ryerson's interest in the "contract value," albeit contingent at the time of filing and not payable until such time as his appointment is terminated or cancelled, is includable within the bankruptcy estate pursuant to section 541(a)(1).[1]

Having concluded that Ryerson's right to "contract value" is property of the bankruptcy estate, we have no difficulty concluding that any payments paid upon termination of Ryerson's appointment are also property of the bankruptcy estate although paid after commencement of the case, at least to the extent the payments are related to prebankruptcy services. Section 541(a)(6) of the Code includes in the bankruptcy estate after-acquired property consisting of "[p]roceeds, product, offspring, rents, and profits of or from property of the estate, except such as are earnings from services performed by an individual debtor after the commencement of the case." § 541(a)(6). It follows therefore that earnings from services performed prior to bankruptcy are includable within the bankruptcy estate. Under the Act, the test was whether the after-acquired property was "sufficiently rooted in the prebankruptcy past and so little entangled in the debtor's ability to make a fresh start that it should not be excluded from property of the estate." *Segal v. Rochelle*, 382 U.S. 375, 380 (1966). The Code follows *Segal* insofar as it includes after-acquired property "sufficiently rooted in the pre-bankruptcy past" but eliminates the requirement that it not be entangled with the debtor's ability to make a fresh start. See S.Rep. No. 989, supra at 82. We think that the termination payments representing value for years of service completed prior to bankruptcy, and not being an arbitrary amount arising after bankruptcy, are "sufficiently rooted in the pre-bankruptcy past" as to be included within the bankruptcy estate. * * *

Our ruling does not necessarily mean that all of the $18,588 is property of the bankruptcy estate. The Bankruptcy Appellate Panel determined that only the debtor's interest at the time of bankruptcy is property of the

---

[1] The debtor makes much of the fact that "contract value" is payable only at the option of the Company. Even if the payment of the "contract value" were truly optional, the fact that the contingency may not occur would not render the debtor's interest unenforceable at common law. It is the nature of a contingent interest that it may never take effect in possession because of the failure of the specified event to occur. 2 Powell on Real Property § 274 (1950). However, Ryerson's right to the "contract value" is not truly contingent. First, the termination or cancellation of the appointment is an event certain to occur. Therefore, Ryerson's right to the "contract value" is not made contingent by the fact that the appointment had not yet terminated at the time of bankruptcy filing. Second, the fact that the Company may elect not to pay the "contract value" does not necessarily have the effect of denying him the right to collect it: the Appointment Agreement permits Ryerson to recover the "contract value" from his successor in the event that the Company elects not to pay it. We therefore attach no significance to the fact that payment of the "contract value" is stated to be at the option of the Company.

estate; any interest attributable to post-filing services was expressly excluded from the estate. We agree. Section 541(a)(6) excludes from the estate "earnings from services performed by an individual debtor after the commencement of the case." Thus any portion of the $18,588 related to services performed after February 10, 1981 are not includable within the bankruptcy estate.

The judgment of the Bankruptcy Appellate Panel is therefore affirmed.

## NOTE

As we see in *Ryerson*, some of a debtor's rights to payment are beyond the reach of creditors because they are not property of the estate, e.g., postpetition earnings under § 541(a)(6). Other rights to payment, though within the bankruptcy estate, may be claimed as exempt property by the debtor, e.g. the debtor's right to receive social security, unemployment, disability and welfare benefits; veterans' benefits; and, to the extent necessary for the support of the debtor and dependents, support and maintenance payments, pensions, annuities, and insurance payments. § 522(d)(10). We will discuss exemptions later in this Chapter.

## PROBLEM

Debtor is employed at a salary of $2,000 per month. Debtor's employer withheld income tax at the rate of $400 a month. Debtor filed a petition in Chapter 7 on August 1 and continued employment at the same salary and the same withholding for the remainder of the year. Debtor filed a tax return in March of the following year. Debtor had no income other than the $24,000 of salary and the total tax payable was $4,500. Since Debtor's employer had withheld $4,800 during the year, Debtor received a tax refund of $300 in April. To what part of the refund is the trustee in bankruptcy entitled?

## D. EXEMPT PROPERTY

### 1. INTRODUCTION

We have seen that the property of a judgment debtor can be seized and sold to satisfy the judgment. There are, however, some limitations on this right of the judgment creditor. Both state and federal law protect certain property of individuals from claims of creditors. These laws are usually referred to as exemption laws and the protected property is called exempt property. This law, with one large exception, is primarily a matter of state law. The exception is wage garnishment which is primarily protected by federal law. Although there is general consensus that individual debtors should be permitted to retain some property as exempt from creditor claims, widely varying state law suggests that there is little consensus on how much or what kinds of property should be exempt.

A creditor seeking payment of a judgment against an individual often looks to the debtor's wages as the best source of payment. The creditor garnishes the debtor's wages by directing the sheriff or other levying officer to serve a document on the debtor's employer directing payment of the debtor's wages to the levying officer for the benefit of the creditor. Wage garnishment is a powerful collection device that is often onerous to the debtor, and it has been curtailed by both court decision and legislation. On due process grounds, *Sniadach v. Family Finance Corp.*, 395 U.S. 337 (1969), prejudgment garnishment of wages has been eliminated as a normal creditor's remedy. Postjudgment garnishment has been severely limited legislatively by the Consumer Credit Protection Act, 15 U.S.C. §§ 1671–1677. With some exceptions, e.g., child and spouse support creditors, a creditor can garnish no more than 25 percent of the debtor's disposable earnings. Disposable earnings are defined as wages and similar earnings after deduction of amounts required by law to be withheld such as federal and state income taxes and social security taxes. More severe restrictions apply to debtors with very low incomes. The federal limitations represent the maximum amount of earnings that can be reached by creditors. State law may impose additional restrictions on wage garnishment. *See, e.g.*, Cal.Code Civ.Proc. § 706.051(b)(West 2000), which allows the debtor in some cases to protect any wages "necessary for the support of the judgment debtor or the judgment debtor's family supported in whole or in part by the judgment debtor."

Outside of bankruptcy and except for wage garnishment, state law is the primary source of protection of a debtor's property from the claims of creditors. However, most pensions and retirement accounts, social security benefits and some other federal payments are exempt from garnishment or attachment under federal law. The statutes of all of the states provide that some property of the individual debtor is exempt from execution. Some states allow the debtor to retain little more than the bare necessities of life. Other states allow the debtor to retain property of very substantial value.

State exemption laws define property that may not be seized by a creditor in the judicial debt collection process. These laws define property that can be protected from the imposition of a judicial lien, but exempt property is not exempt from claims of all creditors. Certain creditors that the state recognizes as having particularly meritorious claims may be able to seize property otherwise exempt. A very common example is a claim for spousal or child support. Exemption laws usually do not apply to enforcement of security interests and certain statutory liens. For example, the state exemption law may provide that the debtor's automobile is exempt property. The debtor could prevent a judgment creditor from levying on the automobile, but a creditor with a security interest in the automobile could seize it if the debtor defaulted on the debt secured by the security interest. By the same token, the exempt status of the automobile would not prevent an unpaid mechanic who performed work on the automobile from enforcing a garageman's lien in the automobile by resorting to the procedure for sale provided by the state statute.

Although the state exemption statutes vary widely in the type of property that is exempt, the following categories of property are frequently covered by exemption laws: the family residence and household furnishings, the clothing and personal effects of the debtor and the debtor's family, the family car, and the tools and other personal property used in the debtor's occupation. Since insurance on the life of the debtor is an important protection for the debtor's dependents, it is also frequently covered by exemption statutes. Within these categories there are usually dollar limitations on the amount of property that may be exempted. However, there are some glaring exceptions to this rule. For instance, in Florida, Iowa, Kansas, South Dakota and Texas, there is *no* ceiling on the amount of homestead exemptions. National Bankruptcy Review Commission Rep. at 299 (1997).

Although state exemption law is important in state proceedings in which a creditor is attempting to enforce a claim against the debtor, it is more commonly invoked in bankruptcy. When a debtor is unable to pay creditors and is faced with immediate or eventual execution against the debtor's property, the typical remedy sought is the protection of the bankruptcy law, with its automatic stay. Under the Bankruptcy Act, determination of the debtor's assets that were subject to distribution in bankruptcy was made according to the state law of exemptions. The result was a nonuniform bankruptcy law. Debtors from states with generous exemption laws were treated far better than debtors from states which granted minimal exemptions to their citizens.

Strong arguments were made in favor of a uniform system of exemptions provided by federal bankruptcy law itself that would override state exemption laws. This view was reflected in early versions of the Bankruptcy Code, which contained a schedule of exemptions falling between the extremes represented by state law. But opposition to a uniform system arose on the part of creditors who wanted to preserve the law in states that had low exemptions and consumers in states that had more generous ones. The result was the compromise that appears in § 522(b). Pursuant to subsection (b)(1), the debtor may elect either the schedule of federal exemptions under (b)(2), which includes those appearing in subsection (d), or, in the alternative, the state exemptions under subsection (b)(3). But the debtor's right to elect the more favorable schedule has been greatly restricted by § 522(b)(2), which allows any state to opt out of the federal exemptions by enacting a law taking away from its citizens the right to elect the § 522(d) exemptions. Thus, in the 34 opt-out states, each state determines its own schedule of exemptions and debtors are unable to elect the federal exemptions. *Collier on Bankruptcy* ¶ 522.02[1] (15th ed. rev. 2004). An important new qualification on the states' opt-out power is that the 2005 Act made retirement funds exempt under both federal and state law. § 522(b)(3)(C) and (d)(12).        Frequently, a husband and wife in bankruptcy have joint debts and own most of their property jointly. To accommodate that kind of situation, § 302 provides for the filing of a single petition for relief in bankruptcy by the husband and wife. This is known as a "joint case." Under the Bankruptcy Code, as originally enacted, one spouse could elect the § 522(b) exemptions and the other spouse the § 522(d) exemptions. By that device, it was possible to exempt more property than could be exempted if either system alone was used. In 1984, § 522(b) was amended to prohibit a split election in a joint case.

Insulation of exempt property from claims of creditors with respect to liability on prebankruptcy debts carries over to the postbankruptcy period. § 522(c). In a Chapter 7 case, an individual normally will receive a discharge under § 727(a) that relieves the debtor of personal liability on all prebankruptcy debts. § 727(b). But some debts are not dischargeable in bankruptcy. § 523(a). Section 522(c) applies to those debts. The creditor on a nondischargeable debt is entitled to share in the distribution of assets of the bankruptcy estate, and postbankruptcy assets of the debtor are also liable for payment of that debt. But, in general, exempt property is not available for distribution to creditors in bankruptcy, and by virtue of § 522(c) remains exempt after bankruptcy. An exception is found in § 522(c)(1), as amended by the 2005 Act, which provides that notwithstanding nonbankruptcy exemption laws, a debtor's postpetition assets remain liable for domestic support claims (§ 101(10A)).The primary effect of § 522(c) is to allow a debtor who claimed the federal exemptions under § 522(d) to preserve in the postbankruptcy period the status of the exempt property with respect to a claim to enforce the personal liability of the debtor on a nondischargeable debt.

## 2. Procedure for Claiming Exempt Property

Under the Bankruptcy Code, all the debtor's property is property of the estate until the debtor acts to exempt it under § 522(*l*) by filing "a list of property that the debtor claims as exempt under subsection (b)" of § 522. Rule 4003(a) requires the debtor to list the property claimed as exempt in the schedule of assets that is filed with the petition in bankruptcy or in some cases within 30 days of the date the petition is filed. Section 522(*l*) goes on to state: "Unless a party in interest objects, the property claimed as exempt on such list is exempt." Under Rule 4003(b), the trustee or creditors "may file an objection to the list of property claimed as exempt only within 30 days after" the § 341 meeting of creditors, which must be held not less than 20 nor more than 40 days after the petition is filed. Rule 2003(a). The objecting party has the burden of proving that exemptions are not properly claimed. Rule 4003(c).

What happens if a debtor lists property as exempt, even though there is no colorable basis for claiming the exemption, and there is no objection by a trustee or creditor within the required 30-day period? Some cases held that unless the debtor had a colorable basis for claiming the exemption, the 30-day limitation does not apply; otherwise debtors would be encouraged to claim meritless exemptions in the hope that no one would object. In *Taylor v. Freeland & Kronz*, 503 U.S. 638 (1992), the Court rejected this line of authority. Section 522(*l*) provides that unless a party in interest objects, the property claimed as exempt is automatically exempt, and Rule 4003(b) gives the parties 30 days from the initial creditors' meeting to object unless further time is granted by the court within that period. In the light of these provisions, the Court decided that it did not have the authority to limit § 522(*l*) to claims for exemptions having some colorable basis. "Deadlines may lead to unwelcome results, but they prompt parties to act and they produce finality." 503 U.S. at 644.

The strict deadline rule applies to debtors as well as trustees and creditors. Rule 4003(a) requires a debtor to file a list of property claimed as exempt within the time specified in Rule 1007 for filing the schedule of assets, and Rule 1007(c) sets this time as within 15 days after the petition is filed. In *Petit v. Fessenden*, 80 F.3d 29 (1st Cir.1996), the debtor was late in filing her schedules; the court, quoting the "deadlines" language from *Taylor*, held that the debtor could not rely on the failure of the trustee to object within the 30-day period of Rule 4003(b) for automatic allowance of the exemptions claimed. She cannot benefit from Rule 4003(b) unless she abides by Rule 1007(c).

## 3. RETIREMENT PLANS

A retirement plan may be a debtor's most valuable asset. Tax legislation increasing the maximum annual contributions that employees can make to tax-deferred retirement plans will increase the already vast pool of pension assets. A question that has plagued the courts since 1978 is the extent to which funds in retirement plans are available to creditors in bankruptcy. The 1978 Code mentioned retirement plans only in § 522(d)(10)(E), which, for purpose of federal exemptions under § 522(b)(2), exempts payments to a debtor under a retirement plan to the extent reasonably necessary for the support of the debtor and dependents. Although most states have opted out of the federal exemptions, some of these opt-out states have enacted statutes exempting retirement funds. Some courts used § 541(c)(3) to exclude employer-sponsored retirement plans from the debtor's estate in the common situation in which federal law, e.g., ERISA, prohibits the transfer of the employee's interest under the plan. *See, e.g., Patterson v. Shumate*, 504 U.S. 754 (1992).

On the eve of passage of the 2005 Act, it was clear that qualified employer-sponsored retirement plans were protected from creditors in bankruptcy by federal law. But there was a division of authority as to the exempt status of the hugely popular IRAs in bankruptcy. IRAs are investment accounts that are entirely funded by the contributions of individuals; the funds grow tax-deferred, and the contributions are in some instances deductible. They resemble tax-free bank accounts: the owner may withdraw funds at will, paying only a 10% penalty if withdrawal occurs before the age of 59 1/2. IRA funds are taxed as they are distributed; distributions must begin no later than the year the account holder turns 70 1/2. By the end of 2003, nearly $3 trillion was invested in IRAs, and this staggering amount grew significantly in 2004. Christopher Conkey & Rachel Emma Silverman, *High Court Rules IRAs Untouchable*, Wall St.J., April 5, 2005, at D1.

Exemption of IRAs is an especially important issue because of the use of these plans as repositories for tax-free rollovers from exempt employer-sponsored 401(k) or 403(b) plans when employees change jobs or retire. Some account holders were reluctant to roll their funds over into IRAs as long as the exempt status of IRAs was uncertain.

A few days before enactment of the 2005 Act, the Supreme Court in *Rousey v. Jacoway*, 125 S.Ct. 1561 (2005), held that debtors can exempt IRAs under § 522(d)(10)(E). It decided that IRAs fulfill the requirements under § 522(d)(10)(E) for exemption in that they are similar plans or contracts to the plans specified in that section and are on account of age. The Court did not address the additional statutory requirement that funds are exempt only "to the extent reasonably necessary for the support of the debtor and any dependent of the debtor" because the issue was not raised on appeal. Since very substantial 401(k) balances are being rolled over into IRAs on the retirement of employees, the "reasonably necessary" issue was likely to become a matter of contention post-*Rousey*. But the new Act changed things.

The 2005 Act has boldly reformed the law on exemption of retirement plans in bankruptcy and has done so in a manner that is very favorable to debtors. It permits a debtor to exempt retirement funds "to the extent that those funds are in a fund or account that is exempt from taxation under section 401 [qualified plans], 403 [annuities], 408 [IRAs], 408(A) [Roth IRAs], 414 [hybrid plans], 457 [deferred compensation plans], or 501(a) [employee contribution plans] of the Internal Revenue Code." The specified retirement funds or accounts are exempt in bankruptcy under both the state (§ 522(b)(3)(C)) and the federal (§ 522(d)(12)) exemptions. Among the assets protected under these provisions are the popular defined contribution 401(k) plans, set up by employers, under which employees are allowed to contribute, under certain dollar amount limits, a percentage of their annual pay into investment accounts, with employers sometimes contributing matching amounts; the fund grows tax-deferred. Both the basic IRA (IRC § 408) and the Roth IRA (IRC § 408(A)) are also protected. Section 522(n) places a $1 million dollar (inflation adjusted) cap on the amount exempted for both IRAs and Roth IRAs, but the amount "may be increased if the interests of justice so require." There is no limitation on funds contributed to or contained in plans provided by the debtor's employer. Section § 522(n) goes even further in excluding from consideration in calculating the $1 million cap funds rolled over into an IRA or Roth IRA from other exempt plans, like 401(k) and 403(b) plans. It is unusual for an IRA to contain over $1 million without rollovers. Loans made to debtors from their retirement plans are not to be construed as claims or debts under the Code (§§ 362(b)(19), 523(a)(18)), and are not dischargeable under § 523(a)(18)). Automatic deductions from a debtor's wages to repay a loan from a retirement plan are not stayed by the debtor's filing (§ 362(b)(19)). All told, the 2005 Act is remarkably generous to debtors in safeguarding their retirement funds in bankruptcy.

Funds placed in education IRAs and qualified state tuition programs under IRC § 529 are, under certain conditions, excluded from the debtor's estate by § 541(b)(5) and (6). The maximum annual contribution to educational IRAs is $2,000. To qualify for exclusion, funds in educational IRAs must have been deposited not less than a year before the date of filing, and the exclusion applies only to the extent of $5,000 for contributions made not earlier than 720 days or later than 365 days before filing. The requirements for the exclusion of state tuition accounts under IRC § 529 are similar. These provisions treat educational savings accounts differently from retirement savings accounts by excluding them from the estate rather than exempting them. Funds withheld by employers from employee wages as contributions to the plans exempted by the statute or received by employers from employees for these purposes are excluded from the debtor-employee's estate by § 541(b)(7).

### 4. IMPAIRMENT OF EXEMPTIONS

#### a. Avoidance of Security Interests under § 522(f)(1)(B)

Creditors bargain for security interests in order to make collection of the debt easier and more certain. The security interest, however, may serve different functions in different cases in carrying out the creditor's desire to assure payment of the debt. In most cases the security interest assures that on default by the debtor the creditor will have property of value that can be sold to pay the debt. But this is not always the case. Some property has little or no value to a creditor, but may have high value to the debtor. This difference in value usually arises because of a difference between resale value and replacement cost of the property concerned. For example, some property of the debtor such as clothing and household goods may be indispensable to the debtor and may be expensive to replace. At the same time it may have very little resale value. This kind of property is usually exempt from execution. To allow unlimited levy on this kind of property is to deprive the debtor of basic necessities while the creditor would receive property of little value. This disparity between cost to the debtor and benefit to the creditor militates against permitting levy.

But because exempt property can be voluntarily transferred, a creditor can, and often does, bargain for a security interest in property of this kind. Even if the property involved has a very low resale value, the threat of the creditor on default to seize the property and impose on the debtor the cost of replacing it or the pain of simply doing without the property constitutes powerful leverage in obtaining repayment of the debt. This is particularly true in cases of small loans to debtors who are unable to provide valuable collateral and who rely primarily on their earning capacity to repay the debt. Although in bankruptcy a debtor can obtain a discharge of a secured debt, the creditor is entitled to enforce the security interest; the debtor may avoid personal liability on the discharged debt, but the property that was collateral for the debt is lost. Before the Bankruptcy Code, the threat of seizing the collateral was often used to discourage the debtor from filing in bankruptcy or to induce the debtor to "reaffirm" the discharged debt after bankruptcy. Reaffirmation reinstates the debt. Exemption laws normally make unenforceable an agreement by a debtor at the time an unsecured debt is incurred to waive rights to protect exempt property. They do not, however, prevent a debtor from granting a security interest in exempt property. In each case, however, the creditor is bargaining for the right to reach exempt property, and the difference between an agreement to waive exemptions and an agreement to give a security interest may be no more than a matter of form. Section 522(f)(1)(B) deals with this issue. It assumes that some kinds of security interests frustrate the bankruptcy objective of providing debtors a fresh start free of onerous debts, and it allows the debtor to nullify those security interests. In 1994, § 522(f) was amended. The provision discussed in the case below as § 522(f)(2)(B) is now § 522(f)(1)(B)(ii).

## In re Liming
United States Court of Appeals, Tenth Circuit, 1986.
797 F.2d 895.

■  LOGAN, Circuit Judge.

Harold Gregg Liming, an Oklahoma farmer, obtained a $15,000 loan from the Central National Bank of Enid, Oklahoma, in April 1980. Liming's loan application stated that he had a net worth of $183,000 and total debts of $88,000. He pledged a John Deere tractor worth $30,000 as collateral.

Seventy-six days later, in June 1980, Liming gave Central National a revised financial statement. The impetus for the new statement is unclear, but it listed a net worth of only $33,000 and total debts of $264,000. Instead of calling its loan, Central National accepted a $3,000 payment on the existing debt and a renewal note on the balance at a lower rate of interest. Less than eight months later, in February 1981, Liming declared bankruptcy.

Central National's complaint asked that Liming's debt be held nondischargeable under § 523(a)(2)(B), because it arose from a materially false statement of his financial condition. Liming argued that the debt was dischargeable and that Central National's security interest in his tractor was avoidable under § 522(f)(2)(B), because it was a lien on an "implement" of his trade exempt under Oklahoma law. The bankruptcy court held that Liming's debt to the bank was nondischargeable but that the lien on Liming's tractor was avoidable. Both parties appealed directly to this court under 28 U.S.C. § 1293(b). * * *

[Omitted is the portion of the opinion in which the court affirmed the ruling that Liming's debt was nondischargeable under § 523(a)(2)(B).]

As the bankruptcy court correctly noted, a debtor may bring an action to avoid a lien under § 522(f) even if the debt secured by that lien is declared nondischargeable. Liming argues that Central National's security interest in his tractor can be avoided under § 522(f), which provides that:

> "(f) Notwithstanding any waiver of exemptions, the debtor may avoid the fixing of a lien on an interest of the debtor in property to the extent that such lien impairs an exemption to which the debtor would have been entitled under subsection (b) of this section, if such lien is—
>
> (1) a judicial lien; or
>
> (2) a nonpossessory, nonpurchase-money security interest in any—
>
> > (B) *implements,* professional books, or tools, *of the trade of the debtor* * * *." (emphasis added).

The first issue is whether the lien on Liming's tractor impaired "an exemption to which the debtor would have been entitled." * * *

The pertinent federal exemption provides that a debtor may exempt an "aggregate interest, not to exceed $750 in value, in any implements, professional books, or tools, of the trade of the debtor * * *." § 522(d)(6). The pertinent Oklahoma exemption provides that:

> "A. Except as otherwise provided in this title and notwithstanding subsection B of this section, the following property shall be reserved to every person residing in the state, exempt from attachment or execution of every other species of forced sales for the payment of debts, except as herein provided:

* * *

> 5. Implements of husbandry necessary to farm the homestead;"

Okla.Stat.Ann. tit. 31, § 1.A.5 (West Supp.1985). Unlike the federal exemption, this state exemption has no dollar limitation.

The Oklahoma courts have held that a farm tractor is "an implement of husbandry" within the Oklahoma exemption. *Davis v. Wright*, 152 P.2d 921, 922 (1944) (construing prior version of the statute with virtually identical language). Central National tries to distinguish *Davis* by noting that it involved an attempted forced sale of a tractor passing through probate, which was needed to pay off estate debts. The tractor was the only means a widow would have had to work her probate homestead. But we see no significant distinction. As a federal court construing Oklahoma law, we must follow *Davis* and find that Liming's tractor was an exempt item under 31 Okla.Stat. § 1.A.5. We therefore agree with the bankruptcy court that Central National's lien on Liming's tractor did "impair" a bankruptcy exemption to which Liming "would have been entitled," as the bankruptcy exemptions are invoked in the avoidance provisions in § 522(f).

Central National, however, contends that Liming's tractor was not a protected "implement" under § 522(f)(2)(B), because such "implements" include only those listed for exemption in § 522(d)(6), which contains a $750 value limitation.

The federal bankruptcy cases are divided over whether the avoiding authority for "implements" in § 522(f)(2)(B) is limited solely to implements exempted under § 522(d)(6). * * *

In the spirit of allowing a fresh start, undoing the consequences of adhesion contracts, and countering creditors' practices of using threats to repossess debtors' household goods to obtain payment, Congress enacted § 522(f) to give debtors the right to avoid liens on exempt property.

"In addition, the bill gives the debtor certain rights not available under current law with respect to exempt property. The debtor may void any judicial lien on exempt property, and any nonpurchase money security interest in certain exempt property such as household goods. The first right allows the debtor to undo the actions of creditors that bring legal action against the debtor shortly before bankruptcy. Bankruptcy exists to provide relief for an overburdened debtor. If a creditor beats the debtor into court, the debtor is nevertheless entitled to his exemptions. The second right will be of more significance for the average consumer debtor. Frequently, creditors lending money to a consumer debtor take a security interest in all of the debtor's belongings, and obtain a waiver by the debtor of his exemptions. In most of these cases, the debtor is unaware of the consequences of the forms he signs. The creditor's experience provides him with a substantial advantage. If the debtor encounters financial difficulty, creditors often use threats of repossession of all of the debtor's household goods as a means of obtaining payment.

In fact, were the creditor to carry through on his threat and foreclose on the property, he would receive little, for household goods have little resale value. They are far more valuable to the creditor in the debtor's hands, for they provide a credible basis for the threat, because the replacement costs of the goods are generally high. Thus, creditors rarely repossess, and debtors, ignorant of the creditors' true intentions, are coerced into payments they simply cannot afford to make.

The exemption provision allows the debtor, after bankruptcy has been filed, and creditor collection techniques have been stayed, to undo the consequences of a contract of adhesion, signed in ignorance, by permitting the invalidation of nonpurchase money security interests in household goods. Such security interests have too often been used by overreaching creditors. The bill eliminates any unfair advantage creditors have."

H. R. Rep. No. 595, 95th Cong., 2d Sess. at 126–27 (footnotes omitted) * * *.

Those courts that have interpreted the scope of the avoidance provisions of § 522(f) restrictively emphasize the references to "household goods," to the items having "little resale value," and the overriding power of the creditors.[6]

We do not accept that limitation, in part because the legislative history exhibits a partially pro-debtor stance, but principally because it would require us to read into the statute provisions contrary to its plain words. Section 522(f) permits the debtor, "notwithstanding any waiver of exemption," to avoid any lien that impairs "an exemption to which the debtor would have been entitled under subsection (b)" on "implements" of the debtor's trade. Id. § 522(f)(2)(B). We cannot read the reference to "subsection (b)" as pertaining only to subsection (b)(1), which encompasses the limited ($750) *federal* implements exemption, to the exclusion of (b)(2), which encompasses the state law exemptions. And, although the wording of the subsection (f) avoidances closely follows the wording of the subsection (d) exemptions, subsection (f) contains no express dollar limitations on the value of the items that the debtor may avoid. Indeed, that the wording is identical but for the dollar limitations suggests a deliberate omission.

Under different circumstances, we have refused to read the avoidance provisions of § 522(f) expansively. In *In re Reid*, 757 F.2d 230 (10th Cir.1985), we denied a debtor avoidance of a lien on paintings worth more than $180,000 as items held primarily for household use. In so holding we stressed that the purpose of the federal and Oklahoma exemptions is to avoid depriving debtors of the "necessities of life." Id. at 236. But a tractor is a necessary "implement" of a farmer's trade under any historical or common sense understanding of the term. We cannot place a more restric-

---

[6] *In re Thompson*, 750 F.2d 628, 631 (8th Cir.1984), did not permit lien avoidance of a security interest in 210 pigs worth $4,500. It found that the pigs were not held primarily for the personal, family, or household use of the farmer as required by § 522(f)(2)(A) for avoidance of liens on animals. Thus the case is distinguishable from the one before us, which involves a (2)(B) exemption and has no use requirement. Nevertheless, in reaching its conclusion the Eighth Circuit made statements contrary to the approach we take here: "In conclusion, we hold that only those personal goods necessary to the debtor's new beginning and of little resale value fit the federal bankruptcy philosophy embodied in section 522(f)(2). We concur with the bankruptcy judge that the Thompsons' pigs were not the sort of low value personal goods in which 'adhesion contract' security interests are taken." *Thompson,* 750 F.2d at 631 (footnote omitted).

tive dollar value limitation on the "implement" exemption than state law imposes, given the wording of § 522.

Some courts have reasoned that a nonrestrictive reading of this avoidance section hurts debtors: If security interests in valuable implements like tractors are avoidable, lenders will refuse to make loans they otherwise might make. * * * That may be so, but arguably farmers are more often already in debt to the lender and, like the average consumer debtor, are subject to threats, pressures, and disadvantages similar to those mentioned in the legislative history. This policy decision is for Congress, not the courts.

Central National argued finally that Liming's tractor was not used in Liming's "trade," as also required for avoidance under § 522(f)(2)(B). It points out that, at the time of bankruptcy hearings, Liming farmed only 160 acres and worked full-time at Northrop Worldwide Aircraft Services in Enid. It further asserts that this particular tractor was larger than Liming needed to farm his quarter section.

Whether an implement is used in a bankrupt's "trade" is a fact question based on an individual's particular circumstances. * * * A temporary abatement of work in a trade is not fatal to a claim for an exemption for tools or implements of that trade. * * * Further, the statutory definition of "farmer" in § 101 is not controlling for purposes of the tool of the trade provisions. * * * The bankruptcy court found that Liming's tractor was used in his trade. We do not think this determination was clearly erroneous. Liming farmed the quarter section that he owned; he previously had been a full-time farmer on a much larger acreage.

## NOTES

**1.** In 1994, § 522(f)(3) was added. What effect would this provision have had on *Liming* if it had been in force at the time this case was decided? What is the justification for this provision? If you are having difficulty understanding § 522(f)(3), you are not alone. The court in *In re Ehlen*, 202 B.R. 742 (Bankr.W.D.Wis.1996), concluded:

> After careful consideration of § 522(f)(3) * * * the Court must conclude that this is indeed one of those 'rare cases' in which the statute is truly ambiguous and subject to a variety of interpretations. * * * While the section clearly places a cap on the lien avoidance powers available to debtors, it is difficult, if not impossible, to ascertain the particular class of debtors subject to this cap from an examination of the statute alone.

202 B.R. at 746.

**2.** Section 522(f)(1)(B) provides that a debtor may avoid a nonpossessory, non-purchase money security interest in "household goods" to the extent that the lien impairs an exemption that the debtor would have been entitled to under § 522(b). Section 522(f)(4) was added by the 2005 Act to define "household goods" for the purpose of § 522(f)(1)(B). The definition is a modified version of the Federal Trade Commission's definition of the term that was adopted with the intention of bringing some certainty to that broad term. It limits the goods subject to the debtor's avoidance power, *e.g.*, with respect to electronic entertainment equipment, only one radio, one TV, one VCR, and one computer qualify as household goods. To the extent that § 522(f)(4) broadens the definition that courts have given to "household goods," it favors debtors in that nonpurchase money, nonpossessory security interests in such property are avoidable. Rapid developments in electronic products will surely make the original list look quaint in a few years, but the U.S. Trustee's Office is directed to report back on the effect of these definitions in 2007, which, one may hope, will lead to more sensible and durable limitations.

**3.** One shortcoming of exemption statutes that state dollar limits on the property exempted is that inflation inexorably reduces the value of the property exempted unless legislatures periodically adjust the dollar limits. In 1994, 15 years after the Code became effective, Congress addressed this concern. All the dollar amounts of exemptions in § 522(d), as well as most of the other dollar amounts throughout the Code, were doubled, and § 104(b) was added providing for adjustments of most of the dollar amounts in the Code by the Judicial Conference each three years to reflect changes in the Department of Labor's Consumer Price Index. The most recent adjustment of the dollar amounts in § 522(d) was made in 2004.

**4.** When is a security interest nonpurchase money? In *In re Matthews*, 724 F.2d 798 (9th Cir.1984), Debtor bought a piano and stereo with the proceeds of a loan from Finance Co. payable in installments. The loan agreement provided that the loan from Finance Co. was secured by a security interest in all of Debtor's household goods including the piano and stereo. Did Finance Co. acquire a purchase money security interest in the piano and stereo? Did Finance Co. acquire a purchase money security interest in Debtor's household goods other than the piano and stereo? About a year later Finance Co. and Debtor entered into a refinancing agreement under which Debtor's obligation under the loan agreement was satisfied and was replaced by a new obligation under the refinancing agreement. The obligation under the refinancing agreement comprised the amount of the obligation under the loan agreement, additional finance charges, insurance charges, and $63 paid in cash to Debtor. The obligation under the refinancing agreement was payable in installments over a period of time longer than that provided in the loan agreement. The refinancing agreement provided that the obligation was secured by a security interest in all of Debtor's household goods including the piano and stereo. Later, Debtor filed in bankruptcy and sought to avoid the security interest under § 522(f)(1)(B). Did Finance Co. have a purchase money security interest in the piano and stereo? Did Finance Co. have a purchase money security interest in Debtor's household goods other than the piano and stereo? The court in *Matthews* held that Debtor could avoid the security interest in all of Debtor's household goods including the piano and stereo. According to the court, even if Finance Co. had a purchase money security interest in the piano and stereo under the loan agreement, the purchase money nature of the lien was lost when the obligation under the loan agreement was satisfied and replaced by the obligation under the refinancing agreement. Do you agree? UCC § 9-103(f) rejects the view of *Matthews*, but only in nonconsumer transactions. Section 9-103(h) states that for consumer transactions courts may continue to apply "established approaches." Why does UCC § 9-103 make the distinction between consumer and nonconsumer transactions? Why is avoidability of a lien under § 522(f)(1)(B) limited to nonpurchase money security interests?

**5.** As originally enacted § 522(d)(3) provided as follows:

The debtor's interest, not to exceed $200 in value in any particular item, in household furnishings, household goods, wearing apparel, appliances, books, animals, crops, or musical instruments, that are held primarily for the personal, family, or household use of the debtor or a dependent of the debtor.

This exemption was the only § 522(d) exemption in which the dollar limitation was an item limitation rather than an aggregate limitation. It proved to be a provision that allowed property of substantial value to be shielded by the debtor. For example, in *In re Wahl*, 14 B.R. 153 (Bankr.E.D.Wis.1981), the debtor was allowed to exempt a set of sterling silver tableware with a value of over $6,000. The court held that each knife, fork and spoon was a "particular item" for the purpose of applying the $200 limitation. In 1984 § 522(d)(3) was revised to impose an overall dollar limitation of $4,000. The amounts have since been raised to $475 for each item and $9850 for the aggregate limitation.

### b.    Avoidance of Judicial Liens under § 522(f)(1)(A)

#### (i)    Impairment

In the preceding section we saw Congress taking an extraordinary action in § 522(f)(1)(B) in providing that a trustee may avoid consensual security interests in certain types of the debtor's exempt property. Normally, in a conflict between a debtor's exemption and a consensual security interest, the latter prevails for the debtor is allowed to create a security interest in exempt property that is prior to any exemption that the debtor may assert. However, in providing in § 522(f)(1)(A) that a debtor may avoid judicial liens that impair a debtor's exemption, Congress is on more familiar ground, for outside bankruptcy a debtor's exempt property cannot be reached by judicial lien creditors. Thus, in the conflict between a debtor's exemption and a judicial lien, the exemption prevails. There is no explanation in the legislative history why the § 522(f)(1) avoiding power is given the debtor beyond the general statement that "[s]ubsection (f) protects the debtor's exemptions, his discharge, and thus his fresh start by permitting him to avoid certain liens on exempt property." H.R.Rep. No. 95-595 at 362.

Section 522(f)(1) provides that a debtor may avoid a judicial lien on property "to the extent that such lien impairs an exemption" on that property. The courts have struggled with the meaning of impairment since enactment of the Code. In *Owen v. Owen*, 500 U.S. 305, 310–11 (1991), the Court said: "To determine the application of § 522(f) they ask not whether the lien impairs an exemption to which the debtor is in fact entitled, but whether it impairs an exemption to which he *would have been* entitled but for the lien itself." The following Problem illustrates the operation of *Owen*.

## PROBLEM

In September 2000, a judgment lien was recorded on Debtor's residence, which she had owned for two decades. In January 2001, Debtor recorded a declaration of homestead that under state law created an exemption in the property to the extent of $55,000. However, state law provided that no homestead affects a previously existing mortgage, lien or other encumbrance. When Debtor filed in Chapter 7 in July 2001, she claimed the exemption on the ground that state law provisions excepting preexisting liens were preempted by § 522(f) under the holding in *Owen* because, absent the lien, Debtor would have been entitled to the homestead exemption. What result? The facts are based on *In re Weinstein*, 164 F.3d 677 (1st Cir.1999).

-------

The *Silveira* case below discusses the division of authority on the meaning of impairment and the 1994 amendment of § 522(f) that resolves the issue. Before assessing what happens to judicial liens on exempt property in bankruptcy, we first sketch out the usual course of events outside bankruptcy when a mortgagee forecloses on property in which a debtor claims an exemption and a creditor asserts a judicial lien. Assume the value of the Debtor's residence is $100,000, Debtor's exemption in the residence is $45,000, and a judgment lien on the residence secures a debt of $60,000 owed by Debtor to Judgment Creditor (JC). Mortgagee holds a mortgage on the residence recorded prior to the time the judgment lien arose, and Debtor is in default on the mortgage debt.

**Case #1.** Assume that the residence is subject to a mortgage of $100,000. If Mortgagee foreclosed, joining Debtor and JC, the $100,000 proceeds would go entirely to Mortgagee. Debtor and JC would receive no proceeds of the sale and JC's judgment lien would be cut off by the foreclosure sale.

**Case #2.** Assume that the mortgage debt is $60,000. Mortgagee would be fully paid; Debtor would receive $40,000; JC would receive nothing and its lien would be cut off.

**Case #3.** Assume that the mortgage debt is $30,000. Mortgagee would be fully paid; Debtor would receive $45,000; JC would receive $25,000 and its lien would be cut off.

In Note 1 following *Silveira*, we inquire to what extent under the 1994 amendment in § 522(f)(2)(A) there would be impairment of the exemption in bankruptcy in these three cases.

## In re Silveira
United States Court of Appeals, First Circuit, 1998.
141 F.3d 34.

■  STAHL, Circuit Judge.

This bankruptcy appeal requires us to decide the extent to which a Chapter 7 debtor may, pursuant to § 522(f)(1) and (f)(2)(A), avoid the fixing of a judicial lien on the debtor's property, when the market value of the property *exceeds* the sum of (1) all consensual (non-judicial) liens on the property and (2) the amount of the debtor's exempt interest under § 522(d). We hold that, in such a situation, section 522(f)(1) permits the avoidance of the targeted judicial lien only in part, not in its entirety. Because the district court concluded otherwise, we vacate the judgment and remand for further proceedings.

### I.

The debtor and appellee in this action, Thomas J. Silveira, owns, as his primary residence, a property that has been stipulated for purposes of this appeal to have a fair market value of $157,000. The property is subject to a mortgage of $117,680. The appellant, East Cambridge Savings Bank ("the Bank"), holds a $209,500 judicial lien * * * on the property.

On May 9, 1995, Silveira filed a voluntary petition under Chapter 7 of the Bankruptcy Code. He claimed an exemption of $15,000 in the property pursuant to § 522(d)(1).[1] Silveira then filed a motion to avoid the Bank's $209,500 judicial lien pursuant to § 522(f)(1) and § 522(f)(2)(A). The bankruptcy court ruled that those provisions permitted the debtor to avoid the Bank's lien in its entirety and thus granted Silveira's motion. The Bank appealed to the district court, arguing that on the facts of this case, § 522(f)(1) & (f)(2)(A) permitted only a *partial* avoidance of its judicial lien. The district court disagreed and entered an order affirming the bankruptcy court's determination. This appeal followed.

### II.

The Bankruptcy Code provides every debtor with a personal power to avoid certain types of liens that would impinge upon interests that the debtor would otherwise be entitled to claim as exemptions from the bankruptcy estate. § 522(f)(1). Judicial liens are principal targets for this avoidance power:

---

[1] As the Supreme Court has explained, "[a]n exemption is an interest withdrawn from the [bankruptcy] estate (and hence from the creditors) for the benefit of the debtor." *Owen v. Owen*, 500 U.S. 305, 308 (1991).

**(f)(1)**   . . . [T]he debtor may avoid the fixing of a lien on an interest of the debtor in property to the extent that such lien
impairs an exemption to which the debtor would have been
entitled under [§ 522(b)], if such lien is—

**(A)** a judicial lien, other than a judicial lien that secures a
debt. . ..

In the years leading up to the Bankruptcy Reform Act of 1994 ("1994
Act"), a wide divergence of views developed concerning the circumstances in which a judicial lien could be deemed to "impair" an exemption
within the meaning of § 522(f)(1), and the precise extent to which liens
causing such impairment could be avoided. See, e.g., 2 David G. Epstein,
Steve H. Nickles & James J. White, Bankruptcy § 8-28, at 560 (West
1992) (describing various approaches). In an effort to resolve this discord,
Congress included in the 1994 Act an amendment to § 522(f), which
added the following new subsection:

For the purposes of this subsection, a lien shall be considered to impair
an exemption to the extent that the sum of—

**(i)** the lien;

**(ii)** all other liens on the property; and

**(iii)** the amount of the exemption that the debtor could claim if there
were no liens on the property;

exceeds the value that the debtor's interest in the property would have
in the absence of any liens.

§ 522(f)(2)(A).

In this case, it is undisputed that the sum of the targeted judicial lien
($209,500), all other liens ($117,680) and the amount of the debtor's exemption ($15,000) *exceeds* the (stipulated) value of the debtor's property
($157,000), by $185,180. Thus, the Bank's judicial lien clearly does "impair" an exemption of the debtor within the meaning of § 522(f)(2)(A).
The question here concerns the extent of the debtor's power under
§ 522(f)(1) to alleviate this "impairment."

The district court concluded that once a debtor's power of avoidance
is triggered by the fact of an impairment of whatever size, that power permits the debtor to avoid the judicial lien causing the impairment in its entirety. The court thus held that Silveira was entitled to avoid the entire
amount of the Bank's $209,500 lien. The Bank now argues that the district
court misapplied § 522(f)(1)(A), and that Silveira is in fact entitled to
avoid only so much of the Bank's lien as necessary to prevent impairment
of the debtor's exemption within the meaning of § 522(f)(2)(A). We agree.

As an initial matter, we find unpersuasive Silveira's argument that the
"plain language" of the statute supports the district court's view. On the
contrary, the language of the relevant provisions seems to us to support the
Bank's position. Section 522(f)(1) permits a debtor to "avoid the fixing of

a lien on an interest of the debtor in property *to the extent that* such lien impairs an exemption [of the debtor]." § 522(f)(1) (emphasis added). Section 522(f)(2)(A), similarly, provides that a judicial lien "impair[s] an exemption *to the extent that* "the targeted lien, in combination with other liens and the value of the debtor's exemption, exceeds the value of the debtor's property. § 522(f)(2)(A) (emphasis added). If Congress intended for avoidance of judicial liens to be an "all-or-nothing" matter, one might wonder why the provisions' drafters chose to use the connective phrase "to the extent that," in lieu of the word "if," which obviously would have been a simpler construction. *See In re Furkes*, 65 B.R. 232, 235 (D.R.I.1986) ("The 'to the extent that' clause cannot be seen as some sort of legislative slip of the pen. . .. [H]ad Congress intended. . . an all-or-nothing proposition, it would have drafted the statutory language more infrangibly. . ..") The statutory directive that a debtor may avoid a judicial lien "to the extent that" the lien impairs an exemption favors—or is at least readily amenable to—reading the definition of "impairment" in § 522(f)(2)(A) not only as a *condition* of avoidability, but also as a *proportional measure* of the scope of the debtor's avoidance power.

But even if the statute's language does not settle the issue, the debtor's proposed interpretation is unacceptable in view of the statute's intended purposes. Consider the following two hypothetical scenarios:

> *Hypothetical A*: The debtor owns a primary residence with a market value of $100,000, subject to an outstanding mortgage balance of $55,000, a judicial lien of $30,000 (not securing a debt), and no other liens. The debtor is entitled, under § 522(d)(1), to claim an exemption of $15,000 with respect to the property.
>
> *Hypothetical B*: Same as Hypothetical A, except that the debtor's property is subject to a judicial lien of $30,001 instead of $30,000.

In Hypothetical A, we can see that the sum of the judicial lien ($30,000), other liens ($55,000) and the debtor's exemption ($15,000) does *not* exceed the value of the debtor's property ($100,000). Thus the judicial lien in Hypothetical A does *not* impair the debtor's exemption within the meaning of § 522(f)(2)(A), and the debtor is *not* entitled to avoid any portion of that lien under § 522(f)(1).

In Hypothetical B, however, the sum of the judicial lien ($30,001), other liens ($55,000) and the debtor's exemption ($15,000) *does* exceed the property's value (by $1), and so the targeted judicial lien is deemed under § 522(f)(2)(A) to impair the debtor's exemption. Under Silveira's proposed interpretation, the fact of this impairment requires that the debtor in Hypothetical B be permitted to avoid the $30,001 judicial lien *in its entirety*. Thus, as Silveira would have it, a $1 *increase* in the amount of the (unavoidable) judicial lien in Hypothetical A would result in the debtor's acquiring the power to avoid the lien in full.[4]

We find it difficult to conceive of any reason that would counsel in favor of interpreting § 522(f)(1)(A) and (f)(2)(A) to produce such a result. The district court, in siding with Silveira, suggested that denying debtors the right to avoid *in full* any judicial lien that impairs an exemption would "circumvent" Congress's goal of providing debtors with a "fresh start" after bankruptcy and would thus frustrate the basic purpose of § 522(f)(1). The problem with this argument, however, is that it proves too much.

The implication of the district court's reasoning is that the statute effects a general policy against the fixing of judicial liens with respect to property in which the debtor holds an exempt interest. Clearly, however, the statute cannot be read so broadly. Section 522(f) unquestionably contemplates that in some circumstances—see, for example, Hypothetical A above—a judicial lien up to some calculable amount will *not* be deemed to impair the debtor's exemption and hence will not be subject to the debtor's avoidance power. But if, in such a circumstance, the statute would not permit the debtor to avoid any judicial lien *smaller* than that calculable amount, it would seem arbitrary and unfair to permit a creditor to avoid the *entirety* of a judicial lien that was *larger* than that amount. Thus, if § 522(f)(1) would permit the fixing of a $30,000 judicial lien on the facts of Hypothetical A above, then it would border on the absurd not to permit the holder of a $30,001 judicial lien, on otherwise identical facts, to pursue the fixing of its lien *up to* the amount of $30,000.

This reasoning compels an analogous result in this case. Here, the sum of the debtor's exemption ($15,000) and all consensual liens on his property ($117,680) is $24,320 *less* than the value of the property ($157,000); in other words, there is $24,320 of excess equity available. This means that if the Bank's judicial lien here had been for $24,320 or less, that lien would have been absolutely unavoidable under § 522(f)(1), because there would have been no "impairment" within the meaning of § 522(f)(2)(A).[5] The fact that the Bank's actual lien is for more than $24,320 surely provides no reason to place the Bank in a position *worse* than it would have been had its lien originally been limited to that amount. Fairness requires, therefore, that the Bank be permitted to pursue the fixing of its $209,500 judicial lien *up to* the amount of $24,320.

In more intuitive terms, it is obvious that the value of the debtor's property in this case is sufficient to cover the entire amount of the debtor's

---

[4] The debtor in Hypothetical A would also acquire full avoidance power (according to Silveira's approach) if the value of the debtor's property were reduced, or the amount of consensual liens were increased, by $1.

[5] That is, the sum of (i) the judicial lien ($24,320), (ii) other liens ($117,680), and (iii) the debtor's exemption ($15,000) would *not* have exceeded the value of the debtor's property ($157,000). See § 522(f)(2)(A).

mortgage ($117,680) plus his claimed exemption ($15,000), with $24,320 of equity to spare. Nothing in § 522(f)(1) or § 522(f)(2) can be read to require that this excess equity be preserved either for the debtor or the bankruptcy estate, rather than being made available for the partial satisfaction of a judicial lien. And, as shown above, the fixing of a judicial lien in an amount equal to this excess equity would not create any impairment of the debtor's $15,000 exemption. See § 522(f)(2)(A). It follows that no legitimate purpose underlying the statute would be served by permitting Silveira to avoid so much of the Bank's lien—$24,320—as could be covered by the excess equity available in the property.

In summary, we apply § 522(f)(1)(A) and § 522(f)(2)(A) to the facts of this case as follows. First, pursuant to § 522(f)(2)(A), we determine that the sum of (i) the targeted judicial lien ($209,500), (ii) all other liens ($117,680), and (iii) the amount of the debtor's exemption ($15,000)—which sum equals $342,180—*exceeds* the value that the debtor's property would have in an unencumbered state ($157,000), and exceeds that value by $185,180. Thus, the Bank's judicial lien impairs the debtor's exemption to the extent of $185,180. Because Silveira is entitled to avoid the Bank's lien to the extent of any impairment, Silveira is entitled to avoidance in the amount of $185,180. See § 522(f)(1)(A). The remainder of the Bank's judicial lien, in the amount of $24,320 ($209,500 minus $185,180), is not subject to avoidance by the debtor under § 522(f)(1)(A).[6]

We note that this result follows the approach recently adopted by this Circuit's Bankruptcy Appellate Panel. * * *; *see also* 2 Norton Bankruptcy Law & Practice 2d § 46:23, at 334–35 (Supp.1997) (applying same approach); David G. Carlson, Security Interests on Exempt Property After the 1994 Amendments to the Bankruptcy Code, 4 Am.Bankr.Inst.L.Rev. 57, 65 (1996) (same).

* * *

## IV.

The interpretation of § 522(f)(1)(A) and § 522(f)(2)(A) advocated by the Bank is consistent with the text of those provisions, fully vindicates the statute's basic purpose, and averts the unfair consequences that the debtor's interpretation would entail. Because the district court rejected the approach we adopt here, we vacate the judgment below and remand this case for further proceedings consistent with the principles set forth herein.

---

[6] These figures would change, of course, if the actual value of the debtor's property were determined, on remand, to be different from the stipulated value of $157,000.

## NOTES

**1.** How would Cases #1 through #3 on p. 53 be decided under *Silveira*? In Case #1, how can the judgment lien impair Debtor's exemption when Debtor has no property to which an exemption can attach at the time of bankruptcy? Impairment is extensively discussed in Charles Jordan Tabb, *The Law of Bankruptcy* § 9.9 (1997).

**2.** Arthur and Bertha owned a home valued at $225,000 as tenants in common, subject to a first-priority mortgage securing an obligation of $165,000. Judgment Creditor (JC) obtained a judgment lien on the home in the amount of $53,878. Arthur (but not Bertha) filed in Chapter 7 and sought complete avoidance of the lien. He claimed an exemption of $5,312. On these facts, the court in *In re Lehman*, 205 F.3d 1255 (11th Cir.2000), opined that strict application of the formula in § 522(f)(2)(A) to these facts would allow Arthur to avoid all of JC's lien: the calculation would be $53,878 plus $165,000 plus $5,312 total $224,190, which exceeds the value of Arthur's interest in the property, in the absence of liens, of $112,500 by $111,690, an amount greater than all of JC's lien.

The court concluded that this result was "absurd" because it would leave Arthur an equity of $30,000 in the property ($225,000 minus $165,000 equals $60,000, divided in half) that would be entirely free from JC's lien, even though Arthur was entitled to an exemption of only $5,312. In a case in which the debtor owns less than all of the property, the statutory formula yields a fair result only if it is tweaked somewhat. According to the court, a fair result under the facts of this case could be reached if the amount of the mortgage proportional to the debtor's share of the property ($82,500) is used in place of the amount of the mortgage on the whole property ($165,000). This would leave JC with a lien of $24,688 ($30,000 less $5,312) on the property. The court's interpretation of the statute is in accord with *Nelson v. Scala*, 192 F.3d 32 (1st Cir.1999). *But see In re Cozad*, 208 B.R. 495 (10th Cir.B.A.P 1997).

## PROBLEM

First Mortgagee lent Debtor money to purchase a homestead and recorded the mortgage on the homestead in 1998. In the fall of 2000, JC obtained a judgment for $134,000 against Debtor and recorded the judgment as a judicial lien against the homestead. In December 2000, Debtor borrowed $80,000 from Second Mortgagee who recorded the mortgage on the homestead. When JC began proceedings to collect its judgment in the spring of 2001, Debtor filed in Chapter 7. At this time the homestead's fair market value was $275,000 and First Mortgagee's outstanding loan had a balance of $219,000. Debtor's obligations to JC and Second Mortgagee were unpaid. The state homestead exemption was $8,000. If 522(f)(2)(A) is applied literally and the second mortgage is counted as one of the liens, JC's lien must be avoided because the impairment exceeds the value of its lien. That is, the sum of the judicial lien ($134,000), the two mortgage liens ($299,000) and the homestead exemption ($8,000) is $441,000, which exceeds Debtor's $275,000 interest in the property in the absence of any liens by $166,000, more than the total value of the judicial lien. But the bankruptcy court concluded that the second mortgage lien should be excluded from the calculation because under state law it was junior to the earlier judicial lien. If this were done, the impairment would be reduced from $166,000 to $86,000, thus only $86,000 of Debtor's judicial lien would be avoided, while the remaining $48,000 would remain an unavoided lien on Debtor's homestead. It based its refusal to read the statute literally on *Nelson* and *Lehman* in the previous Note, which held that when the statute produces an absurd result adjustments can be made. Should the appellate court overturn this decision? *See In re Kolich*, 328 F.3d 406 (8th Cir. 2003), *accord*: *In re Brinley*, 403 F.3d 415 (6th Cir. 2005).

### (ii) The "Fixing of a Lien"

In *Farrey v. Sanderfoot*, 500 U.S. 291 (1991), the Court was faced with a common fact situation. In a property settlement upon divorce, it is common for one spouse, here Husband, to take the residence and agree to pay the other spouse, Wife, her share of the house's value over a period of time. If all Wife received from Husband was an unsecured note, Husband's subsequent bankruptcy might discharge his debt on the note and leave Wife with nothing. Usually, Wife will demand a security interest in the residence to safeguard her interest. In *Farrey,* Wife did not obtain a consensual security interest in the residence, but the divorce decree granted Wife a lien on the residence to secure Husband's obligation to pay the debt. A few months after the decree was issued, Husband filed in bankruptcy, claimed the residence as exempt property and moved to avoid Wife's judicial lien under § 522(f)(1). Congress could not have intended to allow debtors to avoid liens in a case of this sort, and the 1994 amendments except from avoidance judicial liens securing debts to spouses and children for alimony, maintenance or support.

It is clear that the facts of *Farrey* cried out for relief for Wife, and the Court delivered. It said:

> The statute does not say that the debtor may undo a lien on an interest in property. Rather, the statute expressly states that the debtor may avoid "the fixing" of a lien on the debtor's interest in property. The gerund "fixing" refers to a temporal event. That event—the fastening of a liability—presupposes an object onto which the liability can fasten. The statute defines this pre-existing object as "an interest of the debtor in property." Therefore, unless the debtor had the property interest to which the lien attached at some point *before* the lien attached to that interest, he or she cannot avoid the fixing of the lien under the terms of § 522(f)(1).

500 U.S. at 296. But Husband countered that he had owned the residence with Wife before the judicial lien attached. No, replied the Court, Hus-

band's current interest in the property came into being at the time of the divorce decree, which both awarded him the residence and affixed Wife's lien to the property. Since he had not owned his current interest in the residence before the judicial lien attached, Husband cannot use § 522(f)(1) to avoid Wife's lien.

## PROBLEM

Under New York law, an unsatisfied money judgment automatically becomes a lien on real property thereafter acquired by the judgment debtor in the county in which the judgment has been docketed. Bank obtained a judgment against Debtor for $16,000, which was docketed in 1990 in Monroe County, New York. In 1994, Debtor purchased land in that county valued at $86,000; the judgment was never satisfied. In 1995, Debtor filed in bankruptcy, claimed his $10,000 homestead exemption in the Monroe County land and moved to avoid Bank's judicial lien on that property under § 522(f)(1)(A). Under *Farrey* is Debtor entitled to avoidance? Did Debtor have an interest in the property at the time the lien attached? This Problem is based on the facts of *In re Scarpino*, 113 F.3d 338 (2d Cir.1997). "Fixing" is discussed in Charles Jordan Tabb, *The Law of Bankruptcy* § 9.8 (1997).

## 5. PREBANKRUPTCY PLANNING

### a.   Introduction

What is the proper purpose of state exemption laws and how should they be used in bankruptcy? This question was considered by Delmar Karlen in an article in 22 Bus. Law. 1167 (1967). He made the following statement:

> As a matter of common sense and fairness, it would seem that the governing policy should be that a man ought to pay his just debts and if he fails or refuses to do so, his property and income should be taken by law and devoted to that purpose. The only qualification to this principle would be that the debtor and his family should not be pauperized and thrown on relief; they should be left enough property and income to keep going and to make a fresh start toward solvency.

Id. at 1169.

Some exemption laws may reflect that policy but many do not. The federal Consumer Credit Protection Act, 15 U.S.C. § 1673, prevents wage garnishment of more than 25% of the disposable earnings of the debtor, but it applies alike to a debtor with earnings of $200 a week and one who earns $2,000 a week. In Florida and a few other states, a debtor may exempt equity in the family home whether that equity is worth $1,000 or $1,000,000. Fla.Const. Art. 10, § 4 (West 1995). Moreover, debtors with equal assets may be allowed to retain more or less property depending upon the type of assets held. For example, consider two debtors in California with $70,000 to invest in property. Debtor A chose to invest the $70,000 in investment securities and to pay rent on the family home. Debtor B used the $70,000 to buy a house used as the family home. Debtor A can lose the entire $70,000 of securities if a creditor levies on them. Debtor B can protect all of the $70,000 invested in the family home. Cal.Code Civ.Proc. § 704.730(a)(2) (1987 and 2000 Supp.).

### b.  Homestead Exemption

A matter of great contention in the drafting of the 2005 Act was the extent to which debtors in bankruptcy should be allowed to exempt the land and buildings that make up their family residence, their homestead. The homestead exemption, the most basic of exemptions, is intended to protect debtors' homes from being seized by their creditors. Supposedly, the state benefits from the sense of security in the community engendered by homestead laws and by the reduction in demand for state services. *See In re Drenttel*, 403 F.3d 611 (8th Cir. 2005). Most states place dollar limits on homestead exemptions, which vary widely. But a few, notably Florida and Texas, have *no* limits. In 1997, the NBRC Report recommended that state laws should govern the amount of the exemption which should be not less than $20,000 nor more than $100,000. The Report noted that few states exempted more than $100,000 or less than $20,000. NBRC Rep. 125 (1997).

There was Congressional support for an across-the-board cap of $125,000 on homestead exemptions. This would exceed the caps in almost all states but would limit the amount of homestead exemptions in Florida and Texas and the other states with unlimited exemptions. At times the dispute in Congress on this issue was so heated that it stalled the entire bill: "Don't mess with Texas." The tortuous compromise that resulted is a product of its time, a time of corporate scandals featuring multimillionaire executives in no-limit states who were on trial for  securities law violations, fraud in a fiduciary capacity and the like, and who lived in or were constructing valuable residences that were protected from aggrieved creditors and shareholders by exemption laws.

Section 522(q) provides that a debtor electing the state exemptions under (b)(3)(A) may not exempt any amount of an interest in property that the debtor uses as a residence or claims as a homestead that exceeds $125,000 if (i) the debtor has been convicted of a felony under circumstances that demonstrate that the filing of the case was an abuse of the provisions of the Bankruptcy Code, or (ii) the debtor owes a debt arising from violations of securities laws, or fraud in a fiduciary capacity or in connection with securities sales or purchases. Previously, exemption laws have drawn rules for different kinds of property; here the rule is drawn on the basis of the conduct of the debtor: debtors cannot exempt more than $125,000, whatever the state homestead exemption statutes provide, if they have been bad actors, unless under § 522(q)(2), the property is reasonably necessary for the support of the debtor and dependants. Moreover, §§ 727(a)(12) and 1328(h) allow courts to hold up the discharge of a debtor if there is reasonable cause to believe that the debtor has engaged in the reprehensible conduct described in § 522(q).

### c. Domicile

Since state homestead exemptions vary widely among the states, debtors may engage in opportunistic behavior to take advantage of these differences by moving to states with greater exemptions. Section 522(b)(3)(A), added by the 2005 Act, requires a two-year residence in a state before debtors are protected by the exemption laws of that state. Section 522(p) requires roughly a 40-month residence for a debtor to claim an exemption in a homestead that exceeds the $125,000 cap discussed above. But nothing stops savvy debtors from planning years in advance. The following Problem illustrates § 522(b)(3)(A).

## PROBLEM

Debtor has lived in State A, which has a $25,000 homestead exemption, for 30 years before retiring and moving to State B, which has a $100,000 exemption and a much better climate, on January 2, 2006. After moving, Debtor sold his home in State A and bought one in State B. On January 2, 2007, Debtor filed in Chapter 7 in State B and claimed a $100,000 exemption in the new residence. Under the law of both states, homestead exemption laws apply only to real property within the state. If Debtor chooses the state exemptions, how much of the value of the residence can Debtor exempt under § 522(b)(3)(A): (a) $100,000? (b) $25,000? (c) $0? or (d) none of the above? Should Debtor choose the federal exemptions under § 522 (d)(1)?

### d. Fraudulent Use of Exemptions

If a debtor contemplating bankruptcy holds substantial property that is not exempt under the state exemption law, is it proper to sell the nonexempt property and use the proceeds to buy property that is exempt? Is it ethical for a lawyer to advise a client contemplating bankruptcy to do so? Is it malpractice if the lawyer does not advise the client that the exemption laws can be used to the client's advantage?

*Hanson* and *Tveten*, which follow, shed light on these questions. These cases were decided by the Eighth Circuit as companion cases. The debtors in *Hanson* were domiciled in South Dakota and the debtor in *Tveten* was domiciled in Minnesota. At the time the relevant events occurred, the Uniform Fraudulent Conveyance Act (UFCA) was in effect in both states. UFCA § 7 states: "Every conveyance made * * * with actual intent, as distinguished from intent presumed in law, to hinder, delay, or defraud either present or future creditors, is fraudulent as to both present and future creditors." UFCA § 4 provides: "Every conveyance made * * * by a person who is or will be thereby rendered insolvent is fraudulent as to creditors without regard to his actual intent if the conveyance is made. . . without a fair consideration." Suppose an insolvent debtor was faced with creditors who were about to levy on the debtor's real property. Before levy was made, the debtor conveyed title to the property to a relative without consideration. Under the UFCA, the conveyance was fraudulent under § 4, and, if the purpose of the conveyance was to prevent the levy and thus avoid payment of the debt, the conveyance was fraudulent under § 7 as well. Under UFCA § 9 fraudulent conveyances can be nullified with the effect of returning the conveyed property to the debtor's estate. If a debtor made a fraudulent conveyance before bankruptcy, the trustee in bankruptcy can, if certain conditions are met, nullify the conveyance either on the basis of the state law or under § 548. Fraudulent transfers are discussed at length in chapter 7, *infra.*

The effect of converting nonexempt assets into exempt assets on the eve of bankruptcy is similar to that of a fraudulent transfer. If the exemption is allowed, the ability of creditors to reach assets of the debtor has been frustrated. But the analogy to fraudulent transfer law is imperfect. The public policy of that law in favor of protecting creditors from actions by a debtor that avoid payment of debts collides with another public policy represented by the exemption laws in favor of allowing the debtor to protect certain property from the claims of creditors. How is the conflict to be resolved?

The 2005 Act intervened in this dispute by providing in § 522(o) that if a debtor within the 10-year period before filing has fraudulently converted nonexempt property into property that the debtor claims as a homestead the value of the homestead must be reduced by the amount of the nonexempt property fraudulently transferred. The amendment extends the period of limitations for fraudulent transfer from two years under § 548(a) to 10 years but does not deal with the troublesome substantive issue treated by the following material with respect to circumstances under which such a conversion is deemed fraudulent.

One of the principal reasons the National Bankruptcy Review Commission recommended a uniform federally prescribed lump-sum $20,000 nonhomestead exemption, NBRC Rep. § 1.2.1 & § 1.2.3, was to minimize the need for what has come to be called "prebankruptcy planning." These recommendations would enable the debtor, at the time of bankruptcy, to select any personal property to claim as exempt, so long as the value was under the ceiling. Debtors who are too ill-informed to engage in sophisticated transfers from nonexempt to exempt property on the eve of bankruptcy could enjoy the full measure of their exemptions, free from creditor challenges.

# Hanson v. First National Bank in Brookings

United States Court of Appeals, Eighth Circuit, 1988.
848 F.2d 866.

■ TIMBERS, Circuit Judge.

A creditor bank appeals from a district court order * * * affirming the bankruptcy court's order which rejected the creditor's challenge to the debtors' claimed exemptions. On appeal, the creditor asserts that there was extrinsic evidence establishing the debtors' intent to defraud their creditors. We disagree. We hold that the bankruptcy court was not clearly erroneous in finding no fraudulent intent. We affirm.

## I.

We summarize only those facts and prior proceedings believed necessary to an understanding of the issues raised on appeal.

On November 30, 1983 appellees Kenneth Hanson and his wife Lucille Hanson (the "Hansons" or "debtors"), residents of South Dakota, filed a voluntary joint bankruptcy petition pursuant to Chapter 7 of the Bankruptcy Code. Appellant First National Bank in Brookings ("First National") is the principal creditor of appellees. The instant appeal arises out of First National's objections to the exemptions claimed by the Hansons.

First National loaned money to the Hansons who were farmers. The Hansons sustained financial problems which led to their default on the loans. Before filing for bankruptcy, the Hansons consulted an attorney. On the advice of counsel, the Hansons had appraised and sold certain of their property which would not be exempt under South Dakota law. They sold to their son, Ronald Hanson, a car, two vans, and a motor home for a total of $27,115, the amount for which the property was appraised. Ronald had purchased the property with money he obtained from a bank loan. The debtors also sold some of their household goods and furnishings to Kenneth's brother, Allen Hanson, for $7,300, the appraised value.

A couple weeks prior to filing their bankruptcy petition, the Hansons used these proceeds to purchase life insurance policies with cash surrender values of $9,977 and $9,978 and, two days before filing their petition had prepaid $11,033 on their homestead real estate mortgage which was held by First National. This property was exempt from their creditors' reach. Under South Dakota law, a debtor may exempt the proceeds of life insurance policies up to a total of $20,000 * * * and he also may exempt his homestead. * * *

First National objected to these exemptions, claiming that the debtors had converted non-exempt property to exempt property on the eve of bankruptcy with intent to defraud their creditors. At the hearing before the bankruptcy court on September 10, 1984, First National asserted that none of the property allegedly sold ever was transferred to the buyers. The debtors testified that the vehicles sold to their son, Ronald, were stored at their home because Ronald still lived with them while he was working part time and attending school part time. Part of the agreement, the debtors testified, included their permission to store the vehicles on their property. While the debtors said they occasionally used the vehicles, they did so only with express permission of their son. Ronald subsequently sold the motor home to a third party. The household goods and furnishings were stored in the Hansons' home, they said, because Allen Hanson, Kenneth's brother, was then living in Anchorage, Alaska, and could not retrieve the property immediately after the sale. First National did not assert, nor does it assert on appeal before us, that the transfers were for less than fair market value. The bankruptcy court from the bench denied First National's motion which objected to the exemptions. The court found that the Hansons had done what was permissible under the law and that their actions did not constitute extrinsic evidence of fraud.

First National appealed to the federal district court. Oral argument was heard on June 8, 1987. In a memorandum opinion and order entered June 15, 1987, the district court affirmed the bankruptcy court's order, concluding that it was not clearly erroneous. The instant appeal followed. The sole issue on appeal is whether the Hansons should not be allowed to claim their life insurance and homestead exemption as a product of fraudulent conveyances. We affirm.

## II.

\* \* \*

Under the Bankruptcy Code (the "Code"), a debtor is entitled to exempt certain property from the claims of his creditors. The Code permits a debtor to exempt either under the provisions of the Code itself if not forbidden by state law, § 522(b) & (d), or under the provisions of state law and federal law other than the minimum allowances in the Code. § 522(b)(2). When the debtor claims a state-created exemption, the scope of the claim is determined by state law.

It is well established that under the Code, a debtor's conversion of non-exempt property to exempt property on the eve of bankruptcy for the express purpose of placing that property beyond the reach of creditors, without more, will not deprive the debtor of the exemption to which he otherwise would be entitled. \* \* \* A leading bankruptcy commentator explains that this rule is just because "The result which would obtain if debtors were not allowed to convert property into allowable exempt property would be extremely harsh, especially in those jurisdictions where the exemption allowance is minimal." 3 Collier on Bankruptcy ¶ 522.08[4], at 40 (15th ed.1984). Nevertheless, this rule is not absolute. Where the debtor acts with actual intent to defraud creditors, his exemptions will be denied. Since fraudulent intent rarely is susceptible of direct proof, courts long have accepted extrinsic evidence of fraud. Absent extrinsic evidence of fraud, however, the debtor's mere conversion of non-exempt property to exempt property, even while insolvent, is not evidence of fraudulent intent as to creditors.

The crux of the issue on the instant appeal is whether there was extrinsic evidence to establish that the Hansons transferred the property with intent to defraud their creditors. We may reverse the bankruptcy court's finding as to the debtors' actual intent only if it is clearly erroneous. * * * *In re Cadarette*, 601 F.2d 648, 650 (2d Cir.1979).

In *In re Olson*, 45 B.R. 501 (1984), debtors with a defunct business had placed non-exempt funds into their homestead asset, which was exempt property, just prior to filing their bankruptcy petition. The debtors, 55 and 56 years old, testified, on the advice of their attorney, that the reason they paid off the mortgages was to protect their homestead and to reduce their monthly living expenses, since they believed they would have difficulty finding employment after terminating their business. The bankruptcy court found that the debtors did not commit a fraudulent conveyance. The court permitted the debtors to exempt their entire homestead after finding that the debtors prior to bankruptcy used their savings to satisfy their mortgages, no business assets having been used and no debts having been incurred.

First National asserts here that the Hansons while insolvent committed a "classic badge of fraud" by transferring their property to family members and at the same time retaining the use and enjoyment of that property. First National asserts that the controlling case is *Cadarette,* supra. We disagree.

In *Cadarette,* the debtor, whose business was on the brink of financial collapse, transferred title to his expensive automobile, boat and trailer to his fiancee without consideration three weeks before filing his bankruptcy petition. The district court, reversing the decision of the bankruptcy court, held that the debtor's discharge was denied because of his fraudulent intent to shield his assets from his creditors. The Second Circuit, in affirming the district court, found a number of factors clearly evidencing the debtor's fraudulent intent. The court found significant, among other things, that "someone facing dire financial straits would choose to make a gift of a valuable and highly marketable automobile"; that eight days after the alleged transfer of the car a service charge of $399 was paid not by the alleged new owner but by the debtor, who further depleted his business assets by paying with a company check; that the debtor's fiancee lived only two houses away from him; and that he retained a key to the car and continued to use the car to the same extent as he previously had used it.

We find the instant case quite different from the situation in *Cadarette.* First National does not dispute the fact that the purchasers paid fair market value. The vehicles and household goods were not gifts. Title appears to have been transferred correctly. In the instant case, the debtors had reasonable explanations as to why the property they sold remained on their premises. Of particular significance, their son purchased the vehicles with a bank loan taken in his name and he subsequently resold the motor home to a third party, keeping all of the proceeds himself. The sale to family members, standing on its own, does not establish extrinsic evidence of fraud. First National also asserts that the Hansons' schedules filed in the bankruptcy proceeding listing their assets contained numerous items identical to those they purportedly sold to Allen Hanson. This issue was not raised in the bankruptcy court, the finder of fact; nor is there any indication in the record that it was brought to the attention of the district court. Accordingly, First National has waived its right to raise this additional issue. We decline to address it on appeal.

The bankruptcy court found that First National did not establish any indicia of fraud: the Hansons did not borrow money to place into exempt properties; they accounted for the cash they received from the sales; they had a preexisting homestead; and they did not obtain goods on credit, sell them, and then place the money into exempt property. They sold the property for its fair market value and then used this money to take advantage of some of the limited exemptions available under South Dakota law on the advice of counsel.

### III

To summarize:

We hold that the bankruptcy court was not clearly erroneous in finding no fraudulent intent by the Hansons and permitting them to claim their full exemptions. We believe that the instant case falls within the myriad of cases which have permitted such a conversion.

Affirmed.

■ ARNOLD, Circuit Judge, concurring.

I agree with the result reached by the Court and with almost all of its opinion. I write separately to indicate some variation in reasoning and also to compare this case with the companion case of *Norwest Bank Nebraska, N.A. v. Tveten*, 848 F.2d 871, also decided today by this panel.

* * *

The Court is entirely correct in holding that there is no extrinsic fraud here. The money placed into exempt property was not borrowed, the cash received from the sales was accounted for, and the property was sold for fair market value. The fact that the sale was to family members, "standing on its own, does not establish extrinsic evidence of fraud."

With all of this I agree completely, but exactly the same statements can be made, just as accurately, with respect to Dr. Tveten's case. So far as I can tell, there are only three differences between Dr. Tveten and the Hansons, and all of them are legally irrelevant: (1) Dr. Tveten is a physician, and the Hansons are farmers; (2) Dr. Tveten attempted to claim exempt status for about $700,000 worth of property, while the Hansons are claiming it for about $31,000 worth of property; and (3) the Minnesota exemption statute whose shelter Dr. Tveten sought had no dollar limit, while the South Dakota statute exempting the proceeds of life-insurance policies * * * is limited to $20,000. The first of these three differences—the occupation of the parties—is plainly immaterial, and no one contends otherwise. The second—the amounts of money involved—is also irrelevant, in my view, because the relevant statute contains no dollar limit, and for judges to set one involves essentially a legislative decision not suitable for the judicial branch. The relevant statute for present purposes is § 522(b)(2)(A), which authorizes debtors to claim exemptions available under "State or local law," and says nothing about any dollar limitations, by contrast to § 522(d), the federal schedule of exemptions, which contains a number of dollar limitations. The third difference—that between the Minnesota and South Dakota statutes—is also legally immaterial, and for a closely related reason. The federal exemption statute, just referred to, simply incorporates state and local exemption laws without regard to whether those laws contain dollar limitations of their own.

The Court attempts to reconcile the results in the two cases by characterizing the question presented as one of fact—whether the conversion was undertaken with fraudulent intent, or with an intent to delay or hinder creditors. In *Tveten*, the Bankruptcy Court found fraudulent intent, whereas in *Hanson* it did not. Neither finding is clearly erroneous, the Court says, so both judgments are affirmed. This analysis collapses upon examination. For in *Tveten* the major indicium of fraudulent intent relied on by the Bankruptcy Court was Dr. Tveten's avowed purpose to place the assets in question out of the reach of his creditors, a purpose that, as a matter of law, cannot amount to fraudulent intent, as the Court's opinion in *Hanson* explicitly states. The result, in practice, appears to be this: a debtor will be allowed to convert property into exempt form, or not, depending on findings of fact made in the court of first instance, the Bankruptcy Court, and these findings will turn on whether the Bankruptcy Court regards the amount of money involved as too much. With all deference, that is not a rule of law. It is simply a license to make distinctions among debtors based on subjective considerations that will vary more widely than the length of the chancellor's foot.


## Norwest Bank Nebraska v. Tveten

United States Court of Appeals, Eighth Circuit, 1988.
848 F.2d 871.

■ TIMBERS, Circuit Judge.

Appellant Omar A. Tveten, a physician who owed creditors almost $19,000,000, mostly in the form of personal guaranties on a number of investments whose value had deteriorated greatly, petitioned for Chapter 11 bankruptcy. He had converted almost all of his non-exempt property, with a value of about $700,000, into exempt property that could not be reached by his creditors. The bankruptcy court, on the basis of its findings of fact and conclusions of law, entered an order on February 27, 1987, denying a discharge in view of its finding that Tveten intended to defraud, delay, and hinder his creditors. The district court * * * affirmed the bankruptcy court's order. On appeal, Tveten asserts that his transfers merely constituted astute pre-bankruptcy planning. We hold that the bankruptcy court was not clearly erroneous in inferring fraudulent intent on the part of Tveten. We affirm.

**I**

\* \* \*

Tveten is a 59-year-old physician in general practice. He is the sole shareholder of Omar A. Tveten, P.A., a professional corporation. He has no dependents. He began investing in various real estate developments. These investments initially were quite successful. Various physician friends of Tveten joined him in organizing a corporation to invest in these ventures. These investments were highly leveraged. The physicians, including Tveten, personally had guaranteed the debt arising out of these investments. In mid–1985, Tveten's investments began to sour. He became personally liable for an amount close to $19,000,000—well beyond his ability to pay. Appellees Norwest Bank Nebraska, N.A. ("Norwest Bank"), Business Development Corporation of Nebraska ("Business Development"), and Harold J. Panuska ("Panuska") as trustee of the Harold J. Panuska Profit Sharing Trust and the Harold J. Panuska Employee Trust Fund, became creditors of Tveten as a result of his various investment ventures.

Tveten filed a Chapter 11 petition on January 7, 1986. Meanwhile, several creditors already had commenced lawsuits against him. Panuska had obtained a $139,657 judgment against him on October 9, 1985. Norwest Bank and Business Development had commenced an action against him but had not obtained judgment when Tveten filed for bankruptcy. On the date the Chapter 11 petition was filed, Tveten owed his creditors close to $19,000,000.

Before filing for bankruptcy, Tveten consulted counsel. As part of his pre-bankruptcy planning, he liquidated almost all of his non-exempt property, converting it into exempt property worth approximately $700,000. This was accomplished through some seventeen separate transfers. The non-exempt property he liquidated included land sold to his parents and his brother, respectively, for $70,000 and $75,732 in cash; life insurance policies and annuities with a for-profit company with cash values totalling $96,307.58; his net salary and bonuses of $27,820.91; his Keogh plan and individual retirement fund of $20,487.35; his corporation's profit-sharing plan worth $325,774.51; and a home sold for $50,000.[1] All of the liquidated property was converted into life insurance or annuity contracts with the Lutheran Brotherhood, a fraternal benefit association, which, under Minnesota law, cannot be attached by creditors. Tveten concedes that the purpose of these transfers was to shield his assets from creditors. Minnesota law provides that creditors cannot attach *any* money or other benefits payable by a fraternal benefit association. \* \* \* Unlike most exemption provisions in other states, the Minnesota exemption has no monetary limit. Indeed, under this exemption, Tveten attempted to place $700,000 worth of his property out of his creditors' reach.

---

[1] There were no claims that these transfers were for less than market value.

Tveten sought a discharge with respect to $18,920,000 of his debts. Appellees objected to Tveten's discharge. In its order of February 27, 1987, the bankruptcy court concluded that, although Tveten's conversion of non-exempt property to exempt property just before petitioning for bankruptcy, standing alone, would not justify denial of a discharge, his inferred intent to defraud would. The bankruptcy court held that, even if the exemptions were permissible, Tveten had abused the protections permitted a debtor under the Bankruptcy Code (the "Code"). His awareness of Panuska's judgment against him and of several pending lawsuits, his rapidly deteriorating business investments, and his exposure to extensive liability well beyond his ability to pay, all were cited by the court in its description of the circumstances under which Tveten converted his property. Moreover, the court concluded that Tveten intended to hinder and delay his creditors. Accordingly, the bankruptcy court denied Tveten a discharge.

Tveten appealed from the bankruptcy court order to the federal district court. In a memorandum opinion and order entered July 10, 1987, the district court affirmed the denial of a discharge, concluding that the bankruptcy court's finding as to Tveten's intent was not clearly erroneous.[3]

The instant appeal followed. Basically, Tveten asserts on appeal that as a matter of law we should reject the factors relied on by the bankruptcy court to infer that Tveten intended to delay, hinder and defraud creditors. We disagree. We affirm.

## II

The sole issue on appeal is whether Tveten properly was denied a discharge in view of the transfers alleged to have been in fraud of creditors.

At the outset, it is necessary to distinguish between (1) a debtor's right to exempt certain property from the claims of his creditors and (2) his right to a discharge of his debts. * * * When the debtor claims a state-created exemption, the scope of the claim is determined by state law. It is well established that under the Code the conversion of non-exempt to exempt property for the purpose of placing the property out of the reach of creditors, without more, will not deprive the debtor of the exemption to which he otherwise would be entitled. E.g., *Ford v. Poston*, 773 F.2d 52, 54 (4th Cir.1985); * * * *In re Reed*, 700 F.2d 986, 990 (5th

---

[3] Before the district court entered its order, the Supreme Court of Minnesota held in a decision entered March 27, 1987, that annuities and life insurance contracts issued by a fraternal benefit society were exempt under Minnesota law, but that these statutory provisions violated the Minnesota Constitution. *In re Tveten*, 402 N.W.2d 551 (Minn.1987). Accordingly, Tveten no longer will be able to claim these exemptions. Following the opinion of the Supreme Court of Minnesota, Tveten claimed an exemption for his pension in the amount of approximately $200,000. He and his creditors settled this issue before the bankruptcy court. He will retain this property as exempt.

Cir.1983) * * *. Both the House and Senate Reports regarding the debtor's right to claim exemptions state:

> "As under current law, the debtor will be permitted to convert non-exempt property into exempt property before filing a bankruptcy petition. The practice is not fraudulent as to creditors, and permits the debtor to make full use of the exemptions to which he is entitled under the law."

H.R.Rep. No. 595, 95th Cong., 1st Sess. 361 (1977); S.Rep. No. 989, 95th Cong., 2d Sess. 76 (1978). * * *

A debtor's right to a discharge, however, unlike his right to an exemption, is determined by *federal,* not state, law. The Code provides that a debtor may be denied a discharge under Chapter 7 if, among other things, he has transferred property "with intent to hinder, delay, or defraud a creditor" within one year before the date of the filing of the petition. § 727(a)(2). Although Tveten filed for bankruptcy under Chapter 11, the proscription against discharging a debtor with fraudulent intent in a Chapter 7 proceeding is equally applicable against a debtor applying for a Chapter 11 discharge. The reason for this is that the Code provides that confirmation of a plan does not discharge a Chapter 11 debtor if "the debtor would be denied a discharge under section 727(a) of this title if the case were a case under Chapter 7 of this title." § 1141(d)(3)(C).

Although the determination as to whether a discharge should be granted or denied is governed by federal law, the standard applied consistently by the courts is the same as that used to determine whether an exemption is permissible, i.e. absent extrinsic evidence of fraud, mere conversion of non-exempt property to exempt property is not fraudulent as to creditors even if the motivation behind the conversion is to place those assets beyond the reach of creditors. * * * *Forsberg v. Security State Bank,* 15 F.2d 499 (8th Cir.1926).

As the bankruptcy court correctly found here, therefore, the issue in the instant case revolves around whether there was extrinsic evidence to demonstrate that Tveten transferred his property on the eve of bankruptcy with intent to defraud his creditors. The bankruptcy court's finding that there was such intent to defraud may be reversed by us only if clearly erroneous. * * *

There are a number of cases in which the debtor converted non-exempt property to exempt property on the eve of bankruptcy and was granted a discharge because there was no extrinsic evidence of the debtor's intent to defraud. In *Forsberg,* supra, an old decision of our Court, a debtor was granted a discharge despite his trade of non-exempt cattle for exempt hogs while insolvent and in contemplation of bankruptcy. Although we found that the trade was effected so that the debtor could increase his exemptions, the debtor "should [not] be penalized for merely doing what the law allows him to do." 15 F.2d at 501. We concluded that "before the existence of such fraudulent purpose can be properly found, there must appear in evidence some facts or circumstances which are extrinsic to the mere facts of conversion of nonexempt assets into exempt and which are indicative of such fraudulent purpose." Id. at 502. * * *

There also are a number of cases, however, in which the courts have denied discharges after concluding that there was extrinsic evidence of the debtor's fraudulent intent. In *Ford,* supra, the debtor had executed a deed of correction transferring a tract of land to himself and his wife as tenants by the entirety. The debtor had testified that his parents originally had conveyed the land to the debtor alone, and that this was a mistake that he corrected by executing a deed of correction. Under relevant state law, the debtor's action removed the property from the reach of his creditors who were not also creditors of his wife. The Fourth Circuit, in upholding the denial of a discharge, found significant the fact that this "mistake" in the original transfer of the property was "corrected" the day after an unsecured creditor obtained judgment against the debtor. The Fourth Circuit held that the bankruptcy court, in denying a discharge, was not clearly erroneous in finding the requisite intent to defraud, after "[h]aving heard * * * [the debtor's] testimony at trial and having considered the circumstances surrounding the transfer." Id. In *In re Reed,* supra, shortly after the debtor had arranged with his creditors to be free from the payment obligations until the following year, he rapidly had converted non-exempt assets to extinguish one home mortgage and to reduce another four months before bankruptcy, and had diverted receipts from his business into an account not divulged to his creditors. The Fifth Circuit concluded that the debtor's "whole pattern of conduct evinces that intent." 700 F.2d at 991. The court went further and stated:

> "It would constitute a perversion of the purposes of the Bankruptcy Code to permit a debtor earning $180,000 a year to convert every one of his major nonexempt assets into sheltered property on the eve of bankruptcy with actual intent to defraud his creditors and then emerge washed clean of future obligation by carefully concocted immersion in bankruptcy waters."

Id. at 992.

In most, if not all, cases determining whether discharge was properly granted or denied to a debtor who practiced "pre-bankruptcy planning", the point of reference has been the state exemptions if the debtor was claiming under them. Although discharge was not denied if the debtor merely converted his non-exempt property into exempt property as permitted under state law, the exemptions involved in these cases comported with federal policy to give the debtor a "fresh start"—by limiting the monetary value of the exemptions. This policy has been explicit, or at least implicit, in these cases. In *Forsberg,* supra, for example, we stated that it is not fraudulent for an individual who knows he is insolvent to convert non-exempt property into exempt property, thereby placing the property out of the reach of creditors "because the statutes granting exemptions have made no such exceptions, and because the policy of such statutes is to favor the debtors, at the expense of the creditors, *in the limited amounts allowed to them, by preventing the forced loss of the home and of the necessities of subsistence,* and because such statutes are construed liberally in favor of the exemption."

*Forsberg,* supra, 15 F.2d at 501 (emphasis added). Similarly, in *In re Ellingson,* supra, 63 B.R. 271, in holding that the debtors' conversion of non-exempt cash and farm machinery did not provide grounds for denial of a discharge, the court relied on the social policies behind the exemptions. The court found that the debtors' improvement of their homestead was consistent with several of these policies, such as protecting the family unit from impoverishment, relieving society from the burden of supplying subsidized housing, and providing the debtors with a means to survive during the period following their bankruptcy filing when they might have little or no income. The court held that exemptions should further one or more of the following social policies:

"'(1) To provide the debtor with property necessary for his physical survival; (2) To protect the dignity and the cultural and religious identity of the debtor; (3) To enable the debtor to rehabilitate himself financially and earn income in the future; (4) To protect the debtor's family from the adverse consequences of impoverishment; (5) To shift the burden of providing the debtor and his family with minimal financial support from society to the debtor's creditors.'"

Id. at 277–78 (quoting Resnick, *Prudent Planning or Fraudulent Transfer?,* 31 Rutgers L.R. 615, 621). * * *

In the instant case, however, the state exemption relied on by Tveten was unlimited, with the potential for unlimited abuse. Indeed, this case presents a situation in which the debtor liquidated almost his entire net worth of $700,000 and converted it to non-exempt property in seventeen transfers on the eve of bankruptcy while his creditors, to whom he owed close to $19,000,000, would be left to divide the little that remained in his estate. Borrowing the phrase used by another court, Tveten "did not want a mere *fresh* start, he wanted a *head* start." *In re Zouhar,* supra, 10 B.R. at 156 (emphasis in original). His attempt to shield property worth approximately $700,000 goes well beyond the purpose for which exemptions are permitted. Tveten's reliance on his attorney's advice does not protect him here, since that protection applies only to the extent that the reliance was reasonable. * * *

The bankruptcy court, as affirmed by the district court, examined Tveten's entire pattern of conduct and found that he had demonstrated fraudulent intent. We agree. While state law governs the legitimacy of Tveten's exemptions, it is federal law that governs his discharge. Permitting Tveten, who earns over $60,000 annually, to convert all of his major non-exempt assets into sheltered property on the eve of bankruptcy with actual intent to defraud his creditors "would constitute a perversion of the purposes of the Bankruptcy Code." *In re Reed*, supra, 700 F.2d at 992. Tveten still is entitled to retain, free from creditors' claims, property rightfully exempt under relevant state law.

We distinguish our decision in *Hanson v. First National Bank*, 848 F.2d 866 (8th Cir.1988), decided today. *Hanson* involves a creditor's objection to two of the debtors' claimed exemptions under South Dakota law, a matter governed by state law. The complaint centered on the Hansons' sale, while insolvent, of non-exempt property to family members for fair market value and their use of the proceeds to prepay their preexisting mortgage and to purchase life insurance policies in the limited amounts permissible under relevant state law. The bankruptcy court found no extrinsic evidence of fraud. The district court, in a memorandum opinion and order entered June 15, 1987, affirmed. We also affirmed, concluding that the case fell within the myriad of cases which have permitted such a conversion on the eve of bankruptcy.

## III

To summarize:

We hold that the bankruptcy court was not clearly erroneous in inferring fraudulent intent on the part of the debtor, rather than astute pre-bankruptcy planning, with respect to his transfers on the eve of bankruptcy which were intended to defraud, delay and hinder his creditors.

■  ARNOLD, Circuit Judge, dissenting.

The Court reaches a result that appeals to one's general sense of righteousness. I believe, however, that it is contrary to clearly established law, and I therefore respectfully dissent.

Dr. Tveten has never made any bones about what he is doing, or trying to do, in this case. He deliberately set out to convert as much property as possible into a form exempt from attachment by creditors under Minnesota law. Such a design necessarily involves an attempt to delay or hinder creditors, in the ordinary, non-legal sense of those words, but, under longstanding principles embodied both in judicial decisions and in statute, such a purpose is not unlawful. The governing authority in this Court is *Forsberg v. Security State Bank*, 15 F.2d 499 (8th Cir.1926).

* * *

To be sure, if there is extrinsic evidence of fraud, or of a purpose to hinder or delay creditors, discharge may and should be denied, but "extrinsic," in this context, must mean something beyond the mere conversion of assets into exempt form for the purpose of putting them out of the reach of one's creditors. If Tveten had lied to his creditors, like the debtor in *McCormick v. Security State Bank*, 822 F.2d 806 (8th Cir.1987), or misled them in some way, like the debtor in *In re Reed*, 700 F.2d 986 (5th Cir.1983), or transferred property for less than fair value to a third party, like the debtor in *Ford v. Poston*, 773 F.2d 52 (4th Cir.1985), we would have a very different case. There is absolutely no evidence of that sort of misconduct in this record, and the Court's opinion filed today cites none.

One is tempted to speculate what the result would have been in this case if the amount of assets converted had been $7,000, instead of $700,000. Indeed, the large amount of money involved is the only difference I can see between this case and *Forsberg.* It is true that the *Forsberg* opinion referred to "the limited amounts allowed to" debtors by exemptions, 15 F.2d at 501, but whether exemptions are limited in amount is a legislative question ordinarily to be decided by the people's elected representatives, in this case the Minnesota Legislature. Where courts punish debtors simply for claiming exemptions within statutory limits, troubling problems arise in separating judicial from legislative power.

* * *

If there ought to be a dollar limit, and I am inclined to think that there should be, and if practices such as those engaged in by the debtor here can become abusive, and I admit that they can, the problem is simply not one susceptible of a judicial solution according to manageable objective standards. A good statement of the kind of judicial reasoning that must underlie the result the Court reaches today appears in *In re Zouhar*, 10 B.R. 154 (Bankr.D.N.M.1981), where the amount of assets converted was $130,000. The Bankruptcy Court denied discharge, stating, among other things, that "'there is a principle of too much; phrased colloquially, when a pig becomes a hog it is slaughtered.'" Id. at 157. If I were a member of the Minnesota Legislature, I might well vote in favor of a bill to place an over-all dollar maximum on any exemption.[3] But sitting as a judge, by what criteria do I determine when this pig becomes a hog? If $700,000 is too much, what about $70,000? Would it matter if the debtor were a farmer, as in *Forsberg,* rather than a physician? (I ask the question because the appellee creditor's brief mentions the debtor's profession, which ought to be legally irrelevant, several times.)

Debtors deserve more definite answers to these questions than the Court's opinion provides. In effect, the Court today leaves the distinction between permissible and impermissible claims of exemption to each bankruptcy judge's own sense of proportion. As a result, debtors will be unable

---

[3] There is some irony in the fact that the exemption sought by the debtor in this case, that for benefits under annuities or life-insurance policies issued by fraternal associations, has been held unconstitutional under two provisions of the Minnesota Constitution. One such provision, Article 1, Section 12, provides that "[a] reasonable amount of property shall be exempt * * *." The Supreme Court of Minnesota has held that the exemption statute involved in the present case is unconstitutional precisely because it contains no dollar limit. So the principle of limitation has been upheld, the debtor has in any event lost the exemption he sought, but he also loses his discharge under today's decision.

to know in advance how far the federal courts will allow them to exercise their rights under state law.

Where state law creates an unlimited exemption, the result may be that wealthy debtors like Tveten enjoy a windfall that appears unconscionable, and contrary to the policy of the bankruptcy law. I fully agree with Judge Kishel, however, that

> [this] result * * * cannot be laid at [the] Debtor's feet; it must be laid at the feet of the state legislature. Debtor did nothing more than exercise a prerogative that was fully his under law. It cannot be said that his actions have so tainted him or his bankruptcy petition as to merit denial of discharge.

*In re Johnson*, 80 B.R. 953, 963 (Bankr.D.Minn.1987). I submit that Tveten did nothing more fraudulent than seek to take advantage of a state law of which the federal courts disapprove.

I would reverse this judgment and hold that the debtor's actions in converting property into exempt form do not bar a discharge in bankruptcy.

## NOTES

**1.** Under the prevailing view, mere conversion of the debtor's property in contemplation of bankruptcy from nonexempt assets to exempt assets does not prevent recognition of the exemption unless the conversion involves actual fraud by the debtor. If all cases in which an exemption is denied must involve actual fraud, shouldn't the result be that there has also been a fraudulent transfer that triggers § 727(a)(2)?

**2.** One court's effort to reconcile *Tveten* and *Hanson* follows:

> We read *Tveten* and *Hanson* to reaffirm the rule that conduct sufficient to defeat discharge requires indicia of fraud beyond mere use of the exemptions. Under *Tveten, Hanson,* and the cases they discuss, extrinsic evidence can be composed of: further conduct intentionally designed to materially mislead or deceive creditors about the debtor's position; conveyances for less than fair value; or, the continued retention, benefit or use of property allegedly conveyed together with evidence that the conveyance was for inadequate consideration. In addition, *Tveten* establishes that where an exemption, other than a homestead exemption, is not limited in amount, the amount of property converted into exempt forms and the form taken may be considered in determining whether fraudulent intent exists.

*In re Johnson*, 880 F.2d 78, 82 (8th Cir.1989).

**3.** The latest Eighth Circuit opinion involving conversion of nonexempt property into property exempt under Minnesota law is *In re Sholdan*, 217 F.3d 1006 (8th Cir.2000). In that case, Debtor, a 90–year old retired farmer, who had lived alone in an apartment for many years before moving to an assisted-care facility, liquidated all his assets (bank account, CDs, rights in a mortgage). He used the resulting proceeds to buy a newly built house that far exceeded his housing needs. Immediately after his purchase of the house, he filed in Chapter 7 and listed the house as exempt under Minnesota's homestead exemption. Before these transactions, Debtor had been named a defendant in a personal injury suit with damages claimed well in excess of his liability insurance coverage. After discussing *Tveten* and *Hanson*, a majority of the panel affirmed the bankruptcy court opinion that found that there was ample evidence extrinsic to the mere conversion of the assets from nonexempt to exempt that showed fraudulent intent on the part of the debtor. Judge Richard Arnold again dissented on the ground that the court had failed to identify any evidence of fraud extrinsic to the Debtor's conversion of assets for the purpose of protecting his assets from creditors, a practice that is allowed by law. In an exhaustive analysis of the case law in the field, the court in *In re Crater*, 286 B.R. 756, 771 (Bankr. D. Ariz. 2002), concluded that the Arnold dissent in *Sholdan* was a correct statement of the majority view nationwide.

**4.** One court suggests degree is as a factor in evaluating the legality of prepetition bankruptcy planning:

> One approach that appears appropriate in this instance is the "pig to hog" analysis: "when a pig becomes a hog it is slaughtered." * * * This analysis recognizes that while some prebankruptcy planning is appropriate, the wholesale expenditure of non-exempt assets on the eve of bankruptcy, including conversion to exempt assets (especially where there are liberal state law exemptions), may not be.

*In re Bowyer*, 916 F.2d 1056, 1060 (5th Cir. 1990).

**5.** In *Havoco of America, Ltd. v. Hill*, 197 F.3d 1135 (11th Cir.1999), the Circuit Court certified to the Florida Supreme Court the question whether the state constitution exempts a Florida homestead acquired by the debtor with nonexempt funds with the specific intent of hindering, delaying or defrauding creditors in violation of state fraudulent conveyance law. In a subsequent opinion in the case, 255 F.3d 1321 (11th Cir.2001), the court reported that the Florida court answered the question in the affirmative so long as the funds were not obtained through fraud or egregious conduct.

## 6. ASSET PROTECTION

Asset protection trusts are used by persons seeking to shelter their assets from their creditors. Several jurisdictions have sought to become havens for these trusts. What is the status of these trusts in bankruptcy? If Settlor grants property to Trustee to hold in trust for Beneficiary and provides that the beneficial interest cannot be voluntarily or involuntarily transferred, the restriction on transfer prevents Beneficiary's interest from being taken by its creditors under state common law because creditor process is considered to be an involuntary transfer. This is the familiar "spendthrift trust." Section 541(c)(2) provides that this restriction on transfer is enforceable in bankruptcy because it is enforceable under non-bankruptcy law; the effect is that the beneficial interest under the trust is not property of the estate. But if Settlor grants property to Trustee to hold in trust for Settlor, state common law has long held that a restriction on transfer is invalid. Historically, spendthrift self-settled trusts were void as against public policy; owners should not be allowed to free their assets from liability to their creditors in this manner. *See In re Brown*, 303 F.3d 1261 (11th Cir. 2002). Since such a trust is ineffective for asset protection under nonbankruptcy law, it is ineffective in bankruptcy as well. Jurisdictions seeking to become havens for asset protection trusts have principally done so by changing their law to validate spendthrift clauses in self-settled trusts. In these jurisdictions, restrictions against involuntary transfers are valid in bankruptcy with respect to self-settled trusts under § 522(c)(2) because they are effective under nonbankruptcy law, the law of the haven state.

In *The Death of Liability*, 106 Yale L.J. 1, 32–34 (1996), Professor Lynn LoPucki describes the use of asset protection trusts:

More than a half-dozen nations compete for foreign investment by refusing comity with respect to the enforcement of judgments and providing havens for judgment debtors from their foreign creditors. They implement the latter policy principally by validating self-settled spendthrift trusts under which the settlor is a beneficiary. In the United States, such a trust is ineffective against creditors as against public policy. A self-settled spendthrift trust amounts, in essence, to a declaration that one wishes to own one's assets free of the claims of one's judgment creditors—that is, free of liability. One commentator estimates that this offshore trust industry already administers a trillion dollars in assets.

To understand the strategy of removing assets to a spendthrift trust jurisdiction, consider the example of a medical doctor who lives and practices medicine in the United States. Assume that the doctor owns a nonexempt home, a medical practice, and liquid assets in a brokerage account. Each of the three assets is worth approximately one million dollars. . ... All of the assets are located in the United States. . ... Through a U.S. lawyer who specializes in such transactions. . . the doctor establishes a spendthrift trust [in the Cook Islands]. . . . Cook Islands law permits the doctor to serve as the "protector" of the trust assets with the power to remove and replace trustees and to veto investment decisions. Over one aspect of trust management, the doctor retains no control or power of revocation: Whoever is trustee may not expose trust assets to the claims of the doctor's creditors. The standard trust documents also mandate that the trustee ignore instructions made by the doctor under duress, such as an order from a U.S. court that the doctor cause the trust to return assets so that they may be applied to the claim of a creditor.

Once the trust has been established, the doctor deeds his home and transfers ownership of his medical practice into it. Though both are now foreign owned, the home and the medical practice remain physically in the United States. The trust will permit the doctor to use them without charge. . .. The doctor also transfers the liquid assets. . . to the Cook Islands trustee, who then proceeds to invest them in accord with nonbinding instructions furnished by the doctor.

Although, as Professor LoPucki indicates, the movement toward asset protection trusts began in offshore venues—the Channel Islands, the Cook Islands, Jersey, and the like—those seeking asset protection no longer need go abroad. Alaska, Delaware, Nevada, Rhode Island, and Utah have become the first United States jurisdictions to permit self-settled spendthrift trusts. These American cousins of the offshore asset protection trust are subject to attack if created with the intent to defraud creditors and, in Delaware, the trusts are not effective against tort creditors. The 2005 Act § 548(e) provides for a 10-year look-back provision in place of the two-year period in § 548(a) if the debtor has transferred assets to a self-settled trust for the benefit of the debtor with fraudulent intent, which may be to shelter the assets from any liability that might be incurred for violating securities laws or fraud in a fiduciary capacity or in connection with the purchase or sale of certain securities. Since such acts would likely have been considered fraudulent under the prior law, the only significant change in the law made by the 2005 Act is to give trustees eight more years of look-back time to seek out fraud. Thus, efforts by some to use the 2005 Act to abolish asset protection trusts in the United States clearly failed.

Another issue of asset protection is raised by the practice of segregating rights to payment, such as accounts receivables or mortgages, into "bankruptcy remote vehicles" to serve as security for bonds issued to investors. For example, assume that if Originator, a financial institution, buys accounts receivables from retail stores, pools these accounts and issues bonds secured by them, the credit rating agencies would award these bonds a single A credit rating. Originator may seek a higher bond rating by engaging in a transaction referred to as "asset securitization" under which Originator transfers the accounts to a trust or limited liability company that engages in no business other than ownership and management of the segregated assets, a "special purpose vehicle," in which the transferred assets would be structurally isolated from Originator's general assets. The intended result of this transaction is that the bond obligation is not considered a liability of Originator and therefore is not reflected on Originator's balance sheet; moreover, in the event of Originator's bankruptcy, the accounts have been removed from Originator's estate and are not available to its creditors. Since investors buying the bonds are relieved of the risk of Orginator's bankruptcy, this allows credit rating agencies to rate the bonds on the basis of the value of the assets transferred rather than the general credit of Originator, the transferor: AA or AAA credit ratings may result.

Bankruptcy lawyers have long been skeptical of this stratagem for making assets bankruptcy-proof. They have attacked securitization transactions in which the transferor remains involved in the management of the assets after transfer, in which the transferor has issued guarantees or similar credit enhancements, or has retained a residual interest in the entity holding the transferred assets. More will be said about strategies for attacking asset securitization transactions in Chapter 8 with respect to the substantive consolidation doctrine on pp. 504-505.

# CHAPTER 3

# CLAIMS

---

## A. INTRODUCTION

### 1. TERMINOLOGY

In the Bankruptcy Code the terms "debt" and "claim" are correlatives. Debt is defined in § 101 as "liability on a claim." Section 727(b) provides that, subject to the exceptions stated in § 523, a discharge in bankruptcy "discharges the debtor from all debts" that arose before bankruptcy. Thus, the debtor cannot be discharged from an obligation unless the obligation is on a claim. Claim serves the double function of defining the obligations that will receive distributions in bankruptcy and the kind of obligations that will be discharged.

Claim is defined in § 101 in very broad terms as any "right to payment, whether or not such right is reduced to judgment, liquidated, unliquidated, fixed, contingent, matured, unmatured, disputed, undisputed, legal, equitable, secured, or unsecured," and also includes a "right to an equitable remedy for breach of performance if such breach gives rise to a right to payment." The bankruptcy court can therefore discharge any obligation of the debtor that gives the creditor a right to payment. Obligations that give rise to equitable remedies such as specific performance can be discharged in bankruptcy if the breach that gives rise to the equitable remedy also gives rise to a right to payment. *See In re Ward, infra* p. 107

A claim is the basis for a distribution from the bankruptcy estate. A "proof of claim," which is a written statement setting forth a creditor's claim, is usually filed by the creditor having the claim. § 501 and Bankruptcy Rule 3001. However, in Chapter 7 if it appears that there are no assets from which a dividend can be paid to creditors, Rule 2002(e) provides that creditors may be notified that it is unnecessary to file claims. Creditor is defined in § 101 to mean an entity holding a claim that arose before the filing of the petition in a voluntary case or before the order for relief in an involuntary case. Thus, if a debtor files in Chapter 7, rights against the debtor that arise after bankruptcy are not treated as claims in bankruptcy. Holders of such postpetition claims cannot share in the distribution of the estate and their claims are not discharged.

A claim is entitled to distributions only if it is "allowed." § 726(a). Allowance of a claim means simply that it has been recognized by the court as valid in the amount claimed. In many cases there is no dispute concerning the claim. For that reason § 502(a) provides that a claim, proof of which has been filed, is allowed unless a party in interest objects. Party in interest, which is a term used in various parts of the Bankruptcy Code, is not defined. Its meaning may vary depending upon the kind of dispute involved in the particular case. With respect to objecting to a creditor's claim, it always includes the trustee, and in some instances other creditors and the debtor. *See In re I & F Corp.*, 219 B.R. 483 (Bankr.S.D.Ohio 1998). If there is an objection, the court must determine whether the claim is allowable. § 502(b).

Although under § 726(a) a claim cannot share in the distribution of the estate unless is it allowed under § 502, claims that are not allowed are nevertheless discharged under § 727(b): "[A] discharge under subsection (a) of this section discharges the debtor from all debts that arose before the date of the order for relief under this chapter, * * * whether or not a claim based on any such debt or liability is allowed under section 502 * * *."

## 2.  TIME LIMITS FOR FILING PROOF OF CLAIM

### a.    Cases under Chapters 7, 12 and 13

*Section 502(b)(9).* Creditors whose claims are scheduled by the debtor should receive notice of the commencement of the bankruptcy case, the date of the statutory first meeting of the creditors, and the deadline to file a proof of claim, often called the bar date. Rule 2002. For Chapters 7, 12 and 13, Rule 3002(c) prescribes that this date will be not later than 90 days after "the first date set for the meeting of the creditors called under § 341(a)," subject to five stated exceptions. The question dividing the courts before 1994 was whether a claim that was filed after the 90–day period prescribed in Rule 3002 was allowable.

In 1994, Congress added § 502(b)(9), which provides that a tardily filed claim must be disallowed if an objection to the claim is filed except to the extent that the holder of the claim is entitled to distribution under § 726(a)(1), (2) or (3). A special rule is prescribed allowing 180 days after the date of the order for relief for governmental claims to be filed. With respect to priority claims, § 726(a)(1) was amended to allow distribution to a tardily filed claim so long as the filing takes place before the date on which the trustee commences distribution under § 726. This is the date on which a court approves the trustee's final report allowing the trustee to commence final distribution of the estate. *See In re Van Gerpen*, 267 F.3d 453 (5th Cir.2001).

Although the Section-by-Section Description § 213, 140 Cong.Rec. H10768 (Oct. 4,1994), says that the addition of § 502(b)(9) was intended to disallow claims that are not timely filed, in Chapter 7 cases the amendment actually subordinates rather than disallows unsecured, nonpriority claims that are tardily filed. The first "except" clause in § 502(b)(9) provides that late claims are allowable only to the extent that they qualify for distribution as tardily filed claims under § 726(a)(1) which governs priority claims, § 726(a)(2) which allows payment at the second tier level of claims that were not timely filed because the creditor didn't know of the case in time to file, and § 726(a)(3) which provides for payment at the third tier level of all other tardily filed claims. Thus, although § 502(b)(9) does not disallow tardily filed nonpriority unsecured claims, it achieves the same result by awarding them a place at the end of the line under § 726(a)(3). Only rarely are all the nonpriority unsecured claims paid in full. *See In re Outboard Marine*, 386 F.3d 824 (7th Cir. 2004), where the effect of subordination was to disallow the claim.

*Application of § 502(b)(9) in Chapters 12 and 13.* The fact that § 502(b)(9) deals with late filed claims by subordinating them pursuant to § 726 raises problems in Chapters 12 and 13 cases because, on its face, § 726 applies only to Chapter 7 cases. § 103(b). The first case to deal with this question with respect to Chapter 13, *In re Lang*, 196 B.R. 528, 530 (Bankr.D.Ariz.1996), posed the question: "[T]he issue is whether § 726(a)(1)-(3) applies to all chapters because it is referenced in § 502(b) or whether the exception contained in § 502(b) is limited to claims that independently fall within the explicit provisions of § 726(a)." The court adopted the latter interpretation. *In re Gardenhire*, 209 F.3d 1145, 1147 n. 6 (9th Cir.2000), agrees that § 726(a) does not apply to Chapter 13 cases. *In re Greenig*, 152 F.3d 631, 633 n. 3 (7th Cir.1998), reaches the same conclusion with respect to Chapter 12.

*Notice of filing.* All creditors whose claims are scheduled by the debtor should be notified by the clerk of the court of the filing in bankruptcy and the meeting of creditors. Rule 2002. If a debt is not scheduled, the creditor will not receive notice under Rule 2002. If the creditor does not learn of the bankruptcy until after the 90–day period has expired, the claim may be disallowed unless the case falls within one of the exceptions to the 90–day rule set out in Rule 3002(c). As stated above, § 502(b)(9) provides some relief by its reference to § 726(a)(2)(C), which allows a creditor in a Chapter 7 case to share in the estate at the second-tier level if the creditor did not have notice of the bankruptcy that would have allowed timely filing of a claim and if the late claim is filed in time to permit payment. Though a claim may be disallowed if it was not scheduled and the creditor did not have notice of the bankruptcy in time to allow for timely filing of the claim, the claim is not discharged. § 523(a)(3).

### b. Cases under Chapter 11

Cases under Chapter 11 are governed by Rule 3003; the 90–day rule of Rule 3002(c) doesn't apply in Chapter 11. Rather, the time within which proofs of claim must be filed (the bar date) is fixed by the court. The bar date may be extended by the court for cause. Rule 3003(c). Late filed claims under Chapter 11 are governed by Rule 9006(b)(1). In the context of the filing of a proof of claim after a bar date, the rule provides that a bankruptcy court "for cause shown may * * * in its discretion * * * on motion made after the [bar date] permit [a proof of claim to be filed] where the failure to act was the result of excusable neglect." The circuits were divided on the meaning of "excusable neglect." The majority took a narrow view of the term as requiring a showing that the delay was caused by circumstances beyond the claimant's control. Others used a more flexible analysis.

In *Pioneer Investment Services Co. v. Brunswick Associates Limited Partnership*, 507 U.S. 380 (1993), the Court resolved the split in the circuits by embracing the more flexible view. In *Pioneer Investment* the notice of the bar date was rather inconspicuously appended to the notice for the § 341 meeting of creditors instead of being set out in a separate notice. The president of the corporate general partner of the claimant received and read the notice and passed it on to an experienced bankruptcy lawyer. When asked later by the president whether there was a deadline for filing claims, the lawyer replied that no bar date had been set and that there was no urgency about filing a proof of claim. The claimant filed a claim 20 days after the bar date, but the bankruptcy court declined to allow the late filing on the ground of excusable neglect, citing the lawyer's indifference and negligence. The Court held that there was excusable neglect in this case and that the bankruptcy court had abused its discretion in refusing the late filing. The Court held further that the strict Chapter 7 rule on late filing is different from the more flexible Chapter 11 rule. Equitable balancing of interests of the parties is more appropriate in Chapter 11. The Court identified several factors to be taken into consideration in determining excusable neglect in tardy filing cases: the danger of prejudice to the debtor, the length of the delay and its potential impact on judicial proceedings, the reason for the delay, including whether it was within the reasonable control of the claimant, and whether the claimant acted in good faith. Moreover, the Court considered it significant that the notice of the bar date was given in an unusual manner.

The post-*Pioneer Investment* cases on excusable neglect have been a mixed bag. On the issue of attorney negligence, some cases have virtually ignored *Pioneer Investment* in adhering to the old narrow rule. *E.g., In re Plunkett*, 82 F.3d 738 (7th Cir.1996) (Easterbrook, J.). But most have acknowledged that "[t]here is not a 'hard and fast' rule * * * which bars a trial judge from exercising discretion to determine whether attorney negligence in missing a filing deadline may be deemed 'excusable neglect.'" *Robb v. Norfolk & Western Railway Co.*, 122 F.3d 354, 361 (7th Cir.1997) (marshaling the authorities).

## B. RIGHTS TO PAYMENT

### 1. LEGAL RIGHTS

Although a claim is defined as a right to payment, it is not necessary that there be a present right to receive money. Unmatured claims are specifically covered in the definition of claim. Nor is it necessary that there be any certainty that a right to payment will ever mature. The definition of claim includes contingent claims. A contingent claim is "one which the debtor will be called upon to pay only upon the occurrence or happening of an extrinsic event which will trigger the liability of the debtor to the alleged creditor and if such triggering event or occurrence was one reasonably contemplated by the debtor and creditor at the time the event giving rise to the claim occurred." *In re All Media Properties, Inc.*, 5 B.R. 126, 133 (Bankr.S.D.Tex.1980); *In re B.D. International Discount Corp.*, 701 F.2d 1071, 1073 n.2 (2d Cir.1983) (Friendly, J.). For example, the debtor may have guaranteed some performance by X that is due to Y in the future. Does Y have a claim in the bankruptcy of the debtor if the performance by X is not yet due and there is no basis for determining whether X will or will not perform? There are two aspects to the problem: First, if Y has a claim, the court must determine the amount that Y is entitled to receive. Second, if Y has a claim, it is subject to discharge in bankruptcy. Under § 727(b) the debtor is discharged "from all debts that arose before the date of the order for relief." In many cases estimating the amount of a contingent liability is speculative. Under the Bankruptcy Act a contingent claim not capable of reasonable estimation within a time that did not unduly delay administration of the estate was not allowable, with the effect that a contingent claim incapable of reasonable estimation was not dischargeable and not entitled to share in the estate. If the debtor was an individual, the claim was payable from postbankruptcy property of the debtor if it ever ripened into a right to payment. If the debtor was a corporation, the effect was to deny any payment to the holder of the claim if the corporation was liquidated. Section 502(c) rejects this approach. Any contingent claim must be estimated by the court and it is dischargeable.

As we shall see, under the Bankruptcy Code much turns on when a claim arises. We use Judge Mark's lucid and informative opinion in *Piper Aircraft* to explore this issue.

## In re Piper Aircraft Corporation
United States Bankruptcy Court, S.D. Florida, 1994.
162 B.R. 619.

■ ROBERT A. MARK, Bankruptcy Judge.

Piper Aircraft Corporation has been designing, manufacturing and selling general aviation aircraft and associated spare parts since 1937. Approximately 50,000 to 60,000 aircraft are still operational in the United States. Piper is attempting to reorganize under Chapter 11 of the Bankruptcy Code. Following confirmation of a plan, some of these planes will crash. People will be killed or injured. Others will suffer property damage. Some of the crashes may be caused in whole or in part by design or construction defects in the planes or in their parts. The Court must determine whether these presently unknown persons who will suffer personal injury or property damage in the future have "claims" in this bankruptcy case.

The specific issue before the Court is framed by an objection by the Official Committee of Unsecured Creditors to the claim filed by a court-appointed legal representative on behalf of this broad class of potential future claimants. The Court concludes that these future claimants do not have "claims" as defined by § 101(5) of the Bankruptcy Code.

## BACKGROUND FACTS AND PROCEDURAL HISTORY

\* \* \*

Over the years, Piper has been a defendant in several lawsuits based on its manufacture, design, sale, distribution and support of aircraft and parts. Although it has never acknowledged that its products are harmful or defective, Piper has suffered from the economic drain of escalating litigation costs in connection with defending these product liability claims. In large part because of this financial burden, on July 1, 1991, Piper filed a voluntary petition for relief under Chapter 11 of Title 11 of the United States Code.

With 50,000 to 60,000 Piper aircraft still in operation, accidents involving these aircraft undoubtedly will occur. Thus, additional though presently unidentifiable individuals will have similar product liability, property damage, or other claims as a result of incidents occurring after confirmation of the Debtor's Chapter 11 plan of reorganization, but arising out of or relating to aircraft or parts manufactured, sold, designed, or distributed by the Debtor prior to confirmation.

The Debtor's anticipated plan of reorganization contemplates finding a purchaser of substantially all of the Debtor's assets or obtaining investments from outside sources with the proceeds of such transactions serving to fund distributions to creditors. On April 8, 1993, the Debtor and Pilatus Aircraft Limited ("Pilatus") signed a letter of intent ("Letter of Intent") pursuant to which the Debtor agreed to sell to Pilatus, and Pilatus agreed to purchase from the Debtor, substantially all of the Debtor's assets. The Letter of Intent required the Debtor to seek the appointment of a legal representative (the "Legal Representative") for future claimants to represent their interests in arranging a set-aside of monies generated by the sale to pay off future product liability claims. On May 19, 1993, the Court entered an order authorizing the appointment of David G. Epstein as Legal Representative of the "Future Claimants."[1] However, the Court specifi-

---

[1] The May 19 Order specifically defines "Future Claimants" to include:

All persons, whether known or unknown, born or unborn, who may, after the date of confirmation of Piper's chapter 11 plan of reorganization, assert a claim or claims for personal injury, property damage, wrongful death, damages, contribution and/or indemnification, based in whole or in part upon events occurring or arising after the Confirmation Date, including claims based on the law of product liability, against Piper or its successor arising out of or relating to aircraft or parts manufactured and sold, designed, distributed or supported by Piper prior to the Confirmation Date.

cally excluded from the appointment order any finding on whether the Future Claimants hold claims against the Debtor under § 101(5) of the Bankruptcy Code.

On July 12, 1993, the Legal Representative filed a proof of claim on behalf of the Future Claimants (the "Claim"). In the Claim, the Legal Representative asserts that the Debtor is indebted to the Future Claimants in the approximate amount of $100,000,000. The Claim purports to be based on statistical assumptions regarding the number of people who are likely to suffer personal injury or property damage after the confirmation of a reorganization plan, which is caused by Debtor's pre-confirmation manufacture, sale, design, distribution or support of aircraft and spare parts.

In conjunction with the Claim, the Legal Representative filed a motion requesting estimation of the Claim for voting purposes. At the July 26, 1993 preliminary hearing on this motion, the Debtor, the Official Committee of Unsecured Creditors (the "Committee") and the Legal Representative urged the Court to determine whether the Future Claimants hold "claims" as defined in § 101(5) of the Bankruptcy Code before conducting an evidentiary hearing on the estimation motion. The Court agreed and set a briefing and hearing schedule, with the issue to be framed by a formal objection to the Claim. In turn, on July 28, 1993, the Committee filed an Objection to the Legal Representative's Claim.

The Legal Representative and Committee submitted memoranda on the objection, as did three potential purchasers of Piper's assets: Pilatus; 2I, Inc.; and Alberta, Limited. A hearing on the Objection to Claim was held on September 2, 1993. At the hearing, the Debtor joined the Committee in objecting to the Claim.[3] Various issues arose at the hearing, including whether or not the claims could be estimated and provided for in a plan and whether or not the claims, if they existed, were dischargeable. These issues are relevant to but distinct from the narrow and only issue the Court decides here: whether the Future Claimants hold "claims" as defined in § 101(5) of the Bankruptcy Code.

On September 10, 1993, the Court announced its ruling that the Future Claimants do not hold claims within the meaning of § 101(5). Detailed findings and conclusions pursuant to Fed.R.Bankr.P. 7052 were stated on the record. The Court advised that its written order disallowing the Claim, together with a Memorandum Opinion, would be entered subsequently.

* * *

---

[3] When the Debtor sought appointment of the Legal Representative, it believed that a plan of reorganization based upon a sale of assets would have to make provision for the interests of Future Claimants, whether or not they had "claims." The Debtor and the Committee now believe that providing for Future Claimants is unnecessary to attract viable purchase offers and legally impermissible if, as the Legal Representative argues, the Future Claimants can be treated under a plan only if they have "claims."

## DISCUSSION

### A. Statute and Legislative History

The Bankruptcy Code [§ 101] defines claim as follows:

"claim" means—

**(A)** right to payment, whether or not such right is reduced to judgment, liquidated, unliquidated, fixed, contingent, matured, unmatured, disputed, undisputed, legal, equitable, secured or unsecured; or

**(B)** right to an equitable remedy for breach of performance if such breach gives rise to a right to payment, whether or not such right to an equitable remedy is reduced to judgment, fixed, contingent, matured, unmatured, disputed, undisputed, secured or unsecured * * *.

When Congress promulgated § 101(5), it intended to define "claim" more broadly than the term was defined under prior bankruptcy law.

Under the former Bankruptcy Act of 1898, a corporation could reorganize under Chapter X or Chapter XI. Chapter XI defined claim very narrowly. Under Chapter XI, a claim had to be both "proved" and "allowed." Contingent obligations were theoretically "provable" under § 63 of the Bankruptcy Act. However, a contingent or unliquidated claim would not be "allowed" under § 57(d) of the Bankruptcy Act unless the claim could be estimated or liquidated. If the court believed a claim was not susceptible to liquidation or estimation, or that such liquidation or estimation would unduly delay the administration of the bankrupt's estate, the claim would be disallowed, and in turn be deemed unprovable under § 63(d) of the Act. Disallowed or unprovable claims were not subject to discharge.

As a result of this narrow definition, Chapter XI of the Bankruptcy Act prevented a debtor from treating under its plan certain contingent claims that were not "provable," including contingent tort claims. Thus, the Act allowed such claims to be asserted against the reorganized debtor and caused two potential results which contravened established bankruptcy policy: first, it allowed similarly situated creditors to be treated differently; and second, it often led to the failure of the reorganization process. * * *

In enacting the current Bankruptcy Code, Congress intentionally eliminated the "provability" requirement to broaden the range of claims that could be dealt with in bankruptcy and thereby avoid the inequities occurring under the Bankruptcy Act. The legislative history of § 101(5) reflects the intent of Congress in revising the definition of "claim," providing:

By this broadest possible definition, and by the use of the term throughout title 11, especially in subchapter I of Chapter 5, the bill contemplates that all legal obligations of the debtor, no matter how remote or contingent, will be able to be dealt with in the bankruptcy case. It permits the broadest possible relief in the Bankruptcy Court.

Based upon the statutory language and legislative history, virtually all courts agree that the definition of claim is expansive. * * * The question is, how far can the concept of "claim" be expanded? In referring to the legislative history, one court has observed, "That language surely points us in a direction, but provides little indication of how far we should travel," *In re Chateaugay Corp.*, 944 F.2d 997, 1003 (2d Cir.1991).

Pilatus and the Legal Representative argue that any right to payment arising out of the prepetition conduct of the Debtor, no matter how remote, should be deemed a claim and provided for in this case. Specifically, they argue that because Piper aircraft and parts manufactured, designed, sold or distributed prepetition will be involved in post-confirmation accidents causing injury, death and property damage, those individuals who suffer damages, although not yet identifiable, hold claims cognizable in this bankruptcy case. The Committee and the Debtor argue that while Congress intended to expand the definition of claim, the definition is not so broad as to include unidentified, and presently unidentifiable, individuals with no discernible prepetition relationship to Piper. For the reasons set forth below, the Court agrees with the Committee and the Debtor.

### B. Accrued State Law Claim Theory

The issue before the Court is defining the extent to which a "contingent," "unmatured," and "unliquidated" potential right to payment is a claim under § 101(5). Several theories have emerged in the relevant case law. Under the most narrow interpretation, there is no claim for bankruptcy purposes until a claim has accrued under state law. Most notable among cases adopting this approach is the Third Circuit's decision in *In re M. Frenville Co.*, 744 F.2d 332 (3d Cir.1984). In *Frenville*, the court held that an indemnification claim which did not arise under state law until after the petition date was not a claim under § 101(5).

The problem with the *Frenville* decision and its progeny is that exclusive reliance on the accrual of a state law cause of action ignores the intent of Congress to define claim broadly in bankruptcy cases. State or non-bankruptcy law does not and should not override the bankruptcy policies of equitable distribution to creditors and a fresh start to the debtor. Defining the right to payment under § 101(5) ["claim"] by tying it to state law is inappropriate and the Court thus rejects the accrued state law claim theory, as have most courts that have considered it in the context of both mass tort cases and indemnification cases. * * *

### C. Conduct Test Theory

Recognizing the shortcomings of the standard espoused in *Frenville*, several courts, including those addressing mass tort issues, devised a theory commonly referred to as the "Conduct Test." Under this test, a right to payment arises when the conduct giving rise to the alleged liability occurred. The leading Circuit Court of Appeals case describing and adopting the Conduct Test is *Grady v. A.H. Robins Co.*, 839 F.2d 198 (4th Cir.1988). In *A.H. Robins*, the claimant, Grady, was inserted with a Dalkon Shield contraceptive intra-uterine device (IUD) a number of years prior to the petition date. After the petition was filed, Grady manifested injuries related to the Dalkon Shield. Relying on California's "discovery rule"[7] statute of limitations provision, Grady argued that she was not stayed from bringing suit against the debtor because her claim arose post-petition.

The *A.H. Robins* court disagreed. Applying the Conduct Test, the Fourth Circuit held that Grady's claim was a prepetition contingent claim, since all of the acts constituting the tort other than the manifestation of injury had occurred prior to the petition date. The court stated that Grady's claim was undoubtedly contingent as that term is defined in Black's Law Dictionary, and continued:

> [The claim] depends upon a future uncertain event, that event being the manifestation of injury from use of the Dalkon Shield. We do not believe that there must be a right to the immediate payment of money in the case of a tort or allied breach of warranty or like claim, as present here, when the acts constituting the tort or breach of warranty have occurred prior to the filing of the petition. . .

Using this analysis, the court held that Grady had a claim that arose before the commencement of the case.

Essentially the same test was applied in the asbestos case of *In re Waterman S.S. Corp.*, 141 B.R. 552 (Bankr.S.D.N.Y.1992), vacated on other grounds, 157 B.R. 220 (S.D.N.Y.1993). In *Waterman*, former employees of the debtor sought a declaratory judgment holding that their asbestosis claims, which were manifested post-confirmation, were not discharged by the confirmation order. In reaching his decision, Bankruptcy Judge Conrad bifurcated the analysis into two issues: first, whether the individuals held claims, and second, if they did hold claims, whether these claims were dischargeable.

In answering the first question, Judge Conrad followed the lead of the Johns–Manville asbestosis cases and reasoned that, in determining whether or not a claim exists, "the focus should be on the time when the acts giving rise to the alleged liability were performed," In re Johns–Manville Corp., 57 B.R. 680, 690 (Bankr.S.D.N.Y.1986). Since the asbestos was manufactured prepetition, and since the individuals suffering injuries were exposed prepetition, the former employees held "claims" under § 101. However, because the debtor failed to include this known class of creditors in its schedules and failed to provide adequate notice to this

---

[7] Under California law, actions based on progressively developing or continuing wrongs where the nature, extent or permanence of the harm are difficult to discover, do not accrue until the injured party knows or should have known of the cause of injury.

known class, Judge Conrad held that the claimants did not have notice sufficient to meet due process requirements for discharging their claims.[8]

At least one case has used a similar application of the Conduct Test outside the mass tort context. In *In re Edge*, 60 B.R. 690 (Bankr.M.D.Tenn.1986), the debtor was a dentist. After the debtor filed his Chapter 7 petition, a former patient sought a declaration that a "claim" based on negligent treatment received prior to the debtor's filing, but discovered afterwards, was a postpetition claim and thus not subject to the § 362 automatic stay. The court, applying a broad interpretation of claim as guided by the legislative history, concluded that the claim arose at the time of the debtor's prepetition misconduct and thus was subject to the automatic stay. As in *Waterman* and *A.H. Robins*, the claimant had already been exposed to or had contact with the cause of injury (in *Edge*, the dentist's negligent treatment; in *Waterman* and *A.H. Robins*, known defective and dangerous products), but simply had not manifested injury as of the commencement of the case.

The Legal Representative urges a similar application of the Conduct Test in this case, with the relevant conduct being Piper's prepetition manufacture, design, sale and distribution of allegedly defective aircraft. However, unlike the asbestos and Dalkon Shield cases, the Legal Representative cannot pinpoint which aircraft or parts are defective or, more significantly, who will be exposed to the defective product in the future. In effect, under the Conduct Test, everyone in the world would hold a claim against Piper simply by virtue of their potential future exposure to any plane in the existing fleet. The conduct of Piper purporting to support the existence of prepetition "claims" is readily distinguishable from the conduct of the asbestos and Dalkon Shield manufacturers.[9] Thus, the Court rejects application of a Conduct Test that would give rise to "claims" simply because the design and manufacture of products occurred prepetition.

---

[8] On appeal, the District Court found that known potential claimants were entitled to actual personal notice; that potential claimants who could not be personally identified were entitled to reasonable notice by publication; and that potential future claims of individuals who had not manifested any detectable signs of disease when notice of the bar date was given were not discharged in the bankruptcy case.

[9] There is also no "great wrong" to be redressed in this case which mandates that present provisions be made for potential future claimants. In the asbestos and Dalkon Shield cases, manufacturers had produced and distributed products known to be harmful from well-documented and overwhelmingly accepted scientific evidence, and a defined group of individuals were exposed to these harmful products and could be expected to manifest injuries as a result. Here, although Piper has been involved in product liability litigation related to its manufacture, design, sale and distribution of aircraft and parts, and has expended considerable funds in such litigation, only a very small percentage of Piper aircraft will be involved in crashes, and only a fraction of those crashes are likely to result from prepetition manufacturing or design defects.

### D. Prepetition Relationship Theory

Recognizing that the Conduct Test may define a § 101(5) claim too broadly in some situations, several courts have recognized "claims" only for those individuals with some type of prepetition relationship with the Debtor. In *In re Pettibone Corp.*, 90 B.R. 918 (Bankr.N.D.Ill.1988), the debtor was sued for injuries sustained by the operator of a forklift designed and manufactured by the debtor before it filed its bankruptcy case. The claimant's employer purchased the forklift postpetition and therefore the claimant had no prepetition contact with the debtor or the forklift. The accident and the resulting injuries all occurred postpetition. The *Pettibone* court found that the facts before it were distinguishable from the asbestos and other mass tort cases where the injuries sustained could be tied to some type of prebankruptcy privity, contact, impact or hidden harm. Because the operator's injury occurred postpetition without any prepetition relationship or exposure to tie the claimant to the debtor, the court held there was no "claim" as of the petition date.

The Second Circuit suggested a similar analysis in *In re Chateaugay Corp.*, 944 F.2d 997 (2d Cir.1991). The issue in that case was whether the Environmental Protection Agency ("EPA") had a prepetition (and thus dischargeable) claim for environmental cleanup costs which would not be incurred until after confirmation, but which concerned environmental hazards related to prepetition conduct of the debtor.[10] The court tied the concept of "claim" to the prepetition relationship between debtor and claimant, finding that the relationship between environmental regulating agencies and the parties subject to regulation makes those contingent obligations based on prepetition conduct "claims" under the Code's definition. Thus, even though the EPA could not identify all of the sites or the full extent of the removal costs, the future environmental response costs for sites contaminated prior to filing of the bankruptcy petition were prepetition claims under the Bankruptcy Code.[11]

The finding in *Chateaugay* of a sufficient relationship is a narrow one, and that court expressly excluded several other scenarios from its holding. The court noted,

---

[10] Under the Comprehensive Environmental Response, Compensation and Liability Act ("CERCLA"), the EPA, upon discovery of a release or substantial threat of release of hazardous substances into the environment, may either order the potentially responsible party to take remedial measures, or take such measures itself and then seek reimbursement for such response costs after they are incurred.

[11] The court expressly noted that not all prepetition conduct would necessarily give rise to a prepetition claim, but only that conduct expressly contemplated by CERCLA to give rise to liability: "[T]he District Court did not go so far as to include CERCLA response costs attributable to any action of the debtor that occurred pre-petition, such as the construction of a storage facility. Instead, the Court carefully limited its ruling to pre-petition releases or threatened releases of hazardous substances."

We need not decide how the definition of "claim" applies to tort victims injured by pre-petition conduct, especially as applied to the difficult case of pre-petition conduct that has not yet resulted in detectable injury, much less the extreme case of pre-petition conduct that has not yet resulted in any tortious consequence to a victim.

In concluding that the degree of relationship between the debtor and the EPA was sufficient, the court found it "far closer than that between future tort claimants totally unaware of injury and a tort-feasor." Id. at 1005.[12]

Indeed, the *Chateaugay* court noted that defining claims to include any ultimate right to payment arising out of prepetition conduct by the debtor would yield questionable results. In pursuing this discussion, the court presented a hypothetical example of a company in bankruptcy which estimates that one out of the ten thousand bridges it built prepetition eventually will fail, causing the death of ten individuals. The court explored the problems inherent in attempting to recognize these "claims" pursuant to the Conduct Test:

> Is there a "claim" on behalf of the 10 people who will be killed when they drive across the one bridge that will fail someday in the future? If the only test is whether the ultimate right to payment will arise out of the debtor's pre-petition conduct, the future victims have a "claim." Yet it must be obvious that enormous practical and perhaps constitutional problems would arise from recognition of such a claim. The potential victims are not only unidentified, but there is no way to identify them. Sheer fortuity will determine who will be on that one bridge when it crashes.

The problem posed by this hypothetical has become reality here. We know that some planes in the existing fleet of Piper aircraft will crash, and we know that there may be injuries, deaths and property damage as a result. We also know that under theories of negligence and products liability, Piper, if it remains in existence, would be liable for some of these damages. Even so, there is no way to identify who the victims will be or to identify any particular prepetition contact, exposure, impact, privity or other relationship between Piper and these potential claimants that will give rise to these future damages.

### E. Analysis and Application

The Conduct Test and the Relationship Test are not mutually exclusive theories. Requiring that there be some prepetition relationship between the Debtor and claimant would not change the analysis or results of

---

[12] At least one court has found that even the test applied in *Chateaugay* was too broad. See *In re Jensen*, 995 F.2d 925 (9th Cir.1993). In *Jensen*, the Ninth Circuit found that there must not only be a relationship between the claimant and the debtor, but that their prepetition interaction must be such that the claim is within the "fair contemplation" of the parties at the time of the bankruptcy. Id. at 930.

the Conduct Test cases. In fact, such a requirement appears to be implicit in those decisions. In the asbestos cases, the future claimants were individuals who were known to have had prepetition exposure to the dangerous product. See, e.g., *Waterman*, 141 B.R. at 556 (claims arose "at the moment the asbestos claimants came into contact with the asbestos"). Likewise, in *A.H. Robins*, the court determined that the claim arose when the claimant was inserted with a Dalkon Shield. And in *Edge*, the court noted that the Bankruptcy Code recognizes a claim for the victim of prepetition misconduct "at the earliest point in the relationship between victim and wrongdoer." *Edge*, 60 B.R. at 699. Thus, the Conduct Test cases presume not only that there was prepetition conduct, but also that there was some prepetition relationship between the debtor's conduct and the claimant.

The theories advanced by prior cases exploring the outer limits of the concept of claim, when thus reconciled, lead to the conclusion that in order for a future claimant to have a "claim" under § 101(5), there must be some prepetition relationship, such as contact, exposure, impact, or privity, between the debtor's prepetition conduct and the claimant. This is not to suggest that any and every prepetition relationship will give rise to a claim.[13] Rather, a prepetition relationship connecting the conduct to the claimant is a threshold requirement.

In the instant case, the Claim advanced by the Legal Representative on behalf of the Future Claimants fails to fulfill this minimum requirement: the conduct upon which the claim is based, in its entirety, is merely the prepetition design, manufacture and sale of aircraft, without any discernible connection between that conduct and the Legal Representative's constituency.[14] There is no prepetition exposure to a specific identifiable defective product or any other prepetition relationship between the Debtor and the broadly defined class of Future Claimants. Since there is no way to connect the future claims to some prepetition relationship, there is also no way to identify a discrete class of individuals who will have claims arising out of prepetition conduct. In short, the Claim in this case fails even the broadest test for recognition of a "claim".

---

[13] Thus, the Court makes no finding that the relationship between Piper and prepetition owners of Piper aircraft would give rise to "claims" even for this relatively small and identifiable subclass of Future Claimants.

[14] If the Legal Representative's proposed application of the Conduct Test had been adopted in the earlier cases, the claims in the asbestos and Dalkon Shield cases would have arisen at the time of manufacture or design of the dangerous products, rather than at the time of contact between the products and the future claimants. The Conduct Test cases clearly did not reach such results on their facts, nor would they require the result sought by the Legal Representative here.

### F. Policy Considerations

Since no binding case law exists mandating the result here, the Court has also considered the policy implications of its decision. The Legal Representative and Pilatus argue that tying the issue of "claim" solely to whether the Debtor's conduct occurred prepetition would foster two primary policies of the Bankruptcy Code: (1) the effective reorganization of the Debtor, and (2) the equal treatment of similarly situated creditors. The Court disagrees.

Focusing on reorganization issues, Pilatus and the Legal Representative assert that an effective reorganization depends on Piper being relieved from liability arising out of the prepetition manufacture, design, sale or distribution of defective aircraft. They argue that this Court should therefore find that the Future Claimants hold dischargeable prepetition claims. This argument has several weak links.

First, unlike the Dalkon Shield and asbestos cases, the Debtor in this case does not believe that recognition of these future interests in the plan is necessary for its reorganization. Indeed, both the Debtor and the Committee conclude that allowing the Claim will hinder, not promote reorganization. Second, as revealed by the *Waterman* case, a determination that the Future Claimants hold "claims" would not necessarily mean that the claims are dischargeable. If they are not dischargeable, calling them "claims" would not in any way facilitate Piper's reorganization. Here, significant and possibly insurmountable due process problems exist in providing notice to this vast class of Future Claimants sufficient to allow the discharge of their claims, regardless of the appointment of, and diligent efforts by, the Legal Representative. In sum, the Court cannot and does not find that recognizing the Future Claimants' "claims" will aid in an effective reorganization.[15]

Pilatus and the Legal Representative also argue that all individuals injured from Piper aircraft manufactured before confirmation should be treated equally, regardless of whether their injuries occur pre-confirmation or post-confirmation. Determining that the Future Claimants do not hold "claims," they argue, would cause disparate treatment based solely on the fortuity of when a crash occurs. This argument is framed by a hypothetical: Should crash victim Jones be able to share in plan distributions if his

---

[15] The Legal Representative argues, correctly, that a plan could provide for the Future Claimants by setting aside some portion of the plan distributions for their benefit. However, the Legal Representative also has steadfastly asserted that Future Claimants must be found to have "claims" to be treated under a plan in the instant case. Compare, *Matter of Johns–Manville Corp.*, 68 B.R. 618, 628 (Bankr.S.D.N.Y.1986), aff'd in part, rev'd in part, 78 B.R. 407 (S.D.N.Y.1987), aff'd sub nom. *Kane v. Johns–Manville Corp.*, 843 F.2d 636 (2d Cir.1988), in which the plan provided for future asbestosis victims without determining that they had claims. The theoretical ability to provide a fund for the Future Claimants does not help resolve the independent and threshold issue of whether or not they have "claims".

plane crashes pre-confirmation, while crash victim Smith receives nothing under the plan if his plane crashes post-confirmation?

The Court concludes that the answer is yes, their treatment can and should be different. In bankruptcy, as in life, timing matters.[16] There is a major distinction between Jones and Smith. Jones can be identified presently; Smith cannot. Only future events, impossible to predict at the time of confirmation of a plan, will determine who the future claimants will be, and whether Smith in fact will be one of them. Were Smith and his fellow claimants presently ascertainable and identifiable, the answer might be different; but in the instant case it is impossible to determine who ultimately will belong to the class of creditors, and whether any prepetition relationship to the Debtor gives rise to their potential future causes of action.

Thus, the Court's decision today is not inconsistent with the statutory language, legislative history, or policies suggesting the "broadest possible definition" of claim. The concept of "claim" cannot be extended to include unidentified and presently unidentifiable potential claimants against this Debtor, claimants whose rights depend entirely on the fortuity of future occurrences and not on any prepetition relationship to the Debtor. Congress may have intended the broadest possible definition of claim, but that definition still has limits. One such limit is present here.

### EFFECT OF COURT'S RULING

In determining that the Future Claimants do not hold claims under the Bankruptcy Code, the Court is not determining whether any or all of the future victims may have a non-bankruptcy future remedy. The nature of the reorganization plan eventually confirmed in the case may affect the result as will, in the event of a sale of Piper's assets, application of successor liability laws which may vary among the states. The ruling simply means that the future claims are not bankruptcy "claims" that will be administered in this case.[17]

---

[16] The simple truth that timing matters is evident in numerous provisions of the Bankruptcy Code, including the avoidance provisions in § 547 and § 548. Creditor Jones, paid in full 91 days before the petition, may keep his money while creditor Smith, paid the very next day, will have to disgorge the entire amount and share in any distributions to unsecured creditors. If timing was irrelevant, then Congress would have allowed the Trustee to reach back indefinitely to recover all prepetition payments made by insolvent debtors. Instead, Congress created a relatively arbitrary period of backward reach. Similarly, the Code does not permit or contemplate the indefinite, unlimited forward reach urged by the Legal Representative, even though it might foster the theoretical goal of equitable distribution.

[17] Since postpetition, pre-confirmation claims are not within the defined group of Future Claimants, this decision does not determine the nature or treatment of such claims.

**CONCLUSION**

The definition of "claim" in the Bankruptcy Code is intentionally broad and sweeps within its scope remote and contingent obligations not necessarily actionable under state law at the commencement of a bankruptcy case. Still, the definition must and does have limits. Based upon the nature of Piper's prepetition conduct and the absence of any relationship between the class and Piper's prepetition activities, Piper's Future Claimants do not have "claims" in this case. The Committee's Objection is sustained, and the Claim filed by the Legal Representative is disallowed.

## NOTES

**1.** Although the bankruptcy court's decision was affirmed in *Epstein v. Official Committee of Unsec. Creditors*, 58 F.3d 1573 (11th Cir.1995), we have not replaced the bankruptcy court opinion's more extensive analysis of the future claims issue. In Footnote 17 of the bankruptcy court opinion, Judge Mark stated that he does not determine the rights of parties who were injured after the petition was filed but before confirmation of the plan. But only a few months later this issue came before him in *Piper Aircraft Corp. v. Calabro*, 169 B.R. 766 (Bankr. S.D. Fla. 1994), and he held that it is enough if at the time of confirmation the members of the class are identifiable, and the postpetition crash provided sufficient identification. The court admitted to being influenced by the absurdity of not allowing Debtor's plan to deal with the some 200 incidents regarding Piper airplanes, involving identifiable potential claimants, that had arisen after Debtor filed. Since Debtor was liquidating, these parties could not share in the estate unless they had claims, and, if these claims were not discharged under § 1141(d), the cloud of potential successor liability might hang over any entity that bought Debtor's assets.

The circuit court agreed with this view and stated:

> We * * * adopt what we will call the "Piper test" in determining the scope of the term claim under § 101(5): an individual has a § 101(5) claim against a debtor manufacturer if (i) events occurring before confirmation create a relationship, such as contact, exposure, impact, or privity, between the claimant and the debtor's product; and (ii) the basis for liability is the debtor's prepetition conduct in designing, manufacturing and selling the allegedly defective or dangerous product. The debtor's prepetition conduct gives rise to a claim to be administered in a case only if there is a relationship established before confirmation between an identifiable claimant or group of claimants and that prepetition conduct.

58 F.3d at 1577.

**2.** In *Fogel v. Zell*, 221 F.3d 955 (7th Cir.2000), the debtor's predecessor, Interpace manufactured and sold defective prestressed concrete pipe to 10,000 end users including the the City of Denver. Interpace was sold to the debtor. By the time of the debtor's bankruptcy in 1991, eight purchasers of Interpace pipe had filed suit against the debtor asserting damages of $300 million. Denver was not among the eight because its Interpace sewer pipes had not yet burst. By the time the pipes did burst (causing $17 million in damages) it was 1997, long after the April 5, 1993 claims bar date fixed by the bankruptcy court in the debtor's case. Chief Judge Posner expressed doubt that Denver held a claim subject to discharge at the time of the bar date:

> Suppose a manufacturer goes bankrupt after a rash of products liability suits. And suppose that ten million people own automobiles manufactured by it that may have the same defect that gave rise to those suits but, so far, only a thousand have had an accident caused by the defect. Would it make any sense to hold that all ten million are tort creditors of the manufacturer * * * ? Does a pedestrian have a contingent claim against the driver of every automobile that might hit him? We are not alone in thinking that the answer to those questions is "no."

* * *

> There has been, however, understandable pressure to expand the concept of a "claim" in bankruptcy in order to enable a nonarbitrary allocation of limited assets to be made between present and future claimants

* * *

> However, mindful of the problem flagged by our automobile hypotheticals, the courts in these cases have suggested various limiting principles. We needn't go through them, for a reason that will appear in a moment; and anyway we greatly doubt that the issue is one that lends itself to governance by formula. It may not be possible to say anything more precise than that if it is reasonable to do so, bearing in mind the cost and efficacy of notice to potential future claimants and the feasibility of estimating the value of their claims before, perhaps long before, any harm giving rise to a matured tort claim has occurred, the bankruptcy court can bring those claimants into the bankruptcy proceeding and make provision for them in the final decree. This "test," if it can be dignified by such a term, would exclude the automobile hypotheticals; given that so far only one of every thousand pipes sold by Interpace have burst, this case may be closer to those hypotheticals than to asbestos and Dalkon Shield.

*Id.* at 960-962.

**3.** In *Piper Aircraft* the court declined to discuss the consequences of its decision with respect to the nonbankruptcy remedies of any future victims. This issue was before the court in *Lemelle v. Universal Mfg. Corp.*, 18 F.3d 1268 (5th Cir.1994), and its resolution shows the great importance of whether the court chooses the Conduct test or the Relationship test in determining the existence of a claim. In *Lemelle* the victims died in a fire in a mobile home manufactured by Debtor before it filed in Chapter 11. The fire occurred two years after Debtor's reorganization plan had been confirmed and a discharge entered. The question was whether the victim's personal representative could bring a wrongful death action against the corporation into which Debtor's reorganized entity had been merged. The court, relying on *Piper Aircraft*, held that the cause of action for wrongful death was not a claim that was discharged in Debtor's bankruptcy; hence, the successor corporation was potentially liable on the wrongful death claim.

> [A]t a minimum, there must be evidence that would permit the debtor to identify, during the course of the bankruptcy proceeding, potential victims and thereby permit notice to these potential victims of the pendency of the proceedings. * * * This record is devoid of any evidence of any pre-petition contact, privity, or other relationship between [Debtor] * * * [and the decedents]. We think the absence of this evidence precludes a finding * * * that the claims asserted * * * were discharged * * *.

18 F.3d at 1277.


## NOTE: DEALING WITH MASS FUTURE CLAIMS IN BANKRUPTCY

*The Asbestos Cases.* In recent years methods of dealing with mass future claims in bankruptcy have been explored by the courts in cases involving mass products liabilities torts. Prototypic cases are those involving claimants exposed to asbestos fibers. Exposure to asbestos may cause asbestosis, a disease of the lungs, lung cancer, and mesothelioma, an asbestos-related cancer of chest and abdominal membranes, as well as other pleural disorders. But these diseases normally have a long incubation period. Symptoms may not appear until many years after asbestos fibers were inhaled by the victim. In the 1970s and 1980s, thousands of lawsuits were brought against asbestos producers based on injuries caused by asbestos. Many plaintiffs were employees of shipyards and other industries in which workers were exposed to asbestos in their employment. Faced by the prospect of unending personal injury and wrongful death suits, Johns Manville and UNR Industries, both asbestos producers, filed in Chapter 11 in 1982.

At the time the asbestos producers filed for bankruptcy, many people who had been exposed to asbestos were already suffering from injuries attributable to these products. Others had not developed symptoms of injury but would develop symptoms in the future. What impact would bankruptcy have on the people who would eventually develop symptoms but who were without symptoms at the time of the Chapter 11 filings? To share in a debtor's bankruptcy, one must have a claim under § 101. The effect of recognizing or not recognizing a claim in bankruptcy by a person who has inhaled asbestos fibers but who has not yet developed symptoms of injury will differ depending on whether the manufacturer is liquidating in Chapter 7 or reorganizing in Chapter 11. In Chapter 7, nonrecognition of a claim means that the victim will get no compensation for injury that becomes manifest after bankruptcy because the bankruptcy estate will have been liquidated and distributed to creditors. In Chapter 11, nonrecognition of the claim means that the manufacturer's potential liability is not discharged under § 1141(d)(1)(A). Under that provision, confirmation of a plan of reorganization discharges the debtor from any "debt" that arose before the date of the confirmation of the plan of reorganization. Since debt means liability on a claim, § 101(12), if a victim is held to have no claim because symptoms of injury do not develop until after confirmation, the victim is not barred from asserting a cause of action against the reorganized debtor. As a practical matter it may be impossible to successfully reorganize a business that has massive undischarged future claims hanging over it. Since the asbestos producers desired to stay in business, they chose Chapter 11 reorganization. Thus, it was in their interest that all persons with potential causes of action be classified as holders of claims so that their rights could be terminated by the § 1141 discharge. But it may not be possible to stretch the definition of claim to include all potential claimants. Although the "relationship test" may be sufficiently broad to accord claim status to all who were exposed to asbestos fibers prepetition, it would not include those exposed afterwards.

*Trust for Future Claims.* The central question raised by these cases is how might a successful reorganization occur under these circumstances and on what terms? In the belief that a bankruptcy court's equitable powers might be broad enough to make provision for future claims whether or not they meet the definition of "claim" under § 101, the Manville reorganization plan established a trust from which claimants might collect compensatory damages by mediation, arbitration or traditional tort litigation. In confirming the plan, the court in *Kane v. Johns–Manville Corp.*, 843 F.2d 636, 640 (2d Cir.1988), described the trust fund device as follows:

> The purpose of the Trust is to provide a means of satisfying Manville's ongoing personal injury liability while allowing Manville to maximize its value by continuing as an ongoing concern. To fulfill this purpose, the Plan seeks to ensure that health claims can be asserted only against the Trust and that Manville's operating entities will be protected from an onslaught of crippling lawsuits that could jeopardize the entire reorganization effort. To this end, the parties agreed that as a condition precedent to confirmation of the Plan, the Bankruptcy Court would issue an injunction channeling all asbestos-related personal injury claims to the Trust (the "Injunction"). The Injunction provides that asbestos health claimants may proceed only against the Trust to satisfy their claims and may not sue Manville, its other operating entities, and certain other specified parties, including Manville's insurers.

Significantly, the Injunction applies to all health claimants, both present and future, regardless of whether they technically have dischargeable "claims" under the Code. The Injunction applies to any suit to recover "on or with respect to any Claim, Interest or Other Asbestos Obligation." "Claim" covers the present claimants, who are categorized as Class–4 unsecured creditors under the Plan and who have dischargeable "claims" within the meaning of § 101(4). The future claimants are subject to the Injunction under the rubric of "Other Asbestos Obligation," which is defined by the Plan as asbestos-related health liability caused by pre-petition exposure to Manville asbestos, regardless of when the individual develops clinically observable symptoms. Thus, while the future claimants are not given creditor status under the Plan, they are nevertheless treated identically to the present claimants by virtue of the Injunction, which channels all claims to the Trust.

The Manville Trust, established in 1986 under the Manville plan of reorganization, was given about $2 billion in assets, which included a substantial amount of Manville's common stock, and the right to receive 20% of Manville's profits, for payment of claims. In 2000, Berkshire Hathaway agreed to buy the operating company, Johns Manville, for $1.96 billion in cash and the assumption of $300 million in debt. Devon Spurgeon, *Berkshire to Buy Manville for $1.96 Billion*, Wall St.J., Dec. 21, 2000, at A3.

The Trust encountered no end of legal and financial troubles. The aggregate amount of future claims was greatly underestimated. It was initially anticipated that 83,000 to 100,000 claimants would be compensated, but within a few years it became apparent that the Trust would run out of assets before all the present claimants were paid, leaving nothing for future claimants, and payments were suspended. By 1994, some 240,000 claims had been filed. After class action litigation over the restructuring of the Trust and payment schedule, settlement was reached in 1996 in which the company gave more of its stock to the Trust and an additional $772 million in exchange for the Trust's giving up its right to receive a share of Manville's profits. After the settlement, the Trust owned nearly 80% of Manville's stock; $1.2 billion in cash and securities and $2.3 billion in other assets were also added. At that time, the Trust expected to pay 10% of an estimated $18 billion in present and future claims to 275,000 people who had already filed claims and as many as 400,000 who might have symptoms appearing in the future. Carlos Tejada, *Manville Settlement Gives Trust Enough Cash for Asbestos Claims*, Wall St.J., Mar. 29, 1996, at B4. But claims have soared: 58,059 in 2000 and 69,784 in the first 11 months of 2001. And, in order to deal with the unanticipated rise in claims, in mid–2001 the Trust had to reduce the amount paid on each claim to five cents on the dollar instead of 10 cents. A disturbing trend has been that a disproportionate share of the settlement dollars are going to the least injured claimants, many of whom have no discernible asbestos-related physical impairment, at the expense of other claimants who are seriously ill with cancer. Queena Sook Kim, *Asbestos Trust Says Assets*

*Are Reduced as the Medically Unimpaired File Claims,* Wall. St.J., Dec. 14, 2001, at B6. The Trust has had to slash payments to claimants dying of cancer to $10,000 or less, in contrast to the hundreds of thousand dollars per claimant in the late 1980s. Lisa Girion, *Firms Hit Hard as Asbestos Claims Rise*, L.A.Times, Dec. 17, 2001, at A1.

The trust device has been used in other future claims cases. In the best known of these, the claimants were women who had used the Dalkon Shield intrauterine device manufactured by A.H. Robins Co. By the middle 1970s, millions of women were using IUDs, and the Dalkon Shield was one of the most prominent of these devices. By the end of the 1970s, hundreds of lawsuits had been brought against Robins for damages for health problems attributed to use of the Dalkon Shield. Some of the suits resulted in multi-million dollar punitive damage awards. Robins faced a problem similar to that of the asbestos producers. Symptoms of injury from use of the Dalkon Shield might not become manifest until passage of a substantial period of time after use of the device had terminated. Beset by negative publicity and fearing that it would not be able to pay the punitive damage awards sure to lie ahead, Robins filed in Chapter 11 in 1985. The Dalkon Shield saga is recounted in Richard B. Sobol, *Bending the Law, The Story of the Dalkon Shield Bankruptcy* (1991) (hereafter cited as "Sobol").

The trust set up in the *Robins* bankruptcy seems to have processed claims more efficiently than that in *Manville*. In 2000, after paying over 100,000 claims, and having disbursed the bulk of its $2.255 billion, the Robins trust terminated. Georgene Vairo, *More Tort Bankruptcies, The Who, The Why and The How*, 78 Am. Bankr. L.J. 93, 121 (2004).

A more recent example of use of a trust is the Dow Corning bankruptcy in which a Chapter 11 plan was confirmed to compensate women injured by breast implants containing Dow Corning silicone gel. The plan set up a trust including $3.2 billion for payments to 175,000 women who had filed claims and an additional 125,000 expected to file in the future. 11 Bankr. L. Rep. (BNA) 1073 (1999).

*Channeling Injunctions.* A major purpose of creating a trust to pay future claims is to safeguard the reorganized debtor from postbankruptcy lawsuits by future claimants. As indicated above, in the Manville bankruptcy the bankruptcy court faced the issue squarely by issuing a "channeling" injunction compelling all future claimants to seek compensation solely from the trust rather than from the reorganized debtor. The Second Circuit upheld confirmation of the plan but declined to pass on the validity of the injunction. Part of the bankruptcy court's purpose in enjoining claims against the reorganized debtor was to allow the reorganized debtor to attract investment and generate sufficient profits to meet the requirements of future claimants. Uncertainties about the validity of the injunction have clouded Manville's prospects, and Manville management pressed for new legislation explicitly authorizing courts to issue channeling injunctions. In 1994 Congress generously responded to Manville's entreaties by enacting an elaborate piece of special legislation, § 524(g), that applies only to asbestos claims and validates the injunctions issued in *Manville* and other asbestos cases. It authorizes similar injunctions to be issued in the future in other asbestos cases so long as the debtors in those cases have taken the same precautions to safeguard the rights of victims observed by Manville in its trust/injunction mechanism. The injunctions may even enjoin litigation against third parties (e.g., officers, directors, and insurance companies) if those parties may be liable for the claims or demands made on the debtor. In order to assure that Manville and UNR, "both of which have met and surpassed the standards imposed in this section, will be able to take advantage of the certainty it provides without having to reopen their cases" (Section-by-Section Description § 111, 140 Cong.Rec. H10765 (Oct. 4, 1994)), § 524(g) applies to cases already filed.

*A Federal "Global Solution"?* Asbestos litigation has transcended the status of merely posing challenging legal issues of management of mass tort claims and assumed the condition of a national economic crisis, if not scandal. Insurance companies predict that a million asbestos claims would ultimately be filed; according to a RAND study, 600,000 already have, and the number of claims increases each year. Shailagh Murray & Kathryn Kranhold, *Unsettling Dust: Asbestos Factions Struggle to Settle Their 30-Year War*, Wall St. J., Oct. 15, 2003, at A1. Labor unions complained that asbestos litigation was closing down businesses and costing jobs. Some studies claim that as many as 60,000 workers have lost jobs as a direct result of asbestos-related bankruptcies. *See* 15 Bankr. L. Rep.(BNA), 195-196 (Feb. 20, 2003). Law firms devoted entirely to representing asbestos claimants have sprung up as courts found liability not just against entities that had manufactured products containing asbestos but also against those using or selling such products. Some individuals brought multiple claims against every conceivable defendant; one brought 62 claims. *See* Michelle J. White, *Why the Asbestos Genie Won't Stay in the Bankruptcy Bottle*, 70 U. Cin. L.Rev. 1319 (2002). Sick claimants stood by anxiously as an increasing share of litigation proceeds went to claimants with no symptoms of asbestosis or cancer as courts allowed recoveries even by those who claimed mental anguish damages resulting from fear of developing cancer caused by work-related exposure to asbestos with no proof of physical manifestation of the claimed emotional distress. *Norfolk & Western Railway Company v. Ayers*, 538 U.S. 135 (2004). Business entities found themselves blindsided by asbestos claims arising from activities of acquired companies that occurred many years before the acquisition. Only trial lawyers were happy with the situation. White quotes a RAND study that concluded that only about one-third of compensation expenditures reached the claimants, with the remainder going to administrative expenses and lawyers. White, *supra*, at 1327.

Business entities have stampeded into bankruptcy in an attempt to limit their asbestos liability. White counted 48 firms that filed between 1982 and 1999, and an additional 30 firms that filed between 2000 and 2002. *See* White, *supra,* at 1320. Chapter 11 filing gives debtor entities a few years delay, but companies that filed hoping to retain some equity in the reorganized entity were often disappointed. On the other hand managers, contract creditors and asbestos trial lawyers discovered a community of interest in discharging the debtor firms while establishing a largely insurer funded trust to handle asbestos claims.

Coalitions of interested parties began to lobby Congress for a "global" settlement. A $140 billion trust fund has been proposed, financed by defendants and insurers; the federal government would not contibute. Murray & Kranhold, *supra*, chronicles developments in the effort to persuade Congress to set up such a trust fund, similar to the toxic waste superfund, from which payments would be made to claimants. At the time this book went to press, the Senate Judiciary Committee had approved a bill under which workers injured from asbestos exposure would receive monetary awards based on the severity of their injury. The largest award of $1.1 million would go to workers with mesothelioma, a deadly form of lung cancer. When the trust fund is set up, all lawsuits alleging injury from asbestos exposure would be barred unless the fund runs out of money. Businesses and insurers would pay into the fund for an estimated 30 years. Controversy over which industries would have to contribute and how much they would have to contribute has not been resolved, and it is unlikely that the bill can be enacted in its present state. *BNA Bankr. L. Rep.*, Vol. 17, No. 26, at 580, June 30, 2005.

*Due Process Requirements. Mullane v. Central Hanover Bank & Trust Co.*, 339 U.S. 306 (1950), held that before a court can deprive a person of property, due process requires notice and opportunity for hearing; notice by publication may meet this standard if persons to be notified are unknown. Such notice was given in *Robins.* There the court dealt with the future claims issue by ruling that a woman's claim arose for purposes of bankruptcy law at the time she began use of the Dalkon Shield even though injury might not occur until after the date of confirmation of the Robins' plan. Sobol, at 113–114. This ruling was upheld in *Grady v. A.H. Robins Co.*, 839 F.2d 198 (4th Cir.1988), which described future claims as "contingent." A notice of the bar date, which was published widely, said:

> "IF YOU * * * may have used the Dalkon Shield but have not yet experienced an injury * * * and if you wish to assert a claim against [Robins], the United States Bankruptcy Court * * * must receive your claim * * * on or before April 30, 1986 or you will lose the right to make a claim."

Sobol, at 110. Women who had not submitted claims by the bar date were allowed to claim from the trust by showing that they first manifested injury after the bar date and that they lacked knowledge either of the bar date or of the fact that the IUD that she used was a Dalkon Shield. Sobol, at 223. The plan enjoined all persons holding claims from commencing or continuing any action on the claims outside the plan. The injunction was vacated in *In re A.H. Robins Co.*, 972 F.2d 77 (4th Cir.1992). Given the likelihood that many women either would not see the bar date notice or, if free of symptoms, would not act on it, the *Robins* plan provisions dealing with future claims raise due process concerns.

In order to address the due process issue, some courts appointed a legal representative to act in a fiduciary capacity on behalf of future claimants. Such a representative should be empowered to file claims, investigate, negotiate, cast votes, and exercise the powers of a creditors' committee. The National Bankruptcy Review Commission Report § 2.1.2 (1997) recommends that that the Bankruptcy Code be amended to require appointment of such legal representative, and commentators, e.g., Alan N. Resnick, *Bankruptcy As a Vehicle For Resolving Enterprise–Threatening Mass Tort Liability*, 148 U. Pa. L. Rev. 2045, 2078 (2000), concur. Both the NBRC Report (§ 2.1.4) and Professor Resnick also recommend empowering courts to issue channeling injunctions in appropriate cases to preserve assets for future claimants.

Although courts and litigants are becoming more sure-footed in dealing with future tort claims, the subject will be clouded with doubt until substantial amendments are made to the Bankruptcy Code. The Resnick article cited above is a helpful guide to the nature of such amendments.

## 2. EQUITABLE RIGHTS

Claim is defined in § 101 to include "a right to an equitable remedy for breach of performance if such breach gives rise to a right to payment." The apparent meaning of the quoted language is that the equitable remedy need not give rise to a right to payment, but the right to the remedy must be based on breach of an obligation to the claimant on which a right to payment could be based. The most common example is a breach of contract that gives rise not only to a legal right to recover damages but also to an equitable right to specific performance of the contract. The definition would appear to mean that the right to obtain the equitable remedy of specific performance is a claim. Under this reading of the quoted language, a debtor could discharge an obligation to make specific performance. The claimant who loses the remedy for specific performance can have the claim valued under § 502(c)(2) as a right to payment. But the court in *In re Udell*, 18 F.3d 403 (7th Cir.1994), read the quoted language differently and cast doubt on the dischargeability of specific performance obligations arising out of contracts. *Udell* is critically discussed in the following case.

## In re Ward

United States Bankruptcy Court, D. Massachusetts, 1996.
194 B.R. 703.

■ JAMES F. QUEENAN, JR., Bankruptcy Judge.

Seeking to enforce a noncompetition clause in its franchise agreement, The Maids International, Inc. ("Maids") has brought this complaint to enjoin Michael E. Ward and Angela L. Ward (the "Debtors") from owning or operating a maintenance and cleaning service within a fifty mile radius of the franchised territory. Maids contends neither the Debtors' bankruptcy filing nor rejection of their covenant not to compete affects its right to an injunction against the Debtors' competition. I am thus faced with the question of whether Maids' right to injunctive relief is a "claim" within the meaning of the Bankruptcy Code and hence subject to being discharged. * * *

### I. FACTS

The facts are not in dispute. Maids has developed a system for establishing and operating a household maintenance and cleaning service. Having a principal office in Omaha, Nebraska, Maids franchises its rights in the system to numerous parties throughout the United States.

On April 10, 1989, Maids signed a franchise agreement with a corporation owned and operated by the Debtors named Award Services, Inc. ("Award"). In addition to signing on behalf of Award, the Debtors signed the agreement personally as guarantors of Award's performance thereunder. The agreement also includes the Debtors within the meaning of the term "Franchise", thereby making them jointly responsible with Award. Under the agreement, Maids gave Award the exclusive right to use its system and the name "Maids" in Concord, Massachusetts and in several nearby towns. In return, Award paid Maids $15,900 and obligated itself (and the Debtors) to pay Maids a royalty based on a percentage of its gross sales at rates which range from 4.5% to 7%, depending upon the amount of weekly gross sales. The agreement was for an initial term of five years.

The following provisions of the franchise agreement are of relevance to the present proceeding:

### XV. COVENANTS

. . . . .

C. FRANCHISEE further covenants that for a period of two (2) years after the termination or nonrenewal of the franchise, regardless of the cause of termination, it shall not, either directly or indirectly, for itself, or on behalf of or in conjunction with any other person, persons, partnership or corporation, own, maintain, engage in, or participate in the operation of a maintenance and cleaning service system within a radius of fifty (50) miles of the area designated hereunder or any then existing The Maids Unit Franchise.

. . . . .

E. FRANCHISEE acknowledges that a violation of any covenant in this Paragraph will cause irreparable damage to FRANCHISOR, the exact amount of which may not be subject to reasonable or accurate ascertainment, and therefore, FRANCHISEE does hereby consent that in the event of such violation, FRANCHISOR shall as a matter of right be entitled to injunctive relief to restrain FRANCHISEE, or anyone acting for or on behalf (sic), from violating said covenants, or any of them. Such remedies, however, shall be cumulative and in addition to any other remedies to which FRANCHISOR may then be entitled. FRANCHISEE represents and acknowledges that in the event of the termination of this Agreement for whatever cause, its experience and capabilities are such that it can obtain employment in business engaged in other lines or of a different nature than that of the operation of a maintenance and cleaning service franchise and that the enforcement of a remedy by way of injunction will not prevent it from earning a livelihood. In the event FRANCHISOR brings suit to enforce any provision hereof, FRANCHISOR shall be entitled to receive, in addition to any relief or remedy granted, the cost of bringing such suit, including reasonable attorney's fees. The covenants set forth in this Paragraph XV shall survive the termination or expiration of this Agreement.

.. . . .

### XVIII. RESOLUTION OF DISPUTE

Except as to a breach for non-payment of any fee for royalty or advertising as set forth heretofore, any controversy or claim arising out of or relating to this Agreement, or the breach thereof, shall be settled by arbitration conducted in Omaha, Nebraska in accordance with the commercial Arbitration Rules of the American Arbitration Association and judgement upon any award rendered by the Arbitrator may be entered in any court having jurisdiction thereof.

.. . . .

### XXVIII. LIABILITY FOR BREACH

In the event of any default on the part of either party hereto, in addition to any other remedies of the aggrieved party, the party in default shall pay to the aggrieved party all amounts due and all damages, costs and expenses, including reasonable attorneys fees, incurred by the aggrieved party as a result of any such default.

.. . . .

### XXXIII. EQUITABLE RELIEF

Nothing herein contained shall bar the right of either party to obtain injunction relief against threatened conduct that will cause loss or damages under the usual equity rules, including the applicable rules for obtaining preliminary injunctions, provided an appropriate bond against damages be provided.

.. . . .

The franchisee agreement expired on April 9, 1994, the end of its five year term. Thereafter, the Debtors commenced operation of a cleaning service within the franchised territory. They operate the business under the name "Mops" and do not hold themselves out as operating a franchise of Maids.

Maids responded to this competition with a series of legal actions. It first commenced an arbitration proceeding in Omaha with the American Arbitration Association. This was uncontested by the Debtors. On March 31, 1995, the arbitrator awarded Maids damages (including interest) of $29,232. He also ordered the Debtors to cease and desist the ownership or operation of a maintenance and cleaning service until April 9, 1996, within a radius of fifty miles from the franchised area or within a radius of fifty miles from any Maids franchise existing on April 9, 1994. Maids then brought suit in the District Court of Douglas County, Nebraska. On July 20, 1995, that court entered a default judgment against the Debtors in the sum of $61,056. Apparently this was in part a confirmation of the arbitration award. At no time has any court entered an injunction against the Debtors competing, in confirmation of the arbitration award or otherwise. Maids next brought its attack closer to home. On November 1, 1995, it filed suit on the judgment in the District Court of Concord, Massachusetts. That court authorized attachments of the Debtors' residence and bank accounts.

Shortly thereafter, on November 13, 1995, the Debtors filed a petition with this court requesting entry of an order for relief under chapter 7 of the Bankruptcy Code. Undeterred, Maids on January 25, 1996 filed its complaint commencing the present adversary proceeding. In its complaint Maids requested an injunction against the Debtors owning or operating a maintenance and cleaning establishment within a fifty mile radius of the franchised territory. At the same time, Maids filed a motion for a temporary restraining order and asked for an emergency hearing. At the hearing on February 5, 1996, I denied the motion, dismissed the complaint and ordered Maids to file a proof of claim. Maids thereafter filed a proof of claim within the permissible filing period.

### II. VALIDITY OF DEBTORS' COVENANT NOT TO COMPETE

* * *

Covenants not to compete are often made by sellers of small businesses, key employees, franchisees and partners. The covenant is generally valid under state law so long as its time period, geographic area and covered activities go no further than what is reasonably necessary to protect the other's business and goodwill. For this reason, the wording of the covenant is usually restricted in time and area, and sometimes in scope of activity. The Debtors' covenant was so restricted. It is valid and enforceable.

### III. MAIDS' INJUNCTIVE RIGHTS AS A "CLAIM"

The Debtors are clearly in breach of their covenant not to compete. Breach of the ordinary contract gives rise only to a claim for damages. Maids, however, has the additional right under state law to obtain an injunction against the Debtors' competition, without regard to the provision in the agreement permitting such relief. Although many of the decisions do not reach the issue, engaging instead in what is often a mechanical search for "executoriness," breach of a covenant not to compete presents a question which has proven difficult for the courts: Do the nondebtor's injunctive rights constitute a "claim" so as to be subject to discharge? The Debtors' discharge hinges upon this issue. A discharge in bankruptcy releases a debtor only as to liability on a "debt,"[7] which is defined as "liability on a claim."[8]

The Code defines "claim" as follows:

**(A)** right to payment, whether or not such right is reduced to judgment, liquidated, unliquidated, fixed, contingent, matured, unmatured, disputed, undisputed, legal, equitable, secured, or unsecured; or

**(B)** right to an equitable remedy for breach of performance if such breach gives rise to a right to payment, whether or not such right to an equitable remedy is reduced to judgment, fixed, contingent, matured, unmatured, disputed, undisputed, secured, or unsecured.[9]

Maids unquestionably has a "right to an equitable remedy" for breach of the Debtors' covenant. But does the breach also give rise to a "right to payment" within the meaning of the statute? That question is not answered by Maids having obtained a damage judgment. As shall be explained, the damages available for breach of the covenant must be an alternative to an equitable remedy if "a right to payment" is to be present. For all we know, the arbitration award and default judgment Maids obtained were only for damages accrued to the date of the hearings, and did not include the future damages that are an alternative to equitable relief.

The only order issued against the Debtors competing is the arbitrator's cease and desist order. No court has entered an injunction against the competition. Even if one had, it would make no difference on the claim issue. The inclusion of an equitable remedy within the definition of "claim" applies "whether or not such right to an equitable remedy is reduced to judgment. . .."[10]

* * *

Focussing more on the statutory definition, some courts hold the nondebtor party's injunctive right is not a claim because it is present only if the remedy at law is "inadequate," or only if the threatened harm is "irreparable," concluding from this that the nondebtor has no right to payment within the meaning of the statutory definition. Although these courts are correct in ruling a right to payment must exist under nonbankruptcy law, their holding that there is no right to payment for breach of a cove-

---

[7] § 524(a).

[8] § 101(12).

[9] § 101(5).

[10] Id.

nant not to compete conflicts with the damage rights of the beneficiary of a covenant as well as with the general standard employed by courts in determining whether a party's remedy at law is adequate. This requires some explanation.

An injunction against breach of the covenant is a grant of specific performance. As a result of the historical separation of courts of law and equity, such an equitable remedy is available only if the remedy at law, typically damages, is "inadequate." Courts take into account a number of factors in determining whether damages are inadequate. Principal among them are difficulty in proving the existence and amount of damages with reasonable certainty, difficulty in collecting a monetary judgment, and uncertainty that the benefits of a monetary judgment would be equivalent to the promised performance.[24] The rule has been stated as follows: "The adequate remedy at law, which will preclude the grant of specific performance of a contract by a court of equity, must be as certain, prompt, complete, and efficient to attain the ends of justice as a decree of specific performance."[25] Put another way, "the remedy at law, in order to exclude a concurrent remedy at equity, must be as complete, as practical and as efficient to the ends of justice and its prompt administration, as the remedy at equity."[26]

Courts thus compare the remedies at law and equity to see which is more effective in serving the ends of justice. Difficulty in fixing damages is only one factor in that equation. In any event, damages need only be difficult, not impossible, to prove for equitable relief to be available. Comparison of the two remedies usually leads to the grant of equitable relief. Doubts as to the adequacy of the remedy at law are resolved in favor of granting equitable relief. In sum, courts look quite favorably upon equitable relief. This has led one author to conclude that the adequate remedy rule is essentially dead.[30]

Loss of future profits is typically a principal element of damages for breach of a covenant not to compete. The evidentiary problems here for Maids and other covenant beneficiaries are obvious. The proof involves futuristic projections which are especially subject to contest. Courts therefore readily grant an injunction for breach of a covenant not to compete. Indeed, the injured party invariably requests injunctive relief because an injunction gives strong assurance he will receive precisely what was bargained for. This avoids the trauma of future injury, the need to prove dam-

---

[24] *E.g.*, ARTHUR L. CORBIN, 5A CORBIN ON CONTRACTS § 1142 (1964); RESTATEMENT (SECOND) OF CONTRACTS § 360 (1981).

[25] *National Marking Mach. Co. v. Triumph Mfg. Co.*, 13 F.2d 6, 9 (8th Cir.1926) * * *.

[26] *Walla Walla City v. Walla Walla Water Co.*, 172 U.S. 1, 12, 19 S.Ct. 77, 82, 43 L.Ed. 341 (1898).

[30] Douglas Laycock, *The Death of the Irreparable Injury Rule,* 103 Harv.L.Rev. 688 (1990).

ages, and problems in collecting a money judgment. The request for equitable relief has historically been regarded as the election of a preferred remedy.

If the beneficiary of a covenant not to compete elects to receive damages for loss of future profits, he gets the lost profits. Lost profits are a proper element of damages for any breach of contract so long as at the time of the contract the breaching party had reason to know they would be the probable result of breach.[34] The Debtors certainly had that knowledge. The purpose of their covenant was to protect Maids' business. Although damages must be established with reasonable certainty,[35] an approximation rather than mathematical accuracy is all that is required.[36] The perceived difficulty in proving lost profits is less present today because of the receptive attitude of modern courts toward proof of sophisticated financial data through expert testimony.[37] The award of damages for lost future profits is now a commonplace remedy for breach of all kinds of contracts.

Maids therefore has the right to obtain either damages for the Debtors' future competition or an injunction against the competition.[39] As a result, in the words of the statute, Maids has a "right to an equitable remedy for breach of performance. . . [which] breach gives rise to a right to payment. . . ."[40] As an alternative remedy, this right to payment permits a dollar sign to be placed on the equitable remedy, as is done with other claims. Including equitable remedies within the statute's definition of "claim" is therefore supported by a strong bankruptcy policy—equal treatment of similar rights. And because a "claim" is subject to discharge, another important bankruptcy policy is promoted—the policy favoring a debtor's fresh start, unencumbered by past commitments.

In *In re Udell*,[42] the Seventh Circuit came to the opposite conclusion, and in the process added greatly to the confusion in this troubled area of the law. The debtor there had signed an agreement not to compete with his former employer, Standard Carpetland USA, Inc. The covenant was for three years, commencing on termination of employment, and covered a fifty mile radius from the store where the debtor worked. It further provided: "In the event of [the debtor's] actual or threatened breach of the [covenant], Carpetland shall be entitled to an injunction restraining [the debtor] as well as reimbursement for reasonably [sic] attorneys fees in-

---

[34] RESTATEMENT (SECOND) OF CONTRACTS § 351 (1981).

[35] RESTATEMENT (SECOND) OF CONTRACTS § 352 (1981).

[36] Id., cmt. a.

[37] Id.

[39] He is also entitled to compensation for any damages already incurred. * * *

[40] § 101(5); see National Bankruptcy Conference, Reforming The Bankruptcy Code 202 (1994), which adopts this view.

[42] 18 F.3d 403 (7th Cir.1994).

curred in securing said judgment and stipulated damages in the sum of $25,000." Soon after leaving his employment, the debtor purchased a carpet store which he claimed did not compete in the same market as Carpetland's. He sued Carpetland in state court, seeking past due commissions and other compensation. Contending the debtor had breached his agreement not to compete, Carpetland counterclaimed for damages and an injunction against the debtor operating his new store. The state court issued the requested preliminary injunction. The debtor appealed and then filed a chapter 13 petition. Carpetland moved for relief from the automatic stay in order to pursue the state court litigation.

In approving relief from stay as a proper exercise of discretion, the Seventh Circuit in *Udell* held Carpetland's injunctive rights were not a "claim" and hence were not dischargeable in bankruptcy. Although not finding the statutory definition of claim ambiguous, the court nevertheless looked to the legislative history that accompanied the final version of the definition, which reconciled differences in the House and Senate bills.[45] It saw significance in the following statement made on the floors of both houses of Congress:

> Section 101(4)(B) [now § 101(5)(B)] represents a modification of the House-passed bill to include [sic] the definition of "claim" a right to an equitable remedy for breach of performance if such breach gives rise to a right to payment. This is intended to cause the liquidation or estimation of contingent rights of payment for which there may be an alternative equitable remedy with the result that the equitable remedy will be susceptible to being discharged in bankruptcy. For example, in some States, a judgment for specific performance may be satisfied by an alternative right to payment, in the event performance is refused; in that event the creditor entitled to specific performance would have a "claim" for purposes of proceeding under title 11.
>
> On the other hand, rights to an equitable remedy for breach of performance with respect to which such breach does not give rise to a right to payment are not "claims" and would therefore not be susceptible to discharge in bankruptcy.[46]

The *Udell* court constructed a confusing alternative test from this floor statement. It seized on the awkward phrase "with respect to which such breach does not give rise to a right to payment" appearing in the last sen-

---

[45] The definition in the Senate bill included only "right to payment", with no reference to an equitable remedy. S. 2266, 95th Cong., 2d Sess. § 101(4) (1978). The House bill referred to an equitable remedy in these words: "right to an equitable remedy for breach of performance if such breach does not give rise to a right to payment. . .." H.R. 8200, 95th Cong. 1st Sess. § 101(4)(B) (1977).

[46] 124 CONG.REC. H11090 (daily ed. Sept. 28, 1978); S17406 (daily ed. Oct. 6, 1978) (statements of Rep. Edwards and Sen. DeConcini).

tence. Because the phrase arguably modifies "equitable remedy" rather than "breach of performance," the court concluded equitable rights are a claim if payment arises from their exercise. This is opposed to the wording of the statute, which clearly requires that the breach, not the equitable remedy, give rise to a right to payment. And the test makes no sense because equitable remedies are typically designed to provide nonmonetary relief. Having thus created a virtually unpassable test, the court ruled it was flunked by the facts before it because the right to obtain liquidated damages arose from the contract, not from an equitable remedy under it.

The *Udell* court also fashioned another test which, if passed, would make an equitable remedy a claim. It here focussed on the reference in the floor statement to a right to payment being an "alternative" to the equitable remedy. From this the court concluded *all* right to payment must be an alternative to the equitable remedy. Because state courts would enforce the parties' agreement by granting both damages and an injunction, the court ruled an alternative right to payment was not present, so Carpetland's rights failed this test as well. This reasoning ignores Carpetland's right to damages for future loss, which is an alternative to its equitable remedy. The floor statement's reference to a right to payment being an alternative to equitable relief is understandable because the claim for future loss is the monetary equivalent to the right to an injunction against further competition. Nor is there any reason to believe Congress intended that this alternative right to payment be the only right to payment. The statute does not say so. The injured party is obviously entitled to compensation for damages already incurred by the time of trial, as well as to an injunction against future competition. The liquidated damage clause before the court was presumably designed to provide this compensation because the parties also agreed upon an injunction to prevent future loss. *Udell* thus commits the double sin of elevating legislative history above the statute's plain wording and then misunderstanding the legislative history.

The real basis for the *Udell* court's holding emerges from the concurring opinion of Judge Flaum. He thought the majority opinion "dodges this statute's plain language in an effort to reach a sensible result."[49] To Judge Flaum, and one suspects to the other panel members, discharge in bankruptcy of an injunction against competition is like a bankruptcy discharge of an injunction against trespassing, polluting, stalking or battering. Because he thought the debtor's discharge would have similar "patently absurd consequences,"[50] Judge Flaum believed the plain language of the statute should not be followed.

Judge Flaum's reasoning leaves much to be desired as well, quite apart from his willingness to elide what he admits to be the statute's plain word-

---

[49] 18 F.3d at 410.

[50] Id. at 411.

ing. The case concerned breach of contract, not trespass, pollution, stalking or battery. Moreover, trespass and the like is prohibited by law, without regard to the existence of an injunction. So a bankruptcy discharge does not terminate the obligation to refrain from such conduct. In the final analysis, the decision in *Udell* comes down to this: The court could not bring itself to equate an injunction against breach of contract with a monetary judgment for breach of contract which is routinely discharged in bankruptcy.

### IV. CONCLUSION

In summary, although the decisions are in disarray, Maids' alternative right to damages from the Debtors' future competition in breach of their covenant not to compete is a "right to payment" within the meaning of the statutory definition of an equitable claim. Hence, under the definition, Maids' injunctive rights constitute a claim. That state courts consider damages inadequate when compared to the equitable remedy of an injunction is beside the point. Although damages for breach of the covenant, particularly damages for lost future profits, are difficult to fix, courts are perfectly capable of doing so. This alternative right to damages fits into the statutory definition of an equitable claim very well. The same breach, a debtor's competition and threat of further competition, "gives rise" to both a damage claim and injunctive rights. The definition imposes no requirement that the claimant elect to receive a monetary payment, that compliance with the injunction require an expenditure of funds, or that the equitable remedy, as opposed to the breach, give rise to a right to payment. Following the statute's plain meaning promotes two fundamental policies of the Bankruptcy Code—the policy favoring a debtor's fresh start and the policy favoring equality among holders of similar rights.

## NOTES

**1.** *Kennedy v. Medicap Pharmacies, Inc.,* 267 F.3d 493 (6th Cir.2001), adopts the *Udell* interpretation of the statute and holds that the right to equitable relief constitutes a claim only if it is an alternative to a right to payment or if compliance with the equitable order will itself require payment of money. We join with Judge Queenan in *Ward* in believing that neither the wording of § 101(5)(B) nor the policy of the statute supports this view.

**2.** The prototypic case for finding a right to an equitable remedy to be a claim in bankruptcy is specific performance for breach of a contract to convey real estate in which the seller is the debtor in bankruptcy. Even though under state law damages for the breach of a land sale contract is an inadequate remedy because land is unique, it has been thought that strong bankruptcy policies of equality of treatment for creditors and a fresh start for debtors lead to the conclusion that the buyer's only right in bankruptcy should be a claim for money damages instead of a right to specific performance. National Bankruptcy Conference, *Reforming the Bankruptcy*

*Code* 132 (Rev.ed.1997), takes the view that these bankruptcy policies, on balance, "outweigh any nonbankruptcy policies that support specific performance" of covenants not to compete. But some fact situations regarding noncompete covenants raise difficult problems.

To enjoin former franchisees like Barry Udell from selling carpets or Michael and Angela Ward from providing maintenance and cleaning services seems harsh. There is no indication that their breach of the noncompete covenant threatened their former franchisors' businesses. Thus, without paying very much for the noncompete covenant, their former franchisors would be making it very difficult for them to start over after bankruptcy. But what of the case in which the noncompete covenant was a key element in the sale of a business, the existence of which was essential to protect the good will the buyer was purchasing? For example Likeable Phil, who had built his pricey fish market, "Phil's Phish," on his sparkling personality over the years, sold to Dull Don who was willing to pay three times the value of the tangible assets for the business if Phil would sign an ironclad ten-year, 25–mile noncompete covenant and go away. Phil took the money and ran. Within a year he had lost everything in a Borneo gold mine venture, filed in Chapter 7, scheduled the noncompete covenant obligation as a debt owing to Don, obtained postpetition financing and opened a fish store down the street from Don which he named "Phresh Phish." You may assume that any claim for damages against Phil would be valueless and that Don's business was sinking fast. Should Don be able to enjoin Phil from proceeding with his new store? Phresh start or head start?

**3.** Toward the end of the opinion in *Ward*, the court discussed Judge Flaum's view in *Udell* that a literal interpretation of the statutory definition of "claim" would result in a "patent absurdity" is apparently based on the intentional tort and criminal examples that he mentions. Here the judge is on solid ground. It would be absurd to allow a person to avoid having to comply with an injunction or order against such tortious conduct as maintaining a nuisance or such criminal conduct as stalking or battering a victim merely by filing a petition in bankruptcy. Indeed, criminal and regulatory orders obtained by governmental units are specifically excepted from the automatic stay provisions of the Code. § 362(b)(1) and (4). Even money damages arising out of such conduct are generally nondischargeable in Chapter 7 cases. § 523(a)(6). And there is no dispute, generally speaking, that equitable remedies restraining acts that prospectively endanger public health and safety should not be dischargeable.

Most of the litigation in the area of equitable remedies in bankruptcy has arisen from environmental cases in which public health and safety are implicated. *In re Torwico Electronics*, 8 F.3d 146 (3d Cir.1993), is an example of a case in which a debtor was not allowed to avoid complying with a state environmental order regarding cleaning up hazardous wastes by filing in bankruptcy, while *Ohio v. Kovacs*, 469 U.S. 274 (1985), shows that circumstances may exist even in environmental cases in which discharge may be appropriate. But *Udell* is a contract case, and here a literal interpretation of § 101 ("claim") would not result in a "patent absurdity." Carpetland has been harmed by Udell's breach (its business is not worth as much as it would have been had Udell not broken the contract), and presumably Udell would have to answer in damages for the breach but for the state law rule that damages are considered to be too speculative in cases of breach of noncompete covenants. David G. Epstein, Steve H. Nickles & James J. White, *Bankruptcy* § 11–2 (1992), views breach of a covenant not to compete as giving the nondebtor "not only a right to equitable injunctive relief but also a right to payment, i.e., [the nondebtor] would have a 'claim'." For an argument that bankruptcy courts are compelled by § 502(c)(2) to monetize equitable remedies, however contingent or unliquidated, so that creditors can be dealt with equally and debtors can be given a fresh start, whatever limitations state law places on remedies available outside bankruptcy, see Jay L. Westbrook, *A Functional Analysis of Executory Contracts*, 74 Minn.L.Rev. 227, 255–57, 277–78 (1989).

## C. DETERMINING THE AMOUNT OF A CLAIM

Section 502(b) directs the bankruptcy court to determine the amount of each claim in dollars. If the claim is for a fixed amount and the claim is not disputed, the bankruptcy court does not have to act on the claim, for a claim is deemed allowed unless there is an objection to it. § 502(a). But many claims, such as tort claims, may be unliquidated or there may be a dispute concerning the extent to which the debtor is liable. Upon objection, the bankruptcy court must determine whether the claim is valid and its amount in a summary hearing. A personal injury tort or wrongful death claim must be tried in a federal district court rather than in the bankruptcy court. 28 U.S.C. § 157(b)(2)(B) and § 157(b)(5). With respect to personal injury and wrongful death claims, bankruptcy does not affect any right to trial by jury that an individual has under applicable nonbankruptcy law. 28 U.S.C. § 1411. By filing proof of other kinds of claims, the creditor brings itself within the equitable jurisdiction of the bankruptcy court and relinquishes any right to trial by jury with respect to the determination of that claim.

Section 502(c)(1) directs the bankruptcy court to estimate the amount of a contingent or unliquidated claim. This is a major change from pre-Code law. Under the Bankruptcy Act, if liquidation or estimation of a claim "would unduly delay administration of the estate," the claim was not allowable. The impact of this provision on unliquidated claims is illustrated by a well known pre-Code case, *In re Cartridge Television, Inc.*, 535 F.2d 1388 (2d Cir.1976), in which stockholders of a corporation in liquidation bankruptcy filed proof of claims of about $60 million. The claims were based on alleged fraud by the corporation in the sale of its stock. Liquidation of these claims might have required litigation of several years. Even though the consequence of disallowing the stockholders' claims was to leave them with a worthless claim against an asset-less corporate shell, the court disallowed the claims because they would unduly delay the administration of the estate. Disallowance of these claims resulted in a windfall to other creditors. Section 502(c) rejects this approach: any contingent or unliquidated claim must be estimated by the court and is subject to discharge.

> No longer will some creditors enjoy a windfall or effectively be denied any recovery based upon the provability or allowability of their claims and the financial status of the debtor after bankruptcy. Equally important, Congress has insured that the debtor will receive a complete discharge of his debts and a real fresh start, without the threat of lingering claims "riding through" the bankruptcy.

*In re Baldwin–United Corp.*, 55 B.R. 885, 898 (Bankr.S.D.Ohio 1985).

The bankruptcy court may determine the amount of an unliquidated claim under § 502(b) itself, or, as we will see with respect to stays and injunctions in Chapter 5 of this book, it may lift the automatic stay against proceedings against the debtor in order to allow the creditor to proceed against the debtor in a state court. The effect of the state court judgment is to give the creditor a liquidated claim in bankruptcy.

In Chapter 11 cases, the bankruptcy court must determine that the reorganization plan is feasible. In making the feasibility finding, the court may make a preliminary estimation of the amount of claims and reserve final determination of the value of the claim for later. Moreover, claims may be temporarily allowed for the purpose of establishing voting rights in connection with confirmation of a proposed plan. Bankruptcy Rule 3018(a). Although the bankruptcy court may not fix the amount of personal injury tort or wrongful death claims for purposes of distribution, it may estimate the claims for purposes of determining the feasibility of a Chapter 11 plan or establishing voting rights. *A.H. Robins Co. v. Piccinin*, 788 F.2d 994 (4th Cir.1986).

Section 502(c) gives no hint to courts of how they are to go about estimating the amount of contingent or unliquidated claims. *Collier* advises: "In estimating a claim, the bankruptcy court should use whatever method is best suited to the particular circumstances." *Collier on Bankruptcy* ¶ 502.04[2] (15th ed. rev. 2004). In *Baldwin-United*, which involved hundreds of millions of dollars in complicated indemnity and contribution claims, the court noted that "a formal trial on the merits would eviscerate the purpose underlying § 502(c)" and held that a summary two-day hearing which allowed one witness per party met the requirements of due process in estimating the value of these claims. At that hearing the court estimated these claims at $0. 55 B.R. at 899.

## D. SECURED CLAIMS

### 1. INTRODUCTION

The holder of a secured claim enjoys the top priority in the hierarchy of claims. A secured claim is a right to specific property, the collateral in which the creditor has a security interest; an unsecured claim is a right to what is left in the bankruptcy estate after the secured claims are fully paid. Since it is so easy under Article 9 of the Uniform Commercial Code for a creditor to take a security interest in all of a debtor's personal property, now owned and hereafter obtained, there is often nothing left in the estate for unsecured claims.

Some creditors don't take security interests at all because they deal with debtors of such high credit reputation and capacity to repay that security interests in their assets are unnecessary. This is true of loans by major commercial banks to very large corporate borrowers. These lenders can reduce credit risks by carefully monitoring their borrowers' activities against a background of covenants in the loan agreement that forbid encumbering or transferring assets, exceeding loan-to-asset ratios, engaging in novel endeavors, and the like. Other creditors extend unsecured credit to less credit worthy borrowers, but may demand high interest rates or other rights to compensate them for the greater risk of nonpayment. But many creditors, both lenders and sellers, routinely demand security interests in their debtors' assets. Sellers often take security interests in the goods they sell. Lenders operating beneath the rarified level of billion dollar transactions usually take security interests in some or all of their borrowers' assets. However, trade creditors (suppliers of goods or services) often do not take security interests and are, in consequence, subordinated to secured creditors in bankruptcy.

Why do we allow a debtor to contract with one creditor to award that creditor a priority over the debtor's other creditors, past and future, however meritorious their claims and whenever they extended credit, by taking a security interest in the debtor's assets? UCC Article 9 not only allows creditors to take security interests in all of a debtor's present and future tangible property, such as inventory or equipment, but also in the debtor's stream of earnings or cash flow, that is, the proceeds of sales of inventory or services from which unsecured creditors such as trade creditors expect to be paid. Although, in theory, voluntary creditors can use caution in dealing with debtors whose assets are or may be covered by security interests, an involuntary creditor like a tort claimant cannot, and may find its judgment debtor judgment-proof because all its assets are subject to security interests. *Compare* Thomas H. Jackson & Anthony T. Kronman, *Secured Financing and Priorities Among Creditors*, 88 Yale L.J. 1143 (1979), supporting secured credit, *with* Lynn LoPucki, *The Unsecured Creditor's Bargain*, 80 Va.L.Rev. 1887 (1994), challenging it.

*Enforcing a secured claim in bankruptcy.* When a debtor files in bankruptcy, the holder of a secured claim in that debtor's property is automatically stayed by § 362(a)(4) from enforcing the claim by foreclosure or other state law proceedings. The secured party is limited to its rights under the Bankruptcy Code to enforce its security interest. Under § 506(a) a secured party has a secured claim to the extent of the value of its collateral; if the collateral is worth less than the amount of the claim, the secured party has a secured claim to the extent of the value of the collateral and an unsecured claim for the rest of the debt. In Chapter 7 proceedings, the task of the debtor's trustee in bankruptcy is (1) to dispose of property of the estate in which there are security interests (§ 725), and (2) to liquidate the remaining assets of the estate and distribute proceeds to claimants pro rata according to the priorities set out in § 726.

If a secured creditor is oversecured (the collateral is worth more than the amount of the secured party's claim), the trustee will sell the collateral, pay the secured party the amount of its claim, and distribute the surplus in payment of the unsecured claims. If a creditor is undersecured (its collateral is worth less than the amount of the secured party's claim), all the proceeds of the sale of the collateral must go to the secured party, who will be left with an unsecured claim for any remaining deficiency. Since, in the case of an undersecured claim, the estate can't benefit from the trustee's sale of the collateral, the trustee may choose to save expenses by abandoning the property under § 554(a) to the debtor or agreeing to a lifting of the stay under § 362(d). If the property is abandoned or the stay is lifted, the secured party may proceed under state law to foreclose on its collateral; if a deficiency results, the creditor may file an unsecured claim in debtor's bankruptcy for the amount of the deficiency.

In Bankruptcy Code Chapters 11, 12 and 13, the debtor seeks to avoid liquidation under Chapter 7 by gaining approval of a plan of rehabilitation or reorganization that will allow the debtor to retain most of the property of the estate (including assets subject to security interests) by payment over time of part or all the claims of its creditors. The Code requires that the secured party's economic interest in the value of its collateral be respected throughout. As we will see in detail, the holders of secured claims are entitled to adequate protection of their rights during the preconfirmation period (§ 362(d)(1)) and compensation for the present value of their secured claims under the confirmed plan. §§ 1129(b)(2)(A), 1225(a)(5), and 1325(a)(5).

*Effect of discharge on secured claims.* If the property of the estate subject to the lien is abandoned to the debtor under § 554, or the stay is lifted under § 362(d) and the debtor is given a discharge under § 727(b), the effect is to discharge the debtor from liability on the debt that is secured by the lien. How does this affect the rights of the lienholder? The theory of discharge has always been that it affects only the personal liability of the debtor. It does not affect the debt itself, which remains unpaid. If third parties are liable on the debt, they remain liable. For example, a surety or other guarantor is liable even though the principal debtor is released as a result of the discharge. Nor is an insurance carrier's liability affected by the discharge of the insured. Similarly, if the debt is secured by property of a third party, that property can be reached to the full extent of the security agreement. This theory of discharge is specifically recognized in § 524(e).

The same rule applies if the discharged debt was secured by a lien in the debtor's property. As we shall see, liens may be modified in connection with confirmation of reorganization plans under Chapters 11, 12 and 13. But, otherwise, the debt and the lien continue to exist after bankruptcy even though the debtor may have been discharged from personal liability to pay the debt and even though the creditor did not file a proof of claim in bankruptcy. This principle was recognized in *Long v. Bullard*, 117 U.S. 617 (1886), a case antedating the Bankruptcy Act of 1898. In that case, Long received a discharge in bankruptcy and retained as exempt property a homestead that was subject to a mortgage in favor of Bullard. Bullard did not file proof of the mortgage debt in the bankruptcy. After bankruptcy, Bullard brought a foreclosure action. Long defended on the ground that the discharge prevented foreclosure under the mortgage. This defense was rejected in the trial court which charged the jury that "there could be no personal recovery against [Long] upon the note, but that the property could be subjected to the payment of the amount due, as the discharge of Long in bankruptcy did not release the lien of the mortgage." The court entered a decree for sale of the property. The Supreme Court of the United States affirmed the decree. Chief Justice Waite stated:

> [T]he discharge releases the bankrupt only from debts which were or might have been proved, and * * * debts secured by mortgage or pledge can only be proved for the balance remaining due after deducting the value of the security, unless all claim upon the security is released. Here the creditor neither proved his debt in bankruptcy nor released his lien. Consequently his security was preserved notwithstanding the bankruptcy of his debtor. * * * The dispute in the court below was as to the existence of the lien at the time of the commencement of the proceedings in bankruptcy. That depended entirely on the state laws, as to which the judgment of the state court is final and not subject to review here.

117 U.S. at 620–621.

## 2.  VALUING A SECURED CLAIM

In several bankruptcy contexts courts are required to value secured claims. Section 506(a)'s vague directive to value the claim in the light of the purposes of the valuation and the proposed disposition or use of the property, has led courts to adopt widely disparate methods of determining value. The following case addresses and purports to resolve the long-standing division of authority on valuation methodology. Although it arises under Chapter 13, its interpretation of § 506(a) should inform valuation in reorganization cases under Chapters 11 and 12 as well.

# Associates Commercial Corporation v. Rash

Supreme Court of the United States, 1997.
520 U.S. 953.

■ Justice GINSBURG delivered the opinion of the Court.

We resolve in this case a dispute concerning the proper application of § 506(a) of the Bankruptcy Code when a bankrupt debtor has exercised the "cram down" option for which Code § 1325(a)(5)(B) provides. Specifically, when a debtor, over a secured creditor's objection, seeks to retain and use the creditor's collateral in a Chapter 13 plan, is the value of the collateral to be determined by (1) what the secured creditor could obtain through foreclosure sale of the property (the "foreclosure-value" standard); (2) what the debtor would have to pay for comparable property (the "replacement-value" standard); or (3) the midpoint between these two measurements? We hold that § 506(a) directs application of the replacement-value standard.

## I

In 1989, respondent Elray Rash purchased for $73,700 a Kenworth tractor truck for use in his freight-hauling business. Rash made a downpayment on the truck, agreed to pay the seller the remainder in 60 monthly installments, and pledged the truck as collateral on the unpaid balance. The seller assigned the loan, and its lien on the truck, to petitioner Associates Commercial Corporation (ACC).

In March 1992, Elray and Jean Rash filed a joint petition and a repayment plan under Chapter 13 of the Bankruptcy Code (Code). At the time of the bankruptcy filing, the balance owed to ACC on the truck loan was $41,171. Because it held a valid lien on the truck, ACC was listed in the bankruptcy petition as a creditor holding a secured claim. Under the Code, ACC's claim for the balance owed on the truck was secured only to the extent of the value of the collateral; its claim over and above the value of the truck was unsecured. See § 506(a).

To qualify for confirmation under Chapter 13, the Rashes' plan had to satisfy the requirements set forth in § 1325(a) of the Code. The Rashes' treatment of ACC's secured claim, in particular, is governed by subsection (a)(5). Under this provision, a plan's proposed treatment of secured claims can be confirmed if one of three conditions is satisfied: the secured creditor accepts the plan, see § 1325(a)(5)(A); the debtor surrenders the property securing the claim to the creditor, see § 1325(a)(5)(C); or the debtor invokes the so-called "cram down" power, see § 1325(a)(5)(B). Under the cram down option, the debtor is permitted to keep the property over the objection of the creditor; the creditor retains the lien securing the claim, see § 1325(a)(5)(B)(i), and the debtor is required to provide the creditor with payments, over the life of the plan, that will total the present value of the allowed secured claim, i.e, the present value of the collateral, see § 1325(a)(5)(B)(ii). The value of the allowed secured claim is governed by § 506(a) of the Code.

The Rashes' Chapter 13 plan invoked the cram down power. It proposed that the Rashes retain the truck for use in the freight-hauling business and pay ACC, over 58 months, an amount equal to the present value of the truck. That value, the Rashes' petition alleged, was $28,500. ACC objected to the plan and asked the Bankruptcy Court to lift the automatic stay so ACC could repossess the truck. ACC also filed a proof of claim alleging that its claim was fully secured in the amount of $41,171. The Rashes filed an objection to ACC's claim.

The Bankruptcy Court held an evidentiary hearing to resolve the dispute over the truck's value. At the hearing, ACC and the Rashes urged different valuation benchmarks. ACC maintained that the proper valuation was the price the Rashes would have to pay to purchase a like vehicle, an amount ACC's expert estimated to be $41,000. The Rashes, however, maintained that the proper valuation was the net amount ACC would realize upon foreclosure and sale of the collateral, an amount their expert estimated to be $31,875. The Bankruptcy Court agreed with the Rashes and fixed the amount of ACC's secured claim at $31,875; that sum, the court found, was the net amount ACC would realize if it exercised its right to repossess and sell the truck. The Bankruptcy Court thereafter approved the plan, and the United States District Court for the Eastern District of Texas affirmed.

A panel of the Court of Appeals for the Fifth Circuit reversed. On rehearing en banc, however, the Fifth Circuit affirmed the District Court, holding that ACC's allowed secured claim was limited to $31,875, the net foreclosure value of the truck.

In reaching its decision, the Fifth Circuit highlighted, first, a conflict it perceived between the method of valuation ACC advanced, and the law of Texas defining the rights of secured creditors. Tex. Bus. & Com.Code Ann. §§ 9.504(a), (c), 9.505 (1991). In the Fifth Circuit's view, valuing collateral in a federal bankruptcy proceeding under a replacement-value standard—thereby setting an amount generally higher than what a secured creditor could realize pursuing its state-law foreclosure remedy—would "chang[e] the extent to which ACC is secured from what obtained under state law prior to the bankruptcy filing." *In re Rash*, 90 F.3d 1036, 1041 (5th Cir.1996). Such a departure from state law, the Fifth Circuit said, should be resisted by the federal forum unless "clearly compel[led]" by the Code.

The Fifth Circuit then determined that the Code provision governing valuation of security interests, § 506(a), does not compel a replacement-value approach. Instead, the court reasoned, the first sentence of § 506(a) requires that collateral be valued from the creditor's perspective. And because "the creditor's interest is in the nature of a security interest, giving the creditor the right to repossess and sell the collateral and nothing more[,]. . .. the valuation should start with what the creditor could realize by exercising that right." This foreclosure-value standard, the Fifth Circuit found, was consistent with the other relevant provisions of the Code, economic analysis, and the legislative history of the pertinent provisions. Judge Smith, joined by five other judges, dissented, urging that the Code dictates a replacement-value standard.

Courts of Appeals have adopted three different standards for valuing a security interest in a bankruptcy proceeding when the debtor invokes the cram down power to retain the collateral over the creditor's objection. In contrast to the Fifth Circuit's foreclosure-value standard, a number of Circuits have followed a replacement-value approach.[2] * * * Other courts have settled on the midpoint between foreclosure value and replacement value. *See In re Hoskins*, 102 F.3d 311, 316 (7th Cir.1996) * * *. We granted certiorari to resolve this conflict among the Courts of Appeals * * * and we now reverse the Fifth Circuit's judgment.

## II

The Bankruptcy Code provision central to the resolution of this case is § 506(a), which states:

> An allowed claim of a creditor secured by a lien on property in which the estate has an interest. . . is a secured claim to the extent of the value of such creditor's interest in the estate's interest in such property,. . . and is an unsecured claim to the extent that the value of such creditor's interest. . . is less than the amount of such allowed claim. Such value shall be determined in light of the purpose of the valuation and of the proposed disposition or use of such property. . ..

Over ACC's objection, the Rashes' repayment plan proposed, pursuant to § 1325(a)(5)(B), continued use of the property in question, i.e., the truck, in the debtor's trade or business. In such a "cram down" case, we hold, the value of the property (and thus the amount of the secured claim under § 506(a)) is the price a willing buyer in the debtor's trade, business, or situation would pay to obtain like property from a willing seller.

Rejecting this replacement-value standard, and selecting instead the typically lower foreclosure-value standard, the Fifth Circuit trained its attention on the first sentence of § 506(a). In particular, the Fifth Circuit relied on these first sentence words: a claim is secured "to the extent of the value of such *creditor's interest* in the estate's interest in such property." The Fifth Circuit read this phrase to instruct that the "starting point for the valuation [is] what the creditor could realize if it sold the estate's interest in the property according to the security agreement," namely, through "repossess[ing] and sell [ing] the collateral."

---

[2] * * * By using the term "replacement value," we do not suggest that a creditor is entitled to recover what it would cost the debtor to purchase the collateral brand new. Rather, our use of the term replacement value is consistent with the * * * meaning of fair-market value; by replacement value, we mean the price a willing buyer in the debtor's trade, business, or situation would pay a willing seller to obtain property of like age and condition.

We do not find in the § 506(a) first sentence words—"the creditor's interest in the estate's interest in such property"—the foreclosure-value meaning advanced by the Fifth Circuit. Even read in isolation, the phrase imparts no valuation standard: A direction simply to consider the "value of such creditor's interest" does not expressly reveal *how* that interest is to be valued.

Reading the first sentence of § 506(a) as a whole, we are satisfied that the phrase the Fifth Circuit considered key is not an instruction to equate a "creditor's interest" with the net value a creditor could realize through a foreclosure sale. The first sentence, in its entirety, tells us that a secured creditor's claim is to be divided into secured and unsecured portions, with the secured portion of the claim limited to the value of the collateral. * * * To separate the secured from the unsecured portion of a claim, a court must compare the creditor's claim to the value of "such property," i.e., the collateral. That comparison is sometimes complicated. A debtor may own only a part interest in the property pledged as collateral, in which case the court will be required to ascertain the "estate's interest" in the collateral. Or, a creditor may hold a junior or subordinate lien, which would require the court to ascertain the creditor's interest in the collateral. The § 506(a) phrase referring to the "creditor's interest in the estate's interest in such property" thus recognizes that a court may encounter, and in such instances must evaluate, limited or partial interests in collateral. The full first sentence of § 506(a), in short, tells a court what it must evaluate, but it does not say more; it is not enlightening on how to value collateral.

The second sentence of § 506(a) does speak to the *how* question. "Such value," that sentence provides, "shall be determined in light of the purpose of the valuation and of the proposed disposition or use of such property." § 506(a). By deriving a foreclosure-value standard from § 506(a)'s first sentence, the Fifth Circuit rendered inconsequential the sentence that expressly addresses how "value shall be determined."

As we comprehend § 506(a), the "proposed disposition or use" of the collateral is of paramount importance to the valuation question. If a secured creditor does not accept a debtor's Chapter 13 plan, the debtor has two options for handling allowed secured claims: surrender the collateral to the creditor, see § 1325(a)(5)(C); or, under the cram down option, keep the collateral over the creditor's objection and provide the creditor, over the life of the plan, with the equivalent of the present value of the collateral, see § 1325(a)(5)(B). The "disposition or use" of the collateral thus turns on the alternative the debtor chooses—in one case the collateral will be surrendered to the creditor, and in the other, the collateral will be retained and used by the debtor. Applying a foreclosure-value standard when the cram down option is invoked attributes no significance to the different consequences of the debtor's choice to surrender the property or retain it. A replacement-value standard, on the other hand, distinguishes retention from surrender and renders meaningful the key words "disposition or use."

Tying valuation to the actual "disposition or use" of the property points away from a foreclosure-value standard when a Chapter 13 debtor, invoking cram down power, retains and uses the property. Under that option, foreclosure is averted by the debtor's choice and over the creditor's objection. From the creditor's perspective as well as the debtor's, surrender and retention are not equivalent acts.

When a debtor surrenders the property, a creditor obtains it immediately, and is free to sell it and reinvest the proceeds. We recall here that ACC sought that very advantage. If a debtor keeps the property and continues to use it, the creditor obtains at once neither the property nor its value and is exposed to double risks: The debtor may again default and the property may deteriorate from extended use. Adjustments in the interest rate and secured creditor demands for more "adequate protection," § 361, do not fully offset these risks. *See* 90 F.3d, at 1066 (Smith, J., dissenting) ("vast majority of reorganizations fail. . . leaving creditors with only a fraction of the compensation due them"; where, as here, "collateral depreciates rapidly, the secured creditor may receive far less in a failed reorganization than in a prompt foreclosure") (internal cross–reference omitted) * * *.[3]

Of prime significance, the replacement-value standard accurately gauges the debtor's "use" of the property. It values "the creditor's interest in the collateral in light of the proposed [repayment plan] reality: no foreclosure sale and economic benefit for the debtor derived from the collateral equal to. . . its [replacement] value." *In re Winthrop Old Farm Nurseries*, 50 F.3d 72, 75 (1st Cir.1995). The debtor in this case elected to use the collateral to generate an income stream. That actual use, rather than a foreclosure sale that will not take place, is the proper guide under a prescription hinged to the property's "disposition or use." *See ibid.*

The Fifth Circuit considered the replacement-value standard disrespectful of state law, which permits the secured creditor to sell the collateral, thereby obtaining its net foreclosure value "and nothing more." In allowing Chapter 13 debtors to retain and use collateral over the objection of secured creditors, however, the Bankruptcy Code has reshaped debtor and creditor rights in marked departure from state law. *See, e.g.*, Uniform Commercial Code §§ 9-504, 9-505. The Code's cram down option displaces a secured creditor's state-law right to obtain immediate foreclosure upon a debtor's default. That change, ordered by federal law, is attended by a direction that courts look to the "proposed disposition or use" of the

---

[3] On this matter, amici curiae supporting ACC contended: " 'Adequate protection' payments under §§ 361, 362(d)(1) typically are based on the assumption that the collateral will be subject to only ordinary depreciation. Hence, even when such payments are made, they frequently fail to compensate adequately for the usually more rapid depreciation of assets retained by the debtor." Brief for American Automobile Manufacturers Association, Inc., et al. as Amici Curiae 21, n. 9.

collateral in determining its value. It no more disrupts state law to make "disposition or use" the guide for valuation than to authorize the rearrangement of rights the cram down power entails.

Nor are we persuaded that the split-the-difference approach adopted by the Seventh Circuit provides the appropriate solution. Whatever the attractiveness of a standard that picks the midpoint between foreclosure and replacement values, there is no warrant for it in the Code.[5] Section 506(a) calls for the value the property possesses in light of the "disposition or use" in fact "proposed," not the various dispositions or uses that might have been proposed. * * * The Seventh Circuit rested on the "economics of the situation," *In re Hoskins*, 102 F.3d, at 316, only after concluding that the statute suggests no particular valuation method. We agree with the Seventh Circuit that "a simple rule of valuation is needed" to serve the interests of predictability and uniformity. Id., at 314. We conclude, however, that § 506(a) supplies a governing instruction less complex than the Seventh Circuit's "make two valuations, then split the difference" formulation.

In sum, under § 506(a), the value of property retained because the debtor has exercised the § 1325(a)(5)(B) "cram down" option is the cost the debtor would incur to obtain a like asset for the same "proposed... use."[6]

* * *

For the foregoing reasons, the judgment of the Court of Appeals is reversed, and the case is remanded for further proceedings consistent with this opinion.

It is so ordered.

---

[5] As our reading of § 506(a) makes plain, we also reject a ruleless approach allowing use of different valuation standards based on the facts and circumstances of individual cases. *Cf. In re Valenti*, 105 F.3d 55, 62–63 (C.A.2 1997) (permissible for bankruptcy courts to determine valuation standard case-by-case).

[6] Our recognition that the replacement-value standard, not the foreclosure-value standard, governs in cram down cases leaves to bankruptcy courts, as triers of fact, identification of the best way of ascertaining replacement value on the basis of the evidence presented. Whether replacement value is the equivalent of retail value, wholesale value, or some other value will depend on the type of debtor and the nature of the property. We note, however, that replacement value, in this context, should not include certain items. For example, where the proper measure of the replacement value of a vehicle is its retail value, an adjustment to that value may be necessary: A creditor should not receive portions of the retail price, if any, that reflect the value of items the debtor does not receive when he retains his vehicle, items such as warranties, inventory storage, and reconditioning. Nor should the creditor gain from modifications to the property—e.g., the addition of accessories to a vehicle—to which a creditor's lien would not extend under state law.

■ Justice STEVENS, dissenting. [Opinion omitted.]

## NOTE

How would *Rash* be decided under the current version of § 506(a)(2) quoted below?

(2)  If the debtor is an individual in a case under chapter 7 or 13, such value with respect to personal property securing an allowed claim shall be determined based on the replacement value of such property as of the date of filing the petition without deduction for costs of sale or marketing. With respect to property acquired for personal, family, or household purpose, replacement value shall mean the price a retail merchant would charge for property of that kind considering the age and condition of the property at the time value is determined.

We reserve for Chapter 9 on consumer debtors a discussion of valuation in consumer cases. Since § 506(a)(2) doesn't apply to cases concerning corporate or partnership debtors or to Chapter 11 or 12 cases, *Rash* remains good authority in commercial cases. What guidance does it offer on how to determine the "replacement value" of important types of collateral in business reorganization cases involving inventory or accounts receivable?

## PROBLEM

Secured Creditor (SC) repossessed defaulting Debtor's car. Debtor filed in Chapter 7 and petitioned to redeem the car under § 722, which allows the Debtor to retain the car free of SC's security interest "by paying the holder of such lien the amount of the allowed secured claim of such holder that is secured by such lien." Assume that the wholesale value of the car is $4,400 and the replacement value is $8,900. Debtor contends that the holding in *Rash*, which was a Chapter 13 cramdown case, does not control in a redemption case, and that she should be able to redeem by paying $4,400. She relies on the language in 506(a)(1) emphasized by the Court in *Rash* stating that value is to be determined "in the light of the purpose of the valuation and proposed disposition or use of such property." Should a different rule apply for valuation in redemption cases than for cramdown? *See In re Bouzek*, 311 B.R. 239 (Bankr. E.D.Wis.2004); *In re Smith*, 307 B.R. 912 (Bankr. N.D. Ill.2004).

## NOTES

**1.**  In footnote 6 to *Rash*, the Court directs that the replacement value should not include certain enumerated items. How does such a reduced replacement value vary from a wholesale price?

**2.** In the dissent, Justice Stevens points out that by according a secured creditor the replacement value of collateral in a cramdown, the creditor gets a better deal in bankruptcy than it would under state law, under which the creditor would only be able to exercise its lien and foreclose. The result is a windfall to undersecured creditors at the expense of unsecured creditors. Why didn't the majority opinion see it that way?

### 3. AVOIDING LIENS UNDER § 506(d)

Section 506(d) was meant to preserve the rule of *Long v. Bullard*, 117 U.S. 617 (1886). The House Report on the Bankruptcy Reform Act of 1978 states with respect to the original version of § 506(d):

> Subsection (d) permits liens to pass through the bankruptcy case unaffected. However, if a party in interest requests the court to determine and allow or disallow the claim secured by the lien under section 502 and the claim is not allowed, then the lien is void to the extent that the claim is not allowed.

1978 U.S.C.C.A.N. 6313. But on its face § 506(d) states only when a lien is void. Only by negative implication does it indicate that a lien not void under § 506(d) will "pass through the bankruptcy case unaffected." The unstated assumption is that the rule of *Long v. Bullard* governs if the lien is not avoided under § 506(d) and is not avoided by some other provision of the Code. Section 506(d) is illustrated by the hypothetical cases that follow. Assume in each case that the debtor has filed in Chapter 7.

> **Case #1.** Debtor owes Creditor $100,000 secured by a lien on land worth $75,000. If Creditor files a claim in Debtor's bankruptcy, under § 506(a) it would have an allowed secured claim of $75,000 and an allowed unsecured claim for $25,000. Debtor is convinced that property values will increase and wishes to retain ownership of the land. In pursuance of this plan, Debtor files a proceeding to limit or "strip down" Creditor's lien to the value of the land, $75,000, on the ground that under § 506(d) Creditor's lien is void to the extent it is not an allowed secured claim. Since the unless clause is not applicable, literally read, § 506(d) allows the court to strip down the lien to $75,000, the amount of the secured claim. If Debtor can borrow enough money to redeem the land by paying off the remaining amount of the lien, it will gain the advantage of any subsequent increase in the value of the land. Creditor would lose the potential future appreciation that it might have been able to realize under state law that would allow the debtor to redeem property subject to a lien only by paying the full amount of the debt—$100,000.

**Case #2.** Debtor owes Creditor $100,000 secured by a first lien on land owned by Debtor. Debtor owes Lender $25,000 secured by a second lien on the same land. At the time of bankruptcy the land is worth $100,000. Debtor is willing to reaffirm the $100,000 debt under § 524(c); this would allow Debtor to keep the land as long as the installment payments were made to Creditor. As Debtor reduces the first mortgage debt by payments after bankruptcy or as the value of the land increases, Debtor can build a substantial equity in the land. But for Debtor to receive the full benefit of the reaffirmation with Creditor, it must avoid the second lien in bankruptcy. If the second lien is not avoided, the first $25,000 of any postbankruptcy equity will be captured by the Lender. Literally read § 506(d) allows Debtor to void the "underwater" second lien because it had no present value at the time of the bankruptcy and, therefore, does not secure an allowed secured claim. Debtor could then capture all postbankruptcy equity upon reaffirming its obligation to Creditor.

Most courts adopted the foregoing literal interpretation of § 506(d), e.g., *Gaglia v. First Federal Savings & Loan Ass'n*, 889 F.2d 1304 (3d Cir.1989), but the Supreme Court in *Dewsnup v. Timm*, 502 U.S. 410 (1992), rejected this reading of § 506(d) in a case similar to Case #1. In the majority opinion, Justice Blackmun noted that before enactment of the Bankruptcy Code of 1978, liens on property passed through bankruptcy unaffected. *Long v. Bullard*. Under this rule, debtors could not redeem property from a mortgagee unless the debt was paid in full. Congress fully understood this pre-Code rule. The Court found that the new Code did not unambiguously repeal this rule and would not assume that Congress intended to grant to debtors a broad new remedy to strip down liens to the amount of the allowed secured claim as defined in § 506(a). In the view of the majority, all § 506(d) does is avoid liens that secured disallowed claims; that is, if the debtor doesn't legally owe the debt, the lien securing the debt is void. The majority read § 506(d) as though the word "secured" in the phrase "allowed secured claim" were deleted. Thus, after *Dewsnup*, in Case #1, Debtor's attempt to strip down liens would fail. Future appreciation belongs to the secured creditor.

The majority opinion left most commentators surprised and Justice Scalia sputtering in dissent. Although on a policy basis leaving any future appreciation in the collateral with the secured creditor is, as Justice Scalia conceded, quite defensible, on statutory interpretation grounds the majority opinion is of questionable legitimacy. On its face § 506(d) voids a lien to the extent the claim it secures is not both an "allowed claim" and a "secured claim" under § 506(a). The premise of the majority opinion is that somehow "allowed secured claim" in § 506(d) means something different from the definition of allowed secured claim in § 506(a), a proposition that Justice Scalia derided as the one-subsection-at-a-time technique of statutory interpretation. While the statutory construction technique of looking to pre-Code precedents to decide the meaning of ambiguous provisions is well established, it seems inappropriate in a case involving a provision as clearly stated as § 506(d), using an obviously technical term defined earlier in the very same code section. The Court's assertion that the term "secured claim" may, chameleon like, change meaning in different sections of the Code casts doubt on the meaning of the many provisions of the Code using the term. As we shall see in our consideration of Chapters 11 and 13, lien stripping plans are confirmable. *In re Hernandez*, 175 B.R. 962 (N.D.Ill.1994), collects the authorities on this issue. The following case discusses the issue of the completely underwater second lien.

## In re Talbert

United States Court of Appeals, Sixth Circuit, 2003.
344 F.3d 555.

■ SILER, Circuit Judge.

This bankruptcy appeal presents purely a legal question that has split the bankruptcy and federal district courts, namely, whether a debtor who has filed for Chapter 7 bankruptcy may avoid a valueless lien under § 506(d) of the Bankruptcy Code, 11 U.S.C. § 506(d). Because the Supreme Court's reasoning in *Dewsnup v. Timm,* 502 U.S. 410 (1992), applies with equal force and logic to the issue at hand, we hold that a Chapter 7 debtor may not use § 506 to "strip off" an allowed junior lien where the senior lien exceeds the fair market value of the real property in question. Accordingly, we AFFIRM the judgment of the district court.

Debtors Terry and Lahna Talbert (the "Talberts") filed an adversary proceeding against Defendant City Mortgage Services ("City Mortgage") to avoid City Mortgage's lien on their residence pursuant to 11 U.S.C. § 506(d). Although properly served with process, City Mortgage failed to file an answer or other responsive filing in the bankruptcy court, a strategy to which City Mortgage adhered before the district court, and continues to employ before this court. At the hearing for default judgment, the bankruptcy court raised *sua sponte* the issue of whether, as a legal matter, § 506(d) permits the "strip off" of an allowed unsecured lien.[1]

For purposes of its analysis, the court accepted as true that at the time of the Talberts' bankruptcy filing, they owned a residence located in Lans-

---

[1] "The term "strip off" is used when a junior mortgage is totally unsecured, whereas the term "strip down" is used when a mortgage is partially unsecured and partially secured."

ing, Michigan, which had a fair market value of $88,000. The court also accepted that the residence was encumbered by a first mortgage in the amount of $90,633, and that City Mortgage held a junior mortgage in the amount of approximately $33,110. It was thus undisputed that City Mortgage held a "valueless" lien since the Talberts' property had a market value that was $2,633 less than the amount of the lien securing the first mortgage. * * *

### E. "Strip Off" in Chapter 7

The question of whether a Chapter 7 debtor may use § 506(d) to "strip off" a valueless junior lien from real property has divided the bankruptcy and federal district courts.* * * The Fourth Circuit is the only federal appellate court to discuss this debate, and it has sided with those courts that hold that § 506 does not permit the "stripping off" of liens in Chapter 7 proceedings. *See Ryan,* 253 F.3d at 783 ("[W]e hold that an allowed unsecured consensual lien may not be stripped off in a Chapter 7 proceeding pursuant to the provisions of § 506(a) and (d)."). We agree with the Fourth Circuit.

As did the debtors in *Ryan,* the Talberts argue that the secured status of a claim is determined by the security-reducing provision of § 506(a), and that pursuant to this provision, their junior lien is completely unsecured, and, thus, according to § 506(d), may be "stripped off." A similar argument was rejected by the Supreme Court in the analogous context of a debtor's attempt to "strip down" an under-collateralized creditor's lien in a Chapter 7 case. In *Dewsnup,* the debtors owned farmland encumbered by deed of trust securing a debt of $120,000. The farmland was valued at approximately $39,000. This arrangement left an unsecured deficiency of approximately $81,000, which the debtors sought to avoid pursuant to § 506(d). The lower courts would not grant this relief, and the Supreme Court affirmed.

In its analysis, the [*Dewsnup*] Court laid out in detail the different readings that could be given to the thorny statutory interpretation question presented by the perceived interplay of §§ 506(a) and 506(d). One interpretation, which was urged by the debtors, was that "§§ 506(a) and 506(d) are complementary and to be read together." 502 U.S. at 414. According to this argument, "[b]ecause, under § 506(a), a claim is secured only to the extent of the judicially determined value of the real property on which the lien is fixed, a debtor can void a lien on the property pursuant to § 506(d) to the extent the claim is no longer secured and thus is not 'an allowed secured claim.'" *Id.* Although not without merit, this argument was rejected in favor of an analysis advanced by the creditors, and joined by the United States as *amicus curiae,* namely, that the words "'allowed secured claim' in § 506(d) need not be read as an indivisible term of art defined by reference to § 506(a), which by its terms is not a definitional provision." *Id.* at 415.

Under this construction, "allowed secured claim" "should be read term-by-term to refer to any claim that is, first, allowed,[5] and, second, secured." *Id.* (footnote added). The Court continued, "[b]ecause there is no question that the claim at issue here has been 'allowed' pursuant to § 502 of the Code and is secured by a lien with recourse to the underlying collateral, it does not come within the scope of § 506(d), which voids only liens corresponding to claims that have *not* been allowed and secured." *Id.* (emphasis in original). This reading, the Court explained, "gives the provision the simple and sensible function of voiding a lien whenever a claim secured by the lien itself has not been allowed." *Id.* at 415-16. Thus, although limited to the facts of the case, the Court's holding was quite clear: "[w]e hold that § 506(d) does not allow petitioner to 'strip down' respondent's lien, because respondents' claim is secured by a lien and has been fully allowed pursuant to § 502." *Id.* at 417.

Three considerations constituted the analytical underpinnings of the Court's holding, namely, that: (1) any increase in the value of the property from the date of the judicially determined valuation to the time of the foreclosure sale should accrue to the creditor; (2) the mortgagor and mortgagee bargained that a consensual lien would remain with the property until foreclosure; and (3) liens on real property survive bankruptcy unaffected. *Id.* at 417-18. In the Court's own words

The practical effect of petitioner's argument is to freeze the creditor's secured interest at the judicially determined valuation. By this approach, the creditor would lose the benefit of any increase in the value of the property by the time of the foreclosure sale. The increase would accrue to the benefit of the debtor, a result some of the parties describe as a "windfall."

We think. . . that the creditor's lien stays with the real property until the foreclosure. That is what was bargained for by the mortgagor and the mortgagee. The voidness language sensibly applies only to the security aspect of the lien and then only to the real deficiency in the security. Any increase over the judicially determined valuation during bankruptcy rightly accrues to the benefit of the creditor, not to the benefit of the debtor and not to the benefit of other unsecured creditors whose claims have been allowed and who had nothing to do with the mortgagor-mortgagee bargain. . . ..

This result appears to have been clearly established before the passage of the 1978 Act. Under the Bankruptcy Act of 1898, a lien on real property passed through bankruptcy unaffected. This Court recently

---

[5] A claim or interest is deemed "allowed" if proof thereof is timely filed pursuant to Code § 501, and (1) no objection is made by a party in interest, or (2) the bankruptcy court, after notice and a hearing, determines the validity of the claim, thereby overruling the objection of a party in interest.  § 502.

acknowledged that this was so. See *Farrey v. Sanderfoot,* 500 U.S. 291, 297 (1991) ("Ordinarily, liens and other secured interests survive bankruptcy"); *Johnson v. Home State Bank,* 501 U.S. 78, 84 (1991) ("Rather, a bankruptcy discharge extinguishes only one mode of enforcing a claim—namely, an action against the debtor *in personam*—while leaving intact another—namely, an action against the debtor *in rem* ")....

Congress must have enacted the Code with a full understanding of this practice. See H.R.Rep. No. 95-595, p. 357 (1977), U.S.Code Cong. & Admin. News 1978, pp. 5787, 6313 ("Subsection (d) permits liens to pass through the bankruptcy case unaffected").

When Congress amends the bankruptcy laws, it does not write "on a clean slate.".... [T]o attribute to Congress the intention to grant a debtor the broad new remedy against allowed claims to the extent that they become "unsecured" for purposes of § 506(a) without the new remedy's being mentioned somewhere in the Code itself or in the annals of Congress is not plausible, in our view, and is contrary to basic bankruptcy principles.

*Id.* at 417-20.

The Supreme Court's reasoning for not permitting "strip downs" in the Chapter 7 context applies with equal validity to a debtor's attempt to effectuate a Chapter 7 "strip off." *See Ryan,* 253 F.3d at 782 ("[W]e discern no principled distinction to be made between the case *sub judice* and that decided in *Dewsnup.* The Court's reasoning in *Dewsnup* is equally relevant and convincing in a case like ours where a debtor attempts to strip off, rather than. . . strip down, an approved but unsecured lien.") * * * .

As in the case of a "strip down," to permit a "strip off" would mark a departure from the pre-Code rule that real property liens emerge from bankruptcy unaffected. Also, as in the case of a "strip down," a "strip off" would rob the mortgagee of the bargain it struck with the mortgagor, i.e., that the consensual lien would remain with the property until foreclosure. In fact, in *Dewsnup,* the Court was persuaded by the creditors' argument that "'the fresh start' policy cannot justify an impairment of respondents' property rights, for the fresh start does not extend to an *in rem* claim against property but is limited to a discharge of personal liability." 502 U.S. at 416. Finally, as was true in the context of "strip downs," Chapter 7 "strip offs" also carry the risk of a "windfall" to the debtors should the value of the encumbered property increase by the time of the foreclosure sale. As one court observed, "[w]ho knows what the real estate market will be tomorrow? By the time of sale in the future, a piece of real estate may have increased in value to cover a second-mortgage lien not covered by the property's value today." *In re Cater,* 240 B.R. at 424; *see also Ryan,* 253 F.3d at 783 ("[W]e are acutely aware that in the volatile, modern real estate market, substantial price variations occur with weekly or monthly regularities.").

It is true that the Court's opinion has not escaped scholarly criticism, *see Cunningham,* 246 B.R. at 246 (compiling law review articles that have criticized the *Dewsnup* decision), and that some courts have been unwilling to extend *Dewsnup* to its logical conclusion * * *. However, notwithstanding the dissatisfaction of some, we are not at liberty to ignore the Supreme Court's reasoning, which Congress has made no apparent attempt to modify or correct through legislative action. * * *

In the instant case, the Talberts do not challenge that City Mortgage's claim is allowed pursuant to § 502. Also, regardless of the fact that the current value of the real property is insufficient to recover City Mortgage's junior lien, the claim is nonetheless "secured in the ordinary sense, that is,... [it] is backed up by a security interest in property, whether or not the value of the property suffices to cover the claim." *Cater,* 240 B.R. at 422. As *Dewsnup* teaches, that is all that is required; the Talberts may not utilize § 506(a) and (d) to "strip off" City Mortgage's lien. *See Dewsnup,* 502 U.S. at 415 ("Because there is no question that the claim at issue here has been 'allowed' pursuant to § 502 of the Code and is secured by a lien with recourse to the underlying collateral, it does not come within the scope of § 506(d), which voids only liens corresponding to claims that have not been allowed and secured.") (emphasis removed); *see also Cater,* 240 B.R. at 423 ("[B]ecause [the creditor's] claim is allowed under § 502 and is secured by a valid lien, the same result obtains. The fact that the value of the property is insufficient to cover the debt does not warrant a different result.").

"Section 506 was intended to facilitate valuation and disposition of property in the reorganization chapters of the Code, not to confer an additional avoiding power on a Chapter 7 debtor." *Ryan* 253 F.3d at 783 (quoting *Laskin,* 222 B.R. at 876). When a debtor proceeds under Chapter 7, creditors are "entitled to their lien position until foreclosure or other permissible final disposition is had." *Id.* Thus, we conclude that a Chapter 7 debtor may not use § 506 to "strip off" an allowed junior lien where the senior lien exceeds the fair market value of the real property.
AFFIRMED.

### 4. AFTER-ACQUIRED PROPERTY AND CASH COLLATERAL

The postpetition effect of prepetition security interests is an important issue in business bankruptcies. UCC § 9–204(a) allows a security interest to attach to personal property to be acquired by the debtor in the future. In inventory and accounts financing, secured creditors commonly take a "floating lien" on all of the debtor's inventory, accounts, general intangibles, and the proceeds thereof, then owned or thereafter acquired. In commercial real estate financing, mortgagees take a security interest in all future rents and profits as well as in the real estate itself. But secured creditors are dealt a jarring blow by § 552(a), which invalidates prepetition security interests in property acquired postpetition. Since inventory and accounts constantly turn over, if, under this provision, newly acquired property is not covered by the existing security interest, a creditor's floating lien may dwindle to insignificance within weeks after the debtor files.

Of what use, then, is a security interest covering after-acquired property if it may be ineffective at the very time the creditor most needs it, the debtor's filing in bankruptcy? Section 552(b) significantly limits the effect of § 552(a)'s invalidation of after-acquired property clauses. Section 552(b)(1) assures us that secured creditors do have effective security interests in the *proceeds* of property in which the creditor had a security interest at the time of bankruptcy, and § 552(b)(2) was added in 1994 to make clear that assignments of real property rents are effective with respect to postpetition rents.

While § 552(b) preserves the secured creditor's lien in proceeds of prepetition collateral in general, § 363 affords additional protection for a security interest in proceeds in the form of money, checks or deposit accounts, described in § 363(a) as "cash collateral," because of the risk that the debtor may misappropriate or squander this ephemeral form of collateral. Under § 363(c) the debtor in possession (or Chapter 11 trustee if one is appointed) may not use or dispose of cash collateral unless either the secured creditor consents or the court authorizes such use or disposition subject to the secured creditor's right under § 363(e) to "adequate protection" of its interest in the cash collateral. Ordinarily a debtor in possession that cannot use the cash proceeds from the sale of its inventory, the collection of its accounts, or the rentals from its commercial real estate, cannot operate its business, much less reorganize. Hence, the secured creditor whose lien extends to the cash proceeds of prepetition inventory, accounts and real property rents is often in a strong bargaining position. Without the creditor's consent or a court order affording the creditor adequate protection of its interest, the debtor may not be able to buy essential raw materials, pay its employees or meet other essential operating expenses. The less able the debtor is to provide the secured creditor "adequate protection," the more powerful the creditor's threat to shut down the business by withholding its consent to the use of cash collateral. Issues of cash collateral are explored in greater detail in the section entitled "Use of Deposit Accounts and Other Cash Collateral" in chapter 11 on pages 616-619.

What is the reach of § 552(a)? In inventory or accounts financing, in which the collateral turns over frequently, after-acquired property clauses are vital to the effectiveness of "floating liens." Does § 552(a) render these clauses inoperative in bankruptcy, the very situation in which the secured party most needs the protection of a perfected security interest? The following case addresses this important issue.

# In re Bumper Sales, Inc.

United States Court of Appeals, Fourth Circuit, 1990.
907 F.2d 1430.

■ CHAPMAN, Circuit Judge:

This appeal stems from the district court's affirmance of the bankruptcy court's order granting to the appellee/cross-appellant Marepcon Financial Corporation (Marepcon), a post-petition security interest in the inventory, receivables and other assets of debtor Bumper Sales, Inc. (Bumper Sales), to the detriment of appellant/cross-appellee Unsecured Creditors' Committee (the Committee). We affirm.

In order to expand its inventory of car and truck bumpers, Bumper Sales borrowed from Marepcon, a small asset-based lender, about $510,000 in the form of two promissory notes, one for $110,000 dated December 8, 1987, and another for $400,000 dated March 9, 1988. In return, Bumper Sales agreed to give Marepcon a security interest in "all of. . . [Bumper Sales'] inventory, accounts receivable, contract rights, furniture, fixtures and equipment, general intangibles, now owned or hereafter-acquired and the proceeds from said collateral," as stipulated by the parties. * * *

When Bumper Sales filed for Chapter 11 bankruptcy on July 22, 1988, the principal remaining due to Marepcon was $499,964.88. At that time, the value of Bumper Sales' inventory, which consisted solely of finished bumpers, was $769,000. Bumper Sales continued to operate the business as debtor-in-possession. On August 12, 1988, Bumper Sales' counsel, Jonathan L. Hauser, wrote to Ronald M. Gates of Marepcon, stating that he

> assumed that our [Bumper Sales'] previous understanding with Mr. Waters [the former Executive Vice President of Marepcon] remains, i.e., that [Bumper Sales] may continue to use the cash collateral subject to the security interest of [Marepcon] in the ordinary course of business, so long as it continues to keep. . . [Marepcon's] loan current and complies with all of the other usual covenants contained in the loan documents.

In other words, Marepcon consented to Bumper Sales' use of the cash proceeds of pre-petition inventory and accounts to finance post-petition inventory. No order conditioning such use of cash collateral on the grant of a post-petition lien in the collateral was entered.

However, on August 19, 1988, Bumper Sales' owner and president, Joel B. Campbell, and Bumper Sales' counsel, Mr. Hauser, met with Joseph R. Mayes, counsel for the Committee, and had the following exchange:

> Mr. Mayes: Q.      What arrangements have been made with [Marepcon] for the use of cash collateral?
>
> Debtor (Mr. Campbell):A.    We've provided them with security.

| Mr. Mayes: Q. | Is this cash collateral arrangement in effect or about to come into effect? |
| Mr. Hauser: A. | Yeah. I've discussed it with counsel and basically so long as the terms and so long as we provide them with certain information, they'll be reasonably happy. |
| Mr. Mayes: Q. | Will there be a post petition lien in effect? |
| Mr. Hauser: A. | Yes. Most assuredly. |

The parties stipulated that, during the post-petition period, Bumper Sales did not borrow any outside funds or incur any outside debt; that Bumper Sales used *only* Marepcon's cash collateral—the cash proceeds of inventory secured under Marepcon's security interest—to finance new inventory; and that Bumper Sales would not have been able to reorganize without the use of the cash collateral.

On March 31, 1989, Marepcon filed a Motion to Condition Use, Sale or Lease of Collateral and Proceeds, declaring a claim of $500,000 against Bumper Sales and asserting a security interest in Bumper Sales' inventory, accounts receivable, general intangibles, furniture, fixtures, equipment, and proceeds. The motion sought adequate protection for this security interest.[2] The Committee filed an objection to the motion challenging the proper perfection of Marepcon's security interest and contending that any post-petition lien had been lost by Marepcon's failure to condition use of the collateral. The bankruptcy court held that Marepcon had a valid and properly perfected security interest in Bumper Sales' pre-petition inventory and receivables, among other assets, and their proceeds, and that this security interest continued post-petition to the extent of Marepcon's unpaid claim. As a result, the court granted Marepcon a lien on Bumper Sales' pre-and post-petition collateral. The U.S. District Court for the Eastern District of Virginia affirmed the bankruptcy court, and the Committee appeals. * * *

We now address the crux of the Committee's appeal: whether Marepcon has a security interest in Bumper Sales' post-petition assets. This issue is partly answered easily, because the Committee does not contest that Marepcon holds a security interest in the pre-petition collateral (i.e., that held as of the bankruptcy filing on July 22, 1988) remaining in Bumper Sales' hands at the time of Marepcon's motion for adequate protection on

---

[2] Marepcon moved pursuant to Section 363(e) of the Bankruptcy Code, which states that

[n]otwithstanding any other provision of. . . [Section 363], at any time, on request of an entity that has an interest in property used. . . or proposed to be used. . . by the trustee, the court, with or without a hearing, shall prohibit or condition such use. . . as is necessary to provide adequate protection of such interest. § 363(e).

March 31, 1989. It was stipulated that the total amount of inventory at the time of the filing was $769,000. Mr. Waters, the former Executive Vice President of Marepcon, testified that the total cost of goods sold, and hence total amount of inventory released, during this period was at most $464,000 and at least $168,000, making the inventory remaining at the time of the motion between $305,000 ($769,000–$464,000) and $601,000 ($769,000–168,000). Adding the undisputed value of pre-petition equipment of $74,000 and pre-petition receivables of $11,215.57, Marepcon's security interest extends to at least $390,215.57 ($305,000 + $74,000 + $11,215.57) of Bumper Sales' post-petition assets. Given that Marepcon's total claim against Bumper Sales amounts to $486,957.69, the remainder of this opinion is devoted to the issue whether the $96,742.12 balance is secured.

The Committee maintains that Marepcon's security interest does not cover Bumper Sales' post-petition inventory and accounts, because Section 552(a) of the Bankruptcy Code invalidates the operation of after-acquired clauses in bankruptcy. Section 552(a) states as follows:

> Except as provided in subsection (b) of this section, property acquired by the estate or by the debtor after the commencement of the case is not subject to any lien resulting from any security agreement entered into by the debtor before the commencement of the case.

This subsection was "designed to facilitate the debtor's "fresh start" by allowing the debtor to acquire postpetition assets free of prepetition liabilities" and thereby offer "postpetition accounts receivable and inventory as collateral" to new creditors. In re Photo Promotion Associates, Inc., 53 B.R. 759, 763 (Bankr.S.D.N.Y.1985).

In response, Marepcon asserts that Section 552(b), which carves out an exception to Section 552(a), applies:

> **(b)** Except as provided in section[ ] 363. . . of this title, if the debtor and an entity entered into a security agreement before the commencement of the case and if the security interest created by such security agreement extends to property of the debtor acquired before the commencement of the case and to proceeds. . . of such property, then such security interest extends to such proceeds. . . acquired by the estate after the commencement of the case to the extent provided by such security agreement and by applicable nonbankruptcy law, except to any extent that the court, after notice and a hearing and based on the equities of the case, orders otherwise.

Marepcon correctly explains that, according to Section 552, "[p]roceeds coverage, but not after-acquired property clauses, are valid under title 11." In re Gross–Feibel Co., Inc., 21 B.R. 648, 649 (Bankr.S.D.Ohio 1982) (quoting 124 Cong.Rec. H11, 097–98 (Sept. 28, 1978) (remarks of Rep. Edwards); S17,414 (Oct. 6, 1978) (remarks of Sen. DeConcini)). Marepcon contends that its security interest extends to Bumper Sales' post-petition inventory and accounts because they are proceeds of Bumper Sales' pre-petition inventory and accounts, pointing out that Bumper Sales' post-petition inventory was financed solely by the proceeds of its pre-petition inventory and accounts.[8]

The issue before us, then, is whether Bumper Sales' post-petition inventory and accounts are after-acquired property or proceeds. In order to determine the applicability of the exception in Section 552(b), we must undertake a four-part inquiry. First, is there a pre-petition security agreement that by its terms extends to Bumper Sales' pre-petition inventory, accounts and proceeds? Second, did Bumper Sales receive the proceeds of the pre-petition inventory and accounts after the filing of the petition? Third, is Bumper Sales' post-petition inventory second generation proceeds of pre-petition inventory and accounts, and are Bumper Sales' post-petition accounts proceeds of post-petition inventory? Fourth, did Marepcon's consent to Bumper Sales' use of the proceeds of pre-petition inventory and accounts to purchase post-petition inventory destroy Marepcon's security interest?

Under the first inquiry, it is clear that Marepcon has a security interest that was created before Bumper Sales filed its petition for bankruptcy and that covers inventory, accounts and proceeds. Under the second inquiry, the parties do not deny that Bumper Sales received the proceeds of pre-petition inventory after the filing of the petition. Thus, the basic factual prerequisites of Section 552(b) are met.

Under the third inquiry, we encounter difficulties in construing the Bankruptcy Code, because Section 552(b) fails to establish the parameters of "proceeds." Two interpretations are possible. One infers from the absence of a Code definition and from Section 552(b)'s language limiting any security interest "to the extent provided by. . . applicable nonbankruptcy law" that Congress intended to defer to state law, i.e., to the UCC. The other interpretation relies primarily on the legislative history stating that "[t]he term "proceeds' is not limited to the technical definition of that term in the UCC, but covers any property into which property subject to the security interest is converted." H.R.Rep. No. 95–595, 95th Cong., 1st Sess. 377 (1977). This view encourages a broader coverage of proceeds than in the UCC. See, e.g., 2 Norton Bankr.L. and Prac. § 38.03 at 38–2 (1981) (proceeds includes "property into which the prepetition property is converted, property derived from the prepetition property, and income from the prepetition property that is acquired by the estate after the commencement of the case."). However, we believe that Section 552(b)'s ex-

---

[8] While the Committee challenges Marepcon's security interest in post-petition accounts arising from post-petition inventory, the Committee concedes that Marepcon has a security interest in any accounts and cash arising from pre-petition inventory. Nothing in the record enables us to distinguish these two forms of post-petition accounts.

press reference to "nonbankruptcy law" should take priority over a vague and isolated piece of legislative history. We also note that the judicial creation of a definition for "proceeds," broader post-petition than pre-petition, would produce arbitrary and potentially inequitable results. As a result, we hold that the UCC's definition and treatment of proceeds applies to Section 552 of the Bankruptcy Code. This is consistent with the unstated rule of the many courts that have looked to the UCC in applying Section 552 of the Code. * * *

Turning to the UCC, we start with Section 9–306(2), which states that a security interest in collateral continues in any proceeds of such collateral: "Except where this title otherwise provides, a security interest... continues in any identifiable proceeds including collections received by the debtor." Section 9–306(1) explains what is included: "'Proceeds' includes whatever is received upon the sale, exchange, collection or other disposition of collateral or proceeds. . ... Money, checks, deposit accounts, and the like are "cash proceeds.'" Thus, the funds received by Bumper Sales from the sale of its inventory and collection of accounts are cash proceeds, and Marepcon's security interest in Bumper Sales' pre-petition inventory and accounts continues in the cash proceeds, so long as they are identifiable. But there is no doubt that the cash proceeds are identifiable, because the parties have stipulated that Bumper Sales used only these cash proceeds to finance its operations during bankruptcy. Since only these proceeds were used, they are conclusively identifiable. * * *

Under Section 9–306(3)(b), a security interest in proceeds remains perfected [more than ten] days after receipt by the debtor if "a filed financing statement covers the original collateral and the proceeds are identifiable cash proceeds." In this case, we have already shown that Marepcon has a security interest in the pre-petition inventory and accounts and that the cash proceeds of such inventory and accounts are identifiable. As a result, Marepcon has a security interest in the cash proceeds. However, Bumper Sales subsequently used the cash proceeds to finance new inventory, which was both after-acquired property and proceeds. This presents an apparent conflict between Section 552(a), which cuts off after-acquired property clauses, and Section 552(b), which continues security interests in proceeds. Professor Clark describes this collision and offers a solution:

> What happens when the proceeds or final products are sold by the estate and the cash is used to manufacture new inventory, particularly in a rehabilitation proceeding? A literal reading of § 552 would suggest that the general rule applies and the floating lien is cut off. In other words, a bright line is drawn between first-generation proceeds and after-acquired property. Such a result, however, could completely deprive the secured party of his pre-petition perfected security interest. Therefore, the term "proceeds" should be read broadly—as in U.C.C. § 9–306—to include after-acquired property, at least where inventory and accounts are concerned and there is no improvement in position. This is nothing more than a post-petition substitution of collateral.

Clark, The Law of Secured Transactions under the Uniform Commercial Code, ¶ 6.6[3] at 6–47 (1980).

We agree that Section 552(b) covers second generation proceeds, even if they are in the form of inventory, because such proceeds are clearly contemplated by the UCC. Section 9–306(1) states that proceeds includes the proceeds of proceeds:

> "'Proceeds' includes whatever is received upon the sale, exchange, collection or other disposition of collateral *or proceeds*." As a result, "after-acquired property will frequently qualify as second-generation proceeds, as when a dealer sells an appliance and reinvests the cash proceeds in new inventory." Clark, The Law of Secured Transactions under the Uniform Commercial Code, ¶ 10.1[2] at 10–4 (1980). The fact that Section 552(a) denies the validity of after-acquired property clauses in bankruptcy does not affect this reasoning. Accordingly, the courts have held that, when a secured party has a pre-petition security interest in a crop in Year 1, its security interest extends to the post-petition proceeds of that crop as well as to the post-petition crop in Year 2 and its proceeds if the Year 2 crop is financed with the proceeds of the Year 1 crop. * * * The only requirement is that the second generation proceeds be traceable to the original collateral, which, as discussed above, the parties have stipulated is true in this case. Therefore, we hold that Marepcon has a properly perfected security interest in Bumper Sales' post-petition inventory as well as in any post-petition accounts and cash generated therefrom.[12]

Under the fourth inquiry, the Committee argues that Marepcon's consent to Bumper Sales' use of the proceeds to purchase inventory destroyed Marepcon's security interest in the proceeds. In particular, the Committee claims that Marepcon's consent precludes its right to trace proceeds under Section 9–306(2) of the UCC. In effect, the Committee argues that Marepcon's failure to condition its consent on the grant of a post-petition lien on Bumper Sales' inventory under Section 363 precludes its security interest in the post-petition inventory and the proceeds thereof. We disagree.

In this case, Marepcon is claiming only an interest in the proceeds of the use of the cash collateral, i.e., the post-petition inventory and its proceeds, not the cash collateral itself. Thus, Section 9–306(2) preserves

---

[12] Our holding is further supported by the fact that Marepcon's security interest in post-petition inventory does not prejudice the Committee in any way, again because the post-petition inventory was produced entirely with the proceeds of Marepcon's pre-petition collateral, not with any of the debtor's unencumbered assets to which the Committee, as unsecured creditors, might have had a claim in bankruptcy.

Marepcon's security interest in the post-petition inventory, regardless of Marepcon's consent to Bumper Sales' use of the cash collateral.[13]

The Committee's argument under Section 363 is premised on the fact that Section 552(b) is expressly subject to the provisions of Section 363 of the Code. This section deals in part with the use of cash collateral, which includes the proceeds of property subject to a pre-petition security interest;[14] under this definition, the cash proceeds of Bumper Sales' pre-petition inventory and accounts secured by Marepcon are cash collateral. In particular, the Committee claims that Marepcon consented to the use of its cash collateral pursuant to section 363(c)(2), which states that a debtor may not use cash collateral without the secured party's consent. The Committee insists that Marepcon's failure to seek a court order conditioning the use of cash collateral under Section 363(e) is fatal to its claim.

However, we see nothing in Section 363 that alters the rule established under Section 9–306 of the UCC by requiring a secured party to obtain a court order to preserve rights in the proceeds of cash collateral. Indeed, Section 363 deals with the antecedent issue whether the debtor may even use the cash collateral in the first place, an important determination because the use of cash collateral "may involve a complete consumption of the [secured party's] collateral." 3 Collier Bankruptcy Practice Guide, ¶ 41.04 at 41–13 (1990). However, Section 363 does not concern the issue whether the debtor's use affects the secured party's interest in the proceeds of the cash collateral. The latter issue depends on the application of Section 9–306. As a result, Marepcon's consent to Bumper Sales' use of the cash collateral under Section 363(c)(2) does not affect Marepcon's security interest in the proceeds of the cash collateral. Of course, Marepcon could have prevented the litigation of this issue by seeking a court order under Section 363(e), but Marepcon did not lose its security interest by failing to do so.

For the above reasons, the holding of the district court is
AFFIRMED.

---

[13] For this reason, we disagree with In re Lovelady, 21 B.R. 182 (Bankr.D.Or.1982), where the court held that the secured party's consent to the use of cash collateral causes the secured party to lose his right to trace proceeds under Section 9–306(2). This court failed to distinguish between rights in the collateral, which are lost if consent is given, and rights in the proceeds, which are retained regardless of consent.

[14] Section 363(a) states that cash collateral means cash, negotiable instruments, documents of title, securities, deposit accounts, or other cash equivalents whenever acquired in which the estate and an entity other than the estate have an interest and includes the proceeds. . . of property subject to a security interest as provided in section 552(b) of this title, whether existing before or after the commencement of a case under this title. § 363(a).

## NOTE

Although § 552(a) was designed to offer debtors a fresh start by allowing them to acquire postpetition assets free of prepetition security interests that they can use as collateral for postpetition financing, in some cases § 363(e) cuts against this policy by requiring adequate protection for a secured creditor's interest in cash collateral as a prerequisite to granting a debtor the right to use the cash collateral. As we will see in other contexts, adequate protection is a flexible concept. § 361. It may take the form of a grant to the secured party of a lien on a debtor's unencumbered assets in order to replace collateral that is used or sold. The debtor in *Bumper Sales* could not operate its business without being able to use the cash proceeds from the sale of inventory and the collection of accounts to buy new inventory. It is likely that if Marepcon had filed its motion to condition use of cash collateral immediately after Bumper Sales' filing, it could have obtained by way of court-ordered adequate protection a replacement lien on inventory and accounts acquired after the filing. And, to the dismay of the Creditors' Committee, such a lien could extend to postpetition collateral that was not proceeds of prepetition collateral. In the last sentence of the opinion, the court notes that if Marepcon had done so, it would have prevented the litigation that followed. We will deal further with cash collateral issues in Chapter 10.

## 5. POSTFILING INTEREST ON SECURED CLAIMS

Section 502(b) states that the amount of a claim shall be determined by the court "as of the date of the filing of the petition, and shall allow such claim * * * in such amount." Claims for postpetition interest are normally disallowed under § 502(b)(2). Under this general rule a creditor is not entitled to compensation for the delay in payment which results from the bankruptcy proceedings. In a Chapter 7 case, postfiling interest on unsecured claims is allowed only in the rare case in which the debtor is solvent and all claims are paid in full. Section 726(a)(5) states that in that case interest at the "legal rate" is payable from the date of filing of the petition. Legal rate is not defined. There is a special rule, however, for secured claims. Section 506(b) allows an oversecured creditor, to the extent of the value of the collateral, to recover in addition to the secured claim "interest on such claim, and any reasonable fees, costs, or charges provided for under the agreement under which such claim arose."

In the famous "comma" case, *United States v. Ron Pair Enterprises, Inc.*, 489 U.S. 235 (1989), the Supreme Court held that the language quoted above meant that oversecured involuntary secured claims, such as judicial or statutory liens, were also entitled to postpetition interest. The position of the comma between "claim" and "and" showed that no agreement is necessary for recovery of interest; an agreement is needed only for recovery of fees, costs, and charges.

Although § 506(b) awards the oversecured creditor postfiling interest, it is silent on the rate at which the interest is payable, at least after *Ron Pair* which divorces § 506(b)'s reference to "the agreement" from the statutory right to interest. In general, courts have nevertheless continued to apply the contract rate of interest in the case of consensual security interests while necessarily looking to the statutory rate with respect to judicial or statutory liens. *Collier on Bankruptcy*, ¶ 506.04[2][b] (15th ed. rev. 2004). If bankruptcy is seen as essentially a specialized federal procedure for honoring substantive rights created by state law, which is more efficient than the state law race-to-the-courthouse collection system in the case of insolvent debtors, it is appropriate that substantive state law rights be left unaltered to the extent possible under bankruptcy procedures. Under this view, oversecured creditors should earn the same interest rates that they enjoyed under the contract before filing. But if bankruptcy law is seen as having its own redistributive and rehabilitative imperatives, state created substantive rights may have to yield. Both views of bankruptcy law find some support in the Code. Katherine R. Heidt, *Interest Under Section 506(b) of the Bankruptcy Code: The Right, the Rate and the Relationship to Bankruptcy Policy*, 1991 Utah L.Rev. 361. The tension between recognition of state law substantive rights and applying bankruptcy law notions of equity is manifested in *In re Laymon*, 958 F.2d 72 (5th Cir.1992). There the court of appeals reviewed an innovative bankruptcy court holding granting to an oversecured consensual creditor the federal judgment rate of interest. It reversed in favor of the contract rate on the ground that this was the prevailing pre-Code law and was not changed by the Code. But the contract called for 10% pre-default interest and 18% post-default interest. Respect for state substantive law would call for awarding the creditor the 18% rate. The court waffled, stating: "Under pre-Code law, courts were 'not required in all cases to apply a contractual default rate of interest * * *.' Most courts took a flexible approach, recognizing situations in which 'the higher rate would produce an inequitable or unconscionable result * * *'." 958 F.2d at 75. It remanded the issue to the bankruptcy court with a vague mandate to examine the equities in deciding what rate to apply.

## E.  PRIORITY CLAIMS

We have seen that before the final distribution of the bankruptcy estate in a Chapter 7 case the bankruptcy court or the trustee in bankruptcy will already have satisfied secured claims. § 362(d), § 554 and § 725. Section 726(a) states a schedule of priorities for the final distribution of the estate to the holders of unsecured claims.

Unsecured claims are divided into two groups: those entitled to priority under § 507 and those not entitled to priority. Priority claims must be paid in full before any payment is made to nonpriority claims. Priority claims are now divided into ten orders of priority. Claims within any order of priority must be paid in full before any payment is made to a claim in a lower order of priority. If all claims of the same order of priority cannot be fully paid, payment is made pro rata. The § 507 priorities are also recognized in reorganizations under Chapters 11, 12 and 13.

Priority claim status is of some importance because in most liquidation cases there is little or nothing paid to nonpriority claims, and in reorganization cases priority claims must be paid in full in order to confirm reorganization plans under Chapters 11, 12 and 13. Nonpriority claims are paid pro rata, except that certain claims are subordinated by subsections (a)(3) and (a)(4) of § 726. Section 726(a)(4), subordinating fines and penalties (including punitive damage claims), applies both to secured and unsecured claims. If a creditor has a claim described in § 726(a)(4) that is secured by a lien, the claim is not treated as a secured claim. The trustee may avoid the lien under § 724(a). The claim is then paid only if all other unsecured claims are first paid. The rationale is that claims designed to punish the debtor should be disfavored if the effect of enforcement would be to punish other creditors by reducing the amount payable to them.

### 1. DOMESTIC SUPPORT OBLIGATIONS (DSO)

The first priority is accorded to domestic support obligations. § 507(a)(1). As the drafting of the 2005 Act progressed, women's and children's advocates became alarmed that rights to alimony, maintenance and support were being squeezed out by amendments giving automobile financers additional rights, both before and after discharge, by making credit card claims nondischargeable in more transactions, and by not cracking down on reaffirmation of otherwise dischargeable consumer debts. If the position of other creditors was being enhanced by these amendments, that of women and children was being correlatively reduced, particularly with respect to the competition for the debtor's postpetition earnings, usually the only source from which domestic support obligations (DSOs) could be satisfied. Congress responded to these concerns with a panoply of amendments designed to shore up claims for domestic support obligations, both with respect to assets of the debtor's estate and, more importantly, the debtor's postpetition assets. These changes will be discussed in context throughout the book, most extensively in chapter 4 on discharge and chapter 9 on consumer debtors.

Since Chapter 7 debtors have nonexempt assets to distribute to unsecured creditors in only a small percentage of cases, the extraordinary promotion of DSO claims from a seventh priority to a first priority in the 2005 Act, ahead of even administrative expense claims (§ 507(a)(2)), may not be as helpful as it appears. Nonetheless, short of awarding such claims lien status, Congress has done all it can to give DSO claimants first call on assets of the estate that are neither exempt nor burdened by security interests. It is difficult to predict how the subordination of administrative expenses to DSOs will play out. Lawyers handling cases with limited assets and substantial DSO claims can expect no compensation from the estate setting up a potentially interesting set of negotiations between the debtor, the debtor's bankruptcy lawyer and the debtor's former spouse.

The definition of DSOs is found in § 101(14A) of the 2005 Act and expressly covers not only debts in the nature of alimony, maintenance and support that are owed to a spouse, former spouse or child of the debtor but also those owed to a governmental unit. Governments become involved because as a condition to obtaining Aid to Families with Dependent Children (now Temporary Assistance to Needy Families) under § 408(a)(3) of the Social Security Act, any child support obligation must be assigned to the state. 4 *Collier on Bankruptcy* ¶ 523.11[8] (15th ed. rev. 2004). Unlike the prior law, § 507(a)(1) grants a priority not only to obligations owed to a spouse or child ((a)(1)(A)), but also to governmental units to which such obligations have been assigned ((a)(1)(B)), though subparagraph (1)(B) subordinates obligations owed to governmental units to those owed to spouses or children. These priorities are, in turn, subordinated to certain administrative expenses of a trustee who administers assets available for payment of DSOs. § 507(a)(1)(C). Section 1322(a)(4), added by the 2005 Act, provides that if the debtor's repayment plan provides for less than full payment of the § 507(a)(1)(B) governmental priority claims, the plan must have a five-year duration. Considering the large percentage of failure of even three-year plans, such a requirement will make Chapter 13 plans more difficult to carry out.

## 2. ADMINISTRATIVE EXPENSES

The second priority is administrative expenses allowed under § 503. § 507(a)(2).

## In re Jartran, Inc.

United States Court of Appeals, Seventh Circuit, 1984.
732 F.2d 584.

■ CUDAHY, Circuit Judge.

Appellants Reuben H. Donnelley Corporation ("Donnelley") and Sandra C. Tinsley, Inc. ("Tinsley") filed a claim for administrative priority against appellee Jartran, Inc.'s ("Jartran") estate. The bankruptcy judge denied the claim and, on appeal, the district court affirmed. Our appellate jurisdiction was properly invoked * * * and, for the reasons set forth below, we affirm.

The facts are undisputed and can be stated briefly. Jartran is in the business of leasing trucks to consumers nationwide. Pursuant to an agreement dated September 11, 1979 (the "Agreement"), Tinsley, an advertising agency, placed Jartran's orders for classified advertisements in telephone directories (the "Yellow Pages") with Donnelley. Donnelley, in turn, arranged with the Yellow Pages' publishers nationwide for Jartran's ads to appear. Under the Agreement, Tinsley and Jartran were liable to Donnelley for the cost of the advertising. Donnelley was liable to the publishers of the various directories. Although the parties were irrevocably committed to pay for the advertising several months before the ads were to appear,[1] the Agreement provided that Tinsley and Jartran would be billed for the ads only after they were published.

On December 31, 1981, Jartran filed for reorganization under Chapter 11 of the Bankruptcy Code, 11 U.S.C. §§ 1101–1174. At that time, the closing date had passed for many directories which had not yet been published. Appellants claim that the amount owing for ads placed in such directories, $1,311,695.50, should be treated as an administrative expense.[2] As is apparent from our discussion of the law relating to the allowance of administrative expenses, the key fact is that the irrevocable commitment by Jartran, Donnelley and Tinsley to place the ads was made before the filing of the petition in bankruptcy.

Section 503 of the Bankruptcy Code provides as follows:

\* \* \*

**(b)** After notice and a hearing, there shall be allowed, administrative expenses \* \* \* including—

**(1)(A)** the actual, necessary costs and expenses of preserving the estate, including wages, salaries or commissions for services rendered after the commencement of the case[.]

It is well settled that expenses incurred by the debtor-in-possession in attempting to rehabilitate the business during reorganization are within the ambit of § 503. \* \* \* Appellants claim that, because the ads involved in the case were not published until after the "commencement of the case" and presumably aid Jartran in its efforts to rejuvenate its business, the cost of those ads should be treated as an administrative expense. As an administrative expense, the fees for the ads would be afforded priority ahead of certain pre-petition creditors.

The policies underlying the provisions of § 503 (and its predecessor, § 64(a)(1) of the Bankruptcy Act) are not hard to discern. If a reorganization is to succeed, creditors asked to extend credit after the petition is filed must be given priority so they will be moved to furnish the necessary credit to enable the bankrupt to function. *See In re Mammoth Mart, Inc.,* 536 F.2d 950, 954 (1st Cir.1976) (Coffin, Chief Judge). Thus, "[w]hen

---

[1] The date upon which ads were irrevocably placed is referred to in the Agreement and by the parties as the "closing date." On that date, up to six months prior to actual publication, ads could no longer be withdrawn from the directory. Each directory had its own closing date, but Donnelley uniformly billed the advertisers after publication. The Agreement provided that cancellations were effective only with respect to directories for which the closing date had not passed.

[2] Appellants agree that billing for ads published before the petition for reorganization was filed should be treated as non-priority, pre-petition debts. The parties also agree that expenses for ads for which the closing date occurred after the petition was filed are entitled to § 503 priority. \* \* \*

third parties are *induced* to supply goods or services to the debtor-in-possession * * * the purposes of [§ 503] plainly require that their claims be afforded priority." Id. (emphasis added; footnote omitted). Without a provision like § 503, efforts to reorganize would be hampered by the necessity of advance payment for all goods and services supplied to the estate since presumably no creditor would willingly assume the status of a non-priority creditor to a debtor undergoing reorganization.

This involves no injustice to the pre-petition creditors because it is for their benefit that reorganization is attempted. If reorganization successfully rehabilitates the debtor, presumably the pre-petition creditors will be better off than in a liquidation.

* * *

Recognizing the need for careful criteria in granting priority, the court in *Mammoth Mart* established a two part test for determining whether a debt should be afforded administrative priority. Under these criteria a claim will be afforded priority under § 503 if the debt both (1) "arise[s] from a transaction with the debtor-in-possession" and (2) is "beneficial to the debtor-in-possession in the operation of the business." *In re Mammoth Mart, Inc.*, 536 F.2d at 954. This test is, of course, essentially an effort to determine whether the underlying statutory purpose will be furthered by granting priority to the claim in question, and we will apply it in that spirit.

There is no question that the appearance of ads in Yellow Page directories throughout the country is beneficial to Jartran, as a debtor-in-possession, in the operation of its business. After filing the petition in bankruptcy, Jartran continued to place new ads in directories throughout the nation, thus evidencing the importance of Yellow Pages advertising to the success of the Jartran business. Therefore, the only serious question on appeal is whether the district court incorrectly concluded that the claim did not arise from a transaction with the debtor-in-possession.

Stated this simply, we believe that the district court's conclusion was correct: the agreement among the parties was entered into, and the ads were placed without possibility of revocation, before the petition was filed. Appellants urge, however, that the *publication date* rather than the closing date is the key date for § 503 purposes. They argue forcefully that, because the ads were *published* after the petition in bankruptcy was filed, appellants "supplied [consideration] to the debtor-in-possession in the operation of the business." *Mammoth Mart,* supra, 536 F.2d at 954. Appellants support this argument by pointing out that appellants provided additional services after the closing date, and, presumably, after the petition was filed, including "review of advertising copy for correctness, size of advertisement, placement by page and category, accuracy of telephone listings and addresses, review of art work, and response to numerous queries from publishers concerning the advertisements." It was also necessary for Donnelley and Tinsley (presumably after the filing of the petition) to examine the final, published ads to ascertain their correctness. Then, and only then, would Jartran be billed for the advertisements.

We recognize that the services performed by appellants after the closing date, and after the filing of the petition, were significant and of value to Jartran. However, appellants do not allege that Jartran, after the filing of the petition, requested that appellants continue work on ads for which the closing date had passed. Nor is it claimed that Jartran had a duty to take affirmative steps to prevent Donnelley from engaging in post-petition performance. Thus, it was the pre-petition Jartran and not Jartran as debtor-in-possession that *induced* appellants to perform these services. To serve the policy of the priority, inducement of the creditor's performance *by the debtor-in-possession* is crucial to a claim for administrative priority in the context of the furnishing of goods or services to the debtor. * * * Because the closing date occurred before the debtor-in-possession came into existence (through the filing of the Chapter 11 petition), the bankruptcy court in the case before us held that the debtor-in-possession did not induce appellants' performance. * * *

As noted, the reason that *inducement* of the creditor's performance by the debtor-in-possession is crucial to a claim for administrative priority is rooted in the policies that gave rise to the creation of the priority. Thus, administrative priority is granted to post-petition expenses so that third parties will be moved to provide the goods and services necessary for a successful reorganization. * * * In the case before us, no inducement by the debtor-in-possession was required because the liability for the costs of the ads was irrevocably incurred before the petition was filed. This construction of the requirements for the administrative priority provides as full an opportunity as can be furnished for rehabilitation of the debtor. And this approach simply carries out the teaching of the Supreme Court, "that fairness requires that any claims incident to the debtor-in-possession's operation of the business be paid before those for whose benefit the continued operation of the business was allowed." *Mammoth Mart,* supra, 536 F.2d at 954 citing *Reading Co. v. Brown,* 391 U.S. 471, 478 (1968) (first priority for tort claims based upon negligence attributable to debtor-in-possession). It is clear, however, that appellants' claim here arises out of commitments made before the debtor-in-possession came into existence.

## PROBLEM

Carly had achieved success as merchandising manager of GoodCo, a solvent, well regarded retailer. She agreed to leave her good job at GoodCo and join NewCo as general manager at an annual salary of $500,000, generous fringe benefits, stock options, etc. But NewCo was somewhat shaky financially and she was not finally won over by its blandishments until NewCo agreed to a "golden parachute" deal for her, referred to as the "Retention Agreement," which provided that should

Carly's employment terminate without cause following a "Change of Control" she would receive three years' salary plus other benefits, including legal fees and expenses. Two years later, NewCo filed in Chapter 11; during the attempted reorganization Carly continued to work and was paid her prepetition salary. The reorganization failed, the assets were sold and Carly was terminated. She sought an administrative priority under 503(b)(1)(A) for her claim for severance pay under the Retention Agreement on the ground that her employment was terminated without cause after the bankruptcy, which qualified as a change of control under the agreement. The bankruptcy court denied administrative expense status for her claim on the ground that the consideration for the Retention Agreement was entirely performed by Carly at the time she left the employment of GoodCo and joined NewCo; thus the severance pay was earned prepetition. She received reasonable compensation for her postpetition services and may make a prepetition claim for breach of the Retention Agreement. How should the appellate court rule on this case on appeal under the principles that you learned in *Jartran*? *See In re FBI Distribution Corp.*, 330 F.3d 36 (1st Cir. 2003).

# CHAPTER 4

# DISCHARGE

## A. INTRODUCTION

This Chapter discusses discharge in Chapter 7 bankruptcy. Chapters 11 and 13 each contains separate—and distinctive—discharge provisions, and we will discuss these further in the material dealing with those Chapters. In Chapter 7 the debtor, if an individual, is entitled to a discharge of personal liability on prebankruptcy debts. Liquidating corporations don't need a bankruptcy discharge; after Chapter 7 liquidation, they can dissolve under state law. If individuals do not receive a discharge from prebankruptcy debts, they would be burdened with these debts indefinitely. In return for a discharge, the debtor must make available for distribution to creditors all assets that are not exempt. However, in a large percentage of Chapter 7 bankruptcies of individuals, there are no assets available for payment to unsecured creditors. For most individuals the primary purpose of filing in bankruptcy is to obtain a discharge. Section 727(a) provides for the grant of a discharge to debtors, and § 727(b) declares that the effect of a discharge is to free the debtor from all debts that arose before bankruptcy. Other effects of the discharge are stated in § 524.

In some cases debtors are not entitled to a discharge. The various grounds for denying a discharge are set forth in § 727(a). Most of the grounds refer to misconduct by the debtor. But an important ground for denying discharge, § 727(a)(8), is not directly related to any misconduct by the debtor. That provision denies a Chapter 7 discharge if the debtor has previously received a discharge under Chapter 7 in a case commenced within eight years before the date of the filing of the petition. Before the 2005 Act the period was six years. The most commonly stated rationale for this rule, which was also part of the Bankruptcy Act, is that given by Justice Clark in *Perry v. Commerce Loan Co.*, 383 U.S. 392, 399 (1966): "The unmistakable purpose of the six-year provision was to prevent the creation of a class of habitual bankrupts—debtors who might repeatedly escape their obligations as frequently as they chose by going through repeated bankruptcy."

Section 727(a)(9) provides that if a debtor has received a Chapter 13 discharge, she cannot receive a subsequent Chapter 7 discharge in a case filed within six years (the six-year period was not changed in this provision) after the Chapter 13 discharge. The exception to that rule is that if, in the Chapter 13 case, the debtor paid under the plan either all of the unsecured claims or 70% of such claims and proposed the plan in good faith and gave her best effort, she is not barred by the six-year rule in receiving a Chapter 7 discharge.

Even if a debtor is entitled to a discharge in Chapter 7, the discharge may not apply to all of the debts of the debtor. Discharge benefits the debtor at a cost to the creditor. A qualified debtor is generally entitled to the "fresh start" given by a discharge, but Congress determined that some types of creditors holding certain types of claims generally have equities that are greater than those of the debtor. These enumerated types of claims are "nondischargeable." § 523(a). Creditors holding such claims may file a claim in the bankruptcy and can participate in the distribution of the bankruptcy estate, but, to the extent the creditor's claim has not been satisfied, the creditor's claim will survive bankruptcy.

Section 727(c)(1) provides that objection to a discharge of a Chapter 7 debtor may be made by the trustee, a creditor or the U. S. Trustee, but there is no provision in the Code setting time limits within which the objection must be made. This is found in Rule 4004(a), which requires that the objection must be filed within 60 days after the first date set for the § 341 meeting of creditors, unless the court extends the time to file the objection for cause under Rule 4004(b). As with other statute of limitations type defenses, however, a debtor that fails to timely assert the time-bar issue may waive the defense. *Kontrick v. Ryan*, 540 U.S. 443 (2004).

## B. DENIAL OF DISCHARGE BECAUSE OF DEBTOR'S MISCONDUCT

A fresh start by discharge is denied to some debtors that are guilty of inequitable conduct. This policy is detailed in § 727(a). Depriving individual debtors of a discharge in Chapter 7 is a very serious sanction. It leaves debtors with the dismal prospect of having their postpetition assets, including future earnings, subject to seizure under state law to pay the deficiencies remaining on prepetition debts.

Section 727(a)(2)(A) denies a discharge to debtors who, within a year of filing, transfer or conceal their property with "intent to hinder, delay, or defraud" creditors. Perhaps the most common example of this conduct is the foolish attempt of debtors faced with bankruptcy to hide assets by transferring them to relatives for little or no consideration in the belief that the worst that can happen to them is that, if bankruptcy ensues, the property will be brought back into the bankruptcy estate and distributed to creditors. What do such debtors have to lose? Answer: their discharge, if they find themselves in bankruptcy within a year of the transfer. We have a full treatment of fraudulent transfers in chapter 7. Debtors making fraudulent transfers may be smoked out by their response to Question 10 in Official Form 7 (Statement of Financial Affairs) which requires a description of any property transferred out of ordinary course within one year of filing and a statement of the value received and the relationship of the transferee.

If a debtor fails to disclose such a transfer or makes other false statements in the schedules required at the time of filing, the debtor forfeits a discharge under § 727(a)(4)(A) for making a "false oath or account." Section 521(1) requires debtors to file schedules listing creditors, assets, liabilities and other matters, including a statement of the debtor's financial affairs, and the Official Forms for the schedules require that debtors sign a declaration under penalty of perjury that the information given is "true and correct." The false oath ground for denial of discharge addresses one of the most common ploys of dishonest debtors: their failure to disclose assets. Some assets are easy to hide and hard to find. This type of cheating is probably endemic but is sometimes discovered by comparing bullish financial statements made by debtors applying for credit with the meager assets listed on bankruptcy schedules only a few months later. Unless the debtor can satisfactorily describe what happened to the missing assets, § 727(a)(5) denies a discharge to the memory-challenged debtor.

A controversial ground for denial of discharge is that in § 727(a)(3) regarding the debtor's failure to keep records "from which the debtor's financial condition or business transactions might be ascertained." Understandably, the policy of restricting discharges to honest debtors can be implemented only by requiring debtors to come clean with the bankruptcy system. If they can't produce intelligible records so that trustees and creditors can trace their dealings, vital issues concerning their entitlement to receive a discharge may remain unsolved. But judicial determination of what is adequate recordkeeping may be difficult in the extreme. It is an easy case if the debtor is known to have destroyed or concealed relevant records, but what if the debtor is just a sloppy bookkeeper who is the only person who can readily interpret the chicken tracks in her ledgers? The following problem is based on one of a number of cases raising the adequate records issue.

## PROBLEM

Debtor operated a trucking business. He bought grain from Supplier and hauled the grain to three buyers. He reported over $5 million in sales for the period in question. He filed in bankruptcy owing Supplier over $200,000, and Supplier objected to his discharge under § 727(a)(3) on the ground that he failed to keep or preserve records adequately disclosing his business operations. Debtor ran his business through a single checking account. He deposited all grain sales proceeds into the account and made all grain purchases and paid all expenses from that account. The records he produced during the bankruptcy proceedings included checking account ledgers, cancelled checks, deposit slips, bank statements and a federal income tax return for the relevant period.

These records did not show: the source of the funds deposited; how much grain was purchased from whom or sold to whom at what price; substantiation for his business expenses; or employee payroll deductions or taxes. Debtor's expert witness, a veteran accountant, testified that many of his small business clients kept records in a similar manner, although he conceded that his trucking clients usually retained invoices of their sales and expenses because the IRS requires these for substantiation. There was no evidence that Debtor destroyed or concealed any records. Debtor offered testimony by an accountant reconstructing Debtor's business transactions on the basis of the paper records together with his oral explanations of the transactions giving rise to the records. If Debtor's records can be understood only through Debtor's oral explanations, has Debtor met the requirement imposed by § 727(a)(3) for keeping adequate records? Is it relevant that Debtor had no intent to defraud and destroyed and concealed no records? The facts are based on *In re Juzwiak*, 89 F.3d 424 (7th Cir.1996). *See also In re Kowalski,* 316 B.R. 596 (Bankr.E.D.N.Y. 2004), for an enumeration of factors considered in determining a debtor's circumstances.

## C. Nondischargeable Debts

### 1. Unscheduled Debts

### In re Madaj

United States Court of Appeals, Sixth Circuit, 1998.
149 F.3d 467.

■ BATCHELDER, Circuit Judge.

**"How sharper than a serpent's tooth it is to have a thankless child!"**
**WILLIAM SHAKESPEARE, KING LEAR, act I, sc. 4**

Before us on appeal are a husband and wife ("the Creditors"), who have felt the bite of their thankless foster child. With his wife, this foster child ("the Debtors") borrowed a substantial sum of money from his foster parents, promising to repay the loan within a few months out of anticipated insurance proceeds from a fire loss. Instead of repaying the loan, however, the Debtors filed a petition in bankruptcy under Chapter 7 and failed to include the foster parents in the list of creditors filed with the petition. Their no-asset case was duly administered, the Debtors eventually obtained a discharge pursuant to § 727, and their case was closed. The Creditors, unaware of the bankruptcy proceeding, and having repeatedly importuned the Debtors to repay the loan according to their promise, filed suit in state court and obtained a judgment against the Debtors for the unpaid balance of the loan.

The Debtors moved to reopen their Chapter 7 proceeding in order to list the debt, claiming that their failure to include it initially had been due to forgetfulness and inadvertence. The Creditors objected to the motion to reopen, claiming that in light of their repeated requests for payment and the Debtors' protests of poverty, the Debtors' memory lapse was not credible, and that the Debtors had failed to list the debt because they intended to defraud the Creditors. The Creditors opposed the reopening of the Chapter 7 proceeding because they believed, and still believe, that an unlisted debt is not discharged, and that the Debtors ought not be permitted to now list this debt and obtain its discharge. The parties agree that if this debt had been timely scheduled, it would have been dischargeable under § 523, and that even if the debt had been listed and a proof of claim had been filed, because this was a no-asset case, there would have been no payment on the debt. The Bankruptcy Court denied the Debtors' motion to reopen, but held that the debt to the Creditors was nonetheless discharged, and the District Court affirmed. The Creditors timely appealed. We now AFFIRM.

\* \* \*

The confusion in the district and circuit courts concerning unlisted Chapter 7 debts in a no-asset case, including the dischargeability of such debts, the effect of an order of discharge on such debts, and the efficacy of reopening a bankruptcy case to include them, is widespread. This confusion is due, in part, to a line of cases that perpetuates the erroneous view that once his case is closed, the debtor must have his case reopened in order to discharge a pre-petition debt not listed in the bankruptcy petition; once the case is reopened, the debtor amends his schedules to list the debt, and the now-scheduled debt is covered by the discharge. But this is not the law.

In a Chapter 7 no-asset case such as this, "reopening the case merely to schedule [an omitted] debt is for all practical purposes a useless gesture." *In re Hunter*, 116 B.R. 3, 5 (Bankr.D.D.C.1990). \* \* \* Under these circumstances, amending the schedule is pointless because, as we shall explain, this debt is discharged and reopening the case and scheduling the debt cannot affect that fact.

The law in this area is counter-intuitive, and requires a careful fitting together of the relevant sections of the Bankruptcy Code and Rules. Because of the confusion in this area, a review of the provisions governing dischargeability of debts and the effect of a discharge in a Chapter 7 proceeding is in order. At the risk of appearing simplistic, we can summarize the relevant provisions as follows:

A discharge under § 727 discharges every prepetition debt, without regard to whether a proof of claim has been filed, unless that debt is specifically excepted from discharge under § 523. Section 523(a)(3) contains the only exceptions for unlisted and unscheduled debts. Section 523(a)(3)(B) excepts from discharge those debts originally incurred by means of fraud, false pretenses, or malicious conduct, as enumerated in §§ 523(a)(2), (4), and (6), (hereinafter "fraudulent" or "fraudulently incurred" debts).

Section 523(a)(3)(A) excepts from discharge all other debts—i.e., debts other than those fraudulent debts specified in § 523(a)(2), (4), or

(6)—which are not listed by the debtor in his petition and schedules in time for the creditor to file a timely proof of claim. However, even § 523(a)(3)(A) does not except an unscheduled debt from discharge if the creditor had notice or actual knowledge of the bankruptcy case in time for timely filing of a proof of claim.

In a Chapter 7 no-asset case the court does not set a deadline for the filing of proofs of claim. Rather, the court may notify creditors that there are no assets, that it is not necessary to file claims, and that if sufficient assets become available for payment of a dividend, further notice will be given for filing of claims. See Fed. R. Bankr.P. 2002(e). Therefore, there is no date by which a proof of claim must be filed to be "timely," and whenever a creditor receives notice or knowledge of the bankruptcy, he may file a proof of claim.

The operation of § 523 is obscured somewhat by its convoluted structure, but most of the twists and turns affecting dischargeability have to do with the fraudulent types of debts enumerated in §§ 523(a)(2), (4), and (6).

The statutory language relevant to debts not fraudulently incurred reads as follows:

A discharge under section 727. . . does not discharge an individual debtor from any debt. . . neither listed nor scheduled. . . in time to permit. . . timely filing of a proof of claim, unless such creditor had notice or actual knowledge of the case in time for such timely filing.

§ 523(a)(3)(A). Thus, § 523(a)(3)(A) excepts a debt from discharge if the debt was not scheduled in time for a timely filing of the proof of claim, *but not if,* despite the debt's not having been scheduled, the creditor nevertheless received notice of the bankruptcy in time to file a timely proof of claim. Put another way, the debt is discharged so long as it is scheduled in time for the creditor to file a proof of claim or the creditor finds out about the bankruptcy case in time to do so. Scheduling the debt enables the bankruptcy court to provide the creditor with notice. Where the creditor, through some other means, finds out about the bankruptcy in time to assert his right to a portion of the proceeds of the estate, there is no reason to except an otherwise dischargeable debt from the effect of the discharge. But where the creditor is not aware of the bankruptcy, he cannot assert his right. Without the exception in § 523(a)(3)(A), the debtor could simply deny his uninformed creditors the opportunity to recover from the bankruptcy estate by omitting their debts from the schedule.

In a Chapter 7 no-asset case, however, the creditors cannot recover from the estate because there is nothing to recover. For this reason, there is no deadline for filing a timely proof of claim in a no-asset case. Technically speaking, therefore, no matter when the creditor learns of the bankruptcy, he is able to file a timely claim. Because § 523(a)(3)(A) excepts the unscheduled debt from discharge "unless such creditor had notice or actual knowledge of the case in time for such timely filing," the moment the creditor receives notice or knowledge of the bankruptcy case,

§ 523(a)(3)(A) ceases to provide the basis for an exception from discharge. Consequently, the debt is at that point discharged.

The result may seem strange at first blush, but it makes sense when one considers both the type of debt involved and the nature of a no-asset case. Unlike the fraudulent debts covered by §§ 523(a)(2), (4) and (6), the debts excepted from discharge by § 523(a)(3)(A) are not excepted because of their nature, but because an injustice will result if the debt is discharged in a situation where the creditor never had the opportunity to participate in the distribution of the assets of the estate.

Yet, there are no proceeds to be distributed to the creditors in a no-asset case, which renders the notice function served by the scheduling of debts far less important. For precisely this reason, there is no deadline for the filing of proofs of claim in a no-asset case. For the most part, creditors in a no-asset case do not stand to gain by having their debts scheduled, nor do they stand to lose by having their debts omitted from the schedules. Thus, it should come as no surprise that the exception contained in § 523(a)(3)(A)—designed as it is to prevent an ignorant creditor from suffering an unjust loss by having a debt discharged without his knowing it—operates differently in no-asset cases where there is little risk that a creditor will suffer a disadvantage resulting from an unscheduled debt.

* * *

In the case before us, it is undisputed that the debt at issue, *had it been timely filed*, would not have been included in any category of debts that are excepted from discharge by § 523. It is undisputed that the Debtors' bankruptcy was a no-asset Chapter 7 case. In order to determine whether the bankruptcy court erred in denying the Debtors' motion to reopen their Chapter 7 case to amend the schedule of debts and in holding that the debt at issue here was nevertheless discharged, we must answer one question: when an otherwise dischargeable debt is omitted from the schedule in a Chapter 7 no-asset case and the debtor receives a discharge, what is the effect of re-opening the case to permit the debtor to schedule the omitted debt?

The answer is "there is no effect." The reason that the reopening has no effect is clear. A debtor cannot change the nature of the debt by failing to list it in his petition and schedules. Section 523(a)(3)(A) excepts from discharge only those debts as to which a timely proof of claim cannot be filed because the debts were not listed and the creditor had neither notice nor actual knowledge of the bankruptcy in time to file a timely a proof of claim. In a no-asset Chapter 7 case, there is no date by which a proof of claim must be filed in order to be "timely." Whenever the creditor receives notice or acquires actual knowledge of the bankruptcy, he may file a proof of claim, that claim will be timely, and the fact that the debts were not listed becomes irrelevant. Section 523(a)(3)(A) simply provides no basis for excepting an unlisted debt from discharge if the creditor has actual knowledge such that he can file a proof of claim. And once the § 727 order of discharge is entered, all of the debtor's prepetition debts are either discharged or they are not discharged; nothing the debtor does after the entry of the order of discharge can change the character of those debts.

If the Creditors before us had acquired knowledge of the bankruptcy prior to the entry of the discharge order, the debt would not have been excepted from discharge because the Creditors had actual knowledge in time to file a proof of claim. Their learning of the bankruptcy after the entry of the discharge order did not transmogrify the debt into one that is excepted from discharge under some provision of the Code other than § 523(a)(3)(A). Whether or not the Debtors reopen their case and amend their schedules to list this debt, there will still be no date by which proofs of claim would have to be filed in order to be timely; because the Creditors have actual knowledge of the bankruptcy, § 523(a)(3)(A) does not except this debt from discharge. Hence, the reopening of the Debtors' Chapter 7 case to permit the amendment of the schedules can have no effect whatsoever. The debt in question, listed or not, is discharged.

For these reasons, the order of the bankruptcy court denying the Debtors' motion to reopen and holding that the debt to the Creditors has been discharged is AFFIRMED.

## NOTES

**1.** Does the view of the court in *Madaj* offer incentive for debtors to intentionally fail to schedule debts?

**2.** *Collier on Bankruptcy* ¶ 523.09[5] (15th ed. rev. 2004) endorses the view that it is unnecessary to reopen a case in order to obtain discharge of an unscheduled debt in a no-asset case; however, a bankruptcy court has the discretion to reopen a case to allow a debtor to add a creditor in order to promote the debtor's fresh start by having a complete list of all discharged debts.

## 2. DOMESTIC SUPPORT OBLIGATIONS (DSO)

### a. Section 523(a)(5)

Ex-spouses often incur obligations arising from alimony, maintenance, child support, property settlements, assumption of marital debts, or the like. It has long been bankruptcy policy that dependent spouses and children should receive protection against being deprived of the benefits of support obligations by the discharge of the obligated spouse in bankruptcy. *Wetmore v. Markoe*, 196 U.S. 68 (1904). This policy has been carried forward in the 1978 Bankruptcy Code, and the 2005 Act further expanded the protection from discharge of inter-spousal obligations.

Section 523(a)(5) provides that "domestic support obligations" (DSOs) are nondischargeable in Chapters 7, 11, 12 and 13. DSO is defined in § 101(14A) as a debt owing to a spouse, former spouse or child of the debtor or governmental unit that is in the nature of alimony, maintenance or support and that is established by a separation agreement, divorce decree, or property settlement agreement, a court order, or a determination made under nonbankruptcy law by a governmental unit. Support obligations do not qualify as DSOs if they are assigned to a nongovernmental entity unless they are voluntarily assigned for collection. DSOs are often assigned to governmental units as a condition to obtaining Temporary Assistance to Needy Families (formerly Aid to Families with Dependent Children) under § 408(a)(3) of the Social Security Act. The Code does not define the terms alimony, maintenance or support of spouses or children. State court decrees or settlement agreements may label obligations as alimony, child support or property settlements, and these designations are given weight in determining the nature of the obligation, but they are not conclusive. Section 101(14A)(B) provides that a debt may be held to be one "in the nature of alimony, maintenance, or support * * * whether such debt is expressly so designated."

Under the original version of the 1978 Code, debts relating to marital dissolutions that were essentially support obligations of one kind or another (alimony, maintenance or child or spousal support) were nondischargeable under former § 523(a)(5), but those that merely divided up the assets of the marital estate (property settlements) were dischargeable. This distinction was the subject of much litigation. *Collier* attempts to distill the case law into a series of factors. Among these are: (1) labels are given some weight; (2) if the spouse or children benefited by the payments have a strong need for support, the obligations are nondischargeable; (3) if the obligation terminates on the death or remarriage of the receiving spouse, it is usually nondischargeable; (4) if the term of payments is for a fixed period of time, particularly a short period of time, this tends to show a property settlement that is dischargeable; (5) if the obligation is subject to modification by a court, it looks more like a suport obligation and less like a property equalization obligation; and (6) if tax law treats the payments as alimony, maintenance or support, bankruptcy courts may be influenced to follow. *Collier on Bankruptcy* ¶ 523.11[5] (15th ed. rev. 2004).

The following opinion reflects the exasperation of a leading jurist in attempting to distinguish support obligations and property settlements. As we will see, the distinction is still important under the 2005 Act.

## In re Werthen

United States Court of Appeals, First Circuit, 2003.
329 F.3d 269.

■ BOUDIN, Chief Judge.

Paul Werthen, the debtor in this chapter 7 bankruptcy proceeding, appeals from a judgment of the Bankruptcy Appellate Panel ("BAP") for the First Circuit affirming an order of the bankruptcy court. That order determined that two obligations of Paul to his ex-wife Kathleen Werthen, incurred in their state-court divorce proceeding, were alimony or support rather than property division, and therefore nondischargeable in bankruptcy under § 523(a)(5) (2000). We affirm, conceding the case to be a close one under a badly muddled statute.

Paul and Kathleen were married in 1982 and separated in 1995, when Kathleen filed for divorce. During the marriage, Kathleen was the primary caretaker of the home and the couple's four children. Paul was the primary earner, working full time at Whitman Tool & Die Co. ("Whitman"), his family's business in which he held a considerable equity interest. The Massachusetts Probate and Family Court issued an initial divorce decree on March 7, 2000, and entered an amended judgment together with a supporting memorandum on May 2, 2000.

The picture painted by the state court was not favorable to Paul. He had drinking problems, he physically abused his wife and children during the marriage, and he frustrated Kathleen's efforts to obtain a college degree and a measure of financial independence while strictly limiting her allowance. During the divorce proceedings, he and other family members engaged in obfuscatory tactics or worse, aiming to diminish the award against him. The state court noted these circumstances as supporting a generous award, but they do not by themselves explain which portion of the award was alimony and support.

More pertinent to the level of alimony and support were other findings: that the Werthens were a "middle-to-high income family;" that she would have custody of the children who were still relatively young; that her ability to work was affected by a back injury and limited by her curtailed education; that his past income and the value of his family-company stock were large; and that he had understated income and value to decrease the award. On this last issue, the state court found: "Any which way the Husband could avoid his financial obligations to his wife and children, obfuscate his financial condition, and shrink the marital pool of assets, he tried with all his might."

The final decree awarded Kathleen—under the rubric of "Child Support and Alimony"—one-third of Paul's future bonuses and $450 a week in child support. The former payments are to continue until Paul's death or Kathleen's death or remarriage; and the latter payments are to continue until the youngest child (born in 1989) is emancipated, graduates from college, or reaches the age of twenty-three. Paul does not dispute that these awards are not dischargeable in bankruptcy. The dischargeability issue, which alone concerns us, arises from two items contained in the balance of the state court award.

Under the rubric of "Property Division," the state court awarded Kathleen *inter alia* (1) $222,000, representing 60 percent of the gross bonuses received by Paul in the years 1996-99, reduced to $124,485.84 by amounts in savings accounts already awarded Kathleen (the "past bonus award"); and (2) $611,163.20, representing Kathleen's 40 percent marital share of Paul's 22 percent equity interest in Whitman (the "stock award"). With respect to these two awards, the court structured Paul's payment schedule as yearly installments of $50,000 for nine years beginning in 2000, with the remaining balance due in two separate payments in the tenth and the eleventh years (plus interest on unpaid balances).

On July 28, 2000, less than 90 days after the final judgment, Paul filed a voluntary petition for chapter 7 bankruptcy. In that proceeding Kathleen sought a ruling that the past bonus and stock awards—largely or entirely yet unpaid—were not subject to discharge. Her first claim was based on the above-quoted paragraph (5) of subsection 523(a), which prevents discharge of obligations for alimony or support. Alternatively, she relied on paragraph (15), which prevents discharge of other debts incurred in a divorce—even where not within the scope of paragraph (5)—unless the hardship from such a discharge is outweighed by the interests of the debtor. Kathleen bore the burden of showing that the debts were nondischargeable.* * *

The bankruptcy court held a trial on October 2, 2001, and then ruled in a bench opinion that both the bonus and stock awards were nondischargeable under paragraph (5). Thereafter, the court initially altered its position as to the stock award, raising the possibility that it might instead be separately analyzed under paragraph (15); but in a final written decision, the court returned to its original ruling, holding both the bonus and stock awards to be nondischargeable under paragraph (5). The bankruptcy court treated the issue as one turning on the intent of, but not necessarily the label employed by, the state court judge in making the awards.

To discern this intent, the bankruptcy court invoked a set of factors set forth in *Altavilla v. Altavilla* (*In re Altavilla* ), 40 B.R. 938, 941 (Bankr.D.Mass.1984). In viewing the awards as intended "to provide support" for Kathleen and the children rather than as division of property, the court stressed in its final decision Kathleen's otherwise limited resources and earning capacity, the lengthy pay-out period of the two awards, and several other factors. On Paul's appeal, the BAP affirmed, holding that intent was a question of fact and concluding that the bankruptcy court's decision was not plainly wrong. It too mentioned the payment structure and the lack of other assured income to support the family, the future bonus payments being uncertain.

* * * The issue presented is a recurring one with a long history of case-law and legislative development. Unfortunately, the statutory bifurcation in paragraph (5) rests on an unstable assumption.

Paragraph (5) turns upon a supposed distinction between "support" payments for spouse and children (what the statute calls "alimony to, maintenance for, or support of such spouse or child") and other kinds of divorce awards—for example, a division of jointly owned property. A similar distinction is used to determine the federal tax consequences of such payments and may have other effects under state law.[4] But the concepts are not necessarily identical in each context, and we are concerned here only with the meaning of the terms in section 523(a)(5), which is a matter of federal bankruptcy law.* * *

The underlying concept is easy to grasp: support payments are, roughly speaking, what is given to provide for the upkeep of the recipient spouse and children, *see, e.g.,* 4 *Collier,* ¶ 523.11, at 523-81, while other divisions or payments serve different purposes. The central problem is that the two supposedly separate categories overlap because the need for ongoing support will often depend on how much property the less well-off spouse is given outright. Indeed, under Massachusetts law, courts are authorized expressly to award property "[i]n addition to or *in lieu of* a judgment to pay alimony." Mass. Gen. Laws ch. 208, § 34 (2000) (emphasis added).

The federal courts have been unwilling to treat the label applied by the divorce court as controlling for Bankruptcy Code purposes.* * *

Nominally, the critical issue is whether the divorce court judge "intended" a particular award to be for support or for something else. * * * In practice, courts look at a range of factors, including the language used by the divorce court and whether the award seems designed to assuage need, as discerned from the structure of the award and the financial circumstances of the recipients. 4 *Collier,* ¶ 523.11.

Here, as usual in cases worth litigating, the factors do not all line up on one side. One of those helpful to Kathleen is that the award of formal alimony and support to her seems quite limited for an upper middle-class household with several children: $450 per week for the four children (roughly $23,400 per year), plus the evanescent obligation that Paul pay Kathleen one-third of his future "bonuses"—a form of compensation that the state court recognized could easily be manipulated downward within a family company. Kathleen did have real earning capacity but it was capped by her frustrated education, childcare obligations and her back injury.

In this situation, it is no great leap to suppose that $50,000 per year for the next decade, representing the structured pay-out of the past bonus and stock awards, was intended in some measure to close the gap. As the bankruptcy court pointed out, the main pay-out period corresponded roughly to the time in which Kathleen would be supporting the children and would be responsible as well, under the decree, for a portion of their college tuition. That the payment period did not end with anyone's death or exact majority could be a point in Paul's favor, 4 *Collier,* ¶ 523.11[d],

---

[4] In general, alimony is deductible to the payor and taxable to the payee, 26 U.S.C. § § 61(a)(8), 62(a)(10) (2000); and in Massachusetts, alimony is modifiable, but property divisions are not * * * .

at 523-85, but a payout of fixed property in installments is another way to recognize resources available from the payor in fixing support.

The Tenth Circuit took such a view in *Goin v. Rives* (*In re Goin* ), 808 F.2d 1391 (10th Cir.1987) (*per curiam* ). There, a state court awarded the wife $350 per month in child support and the sum of $80,000 to be paid in annual increments of $5,000. The decree said that the $80,000 represented the wife's "one-half interest in certain real estate and stock." *Id.* at 1392. The Tenth Circuit affirmed a finding of nondischargeability, in part because the state decree did not provide for any alimony, and because the bankruptcy court found that $350 a month was insufficient to support both the spouse and the children in conformity with the lifestyle to which they had become accustomed. *Id.* at 1392-93.

Paul's first argument for an out-and-out discharge is the state court's formal division of its assessments into two boxes; but under paragraph (5), payments intended for the support of spouse and child are not dischargeable and the Massachusetts statute quoted above says that an award of property can be made "in lieu" of alimony. Perhaps a more useful point—which Paul does not stress—is that, although $50,000 a year for alimony might not seem outlandish for a man who averaged roughly $150,000 a year during 1996-99, the final catch-up payments in years 10-11 appear to total over $200,000 apart from accrued interest, which does not sound like annual alimony or support outside the world of the super-rich.

Paul also argues in his brief that a precise calculation of Kathleen's income and needs shows that she was well-off without the disputed awards, but Kathleen's own detailed figures and analysis suggest that she was underfunded. Neither the state court nor the bankruptcy court made a systematic assessment of the numbers in terms of "need." Our own assessment suggests that without the awards, Kathleen would be underfunded at least to some extent in relation to her own description of expenses.

Accordingly, we see no basis to disturb the conclusion of the bankruptcy court. Just how much deference is due to its assessment is debatable * * * but there is substantial reason to believe that the state court in some measure intended the property division to assure adequate support for Kathleen and her children. The raw numbers, the uncertainty of future bonus payments, and the lengthy payout period all support this conclusion. The property-division label applied by the court seems most likely to have reflected no more than the mechanical fact that the payments were to come from identified existing resources.

This could be a different case had Paul argued for a remand. A position neither side has taken is that the two disputed awards were partly intended as support and partly as an equitable division of joint property over and above the amount needed for adequate support. Some allocation of the awards between the two categories might reflect the "right" answer; and some courts have so analyzed such problems. * * *

But in this case such a division would be very hard to calculate and would consume more time and lawyer expense—not to speak of the need then to decide the residual paragraph (15) issue. Nor is it clear that the result would better correspond to the "intent" of the state judge who was not completing a bankruptcy schedule but trying to solve a down-to-earth problem of allocating assets and income streams in a divorce. Paul was entitled to make this appeal an all or nothing choice; we see no reason to inject further options that he did not seek. * * *

The larger problem remains that the present statute needs revision. It is no accident that the 1970 Commission on the Bankruptcy Laws of the United States recommended that the line-drawing approach between alimony and property division be abandoned. The competing interests are for Congress to sort out; but a more administrable solution is overdue.

*Affirmed.*

## NOTE

Why didn't Chief Judge Boudin decide *Werthen* under § 523(a)(15), discussed below?

### b.　Section 523(a)(15)

Until 1994, former § 523(a)(5), which provided that support obligations substantially similar to those now included in the definition of DSOs in § 101(14A) were nondischargeable, was the only provision dealing with the dischargeability of marital claims in the Code. A major shortcoming of § 523(a)(5) is that it requires courts to draw lines in very ambiguous situations. Negotiations surrounding a divorce may result in the debtor undertaking obligations that benefit the nondebtor spouse or child but are, arguably, not for alimony, maintenance or support. The most common example of this is property settlement agreements dividing the marital property between the spouses. Another is "hold harmless" agreements in which the debtor agrees to pay a debt on which both spouses are liable and hold the nondebtor spouse harmless against liability on that debt. But debts for support falling within § 523(a)(5) and debts arising from property settlements or hold harmless agreements falling outside that section may be strongly interrelated: the debtor may be willing to make a more generous property settlement in exchange for lower support payments.

By adding § 523(a)(15) in 1994, Congress showed its dissatisfaction with the existing system that required judges to declare certain kinds of debts relating to marriage dissolution nondischargeable and other (often interdependent) dissolution-related debts dischargeable. After § 523(a)(15), as amended by the 2005 Act, a broad array of inter-spousal debts are nondischargeable in Chapter 7. Such obligations are:

> to a spouse, former spouse, or child of the debtor and not of the kind
> described in paragraph (5) that is incurred by the debtor in the course

of a divorce or separation or in connection with a separation agreement, divorce decree or other order of a court of record, or a determination made in accordance with State or territorial law by a governmental unit;

What is the breadth of this provision?

## PROBLEMS

**1.** Husband (H) is a lawyer; Wife (W) is a doctor. They decided to dissolve their marriage amicably and to remain good friends. How does § 523(a)(15) apply to the following cases?

**a.** As part of the dissolution settlement, W agreed to pay H $100,000 in five annual installments in order to equalize the division of their assets. A year after dissolution of the marriage, a recession struck, and the HMO whose members W treated filed in bankruptcy, leaving W with several hundred thousand dollars of worthless claims against the HMO for services rendered to its members for which W was entitled to reimbursement. W had insufficient assets to deal with her creditors and filed in Chapter 7. At the time of dissolution, W and H each had incomes of roughly $150,000 per year, but by the time of W's filing, W had an income of no more than $30,000; H, an insolvency lawyer, had an income that had burgeoned to $400,000 annually. Is W's debt to H nondischargeable? What policy would be furthered by making such a debt nondischargeable?

**b.** During their marriage, H and W had always shared investment opportunities. After they had reached a property settlement and had a court date set for final dissolution, H told W of an initial public offering of stock that his broker had made available to him in the amount of $100,000 and inquired whether she wished to share his allotment. She agreed to go in on the deal but was short of cash. H lent her $50,000 to purchase her half of the allotment. If W files for Chapter 7 bankruptcy after dissolution of the marriage, will W's debt to H be considered to have been "incurred by the debtor in the course of a divorce" and therefore nondischargeable under § 523(a)(15)? What policy would be furthered by making such a debt nondischargeable?

**2.** Husband (H) and Wife (W) were both employed at the time of the amicable dissolution of their marriage. In the dissolution settlement, H agreed to assume liability for approximately $25,000 that W owed on her automobile, credit cards and other personal debts. After dissolution, H lost his job and filed in Chapter 13. Which provision applies to H's assumption of W's debts, § 523(a)(5) or (15)? Why does it matter? § 1328(a)(2).

With respect to Problem 2, amendments to § 1328(a)(2) in 2005 expanded the kinds of debts that are nondischargeable in Chapter 13 cases, but the expansion does not include debts falling within § 523(a)(15). Since H filed in Chapter 13, the court must work through the traditional analysis of whether his assumption of W's personal debts was in the nature of a support payment within the DSO definition in § 101(14A). In a number of other provisions throughout the 2005 Act, special treatment is given DSOs that is not accorded the kinds of debts included in § 523(a)(15), e.g., priority under § 507(a)(1). The issue of whether a dissolution-related debt falls within the DSO definition must be faced with respect to a number of provisions throughout the Code, but § 523(a)(15) operates only with respect to Chapter 7 discharges.

### 3.   WILLFUL AND MALICIOUS INJURY

Section 523(a)(6) makes nondischargeable a debt "for willful and malicious injury by the debtor to another entity or to the property of another entity." Since a discharge in bankruptcy is an equitable remedy for the relief of debtors it may be inequitable to allow discharge in cases in which the debt represents liability for conduct of the debtor involving moral turpitude. This exception from discharge means, for example, that a debtor who assaults a neighbor or deliberately burns down the neighbor's house cannot get absolution in Chapter 7 from the liability resulting from those acts. But not many cases of that kind reach the bankruptcy courts. Most cases of injury to person or property involve a degree of moral culpability by the debtor that is much lower. To define the line between dischargeability and nondischargeability, the Bankruptcy Code uses two rather imprecise terms: willful and malicious. Most of the litigated cases have fallen into two groups: those involving personal injuries, particularly injuries resulting from automobile accidents caused by the debtor while intoxicated, and those involving conversion of property. The drunken driving issue was resolved by the addition in 1984 of § 523(a)(9) at the behest of Mothers Against Drunken Driving, making such debts nondischargeable. The Supreme Court has spoken on personal injuries in the next case, and we follow that case with material on property conversion.

## Kawaauhau v. Geiger
Supreme Court of the United States, 1998.
523 U.S. 57.

■   Justice GINSBURG delivered the opinion of the Court.

Section 523(a)(6) of the Bankruptcy Code provides that a debt "for willful and malicious injury by the debtor to another" is not dischargeable. § 523(a)(6). The question before us is whether a debt arising from a medical malpractice judgment, attributable to negligent or reckless conduct, falls within this statutory exception. We hold that it does not and that the debt is dischargeable.

I

In January 1983, petitioner Margaret Kawaauhau sought treatment from respondent Dr. Paul Geiger for a foot injury. Geiger examined Kawaauhau and admitted her to the hospital to attend to the risk of infection resulting from the injury. Although Geiger knew that intravenous penicillin would have been more effective, he prescribed oral penicillin, explaining in his testimony that he understood his patient wished to minimize the cost of her treatment.

Geiger then departed on a business trip, leaving Kawaauhau in the care of other physicians, who decided she should be transferred to an infectious disease specialist. When Geiger returned, he canceled the transfer and discontinued all antibiotics because he believed the infection had subsided. Kawaauhau's condition deteriorated over the next few days, requiring the amputation of her right leg below the knee.

Kawaauhau, joined by her husband Solomon, sued Geiger for malpractice. After a trial, the jury found Geiger liable and awarded the Kawaauhaus approximately $355,000 in damages.[1] Geiger, who carried no malpractice insurance, moved to Missouri, where his wages were garnished by the Kawaauhaus. Geiger then petitioned for bankruptcy. The Kawaauhaus requested the Bankruptcy Court to hold the malpractice judgment nondischargeable on the ground that it was a debt "for willful and malicious injury" excepted from discharge by § 523(a)(6). The Bankruptcy Court concluded that Geiger's treatment fell far below the appropriate standard of care and therefore ranked as "willful and malicious." Accordingly, the Bankruptcy Court held the debt nondischargeable. * * * In an unpublished order, the District Court affirmed.

A three-judge panel of the Court of Appeals for the Eighth Circuit reversed, and a divided en banc court adhered to the panel's position. Section 523(a)(6)'s exemption from discharge, the en banc court held, is confined to debts "based on what the law has for generations called an intentional tort." On this view, a debt for malpractice, because it is based on conduct that is negligent or reckless, rather than intentional, remains dischargeable.

The Eighth Circuit acknowledged that its interpretation of § 523(a)(6) diverged from previous holdings of the Sixth and Tenth Circuits. We granted certiorari to resolve this conflict and now affirm the Eighth Circuit's judgment.

## II

Section 523(a)(6) of the Bankruptcy Code provides:

"(a) A discharge under Section 727, 1141, 1228(a), 1228(b), or 1328(b) of this title does not discharge an individual debtor from any debt—

. . ..

   "(6)   for willful and malicious injury by the debtor to another entity or to the property of another entity."

---

[1] The jury awarded Margaret Kawaauhau $203,040 in special damages and $99,000 in general damages. In addition, the jury awarded Solomon Kawaauhau $18,000 in general damages for loss of consortium and $35,000 for emotional distress.

The Kawaauhaus urge that the malpractice award fits within this exception because Dr. Geiger intentionally rendered inadequate medical care to Margaret Kawaauhau that necessarily led to her injury. According to the Kawaauhaus, Geiger deliberately chose less effective treatment because he wanted to cut costs, all the while knowing that he was providing substandard care. Such conduct, the Kawaauhaus assert, meets the "willful and malicious" specification of § 523(a)(6).

We confront this pivotal question concerning the scope of the "willful and malicious injury" exception: Does § 523(a)(6)'s compass cover acts, done intentionally,[3] that cause injury (as the Kawaauhaus urge), or only acts done with the actual intent to cause injury (as the Eighth Circuit ruled)? The words of the statute strongly support the Eighth Circuit's reading.

The word "willful" in (a)(6) modifies the word "injury," indicating that nondischargeability takes a deliberate or intentional *injury*, not merely a deliberate or intentional *act* that leads to injury. Had Congress meant to exempt debts resulting from unintentionally inflicted injuries, it might have described instead "willful acts that cause injury." Or, Congress might have selected an additional word or words, i.e., "reckless" or "negligent," to modify "injury." Moreover, as the Eighth Circuit observed, the (a)(6) formulation triggers in the lawyer's mind the category "intentional torts," as distinguished from negligent or reckless torts. Intentional torts generally require that the actor intend "the *consequences* of an act," not simply "the act itself." Restatement (Second) of Torts § 8A, comment a, p. 15 (1964) (emphasis added).

The Kawaauhaus' more encompassing interpretation could place within the excepted category a wide range of situations in which an act is intentional, but injury is unintended, i.e., neither desired nor in fact anticipated by the debtor. Every traffic accident stemming from an initial intentional act—for example, intentionally rotating the wheel of an automobile to make a left-hand turn without first checking oncoming traffic—could fit the description. A "knowing breach of contract" could also qualify. A construction so broad would be incompatible with the "well-known" guide that exceptions to discharge "should be confined to those plainly expressed." *Gleason v. Thaw*, 236 U.S. 558, 562 (1915).

Furthermore, "we are hesitant to adopt an interpretation of a congressional enactment which renders superfluous another portion of that same law." *Mackey v. Lanier Collection Agency & Service, Inc.*, 486 U.S. 825, 837 (1988). Reading § 523(a)(6) as the Kawaauhaus urge would obviate the need for § 523(a)(9), which specifically exempts debts "for death or personal injury caused by the debtor's operation of a motor vehicle if such

---

[3] The word "willful" is defined in Black's Law Dictionary as "voluntary" or "intentional." Black's Law Dictionary 1434 (5th ed.1979). Consistently, legislative reports note that the word "willful" in § 523(a)(6) means "deliberate or intentional."

operation was unlawful because the debtor was intoxicated from using alcohol, a drug, or another substance." § 523(a)(9); see also § 523(a)(12) (exempting debts for "malicious or reckless failure" to fulfill certain commitments owed to a federal depository institutions regulatory agency).

The Kawaauhaus heavily rely on *Tinker v. Colwell*, 193 U.S. 473 (1904), which presented this question: Does an award of damages for "criminal conversation" survive bankruptcy under the 1898 Bankruptcy Act's exception from discharge for judgments in civil actions for "'willful and malicious injuries to the person or property of another'"? Id., at 481. The *Tinker* Court held such an award a nondischargeable debt. The Kawaauhaus feature certain statements in the *Tinker* opinion, in particular: "[An] act is willful. . . in the sense that it is intentional and voluntary" even if performed "without any particular malice," id., at 485; an act that "necessarily causes injury and is done intentionally, may be said to be done willfully and maliciously, so as to come within the [bankruptcy discharge] exception," id., at 487. See also id., at 487 (the statute exempts from discharge liability for "'a wrongful act, done intentionally, without just cause or excuse'") (quoting from definition of malice in *Bromage v. Prosser*, 4 Barn. & Cress. 247, 107 Eng. Rep. 1051 (K.B.1825)).

The exposition in the *Tinker* opinion is less than crystalline. Counterbalancing the portions the Kawaauhaus emphasize, the *Tinker* Court repeatedly observed that the tort in question qualified in the common law as trespassory. Indeed, it ranked as "trespass *vi et armis*." 193 U.S., at 482, 483. Criminal conversation, the Court noted, was an action akin to a master's "action of trespass and assault. . . for the battery of his servant," id., at 482. *Tinker* thus placed criminal conversation solidly within the traditional intentional tort category, and we so confine its holding. That decision, we clarify, provides no warrant for departure from the current statutory instruction that, to be nondischargeable, the judgment debt must be "for willful and malicious *injury*."

Subsequent decisions of this Court are in accord with our construction. In *McIntyre v. Kavanaugh*, 242 U.S. 138 (1916), a broker "deprive[d] another of his property forever by deliberately disposing of it without semblance of authority." Id., at 141. The Court held that this act constituted an intentional injury to property of another, bringing it within the discharge exception. But in *Davis v. Aetna Acceptance Co.*, 293 U.S. 328 (1934), the Court explained that not every tort judgment for conversion is exempt from discharge. Negligent or reckless acts, the Court held, do not suffice to establish that a resulting injury is "wilful and malicious." See id., at 332.

Finally, the Kawaauhaus maintain that, as a policy matter, malpractice judgments should be excepted from discharge, at least when the debtor acted recklessly or carried no malpractice insurance. Congress, of course, may so decide. But unless and until Congress makes such a decision, we must follow the current direction § 523(a)(6) provides.

* * *

We hold that debts arising from recklessly or negligently inflicted injuries do not fall within the compass of § 523(a)(6). For the reasons stated, the judgment of the Court of Appeals for the Eighth Circuit is

Affirmed.


## NOTES

**1.** *Geiger* established that § 523(a)(6) does not apply to debts arising from unintentionally inflicted injuries but did not decide whether actual knowledge is necessary to satisfy the willful injury requirement. The circuits are divided on the matter. The Sixth Circuit adopts a subjective standard: a debt is nondischargeable under § 523(a)(b) only if the debtor intended to cause harm or actually knew that harm was a substantially certain consequence of her behavior. *In re Markowitz*, 190 F.3d 455 (6th Cir. 1999). The Ninth Circuit is in accord: *In re Su*, 290 F.3d 1140 (9th Cir. 2002). The Fifth Circuit adopts an objective standard: *In re Miller*, 156 F.3d 598 (5th Cir. 1998). The objective standard disregards the debtor's state of mind and considers whether an objective, reasonable person would have known that the actions in question were substantially certain to injure the creditor.

**2.** Courts have not known what to make of *Tinker v. Colwell*, 193 U.S. 473 (1904), in which Colwell's judgment for $50,000 against Tinker for criminal conversation with his wife was held to be nondischargeable within the willful and malicious exception even though Tinker's act was done without "any particular malice." *Mellinkoff's Dictionary of American Legal Usage* 140 (1992) defines criminal conversation as "the waning civil action for damages for adultery with plaintiff's spouse." The Court in *Kawaauhau* makes clear that *Tinker* is a waning authority, confined, in effect, to its facts.

**3.** A second group of cases involving conversion of property is an important focus of § 523(a)(6) and has significant commercial importance. There is ample authority for holding that conversion of property can qualify as a "willful and malicious injury" to property under § 523(a)(6). The clearest example is a theft of property by the debtor. But that kind of case is not typical. The most common cases under § 523(a)(6) are those in which the debtor in a secured transaction converts the collateral of the secured party by selling it and spending the proceeds of the sale for the benefit of the debtor or a third party. For example, a finance company has a security interest in the debtor's inventory and any proceeds of the sale of the inventory. Under the security agreement the debtor is required to pay over to the finance company the cash proceeds of any sale of the inventory. If the debtor sells inventory and, in violation of the security agreement, uses the proceeds of the sale to pay other debts of the debtor, there is a clear conversion of property of the finance company. This kind of conversion is sometimes referred to as a "sale out of trust."

The conversion, however, is not necessarily "willful and malicious" as required by § 523(a)(6). Conversion can occur in cases in which the debtor has exercised unauthorized control over somebody else's property without being aware of the fact that the conduct was unlawful. This exercise of control may be willful in the sense that the debtor intended to do the act that constituted the exercise of control. But the act is clearly not "willful and malicious" under § 523(a)(6) if the debtor thought that the exercise of control was lawful. This point was made by Justice Cardozo in *Davis v. Aetna Acceptance Co.*, 293 U.S. 328 (1934). He took the view that, though a sale by a dealer "out of trust" is a conversion, it is not, without more, willful and malicious conduct. "There may be a conversion which is innocent or technical, an unauthorized assumption of dominion without willfulness or malice. * * * There may be an honest, but mistaken belief, engendered by a course of dealing, that powers have been enlarged or incapacities removed. In these and like cases, what is done is a tort, but not a willful or malicious one." 293 U.S. at 332. But cases of innocent conversion of collateral by the debtor are not usually litigated under § 523(a)(6). In the typical litigated case the debtor knows that the use of the cash proceeds of the sale of collateral is a violation of the property rights of the secured party. In those cases the conversion is certainly willful. Is such a conversion necessarily also malicious?

## PROBLEM

Corporation borrowed $50,000 from Bank in order to purchase a piece of business equipment. Bank took a perfected a security interest in the equipment. The security agreement forbids sale of the equipment or its removal from the state in which Corporation's place of business was located without permission of Bank. Debtor, an individual who is the principal stockholder of Corporation, guaranteed payment of the Bank's loan.

A few months after the loan was made, a sudden downturn in Corporation's sales caused a severe cash shortage. In order to raise cash Debtor, acting for Corporation, removed the equipment to another state and sold it to Buyer for $40,000, its fair value. Debtor, knowing that the sale violated Bank's security agreement, told Buyer that the equipment was unencumbered. Bank had no knowledge of the transaction. Corporation's business did not improve, and eventually Corporation filed in bankruptcy. Debtor also filed in bankruptcy at the same time. At that time: (i) Corporation owed $50,000 to Bank, (ii) Corporation was insolvent and all of its assets were encumbered by liens that secured debts (other than Bank's claim) in excess of the value of the assets, and (iii) Debtor was also insolvent and had no nonexempt assets.

Assume that under state law Bank has no right to assert its security interest against Buyer. Is Bank's claim against Debtor for conversion nondischargeable under § 523(a)(6)? Would it matter if Debtor's conversion was done solely for the purpose of raising funds to keep Corporation afloat and all of the $40,000 was invested in Corporation? *See* Charles Jordan Tabb, *The Scope of the Fresh Start in Bankruptcy: Collateral Conversions and the Dischargeability Debate*, 59 Geo. Wash. L. Rev. 56 (1990).

## 4. EDUCATIONAL LOANS

Federally guaranteed student loans have played an essential role in making it possible for many students to pay the ever-rising costs of higher education. Loans outstanding under this program have tripled over the past decade to $357 billion. John Hechinger, *U.S. Gets Tough on Failure to Repay Student Loans,* Wall St.J. Jan. 6, 2005, at A1. According to this article, in 2004 two-thirds of students at private four-year colleges had guaranteed loans, averaging $17,000 at graduation, and graduates of private medical and law schools owed an average of $74,000. These loans are usually made by banks and other private lenders with state agencies administering the program and initially guaranteeing the loans. The Department of Education both subsidizes interest rates on educational loans and ultimately guarantees payment of loans in default. Repayment is made in installments, commencing six months after graduation usually for a ten-year term. See the following case for a discussion of alternative repayment plans. A major player in educational lending is SLM Corp., known as Sallie Mae, formerly a federal agency but now a private corporation, which buys and packages student loans for securitization purposes. Sallie Mae securitizes student loans for the public debt markets, and, in some instances, makes, services, and collects student loans.

An enduring policy dispute has centered around what to do about educational loans in bankruptcy. The current law provides broadly that educational loans are nondischargeable, § 523(a)(8), except in cases of "undue hardship." A starry-eyed undergraduate receiving a student loan may have no comprehension that she is undertaking a lifetime obligation—there is no statute of limitations—that in default, even under subsidized interest rates, can grow substantially over time and that, under current practices, may be enforced against her at any point during her life by collection agencies to which the Department of Education has outsourced delinquent debts for a 20% commission. Opponents of § 523(a)(8) argue that there is no evidence that use of bankruptcy to avoid payment would be any greater with respect to student loans than with ordinary consumer loans. According to Hechinger, the default rate in 2004 for private universities with four-year undergraduate and graduate programs was only 3.1%, but the default rate was much higher for students of community colleges or trade schools. The overall default rate was 5.2%, about the same as defaults on credit cards.

Nevertheless, Congress has rejected the view that educational loans should be dischargeable to deter perceived abuse. Proponents of nondischargeability argue that these loans are not granted on the same basis as other loans. Students who could not qualify for an ordinary consumer loan are able to obtain generous educational loans. Interest rates and repayment terms are very favorable and no security is required. These educational loans are likely to be the principal unsecured debt of a student. Upon graduation the typical student has little or no nonexempt property but may have very substantial future earning potential. If discharge is unrestricted, bankruptcy provides a tempting low cost method of unencumbering these future earnings. Section 523(a)(8) is designed to remove the temptation.The policy basis of § 523(a)(8) is more easily understood in the case of graduates of elite universities on their way to riches, but it can be a heavy burden for students who attend vocational schools of questionable quality.

The debtor has only one way out: § 523(a)(8) provides an exception if nondischargeability of an educational debt "will impose an undue hardship on the debtor and the debtor's dependents." There is no definition in the statute of "undue hardship." Since many debtors are desperate to escape nondischargebility of their educational loans, predictably, a large body of case law has grown around the meaning of these words. It is fair to conclude that courts have not been generous to debtors seeking undue hardship discharges of educational loans. The prevailing view is expressed in *In re Roberson*, 999 F.2d 1132, 1137 (7th Cir. 1993): "The government is not twisting the arms of potential students. The decision of whether or not to borrow for a college education lies with the individual; absent an expression to the contrary, the government does not guarantee the student's future financial success. If the leveraged investment of an education does not generate the return the borrower anticipated, the student, not the taxpayers, must accept the consequences of the decision to borrow."

We include the following case for its discussion of (i) "undue hardship," (ii) partial discharge and (iii) alternative repayment plans.

## In re Tirch

United States Court of Appeals, Sixth Circuit, 2005.
409 F.3d 677.

■ BATCHELDER, Circuit Judge.

Defendant-Appellant Pennsylvania Higher Education Assistance Agency ("PHEAA") appeals the Bankruptcy Appellate Panel's ("BAP") order affirming the bankruptcy court's order granting partial discharge of Plaintiff-Appellee Rose Tirch's student loan debt. Because the record does not support the bankruptcy court's findings that Tirch's ailments preclude her return to work and are likely to persist for a significant portion of the repayment period, or that she made a good faith effort to pay back her student loans, we will REVERSE.

Tirch, a single female in her mid-40s, holds a B.A. in Counseling, which she received in the mid-1980's and a Master's Degree in Counseling, which she received in 1998. Tirch financed her education through a total of 17 loans provided by PHEAA and owed an aggregate balance of

$84,604.65 as of June 19, 2001, with interest accruing at a rate of $558.08 per month. As of the filing of this appeal, Tirch, who first defaulted on her loans on October 24, 2000, had made $3,072.75 in payments on the loans and had arranged for her alma mater, Franciscan University of Steubenville, to make a charitable payment of $1,850.77.

After receiving her Master's Degree, Tirch worked in various counseling positions and earned about $27,000 in 1999, $28,500 in 2000, and $27,500 in 2001. Claiming various long-term medical and emotional problems, including attention deficit disorder, chronic anxiety and depression, as well as colorectal surgery in December 2001, from which she has had a slow recovery, Tirch stopped working at the end of 2001. Apparently as a result of anaesthetics administered during the surgery, Tirch lost her sense of taste, which has affected her appetite and which she contends has made a return to work impossible. For a period of 24 months, Tirch received $1,400 per month in disability benefits based on her allegedly debilitating mental condition.

Sometime in 2000—Tirch does not provide us with the date—Tirch filed for protection under Chapter 7 of the Bankruptcy Code. In August of 2000, some sixteen months before she stopped working, Tirch filed an adversary proceeding against PHEAA in her Chapter 7 case, seeking a discharge of her student loan debt for "undue hardship" pursuant to § 523(a)(8). The bankruptcy court held a trial on August 16, 2002, at which Tirch was the only witness. During the trial, Tirch described her medical and emotional problems and produced unauthenticated records from her treating doctors, which the bankruptcy court admitted solely as evidence that she had sought medical help, but not as evidence of the underlying medical diagnoses. She also testified that she did not apply to participate in the William D. Ford Federal Direct Consolidation Program. This program includes an Income Contingent Repayment ("ICR") plan whereby the lenders and loan guarantors are repaid by the Program, and the borrower becomes obligated to repay the Program a reduced amount for a period of up to 25 years, after which time any unpaid portion is discharged. Tirch admitted that she was aware of the program's existence but elected not to avail herself of its benefits.

Applying the three-part test announced by the Second Circuit in *Brunner v. New York State Higher Education Services Corp.*, 831 F.2d 395 (2d Cir.1987), the bankruptcy court granted Tirch a partial discharge of her student loan debt, holding that requiring Tirch to pay her student loans in an amount in excess of $200 per month once she returns to work and earns a salary of at least $20,000 per year would impose an undue hardship. The bankruptcy court's order allows Tirch to discontinue payments at age 65 in any eventuality. The BAP affirmed the bankruptcy court's order. PHEAA timely appealed. * * *

The Bankruptcy Code provides for the complete discharge of educational loans whose repayment would impose an "undue hardship" on the debtor. § 523(a)(8). Despite the fact that § 523(a)(8) makes no mention of partial discharges, we have held that the bankruptcy court may grant a partial discharge of such a debt pursuant to the equitable powers enumerated in § 105(a). *In re Miller*, 377 F.3d 616, 620-21 (6th Cir.2004) (citing *Tenn. Student Assistance Corp. v. Hornsby*, 144 F.3d 433, 439-40 (6th Cir.1998)). *Miller* held that "the requirement of undue hardship must always apply to the discharge of student loans in bankruptcy—regardless of whether a court is discharging a debtor's student loans in full or only partially." Id. at 622.

Because "undue hardship" is not defined by the Bankruptcy Code, this circuit has traditionally looked to the *Brunner* test for guidance. * * * Very recently, however, we explicitly adopted the *Brunner* test. *In re Oyler*, 397 F.3d 382, 385 (6th Cir.2005). Accordingly, in this circuit, a debtor seeking a partial discharge of student loans due to "undue hardship" must make a three-part showing:

(1)  that the debtor cannot maintain, based on current income and expenses, a "minimal" standard of living for herself and her dependents if forced to repay the loans;

(2)  that additional circumstances exist indicating that this state of affairs is likely to persist for a significant portion of the repayment period of the student loans; and

(3)  that the debtor has made good faith efforts to repay the loans.

*Brunner*, 831 F.2d at 396. Because PHEAA concedes that under her current circumstances, Tirch cannot maintain a minimal standard of living if forced to repay the loans, this case turns on the second and third prongs of the *Brunner* test. After examining the record of the proceedings in the bankruptcy court, we conclude that Tirch failed to carry her burden on either of these prongs.

To demonstrate that the debtor's current "state of affairs is likely to persist for a significant portion of the repayment period of the student loans," as required by *Brunner* 's second prong, the debtor must precisely identify her problems and explain how her condition would impair her ability to work in the future. * * * The dischargeability of loans should be based upon "a certainty of hopelessness, not merely a present inability to fulfill financial commitment." *Oyler*, 397 F.3d at 386 * * *. Tirch has not made this showing.

Tirch testified that she continues to experience problems arising from her rectal surgery, including irregularity and loss of taste, but she did not provide evidence that these physical problems would preclude her from working. Instead, she explained that "[a]t this point I can't help somebody else when I can't help myself and no one can help me. So I don't feel I can be in the counseling field or social work field at this time and I'm not even functioning in my own home." When pressed, she explained further,

> If my taste returns, which is my biggest difficulty that I'm having, which people may see as simple, but it's not. . ... So I don't believe I can return to work any time soon. If I don't have the—the return of my

taste, I don't know how I'm going to cope long term to be able to get back to work in any capacity, I don't know.

Neither has Tirch provided evidence sufficient to demonstrate that her psychological conditions preclude her return to work. Her assertion that "I went through post-traumatic stress when I went to work at the State of West Virginia as a social worker" is certainly not sufficient. Tirch should have sought employment in another field when the stress of clinical social work became debilitating. *See In re Paolini* , 1997 WL 476515, at *6 (6th Cir. 1997) ("while [the debtor's] struggle with [obsessive compulsive disorder] makes her unsuited for work in the stressful environment of a large law firm, there are a plethora of legal jobs [the debtor] has not yet explored")* * * . The remainder of Tirch's testimony relating to her claim that she is unable to work is simply a recitation of incidents of stress occurring over a period of several years, unsupported by competent medical or psychological evidence. * * * [T]he bankruptcy court provided no factual basis whatsoever for its bald conclusion that Tirch had met all three prongs of the *Brunner* test.

Nor did Tirch provide evidence that these problems would "persist for a significant portion of the repayment period of the student loans." *Brunner*, 831 F.2d at 396. When asked if she would be able to return to work, Tirch responded,

> Not at this time. And I don't know when this would be. It could be a year, it could be two years. I don't know how I'm going to cope if I have complete [loss of taste] forever. I really at this time can't and I know it's—it could be six months to a year if I don't—if [my sense of taste] returns, I could.

Nothing in Tirch's statements and nothing in the record as a whole provides any "certainty of hopelessness," *Oyler*, 397 F.3d at 386, or any basis for concluding that Tirch's current condition will persist for any appreciable period. Indeed, we are hard-pressed to discern, either from any of these statements or from the entire record, how her condition prevents her from working now, let alone in the future.

The facts of Tirch's case are similar to those in *In re Burton*, 117 B.R. 167 (Bankr.W.D.Pa.1990), in which a 33-year-old debtor with a four-year college degree testified that he suffered from Epstein-Barr Syndrome (the virus that causes, among other things, infectious mononucleosis), a severe bowel disorder, depression, and a lack of concentration, and presented unauthenticated letters from a doctor, which purported to corroborate his testimony. The court held that the debtor did not demonstrate undue hardship because he "failed to show what the long-term deleterious effects of the disease are; that he can be expected to suffer those effects during the next ten (10) years or so; or, that this condition will prevent him from being gainfully employed during that time." *Id*. at 171. Like the debtor in *Burton*, Tirch has failed to prove that her ailments preclude her return to work and will persist for a significant portion of the repayment period.

Tirch has also failed to show that she made a good faith effort to repay the loans, as required by the third prong of the *Brunner* test. We begin our good faith analysis with Tirch's decision not to avail herself of the William D. Ford ICR. The bankruptcy court in *In re Korhonen*, 296 B.R. 492, 496 (Bankr.D.Minn.2003), explained the mechanics of the ICR:

> The Income Contingent Repayment Program permits a student loan debtor to pay twenty percent of the difference between his adjusted gross income and the poverty level for his family size, or the amount the debtor would pay if the debt were repaid in twelve years, whichever is less. Under the program, the borrower's monthly repayment amount is adjusted each year to reflect any changes in these factors. The borrower's repayments may also be adjusted during the year based on special circumstances. See 34 C.F.R. § 685.209(c)(3). At the end of the twenty five year payment period, any remaining loan balance would be cancelled by the Secretary of Education. However, the amount discharged would be considered taxable income.

While not a per se indication of a lack of good faith, * * * Tirch's decision not to take advantage of the ICR is probative of her intent to repay her loans. See *Brunner*, 831 F.2d at 397. In cases involving a partial discharge of student loans, "it is a difficult, although not necessarily an insurmountable burden for a debtor who is offered, but then declines the government's income contingent repayment program, to come to this Court and seek an equitable adjustment of their student loan debt." *In re Swinney*, 266 B.R. 800, 806-07 (Bankr.N.D.Ohio 2001) * * * .

The BAP determined that Tirch's failure to avail herself of the ICR was not probative of her good faith because her payments under the plan would be $597.34 per month, and the bankruptcy court had found that it would work an undue hardship on Tirch to require her to pay more than $200 per month once she attained an annual income level of $20,000. According to the BAP, the ICR therefore provided no effective relief. The BAP, however, misapplied the formula that calculates a debtor's payments under the ICR. As we will explain, Tirch would have had to pay only $183.66 per month had she taken advantage of the ICR.

Under the ICR, the annual amount payable by the student is the lesser of,

**(i)**  the amount the borrower would repay annually over 12 years using standard amortization multiplied by an income percentage factor that corresponds to the borrower's adjusted gross income (AGI) as shown in the income percentage factor table in a notice published annually by the Secretary in the Federal Register; or

**(ii)**  20 percent of discretionary income.

34 C.F.R. § 685.209(a)(2). Under subsection (a)(2)(i), Tirch would have to pay $597.34 per month (while there is a discrepancy in the BAP's opinion over whether the monthly total under subsection (a)(2)(i) is

$597.37 or $597.34, this discrepancy makes no difference in the analysis). In Tirch's case, however, her payments under subsection (a)(2)(ii), twenty percent of her discretionary income, would be far less than $597.34 per month. According to 34 C.F.R. § 685.209(a)(3), a borrower's discretionary income is her AGI minus the Health and Human Services Poverty Guideline Amount. The BAP calculated Tirch's discretionary income as $11,020 by subtracting $8,980 (the HHS poverty guideline for a single person living in the continental 48 states) from $20,000 (Tirch's estimated AGI). Next, the BAP divided $11,020 by 12 months and concluded that the ICR monthly payment under subsection (a)(2)(ii) would be $918.33 per month. However, the BAP did not consider that 34 C.F.R. § 685.209(a)(2)(ii) requires the debtor to pay only 20% of her discretionary income. Twenty percent of Tirch's discretionary income of $11,020 equals $2,204 Tirch's resulting monthly payment under the ICR is $183.66, which is even less than the $200 monthly payment that the bankruptcy court ordered and the BAP upheld.

Because Tirch declined to take advantage of an ICR that would have been advantageous, she failed to sustain the heavy burden of proving that she made a good faith effort to repay her loans. Since the mid-1980's (when she received a B.A. financed by PHEAA loans), Tirch had paid only $4,093.52 (including Franciscan University's contribution) on a series of loans which reached an aggregate balance of $84,604.65 by June of 2001. Despite receiving her Master's Degree in 1998 (also financed by PHEAA loans) and making roughly $27,000 in 1999, $28,500 in 2000 and $27,500 in 2001, she defaulted on her loans by October of 2001. When viewed in the context of her demonstrable earned-income potential, the $4,093.52 that Tirch paid on her student loans in the 20 years since she received her B.A. is meager. Tirch has failed to satisfy the third prong of the *Brunner* test.

Because Tirch has failed to demonstrate that her circumstances meet the *Brunner* standard to qualify for an "undue hardship" partial discharge of her student loans, we REVERSE the decision of the BAP affirming the judgment of the bankruptcy court.

## NOTE

The *Brunner* test is now generally accepted. *Collier on Bankruptcy* ¶ 523.14[2] (15th ed. rev. 2004). As set out in *Tirch*, this test requires the debtor to prove that (1) she cannot maintain a minimal standard of living if forced to repay, (2) this state of affairs is likely to persist for a significant portion of the repayment period of the loans, and (3) that she has made good faith efforts to repay the loans. In 1987, when *Brunner* was decided courts saw the issue to be whether the debtor's obligation to pay the entire debt over the conventional 10-year period constituted undue hardship. Today courts are faced by a more complex determination because of the acceptance of partial discharges and the adoption by the Department of Education of a program, referred to in *Tirch* as the Ford Program, allowing debtors to opt for a longer repayment period. *See* 34 C.F.R. § 685.209. The following Problems concern these developments.

## PROBLEMS

**1. a.** Debtor owes Lender an educational loan of $100,000. Under *Brunner* his circumstances are such that he meets the test for undue hardship under § 523(a)(8); therefore, Debtor qualifies for discharge of the full amount of his loan. However, Lender proposed that Debtor be discharged for only $45,000 of his loans but not for the $55,000 balance, which Debtor could repay without undue hardship. Does § 523(a)(8) empower a bankruptcy court to grant a partial discharge in such a case? Some cases say no, *e.g.*, *In re Cox*, 338 F.3d 1238 (11th Cir. 2003). Others say yes, *e.g.*, *In re Saxman*, 325 F.3d 1168 (9th Cir. 2003), which held that bankruptcy courts may exercise their equitable authority under § 105(a) to partially discharge student loans. Which view is the correct interpretation of § 523(a)(8)? Note that although § 523(a)(2) and (7) include the phrase "to the extent," those words do not appear in § 523(a)(8).

**b.** Is the emergence of partial discharge a pro-debtor or pro-creditor development? Do partial discharges further the policy objective of § 523(a)(8)?

**2.** The Educational Credit Management Corporation (ECMC) offers education loan debtors the Department of Education's program pursuant to which the debtor is given the option of choosing one of the following repayment plans: (1) the standard 10-year plan; (2) the extended 30-year plan (ranging from 12 years for a loan less than $10,000 to 30 years for a loan in excess of $60,000); (3) the graduated 30-year plan; and (4) the Income Contingent Repayment Plan (ICRP), which allows a borrower to remain current on her loan obligation by paying an amount based on income, debt, and family size. *See* 34 C.F.R. § 685.208 ((Repayment Plans) and § 685.209 (Income Contingent Repayment Plan). *See also In re Rose*, 324 B.R. 709 (8th Cir. B.A.P. 2005). What problems do these regulations pose for debtors seeking an undue hardship discharge? *See* the discussion in *Tirch*.

### 5. FRAUDULENTLY INCURRED DEBTS

A debtor who has engaged in certain kinds of fraudulent conduct such as concealing or transferring assets with intent to hinder or defraud creditors or falsifying information from which the debtor's financial condition might be ascertained may be denied a discharge in bankruptcy. § 727(a)(2) and (3). Debts resulting from a debtor's fraudulent conduct may be nondischargeable under § 523(a)(2). Section 523(a)(2)(A) provides that debts obtained by "false pretenses, a false misrepresentation, or actual fraud" are nondischargeable but is silent on the degree of reliance required on the part of creditors for nondischargeability. The following case resolves this oft-litigated issue.

## Field v. Mans

Supreme Court of the United States, 1995.
516 U.S. 59.

■   Justice SOUTER delivered the opinion of the Court.

The Bankruptcy Code's provisions for discharge stop short of certain debts resulting from "false pretenses, a false representation, or actual fraud." § 523(a)(2)(A). In this case we consider the level of a creditor's reliance on a fraudulent misrepresentation necessary to place a debt thus beyond release. While the Court of Appeals followed a rule requiring reasonable reliance on the statement, we hold the standard to be the less demanding one of justifiable reliance and accordingly vacate and remand.

**I**

In June 1987 petitioners William and Norinne Field sold real estate for $462,500 to a corporation controlled by respondent Philip W. Mans, who supplied $275,000 toward the purchase price and personally guaranteed a promissory note for $187,500 secured by a second mortgage on the property. The mortgage deed had a clause calling for the Fields' consent to any conveyance of the encumbered real estate during the term of the secured indebtedness, failing which the entire unpaid balance on the note would become payable upon a sale unauthorized.

On October 8, 1987, Mans's corporation triggered application of the clause by conveying the property to a newly formed partnership without the Fields' knowledge or consent. The next day, Mans wrote to the Fields asking them not for consent to the conveyance but for a waiver of their rights under the due-on-sale clause, saying that he sought to avoid any claim that the clause might apply to arrangements to add a new principal to his land development organization. The letter failed to mention that Mans had already caused the property to be conveyed. The Fields responded with an offer to waive if Mans paid them $10,500. Mans answered with a lower bid, to pay only $500, and again failed to disclose the conveyance. There were no further written communications.

The ensuing years brought a precipitous drop in real estate prices, and on December 10, 1990, Mans petitioned the United States Bankruptcy Court for the District of New Hampshire for relief under Chapter 11 of the Bankruptcy Code. On the following February 6, the Fields learned of the October 1987 conveyance, which their lawyer had discovered at the registry of deeds. In their subsequent complaint in the bankruptcy proceeding, they argued that some $150,000 had become due upon the 1987 conveyance for which Mans had become liable as guarantor, and that his obligation should be excepted from discharge under § 523(a)(2)(A) of the Bankruptcy Code, § 523(a)(2)(A), as a debt resulting from fraud.[1]

The Bankruptcy Court found that Mans's letters constituted false representations on which petitioners had relied to their detriment in extending credit. The court followed Circuit precedent, however * * * in requiring the Fields to make a further showing of reasonable reliance, defined as "what would be reasonable for a prudent man to do under those circumstances." The court held that a reasonable person would have checked for any conveyance after the exchange of letters, and that the Fields had unreasonably ignored further reason to investigate in 1988, when Mr. Field's boss told him of a third party claiming to be the owner of the property.[3] Having found the Fields unreasonable in relying without further enquiry on Mans's implicit misrepresentation about the state of the title, the court held Mans's debt dischargeable.

The District Court affirmed, likewise following Circuit precedent in holding that § 523(a)(2)(A) requires reasonable reliance to exempt a debt from discharge, and finding the Bankruptcy Court's judgment supported by adequate indication in the record that the Fields had relied without sufficient reason. The Court of Appeals for the First Circuit affirmed judgment for the Bankruptcy Court's reasons. * * *

We granted certiorari * * * to resolve a conflict among the Circuits over the level of reliance that § 523(a)(2)(A) requires a creditor to demonstrate.

## II

The provisions for discharge of a bankrupt's debts, §§ 727, 1141, 1228, and 1328(b), are subject to exception under § 523(a), which carries 16 subsections setting out categories of nondischargeable debts. Two of these are debts traceable to falsity or fraud or to a materially false financial statement, as set out in § 523(a)(2):

> "(a) A discharge under section 727, 1141, 1228(a), 1228(b), or 1328(b) of this title does not discharge an individual debtor from any debt—

.. . . .

> "(2) for money, property, services, or an extension, renewal, or refinancing of credit, to the extent obtained by—

---

[1] Although we observe the distinction between Mans and his corporations, the record before us does not indicate that the parties thought anything should turn on treating them separately. As the case comes to us, Mans is presented as the originator of both debt and misrepresentation.

[3] Mr. Field testified in the Bankruptcy Court proceeding that he asked Mans in 1988 about the report of a conveyance and that Mans indicated he had not conveyed the property, but Mr. Field later testified that he had not confronted Mans on the issue. The Bankruptcy Court made no finding about any such conversation.

"(A) false pretenses, a false representation, or actual fraud, other than a statement respecting the debtor's or an insider's financial condition; [or]

"(B)   use of a statement in writing—

"(i)   that is materially false;

"(ii)   respecting the debtor's or an insider's financial condition;

"(iii)   on which the creditor to whom the debtor is liable for such money, property, services, or credit reasonably relied; and

"(iv)   that the debtor caused to be made or published with intent to deceive."

These provisions were not innovations in their most recent codification, the Bankruptcy Reform Act of 1978 (Act), but had obvious antecedents in the Bankruptcy Act of 1898 (1898 Act). The precursor to § 523(a)(2)(A) was created when § 17(a)(2) of the 1898 Act was modified by an amendment in 1903, which provided that debts that were "liabilities for obtaining property by false pretenses or false representations" would not be affected by any discharge granted to a bankrupt, who would still be required to pay them. This language inserted in § 17(a)(2) was changed only slightly between 1903 and 1978, at which time the section was recodified as § 523(a)(2)(A) and amended to read as quoted above. Thus, since 1903 the statutory language at issue here merely progressed from "false pretenses or false representations" to "false pretenses, a false representation, or actual fraud, other than a statement respecting the debtor's or an insider's financial condition."

Section 523(a)(2)(B), however, is the product of more active evolution. The germ of its presently relevant language was also inserted into the 1898 Act by a 1903 amendment, which barred any discharge by a bankrupt who obtained property by use of a materially false statement in writing made for the purpose of obtaining the credit. The provision did not explicitly require an intent to deceive or set any level of reliance, but Congress modified its language in 1960 by adding the requirements that the debtor intend to deceive the creditor and that the creditor rely on the false statement, and by limiting its application to false financial statements.[6] In

---

[6] The 1960 amendments also transferred the language on false financial statements by individuals from § 14 (where it barred any discharge) to § 17(a)(2) (where it barred discharge of only the specific debt incurred as a result of the false financial statement). Thus, as of 1960 the relevant portion of § 17(a)(2) provided that discharge would not release a bankrupt from debts that "are liabilities for obtaining money or property by false pretenses or false representations, or for obtaining money or property on credit or obtaining an extension or renewal of credit in reliance upon a materially false statement

1978, Congress rewrote the provision as set out above and recodified it as § 523(a)(2)(B). Though the forms of the 1960 and 1978 provisions are quite different, the only distinction relevant here is that the 1978 version added a new element of reasonable reliance.

The sum of all this history is two close statutory companions barring discharge. One applies expressly when the debt follows a transfer of value or extension of credit induced by falsity or fraud (not going to financial condition), the other when the debt follows a transfer or extension induced by a materially false and intentionally deceptive written statement of financial condition upon which the creditor reasonably relied.

## III

The question here is what, if any, level of justification a creditor needs to show above mere reliance in fact in order to exempt the debt from discharge under § 523(a)(2)(A). The text that we have just reviewed does not say in so many words. While § 523(a)(2)(A) speaks of debt for value "obtained by... false pretenses, a false representation, or actual fraud," it does not define those terms or so much as mention the creditor's reliance as such, let alone the level of reliance required. No one, of course, doubts that some degree of reliance is required to satisfy the element of causation inherent in the phrase "obtained by," but the Government, as amicus curiae (like petitioners in a portion of their brief), submits that the minimum level will do. It argues that when § 523(a)(2)(A) is understood in its statutory context, it requires mere reliance in fact, not reliance that is reasonable under the circumstances. Both petitioners and the Government note that § 523(a)(2)(B) expressly requires reasonable reliance, while § 523(a)(2)(A) does not. They emphasize that the precursors to §§ 523(a)(2)(A) and (B) lacked any reasonableness requirement, and that Congress added an element of reasonable reliance to § 523(a)(2)(B) in 1978, but not to § 523(a)(2)(A). They contend that the addition to § 523(a)(2)(B) alone supports an inference that, in § 523(a)(2)(A), Congress did not intend to require reasonable reliance, over and above actual reliance. But this argument is unsound.

The argument relies on the apparent negative pregnant, under the rule of construction that an express statutory requirement here, contrasted with statutory silence there, shows an intent to confine the requirement to the specified instance. *See Gozlon–Peretz v. United States*, 498 U.S. 395, 404 (1991) (" "[W]here Congress includes particular language in one section of a statute but omits it in another section of the same Act, it is generally presumed that Congress acts intentionally and purposely in the disparate inclusion or exclusion"") * * *. Thus the failure of § 523(a)(2)(A) to require the reasonableness of reliance demanded by § 523(a)(2)(B) shows that (A) lacks such a requirement. Without more, the inference might be a

---

in writing respecting [the bankrupt's] financial condition made or published or caused to be made or published in any manner whatsoever with intent to deceive."

helpful one. But there is more here, showing why the negative pregnant argument should not be elevated to the level of interpretive trump card.

First, assuming the argument to be sound, the most it would prove is that the reasonableness standard was not intended. But our job does not end with rejecting reasonableness as the standard. We have to discover the correct standard, and where there are multiple contenders remaining (as there are here), the inference from the negative pregnant does not finish the job.

There is, however, a more fundamental objection to depending on a negative pregnant argument here, for in the present circumstances there is reason to reject its soundness even as far as it goes. Quite simply, if it proves anything here, it proves too much. If the negative pregnant is the reason that § 523(a)(2)(A) has no reasonableness requirement, then the same reasoning will strip (A) of any requirement to establish a causal connection between the misrepresentation and the transfer of value or extension of credit, and it will eliminate scienter from the very notion of fraud. Section 523(a)(2)(B) expressly requires not only reasonable reliance but also reliance itself; and not only a representation but also one that is material; and not only one that is material but also one that is meant to deceive. Section 523(a)(2)(A) speaks in the language neither of reliance nor of materiality nor of intentionality. If the contrast is enough to preclude a reasonableness requirement, it will do as well to show that the debtor need not have misrepresented intentionally, the statement need not have been material, and the creditor need not have relied. But common sense would balk.[7] If Congress really had wished to bar discharge to a debtor who made unintentional and wholly immaterial misrepresentations having no effect on a creditor's decision, it could have provided that. It would, however, take a very clear provision to convince anyone of anything so odd, and nothing so odd has ever been apparent to the courts that have previously construed this statute, routinely requiring intent, reliance, and materiality before applying § 523(a)(2)(A). * * *

The attempt to draw an inference from the inclusion of reasonable reliance in § 523(a)(2)(B), moreover, ignores the significance of a different and historically persistent textual difference between the substantive terms

---

[7] The fact that § 523(a)(2) uses the term "obtained by" does not avoid this problem, for two reasons. First, "obtained by" applies to both §§ 523(a)(2)(A) and (B); if it supplies the elements of materiality, intent to deceive, and actual reliance it renders § 523(a)(2)(B)'s inclusion of materiality and intent to deceive redundant. More to the point, it renders Congress's addition of the requirements of actual reliance and intent to deceive to the precursor of § 523(a)(2)(B) (§ 17(a)(2) of the 1898 Act) in 1960 nonsensical, since that provision also had the "obtained by" language. Second, it seems impossible to construe "obtained by" as encompassing a requirement of intent to deceive; one can obtain credit by a misrepresentation even if one has no intention of doing so (for example, by unintentionally writing that one has an annual income of $100,000, rather than $10,000, in applying for a loan).

in §§ 523(a)(2)(A) and (B): the former refer to common-law torts, and the latter do not. The principal phrase in the predecessor of § 523(a)(2)(B) was "obtained property. . . upon a materially false statement in writing," in the current § 523(a)(2)(B) it is value "obtained by. . . use of a statement in writing." Neither phrase is apparently traceable to another context where it might have been construed to include elements that need not be set out separately. If other elements are to be added to "statement in writing," the statutory language must add them (and of course it would need to add them to keep this exception to dischargeability from swallowing most of the rule). The operative terms in § 523(a)(2)(A), on the other hand, "false pretenses, a false representation, or actual fraud," carry the acquired meaning of terms of art. They are common-law terms, and, as we will shortly see in the case of "actual fraud," which concerns us here, they imply elements that the common law has defined them to include. * * * Congress could have enumerated their elements, but Congress's contrary drafting choice did not deprive them of a significance richer than the bare statement of their terms.

## IV

"It is. . . well established that "[w]here Congress uses terms that have accumulated settled meaning under. . . the common law, a court must infer, unless the statute otherwise dictates, that Congress means to incorporate the established meaning of these terms.'" *Community for Creative Non–Violence v. Reid*, 490 U.S. 730, 739, * * *. In this case, neither the structure of § 523(a)(2) nor any explicit statement in § 523(a)(2)(A) reveals, let alone dictates, the particular level of reliance required by § 523(a)(2)(A), and there is no reason to doubt Congress's intent to adopt a common-law understanding of the terms it used.

Since the District Court treated Mans's conduct as amounting to fraud, we will look to the concept of "actual fraud" as it was understood in 1978 when that language was added to § 523(a)(2)(A).[8] Then, as now, the most widely accepted distillation of the common law of torts[9] was the Restatement (Second) of Torts (1976), published shortly before Congress passed the Act. The section on point dealing with fraudulent misrepresentation states that both actual and "justifiable" reliance are required. Id., § 537. The Restatement expounds upon justifiable reliance by explaining that a person is justified in relying on a representation of fact "although he might have ascertained the falsity of the representation had he made an investigation." Id., § 540. Significantly for our purposes, the illustration is given

---

[8] Although we do not mean to suggest that the requisite level of reliance would differ if there should be a case of false pretense or representation but not of fraud, there is no need to settle that here.

[9] We construe the terms in § 523(a)(2)(A) to incorporate the general common law of torts, the dominant consensus of common-law jurisdictions, rather than the law of any particular State. * * *

of a seller of land who says it is free of encumbrances; according to the Restatement, a buyer's reliance on this factual representation is justifiable, even if he could have "walk[ed] across the street to the office of the register of deeds in the courthouse" and easily have learned of an unsatisfied mortgage. Id., § 540, Illustration 1. The point is otherwise made in a later section noting that contributory negligence is no bar to recovery because fraudulent misrepresentation is an intentional tort. Here a contrast between a justifiable and reasonable reliance is clear: "Although the plaintiff's reliance on the misrepresentation must be justifiable. . . this does not mean that his conduct must conform to the standard of the reasonable man. Justification is a matter of the qualities and characteristics of the particular plaintiff, and the circumstances of the particular case, rather than of the application of a community standard of conduct to all cases." Id., § 545A, Comment b. Justifiability is not without some limits, however. As a comment to § 541 explains, a person is

> "required to use his senses, and cannot recover if he blindly relies upon a misrepresentation the falsity of which would be patent to him if he had utilized his opportunity to make a cursory examination or investigation. Thus, if one induces another to buy a horse by representing it to be sound, the purchaser cannot recover even though the horse has but one eye, if the horse is shown to the purchaser before he buys it and the slightest inspection would have disclosed the defect. On the other hand, the rule stated in this Section applies only when the recipient of the misrepresentation is capable of appreciating its falsity at the time by the use of his senses. Thus a defect that any experienced horseman would at once recognize at first glance may not be patent to a person who has had no experience with horses."

Id., § 541, Comment a.

A missing eye in a "sound" horse is one thing; long teeth in a "young" one, perhaps, another.

Similarly, the edition of Prosser's Law of Torts available in 1978 (as well as its current successor) states that justifiable reliance is the standard applicable to a victim's conduct in cases of alleged misrepresentation and that "[i]t is only where, under the circumstances, the facts should be apparent to one of his knowledge and intelligence from a cursory glance, or he has discovered something which should serve as a warning that he is being deceived, that he is required to make an investigation of his own." W. Prosser, Law of Torts § 108, p. 718 (4th ed. 1971); accord, W. Keeton, D. Dobbs, R. Keeton, & D. Owen, Prosser and Keeton on Law of Torts § 108, p. 752 (5th ed. 1984) (Prosser & Keeton). Prosser represents common-law authority as rejecting the reasonable person standard here, stating that "the matter seems to turn upon an individual standard of the plaintiff's own capacity and the knowledge which he has, or which may fairly be charged against him from the facts within his observation in the light of his individual case." Prosser, supra, § 108, at 717; accord, Prosser &

Keeton, supra, § 108, at 751; see also 1 F. Harper & F. James, Law of Torts § 7.12, pp. 581–583 (1956) (rejecting reasonableness standard in misrepresentation cases in favor of justifiability and stating that "by the distinct tendency of modern cases, the plaintiff is entitled to rely upon representations of fact of such a character as to require some kind of investigation or examination on his part to discover their falsity, and a defendant who has been guilty of conscious misrepresentation can not offer as a defense the plaintiff's failure to make the investigation or examination to verify the same") (footnote omitted); accord, 2 F. Harper, F. James, & O. Gray, Law of Torts § 7.12, pp. 455–458 (2d ed.1986).

These authoritative syntheses surely spoke (and speak today) for the prevailing view of the American common-law courts. Of the 46 States that, as of November 6, 1978 (the day the Act became law), had articulated the required level of reliance in a common-law fraud action, 5 required reasonable reliance, 5 required mere reliance in fact, and 36 required an intermediate level of reliance, most frequently referred to as justifiable reliance. Following our established practice of finding Congress's meaning in the generally shared common law when common-law terms are used without further specification, we hold that § 523(a)(2)(A) requires justifiable, but not reasonable, reliance. * * *

It should go without saying that our analysis does not relegate all reasoning from a negative pregnant to the rubbish heap, or render the reasonableness of reliance wholly irrelevant under § 523(a)(2)(A). As for the rule of construction, of course it is not illegitimate, but merely limited. The more apparently deliberate the contrast, the stronger the inference, as applied, for example, to contrasting statutory sections originally enacted simultaneously in relevant respects, see *Gozlon–Peretz v. United States*, 498 U.S., at 404 (noting that a single enactment created provisions with language that differed). Even then, of course, it may go no further than ruling out one of several possible readings as the wrong one. The rule is weakest when it suggests results strangely at odds with other textual pointers, like the common-law language at work in the statute here. * * *

As for the reasonableness of reliance, our reading of the Act does not leave reasonableness irrelevant, for the greater the distance between the reliance claimed and the limits of the reasonable, the greater the doubt about reliance in fact. Naifs may recover, at common law and in bankruptcy, but lots of creditors are not at all naive. The subjectiveness of justifiability cuts both ways, and reasonableness goes to the probability of actual reliance.

## V

There remains a fair question that ought to be faced. It makes sense to protect a creditor even if he was not quite reasonable in relying on a fraudulent representation; fraudulence weakens the debtor's claim to consideration. And yet, why should the rule be different when fraud is carried to the point of a written financial statement? Does it not count against our reading of the statute that a debtor who makes a misrepresentation with the formality of a written financial statement may have less to bear than the debtor who commits his fraud by a statement, perhaps oral, about something other than his bank balance? One could answer that the question does have its force, but counter it by returning to the statutory history and asking why Congress failed to place a requirement of reasonable reliance in § 523(a)(2)(A) if it meant all debtors to be in the same boat. But there may be a better answer, tied to the peculiar potential of financial statements to be misused not just by debtors, but by creditors who know this bankruptcy law. The House Report on the Act suggests that Congress wanted to moderate the burden on individuals who submitted false financial statements, not because lies about financial condition are less blameworthy than others, but because the relative equities might be affected by practices of consumer finance companies, which sometimes have encouraged such falsity by their borrowers for the very purpose of insulating their own claims from discharge.[13] The answer softens the ostensible anomaly.

## VI

In this case, the Bankruptcy Court applied a reasonable person test entailing a duty to investigate. The court stated that

> "the case law establishes an objective test, and that is what would be reasonable for a prudent man to do under those circumstances. At a minimum, a prudent man, I think, would have asked his attorney, could he transfer it without my consent? And the answer would have to be yes, and then the next question would be, well, let's see if he's done it? And those questions simply were not asked, and I don't think on balance that was reasonable reliance."

Because the Bankruptcy Court's requirement of reasonableness clearly exceeds the demand of justifiable reliance that we hold to apply under § 523(a)(2)(A), we vacate the judgment and remand the case for proceedings consistent with this opinion.[14]

---

[13] "It is a frequent practice for consumer finance companies to take a list from each loan applicant of other loans or debts that the applicant has outstanding. While the consumer finance companies use these statements in evaluating the credit risk, very often the statements are used as a basis for a false financial statement exception to discharge. The forms that the applicant fills out often have too little space for a complete list of debts. Frequently, a loan applicant is instructed by a loan officer to list only a few or only the most important of his debts. Then, at the bottom of the form, the phrase 'I have no other debts' is either printed on the form, or the applicant is instructed to write the phrase in his own handwriting." H.R.Rep. No. 95–595, pp. 130–131.

[14] Justice Breyer would not remand, for essentially two reasons: in substance the Bankruptcy Court applied the right standard, looking to the individual capacity of Mr. Field in testing whether the Fields relied at all; and the Fields do not deserve a remand, having failed to get their own terminology right below and having no real prospect of anything but needless expense even if there is a remand. The first reason takes a bit of kind reading, since the Bankruptcy Judge spoke in terms of an objective standard and expressly found that the Fields had in fact relied, however imprudently. The

## NOTES

**1.** In concurring, Justice Ginsburg questioned whether the debt in question was actually "obtained by" the alleged fraud, as required by § 523(a)(2). The subsequent fraud could not have caused the Fields to grant the credit to Mans represented by the promissory note of an earlier date. The requisite causation is present only if some form of grant of credit took place after the misrepresentation was made. Thus, one issue the bankruptcy court should decide on remand is whether the Fields' failure to invoke the due-on-sale clause (because they didn't know it had been violated) amounted to an extension of credit within the meaning of the statute.

In dissent, Justice Breyer thought the case should not have been remanded, for the facts show that the bankruptcy judge got the result that would have obtained under the correct justifiable reliance standard. Mr. Fields was in touch with the development project, had discussed the project with Mans over the years and had been told that De Felice had been on the premises claiming to be "the new owner." Under the justifiable reliance standard, Field should have asked more questions, not because of any general duty to investigate, but because of the particular circumstances of the case. Mr. Field had learned enough to serve as a warning that he had been deceived. Justice Breyer concluded : (i) the majority opinion correctly cleared up the issue of the standard of reliance on which the circuits had been divided; (ii) in holding that the debt was dischargeable, the bankruptcy court got the right result even under the "new" standard; (iii) thus there was no reason to require the parties to spend more money on further proceedings.

**2.** On remand, the initial bankruptcy judge recused himself and the new judge ruled that the Fields had justifiably relied upon the misrepresentation of Mans and entered judgment declaring his debt to the Fields nondischargeable. 200 B.R. 293 (Bankr.D.N.H.1996). Mans appealed to the Bankruptcy Appellate Panel which reversed on the ground that Justice Ginsburg, in her concurring opinion, pointed out had been left open, that is, whether the debt had been "obtained by" the fraud. 210 B.R. 1 (1st Cir.B.A.P. 1997). The BAP held that the requirement in § 523(a)(2) that "any debt * * * for money, property, services, or an extension, renewal, or refinancing of credit, to the extent obtained by. . . false pretenses, a false representation, or actual fraud" had not been met because Fields' failure to accelerate the debt was not the equivalent of an extension of that debt. Id. at 5. The First Circuit disagreed and held that Mans's fraudulent concealment that a sale had occurred frustrated the Fields' option to accelerate the

---

second may indicate that we would have been justified in denying certiorari, but after taking the case and declaring the correct standard in response to the Fields' argument in this Court, we think they are entitled to decide how Pyrrhic a victory to declare.

debt and amounted to an involuntary extension of credit induced by fraud. 157 F.3d 35 (1st Cir.1998).

## PROBLEMS

**1.** Seller sold a machine to Buyer for $200,000 to be paid for in installment payments. Seller reserved a security interest in the machine. When Buyer defaulted with $100,000 still owing, Seller sued Buyer for the unpaid indebtedness in state court. While suit was pending, Seller transferred ownership of the machine to his sister, Debby, for $10. In "buying" the property, it is clear that Debby willingly colluded with Buyer to frustrate Seller's collection efforts. After Seller joined Debby as a defendant in his suit, she filed in bankruptcy. Is Seller's claim against Debby nondischargeable under either § 523(a)(2)(A) ("actual fraud") or § 523(a)(6) ("willful and malicious injury")? The facts are based on *McClellan v. Cantrell*, 217 F.3d 890 (7th Cir.2000).

**2.** The question of overlap among the various provisions of § 523(a) has arisen in a number of cases. The following facts raise this issue. Debtor orally induced Creditor to pay money on his behalf to a construction project by promising to reimburse Creditor soon after. Debtor knew that he had no realistic prospect of repaying the money, and his statements amounted to a false statement of financial condition. Creditor obtained a judgment against Debtor for the amount of the loan and Debtor filed in Chapter 7. Creditor objected to discharge of the debt. Since § 523(a)(2)(B) has a writing requirement, Creditor relied on § 523(a)(6), which has no such requirement. Is that provision applicable in this case? The facts are based on *In re Gulevsky*, 362 F.3d 961 (7th Cir. 2004).

## 6. CREDIT CARD FRAUD

The growth of credit cards issued by financial institutions has been phenomenal. The first bank credit cards were issued in the 1950s. By 2003, VisaUSA had passed the $1 trillion mark in transactions per year; it had reached the $1 billion mark in 1971. Eileen Alt Powell, *Use of "Plastic" Changing Rapidly*, LA Times, Aug. 29, 2003, at C2. Credit cards have been so wildly successful in expanding the volume of consumer credit that they are viewed as posing serious social problems for consumers, particularly in the area of bankruptcy.

Before credit cards, credit was usually given by the creditor only after a face-to-face meeting with the debtor in which the debtor's creditworthiness was assessed. The creditor had complete control over the amount of the credit extension and could assess the debtor's current financial position. This control is substantially lessened in credit card transactions in which the cardholder may use the card to buy goods or obtain cash advances from merchants or banks other than the issuer of the card. Moreover, cardholders may continue to use (indeed increase usage of) their cards after their financial condition has, unknown to the card issuer, worsened. Card issuers have attempted to reduce these risks by imposing limits on the amount the cardholder can charge on a card and by requiring merchants and others honoring cards to seek approval from the card issuer for amounts exceeding specified amounts. Improved information systems offer vendors and lenders more information about cardholders' accounts through credit card networks like VisaUSA or MasterCard International, but these systems provide information only with respect to the account being charged and not the cardholders' other credit card accounts.

Consumers often obtain very large amounts of approved credit by accepting offers of credit cards from several different issuers. Consumers may receive many unsolicited offers from issuers to accept credit cards with pre-approved lines of credit. A frequent element in personal bankruptcy cases is a large amount of debt owing on a number of credit cards that have been used up to or beyond their credit limits. In some instances the cards have been heavily used during the period immediately before the debtor filed in bankruptcy. Courts often characterize such use as a "credit card spree."

Credit card issuers have invoked § 523(a)(2)(A) to challenge the dischargeability of debts incurred by cardholders. A debtor who contracts a debt intending not to pay the debt is guilty of actual fraud. Credit card issuers maintain that actual fraud is also involved in cases in which the card is used by an insolvent cardholder who could not reasonably have believed that repayment was possible. In resisting nondischargeability motions, cardholders assert that no fraud is present in these cases unless the card issuer can prove that the cardholder did not intend to pay at the time the credit card debt was incurred. Some courts see nondischargeability proceedings as attempts by card issuers to cut losses from abnormal credit risks knowingly created by themselves in order to gain greater market share by issuing large numbers of cards without regard to creditworthiness.

The *Hashemi* case that follows reflects the orthodox view of focusing on the intent of the cardholder. In the Note following *Hashemi*, *Ellingsworth* presents a revisionist approach which calls into question whether there is justifiable reliance on the part of the card issuer.


# American Express Travel Related Services Company, Inc. v. Hashemi

United States Court of Appeals, Ninth Circuit, 1996.
104 F.3d 1122.

■ KOZINSKI, Circuit Judge.

Appellant didn't leave home without his American Express cards. In fact, he and his family traveled to Europe in style, and charged it all. On his return, appellant owed American Express more than $60,000, the bulk of which represented charges made during the six-week trip. He promptly filed for bankruptcy, and American Express petitioned to have his debt declared nondischargeable under § 523(a)(2)(A), which precludes discharge of debts obtained through "actual fraud." The bankruptcy court denied appellant's request for a jury trial, ruled the debt nondischargeable and ordered appellant to pay American Express $69,793.67 plus interest. The district court affirmed the bankruptcy court's judgment and Dr. Hashemi appeals again. * * *

* * *

* * * [A]ppellant claims the bankruptcy court erred in finding that he defrauded American Express. Section 523(a)(2)(A) precludes discharge of any debt obtained by "false pretenses, a false representation, or actual fraud." In order to establish a debt's nondischargeability under this section, the creditor must show:

**(1)**   the debtor made. . . representations;

**(2)**   that at the time he knew they were false;

**(3)**   that he made them with the intention and purpose of deceiving the creditor;

**(4)**   that the creditor relied on such representations; [and]

**(5)**   that the creditor sustained the alleged loss and damage as the proximate result of the misrepresentations having been made.

* * * These requirements mirror the elements of common law fraud, see In re Eashai, 87 F.3d 1082, 1087 (9th Cir.1996), and the creditor is required to prove each by a preponderance of the evidence. * * * Appellant contends that American Express failed to establish his intent to defraud, that he made no false representations to American Express, and that if any such representations were made, American Express did not justifiably rely on them.

a. *Fraudulent Intent.* "[A] court may infer the existence of the debtor's intent not to pay if the facts and circumstances of a particular case present a picture of deceptive conduct by the debtor." *In re Eashai*, 87 F.3d at 1087. In *In re Dougherty*, 84 B.R. 653 (9th Cir.B.A.P. 1988), our Bankruptcy Appellate Panel enumerated twelve factors relevant to determining a debtor's intent.[2] These factors are nonexclusive; none is dispositive, nor

---

[2] The factors are: (1) the length of time between the charges and the bankruptcy filing; (2) whether or not an attorney had been consulted concerning the filing of bankruptcy before the charges were made; (3) the number of charges made; (4) the amount of the charges; (5) the financial condition of the debtor at the time the charges were made; (6) whether the charges were above the credit limit of the account; (7) whether the debtor made multiple charges on the same day; (8) whether or not the debtor was employed; (9) the debtor's prospects for employment; (10) the financial sophistication of the debtor; (11) whether there was a sudden change in the debtor's buying habits; and (12) whether the purchases made were luxuries or necessities. * * *

must a debtor's conduct satisfy a minimum number in order to prove fraudulent intent. So long as, on balance, the evidence supports a finding of fraudulent intent, the creditor has satisfied this element. * * * We adopted *Dougherty's* twelve-factor test as the law of the circuit in *In re Eashai*, 87 F.3d at 1087–88.

Applying the test set out in *Dougherty* and *Eashai*, as did the bankruptcy court, there is ample evidence to support the finding that appellant intended to defraud American Express. Appellant made nearly 170 charges totaling more than $60,000 during a six-week trip with his family to France. These charges exceeded appellant's annual income and, even before the trip, appellant already owed more than $300,000 in unsecured credit card debt. Appellant did have one major asset when he made the charges—a one-half ownership interest in an eight-unit condominium project. He claims the purpose of his trip was to borrow money from his mother-in-law to support this real estate venture. This does not explain why appellant stayed in France for six weeks, took his wife and two children with him, took a side-trip to the French Riviera, purchased cosmetics, expensive meals and other luxury items, and ultimately charged almost as much on his credit cards as he claims he planned to borrow. Moreover, while appellant was away, the holder of the second mortgage on his condominium project initiated foreclosure proceedings. This should have alerted appellant that he would not be able to repay his debt by selling his interest in the property. Given these facts, the bankruptcy court could reasonably infer that appellant tried to have a last hurrah at American Express's expense.

b. *False Representations.* Appellant also complains that he never made any fraudulent misrepresentations to American Express because American Express extended him an unlimited line of credit. We rejected the identical argument in *In re Anastas*, 94 F.3d 1280 (9th Cir.1996). Each time a "card holder uses his credit card, he makes a representation that he intends to repay the debt. . . .. When the card holder uses the card without an intent to repay, he has made a fraudulent representation to the card issuer." Id. at 1285. Because the bankruptcy court found that appellant had no intention of repaying his debt, each time he used his cards he made a fraudulent representation to American Express.

c. *Justifiable Reliance.* "[T]he credit card issuer justifiably relies on a representation of intent to repay as long as the account is not in default and any initial investigations into a credit report do not raise red flags that would make reliance unjustifiable." Id. at 1286. At the time appellant began his spending spree, his account was not in default. In fact, he owed American Express only $227. Moreover, appellant himself testified that he had repaid American Express balances of up to $60,000 "numerous times" before. American Express therefore had no reason to question the good faith of appellant's promise to repay. Because American Express provided ample evidence of each element of common law fraud, the bankruptcy court was fully justified in declaring appellant's debt nondischargeable.

\* \* \*

AFFIRMED AND REMANDED.

## NOTES

**1.** In *In re Ellingsworth*, 212 B.R. 326 (Bankr.W.D.Mo.1997), the court held that even if the cardholders misrepresented their intention to repay, the debt was dischargeable because the card issuer did not make an adequate inquiry into their financial position and could not be found to have justifiably relied on their representation to repay. The court was critical of *Hashemi* and characterized the case as follows:

> A woman walks in one day and says she wants to borrow $60,000 on her signature. She willingly fills out a financial statement which shows that she already has $300,000 in unsecured debt, but she needs these additional funds for a business trip. She also shows one asset, a heavily encumbered apartment building that is being foreclosed. Of course, she promises to repay the loan if one is made to her. Would a bank that makes such a loan be found to have justifiably relied on her promise? Of course not. But, what if, instead, the bank made the loan without bothering to ask her basic information about assets, liabilities, and income? And what if she did not make an express promise to repay the loan? Should this bank be allowed to claim that it justifiably relied on her implied promises to pay? One would think not. However, these are the very facts of a recent bankruptcy opinion [*Hashemi*], except that rather than a face to face encounter with a bank officer, the debt was incurred through use of a credit card.

212 B.R. at 329.

*Ellingsworth* involved Debtors who owed over $65,000 in unsecured debts, mostly on 16 credit cards, at the time Issuer offered them a pre-approved card with a $4,000 limit. Debtors used their new card for cash advances after they had "maxed out" on their other cards. When they reached the credit limit, they ceased use of the new card and, without making a single payment on it, filed in bankruptcy. Noting that their monthly obligations far exceeded their income, the court concluded that Debtors knew that they would be unable to repay the $4,000 debt and thus should be considered to have misrepresented their intent to repay.

The Issuer offered Debtors a pre-approved card on the basis of a credit scoring formula that emphasized their history of not defaulting on their debts. Debtors verified by telephone their income and employment. No information was sought about the amount of their liabilities, assets or monthly expenses. A full credit bureau report would have listed their obligations in detail and implied their insolvency. The court concluded that offering a customer a pre-approved credit card without making a full inquiry into the customer's financial status was the equivalent of buying Justice Souter's one-eyed horse in *Field*. If Debtors had applied to a bank for an unsecured loan for $4,000 and had revealed their true financial position on their credit application, the bank could not be held to have justifiably relied on Debtors' promise to repay the loan. Why should credit cards be treated differently?

In a far-ranging discussion of the economics of the credit card business, the court conjectured that even with a six percent charge-off rate credit cards are highly profitable because issuers charge high rates and enjoy a vast customer base. The court observed:

> In their eagerness to capture market share, banks spend little time gathering financial information about their potential credit card customers. Prior to a mass mailing, creditors such as [Issuer] obtain lists from credit bureaus with the names of candidates and a "credit score" for each person on the list. These scores relate generally to past card use, whether the candidate pays the minimum monthly balance on current cards, and whether there are any delinquencies or bankruptcies on record. Car loans, medical bills, and mortgages are not included in the credit score, nor are income, job history, marital status, and assets.

212 B.R. at 330–331.

**2.** In § 1229 of the 2005 Act, Congress reacted to the concerns expressed in *Ellingsworth* with a Sense-of-the-Congress provision noting, gingerly, that "(1) certain lenders may sometimes offer credit to consumers indiscriminately, without taking steps to ensure that consumers are capable of repaying the resulting debt, and in a manner which may encourage certain consumers to accumulate additional debt; and (2) resulting consumer debt may increasingly be a major contributing factor to consumer insolvency." The Board of Governors of the Federal Reserve System was directed to conduct a study of this problem, make a report and issue regulations prescribing additional disclosures for consumers and take any other appropriate action consistent with its statutory authority. What kind of disclosure do you think would help credit card users? What "other appropriate action" should be taken?

**3.** Credit card issuers significantly gained ground on cardholders on the discharge front in the 2005 Act by an amendment to § 523(a)(2)(C) that presumes nondischargeable all consumer debts to a single creditor aggregating more than $500 (formerly $1,225) incurred on or within 90 (formerly 60) days of filing if for "luxury goods or services." § 523 (a)(2(C)(i)(I). The quoted term "does not include goods or services reasonably necessary for the support or maintenance of the debtor or a dependent of the debtor." § 523 (a)(2(C)(ii)(II). There is no positive definition of "luxury;" the extent to which goods and services not reasonably necessary for support or maintenance should be deemed luxury goods or services is not clear. Cash advances aggregating more than $750 (formerly $1,225) obtained on or within 70 (formerly 60) days before filing are presumed nondischargeable, but only if made in an open end credit transaction, which is the kind of transaction used for cash advances on credit cards. So long as the loan transaction is an extension of consumer credit, that is, the loan was obtained for a personal, family or household purpose, there are no limits on the use of the loan proceeds. Thus, the original, sensible concept that card issuers deserve some protection against the excesses of "credit card sprees" that allow debtors to acquire expensive "luxury goods" on the eve of bankruptcy, now, as amended, potentially applies to the huge volume of consumer sales transactions made by use of credit cards within three months before filing and cash advances made pursuant to credit cards 70 days before filing. This provision enhances the procedural advantage enjoyed by credit card issuers described in the following Note.

**4.** Since *Hashemi* and *Ellingsworth*, a number of cases have been decided on the nondischargeability problem, roughly divided between the views of these two cases, with no clear pattern prevailing. *See In re Mercer*, 246 F.3d 391 (5th Cir. 2001), in which there were *three* views on the issue within the *en banc* court itself. The National Bankruptcy Review Commission Report viewed the law governing the dischargeability of credit card debts as chaotic and unfair. NBRC Rep. at 180–196. Creditors are increasingly challenging discharge of credit card debts on the basis of fraud. Impoverished debtors lack the resources to litigate the issue, and the law is so unsettled that it is difficult for debtors to avail themselves of the remedy offered by § 523(d) to force creditors to pay costs and attorney's fees in cases in which the creditors' challenge to discharge fails "if the court finds that the position of the creditor was not substantially justified." This is true because in the muddle of conflicting case law on the subject creditors can find some legal justification for almost any position they may take. NBRC Rep. at 193.

**5.** Some consumers abuse credit cards: They apply for cards from multiple grantors with similar credit limits, thereby greatly amplifying their capacity to obtain more credit than they can repay. When their cards are maxed out, they apply for additional cards from other grantors. They continue to use their cards after their credit position has weakened, including heavy use in the period immediately before bankruptcy. These practices are well known to credit card issuers; why do they tolerate them? In the early years of credit cards, information systems were so primitive that information about consumer use was virtually unobtainable. Even after the arrival of electronic data retrieval, timely information was difficult and expensive to obtain. This is no longer true; new technology allows lenders to get *daily* reports on their customers from the major credit bureaus. Ron Lieber, *Careful, Your Bank Is Watching*, Wall St. J., July 22, 2003, at D1, notes that credit grantors can receive daily reports on when customers are applying for new credit cards or new loans, when their credit cards are maxed out, how much credit they are using, and whether they have fallen behind on insurance premiums or other bills. How does this greatly enhanced monitoring capacity on the part of card issuers affect your views on *Hashemi, Ellingsworth* and the Commission Report, which proposed allowing debtors to discharge credit card debts that did not exceed the debtor's credit limit unless the debts were incurred within 30 days of bankruptcy?

## 7. FINE, PENALTY OR FORFEITURE

### a. Punitive Damages

"Claim" is a very broad term designed to encompass virtually all rights to payment without regard to the identity of the entity having the right to payment or the reason why the law creates the right. Some rights to payment are created in order to punish the person against whom the right can be asserted. Examples are causes of action for punitive damages in a tort case or for treble damages under the antitrust laws. Another example is a civil penalty imposed by a state or the United States under the tax laws. These rights to payment are specially treated under the Bankruptcy Code. If an insolvent debtor is in Chapter 7, and the holder of a punitive right to payment is entitled to pro rata distribution of the estate along with holders of compensatory rights of payment, the punitive claim would in effect be paid from the pockets of other creditors rather than from the pocket of the debtor. This inequity is prevented by § 726(a)(4), which subordinates a punitive and multiple damage claim or a claim for a "fine, penalty or forfeiture" to the extent the claim is not "compensation for actual pecuniary loss suffered by the holder of such claim." The result is that punitive damages claimants seldom receive anything from the bankruptcy estate. Hence, unless punitive damages debts are nondischargeable under § 523, a Chapter 7 filing effectively defeats these claims in most cases.

The circuits are divided over the issue of whether punitive damages are made nondischargeable by § 523(a). Courts agreed that § 523(a)(6) ("any debt * * * for willful and malicious injury by the debtor to another entity or to the property of another entity") clearly encompassed punitive damages, e.g., *In re Bugna*, 33 F.3d 1054 (9th Cir.1994). But § 523(a)(2)(A) ("any debt * * * for money, property, services * * * to the extent obtained by * * * fraud") is drafted in a manner that led some courts to hold that the portion of a damages award rendered nondischargeable is limited to the value of the "money, property, services." Hence, the amount of the damages award allocable to punitive damages remains dischargeable. This view gained some support from the maxim that, in order to protect the debtor's interest in a fresh start, exceptions from discharge should be narrowly construed. Other courts, in the belief that Congress could not have intended such a distinction, held that all liability arising from the fraud, whether in the form of compensatory or punitive damages, should be nondischargeable. The interest in giving debtors a fresh start applies to honest debtors and not perpetrators of fraud.

The issue was resolved in *Cohen v. de la Cruz*, 523 U.S. 213 (1998), which involved the following facts: a landlord fraudulently overcharged his tenants $31,282 in excess rents; pursuant to the provisions of the state consumer fraud act, judgment was entered for the amount of the excess rents and treble damages. The landlord filed in bankruptcy and contended that only the compensatory portion of the damages award was nondischargeable. The Court held that once it is established that property has been obtained by fraud, any claim arising therefrom—punitive as well as compensatory—is nondischargeable. The issue decided in *Cohen*, whether the scope of the discharge is broad enough to encompass punitive damage claims, does not affect other creditors holding dischargeable claims, but it does bear on other creditors with nondischargeable claims who must compete for payment out of the debtor's future earnings and after-acquired property.

### b. Criminal Penalties

The status of rights to payment arising out of criminal proceedings is not completely clear. A crime may be punished by a judgment of the court providing for a fine or imprisonment or both. If a fine is imposed, the judgment represents a right to payment in favor of the state against the criminal. If the fine is not paid the judgment usually may be satisfied by imprisonment in lieu of payment. The state law might also provide that the judgment may be enforced in the same manner as a civil judgment. *See, e.g.* Cal. Penal Code § 1214(a) (West 2004). Thus, the obligation to pay a fine imposed in a criminal proceeding would seem to fall within the definition of "debt" in § 101(13). In any event it is clear under § 523(a)(7) that an obligation to pay a fine imposed in a criminal proceeding is not dischargeable in bankruptcy.

Conviction of a crime may give rise to other rights to payment that have some similarity to fines but which also differ in that they are payable for the benefit of someone other than the state. For example, if the crime resulted in an injury or loss to a victim, the culprit may be ordered to make restitution to the victim. Normally, the restitution is payable to the state for the benefit of the victim. Does the restitution order give status to the state as a creditor having a claim in bankruptcy if the culprit files a petition in bankruptcy? Is the obligation to make restitution a debt? If it is a debt, is it made nondischargeable by § 523(a)(7)? These questions were considered in *Kelly v. Robinson*, 479 U.S. 36 (1986). Debtor pleaded guilty to larceny resulting from wrongful receipt of welfare benefits. She was sentenced to a suspended prison term and was then placed on probation. As a condition to probation, she was ordered to make restitution of the welfare benefits in monthly installments over the probation period. Three months later she filed a petition in Chapter 7 bankruptcy. She listed the restitution obligation as a debt. The State of Connecticut, which was entitled to receive the restitution payments, did not file a claim in the bankruptcy and did not oppose discharge. It took the position that discharge did not affect the restitution debt. Debtor was granted a discharge, but the bankruptcy court held that the restitution obligation was excepted from discharge under § 523(a)(7).

The Second Circuit reversed the bankruptcy court's determination that the restitution obligation was excepted from discharge. It held that the obligation was a debt under § 101 and that § 523(a)(7) did not apply because the restitution order was intended as "compensation for actual pecuniary loss" of the State of Connecticut. The Supreme Court reversed. It relied on the fact that under the Bankruptcy Act fines, forfeitures and obligations to pay restitution were not allowable claims and thus were not subject to discharge. The Supreme Court also relied on a "fundamental policy against federal interference with state criminal prosecutions." To allow discharge of an obligation to pay restitution in a criminal case could interfere with the ability of the state courts to choose the best combination of imprisonment, fine or restitution to further the rehabilitative and deterrent goals of the state criminal justice system. In the Court's view the phrase "compensation for actual pecuniary loss" does not apply to restitution orders because compensation of the victim for loss is only an incidental result of a restitution order. The primary function of the order is to carry out the penal goals of the state. In the course of the opinion the Court expressed "serious doubts" whether criminal penalties were debts within § 101, but found it unnecessary to decide the issue.

The doubts about whether criminal penalties were debts were removed in *Pennsylvania Department of Public Welfare v. Davenport*, 495 U.S. 552 (1990), in which the Court held that a restitution obligation imposed as a condition of probation in a state criminal action is a debt for bankruptcy purposes and was dischargeable in Chapter 13 under § 1328(a), which did not except fines or penalties from discharge. Congress moved with rare alacrity in adding § 1328(a)(3), which excepted from discharge any debt "for restitution included in a sentence on the debtor's conviction of a crime." In 1994, § 1328(a)(3) was amended to include criminal fines.

### c.   Restitution Settlements

Restitution settlements are common in fraud and embezzlement cases. How are these agreements treated in bankruptcy? Debtor embezzled $100,000 while working as Creditor's bookkeeper. Creditor demanded restitution but Debtor had already spent the money. Ultimately a settlement was reached in which Debtor executed a note to Creditor for $75,000, in consideration for which Creditor executed a general release and covenant not to sue Debtor for any obligations other than her obligation as maker of the note. When Debtor filed in Chapter 7 a few months later, Creditor contended that the debt on the note was nondischargeable under § 523(a)(4). On these facts, the court in *Matter of West*, 22 F.3d 775 (7th Cir.1994), held the debt to be dischargeable on the ground that the obligation was based on the note rather than on the fraudulent conduct that gave rise to the note. The court relied on the fact that Creditor had given Debtor a full release; in the view of the court, the release extinguished the underlying debt based on the embezzlement. In *United States v. Spicer*, 57 F.3d 1152 (D.C.Cir.1995), another full release case, the court disagreed on the ground that the settlement obligation was wholly attributable to Debtor's admittedly fraudulent conduct. The Supreme Court resolved the issue in *Archer v. Warner*, 538 U.S. 314 (2003), in which the Court concluded that the settlement debt arose out of fraud and was nondischargeable.

### 8. TAXES

The "fresh start" policy of bankruptcy law must be balanced against the government's insatiable need for tax revenue. We shall not delve into the complex rules regarding the dischargeability of the numerous varieties of taxes. A brief treatment of the income tax demonstrates how the Bankruptcy Code balances the policies of discharge against those of protection of the public fisc. Before 1966, tax debt was not dischargeable in bankruptcy; the IRS could allow unpaid taxes to accumulate and, limited only by the statute of limitations, collect these taxes from the debtor's bankruptcy estate. By the time of the 1978 Act, a compromise had been reached in which only tax debts for which the return was due three years or less before the petition was filed were nondischargeable. This forced the IRS to act within the three-year period to assess the taxes and obtain a lien that would be nondischargeable in bankruptcy for tax debts without respect to the three-year lookback provision. Under the current law this policy is implemented by § 523(a)(1)(A), which excepts from discharge income taxes, among others, for which a priority is given under § 507(a)(8), meaning income taxes for which returns were due within three years of the debtor's bankruptcy. Section 523(a)(1)(B) excepts from discharge taxes whenever due for which the debtor either filed no return or filed a return late and within two years of bankruptcy. Hence, a debtor who has not been filing returns cannot avoid nondischargeability by filing shortly before bankruptcy.

In *Young v. United States*, 535 U.S. 43 (2002), the Court held that the three-year lookback period is tolled during the pendency of a debtor's Chapter 13 case. Although § 507(a)(8) says nothing about tolling, the Court held that equitable tolling is appropriate when a debtor files a Chapter 13 case during the three-year lookback period, thereby precluding the IRS from proceeding to collect the tax, owing to the automatic stay of § 362. A tax loophole would result if a debtor remains in Chapter 13 until the three-year period has run on an unpaid tax and then voluntarily dismisses the case and files in Chapter 7. By equitably tolling the three-year lookback period while the debtor was in bankruptcy, the Court closed the loophole.

Controversy has surrounded the meaning of § 523(a)(1)(C), which excepts from discharge taxes whenever due "with respect to which the debtor made a fraudulent return or willfully attempted in any manner to evade or defeat such a tax." How would you apply this provision to the facts in the following Problem?

## PROBLEM

The IRS contended that Debtor's income tax for which a return was due more than three years before bankruptcy was nondischargeable under § 523(a)(1)(C) in each of the following situations. In each case, Debtor filed a timely and accurate return but, although she was fully aware of her legal obligation, did not pay the tax.

> **Case #1.** Debtor did not pay the tax because she had no money beyond that required to support her and her family at a subsistence level.

> **Case #2.** Debtor did not pay the tax because she needed the money to keep her business going. She chose to use the money to buy supplies and pay her employees. By this choice she was able to avoid closing the business and impoverishing her employees.

> **Case #3.** Debtor used the money to buy a residence with her husband as tenants in the entirety. Under relevant state law, assets held in tenancy in the entirety are exempt from levy without a judgment against both owners.

Debtor contended that the tax claims were dischargeable in all three cases because, under the literal wording of § 523(a)(1)(C), the phrase "attempted in any manner to evade or defeat such tax" does not imply attempts to evade or defeat *payment* of the tax. Since mere nonpayment of taxes should not make taxes nondischargeable under § 523(a)(1)(C), the language of the statute must require the debtor to engage in affirmative acts other than nonpayment of taxes in order to establish the exception. This view was taken by *In re Haas*, 48 F.3d 1153 (11th Cir.1995). But in *In re Griffith*, 206 F.3d 1389 *en banc* (11th Cir. 2000), the Eleventh Circuit overruled *Haas*, and reinterpreted the quoted language to mean: (1) mere nonpayment of taxes is insufficient to establish the § 523(a)(1)(C) exception; but (2) tax debts are nondischargeable if the debtor engages in affirmative acts seeking to evade or defeat the collection of taxes. How would you apply this test to the three cases? What if the debtor had failed to file a return? *See In re Fretz*, 244 F.3d 1323 (11th Cir.2001).

## D. PROTECTION OF THE DISCHARGE

Under § 727 the debtor in a Chapter 7 case is granted a discharge from all prebankruptcy debts. But the effect of the discharge may be uncertain because specific debts described in § 523 are excepted from the discharge. As we have seen, the issue of whether a particular debt is or is not dischargeable in many cases cannot be determined except by a fact-finding process. Suppose a creditor who has a prebankruptcy claim waits until after the bankruptcy case has been closed and then brings an action on the claim in a state court. This was a frequent scenario under the Bankruptcy Act before 1970. Under that regime, if the claim of the creditor had been discharged in bankruptcy, the discharge was simply an affirmative defense to the subsequent state court action that the debtor had to assert. A debtor who had just gone through bankruptcy might not have the resources to bear the litigation expenses involved in asserting the defense. Or, the debtor might erroneously believe that there was no need to defend because the debt had already been discharged. If the debtor did not assert the defense it was waived, and any subsequent judgment was conclusive on the question of liability. Thus, a creditor was sometimes able to get a judgment on a discharged debt even in cases in which there was no doubt about dischargeability.

Even if the debtor defended the state court action, the question of whether the claim was or was not discharged was determined by the state court rather than the bankruptcy court. In the state court the creditor sometimes found a forum more favorable to debt collection than to the bankruptcy policy of providing a fresh start for debtors. But apart from any question of bias, determination of dischargeability in the state court may have been less efficient than having the bankruptcy court determine all matters regarding the bankruptcy in the original bankruptcy proceedings. Moreover, uniform application of bankruptcy policies was not furthered by state court adjudication of these questions.

In some cases a creditor was able to collect a discharged debt without resort to judicial process. A creditor dealing with an unsophisticated debtor could sometimes induce payment by misrepresentations about the effect of discharge or by simply dunning the debtor or threatening to take legal action. In 1970 the Bankruptcy Act was amended to address some of the problems just outlined. These provisions were modified and expanded and became part of the Bankruptcy Code as § 524(a)(1) and (2) and § 523(c). *See* Charles Jordan Tabb, *The Law of Bankruptcy* § 10.30 (1997).

The National Bankruptcy Review Commission found that creditor misconduct in violation of the discharge injunction of § 524(a)(2) was so widespread that it recommended in § 1.3.2, NBRC Rep. at 161:

> An additional subsection should be added to section 524 to provide that the court shall grant judgment in favor of an individual who has received a discharge under section 727, 1141, 1228, or 1328 of this title for costs and attorney's fees, plus treble damages, from a creditor who threatens, files suit, or otherwise seeks to collect any debt that was discharged in bankruptcy and was not the subject of an agreement in accordance with subsections (c) and (d) of section 524.

Congress did not respond to the Commission's recommendation in the 2005 Act but did amend § 524 to add one mildly pro-consumer provision and one sensible pro-creditor provision. Section 524(i) provides that the willful failure on the part of a creditor to credit payments received under a confirmed plan (this includes plans under Chapters 11, 12 and 13) is a violation of the injunction under § 524(a)(2), but only if this failure "caused material injury to the debtor." Section 524(j) addresses concerns that home mortgage lenders have about how to deal with debtors who have been discharged but who remain on the land. Do such lenders violate § 524(a)(2) if they send the debtor notices requesting payments and explaining the consequences if the debtor falls behind in her payments? Section 524(j) provides a safe harbor that allows home mortgage lenders to deal with discharged debtors in the ordinary manner to induce them to keep their payments current. Certainly mortgagees can communicate with debtors about the consequences of falling into default.

## PROBLEMS

**1.** Debtor owed $4,000 to Finance Co. on an unsecured loan. Debtor filed in bankruptcy and scheduled the debt to Finance Co. Debtor received a § 727(b) discharge. Finance Co. did not file a bankruptcy claim or otherwise take part in the bankruptcy because Debtor had no nonexempt assets and Finance Co. had received notice pursuant to Rule 2002(e) that it was unnecessary to file a claim. After the bankruptcy case was closed Finance Co. brought an action on the loan debt in a state court. Debtor pleaded the discharge in bankruptcy. Finance Co. alleged that the loan was obtained by Debtor by written fraudulent statements concerning Debtor's financial condition and was therefore nondischargeable under § 523(a)(2). Debtor moved for summary judgment. What result? § 523(c)(1); Bankruptcy Rule 4007(c). Can Finance Co. be cited for contempt? § 524(a)(2).

**2.** Assume the facts in Problem 1 except for the following changes: The loan was an educational loan described in § 523(a)(8) and the creditor was a university. Debtor alleged that repayment of the loan would impose an undue hardship on Debtor. Can the state court dispose of the case? Can the bankruptcy court dispose of the case? § 350(b) and Bankruptcy Rule 4007(a) and (b).

**3.** Suppose in Problem 1 that Debtor did not answer the complaint and that Finance Co. was given a default judgment. Finance Co. then garnished Debtor's wages to pay the judgment. What are the rights of Debtor? § 524(a)(1) and (2).

**4.** Suppose in Problem 1 that Finance Co. took no legal action against Debtor. Instead, it obtained voluntary repayment of the debt by Debtor by convincing Debtor that the debt was not discharged in bankruptcy because of Debtor's fraudulent statements. What are Debtor's rights? § 524(a)(2) and (f).

## E. DISCRIMINATION AGAINST DEBTORS

*Perez v. Campbell*, 402 U.S. 637 (1971), involved an Arizona statute that suspended the debtor's driver license for nonpayment of a judgment for damages resulting from an automobile accident. The statute specifically provided that a discharge in bankruptcy of the judgment debt did not relieve the judgment debtor from the effects of the statute. The Arizona statute was based on a uniform act adopted in most of the states. A divided

Court held that the statute was unconstitutional under the Supremacy Clause. The majority opinion described the issue as "whether a state statute that protects judgment creditors from 'financially irresponsible persons' is in conflict with a federal statute that gives discharged debtors a new start 'unhampered by the pressure and discouragement of preexisting debt.'" 402 U.S. at 649. The majority opinion saw the principal purpose of the statute to be the protection of the public from "financial hardship which may result from the use of automobiles by financially irresponsible persons." *Id.* at 644. It stated that the "sole emphasis of the [statute] is one of providing leverage for the collection of damages from drivers who either admit that they are at fault or are adjudged negligent." *Id.* at 646–647. Thus, the decision may be merely an example of invalidation of an indirect attempt to force payment of a discharged debt. But from this case there has developed a broader policy prohibiting certain kinds of discrimination against bankrupts. The policy is embodied in § 525. Subsection (a) relates to action by governmental units (§ 101). It codifies the result of *Perez*, but the focus of the provision is against discrimination rather than coercion to pay a discharged debt. It expands protection substantially beyond *Perez* in protecting the debtor from loss of employment as a result of bankruptcy. The reason for this provision is obvious. The most dramatic frustration of the fresh start that discharge gives the debtor is to deny the debtor employment that may be vital to that fresh start.

Before 1984, and except for § 366, there were no provisions preventing discrimination against bankrupts by nongovernmental action unless the discrimination was an attempt to enforce payment of a discharged debt prohibited by § 524(a)(2). Although *Perez* might be read to protect a debtor from discriminatory state action that frustrates the fresh start, that case has no application to purely private action. In *McLellan v. Mississippi Power & Light Co.*, 545 F.2d 919 (5th Cir.1977), a case arising under the Bankruptcy Act, the court held that a private employer could fire an employee for violating company policy by filing a voluntary petition in bankruptcy. The court stated:

> We find no law which restrains [the employer] from firing an employee because he has filed a petition in voluntary bankruptcy. No statutory provision shields a bankrupt from later economic consequences visited upon him by private individuals, whether acting alone or in concert. A thorough examination of the Bankruptcy Act and its legislative history discloses no explicit provision or intent to prohibit discriminatory action against an individual on the basis of his declaring bankruptcy. In addition, no such Congressional intent can be reasonably inferred from the statute as it is now enacted. Nor can such a right be legitimately implied from the Constitution's Bankruptcy Clause itself. As has been pointed out, that empowering provision speaks only in discretionary terms and does not afford any individual a right which Congress has not specifically legislated.

545 F.2d at 929. In 1984, Subsection (b) of § 525 was added. By virtue of that amendment a bankrupt is now protected from discrimination in employment by private as well as public employers.

## PROBLEM

David registered with an employment agency that sent him to Bank to be interviewed for a position as a teller. There he was interviewed by a hiring officer who asked a number of questions about his credit history. When David disclosed that he had filed for Chapter 7 bankruptcy five years before, the hiring officer abruptly terminated the interview, saying: "I know you'll understand, but we can't hire bankrupts here at the Bank." David sued Bank for violation of § 525(b), but the court, comparing the language of § 525(b) with that of § 525(a), held for Bank. Do you agree with the court? *See Fiorani v. CACI*, 192 B.R. 401 (E.D.Va.1996). *But see Leary v. Warnaco, Inc.*, 251 B.R. 656 (S.D.N.Y.2000).

———

Since enactment of § 525, the clash has continued between state statutes whose purpose is to impose financial responsibility on motor vehicle operators and the bankruptcy laws whose purpose it is to free debtors from the onus of debts they cannot pay. *Duffey v. Dollison*, 734 F.2d 265 (6th Cir.1984), concerned the constitutionality of an Ohio statute relating to judgments for damages arising from motor vehicle accidents. Under that statute, if the judgment debtor does not satisfy the judgment within 30 days, the court, upon request of the judgment creditor, must forward the judgment to the Registrar of Motor Vehicles who must suspend the judgment debtor's driving privileges for seven years. The suspension can be vacated upon proof that the judgment was stayed or satisfied and upon filing of proof of financial responsibility, which usually means filing a certificate of liability insurance. The judgment debtor whose driving privileges have been suspended does not have to satisfy the judgment if the debt has been discharged in bankruptcy, but whether or not the judgment is satisfied the debtor must file proof of financial responsibility to regain driving privileges. Thus, the requirement of filing proof of financial responsibility applies alike to a debtor who has paid the judgment debt and a debtor who has discharged the debt in bankruptcy. In sustaining the statute, the court pointed out that Ohio could have required proof of financial responsibility as a condition of granting driving privilege initially. The state can validly require that only financially responsible drivers be allowed to use the public highways. The one-bite approach, which requires proof of future financial responsibility only after a driver has demonstrated lack of financial responsibility by failure to pay a judgment, is equally valid. In both cases the same state policy is being carried out and in neither case are bankrupts singled out for special treatment.

## Toth v. Michigan State Housing Development Authority

United States Court of Appeals, Sixth Circuit, 1998.
136 F.3d 477.

■  ALAN E. NORRIS, Circuit Judge.

Plaintiff Sue Toth appeals from the district court's grant of summary judgment to the Michigan State Housing Development Authority and two of its officers in an action alleging discrimination in violation of § 525(a) of the Bankruptcy Code. She contends that the denial of her application for a low income home improvement loan based upon a recent discharge in bankruptcy was contrary to the language of § 525(a) of the Code. Plaintiff further claims that the violation of § 525(a) gives rise to a 42 U.S.C. § 1983 claim. Because we conclude that § 525(a) does not forbid consideration of a prior bankruptcy in post-discharge credit arrangements with state entities, we affirm.

### I.

Plaintiff received a discharge in bankruptcy in June 1995. Several months later, she applied to the Michigan State Housing Development Authority ("MSHDA") for a home improvement loan. That agency administers a home improvement loan program of the United States Department of Housing and Urban Development designed to assist eligible low income participants. Thereafter, in November 1995, MSHDA notified plaintiff that her loan application had been denied due to the agency's policy of requiring at least three years to lapse after the date of a bankruptcy discharge before a loan application will be processed.

Plaintiff filed suit in February 1996 in United States District Court for the Western District of Michigan alleging that MSHDA and two of its officials unlawfully discriminated against her in violation of § 525(a) of the Bankruptcy Code. She sued the two officials, James Logue III, executive director of MSHDA, and Robert Brown, manager of MSHDA's home improvement loan program, in both their official and individual capacities. Plaintiff contended that § 525(a) prohibits a state's denial of a low-interest home improvement loan based solely upon a prior discharge in bankruptcy, and that the violation of § 525(a) gave rise to a cause of action under 42 U.S.C § 1983.

The parties consented to the exercise of jurisdiction by a magistrate judge, who issued the district court's opinion and order holding that the court had jurisdiction over the case notwithstanding the Eleventh Amendment, and granted defendants' motion for summary judgment on the merits.

### II.

The primary issue raised by this appeal is whether the denial by MSHDA of a home improvement loan solely because the applicant had been discharged in bankruptcy within three years of the loan application violates § 525(a) of the Bankruptcy Code. Plaintiff asserts that the strictures of § 525(a) apply to the home improvement loan program operated by the Michigan agency to prohibit implementation of the agency's policy to deny her a loan based solely upon her prior discharge in bankruptcy. We disagree.

**A.**

Section 525(a) provides:

**(a)** . . . a governmental unit may not deny, revoke, suspend, or refuse to renew a license, permit, charter, franchise, *or other similar grant to*, condition such a grant to, *discriminate with respect to such a grant* against, deny employment to, terminate the employment of, or discriminate with respect to employment against, a person that is or has been a debtor under this title or a bankrupt or a debtor under the Bankruptcy Act, or another person with whom such bankrupt or debtor has been associated, *solely because* such bankrupt or debtor is or has been a debtor under this title or a bankrupt or debtor under the Bankruptcy Act, has been insolvent before the commencement of the case under this title, or during the case but before the debtor is granted or denied a discharge, or has not paid a debt that is dischargeable in the case under this title or that was discharged under the Bankruptcy Act.

To the extent that it may apply to the circumstances of this case, § 525(a) prohibits a governmental entity from denying a "license, permit, charter, franchise, or other similar grant" or discriminating "with respect to such a grant" solely on the basis that the person seeking such a boon has been a bankrupt.

**B.**

One could, of course, argue that the scope of § 525(a)'s "other similar grant" language should be construed broadly, relying upon the general policy underlying bankruptcy, that a debtor should be able to have a "fresh start," to preclude conduct that would frustrate that policy. However, the courts of appeals that have approached the question have read the statute's reach narrowly, focusing upon the specific language of the statute. See, *e.g., Watts v. Pennsylvania Hous. Fin. Co.*, 876 F.2d 1090, 1093–94 (3d Cir.1989); *In re Goldrich*, 771 F.2d 28, 30 (2d Cir.1985). *Watts* involved an emergency mortgage assistance program designed by the State of Pennsylvania to prevent imminent mortgage foreclosures by providing for loans to distressed borrowers in the form of direct payments to their mortgage lenders, keeping their mortgages current. When plaintiff borrowers filed for bankruptcy, the program suspended these payments for the duration of the Bankruptcy Code's automatic stay. Plaintiffs contended this suspension violated § 525(a). In response, the court of appeals noted that a loan from the Pennsylvania program simply was not a "license, permit, charter [or] franchise," and that since those terms "are in the nature of indicia of authority from a governmental unit to. . . pursue some endeavor," the term "similar grant" should be given the same meaning. *Watts*, 876 F.2d at 1093. Similarly, the court in *In re Goldrich* concluded that § 525(a) did not prohibit consideration of prior bankruptcies in credit decisions, since "the language of section 525 may not properly be stretched so far beyond its plain terms." *Goldrich*, 771 F.2d at 29. We agree with the analysis employed by our sister courts.

The items enumerated in the statute—licenses, permits, charters, and franchises—are benefits conferred by government that are unrelated to the extension of credit. They reveal that the target of § 525(a) is government's role as a gatekeeper in determining who may pursue certain livelihoods. It is directed at governmental entities that might be inclined to discriminate against former bankruptcy debtors in a manner that frustrates the "fresh start" policy of the Bankruptcy Code, by denying them permission to pursue certain occupations or endeavors. The intent of Congress incorporated into the plain language of § 525(a) should not be transformed by employing an expansive understanding of the "fresh start" policy to insulate a debtor from all adverse consequences of a bankruptcy filing or discharge. A reckoning of an applicant's financial responsibility is an essential part of any lender's evaluation of a post-discharge application for a loan or extension of credit.

Accordingly, the district court correctly concluded that plaintiff failed to make out a case of discrimination under § 525(a), since that section does not include within its purview either the extension of credit by home loan programs of the nature involved in this case, or the specific conduct of defendants about which plaintiff complains.

\* \* \*

## V.

The judgment of the district court is affirmed.

## NOTES

**1.** The court cites *In re Goldrich*, 771 F.2d 28 (2d Cir.1985), as one of the cases supporting its view that § 525(a) should be read narrowly. In that case Debtor defaulted on a student loan guaranteed by an agency of New York State that has a statute providing that no student in default under a guaranteed student loan is eligible for another guaranteed loan so long as the default is not cured. The court held that a grant of credit is not included in the phrase "license, permit, charter, franchise, or other similar grant" appearing in § 525(a). In 1994, § 525(c) was added which, according to the Section-by-Section Description § 313, 140 Cong. Rec. H10771 (Oct. 4, 1994), was intended to overrule *Goldrich* because it "gave an unduly narrow interpretation to Code section 525." Is the interpretation of § 525(a) in *Toth* also unduly narrow?

**2.** The most spectacular use of § 525(a) occurred in *Federal Communications Commission v. NextWave Personal Communications, Inc.*, 537 U.S. 293 (2003), in which billions of dollars of worth of broadband wireless spectrum licenses were in issue. In this case, NextWave, the debtor, was awarded exclusive licenses for broadband personal communications services by the Federal Communications Commission (FCC) pursuant to a set of auction procedures designed to limit the spectrum licenses to "small businesses." In accordance with FCC regulations, NextWave made a small downpayment on the purchase price and signed promissory notes for the balance to be paid in installments, secured by a security interest in NextWave's rights in the licenses. The licenses recited that they were conditioned on compliance with terms of the installment plan and failure to comply with these conditions would result in automatic cancellation of the licenses. When NextWave had difficulty in obtaining financing for its operations, the FCC suspended the installment payments schedule pending NextWave's adoption of restructuring options. When NextWave saw that it would be unable to restructure within the deadline set by the FCC, it sought to obtain further extensions of the deadline from the Commission and courts, to no avail. NextWave filed in Chapter 11 in June 1998 and suspended payments to all creditors, including the FCC, pending confirmation of a reorganization plan.

The FCC objected to the proposed Chapter 11 plan on the ground that NextWave's licenses had been cancelled automatically when the company missed its first payment deadline in October 1998, after NextWave filed in Chapter 11. NextWave contended that the FCC's cancellation of the licenses violated § 525(a). The Court agreed with NextWave, holding that the case fell squarely within the language of § 525(a): a governmental unit, the FCC, revoked licenses of the the debtor, NextWave, solely because the debtor had not paid a dischargeable debt. The fact that the FCC may have had a valid regulatory motive for the cancellation is irrelevant; there is no regulatory exception to § 525(a).

In his dissent, Justice Breyer criticized the result in this case as inconsistent with the purpose of § 525, which was to prevent discrimination against persons on account of their status as bankrupts. Granted that a state or federal governmental unit should not be able to deny or revoke a license solely because a person has filed in bankruptcy, § 525(a) was intended to protect debtors from discriminatory license terminations. But that's not this case. There was no discrimination against NextWave based on its status as a bankrupt, rather NextWave lost its license because it didn't pay a debt secured by the licenses at issue. This has nothing to do with discrimination based on bankruptcy. He urged that the language of the statute be interpreted in conformity with the statute's purposes, and he suggested some interpretations that would reach that goal. He cited *Toth* as being consistent with his views about a more limited view of the statute.

# CHAPTER 5

# STAYS AND INJUNCTIONS

## A. INTRODUCTION

Stays and injunctions in bankruptcy arise under two sections of the Bankruptcy Code: Section 105 allows a bankruptcy court to "issue any order, process, or judgment that is necessary or appropriate to carry out the provisions of this title." Under § 105 the bankruptcy court has wide discretion to issue injunctions to facilitate the bankruptcy process. Under § 362(a) the filing of a petition in bankruptcy operates as a stay against a variety of acts affecting the debtor, property of the debtor, property of the estate or property held by the estate. This stay is known as the automatic stay.

> The automatic stay is one of the fundamental debtor protections provided by the bankruptcy laws. It gives the debtor a breathing spell from his creditors. It stops all collection efforts, all harassment, and all foreclosure actions. It permits the debtor to attempt a repayment or reorganization plan, or simply to be relieved of the financial pressures that drove him into bankruptcy.
>
> The automatic stay also provides creditor protection. Without it, certain creditors would be able to pursue their own remedies against the debtor's property. Those who acted first would obtain payment of the claims in preference to and to the detriment of other creditors. Bankruptcy is designed to provide an orderly liquidation procedure under which all creditors are treated equally. A race of diligence by creditors for the debtor's assets prevents that.

H. Rep. No. 95–595, 1978 U.S.C.C.A.N. 6296–6297.

This oft-quoted passage from the legislative history justifies the automatic stay of § 362 as a fundamental protection for both debtors (safeguard against dismembering the bankrupt's estate) and creditors (insuring ratable distribution). Evidence of the importance of the automatic stay is the extraordinary volume of litigation regarding its scope, effect, and duration.

The automatic stay pervades bankruptcy law and we refer to it throughout the book. The overview of bankruptcy in chapter 1 presented a very brief description of the automatic stay intended to allow students to understand references to it in chapters 2 through 4. In this chapter we offer a more detailed treatment of the stay, but important issues concerning stays and injunctions are raised in context in other chapters of the book as well. Under state law the property of a defaulting debtor may be seized by unsecured creditors in an unruly "race of diligence" to obtain judicial liens on the debtor's assets; the first person to obtain a lien on the property prevails to the exclusion of other creditors. Liquidation bankruptcy offers debtors respite from seizure of their assets under state law and assures unsecured creditors ratable distribution of the debtor's estate. The automatic stay is the instrument that protects the debtor and its assets from prepetition creditor collection activity during the bankruptcy case.

## B. APPLICABILITY OF THE STAY

### 1. CREDITOR PROCESSES STAYED

The date of filing a petition in bankruptcy is the Greenwich Meridian of bankruptcy law. As we have seen, this date is important in determining what is property of the estate (§ 541) and which claims are discharged (§ 727(b)). It also governs the applicability of the automatic stay (§ 362(a)). The rules are relatively simple: all proceedings to collect prepetition claims are stayed if these claims are against the debtor, the property of the debtor or the property of the estate; the stay is automatic, no injunction need be sought, and it is immediately binding on claimants, whether they have notice of the bankruptcy petition or not. We pose a series of basic questions that are intended to illustrate these general principles.

**Problem 1.**

What creditor processes are stayed by § 362(a)? In each of the following questions, assume that Debtor filed a petition in Chapter 7 bankruptcy on July 1. The inquiry in each case is whether Creditor's conduct violated § 362(a) and, if so, which, if any, paragraph or paragraphs of subsection (a) was violated .

**Question #1.**    Creditor held a perfected security interest in Debtor's equipment that secured a promissory note on which Debtor defaulted on May 1. Creditor gave Debtor appropriate notice that the equipment would be sold on July 10 pursuant to Article 9 of the UCC. Although Creditor learned of Debtor's bankruptcy filing, it proceeded to sell the property on July 10 at a nonjudicial sale conducted by Creditor.

**Question #2.**    Same facts as Question #1 except that Creditor notified Debtor that the sale would be held on July 2. At the time the sale was held, Creditor knew nothing of Debtor's status as a debtor in bankruptcy.

**Question #3.**    On July 1, Creditor held a judgment against Debtor that was duly recorded in the land records of the county where the land owned by the Debtor is located. Hence, Debtor has a valid judicial lien on the property, indefeasible in bankruptcy. On July 15, Debtor obtained a writ of execution ordering the appropriate judicial officer to foreclose on the land. No further action was taken.

**Question #4.**    Creditor performed successful surgery on Debtor who still owed Creditor $10,000 on July 1 for the surgery. Creditor was outraged to learn of Debtor's bankruptcy and had his assistant call the ungrateful Debtor at least once a day in the period following July 1, demanding payment of his fee. The calls became more irate each day.

**Question #5.** Same facts as Question above except that Creditor called Debtor and told her that he would no longer perform services for her until she paid her bill.

**Question #6.** On June 29, Creditor repossessed Debtor's automobile in which Creditor held a validly perfected security interest. Debtor was clearly in default and Creditor complied with all requirements for a valid repossession. On July 10, while Creditor was still in possession of the car, Debtor's trustee in bankruptcy demanded that Creditor return the vehicle, in which under the law of the jurisdiction the Debtor held legal title until its ownership rights were cut off by a resale by Creditor. Creditor refused.

In 2005 a change was made in the traditional rule that the automatic stay becomes effective on the date the debtor files without respect to whether creditors know of the filing. See Question #2 above. Under Bankruptcy Rule 1007(a)(1), when a debtor files in bankruptcy she must supply the court with the names and addresses of her creditors, and notice of the filing is sent to these addresses. But addresses supplied by the debtor may be the addresses to which she was required to send her monthly payments, so-called "lockbox" accounts that did nothing but process payments, and creditors complained that they should not be penalized for violating the automatic stay in such cases until they received actual notice of the bankruptcy. Under the 2005 Act, § 342(f) and (g) allows creditors to protect themselves in such cases by filing with any bankruptcy court a notice of address that must be used by all bankruptcy courts in notifying that entity. If the creditor has filed the prescribed notice of bankruptcy with the court, no notice to a creditor at a different address is effective until it is "brought to the attention" of such creditor. § 342(g)(1). No monetary penalty may be imposed on a creditor for acts violating the stay committed before the creditor is given an effective notice. § 342(g)(2). Prudent bankruptcy counsel will make sure that the addresses of creditors on the schedule are consistent with any notice of address filed by the creditor. More work for bankruptcy attorneys.

## 2. PARTIES AND PROPERTY PROTECTED

### Problem 2.

What parties and property are protected by the stay? Same instructions as those for Problem 1 above.

**Question #1.** Debtor borrowed $1,000 from Creditor who insisted that Guarantor co-sign the note evidencing the obligation. When Debtor defaulted on the note, Creditor, with full knowledge of Debtor's bankruptcy, brought suit on the note on July 10 against Guarantor to collect the amount of the note. Under the law of the state, if Guarantor pays the note it has a right of action for reimbursement against Debtor.

**Question #2.**     Creditor, a lender who deals in the sub-prime market, prefers to lend money to debtors who have recently filed in bankruptcy because these debtors cannot receive a discharge in Chapter 7 in a case filed within eight years of their prior discharge. On July 15, Creditor lent $1,000 to Debtor who missed her first payment on the loan that was due on August 15. Creditor immediately filed suit against Debtor for a money judgment. Under 362(c)(2), the stay was still in effect because the case was not closed.

**Question #3.**     Same facts as in Question #2 except that in connection with its suit on the postpetition claim, Creditor attached property in Debtor's possession that she had owned at the time of bankruptcy.

**Question #4.**     Section 541(a)(6) provides that earnings of a debtor for services performed postpetition are not property of the estate. On July 1, Creditor held a prepetition claim of $1,000. Knowing that Debtor's deposit account was entirely made up of postpetition earnings of Debtor, Creditor attached the account on July 20 in an attempt to collect the debt.

## 3. EXCEPTIONS TO THE STAY

### a.   Section 362(b)

The sweep of the automatic stay under § 362(a) is so broad and its impact so great that over the years numerous interests have sought and obtained exceptions; these are enumerated in § 362(b). Most of these are specific to the  needs of the parties seeking relief and need not concern us, *e.g.*, § 362(b)(3) allows secured creditors to maintain perfection of security interests by an act such as filing a UCC continuation statement during the stay; § 362(b)(9) was significantly broadened to allow tax authorities during the stay to conduct tax audits, make demands for tax returns, and make certain assessments for tax liabilities and issue notice and demand for payment of these assessments; and § 362(b)(18) was added allowing for the creation or perfection of ad valorem tax liens during the stay. This last amendment resolves an issue that illustrates the inexorable law of unintended consequences that faces all statutory drafters. In *In re Parr Meadows Racing Association, Inc.*, 880 F.2d 1540 (2d Cir. 1989), the court held that § 362(a)(4), staying "any act to create, perfect, or enforce any lien against property of the estate," precluded local government units from imposing liens for ad valorem property taxes that became due after the petition in bankruptcy. Local government tax authorities were shocked to learn that the operation of the stay deprived them of the priority over mortgages that they enjoyed under nonbankruptcy law and relegated them to the status of unsecured claimants for the amount of taxes owed. Their cries were heard and § 362(b)(18)  resulted.

The amendments to § 362 in the 2005 Act go beyond merely correcting oversights in the original statute and move toward limiting the automatic stay in order to enable favored groups of creditors to proceed against debtors unhindered by the stay. For instance, the stay is broadened to preclude bankruptcy from interfering with rights of spouses and children to receive domestic support payments from debtor spouses, *e.g.*, § 362(b)(2)(C). Other examples are the provisions strengthening the rights of secured creditors and lessors, *e.g.* § 362(b)(22), which excepts from the stay the continuation of eviction proceedings involving residential property if the lessor has obtained a judgment for possession before the tenant filed in bankruptcy. Under § 362(h), the stay is terminated if the debtor who has retained possession of personal property subject to a security interest or lease without the consent of the creditor fails to redeem (§ 722) the property or reaffirm the contract (§ 524(c)) within statutory time limits. Limitations on the stay are used to deal with the abuse of repeated filings: § 362(c)(3) provides that if an individual debtor has had a prior case dismissed in the preceding one-year period, the automatic stay in the second case terminates within 30 days after filing unless the debtor can rebut a heavy presumption that her case was not filed in good faith. If two or more cases have been pending within the previous year, there is no stay at all in the second case unless the bad faith presumption described in the preceding sentence is rebutted. § 362(c)(4). If a court finds that the transfer of real property or multiple bankruptcy filings affecting real property is part of a scheme to defraud creditors, the court order may be recorded and is binding *in rem* in any bankruptcy case affecting the property within the next two years, (§ 362(d)(4)), and in such a case, the automatic stay does not apply to actions to enforce a lien or security interest for a period of two years after entry of the order. § 362(b)(20).

Section 362(b)(1) states the obvious: a debtor cannot avoid criminal proceedings by filing in bankruptcy. But what if the purpose of the criminal proceeding is to collect a debt?

## PROBLEM

Debtor was delinquent in his child support payments and filed in bankruptcy. When his former wife stopped receiving the payments, she complained to the district attorney in an effort to make Debtor resume payments. As a result, criminal charges were brought in state court aginst Debtor for his dereliction. After his conviction, Debtor requested the bankruptcy court to declare the state criminal proceedings void as a violation of the automatic stay. Are state criminal proceedings excepted from the application of the automatic stay even if the prosecution is motivated by the complaining witness's desire to collect a debt? See *In re Gruntz*, 202 F.3d 1074 (9th Cir. 2000).

### b. Police and Regulatory Power Exception

The major exception to § 362(a) is the police and regulatory power exception of § 362(b)(4), which allows a governmental unit to sue a debtor in bankruptcy to prevent or stop violations of fraud, environmental protections, consumer protection, safety, or similar police or regulatory laws, or to fix damages for violation of such laws. Clearly, filing bankruptcy cannot be a license to avoid compliance with all manner of generally applicable environmental, zoning, safety, criminal, antitrust and licensing statutes and regulations. Unfortunately, the wording of § 362(b)(4) was cobbled together in 1998 in the dying days of the 105th Congress in omnibus appropriation legislation. Its ostensible purpose was to exempt agencies having authority under an international convention prohibiting chemical weapons. Since it is unimaginable that any bankruptcy judge would not allow chemical weapons inspections and regulations to proceed notwithstanding the automatic stay, the chemical weapons provision is of no import. But the 1998 redraft of § 362(b)(4) was not carefully done and courts have struggled with its meaning.

Section 362(b)(4) exempts from the automatic stay actions or proceedings of governmental units or organizations "to enforce such governmental unit's or organization's police and regulatory power, including the enforcement of a judgment *other than a money judgment*, obtained in an action or proceeding by the governmental unit's or organization's police or regulatory power." The money judgment exclusion from the police and regulatory power exception is intended to prevent governmental units from using their police and regulatory powers to gain preferential treatment at the expense of other creditors in bankruptcy. The governmental unit may obtain a judgment against the debtor but cannot enforce it. The distinction is between the governmental unit acting as a regulator, which is exempted from the stay, and acting as a creditor, which is not. As we see in the case discussed below, this distinction is not easy to make.

This is the issue in *Securities & Exchange Commission v. Brennan*, 230 F.3d 65 (2d Cir. 2000), in which the district court held that Brennan had defrauded brokerage customers by inducing them to buy securities at excessive prices in violation of federal securities law and entered a judgment ordering him to disgorge $75 million in ill-gotten gains. Brennan filed in Chapter 11 bankruptcy. Later the SEC sought from the district court an order to show cause why Brennan should not be held in contempt of the disgorgement judgment, and ancillary relief requiring Brennan to repatriate $5 million held in an offshore asset protection trust. Brennan resisted the repatriation order on the ground that it was an invalid use of the the SEC's police and regulatory powers to enforce a money judgment and thus was not excepted from the automatic stay by § 363(b)(4). The SEC contended that it was not seeking to collect the judgment, rather it was seeking the return of assets transferred by Brennan "so as to preserve them for the benefit of all potential [bankruptcy] claimants." 230 F.3d at 69. The funds would be held in the district court's registry to be at the disposal of the bankruptcy court to be distributed later to the claimants; the SEC would receive only its pro rata share.

By a divided panel the Second Circuit vacated the repatriation order as a violation of the automatic stay because it amounted to the enforcement of a money judgment. The majority opinion stated that although § 362(b)(4) permits entry of a money judgment against a debtor, anything beyond mere entry of a money judgment is prohibited by the automatic stay; the repatriation order crossed the line because it was sought to make it easier for the SEC to collect its judgment in bankruptcy. In the court's view, the SEC's action in obtaining a judgment was taken in exercise of its police or regulatory power to deter the debtor's conduct, but once the judgment was entered, the SEC was no longer acting in its police or regulatory capacity, it was merely trying to collect the judgment at the expense of the other bankruptcy claimants. The dissent saw nothing in either the statute or the policies underlying it that supports the majority view. In Judge Calabresi's view, the question in the application of § 362(b)(4) should be whether the government's action enables the government to enrich itself at the expense of the nongovernment creditors, but in this case no nongovernmental creditors would suffer any harm as a result of the repatriation order. Is the majority saying that any governmental action that takes place between the entry of judgment and collection of the judgment—like the repatriation order in this case—is an act of enforcement? If so line drawing becomes very difficult. What about deposing or examining the judgment debtor concerning its assets?

## 4. TERMINATION OF THE STAY

Termination of the stay is governed by § 362(c). If the stay is of an act against property of the estate, the stay terminates when the property ceases to be property of the estate. With respect to any other act, the stay terminates when the bankruptcy case is closed or dismissed or the debtor is granted or denied a discharge, whichever occurs first. Under § 362(d) the bankruptcy court may lift the stay or grant other relief from the stay.

## C. EFFECT OF VIOLATION OF STAY

## 1. DAMAGES

The filing of a bankruptcy petition automatically operates as a stay; no formal order of a stay need be entered. The automatic stay is a form of an injunction; violators may in the discretion of the court be held in contempt and assessed damages. Section 362(h) allows an "individual" injured by a willful violation of the stay to recover actual damages, costs and attorney's fees, and, under appropriate circumstances, punitive damages. The term "individual," although not defined in the Bankruptcy Code, is consistently used in the Code to refer to natural persons in contrast to legal entities such as corporations and partnerships. Examples are § 109(e) and

§ 101(30) ("individual with regular income"), which limit the use of Chapter 13 to natural persons, and § 101(18) ("family farmer"), which distinguishes between farmers who are individuals and those that are corporations or partnerships. A similar distinction is made in § 101(31) ("insider"). Under § 101(41), "person" includes individual, partnership, and corporation. Thus, the apparent meaning of § 362(h) is that a corporation or partnership that is in bankruptcy is not entitled to the cause of action provided by that section.

Some courts, however, have refused to infer that Congress intended to incorporate a distinction between natural persons and other debtors into § 362(h). Currently the circuits are divided on the issue with four holding that the term "individual" does not include corporations and two holding that it does. The authorities are marshaled in *In re Spookyworld, Inc.*, 346 F.3d 1 (1st Cir. 2003). The Second Circuit justifies the majority view:

> After Congress in 1978 passed the automatic stay provisions of § 362 along with the rest of the code, including § 105(a). . ., it is entirely possible that Congress then chose to expand the remedies for violations one step at a time. Congress may well have thought that individual debtors were particularly vulnerable to violations of the stay by debt-collection agencies and others who may be tempted to believe that individuals are less likely than corporations to be aware of their rights under the automatic stay.

*In re Chateaugay Corp.*, 920 F.2d 183, 186 (2d Cir. 1990).

Majority view courts point out that corporations are free to petition bankruptcy courts to award damages for automatic stay violations pursuant to their § 105(a) power, a practice that was routine prior to the enactment of § 362(h). See *Spookyworld*, 346 F.3d at 8.

Another issue on which the circuits are divided is whether "actual damages" in § 362(h) includes emotional distress. The Seventh Circuit in *Aiello v. Providian Financial Corp.*, 239 F.3d 876, 880 (7th Cir. 2001), saw the protection of the automatic stay as primarily financial in character and required proof of financial loss in order to claim emotional distress damages. Other circuits have disagreed. The Ninth Circuit in *In re Dawson*, 390 F.3d 1139 (9th Cir. 2004), ruled that damages for emotional distress may be recovered if it is established that the individual debtor suffered significant harm as a result of the violation of the stay. No proof of pecuniary loss is required and the debtor may prove entitlement to damages even in the absence of corroborating evidence if the debtor in fact suffered significant emotional harm and the circumstances surrounding the violation make it obvious that a reasonable person would suffer significant emotional harm. *See also Fleet Mortgage Group, Inc. v. Kaneb*, 196 F.3d 265 (1st Cir. 1999).

## 2. VOID OR VOIDABLE?

Another long-standing division of authority concerns whether acts in violation of the automatic stay are void or voidable. In *Kalb v. Feuerstein*, 308 U.S. 433, 438 (1940), the Court, in construing the effect of a stay under a prior bankruptcy statute, held a postpetition state court real property foreclosure to be "not merely erroneous but * * * beyond its power, void, and subject to collateral attack." The Bankruptcy Code does not directly speak to the issue. Some courts believe that § 362(d), which empowers courts to annul the stay, undermines *Kalb*: if an act in violation of the stay is a nullity, how can it be subsequently ratified by annulment of the stay? See a discussion of this view in *Bronson v. United States*, 46 F.3d 1573 (Fed.Cir.1995) (a strong holding that acts violating the stay are voidable). The confines of the automatic stay and the consequences of the void/voidable distinction are discussed in the following case.

## In re Soares

United States Court of Appeals, First Circuit, 1997.
107 F.3d 969.

■ SELYA, Circuit Judge.

"[T]he dead tree gives no shelter." T.S. Eliot, *The Waste Land, I, The Burial of the Dead* (1922). Like a shade tree, the automatic stay which attends the initiation of bankruptcy proceedings, § 362(a), must be nurtured if it is to retain its vitality. This appeal, which pits a Chapter 13 debtor bent on saving his home against a creditor bent on enforcing its rights under a mortgage, raises issues which touch upon the degree of judicial protection that the automatic stay invites. These issues are whether the automatic stay precludes a state court from undertaking ministerial acts after a bankruptcy filing; if not, what acts are exempt under that rubric; whether a bankruptcy court may grant retroactive relief from the automatic stay; and if so, what legal standard it should apply in prescribing such an anodyne.

### I. LAYING THE FOUNDATION

We begin by retracing the labyrinthine corridors through which this litigation has passed. In 1990 the debtor, Napoleon G. Soares, purchased a home in Brockton, Massachusetts. He executed a $70,000 promissory note to the Brockton Credit Union (BCU) and secured the note by a first mortgage on the real estate. After sustaining injuries in a motorcycle accident, Soares lagged in his monthly payments. BCU grew restive and commenced foreclosure proceedings in the state superior court. Soares did not file an answer. On March 22, 1995, BCU sent a letter to the clerk of court seeking an order of default and a judgment authorizing foreclosure. Two days later Soares filed a bankruptcy petition, thus triggering the automatic stay. He immediately gave notice to BCU, but neither party alerted the state court. On April 10, with the stay still firmly in place, a judge of that court issued the requested default order. One week later, she authorized the entry of a foreclosure judgment.

Soares missed some post-petition mortgage payments. On June 14, 1995, BCU, without apprising the bankruptcy court of the orders previously obtained in the state proceedings, filed a motion seeking relief from the automatic stay. The debtor's then-counsel, Gerard Williamson, neglected to oppose BCU's motion. The bankruptcy court granted the unopposed motion on June 29 (the same day, coincidentally, that Soares, unbeknownst to the judge, paid the post-petition arrearage). The court subsequently refused to entertain a belated objection filed by Williamson.

When Soares missed his November payment, BCU activated the state court judgment. At the ensuing foreclosure sale, held on November 29, BCU itself bid in the mortgaged premises and paid approximately $14,200 in overdue municipal taxes to clear the title. Soares thereafter sought relief in the state court on the ground that the foreclosure judgment had been issued in contravention of the automatic stay. The court denied the motion, saying that its post-petition actions had been "ministerial" and that any error was harmless.

Soares' unsuccessful foray apparently rang warning bells for BCU, which asked the bankruptcy court to clarify whether the June 29 order (lifting the automatic stay) ratified the earlier state court judgment. BCU served this so-called clarification motion on the attorney, Williamson, but not on Soares. In a margin order entered on February 9, 1996, Judge Kenner addressed the question of retroactivity for the first time and vacated the automatic stay retroactive to March 24, 1995, "such that the [state] judgment and movant's foreclosure shall not be deemed to have violated the automatic stay."

Less than three weeks later Soares, through newly retained counsel, filed a motion to reconsider both the February 9 order and the original grant of relief from the automatic stay. Judge Kenner denied the reconsideration motion on the merits and also denied a companion motion to void the foreclosure sale. The judge advanced three reasons for having lifted the automatic stay retroactively on February 9. First, because BCU "had done everything right," it would be inequitable to upset its expectations. Second, because the foreclosure had wiped out junior lienholders, it would be too complicated to "unscramble the egg." Third, because Soares could not immediately repay the funds that BCU had expended to clear title to the property, the economic realities favored ratification of the foreclosure.

Soares appealed. The district court temporarily stayed further proceedings (blocking both a planned eviction and a possible resale of the property). Eventually, however, the district court—although finding that BCU had neglected its responsibility to apprise the state tribunal of Soares' bankruptcy (an error which it termed "harmless")—determined that the retroactive lifting of the automatic stay did not constitute an abuse of discretion.

Soares again appealed. We enlarged the earlier stay on condition that Soares make monthly payments to BCU for use and occupancy of the premises (to be credited against the mortgage indebtedness, should Soares prevail on appeal).

## II. DISCUSSION

To the extent that the threshold inquiries in this case involve questions of statutory interpretation, we exercise plenary review.[4] * * * From this vantage point we first address the purported exemption for "ministerial acts," as it is only necessary to reach the retroactivity question if a violation of the automatic stay in fact occurred.

### A. The Nature of the State Court's Actions.

The parties clash head-on in respect to classification of the state court's actions. The debtor claims that the state court order and judgment transgressed the automatic stay. The creditor claims that these entries, though occurring post-petition, were purely ministerial and, thus, not offensive to the stay. The debtor has the better argument.

Section 362(a)(1) of the Bankruptcy Code provides that the filing of a bankruptcy petition stays the commencement or continuation of all non-bankruptcy judicial proceedings against the debtor. Here, the state court default order eventuated more than two weeks *after* Soares filed for bankruptcy and the foreclosure judgment one week later. The issue, then, is whether these entries contravened the mandate of section 362(a)(1). BCU asserts that they did not because the stay was not in effect when the creditor requested the state court to act and because the state court's actions, when taken, constituted ministerial acts.

The creditor's first assertion is mere buzznacking. The focus here is whether or not the state court's actions, when effected, transgressed the automatic stay. The date on which the creditor asked the state court to act, while material to an assessment of the creditor's good faith (which is not seriously questioned here), does not bear on whether the activities themselves constituted the forbidden continuation of a judicial proceeding.

BCU's second assertion is more substantial. Ministerial acts, even if undertaken in a state judicial proceeding subsequent to a bankruptcy filing, do not fall within the proscription of the automatic stay. * * * But the state court's actions in this case cannot properly be characterized as ministerial.

A ministerial act is one that is essentially clerical in nature. *See Black's Law Dictionary* 996 (6th ed. 1990). Thus, when an official's duty is delineated by, say, a law or a judicial decree with such crystalline clarity that nothing is left to the exercise of the official's discretion or judgment,

---

[4] A different standard of review applies to the bankruptcy court's discretionary decision to lift the automatic stay retroactively. We review that ruling for abuse of discretion. * * *

the resultant act is ministerial. *See United States ex rel. McLennan v. Wilbur*, 283 U.S. 414, 420 (1931) (indicating that a duty is ministerial if "the obligation to act [is] peremptory, and plainly defined"); *Neal v. Regan*, 587 F.Supp. 1558, 1562 (N.D.Ind.1984) (describing a ministerial act as "one which "the law prescribes and defines. . . with such precision as to leave nothing to the exercise of discretion or judgment'") (citation omitted). Such acts can usefully be visualized as the antithesis of judicial acts, inasmuch as the essence of a judicial act is the exercise of discretion or judgment. *See Black's Law Dictionary*, supra, at 846.

Virtually by definition, a judicial proceeding does not conclude until the judicial function is completed, that is, until the judicial decision is made. *See*, e.g., *Bidermann*, 21 F.3d at 528 (holding that the judicial function is completed "at the moment the judge direct[s] entry of judgment"). Frequently, routine scrivening, such as recordation or entry on the docket, follows on the heels of a judicial decision. Such actions—taken in obedience to the judge's peremptory instructions or otherwise precisely defined and nondiscretionary—are ministerial and, consequently, do not themselves violate the automatic stay even if undertaken after an affected party files for bankruptcy. *See, e.g., Knightsbridge Dev.*, 884 F.2d at 148 (suggesting that merely recording a previously decided award would be a "clerical act" and therefore would not infract the automatic stay); *In re Capgro Leasing Assocs.*, 169 B.R. 305, 315–16 (Bankr.E.D.N.Y.1994) (stating that "entry of a judgment will constitute a "ministerial act' where the judicial function has been completed and the clerk has merely to perform the rote function of entering the judgment upon the court's docket"). By the same token, however, acts undertaken in the course of carrying out the core judicial function are not ministerial and, if essayed after bankruptcy filing, will be deemed to violate the automatic stay.

*Bidermann* captures this distinction. There, the district judge ruled *ora sponte* and endorsed the motion papers. The defendant then sought refuge in bankruptcy. The Second Circuit held the clerk's subsequent, post-petition entry of the judgment on the docket to be ministerial (and, therefore, unaffected by the automatic stay). Other cases are to the same effect. *See Heikkila v. Carver (In re Carver)*, 828 F.2d 463, 464 (8th Cir.1987) (holding that a "routine certification" by the clerk, entered post-petition, did not transgress the automatic stay); *Capgro Leasing*, 169 B.R. at 315–16 (holding the clerk's entry of judgment on the docket to be ministerial when, prior to the bankruptcy filing, the court had ordered summary judgment). A parallel line of cases reinforces the notion that the compendium of ministerial acts excludes those involving deliberation, discretion, or judicial involvement. *See, e.g., Ellis v. Consolidated Diesel Elec. Corp.*, 894 F.2d 371, 372–73 (10th Cir.1990) (invalidating a judicial decision that granted summary judgment two weeks after a bankruptcy filing); *Knightsbridge Dev.*, 884 F.2d at 148 (voiding an arbitration award because the bulk of the panel's deliberations occurred after the stay arose); *Ellison v. Northwest Eng'g Co.*, 707 F.2d 1310, 1311 (11th Cir.1983) (holding that while the automatic stay was in effect a court could not render a decision in a case which had been briefed and argued pre-petition).

This line of demarcation makes perfectly good sense. The statutory proviso which gives rise to the automatic stay says what it means and means what it says. * * * Confining the exemption for ministerial acts to those actions which are essentially clerical, as opposed to judicial, honors this principle because such an interpretation comports precisely with the text of section 362(a)(1). In the bargain, this interpretation also facilitates the statute's due administration.

Silhouetted against this legal landscape, it is readily apparent that the state court's actions in ordering a default and directing the entry of a judgment possess a distinctly judicial, rather than a ministerial, character. The record is totally barren of any evidence that the state court judge decided to grant BCU's request prior to the date of the bankruptcy filing, and all visible signs point in the opposite direction. The judge did not enter the default order until more than two weeks after Soares sought the protection of the bankruptcy court and she did not direct the entry of a judgment authorizing foreclosure until another week had elapsed. Moreover, the judge indicated after the fact that she waited to confirm Soares' nonmilitary status before directing the entry of judgment. This indicates deliberativeness and a concomitant willingness to exercise discretion.

Nor does the fact that the judge later characterized her entry of the foreclosure judgment as "ministerial" require a different result. An appellate court is not bound by a trial judge's unsupported description, * * * and we are aware of no reason why that salutary principle would not apply with equal vigor to our assessment of a state court's actions when the underlying question relates to the effect of those actions *under federal law*. Hence, we decline to adopt the label that the state court judge chose in hindsight to affix to her activities.

We summarize succinctly. Because the decision which animated the entry of the order and judgment occurred after the stay was in force, those actions continued the state judicial proceeding within the meaning of section 362(a)(1). Consequently, the actions violated the automatic stay. Given this infraction, we now must assess the availability of a retroactive cure.

**B. The Operation of the Automatic Stay.**

We subdivide this part of our discussion into four segments. In each segment, our comments reflect our awareness that bankruptcy courts traditionally pay heed to equitable principles. * * *

**1.** The Nature of the Stay. The automatic stay is among the most basic of debtor protections under bankruptcy law. * * * It is intended to give the debtor breathing room by "stop[ping] all collection efforts, all harassment, and all foreclosure actions." H.R. Rep. No. 95–595, at 340 (1977). * * *

The stay springs into being immediately upon the filing of a bankruptcy petition: "[b]ecause the automatic stay is exactly what the name implies—'automatic'—it operates without the necessity for judicial intervention." *Sunshine Dev., Inc. v. FDIC*, 33 F.3d 106, 113 (1st Cir.1994). It remains in force until a federal court either disposes of the case, see § 362(c)(2), or lifts the stay, see id. § 362(d)-(f). This respite enables debtors to resolve their debts in a more orderly fashion, *see In re Siciliano*, 13 F.3d 748, 750 (3d Cir.1994), and at the same time safeguards their creditors by preventing "different creditors from bringing different proceedings in different courts, thereby setting in motion a free-for-all in which opposing interests maneuver to capture the lion's share of the debtor's assets." *Sunshine Dev.*, 33 F.3d at 114; *see generally* 3 *Collier on Bankruptcy* ¶ 362.03 (15th rev. ed. 1996).

In order to secure these important protections, courts must display a certain rigor in reacting to violations of the automatic stay. * * * The circuits are split on whether actions taken in derogation of the automatic stay are merely "voidable" or, more accurately, "void." Some courts characterize unauthorized postpetition proceedings as "voidable." * * * Other courts—a majority, insofar as we can tell—call such actions "void," but recognize that equitable considerations may alter some outcomes. * * *

Our earlier opinions—which we today reaffirm—align us with the majority view. * * * This semantic difference has practical consequences because the characterization of an infringing action as "void" or "voidable" influences the burden of going forward. Treating an action taken in contravention of the automatic stay as void places the burden of validating the action after the fact squarely on the shoulders of the offending creditor. In contrast, treating an action taken in contravention of the automatic stay as voidable places the burden of challenging the action on the offended debtor. We think that the former paradigm, rather than the latter, best harmonizes with the nature of the automatic stay and the important purposes that it serves. *See generally* 3 *Collier on Bankruptcy*, supra, ¶ 362.11[1] & n.1 (observing that most courts hold violations void and terming this the better view).

**2.**   The Availability of Retroactive Relief. While the automatic stay is significant, it is not an immutable article of faith. Indeed, the Bankruptcy Code, § 362(d), expressly authorizes courts to lift it in particular situations. Whether this statutory authorization encompasses retroactive relief is not entirely clear. We previously hinted that a court may set aside the automatic stay retroactively in an appropriate case. *See Smith Corset Shops*, 696 F.2d at 976–77. We now confirm *Smith's* adumbration, holding that § 362(d) permits bankruptcy courts to lift the automatic stay retroactively and thereby validate actions which otherwise would be void.

Section 362(d) confers upon courts discretionary power in certain circumstances to terminate, annul, modify, or place conditions upon the automatic stay.[6] In drafting the law, Congress chose to include both the power to terminate the stay and the power to annul it. When construing this language, we must try to give independent meaning to each word. * * * The only plausible distinction between the two verbs in this context is that terminating the stay blunts it prospectively, from the moment the court's order enters, whereas annulling the stay erases it retrospectively, as of some date prior to the entry of the court's order (reaching as far back as the date when the debtor filed the bankruptcy petition, if the court so elects).

Seen from this perspective, Congress' grant of a power of annulment is meaningful only if the court may thereby validate actions taken *before* the date on which the court rules. On any other construction, annulment lacks any independent significance; it merely replicates termination. It follows, therefore, that section 362(d) authorizes retroactive relief from the automatic stay. * * *

**3.** The Limiting Principle. Recognizing the discretionary authority of bankruptcy courts to relieve creditors and other interested parties retroactively from the operation of the automatic stay tells us nothing about the yardstick by which attempts to secure such relief should be measured. We turn next to this inquiry.

Once again, the overarching purpose of the automatic stay informs our analysis. Because the stay is a fundamental protection for all parties affected by the filing of a petition in bankruptcy, it should not be dismantled without good reason. * * * Undoing the stay retroactively should require a measurably greater showing. Congress intended the stay to afford debtors breathing room and to assure creditors of equitable distribution. *See* H.R.Rep. No. 95–595, supra, at 340. If retroactive relief becomes commonplace, creditors—anticipating post facto validation—will be tempted to pursue claims against bankrupts heedless of the stay, leaving debtors with no choice but to defend for fear that post-petition default judgments routinely may be resuscitated.

We believe that Congress created the automatic stay to ward off scenarios of this sort. Thus, if congressional intent is to be honored and the integrity of the automatic stay preserved, retroactive relief should be the long-odds exception, not the general rule. In our view, only a strict standard will ensure the accomplishment of these objectives. * * * We conclude, therefore, that although courts possess a limited discretion to grant retroactive relief from the automatic stay, instances in which the exercise of that discretion is justified are likely to be few and far between.

---

[6] The statute provides in pertinent part:

On request of a party in interest and after notice and a hearing, the court shall grant relief from the stay. . ., such as by terminating, annulling, modifying, or conditioning such stay—

(1) for cause, including the lack of adequate protection of an interest in property of such party in interest;. . ..

We do not suggest that we can write a standard that lends itself to mechanical application. Each case is sui generis and must be judged accordingly. But, while it is not practical to anticipate and catalogue the varied circumstances in which retroactive relief from the automatic stay may be warranted, some examples may be helpful.

When a creditor inadvertently violates the automatic stay in ignorance of a pending bankruptcy, courts sometimes have afforded retroactive relief. *See, e.g., In re Jones*, 63 F.3d 411, 412–13 (5th Cir.1995) (affirming retroactive validation of a foreclosure sale where the mortgagee had no notice of the bankruptcy filing); * * * . By like token, debtors who act in bad faith may create situations that are ripe for retroactive relief. * * *

These examples—a creditor's lack of notice or a debtor's bad faith—clearly do not exhaust the possibilities. But they illustrate that a rarely dispensed remedy like retroactive relief from the automatic stay must rest on a set of facts that is both unusual and unusually compelling. The case law echoes this conclusion. * * *

**4.** Applying the Standard. Having constructed the limiting principle, we now consider whether the bankruptcy court erred in validating the foreclosure judgment which had been obtained in violation of the automatic stay. We conclude that no proper predicate existed for doing so and that the bankruptcy court therefore abused its discretion in ordering retroactive relief. * * *

Contrary to BCU's importunings, it is the creditor's knowledge, not the state court's nescience, that is relevant to the question at hand. Bankruptcy law forbids creditors from continuing judicial proceedings against bankrupts, see § 362(a)(1), and, accordingly, it is the creditor's obligation to inform other courts of the situation * * *. Here, both BCU's knowledge and its failure to act are undisputed; the debtor immediately notified BCU of the bankruptcy filing, but BCU kept quiet and permitted the superior court to proceed in ignorance of the stay. We are reluctant to reward creditors who, despite notice of a bankruptcy filing, fail for no discernible reason to notify courts in which they have initiated proceedings of the changed circumstances.

The other facts are no more conducive to the bestowal of retroactive relief. The creditor was represented by counsel throughout and does not claim that it misapprehended the effect of the filing. The bankruptcy court made no finding that Soares acted in bad faith, and, at any rate, the record does not contain any basis for such a finding. The procedural errors committed by both parties, such as BCU's failure to serve Soares with the so-called clarification motion and Soares' failure to lodge timely objections at various points in the proceedings, seemingly cancel each other out. And BCU's entreaty that the equities favor retroactive relief rings unmistakably hollow; though BCU expended funds to clear title and maintain the property after foreclosing, this financial hardship is the natural consequence of its own failure to abide by the terms of the automatic stay. Thus, it is unredressable. *See K–Mart Corp. v. Oriental Plaza, Inc.*, 875

F.2d 907, 916 (1st Cir.1989) (declining to deny permanent injunctive relief which would require substantial demolition of an expensive structure where "appellant's wound, deep as it appears, was self-inflicted"). In the last analysis, BCU is the author of its own misfortune.

### III. CONCLUSION

To sum up, we hold that the state court's post-petition issuance of a foreclosure judgment violated the automatic stay; that bankruptcy courts ordinarily must hold those who defile the automatic stay to the predictable consequences of their actions and can grant retroactive relief only sparingly and in compelling circumstances; and that, because this case involves no sufficiently unusual circumstances, the bankruptcy court abused its discretion ingranting retroactive relief from the automatic stay.[7]

In an abundance of caution, we note that our review is confined to the order granting the so-called clarification motion and the retroactive relief awarded therein. Although Soares may ask the bankruptcy court to reconsider its decision to lift the automatic stay, BCU can request a new foreclosure judgment in the state court unless and until the bankruptcy court reinstates the stay. For our part, we need go no further.

Reversed and remanded.

## NOTES

**1.** Why was it important whether the judge's entry of the foreclosure judgment in *Soares* was ministerial? What is a ministerial act?

**2.** What is the court's view of the functional difference between void or voidable with respect to actions taken in violation of the stay? Can a void act be cured or validated? See § 362(d).

**3.** In *Easley v. Pettibone Michigan Corp.*, 990 F.2d 905, 909 (6th Cir.1993), the court found the term "void" to be so indeterminate as to be almost useless as a guide to courts and rejected the voidness rule. The same courts that embrace the voidness rule readily recognize exceptions to it based on the equities in the case. The *Easley* court scrapped the void/voidable terminology:

> We think that "invalid" is a more appropriate adjective to use when defining an action taken against a debtor during the duration of the automatic stay. Like the word "void," "invalid" describes something that is without legal force or effect. However, something that is invalid is not incurable, in contrast to a void action which is incapable of being ratified.

---

[7] We recognize the difficulties that attend the undoing of the foreclosure sale and the restoration of the pre-petition status quo, but that problem cannot in and of itself justify overlooking BCU's unexcused violation of the automatic stay. * * *

## D. SECURED CLAIMS

The automatic stay functions differently for secured creditors than for unsecured creditors. In liquidation bankruptcy secured creditors are entitled to the value of their secured claims. The stay gives the trustee time to sell the collateral and turn the proceeds over to the secured creditor. If the proceeds of the sale exceed the amount of the secured claim, the excess is available for distribution to the unsecured creditors when the case closes. If the trustee sees no likelihood of there being equity in the collateral, it may abandon the property to the debtor under § 554, subject to the secured creditor's security interest. Any sale by the trustee in such a case would be entirely for the benefit of the secured creditor and not worth incurring the expenses of a sale. In rehabilitation or reorganization bankruptcy, the stay may allow the debtor to retain the property if it is necessary for an effective reorganization.

Section 362(a) stays any act of a prepetition secured creditor to enforce its security interest in property of the estate or of the debtor. Accordingly, a creditor having a UCC Article 9 security interest in personal property is barred by the stay from availing itself of its rights under UCC § 9-609 to repossess by either self-help or judicial process. If the creditor is a pledgee or has retaken possession of the collateral before the debtor's petition, it may not realize on the collateral by either a judicial sale or nonjudicial creditor's sale under the UCC after the petition. If sale of the collateral had already been completed before the petition, the debtor has no right under the UCC to redeem and the stay is inapplicable because the property sold is no longer either property of the estate or of the debtor.

The real property secured creditor is stayed from foreclosing its mortgage by either judicial action or extrajudicial process, which usually would be exercise of a power of sale. The creditor must halt its judicial action or extrajudicial proceeding at any stage of the foreclosure process as soon as the debtor's petition is filed. However, if the foreclosure sale is completed before the petition and the debtor has no right to redeem under the law of the jurisdiction, the real property does not become property of the bankruptcy estate, and the stay is inapplicable.

Much litigation concerns the effect of § 362 on the debtor's right to redeem from the foreclosure sale of real property when the petition was filed after the sale but before the expiration of a statutory redemption period. In that case, the bankruptcy estate includes the debtor's right to redeem the property. Was § 362 intended to halt the running of the time for redemption and other limitation periods? The next case discusses the impact of § 105(a), § 108(b), and § 362 on the mortgagor's right of redemption.

# Johnson v. First National Bank

United States Court of Appeals, Eighth Circuit, 1983.
719 F.2d 270.

■ Ross T. Roberts, District Judge.

This case presents a troublesome question concerning whether a bankruptcy court possesses the authority to toll or suspend the running of a statutory redemption period created by state law in connection with real estate mortgage foreclosures.

The First National Bank of Montevideo ("First National") appeals from an order of the District Court for the District of Minnesota. That District Court order affirmed a bankruptcy court order which enjoined First National from taking further action to foreclose a lien on certain real estate, and stayed the expiration of the redemption period allowed by Minnesota law. For the reasons set forth below we reverse the judgment of the district court, and remand for further proceedings consistent with this opinion.

The relevant facts are undisputed. Curtis H. Johnson and Gloria Jean Johnson ("debtors") are the principal officers and shareholders of Oak Farms, Inc., and Oak Farms Service Co., both Minnesota corporations engaged in agricultural business pursuits. In 1978 Oak Farms, Inc. executed a mortgage on certain parcels of real estate located in Yellow Medicine and Lac qui Parle counties, Minnesota, to secure a $300,000 promissory note in favor of First National. In 1979, Oak Farms, Inc., Oak Farms Service Co., and the Johnsons executed a second mortgage to First National on the same property to secure nineteen additional promissory notes totaling approximately $650,000. Each mortgage contained a clause allowing First National to sell the mortgaged property at public auction in the event of default.

Following the debtor's default in September of 1980, First National commenced foreclosure proceedings. A sheriff's auction was held on October 31, 1980, in conformity with the requirements of Minnesota statutes. At that auction First National purchased the mortgaged property for the sum of $566,355.34.

Minn. Stat. § 580.23(2) provides that a mortgagor shall have twelve months following the sale of real estate within which to redeem the property by paying the sale price plus interest from the date of the sale. In this instance that redemption period would have expired on or about October 31, 1981. Approximately three weeks prior to the expiration date, however, without having redeemed the property, the debtors filed a joint petition for reorganization under Chapter 11 of the Bankruptcy Code (the "Code"), and an adversary complaint alleging, in part, that they had substantial equity in the mortgaged property and were entitled to an order staying the expiration of the redemption period.

At a hearing convened before the bankruptcy court on October 16, 1981, Curtis Johnson testified that he estimated the value of the mortgaged property at $2,720,000 and that the encumbrances against the property totaled $2,043,000. Based upon Johnson's testimony, on October 20, 1981, the bankruptcy judge found that "an exigency exists, and that the debtors have substantial equity in [the] real property." Upon these findings, he enjoined First National from taking any further action to foreclose the property and ordered that the running of the statutory redemption period be stayed until further order or until the bankruptcy cases concerning the property were closed, all pursuant to 11 U.S.C. § 105. On March 17, 1982, the district court affirmed the bankruptcy court's order.

\* \* \*

The issue as to whether the broad powers granted the bankruptcy court by § 105(a)—to "issue any order \* \* \* necessary or appropriate to carry out the provision of [the Code]"—empowers the court to suspend the running of a statutory period of redemption in a matter of first impression among the circuit courts. An examination of the reported decisions of those district courts and bankruptcy courts which have considered the matter reveals a wide divergence of opinion.

Section 2(a)(15) of the Bankruptcy Act, from which § 105(a) is derived, allowed a bankruptcy court to issue such orders as might be necessary to prevent the defeat or impairment of its jurisdiction and to protect the integrity of the bankruptcy estate. \* \* \* Although § 105(a) is in certain respects broader in scope than its predecessor, the general equitable powers granted to the bankruptcy court by the statute are not unlimited, particularly in instances where property rights created and defined by state law are involved.

\* \* \*

\* \* \* [I]t follows that, absent a specific grant of authority from Congress or exceptional circumstances, a bankruptcy court may not exercise its equitable powers to create substantive rights which do not exist under state law. \* \* \* To conclude otherwise, and thus to hold that a bankruptcy court may, as a matter of course, suspend the running of a statutory period of redemption pursuant to § 105(a), would be to enlarge the debtor's property rights beyond those specifically set forth by the Minnesota legislature and by Congress in § 108(b). Despite the broad equitable powers bestowed by § 105(a), we therefore find ourselves in agreement with those courts which have held that § 105(a) may not be invoked to toll or suspend the running of a statutory period of redemption absent fraud, mistake, accident, or erroneous conduct on the part of the foreclosing officer. \* \* \*

Although the bankruptcy court here did not purport to create a uniform rule that the redemption period is tolled whenever a petition in bankruptcy is filed, we cannot agree with the district court that the bankruptcy court's order was a proper exercise of its equitable authority to deal with a "particular, individualized problem" under the standards outlined above. The bankruptcy court, after hearing certain evidence, found only "that an exigency exists, and that the debtors have substantial equity" in the property. One might well anticipate that in many instances the debtor will indeed enjoy substantial equity in the property in question. It is precisely this concern, however, which the Minnesota legislature addressed by providing for a one-year period of redemption. As will be developed in detail below, whatever "exigency" may be said to have existed due to the timing of the expiration of that period was susceptible to alleviation by the specific provisions of § 108(b). There is no claim that First National or any other party was guilty of any wrongdoing which adversely affected the debtors' ability to redeem the property within the statutory period. "[E]quity is available to protect property rights of the innocent debtor from the wrongful acts of other persons; however, equity does not extend to situations in which the debtor is simply unable to make the required payment within the prescribed time." *In re Headley*, [13 B.R. 295, 297 (Bankr.D.Colo.1981).] Nor have the debtors identified any federal interest which would * * * justify interference with clearly expressed state law and thwart First National's reasonable expectation that, upon expiration of the redemption period, it would obtain full title to the property. Given these circumstances, we hold that the bankruptcy court erred in ordering that the running of the statutory period of redemption be stayed pursuant to § 105(a).

Although the district court rested its decision solely upon § 105(a), the potential application of two other statutes—namely, § 362(a) and § 108(b)—has been briefed and argued on appeal by the parties. Since an appellate court is entitled to affirm a district court's judgment on grounds other than those relied upon by the district court, * * * a complete disposition of the present appeal therefore requires us to determine whether the decision below may be sustained by virtue of either of these two statutes.

Courts which have considered the present question under § 362(a) and § 108(b) have been virtually unanimous in concluding that, upon the filing of a petition in bankruptcy by a debtor, one of the two sections operates to stay the expiration of a statutory redemption period. The courts are in sharp disagreement, however, as to which section is the fount of such authority, and as to the extent of the relief granted. One line of cases * * * stands for the proposition that the automatic stay provisions of § 362(a) should be liberally construed to suspend the running of a statutory period of redemption. Other decisions, holding to the contrary with respect to § 362(a), have instead found that § 108(b) is the sole applicable statute, and that its automatic extension of a redemption period provides the only relief available. * * * We conclude that the latter group of cases more accurately construe the language and legislative history of the two sections.

Preliminary to an examination of § 362(a), it is important to identify the debtors' remaining interest in mortgaged property following a foreclosure sale, and to determine whether that interest constitutes property of the bankruptcy estate. It is long-settled under Minnesota law that foreclosure extinguishes the mortgage and that the purchaser at the foreclosure sale acquires a vested right to become the absolute owner of the property upon expiration of the redemption period, or, in lieu thereof, to receive the payment of the purchase price plus interest. * * * The mortgagor, on the other hand, retains only the equity of redemption, plus the rights to possessions, rents, and profits of the property during the period of redemption. Accordingly, it is only the right of redemption, rather than the property itself, which passes into the bankruptcy estate if the redemption period has not expired at the time the bankruptcy petition is filed. * * *

Section 362(a) prohibits the "commencement or continuation * * * of a judicial, administrative, or other proceeding," the "enforcement" of a judgment obtained prior to bankruptcy, or any other "act" to obtain possession of property of the estate or to create, perfect, or enforce any lien against property of the estate. The fundamental purposes of the automatic stay imposed by § 362(a) against such actions are two-fold: to provide the debtor with a breathing spell from the collection efforts of creditors, and to protect creditors by insuring that the assets of the estate will not be dissipated in a number of different proceedings. * * * Although a stay under the circumstances involved here would be consistent with these broad policies, we are of the view that § 362(a) cannot be read to stay the mere running of a statutory time period.

We respectfully disagree with those courts which have held that an automatic transfer of property, following the expiration of a period of redemption, constitutes either an "act" or "proceeding," or the "enforcement" of a right, within the meaning of § 362(a). * * * That Congress intended § 362(a) to prohibit only certain types of *affirmative actions* is evidenced by its use of the terms referenced above and by a corresponding failure to use terms which appropriately describe the suspension or extension of a statutory time period. * * * It is also instructive to note that although Congress did not, in § 362(a), specifically empower the bankruptcy court to suspend the running of a statutory period of redemption, it had no difficulty expressing such authority when it amended § 203 of the Bankruptcy Act in 1935 to provide for the tolling of statutory redemption periods in cases involving the reorganization of family farming operations.

Section 362(a) was designed to codify, in a single section, the scattered provisions of the Act and the former Bankruptcy Rules which governed the stay of various actions. 2 *Collier on Bankruptcy* ¶ 362.01 at 362–5 (15th ed.1983). The clear majority of cases decided under the prior provisions relating to automatic stays held that the filing of a petition in bankruptcy did not toll or extend the running of a statutory period of redemption. * * * If we assume, as it is proper to do, that Congress acts with knowledge of existing law, * * * it follows that, absent a clear manifestation of contrary intent, a newly-enacted or revised statute is presumed to be harmonious with existing law and its judicial construction. * * * This presumption is especially valid where, as in the present case, the language of the statute under consideration is substantially identical to that of the previous statutes. * * * We conclude, therefore, that § 362(a) does not operate to toll or suspend the running of the one-year statutory period of redemption created by Minn. Stat. § 580.23(2).

The opposite result has been reached in jurisdictions which require that some affirmative action be taken by a creditor or by a third party in order to transfer full title to property upon the expiration of the period of redemption. * * * Under the statutory scheme adopted by Minnesota, however, once the sheriff's certificate is issued to the successful bidder following the foreclosure sale, no further proceedings are required to vest absolute title to the property in the holder of the sheriff's certificate, assuming the debtor takes no steps to redeem the property.[10] * * * First National, as purchaser at the foreclosure sale, thus had the right to expect either full title upon the expiration of the redemption period or, in lieu thereof, payment of the full purchase price plus accrued interest. Even accepting the debtors' argument that § 362(a) is designed in part to preserve the status quo as of the date of the petition in bankruptcy, their right remains only to redeem the property within the period established by statute. To hold that § 362(a) operates as an automatic stay of the running of the statutory period of redemption would be to enlarge property rights created by state law, a result we view as unjustified by the language of § 362(a) and as unintended by Congress.

Our conclusion regarding § 362(a) is also based in part upon the presence in the Code of § 108(b). That latter section, derived from § 11(e) of the Act, provides that where the debtor "may file any pleading, demand, notice, or proof of claim or loss, cure a default, or perform any other similar act," and the period for so doing has not expired as of the filing of the petition in bankruptcy, the trustee is given until the end of such period, "including any suspension of such period occurring on or after the commencement of the case," or 60 days, whichever is later, to perform that act. The relationship between § 362(a) and § 108(b) was treated at length in *Bank of Commonwealth v. Bevan*, [13 B.R. 989 (E.D.Mich.1981).] the case which underlies the district court's opinion below and one of the few cases to consider all three statutes involved in this controversy (i.e., §§ 362(a), 108(b), and 105(a)). In *Bevan*, the mortgagor filed a petition for reorganization under Chapter 11 of the Code following foreclosure of the mortgaged property. The bankruptcy court subsequently entered an order pursuant to § 362(a), indefinitely extending the statutory redemption period. In reviewing the bankruptcy court's order the district court noted that, unlike the language of § 362(a), which does not appear to affect the running of specific time periods, § 108(b) explicitly grants the trustee additional time in which to perform an act such as that of redemption. Reading the two sections together, the court held that the automatic stay provisions of § 362(a) do not override the extension of time provision contained in § 108(b). "While a stay tolling the running of the statutory period would give the debtor greater protection than that contemplated by § 108," the

---

[10] It may also be noted that apparently Minnesota law contains no provision for extension of the statutory period of redemption.

court reasoned, "where one section of the Bankruptcy Code explicitly governs an issue, another section should not be interpreted to cause an irreconcilable conflict." Id., at 994. Thus, the court concluded:

"An interpretation of § 362(a) as an indefinite stay of the statutory period of redemption would render § 108(b) superfluous. If § 362(a) automatically stays the running of the statutory right to redeem until the stay is lifted pursuant to § 362(c) or (d), the pertinent time allotments of § 108(b) are completely extraneous as statutory time periods designed to control the trustee's activity. Moreover, if § 362(a) is interpreted to provide for the automatic stay of time periods for an indefinite amount of time, then subsections (a) and (b) of § 108, which define minimum and maximum time periods for the trustee to act, directly conflict with § 362(a)." Id., at 994.

A number of other courts have agreed * * * as does the leading authority in the field, see 4 *Collier on Bankruptcy*, ¶ 541.07[3] at 541–30 (15th ed.1983).

Given our conclusion that the bankruptcy court lacked authority under either § 105(a) or § 362(a), to stay indefinitely the expiration of the statutory period of redemption, it becomes apparent that the only extension of time available to the debtors was that provided by the express terms of § 108(b). Since their petition in bankruptcy was filed on October 8, 1981, some three weeks prior to the expiration of the one-year statutory period of redemption, the debtors had sixty days from the former date, or until December 8, 1981, within which to redeem the mortgaged property. That sixty-day period having passed without the debtors redeeming the property, full title vested automatically in First National in accordance with Minnesota law.

The decision of the district court is reversed and the case is remanded to the district court for further proceedings consistent with this opinion.

## PROBLEM

On November 1, Debtor filed a petition in bankruptcy under Chapter 11. On June 1 of that year Debtor had obtained an option under which Debtor had the right to purchase a tract of real property for $100,000 at any time before December 1. At the time Debtor filed in bankruptcy the option had not yet been exercised. Does Debtor, as debtor in possession, have any right to exercise the option on or after December 1? Does § 108(b) apply? *See Good Hope Refineries, Inc. v. Benavides*, 602 F.2d 998 (1st Cir.1979); *In re Santa Fe Development & Mortgage Corp.*, 16 B.R. 165 (9th Cir. B.A.P. 1981); *Collier on Bankruptcy* ¶ 108.03[1] (15th ed. rev. 2004).

## E. ACTIONS AGAINST NONDEBTORS

### 1. CO-DEFENDANTS IN LAWSUITS

Section 362(a)(1) applies to actions and other proceedings against the debtor. It does not apply to actions or proceedings against anybody other than the debtor. But § 105(a) gives the bankruptcy court broad authority to "issue any order, process, or judgment that is necessary or appropriate to carry out the provisions of this title." Can § 105(a) be used to provide relief to anyone other than the debtor? *Lynch v. Johns–Manville Sales Corp.*, 710 F.2d 1194 (6th Cir.1983), concerns that problem. Thousands of personal-injury actions had been brought against two major asbestos manufacturers, Johns–Manville and Unarco. While the cases were pending, Johns–Manville and Unarco filed in bankruptcy under Chapter 11. As a result, all of these actions were stayed by § 362(a)(1) and relief from the stay under § 362(d) was not available. Since an asbestos victim does not normally know the identity of the manufacturer of the asbestos that caused the injury, the practice is for the victim to file an action in which all available asbestos manufacturers are joined as co-defendants. Thus, in the actions against Johns–Manville and Unarco there were other defendants, and some were not in bankruptcy. Since the nonbankrupt defendants are not covered by § 362(a)(1), the pending actions, although stayed so far as Johns–Manville and Unarco were concerned, could continue against the nonbankrupt defendants. Some of these defendants asked the bankruptcy court to use its equity powers to stay continuation of these actions against them. Their arguments were summarized in *Lynch* as follows:

> Particularly, the solvent co-defendants conjecture that a continuation of proceedings in the absence of J–M and Unarco will result in multiple and piecemeal litigation on a scale heretofore unknown in the history of American jurisprudence; initial litigation would transpire in the state and federal forums and then duplicative litigation would issue in the respective bankruptcy forums for indemnity or contribution thereby adversely impacting upon valuable judicial resources and generating a risk of inadequate and conflicting adjudications. Additionally the solvent co-defendants assert that the automatic stay of . . . § 362 precludes discovery upon J–M and Unarco thereby seriously compromising their ability to successfully defend pending actions.

710 F.2d at 1199. The court denied relief and gave the following response to the arguments stated above:

> Confronting these arguments, it is initially observed that any duplicative or multiple litigation which may occur is a direct by-product of bankruptcy law. As such, the duplication, to the extent that it may exist, is congressionally created and sanctioned. More importantly, however, any benefits which may derive to the solvent co-defendants

from a stay are clearly outweighed by the countervailing interests of the plaintiffs. As the First Circuit has cogently observed:

> In a number of those [asbestos] cases, plaintiffs and crucial witnesses are dying. We are not persuaded that the hardship to defendants of having to go forward on this appeal without Unarco, or the interests of judicial economy in avoiding relitigation of the issues, are strong enough to justify forcing plaintiff and a number of other plaintiffs to wait until bankrupt defendants are successfully reorganized in order to be able to pursue their claims.

[*Austin v. Unarco Industries, Inc.*, 705 F.2d 1, 5 (1st Cir.1983).] The First Circuit's implicit concern that time is of the essence in the prosecution of asbestos cases is further amplified by the unknown and potentially unlimited duration of the stay which, to successfully avoid duplicative litigation, must necessarily issue until reorganization is effected:

> A "temporary" stay which was keyed to the resolution of the pending "relief-from-stay" petitions in the bankruptcy courts could, indeed, become one of nearly "indefinite," or, at least, unpredictable duration. These plaintiffs should not be thus denied a forum in which to pursue their claims against those defendants who remain unshielded by the bankruptcy laws. *In re Related Asbestos Cases*, [23 B.R. 523, 532 (N.D.Cal.1982)].

710 F.2d at 1199.

Although courts have generally been unwilling to use § 105(a) to protect the interest of a nondebtor, actions against nondebtors have been stayed in a number of Chapter 11 cases on the ground that reorganization of the debtor could be jeopardized by continuation of an action against a third party that affects the debtor. An example is the following case.

## A.H. Robins Co. v. Piccinin
United States Court of Appeals, Fourth Circuit, 1986.
788 F.2d 994.

■  Donald Russell, Circuit Judge:

Confronted, if not overwhelmed, with an avalanche of actions filed in various state and federal courts throughout the United States by citizens of this country as well as of foreign countries seeking damages for injuries allegedly sustained by the use of an intrauterine contraceptive device known as a Dalkon Shield, the manufacturer of the device, A.H. Robins Company, Incorporated (Robins) filed its petition under Chapter 11 of the Bankruptcy Code in August, 1985.

The device, which is the subject of these suits, had been developed in the 1960's by Dr. Hugh Davis at the Johns Hopkins Hospital in Baltimore, Maryland. In mid–1970 Robins acquired all patent and marketing rights to the Dalkon Shield and engaged in the manufacture and marketing of the device from early 1971 until 1974, when it discontinued manufacture and sale of the device because of complaints and suits charging injuries arising allegedly out of the use of the device. The institution of Dalkon Shield suits did not, however, moderate with the discontinuance of manufacture of the device, since Robins did not actually recall the device until 1984. By the middle of 1985, when the Chapter 11 petition was filed the number of such suits arising out of the continued sale and use of the Dalkon Shield device earlier put into the stream of commerce by Robins had grown to 5,000. More than half of these pending cases named Robins as the sole defendant; a co-defendant or co-defendants were named in the others. Prior to the filing, a number of suits had been tried and, while Robins had prevailed in some of the actions, judgments in large and burdensome amounts had been recovered in others. Many more had been settled.[4] Moreover, the costs of defending these suits both to Robins and to its insurance carrier had risen into the millions. A large amount of the time and energies of Robins' officers and executives was also being absorbed in preparing material for trial and in attending and testifying at depositions and trials. The problems arising out of this mounting tide of claims and suits precipitated this Chapter 11 proceeding.

The filing of the Chapter 11 petition automatically stayed all suits against Robins itself under section 362(a) of the Bankruptcy Code * * *. But a number of plaintiffs in suits where there were defendants other than Robins, sought to sever their actions against Robins and to proceed with their claims against the co-defendant or co-defendants. Robins responded to the move by filing an adversary proceeding in which it named as defendants the plaintiffs in eight such suits pending in various state and federal courts. In that proceeding, the debtor sought (1) declaratory relief adjudging that the debtor's products liability policy with Aetna Casualty and Insurance Company (Aetna) was an asset of the estate in which all the Dalkon Shield plaintiffs and claimants had an interest and (2) injunctive relief restraining the prosecution of the actions against its co-defendants. * * *

* * *

At the hearing on the motion for a preliminary injunction, a number of defendants as well as the Committee constituted by the court to represent Dalkon Shield Claimants appeared by counsel. At the commencement of the hearing the defendant Piccinin, a plaintiff in one of the Dalkon Shield actions which Robins sought to stay, filed through her attorney a written motion to dismiss as against her. No other defendant filed a motion in response to the motion for a preliminary injunction. After receiving certain testimony, admitting various records, and hearing arguments of parties, the district court granted Robins' request for a preliminary injunction.

---

[4] * * * A recent article in the Nat.L.J., p. 10, (March 17, 1986), states that by mid 1985, Robins, along with its insurer, Aetna Casualty & Surety Company, "had paid roughly $517 million for 25 trial judgments and 9,300 settlements since the first verdict in 1975."

In his order granting the preliminary injunction, the district judge found (1) that continuation of litigation in the civil actions threatened property of Robins' estate, burdened and impeded Robins' reorganization effort, contravened the public interest, and rendered any plan of reorganization futile; (2) that this burden on Robins' estate outweighed any burden on the Dalkon claimants caused by enjoining their civil actions; and (3) that all remaining insurance coverage in favor of the debtor under its liability policy issued by Aetna was property of the Robins' Chapter 11 estate. The district judge then held that all actions for damages that might be satisfied from proceeds of the Aetna insurance policy were subject to the stay pursuant to § 362(a)(3) and enjoined further litigation in the eight civil actions, pursuant to § 362(a)(1), (3) as supplemented by § 105.

\* \* \*

## I

The initial question in the appeal of the first issue relates to the court's jurisdiction to grant a stay or injunction of suits in other courts against co-defendants of the debtor or of third parties; none of the parties herein contest the jurisdiction of the bankruptcy court to stay actions against the debtor itself in any court. Jurisdiction over suits involving co-defendants or third-parties may be bottomed on two statutory provisions of the Bankruptcy Act itself as well as on the general equitable powers of the court. The first of these statutory grants of jurisdiction is found in section 362 \* \* \*.

\* \* \*

### (a)

[Section 362](a)(1) is generally said to be available only to the debtor, not third party defendants or co-defendants. \* \* \* However, as the Court in *Johns–Manville Sales Corp.*, 26 B.R. 405, 410 (S.D.N.Y.1983) remarked, \* \* \* "there are cases [under § 362(a)(1)] where a bankruptcy court may properly stay the proceedings against non-bankrupt co-defendants" but, it adds, that in order for relief for such non-bankrupt defendants to be available under § 362(a)(1), there must be "unusual circumstances" and certainly " "[s]omething more than the mere fact that one of the parties to the lawsuit has filed a Chapter 11 bankruptcy must be shown in order that proceedings be stayed against non-bankrupt parties." This "unusual situation," it would seem, arises when there is such identity between the debtor and the third-party defendant that the debtor may be said to be the real party defendant and that a judgment against the third-party defendant will in effect be a judgment or finding against the debtor. An illustration of such a situation would be a suit against a third-party who is entitled to absolute indemnity by the debtor on account of any judgment that might result against them in the case. To refuse application of the statutory stay in that case would defeat the very purpose and intent of the statute. \* \* \*

\* \* \*

**(b)**

But [§ 362](a)(1), which stays actions against the debtor and arguably against those whose interests are so intimately intertwined with those of the debtor that the latter may be said to be the real party in interest, is not the only part of section 362 providing for an automatic stay of proceedings. Subsection (a)(3) directs stays of any action, *whether against the debtor or third-parties,* to obtain possession or to exercise control over property of the debtor. A key phrase in the construction and application of this section is, of course, "property" as that term is used in the Act. Section 541(a)(1) \* \* \* provides that the "estate is comprised of all the following property, wherever located \* \* \* all legal or equitable interests of the debtor in property as of the commencement of the case." \* \* \*

Under the weight of authority, insurance contracts have been said to be embraced in this statutory definition of "property." *In re Davis,* 730 F.2d 176, 184 (5th Cir.1984). For example, even the right to cancel an insurance policy issued to the debtor has uniformly been held to be stayed under section 362(a)(3). \* \* \* A products liability policy of the debtor is similarly within the principle: it is a valuable property of a debtor, particularly if the debtor is confronted with substantial liability claims within the coverage of the policy in which case the policy may well be, as one court has remarked in a case like the one under review, "the most important asset of [i.e., the debtor's] estate," *In re Johns–Manville Corp.,* 40 B.R. 219, 229 (S.D.N.Y.1984). Any action in which the judgment may diminish this "important asset" is unquestionably subject to a stay under this subsection. Accordingly actions "related to" the bankruptcy proceedings against the insurer or against officers or employees of the debtor who may be entitled to indemnification under such policy or who qualify as additional insureds under the policy are to be stayed under section 362(a)(3).

**(c)**

The statutory power of the bankruptcy court to stay actions involving the debtor or its property is not, however, limited to section 362(a)(1) and (a)(3). It has been repeatedly held that § 105 which provides that the bankruptcy court "may issue any order, process, or judgment that is necessary or appropriate to carry out the provisions of this title," "empowers the bankruptcy court to enjoin parties other than the bankrupt" from commencing or continuing litigation. *In re Otero Mills, Inc.,* 25 B.R. 1018, 1020 (D.N.M.1982).

\* \* \*

[In *In re Johns–Manville Corp.,* 40 B.R. 219 (S.D.N.Y.1984),] the Court phrased somewhat fuller the circumstances when section 105 may support a stay:

> In the exercise of its authority under § 105, the Bankruptcy Court may use its injunctive authority to "protect the integrity of a bankrupt's estate and the Bankruptcy Court's custody thereof and to preserve to

that Court the ability to exercise the authority delegated to it by Congress" [citing authority]. Pursuant to the exercise of that authority the Court may issue or extend stays to enjoin a variety of proceedings [including discovery against the debtor or its officers and employees] which will have an adverse impact on the Debtor's ability to formulate a Chapter 11 plan.

40 B.R. at 226.

**(d)**

Beyond these statutory powers under section 362 and section 105 to enjoin other actions whether against the debtor or third-parties and in whatsoever court, the bankruptcy court under its comprehensive jurisdiction as conferred by [28 U.S.C.] § 1334 has the "inherent power of courts under their general equity powers and in the efficient management of the dockets to grant relief" to grant a stay. * * * In exercising such power the court, however, must "weigh competing interests and maintain an even balance" and must justify the stay "by clear and convincing circumstances outweighing potential harm to the party against whom it is operative." * * *

* * *

**(g)**

* * * In the three situations in which the defendants have challenged the injunction granted by the district judge * * * the only defendants other than the debtor, are the two Robins, Dr. Frederick A. Clark, Jr., Dr. Hugh J. Davis, and the debtor's insurer Aetna. So far as the suits against the two Robins and Dr. Clark, those defendants were entitled to indemnification by the debtor under the corporate by-laws and the statutes of Virginia, the State of debtor's incorporation, and were, in addition, additional insureds under the debtor's insurance policy. Dr. Davis was the beneficiary of an express contract of indemnification on the part of Robins and was, under a compromise agreement with Robins and Aetna, an additional insured under Robins' insurance policy. The *Manville* court had granted a preliminary injunction in favor of defendants in the same position as these defendants, as we have seen, on facts similar to those here, finding that the requirements of possible irreparable harm "had been satisfied by the showing * * * [that the suits against the defendants would represent] an immediate and irreparable impact on the pool of insurance assets, of the existence of sufficiently serious questions going to the merits," and of the tipping in the defendants' favor in the hardships in a balancing of the debtor's and the plaintiffs'. That court had previously disposed of the public interest being weighted in the debtor's favor: "Indeed, this Court finds the goal of removing all obstacles to plan formulation eminently praiseworthy and supports every lawful effort to foster this goal while protecting the due process rights of all constituencies." 26 B.R. at 428.

## II

The district court in this case applied the test for a grant of preliminary injunctive relief * * *. It found, as had the Johns–Manville courts, that irreparable harm would be suffered by the debtor and by the defendants since any of these suits against these co-defendants, if successful, would reduce and diminish the insurance fund or pool represented in Aetna's policy in favor of Robins and thereby affect the property of the debtor to the detriment of the debtor's creditors as a whole. The likelihood of success by the debtor under these circumstances appeared indisputable. The hardships which would be suffered irreparably by the debtor and by its creditors generally in permitting these plaintiffs to secure as it were a preference in the distribution of the insurance pool herein to which all creditors were entitled, together with the unquestioned public interest in promoting a viable reorganization of the debtor can be said to outweigh any contrary hardship to the plaintiffs. Such was the finding in the *Manville* cases and that finding does not appear unreasonable here.

The appellants, however, suggest that the record is insufficient to support such findings by the district judge. We disagree. The record is not extensive but it includes every fact considered by the courts in the *Manville* cases to be necessary for their decision. The rights of Dr. Davis, Dr. Clark and the two Robins to indemnity and their status as additional insureds under Robins' insurance policy are undisputed on the record. That there are thousands of Dalkon Shield actions and claims pending is a fact established in the record and the limited fund available under Robins' insurance policy is recognized in the record. It seems incontestable that, if the suits are permitted to continue and discovery allowed, any effort at reorganization of the debtor will be frustrated, if not permanently thwarted. It is obvious from the record that if suits are permitted to proceed against indemnitees on claims on which the indemnitees are entitled to indemnity by Robins, either a binding judgment against the debtor will result or * * * inconsistent judgments will result, calling for the exercise of the court's equitable powers. In our opinion, the record was thus more than adequate to support the district court's grant of injunctive relief. Certainly, the district court did not commit an abuse of discretion in granting the injunction herein.

The appellants add a final complaining note that the district judge stated in his decision that the "Conclusions of Law" made by him should apply "with equal force to all defendants similarly situated who are brought to the attention of the court." This is little different, however, from the language of the court in the *Manville* cases in which there was a broad, general injunction against all present or future suits.

In summary, we have no difficulty in sustaining the grant of a preliminary injunction herein. We are sustained in this conclusion by the fact, recognized by the district judge on the record, that any Dalkon Shield plaintiff may at any time petition for the vacation of the stay as it affects his or her suit and he or she is entitled to a hearing on such petition. Actually, there is one such petition pending and the district judge has agreed to set a hearing on that petition.

\* \* \*

## NOTES

**1.** In *In re Minoco Group of Companies, Ltd.*, 799 F.2d 517 (9th Cir.1986), Minoco owned insurance policies that covered claims by directors and officers for indemnification for legal expenses and judgments arising from their activities as directors and officers. The policies covered claims made through July 1, 1984. The policies were prepaid, but they allowed either Minoco or the insurers to cancel at any time upon 30 days notice. Minoco filed in Chapter 11 in September 1983. Two months later the insurers cancelled the policies. Minoco brought an action seeking a declaratory judgment that cancellation of the policies was automatically stayed by § 362(a). The court held that § 362(a)(3) applied. The court explained:

> The reasoning of the Fourth Circuit in *A.H. Robins* applies to this case with full force. For the purposes of the automatic stay, we see no significant distinction between a liability policy that insures the debtor against claims by *consumers* and one that insures the debtor against claims by *officers and directors*. In either case, the insurance policies protect against diminution of the value of the estate. As the Fourth Circuit understood, liability policies meet the fundamental test of whether they are 'property of the estate' because the debtor's estate is worth more with them than without them. *See* Jackson, *Translating Assets and Liabilities to the Bankruptcy Forum*, 14 J.Legal Stud. 73, 99 (1985). Accordingly, cancellation of the insurance policies by First State was automatically stayed by section 362(a)(3).

799 F.2d at 519.

**2.** Assume the common case in which Debtor has a liability policy with Insurer to pay personal injury and property damages claims stemming from Debtor's use of an automobile up to a limit of $500,000? Debtor negligently injured Plaintiff who sued Debtor and Insurer for $200,000. Debtor filed in Chapter 7 and Debtor and Insurer sought to stay Plaintiff's suit under § 362(a)(3) and § 105(a) on the ground that the insurance policy was property of Debtor's estate. Should Plaintiff's suit against Insurer be enjoined? *Matter of Edgeworth*, 993 F.2d 51 (5th Cir.1993), held in a comparable case that the insurance proceeds were not property of the estate because they were entirely payable to Plaintiff; Debtor has no right to receive and keep any of the proceeds. Liability insurance policies differ from those covering collision and fire insurance in which the proceeds go to Debtor as beneficiary and inure to the creditors of the estate. The court distinguished the facts in this Note from those of cases like *Piccinin* in which liability insurance proceeds would be exhausted by the claims of the many plaintiffs if the proceeds were not marshaled in a bankruptcy proceeding. The Fifth Circuit subsequently retreated somewhat from this view. *In re Vitek*, 51 F.3d 530, 535 (5th Cir. 1995). These issues are discussed further in *In re Sfuzzi, Inc.*, 191 B.R. 664 (Bankr.N.D.Tex.1996).

## 2. THIRD PARTIES LIABLE TO PAY THE DEBTOR'S OBLIGATIONS

### a.   Guarantors

## Credit Alliance Corp. v. Williams
United States Court of Appeals, Fourth Circuit, 1988.
851 F.2d 119.

■ WILKINSON, Circuit Judge:

\* \* \*

### I.

On February 22, 1980, Penn Hook Coal Co. signed a three year conditional sales contract note with Croushorn Equipment Co. for the purchase of a John Deere wheel loader. Croushorn assigned Penn Hook's note to Credit Alliance Corp. and Gary Williams and Malcolm C. Williams executed a guaranty of Penn Hook's obligation in favor of Credit Alliance.

Penn Hook subsequently defaulted on its obligation. On January 14, 1981, Credit Alliance filed suit in the United States District Court for the Southern District of New York against Penn Hook and the guarantors, Gary and Malcolm Williams. Credit Alliance sought judgment in the amount of $54,018.07, the balance due on the note after crediting the proceeds realized from the sale of the collateral, plus attorneys' fees, interest, and costs. Defendants failed to respond to the summons and complaint, and on March 4, 1981, Penn Hook petitioned for bankruptcy under Chapter 11 of the Bankruptcy Code in the District Court for the Western District of Virginia. On April 15, 1981, the District Court for the Southern District of New York entered a default judgment in the amount of $62,866.70 against the three defendants.

On October 5, 1984, Credit Alliance instituted garnishment proceedings against Penn Hook and the guarantors in the Western District of Virginia. The matter was referred to the bankruptcy court which held that the automatic stay provision of the Bankruptcy Code, § 362, rendered void the default judgment against the debtor and the non-debtor guarantors, entered after Penn Hook petitioned for bankruptcy. The district court reversed the decision of the bankruptcy court with respect to the guarantors, and held that Credit Alliance's claim against Gary Williams and Malcolm Williams was not stayed or void. Guarantor Gary Williams now appeals.

## II.

Appellant seeks to invoke the automatic stay provision of § 362 to invalidate the New York judgment entered against him in his capacity as guarantor of the now bankrupt debtor's note with Credit Alliance.

The plain language of § 362, however, provides only for the automatic stay of judicial proceedings and enforcement of judgments "against the debtor or the property of the estate." * * *

Nothing in § 362 suggests that Congress intended that provision to strip from the creditors of a bankrupt debtor the protection they sought and received when they required a third party to guaranty the debt. Congress knew how to extend the automatic stay to non-bankrupt parties when it intended to do so. Chapter 13, for example, contains a narrowly drawn provision to stay proceedings against a limited category of individual co-signers of consumer debts. *See* § 1301(a). No such protection is provided to the guarantors of Chapter 11 bankrupts by § 362(a). * * *

Guarantors of debtors proceeding in bankruptcy under Chapter 11 are limited to claims for reimbursement or contribution to the extent allowed under § 502(e) or subrogation to the rights of the creditor under § 509. This scheme protects the assured creditor "to the extent that a surety or codebtor is not permitted to compete with the creditor he has assured until the assured party's claim has been paid in full." 124 Cong.Rec. H11089 (Sept. 28, 1978) (statement of Rep. Edwards). A reading of § 362 restricting a creditor's ability to proceed against its guarantor would eliminate the protection of assured creditors contemplated by the Bankruptcy Code.

*A.H. Robins Co. v. Piccinin*, 788 F.2d 994 (4th Cir.1986), is not to the contrary. We recognized in *Robins* that in "unusual circumstances" a court, pursuant to § 362, may properly stay proceedings against non-bankrupt codefendants of the bankrupt debtor. Such unusual circumstances might arise where "there is such identity between the debtor and the third-party defendant that the debtor may be said to be the real party defendant and that a judgment against the third-party defendant will in effect be a judgment or finding against the debtor," id. at 999, or where proceedings against non-debtor codefendants would reduce or diminish "the property of the debtor [such as the debtor's insurance fund or pool] to the detriment of the debtor's creditors as a whole." Id. at 1008.

There is nothing "unusual" about this guaranty agreement that would permit the guarantor, Williams, to invoke the statutory protection of § 362 or that would permit us to stay the enforcement of the New York judgment against him on equitable grounds. *See A.H. Robins,* 788 F.2d at 1000. It is unnecessary to stay proceedings or void the judgment against the non-bankrupt guarantor to protect Penn Hook or to prevent the dissipation of its assets, since neither Penn Hook nor its estate is jeopardized by the judgment against Williams. "The very purpose of a guaranty is to assure the [creditor] that in the event the [debtor] defaults, the [creditor] will have someone to look to for reimbursement." *Rojas v. First Bank National Ass'n,* 613 F.Supp. 968, 971 (E.D.N.Y.1985). The purpose of the guaranty would be frustrated by interpreting § 362 so as to stay Credit Alliance's action against the non-bankrupt guarantor when the defaulting debtor petitioned for bankruptcy.

* * *

We conclude that the judgment against Gary Williams is valid and enforceable. The judgment of the district court is therefore

Affirmed.

## NOTES

**1.** *In re Otero Mills, Inc.*, 25 B.R. 1018 (D.N.M.1982), involved the use of § 105(a) with respect to a guaranty. Otero executed two promissory notes for a total principal amount of $650,000 in favor of Bank. The obligation of Otero to pay the notes was guaranteed by Dugan, a stockholder and the president of Otero. Otero defaulted on the notes and filed in Chapter 11. Dugan did not file in bankruptcy. Bank brought an action in state court against Dugan on the guaranty and obtained judgment. The bankruptcy court issued an injunction pursuant to § 105(a) against enforcement of the judgment against Dugan, but it allowed Bank to domesticate the judgment in states in which Dugan had assets. Bank appealed to the district court, which affirmed. The district court held that an injunction could issue only if there was proof that irreparable harm to the bankruptcy estate would result from enforcement of the judgment. Otero argued that irreparable harm would result because Otero's reorganization plan would require Dugan to contribute assets to the reorganized corporation. The bankruptcy court found that if Bank were allowed to reach Dugan's property the ability of Otero to implement its reorganization plan would be impaired.

Since in most cases, a personal guarantor of the debt of a corporation is a principal stockholder, it is likely that an argument such as that made in *Otero* will be made routinely in any instance in which the guarantor might contribute assets to the reorganization. What about the potential for harm to Bank? If Otero is unable to pay Bank and Dugan is allowed to divert assets to Otero that otherwise would be paid to Bank under the guaranty, Bank will be injured if Dugan has insufficient assets to pay Bank after contributing to the reorganization.

A debt that is secured by a personal guaranty can be compared to a debt secured by a lien in property of the debtor. If a debt is secured by a lien in property of the debtor, the creditor does not have an unqualified right to resort to the collateral when the debtor goes into bankruptcy. The secured creditor can be stayed from enforcing the lien if the collateral is necessary to the Chapter 11 reorganization and the secured claim is adequately protected. Does the same analysis apply to a personal guaranty? If resort to the guaranty will jeopardize the reorganization it may be proper to enjoin enforcement of the guaranty so long as the creditor's claim is adequately protected. The bankruptcy court in *Otero* recognized that Bank had a right to adequate protection of its claim and found that Bank was adequately protected. The loan was secured by assets of Debtor and Bank apparently stipulated that it was adequately protected "until at least August 26, 1982." The bankruptcy court indicated that it would consider lifting the stay when Bank was no longer adequately protected. Adequate protection is considered in chapter 10.

**2.** In *Matter of Supermercado Gamboa, Inc.,* 68 B.R. 230 (Bankr.D.Puerto Rico 1986), the court indicated that it would require a clear showing that making the nondebtor guarantor pay would have a detrimental impact on the debtor's reorganization before it would stay action against the guarantor. The court said, "I believe the more relaxed approach initiated in *In re Otero Mills, Inc.,* * * * and its progeny is simply bad law." 68 B.R. at 234. In *Supermercado* the court rejected the contention that the creditor's suit against the guarantor indirectly involved property of the estate and was stayed by § 362 because the guarantor might claim indemnity against the bankruptcy estate. It should not make any difference whether the guarantor had paid the creditor and had a claim for indemnity against the estate or the creditor remained unpaid and had its original claim. *Otero* is criticized in Howard C. Buschman, III, and Sean P. Madden, *The Power and Propriety of Bankruptcy Court Intervention in Actions Between Nondebtors,* 47 Bus.Law. 913 (1992).

**3.** The courts are divided on the extent to which injunctions against non-debtors are permissible on the ground that they are necessary to protect the debtor's ability to formulate a reorganization plan. For an exhaustive analysis of the subject, see Ralph Brubaker, *Bankruptcy Injunctions and Complex Litigation: A Critical Reappraisal of Non–Debtor Releases in Chapter 11 Reorganizations,* 1997 U. Ill. L.Rev. 959 (1997). He cites a number of cases permitting injunctions in such cases. *Id.* at 1055, n.363. In *Celotex Corp. v. Edwards,* 514 U.S. 300 (1995), the Supreme Court found that the bankruptcy court had jurisdiction to temporarily stay a non-debtor from execution on a supersedeas bond that could impede the debtor's ability to reorganize. Professor Brubaker distinguishes between temporary injunctions and permanent ones that amount to extinction of the non-debtor's rights; he finds no statutory predicate for the latter in the Code. Brubaker, *supra,* at 1077 *et seq.*

### b.  Issuers of Letters of Credit

There are three principal consensual security devices that can be used to assure payment of a debt. First, the debtor can grant the creditor a security interest in property of the debtor. Second, a third party can guarantee payment of the debt by either a personal guaranty or by providing collateral to secure payment of the debt. Third, the debtor can obtain a standby letter of credit from a bank for the benefit of the creditor. The bank that issues the letter of credit obligates itself to pay the creditor the amount of the debt if certain conditions stated in the letter of credit are met. The conditions usually require the creditor to demand payment from the bank and to provide a certificate or other evidence that the debt is due and has not been paid. In most cases the debtor grants a security interest in property to the bank or obtains a third-party guarantee to secure the debtor's obligation to reimburse the bank in the event the bank pays the creditor under the letter of credit.

A creditor dealing with a debtor with adequate collateral may have a choice of security devices. The creditor may obtain a security interest in the debtor's collateral, or the creditor may induce the debtor to cause a bank to issue a letter of credit for the benefit of the creditor. In the latter case, assume that the bank obtains a security interest in the debtor's property as security for its right of reimbursement. If the debtor is unable to pay the debt and files in bankruptcy, what are the rights of the creditor in each of the two cases? If the creditor was granted a security interest in the debtor's collateral, § 362(a)(4) stays any act by the creditor to enforce the security interest. If, instead, a letter of credit was issued to the creditor, does § 362(a) prevent the creditor from obtaining payment from the bank under the letter of credit? This issue was presented in *In re Page*, 18 B.R. 713 (D.D.C.1982). In that case the bankruptcy court enjoined payment of a letter of credit issued for the benefit of a creditor of a Chapter 11 debtor. In the opinion of the bankruptcy court, payment under the letter of credit would violate § 362(a)(3) and (4). On appeal, the district court reversed the bankruptcy court. Judge Gesell stated:

> With respect to § 362(a)(3), cashing the letter of credit will not divest the estate of property since neither the letter of credit nor its proceeds are property of the estate under the Bankruptcy Code. Section 541 defines property of the estate as "all legal or equitable interests of the debtor" (subject to various limitations not relevant in this case). In issuing the letter of credit the Bank entered into an independent contractual obligation to pay [the beneficiary of the letter of credit] out of its own assets. Although cashing the letter will immediately give rise to a claim by the Bank against the debtors pursuant to the latter's indemnification obligations, that claim will not divest the debtors of any property since any attempt to enforce that claim would be subject to an automatic stay pursuant to § 362a(4).
>
> Nor would cashing the letter of credit "create, perfect or enforce" a lien in the property securing the debtors' obligation to indemnify the Bank. The Bank's liens on property of the debtors to secure the letter of credit arrangement were created prior to the initiation of Chapter 11 proceedings and remain valid in bankruptcy whether or not the letter of credit is cashed. * * *
>
> It is uncontested that the Bank's liens were perfected prior to the Chapter 11 filing. Appellees acknowledge that the "security interest in favor of First National Bank was perfected when the Letter of Credit was initially provided." * * * Since the liens have already been perfected and the Bank is under a contractual obligation to fund the letter

of credit, the Bank has perfected liens valid in a Chapter 11 proceeding. Since perfected liens already exist cashing of the letter of credit cannot have the effect of either creating or perfecting a lien.

Cashing of the letter of credit is not an act to "enforce" a lien. The Bank will, of course, have a claim against the debtors under the indemnification agreement once the letter of credit is funded. But the filing of the Chapter 11 petition automatically stays any attempt to enforce that claim. Funding of the letter is therefore not an act to "enforce" a lien.

18 B.R. at 715–716. This statement of the law is generally accepted. See also *In re Prime Motor Inns, Inc.*, 130 B.R. 610 (S.D.Fla.1991).

### c.  Partners of Bankrupt Partnership

Partners of a general partnership are personally liable to pay the debts and obligations of the partnership. Revised Uniform Partnership Act § 306. In addition to having liability to partnership creditors, a partner is obliged to contribute toward the losses sustained by the partnership according to the partner's share in the profits. Revised Uniform Partnership Act § 401(b). Under § 807 of the Act, the assets of the partnership include the contributions of the partners necessary for the payment of all the liabilities of the partnership. Thus, the right of the partnership to obtain contribution from the partners is property of the bankruptcy estate under § 541(a)(1) if the partnership is in bankruptcy. Suppose a partnership has filed for relief under Chapter 11, but the partners of the firm have not filed in bankruptcy. If, after bankruptcy, a prepetition creditor of the partnership brings an action against a partner to enforce the claim, can the bankruptcy court use § 105(a) to enjoin the action? This issue was raised in the case that follows.

## Patton v. Bearden
United States Court of Appeals, Sixth Circuit, 1993.
8 F.3d 343.

■ KENNEDY, Circuit Judge.

In this contract case for royalties allegedly due, defendants Richard Bearden, Robert Bearden, and J.M. Bearden, individually and d/b/a Bearden Fish Farms (collectively referred to as "the Beardens") appeal the grant of summary judgment for Nicolas M. Patton, the plaintiff. The Beardens assert the following errors: * * * (3) the judgment against the Beardens violated the automatic bankruptcy stay of claims against the Bearden & Sons Fish Farm partnership. For the reasons stated below, we affirm.

Patton developed a process for a catfish breading mix and in 1982 entered into a licensing agreement with Anthony Pizzolato. This licensing agreement granted Pizzolato the exclusive right to produce Patton's breading mix. Subsequently, Pizzolato granted a sub-license for the breading mix to Richard Bearden, Robert Bearden and J.M. Bearden, individually and d/b/a Bearden Farms.

After production commenced, the Beardens issued several royalty checks directly to Patton as provided by the sub-license agreement. After the payments were sent to Patton, Patton then divided up the royalties between Pizzolato and himself. However, a dispute arose between Patton on the one hand and Pizzolato and the Beardens on the other regarding the production costs of the breading mix. Consequently, the Beardens stopped selling Patton's breading mix and contracted for a similar breading mix made by a different manufacturer and stopped making royalty payments to Patton.

In accord with the licensing agreement, Pizzolato and Patton settled their disagreement, regarding the production costs of the mix, by arbitration. As a result of this arbitration, Pizzolato assigned any rights he had to royalty payments from the Beardens to Patton.

Patton, the assignee, filed this action against the Beardens, individually and d/b/a Bearden Fish Farms, to recover unpaid royalties allegedly due under the sub-license agreement in the United States District Court for the Western Division of Tennessee. Patton then moved for summary judgment. * * * The District Court * * * granted Patton summary judgment.

\* \* \*

Finally, the Beardens filed a Notice of Bankruptcy indicating that Bearden & Sons Fish Farms d/b/a Bearden Farms, a partnership, had filed for chapter 11 reorganization. The Beardens argued that Richard Bearden, Robert Bearden and J.M. Bearden were partners of Bearden & Sons Fish Farm and that entry of judgment against the individuals, who are the partners of the debtor-partnership, violated the automatic stay of § 362.

The District Court rejected this argument because the automatic stay does not protect a partner of a partnership. * * *

\* \* \*

The District Court concluded that the automatic stay of claims against the debtor-partnership did not protect the Beardens. We agree that defendants' mere status as general partners does not entitle them to protection under the automatic stay of the debtor-partnership. * * *

The automatic stay provision of the Bankruptcy Code, § 362(a)(1) stays an "action or proceeding against the debtor that was or could have been commenced before the commencement of the case under this title, or to recover a claim against the debtor that arose before the commencement of the case under this title...." Clearly, § 362(a)(1) stays any actions against the *debtor*. The Beardens argue the stay should be extended to protect non-debtor partners, merely because of their partner status.

Under chapter 11, a partnership may file a petition in bankruptcy even though its partners have not. This Court sees no reason to ignore the formal distinctions between the partners and the partnership in this case. Because the partners are jointly and severally liable, Patton's action operates against individual assets of the partners, not partnership assets. Indeed, "[t]he stay of § 362 is extremely broad in scope. . . and should apply to almost any type of formal or informal action against the debtor or the property of the estate. . .. [The stay] does not extend, however, to separate legal entities such as corporate affiliates, *partners in debtor partnerships* or to codefendants in pending litigation." 2 *Collier on Bankruptcy* ¶ 362.04 (15th ed.1993) (emphasis added).

Some courts have held that the debtor's stay may be extended to non-bankrupt parties in "unusual circumstances." * * * Such circumstances usually include when the debtor and the non-bankrupt party are closely related or the stay contributes to the debtor's reorganization. It should be noted that such extensions, although referred to as extensions of the automatic stay, were in fact injunctions issued by the bankruptcy court after hearing and the establishment of unusual need to take this action to protect the administration of the bankruptcy estate.

Even if we were to adopt the unusual circumstances test, the bankruptcy court would first need to extend the automatic stay under its equity jurisdiction pursuant to § 105. Moreover, the Beardens have not brought forth any evidence of unusual circumstances which would justify extending the automatic stay to their protection.

Under § 362(a)(3), filing a chapter 11 petition stays "any act to obtain possession of property of the estate or of property from the estate or to exercise control over property of the estate." The Beardens argue that the partnership is entitled to compel contributions from the partners for partnership debt. This chose in action constitutes partnership property, and under § 541(a), this power to compel contributions became the property of the estate upon the filing of the bankruptcy petition and may be enforced against the partners to the extent of any deficiency in the debtor's property. The Beardens argue that § 362(a)(3) prevents the prosecution of the action against them because this action is "an act to obtain possession of property of the estate or to exercise control over property of the estate," and any proceeding against the general partners would necessarily impair the debtor's right to compel contribution from its partners, thus interfering with the debtor's property.

The court in *In re Litchfield Co. of South Carolina Limited Partnership*, 135 B.R. 797 (W.D.N.C.1992), adopted the argument urged by the defendants. However, in *Litchfield*, the partner promised to devote assets to the reorganizational efforts and testified that entry of the judgment could render the partner insolvent or impair his ability to pay the debtor's creditors if liquidation ensued. *Id.*, at 801; see also *In re Marley Orchards Income Fund I, Limited Partnership*, 120 B.R. 566 (Bankr.E.D.Wash.1990) (Court refused to extend the automatic stay to general partners of a debtor-partnership under § 362(a)(3) absent evidence of a potential deficiency in partnership assets.).

In the present case, the defendants do not even allege that the judgments here will render them insolvent or impair their ability to help with reorganizational efforts. Rather, the Beardens merely rely on their status as general partners to urge extension of the automatic stay for their benefit.

Thus, even if a debtor-partnership may under unusual circumstances seek an injunction prohibiting action against its partners, requests for such relief can only be presented to the bankruptcy court.

For the reasons stated above, we AFFIRM the District Court's decision.

## NOTES

**1.** *Patton* represents the prevailing view that § 362 should not be stretched to protect partners against partnership creditors. Partners have had somewhat better success in seeking a § 105(a) injunction on the ground that allowing suits against them will irreparably harm the partnership's attempt to reorganize. Factors courts have considered in § 105(a) cases are whether general partners' plans to contribute capital to the reorganized entity would be frustrated by allowing creditor suits against them and whether partners' efforts to defend themselves against creditors would divert their attention from the reorganization. *Litchfield*, discussed in *Patton*, is an example of the use of § 105 in conjunction with § 362(a)(3) in a partnership reorganization case. In that case a limited partnership had a general partner that was itself a partnership having two general partners (Partners). The limited partnership (Debtor) filed in Chapter 11 after a workout plan failed owing to Bank's refusal to agree to a stretchout and lowering of interest rate on its debt. Before Debtor filed, Bank had brought an action on its debt in state court against Debtor and Partners. Debtor's other creditors were unwilling to agree to a reorganization plan if Bank was able to recover against Partners. Debtor elicited an agreement from Partners to make their property available to help in funding the plan and filed a complaint seeking to stay Bank's suit against Partners. The court affirmed the bankruptcy court's grant of a stay under § 362(a)(3) and an injunction under § 105(a). Under the state law in question, a partnership had a right to compel its partners to contribute to it if necessary to pay its debts. The court held that this right is property of the partnership's estate in bankruptcy, and a suit by a partnership creditor against a partner is stayed under § 362(a)(3) because it is an act to obtain possession of property of the estate or to exercise control over property of the estate. The bankruptcy court properly exercised its discretion to enjoin the action of Bank against Partners under § 105(a) because of the likelihood of irreparable harm that would result were Bank allowed to recover from Partners. A judgment by Bank against Partners would block a successful reorganization because their assets, already pledged to the plan, were essential to success of the plan which called for paying all creditors in full over an extended period of time. With the injunction, the court believed Debtor had a reasonable likelihood of a successful reorganization.

**2.** The National Bankruptcy Review Commission proposed an elaborate restatement of bankruptcy law as it relates to partnerships, NBRC Rep. at 371–449. With respect to the issue of enjoining suits against nondebtor partners, the Commission recommendations permit a court to "temporarily enjoin" creditor actions against nondebtor partners on partnership claims for a limited period of time. The object is "to preserve asset values from dissipation through creditor action and provide nondebtor partners with a breathing spell in order to focus on rehabilitation or reorganization." NBRC Rep. at 405. Such an injunction does not operate automatically; the party requesting relief must demonstrate its entitlement to this protection. As a condition to this relief, a nondebtor partner must make disclosure of its financial condition. Since a delay may afford the nondebtor partner the opportunity to transfer or hide assets, the order granting the injunction may preclude the partner from incurring obligations or transferring property except under specified conditions. National Bankruptcy Conference, Reforming the Bankruptcy Code 218–222 (Rev.ed.1997), recommended a similar approach.

## G. RELIEF FROM AUTOMATIC STAY FOR CAUSE

Relief from the automatic stay pursuant to § 362(d) is an issue of great importance that has been heavily litigated. In this Chapter we briefly considered the issue as it relates to secured creditors in liquidation bankruptcy. In Chapters 9 and 10 we consider the issue in greater detail as it relates to secured creditors in rehabilitation and reorganization proceedings. In the present section we deal with but a limited part of the issue. We examine when a claimant barred by the automatic stay of § 362 is entitled to relief from the stay to allow a lawsuit pending against the debtor to proceed to judgment.

## In re Holtkamp

United States Court of Appeals, Seventh Circuit, 1982.
669 F.2d 505.

■ BAUER, Circuit Judge.

Defendants-appellants Charles Holtkamp and Holtkamp Farms, Inc. (collectively Holtkamp) appeal from an order of the bankruptcy court lifting an automatic stay and permitting a pending civil action to proceed. We affirm.

The pending civil action was a personal injury suit initiated by plaintiff-appellee Ronald E. Littlefield in 1979 and set for trial in May 1980. Five days before the trial was scheduled to begin, Holtkamp filed voluntary bankruptcy petitions under Chapter 11 of the Bankruptcy Code designating Littlefield's personal injury claim as an unsecured debt. The personal injury suit was stayed automatically pursuant to § 362(a). Littlefield immediately filed adversary proceedings in the bankruptcy court seeking an emergency hearing to lift the stay. Holtkamp had only three hours notice of this hearing. The bankruptcy court granted Littlefield's request to permit the personal injury suit to proceed to judgment, but prohibited Littlefield from attempting to collect any judgment he might receive. After a jury trial, a $5,025,000 judgment was entered in Littlefield's favor.

Holtkamp contends that the modification of the automatic stay arising under § 362 constitutes reversible error because it contravenes the express provisions of the statute. * * *

### I

Section 362(d) provides for relief from the automatic stay "for cause, including the lack of adequate protection of an interest in property of such party in interest." Since the statute commits the decision of whether to lift the stay to the discretion of the bankruptcy judge, his decision may be overturned only upon a showing of abuse of discretion. * * *

Citing no authority to support his contention, Holtkamp argues that § 362(d) applies only to secured creditors and, thus, has no relevance to Littlefield's unsecured claim. He maintains that Congress intended the automatic stay provisions to be broadly applied to cover all situations not specifically exempted by the statute and asserts that because none of the enumerated exceptions in § 362(d) apply here the lifting of the stay is contrary to both the spirit and the policy of the new Code. Holtkamp maintains that by permitting the litigation to proceed Littlefield, as an unsecured creditor, has improved his position at the expense of other creditors.

Holtkamp's contention that § 362(d) applies only to secured creditors is not supported by the statutory language or case-law. Subsection (d) grants relief from the automatic stay, under certain conditions, to "a party in interest." Had Congress intended the section to apply only to secured creditors, it undoubtedly would have so stated. Further, nothing in the legislative history implies that Congress intended the restrictive application Holtkamp urges. Moreover, although the scope of subsection (d) is an issue of first impression in this Circuit, courts from other jurisdictions have applied subsection (d) in analogous situations. Thus, previously filed actions involving unsecured creditors have been allowed to continue despite the automatic stay provisions in § 362(a). * * *

While we agree that Congress intended that the automatic stay have broad application, the legislative history to § 362 clearly indicates that Congress recognized that the stay should be lifted in appropriate circumstances. It states:

> [I]t will often be more appropriate to permit proceedings to continue in their place of origin, when no great prejudice to the bankruptcy estate would result, in order to leave the parties to their chosen forum and to relieve the bankruptcy court from many duties that may be handled elsewhere.

* * * S.Rep. No. 989, 95th Cong., 2d Sess. 50.

Holtkamp's claim that permitting the trial to go forward enabled Littlefield to gain a superior position over other creditors is belied by the facts. Holtkamp argues that by obtaining a judgment Littlefield can now enforce that judgment by securing a lien against Holtkamp's property. This contention is erroneous, for the bankruptcy's court's order expressly prohibited Littlefield from attempting to enforce his judgment. Allowing the pending action to proceed merely determined Holtkamp's liability but did not change Littlefield's status in relation to other creditors. * * *

Indeed, contrary to Holtkamp's assertion that the order of the bankruptcy court frustrated the policy of the Code, the lifting of the stay in this case is in complete harmony with the Code's policy of quickly and efficiently formulating plans for repayment and reorganization. The purpose of the automatic stay is to preserve what remains of the debtor's insolvent estate and to provide a systematic equitable liquidation procedure for all creditors, secured as well as unsecured * * * thereby preventing a "chaotic and uncontrolled scramble for the debtor's assets in a variety of uncoordinated proceedings in different courts." *In re Frigitemp Corp.*, 8 B.R. 284, 289 (S.D.N.Y.1981), citing *Fidelity Mortgage Investors v. Camelia Builders, Inc.*, 550 F.2d 47, 55 (2d Cir.1976).

However, where, as here, the pending action is neither connected with nor interfering with the bankruptcy proceeding, the automatic stay in no way fosters Code policy. * * * Allowing the civil action to go forward did not jeopardize Holtkamp's bankrupt estate because his insurance company assumed full financial responsibility for defending that litigation. On the other hand, the interests of judicial economy militated in favor of permitting the suit to go forward, for the trial date had been set and witnesses, including Littlefield who is a quadriplegic and several out of state witnesses, had been subpoenaed. Additionally, determination of the issues in the personal injury action did not require the expertise of the bankruptcy court. Under these circumstances, the lifting of the stay was proper.

* * *


## NOTES

**1.** A portion of the legislative history with respect to § 362 follows:

The lack of adequate protection of an interest in property of the party requesting relief from the stay is one cause for relief, but is not the only cause. [A] desire to permit an action to proceed to completion in another tribunal may provide another cause. Other causes might include the lack of any connection with or interference with the pending bankruptcy case. For example, a divorce or child custody proceeding involving the debtor may bear no relation to the bankruptcy case. In that case, it should not be stayed. A probate proceeding in which the debtor is the executor or administrator of another's estate usually will not be related to the bankruptcy case, and should not be stayed. Generally, proceedings in which the debtor is a fiduciary, or involving post-petition activities of the debtor, need not be stayed because they bear no relationship to the purpose of the automatic stay, which is debtor protection from his creditors. The facts of each request will determine whether relief is appropriate under the circumstances.

H.Rep. No. 95–595, 1978 U.S.C.C.A.N. 6300.

**2.** The statement in the above-quoted legislative history that "a desire to permit an action to proceed to completion in another tribunal" may be a cause for lifting the stay has proved prophetic. A strong body of authority is developing to the effect that a plaintiff in a nonbankruptcy proceeding against the debtor may have the stay lifted if it is ordered or stipulated that the plaintiff will use the nonbankruptcy forum only to liquidate the claim and not to satisfy any judgment obtained from the assets of the estate. The factors a court should consider in deciding whether cause has been shown under § 362(d)(1) are stated in *In re Robbins*, 964 F.2d 342, 345 (4th Cir.1992):

> **(1)** whether the issues in the pending litigation involve only state law, so the expertise of the bankruptcy court is unnecessary; **(2)** whether modifying the stay will promote judicial economy and whether there would be greater interference with the bankruptcy case if the stay were not lifted because matters would have to be litigated in bankruptcy court; and **(3)** whether the estate can be protected properly by a requirement that creditors seek enforcement of any judgment through the bankruptcy court.

## PROBLEM

Plaintiff sued Debtor in a state court in tort for negligence. The claim against Debtor was fully covered by Debtor's liability insurance. Before trial Debtor filed a petition in Chapter 7 and listed Plaintiff as an unsecured creditor with an unliquidated claim. Plaintiff did not attempt to obtain relief from the automatic stay to pursue the tort claim against Debtor under the *Holtkamp* doctrine. Debtor received a discharge, which applied to the debt on the tort claim. When Debtor was discharged, the automatic stay expired under § 362(c)(2)(C) and, at the same time, the discharge operated "as an injunction against the commencement or continuation of an action * * * to collect, recover or offset any such debt as a personal liability of the debtor." § 524(a)(2). Plaintiff wishes to continue the state court tort action against Debtor for the purpose of recovering against Debtor's insurer. § 524(e). Does § 524(a)(2) prohibit Plaintiff from continuing the state court action? If Plaintiff were to obtain a judgment in the action, would the judgment be void under § 524(a)(1)? *See Green v. Welsh*, 956 F.2d 30 (2d Cir.1992); *Matter of Hendrix*, 986 F.2d 195 (7th Cir.1993).

## F.  PREPETITION WAIVER OF STAY

We started this Chapter by reciting what is perhaps the most quoted piece of legislative history on any provision of the Bankruptcy Code: "The automatic stay is one of the fundamental debtor protections provided by the bankruptcy laws." H. Rep. No. 95–595, 1978 U.S.C.C.A.N. 6296. It has long been the law that debtors cannot waive the right to file for bankruptcy in the future. *In re Weitzen*, 3 F.Supp. 698 (S.D.N.Y.1933). Many assume that this anti-waiver view carries over to such a fundamental debtor protection as the automatic stay as well, and some courts have held that prepetition waivers of the automatic stay are unenforceable per se as undermining the carefully drawn statutory scheme of the Bankruptcy Code, e.g., *Matter of Pease*, 195 B.R. 431 (Bankr.D.Neb.1996). But an increasing number of courts are enforcing these waivers in varying degrees in appropriate cases, *e.g.*, *In re Excelsior Henderson Motorcycle Mfg. Co.*, 273 B.R. 920 (Bankr. S.D. Fla. 2002).  How can this be?

The real estate recession of the 1980's chastened trusting secured lenders who had agreed in workout agreements to give defaulting debtors another chance, only to be met with subsequent defaults leading to a Chapter 11 filing on the part of the debtors who then strenuously resisted foreclosure for protracted periods by reliance on the automatic stay. Although they had doubts about the enforceability of waiver-of-stay clauses, lenders began to demand waivers on a routine basis as a part of the consideration for workout deals with real property developers: if the debtor can't meet its obligations under the workout agreement, the lender claims the right to foreclose immediately upon postpetition default. No more stalling. To the surprise of most lawyers and academics, some courts began to enforce these clauses, and this view is gathering strength. *See* Daniel B. Bogart, *Games Lawyers Play: Waivers of the Automatic Stay in Bankruptcy and the Single Asset Loan Workout*, 43 UCLA L.Rev. 1117, 1127 n.20 (1996) ("Interviews with many attorneys indicate what might be deemed amazement at courts' enforcement of these provisions. This reaction is also found in published materials in bar journals and the like.")

In *In re Cheeks*, 167 B.R. 817, 819 (Bankr.D.S.C.1994), a Chapter 13 case, the Resolution Trust Corp. (RTC) agreed to forbear from foreclosure and, in partial consideration, Debtor agreed that if bankruptcy ensued she would not oppose RTC's motion for relief from the automatic stay. In upholding the waiver, the court opined:

> Perhaps the most compelling reason for enforcement of the forbearance [waiver] agreement is to further the public policy in favor of encouraging out of court restructuring and settlements. * * * Bankruptcy courts may be an appropriate forum for resolving many of society's problems, but some disputes are best decided through other means.

Scholars have found some favor with this view, *e.g.*, Marshall E. Tracht, *Contractual Bankruptcy Waivers: Reconciling Theory, Practice and Law*, 82 Cornell L.Rev. 301 (1997).

Some courts have taken a middle view in holding that although waiver-of-stay clauses are not self-executing, they may be weighed as a factor in the court's decision whether to lift the automatic stay for cause under § 362(d), *e.g.*, *In re Desai*, 282 B.R. 527 (Bankr. M.D. Ga. 2002), a single-asset case in which, in the context of a consensual plan in a previous case, debtor agreed not to oppose a motion for relief from the stay by the secured creditor if debtor defaulted and filed in bankruptcy again. The court held that such waivers are not self-executing and that in deciding whether a stay should be granted based on the waiver several factors should be considered: the sophistication of the party making the waiver; the consideration for the waiver, including the creditor's risk and the length of time the waiver covers; whether other parties are affected, including unsecured creditors and junior lienholders; the feasibility of the debtor's plan; and whether the debtor has any equity in the property.

The National Bankruptcy Review Commission has taken a strong position in opposition to any prepetition agreement by a debtor that waives, terminates, restricts, conditions, or otherwise modifies "any rights or defenses provided by" the Bankruptcy Code. NBRC Rep. at 478. "The ability of one creditor to negotiate privately with the debtor for special treatment in bankruptcy runs counter to the principle of equitable treatment and could have significant distributional consequences for all other creditors." *Id.* at 481.

# CHAPTER 6

# EXECUTORY CONTRACTS AND LEASES

## A. EXECUTORY CONTRACTS

### 1. INTRODUCTION

Suppose a contract for a sale of goods with Buyer to pay at the time of delivery. What are the rights and obligations of the parties if either goes into bankruptcy before delivery (and payment) is due? This question can arise in a Chapter 7 case as well as in all types of reorganization cases, but typically the issue arises in Chapter 11 cases and we assume Chapter 11 filing in this discussion. Suppose Seller is the debtor in bankruptcy. Because "claim" is defined in § 101 in very broad terms to include any right to enforce an obligation of the debtor so long as breach of that obligation gives rise to a right to payment, Buyer has a claim in the bankruptcy even though the claim is unmatured. But it is not possible to know at the time of bankruptcy whether this claim will ever ripen into a right to payment. Bankruptcy is not treated as an automatic repudiation of the obligations of the debtor. If Seller continues its business as debtor in possession, Seller in many cases would want to perform the contract and obtain payment as though bankruptcy had not occurred. If Seller is able to perform and the contract is favorable to Seller, Seller will normally want to perform the contract. If the contract is unfavorable, Seller will want to refuse to perform.

Section 365 governs this situation. It allows the trustee in bankruptcy (including a debtor in possession), subject to approval of the bankruptcy court, to "assume or reject any executory contract or unexpired lease of the debtor." § 365(a).

Fundamental to the treatment of executory contracts under § 365 is the notion that an unperformed contract is a "package deal" that must be assumed or rejected in its entirety. If the bankruptcy trustee wishes to retain the benefit of the agreement or lease for the estate, the estate must accept the burden of performance in accordance with the original terms of the contract. In our sale of goods example, the trustee must deliver the goods to earn the sale price. What the trustee cannot do is demand Buyer's future performance (payment) without binding the estate to the perform its obligations as Seller (delivery).

If the trustee decides to have the estate perform the contract (in order to gain the benefit of a favorable agreement), the contract must be assumed. The effect of assumption is to convert the obligations of Seller under the contract into obligations of the bankruptcy estate. After assumption, if the debtor in possession fails to perform in compliance with the contract, Buyer has a right to payment of an administrative expense for damages for breach of contract.

If the trustee decides not to perform under the contract, the contract must be rejected. "Reject" is perhaps an inapt word to express the intent of § 365(a) and the courts sometimes have given the word surprising interpretations. Rejection can best be understood as the opposite of assumption. It is a formal declaration not to assume the contract. Rejection is treated by § 365(g) as a breach of Seller's contract because rejection means that Seller's obligations under the contract will not be performed. Buyer has a prepetition claim in bankruptcy for breach of contract and is released from the obligation to render any further performance under the contract. § 502(g).

The following cases illustrate the advantages § 365(a) gives to the bankruptcy estate.

> **Case #1.** On February 1, Seller and Buyer agreed to a sale of goods at $20 a unit with delivery and payment to be made on April 1. On March 1, Buyer filed a Chapter 11 petition. Because similar goods can be purchased from another supplier for $15 a unit Buyer, as debtor in possession, seeks to reject the contract.

> **Case #2.** Under the same contract described in Case #1, Seller rather than Buyer filed a Chapter 11 petition in bankruptcy under Chapter 11. Seller can sell the goods to others for $25 a unit. Seller, as debtor in possession, seeks to reject the contract.

Assume that nonpriority creditors in each case will receive less than the full amount of their claims. If Buyer is allowed to reject in Case #1, the bankruptcy estate will normally benefit because the goods can be bought more cheaply from another supplier. If Seller is allowed to reject in Case #2, the estate will normally benefit because the goods can be sold at a higher price to other buyers. In either case the nonbankrupt party to the contract is entitled to damages for breach of contract. If damages are measured only by a $5 per unit loss of bargain in each case, there is a net benefit to the estate because the claim will be paid at less than face amount and the estate will receive a full $5 per unit benefit in the substitute transactions. If the nonbankrupt party has damages in addition to the $5 per unit loss of bargain, the estate may or may not benefit from rejection, depending upon the amount of the additional damages and the extent to which payment of claims is discounted below 100% of face amount.

The National Bankruptcy Review Commission proposed several changes in § 365 and related provisions. Among these are recommendations to replace the concept of "rejection" with "election to breach," which the Commission describes as "a common-sense clarification," and "assumption" with "election to perform," a concept parallel to "election to breach." NBRC Rep. at 459–465. We will comment on the substantive consequences of these recommendations at appropriate places in this Chapter.

## 2. DECISION TO ASSUME OR REJECT

A trustee or debtor in possession must obtain the court's approval in order to assume or reject a contract. § 365(a). The statute is silent on what standards a court should apply in granting its approval. The prevailing view, which accords great deference to the decision of the trustee, is that the trustee's decision to assume or reject because of belief that there is a business advantage in doing so must be accepted by the court unless it is shown that the decision was made in bad faith or in abuse of discretion. *In re Minges*, 602 F.2d 38 (2d Cir.1979). This is similar to the business judgment rule of corporation law which protects directors from liability when decisions made by them on matters entrusted to their business judgment turn out badly. Ordinarily the trustee should reject a contract if the trustee believes that the estate's costs of taking over the debtor's remaining burdens exceed the value of the nondebtor party's remaining performance.

Occasionally courts refuse to go along with the trustee's business judgment either because the contract is not "burdensome" or because the cost of rejection to the nondebtor party is disproportionate to the benefit to the estate—the "balancing of equities" rule. These rules are discussed in Jesse M. Fried, *Executory Contracts and Performance Decisions in Bankruptcy*, 46 Duke L.J. 517, 540–544 (1996). Under the burdensomeness test a trustee would not be allowed to reject a contract on the ground that although performance of the original contract would increase the value of the estate, the estate could make more money devoting its resources to another contract. Under the balancing test, if rejection would benefit the bankruptcy estate only slightly but would destroy the nondebtor's business, the court may withhold its approval. In *In re Chi–Feng Huang*, 23 B.R. 798, 801 (B.A.P. 9th Cir.1982), the court held that it is "proper for the court to refuse to authorize rejection of a lease or executory contract where the party whose contract is to be rejected would be damaged disproportionately to any benefit that would be derived by the general creditors of the estate * * *." In *In re Petur U.S.A. Instrument Co.*, 35 B.R. 561 (Bankr.W.D.Wash.1983), the court would not allow rejection of a licensing agreement because the rejection threatened to ruin the nondebtor's profitable business. Unpersuaded, the court in *In re Riodizio, Inc.*, 204 B.R. 417, 425 n. 9 (Bankr.S.D.N.Y.1997), declared "Section 365 does not require any balancing of the equities." The National Bankruptcy Conference recommends replacing the business judgment standard with an "interest-of-the-estate" test that would give less deference to the judgment of the trustee. Reforming the Bankruptcy Code 126 (Rev.ed.1997).

Section 365(g) treats the rejection of a contract as a prepetition breach, and as a result the damages for the breach to the nondebtor party are considered a prepetition claim. This claim of the nondebtor party will be treated like other prepetition claims, and the nondebtor will receive only a ratable share of the assets of the estate available to general creditors. These pro-rata "bankruptcy dollars" can be pretty small. Estimates are that 80% of liquidation cases yield no distribution to general creditors, and in the cases in which there is a payout creditors often receive a small fraction of their claims. Even in reorganization cases involving the largest corporations the payout rate often doesn't exceed 50%. Professor Fried argues that under the present ratable share rule, trustees have too much incentive to reject and proposes reforms that would limit the rights of trustees to reject value producing contracts, that is, cases in which rejection makes the estate better off but makes the other party worse off by a greater amount.

### 3. MEANING OF "EXECUTORY CONTRACT"

The term "executory contract" is not defined in the Bankruptcy Code and may not be definable, except in an arbitrary way. Long ago Professor Williston counseled against the use of the terms "executed contract" and "executory contract" on the ground that they were vague and misleading. He stated: "All contracts to a greater or lesser extent are executory. When they cease to be so, they cease to be contracts." *Williston on Contracts* § 14 (1920). More recently, Professor Jay Westbrook has said with respect to § 365(a):

> It is obvious that a contract must be executory to be assumed or rejected, if the term is used in its ordinary sense to mean merely that aspects of the contract were not fully performed or satisfied on Bankruptcy Day. But if executoriness had such a simple meaning, the requirement would be trivial. The trustee need not, and could not, assume or reject a contract fully performed a year before bankruptcy— nor would anyone dream of doing so. Speaking of a "nonexecutory" contract in that sense is like discussing a sunset after dark.

Jay L. Westbrook, *A Functional Analysis of Executory Contracts*, 74 Minn.L.Rev. 227, 243 (1989). The courts, however, treat the adjective "executory" in § 365 as a limitation on the contracts to which the section applies. In this regard the courts have been strongly influenced by a definition of executory contract proposed by Professor Vern Countryman in *Executory Contracts in Bankruptcy: Part I*, 57 Minn.L.Rev. 439, 460 (1973). He states that an executory contract is:

> [A] contract under which the obligation of both the bankrupt and the other party to the contract are so far unperformed that the failure of either to complete performance would constitute a material breach excusing the performance of the other.

Countryman defined executory contract as requiring performance due on both sides because he believed that it furthered the purpose for which the trustee is given the option to assume or reject. This purpose is to benefit the estate. If the creditor has already performed, the estate has already received the full benefit, and rejection would have no function for it would change neither the creditor's claim nor the estate's liability. According to Countryman, assumption would in no way benefit the estate and would convert the debtor's obligation on the contract into an administrative expense. If the debtor has performed, rejection would not be a breach and assumption would add nothing to its right to have the other party perform.

Under the Countryman definition a contract cannot be "executory" under § 365(a) if either the debtor or the other party to the contract has fully performed its obligations under the contract. The following Case #3 and Case #4 are examples.

> **Case #3.**  Seller and Buyer agree to a sale of goods with payment to be made six months after delivery of the goods. After Seller delivers the goods but before payment is due, either Seller or Buyer files in Chapter 11 bankruptcy.

If Seller is the bankrupt in Case #3, the right to payment of the price of the goods from Buyer is property of the bankruptcy estate that can be enforced by the debtor in possession. Buyer has a claim in bankruptcy if there was a breach of contract with respect to Seller's performance, such as breach of warranty. There is no reason for § 365 to apply because assumption or rejection of the contract can't affect the rights of Buyer or the estate. Seller has fully performed. A decision to assume or not to assume can't relate to performance that has already occurred.

If Buyer is the bankrupt in Case #3, Seller has a claim in bankruptcy for the price of the goods. Since the only obligation of Buyer under the contract was to pay money, there is no need for § 365. The estate already has the goods and cannot obtain any benefit through § 365.

Under the Countryman definition, § 365(a) cannot be applied to Case #3, and that is the right result. But that result should follow even if the word "executory" were deleted from § 365(a). Assumption or rejection is irrelevant in Case #3.

> **Case #4.**  On February 1, Seller and Buyer agreed to a sale of goods with delivery to be made on April 1. Buyer paid Seller the price of the goods at the time the agreement was signed as required by the agreement. On March 1, before the time for Seller's performance, either Buyer or Seller filed a petition in bankruptcy under Chapter 11.

Under the Countryman definition, § 365(a) cannot be applied to Case #4 because Buyer has fully performed. If Buyer is the bankrupt, there is no obligation that the debtor in possession can assume or reject. The right of the bankruptcy estate to receive goods from Seller can be enforced by the debtor in possession. Section 365 is irrelevant. The Countryman definition produces the right result, but it is not necessary. The analysis is the same as in Case #3 if Buyer is the bankrupt.

But suppose Seller is the bankrupt in Case #4 and the contract is unfavorable to Seller. Why shouldn't the debtor in possession be able to reject the contract under § 365? The case is essentially the same as Case #2 and there is no apparent reason to treat Case #4 differently. What happens if Case #4 is excluded from § 365(a)? Seller's filing in bankruptcy does not oblige the bankruptcy estate to perform the contract. The estate hasn't agreed to perform it. If the contract isn't assumed the estate has no liability on the contract. But if the contract isn't performed, Buyer should have a claim in bankruptcy for damages. Even if § 365(a) is held not to apply, the result should be the same as if the contract had been rejected under § 365(a). Thus, the Countryman definition does not affect nonperformance of the contract, but that definition would prevent assumption of the contract. Although, in most cases, performance by the estate will not benefit the estate if Buyer has prepaid, there may be cases in which the estate might suffer loss by reneging on the obligation. The Countryman definition prevents the trustee or debtor in possession from avoiding such a loss by assuming the contract.

Several courts have questioned whether assumption or rejection by the trustee should depend upon performance or nonperformance by the non-bankrupt party. In *In re Norquist*, 43 B.R. 224 (Bankr.E.D.Wash.1984), the debtor was a partner in a firm of doctors carrying on a medical practice. The debtor withdrew from the firm and, upon withdrawal, was bound by a covenant not to compete with the firm for two years in the city in which the firm's practice was carried on. As debtor in possession, the debtor wanted to avoid the burden of the covenant by rejecting the partnership agreement. The court said with respect to the Countryman test, "The logic of this approach escapes me. I believe that the requirement of a remaining material obligation on the part of the nondebtor serves no useful purpose. It eliminates from the category of executory contracts some obligations which may prove extremely burdensome and, in some cases, obligations which may be prohibitive to the reorganization efforts of the debtor." 43 B.R. at 227. In *In re Oxford Royal Mushroom Products, Inc.*, 45 B.R. 792 (Bankr.E.D.Pa.1985), Judge Goldhaber concluded that an executory contract is one that requires substantial performance by either party to the contract other than the payment of money.

Although the Countryman definition is widely cited by almost all of the courts that have decided § 365 cases, the use of that definition has been severely criticized in recent years. The primary attack began in Professor Westbrook's article cited above and in two articles by Michael T. Andrew: *Executory Contracts in Bankruptcy: Understanding "Rejection,"* 59 U.Colo.L.Rev. 845 (1988), and *Executory Contracts Revisited: A Reply to Professor Westbrook*, 62 U.Colo.L.Rev. 1 (1991). These articles have been very influential and they contend that "executoriness" of a contract should not be a precondition to assuming or rejecting a contract under § 365(a).

The National Bankruptcy Conference, Reforming the Bankruptcy Code 124 (Rev.ed.1997), explains:

> The terms used in section 365, especially "rejection" and "executory contract," should be retired from use, as they carry the accumulated baggage of too many erroneous preconceptions. A fundamental change of mind set is necessary. This will be difficult to accomplish unless these terms are replaced by others conveying more precisely that the decision facing the trustee is whether to perform the contract as an administrative expense, or breach it and pay in bankruptcy dollars (absent equitable remedies). Also, the trustee, acting in the interest of the estate, should be free to decide not to perform future contractual obligations without first having to show that the contract is "executory." The trustee must determine either to perform or breach, according to whichever is better calculated to achieve the maximum economic net value for the estate. An inquiry into whether the contract is "executory" is beside the point.

The National Bankruptcy Review Commission agreed. It recommended that "all references to 'executory' be deleted from § 365 and related provisions, and that 'executoriness' be eliminated as a prerequisite to the trustee's election to assume or breach a contract." NBRC Rep. at 472. The Report explains on p. 475:

> A growing case law trend de-emphasizes a strict analysis of the term "executory" in favor of a "functional" analysis, an approach articulated by Professor Jay Westbrook, Michael Andrew, and others. Using a functional analysis, a court does not consider remaining mutual material performance but instead considers the goals that assumption or rejection were expected to accomplish: enhancement of the estate. * * * [A] few courts taking the functional approach have declined to make the threshold finding of executoriness at all and simply have focused on whether the estate would be benefited by performance or breach.

## PROBLEM

On May 1 Seller sold Buyer an option to buy real property from Seller for the price of $200,000 at any time within the following six months. Buyer paid $5,000 for the option. Although market conditions caused the value of the property to rise, Buyer's business faltered and it filed in Chapter 11 on September 1. Buyer as Debtor in Possession sought to exercise the option contract in order to resell the property to another purchaser for $250,000. Is the option contract an executory contract that can be lost if not assumed by the estate? Or is the option simply an asset of Buyer's bankruptcy estate that can be exercised in accordance with its terms? Jay L. Westbrook, *A Functional Analysis of Executory Contracts*, 74 Minn.L.Rev. 227, 316 (1989); Michael T. Andrew, *Executory Contracts Revisited: A Reply to Professor Westbrook*, 62 U.Colo.L.Rev. 1, 32 (1991). *See In re Robert L. Helms Construction and Development Co., Inc.*, 139 F.3d 702, 706 *en banc* (9th Cir., 1998), in which the court held that an option was not an executory contract and therefore remained an asset of the bankruptcy estate notwithstanding the debtor's rejection of all its executory contracts. With respect to option contracts "[t]he question thus becomes: At the time of filing, does each party have something it must do to avoid materially breaching the contract? Typically, the answer is no; the optionee commits no breach by doing nothing." Compare *In re Riodizio, Inc.*, 204 B.R. 417, 424 (Bankr.S.D.N.Y.1997), which held a stock option to be an executory contract because "each party must perform under the Warrant to obtain the benefits under the contingent bilateral contract of sale." If you agree with the *Helms Construction* view, what result if the bankrupt is the Seller/Optionor and the option price is unfavorable to Seller? Would Seller be precluded from rejecting its obligation to deliver the land for a below-market price?

### 4. REJECTION OF LICENSES OF INTELLECTUAL PROPERTY

## Lubrizol Enterprises, Inc. v. Richmond Metal Finishers, Inc.

United States Court of Appeals, Fourth Circuit, 1985.
756 F.2d 1043.

■ JAMES DICKSON PHILLIPS, Circuit Judge:

The question is whether Richmond Metal Finishers (RMF), a bankrupt debtor in possession, should have been allowed to reject as executory a technology licensing agreement with Lubrizol Enterprises (Lubrizol) as licensee. The bankruptcy court approved rejection pursuant to § 365(a) * * * but the district court reversed on the basis that within contemplation of § 365(a), the contract was not executory * * *. We reverse and remand for entry of judgment in conformity with that entered by the bankruptcy court.

### I

In July of 1982, RMF entered into the contract with Lubrizol that granted Lubrizol a nonexclusive license to utilize a metal coating process technology owned by RMF. RMF owed the following duties to Lubrizol under the agreement: (1) to notify Lubrizol of any patent infringement suit and to defend in such suit; (2) to notify Lubrizol of any other use or licensing of the process, and to reduce royalty payments if a lower royalty rate agreement was reached with another licensee; and (3) to indemnify Lubrizol for losses arising out of any misrepresentation or breach of warranty by

RMF. Lubrizol owed RMF reciprocal duties of accounting for and paying royalties for use of the process and of cancelling certain existing indebtedness. The contract provided that Lubrizol would defer use of the process until May 1, 1983, and in fact, Lubrizol has never used the RMF technology.

RMF filed a petition for bankruptcy pursuant to Chapter 11 of the Bankruptcy Code on August 16, 1983. As part of its plan to emerge from bankruptcy, RMF sought, pursuant to § 365(a), to reject the contract with Lubrizol in order to facilitate sale or licensing of the technology unhindered by restrictive provisions in the Lubrizol agreement. On RMF's motion for approval of the rejection, the bankruptcy court properly interpreted § 365 as requiring it to undertake a two-step inquiry to determine the propriety of rejection: first, whether the contract is executory; next, if so, whether its rejection would be advantageous to the bankrupt.

Making that inquiry, the bankruptcy court determined that both tests were satisfied and approved the rejection. But, as indicated, the district court then reversed that determination on the basis that neither test was satisfied and disallowed the rejection. This appeal followed.

## II

We conclude initially that, as the bankruptcy court ruled, the technology licensing agreement in this case was an executory contract, within contemplation of § 365(a). Under that provision a contract is executory if performance is due to some extent on both sides. * * * This court has recently adopted Professor Countryman's more specific test for determining whether a contract is "executory" in the required sense. * * * This issue is one of law that may be freely reviewed by successive courts.

Applying that test here, we conclude that the licensing agreement was at the critical time executory. RMF owed Lubrizol the continuing duties of notifying Lubrizol of further licensing of the process and of reducing Lubrizol's royalty rate to meet any more favorable rates granted to subsequent licensees. By their terms, RMF's obligations to give notice and to restrict its right to license its process at royalty rates it desired without lowering Lubrizol's royalty rate extended over the life of the agreement, and remained unperformed. Moreover, RMF owed Lubrizol additional contingent duties of notifying it of suits, defending suits and indemnifying it for certain losses.

The unperformed, continuing core obligations of notice and forbearance in licensing made the contract executory as to RMF. In *Fenix Cattle Co. v. Silver (In re Select–A–Seat Corp.)*, 625 F.2d 290, 292 (9th Cir.1980), the court found that an obligation of a debtor to refrain from selling software packages under an exclusive licensing agreement made a contract executory as to the debtor notwithstanding the continuing obligation was only one of forbearance. Although the license to Lubrizol was not exclusive, RMF owed the same type of unperformed continuing duty of forbearance arising out of the most favored licensee clause running in favor of Lubrizol. Breach of that duty would clearly constitute a material breach of the agreement.

Moreover, the contract was further executory as to RMF because of the contingent duties that RMF owed of giving notice of and defending infringement suits and of indemnifying Lubrizol for certain losses arising out of the use of the technology. Contingency of an obligation does not prevent its being executory under § 365. See *In re Smith Jones, Inc.*, 26 B.R. 289, 292 (Bankr.D.Minn.1982) (warranty obligations executory as to promisor); *In re O.P.M. Leasing Services, Inc.*, 23 B.R. 104, 117 (Bankr.S.D.N.Y.1982) (obligation to defend infringement suits makes contract executory as to promisor). Until the time has expired during which an event triggering a contingent duty may occur, the contingent obligation represents a continuing duty to stand ready to perform if the contingency occurs. A breach of that duty once it was triggered by the contingency (or presumably, by anticipatory repudiation) would have been material.

Because a contract is not executory within the meaning of § 365(a) unless it is executory as to both parties, it is also necessary to determine whether the licensing agreement was executory as to Lubrizol. * * * We conclude that it was.

Lubrizol owed RMF the unperformed and continuing duty of accounting for and paying royalties for the life of the agreement. It is true that a contract is not executory as to a party simply because the party is obligated to make payments of money to the other party. * * * Therefore, if Lubrizol had owed RMF nothing more than a duty to make fixed payments or cancel specified indebtedness under the agreement, the agreement would not be executory as to Lubrizol. However, the promise to account for and pay royalties required that Lubrizol deliver written quarterly sales reports and keep books of account subject to inspection by an independent Certified Public Accountant. This promise goes beyond a mere debt, or promise to pay money, and was at the critical time executory. See *Fenix Cattle*, 625 F.2d at 292. Additionally, subject to certain exceptions, Lubrizol was obligated to keep all license technology in confidence for a number of years.

Since the licensing agreement is executory as to each party, it is executory within the meaning of § 365(a), and the district court erred as a matter of law in reaching a contrary conclusion.[*]

---

[*] We disagree with the district court's characterization of the transaction as effectively a completed sale of property. If an analogy is to be made, licensing agreements are more similar to leases than to sales of property because of the limited nature of the interest conveyed. Congress expressly made leases subject to rejection under § 365 in order to "preclude any uncertainty as to whether a lease is an executory contract" under § 365. 2 Collier on Bankruptcy ¶ 365.02 (L.King 15th ed.1984).

### III

There remains the question whether rejection of the executory contract would be advantageous to the bankrupt. * * * Courts addressing that question must start with the proposition that the bankrupt's decision upon it is to be accorded the deference mandated by the sound business judgment rule as generally applied by courts to discretionary actions or decisions of corporate directors. * * *

As generally formulated and applied in corporate litigation the rule is that courts should defer to—should not interfere with—decisions of corporate directors upon matters entrusted to their business judgment except upon a finding of bad faith or gross abuse of their "business discretion." Transposed to the bankruptcy context, the rule as applied to a bankrupt's decision to reject an executory contract because of perceived business advantage requires that the decision be accepted by courts unless it is shown that the bankrupt's decision was one taken in bad faith or in gross abuse of the bankrupt's retained business discretion.

* * *

Here, the bankruptcy judge had before him evidence not rebutted by Lubrizol that the metal coating process subject to the licensing agreement is RMF's principal asset and that sale or licensing of the technology represented the primary potential source of funds by which RMF might emerge from bankruptcy. The testimony of RMF's president, also factually uncontested by Lubrizol, indicated that sale or further licensing of the technology would be facilitated by stripping Lubrizol of its rights in the process and that, correspondingly, continued obligation to Lubrizol under the agreement would hinder RMF's capability to sell or license the technology on more advantageous terms to other potential licensees. On the basis of this evidence the bankruptcy court determined that the debtor's decision to reject was based upon sound business judgment and approved it.

On appeal the district court simply found to the contrary that the debtor's decision to reject did not represent a sound business judgment. The district court's determination rested essentially on two grounds: that RMF's purely contingent obligations under the agreement were not sufficiently onerous that relief from them would constitute a substantial benefit to RMF; and that because rejection could not deprive Lubrizol of all its rights to the technology, rejection could not reasonably be found beneficial. We conclude that in both of these respects the district court's factual findings, at odds with those of the bankruptcy court, were clearly erroneous and cannot stand.

### A

In finding that the debtor's contingent obligations were not sufficiently onerous that relief from them would be beneficial, the district court could only have been substituting its business judgment for that of the debtor. There is nothing in the record from which it could be concluded that the debtor's decision on that point could not have been reached by the exercise of sound (though possibly faulty) business judgment in the normal process of evaluating alternative courses of action. If that could not be concluded, then the business judgment rule required that the debtor's factual evaluation be accepted by the court, as it had been by the bankruptcy court. * * *

## B

On the second point, we can only conclude that the district court was under a misapprehension of controlling law in thinking that by rejecting the agreement the debtor could not deprive Lubrizol of all rights to the process. Under § 365(g), Lubrizol would be entitled to treat rejection as a breach and seek a money damages remedy; however, it could not seek to retain its contract rights in the technology by specific performance even if that remedy would ordinarily be available upon breach of this type of contract. See In re Waldron, 36 B.R. 633, 642 n. 4 (Bankr.S.D.Fla.1984). Even though § 365(g) treats rejection as a breach, the legislative history of § 365(g) makes clear that the purpose of the provision is to provide only a damages remedy for the non-bankrupt party. * * * For the same reason, Lubrizol cannot rely on provisions within its agreement with RMF for continued use of the technology by Lubrizol upon breach by RMF. Here again, the statutory "breach" contemplated by § 365(g) controls, and provides only a money damages remedy for the non-bankrupt party. Allowing specific performance would obviously undercut the core purpose of rejection under § 365(a), and that consequence cannot therefore be read into congressional intent.

## IV

Lubrizol strongly urges upon us policy concerns in support of the district court's refusal to defer to the debtor's decision to reject or, preliminarily, to treat the contract as executory for § 365(a) purposes. We understand the concerns, but think they cannot control decision here.

It cannot be gainsaid that allowing rejection of such contracts as executory imposes serious burdens upon contracting parties such as Lubrizol. Nor can it be doubted that allowing rejection in this and comparable cases could have a general chilling effect upon the willingness of such parties to contract at all with businesses in possible financial difficulty. But under bankruptcy law such equitable considerations may not be indulged by courts in respect of the type of contract here in issue. Congress has plainly provided for the rejection of executory contracts, notwithstanding the obvious adverse consequences for contracting parties thereby made inevitable. Awareness by Congress of those consequences is indeed specifically reflected in the special treatment accorded to union members under collective bargaining contracts * * * and to lessees of real property, see § 365(h). But no comparable special treatment is provided for technology licensees such as Lubrizol. They share the general hazards created by § 365 for all business entities dealing with potential bankrupts in the respects at issue here.

The judgment of the district court is reversed and the case is remanded for entry of judgment in conformity with that entered by the bankruptcy court.

## NOTES

**1.** In *Lubrizol,* the difference of opinion between Judge Phillips and Judge Warriner, the District Court judge whose judgment was reversed, reflects a fundamental disagreement about the nature of rejection under § 365. Judge Warriner assumed that the only effect of rejection was to relieve RMF of future performance under the contract. In Judge Warriner's view, the only significant executory performance was that of defending Lubrizol in infringement suits. Since RMF had already granted to Lubrizol the right to use the technology, RMF couldn't take back that right by rejecting the contract. Judge Warriner saw the licensing agreement as the grant of a property right. One analogy is the conveyance of real property under a warranty deed. The grantor conveys title to the grantee and covenants to defend the grantee against any suits that question the grantee's title. If the grantor goes into bankruptcy after conveying the property the grantor might reject the executory obligation to defend the grantee's title, but no court would hold that the grantor can rescind the conveyance of the property. A closer analogy is that of a real property lease. A lease is a type of executory contract but it is separately treated in § 365. If a lessor goes into bankruptcy, the lessor can, by rejecting the lease, relieve itself of executory duties under the lease such as providing heat, utilities, repair services and the like, but it cannot take away from the lessee the right to possession of the premises granted by the lease. § 365(h). Judge Warriner's view is consistent with the policy that underlies § 365(h). The view of Judge Phillips is not.

Judge Phillips apparently differentiates between a contract right and a property right, and places licenses in the first category. Suppose X conveyed to Y ownership of intellectual property such as a patent or a copyright. X also agreed to defend Y against infringement suits. This case is like that of the warranty deed discussed above. Even Judge Phillips would not allow X to rescind Y's ownership by rejecting under § 365. But suppose X had licensed to Y the right to use the patent or copyright and further covenanted to license no other. *Select–A–Seat* which is discussed in *Lubrizol* involved this sort of exclusive license. In that case the Ninth Circuit treated the case as involving an executory contract because the bankrupt licensor had an unperformed obligation to refrain from licensing others. The court recognized that the bankrupt could not use § 365 to prevent the licensee from using the intellectual property, but the court allowed the bankrupt to convert the exclusive license into a nonexclusive license by rejecting the contract, i.e. repudiating its obligation not to license others. The court argued that the obligation not to license others was like the obligation of a lessor under § 365(h) with respect to heat and utilities discussed above; either obligation can be rejected by the debtor in possession under § 365. In our opinion, the lease case is not a valid analogy to the exclusive license case. The grant of an exclusive license to use intellectual property is the practical equivalent of an outright transfer of intellectual property. A principal reason for expressing a transfer of intellectual property as an exclusive license rather than a sale is that the price is normally not a fixed amount that can be determined at the inception of the transaction. Rather, it is usually calculated by a formula based on the income that will be generated by the intellectual property over the life of the property. Expression of the price as a license fee that varies with the eventual economic value of the property is a more convenient way of setting up the transaction. In *Select–A–Seat* there was an additional reason. The transaction had to take the form of an exclusive license because exclusivity was geographical. The exclusive license applied to all but five areas of the world in which others had been granted licenses. But with respect to the areas of the world to which the exclusive license applied the licensor had no residual rights. It had granted everything to the licensee. *Select–A–Seat* is more like the conveyance of real property by warranty deed discussed above. It is meaningless to say that the contract by which the real property was conveyed is executory because the bankrupt had an unperformed obligation not to convey the real property to somebody else. The bankrupt has already disposed of the real property. In our opinion the same analysis should apply to an exclusive license which effectively disposes of the intellectual property. The licensor has already fully performed. There is nothing left to repudiate.

*Select–A–Seat* was bad enough. *Lubrizol* is worse. *Lubrizol* treats rejection as a strange variety of contract rescission that enables the debtor in possession to nullify rights already granted, and in return gives to the licensee damages for the wrongful nullification. In *Lubrizol* the court concedes that allowing debtors to take back the right to use a technology "could have a general chilling effect on the willingness * * * to contract at all with businesses in possible financial difficulty." 756 F.2d at 1048. Experience in high-technology fields is that important technology is often developed by small, unseasoned companies that are candidates for bankruptcy. It is common for these start-up companies to grant licenses to more established firms to develop marketable products based on the licensed technology. The licensed companies may invest large sums of money that would be lost if the licensor's bankruptcy allows the licensee to be deprived of its right to exploit the technology. The "Intellectual Property Protection Act" was introduced in Congress in 1987 and enacted in 1988. Its sponsors were an industry coalition of the largest high-technology companies. This Act overturns *Lubrizol* with respect to intellectual property by adding subsection (n) to § 365, which allows licensees to retain rights in intellectual property conveyed to them before the licensor's bankruptcy.

**2.** The National Bankruptcy Review Commission recommended that § 365 be amended to provide that rejection is merely a breach of a contract and does not nullify, rescind or "vaporize" the contract or terminate the rights of the parties. It is not an avoiding power that enables a trustee to retrieve property already transferred. The effect of rejection in most cases is merely that the nondebtor party is entitled to recover money damages, paid ratably with other general creditors, and the creditor's claim is discharged. *Lubrizol* led the list of cases disapproved. NBRC Rep. at 460–463.

## 5. CONTRACTS NOT ASSIGNABLE UNDER NONBANKRUPTCY LAW

### a. Assumption

Suppose Corporation entered into a three-year employment contract with Executive at $250,000 per year. Two years remained on the contract when Corporation filed a petition in bankruptcy under Chapter 11. Corporation continued to operate the business as debtor in possession. The debtor in possession can replace Executive with a competent person who will work for less than $250,000 per year. Executive will probably not be able to find a position elsewhere at a salary that high. The debtor in possession can, with the approval of the bankruptcy court, reject the contract. § 365(a). Executive has a claim in bankruptcy for breach of contract. § 365(g) and § 502(g). But the damages of Executive are limited by § 502(b)(7).

Suppose, instead, that the debtor in possession wishes to assume Executive's contract, but Executive doesn't want to work for a company that is in bankruptcy. Can the debtor in possession assume the contract if Executive is unwilling? Outside of bankruptcy, Executive could be held to the employment contract. The contract is not specifically enforceable, but Executive could be held liable for damages for refusing to perform or in an appropriate case Corporation might be able to obtain an injunction against Executive's employment by somebody else. But Corporation couldn't assign the contract to a third party without consent of Executive. If Corporation files in bankruptcy are the rights of Executive and Corporation changed? This question is dealt with by § 365(c)(1). Subsection (c)(1)(A) has been amended twice. As originally enacted it read, "applicable law excuses a party, other than the debtor, to such contract or lease from accepting performance from or rendering performance to *the trustee or an assignee of such contract or lease* * * *." (Emphasis added.) In 1984 the words in italics were changed to "an entity other than the debtor or the debtor in possession or an assignee of such contract or lease." In 1986 "or an assignee of such contract or lease" was deleted from the 1984 version. What were these amendments intended to achieve?

*Catapult Entertainment*, which follows, interprets the 1986 version of § 365(c)(1)(A) as posing a "hypothetical test." Three other Circuits take this view: *In re West Electronics, Inc.*, 852 F.2d 79 (3d Cir.1988); *In re Sunterra Corporation*, 361 F.3d. 257 (4th Cir. 2004), and *In re James*

*Cable Partners*, 27 F.3d 534 (11th Cir. 1994). The First Circuit adopted the competing "actual test" favored by most bankruptcy courts and commentators in *Summit Investment and Development Corp. v. Leroux*, 69 F.3d 608 (1st Cir. 1995). The 2005 Act failed to clear up this long-running dispute that has such important consequences, particularly in the field of intellectual property.

## In re Catapult Entertainment, Inc.

United States Court of Appeals, Ninth Circuit, 1999.
165 F.3d 747.

■ FLETCHER, Circuit Judge.

Appellant Stephen Perlman ("Perlman") licensed certain patents to appellee Catapult Entertainment, Inc. ("Catapult"). He now seeks to bar Catapult, which has since become a Chapter 11 debtor in possession, from assuming the patent licenses as part of its reorganization plan. Notwithstanding Perlman's objections, the bankruptcy court approved the assumption of the licenses and confirmed the reorganization plan. The district court affirmed the bankruptcy court on intermediate appeal. Perlman appeals that decision. We are called upon to determine whether, in light of § 365(c)(1) of the Bankruptcy Code, a Chapter 11 debtor in possession may assume certain nonexclusive patent licenses over a licensor's objection. We conclude that the bankruptcy court erred in permitting the debtor in possession to assume the patent licenses in question.

### I.

Catapult, a California corporation, was formed in 1994 to create an online gaming network for 16–bit console videogames. That same year, Catapult entered into two license agreements with Perlman, wherein Perlman granted to Catapult the right to exploit certain relevant technologies, including patents and patent applications.

In October 1996, Catapult filed for reorganization under Chapter 11 of the Bankruptcy Code. Shortly before the filing of the bankruptcy petition, Catapult entered into a merger agreement with Mpath Interactive, Inc. ("Mpath"). This agreement contemplated the filing of the bankruptcy petition, followed by a reorganization via a "reverse triangular merger" involving Mpath, MPCAT Acquisition Corporation ("MPCAT"), and Catapult. Under the terms of the merger agreement, MPCAT (a wholly-owned subsidiary of Mpath created for this transaction) would merge into Catapult, leaving Catapult as the surviving entity. When the dust cleared, Catapult's creditors and equity holders would have received approximately $14 million in cash, notes, and securities; Catapult, in turn, would have become a wholly-owned subsidiary of Mpath. The relevant third party creditors and equity holders accepted Catapult's reorganization plan by the majorities required by the Bankruptcy Code.

On October 24, 1996, as part of the reorganization plan, Catapult filed a motion with the bankruptcy court seeking to assume some 140 executory contracts and leases, including the Perlman licenses. Over Perlman's objection, the bankruptcy court granted Catapult's motion and approved the reorganization plan. The district court subsequently affirmed the bankruptcy court. * * * *

## II.

Section 365 of the Bankruptcy Code gives a trustee in bankruptcy (or, in a Chapter 11 case, the debtor in possession) the authority to assume, assign, or reject the executory contracts and unexpired leases of the debtor, notwithstanding any contrary provisions appearing in such contracts or leases. See § 365(a) & (f). This extraordinary authority, however, is not absolute. Section 365(c)(1) provides that, notwithstanding the general policy set out in § 365(a):

**(c)**   The trustee may not assume or assign any executory contract or unexpired lease of the debtor, whether or not such contract or lease prohibits or restricts assignment of rights or delegation of duties, if

**(1)(A)** applicable law excuses a party, other than the debtor, to such contract or lease from accepting performance from or rendering performance to an entity other than the debtor or the debtor in possession, whether or not such contract or lease prohibits or restricts assignment of rights or delegation of duties; and

**(B)** such party does not consent to such assumption or assignment. . ..

Our task, simply put, is to apply this statutory language to the facts at hand and determine whether it prohibits Catapult, as the debtor in possession, from assuming the Perlman licenses without Perlman's consent.

While simply put, our task is not so easily resolved; the proper interpretation of § 365(c)(1) has been the subject of considerable disagreement among courts and commentators. On one side are those who adhere to the plain statutory language, which establishes a so-called "hypothetical test" to govern the assumption of executory contracts. * * * In re West Elec., Inc., 852 F.2d 79, 83 (3d Cir.1988) * * *. On the other side are those that forsake the statutory language in favor of an "actual test" that, in their view, better accomplishes the intent of Congress. See Institut Pasteur v. Cambridge Biotech Corp., 104 F.3d 489, 493 (1st Cir.1997). . ..[2] Although we have on two occasions declined to choose between these competing visions, today we hold that we are bound by the plain terms of the statute

---

[2] The weight of lower court authority appears to favor the "actual test." * * * *

and join the Third and Eleventh Circuits in adopting the "hypothetical test."

## III.

We begin, as we must, with the statutory language.... The plain language of § 365(c)(1) "link[s] nonassignability under 'applicable law' together with a prohibition on assumption in bankruptcy." 1 DAVID G. EPSTEIN, STEVE H. NICKLES & JAMES J. WHITE, BANKRUPTCY § 5–15 at 474 (1992). In other words, the statute by its terms bars a debtor in possession from *assuming* an executory contract without the nondebtor's consent where applicable law precludes *assignment* of the contract to a third party. The literal language of § 365(c)(1) is thus said to establish a "hypothetical test": a debtor in possession may not assume an executory contract over the nondebtor's objection if applicable law would bar assignment to a hypothetical third party, even where the debtor in possession has no intention of assigning the contract in question to any such third party.

Before applying the statutory language to the case at hand, we first resolve a number of preliminary issues that are either not disputed by the parties, or are so clearly established as to deserve no more than passing reference. First, we follow the lead of the parties in assuming that the Perlman licenses are executory agreements within the meaning of § 365. Second, it is well-established that § 365(c)'s use of the term "trustee" includes Chapter 11 debtors in possession. Third, our precedents make it clear that federal patent law constitutes "applicable law" within the meaning of § 365(c), and that nonexclusive[3] patent licenses are "personal and assignable only with the consent of the licensor." *Everex*, 89 F.3d at 680.

When we have cleared away these preliminary matters, application of the statute to the facts of this case becomes relatively straightforward:

(c)   *Catapult* may not assume... the *Perlman licenses*,.... if

      (1)(A)   *federal patent* law excuses *Perlman* from accepting performance from or rendering performance to an entity other than *Catapult*...; and

(B)   *Perlman* does not consent to such assumption. . ..

11 U.S.C. § 365(c) (substitutions in italics).

---

[3] One of the two Perlman licenses began its life as an exclusive license. Perlman in a sworn declaration stated that, pursuant to its terms, the license has since become nonexclusive. Because Catapult has not offered any rebuttal evidence, and because neither party raised the issue in connection with the issues raised in this appeal, we will assume that the Perlman licenses are nonexclusive. Accordingly, we express no opinion regarding the assignability of exclusive patent licenses under federal law, and note that we expressed no opinion on this subject in *Everex*. See *Everex*, 89 F.3d at 679 ("Federal law holds a nonexclusive patent license to be personal and nonassignable. . ..") (emphasis added).

Since federal patent law makes nonexclusive patent licenses personal and nondelegable, § 365(c)(1)(A) is satisfied. Perlman has withheld his consent, thus satisfying § 365(c)(1)(B). Accordingly, the plain language of § 365(c)(1) bars Catapult from assuming the Perlman licenses.

## IV.

Catapult urges us to abandon the literal language of § 365(c)(1) in favor of an alternative approach, reasoning that Congress did not intend to bar debtors in possession from assuming their own contracts where no assignment is contemplated. In Catapult's view, § 365(c)(1) should be interpreted as embodying an "actual test": the statute bars assumption by the debtor in possession only where the reorganization in question results in the nondebtor actually having to accept performance from a third party. Under this reading of § 365(c), the debtor in possession would be permitted to assume any executory contract, so long as no assignment was contemplated. Put another way, Catapult suggests that, as to a debtor in possession, § 365(c)(1) should be read to prohibit assumption and assignment, rather than assumption or assignment.

Catapult has marshalled considerable authority to support this reading. The arguments supporting Catapult's position can be divided into three categories: (1) the literal reading creates inconsistencies within § 365; (2) the literal reading is incompatible with the legislative history; and (3) the literal reading flies in the face of sound bankruptcy policy. Nonetheless, we find that none of these considerations justifies departing from the plain language of § 365(c)(1).

## A.

Catapult first argues that a literal reading of § 365(c)(1) sets the statute at war with itself and its neighboring provisions. Deviation from the plain language, contends Catapult, is necessary if internal consistency is to be achieved. We agree with Catapult that a court should interpret a statute, if possible, so as to minimize discord among related provisions. See 2A NORMAN J. SINGER, SUTHERLAND STATUTORY CONSTRUCTION § 46.06 (5th ed. 1992) ("A statute should be construed so that effect is given to all its provisions, so that no part will be inoperative or superfluous, void or insignificant, and so that one section will not destroy another unless the provision is the result of obvious mistake or error."). However, the dire inconsistencies cited by Catapult turn out, on closer analysis, to be no such thing.

Catapult, for example, singles out the interaction between § 365(c)(1) and § 365(f)(1) as a statutory trouble spot. See In re Catron, 158 B.R. at 636 (exploring apparent conflict between subsections (c)(1) and (f)(1)); In re Cardinal Indus., 116 B.R. at 976–77 (same). Subsection (f)(1) provides that executory contracts, once assumed, may be assigned notwithstanding any contrary provisions contained in the contract *or applicable law*:

(**f)(1)** Except as provided in subsection (**c**) of this section, notwithstanding a provision in an executory contract or unexpired lease of the debtor, *or in applicable law*, that prohibits, restricts, or conditions the assignment of such contract or lease, the trustee may assign such contract or lease under paragraph **(2)** of this subsection. . ..

§ 365(f)(1) (emphasis added).

The potential conflict between subsections (c)(1) and (f)(1) arises from their respective treatments of "applicable law." The plain language of subsection (c)(1) bars assumption (absent consent) whenever "applicable law" would bar assignment. Subsection (f)(1) states that, *contrary provisions in applicable law notwithstanding,* executory contracts may be assigned. Since assumption is a necessary prerequisite to assignment under § 365, see § 365(f)(2)(A), a literal reading of subsection (c)(1) appears to render subsection (f)(1) superfluous. In the words of the Sixth Circuit, "[S]ection 365(c), the recognized exception to 365(f), appears at first to resuscitate in full the very anti-assignment 'applicable law' which 365(f) nullifies." In re Magness, 972 F.2d 689, 695 (6th Cir.1992) (Guy, J., concurring). Faced with this dilemma, one district court reluctantly concluded that the "[c]onflict between subsections (c) and (f) of § 365 is inescapable." See In re Catron, 158 B.R. at 636.

Subsequent authority, however, suggests that this conclusion may have been unduly pessimistic. The Sixth Circuit has credibly reconciled the warring provisions by noting that "each subsection recognizes an 'applicable law' of markedly different scope." Subsection (f)(1) states the broad rule–a law that, as a general matter, "prohibits, restricts, or conditions the assignment" of executory contracts is trumped by the provisions of subsection (f)(1). Subsection (c)(1), however, states a carefully crafted exception to the broad rule–where applicable law does not merely recite a general ban on assignment, but instead more specifically "excuses a party. . . from accepting performance from or rendering performance to an entity" different from the one with which the party originally contracted, the applicable law prevails over subsection (f)(1). In other words, in determining whether an "applicable law" stands or falls under § 365(f)(1), a court must ask why the "applicable law" prohibits assignment. Only if the law prohibits assignment on the rationale that the identity of the contracting party is material to the agreement will subsection (c)(1) rescue it.[4] We agree with the Sixth and Eleventh Circuits that a literal reading of subsection (c)(1) does not inevitably set it at odds with subsection (f)(1).

Catapult next focuses on the internal structure of § 365(c)(1) itself. According to Catapult, the literal approach to subsection (c)(1) renders the phrase "or the debtor in possession" contained in § 365(c)(1)(A) superflu-

---

[4] We note that, in the instant case, the federal law principle against the assignability of nonexclusive patent licenses is rooted in the personal nature of a nonexclusive license–the identity of a licensee may matter a great deal to a licensor. See In re CFLC, 89 F.3d at 679 (explaining rationale behind federal law rule against assignability).

ous.[5] In the words of one bankruptcy court, "[i]f the directive of Section 365(c)(1) is to prohibit assumption whenever applicable law excuses performance relative to any entity other than the debtor, why add the words 'or debtor in possession?' The [hypothetical] test renders this phrase surplusage." In re Hartec, 117 B.R. at 871–72.

A close reading of § 365(c)(1), however, dispels this notion. By its terms, subsection (c)(1) addresses two conceptually distinct events: assumption and assignment. The plain language of the provision makes it clear that each of these events is contingent on the nondebtor's separate consent. Consequently, where a nondebtor consents to the assumption of an executory contract, subsection (c)(1) will have to be applied a second time if the debtor in possession wishes to assign the contract in question. On that second application, the relevant question would be whether "applicable law excuses a party from accepting performance from or rendering performance to an entity other than. . . *the debtor in possession.*" § 365(c)(1)(A) (emphasis added). Consequently, the phrase "debtor in possession," far from being rendered superfluous by a literal reading of subsection (c)(1), dovetails neatly with the disjunctive language that opens subsection (c)(1): "The trustee may not assume or assign. . .." § 365(c) (emphasis added); cf. In re Catron, 158 B.R. at 636 (rejecting argument that literal reading of § 365(c) makes "or assign" superfluous insofar as assumption is a prerequisite to assignment).

A third potential inconsistency identified by Catapult relates to § 365(c)(2). According to Catapult, a literal reading of subsection (c)(1) renders subsection (c)(2) a dead letter. Subsection (c)(2) provides:

> **(c)** The trustee may not assume or assign any executory contract or unexpired lease of the debtor, whether or not such contract or lease prohibits or restricts assignment of rights or delegation of duties, if
>
> > **(2)** such contract is a contract to make a loan, or extend other debt financing or financial accommodations, to or for the benefit of the debtor, or to issue a security of the debtor. . ..

§ 365(c)(2). According to Catapult, the contracts encompassed by subsection (c)(2) are all nonassignable as a matter of applicable state law. As a result, a literal reading of subsection (c)(1) would seem to snare and dis-

---

[5] The phrase in question was added by Congress in 1984, replacing an earlier formulation focusing on the "trustee or an assignee":

(1)(A) applicable law excuses a party, other than the debtor, to such contract or lease from accepting performance from or rendering performance to an entity other than the ~~trustee or an assignee of such contract or lease~~ *the debtor or the debtor in possession*, whether or not such contract or lease prohibits or restricts assignment of rights or delegation of duties.

§ 365(c)(1)(A) (prior language stricken through).

pose of every executory contract within subsection (c)(2)'s scope. Perlman, however, persuasively rebuts this argument, noting that even if the state law governing the assignability of loan agreements and financing contracts is relatively uniform today, Congress by enacting subsection (c)(2) cemented nationwide uniformity in the bankruptcy context, effectively ensuring creditors that these particular contracts would not be assumable in bankruptcy. Put another way, it is the national uniformity of applicable state law that has rendered subsection (c)(2) superfluous, not the terms of subsection (c)(1).

In any event, subsection (c)(1) does not completely swallow up subsection (c)(2). Subsection (c)(1) by its terms permits assumption and assignment of executory loan agreements *so long as the nondebtor consents.* See § 365(c)(1)(B). Subsection (c)(2), in contrast, bans assumption and assignment of such agreements, *consent of the nondebtor notwithstanding.* See Transamerica Commercial Fin. Corp. v. Citibank, N.A. (In re Sun Runner Marine, Inc.), 945 F.2d 1089, 1093 (9th Cir.1991) ( "Section 365(c)(2) unambiguously prohibits the assumption of financial accommodation contracts, regardless of the consent of the non-debtor party."); 2 WILLIAM L. NORTON, JR., NORTON BANKRUPTCY LAW AND PRACTICE 2D § 39:19 ("[T]he correct view is that executory credit contracts may not be assumed in bankruptcy regardless of the desires of the parties."). Accordingly, contrary to Catapult's assertion, subsection (c)(1) does not necessarily catch upriver all the fish that would otherwise be netted by subsection (c)(2). Once again, the "inconsistency" identified by Catapult proves evanescent under close scrutiny. We see no reason why these two provisions cannot happily coexist.[6]

We conclude that the claimed inconsistencies are not actual and that the plain language of § 365(c)(1) compels the result Perlman urges: Catapult may not assume the Perlman licenses over Perlman's objection. Catapult has not demonstrated that, in according the words of subsection (c)(1) their plain meaning, we do violence to subsection (c)(1) or the provisions that accompany it.

### B.

Catapult next urges that legislative history requires disregard of the plain language of § 365(c)(1). First off, because we discern no ambiguity in the plain statutory language, we need not resort to legislative history.

We will depart from this rule, if at all, only where the legislative history clearly indicates that Congress meant something other than what it said. Here, the legislative history unearthed by Catapult falls far short of

---

[6] Catapult also advances what it claims is a fourth inconsistency by contrasting the plain language of § 365(c)(1) with the provisions of § 365(e)(1), which nullifies "ipso facto" clauses. In rejecting this contention, it is enough to note that § 365(e)(2)(A) expressly revives "ipso facto" clauses in precisely the same executory contracts that fall within the scope of § 365(c)(1).

this mark. The legislative history behind § 365(c) was exhaustively analyzed by the bankruptcy court in *In re Cardinal Industries*, 116 B.R. at 978–80. Its discussion makes it clear that there exists no contemporaneous legislative history regarding the current formulation of subsection (c)(1). *Id.* at 978 ("[T]here is no authoritative legislative history for BAFJA as enacted in 1984."). Catapult, however, argues that the language as ultimately enacted in 1984 had its genesis in a 1980 House amendment to an earlier Senate technical corrections bill. The amendment was accompanied by "a relatively obscure committee report." 1 DAVID G. EPSTEIN, STEVE H. NICKLES & JAMES J. WHITE, BANKRUPTCY § 5–15 (1992). In explaining the amendment, the report stated:

> This amendment makes it clear that the prohibition against a trustee's power to assume an executory contract does not apply where it is the debtor that is in possession and the performance to be given or received under a personal service contract will be the same as if no petition had been filed because of the personal service nature of the contract.

In re Cardinal Indus., 116 B.R. at 979 (quoting H.R.Rep. No. 1195, 96th Cong., 2d Sess. § 27(b) (1980)). However, since the report relates to a different proposed bill, predates enactment of § 365(c)(1) by several years, and expresses at most the thoughts of only one committee in the House, we are not inclined to view it as the sort of clear indication of contrary intent that would overcome the unambiguous language of subsection (c)(1).

## C.

Catapult makes the appealing argument that, as a leading bankruptcy commentator has pointed out, there are policy reasons to prefer the "actual test." See 3 LAWRENCE P. KING, COLLIER ON BANKRUPTCY § 365.06[1][d][iii] (15th ed. revised) (arguing that sound bankruptcy policy supports the actual test). That may be so, but Congress is the policy maker, not the courts.

Policy arguments cannot displace the plain language of the statute; that the plain language of § 365(c)(1) may be bad policy does not justify a judicial rewrite. And a rewrite is precisely what the actual test requires. The statute expressly provides that a debtor in possession "may not assume *or* assign" an executory contract where applicable law bars assignment and the nondebtor objects. § 365(c)(1) (emphasis added). The actual test effectively engrafts a narrow exception onto § 365(c)(1) for debtors in possession, providing that, as to them, the statute only prohibits assumption and assignment, as opposed to assumption or assignment. *See In re Fastrax*, 129 B.R. at 277 (admitting that, by adopting the actual test, the court reads the word "assume" out of subsection (c) with respect to debtors in possession).

## V.

Because the statute speaks clearly, and its plain language does not produce a patently absurd result or contravene any clear legislative history, we must "hold Congress to its words." Accordingly, we hold that, where applicable nonbankruptcy law makes an executory contract nonassignable because the identity of the nondebtor party is material, a debtor in possession may not assume the contract absent consent of the nondebtor party. A straightforward application of § 365(c)(1) to the circumstances of this case precludes Catapult from assuming the Perlman licenses over Perlman's objection. Consequently, the bankruptcy court erred when it approved Catapult's motion to assume the Perlman licenses, and the district court erred in affirming the bankruptcy court.

REVERSED.

## NOTES

**1.** Consider the following passages from Daniel J. Bussel and Edward A. Friedler, *The Limits on Assuming and Assigning Executory Contracts*, 74 Am. Bankr.L.J. 321 (2000):

> Section 365 gets off on the wrong foot by equating assumption and assignment notwithstanding sharp policy distinctions between the two. Assumption involves performance of the agreement by and to the bankruptcy estate. Assignment involves performance by and to a third party and a release of the bankruptcy estate from further liability. Assignment does not merely substitute the bankruptcy estate as a successor to the prebankruptcy debtor–it allows the bankruptcy estate greater rights than those held by the prebankruptcy debtor, that is, the additional right to assign an otherwise nonassignable agreement. Yet § 365 appears to authorize assignment and limit assumption as if the two involved the same balance of interests. Most bankruptcy courts and a few higher courts have sought to repair the damage by decoupling the two, finding that a nonassignable contract outside of bankruptcy was nonassumable only where under the particular circumstances the assumption would amount to a forbidden assignment under otherwise applicable law. This "actual test" yields correct results from the point of view of bankruptcy policy and allows results in bankruptcy to effectively mirror the results outside of bankruptcy.
>
> But most courts of appeals have followed the literal language of § 365(c) to the conclusion that the bankruptcy estate loses the rights of the prebankruptcy debtor to valuable contracts that would not be assignable under otherwise applicable law even when no assignment is contemplated, and the nondebtor party to the contract, under nonbankruptcy law, could not refuse the performance that is actually offered. Under this "hypothetical test" contracts governed by § 365(c)(1) be-

come one of the very few instances where the debtor's valuable rights against nondebtors are legally forfeited simply because of a bankruptcy filing. This kind of forfeiture is generally inconsistent with current bankruptcy policy as indicated by provisions invalidating the *ipso facto* or "bankruptcy default" clauses that commonly resulted in such forfeitures under the Bankruptcy Act of 1898. §§ 365(e)(1), 541(c)(1) and 545(1).

\* \* \*

[The] hypothetical test flies in the face of (i) the pro-reorganization policy of the Code, (ii) the policy that bankruptcy entitlements should generally mirror nonbankruptcy entitlements subject to the exigencies of the collective bankruptcy proceeding itself, and (iii) principles favoring equal treatment of creditors with similar nonbankruptcy law entitlements. It could not be what the Congress that enacted the Bankruptcy Reform Act of 1978 and the two subsequent amendments to § 365(c)(1) intended.

\* \* \*

Most nonbankruptcy law regulating assignment of contract rights does not flatly prohibit or authorize assignment. Only a few types of contracts are always, or never, assignable under nonbankruptcy law. Contracts governed by nonbankruptcy law that does not flatly prohibit assignment cannot fit within the framework of the hypothetical test because it is impossible to know in the abstract whether or not such an agreement is assignable under otherwise applicable law. The answer otherwise applicable law gives to the question "Is it assignable?" is "It depends upon particular facts and circumstances." In order to determine if a contract could be assigned to some hypothetical third party under an applicable law that allows assignment under certain conditions, it is necessary to know whether the proposed assignee meets those conditions. If there is no proposed assignee, this is impossible to do and the hypothetical test completely breaks down. The literal "hypothetical" construction of § 365(c) when applied to contracts assignable only under particular circumstances is simply incoherent. Only contracts subject to a flat ban on assignment fail the § 365(c) test whether construed literally as a hypothetical test or as an actual test.

\* \* \*

[T]he purpose of § 365(c)(1) is to simply preserve the nonbankruptcy law consent requirement in the few instances that nonbankruptcy law requires consent as a condition to assignment, and not to impose an independent and higher bankruptcy law bar to assumption or assignment. Given the function of § 365(c)(1), and its relationship to § 365(f), it is error to construe § 365(c)(1) to preclude assumption of an executory contract by a Chapter 11 debtor in possession. . .. There is no nonbankruptcy law that requires express consent to the continued performance or receipt of performance of the original contracting party. Section 365(c)(1) simply has no application in the case of assumption of an executory contract or lease by the debtor in possession.

**2.** Even if the "actual test" rejected in *Catapult Entertainment* is the correct interpretation of § 365(c)(1), non-debtor parties to contracts that fall under § 365(c)(1) have argued that they are entitled to enforce ipso facto clauses in such agreements. These ipso facto clauses are extremely common and they provide that the contract is terminated upon the bankruptcy of a party to the agreement. The effect of accepting this argument is equivalent to denying the debtor-in-possession the right to assume the contract—it frees the non-debtor party from any obligation to perform for or accept performance from the debtor in the event of bankruptcy. Non-debtors argue that even if § 365(c)(1) imposes an "actual test," the plain language of § 365(e)(2), which is an exception to the general rule that such ipso facto clauses are invalid in bankruptcy, imposes a *Catapult Entertainment*-style "hypothetical test." Originally, § 365(c)(1) and § 365(e)(2) were strictly parallel, the apparent notion being that there would be no harm in allowing an ipso facto clause to operate in the case of a contract that could not be assumed without the consent of the non-debtor pursuant to § 365(c)(1). In 1984 and 1986 when Congress amended § 365(c)(1) in the manner described in the introductory note before *Catapult Entertainment* and arguably created the textual basis for the "actual test" interpretation of § 365(c)(1), § 365(e)(2) was left untouched. The language of the two sections is therefore no longer parallel and to the extent that the "actual test" interpretation of § 365(c)(1) critically depends upon the 1984 and 1986 amendments, the "actual test" may not apply to § 365(e)(2). In *Summit Investment and Development Corporation v. Leroux*, 69 F.3d 608 (1st Cir.1995), the Court in an opinion by Judge Cyr (a former bankruptcy judge) nevertheless found that § 365(c) and § 365(e) were necessarily parallel in scope and were both properly construed as imposing an "actual test":

> Given the interrelated concerns addressed by sections 365(c) and 365(e)(2), however, we think Congress contemplated in 1984 that section 365(e)(2) would permit a debtor or a debtor in possession to avoid *automatic termination* of his executory contract rights under the section 365(e)(2)(A) exception. Were this not so, an absurd result would eventuate: there would be no contractual right left for a debtor or debtor in possession to *assume* under section 365(c)(1) because it would already have been terminated automatically under section 365(e). * * *

**3.** Under contract law an assignor remains liable on the assigned contract or lease unless the non-assigning party consents to a release. This rule of contract law is preempted by the Bankruptcy Code—§ 365(k) provides that assignment relieves the trustee and the estate from any liability occurring after assignment. The non-assigning party finds protection in the requirement under § 365(f)(2) that a contract or lease may be assigned only if the debtor assumes the contract or lease and the assignee provides adequate assurance of future performance, whether or not the contract or lease is in default.

Section 365(b)(1) precludes a debtor from assuming an executory contract or lease in default until the debtor has cured the default or provided adequate assurance that it will promptly do so. Certain kinds of defaults are excepted from the cure requirement by § 365(b)(2). The most important of these are those stemming from "bankruptcy clauses" or "ipso facto" clauses which declare the debtor in default upon filing in bankruptcy. These clauses are rendered inoperative by § 365(b)(2)(A)-(C) and (e)(1).

Under the 1994 version of § 365(b)(2), the cure condition to assumption did not apply to a default that is a breach of a provision relating to

**(D)** the satisfaction of any penalty rate or provision relating to a default arising from any failure by the debtor to perform nonmonetary obligations under the executory contract or unexpired lease.

This provision might have been viewed as intended to make it easier for debtors to assume contracts and leases by resolving two separate issues. First, contracts and leases often provide for a higher rate of interest after a default; under (D) debtors can cure without paying the default rate. Second, there may be defaults in the performance of nonmonetary obligations that may be impossible to cure; under (D) no cure of these defaults is required. *Collier on Bankruptcy* ¶ 365.05[4] (15th ed. rev. 2004). However, the first authoritative decision on this provision, *In re Claremont Acquisition Corp., Inc.*, 113 F.3d 1029 (9th Cir.1997), rejected this broad interpretation and held that (D) is limited to excusing debtors from having to pay penalties. The court reached this result by holding that "penalty" modified both "rate" and "provision"; hence, the debtor is excused from curing defaults of nonmonetary obligations only to the extent of penalties that the contract imposes for the default. An example would be a clause calling for the payment of liquidated damages as a penalty for breach of a nonmonetary obligation.

The severe consequences of this holding are seen in *Claremont* which involved an attempt on the part of Debtor, an auto dealer, to assume and assign a General Motors franchise. The GM dealer agreement contained a provision terminating a franchise for failure to operate the business for seven consecutive days; Debtor had failed to operate the dealership for two weeks prior to filing. The District Court held that this was a nonmonetary obligation which need not be cured under § 365(b)(2)(D). The Ninth Circuit, in the belief that this provision was intended by Congress only to relieve debtors of obligations to pay penalties, held (i) Debtor was not excused from its obligation to cure because the exception in (D) did not apply to Debtor's default; and (ii) since the default could not be cured, the contract could not be assumed and assigned. *See* Charles Jordan Tabb, *The Law of Bankruptcy* 614–615 (1997) (discussing the consequences of an incurable default). The *Claremont* holding is particularly devastating for debtors who had leased their places of business under long-term commercial leases which commonly provide for lease termination whenever the tenant ceases operation (in the vernacular, "goes dark") at the leased premises.

The 2005 Act codified *Claremont*. But the amended version of § 365(b)(1)(A) carves out an important exception with respect to unexpired real property leases: the trustee need not cure defaults that relate to breach of nonmonetary obligations in real property leases if it is impossible to do so. However, the trustee must begin performing all nonmonetary obligations under the lease at or after the time of assumption. Moreover, if a lessor of nonresidential real property suffers any pecuniary losses as a result of the debtor's failure to perform its nonmonetary obligations under the lease, these losses must be compensated as part of the cure. The effect of these two amendments is to reverse *Claremont* as to real property leases but to uphold its result as to personal property leases and executory contracts other than unexpired leases of real property. Under § 365(b)(2)(D), those debtors with personal property leases and other executory contracts may not be permitted to assume and assign their agreements if they have committed an incurable nonmonetary default.

### b.   Assignment

Subsections 365(c) and (f) read like Joseph Heller's *Catch–22*. Subsection (f) seems to embody a special bankruptcy "pro-assignment" policy. Section 365(f)(1) allows the trustee to assign an executory contract notwithstanding a provision in the contract or in "applicable law" prohibiting the assignment. But a contract cannot be assigned unless it has been assumed. § 365(f)(2)(A). And what kind of contracts cannot be assumed? Those which "applicable law" makes non-assignable. In short, the debtor can assign non-assignable agreements, but only if it can assume them—which it cannot if they are non-assignable. Both provisions refer to "applicable law" that may prohibit assignment without consent of both parties to the contract. Section 365(c)(1) says that the "applicable law" is controlling while § 365(f)(1) allows assignment notwithstanding that law. Since § 365(c)(1) controls § 365(f)(1) there is great confusion concerning the meaning of § 365(f)(1).

*Pioneer Ford,* which follows, interprets § 365(c)(1)(A) as originally enacted. It also discusses the relationship between § 365(c)(1)(A) and § 365(f)(1) and how they can be harmonized.

# In re Pioneer Ford Sales, Inc.

United States Court of Appeals, First Circuit, 1984.
729 F.2d 27.

■ BREYER, Circuit Judge.

The Ford Motor Company appeals a federal district court decision allowing a bankrupt Ford dealer (Pioneer Ford Sales, Inc.) to assign its Ford franchise over Ford's objection to a Toyota dealer (Toyota Village, Inc.). The district court decided the case on the basis of a record developed in the bankruptcy court. The bankruptcy court had approved the transfer, which ran from Pioneer to Fleet National Bank (Pioneer's principal secured creditor) and then to Toyota Village. Fleet sought authorization for the assignment because Toyota Village will pay $10,000 for the franchise and buy all parts and accessories in Pioneer's inventory at fair market value (about $75,000); if the franchise is not assigned, Ford will buy only some of the parts for between $45,000 and $55,000. Thus, the assignment will increase the value of the estate. Fleet is the appellee here.

The issue that the case raises is the proper application of § 365(c)(1)(A), an exception to a more general provision, § 365(f)(1), that allows a trustee in bankruptcy (or a debtor in possession) to assign many of the debtor's executory contracts even if the contract itself says that it forbids assignment. The exception at issue reads as follows:

(c) The trustee [or debtor in possession] may not assume or assign an executory contract * * * of the debtor, whether or not such contract * * * prohibits assignment if—

(1)(A) applicable law excuses [the other party to the contract] from accepting performance from * * * an assignee * * * whether or not [the] * * * contract * * * prohibits * * * assignment.

The words "applicable law" in this section mean "applicable non-bankruptcy law." * * * Evidently, the theory of this section is to prevent the trustee from assigning (over objection) contracts of the sort that contract law ordinarily makes nonassignable, i.e. contracts that cannot be assigned when the contract itself is silent about assignment. At the same time, by using the words in (1)(A) "whether *or not* the contract prohibits assignment," the section prevents parties from using contractual language to prevent the trustee from assigning contracts that (when the contract is silent) contract law typically makes assignable. Id. Thus, we must look to see whether relevant nonbankruptcy law would allow Ford to veto the assignment of its basic franchise contract "whether or not" that basic franchise contract itself specifically "prohibits assignment."

The nonbankruptcy law to which both sides point us is contained in Rhode Island's "Regulation of Business Practices Among Motor Vehicle Manufacturers, Distributors and Dealers" Act, R.I.Gen.Laws § 31–5.1–4(C)(7). It states that

[N]o dealer * * * shall have the right to * * * assign the franchise * * * without the consent of the manufacturer, except that such consent shall not be unreasonably withheld.

The statute by its terms, allows a manufacturer to veto an assignment where the veto is reasonable but not otherwise. The statute's language also indicates that it applies "whether or not" the franchise contract itself restricts assignment. Thus, the basic question that the case presents is whether Ford's veto was reasonable in terms of the Rhode Island law.

Neither the district court nor the bankruptcy court specifically addressed this question. Their failure apparently arose out of their belief that § 365(c)(1)(A) refers only to traditional personal service contracts. But in our view they were mistaken. The language of the section does not limit its effect to personal service contracts. It refers generally to contracts that are not assignable under nonbankruptcy law. State laws typically make contracts for personal services nonassignable (where the contract itself is silent); but they make other sorts of contracts nonassignable as well. See, e.g., N.Y. State Finance Law § 138 (1974) (making certain government contracts unassignable); N.Y. General Municipal Law § 109 (1977) (same); N.C.Gen.Stat. § 147–62 (1978) (same). The legislative history of § 365(c) says nothing about "personal services." To the contrary, it speaks of letters of credit, personal loans, and leases—instances in which assigning a contract may place the other party at a significant disadvantage. The history thereby suggests that (c)(1)(A) has a broader reach.

The source of the "personal services" limitation apparently is a bankruptcy court case, In re Taylor Manufacturing, Inc., 6 B.R. 370 (Bankr.N.D.Ga.1980), which other bankruptcy courts have followed. The *Taylor* court wrote that (c)(1)(A) should be interpreted narrowly, in part because it believed that (c)(1)(A) conflicted with another section, (f)(1), which states in relevant part:

Except as provided in subsection (c) * * *, notwithstanding a provision * * * in applicable law that prohibits * * * the assignment of [an executory] contract * * * the trustee may assign [it] * * *.

As a matter of logic, however, we see no conflict, for (c)(1)(A) refers to state laws that prohibit assignment "whether or not" the contract is silent, while (f)(1) contains no such limitation. Apparently (f)(1) includes state laws that prohibit assignment only when the contract is *not* silent about assignment; that is to say, state laws that enforce contract provisions prohibiting assignment. See 1 Norton, Bankruptcy Law and Practice § 23.14. These state laws are to be ignored. The section specifically excepts (c)(1)(A)'s state laws that forbid assignment even when the contract *is* silent; they are to be heeded. Regardless, we fail to see why a "conflict" suggests that (c)(1)(A) is limited to "personal services."

The *Taylor* court cites 2 Collier on Bankruptcy § 365.05 and the Commission Report, H.R.Doc. No. 93–137, 93rd Cong., 1st Sess. 199 (1973), in support. Both of these sources speak of personal services. However, they do not say that (c)(1)(A), was intended to be *limited* to personal services. Indeed, since it often is difficult to decide whether or not a particular duty can be characterized by the label "personal service," it makes sense to avoid this question and simply look to see whether state law would, or would not, make the duty assignable where the contract is silent. Thus, the Fifth Circuit has found no reason for limiting the scope of (c)(1)(A) to personal service contracts. In re Braniff Airways, Inc., 700 F.2d 935, 943 (5th Cir.1983). Fleet concedes in its brief that "the exception to assignment [of § 365(c)(1)(A)] is not limited to personal services contracts." We therefore reject the district court's conclusion in this respect.

Although the district court did not explicitly decide whether Ford's veto was reasonable, it decided a closely related question. Under other provisions of § 365 a bankruptcy court cannot authorize assignment of an executory contract if 1) the debtor is in default, unless 2) there is "adequate assurance of future performance," § 365(b)(1)(C). Pioneer is in default, but the bankruptcy and district courts found "adequate assurance." For the sake of argument, we shall assume that this finding is equivalent to a finding that Ford's veto of the assignment was unreasonable. And, we shall apply a "clearly erroneous" standard in reviewing the factual element in this lower court finding. Fed.R.Civ.P. 52. On these assumptions, favorable to Fleet, we nonetheless must reverse the district court, for, in our view, any finding of unreasonableness, based on this record, is clearly erroneous.

Our review of the record reveals the following critical facts. First, in accordance with its ordinary business practice and dealer guidelines incorporated into the franchise agreement, Ford would have required Toyota Village, as a dealer, to have a working capital of at least $172,000, of which no more than half could be debt. Toyota Village, however, had a working capital at the end of 1981 of $37,610; and its net worth was $31,747. Although the attorney for Fleet at one point in the bankruptcy proceedings said Toyota Village could borrow some of the necessary capital from a bank, he made no later reference to the point, nor did he ever specifically state how much Toyota Village could borrow. Since the tax returns of Toyota Village's owner showed gross income of $27,500 for 1981, there is no reason to believe that the owner could readily find the necessary equity capital.

Second, at a time when Japanese cars have sold well throughout the United States, Toyota Village has consistently lost money. * * *

At the same time, the record contains no significant evidence tending to refute the natural inference arising from these facts. The bankruptcy court mentioned five factors that it said showed that Toyota Village gave "adequate assurance" that it could do the job.

**(1)** Toyota Village was an established dealership.

**(2)** Toyota Village was "located within 500 yards of the present Ford dealership."

**(3)** Toyota Village had a proven track record for selling cars.

**(4)** Toyota Village was willing and able to pay $15,000 that Pioneer still owed Ford.

**(5)** The owner and sole stockholder of Toyota Village testified that he was willing and able to fulfill the franchise agreement.

The first of these factors (dealer experience), while favoring Toyota Village, is weak, given the record of continuous dealership losses. The second (location) proves little, considering that Pioneer went bankrupt at the very spot. The third (track record) cuts against Toyota Village, not in its favor, for its track record is one of financial loss. The fourth (willingness to pay a $15,000 debt that Pioneer owed Ford) is relevant, but it shows, at most, that Toyota Village *believed* it could make a success of the franchise. The fifth (ability to act as franchisee) is supported by no more than a simple statement by the owner of Toyota Village that he could do the job.

We do not see how the few positive features about Toyota Village that the record reveals can overcome the problem of a history of losses and failure to meet Ford's capital requirements. In these circumstances, Ford would seem perfectly reasonable in withholding its consent to the transfer. Thus, Rhode Island law would make the franchise unassignable.

\* \* \*

One might still argue that under Rhode Island law the only "reasonable" course of action for Ford is to allow the transfer and then simply terminate Toyota Village if it fails to perform adequately. This suggestion, however, overlooks the legal difficulties that Ford would have in proving cause for termination under the Rhode Island "Regulation of Business Practices Among Motor Vehicle Manufacturers, Distributors and Dealers" Act. R.I.Gen.Laws § 31–5.1–4(D)(2). The very purpose of the statute—protecting dealer reliance—suggests that it ought to be more difficult for a manufacturer to terminate a dealer who has invested in a franchise than to oppose the grant of a franchise to one who has not. In any event, the law does not suggest a manufacturer is "unreasonable" in objecting to a transfer unless he would have "good cause" to terminate the transferee. And, to equate the two standards would tend to make the "unreasonable" provision superfluous. Thus, we conclude that the Rhode Island law would make the franchise unassignable on the facts here revealed. Therefore, neither the bankruptcy court nor the district court had the power to authorize the transfer.

\* \* \*

For these reasons, the judgment of the district court is
Reversed.

## NOTES

**1.** The result in this case is full of irony. Surely the relevant Rhode Island statute was enacted to protect auto dealers from onerous anti-assignment provisions imposed by manufacturers in their agreements. It is a pro-assignment statute. And yet because the legislature acted to limit contractual anti-assignment clauses in these franchise agreements, the franchise in *Pioneer Ford* is rendered non-assignable. Had there been no such statute then any anti-assignment clause in the agreement would have been unenforceable in toto.

**2.** Section 365 is ambiguous on the assignability of otherwise nonassignable contracts in bankruptcy. Under § 365(f)(1) the trustee may assign an executory contract "notwithstanding a provision * * * in applicable law, that prohibits, restricts, or conditions the assignment * * *." Subsection (f)(1) is subject to subsection (c) which states that the trustee may not assign if "applicable law excuses a party, other than the debtor, * * * from accepting performance from or rendering performance to * * * an entity other than the debtor or the debtor in possession." This suggests that there are some contracts that are nonassignable under nonbankruptcy law that can be assigned in bankruptcy in spite of that law (§ 365(f)(1)) and some contracts that are nonassignable under nonbankruptcy law that can't be assigned in bankruptcy. § 365(c)(1)(A). This was the basis of the lower court's conclusion in *Pioneer Ford* that § 365(c)(1)(A) was meant to apply only to personal service contracts and that all other contracts nonassignable under nonbankruptcy law fall under § 365(f)(1).

On appeal, the First Circuit harmonized the two provisions in a different way. It held that (c)(1)(A) applies to cases in which the nonbankruptcy law forbids assignment regardless of whether the contract specifically forbids assignment, while (f)(1) applies to cases in which assignment is prohibited only because the nonbankruptcy law enforces a contract provision that specifically forbids assignment. In other words some contracts, such as personal service contracts, are nonassignable regardless of whether the contract specifically forbids assignment. They cannot be assigned in bankruptcy. A contract such as the nonexclusive patent license in *Catapult Entertainment* falls in this category because assignment without approval of the licensor is forbidden by federal patent law. Other contracts are nonassignable only if the contract specifically forbids assignment. They can be assigned in bankruptcy. The basis of this analysis is the presence in § 365(c) of the phrase "whether or not such contract * * * prohibits or restricts assignment" and the absence of that phrase in subsection (f)(1). In *Pioneer Ford,* (c)(1)(A) applied because the Rhode Island statute prevented assignment without consent of Ford Motor Company regardless of what the contract provided.

**3.** The *Pioneer Ford* reconciliation of § 365(c) and (f) is criticized in Daniel J. Bussel & Edward A. Friedler, *The Limits on Assuming and Assigning Executory Contracts*, 74 Am. Bankr. L.J. 321 (2000):

While *Pioneer Ford*'s reconciliation of subsections (c) and (f) parses the statute cleverly, the policy and legislative intent supporting such a distinction are either obscure or nonexistent. *Pioneer Ford* invites state legislatures to override bankruptcy's pro-assignment policy to protect favored constituencies, thereby undermining the uniformity and coherence of federal bankruptcy law on an *ad hoc* and state-by-state basis. And from the perspective of nonbankruptcy policy, there is no apparent justification for giving priority to statutory restrictions on assignment over bargained-for restrictions on assignment that would be clearly enforceable under otherwise applicable law. Nonbankruptcy policy does not give greater weight to statutory restrictions on alienation than to contractual restrictions. Indeed, under state law parties can almost always override statutory restrictions on alienation by agreement.

The court in *In re Magness*, 972 F.2d 689 (6th Cir.1992), states that *Pioneer Ford* erred in limiting § 365(f) to cases in which there are contractual provisions prohibiting assignment. "There is simply nothing in the language of § 365(f) which supports the limitation read into it by that court." 972 F.2d at 695. If *Pioneer Ford* narrowed the scope of "applicable law" in § 365(f), *Magness* appeared to narrow the scope of these words in § 365(c) to situations in which the common law would permit the nondebtor party to refuse to accept performance from a proposed assignee, even in the absence of an express anti-assignment agreement. *Magness* held a Chapter 7 debtor's "golf membership" in a country club to be nonassignable as a "personal contract" under Ohio common law. The judge writing the majority opinion (a respected former law school dean who is an avid golfer) rhapsodized on the unique relationship created by golf club memberships. Quieting any possible reservations we might have had on the issue, he stated that the memberships "were not in any way commercial" (gulp) and "[t]hey create personal relationships among individuals who play golf, who are waiting to play golf, who eat together, swim and play together." 972 F.2d at 696. To allow a trustee in bankruptcy to confer this idyllic status on the highest bidder was unthinkable, even though no riff-raff need apply because under club rules no one could become a golf member without being or becoming a social (nongolf) club member.

Bussel and Friedler, *supra*, reject the holding and reasoning of *Pioneer Ford*. They argue that nonbankruptcy law restrictions on assignment fall into four categories, and that § 365(f) overrides such restrictions in all but those instances where the restriction forbids all assignments without the consent of the nondebtor party:

> Accordingly, under modern law, there are virtually no absolute prohibitions on assignment of contract rights. A few contract rights are conclusively presumed assignable (the first category). Most other contract rights are rebuttably presumed assignable, that is they are assignable unless the party resisting assignment can point to valid contrac-

tual restrictions or partial statutory or common law restrictions on assignment that apply under the circumstances of the particular case (the second and third categories). These contracts are "somewhat assignable." In a few instances, however, there are contract rights that are presumed nonassignable absent the express consent on the non-assigning party (the fourth category).

Section 365(c)(1) is directed at preserving the consent requirement for the fourth category of contract rights. Section 365(f) overrides otherwise applicable law restricting assignment for the second and third categories. If the assignor is in bankruptcy, the protection for the non-assigning party against material alteration of rights or duties is found in the requirement that the assuming debtor or trustee or any assignee provide adequate assurance of future performance. [§ 365(b)(1)(C), (f)(2)(B)]. The requirements of cure and adequate assurance of future performance replace the conditions under which most "somewhat assignable" contracts could be assigned outside of bankruptcy. Most law limiting contract assignments does so to protect the non-assigning party from adverse material changes on account of performance by or to an assignee. Requiring prophylactic court findings of cure and adequate assurance of future performance meets this important policy concern.

If we understand the limited purpose of § 365(c)(1) to be to preserve the consent requirement in the few instances that nonbankruptcy law requires consent as a condition to assignment, it becomes clear that all contractual and most statutory and common law limitations on assignability are overridden by the pro-assignment policy embodied in § 365(f). Only in those few instances where otherwise applicable law presumes complete nonassignability absent express consent does § 365(c)(1) apply.

This reading of § 365(c) also has the virtue of making sense of the language of § 365(c)(1)(B) which limits the § 365(c)(1)(A) restriction on assumption to cases where the nondebtor "party does not consent to such assumption or assignment." This language is a clear textual indication that the purpose of § 365(c)(1) is to simply preserve the non-bankruptcy law consent requirement in the few instances that non-bankruptcy law requires consent as a condition to assignment, and not to impose an independent and higher bankruptcy law bar to assumption or assignment.

74 Am. Bankr. L.J. at 336-337. The recommendation of the National Bankruptcy Conference in Reforming the Bankruptcy Code 140 (Rev.ed.1997) is that any contract, other than a personal service or credit extension contract, should be assignable so long as adequate assurance of future performance is provided. "The present bankruptcy policy of enforcing nonbankruptcy case law or statutory law prohibitions, restrictions, or

conditions on the assignment of a contract or delegation of performance duties thereunder should not be continued."

**4.** In portions of *Summit Investment and Development Corp. v. Leroux*, not mentioned in the discussion of that case in Note 2 following the *Catapult* opinion, the Court dealt with the problem of the enforcement of statutory bankruptcy termination provisions applicable to executory contracts. Contractual bankruptcy termination provisions ("ipso facto clauses") are invalidated by § 365(e). The First Circuit in *Summit* refused to recognize any distinction between statutory and contractual provisions in the case of bankruptcy termination provisions. In *Summit*, the executory contract at issue was a limited partnership agreement. The debtor in bankruptcy was a general partner with certain management rights under this agreement. The relevant state law, the Massachusetts Limited Partnership Act, provided that in the absence of any contractual provision to the contrary, the general partner's interest was terminated upon the bankruptcy of one of the general partners. The partnership agreement itself provided likewise. The First Circuit held the partnership agreement nevertheless assumable by the debtor in possession and the provisions of both the contract and state law ousting the debtor as general partner unenforceable under § 365(e). After reviewing the plain language of § 365(e) and noting the absence of any legislative history supporting the contractual—statutory distinction, the Court wrote:

> We are left, then, with no rationale which would warrant the categorical conclusion that Congress recognized a State interest sufficiently compelling to outweigh the important rehabilitative policies that section 365(e) was designed to serve. Nor has Summit suggested a sound basis for concluding that Congress considered statutory ipso facto provisions a lesser impediment to chapter 11 rehabilitation efforts than contractual ipso facto clauses.

69 F.3d at 611.

Is there a sound basis for distinguishing state mandated anti-assignment statutes (enforceable under *Pioneer Ford*) from state mandated bankruptcy termination statutes (unenforceable under *Summit*)?

## 6. ENFORCEMENT OF EXECUTORY CONTRACT BY BANKRUPTCY ESTATE BEFORE ASSUMPTION OR REJECTION

We have seen what the rights of the parties are under executory contracts if the debtor (i) rejects, (ii) assumes or (iii) assumes and assigns. But in Chapter 11 reorganizations a debtor in possession may be allowed a considerable period of time in which to decide whether to reject or assume. In this section we examine the rights of the parties during this hiatus. Section 365(d)(2) provides that in a Chapter 11 case the debtor's decision whether to reject or assume may be made "at any time before the confirmation of a plan," but allows the nondebtor party to request that the court fix an earlier time within which the debtor must decide. Since the debtor in possession may not be able to decide whether to assume before its plan of reorganization is formulated, courts have usually been reluctant to force a premature decision. Until the debtor in possession has assumed, an executory contract is not enforceable against the estate. But is it enforceable against the nondebtor party? If the debtor in possession enforces it against the nondebtor party, has the contract been assumed? The following case is a leading case on these questions.

## Matter of Whitcomb & Keller Mortgage Co.

United States Court of Appeals, Seventh Circuit, 1983.
715 F.2d 375.

■ JAMESON, District Judge.

This is an appeal from an order of the district court affirming a decision of the bankruptcy court allowing the debtor, Whitcomb & Keller Mortgage Co., Inc., Appellee, to reject an executory contract with Data–Link Systems, Inc., Appellant, and classifying Data–Link as a general unsecured creditor in the Whitcomb & Keller bankruptcy proceeding for the sum of $12,954.63. We affirm.

### I. Factual and Procedural Background

Whitcomb & Keller, a mortgage banker whose business included servicing mortgage accounts for investors, executed an executory contract with Data–Link, whereby, for a fee, Data–Link was to provide computer services to update and maintain Whitcomb & Keller's customer accounts. The contract provided that upon termination of the contract, Data–Link would return all master files and other occupational data relating to Whitcomb & Keller upon payment in full of any outstanding balance.

On October 27, 1980, Whitcomb & Keller filed for relief under Chapter 11 of the Bankruptcy Code. The bankruptcy court approved Whitcomb & Keller as a debtor in possession. At the time Whitcomb & Keller filed its bankruptcy petition, it owed Data–Link $12,954.63 for computer services previously rendered. Data–Link's claim for that amount was listed in the bankruptcy schedule as a general unsecured claim. Data–Link continued providing computer services, and Whitcomb & Keller paid for all services provided during the administration of the estate.

During the course of the bankruptcy, Whitcomb & Keller determined that it should sell its mortgage servicing contract assets. On February 26, 1981, the bankruptcy court found the bids of Milliken Mortgage Company and Unity Savings Association to be the best for the sale of the assets. As the district court found, on March 4, 1981, Data–Link discontinued computer services to Whitcomb & Keller, paralyzing it, and precipitated the filing of an application for a temporary restraining order and preliminary injunction. Over Data–Link's objections, the bankruptcy court entered an order enjoining Data–Link from terminating the computer services, and the services were resumed.

On March 5, 1981, Data–Link filed its answer which included a counterclaim requesting the bankruptcy court either (1) to declare that Whitcomb & Keller, by its application requesting the court to enforce the executory contract and by its continued receipt of the benefits of the executory contract, had assumed the executory contract, or (2) to require Whitcomb & Keller to decide whether to assume or reject the executory contract within a specified period of time before the confirmation of the plan. After a hearing on March 9, 1981, the bankruptcy court took the matter under advisement and continued the restraining order in effect.

On March 12, 1981, Unity Savings informed the bankruptcy court that Data–Link refused to give either Whitcomb & Keller or Unity Savings essential information stored in the master data base, thereby preventing Unity Savings from purchasing the servicing contract assets. Data–Link contended that the restraining order did not require it to provide Unity Savings with test tapes of information stored in the master data base but only to provide computer services to Whitcomb & Keller. Following a hearing on March 16, 1981, the bankruptcy court directed Data–Link to cooperate and turn over test tapes to expedite the sale of Whitcomb & Keller's mortgage servicing assets. The parties stipulated that any right, lien or other interest Data–Link might have would attached to proceeds of the sale of Whitcomb & Keller's assets. Whitcomb & Keller paid Data–Link in full for all charges relating to the preparation of the master data base.

On April 8, 1981, the bankruptcy court found that Whitcomb & Keller had not assumed the executory contract. The court found further that Whitcomb & Keller had remained current on its post-petition debts and that Data–Link was adequately protected, in that any right, lien or other interest that it might have would attach to the proceeds of the sale of Whitcomb & Keller's assets. Accordingly, the bankruptcy court denied Data–Link's request to require Whitcomb & Keller to assume or reject the executory contract prior to the confirmation of the plan.

Also on April 8, 1981, Whitcomb & Keller requested authority to reject the executory contract. Data–Link objected, and the matter was set for trial. On April 24 the court confirmed the second amended plan of reorganization. Data–Link filed a proof of claim on April 30, asserting priority for the pre-petition claim of $12,954.63.

On July 10, 1981, a trial was held in bankruptcy court on Whitcomb & Keller's request for authority to reject the executory contract. By order dated April 15, 1982, the court found that Whitcomb & Keller had not assumed the executory contract and that the language of the contract did not give rise to an equitable lien or warehouseman's lien on the information stored in Data–Link's computer. Accordingly, the bankruptcy court concluded that (1) Whitcomb & Keller was entitled to reject the executory contract, and (2) Data–Link's prepetition debt of $12,954.63 incurred under the executory contract was an unsecured claim. On appeal the district court affirmed the decision of the bankruptcy court.

## II. Contentions on Appeal

Data–Link contends that:

**(1)** neither the debtor in possession nor the bankruptcy court had authority to enforce the executory contract unless the contract was assumed by the debtor;

**(2)** because of the essential nature of the services provided under the contract, the bankruptcy court should have specified a period of time within which Whitcomb & Keller was required to decide whether to assume or reject the contract;

**(3)** Whitcomb & Keller continued receiving benefits from the executory contract and should have been required to assume its burdens; and

**(4)** Whitcomb & Keller's request for an order prohibiting Data–Link from terminating computer services and the bankruptcy court's restraining orders constituted an assumption by Whitcomb & Keller of the executory contract.

### III. Authority to Enforce Executory Contract Pending Acceptance or Rejection

Acceptance and rejection of executory contracts are governed by Section 365 of the Bankruptcy Code. Section 365(d)(2) provides: In a case under Chapter 9, 11 or 13 of this title, the trustee may assume or reject an executory contract or unexpired lease of the debtor at any time before the confirmation of a plan, but the court, on request of any party to such contract or lease, may order the trustee to determine within a specified period of time whether to assume or reject such contract or lease.[3]

In In re American National Trust, 426 F.2d 1059, 1064 (7 Cir.1970), this court held that a trustee in a reorganization proceeding "is entitled to a reasonable time to make a careful and informed evaluation as to possible burdens and benefits of an executory contract," quoting from 6 Collier on Bankruptcy (14th Ed.) 576–80.

The executory contract between Data–Link and Whitcomb & Keller was in effect on October 27, 1980, when Whitcomb & Keller filed its bankruptcy petition. The contract remained in effect until Whitcomb & Keller made its decision to assume or reject the contract. Before

---

[3] The policy behind § 365(d)(2) was summarized by the bankruptcy court in its April 8, 1981, order as follows:

Since a debtor is in limbo until confirmation of a plan, it is understandably difficult to commit itself to assuming or rejecting a contract much before the time for confirmation of a plan. Thus, the code allows for the debtor to provide for assumption or rejection of the executory contracts in its plan. This procedure insures that the debtor is not in the precarious position of having assumed a contract relying on confirmation of a particular plan, only to find the plan to have been rejected.

Whitcomb & Keller made its decision, however, Data–Link ceased providing essential computer services. Whitcomb & Keller then applied for the restraining order, as it had a right to do. Similarly, the bankruptcy court had the authority to preserve the status quo until Whitcomb & Keller made its decision.[4] The district court held that the bankruptcy court did not err in issuing the restraining order. We agree.

### IV. Requiring Debtors in Possession to Assume or Reject Executory Contract

Data–Link contends that because of the essential nature of the service it provided under the contract, the bankruptcy court, pursuant to Section 365 of the Bankruptcy Code, § 365(d)(2), should have specified a period of time within which Whitcomb & Keller was required to decide whether to assume or reject the executory contract. The parties had, of course, stipulated that the computer services were essential and that the information stored in the computer included information essential to the sale of Whitcomb & Keller's accounts. Data–Link argues that time for further inquiry into the benefits and burdens of the contract was not needed.

Data–Link interprets the purpose of § 365(d) too narrowly. It is not enough that the trustee or debtor in possession recognize that the services provided under the contract are essential. Rather, § 365(d) allows the trustee or debtor in possession a reasonable time within which to determine whether adoption or rejection of the executory contract would be beneficial to an effective reorganization. In re American National Trust, supra, 426 F.2d at 1064 (interpreting § 516(1) (repealed 1979), predecessor to § 365).

The bankruptcy court addressed this issue in its order of April 8, 1981. After discussing the purpose of allowing the trustee a reasonable time to make its decision, the court noted that Data–Link was adequately protected because (1) Whitcomb & Keller had paid for all services received during the administration of its estate, and (2) the parties had stipulated that any right, lien or other interest that Data–Link might have would attach to the proceeds of the sale of Whitcomb & Keller's assets. Accordingly, the court exercised its discretion under § 365(d) in denying Data–Link's request to require Whitcomb & Keller "to assume or reject the contract forthwith." We find no abuse of the bankruptcy court's discretion.

### V. Receipt of Benefits and Assumption of Burdens

Data–Link next contends that a finding that Keller assumed the contract is necessary to avoid the inequitable result of allowing Whitcomb & Keller to derive the benefits of the contract without assuming its burdens.

---

[4] The Bankruptcy Code provides a sufficient legal basis for a bankruptcy court to issue an injunction or restraining order in appropriate situations. Section 105(a) empowers a bankruptcy court to issue any order that is necessary or appropriate to carry out the provisions of the Code.

In the first place, it may be noted that general principles governing contractual benefits and burdens do not always apply in the bankruptcy context. The purpose of the Bankruptcy Code is to "suspend the normal operation of rights and obligations between the debtor and his creditors." Fontainebleau Hotel Corp. v. Simon, 508 F.2d 1056, 1059 (5 Cir.1975). Moreover, successful reorganization under Chapter 11 depends on relieving the debtor of burdensome contracts and pre-petition debts so that "additional cash flow thus freed is used to meet current operating expenses." H.R.Rep. No. 595, 95th Cong., 1st Sess. 221 (1977). The post-petition services provided by Data–Link were operating expenses which Whitcomb & Keller paid in full. But merely providing such services did not alter Data–Link's position as a general unsecured creditor on its pre-petition claim. * * *

The cases upon which appellant relies are factually distinguishable. Here it is undisputed that Whitcomb & Keller paid in full for all services rendered during the administration of the estate, including the preparation of the data base tape. The only alleged breach of the executory contract relates to the indebtedness owed by Whitcomb & Keller when the petition was filed. Data–Link suffered no harm nor prejudice through the continued utilization of its computer services. Rather it presumably earned a profit from the continued use.[5] We agree with district court that Whitcomb & Keller's utilization of the computer services during the administration of the estate did not support a finding that Whitcomb & Keller assumed the contract or that Data–Link was entitled to a priority.

## VI. Requirements for Assumption of Executory Contracts

Finally, Data–Link contends that Whitcomb & Keller's "application for the enforcement of this essential executory contract and the Bankruptcy Court's mandatory order thereon (that Data–Link must perform) constituted an assumption with Court approval."

Under § 365(a) the trustee or debtor in possession, *subject to the court's approval,* may assume or reject any executory contract * * *." § 365(a) (emphasis added). Interpreting similar language in [the Bankruptcy Act] * * * this court declared: "'Assumption or adoption of the contract can only be affected through an express order of the judge.'" [In re American National Trust, supra, 426 F.2d at 1064] (quoting 6 Collier on Bankruptcy 576–80 (14th ed.)). No such order issued in the present case. Neither the bankruptcy court nor Whitcomb & Keller exhibited any intention of assuming the contract when the court enjoined Data–Link's termination of services. We will not infer such intention. Instead, we find

---

[5] As the district court noted, Whitcomb & Keller in effect "assumed the burdens as it received the benefits during the administration of the estate. If Whitcomb & Keller had continued to receive the services of Data–Link during the administration of the estate and not paid for them, the law clearly states that that indebtedness would be entitled to priority status. However, that is not the case here."

the order was directed solely toward maintaining the status quo—a permissible purpose well within the bankruptcy court's power, as we have noted.

### VII. Conclusion

We find no abuse of the bankruptcy court's discretion. We agree with the bankruptcy court and the district court that (1) Whitcomb & Keller did not assume the executory contract; but rather (2) was entitled to and did reject the contract; and (3) Data–Link's pre-petition claim of $12,954.63 is an unsecured claim.

Affirmed.

## NOTES

**1.** If Debtor assumes an executory contract, the contract becomes a postpetition obligation of the estate and Nondebtor is entitled to an administrative expense priority for its performance according to the terms of the contract. This issue is discussed in detail in *In re Klein Sleep Products, Inc., infra.* In this Note we consider the estate's liability to Nondebtor if Nondebtor continues to perform during the gap period and Debtor eventually rejects. In *Whitcomb & Keller* we saw that Debtor's acceptance of Nondebtor's postpetition performance is not assumption of the executory contract. Hence, the extent to which Nondebtor is entitled to an administrative expense priority is governed by benefit conferred on the estate by Nondebtor's performance. § 503(b)(1)(A). The benefit-to-the-estate standard may be difficult to apply in some cases.

Suppose Debtor, a developer, contracted with Nondebtor to serve as project manager in construction of a hotel in 1997. Nondebtor was to provide security services at the construction site. Debtor agreed to indemnify Nondebtor against suits brought against Nondebtor in the performance of its duties under the contract; the indemnification agreement specifically included attorney's fees and expenses. After construction money dried up, Debtor filed in Chapter 11 and asked Nondebtor to continue to perform security services. In the course of doing so, Nondebtor was sued by a subcontractor for allegedly allowing spoliation of certain building materials. Nondebtor spent $125,000 in successfully defending against this claim. When Debtor eventually rejected the prepetition contract, Nondebtor requested administrative expense treatment for the $125,000 postpetition indemnity claim. Debtor opposed the request on the ground that the contract calling for indemnification was not assumed and the debt incurred by Nondebtor in defending the claim did not "directly and substantially" benefit the estate under § 503(b)(1)(A). Neither Debtor nor Nondebtor referred to indemnity when Nondebtor was asked to continue. Nondebtor can show that indemnity agreements are common in situations like this and will testify that it wouldn't have undertaken to continue without indemnity. Should Nondebtor receive administrative expense priority for the $125,000? See *In re Santa Monica Beach Hotel, Ltd.*, 209 B.R. 722

(B.A.P. 9th Cir.1997). Should Nondebtor's legitimate expectations be a factor in this case?

**2.** The National Bankruptcy Review Commission has proposed that the law governing compensation for the performance of the nondebtor during the gap period before the debtor's election to reject be changed to focus on damage to the nondebtor rather than on benefit to the estate. It recommends in NBRC Rep. at p. 465 that a court be authorized to order the nondebtor (i) to continue to perform during the gap period, and (ii) to provide protection of the nondebtor's interests during that period. Compensation awarded to the nondebtor would be based on ordinary contract principles. "Whatever compensation would be awarded to the nondebtor party under similar nonbankruptcy circumstances should be its allowed administrative claim for postpetition performance or breach." NBRC Rep. at p. 468. The current standard of actual benefit to the estate would be abandoned.

**3.** There are major risks to nondebtor parties to executory contracts who take unilateral actions with respect to their relationship with the debtor prior to rejection. *Computer Communications, Inc. v. Codex Corporation*, 824 F.2d 725 (9th Cir.1987), is a leading case in point. The debtor CCI entered into a restated four-year Joint Marketing and Development Agreement (JMDA) relating to complex telecommunications equipment, software and related services with Codex two days before filing under Chapter 11. Codex terminated the agreement asserting its rights under the contract's ipso facto clause were enforceable because the JMDA was a nonassignable agreement that could not be assumed. Unlike Data–Link in *Whitcomb & Keller* CCI did not seek to enjoin the termination. Instead it found itself with a substantial new asset: its damage claim against Codex based on a violation of the automatic stay. In upholding a $5 million judgment in favor of the debtor the Ninth Circuit wrote : "Even if Codex had a valid reason for terminating the Agreement, it still was required to petition the court for relief from the automatic stay. . . .. We need not reach t[he] question [whether the JMDA could be assumed, and, if so, whether it could nevertheless be terminated under the ipso facto clause], however, because we hold that even if § 365(e)(2) allowed Codex to terminate the contract, § 362 automatically stayed termination." 824 F.2d at 730.

## B. LEASES

### 1. REJECTION BY DEBTOR IN POSSESSION AS LESSOR

The rejection of executory contracts allows the debtor in possession or trustee to avoid the burden on the bankruptcy estate of performing contracts that are not beneficial to the estate and gives to the nondebtor party a claim in bankruptcy for breach of contract damages. The predominant view, notwithstanding *Lubrizol*, is that it *does not* allow the debtor in possession to rescind the contract and to take back performance already granted. Thus, if the debtor grantor a patent license or a franchise, the debtor in possession can refuse to perform unperformed obligations under the license agreement or franchise agreement, but should not be able to take away from the nonbankrupt party the right to use the patent or the right to operate the franchise. A similar analysis applies to land sale contracts in which the debtor is the vendor. Land sale contracts are sometimes used as a substitute for the more common installment note secured by a mortgage, particularly in the case of the sale of a home to a low income buyer. Under the contract, the real property title passes to the buyer only when the buyer has made all of the installment payments required by the contract. If the seller were to file in Chapter 11 and the transaction were treated as an executory contract that could be rejected, the debtor in possession would presumably not be required to give the buyer a deed to the property. Some cases decided under the Bankruptcy Act reached that result, but under the Bankruptcy Code the buyer's property interest, which amounts to equitable title to the real property, is protected by § 365(i). The seller, as debtor in possession, can refuse to perform collateral obligations under the contract, but must deliver a deed to the real property as required by the contract if the nondebtor buyer makes all the payments.

In cases involving bankrupt landlords of real property, § 365(h) gives to the lessee rights comparable those of a buyer under a land sale contract. The landlord, as debtor in possession, can refuse to perform collateral obligations such as providing heat, utilities, property maintenance and the like, but the debtor in possession cannot deprive the lessee of the leasehold itself. Under § 365(h)(1) the lessee is given an option to treat the lease as terminated for material breach and assert a claim for damages in the bankruptcy or to remain in possession under the lease. As in the case of the land sale buyer, the lessee exercising its option to remain in possession can recover damages resulting from the failure to perform collateral services, but recovery can be had only by deducting those damages from rent due under the lease. § 365(h)(1)(B). For example, if the landlord is required under the lease to keep the property in good repair, the lessee can cause any required repair to be made and can deduct the cost of the repair from the rent.

What rights does the lessee who remains in possession under a rejected lease have, in addition to the essential right to remain in possession for the duration of the rejected lease? The issue has sometimes been posed in terms of whether rejection by the debtor-landlord terminates the lease, leaving the lessee with nothing but this essential right. *In re Carlton Restaurant, Inc.*, 151 B.R. 353 (Bankr.E.D.Pa.1993), cited in the Section-by-Section Description § 205, 140 Cong. Rec. H10767 (1994), took the view that the debtor-landlord's rejection does terminate the lease and leaves the lessee with only its "personal rights to possession." Therefore, the lessee cannot assign its right to another. Congress disapproved this narrow view and in 1994 added § 365(h)(1)(A) which provides:

> * * * the lessee may retain its rights under such lease (including rights
> such as those relating to the amount and timing of payment of rent and
> other amounts payable by the lessee and any right of use, possession,
> quiet enjoyment, subletting, assignment, or hypothecation) that are in
> or appurtenant to the real property for the balance of the term of such
> lease * * *.

After this amendment, the lessee's rights under a rejected lease are very
similar to those before rejection and it is questionable whether a
debtor-landlord gains much from rejection beyond limiting the lessee's
remedies for post-rejection breaches to an offset against rentals.

The effect of rejection of a personal property lease by the lessor is not
clear. Rejection raises an issue similar to that in the technology licensing
cases. The result in *Lubrizol* has been reversed by § 365(n), but the rationale of the case could be used to deprive the personal property lessee of the
right to continue use of the property under the lease. We disagree with *Lubrizol* and would allow the lessee to retain the right to use the property.
We see no policy reason to differentiate between real property and personal property leases in this respect. Nevertheless, the legislative decision
to limit the statutory safe harbors to real property leases and intellectual
property licenses might be viewed as creating a contrary inference with
respect to personal property leases.

The vast real estate finance industry was rudely jolted by the following
decision, handed down by one of the most prestigious commercial courts
in the land.

## Precision Industries, Inc. v. Qualitech Steel SBQ, LLC

United States Court of Appeals, Seventh Circuit, 2003.
327 F.3d 537.

■  ILANA DIAMOND ROVNER, Circuit Judge.

In this case of first impression at the circuit level, we are asked to reconcile two distinct provisions of the Bankruptcy Code: § 363(f), which
authorizes the sale of a debtor's property free of any "interest" other than
the estate's, and  § 365(h), which protects the rights of the lessee when the
debtor rejects a lease of estate property. The bankruptcy court in this case
construed a sale order issued pursuant to section 363(f) to extinguish the
possessory rights bestowed by a lease of the estate's land. The district
court disagreed, reasoning that sections 363(f) and 365(h) conflict and that
the more specific terms of the latter provision concerning leaseholds
trump those of the former, in this way preserving the lessee's possessory
interest even after a section 363(f) sale. We reverse, concluding that under
the plain terms of section 363(f), the sale order extinguished the lessee's
possessory interest.

# I.

The debtors in the underlying bankruptcy proceedings—Qualitech Steel Corporation and Qualitech Steel Holdings Corporation (collectively, "Qualitech")—owned and operated a steel mill on a 138-acre tract of land in Pittsboro, Indiana. Before it entered bankruptcy, Qualitech had entered into two related agreements with appellees Precision Industries, Inc. and Circo Leasing Co., LLC (collectively, "Precision"). A detailed supply agreement executed on June 29, 1998, provided that Precision would construct a supply warehouse at Qualitech's Pittsboro facility and operate it for a period of ten years so as to provide on-site, integrated supply services for Qualitech. The second agreement, a land lease executed on February 25, 1999, specified that Qualitech would lease to Precision the property underlying the warehouse for a period of ten years. In exchange for nominal rent of $1 per year, the lease granted Precision exclusive possession of the warehouse and any other improvements or fixtures it installed on the land for the term of the lease; and in the event of an early termination or default under either the lease or the supply agreement, Precision had the right to remove all improvements and fixtures from the property. Assuming no default, Qualitech had the right at the end of the lease term to purchase the warehouse, its fixtures, and other improvements for $1. In accordance with the two agreements, Precision built and stocked a warehouse on the leased property and Qualitech began purchasing goods from Precision. The lease was never recorded.

Heavily in debt, Qualitech filed a Chapter 11 bankruptcy petition on March 22, 1999. On June 30, 1999, substantially all of Qualitech's assets were sold at auction for a credit bid of $180 million to a group of senior pre-petition lenders that held the primary mortgage on the Pittsboro property. On August 13, 1999, at the conclusion of a noticed hearing, the bankruptcy court entered an order approving the sale (hereinafter, the "Sale Order"). Precision, which had notice of the hearing, did not object to the Sale Order. That order directed Qualitech to convey its assets to the pre-petition lenders—referred to in the Sale Order collectively as the "purchaser"—"free and clear of all liens, claims, encumbrances, and *interests*," except for specifically enumerated liens, pursuant to section 363(f), among other provisions of the Code. All persons and entities holding interests other than those expressly preserved in the Sale Order were barred from asserting those interests against the purchaser. The pre-petition senior lenders subsequently transferred their interest in the purchased assets to newly-formed Qualitech Steel SBQ, LLC ("New Qualitech"), which assumed the rights of the purchaser under the Sale Order and took title to the Pittsboro property. The Sale Order also reserved for the purchaser the debtor's right to assume and assign executory contracts pursuant to § 365. Although the sale closed on or about August 26, 1999 without assumption of either the lease or the supply agreement with Precision, negotiations toward that end continued and the parties extended the deadline for assumption on four occasions. Those negotiations did not prove successful, however, with the result that Precision's lease and supply agreement were *de facto* rejected.

By December 3, 1999, Precision had completely vacated and padlocked the warehouse. Shortly thereafter, New Qualitech, without Precision's knowledge or consent, hired a locksmith and changed the locks on the building. New Qualitech's takeover of the warehouse led to a dispute over whether Precision's possessory interest in the leased property, pursuant to section 365(h), survived the bankruptcy sale. Finding itself locked out of the warehouse, Precision filed a diversity suit in the district court contending that New Qualitech was guilty of trespass, conversion, wrongful eviction, breach of an implied contract, and estoppel. New Qualitech in turn asked the district court to refer Precision's complaint—which was premised on the notion that Precision retained a possessory interest in the warehouse under the lease—to the bankruptcy court, and New Qualitech also filed a request with the bankruptcy court asking it to clarify that the Sale Order had extinguished Precision's possessory interest. The district court obliged New Qualitech by referring Precision's complaint to the bankruptcy court, and that court in turn resolved the matter of Precision's possessory interest in New Qualitech's favor.

Based on the terms of both section 363(f) and the Sale Order itself, the bankruptcy court determined that New Qualitech had obtained title to Qualitech's property free and clear of any possessory rights that Precision otherwise might have enjoyed under its lease. In relevant part, the court held that Precision's possessory interest was among those interests extinguished by the Sale Order. * * * New Qualitech filed a timely notice of appeal from the district court's decision. * * *

## II.

Our task in this appeal is straightforward. We must decide whether a sale order issued under section 363(f), which purports to authorize the transfer of a debtor's property "free and clear of all liens, claims, encumbrances, and interests," operates to extinguish a lessee's possessory interest in the property, or whether the terms of section 365(h) operate to preserve that interest. This is, of course, a question of law, making our review of the district court's decision de novo. * * *

As in all statutory interpretation cases, we begin with the statutory language.* * * Statutory terms or words will be construed according to their ordinary, common meaning unless they are specifically defined by the statute or the statutory context requires a different definition. * * * We must also have in mind our obligation to construe the two statutory provisions at issue in this case in such a way as to avoid conflicts between them, if such a construction is possible and reasonable. * * *

Section 363 generally provides for the use, sale, or lease of property belonging to the bankruptcy estate. As relevant here, subsections (b) and (c) permit the trustee of a bankruptcy estate to sell estate property either within the normal course of a debtor's business (in which case the sale may take place without prior notice and a hearing) or outside the normal course of business (in which case, as here, notice and hearing are mandatory). Subsection (f) makes clear that the property, under specified conditions, may be sold unencumbered of interests held by others:

> The trustee may sell property under subsection (b) or (c) of this section free and clear of *any interest* in such property of an entity other than the estate, only if—
>
> **(1)** applicable nonbankruptcy law permits sale of such property free and clear of such interest;
>
> **(2)** such entity consents;
>
> **(3)** such interest is a lien and the price at which such property is to be sold is greater than the aggregate value of all liens on such property;
>
> **(4)** such interest is in bona fide dispute; or
>
> **(5)** such entity could be compelled, in a legal or equitable proceeding, to accept a money satisfaction of such interest.

(Emphasis ours.) Finally, subsection (e) provides that "on request of an entity that has an interest in property. . . proposed to be. . . sold. . . by the trustee, the court, with or without a hearing, shall prohibit or condition such. . . sale. . . as is necessary to provide adequate protection of such interest." We note that although section 363(f) refers to the powers and obligations of the "trustee," these are powers and obligations which, in a Chapter 11 case, inure to the debtor-in-possession. *See* § 1107(a). * * *

Because Precision's right to possess the property as a lessee qualifies as an interest for purposes of section 363(f), the statute on its face authorized the sale of Qualitech's property free and clear of that interest. Although the statute conditions such a sale on the satisfaction of one of five conditions, the parties before us do not dispute that at least one of those conditions was satisfied.[3] On the contrary, both parties to the appeal proceed from the premise that section 363(f) standing alone permits the sale of estate property free and clear of a lessee's possessory interest.

Where the parties lock horns is on whether the terms of section 365(h) conflict with and override those of section 363(f). Section 365 generally provides the trustee (and here, the debtor-in-possession, *see* § 1107(a)) with the right to reject executory contracts, a power that serves to relieve the debtor of contractual obligations that are unduly burdensome. * * *

---

[3] New Qualitech asserts in its opening brief that "[p]utting aside the issue of whether § 365(h) somehow trumps a § 363(f) sale, it is not disputed that the Debtor was authorized to sell the property free and clear of Precision's unrecorded lease." Precision does not take issue with this assertion in its response brief. Accordingly, we shall assume, as New Qualitech asserts, that one or more of the statutory criteria were met and that a sale of the property free and clear of Precision's possessory interest as a lessee was permissible.

However, insofar as lessees of the estate's property are concerned, the power of rejection is limited so as to preclude eviction of the lessee. In relevant part, section 365(h)(1)(A)(ii) provides:

If the trustee rejects an unexpired lease of real property under which the debtor is the lessor and—

. . .

(ii) if the term of such lease has commenced, the lessee may retain its rights under such lease. . . that are in or appurtenant to the real property for the balance of the term of such lease and for any renewal or extension of such rights to the extent that such rights are enforceable under applicable non-bankruptcy law.

The terms of section 365(h) thus allow a lessee to remain in possession of estate property notwithstanding the debtor-in-possession's decision to reject the lease. In this way, the statute strikes a balance between the respective rights of the debtor-lessor and its tenant: the lessee retains the right to possess the property for the remainder of the term it bargained for, while the rejection frees the debtor-lessor of other burdensome obligations that it assumed under the lease (as, for example, the duty to provide services to the lessee).* * *

The district court, following the lead of other lower courts, concluded that the limitations imposed by section 365(h) vis à vis rejection of leases necessarily conflict with and override the debtor-in-possession's ability to sell estate property free and clear of a lessee's possessory interest. But for the reasons that follow, we conclude that the terms of section 365(h) do not supersede those of section 363(f).

First, the statutory provisions themselves do not suggest that one supersedes or limits the other. Notably, sections 363 and 365 both contain cross-references indicating that certain of their provisions are subject to other statutory mandates. *See* §§ 363(d), 365(a). But nowhere in either section 363(f) or section 356(h) is there a similar cross-reference indicating that the broad right to sell estate property free of "any interest" is subordinate to the protections that section 365(h) accords to lessees. The omission suggests that Congress did not intend for the latter section to limit the former. * * *

Second, the plain language of section 365(h)(1)(A) suggests that it has a limited scope. By its own terms, that subsection applies "[i]f the trustee [or debtor-in-possession] *rejects* an unexpired lease of real property. . . .." (Emphasis supplied.) Here what occurred in the first instance was a sale of the property that Precision was leasing rather than a rejection of its lease. Granted, if the Sale Order operated to extinguish Precision's right to possess the property—as we conclude it did—then the effect of the sale might be understood as the equivalent of a repudiation of Precision's lease. *See In re Taylor*, 198 B.R. 142, at 166 (Bankr. D.S.C. 1996) ("[t]o allow a sale free and clear of a leasehold interest pursuant to § 363. . . would effectively provide a debtor with means of dispossessing the lessee"). But nothing in the express terms of section 365(h) suggests that it applies to any and all events that threaten the lessee's possessory rights. Section 365(h) instead focuses on a specific type of event—the rejection of an executory contract by the trustee or debtor-in-possession—and spells out the rights of parties affected by that event. It says nothing at all about sales of estate property, which are the province of section 363. The two statutory provisions thus apply to distinct sets of circumstances.* * *

Third, section 363 itself provides for a mechanism to protect the rights of parties whose interests may be adversely affected by the sale of estate property. As noted above, section 363(e) directs the bankruptcy court, on the request of any entity with an interest in the property to be sold, to "prohibit or condition such. . . sale. . . as is necessary to provide adequate protection of such interest." Because a leasehold qualifies as an "interest" in property for purposes of section 363(f), a lessee of property being sold pursuant to subsection (f) would have the right to insist that its interest be protected. "Adequate protection" does not necessarily guarantee a lessee's continued possession of the property, but it does demand, in the alternative, that the lessee be compensated for the value of its leasehold—typically from the proceeds of the sale. * * * Lessees like Precision are therefore not without recourse in the event of a sale free and clear of their interests. They have the right to seek protection under section 363(e), and upon request, the bankruptcy court is obligated to ensure that their interests are adequately protected.

With these points in mind, it is apparent that the two statutory provisions can be construed in a way that does not disable section 363(f) vis à vis leasehold interests. Where estate property under lease is to be sold, section 363 permits the sale to occur free and clear of a lessee's possessory interest—provided that the lessee (upon request) is granted adequate protection for its interest. Where the property is not sold, and the debtor remains in possession thereof but chooses to reject the lease, section 365(h) comes into play and the lessee retains the right to possess the property. So understood, both provisions may be given full effect without coming into conflict with one another and without disregarding the rights of lessees.

We are persuaded that it is both reasonable and correct to interpret and reconcile sections 363(f) and 365(h) in this way. It is consistent with the express terms of each provision, and it avoids the unwelcome result of reading a limitation into section 363(f) that the legislature itself did not inscribe onto the statute. Congress authorized the sale of estate property free and clear of "*any* interest," not "any interest *except* a lessee's possessory interest." The interpretation is also consistent with the process of marshaling the estate's assets for the twin purposes of maximizing creditor recovery and rehabilitating the debtor, which are central to the Bankruptcy Code. * * * Thus, section 363(f), as we interpret that provision, permitted the bankruptcy court to allow the sale of Qualitech's Pittsboro property unencumbered by Precision's possessory interest as a lessee. Precision neither objected to the sale nor sought the protection that was available under section 363(e). Its possessory interest was extinguished by the sale.

## III.

As the sale of Qualitech's property terminated Precision's possessory interest in the property as a lessee, we REVERSE the district court's judgment to the contrary.

## NOTES

**1.** The holding of the principal case is that if debtor-lessor *rejects* an unexpired real estate lease the lessee has a right to retain possession under § 365(h)(1)(A)(ii), but if the debtor-lessor *sells* the leased premises free and clear of the interests of others under § 365(f), the right of the lessee to remain in possession is cut off and the lessee's only remedy is to seek adequate protection under § 363(e). Since the option to sell or reject lies with the debtor-lessor, is not sale of the leased premises free and clear of the lessee's interest a *de facto* rejection of the lease?

**2.** The court in *In re Haskell L.P.*, 321 B. R. 1 (Bankr. D. Mass. 2005), rejected *Qualitech* on the ground that under the sale-rejection distinction "the provisions of § 365(h) would be eviscerated." 321 B. R. at 10. This is the view of Michael S. Baxter, *Section 363 Sales Free and Clear of Interests: Why the Seventh Circuit Erred in Precision Industries v. Qualitech Steel*, 59 Bus. Law. 475 (2004), a withering critique of *Qualitech*. The author points out the "potentially devastating consequences" of this decision in the common transaction in which a lessee enters into a long-term real estate lease (the lease in *Haskell* was 99 years) and constructs an expensive building on the premises. The lender advancing the construction financing takes a security interest in the lease as security for its advances. Both the lessee and the lender rely on the lengthy term of the lease and § 365(h) as protection against the lessor's bankruptcy.

**3.** How could a court arrive at a form of adequate protection under § 363(e) for sale of the premises free of the lessee's interest in a case like *Haskell* in which the lessee might have had a right to possession for decades under § 365(h)? In that case the lessee successfully contended that only continuation of the lessee's right to possession for the remaining term of the lease would constitute adequate protection because its losses cannot be quantified. If the required adequate protection mimics § 365(h) rights, then *Qualitech* is simply a trap for unwary lessees who fail to lodge a timely demand for adequate protection, right?

**4.** Section 365(n) extends licensees rights similar to those extended by § 365(h) to lessees of real property How would *Qualitech* affect the rights of a licensee of intellectual property in case the debtor-licensor sells the property free and clear under § 363(f)?

## 2. REJECTION BY DEBTOR IN POSSESSION AS LESSEE

In the previous section we saw that if a land sale contract vendor files in bankruptcy, § 365(i) treats the transaction, in effect, as a secured transaction rather than as an executory contract. Section 365(i) allows the vendee to remain in possession, make the required installment payments and, upon completion, receive a deed from the vendor. Although no comparable statutory provision applies to cases in which the bankruptcy debtor is the vendee, caselaw holds that the transaction should be treated as a security interest rather than an executory contract for this purpose as well. *See, e.g., In re Heward Brothers*, 210 B.R. 475 (Bank.D.Id.1997) (marshaling the authorities). If a land sale contract were treated as an executory contract, the debtor-vendee could be compelled to elect whether to assume or reject. Rejection as the concept was understood in *Lubrizol*, p. 268, would result in forfeiture of the vendee's equitable interest in the real property notwithstanding the vendor's receipt of prior installment payments, even if the value of the property were substantially greater than the present value of the future installment payments due the vendor. If on the other hand the vendee-debtor were to assume the contract in order to preserve its equity in the property, it must cure all payments in default and give adequate assurance that it will perform the remainder of the contract as written. Modification of the rights of the nondebtor vendor under Chapter 11 would be virtually precluded. But if the transaction is characterized as a secured transaction, as we shall see, a Chapter 11 plan can both preserve the debtor's equity in the property and modify the nondebtor-vendor's rights significantly, even though the debtor remains in possession of the property without the vendor's consent. The *Restatement of Property (Third) Mortgages* § 3.4(b) provides: "A contract for deed creates a mortgage." One of the reasons given for the Restatement rule is the harsh bankruptcy treatment of the vendee if the transaction were viewed as an executory contract rather than a secured transaction.

As is true with respect to executory contracts, a trustee in bankruptcy or debtor in possession may reject an unwanted lease or assume a favorable lease. § 365(a). Rejection of a lease under which the debtor is lessee is a breach of the lease giving the landlord a claim in bankruptcy for damages. § 365(g) and § 502(g). The landlord is entitled to a bankruptcy claim to the extent that it could have recovered compensatory damages under otherwise applicable law. In the case of a lease of real property, however, although the amount of the landlord's bankruptcy claim can be no more than the actual damages under nonbankruptcy law, the claim is further limited by § 502(b)(6). That provision is best understood through an example. Suppose the debtor was the lessee under a 10-year lease of real property, and that the debtor files in bankruptcy at the end of the first year of the lease. At the time of filing the debtor occupies the leased premises, but it subsequently rejects the lease and turns over the premises. The landlord asserts a damage claim under § 365(g) for its actual damages including loss of future rent. Under § 502(b)(6) the landlord can recover no more than one year of future rent, or rent for 15% of the remaining term, whichever is greater. Since 15% of the remaining term of nine years is 1.35 years, the landlord's claim is limited to 1.35 years of rent. If the lease had had a shorter term, say five years, 15% of the remaining term of four years would be 0.6 years. In that case the landlord could claim up to a maximum of one year of rent. The second limitation of § 502(b)(6) applies only to long-term leases. It means that in no event can the landlord claim more than three years of rent. If the term of the lease had been 25 years, 15% of the remaining term of 24 years is 3.6 years. In that case the landlord's claim cannot exceed three years of rent. In addition to its capped claim for future rent, the landlord is entitled to a claim in bankruptcy for any unpaid rent due at the time of the filing and may have a right to payment of an administrative expense for postpetition rent for the period before the lease is rejected.

Section § 502(b)(6) reflects a certain skepticism over landlords' future rent claims. Damages under unfavorable long-term leases can be asserted to be very high, especially if the debtor's bankruptcy occurs at a time when real estate markets are greatly (and perhaps artificially and temporarily) depressed. In a liquidation, if damages are not limited they might so overwhelm other unsecured claims as to effectively deprive anyone but the landlord of any recovery from the estate. In a reorganization, the landlord's uncapped damage claim might be a great impediment to the ability of the debtor to confirm and carry out the plan. These practical difficulties are compounded by the difficulty of assessing future market conditions in order to calculate the damages. Particularly in cases involving long-term leases, a landlord might well receive a windfall if given full damages based on estimates and projections. Finally, the fact that bankruptcy courts do not discount future obligations to present value in calculating claims would lead to greatly inflated claims under long-term leases but for the § 502(b)(6) limitation.

## 3. LIABILITY FOR USE OF LEASED PROPERTY BEFORE REJECTION AND TIME LIMITS FOR ASSUMPTION OR REJECTION

In many cases, a landlord wants to be rid of a lessee that is in bankruptcy. The landlord-tenant relationship can be greatly complicated by the intervention of bankruptcy with its attendant tangle of legal rules. Before the Bankruptcy Code a landlord could often avoid these complications by a clause in the lease that allowed termination of the lease when the lessee went into bankruptcy. Even under the old Bankruptcy Act, however, courts would sometimes refuse to enforce these "ipso facto" or "bankruptcy termination" clauses. Section 365(e) has made clear in all cases that a lease can be assumed notwithstanding an ipso facto clause in the lease. Moreover, § 365(f) allows a lease to be assigned notwithstanding a clause in the lease prohibiting or restricting assignment.

### a.    Real Estate Leases

What are the rights and obligations of the landlord and the bankruptcy estate before the debtor's lease is either rejected or assumed under § 365? Before 1984, the general rule was that the estate was liable only for the reasonable value of the occupancy of the leased premises. There was authority stretching back to the 1898 Bankruptcy Act that, if the trustee in bankruptcy did not occupy the leased premises, no compensation was due to the landlord during a reasonable period taken by the trustee to decide whether to reject or assume the lease. The rationale was that there was no benefit to the estate if the trustee did not occupy the leased premises, even though the bankruptcy stay precluded the landlord from obtaining possession and reletting the premises prior to rejection of the lease. This doctrine when carried forward into cases filed under the Bankruptcy Code and coupled with § 365(d)(2), which allowed the debtor in possession in a Chapter 11 case to elect to assume or reject at any time before confirmation of the plan of reorganization, placed landlords in an unfavorable position. Premises might stand vacant for months while the debtor pondered whether to reject or assume. If the ultimate decision was to reject, the lessor received no compensation. If the debtor occupied the premises, the landlord received rent at reasonable value, an uncertain amount measured by current market rents that might be less than the rent provided for by the lease. The landlord's only legal recourse was to request the court to order the lessee to determine within a specified period of time whether to assume or reject. This state of the law resulted in landlords having to incur legal expenses in litigating the value of occupancy and in obtaining orders compelling the lessee to assume or reject. It meant that landlords might receive no income from the rental property for a period of time during which they had to continue making mortgage and tax payments. Sometimes the landlord's only practical course of action was to attempt to buy a prompt rejection from the debtor in possession. Landlords thought that under the Bankruptcy Code the pendulum had swung too far in favor of the debtor in possession.

The Leasehold Management Bankruptcy Amendments Act formed an important part of the 1984 amendments to the Bankruptcy Code and changed the relative bargaining positions of landlords and commercial tenants in Chapter 11 cases. These amendments apply to all leases of "nonresidential real property," which is generally understood to exclude leases of real property that is used by the debtor as his or her residence as well as personal property leases.

The key amendment is § 365(d)(3) which requires the debtor in possession to "timely perform all the obligations of the debtor * * * arising from and after the order for relief under any unexpired lease of nonresidential real property, until such lease is assumed or rejected * * *." Under a literal reading of this provision, the bankruptcy estate is liable for the rent called for by the lease and other payments, like common area charges in shopping centers, until rejection, regardless of whether the premises are occupied during the period before rejection, and the payments must be made at the time called for by the lease. The landlord need not fall within § 503(b)(1) for the allowance of administrative expenses in order to be entitled to the rent. The court may give the debtor in possession, for cause, a 60–day grace period after the petition during which payments may be postponed so long as all payments falling due within that period are made by the end of the period. The reason for the grace period is to allow the debtor in possession sufficient time to evaluate the situation and to arrange for payment. No more arguments about the fair value of the premises. Until rejection, the bankruptcy estate must pay the rent required by the lease even though it may be above market rates. While not all cases have interpreted § 365(d)(3) literally, the dominant view is that the statute means what it says, at least if the bankruptcy estate is administratively solvent. *In re Pacific–Atlantic Trading Co.*, 27 F.3d 401 (9th Cir.1994).

Some courts go even further and apply the statute literally even in the case of an administratively insolvent estate in which the effect of strict compliance with § 365(d)(3) is to give the landlord's administrative rent claim a priority in payment over other administrative claims. This issue was addressed in *In re Orvco*, 95 B.R. 724 (B.A.P. 9th Cir.1989), as follows:

> Great Western next argues that because section 365(d)(3) requires that the trustee "timely" perform the obligations of the debtor, it is entitled to immediate payment of its claim, without regard to the amount owing other administrative claimants. In other words, Great Western seeks a super-administrative status for its claim. We don't believe the statute supports such a reading.

> Although section 365(d)(3) calls for "timely" performance of the debtor's lease obligations, there is no indication that Congress intended to grant landlords some type of super-priority status. Accordingly, most courts addressing the issue have held that where there are insufficient funds in the estate to satisfy all administrative claims, a landlord is only entitled to its pro rata share with the other allowed administrative claimants. * * *

> [W]e agree with the *Dieckhaus* court that:

>> The enactment of section 365(d)(3) reflects a policy choice comparable to that of section 331. Congress clearly envisioned that debtor-tenants would "pay their rent, common area, and other charges on *time* pending the trustee's assumption or rejection of the lease." In light of this strong expression of legislative intent, I must conclude that a non-residential lessor's administrative expense claim arising under section 365(d)(3) should be paid immediately unless the trustee establishes good cause for withholding the payment.

73 B.R. at 973 (citations omitted) (emphasis in original). Because the record indicates that there may not be sufficient funds in the estate to pay all administrative claimants in full, the bankruptcy court did not err in deferring payment on Great Western's claim pending a determination of the amount of the claim and the ability of the Debtor to pay all administrative claimants.

95 B.R. at 728.

However, in *In re Telesphere Communications*, 148 B.R. 525 (Bankr.N.D.Ill.1992), although the court conceded that *Orvco* represents the majority view on this issue, it held that the requirement of "timely performance" in § 365(d)(3) mandates immediate and full payment of each rental payment when due.

At least one court of appeals has also found that the requirement of timely payment of rent is not subject to pro rata reduction in the case in which rent has been paid in advance and the lease terminated by rejection before the prepaid period has elapsed. In *In re Koenig Sporting Goods, Inc.*, 203 F.3d 986 (6th Cir.2000), the debtor was obligated to pay $8500 in rent monthly in advance on the first day of each month. Debtor rejected the lease, vacated the premises and turned them back to the landlord on December 2. The court held that the December rent payment that was due in full on December 1 constituted an administrative obligation of the estate and would not be prorated.

## PROBLEM

Assume that property taxes on leased commercial real estate are billed to the lessor as owner, and the lease requires the lessee to reimburse the lessor for the amounts paid by the lessor; reimbursement payment must be made at the time the lessor bills the lessee. In *In re Montgomery Ward Holding Corp.*, 268 F.3d 205 (3d Cir.2001), lessor billed the lessee for back taxes after the lessee had filed in bankruptcy but before the lease was rejected. The lessee argued that § 365(d)(3) should not be read to cover the amounts accrued over past years merely because the lessor chose to bill the lessee for these after the lessee's filing; such amounts should be treated as prepetition unsecured claims. The court held that the entire amount for which the lessee was billed fell under § 365(d)(3) as obligations of the debtor arising under a lease after the order of relief (the "billing" test). It recognized that its view leaves room for strategic behavior on the part of lessors. In an earlier case, *Matter of Handy Andy Home Improvement Centers, Inc.*, 144 F.3d 1125 (7th Cir.1998), Judge Posner adopted an "apportionment" test that treats obligations for past taxes as arising when those taxes were due and not when the lessor bills lessee for them. Admitting that the broad wording of § 365(d)(3) gave him some difficulties, he declared that "statutory language like other language should be read in context * * * When context is disregarded, silliness results." 144 F.3d at 1128. To him, § 365(d)(3) required the lessee to pay the full rent under the lease for every day the lessee continued occupancy until rejection, but tax debts for prior years relate to an earlier period and were no different from its debts to trade creditors that arose prepetition. Such debts should be treated as sunk costs (treat "bygones as bygones") and the lessee should be allowed to continue to operate as long as it yields net economic benefit. Which court has the better interpretation of the statute?

### b.   When Rejection Occurs

Since a lessee is liable for rent called for by the lease for the period after filing until it rejects the lease, large sums of money may ride on how quickly a lessee can jettison an expensive lease. Under Bankruptcy Rule 9014 the debtor must obtain court approval for assumption or rejection of a lease under § 365(a) by filing a motion in the bankruptcy court. Notice and opportunity for hearing must be afforded the landlord before the court rules on the motion. The cases have divided on whether the effective date of the lessee's rejection is the motion filing date or the date of court approval. In the first court of appeals decision in point, *In re Thinking Machines Corporation*, 67 F.3d 1021 (1st Cir.1995), the court adopted the date-of-approval view. In that case the lessee occupied only a fraction of the leased space after August 17, the date it filed in Chapter 11. On September 13 it filed a motion to reject and the court approved the motion on October 4. The difference between the rental due on the motion filing date and on the date of court approval was more than $200,000.

Lessee contended that the motion filing date was the proper date of rejection on two grounds: (i) When the Bankruptcy Code makes judicial approval a condition precedent to a trustee's action, it usually says "the trustee, after notice and a hearing" (e.g., § 363(b)(1)), but § 365(a) merely says "the trustee, subject to the court's approval." (ii) Use of the date of court approval departs from Chapter 11 policy in that it burdens the scarce resources of bankruptcy estates with unnecessary expenses, here, $200,000. The court rejected these arguments and held that when the Bankruptcy Code made court approval obligatory for the first time (under the Bankruptcy Act a trustee, acting alone, could reject a lease), Congress intended to involve bankruptcy courts more actively in the decisional process and increased involvement is better served by viewing judicial approval as a condition precedent to the effectiveness of a rejection instead of as a condition subsequent. "We see no reason for allowing a trustee to substitute his voice for that of the court. The trustee may sing all he wants, but it is the court that must call the tune. Cf. W.A. Mozart, Le Nozze di Figaro, Act 1, sc.2 (1786) (Figaro's Aria)." 67 F.3d at 1026.

The court added, however, that bankruptcy courts, as courts of equity, may enter retroactive orders of approval in cases in which the balance of equities favors this result. It made no effort to spell out what circumstances might justify retroactivity. The court in *In re Amber's Stores, Inc.*, 193 B.R. 819 (Bankr.N.D.Tex.1996), expressly relied on this dictum in a case in which the lessee, a month before filing, vacated and turned over the keys to landlord. Lessee served an emergency motion to reject on the lessor on the date of its Chapter 11 petition. It filed this motion with the court three days after its petition; the court approved the motion the same day, effective the date of the petition. It held that retroactive rejection of the lease was justified by the equities of the case.

In *In re At Home Corp.*, 392 F. 3d 1064 (9th Cir. 2004), citing *Thinking Machines*, the Ninth Circuit affirmed a bankruptcy court's decision approving rejection of a real property lease as of the date of the filing of the Chapter 11 debtor's motion to reject basing this exercise of its equitable discretion on the debtor's prompt action seeking rejection, that the debtor was not occupying the premises and that the landlord's opposition was based solely on its desire to claim $1 million in administrative rent notwithstanding the lack of any delay in its ability to repossess the premises.

### c.    Personal Property Leases

Section 365(d)(3) does not apply to personal property leases or to leases of residential real property. With respect to the rights of the lessor when a debtor in possession as lessee rejects a personal property lease, Judge (now Supreme Court Justice) Anthony Kennedy stated in *In re Thompson*, 788 F.2d 560, 563 (9th Cir.1986):

> When a lease is ultimately rejected but its interim continuance was an actual and necessary cost and expense of the estate, the allowable administrative expense is valued not according to the terms of the lease * * * but under an objective worth standard that measures the fair and reasonable value of the lease. * * * The rent reserved in the lease is presumptive evidence of fair and reasonable value * * * but the presumption may be rebutted by demonstrating that the reasonable worth of the lease differs from the contract rate * * *.

> The actual value or benefit conferred on the debtor is not the object of the reasonable worth inquiry. * * * Rather, the fair and reasonable value of the lease upon the open market must control. * * * Fair market value may be determined by expert testimony if, in the discretion of the trial court, it is warranted in the circumstances of a particular case. * * * The debtor's experience and his testimony regarding his actual use of the equipment and the value the equipment conferred upon him would seem in most cases irrelevant, though testimony such as whether the leased equipment operated as promised might bear upon the question whether the equipment was still marketable and acceptable in the industry generally, a matter that in turn would bear upon fair market value. * * * Equating reasonableness with fair market value provides a neutral estimate of the value of the leased property and is therefore the fairest measure of compensation for all concerned. Furthermore, it avoids self-serving testimony by a debtor on the benefit, or lack of benefit, he has experienced.

Personal property lessors were dissatisfied with this state of the law and pressed for the inclusion of personal property leases in § 365(d)(3) so that lessees in bankruptcy would have to make timely payments of contract rentals. They failed, and the tortured compromise that emerged in 1994 was a package of amendments that added § 365(b)(2)(D) and § 365(d)(10), and amended § 363(e). Under § 365(d)(10), the debtor-lessee must make, on a timely basis, rental payments called for by the lease that come due 60 days or more after the petition *unless* the debtor can convince the court "based on the equities of the case" that the amount of payments should be less or the time of making the payments should be delayed. The statute is silent on what the debtor's liability is for the rentals due during the first 60 days after the petition. However, § 363(e) was amended to provide that the lessor is entitled to adequate protection of its interest under an unexpired lease of personal property. Curiously, its right to adequate protection under § 363(e) is "to the exclusion of such property being subject to an order to grant relief from the stay under section 362."

It is not clear that the position of personal property lessors has been appreciably strengthened by these amendments. What a debtor-lessee will be required to pay and when it will be required to pay it seem completely discretionary with the court, with a sort of presumption that the time and amount of payments called for by the lease will control unless the debtor can rebut the presumption, perhaps by showing that current payment of contract rent is too great a burden on the reorganization effort. Note that secured lenders are most certainly not entitled to interim loan payments in accordance with their loan agreements during the pendency of a bankruptcy case. Courts can and do recharacterize personal property leases as secured loans when the lessor fails to retain a meaningful reversionary interest in the leased property either because the lease exhausts the useful economic life of the property or because the lessee has the obligation or option to acquire the property at the expiration of the lease. Section 365(d)(10) makes the power to recharacterize personal property leases as secured loans even more important.

Note that leases of commercial aircraft and related equipment and vessels are a special case in Chapter 11 cases. Under § 1110, unless such a lease is assumed within 60 days of the order for relief, lessors may exercise all their rights under their lease agreement, such rights being "not limited or otherwise affected by any other provision of this title or by any power of the court." *See United Airlines, Inc. v. US Bank, N.A.,* 406 F.3d 918 (7th Cir. 2005).

### d.  Time in Which to Assume or Reject

Before 1984, there were two rules with respect to the amount of time allowed to a trustee or debtor in possession to decide whether to reject or assume an executory contract or unexpired lease of the debtor. In Chapter 7 cases § 365(d)(1) applied. If a decision is not made within 60 days after the order for relief, the contract or lease is rejected. The bankruptcy court, for cause, may give the trustee additional time. In Chapter 11 cases, § 365(d)(2) applied. The debtor in possession could defer the decision until the time of confirmation of the plan of reorganization unless the bankruptcy court orders the debtor in possession to make an earlier decision. In 1984, § 365(d)(1) and (2) were amended so that they no longer apply to leases of nonresidential real property. Section 365(d)(4), added in 1984, governs leases of nonresidential real property and applies to a bankruptcy case under any chapter of the Bankruptcy Code.

The 2005 Act significantly amends § 365(d)(4), requiring the written consent of the lessor to extend the time within which a debtor in possession may assume, assume and assign, or reject an unexpired lease of nonresidential real property beyond seven months after the commencement of a voluntary chapter 11 case, unless the lessor consents in writing. Absent a court order, the debtor-lessee has until the earlier of (1) 120 days (about 4 months) after the order for relief is entered or (2) the date the confirmation order is entered, to assume, assume and assign or reject its leases of nonresidential real property. For cause, the court can extend the 120-day period by 90 days (about 3 months). After the court grants that first 90-day extension, however, it cannot further extend the assumption/rejection period without the consent of the lessor.

These amendments seem likely to change the course of many Chapter 11 cases, particularly cases involving large numbers of retail outlets, where a debtor often seeks to postpone the decision on what to do with its store leases until the very end of the case or at least until it determines the size of the reorganized entity or is able to operate through critical selling seasons, often the Christmas season. Absent striking a deal with their landlords, those debtors may be forced to prematurely assume or reject their leases of nonresidential real property. Premature rejection may result in unnecessary store closures and impair reorganization. Premature assumption may result in potentially catastrophic administrative liabilities in the event the reorganization fails.

### 4. EVICTING THE DEBTOR IN POSSESSION

One of the objectives of the 1984 amendments was to aid landlords in evicting lessees of nonresidential real property when their leases had terminated either before or after commencement of the case. To this end, § 362(b)(10), § 365(c)(3) and § 541(b)(2) were all added. A lease can terminate "by expiration of the stated term of such lease" and § 362(b)(10) and § 541(b)(2) apply to leases that terminate in that way. A lease can also be "terminated under applicable nonbankruptcy law" and § 365(c)(3) applies to termination in that way. Thus, the Code makes a distinction between expiration of a lease and termination for cause before the expiry date. Sections 362(b)(10) and § 541(b)(2) apply to cases in which expiration occurs either before or after commencement of the case. Section

365(c)(3) applies to cases in which termination prior to the lease's expiry date occurs before commencement of the case.

### a.  Expiration of Lease

Suppose that under a five-year lease of nonresidential real property expiring on July 1, 2006 the lessee was not entitled to renew at the end of the term. A few months before the expiry date the landlord informed the lessee that the landlord had found another tenant and that the lessee was required to quit the premises on the expiration date. On June 15, 2006, while still in possession of the premises, the lessee filed a petition in bankruptcy under Chapter 11. On July 1, 2006 the lessee, as debtor in possession, informed the landlord that it refused to quit the premises. If this case had arisen before 1984, the landlord could not have evicted the debtor in possession without first obtaining a bankruptcy court order. Under § 362(a)(3) there is an automatic stay against "any act to obtain possession * * * of property from the estate." The landlord must request relief from the stay under § 362(d). This is changed by § 362(b)(10) which provides that the automatic stay does not apply. Section 362(b)(10) allows the landlord to bring an eviction action in state court without first seeking relief from stay.

Under § 541(a)(1) the lease became property of the estate when the lessee filed in bankruptcy on June 15, 2006 and, under § 541(b)(2), it ceased to be property of the estate on July 1, 2006 when the lease expired. Section 541(b)(2) may be redundant. The same result can be obtained without it. On July 1, 2006 the debtor in possession had no rights under the lease under § 365(a) because that provision applies only to unexpired leases.

### b.  Termination Before Expiration of Lease

Suppose a five-year lease that restricts the use of the premises to the sale of merchandise at retail. Six months after the commencement of the lease the lessee's retail business failed and, acting without the landlord's consent or knowledge, the lessee converted the business to a restaurant. Under the terms of the lease, violating the use covenant constituted a default justifying termination upon notice from the landlord and otherwise applicable law does not allow for reinstatement or cure after notice has been given. Assume that upon discovering the facts shortly after the restaurant opened, the landlord duly notified the lessee that the lease was terminated because of breach of the use covenant. The lessee then files in Chapter 11. What are the rights of the debtor in possession and the landlord in the demised premises?

The debtor in possession cannot assume the lease if, before the lessee filed in bankruptcy, the lease terminated under state law. *In re Maxwell*, 40 B.R. 231 (N.D.Ill.1984). If the lease has been terminated it is not be property of the estate because the debtor had no "legal or equitable interest" at the time of filing. § 541(a)(1). Section 541(b)(2) does not apply because termination of the lease occurred before its expiry date. Section 365(c)(3) applies but it does not affect the result. If the lease has been fully and finally terminated under the state law, the lease cannot be assumed. Section 365(c)(3) is not only redundant, it is confusing as well. A lease of residential real property or a personal property lease that was terminated before filing would also not be assumable under the previous law. To the extent § 365(c)(3) applies specifically to nonresidential real property, one could argue that the negative inference is that other terminated leases or contracts can be assumed. This is not so.

If the landlord brings an action in a state court to evict the debtor in possession, the lessor has violated § 362(a)(3), and § 362(b)(10) does not apply because termination did not occur because of "expiration of the stated term of the lease." Why is § 362(b)(10) limited to cases of expiration? There is not likely to be any question about whether termination is valid if the lease's expiry date has passed. But whether a lease has been terminated for cause before its expiry date depends upon facts that may be disputed. If termination is for violation of a use clause, it is necessary to determine whether the new use conflicts with use permitted under the lease. If a use clause is arbitrary or unreasonable a court may find that the lease may not be terminated for violation of the clause. For example, if a lease restricts use of the premises to operation of a French restaurant it does not necessarily follow that operation of an Italian restaurant allows the lessor to terminate for violation of the use clause. A court would have to look at the context in which the clause was adopted to determine whether it is reasonable to enforce it. If there is no interest of the landlord that is affected by the kind of food served in the restaurant, the violation is innocuous and termination should not be allowed. If there is doubt about whether termination is valid, it is proper to have that determination made by the bankruptcy court before permitting the landlord to exercise its rights under state law. Limiting § 362(b)(10) to cases of lease expiration carries out that policy.

## 5. ASSUMPTION AND ASSIGNMENT

### a.    The Perils of Assumption

If you were advising a debtor in possession or bankruptcy trustee, what concerns would you have about assuming a long-term commercial real estate lease before confirmation of a reorganization plan? Consider the following case.

# In re Klein Sleep Products, Inc.

United States Court of Appeals, Second Circuit, 1996.
78 F.3d 18.

■ CALABRESI, Circuit Judge:

The liquidation provisions of the Bankruptcy Code contained in § 726 distribute a pro-rata share of a debtor's estate to each unsecured creditor so that similarly situated creditors may be treated alike. This pro-rata rule does not, however, always lead to an equitable distribution of the estate. When one claimant is a landlord holding a long-term lease, its single unsecured claim for twenty or thirty years of future rent could devour so much of the debtor's estate that only crumbs could be left for the other unsecured creditors. Recognizing the potentially distorting effect of claims arising out of long-term leases, Congress capped unsecured claims for future rent at one year. § 502(b)(6). This allows landlords to recover some of their losses from a bankrupt tenant, but sees to it that their recovery will not crowd out the claims of competing creditors.

Bankruptcy law also aims to avoid liquidation altogether when that is possible. Although the Code offers no magical potion to restore a debtor's financial health, it does provide some useful medicine designed to help a debtor get back on its feet and heading towards convalescence. It does this by allowing a debtor to attempt to reorganize rather than fold and by creating incentives for creditors to continue to do business with the debtor while reorganization proceeds. The Code does this, at least in part, by assuring these post-bankruptcy creditors that, if the debtor fails to rehabilitate itself and winds up in liquidation, they can move to the front of the distributive line, ahead of the debtor's pre-bankruptcy creditors. Special priority is therefore accorded to expenses incurred under new contracts with the debtor, as "administrative expenses" of the estate. The same priority is given to expenses arising under pre-existing contracts that the debtor "assumes"—contracts whose benefits and burdens the debtor decides, with the bankruptcy court's approval, are worth retaining.

These two competing bankruptcy policies—promoting parity among creditors and yet granting priority to the claims of creditors who continue to do business with an insolvent debtor—collide in the case before us. After entering bankruptcy, Klein Sleep (the debtor) assumed, with court approval, the unexpired lease it had with Nostas Associates (its landlord). Some eighteen months later, when it became apparent that the reorganization had failed, the newly appointed bankruptcy trustee decided to "reject" the lease. The landlord then sought to recover the future rent that was due under the lease. The bankruptcy court held, and the district court agreed, that Nostas was entitled to recover as an administrative expense only the rent that had come due before the trustee rejected the lease. Beyond that, Nostas could recover as a general unsecured claim only one year's worth of the rent coming due after rejection.

Two questions arise on appeal. We must first decide whether the future rent gives rise to a general unsecured claim that receives no priority or whether it is, instead, an administrative expense entitled to priority. If it is an administrative expense, we must then determine whether the claim is nonetheless capped at a year's worth of rent by § 502(b)(6).

Our task would be far easier if Congress had answered these questions explicitly in the Code, but unfortunately it left its intentions ambiguous. In order to resolve this ambiguity, we turn first to the various provisions of the Code that discuss the timing and priority of claims. Since we do not find an unmistakable Code directive, however, we also seek guidance from the practice prevailing under the Code's predecessor, the Bankruptcy Act. Adhering to that practice, we hold that damages arising from future rent under an assumed lease must be treated as an administrative expense, and we therefore reverse in part.

The conclusion we reach seems on its face to be unduly favorable to landlords. But it may in fact do no more than recognize the existence of a default rule, which the bankruptcy court can use in encouraging landlords and tenants alike to renegotiate leases in bankruptcy so as to treat all the parties, including general unsecured creditors, equitably.

## I. FACTS

Nostas Associates, the landlord, appeals from a judgment of the United States District Court * * *, affirming the bankruptcy court's order—which assigned administrative priority to Nostas's claims for past rent accruing under a commercial lease, allowed another year's worth of future rent as a general unsecured claim, and disallowed any recovery for the rest. Before entering bankruptcy, Klein Sleep, Inc. had leased a store from Nostas in Paramus, New Jersey. Shortly after filing for Chapter 11 relief in June 1991, Klein Sleep (acting as debtor-in-possession) assumed the lease with the approval of the bankruptcy court pursuant to § 365, and accordingly cured all rental arrears to that point. Klein Sleep continued to pay rent through October 1992. By January 1993, however, it had become clear that the reorganization had failed so completely that liquidating the firm's assets would not cover even the administrative expenses of the estate. On January 29, 1993, Klein Sleep's newly appointed Chapter 11 trustee, who was assigned the task of liquidating the estate, rejected the lease and surrendered possession of the store to Nostas.

Nostas argued to the bankruptcy court, to the district court, and now to us on appeal that Klein Sleep's court-approved lease assumption converted *all* liability under the lease into administrative expenses that warrant a first priority in repayment under § 507(a)(1) (providing that administrative expenses, as defined by § 503(b), are first in the order of repayment of claims and expenses). Under this theory, Nostas seeks administrative expense status for rent arrearages from November 1992 through January 1993, [and] for future rent accruing after January 1993 * * *.

The bankruptcy court * * * allowed Nostas's claims in the following order of priority: (1) Super-priority administrative expense status for rent during the liquidation period, from December 1, 1992, through January 29, 1993 (approximately $18,000, of which 100% will be paid upon distribution of the estate), as "burial expenses" of winding up the estate; (2) priority administrative expense status for rent during the pre-liquidation period, from November 1, 1992, through December 1, 1992 (approximately $6800, of which approximately 85% will be paid upon distribution of the estate); and (3) general unsecured claim status for future damages arising after the trustee rejected the lease (approximately $80,000[2] or one year's future rent as limited by § 502(b)(6), of which nothing will be paid upon distribution of the estate). * * *

* * * Relying primarily on this court's decision in Trustees of Amalgamated Insurance Fund v. McFarlin's, Inc., 789 F.2d 98, 101 (2d Cir.1986) * * * the district court held that:

> benefit to the estate as required by section 503(b)(1)(A) must be shown for damages arising from the subsequent rejection of an assumed lease to be afforded administrative priority, even if the expenses are considered post-petition expenses under section 365(g)(2)(A). Because the post-surrender damages incurred by Nostas in the instant case conferred no benefit upon Klein Sleep, those expenses are not entitled to administrative priority status.

* * *

## II. DISCUSSION

### A. Administrative Expense Status

According to § 503(b)(1)(A), "the actual, necessary costs and expenses of preserving the estate" constitute administrative expenses entitled to priority status upon distribution of the estate. The crux of Nostas's argument is that a trustee's or debtor-in-possession's assumption of an unexpired lease transforms *all* liability under the lease, including damages that stem from a subsequent rejection of the lease, into administrative expenses. There is strong bankruptcy court precedent directly on point that supports this proposition. See, e.g., * * * 2 COLLIER ON BANKRUPTCY ¶ 365.08[01], at 365–65 (15th ed. 1995) ("[A] trustee must proceed cautiously in electing whether to assume or reject since an assumption will have the effect of making the expenses and liabilities incurred expenses of administration.").

*Multech*, the seminal case on this issue, offers the following rationale for this rule:

> By defining the time at which a rejection of an assumed contract or lease constitutes a breach, § 365(g) clearly indicates that the act of as-

---

[2] Because Nostas relet the premises beginning on July 1, 1993, it claimed the entire rent due under the Klein Sleep lease from January 29, 1993 through June 30, 1993 (totalling approximately $38,000), plus the difference between the rent it would have collected under the remainder of the Klein Sleep lease (approximately $215,000) and the rent due under the new lease (approximately $157,000), for a total claim of $96,000 in post-rejection rent.

sumption creates an administrative expense obligation of the particular proceedings in which the contract or lease was assumed. Consequently, if a lease is assumed in Chapter 11 proceedings, the liabilities flowing from the rejection of that lease will ever after be regarded as a Chapter 11 administrative expense.

47 B.R. at 750 (footnote omitted).

Citing our decision in *McFarlin's*, however, the district court declined to follow *Multech* and its progeny. The court stated that our decision in *McFarlin's* established that expenses fall within § 503(b)(1)(A) if they arise out of a transaction between the debtor and the creditor, and "'only to the extent that the consideration supporting the claimant's right to payment was both supplied to and beneficial to the debtor-in-possession in the operation of the business.'" *McFarlin's*, 789 F.2d at 101 (quoting *In re Mammoth Mart, Inc.*, 536 F.2d 950, 953 (1st Cir.1976)). It then asserted that Klein Sleep derived actual benefit not from its *assumption* of the lease, but only from its *occupation* of the leased premises.

Once the trustee gave the store back to Nostas, the court reasoned, Klein Sleep received no further benefit from the lease. As a result, the damages it sought for future rent did not meet the prerequisites for administrative expense status under § 503(b)(1)(A). * * *

At first glance, the bankruptcy court's approach has much to recommend it. By denying administrative expense status for all future rent under an assumed lease, the court followed our stated policy that priorities in bankruptcy should be narrowly construed and sparingly granted. *McFarlin's*, 789 F.2d at 100. And, the bankruptcy court's relegation of Nostas to the ranks of the unsecured creditors furthered this fundamental policy— based on the notion that individual creditors, whenever possible, should be prevented from seizing a disproportionate share of the estate—in a second way as well. Once future rent is treated merely as an unsecured claim, it is clearly capped by § 502(b)(6) at one year's worth of unpaid rent. As a result, the rent claims cannot absorb all the assets of the estate, no matter how long the lease.

Yet this approach has several deficiencies. First, it relies on an unduly narrow view of the benefit conferred on an estate when a trustee assumes an unexpired lease. Second, it does not adequately account for the Code's timing provisions, which explicitly provide that claims arise "postpetition," and therefore during the administration of the estate, if they are based on breaches of assumed leases. And finally, even if these two considerations did not resolve the matter, the district court's approach does not accord with prior practice under the Bankruptcy Act (practice which, in cases of ambiguity, stands as a decisive guidepost for interpreting today's Bankruptcy Code). Bankruptcy Act practice strongly directs us to treat the entire liability resulting from breach of an assumed lease as a cost of administering the estate.

### 1. Benefit

\* \* \*

The trustee argues that any inquiry as to "benefit" is foreclosed by the district court's factual finding that Klein Sleep did not benefit from its assumption of the lease. The opposite, however, is true: the bankruptcy court's earlier decision to let Klein Sleep assume the unexpired lease—a decision that was not appealed—precluded a subsequent finding that assuming the lease did not benefit Klein Sleep. That decision required a judicial finding—up-front—that it was in the best interests of the estate (and the unsecured creditors) for the debtor to assume the lease, pursuant to § 365(a). It is the same kind of finding that the bankruptcy court is required to make with regard to all *new* contracts entered into by the trustee without prior court approval during the administration of the estate in order for those contracts to qualify for priority pursuant to § 503(b). Compare *In re Orion Pictures Corp.*, 4 F.3d 1095, 1099 (2d Cir.1993) ("[A] bankruptcy court reviewing a trustee's or debtor-in-possession's decision to assume or reject an executory contract [pursuant to § 365] should examine a contract and the surrounding circumstances and apply its best 'business judgment' to determine if it would be beneficial or burdensome to the estate to assume it.") with *Mammoth Mart*, 536 F.2d at 954 (granting administrative expense status to postpetition claim only if consideration "was both supplied to and beneficial to the debtor-in-possession in the operation of the business").

As one bankruptcy court has explained:

> By requiring the court to determine the reasonable necessity of the newly entered contract under § 503(b), Congress has insured some judicial control over the determination of what executory contracts will be granted administrative expense priority. The Code, in order to streamline reorganization procedure, allows a debtor in possession to enter into contracts in the ordinary course of business without seeking court approval. Thus, contracts initially entered into during reorganization, unlike contracts assumed during reorganization, will not have undergone court scrutiny. By limiting automatic administrative expense treatment under § 365(g) to assumed contracts, and by requiring initially entered contracts to qualify under § 503(b) in order to be granted an administrative expense priority, Congress has insured both similar treatment and similar procedural safeguards for these fundamentally similar obligations. \* \* \*

In short, we decline to find that Klein Sleep did not benefit by assuming its lease simply because the lease was no longer profitable at the time it stopped displaying mattresses on the premises. Such a holding would mean that any post-bankruptcy contract, entered into for the benefit of a bankrupt's estate, would cease to be entitled to priority the moment the deal turned sour. When the debtor-in-possession assumed the lease, it retained the right to occupy the leased premises immediately and in the future. Its ability to assign this immediate right of possession, as well as its ability to assign the future right of possession under the lease, had a present value at the time of assumption. Acquisition of those rights clearly constituted a benefit to the estate even if, later, the benefit turned to dust.

### 2. Timing

The Code's timing provisions also tilt in favor of Nostas's position that all future rent is an administrative expense. In allowing and assigning priority to claims arising from unexpired leases, the Code distinguishes between leases that have been assumed, and those that have not. Section 502(g) of the Code clearly instructs us that claims arising from *unassumed* leases are to be allowed as general unsecured claims. Section 502(g) has no analogue that tells us what to do with claims arising from *assumed* leases. But because § 502(g) limits its reach to unassumed leases, it is reasonable to infer that assumed leases are to be treated differently. Since it would be absurd to suppose that such leases would not qualify as claims at all, it follows that they must be considered administrative expenses of the estate. * * *

This inference is further supported by § 365(g), which fixes the time at which a debtor's rejection of an unexpired lease is deemed to constitute a breach of the lease. When a debtor rejects an unassumed lease, breach is deemed to occur at the time the bankruptcy petition was filed. § 365(g)(1). If the lease has been assumed, however, breach is deemed to occur whenever the lease is later rejected. § 365(g)(2)(A).[5] According to the Code's legislative history, the purpose of § 365(g) is to treat claims arising from unassumed leases "as prepetition claims." H.R.REP. NO. 595, 95th Cong., 2d Sess. 349 (1977); S.REP. NO. 989, 95th Cong., 2d Sess. 63 (1978). But the only way in which prepetition claims are treated differently from postpetition claims is that the former are classified as general claims, whereas the latter—arising, for example, from torts committed by the estate in bankruptcy, or from contracts entered into by the trustee or debtor-in-possession—are entitled to administrative expense priority. It would seem to follow that rejection of an assumed lease—that is, breach of contract committed by the trustee or debtor-in-possession while administering the estate—gives rise to a debt entitled to the same administrative expense priority.

The timing provisions of the Code were not, however, directly designed to answer the question we are asking today, and so we are hesitant to read too much into them. Indeed, because all of our previous discussion has essentially required us to read between the lines of Congress's directives, we conclude that the Bankruptcy Code, though it clearly leans in favor of administrative status for assumed leases, is still ambiguous. When

---

[5] When a reorganization case is converted to a liquidation proceeding after the lease has been assumed but before it is rejected, breach is deemed to have occurred immediately before the conversion. § 365(g)(2)(B).

that is the case, we are required to turn for further guidance to the prior practice under the Bankruptcy Act.

### 3. Practice Under the Bankruptcy Act

Were we writing on a clean slate, we might perhaps be persuaded by the district court's analysis—though, as we have discussed above, we think that the structure of the Code favors the landlord's position. We are not, however, permitted to start from scratch. In *Dewsnup v. Timm*, 502 U.S. 410 (1992), the Supreme Court declined to resolve de novo an ambiguous interrelationship between certain Bankruptcy Code provisions, where accepted pre-Code bankruptcy practice existed. The Court stated:

> When Congress amends the bankruptcy laws, it does not write "on a clean slate.".... Furthermore, this Court has been reluctant to accept arguments that would interpret the Code, however vague the particular language under consideration might be, to effect a change in pre-Code practice that is not the subject of at least some discussion in the legislative history.

502 U.S. at 419 (citation omitted).

In the case before us, an ambiguity arguably exists as to whether claims arising from the rejection of assumed contracts by definition meet the "actual and necessary" requirements of § 503(b)(1)(A) and hence automatically enjoy administrative expense priority under § 507(a)(1). * * * Nostas and amicus argue, however, that the pre-Code practice was to grant administrative status automatically to all claims arising from the subsequent rejection of an assumed executory contract—and, therefore, that any ambiguity must be resolved in favor of granting administrative expense status.

* * *

Absent a clear Code directive, or legislative history that directly addresses the issue and reaches a contrary result, the rule of construction set forth in *Dewsnup* dictates that Nostas's claim for post-rejection rental damages should be governed by Bankruptcy Act practice. That practice strongly supports the conclusion that Nostas's claim was entitled to administrative expense status. This result, moreover, agrees with our earlier analysis that the Code's timing provisions, together with the rules governing "benefit," indicate that all future rent accruing under an assumed lease is entitled to the status of an administrative expense. Accordingly, we so hold.

### B. The § 502(b)(6) Cap on Damages for Future Rent

Because it determined that Nostas's claim was not an administrative expense, the district court never reached the issue of whether § 502(b)(6) limits Nostas's claim arising from the assumed leases to one year's worth of future rent. Since we conclude that such future rent is an administrative expense, we must now decide whether § 502(b)(6) caps the rent.

Section 502(b)(6) requires a court to allow a claim except to the extent that it exceeds one year's rent due under the lease.[6] This cap is designed to prevent a landlord's single unsecured claim—which, depending on the length of the lease, may be enormous—to elbow aside the other unsecured creditors. The trustee argues that "[t]he policy underlying Code § 502(b)(6) applies equally to claims arising under leases that have been assumed and those that have not." Indeed, because the drafters of the Code took such care to prevent a monstrous *unsecured* claim from swallowing up the estate, it might seem odd not only to give an analogous type of claim priority over unsecured creditors, but also to allow such a claim in its entirety, merely because it arose from an assumed lease.

Sensible as this policy argument might be, we do not find the Code ambiguous on this point. Section 502, which contains the cap on future rent, applies only to "a claim or interest, proof of which is filed under section 501." § 502(a). Section 501 prescribes the method for filing proofs of prepetition claims against the debtor and certain postpetition claims that are deemed to have arisen prepetition. It does not apply to administrative expenses payable by the debtor, which must be requested pursuant to § 503. See also id. § 507 (referring to "expenses and claims"). And because § 502 does not apply to administrative expenses, it cannot cap future rent due under an assumed lease.

The legislative history of § 502(b)(6) confirms that, at least on this score, Congress said what it meant. H.R.REP. NO. 595, 95th Cong., 2d Sess. 353 (1977); S.REP. NO. 989, 95th Cong., 2d Sess. 63 (1978) (stating that § 502(b)(6) "does not apply to limit administrative expense claims for use of the leased premises to which the landlord is otherwise entitled"); see also *Multech*, 47 B.R. at 751 (explaining that the policy of preventing landlord's unsecured claim from crowding out other unsecured creditors

---

[6] Section 502(b)(6) provides, more fully, that the bankruptcy court shall allow a lessor's claim for damages arising from the termination of a lease of real property, except to the extent that the claim exceeds

(A) the rent reserved by such lease, without acceleration, for the greater of one year, or 15 percent, not to exceed three years, of the remaining term of such lease, following the earlier of—

(i) the date of the filing of the petition; and

(ii) the date on which such lessor repossessed, or the lessee surrendered, the leased property; plus

(B) any unpaid rent due under such lease, without acceleration, on the earlier of such dates. . . .

Because in the case before us § 502(b)(6) operates to limit rent claims to one year—rather than fifteen percent of all future rent capped at three years—we refer to this section as imposing a "one-year cap."

"is no longer germane in the case of an assumed contract or lease, since the resulting obligations and liabilities are elevated to a priority status and no longer fall in the class of general unsecured creditors"); *In re Johnston, Inc.*, 164 B.R. at 555 (stating that § 502(b)(6) does not limit administrative expense claims); 2 COLLIER ON BANKRUPTCY ¶ 365.08, at 365–67 (15th ed. 1995) ("[T]he limitation upon the amount of an allowed claim arising from breach of a lease in section 502(b)(6) of the Code does not apply to leases assumed and thereafter rejected in the case.")

\* \* \*

## III. CONCLUSION

It would surely have been better if Congress had spelled out its intentions as to assumed leases in the Code, rather than leaving it up to the courts to clean up the ambiguities. But, under the circumstances, clean them up we must. The trustee complains that the rule we pick—a rule that accords administrative priority to claims for all future rent under an assumed lease—is overly generous to landlords, since it gives them a lion's share of estates upon liquidation. While that may seem to be the case, we doubt that it will work out that way in practice. Under the rule we adopt, bankruptcy courts will rarely find that assuming liability for all future rent under a long-term lease is in the best interests of the estate—including the interest of the general creditors—unless the rental terms are highly advantageous. They will therefore block assumption of such leases except in unusual cases. As a result, landlords will find themselves with unsecured claims capped at one year's worth of future rent.

This may also seem undesirable, especially since in some such cases the tenant properly wishes to continue the rental. But this too is not quite the end of the story, for bankruptcy courts may have another option open to them. Faced with the unattractive choice of either requiring a bankrupt tenant to reject its long-term lease (and thereby possibly dooming the reorganization to failure) or letting it assume the lease (and leaving the general creditors with a paltry recovery should liquidation ensue), one bankruptcy court suggested that it could instead put off the decision on whether or not to assume a long-term lease. It could delay, the court stated, until the moment of confirmation, when the debtor's chances of rehabilitation would finally be clear. *See In re Monica Scott*, 123 B.R. 990, 993 (Bankr.D.Minn.1991). ("Unless the Congress addresses this situation, cause will undoubtedly be found to exist, as a matter of course, for extending to confirmation the time to assume or reject significant leases in Chapter 11 cases."), *id.* n. 8 (citing § 365(d)(4), which permits bankruptcy courts to extend the 60–day assumption/rejection period "for cause"). The uncertainty engendered by such an approach would give the bankruptcy court significant leverage over both tenant and landlord, and might well lead to a renegotiation of the long-term lease. The tenant who wishes to retain control over the premises has an interest—arising out of fear that the court will force rejection of the original lease—in renegotiating the lease, though perhaps for a shorter term. The landlord also has an interest in renegotiating the lease to escape the limbo between assumption and rejection. In such circumstances the landlord might well prefer to recover some guaranteed amount of future rent, as an administrative expense, under a new contract rather than risk having the lease rejected and the recovery limited to a fractional share of one year's worth of future rent, as an unsecured claim, under the pre-existing contract.[7]

None of this is before us today. But we do note that the rule that we enunciate may not be quite as rigid as it looks. It may well operate, like so many other default rules in contract law, only as a backdrop against which the parties—here the landlord and tenant—can renegotiate to reach a satisfactory, middle solution.

\* \* \*

For the reasons stated above, we hold that claims for future rent arising out of assumed leases are administrative expenses of the debtor's estate, regardless of whether they are subsequently rejected, and that they are not capped at a year's worth of unpaid rent by § 502(b)(6). We reach this conclusion in light of the prior practice under the Bankruptcy Act, the timing provisions of the Code, and an understanding that debtors generally benefit from court-approved assumptions of executory contracts and unexpired leases.

Reversed to the extent that the court disallowed Nostas's claim for future rent as an administrative expense, and remanded for further proceedings consistent with this opinion.

## NOTE

Section 503(b)(7) overrules that portion of *Klein Sleep* that held that the lessor was entitled to an unlimited administrative expense claim. Under the amendment, a lessor with respect to a nonresidential real property lease that was previously assumed and then rejected will have an administrative expense claim for future rent "[f]or the period of 2 years following the later of the rejection date or the date of actual turnover of the premises. . . ." Damages for "going dark" and penalties are expressly excluded from the administrative claim. Mitigation principles will apply only to the extent that the lessor actually receives rent from a nondebtor.

Section 503(b)(7) also reverses that portion of *Klein Sleep* that held that the § 502(b)(6) cap does not apply to these claims, although the cap will apply on a more limited basis. It applies to the lessor's claim for future rent after the first 2 years: "[t]he claim for remaining sums due for

---

[7] In either event, of course, the landlord is entitled to recover as an administrative expense the rent due while the debtor and the bankruptcy court debate whether to assume the lease. § 365(d)(3).

the balance of the term of the lease shall be a claim under section 502(b)(6)."

These amendments will to some degree mitigate the effects of the new 7-month time limit on nonconsensual extensions of the time for assumption or rejection, by limiting the economic consequences of rejecting previously assumed leases. Still the consequences remain severe: the landlord under such a lease will retain its cure payments, its postpetition administrative rent, hold a second-priority administrative claim for up to 2 years future rent, and hold an unsecured, albeit capped, claim for the balance under § 502(b)(6).

### b.   Effect of Violation of Use Clause

# Matter of U.L. Radio Corp.

United States Bankruptcy Court, S.D. New York, 1982.
19 B.R. 537.

■   JOHN J. GALGAY, Bankruptcy Judge.

Debtor, U.L. Radio Corp., has moved for an order, pursuant to Bankruptcy Code section 365(f), authorizing it to assume its lease ("Lease") with Jemrock Realty Company ("Jemrock"), the landlord, and authorizing U.L. Radio to assign the Lease to Just Heaven Restaurant, Ltd. ("Just Heaven"). U.L. Radio operates the leasehold as a television sales and service store. Just Heaven, the prospective assignee, will operate the premises as a small bistro. Jemrock opposes such an assignment, citing a use clause in the Lease which provides that the lessee shall use the premises only for television service and sale of electrical appliances. Jemrock asserts that the assignment of the Lease to Just Heaven would unlawfully modify the Lease by violating the use clause. Such modification, Jemrock avers, is not permitted under section 365 without the landlord's consent, which consent Jemrock withholds.

* * * The Court grants debtor's motion to assume and assign the Lease to Just Heaven.

### I. Background

On September 17, 1979, the debtor entered into the Lease with Jemrock for a store located at 2656 Broadway, New York, New York. The store is located in a building which is also occupied by a grocery store, a Chinese restaurant, a liquor store, and 170 apartments. The term of the Lease is for ten years. The rent required to be paid is as follows: $9,600 per year from November 1, 1979, to October 31, 1982; $10,800 from November 1, 1982, to October 31, 1985; and $12,000 from November 1, 1985 to October 31, 1989. Paragraph 43 of the rider to the Lease provides that the tenant may assign the Lease with the written consent of the Landlord, which consent is not to be unreasonably withheld.

On May 20, 1981, the debtor filed an original petition under Chapter 11 of the Bankruptcy Code and continues to operate its business as debtor in possession. * * * The debtor intends to propose a liquidation plan of reorganization. The debtor is current in the payment of rent and related charges required by the terms of the Lease and is not in default of any of the Lease terms.

In furtherance of its intention to liquidate all of its assets and to propose a plan of reorganization, the debtor, subject to the approval of this Court, entered into an assignment of the Lease to Just Heaven. The proposed assignment provides, *inter alia,* that Just Heaven will pay to the debtor as consideration for the assignment as follows: for the period commencing three months after this Court's approval of the assignment to October 31, 1988, the sum of $2,000 per month. Such payments will fund a plan paying unsecured creditors 100 percent of their claims. Rockwell International, the largest creditor, recommends the assignment.

The president of Just Heaven has executed a personal guarantee for the payment of rent in favor of the landlord for the first two years of the assignment, together with a statement that her net worth exceeds $50,000.

The Lease provides * * * that "any noise emanating from said premises shall be deemed a breach of the terms and conditions of this Lease." Just Heaven has allocated $20,000 for construction, including soundproofing. David Humpal St. James, Vice President and Secretary as well as a director and a shareholder of Just Heaven, is a noted interior designer including the design of commercial restaurants. His design work has involved soundproofing. * * *

### II. Issues

Two issues confront this Court:

**(1)** Have the provisions of section 365, regarding assumption and assignment of leases, been satisfied?

**(2)** Can deviation from a use clause prevent the assignment of a lease, when the assumption and assignment otherwise comport with the requirements of section 365?

### III. Assumption and Assignment Under Section 365

Code section 365 governs the assumption and assignment of executory contracts, providing broad authority to a trustee or debtor in possession to assume and assign an unexpired lease. * * *

Assignment of a lease, which is at issue here, must comply with section 365(f).

* * *

Subsection (f)(1) "partially invalidates restrictions on assignment of contracts or leases by the trustee to a third party." House Report at 349; Senate Report at 59 * * *. Subsection (f)(2) "imposes two restrictions on assignment by the trustee: (1) he must first assume the contract or lease, subject to all the restrictions found in the section; and (2) adequate assurance of future performance must be provided to the other contracting party." House Report at 349; Senate Report at 59.[1] Finally, subsection (f)(3) "invalidates contractual provisions that permit termination or modification in the event of an assignment, as contrary to the policy of this subsection." House Report at 349; Senate Report at 59.

\* \* \*

### B. Adequate Assurance of Future Performance

The second requirement of assignment under section 365(f)(2) is adequate assurance of future performance ("adequate assurance"). \* \* \* The phrase "adequate assurance of future performance" is not found in the Bankruptcy Act.

\* \* \* In the legislative history of section 365(b), Congress while discussing assumption under section 365(b) and the bankruptcy clause under section 365(f), provided this explanation of adequate assurance:

> If a trustee is to assume a contract or lease, the courts will have to insure that the trustee's performance under the contract or lease gives the other contracting party the full benefit of the bargain.

House Report at 348; Senate Report at 59.

Beyond equating adequate assurance with the full benefit of the bargain, Congress offers no definition of adequate assurance except in the case of real property leases in shopping centers. [See Bankruptcy Code § 365(b)(3).] The Lease at issue here is not located in a shopping center. Congress described a shopping center as "often a carefully planned enterprise, and though it consists of numerous individual tenants, the center is planned as a single unit, often subject to a master lease or financing agreement." House Report at 348. The building in which U.L. Radio is located is primarily a residential apartment building, with a liquor store, a grocery store, a restaurant, and U.L. Radio on the first floor. Thus the specific provisions of adequate assurance in the shopping center case do not apply to the assignment at issue here. \* \* \*

\* \* \* Adequate assurance of future performance are not words of art, but are to be given practical, pragmatic construction. What constitutes "adequate assurance" is to be determined by factual conditions. \* \* \* The broad authorization of the trustee or debtor to assume or assign unexpired leases, notwithstanding anti-assignment or bankruptcy clauses, prompted the admonition from Congress that the courts must "be sensitive to the rights of the nondebtor party to \* \* \* unexpired leases." House Report at 348; Senate Report at 59.

The phrase "adequate assurance of future performance" was adopted from Uniform Commercial Code section 2–609. *Report of the Commission*

---

[1] Code section 365(f) does not state which party must provide assurance. However, since Code section 365(k) relieves the debtor-assignor of liability under the lease after assignment, it is sensible that the assignee must provide the assurance of performance.

*on Bankruptcy Laws of the United States* (1973). U.C.C. section 2–609 provides that a party with reasonable grounds for insecurity regarding another party's performance may demand "adequate assurance." * * * Regarding adequate assurance under an assignment pursuant to section 365(f)(2), the Court in *In re Lafayette Radio Electronics Corp.*, 9 B.R. 993 [, 998] (Bankr.E.D.N.Y.1981), stated, "[T]he Court's primary focus will be on the ability of [the assignee] to comply with the financial obligations under the agreement."

In *In re Pin Oaks Apartments*, 7 B.R. 364 (Bankr.S.D.1980), the Court found that changes in financial provisions of a lease, a percentage rental clause and a sublease provision which protected that rental clause, precluded a finding that adequate assurance had been provided because of the drastic effect the changes would have on rentals received.

Thus, the primary focus of adequate assurance is the assignee's ability to satisfy financial obligations under the lease. In this case, the president of the assignee has executed a personal guarantee of the payment of rent in favor of the landlord for the first two years of the assignment, together with a statement that her net worth exceeds $50,000. The assignee has budgeted $20,000 for construction, enhancing the chances of success of the assignee's enterprise. The assignee will have operating capital of an additional $30,000. * * * Upon these facts, the Court rules that adequate assurance of future financial performance has been provided by the assignee.

### IV. Use Clause

However, adequate assurance of future financial performance is not the complete statutory requirement; adequate assurance of future performance is. The financial capability of an assignee may be sufficient for a finding of adequate assurance under an executory sales contract or a similar commercial transaction. In a landlord-tenant relationship, more than an assignee's ability to comply with the financial provisions of a lease may be required. More particularly, will compliance with a use clause be required in order to provide adequate assurance?

Congress indicates that adequate assurance will give the landlord the full benefit of his bargain. In its case-by-case determination of those factors, beyond financial assurance, which constitute the landlord's bargain, the Court will generally consider the provisions of the lease to be assigned. * * *

However, it is equally clear that, by requiring provision of adequate assurance under section 365, i.e., the lessor's receipt of the full benefit of his bargain, Congress did not require the Court to assure literal fulfillment by the lessee of each and every term of the bargain. * * * Section 365, by its own terms, empowers the court to render unenforceable bankruptcy clauses and anti-assignment clauses which permit modification or termination of a lease for filing in bankruptcy or assignment of the lease. § 365(e), (f)(3). Section 365(k) relieves the estate of liability for future breaches of a lease after assignment, notwithstanding lease provisions to the contrary. * * *

The Court in *In re Pin Oaks Apartments* argued that court authority to abrogate lease provisions extends only to those provisions expressly stated by Congress:

> If Congress intended to give this Court or the trustee the power to abrogate any contractual rights between a debtor and non-debtor contracting party other than anti-assignment and "ipso facto" [i.e. bankruptcy] clauses, it would have expressly done so.

7 B.R. at 367.

Such a narrow view of court authority is not supported by the statute or the legislative history. First, such a narrow view would frustrate the express policy of Congress favoring assignment. Under the *Pin Oaks* reasoning, lessors could employ very specific use clauses to prevent assignment and thus circumvent the Code. Section 365(f), in broad language, empowers the Court to authorize assignment of an unexpired lease and invalidate any lease provision which would terminate or modify the lease because of the assignment of that lease. § 365(f)(1), (3). Any lease provision, not merely one entitled "anti-assignment clause", would be subject to the court's scrutiny regarding its anti-assignment effect. The court could render unenforceable any provision whose sole effect is to restrict assignment, "as contrary to the policy of [subsection (f)(3)]." House Report at 349; Senate Report at 59. * * *

* * *

Thus, provision of adequate assurance of future performance does not require an assignee's literal compliance with each and every term of the lease. The court may permit deviations from strict enforcement of any provision including a use clause. * * *

One commentator suggested that the court render completely invalid any use clause in a non-shopping center lease because: (1) "the lessor is seeking to protect his tenant mix with the lease provision, and the Code does not require the court to provide such protection"; and (2) a use clause "invalidly conditions assignment." Fogel, Executory Contracts and Unexpired Leases in the Bankruptcy Code, 64 Minn.L.Rev. 341, 364 (1980). * * * The Court rejects this *"per se* unenforceable" reading of a use clause.

However, the Court will not go to the other extreme and adopt the "insubstantial" breach or disruption standard for non-shopping center cases that is applicable only to shopping center leases. The insubstantial breaches and disruptions language of section 365(b)(3) clearly reflects an attempt to limit the effect of what was understood—and feared—to be the more expansive authority conferred by the balance of [s]ection 365(a). * * * The Court's authority to waive strict enforcement of lease provisions in the non-shopping center cases will permit deviations which would exceed those permitted in the shopping center cases. * * *

Within the range between unenforceability of a use clause and insubstantial breaches of a use clause, the Code provides no specific standard by which to measure permissible deviations in use. Whatever standard is applied must serve the policy aims of Congress.

Section 365 expresses a clear Congressional policy favoring assumption and assignment. Such a policy will insure that potential valuable assets will not be lost by a debtor who is reorganizing his affairs or liquidating assets for distribution to creditors. * * * To prevent an assignment of an unexpired lease by demanding strict enforcement of a use clause, and thereby contradict clear Congressional policy, a landlord or lessor must show that actual and substantial detriment would be incurred by him if the deviation in use was permitted.

In this case, the contemplated deviation in use is from an appliance store to a small bistro. The building in which the unexpired leasehold is located already contains a restaurant, a laundry, and a liquor store. The landlord has failed to demonstrate any actual and substantial detriment which he would incur if the proposed deviation in use is permitted. The Court also notes that the contemplated use, along with the planned soundproofing, will have no adverse effect on other tenants in the building. Thus, this Court rules that the use clause may not be enforced so as to block assignment of this lease to Just Heaven. The fact that Jemrock withholds its consent to the proposed assignment will not prevent the assignment. * * *

Congress, in section 365, has stated a general policy favoring assignment. Balanced against this general policy is the requirement that the non-debtor contracting party receive the full benefit of his bargain. Jemrock Realty will receive the full benefit of its bargain under the proposed assignment of the leasehold from U.L. Radio to Just Heaven. No defaults exist under the lease. The lease has properly been assumed and Just Heaven has provided adequate assurance of future performance. The landlord has shown no actual or substantial detriment to him from the proposed assignment. The statutory requirements have been satisfied. The assignment is authorized.

## NOTE

In a non-shopping center case, Debtor's lease restricted use to the sale of hardware, paint and related items. Upon Debtor's liquidation, the highest bidder for the remaining 12–year term of the lease was a ladies clothing outlet. The court relied on *U.L. Radio* to approve the assignment over the objections of the lessor and another tenant of the lessor in the same building which also sold ladies clothing. The court held that the other tenant had no standing to object: "Section 365 aims to ensure that the landlord receives the benefit of his bargain, and looks, therefore, to the prejudice to the landlord. It does not deal with a third party's benefit of its own bargain with the landlord * * *." *In re Martin Paint Stores*, 199 B.R. 258, 264 (Bankr.S.D.N.Y.1996).

## In re Standor Jewelers West, Inc.
United States Bankruptcy Appellate Panel, Ninth Circuit, 1991.
129 B.R. 200.

■ JONES, Bankruptcy Judge:

* * *

On June 1, 1990 Debtor Standor Jewelers West, Inc. filed a voluntary petition for relief under Chapter 11 of the Bankruptcy Code. At the time, Debtor operated four retail jewelry stores including a store leased at the South Coast Plaza Mall in Costa Mesa, California. On July 30, 1990 Debtor sought to assume and assign the lease for its South Coast Plaza Store (the "Lease") and to sell the assets of the South Coast Plaza Store free and clear of liens, with liens to attach to proceeds, to Sterling, Inc., an Ohio corporation ("Sterling"). South Coast Plaza objected to the assumption and assignment of the Lease because of debtor's alleged refusal to provide it with "adequate assurances" that it would comply with a provision in the Lease requiring the lessee to remit to the landlord 75% of the appreciation in value of the Lease as a condition to the landlord's consent to any assignment.

* * *

The bankruptcy court held that, even if the provision of the Lease allocating 75% of the value of the leasehold to the landlord as a condition of the assignment was valid under state law, that provision constituted a restriction on transfer of the lease which was preempted by and invalid pursuant to § 365(f). * * *

* * * In order to facilitate the assignment of unexpired leases, § 365(f)(1) renders unenforceable provisions in a lease which condition or in any way restrict the assignment of the lease:

> . . . notwithstanding a provision in an. . . unexpired lease of the debtor, or in applicable law, that prohibits, restricts, or conditions the assignment of such contract or lease, the trustee may assign such contract or lease. . ..

* * * The legislative history of § 365(f) states that contractual provisions that modify the terms of a lease upon assignment are invalid, as contrary to the rehabilitative policies of the Bankruptcy Code. * * *

In *In re National Sugar Refining Co.*, 21 B.R. 196 (Bankr.S.D.N.Y.1982) the court invalidated provisions in a lease which required the debtor to transfer a portion of the purchase price to the lessor.[3] South Coast Plaza attempts to distinguish *National Sugar Refining* by claiming that the court in that case misunderstood that it must first determine whether the provision validly allocated the ownership interest under state law. South Coast Plaza contends that in the instant case, the bankruptcy court erred by not initially determining who owns the property at issue: the 75% of the appreciated leasehold estate. In order to do so, South Coast Plaza argues that the court must refer to state law and the language of the Lease.

Under applicable California law, parties to a commercial lease are permitted to condition assignment of that lease upon payment to the landlord of some or all of any consideration the tenant receives upon assignment in excess of the rent provided in the lease. * * * However, the bankruptcy court rejected this reasoning and found *National Sugar Refining* controlling, concluding that because the Lease is an asset of the estate pursuant to § 541, restrictions on its transfer are invalid pursuant to § 365(f).

In *In re Howe*, 78 B.R. 226 (Bankr.S.D.1987) the court struck down a provision in an executory contract which provided that the vendor would consent to an assignment if the debtor paid a 4% assumption fee. The court stated:

> It is clear from the language of the contract that [vendor's] consent to assignment is directly conditioned on its receipt of the four percent assumption fee. . . . Therefore, Section 365(f)(1) governs this matter and precludes enforcement of the four percent assumption fee required in the contract for the deed.

78 B.R. at 230. The court further added that to the extent the 4% assumption fee represented "an attempt by the vendor to extract any profit realized upon the assignment of the contract. . . [S]uch a purpose would frustrate the Congressional policy of assisting the debtor in realizing the eq-

---

[3] The provision under review in *National Sugar Refining,* is virtually identical in effect to Sections 10.01(e) of the Debtor's lease with South Coast Plaza.

The court in *National Sugar Refining* stated:

The clear language of Section 36.01 of the Lease prohibits [the Debtor] from assigning the Lease without [the landlord's] consent. Section 36.02 of the Lease, which applies only to consensual assignment, provides that as a condition precedent to obtaining [the landlord's] consent to an assignment, [the Debtor] must offer to surrender the premises to [the landlord]. If [the Debtor's] offer to surrender is refused by [the landlord]. . . [the landlord] has the right to request the profits realized by [the Debtor] upon an assignment.

21 B.R. at 198.

Compare: Paragraph 10.01(e) states in pertinent part:

*As a condition to Landlord's consent to any assignment or subletting,* Landlord shall be entitled to receive, in the case of an assignment, 75% of all consideration given, directly or indirectly by the assignee to tenant for tenant's leasehold interest hereunder. (Emphasis added.)

uity in all his or her assets. . . [and] would result in a windfall to the vendor" in contravention of Congressional policy. Id. at 230 n. 7.

We find this reasoning persuasive. In this case, enforcement of § 10.01(b) and (e) of the Lease will favor the Landlord by conditioning and restricting assignment of the Lease. Consequently, the enforcement of the allocation provision in § 10.01(e) would adversely affect the ability of the debtor in its rehabilitation effort in contravention of § 365(f).

## VI
## CONCLUSION

Pursuant to § 365(f) of the Bankruptcy Code, a provision which conditions or restricts the ability of a debtor to fully realize the economic value of its lease upon assignment is invalid. Accordingly, the bankruptcy court order denying South Coast Plaza's claim to 75% of the appreciated value of the leasehold estate upon assignment is Affirmed.

## C. Shopping Center Leases

The shopping center industry feared that the general assignment privileges of Chapter 11 lessees threatened to destroy the identity and integrity of shopping centers. Accordingly, they sponsored § 365(b)(3) which sets forth special standards for adequate assurance of future performance in the assumption and assignment of shopping center leases. The Bankruptcy Code does not define "shopping center," but the House Report tells us what Congress had in mind.

> A shopping center is often a carefully planned enterprise, and though it consists of numerous individual tenants, the center is planned as a single unit, often subject to a master lease or financing agreement. Under these agreements, the tenant mix in a shopping center may be as important to the lessor as the actual promised rental payments, because certain mixes will attract higher patronage of the stores in the center, and thus a higher rental for the landlord from those stores that are subject to a percentage of gross receipts rental agreement. Thus, in order to assure a landlord of his bargained for exchange, the court would have to consider such factors as the nature of the business to be conducted by the trustee or his assignee, whether that business complies with the requirements of any master agreement, whether the kind of business proposed will generate gross sales in an amount such that the percentage rent specified in the lease is substantially the same as what would have been provided by the debtor, and whether the business proposed to be conducted would result in a breach of other clauses in master agreements relating, for example, to tenant mix and location.

1978 U.S.C.C.A.N., p. 6305.

Before amendment in 1984, § 365(b)(3) provided as follows:

**(3)** For the purposes of paragraph (1) of this section, adequate assurance of future performance of a lease of real property in a shopping center includes adequate assurance—

**(A)** of the source of rent and other consideration due under such lease;

**(B)** that any percentage rent due under such lease will not decline substantially;

**(C)** that assumption or assignment of such lease will not breach substantially any provision, such as a radius, location, use, or exclusivity provision, in any other lease, financing agreement, or master agreement relating to such shopping center; and

**(D)** that assumption or assignment of such lease will not disrupt substantially any tenant mix or balance in such shopping center.

The word "substantially" in subparagraphs (C) and (D) caused difficulty to shopping center lessors, because it made it possible for a bankruptcy court to permit some assignments that in fact violated agreement terms and tenant mixes. In the amended version of these subparagraphs the word "substantially" was deleted, thus requiring strict compliance by the assuming lessee or assignee of every term of the agreement and barring even minor alterations in the tenant mix. Second, the following was added to subparagraph (A): "and in the case of an assignment, that the financial condition and operating performance of the proposed assignee and its guarantors, if any, shall be similar to the financial condition and operating performance of the debtor and its guarantors, if any, as of the time the debtor became the lessee under the lease." Thus, under this amendment, not only the financial condition of the assignee and any guarantors must pass muster but also their "operating performance" must meet the level of the original lessee at the time it became the lessee.

The 1984 amendments restrict even more than did the 1978 Code the capacity of courts to deal with adequate assurance with respect to shopping center leases on a flexible case-by-case approach. They appear to require strict enforcement of restrictive use clauses against potential assignees. They pose financial and performance standards that will make it more difficult to find qualified assignees. In short, they limit severely the Chapter 11 lessee's ability to assume or assign its shopping center lease and, thereby, to realize on what might be a valuable asset. In so doing they frustrate the original Congressional intent of allowing leases to be preserved and assigned as valuable property of the estate in order to aid in the lessee's reorganization. Hence, in the case of shopping center leases Congress weighed the interest of landlords and the other tenants in the integrity of the center more heavily than the lessee's interest in rehabilitation. In 2000, approximately 51% of all non-automotive retail trade in the country was conducted in shopping centers. International Council of Shopping

Centers, Scope USA (2001) <http://www.icsc.org/srch/rsrch/scope/current/>. Accordingly, the shopping center amendments constitute a major limitation of the rights of Chapter 11 lessees to assign leases. The following case shows the extent of the shopping center industry's victory.

## In re Trak Auto Corporation

United States Court of Appeals, Fourth Circuit, 2004.
367 F.3d 237.

■   MICHAEL, Circuit Judge:

A Chapter 11 debtor-tenant sought to assign its shopping center lease in contravention of a provision that limits use of the premises to the sale of auto parts. The bankruptcy and district courts approved the assignment, and the lessor and owner of the shopping center appeals. We are asked to resolve the conflict between § 365(f)(1) , which generally allows a debtor to assign its lease notwithstanding a provision restricting assignment, and § 365(b)(3)(C), which specifically requires a debtor-tenant in a shopping center to assign its lease subject to any provision restricting use of the premises. We hold that § 365(b)(3)(C), the more specific provision, controls in this case. As a result, we reverse and remand.

### I.

Trak Auto Corporation (Trak Auto) is a retailer of auto parts and accessories that once operated 196 stores in Virginia, eight other states, and the District of Columbia. On July 5, 2001, in the Eastern District of Virginia, Trak Auto filed a petition under Chapter 11 of the Bankruptcy Code and continued in business as debtor in possession. As part of its effort to reorganize, Trak Auto obtained court approval to close its stores in four states, Illinois, Indiana, Michigan, and Wisconsin. Thereafter, Trak Auto sought to assume and assign certain of its leases of retail space where stores had been closed. One of these leases (the West Town lease or the lease) is at West Town Center, a shopping center in Chicago. Trak Auto's lessor and the owner of the shopping center is West Town Center LLC (West Town), the appellant. The West Town lease contains explicit use restrictions. Section 1.1(L) limits "PERMITTED USES" to the "[s]ale at retail of automobile parts and accessories and such other items as are customarily sold by Tenant at its other Trak Auto stores." J.A. 579. In section 8.1 Trak Auto "covenants. . . to use the Leased Premises only as a Trak Auto Store and for the Uses provided in Section 1.1(L)." J.A. 588.

Trak Auto engaged a real estate firm to advertise the availability of the West Town lease and to solicit bids. Of the bids received, none came from an auto parts retailer. The high bidder was A & E Stores, Inc. (A & E), an apparel merchandiser that offered $80,000 to buy out the lease. If A & E obtains the lease, it will open a Pay Half store on the premises, selling brand name family apparel at discount prices.

In a motion filed in the bankruptcy court, Trak Auto sought an order authorizing it to assume the West Town lease and to assign it to A & E. West Town, Trak Auto's lessor, objected on two grounds. First, West Town argued that the proposed assignment would breach the lease provision limiting use to the sale of auto parts and accessories. According to West Town, this use provision was enforceable under § 365(b)(3)(C). (West Town did not rely on the lease restriction that said the premises could be used "only as a Trak Auto Store.") Second, West Town argued that the assignment would disrupt its shopping center's tenant mix in violation of § 365(b)(3)(D). Trak Auto responded that the use restrictions in the lease were unenforceable anti-assignment provisions under § 365(f)(1) and that an assignment to A & E would not, as a matter of fact, disrupt the tenant mix.

The bankruptcy court held an evidentiary hearing and made the following factual findings, which we accept. The West Town shopping center is in an urban area (Chicago) where only fifty-nine percent of the population own cars. The shopping center is surrounded by competing shopping areas not owned by West Town. The twenty-five tenants in West Town Center include clothing stores, food vendors, a K-Mart, a laundromat, a travel agency, a bank, a cash advance (or small loan) agency, an adult entertainment outlet, and a public library branch. Trak Auto was the shopping center's only auto parts retailer, but there are seven auto parts retailers within three miles of the center. After announcing its factual findings, the bankruptcy court issued its conclusions. First, the court concluded that the lease's use restrictions amounted to anti-assignment provisions that were prohibited by § 356(f)(1) of the Bankruptcy Code. Second, the court concluded that West Town did not present sufficient evidence to support a finding that assignment of the lease to A & E would disrupt the tenant mix at West Town Center. Based on these conclusions, the bankruptcy court entered an order granting Trak Auto's motion to assume the West Town lease and, in turn, to assign it to A & E.

West Town filed a notice of appeal to the district court, and the bankruptcy court stayed its order pending appeal. The district court affirmed, and West Town then appealed to our court. We have also granted a stay. On October 7, 2003, three weeks before oral argument, West Town filed a motion to dismiss its own appeal as moot, arguing that its lease to Trak Auto had expired by its own terms on September 30, 2003. We deferred a ruling on the motion, which we take up now. * * *

### III.

Today's substantive issue requires us to deal with the conflict between two provisions in § 365 of the Bankruptcy Code dealing with the assignment of a lease by a debtor (or trustee). Section 365(b)(3)(C) specifically requires a debtor-tenant at a shopping center to assign its store lease subject to any provision restricting the use of the premises. On the other hand, § 365(f)(1) generally allows a debtor to assign its lease notwithstanding a provision restricting assignment. In this case, the bankruptcy court permitted Trak Auto to assign its shopping center lease to the highest bidder, refusing to enforce the restriction that required the premises to be used for the retail sale of auto parts and accessories. The district court affirmed. The legal issue is dispositive of this appeal, and we (like the district court) review the bankruptcy court's legal conclusions de novo. We hold that § 365(b)(3)(C) controls in this case. This means that the bankruptcy court erred in permitting Trak Auto to assign its lease to an apparel merchandiser that would not honor the use restriction. Our analysis follows.

Section 365(a) allows a Chapter 11 debtor to assume an unexpired lease. § 365(a). The debtor may, in turn, assign the lease if the assignee provides "adequate assurance of future performance." *Id.* § 365(f)(2)(B). When a debtor-tenant in a shopping center seeks to assign its lease, the "adequate assurance of future performance" must include specific assurances that are spelled out in the Code. Most important to this case, there must be adequate assurance that assignment of a shopping center lease "is subject to all the provisions thereof, including (but not limited to) provisions such as a radius, location, use, or exclusivity provision, and will not breach any such provision contained in any other lease, financing agreement, or master agreement relating to such shopping center." *Id.* § 365(b)(3)(C). Section 365(f)(1), on the other hand, contains a general provision that prohibits the enforcement in bankruptcy of anti-assignment clauses in leases. This section allows a debtor to assign a lease "notwithstanding a provision. . . that prohibits, restricts, or conditions. . . assignment." *Id.* § 365(f)(1). Again, we must decide whether Congress intends, notwithstanding § 365(f)(1), for a debtor's assignee to provide adequate assurance that it will comply with use restrictions in a shopping center lease, such as the restriction here that limits the use of the space to the sale of auto parts and accessories.

We begin our inquiry with a look at the interesting history of Congress's efforts to protect shopping center landlords in § 365(b)(3) of the Bankruptcy Code. Congress has been interested in the financial well-being of shopping centers since at least the late 1970s. Specifics, such as the importance of a carefully selected tenant mix, have not escaped Congress's attention. The House Judiciary Committee discussed the tenant mix subject in a 1977 report:

> A shopping center is often a carefully planned enterprise, and though it consists of nuemrous [sic] individual tenants, the center is planned as a single unit, often subject to a master lease or financing agreement. Under these agreements, the tenant mix in a shopping center may be as important to the lessor as the actual promised rental payments, because certain mixes will attract higher patronage of the stores in the center.

H.R.Rep. No. 95-595, at 348 (1977), U.S.Code Cong. & Admin.News 1977 at 5963, 6305. To maintain proper tenant mix, that is, store variety, shopping center landlords have routinely placed use restrictions in leases. Before 1978 the bankruptcy of a shopping center tenant with a use restriction did not present an inordinate problem for a landlord; the typical lease provided that the landlord could terminate the lease if the tenant went bankrupt. The termination option allowed the landlord to engage a new tenant that would contribute to an acceptable mix of stores. *See* Jeffrey S. Battershall, *Commercial Leases and Section 365 of the Bankruptcy Code,* 64 Am. Bankr.L.J. 329, 329 (1990). With the enactment of the Bankruptcy Reform Act of 1978 (the 1978 Act), however, landlords "were no longer able to regain control of the leased property in the event of bankruptcy, and the lease routinely became part of the debtor's estate to be administered" in the bankruptcy. *Id.* at 330. *See* § 365(e). Still, shopping center landlords were able to persuade Congress that they needed special protection, which Congress attempted to write into the 1978 Act. The 1978 legislation provided that a debtor-tenant could not assign its shopping center lease unless there was adequate assurance that "assignment of [the] lease [would] not breach *substantially* any provision, such as a radius, location, use, or exclusivity provision, *in any other* lease, financing agreement, or master agreement relating to such shopping center." § 365(b)(3) (1982) (emphases added).

Shopping center landlords soon realized that the 1978 provisions did not provide them with sufficient protection against debtor-tenant lease assignments that were being made in breach of use (and other) restrictions, with the approval of bankruptcy courts. For example, debtors avoided the 1978 provisions by convincing bankruptcy courts that an assignment would not "breach substantially" a use, radius, location, or exclusivity provision in another lease. *See id.* § 365(b)(3)(C) (1982). And, debtors were able to convince courts that even though an assignment would breach a use provision in the lease sought to be assigned, the assignment could proceed because the 1978 Act only prevented assignment if *some other* lease or agreement relating to the shopping center would be breached. *See id.* Shopping center landlords were, as a result, able to convince Congress that bankruptcy courts were too often "creating new [shopping center] leases by changing essential lease terms to facilitate assignments" by debtor-tenants. 130 Cong. Rec. S8891 (daily ed. June 29, 1984) (statement of Sen. Hatch), *reprinted in* 1984 U.S.C.C.A.N. 590, 600. Congress was told that this practice of avoiding use restrictions was creating problems with tenant mix in affected shopping centers. These locations were losing their balance-of-merchandise drawing card, which was a threat to overall sales revenues in the shopping center sector of the economy. *See* Battershall, *supra*, at 334-35.

Congress responded in 1984 by amending the shopping center provisions in the Bankruptcy Code. Among other things, § 365(b)(3)(C) was amended to delete the word "substantially" from the provision previously requiring that assignment of a shopping center lease must not "breach substantially" certain restrictions. This section was also amended to provide that any assigned shopping center lease would remain subject to all of the provisions of the lease and not just the provisions of "any other lease" relating to the center. Again, the amended provision that we interpret today provides: "adequate assurance of future performance of a lease of real property in a shopping center includes adequate assurance. . . that assumption or assignment of such lease is subject to all the provisions thereof, including (but not limited to) provisions such as a radius, location, use, or exclusivity provision." § 365(b)(3).

This background brings us to the matter of resolving the conflict between § 365(f)(1) , a general provision that permits lease assignment notwithstanding anti-assignment clauses, and § 365(b)(3)(C), a more specific provision that requires the assignee of a shopping center lease to honor a clause restricting the use of the premises. For guidance in sorting out the conflict, we turn to the canons of statutory construction. When two provisions in a statute are in conflict, "a specific [provision] closely applicable to the substance of the controversy at hand controls over a more generalized provision." *Sigmon Coal Co. v. Apfel*, 226 F.3d 291, 302 (4th Cir.2000) (internal quotation marks and citation omitted). *See also* Norman J. Singer, 2A Sutherland Statutes and Statutory Construction § 46:05 (6th ed.2000). Under this canon, § 365(b)(3)(C) controls because it speaks more directly to the issue, that is, whether a debtor-tenant assigning a shopping center lease must honor a straightforward use restriction. This construction is consistent with "the purpose[ ] Congress sought to serve." *Norfolk Redevelopment & Hous. Auth. v. Chesapeake & Potomac Tel. Co.*, 464 U.S. 30, 36 (1983) (internal quotation marks and citation omitted). Congress's purpose is clear from the history (recited above) that culminated in the 1984 shopping center amendments to the Bankruptcy Code and from the language of § 365(b)(3)(C) after those amendments. Specifically, when a shopping center lease is assigned in bankruptcy, Congress's purpose in § 365(b)(3)(C) is to preserve the landlord's bargained-for protections with respect to premises use and other matters that are spelled out in the lease with the debtor-tenant. *In re Ames Dep't Stores, Inc.*, 121 B.R. 160, 165 n. 4 (Bankr.S.D.N.Y.1990). We therefore hold that because A & E does not propose to take the West Town lease subject to the specific restriction limiting use of the premises to the sale of auto parts and accessories, Trak Auto's motion to assume and assign the lease must be denied. * * *

Our decision to block Trak Auto's lease assignment is not an attempt on our part to water down one of the important purposes of Chapter 11. That purpose is to give business debtors with some prospects the opportunity to reorganize, revive their operations, and continue in existence. The assumption and assignment of leases can be an important part of this effort. *See In re Shangra-La, Inc.*, 167 F.3d 843, 849 (4th Cir.1999). Shopping center leases are in a special category, however, because Congress has made it more difficult for debtor-tenants to assign these leases in Chapter 11. This special protection for shopping center landlords, as spelled out in § 365(b)(3)(C), dictates the result in today's case. But this does not mean that § 365(f)(1) can never be used to invalidate a clause prohibiting or restricting assignment in a shopping center lease. *But see In re Joshua Slocum Ltd.*, 922 F.2d 1081, 1090 (3d Cir.1990) (concluding that § 365(b)(3) (1982) rendered § 365(f)(1) inapplicable to shopping center leases). A shopping center lease provision designed to prevent any assignment whatsoever might be a candidate for the application of § 365(f)(1). For example, Senator Hatch, in explaining the 1984 amendment to § 365(b)(3)(C), said that the "amendment is not intended to enforce requirements to operate under a specified trade name." 130 Cong. Rec. S8891 (daily ed. June 29, 1984), *reprinted in* 1984 U.S.C.C.A.N. 590, 600. Senator Hatch's comment suggests that Congress did not intend to make § 365(f)(1) completely inapplicable to shopping center leases. Of course, the issue of when § 365(f)(1) might apply is a subject for some future case.

## IV.

In conclusion, we deny West Town's motion to dismiss this appeal as moot. On the merits, we hold that because A & E does not propose to take the West Town lease subject to the restriction limiting premises use to the retail sale of auto parts and accessories, Trak Auto's motion in bankruptcy court to assume and assign the lease must be denied under § 365(b)(3)(C). * * *

# CHAPTER 7

# THE AVOIDING POWERS OF THE TRUSTEE

## A. PREFERENCES

### 1. THE CONCEPT OF A PREFERENCE

Since an insolvent debtor cannot pay all unsecured creditors in full, transfer of property of the debtor to pay or secure the obligations of some creditors may result in preferring those creditors at the expense of others. The transfer, defined in § 101(54), may be payment of a debt in cash or in kind or it may be the granting of a security interest in the debtor's property to secure a previously existing debt. Sometimes the transfer is involuntary. This might occur if a creditor acquires a judicial lien in the debtor's property under a writ of execution or attachment. For the most part, the obtaining of an advantage by one creditor over another in this manner is valid under nonbankruptcy law. State debt Setofcollection law is characterized by a race of diligence among creditors. The first to obtain an interest in the debtor's property is paid in full to the extent of that interest.

In a bankruptcy liquidation secured claims are satisfied first. Then unsecured claims are paid according to a system of priorities stated in § 507. With some exceptions stated in § 726, unsecured claims without priority are paid pro rata. This scheme of distribution cannot be altered by the debtor or creditors after bankruptcy commences. The debtor's property becomes property of the estate under the control of the bankruptcy court, and creditors are prohibited by the automatic stay from taking any action under nonbankruptcy law to obtain payment of their claims. § 362. But the distribution contemplated by the Bankruptcy Code can be frustrated by transactions occurring before bankruptcy. For example, an unsecured creditor who would receive ten cents on the dollar in the impending bankruptcy of the debtor might try to avert that result by obtaining a judicial lien in the debtor's property before the debtor can file the petition in bankruptcy. Or, the debtor might voluntarily favor an unsecured creditor by paying the debt in some measure greater than ten cents on the dollar.

Section 547 is designed to undo certain prebankruptcy transactions the effect of which is to frustrate the distribution scheme set forth in § 726. It allows the trustee in bankruptcy to avoid certain transfers of the debtor's property. These transfers are known as voidable preferences. The five elements of a voidable preference are set forth in § 547(b). Subsection § 547(c) insulates from avoidance certain transfers that are within the definition of voidable preference under subsection (b), but that are deemed not to violate the policy that § 547 is designed to carry out. Section 547(b)(3) provides that the debtor must be insolvent at the time of the transfer. Section 547(f) creates a presumption that the debtor was insolvent during the 90 days immediately preceding the date of filing of the petition in bankruptcy. This means that the recipient of the preference must come forward with some evidence to rebut the presumption. If the presumption is rebutted, the trustee must prove insolvency by a preponderance of the evidence. With respect to § 547(c) defenses, the burden of proof is on the recipient of the preference who is seeking to make out an affirmative defense to liability, § 547(g).

If the trustee in bankruptcy avoids a preferential transfer under § 547(b), the result is that the property transferred to the creditor can be recovered for the benefit of the estate. § 550(a). If the preference occurred when the debtor paid a debt in cash, the trustee is entitled to recover an equivalent amount, which then becomes part of the bankruptcy estate. § 541(a)(3). Suppose the preference occurred when the creditor obtained a lien in the debtor's property to secure the debt either by voluntary act of the debtor, as in the case of a security interest, or against the will of the debtor, as in the case of a judicial lien. Avoidance of a preferential lien usually means that the creditor's lien is nullified, and, if the lien is in property of the estate, the effect of nullification is to increase the value of the estate in the amount of the nullified lien.

The effect of avoidance of a preferential lien may be more complex if there is more than one lien in the property. Assume Blackacre is property of the bankruptcy estate and is worth $150,000. Blackacre is burdened by two liens that are both valid outside of bankruptcy. One lien is held by Creditor A who is owed $100,000 and the other is held by Creditor B who is also owed $100,000. Because the value of Blackacre is less than the amount of debt secured by the liens, Blackacre has no value to the bankruptcy estate unless one or both of the liens can be avoided in bankruptcy. Assume that under the nonbankruptcy law the lien of Creditor A has priority over the lien of Creditor B. Because Creditor A, as senior lienor, is entitled to full payment from the proceeds of a foreclosure sale of Blackacre before Creditor B receives anything, Creditor B's lien is worth only $50,000. Make a third assumption: the lien of Creditor A is avoidable under § 547(b) while the lien of Creditor B is indefeasible in bankruptcy.

If the lien of Creditor A is nullified by avoidance under § 547(b), the effect is to benefit Creditor B because Creditor B's lien becomes the only lien in Blackacre. Before nullification, the junior lien of Creditor B had a value of $50,000; after nullification, it has a value of $100,000. Nullification also means that the value of the estate's interest in Blackacre is increased from zero to $50,000. But the purpose of allowing the trustee to avoid preferential transfers is to benefit the estate, *i.e.*, to increase the value of the estate for the benefit of creditors with unsecured claims who are paid from property of the estate. In this case that purpose has been satisfied only in part. If avoidance of the $100,000 lien of Creditor A means that the lien is nullified, the avoidance results in a benefit of only $50,000 to the estate. To the extent the effect of avoidance is to shift the benefit from one lien creditor to another lien creditor, the purpose of preference law to benefit the estate is not fully carried out. Section 551 addresses that problem by providing that the "transfer avoided * * * is preserved for the benefit of the estate." The "transfer avoided" is Creditor A's lien. That lien is automatically "preserved," that is, it is artificially treated as though it had not been nullified. Section 551 treats the lien as having been taken away from Creditor A and given to the bankruptcy estate. In effect, the bankruptcy estate is subrogated to the rights of Creditor A with respect to the lien under the nonbankruptcy law. Thus, by virtue of § 551, Creditor B's status as holder of a junior lien is not changed by the avoidance of Creditor A's lien. Creditor B is entitled to receive only $50,000, the value of the junior lien before the avoidance occurred. The remaining $100,000 value of Blackacre is retained by the bankruptcy estate.

## PROBLEMS

**1.** On May 1, Smith was indebted to Jones on an overdue unsecured loan made the previous year. On that date Smith paid Jones cash equal to the amount due on the loan. At the time of payment Smith had other unpaid debts that exceeded Smith's assets. On July 15, Smith filed a petition in bankruptcy under Chapter 7.

(a) Is the trustee in bankruptcy entitled to recover from Jones the amount received from Smith? § 547(b) and § 550(a). Does it matter whether Jones knew of Smith's financial condition when Jones received payment? Who has the burden of proving that Smith was insolvent? § 101 ("insolvent") and § 547(f) and (g)?

(b) Suppose that on May 1 Smith had not paid the loan and that Jones on that date had obtained a prejudgment attachment lien on business property of Smith with a value exceeding the amount due on the loan. At the time of filing in bankruptcy on July 15, Smith's assets included the property on which Jones had an attachment lien. What are the rights of the trustee in bankruptcy? § 547(b) and § 101(54) ("transfer").

**2.** Bank made a one-year loan of $10,000 to Debtor on September 1, 2005, and to secure the loan Debtor granted Bank a security interest in equipment owned by Debtor. Bank promptly perfected by filing a financing statement. On September 1, 2006 Debtor paid Bank $10,000 plus interest in discharge of the debt. Debtor filed a petition in bankruptcy on November 1, 2006. Debtor was insolvent on September 1, 2006 and at all times thereafter. Assume that the value of the equipment was greater than the payment made to Bank and that there were no other security interests or liens in the equipment superior to the security interest of Bank. Can the transfer be avoided by the trustee in bankruptcy under § 547(b)? What is the effect of § 547(b)(5)? Would the outcome of the case be different if Bank had been undersecured at the time it received payment from Debtor?

## 2. TRANSFER OF DEBTOR'S INTEREST IN PROPERTY AND THE "EARMARKING" DOCTRINE

Section 547(b) allows the trustee to avoid only transfers of property of the debtor's estate. Questions have arisen over the applicability of § 547(b) when creditors of the debtor have been paid from funds supplied by third parties. The following Problems explore these issues. *Collier on Bankruptcy* at ¶ 547.03[2] (15th ed. rev. 2004) states the guiding principle to be: "The fundamental inquiry is whether the transfer diminished or depleted the debtor's estate."

## PROBLEMS

In each of the following Problems, you may assume that the transfer would have been preferential under § 547 if there had been a transfer of an interest of the debtor in the property.

**1.** D's obligation to C was guaranteed by Guarantor. The contract of guaranty allowed Guarantor to seek reimbursement from D for any payments made on its behalf but granted Guarantor no security interest in D's assets to secure D's reimbursement obligation. When D defaulted on its obligation, Guarantor paid C. May D's trustee in bankruptcy avoid the transfer to C? *In re Corland Corp.*, 967 F.2d 1069 (5th Cir.1992), held that payments on the guaranty were not property of the estate because the funds came from Guarantor and not from D. In view of the fact that D became liable to reimburse Guarantor for the amount of its payment, do you agree with the holding in *Corland*? What if Guarantor's reimbursement claim were secured by property of D?

**2.** D owes C1, C2 and C3 $10,000 each. D obtains a loan from Bank and directs Bank to disburse the loan proceeds by making direct payments of D's debts to C1, C2 and C3. Is there a preference in this case? Has there been a depletion of D's estate?

**3.** D obtains a loan from Bank of $30,000 for the specific purpose of paying its debts to C1, C2 and C3. Bank disburses the loan proceeds by depositing them in D's account in Bank on July 1, and D pays the three creditors by checks drawn on the account on July 2. Has there been a depletion of D's estate?

––––––

Some courts recognize what is called the "earmarking" doctrine and hold that there is no preference in Problem 3 even though while the funds were in D's account D clearly had the power to divert the funds to purposes other than payment to the three creditors and the funds were subject to D's creditors. These courts purport to cut through form to substance and focus on the reality that functionally the transactions in Problems 2 and 3 are the same. In *In re Superior Stamp & Coin Co., Inc.*, 223 F.3d 1004 (9th Cir. 2000), the court justified its holding that there was no preference in a case resembling Problem 3 by stating that even though D was given the *power* to divert the funds it did not have the *right* to do so; hence, D never had *control* of the funds. But are Problems 2 and 3 the same? The earmarking doctrine has been controversial. What policy is served by protecting the preferred creditors (C1, C2 and C3) in cases like Problem 3 at the expense of other creditors of D? *See In re Moses*, 256 B.R. 641, 647 (B.A.P. 10th Cir. 2000), ("[A]pplication of the earmarking doctrine * * * serves to *prefer* the old creditor, the creditor who was likely clamoring for payment. * * * Such a preference is the essence of what § 547(b) was enacted to prevent."); *In re Ludford Fruit Prod., Inc.*, 99 B.R. 18, 21 (Bankr. C.D.Cal. 1989) ("Common sense is stretched to the breaking point when a court finds that funds loaned to a debtor, even for the specified purpose of paying an existing creditor, do not become property of the debtor.")

### 3.  THE PREFERENCE PERIOD

Under § 547(b)(4) a transfer cannot be a voidable preference unless it occurs within what can be called the "preference period." If the transferee is an insider, defined in § 101(31), the preference period is the one year before the date of the filing of the petition in bankruptcy. If the transferee is not an insider, the preference period is the 90 days before the filing of the petition. The same standards for avoidance apply to both insiders and other transferees. The only difference is that the preference period for insiders is longer. We consider the question of preferences to insiders in connection with the material on fraudulent transfers later in this chapter.

There is some confusion concerning how the preference period is calculated. For example, in the case of the 90–day period, the language of the statute suggests that you count back from the date of the petition 90 calendar days excluding the date of the filing of the petition. Thus, if a petition is filed on June 1, the preference period would start on March 3. The statutory period is controlled by Bankruptcy Rule 9006(a), which is identical to Federal Rule of Civil Procedure 6(a), and the meaning of the rule is not completely clear. It provides that "the day of the act, event, or default from which the designated period of time begins to run shall not be included" but the last day of the period shall be included unless it is a Saturday, Sunday or a legal holiday. In that case the period is extended until the next day that is not a Saturday, Sunday or legal holiday.

The court in *In re Nelson Co.*, 959 F.2d 1260 (3d Cir.1992), held that the "event" referred to in Rule 9006(a) is the filing of the petition not the transfer, and said:

> Our research indicates that no other court of appeals has yet to address this issue in a published opinion. The majority view of district courts and bankruptcy courts faced with the necessity of calculating the 90–day preferential period do so by calculating backward from the

date of the filing of the petition in bankruptcy. * * * A minority of courts have calculated the 90–day period from the date of the transfer. 959 F.2d at 1266 n.6.

## 4. PREFERENCES IN EXEMPT PROPERTY

Suppose Debtor, just before bankruptcy, had only two assets: Asset A, which was property not exempt under § 522(b), and Asset B, which was exempt under § 522(b). Debtor had four nonpriority unsecured creditors each of whom had a claim for $10,000. Assume that each of the four creditors files a timely proof of claim in bankruptcy, that Asset A and Asset B comprise the bankruptcy estate, and that Asset A and Asset B each has a value of $10,000 net of any expenses of disposition or bankruptcy administration. Each creditor will receive $2,500, one fourth of the proceeds of sale of Asset A. Asset B will be turned over to Debtor.

**Case #1.** Suppose Asset A had been conveyed to Creditor #1 just before bankruptcy in payment of the $10,000 debt owing to Creditor #1. This would have been a voidable preference. If the transfer is not avoided, Creditor #1 will have been paid in full and the other three creditors will receive nothing. Avoidance of the transfer clearly benefits the estate.

**Case #2.** Suppose the $10,000 debt to Creditor #1 had been paid just before bankruptcy by a conveyance of Asset B rather than Asset A. As a result of the transfer Creditor #1 has been paid in full. Creditor #1 has clearly been preferred over the other three creditors. Is the transfer a voidable preference? Have the other three creditors been hurt? If the transfer to Creditor #1 is not avoided, only $30,000 of claims will be made in bankruptcy and Asset A, worth $10,000, will be available to pay them. Thus, each of the three creditors will receive $3,333.33 rather than the $2,500 that they would have received if no transfer had been made to Creditor #1. Should a preference that benefited all creditors be voidable? The answer to this question may depend upon what happens to Asset B if it is recovered as a preference by the trustee. If Debtor can claim it as exempt property, recovery results in a net loss to all four creditors. Property of the estate is not increased. Each creditor will receive $2,500, an amount less than each would have received if the transfer had not been avoided. If the recovery is for the benefit of the estate, that is, Debtor cannot claim Asset B as exempt, the property of the estate is increased by $10,000. This increase is shared equally by all four creditors with each receiving $5,000.

Under the Bankruptcy Act, the prevailing view was that there was no preference in Case #2 because the transfer of exempt property did not deplete Debtor's estate; Creditors had no right to proceed against Asset B and its transfer did not concern them. *Rutledge v. Johansen*, 270 F.2d 881 (10th Cir.1959).Courts speak of this as the "no harm, no foul" view. How should Case #2 be decided under the Bankruptcy Code? § 547(b), § 541(a)(1) and (3), and § 522(b). If the exempt property is recovered, is the recovery for the benefit of the debtor or for the benefit of the estate? § 550(a) and § 522(g) and (h). These issues are discussed in 1 David G. Epstein, Steve H. Nickles & James J. White, *Bankruptcy* § 6–6 (1993). Potentially exempt property may be the subject of a fraudulent transfer. In *Tavenner v. Smoot*, 257 F.3d 401 (4th Cir.2001), the court took the majority view that transfers of potentially exempt property are amenable to avoidance and recovery. It stated that § 522(g) "apparently anticipates this result. That statute permits the debtor to exempt property recovered by the trustee under certain circumstances, namely if the debtor could have exempted such property had it not been transferred and if the transfer was involuntary and the debtor did not attempt to conceal the property. Section 522(g) is, thus, premised on the notion that a bankruptcy trustee can avoid the transfer of exemptible property and recover the property." 257 F.3d at 406.

## 5. CONTEMPORANEOUS EXCHANGES

One element of a voidable preference is that the transfer be "for or on account of an antecedent debt." § 547(b)(2). Thus, if an insolvent buyer buys goods and pays for them at the time of sale by transferring money or other property to the seller, there is no preference because the buyer's obligation to pay for the goods and the transfer of the buyer's property to satisfy the obligation arise contemporaneously. But suppose there is a short delay between the time the obligation is incurred and the payment of the obligation. Does the short delay make the debt antecedent? The issue was considered by the Supreme Court in the case of *Dean v. Davis*, 242 U.S. 438 (1917). On September 3 the debtor obtained a loan from Dean on the debtor's promise to secure the loan by a mortgage on all of his property. The proceeds of the loan were used by the debtor to pay a debt owed to a bank. The mortgage was executed on September 10 and recorded the next day. Within a few days a petition for involuntary bankruptcy was filed against the debtor. The trustee in bankruptcy brought an action to set aside the mortgage. Both the district court and the court of appeals held that the mortgage was voidable as a fraudulent conveyance. The court of appeals also held that the mortgage could be avoided as a preference under § 60b of the Bankruptcy Act. The Supreme Court, in reversing the court of appeals on the latter point stated:

The mortgage was not voidable as a preference under § 60b. Preference implies paying or securing a pre-existing debt of the person preferred. The mortgage was given to secure Dean for a substantially contempory advance. The bank, not Dean, was preferred. The use of Dean's money to accomplish this purpose could not convert the transaction into a preferring of Dean, although he knew of the debtor's insolvency.

242 U.S. at 443.

Section 547(c)(1) codifies this holding of the Supreme Court: if the parties intend a contemporaneous exchange of a loan for a mortgage and the transfer of the debtor's property represented by the mortgage is delayed only a short time, the exchange is substantially contemporaneous and the mortgage cannot be avoided. Does this analysis apply to the Problems that follow?

## PROBLEMS

**1.** Bank made an unsecured demand loan to Debtor on the morning of April 1. Bank believed that Debtor was financially sound. Later that day Bank received a credit report indicating that Debtor was in financial difficulty and might be insolvent. Bank immediately talked to Debtor who acknowledged the truth of the credit report. When Bank demanded immediate repayment of the loan, Debtor offered instead to secure the loan by a mortgage on real property worth more than the amount of the loan. Bank agreed, and the mortgage was executed on the evening of April 1 and recorded the next day. If Debtor was insolvent on April 1 and filed a petition in bankruptcy on June 1, can the mortgage be avoided as a preference? § 547(b) and § 547(c)(1). *Nat'l City Bank v. Hotchkiss*, 231 U.S. 50 (1913).

**2.** On April 1, Bank loaned $10,000 to Debtor by crediting that amount to Debtor's checking account. The loan agreement signed on that day provided that the $10,000 would be used to buy certain described equipment in which Debtor granted a security interest to Bank. Bank filed a financing statement covering equipment of Debtor on April 1. On April 7, Debtor bought the equipment described in the loan agreement. On June 20, Debtor filed a petition in bankruptcy. Under § 547(e)(2) and (3), when did a transfer of property of Debtor occur? If Debtor was insolvent on April 1 and at all times thereafter, can Bank's security interest be avoided under § 547(b)? Is avoidance prevented under § 547(c)(1)? Is avoidance prevented under § 547(c)(3)? Would your answers be different if Debtor had acquired the equipment on April 30?

## 6. ORDINARY COURSE PAYMENTS

### a. Policy Basis of § 547(c)(2)

Preference law reflects the oft stated, though inconsistently followed, policy in favor of equal treatment of creditors. Justification for taking away from the preferred creditor an advantage that was lawfully obtained under nonbankruptcy law was often expressed in terms of unfair conduct by the debtor and the preferred creditor. We can find this notion as far back as the 16th century *Case of Bankrupts*, discussed in Chapter 1, in which the court stated " * * * there ought to be an equal distribution * * * but if, after the debtor becomes a bankrupt, he may prefer one * * * and defeat and defraud many other poor men of their true debts, it would be unequal and unconscionable, and a great defect in the law * * *." 76 Eng. Rep.441, 473 (K.B. 1584). The court was referring to the conduct of the debtor in that case, but in some cases the preferred creditor, because of a special relationship to the debtor, is able to obtain an advantage not obtainable by others.

The characterization of preference in terms of unconscionability or fraud has had an important influence on the development of preference law. The classic preference situation is that of a privileged creditor—perhaps an insider—with knowledge of and influence over the affairs of the debtor who, seeing that the debtor is sinking in insolvency, obtains payment from the debtor before the debacle becomes manifest. But the typical preference situation today, more often than not, does not fit this classic pattern. A debtor in trouble may try to hide insolvency and often succeeds for an extended period of time. The debtor pays bills as long as possible hoping that somehow the crisis will pass. Many, if not most, creditors who are paid shortly before bankruptcy are not taking advantage of any special status that they have and indeed may not be aware that the debtor is in any financial difficulty. Is there any basis for treating differently the creditor who takes payment of a debt knowing that other creditors will go unpaid and the creditor who receives payment without knowledge that it is being preferred over the others?

This distinction was made in the Bankruptcy Act. Under Bankruptcy Act § 60b a preferential transfer could be avoided by the trustee only if the creditor had at the time when the transfer was made "reasonable cause to believe that the debtor [was] insolvent." Under this standard the preferred creditor could lose the preference only if the creditor was on notice of the fact that receipt of property of the debtor would prejudice the rights of other creditors. Under the Bankruptcy Act preferential transfers resulting from judicial liens obtained against insolvent debtors within the four-month period before filing of the petition were separately treated by § 67a and were nullified. Although it was not necessary to prove that the creditor had reasonable cause to believe that the debtor was insolvent at the time the lien was obtained, any creditor who obtains a judicial lien is not an innocent recipient of payment of a debt. Debtors who allow their property to be subjected to judicial liens are frequently in financial difficulty, and judicial seizure of a debtor's property is often followed by bankruptcy. Thus, under the Bankruptcy Act a creditor whose preference was avoided usually had received notice that an advantage over other creditors was being obtained.

The Commission on the Bankruptcy Laws of the United States recommended to Congress that proof of "reasonable cause to believe" be eliminated as a requirement for the avoidance of a preference. The recommendation was adopted in § 547(b). The reasons for this change have been described as follows:

> The Commission on the Bankruptcy Laws of the United States, in its report submitted to Congress, was first to recommend the elimination of this requirement. During the congressional hearings that were held both on the bill prepared by the Commission and a companion bill, there was testimony critical of the former requirement. The criticism was twofold. First, it was said that reasonable cause to believe was an unnecessary burden to impose upon the trustee in bankruptcy. Invariably, the transferee alleged that he did not know or have reason to know that the debtor was insolvent, thus creating a litigable issue in every case, with the burden of proof resting on the trustee in bankruptcy. As a result, many preferential transfers were not avoided, thereby undermining a basic tenet of the bankruptcy law—equitable distribution of a debtor's assets among its unsecured creditors. Second, it was said that the requirement had no logical basis in the law of voidable preferences. The main elements of a preference were set forth in section 60a: (1) a transfer of the debtor's property, (2) made within four months before bankruptcy, (3) for an antecedent debt, (4) at a time when the debtor was insolvent, and (5) the effect of which was to permit the transferee to receive a greater portion of its debt than other creditors in the same class would receive. When one reviewed these elements, an intention on the part of the debtor, or intention or knowledge on the part of the creditor, seemed to be irrelevant factors.

Chaim J. Fortgang & Lawrence P. King, *The 1978 Bankruptcy Code: Some Wrong Policy Decisions*, 56 N.Y.U.L.Rev. 1148, 1165–1166 (1981).

In spite of the difficulties that the reasonable-cause-to-believe requirement may have caused, it also performed a useful function. Normally, in the 90–day period before bankruptcy, the debtor has paid many unsecured debts of a recurring nature as they become due. An individual debtor, for example, pays utility bills and credit card debts, and may be paying for previously rendered personal services such as those of doctors and dentists. A business debtor normally purchases inventory and supplies, as well as services of employees and other suppliers, on short-term unsecured credit which may call for payment for various periods of time ranging from 10 or 20 days to as long as six months. Under the Bankruptcy Act, preferential payments of this kind were not voidable because the creditor normally would not have any cause to believe that the debtor was insolvent. But under the Code, if the debtor is insolvent when payment is made, all payments become potential preferences if the debtor goes into bankruptcy within 90 days. Is that a desirable result?

One vital goal of any commercial law regime is certainty and finality of transactions. If large numbers of ordinary commercial transactions are subject to being upset by later legal proceedings, all such transactions become more expensive. There is general consensus in favor of avoiding preferences made in out-of-the-ordinary transactions in which a creditor seeks, and is given, favored treatment by a debtor in obvious financial difficulty. It is not so clear that transactions by an insolvent debtor in paying debts as they mature should be avoided solely because an incidental result is that the creditor that received payment was preferred over others who did not have the good fortune of being paid before bankruptcy. If a doctrine designed to obtain equality for all creditors interferes with normal commercial practices and significantly adds to the cost of ordinary commercial transactions, the cost of the equality may be too high.

In the Bankruptcy Code, Congress attempted to alleviate the effects of dropping the reasonable-cause-to-believe requirement by adopting § 547(c)(2). The purpose of that section was to insulate from avoidance preferential transfers resulting from certain ordinary course transactions of the type outlined above. As originally adopted, § 547(c)(2) read as follows:

(c) The trustee may not avoid under this section a transfer—

(2) to the extent that such transfer was—

    (A) in payment of a debt incurred in the ordinary course of business or financial affairs of the debtor and the transferee;

    (B) made not later than 45 days after such debt was incurred;

    (C) made in the ordinary course of business or financial affairs of the debtor and the transferee; and

    (D) made according to ordinary business terms;

The pre-2005 version of § 547(c)(2), was virtually identical to this provision except for the deletion of subparagraph (B), which required that payment be no more than 45 days after the debt was incurred. Pre–1984 § 547(c)(2) was effective in excluding from avoidance many ordinary course payments, but the 45–day provision in subparagraph (B) was deleted from the Code at the instance of participants in the commercial paper market and certain trade creditors who commonly dealt in 60–day or 90–day obligations. The effect of the deletion of the 45–day requirement has proved far broader than remedying an artificial distinction between certain types of commercial paper and certain trade creditors, as suggested by the following problem and case. In the 2005 Act, § 547(c)(2) was materially amended by making new subparagraphs (A) and (B) disjunctive rather than conjunctive. We refer to this important change *infra* at 368, 372.

## PROBLEM

Five years ago Debtor Corporation borrowed $400,000 from Bank to be used for working capital. The loan was unsecured. It bore interest payable monthly and had a maturity of 90 days. It was the understanding of the parties that the loan would be renewed at maturity from time to time for additional 90–day periods if the financial situation of Debtor was satisfactory to Bank. The loan was regularly renewed over the years and was increased from time to time as the business of Debtor expanded. At the most recent maturity date, the outstanding principal balance was $950,000. Shortly before the maturity date, Bank examined the financial affairs of Debtor and discovered that Debtor had suffered grave financial reversals during the previous 90 days. In fact, Bank determined that Debtor was not paying some of its creditors and was probably insolvent at that time. Bank requested that the loan be repaid at the due date, but Debtor was unable to pay. Bank and Debtor then entered into the following transaction on the due date of the loan: Debtor paid the monthly interest of about $11,500 and repaid $450,000 of the principal. Bank renewed the loan for its unpaid principal amount of $500,000 for an additional 90–day period, but the interest rate was increased substantially. The affairs of Debtor continued to decline. Debtor failed to make any further interest payments to Bank. Two months after the renewal, Debtor filed a petition in bankruptcy under Chapter 7. The trustee in bankruptcy brought an action against Bank to recover the $450,000 and $11,500 payments that Debtor had made to Bank when the loan was renewed. Is the trustee entitled to recover under § 547?

## Union Bank v. Wolas

Supreme Court of the United States, 1991.
502 U.S. 151.

■ Justice STEVENS delivered the opinion of the Court.

Section 547(b) of the Bankruptcy Code authorizes a trustee to avoid certain property transfers made by a debtor within 90 days before bankruptcy. The Code makes an exception, however, for transfers made in the ordinary course of business, § 547(c)(2). The question presented is whether payments on long-term debt may qualify for that exception.

On December 17, 1986, ZZZZ Best Co., Inc. (Debtor) borrowed seven million dollars from petitioner, Union Bank (Bank).[1] On July 8, 1987, the Debtor filed a voluntary petition under Chapter 7 of the Bankruptcy Code. During the preceding 90–day period, the Debtor had made two interest payments totalling approximately $100,000 and had paid a loan commitment fee of about $2,500 to the Bank. After his appointment as trustee of the Debtor's estate, respondent filed a complaint against the Bank to recover those payments pursuant to § 547(b).

The Bankruptcy Court found that the loans had been made "in the ordinary course of business or financial affairs" of both the Debtor and the Bank, and that both interest payments as well as the payment of the loan commitment fee had been made according to ordinary business terms and in the ordinary course of business. As a matter of law, the Bankruptcy Court concluded that the payments satisfied the requirements of § 547(c)(2) and therefore were not avoidable by the trustee. The District Court affirmed the Bankruptcy Court's summary judgment in favor of the Bank.

Shortly thereafter, in another case, the Court of Appeals held that the ordinary course of business exception to avoidance of preferential transfers was not available to long-term creditors. *In re CHG International, Inc.*, 897 F.2d 1479 (C.A.9 1990). In reaching that conclusion, the Court of Appeals relied primarily on the policies underlying the voidable preference provisions and the state of the law prior to the enactment of the 1978 Bankruptcy Code and its amendment in 1984. Thus, the Ninth Circuit concluded, its holding in *CHG International, Inc.* dictated a reversal in this case. The importance of the question of law decided by the Ninth Circuit, coupled with the fact that the Sixth Circuit had interpreted § 547(c)(2) in a contrary manner * * * persuaded us to grant the Bank's petition for certiorari. * * *

I

We shall discuss the history and policy of § 547 after examining its text. In subsection (b), Congress broadly authorized bankruptcy trustees to "avoid any transfer of an interest of the debtor in property" *if* five conditions are satisfied and *unless* one of seven exceptions defined in subsection (c) is applicable. In brief, the five characteristics of a voidable preference are that it (1) benefit a creditor; (2) be on account of antecedent debt; (3) be made while the debtor was insolvent; (4) be within 90 days before

---

[1] The Bankruptcy Court found that the Bank and Debtor executed a revolving credit agreement on December 16, 1986, in which the Bank agreed to lend the Debtor $7 million in accordance with the terms of a promissory note to be executed and delivered by the Debtor. * * * On December 17, 1986, the Debtor executed and delivered to the Bank a promissory note in the principal sum of $7 million. The promissory note provided that interest would be payable on a monthly basis and would accrue on the principal balance at a rate of .65% per annum in excess of the Bank's reference rate.

bankruptcy; and (5) enable the creditor to receive a larger share of the estate than if the transfer had not been made. Section 547 also provides that the debtor is presumed to have been insolvent during the 90–day period preceding bankruptcy. § 547(f). In this case, it is undisputed that all five of the foregoing conditions were satisfied and that the interest and loan commitment fee payments were voidable preferences unless excepted by subsection (c)(2).

The most significant feature of subsection (c)(2) that is relevant to this case is the absence of any language distinguishing between long-term debt and short-term debt. * * *

Instead of focusing on the term of the debt for which the transfer was made, subsection (c)(2) focuses on whether the debt was incurred, and payment made, in the "ordinary course of business or financial affairs" of the debtor and transferee. Thus, the text provides no support for respondent's contention that § 547(c)(2)'s coverage is limited to short-term debt, such as commercial paper or trade debt. Given the clarity of the statutory text, respondent's burden of persuading us that Congress intended to create or to preserve a special rule for long-term debt is exceptionally heavy. *United States v. Ron Pair Enterprises, Inc.*, 489 U.S. 235, 241–242 (1989). As did the Ninth Circuit, respondent relies on the history and the policies underlying the preference provision.

## II

The relevant history of § 547 contains two chapters, one of which clearly supports, and the second of which is not inconsistent with, the Bank's literal reading of the statute. Section 547 was enacted in 1978 when Congress overhauled the Nation's bankruptcy laws. The section was amended in 1984. For purposes of the question presented in this case, the original version of § 547 differed in one significant respect from the current version: it contained a provision that the ordinary course of business exception did not apply unless the payment was made within 45 days of the date the debt was incurred. That provision presumably excluded most payments on long-term debt from the exception. In 1984 Congress repealed the 45–day limitation but did not substitute a comparable limitation. * * *

Respondent contends that this amendment was intended to satisfy complaints by issuers of commercial paper[10] and by trade creditors[11] that

---

[10] Because payments to a commercial paper purchaser within 90 days prior to bankruptcy may be preferential transfers under § 547(b), a purchaser could be assured that the payment would not be avoided under the prior version of § 547(c)(2) only if the commercial paper had a maturity of 45 days or less. Commercial issuers thus complained that the 45–day limitation lowered demand for commercial paper with a maturity in excess of 45 days. * * *

[11] Trade creditors stated that normal payment periods in many industries exceeded 45 days and complained that the arbitrary 45–day limitation in § 547(c)(2) deprived these

regularly extended credit for periods of more than 45 days. Furthermore, respondent continues, there is no evidence in the legislative history that Congress intended to make the ordinary course of business exception available to conventional long-term lenders. Therefore, respondent argues, we should follow the analysis of the Ninth Circuit and read § 547(c)(2) as protecting only short-term debt payments. * * *

We need not dispute the accuracy of respondent's description of the legislative history of the 1984 amendment in order to reject his conclusion. For even if Congress adopted the 1984 amendment to redress particular problems of specific short-term creditors, it remains true that Congress redressed those problems by entirely deleting the time limitation in § 547(c)(2). The fact that Congress may not have foreseen all of the consequences of a statutory enactment is not a sufficient reason for refusing to give effect to its plain meaning. * * *

Respondent also relies on the history of voidable preferences prior to the enactment of the 1978 Bankruptcy Code. The text of the preference provision in the earlier Bankruptcy Act did not specifically include an exception for payments made in the ordinary course of business. The courts had, however, developed what is sometimes described as the "current expense" rule to cover situations in which a debtor's payments on the eve of bankruptcy did not diminish the net estate because tangible assets were obtained in exchange for the payment. * * * Without such an exception, trade creditors and other suppliers of necessary goods and services might have been reluctant to extend even short-term credit and might have required advance payment instead, thus making it difficult for many companies in temporary distress to have remained in business. Respondent argues that Congress enacted § 547(c)(2) in 1978 to codify that exception, and therefore the Court should construe § 547(c)(2) as limited to the confines of the current expense rule.

This argument is not compelling for several reasons. First, it is by no means clear that § 547(c)(2) should be construed as the statutory analogue of the judicially crafted current expense rule because there are other exceptions in § 547(c) that explicitly cover contemporaneous exchanges for new value.[13] Those provisions occupy some (if not all) of the territory previously covered by the current expense rule. Nor has respondent directed our attention to any extrinsic evidence suggesting that Congress intended to codify the current expense rule in § 547(c)(2).

---

trade creditors of the protection of the ordinary course of business exception to the trustee's power to avoid preferential transfers. * * *

[13] Thus, for example, § 547(c)(1) exempts a transfer to the extent that it was a "contemporaneous exchange for new value given to the debtor," and § 547(c)(4) exempts a transfer to a creditor "to the extent that, after such transfer, such creditor gave new value to or for the benefit of the debtor * * *."

The current expense rule developed when the statutory preference provision was significantly narrower than it is today. To establish a preference under the Bankruptcy Act, the trustee had to prove that the challenged payment was made at a time when the creditor had "reasonable cause to believe that the debtor [was] insolvent." 11 U.S.C. § 96(b) (1976 ed.). When Congress rewrote the preference provision in the 1978 Bankruptcy Code, it substantially enlarged the trustee's power to avoid preferential transfers by eliminating the reasonable cause to believe requirement for transfers made within 90 days of bankruptcy and creating a presumption of insolvency during that period. * * * At the same time, Congress created a new exception for transfers made in the ordinary course of business, § 547(c)(2). This exception was intended to "leave undisturbed normal financial relations, because it does not detract from the general policy of the preference section to discourage unusual action by either the debtor or his creditors during the debtor's slide into bankruptcy." H.R.Rep. No. 95–595, at 373.

In light of these substantial changes in the preference provision, there is no reason to assume that the justification for narrowly confining the "current expense" exception to trade creditors before 1978 should apply to the ordinary course of business exception under the 1978 Code. Instead, the fact that Congress carefully reexamined and entirely rewrote the preference provision in 1978 supports the conclusion that the text of § 547(c)(2) as enacted reflects the deliberate choice of Congress.[15]

### III

The Bank and the trustee agree that § 547 is intended to serve two basic policies that are fairly described in the House Committee Report. The Committee explained:

"A preference is a transfer that enables a creditor to receive payment of a greater percentage of his claim against the debtor than he would have received if the transfer had not been made and he had participated in the distribution of the assets of the bankrupt estate. The purpose of the preference section is two-fold. First, by permitting the trustee to avoid prebankruptcy transfers that occur within a short period before bankruptcy, creditors are discouraged from racing to the courthouse to dismember the debtor during his slide into bankruptcy. The protection thus afforded the debtor often enables him to work his

---

[15] Indeed, the House Committee Report concludes its discussion of the trustee's avoidance powers with the observation that the language in the preference section of the earlier Bankruptcy Act was "hopelessly complex" and had been "subject to varying interpretations. The bill undoes the numerous amendments that have been heaped on section 60 during the past 40 years, and proposes a unified and coherent section to deal with the problems created by prebankruptcy preferential transfers." H.R.Rep. No. 95–595, p. 179 (1977). Respondent's assumption that § 547(c)(2) was intended to preserve pre-existing law is at war with this legislative history.

way out of a difficult financial situation through cooperation with all of his creditors. Second, and more important, the preference provisions facilitate the prime bankruptcy policy of equality of distribution among creditors of the debtor. Any creditor that received a greater payment than others of his class is required to disgorge so that all may share equally. The operation of the preference section to deter "the race of diligence' of creditors to dismember the debtor before bankruptcy furthers the second goal of the preference section—that of equality of distribution."

Id., at 177–178.

As this comment demonstrates, the two policies are not entirely independent. On the one hand, any exception for a payment on account of an antecedent debt tends to favor the payee over other creditors and therefore may conflict with the policy of equal treatment. On the other hand, the ordinary course of business exception may benefit all creditors by deterring the "race to the courthouse" and enabling the struggling debtor to continue operating its business.

Respondent places primary emphasis, as did the Court of Appeals, on the interest in equal distribution. * * * When a debtor is insolvent, a transfer to one creditor necessarily impairs the claims of the debtor's other unsecured and undersecured creditors. By authorizing the avoidance of such preferential transfers, § 547(b) empowers the trustee to restore equal status to all creditors. Respondent thus contends that the ordinary course of business exception should be limited to short-term debt so the trustee may order that preferential long-term debt payments be returned to the estate to be distributed among all of the creditors.

But the statutory text—which makes no distinction between short-term debt and long-term debt—precludes an analysis that divorces the policy of favoring equal distribution from the policy of discouraging creditors from racing to the courthouse to dismember the debtor. Long-term creditors, as well as trade creditors, may seek a head start in that race. Thus, even if we accept the Court of Appeals' conclusion that the availability of the ordinary business exception to long-term creditors does not directly further the policy of equal treatment, we must recognize that it does further the policy of deterring the race to the courthouse and, as the House Report recognized, may indirectly further the goal of equal distribution as well. Whether Congress has wisely balanced the sometimes conflicting policies underlying § 547 is not a question that we are authorized to decide.

### IV

In sum, we hold that payments on long-term debt, as well as payments on short-term debt, may qualify for the ordinary course of business exception to the trustee's power to avoid preferential transfers. We express no opinion, however, on the question whether the Bankruptcy Court correctly concluded that the Debtor's payments of interest and the loan commitment fee qualify for the ordinary course of business exception, § 547(c)(2). In particular, we do not decide whether the loan involved in this case was incurred in the ordinary course of the Debtor's business and of the Bank's business, whether the payments were made in the ordinary course of business, or whether the payments were made according to ordinary business terms. These questions remain open for the Court of Appeals on remand.

The judgment of the Court of Appeals is reversed and the case is remanded for further proceedings consistent with this opinion.

It is so ordered.

■ Justice SCALIA, concurring.

I join the opinion of the Court, including Parts II and III, which respond persuasively to legislative-history and policy arguments made by respondent. It is regrettable that we have a legal culture in which such arguments have to be addressed (and are indeed credited by a Court of Appeals), with respect to a statute utterly devoid of language that could remotely be thought to distinguish between long-term and short-term debt. Since there was here no contention of a "scrivener's error" producing an absurd result, the plain text of the statute should have made this litigation unnecessary and unmaintainable.

## NOTES

**1.** The Court in *Wolas* does not rest its decision solely on the plain meaning of § 547(c)(2) but finds a policy justification for its decision as well. We explain in the introduction to this section that preference law is based on the creditor equality principle. However, § 547(c)(2) can be repugnant to the creditor equality principle in some cases. The fact that payments are made in ordinary course does not detract from the reality that they may deplete the debtor's estate for the benefit of the creditor receiving payment. If we can understand the basis for the § 547(c)(2) exception, it will be easier to decide whether it should apply to long-term debts. The *CHG International* case read § 547(c)(2) as restricted to short-term credit, thus making it consistent with the creditor equality principle. The court in that case said: "The rationale for both the old 'current expense' rule and for the section 547(c)(2) exception is the same: the payment does not diminish the estate, is not for antecedent debt, and allows the debtor to remain in business." 897 F.2d at 1483. The value given by the creditor and the payment made by the debtor soon after are viewed as a single transaction. Thus, the payment does not harm the other creditors. But this rationale requires that § 547(c)(2) be restricted to short-term trade debt. Section 547(c)(1) protects suppliers selling for cash; § 547(c)(2) protects those selling for short-term credit. In neither instance is the estate truly depleted. If § 547(c)(2) is to be justified as applying only to transactions that don't in substance deplete the estate, it cannot accommodate long-term credit.

**2.** Justice Stevens justifies the inclusion of long-term debt within the purview of § 547(c)(2) by identifying a second policy basis for preference law: to deter the race of diligence among creditors to dismember the debtor. If preference law can be relied on to reverse transfers made on the eve of bankruptcy, creditors will be less motivated to dismember a debtor who is in financial trouble. He states that § 547(c)(2) is consistent with this second policy basis. "[T]he ordinary course of business exception may benefit all creditors by deterring the 'race to the courthouse' and enabling the struggling debtor to continue operating its business." 502 U.S. at 161. Presumably, Justice Stevens is suggesting that the lure of possibly receiving a nonavoidable transfer in the ordinary course will encourage creditors who might otherwise take aggressive collection activity to desist. Viewed in this way, § 547(c)(2) discourages a race of diligence. We question, however, whether a rule making ordinary course payments nonrecoverable actually discourages collection. How many creditors faced with a sinking debtor will knowingly defer collection activity in the hope that (i) the debtor will voluntarily pay the patient creditor before filing bankruptcy, and (ii) such payment will later be found by a court to fall within the uncertain scope of the § 547(c)(2) ordinary course exception? On the other hand, how many arguably "racing" creditors (those with knowledge of the debtor's looming insolvency) who successfully collect payments within the preference period will assert the § 547(c)(2) defense and force the trustee to litigate these issues when they become preference defendants? If preferences generally become harder to recover because defendants routinely can create litigable issues under a broad ordinary course exception, then finding ways to receive preferences in the form of voluntary transfers from the debtor becomes even more attractive to creditors, not less. Commentators have thus questioned Justice Stevens's incentive rationale for the ordinary course exception. *See* Charles Jordan Tabb, *The Law of Bankruptcy* § 6.18 (1997).

**3.** The Court quotes the brief reference to § 547(c)(2) in the House Report, which said that the provision was intended to "leave undisturbed normal financial relations, because it does not detract from the general policy of the preference section to discourage unusual action by either the debtor or his creditors during the debtor's slide into bankruptcy." But the issue is whether payment by an insolvent debtor to a creditor holding a large long-term debt is payment in ordinary course. Although we know of no empirical evidence on the subject, we suspect that a very high percentage of payments made to creditors within the 90–day preference period are payments made in the good faith exercise of the debtor's business judgment concerning how to stay afloat. The debtor is more likely to pay creditors on whom the debtor is dependent and to defer payment to other creditors. There are costs associated with allowing bankruptcy trustees to upset completed transactions. Uncertainty about finality of payment is a disincentive on the part of credit grantors to deal with businesses in distress. In the introductory material to this section we suggest the view that preference law should balance the interest of creditor equality against the cost of upsetting normal transactions. The cost of creditor equality may sometimes be too high. Omitting the reasonable-cause-to-believe test in the Bankruptcy Code gave trustees greater power to upset normal transactions. Clearly § 547(c)(2) was intended to fill part of the gap left by this omission; it has a legitimate role to play in moderating the costs of preference law. The decision to include long-term debt in § 547(c)(2) may be right on policy grounds as well as under the plain meaning rule so long as the payment of the long term debt is in fact in ordinary course. The meaning of § 547(c)(2)(B) in this context was left open in *Wolas.*

### b.   Meaning of Ordinary Course under § 547(c)(2)

Courts have had no end of trouble in deciding what transfers § 547(c)(2) should protect. *Wolas* told us only that payments on long-term debt may qualify for the ordinary course of business exception, but offered no guidance on what ordinary course means. The 2005 Act amended § 547(c)(2) to allow the preferred creditor to defend on either the ground that the payment was in the ordinary course of business affairs of the parties *or* was in accordance with ordinary business terms. Formerly, as we see in *Tolona Pizza*, the defense required that both elements be satisfied to make out the defense. We include the case for its much cited holding on the meaning of ordinary course of business.

## In re Tolona Pizza Products Corp.

United States Court of Appeals, Seventh Circuit, 1993.
3 F.3d 1029.

■  POSNER, Circuit Judge.

When, within 90 days before declaring bankruptcy, the debtor makes a payment to an unsecured creditor, the payment is a "preference," and the trustee in bankruptcy can recover it and thus make the creditor take pot luck with the rest of the debtor's unsecured creditors. § 547. But there is an exception if the creditor can show that the debt had been incurred in the ordinary course of the business of both the debtor and the creditor, § 547(c)(2)(A); that the payment, too, had been made and received in the ordinary course of their businesses, § 547(c)(2)(B); and that the payment had been "made according to ordinary business terms." § 547(c)(2)(C). The first two requirements are easy to understand: *of course* to defeat the inference of preferential treatment the debt must have been incurred in the ordinary course of business of both debtor and creditor and the payment on account of the debt must have been in the ordinary course as well. But what does the third requirement—that the payment have been "made according to ordinary business terms"—add? And in particular does it refer to what is "ordinary" between this debtor and this creditor, or what is ordinary in the market or industry in which they operate? The circuits are divided on this question * * *.

Tolona, a maker of pizza, issued eight checks to Rose, its sausage supplier, within 90 days before being thrown into bankruptcy by its creditors. The checks, which totaled a shade under $46,000, cleared and as a result

Tolona's debts to Rose were paid in full. Tolona's other major trade creditors stand to receive only 13 cents on the dollar under the plan approved by the bankruptcy court, if the preferential treatment of Rose is allowed to stand. Tolona, as debtor in possession, brought an adversary proceeding against Rose to recover the eight payments as voidable preferences. The bankruptcy judge entered judgment for Tolona. The district judge reversed. He thought that Rose did not, in order to comply with § 547(c)(2)(C), have to prove that the terms on which it had extended credit to Tolona were standard terms in the industry, but that if this was wrong the testimony of Rose's executive vice-president, Stiehl, did prove it. The parties agree that the other requirements of § 547(c)(2) were satisfied.

Rose's invoices recited "net 7 days," meaning that payment was due within seven days. For years preceding the preference period, however, Tolona rarely paid within seven days; nor did Rose's other customers. Most paid within 21 days, and if they paid later than 28 or 30 days Rose would usually withhold future shipments until payment was received. Tolona, however, as an old and valued customer (Rose had been selling to it for fifteen years), was permitted to make payments beyond the 21–day period and even beyond the 28–day or 30–day period. The eight payments at issue were made between 12 and 32 days after Rose had invoiced Tolona, for an average of 22 days; but this actually was an improvement. In the 34 months before the preference period, the average time for which Rose's invoices to Tolona were outstanding was 26 days and the longest time was 46 days. Rose consistently treated Tolona with a degree of leniency that made Tolona (Stiehl conceded on cross-examination) one of a "sort of exceptional group of customers of Rose. . . fall[ing] outside the common industry practice and standards."

It may seem odd that paying a debt late would ever be regarded as a preference to the creditor thus paid belatedly. But it is all relative. A debtor who has entered the preference period—who is therefore only 90 days, or fewer, away from plunging into bankruptcy—is typically unable to pay all his outstanding debts in full as they come due. If he pays one and not the others, as happened here, the payment though late is still a preference to that creditor, and is avoidable unless the conditions of § 547(c)(2) are met. One condition is that payment be in the ordinary course of both the debtor's and the creditor's business. A late payment normally will not be. It will therefore be an avoidable preference.

This is not a dryly syllogistic conclusion. The purpose of the preference statute is to prevent the debtor during his slide toward bankruptcy from trying to stave off the evil day by giving preferential treatment to his most importunate creditors, who may sometimes be those who have been waiting longest to be paid. Unless the favoring of particular creditors is outlawed, the mass of creditors of a shaky firm will be nervous, fearing that one or a few of their number are going to walk away with all the firm's assets; and this fear may precipitate debtors into bankruptcy earlier than is socially desirable. * * *

From this standpoint, however, the most important thing is not that the dealings between the debtor and the allegedly favored creditor conform to some industry norm but that they conform to the norm established by the debtor and the creditor in the period before, preferably well before, the preference period. That condition is satisfied here—if anything, Rose treated Tolona more favorably (and hence Tolona treated Rose less preferentially) before the preference period than during it.

But if this is all that the third subsection of 547(c)(2) requires, it might seem to add nothing to the first two subsections, which require that both the debt and the payment be within the ordinary course of business of both the debtor and the creditor. For, provided these conditions are fulfilled, a "late" payment really isn't late if the parties have established a practice that deviates from the strict terms of their written contract. But we hesitate to conclude that the third subsection, requiring conformity to "ordinary business terms," has no function in the statute. We can think of two functions that it might have. One is evidentiary. * * * If the debtor and creditor dealt on terms that the creditor testifies were normal for them but that are wholly unknown in the industry, this casts some doubt on his (self-serving) testimony. Preferences are disfavored, and subsection C makes them more difficult to prove. The second possible function of the subsection is to allay the concerns of creditors that one or more of their number may have worked out a special deal with the debtor, before the preference period, designed to put that creditor ahead of the others in the event of bankruptcy. It may seem odd that allowing late payments from a debtor would be a way for a creditor to make himself more rather than less assured of repayment. But such a creditor does have an advantage during the preference period, because he can receive late payments then and they will still be in the ordinary course of business for him and his debtor.

The functions that we have identified, combined with a natural reluctance to cut out and throw away one-third of an important provision of the Bankruptcy Code, persuade us that the creditor must show that the payment he received was made in accordance with the ordinary business terms in the industry. But this does not mean that the creditor must establish the existence of some single, uniform set of business terms, as Tolona argues. * * * Not only is it difficult to identify the industry whose norm shall govern (is it, here, the sale of sausages to makers of pizza? The sale of sausages to anyone? The sale of anything to makers of pizza?), but there can be great variance in billing practices within an industry. Apparently there is in this industry, whatever exactly "this industry" is; for while it is plain that neither Rose nor its competitors enforce payment within seven days, it is unclear that there is a standard outer limit of forbearance. It seems that 21 days is a goal but that payment as late as 30 days is generally tolerated and that for good customers even longer delays are allowed. The average period between Rose's invoice and Tolona's payment during the preference period was only 22 days, which seems well within the industry norm, whatever exactly it is. The law should not push businessmen to agree upon a single set of billing practices; antitrust objections to one side, the relevant business and financial considerations vary widely among firms on both the buying and the selling side of the market.

We conclude that "ordinary business terms" refers to the *range* of terms that encompasses the practices in which firms similar in some general way to the creditor in question engage, and that only dealings so idiosyncratic as to fall outside that broad range should be deemed extraordinary and therefore outside the scope of subsection C. * * * Stiehl's testimony brought the case within the scope of "ordinary business terms" as just defined. Rose and its competitors pay little or no attention to the terms stated on their invoices, allow most customers to take up to 30 days to pay, and allow certain favored customers to take even more time. There is no single set of terms on which the members of the industry have coalesced; instead there is a broad range and the district judge plausibly situated the dealings between Rose and Tolona within it. These dealings are conceded to have been within the normal course of dealings between the two firms, a course established long before the preference period, and there is no hint either that the dealings were designed to put Rose ahead of other creditors of Tolona or that other creditors of Tolona would have been surprised to learn that Rose had been so forbearing in its dealings with Tolona.

Tolona might have argued that the district judge gave insufficient deference to the bankruptcy judge's contrary finding. The district judge, and we, are required to accept the bankruptcy judge's findings on questions of fact as long as they are not clearly erroneous. * * * But since Tolona did not argue that the district judge had applied an incorrect standard of review, we need not decide whether the district judge overstepped the bounds. Which is not to say that he did. While he did not intone the magic words "clear error," he may well have believed that the record as a whole left no doubt that Tolona's dealings with Rose were within the broad band of accepted practices in the industry. It is true that Stiehl testified that Tolona was one of an exceptional group of Rose's customers with whom Rose's dealings fell outside common industry practice. But the undisputed evidence concerning those dealings and the practices of the industry demonstrates that payment within 30 days is within the outer limits of normal industry practices, and the payments at issue in this case were made on average in a significantly shorter time.

The judgment reversing the bankruptcy judge and dismissing the adversary proceeding is

AFFIRMED.

■ FLAUM, Circuit Judge, dissenting. [opinion omitted]

## NOTE

*Tolona Pizza* minimizes the inquiry that a court must make into "ordinary business terms," and the 2005 Act goes further by giving the debtor the option of proving *either* that payment was made in ordinary course of the debtor's business *or* that it was made according to ordinary business terms. This is a good change; so long as the debtor is making payments in ordinary course of its business relationship between debtor and creditor, preference law is not offended; it should not grab back normal payments.

## 7. THE "SUBSEQUENT ADVANCE" RULE

Section 547(c)(4) creates a "shelter" rule in situations in which a creditor subsequently advances new value after receiving a payment on account of past debt that would otherwise be an avoidable preference. This subsection is designed for, and of special importance in, the case of running accounts between the debtor and its suppliers. In general, suppliers advance trade credit only up to a preset credit limit. As payments are received, commonly fresh credit is extended; this fresh credit ordinarily would not have been extended in the absence of the payment. Keeping these running accounts alive is of great importance to almost all businesses and especially distressed ones. Prior law permitted the creditor to offset all payments and advances made during the preference period in determining the creditor's net preference liability. *Jaquith v. Alden*, 189 U.S. 78 (1903) (adopting the so-called "net result rule"). Section 547(c)(4) is framed in somewhat narrower terms, limiting recovery of prior preferential payments to the extent that the preferred creditor has made subsequent unsecured advances. Applying this narrower "subsequent advance" rule, raises tricky problems, including the issue of repayment of subsequent advances with transfers that are themselves avoidable preferences. One of the earliest decisions on § 547(c)(4), *In re Bishop*, 17 B.R. 180 (Bankr.N.D.Ga.1982), stated the meaning of that section to be: "First, the creditor must extend new value * * * . Secondly, the new value must be unsecured. * * * Finally, the new value must go unpaid." 17 B.R. at 183. *Bishop*'s statement that the value must be "unpaid" has been widely cited as the majority view, but a growing line of cases, of which the following case is the most illuminating, have adopted a more nuanced analysis. *See* Charles Jordan Tabb, *The Law of Bankruptcy* § 6.20 (1997).

# In re IRFM, Inc.

United States Court of Appeals, Ninth Circuit, 1995.
52 F.3d 228.

■ BEEZER, Circuit Judge:

Robert P. Mosier, Chapter 7 Trustee, appeals the district court's grant of summary judgment in favor of creditor Ever–Fresh Food Company ("Ever–Fresh"). Mosier filed this action seeking recovery of $72,895.17 in preferential transfers from the Debtor, IRFM, Inc., to Ever–Fresh. The district court, affirming the bankruptcy court, held that Ever–Fresh was entitled to a full new value offset under section 547(c)(4), notwithstanding the fact that the new value did not remain unpaid.

* * * We affirm the judgment of the district court.

## I

IRFM was a retail grocery with several stores in the Southern California area. The grocery specialized in selling high quality fresh meats and produce to its customers, and charged the customers accordingly. IRFM expanded its operations to other areas of Southern California where the demand for high quality, high priced groceries was not great. As a result, IRFM suffered substantial losses.

Ever–Fresh was a supplier of fresh cheese and dairy products to IRFM. Ever–Fresh delivered the goods to IRFM on a weekly basis. IRFM often paid Ever–Fresh for these goods more than seven days after delivery, frequently writing one check for a series of invoices, and not in accordance with the terms of payment or industry standards.

In July, 1988, IRFM filed a voluntary Chapter 11 bankruptcy petition. This petition was converted to one under Chapter 7 in October 1989. The appointment of Mosier as trustee became final in November 1989.

During the ninety-day period immediately prior to bankruptcy, IRFM and Ever–Fresh engaged in the following transactions:[1]

---

[1] These transactions represent the amount of goods shipped by Ever–Fresh between each payment by IRFM.

| Check Date | Payment Amount | Goods Shipped |
|---|---|---|
| 25-Apr | $18,475.86 | |
| | | $18,849.16 |
| 2-May | $18,095.66 | |
| | | $33,063.18 |
| 11-May | $16,197.93 | |
| | | $16,197.93 |
| 16-May | $14,492.91 | |
| | | $17,280.78 |
| 23-May | $18,056.21 | |
| | | $20,590.11 |

| Check Date | Payment Amount | Goods Shipped |
|---|---|---|
| 30-May | $18,420.07 | |
| | | $23,056.79 |
| 6-Jun | $18,922.37 | |
| | | $17,436.51 |
| 13-Jun | $23,479.03 | |
| | | $15,967.54 |
| 20-Jun | $17,127.20 | |
| 22-Jul | | $113,566.47 |
| **Totals** | **$163,267.24** | **$276,008.47** |

Mosier filed this action in bankruptcy court seeking to avoid and recover $72,895.17 of the payments made by IRFM to Ever–Fresh under § 547. Mosier calculated this amount by first subtracting the total amount of the payments, $163,267.24, from $253,639.31, the amount he calculated as the total new value given by Ever–Fresh. The remainder, $90,372.07, Mosier argues is the amount of new value which remained "unpaid" at the time of bankruptcy and may be retained by Ever–Fresh. Mosier then subtracted this "unpaid" new value from the $163,267.24 in payments made by IRFM. Mosier contends that the resulting $72,895.17 is paid new value and may be avoided.[2]

The bankruptcy court, Judge John Ryan, rejected this argument and held that Ever–Fresh was entitled to a new value offset for the entire $163,267.24. In reaching this conclusion, the bankruptcy court held that new value need not remain unpaid. The district court affirmed this decision and granted summary judgment in favor of Ever–Fresh. Mosier now appeals.

\* \* \*

### III

A trustee is empowered to challenge every transfer made by a debtor to a creditor during the ninety day period immediately prior to the filing of a bankruptcy petition. § 547(b).[4] This avoidance power enables the trustee to protect the estate of the debtor and to ensure an equitable distribution among the unsecured creditors.

---

[2] In computing the amount he seeks to avoid, Mosier erroneously states that the total amount of new value given was $253,639.31. As the table indicates, the amount of new value given was actually $276,008.47. Using this figure and Mosier's method of calculating the allegedly avoidable amount, we arrive at an amount of "unpaid" new value of $112,741.23 and an allegedly avoidable amount of $50,526.01. At a hearing in the bankruptcy court on this issue, Mosier conceded that the $276,008.47 figure was correct and also conceded that the preference amount was approximately $50,000. Mosier's miscalculation is irrelevant to our decision, however, because we hold that Ever–Fresh is entitled to a full new value offset.

[4] \* \* \* For purposes of summary judgment, Mosier and Ever–Fresh agree that the transfers made by IRFM to Ever–Fresh constitute preferences under § 547(b).

Once the trustee has established that a transfer is a preference, a creditor may assert a defense to the preference under § 547(c). Ever–Fresh contends that it is entitled to a "new value" defense under section 547(c)(4). Ever–Fresh asserts that after each preferential transfer, it gave IRFM new value and thus may retain the transfers by IRFM. Mosier argues that in order to qualify for a new value defense a creditor must prove (1) the new value was given to the debtor after the preferential transfer; (2) that the new value is unsecured; and (3) that it remain unpaid. Ever–Fresh has satisfied the first two elements. The parties contest the operation of the third.

For support of his position, Mosier relies upon language in cases to the effect that new value must remain unpaid. While this is the literal holding of these cases, these cases did not intend to reach the result urged by Mosier in this case.[5] More importantly, Mosier's argument is contrary to both the language of section 547(c)(4) and the legislative history of the Bankruptcy Code. The following analysis of the language of section 547(c)(4) demonstrates why Mosier's position is erroneous.

### A

Section 547(c)(4) of the Bankruptcy Code provides:

The trustee may not avoid under this section a transfer which—

**(4)** to or for the benefit of a creditor, to the extent that, after such transfer, such creditor gave new value to or for the benefit of the debtor—

> **(A)** not secured by an otherwise unavoidable security interest; and
>
> **(B)** on account of which new value the debtor did not make an otherwise unavoidable transfer to or for the benefit of such creditor[.]

---

[5] The result which Mosier urges may be best understood by an example. Assume IRFM made a preferential transfer of $50,000 to Ever–Fresh sixty days prior to filing bankruptcy. Subsequent to this transfer, Ever–Fresh gave IRFM new credit valued at $100,000. If bankruptcy were filed on this day, Ever–Fresh would be able to successfully assert a new value defense and retain the $50,000 transferred by the debtor. However, if one week before bankruptcy IRFM made another transfer to Ever–Fresh of $50,000, under Mosier's rule, Mosier would be able to avoid the entire $100,000 transfer by the debtor. This result follows because none of the new value remains "unpaid."

Under this rule, Mosier may "double count" the second preferential transfer. First, Mosier may properly avoid the second $50,000 transfer because Ever–Fresh transferred no new value subsequent to this preference. Second, Mosier may also use this second transfer to "pay" for the new value, allowing Mosier to recoup the first $50,000 which had previously been subject to a valid new value defense.

At oral argument, Mosier argued that this was not the result urged. However, by totaling new value, subtracting the preferential transfers and then allowing a new value defense for only the amount left "unpaid," this is the exact result that would occur.

Courts and commentators agree that the exception contains two key elements. First, the creditor must give unsecured new value and, second, this new value must be given *after* the preferential transfer. * * * The majority of courts have also adopted a short hand approach to section 547(c)(4)(B) and hold that section 547(c)(4) contains a third element, that the new value must remain unpaid. The Eighth Circuit recently followed this approach in *In re Kroh Bros. Development Co.*, 930 F.2d 648, 653 (8th Cir.1991) (creditor who has been paid for the new value by the debtor may not assert a new value defense). * * *

The rationale for this position is (1) if new value has been repaid by the debtor, the estate has not been replenished and; (2) the creditor is permitted the double benefit of a new value defense and the repayment of the new value. However, focusing only on the issue of whether the new value is unpaid may lead to some absurd results, as Mosier's position demonstrates. As a result, an emerging trend has developed where a few courts have reached the contrary result and hold that new value need not remain unpaid. * * *

However, an even more recent trend has developed where courts and commentators have rejected the short hand approach and have undertaken a more thorough analysis of the language of section 547(c)(4)(B). These cases reason that the numerous decisions focusing on the narrow issue of whether the new value remains unpaid are incomplete and inaccurate. * * *

According to this view, the proper inquiry directed by section 547(c)(4)(B) is whether the new value has been paid for by "an otherwise unavoidable transfer." * * * This inquiry follows the *Kroh Bros.* rationale that a creditor should not get double credit for an advance of new value. However, instead of barring the new value defense altogether anytime new value has been repaid, this approach allows the new value defense if the trustee can recover the repayment by some other means.

This analysis fully comports with the statute's plain language. While the phrase "the debtor did not make an otherwise unavoidable transfer" is complicated, it is not ambiguous and its meaning is easily discernible. *See In re Check Reporting Servs.*, Inc., 140 B.R. 425, 434–436 (Bankr.W.D.Mich.1992) (conducting an exhaustive analysis of the phrase "did not make an otherwise unavoidable transfer"). As one commentator has explained:

> If the debtor has made payments for goods or services that the creditor supplied on unsecured credit after an earlier preference, *and if these subsequent payments are themselves voidable as preferences* (or on any other ground), then under section 547(c)(4)(B) the creditor should be able to invoke those unsecured credit extensions as a defense to the recovery of the *earlier* voidable preference. On the other hand, the debtor's subsequent payments might not be voidable on any other ground and not voidable under section 547, because the goods

and services were given C.O.D. rather than on a credit, or because the creditor has a defense under section 547(c)(1), (2), or (3). In this situation, the creditor may keep his payments but has no section 547(c)(4) defense to the trustee's action to recover the earlier preference. In either event, the creditor gets credit only once for goods and services later supplied.

Vern Countryman, The Concept of a Voidable Preference in Bankruptcy, 38 Vand.L.Rev. 713, 788 (1985) (emphasis added and footnotes omitted) * * *.

We agree with this analysis and hold that a new value defense is permitted unless the debtor repays the new value by a transfer which is otherwise unavoidable.

**B**

In addition to its consistency with the language of the statute, this approach meets the policy underlying preference actions. The purpose of section 547 is twofold. First, enabling a trustee to avoid preferential transfers allows the trustee to secure equality of distribution among the unsecured creditors by preventing a debtor from benefiting a particular creditor on the eve of bankruptcy. Second, the new value exception encourages creditors to continue to do business with financially troubled debtors, with an eye toward avoiding bankruptcy altogether.

The rule for which Mosier argues would discourage creditors from having any dealings with a financially troubled debtor. For instance, Ever–Fresh could have sold the goods to another purchaser and been able to retain the payment for those goods. Instead, Ever–Fresh would not only be required to forfeit *all* payments made by IRFM during the preference period, but Ever–Fresh would also lose the new value extended to the debtor. Mosier's rule also makes the creditor worse off vis-a-vis the other creditors. By refusing to permit the creditor to receive some benefit for the transfer of new value, the proposed rule would put the creditor in a worse position than those creditors who chose not to deal with the debtor.

**IV**

We must now decide the proper calculation of the new value offset. The district court adopted the following approach:

| Check Date | Payment Amount | Goods Shipped | Preference |
|---|---|---|---|
| April 25 | $18,475.86 | | $18,475.86 |
| | | $18,849.16 | |
| May 2 | $18,095.66 | | $18,095.66 |
| | | $33,063.18 | |
| May 11 | $16,197.93 | | $16,197.93 |
| | | $16,197.93 | |
| May 16 | $14,492.91 | | $14,492.91 |
| | | $17,280.78 | |

| Check Date | Payment Amount | Goods Shipped | Preference |
|---|---|---|---|
| May 23 | $18,056.21 | | $18,056.21 |
| | | $20,590.11 | |
| May 30 | $18,420.07 | | $18,420.07 |
| | | $23,056.79 | |
| June 6 | $18,922.37 | | $18,922.37 |
| | | $17,436.51 | $1,485.86 |
| June 13 | $23,479.03 | | $24,964.89 |
| | | $15,967.54 | $8,997.35 |
| June 20 | $17,127.20 | | $26,124.55 |
| July 22 | | $113,566.47 | $0.00 |
| | $163,267.24 | $276,008.47 | $0.00 |

This calculation results in a full new value defense for Ever–Fresh and we accept it as correct. This approach is derived from *In re Thomas W. Garland, Inc.*, 19 B.R. 920 (Bankr.E.D.Mo.1982). Under this method, subsequent advances of new value may be used to offset prior (although not immediately prior) preferences. A creditor is permitted to carry forward preferences until they are exhausted by subsequent advances of new value.

The rationale behind this method is twofold. First, it encourages creditors to do business with financially troubled debtors. A creditor will be more likely to continue to advance new value to a debtor if all these subsequent advances may be used to offset a prior preference. If a second advance of new value carries no benefit, the creditor will be unlikely to make it. * * * Second, this approach recognizes the fluid nature of ongoing commercial activity where a creditor looks to a debtor's entire repayment history, instead of one isolated transaction, to decide whether to advance new credit.

A contrary approach was adopted in *Leathers v. Prime Leather Finishes Co.*, 40 B.R. 248 (D.Maine 1984). Under this "transactional approach," the new value given by the creditor may be used to offset only the immediately preceding preference. Here, Mosier would be able to avoid the excess of the June 6 and June 13 transfers over the immediately subsequent advances of new value, resulting in a total recoupment of $8,997.35 from Ever–Fresh.

We reject the *Leathers* approach. First, nothing in the language of section 547(c)(4) requires this result. The statute states only that after a preferential transfer, new value must be given. * * * Second, as discussed above, the *Garland* approach better satisfies the purposes and goals of the preference section.

We adopt the *Garland* approach with a few additional requirements that are necessary given our holding in section III.

First, to calculate the new value defense, consideration must be given to whether an increment of new value has been paid for by something other than an avoidable transfer. If so, this increment of new value may not be included in calculating the amount of the new value defense.

Second, assurance must be given that the creditor will not attempt to obtain double credit for a transfer. This requirement may be satisfied by disallowing a creditor from asserting a separate section 547(c) defense against a preference when the creditor has already used section 547(c)(4) to offset that preference.[6]

Applying these requirements to the present case, we affirm the district court's award of the full new value offset to Ever–Fresh. Under the *Garland* test where new value may offset more than the immediately prior preference, the resulting preference amount is zero. Second, the parties agreed that all transfers by IRFM which are challenged by Mosier are preferences under 547(b). Therefore, none of these transfers are "otherwise unavoidable." Finally, because Ever–Fresh has been granted a new value offset for each of these preferential transfers, no other preference defense is available for these same transfers.

V

The preference section of the Bankruptcy Code requires that new value must not be repaid by an otherwise unavoidable transfer. Because the parties agree that the transfers made in this case are preferences under section 547(b), they are not "unavoidable." We conclude that Ever–Fresh is entitled to a new value defense for the entire amount of preferential transfers made by IRFM.

AFFIRMED.

## NOTE: TIME OF TRANSFER WHEN PAYMENT MADE BY CHECK

If a debtor gives a check to a creditor and the check is paid, the result is a "transfer of an interest of the debtor in property" under Section 547(b). When exactly does the transfer occur? Under the date-of-delivery view, the transfer occurs when the check is delivered to the creditor so long as the check is paid by the bank on which it was drawn within a rea-

---

[6] Alternatively, a creditor may file a waiver of all other preference defenses or may also stipulate to the avoidability, other than under section 547(c)(4), of all transfers it received from the debtor except those made after the last transfer of new value. *Check Reporting Servs.*, 140 B.R. at 438.

Likewise, once a creditor has successfully asserted a defense under section 547(c)(1), (2) or (3), it may not attempt to assert a defense under section 547(c)(4) for the same preferential transfer.

sonable time. Under the date-of-honor view, the transfer occurs when the check is honored, that is, paid by the drawee bank.

Time of transfer is important both under § 547(b) and § 547(c). Under § 547(b)(4) the transfer must occur within the preference period. If a check is delivered to the creditor before the start of the preference period and is paid after the start of the period, under the delivery rule there cannot be a voidable preference, while under the honor rule § 547(b)(4) is satisfied. The Supreme Court in *Barnhill v. Johnson*, 503 U.S. 393 (1992), held that for the purpose of § 547(b)(4) transfer occurs on the date the drawee bank honors the check.

## PROBLEM

In *Barnhill* the Court noted that the courts of appeal had been unanimous in holding that the delivery rule prevailed in § 547(c) cases and made clear that it was not deciding that issue. Do you believe the policies involved in deciding when a transfer takes place under § 547(c) are sufficiently different from those under § 547(b) to justify having different rules for the determining the time of transfer with respect to checks under each subsection? How would you decide the following case?

Debtor was a struggling borrower that "paid when it could." With growing reluctance, Supplier continued to ship ingredients essential for Debtor to continue its manufacturing business. Supplier delivered a $25,000 shipment on March 1. On March 18, Debtor ordered an additional shipment, but Supplier refused to make any more shipments until "I see your money" in payment of the March 1 shipment. On March 20, Supplier received by overnight mail Debtor's check for $25,000; on March 21, Supplier delivered the new order invoiced at $30,000; on March 22, the $25,000 check was honored. Debtor filed in bankruptcy on April 3, and Debtor's trustee sought to recover the $25,000 payment as a preference; Supplier defended under § 547(c)(4). Debtor relied on *Barnhill* to assert that the $30,000 shipment could not be offset against Debtor's $25,000 payment under § 547(c)(4) because the check had not transferred property of Debtor to Supplier until March 22, the date of its honor; hence, the preference was subsequent to the shipment. Supplier contended that the $25,000 payment took place on March 20 when the check was delivered; hence, the $30,000 shipment on March 21 was subsequent to the payment and could be setoff against it. Supplier argued that the purpose of § 547(c)(4) is to encourage creditors to continue to deal with troubled debtors; this purpose was better served by allowing Supplier to rely on delivery of Debtor's check rather than having to wait for the check to clear. Who has the better argument? *See, e.g., In re Tennessee Chemical Co.*, 112 F.3d 234 (6th Cir.1997).

## 8. SECURITY INTERESTS IN INVENTORY AND ACCOUNTS RECEIVABLE

The battle over the validity of floating liens in bankruptcy was the cause celebre of commercial law in the years immediately after enactment of the UCC. The bankruptcy bar had stood by, largely ignored, while Article 9 was drafted in a manner that seemed to give every advantage to the secured creditor: abrogation of the prohibition on the debtor's retention of unrestricted dominion over collateral in §9-205; automatic future advance and after-acquired property clauses in §9-204; first-to-file priority rule in §9-322; notice filing in §9-502. Taken together, these provisions allowed the secured party to take a security interest in all of a debtor's personal property now owned or thereafter acquired to secure both present and future advances. If the floating lien were upheld in bankruptcy, there would be nothing left in a debtor's estate to distribute among unsecured trade creditors who had provided goods and services to the failed debtor.

But bankruptcy counsel believed that the drafters of the 1962 version of Article 9, none of whom was experienced in the nether world of bankruptcy law, had painted themselves into a corner, and that security interests in inventory acquired and accounts that arose during the preference period were potentially voidable as preferences. This view if accepted could have severely affected the inventory and accounts financing industry. And these lawyers had a solid basis for their opinion because the time of transfer for security interests in bankruptcy is the time of perfection of the security interest, not its attachment. § 547(e).

Suppose Debtor, an appliance retailer, signed a security agreement on February 1 granting a security interest to Bank to secure a loan made at the same time. The collateral was all of Debtor's inventory then owned or thereafter acquired. Bank immediately filed a financing statement covering inventory. Under Article 9 the security interest attached, with respect to any item of inventory, when all of the following conditions were met: (1) there was an authenticated security agreement; (2) Bank gave value to Debtor; and (3) Debtor had rights in the item of inventory. §9-203(b). The first two conditions were satisfied on February 1 when the loan was made and the agreement signed. The third condition was satisfied at various times. With respect to inventory owned on February 1 it was satisfied on that date. With respect to after-acquired inventory it was satisfied when the inventory was acquired. Section 9-308(a) states that a security interest is perfected when it has attached and when all of the applicable steps required for perfection have been taken. The step normally taken to perfect a security interest in inventory is the filing of a financing statement. Thus, under Article 9 whenever Debtor acquired an item of inventory after February 1, a security interest in that item attached and was perfected. Filing of the financing statement occurred on February 1 but perfection with respect to the inventory covered by the financing statement could not occur until the inventory was acquired.

Suppose in our example that Debtor's inventory completely turned over every 60 days and that Debtor filed in bankruptcy on December 1. Under this assumption, all inventory on hand at the date of bankruptcy had been acquired during the preference period. Assume further that Bank did not make additional loans to Debtor after February 1 and that the original loan was unpaid at the date of bankruptcy. Under Article 9 the security interest of Bank in inventory at the date of bankruptcy attached and was perfected during the preference period and secured a debt that arose on February 1. Under Bankruptcy Act § 60a(2) (now found in § 547(e)), the apparent result was that the transfer of Debtor's property represented by the security interest was made when the security interest attached and was perfected during the preference period. Thus, if Debtor was insolvent at the time of the transfer, the security interest was voidable as a preferential transfer under Bankruptcy Act § 60b.

For our purposes, it is enough to say that in *Grain Merchants of Indiana, Inc. v. Union Bank & Sav. Co.*, 408 F.2d 209 (7th Cir.1969), the court, in a highly unorthodox reading of the law, upheld the validity of floating lien security interests in inventory and accounts in bankruptcy. The reasoning of this opinion was sufficiently troublesome to drive all parties to resolve the issue by a compromise amendment to the Bankruptcy Code. This provision is now § 547(c)(5). It was drafted against a background that assumed the following: accounts receivable and inventory normally turn over within a short period of time; it is likely that at the date of bankruptcy some receivables or inventory on hand had been acquired by the debtor within the 90-day period; since a security interest in this new collateral was, by virtue of § 547(e)(3), a transfer to the secured party when it was acquired by the debtor, there might have been a voidable preference under § 547(b) if the debtor was insolvent at the time. Section 547(c)(5), set out below, is a limited exemption from this rule.

(c)   The trustee may not avoid under this section a transfer—

(5)   that creates a perfected security interest in inventory or a receivable or the proceeds of either, except to the extent that the aggregate of all such transfers to the transferee caused a reduction, as of the date of the filing of the petition and to the prejudice of other creditors holding unsecured claims, of any amount by which the debt secured by such security interest exceeded the value of all security interests for such debt on the later of

(A) (i)   with respect to a transfer to which subsection (b)(4)(A) of this section applies, 90 days before the date of the filing of the petition; or

    **(ii)** with respect to a transfer to which (b)(4)(B) of this section applies, one year before the date of the filing of the petition; or

  **(B)** the date on which new value was first given under the security agreement creating such security interest;

## PROBLEM

How does § 547(c)(5) work? Secured Party is secured by all accounts receivable of Debtor, now owned or thereafter acquired. At the beginning of the 90-day period the debt was $100,000 and at the date of bankruptcy the debt was $90,000; at the beginning of the 90-day period there were $60,000 in receivables. During the 90-day period Debtor increased its receivables so that on the date of bankruptcy they amounted to $70,000. The test is stated in terms of the amount of the reduction of the amount by which the debt exceeded the value of the security interest from the beginning of the 90-day period to the date of bankruptcy.

**(a)** What result would it give in this case?

**(b)** What result if Secured Party's $100,000 debt was secured by $120,000 in account receivables at the beginning of the 90-day period and $70,000 in receivables on the date of bankruptcy all obtained by Debtor within the 90-day period?

Section 547(c)(5) is a variation of the substitution theory, which was one of the more persuasive bases of the *Grain Merchants* decision. It provides, in effect, that it is not important whether the items making up the mass of inventory or accounts receivable at bankruptcy were identical to the items making up the mass at the beginning of the 90-day period so long as the volume has not changed. Within that limitation any new item that came into existence within the 90-day period is treated as a substitute for an item that was disposed of by the debtor during the same period. Note the extreme difficulty in applying this net "improvement in position" test to a constantly fluctuating inventory (which may include raw materials and work in progress as well as finished goods) in constantly fluctuating market conditions.

## 9.  OTHER PROTECTED TRANSFERS

The equality-of-distribution premise of preference law gives way to strong policy concerns protecting payments made for domestic support obligations. These are obligations owed to spouses or children in the nature of alimony, maintenance or support. § 101(14A). This definition includes debts owed to governmental units that have acquired such rights in exchange for assistance provided to families. Thus, spouses, children and governmental units providing assistance don't have to give back alimony or child support payments received within the preference period from debtors who file in bankruptcy. Section 547(c)(7) precludes recovery of such payments as preferences.

Section 547(c)(8) provides a small transactions exception for payments made on debts that are "primarily consumer debts." If the "aggregate value of all property that constitutes or is affected by such transfer is less than $600," the property cannot be recovered as preferences. The 2005 Act appropriately added a comparable provision excepting property of less than $5,000 made in payment of debts that are "not primarily consumer debts." § 547(c)(9). Recovering preferences in these small-potatoes cases consumes judicial resources better devoted to more important matters. Moreover, creditor recipients of such small transfers commonly find it un-economic to defend the trustee's action. Although § 547(c)(8) and (9) function as jurisdictional minimums, § 547(g) makes them affirmative defenses rather than an element in the trustee's case in chief.

## PROBLEM

Insolvent Debtor made payments of $500 to Bank on her overdue credit card debt on the first day of each month from January through July. She filed in Chapter 7 bankruptcy on July 15, and her trustee in bankruptcy sought to recover $1,500 from Bank as a voidable preference. Bank relied on § 547(c)(8) in its contention that trustee should recover nothing. Does that provision allow the trustee to aggregate all sums paid during the 90–day period to the same creditor? *See In re Hailes*, 77 F.3d 873 (5th Cir.1996).

## 10. LETTERS OF CREDIT

As we saw on pp. 248-250, if Applicant obtains a letter of credit from Issuer Bank to support performance of its obligation to Beneficiary, Applicant's bankruptcy does not affect Beneficiary's right to proceed against Issuer on its independent undertaking under the letter of credit, unimpeded by the automatic stay of § 362. This is an end devoutly to be desired by any obligee, so much so that sometimes clients come to believe that obtaining a letter of credit fully insulates them from the risks attending the bankruptcy of their obligors. The following cases showed the business world the fallacy of that view.

# In re Compton Corp.

United States Court of Appeals, Fifth Circuit, 1987.
831 F.2d 586.

■   JERRE S. WILLIAMS, Circuit Judge:

This is a bankruptcy preference case in which a bankruptcy trustee seeks to recover a transfer made via a letter of credit for the benefit of one of the debtor's unsecured creditors on the eve of bankruptcy. The bankruptcy court and the district court found there to be no voidable preference. We reverse.

## I. Factual Background

In March 1982, Blue Quail Energy, Inc., delivered a shipment of oil to debtor Compton Corporation. Payment of $585,443.85 for this shipment of oil was due on or about April 20, 1982. Compton failed to make timely payment. Compton induced Abilene National Bank (now MBank–Abilene) to issue an irrevocable standby letter of credit in Blue Quail's favor on May 6, 1982. Under the terms of the letter of credit, payment of up to $585,443.85 was due Blue Quail if Compton failed to pay Blue Quail this amount by June 22, 1982. Compton paid MBank $1,463.61 to issue the letter of credit. MBank also received a promissory note payable on demand for $585,443.85. MBank did not need a security agreement to cover the letter of credit transaction because a prior 1980 security agreement between the bank and Compton had a future advances provision. This 1980 security agreement had been perfected as to a variety of Compton's assets through the filing of several financing statements. The most recent financing statement had been filed a year before, May 7, 1981. The letter of credit on its face noted that it was for an antecedent debt due Blue Quail.

On May 7, 1982, the day after MBank issued the letter of credit in Blue Quail's favor, several of Compton's creditors filed an involuntary bankruptcy petition against Compton. On June 22, 1982, MBank paid Blue Quail $569,932.03 on the letter of credit after Compton failed to pay Blue Quail.

In the ensuing bankruptcy proceeding, MBank's aggregate secured claims against Compton, including the letter of credit payment to Blue Quail, were paid in full from the liquidation of Compton's assets which served as the bank's collateral. Walter Kellogg, bankruptcy trustee for Compton, did not contest the validity of MBank's secured claim against Compton's assets for the amount drawn under the letter of credit by Blue Quail. Instead, on June 14, 1983, trustee Kellogg filed a complaint in the bankruptcy court against Blue Quail asserting that Blue Quail had received a preferential transfer under § 547 through the letter of credit transaction. The trustee sought to recover $585,443.85 from Blue Quail pursuant to § 550.

Blue Quail answered and filed a third party complaint against MBank. On June 16, 1986, Blue Quail filed a motion for summary judgment asserting that the trustee could not recover any preference from Blue Quail because Blue Quail had been paid from MBank's funds under the letter of credit and therefore had not received any of Compton's property. On August 27, 1986, the bankruptcy court granted Blue Quail's motion, agreeing that the payment under the letter of credit did not constitute a transfer of debtor Compton's property but rather was a transfer of the bank's property. The bankruptcy court entered judgment on the motion on September 10, 1986. Trustee Kellogg appealed this decision to the district court. On December 11, 1986, the district court affirmed the bankruptcy court ruling, holding that the trustee did not establish two necessary elements of a voidable transfer under § 547. The district court agreed with Blue Quail and the bankruptcy court that the trustee could not establish that the funds transferred to Blue Quail were ever property of Compton. Furthermore, the district court held that the transfer of the increased security interest to MBank was a transfer of the debtor's property for the sole benefit of the bank and in no way benefitted Blue Quail. The district court therefore found no voidable preference as to Blue Quail. The trustee is appealing the decision to this Court.

## II. The Letter of Credit

It is well established that a letter of credit and the proceeds therefrom are not property of the debtor's estate under § 541. * * * When the issuer honors a proper draft under a letter of credit, it does so from its own assets and not from the assets of its customer who caused the letter of credit to be issued. * * * As a result, a bankruptcy trustee is not entitled to enjoin a post petition payment of funds under a letter of credit from the issuer to the beneficiary, because such a payment is not a transfer of debtor's property (a threshold requirement under § 547(b)). A case apparently holding otherwise, *In re Twist Cap, Inc.*, 1 B.R. 284 (Bankr.Fla.1979), has been roundly criticized and otherwise ignored by courts and commentators alike.

Recognizing these characteristics of a letter of credit in a bankruptcy case is necessary in order to maintain the independence principle, the cornerstone of letter of credit law. Under the independence principle, an issuer's obligation to the letter of credit's beneficiary is independent from any obligation between the beneficiary and the issuer's customer. All a beneficiary has to do to receive payment under a letter of credit is to show that it has performed all the duties required by the letter of credit. Any disputes between the beneficiary and the customer do not affect the issuer's obligation to the beneficiary to pay under the letter of credit.

Letters of credit are most commonly arranged by a party who benefits from the provision of goods or services. The party will request a bank to issue a letter of credit which names the provider of the goods or services as the beneficiary. Under a standby letter of credit, the bank becomes primarily liable to the beneficiary upon the default of the bank's customer to pay for the goods or services. The bank charges a fee to issue a letter of credit and to undertake this liability. The shifting of liability to the bank rather than to the services or goods provider is the main purpose of the letter of credit. After all, the bank is in a much better position to assess the risk of its customer's insolvency than is the service or goods provider. It should be noted, however, that it is the risk of the debtor's insolvency and not the risk of a preference attack that a bank assumes under a letter of credit transaction. * * *

The trustee in this case accepts this analysis and does not ask us to upset it. The trustee is not attempting to set aside the post petition payments by MBank to Blue Quail under the letter of credit as a preference; nor does the trustee claim the letter of credit itself constitutes debtor's property. The trustee is instead challenging the earlier transfer in which Compton granted MBank an increased security interest in its assets to obtain the letter of credit for the benefit of Blue Quail. Collateral which has been pledged by a debtor as security for a letter of credit is property of the debtor's estate. * * * The trustee claims that the direct transfer to MBank of the increased security interest on May 6, 1982, also constituted an indirect transfer to Blue Quail which occurred one day prior to the filing of the involuntary bankruptcy petition and is voidable as a preference under § 547. * * *

It is important to note that the irrevocable standby letter of credit in the case at bar was not arranged in connection with Blue Quail's initial decision to sell oil to Compton on credit. Compton arranged for the letter of credit after Blue Quail had shipped the oil and after Compton had defaulted in payment. The letter of credit in this case did not serve its usual function of backing up a contemporaneous credit decision, but instead served as a back up payment guarantee on an extension of credit already in jeopardy. The letter of credit was issued to pay off an antecedent unsecured debt. This fact was clearly noted on the face of the letter of credit. Blue Quail, the beneficiary of the letter of credit, did not give new value for the issuance of the letter of credit by MBank on May 6, 1982, or for the resulting increased security interest held by MBank. MBank, however, did give new value for the increased security interest it obtained in Compton's collateral: the bank issued the letter of credit.

When a debtor pledges its assets to secure a letter of credit, a transfer of debtor's property has occurred under the provisions of § 547. By subjecting its assets to MBank's reimbursement claim in the event MBank had to pay on the letter of credit, Compton made a transfer of its property. The broad definition of "transfer" under § 101 is clearly designed to cover such a transfer. Overall, the letter of credit itself and the payments thereunder may not be property of debtor, but the collateral pledged as a security interest for the letter of credit is.

Furthermore, in a secured letter of credit transaction, the transfer of debtor's property takes place at the time the letter of credit is issued (when the security interest is granted) and received by the beneficiary, not at the time the issuer pays on the letter of credit. * * *

### III. Direct/Indirect Transfer Doctrine

The federal courts have long recognized that "[t]o constitute a preference, it is not necessary that the transfer be made directly to the creditor."
*National Bank of Newport v. National Herkimer County Bank*, 225 U.S.
178, 184 (1912). "If the bankrupt has made a transfer of his property, the
*effect* of which is to enable one of his creditors to obtain a greater percentage of his debt than another creditor of the same class, circuity of arrangement will not avail to save it." *Id.* (emphasis added). To combat such
circuity, the courts have broken down certain transfers into two transfers,
one direct and one indirect. The direct transfer to the third party may be
valid and not subject to a preference attack. The indirect transfer, arising
from the same action by the debtor, however, may constitute a voidable
preference as to the creditor who indirectly benefitted from the direct
transfer to the third party.

This is the situation presented in the case before us. The term "transfer" as used in the various bankruptcy statutes through the years has always been broad enough to cover such indirect transfers and to catch various circuitous arrangements. * * * The new Bankruptcy Code implicitly
adopts this doctrine through its broad definition of "transfer." * * *

In *Palmer v. Radio Corporation of America*, 453 F.2d 1133 (5th
Cir.1971), a third party purchased from the debtor a television station for
$40,000 cash and the assumption of certain liabilities of the debtor, in-
cluding unsecured claims by creditor RCA. This Court found the direct
transfer from the debtor to the third party purchaser constituted an indirect
preferential transfer to creditor RCA. We found that the assumption by the
third party purchaser of the debt owed by the debtor to RCA and the subsequent payments made thereunder constituted a voidable transfer as to
RCA. The court noted that such indirect transfers as this had long been
held to constitute voidable preferences under bankruptcy laws.

* * *

In *Virginia National Bank v. Woodson*, 329 F.2d 836 (4th Cir.1964),
the debtor had several overdrawn accounts with his bank. The debtor
talked his sister into paying off $8,000 of the overdrafts in exchange for an
$8,000 promissory note and an assignment of some collateral as security.
The debtor's sister made the $8,000 payment directly to the bank. The
$8,000 technically was never part of the debtor's estate. The court, how-
ever, held that the payment of the $8,000 by the sister to the bank was a
preference as to the bank to the extent of the value of the collateral held by
the sister. The court noted that the measure of the value of a voidable preference is diminution of the debtor's estate and not the value of the transfer
to the creditor.

In the *Woodson* case the sister was secured only to the extent the
pledged collateral had value; the remainder of her loan to her brother was
unsecured. Swapping one unsecured creditor for another unsecured creditor does not create any kind of preference. The court held that a preference
in such a transaction arises only when a secured creditor is swapped for an

unsecured creditor. Only then is the pool of assets available for distribution to the general unsecured creditors depleted because the secured creditor has priority over the unsecured creditors. Furthermore, the court held that the bank and not the sister had received the voidable preference and had to pay back to the trustee an amount equal to the value of the collateral.

\* \* \*

### IV. The Direct/Indirect Doctrine in the Context of a Letter of Credit Transaction

The case at bar differs from the cases discussed in Part III supra only by the presence of the letter of credit as the mechanism for paying off the unsecured creditor. Blue Quail's attempt to otherwise distinguish the case from the direct/indirect transfer cases does not withstand scrutiny.

In the letter of credit cases discussed in Part II supra, the letters of credit were issued contemporaneously with the initial extension of credit by the beneficiaries of the letters. In those cases the letters of credit effectively served as security devices for the benefit of the creditor beneficiaries and took the place of formal security interests. \* \* \* [I]n those cases \* \* \* there had been no voidable transfers, direct or indirect, in the letter of credit transactions involved. New value was given contemporaneously with the issuance of the letters of credit in the form of the extensions of credit by the beneficiaries of the letters. As a result, the § 547(c)(1) preference exception was applicable.

The case at bar differs from these other letter of credit cases by one very important fact: the letter of credit in this case was issued to secure an antecedent unsecured debt due the beneficiary of the letter of credit. The unsecured creditor beneficiary gave no new value upon the issuance of the letter of credit. When the issuer paid off the letter of credit and foreclosed on the collateral securing the letter of credit, a preferential transfer had occurred. An unsecured creditor was paid in full and a secured creditor was substituted in its place.

The district court upheld the bankruptcy court in maintaining the validity of the letter of credit issued to cover the antecedent debt. The district court held that MBank, the issuer of the letter of credit, could pay off the letter of credit and foreclose on the collateral securing it. We are in full agreement. But we also look to the impact of the transaction as it affects the situation of Blue Quail in the bankrupt estate. We hold that the bankruptcy trustee can recover from Blue Quail, the beneficiary of the letter of credit, because Blue Quail received an indirect preference. This result preserves the sanctity of letter of credit and carries out the purposes of the Bankruptcy Code by avoiding a preferential transfer. MBank, the issuer of the letter of credit, being just the intermediary through which the preferential transfer was accomplished, completely falls out of the picture and is not involved in this particular legal proceeding.

MBank did not receive any preferential transfer—it gave new value for the security interest. Furthermore, because the direct and indirect transfers are separate and independent, the trustee does not even need to challenge the direct transfer of the increased security interest to MBank, or seek any relief at all from MBank, in order to attack the indirect transfer and recover under § 550 from the indirect transferee Blue Quail.

We hold that a creditor cannot secure payment of an unsecured antecedent debt through a letter of credit transaction when it could not do so through any other type of transaction. The purpose of the letter of credit transaction in this case was to secure payment of an unsecured antecedent debt for the benefit of an unsecured creditor. This is the only proper way to look at such letters of credit in the bankruptcy context. The promised transfer of pledged collateral induced the bank to issue the letter of credit in favor of the creditor. The increased security interest held by the bank clearly benefitted the creditor because the bank would not have issued the letter of credit without this security. A secured creditor was substituted for an unsecured creditor to the detriment of the other unsecured creditors.

\* \* \*

The precise holding in this case needs to be emphasized. We do not hold that payment under a letter of credit, or even a letter of credit itself, constitute preferential transfers under § 547(b) or property of a debtor under § 541. The holding of this case fully allows the letter of credit to function. We preserve its sanctity and the underlying independence doctrine. We do not, however, allow an unsecured creditor to avoid a preference attack by utilizing a letter of credit to secure payment of an antecedent debt. Otherwise the unsecured creditor would receive an indirect preferential transfer from the granting of the security for the letter of credit to the extent of the value of that security. Our holding does not affect the strength of or the proper use of letters of credit. When a letter of credit is issued contemporaneously with a new extension of credit, the creditor beneficiary will not be subject to a preferential attack under the direct/indirect doctrine elaborated in this case because the creditor will have given new value in exchange for the indirect benefit of the secured letter of credit. Only when a creditor receives a secured letter of credit to cover an unsecured antecedent debt will it be subject to a preferential attack under § 547(b).

\* \* \*

# In re Powerine Oil Co.

United States Court of Appeals, Ninth Circuit, 1995.
59 F.3d 969.

■  KOZINSKI, Circuit Judge.

Can an unsecured creditor be better off when the debtor defaults rather than paying off the debt? Yes: Law can be stranger than fiction in the Preference Zone.

## I

Powerine Oil Company (the debtor here) obtained a $250.6 million line of credit from a syndicate consisting of several banks and insurance companies; the loan was secured by most of Powerine's personal property. The security agreement provided that the collateral would serve as security for all letters of credit that "have been, or are in the future, issued on the account of Debtor."

Koch Oil Company thereafter agreed to sell crude oil to Powerine. To secure Powerine's obligation, it designated Koch as beneficiary of two irrevocable standby letters of credit issued by First National Bank of Chicago, one of the lenders covered by the security agreement. The letters, which were to expire in April 1984, totaled approximately $8.7 million, an amount at all times sufficient to cover the cost of the oil Koch sold to Powerine.

In January and February 1984, Koch billed Powerine $3.2 million for oil it had delivered in December and January. Powerine eventually paid this amount but, unfortunately for Koch, it also filed a chapter 11 bankruptcy petition less than 90 days later. The Committee of Creditors Holding Unsecured Claims (the Committee) eventually brought an action to recover the payment, claiming it was a preference under § 547(b).[1]

The bankruptcy court held that the transfer was protected by the "contemporaneous exchange for new value" exception of § 547(c)(1) and granted Koch's motion for summary judgment. The Bankruptcy Appellate Panel (BAP) affirmed on a different ground: It held that the payment wasn't a preference because it didn't enable Koch to recover more than it would in a chapter 7 liquidation. Even if Powerine hadn't made the $3.2 million transfer, the BAP reasoned, Koch would have been paid in full because it would have drawn on First National's letters of credit.

---

[1] Pursuant to Powerine's reorganization plan, any preferential transfers recovered for the estate will be divided equally between secured and unsecured creditors. The full amount of the January and February payments was $8.5 million, but only $3.2 million was paid more than 45 days after delivery. We agree with the BAP that Powerine incurred its debts on the date Koch delivered the oil, not (as Koch argues) the first date the exact amount of the debt could be determined. Accordingly, $3.2 million of the transfer wasn't covered by the "ordinary course of business" exception under the version of § 547(c)(2) in effect at the time of the transfer. * * *

## II

Bankruptcy Code section 547(b) sets forth the five elements of a preferential transfer. The parties dispute only whether the last element—section 547(b)(5)—was satisfied here. Under this provision, the Committee must prove that Koch "received more than it would [have] if the case were a chapter 7 liquidation case, the transfer had not been made, and [Koch] received payment of the debt to the extent provided by the provisions of the Code." 4 Collier on Bankruptcy ¶ 547.08, at 547–45 (Lawrence P. King ed., 15th ed. 1995).

Whether section 547(b)(5)'s requirements have been met turns in part on the status of the creditor to whom the transfer was made. Pre-petition payments to a fully secured creditor generally "will not be considered preferential because the creditor would not receive more than in a chapter 7 liquidation." Id. at 547–47. With respect to unsecured creditors, however, the rule is quite different: "[A]s long as the distribution in bankruptcy is less than one-hundred percent, *any* payment "on account' to an unsecured creditor during the preference period will enable that creditor to receive more than he would have received in liquidation had the payment not been made." *In re Lewis W. Shurtleff, Inc.*, 778 F.2d 1416, 1421 (9th Cir.1985).

Vis-a-vis Powerine, Koch was an unsecured creditor as it didn't hold any security interest in Powerine's property. See 11 U.S.C. § 506(a). Because most of Powerine's assets on the date it filed for bankruptcy were subject to the lien held by the secured creditors, Powerine's unsecured creditors could expect to receive much less than one-hundred cents on the dollar in a chapter 7 liquidation. Consequently, Powerine's $3.2 million pre-petition payment enabled Koch to recover more than it would have in a chapter 7 liquidation, and it was therefore a preference.

The BAP came to the contrary conclusion by focusing on the fact that Koch could have drawn down the letters of credit, had Powerine not paid it directly. Since Koch would have recovered the full amount owed to it (albeit from First National) had Powerine defaulted, the BAP reasoned that the $3.2 million payment wasn't a preference.

Courts have long held, however, that the key factor in determining whether a payment is a preference is the "percentage[ ]. . . [creditors'] claims are entitled to draw out of the *estate of the bankrupt*." *Swarts v. Fourth Nat'l Bank*, 117 F. 1, 7 (8th Cir.1902) (emphasis added). Thus, the relevant inquiry focuses "not on whether a creditor may have recovered all of the monies owed by the debtor *from any source whatsoever*, but instead upon whether the creditor would have received less than a 100% payout" from the debtor's estate. *Id.* * * * That Koch had recourse against a third party in case the debtor defaulted thus has no bearing on this issue.

The BAP nonetheless invoked a "rule of reason" to avoid what it viewed as an inequitable result. Koch's right to collect under the letters could be taken into account, the BAP held, because the letters of credit had expired by the time the Committee initiated its preference action.

Koch was thus left far worse off because Powerine paid its bill rather than defaulting. The BAP recognized that a creditor's "rights against a surety are not relevant to whether a transfer is preferential so long as those rights are still in place after the preference action is commenced." It concluded, however, that "when that right of action against the surety no longer exists, it is incumbent upon the court to measure the net recovery that the transferee would have obtained from the surety had the transfer not been made." The BAP cited no authority for this proposition and we construe it to have been an exercise of its equitable powers.

Although bankruptcy courts are sometimes referred to as courts of equity, the Supreme Court has reminded us that "whatever equitable powers remain in the bankruptcy courts must and can only be exercised within the confines of the Bankruptcy Code." *Norwest Bank Worthington v. Ahlers,* 485 U.S. 197, 206 (1988). Equity may not be invoked to defeat clear statutory language, nor to reach results inconsistent with the statutory scheme established by the Code. * * * Because the statutory language here provides no basis for the BAP's "rule of reason," we conclude that it was error to consider the right to draw on third-party letters of credit in deciding whether Koch had received a preference.

### III

Having determined that Powerine's $3.2 million payment to Koch was preferential under section 547(b), we must next determine whether any of section 547(c)'s exceptions apply. Placing heavy reliance on *In re Fuel Oil Supply & Terminaling, Inc.,* 837 F.2d 224 (5th Cir.1988), Koch contends the payment it received is protected by the "contemporaneous exchange for new value" exception of § 547(c)(1).[3] In *Fuel Oil,* the debtor paid one of its unsecured creditors within 90 days of filing for bankruptcy. Like Koch, the creditor was the beneficiary of two letters of credit securing payment if the debtor defaulted. The issuing banks "held a security interest in [debtor]'s assets which at all times was equal to or in excess of [debtor]'s obligation to [the creditor]." *Id.* at 228.

The Fifth Circuit held that the payment was protected by the contemporaneous exchange for new value exception, reasoning that, when the debtor paid the creditor, the banks' exposure under the letters of credit was reduced by a corresponding amount. The banks' contingent reimbursement claim against the debtor's assets was thereby released, giving the debtor new value. "This outcome is consistent with the principle underlying § 547(c)(1)," the Fifth Circuit noted, "because the release of the

---

[3] Section 547(c)(1) provides:

The trustee may not avoid under this section a transfer. . . to the extent that such transfer was—(A) intended by the debtor and the creditor to or for whose benefit such transfer was made to be a contemporaneous exchange for new value given to the debtor; and (B) in fact a substantially contemporaneous exchange.

debtor's collateral offsets the transfer to the creditor, thereby resulting in no depletion to the debtor's estate." Id. * * *

Unlike the banks in *Fuel Oil Supply*, which were fully secured, however, First National was only partially secured. When Powerine filed for bankruptcy, it had $282 million in secured debt and assets of only $66 million. Nor did First National have first claim on the security because the loan agreement provided that Powerine's debts would be secured "equally without preference or priority of any one over the other."

Only a portion of First National's contingent reimbursement claim was thus secured by the blanket lien. When Powerine paid Koch directly, First National's exposure under the letters of credit was reduced by a corresponding amount, and its contingent claim against Powerine's assets was thereby released, but only to the extent the claim was secured. Thus, Powerine received new value equal to the amount of the secured portion of First National's reimbursement claim. * * * As to the unsecured portion of First National's claim, however, Powerine didn't receive new value; the bank couldn't release a security interest in Powerine's assets it didn't in fact have. The contemporaneous exchange for new value exception therefore doesn't protect Koch's $3.2 million payment to the extent First National's reimbursement claim was unsecured.

* * *

We are unable to determine on this record how much of First National's contingent reimbursement claim against Powerine was secured. We therefore remand for the bankruptcy court to determine what portion of the $3.2 million payment may be recovered from Koch.

REVERSED and REMANDED.

■   FARRIS, Circuit Judge, dissenting:

Bankruptcy courts sit as courts of equity, but they may not avoid the plain language of a statute. * * * We must decide whether the Bankruptcy Appellate Panel's interpretation of § 547(b)(5) is plausible.

Section 547(b)(5) states: [T]he trustee may avoid any transfer of an interest of the debtor in property—

.. . . .

(5) that enables such creditor to receive more than such creditor would receive if

(A) the case were a case under chapter 7 of this title;

(B) the transfer had not been made; and

(C) such creditor received payment of such debt to the extent provided by the provisions of this title.

The plain language of the statute does not limit consideration to funds from Powerine's estate. Under a hypothetical chapter 7 liquidation, it could have collected from First National as "provided by the provisions of this title." In its opinion, the BAP ruled that "[n]othing in title 11 would prevent a draw down on the credits here at issue had Powerine filed bankruptcy without paying Koch."

In my opinion, the BAP's decision does not avoid the plain language of section 547(b)(5). I respectfully dissent.

## NOTE

Koch, Powerine, and First Chicago entered into this triangular standby letter of credit relationship on the understanding that Powerine would pay Koch for the oil Koch provided and if Powerine could not or would not pay Koch directly then First Chicago would honor the letter of credit and seek reimbursement from Powerine. The point of this entirely sensible business relationship was to shift the credit risk of Powerine's insolvency from Koch to First Chicago, presumably because First Chicago was better positioned than Koch to assess and monitor Powerine's creditworthiness. As the Ninth Circuit holds in Part III of its opinion, the payment by Powerine to Koch had the effect of depleting the bankruptcy estate within the preference period in order to satisfy an unsecured claim. But the parties had agreed by entering into the standby letter of credit that the risk of non-payment of this unsecured obligation was First Chicago's risk, not Koch's. From a functional point of view the payment to Koch, by eliminating a partially unsecured contingent reimbursement obligation to First Chicago, benefited First Chicago, not Koch, which otherwise would have simply drawn on the standby letter of credit. In short, the true beneficiary of the payment to Koch (the preference sought to be recovered) was First Chicago, not Koch. Nevertheless, the Ninth Circuit in *Powerine Oil* authorizes recovery of the preference from Koch, which left Koch with an unsecured claim against now-bankrupt Powerine. Koch, which bargained to shift this credit risk to First Chicago is left without any recourse against First Chicago. And to add insult to Koch's injury, First Chicago retains the benefit of the preference it indirectly received, and pursuant to the stipulation referred to in footnote 1, First Chicago as one of the stipulating secured lenders also receives a pro rata portion of half of the money recovered from Koch!

After *Powerine Oil*, the safest way to structure this triangular relationship from Koch's perspective is as a commercial letter of credit. Under the terms of a commercial letter of credit, First Chicago would have had to honor a draft under the letter of credit upon Koch's presentation of documents evidencing the shipment of the oil. Standby letters of credit are generally favored over commercial letters because they are less cumbersome to administer and are thought to achieve the same effective shifting of credit risk from beneficiary to issuing bank. As a result the standby letter of credit is a commonplace and valuable tool in commercial transactions. There is no apparent reason why the Bankruptcy Code should require parties to use commercial letters in these situations when they would otherwise prefer to use standby letters.

In *Powerine Oil,* the Ninth Circuit follows the "plain meaning" of § 547(b) to a result it concedes is "stranger than fiction" in the face of clear policy considerations to the contrary and in the absence of any evidence that Congress ever considered the application of the statutory text to standby letters of credit. Is it really so plain that this is the meaning of § 547(b)? If so, was it nevertheless appropriate to use "equitable considerations" or a "rule of reason" (as the bankruptcy appellate panel did) in order to reach a more sensible result?

## 11. FALSE PREFERENCES: DELAYED PERFECTION OF SECURITY INTERESTS

We have already dealt with the problem of a secured creditor who makes a loan to a debtor in what is a secured transaction but in which there is some delay between the time the loan is made and the time that the security interest attaches. Since the attaching of the security interest is a transfer of property of the debtor on account of the antecedent loan debt, there is a prima facie voidable preference if the other elements of § 547(b) are present. If the delay is very short, the security interest may, under some circumstances, be saved by § 547(c)(1). If the loan is made to enable the debtor to acquire the collateral which secures the loan debt, the security interest may be saved if there is compliance with § 547(c)(3). In these cases the problem arises because of a delay in the creation of the security interest.

A problem that is superficially similar but of an entirely different legal category arises when the making of the loan and the creation of the security interest are contemporaneous, but there is a delay between the creation, i.e. attachment, of the security interest and the perfection of the security interest. There is no true preference in these cases because the transfer of the security interest to the creditor is not on account of an antecedent debt. Rather, the problem of delayed perfection is the evil of the secret lien. The classic case is that of a debtor in financial difficulty who wants to conceal from general creditors the true state of its financial condition. The debtor obtains an emergency loan from a creditor and grants to that creditor a mortgage on real property or a security interest in personal property to secure the loan. The property involved might well be most of the debtor's previously unencumbered assets. If public notice of the transaction were given by recording of the mortgage or filing a financing statement with respect to the security interest, the result might be that other creditors will be deterred from giving the debtor further unsecured credit because of the absence of unencumbered assets. To avoid this result the creditor might be induced not to record the mortgage or file the financing statement.

Essentially, the issue is one of fraud on creditors, not whether a transfer for antecedent consideration prefers one creditor over another. Usually an unrecorded real property mortgage has priority over a creditor who subsequently levies on the property. The holder of an unperfected security interest in personal property takes a greater risk by not promptly perfecting because an unperfected Article 9 security interest does not have priority over a subsequent judicial lien. But in either case the creditor can protect the lien by promptly perfecting at the first sign that other creditors may either levy on assets of the debtor or file a petition for involuntary bankruptcy against the debtor. In the classic case, the creditor is an insider with access to information that provides some assurance that the creditor will have sufficient advance notice of facts to allow the creditor to perfect in time.

It is understandable that there should be a policy against secret liens, and such a policy was expressed in the Bankruptcy Act. However, the preferences approach used in the Bankruptcy Act to address the evil was unusual. Instead of dealing with the problem directly as a case of fraud on creditors, the Bankruptcy Act discouraged secret liens by treating a lien as effective at the time it was perfected rather than when it was actually created. Hence, if the creditor gave value at the time the security interest was created but did not perfect until later, the effect was that the lien was treated as having been for an antecedent debt. This technique of turning secret liens into false preferences was carried over into the Bankruptcy Code. The relevant provision is § 547(e)(2). The meaning of § 547(e)(2) is clarified in § 547(e)(1), which defines the term "perfected" and in § 547(e)(3), which states that a transfer cannot occur before the debtor has rights in the property transferred.

Although former § 547(e)(2) was intended to eliminate the evils of the secret lien, unfortunately, it could also ensnare a hapless secured creditor who, through no fault of its own, was unable to perfect within the pre-2005 10–day grace period. This is particularly true in cases involving motor vehicles for which a security interest must be noted on a certificate of title issued by a state agency. Unhappy with the harsh results in cases in which perfection was delayed beyond 10 days, several states attempted to deal with the problem by making special rules for security interests in motor vehicles by providing that if proper documentation is presented to the relevant state agency within a given period of time (usually from 15 to 30 days) after the security interest has attached, the security interest is deemed to have been perfected at the time it attached. Courts divided over whether the extended relation-back period under the state statute could prevail over the 10–day period in former § 547(e)(2). The Supreme Court resolved the issue in *Fidelity Financial Services, Inc.* v. *Fink*, 522 U.S. 211 (1998), by holding that the time period provided in § 547(e)(2) trumped any more expansive relation-back period under state law. In the 2005 Act, the periods in § 547(e)(2)(A),(B) and (C) for refinancing transactions and in § 547(c)(3)(b) for purchase money transactions are extended to 30 days. These amendments should ameliorate the difficulties posed for secured creditors by the *Fink* analysis.

## PROBLEM

Debtor was being pressed by several credit card issuers for payment on her delinquent debts which amounted to $25,000; she also owed a purchase money debt of $5,000 to GMAC, secured by a Saturn auto. She came to Personal Finance (PF) for relief. PF is a "loan consolidator," that is, it paid off Debtor's creditors and took a note from Debtor for the full amount advanced, secured by everything she owned. On March 1, Debtor signed the note and security agreement covering all her property; on that date PF paid the credit card issuers and filed a UCC financing statement to perfect a security interest in all of Debtor's personal property except the Saturn. In the relevant jurisdiction, perfection of a security interest in a motor vehicle can be accomplished only by (i) sending the certificate of title of the vehicle, suitably indorsed, to DMV and (ii) having a new certificate issued with the secured party's lien noted. On March 1, PF sent a check for $5,000 to GMAC which was holding the certificate of title to the Saturn. GMAC indorsed the certificate of title and sent it to PF. When it arrived on March 19, PF sent it to DMV; it arrived on March 24, but DMV did not issue the new certificate until April 1. When Debtor filed in bankruptcy on May 1, Debtor's trustee sued to avoid PF's security interest in the Saturn because PF had failed to perfect within the ten-day relation-back window provided by former § 547(e)(2). PF defended by asserting that there had been a contemporaneous exchange under § 547(c)(1). The parties have stipulated that PF did not have a perfected security interest in the Saturn until the new certificate was issued on April 1 and that PF acted as expeditiously as possible to obtain a perfected security interest in the vehicle. What result? *Compare In re Arnett*, 731 F.2d 358 (6th Cir.1984) (§ 547(e)(2) governs this case of delayed perfection, not § 547(c)(1), which governs delayed attachment cases), *with Pine Top Ins. Co. v. Bank of America, NTSA*, 969 F.2d 321 (7th Cir.1992) ("substantially contemporaneous" is a flexible term and case by case analysis is required). *In re Dorholt, Inc.*, 224 F.3d 871 (8th Cir.2000), and *In re Marino*, 117 F.3d 1425 (9th Cir.1997), follow *Pine Top*. In his prestigious article, *The Concept of a Voidable Preference in Bankruptcy*, 38 Vand. L.Rev. 713, 765 (1985), Professor Vern Countryman agrees with the *Arnett* analysis.

## B. SETOFF

### 1. WHAT IS SETOFF?

# Citizens Bank of Maryland v. Strumpf

Supreme Court of the United States, 1995.
516 U.S. 16.

■ Justice SCALIA delivered the opinion of the Court.

We must decide whether the creditor of a debtor in bankruptcy may, in order to protect its setoff rights, temporarily withhold payment of a debt that it owes to the debtor in bankruptcy without violating the automatic stay imposed by § 362(a).

### I

On January 25, 1991, when respondent filed for relief under Chapter 13 of the Bankruptcy Code, he had a checking account with petitioner, a bank conducting business in the State of Maryland. He also was in default on the remaining balance of a loan of $5,068.75 from the bank. Under § 362(a), respondent's bankruptcy filing gave rise to an automatic stay of various types of activity by his creditors, including "the setoff of any debt owing to the debtor that arose before the commencement of the [bankruptcy case] against any claim against the debtor." § 362(a)(7).

On October 2, 1991, petitioner placed what it termed an "administrative hold" on so much of respondent's account as it claimed was subject to setoff—that is, the bank refused to pay withdrawals from the account that would reduce the balance below the sum that it claimed was due on respondent's loan. Five days later, petitioner filed in the Bankruptcy Court, under § 362(d), a "Motion for Relief from Automatic Stay and for Setoff." Respondent then filed a motion to hold petitioner in contempt, claiming that petitioner's administrative hold violated the automatic stay established by § 362(a).

The Bankruptcy Court ruled on respondent's contempt motion first. It concluded that petitioner's "administrative hold" constituted a "setoff" in violation of § 362(a)(7) and sanctioned petitioner. Several weeks later, the Bankruptcy Court granted petitioner's motion for relief from the stay and authorized petitioner to set off respondent's remaining checking account balance against the unpaid loan. By that time, however, respondent had reduced the checking account balance to zero, so there was nothing to set off.

The District Court reversed the judgment that petitioner had violated the automatic stay, concluding that the administrative hold was not a violation of § 362(a). The Court of Appeals reversed. "[A]n administrative hold," it said, "is tantamount to the exercise of a right of setoff and thus violates the automatic stay of § 362(a)(7)." 37 F.3d [at] 158. We granted certiorari.

## II

The right of setoff (also called "offset") allows entities that owe each other money to apply their mutual debts against each other, thereby avoiding "the absurdity of making A pay B when B owes A." *Studley v. Boylston Nat. Bank*, 229 U.S. 523, 528 (1913). Although no federal right of setoff is created by the Bankruptcy Code, 11 U.S.C. § 553(a) provides that, with certain exceptions, whatever right of setoff otherwise exists is preserved in bankruptcy. Here it is undisputed that, prior to the bankruptcy filing, petitioner had the right under Maryland law to set off the defaulted loan against the balance in the checking account. It is also undisputed that under § 362(a) respondent's bankruptcy filing stayed any exercise of that right by petitioner. The principal question for decision is whether petitioner's refusal to pay its debt to respondent upon the latter's demand constituted an exercise of the setoff right and hence violated the stay.

In our view, petitioner's action was not a setoff within the meaning of § 362(a)(7). Petitioner refused to pay its debt, not permanently and absolutely, but only while it sought relief under § 362(d) from the automatic stay. Whether that temporary refusal was otherwise wrongful is a separate matter—we do not consider, for example, respondent's contention that the portion of the account subjected to the "administrative hold" exceeded the amount properly subject to setoff. All that concerns us here is whether the refusal *was a setoff*. We think it was not, because—as evidenced by petitioner's "Motion for Relief from Automatic Stay and for Setoff"—petitioner did not purport permanently to reduce respondent's account balance by the amount of the defaulted loan. A requirement of such an intent is implicit in the rule followed by a majority of jurisdictions addressing the question, that a setoff has not occurred until three steps have been taken: (i) a decision to effectuate a setoff, (ii) some action accomplishing the setoff, and (iii) a recording of the setoff. * * * But even if state law were different, the question whether a setoff *under § 362(a)(7)* has occurred is a matter of federal law, and other provisions of the Bankruptcy Code would lead us to embrace the same requirement of an intent permanently to settle accounts.

Section 542(b) of the Code, which concerns turnover of property to the estate, requires a bankrupt's debtors to "pay" to the trustee (or on his order) any "debt that is property of the estate and that is matured, payable on demand, or payable on order. . . *except to the extent that such debt may be offset under section 553 of this title against a claim against the debtor*." § 542(b) (emphasis added). Section 553(a), in turn, sets forth a general rule, with certain exceptions, that any right of setoff that a creditor possessed prior to the debtor's filing for bankruptcy is not affected by the Bankruptcy Code. It would be an odd construction of § 362(a)(7) that required a creditor with a right of setoff to do immediately that which

§ 542(b) specifically excuses it from doing as a general matter: pay a claim to which a defense of setoff applies.

Nor is our assessment of these provisions changed by the fact that § 553(a), in generally providing that nothing in the Bankruptcy Code affects creditors' prebankruptcy setoff rights, qualifies this rule with the phrase "[e]xcept as otherwise provided in this section and in sections 362 and 363." This undoubtedly refers to § 362(a)(7), but we think it is most naturally read as merely recognizing that provision's restriction upon *when* an *actual setoff* may be effected—which is to say, not during the automatic stay. When this perfectly reasonable reading is available, it would be foolish to take the § 553(a) "except" clause as indicating that § 362(a)(7) requires immediate payment of a debt subject to setoff. That would render § 553(a)'s general rule that the Bankruptcy Code does not affect the right of setoff meaningless, for by forcing the creditor to pay *its* debt immediately, it would divest the creditor of the very thing that supports the right of setoff. Furthermore, it would, as we have stated, eviscerate § 542(b)'s exception to the duty to pay debts. It is an elementary rule of construction that "the act cannot be held to destroy itself." *Texas & Pacific R. Co. v. Abilene Cotton Oil Co.*, 204 U.S. 426, 446 (1907).

Finally, we are unpersuaded by respondent's additional contentions that the administrative hold violated § 362(a)(3) and § 362(a)(6). Under these sections, a bankruptcy filing automatically stays "any act to obtain possession of property of the estate or of property from the estate or to exercise control over property of the estate," § 362(a)(3), and "any act to collect, assess, or recover a claim against the debtor that arose before the commencement of the case under this title," § 362(a)(6). Respondent's reliance on these provisions rests on the false premise that petitioner's administrative hold took something from respondent, or exercised dominion over property that belonged to respondent. That view of things might be arguable if a bank account consisted of money belonging to the depositor and held by the bank. In fact, however, it consists of nothing more or less than a promise to pay, from the bank to the depositor * * *; and petitioner's temporary refusal to pay was neither a taking of possession of respondent's property nor an exercising of control over it, but merely a refusal to perform its promise. In any event, we will not give §§ 362(a)(3) or (6) an interpretation that would proscribe what § 542(b)'s "except[ion]" and § 553(a)'s general rule were plainly intended to permit: the temporary refusal of a creditor to pay a debt that is subject to setoff against a debt owed by the bankrupt.

The judgment of the Court of Appeals for the Fourth Circuit is reversed.

## NOTES

**1.** The Court states that the act of setoff is not complete until three steps have been taken: (i) the decision to exercise the right, (ii) some action that accomplishes the setoff, and (iii) some record evidencing that the right of setoff has been exercised. What is the action that "accomplishes the setoff"? It is no more than a bookkeeping transaction. The bank debits (reduces) the debtor's deposit account (the bank's debt to the debtor) in the amount of the setoff and credits (reduces) the debtor's loan account (the debtor's debt to the bank) in the same amount. The bookkeeping entries merely reflect the bank's unilateral determination that each of the mutual debts has been reduced by the amount of the setoff. If the bank does not set off, but simply places a hold on (freezes) the account, the bank continues to recognize its debt to the debtor but refuses to pay the debt by allowing withdrawals from the account by check or otherwise. In both setoff and freezing, the debtor loses the use of the deposit account and the bank retains the money. But there are some differences between setoff and freezing. For example, if the deposit account bears interest, a setoff will terminate the running of interest on both the deposit account and the loan from the time of, and to the extent of, the setoff. A freezing of the account allows interest to run on both debts. But differences of this kind may be of minor importance. As a practical matter, the principal benefits of setoff can be obtained by the bank by freezing the account and the burden on the debtor is essentially the same in either case.

**2.** As the Court points out, the Bankruptcy Code does not create the right to set off mutual debts, but § 553 brings the state law doctrine of setoff into bankruptcy. The traditional policy basis for setoff is to avoid "the absurdity of making A pay B when B owes A." Outside bankruptcy, this policy may make sense but in bankruptcy it produces results that fly in the face of the equality-of-distribution rule that we posited as the backbone of preference law. Suppose Debtor in *Strumpf* owed Bank $20,000 and had a balance of $10,000 in its deposit account in Bank when it filed in bankruptcy. Its nonexempt assets were valued at $20,000, including the deposit account balance, and it owed ten other creditors $20,000 apiece. The doctrine of setoff allows Bank to take the full $10,000 balance of the account as an offset to its claim for $20,000, while the other creditors receive distributions of $1,000 each. The right of setoff is accorded the same favorable treatment as a security interest, and § 506(a) recognizes that a claim subject to setoff under § 553 is a secured claim to the extent of the setoff right.

## PROBLEM

**1.** Debtor, a wholesaler, sold goods to Retailer on unsecured credit for a price of $10,000. The goods sold to Retailer had been acquired by Debtor from Manufacturer at a price of $8,000 on unsecured credit. When Manufacturer demanded payment from Debtor of the $8,000 price of the goods, Debtor was unable to pay. Debtor offered to assign, as security for the debt, Debtor's right to receive payment from Retailer. Manufacturer refused after determining that Debtor was insolvent. After Manufacturer explained the situation to Retailer, the claim of Manufacturer against Debtor was assigned to Retailer who paid Manufacturer $4,000 for it. Shortly thereafter, Debtor filed in Chapter 7 bankruptcy. The trustee in bankruptcy demanded payment from Retailer of the $10,000 price of the goods purchased from Debtor. Retailer asserted a right to set off against the $10,000 owed to Debtor the $8,000 claim against Debtor acquired from Manufacturer. As a matter of policy, should the setoff be allowed? Assume that all of the bankruptcy estate will be consumed by secured and priority claims so that nothing will be available to pay ordinary unsecured claims such as the claim assigned to Retailer. Is the setoff permissible? § 553(a)(2).

**2.** Debtor owed Bank $20,000 on a past-due loan. Debtor's checking account was also overdrawn by more than $1,000. When Bank demanded payment of both debts, Debtor was unable to pay because of insolvency. Debtor told Bank that bankruptcy was imminent. Debtor offered to pay the loan by conveying to Bank the title to Blackacre, a small lot that was Debtor's only unencumbered asset of substantial value. Bank refused the offer but urged Debtor to sell Blackacre before going into bankruptcy. Bank reasonably assumed that Debtor would deposit the proceeds of sale in Debtor's checking account with Bank because Debtor had no other bank account. Debtor sold Blackacre and deposited the $15,000 proceeds in Debtor's account with Bank. Shortly thereafter, Debtor filed in bankruptcy. At the date of bankruptcy, Debtor's account with Bank had a credit balance of $13,500. The trustee in bankruptcy and Bank both claim the $13,500 balance in Debtor's bank account. Who wins? Would your answer differ if Debtor had not had the conversation with Bank described above and Debtor simply sold Blackacre and deposited the proceeds in the checking account? § 553(a)(3).

## 2. THE IMPROVEMENT IN POSITION TEST

## PROBLEM

On January 2, 90 days before Debtor's bankruptcy, Debtor owed Bank $10,000 on an unsecured demand promissory note. On that date Debtor's checking account had a $1,000 balance. On March 20, Debtor deposited a check for $15,000 in the checking account. The deposit was made in the ordinary course of business and with the expectation that the proceeds of the check would be available for withdrawal when the check was collected. The check was collected on March 25 and as a result Debtor's credit balance exceeded $15,000. Checks of Debtor were paid by Bank after that date. On March 29, Bank learned that Debtor was in serious financial difficulty, but before that date Bank had had no notice of that fact. Bank immediately demanded payment of the note. Debtor could not pay and, on March 30, Bank exercised its setoff rights given by state law by debiting Debtor's checking account $10,300, the amount then due under the note. After the setoff Debtor's account was reduced to $2,000. On April 2, Debtor filed in Chapter 7 bankruptcy. On March 29 and at all times thereafter, Debtor was insolvent. May the trustee in bankruptcy recover, under § 553(b), any part of the setoff? If Bank had not set off before bankruptcy it would have been able to assert its entire $10,300 setoff in the bankruptcy. § 506(a). Section 553(a) recognizes the right of setoff "except as otherwise provided in this section." Section 553(b) is a limitation on § 553(a) but it applies only to a setoff "on or within 90 days before the date of the filing of the petition." Thus, a postbankruptcy setoff is not affected by § 553(b). What is the policy basis for reducing the rights of creditors that exercise setoff rights within 90 days before bankruptcy while preserving for the benefit of the creditor the value of unexercised setoff rights postbankruptcy?

## NOTE

*Collier on Bankruptcy* ¶ 553.09[2][b] (15th ed. rev. 2004) sets out a series of "Examples" that demonstrate the operation of the improvement-of-position test of § 553(b). One of these, Example 5, is troubling. The facts are that on the 90th day before Debtor's bankruptcy, Debtor owed Bank $100,000 and had $100,000 on deposit in Bank. Thus, the insufficiency was zero. At 50 days before bankruptcy, Debtor borrowed $20,000 more and withdrew $10,000 from the deposit account, leaving an insufficiency of $30,000. At the time of setoff, 30 days before bankruptcy, Debtor had paid down its loan to $40,000 and had $40,000 on deposit. Thus the insufficiency was zero both on the 90th day and the day of the setoff.

*Collier* reads the statute literally and concludes that the trustee may recover $30,000, the amount of the insufficiency on the "first date during the 90 days immediately preceding the date of the filing of the petition on which there was an insufficiency," which was the 50th day. § 553(b)(1)(B). This reading of the statute may produce absurd results. It is clear in this Example that Bank did not improve its position during the 90–day period yet it must disgorge $30,000. But if in the Example the deposit on the 90th day had been $99,999, leaving an insufficiency of $1, according to *Collier*, the 90th day would have become the day of comparison and the trustee could recover $1 instead of $30,000. It is difficult to believe that Congress intended these wildly inconsistent results. Section 553(b)(1)(B) works well if there was no debt owing on the 90th day; in this case there would be no insufficiency on that date because there were no mutual debts. If a debt to Bank arises at a later date, that would be the comparison date because it is the first day on which a setoff situation arises. We would read § 553(b)(1)(B) as applying only to this situation. This interpretation harmonizes § 553(b)(1)(B) with § 547(c)(5)(B), a comparable provision applying an improvement-of-position test to security interests in accounts receivable and inventory arising within the 90–day period. The secured party's "insufficiency" is calculated under that provision on the 90th day unless "new value was first given under the security agreement" at a later time.

## C. FRAUDULENT TRANSFERS

### 1. ACTUAL FRAUD

*Fact Situation.* Debtor owned a residence valued at $100,000. While driving, she negligently collided with Plaintiff's car and badly injured him. Since Debtor carried only the legal minimum of liability insurance for personal injuries, she feared that she might lose her residence if sued by Plaintiff. On the day after the collision, she deeded her residence to her mother for no consideration; her mother recorded the deed. Debtor continued to live in the residence. Plaintiff sued Debtor for damages and obtained a judgment for $1 million.

*State Law.* American law, following English precedents, traditionally gave persons in the position of Plaintiff remedies in such cases. The most recent codification of fraudulent transfer law, which has been adopted by most states, is the Uniform Fraudulent Transfer Act (UFTA). In the case above, the transfer of the residence depleted the Debtor's assets from which Plaintiff could satisfy his judgment. Under UFTA § 4(a)(1), the transfer was made "with actual intent to hinder, delay, or defraud any creditor of the debtor," and Plaintiff can avoid the transfer to the extent necessary to satisfy his claim (§ 7(a)(1)) or, if he has obtained a judgment, as Plaintiff has in this case, move immediately to levy execution on the asset transferred or its proceeds (§ 7(b)). The effect is to treat the residence that was fraudulently transferred as though it remained Debtor's property.

*Federal Law.* Assume that in the fact situation above, before Plaintiff could levy on the residence, Debtor filed in Chapter 7 bankruptcy.

Section 548 provides:

(a)(1) The trustee may avoid any transfer * * * of an interest of the debtor in property, or any obligation * * * incurred by the debtor, that was made or incurred on or within 2 years before the date of filing of the petition, if the debtor voluntarily or involuntarily

    (A) made such transfer or incurred such obligation with actual intent to hinder, delay, or defraud any entity to which the debtor was or became, on or after the date that such transfer was made or such obligation was incurred, indebted; or

* * *

Section 550 provides:

(a) Except as otherwise provided in this section, to the extent that a transfer is avoided under section 544 [or] * * * 548 * * * of this title, the trustee may recover, for the benefit of the estate, the property transferred, or, if the court so orders, the value of such property from—

(1) the initial transferee of such transfer or the entity for whose benefit such transfer was made; or

(2) any immediate or mediate transferee of such initial transferee.

\* \* \*

Thus, § 548(a)(1)(A) allows the bankruptcy trustee to avoid fraudulent transfers, such as the one in the case above, of property by Debtor to her mother made with actual intent to hinder, delay, or defraud creditors. Section 550(a) allows the trustee to recover the residence from Debtor's mother "for the benefit of the estate," and § 541(a)(3) provides that the property recovered regains its status as property of Debtor's estate available for distribution to claimants. The similarities between UFTA and the fraudulent transfer provisions of the Bankruptcy Code, such as § 548(a)(1)(A), are obvious and intentional. The UFTA was drafted after enactment of the Bankruptcy Code in 1978, and the drafters of UFTA strove to make that statute compatible with the fraudulent transfer provisions in the Code.

But there are significant differences. First, in bankruptcy, Plaintiff loses his right under the UFTA to satisfy his in personam judgment out of Debtor's property fraudulently transferred, and the judgment is discharged. Section 550(a) provides that the trustee may recover property fraudulently transferred for the benefit of the estate. Thus, Debtor's filing in bankruptcy relegates Plaintiff to the status of a creditor with an unsecured claim who shares pro rata in the property transferred with the other general creditors. Since in Chapter 11 cases there usually is no trustee, under § 1107(a) the debtor in possession exercises the trustee's rights to proceed under § 550(a). Later in this section we will consider whether courts may authorize creditors' committees to bring avoidance proceedings under § 550(a) when debtors in possession lack incentive to do so.

Another difference is that § 548(a) allows trustees to avoid only fraudulent transfers made within two years of filing in bankruptcy, but the statute of limitations for a transfer avoidable under UFTA § 4(1)(a) is four years pursuant to UFTA § 9. Given the complexities of some bankruptcy cases, empowering the trustee to overturn transactions occurring as far back as four years before the debtor's filing may be of great importance to the trustee. But how does a trustee in bankruptcy operating under the federal Bankruptcy Code take advantage of the four-year state law UFTA statute of limitation? The answer lies in § 544(b), which gives a trustee in bankruptcy derivative rights of creditors under the UFTA.

Section 544

(b)  \* \* \*  [T]he trustee may avoid any transfer of an interest of the debtor in property \* \* \* that is voidable under applicable law by a creditor holding an unsecured claim that is allowable \* \* \*.

Section 550(a) allows the trustee to set aside any transfer avoidable under § 544. Since UFTA §4(a) is "applicable law" under § 544, the trustee may take the rights under § 4(a)(1) of any actual creditor holding an unsecured claim at the time of bankruptcy without regard to whether the claim arose before or after the transfer. With these derivative rights, the trustee can set aside the transfer. Hence, in any actual fraud case, the trustee can fall back on the UFTA four-year reach-back provision because there will always be at least one unpaid creditor at the time of bankruptcy.

In the celebrated case of *Moore v. Bay*, 284 U.S. 4 (1931) (Holmes, J.), the Court held that the action of a trustee in avoiding a transfer is not just for the benefit of creditors who would have been able to set aside the transfer under state law, nor is the avoidance power limited to the amount of such creditors' claims, rather the entire transfer is set aside for the benefit of the estate, *i.e.*, for the benefit of all creditors with unsecured claims in the bankruptcy. The principle of *Moore v. Bay* can have dramatic effects and is applicable to cases brought under either § 544(a) or 548. Assume that the debtor made a transfer of property worth $1,000,000 and that under state law one creditor, with a claim of $100, can avoid the transfer because some duty to that creditor had not been performed. Assume that no other creditor has a right under the state law to attack the transfer, that under the state law the creditor with the $100 claim is entitled to have the claim paid from the property transferred, and that the transfer is otherwise valid. The effect in bankruptcy, if the $100 claim still exists, is that (i) the entire $1,000,000 transfer is voidable by the trustee under § 544(b); (ii) the estate receives the benefit of the avoidance; and (iii) the creditor who, prebankruptcy, had the state law right to avoid the transfer will lose that right and will receive only its pro rata share of the (enhanced) estate in accordance with its rights under bankruptcy law.

*What is Actual Intent to Hinder, Delay, or Defraud?* Courts have struggled for centuries to decide this illusive issue. Sometimes it is obvious, as in the fact situation at the beginning of the section in which a debtor attempts to shield her assets from her creditors by transferring them to a relative for nominal or no consideration. But in other cases it is not so clear. Given the practical difficulty of obtaining direct evidence of the debtor's intent, few cases turn on such proof. Instead, looking to the circumstances surrounding the transfer, courts have identified several objective indicia that, taken together, strongly indicate fraudulent intent. These indicia have been referred to as the "badges of fraud" from the time of *Twyne's Case*, 3 Coke 80b, 76 Eng. Rep. 809 (1601). These indicia include: (1) insider relationships between the parties; (2) retention of possession, benefit or use of the property; (3) the lack or inadequacy of consideration for the transfer; (4) the financial condition of the party sought to be charged both before and after the transaction at issue; (5) the existence or cumulative effect of the pattern or series of transactions or course of conduct after the incurring of debt, onset of financial difficulties, or pendency or threat of suits by creditors; (6) the general chronology of events and transactions under inquiry; and (7) an attempt by the debtor to keep the transfer a secret. *See* UFTA § 4(b). How many of these criteria apply to the fact situation at the beginning of the section? In *In re Watman*, 301 F.3d 3 (1st Cir. 2002), the court added a 21st century indicium: "The shifting of assets by the debtor to a corporation wholly controlled by him is another badge of fraud." 301 F.3d at 8.

*Who Can Sue to Set Aside the Transfer?* In recent years disagreement has arisen on this basic question. Section 550(a) allows trustees to recover property fraudulently transferred under § 548(a), and this power may be exercised by the debtor in possession in Chapter 11 cases. § 1107(a). Section 544(b) also refers only to trustees. But in some situations the transfers may have been made by the management of the debtor now serving as debtor in possession and in other cases the debtor in possession may be attempting to negotiate a plan with the recipients of the alleged fraudulent transfer; in neither instance does the debtor in possession have much incentive to prosecute an avoidance claim. Seeing the debtor in possession dragging its heels, creditors may wish to take matters in their own hands. The accepted remedy has been for the creditors' committee to ask the court to permit it to pursue recovery for the benefit of the estate. This practice was accepted by courts pre-1978 and carried on under the new Code even though there is no specific authorization under § 544(b) or § 550, both of which refer to only trustees and debtors in possession.

A bombshell was exploded by *Official Committee of Unsecured Creditors of Cybergenics Corp. v. Chinery (Cybergenics I),* 310 F.3d 785 (3d Cir.2002), in which a Third Circuit panel decreed that the holding in *Hartford Underwriters Ins. Co. v. Union Planters Bank, N.A.*, 530 U.S. 1 (2000) (reprinted at p. 631), compelled a "plain meaning" reading of § 544(b) that precluded creditors' committees from bringing fraudulent transfer actions. In footnote 5 of *Hartford Underwriters*, the Court had left open the issue before the *Cybergenics* I court. The Third Circuit, besieged by demands from academics and other amici for a rehearing, reversed the panel in Official Committee of *Unsecured Creditors of Cybergenics Corp. v. Chinery, (Cybergenics II),* 330 F.3d 548 *en banc* (3d Cir.2003). The majority held that the equitable power of a bankruptcy court gave it the power to craft a remedy when the Code's "envisioned scheme breaks down." 330 F.3d at 553. A vigorous dissenting opinion saw the case as a simple instance of interpreting the wording of an unambiguous statute, the meaning of which is plain; if Congress had intended to allow creditors' committees to pursue fraudulent transfers, it would have expressly said so in the statute. But the law of fraudulent transfers is of little help to defrauded creditors if there is no one with the incentive to enforce it, and even critics of *Cybergenics II* have difficulty articulating any policy basis for denying standing to bring such suits in appropriate circumstances. *See* Daniel J. Bussel, *Creditors' Committees as Estate Representatives in Bankruptcy Litigation*, 10 Stan. J. L. Bus. & Fin. 28 (2004).

Section 548(e). The 2005 Act added § 548(e) to deal with asset protection trusts. In the last section of chapter 2, we explain how these are used to shelter assets from creditors in and out of bankruptcy. During the drafting process, critics of these devices urged that the legislation that finally became the 2005 Act should do away with them. This was not done. About the only change that § 548(e) made in pre-2005 law was to extend the two-year look-back period in § 548(a) to ten years.

## 2. CONSTRUCTIVE FRAUD

### a.   Introduction

"Constructive fraud" is an oxymoron; fraud generally connotes some degree of evil intent. Professor Tabb observes:

> The promulgation of the [Uniform Fraudulent Conveyance Act] in 1918 marked a watershed in the evolution of fraudulent conveyance law. The objectification of the law, developed over the centuries by courts through the invocation of "badges of fraud" as a means of inferring actual fraudulent intent, was given formal recognition. For the first time, proof of certain specified facts conclusively established that the transfer at issue was a fraudulent conveyance, irrespective of the actual subjective intention of the debtor. This type of fraudulent conveyance has come to be known as *constructive* fraud.

Charles Jordan Tabb, *The Law of Bankruptcy* 423 (1997).

Constructive fraud is a basis for avoidance under both UFTA § 4(a)(2) and § 548(a)(1)(B) of the Bankruptcy Code. Under the latter provision, a trustee can avoid a transfer or obligation by proving (A) that the debtor received less than reasonably equivalent value in exchange for the transfer or obligation, and, (B) that on the date the transfer was made or the obligation was incurred, the debtor was either (i) insolvent or was rendered insolvent by the transfer or obligation, (ii) was engaged in or was about to engage in business or a transaction for which any property remaining with the debtor was unreasonably small capital, or (iii) intended to incur debts beyond the debtor's ability to pay as the debts matured. Dean Robert C. Clark's aphorism sums it up: insolvent debtors must "be just before [they] are generous." *The Duties of the Corporate Debtor to Its Creditors*, 90 Harv.L.Rev. 505, 510 (1977). The metaphor sometimes invoked is that an insolvent debtor holds property in trust for its creditors.

The drafters of the UFCA in 1918 could not possibly have imagined the impact that their modest-appearing constructive fraud provisions would have on common business transactions involving corporate distributions, mergers and acquisitions, guaranties and foreclosures. As we shall see, no lawyer can give competent counsel in these areas without having a good grasp of the law of fraudulent transfers. In order to predict whether a transfer or obligation will stand up in a subsequent bankruptcy, transaction planners must address two inherently fact-intensive, often difficult, issues: whether the transferor or obligor will receive reasonably equivalent value and whether this person is, or will be rendered, insolvent at the time of the transfer. In the following materials we will examine the meaning of these terms.

The rationale of § 548(a)(1)(B) is that a transfer of property by an insolvent debtor for less than reasonably equivalent value is unfair to creditors having claims at the time of the transfer because those creditors are being deprived of assets that would otherwise be available for payment of the debts owed to them. Gratuitous transfers are obviously subject to avoidance under this provision, but sale transactions may also be avoided. If a sale is made at a bargain price to an insider, the debtor may intend to confer a benefit on the buyer. If that is so, the debtor has made a gratuitous transfer to the buyer to the extent the price received is less than the price that would have been received in an arms-length transaction.

If the debtor is not trying to favor the buyer, the interests of the debtor and creditors coincide. There is no advantage to either the debtor or the creditors if the property is not sold for the best price possible. Thus, if the debtor and the buyer arrive at a price in an arms-length uncoerced transaction, that price should represent reasonably equivalent value or at least the best evidence of that value. Opinion concerning what price the property might have brought if it had been sold in a hypothetical transaction involving a different buyer or seller or both may be an unreliable guide to value. Some courts, however, have second-guessed the price received in forced sale scenarios. The most notorious example of this is *Durrett*, discussed later.

### b.   Religious and Charitable Contributions

Bruce and Nancy Young were active church members who made annual contributions to the church in furtherance of their religious beliefs. When they filed in Chapter 7 bankruptcy in 1992, their trustee successfully challenged a $13,450 contribution made by them in the year preceding their bankruptcy on the ground of constructive fraud under § 548(a)(1)(B); the Youngs did not receive reasonably equivalent value from the church in exchange for their gift. *In re Young*, 148 B.R. 886 (Bankr.D.Minn.1992). This set in motion a series of events that culminated in passage of the "Religious Liberty and Charitable Donation Protection Act of 1998." After the bankruptcy court opinion, trustees in other cases began to challenge tithes by insolvent debtors, and the attention of the religious and bankruptcy communities was drawn to this issue. When the case was before the Eighth Circuit, the Justice Department filed a brief in favor of the trustee. In the 18 months between oral argument and the final decision in *In re Young*, 82 F.3d 1407 (8th Cir.1996), Congress enacted the Religious Freedom Restoration Act (RFRA), 42 U.S.C. § 2000bb. In a move that was described by headline writers as "divine intervention," President Clinton ordered the Department of Justice to pull its *Young* brief and campaigned as a protector of religious freedom, highlighting the issue in one of the TV debates with Senator Dole. Mary Jo New-born Wiggins, *A Statute of Disbelief?: Clashing Ethical Imperatives in Fraudulent Transfer Law*, 48 S.C.L.Rev. 771, 774 n.25 (1997).

In *Young,* the Eighth Circuit held that although the debtors' donation was an avoidable transfer under § 548(a)(2) (now § 548(a)(1)(B)), recovery from the church would substantially burden the debtors' free exercise of religion and was not justified by a compelling governmental interest; hence, the church won under RFRA. But in *City of Boerne v. Flores*, 521 U.S. 507 (1997), the Supreme Court held the RFRA unconstitutional insofar as it sought to preempt on free exercise grounds state law that was otherwise consistent with the First Amendment, reopening the possibility that tithes could be avoided as fraudulent transfers under state law notwithstanding RFRA and *Young.* Religious indignation at this turn of events resulted in prompt enactment of the "Religious Liberty and Charitable Donation Protection Act" in 1998 by the unanimous vote of both houses of Congress. Although the impetus for this law came from religious groups, Congress included all charities to head off constitutional objections to the Act based on the establishment of religion.

This measure added § 548(a)(2), which allows individuals to make contributions to qualified religious or charitable entities without fear of avoidance as constructive fraud under § 548 so long as (i) the contribution does not exceed 15% of the debtor's gross annual income for the year in which the transfer is made (there is no limit on the number of such contributions), or (ii) even if it does exceed that amount, the contribution is consistent with the practices of the debtor in making charitable contributions in the past. Section 544(b) was amended to prevent the trustee from using state fraudulent transfer law to avoid these transfers.

Presumably, charities around the nation are rejoicing that they can broaden their solicitations to include a group never before thought to be promising targets—insolvents on the eve of bankruptcy. Astonishingly, on the face of the statute, debtors can clean out their entire estate on the eve of bankruptcy by making gifts of up to 15% of their incomes to each of several qualified donees until their money runs out, without offending the constructive fraud provisions of § 548. Any state law action to recover a contribution to a qualified charity as a fraudulent transfer is preempted by the debtor's filing bankruptcy.

What is left of fraudulent transfer law in the area of charitable giving? The statute speaks only of transfers; obligations to make charitable gifts in the future (the familiar charitable pledge) could still be set aside under § 548's constructive fraud provisions. Since the actual intent fraud provision of § 548(a)(1)(A) is unchanged, presumably a debtor who engages in the abusive conduct described above would face a challenge under this provision, as well as the threat of being barred from discharge by § 727(a)(2). Interestingly, the Act makes no reference to preference law and if payment of a pledge within 90 days of bankruptcy can be characterized as a transfer to a creditor on account of antecedent debt, the payment is arguably avoidable as a preference.

Professor Klee has made an empirical survey of both Chapter 7 and Chapter 13 cases since the Religious Liberty Act and suggests that fraudulent transfer law in practice is not much changed. Before the Act, *de facto* tithes and other charitable gifts were rarely recovered except in cases where the giving appeared fraudulent or abusive or not consistent with the debtor's past practices. After the Act, tithing is *de jure* protected except in cases where the gifts are actually fraudulent and trustees, and bankruptcy courts are likely to view apparently abusive giving not consistent with past practices as actual fraud. Kenneth N. Klee, *Tithing and Bankruptcy*, 75 Am. Bankr. L. J. 157 (2001). Klee suggests that the real effect of the Religious Liberty Act is not in fraudulent transfer law but in Chapter 13 cases since the statute now expressly includes charitable giving as a living expense reducing the net disposable income available for debt repayment. *Id.*, at 192. By including substantial amounts of giving in their Chapter 13 plan budgets, debtors can reduce their obligations to creditors, standing Dean Clark's aphorism on its head: Chapter 13 now presumes one can be generous before being just. *See infra* Chapter 9.

### c.  Insider Transfers or Obligations under Employment Contracts

The 2005 Act adopts a fraudulent transfer approach to excessive compensation for insider employees. Section 548(a)(1) is amended to address the issue by allowing the trustee to recover such payments or avoid such obligations made to insiders under employment contracts by showing (i) that the services rendered by the employee were not reasonably equivalent value for the transfers or obligations, § 548(a)(1)(B)(i), and (ii) that the transfers or obligations were not made "in ordinary course of business," § 548(a)(1)(B)(ii)(IV). The novelty of the amendment is that the trustee can  prove constructive fraud without proof of the of the insolvency of the debtor. Before this amendment, constructive fraud in fraudulent transfer law was present only when the debtor made transfers or incurred obligations that diminished the assets of the debtor to the prejudice of the creditors of the debtor. Generally speaking, creditors are prejudiced only when a debtor, who is insolvent at the time of the transfer or obligation, or is rendered insolvent thereby, doesn't receive reasonably equivalent value from the transferee or obligee. § 548(a)(1)(B)(ii)(I).

It is not clear what, if any, effect this amendment will have. First, the trustee will have a difficult task in proving that the compensation called for by an employment contract, viewed at the time of making the contract, is so excessive that the employee's services would not amount to reasonably equivalent value. Salaries of executives vary widely: the appropriate level of executive compensation is much debated as are the theories of how the level should be determined. Even if the trustee makes this proof, it must still prove that the payments or obligations were not in ordinary course of business. Presumably this means the debtor's course of business. Would the trustee's case fail if the debtor rountinely overpaid all its executives? Nell Hennessey, Marcia Goldstein, Scott Cohen & Matthew Weinstein, *Employee Benefits and Executive Compensation Provisions in the New Bankruptcy Act*, BNA Bankruptcy Law Reporter, Vol. 17, No. 19 (2005), conclude that since most employment contracts can be treated as arguably in the ordinary course of a company's business, the amendment will have little effect. They point out that, perversely, the most vulnerable contracts may be those made with bankruptcy turnaround professionals. Transfers not made in ordinary course of the debtor's business is a new concept in contructive fraudulent transfer law.

### 3. FORECLOSURES

One of the more heated controversies in fraudulent transfer law arose from the holding in *Durrett v. Washington Nat'l Ins. Co.*, 621 F.2d 201 (5th Cir.1980), which decided for the first time that a regularly conducted, noncollusive foreclosure sale of real estate, valid under state mortgage foreclosure statutes, could be set aside in bankruptcy as a fraudulent transfer if the amount paid by the foreclosure sale buyer was found by a bankruptcy court to be less than reasonably equivalent value. The Supreme Court resolved this controversy in the following case.

## BFP v. Resolution Trust Co.
Supreme Court of the United States, 1994.
511 U.S. 531.

■ Justice SCALIA delivered the opinion of the court.

This case presents the question whether the consideration received from a noncollusive, real estate mortgage foreclosure sale conducted in conformance with applicable state law conclusively satisfies the Bankruptcy Code's requirement that transfers of property by insolvent debtors within one year prior to the filing of a bankruptcy petition be in exchange for "a reasonably equivalent value." § 548(a)(2).

### I

Petitioner BFP is a partnership, formed by Wayne and Marlene Pedersen and Russell Barton in 1987, for the purpose of buying a home in Newport Beach, California, from Sheldon and Ann Foreman. Petitioner took title subject to a first deed of trust in favor of Imperial Savings Association (Imperial)[1] to secure payment of a loan of $356,250 made to the Pedersens

---

[1] Respondent Resolution Trust Corporation (RTC) acts in this case as receiver of Imperial Federal Savings Association (Imperial Federal), which was organized pursuant to a June 22, 1990, order of the Director of the Office of Thrift Supervision, and into which RTC transferred certain assets and liabilities of Imperial. The Director previously had appointed RTC as receiver of Imperial. For convenience we refer to all respondents other than RTC and Imperial as the private respondents.

in connection with petitioner's acquisition of the home. Petitioner granted a second deed of trust to the Foremans as security for a $200,000 promissory note. Subsequently, Imperial, whose loan was not being serviced, entered a notice of default under the first deed of trust and scheduled a properly noticed foreclosure sale. The foreclosure proceedings were temporarily delayed by the filing of an involuntary bankruptcy petition on behalf of petitioner. After the dismissal of that petition in June 1989, Imperial's foreclosure proceeding was completed at a foreclosure sale on July 12, 1989. The home was purchased by respondent Paul Osborne for $433,000.

In October 1989, petitioner filed for bankruptcy under Chapter 11 of the Bankruptcy Code. Acting as a debtor in possession, petitioner filed a complaint in Bankruptcy Court seeking to set aside the conveyance of the home to respondent Osborne on the grounds that the foreclosure sale constituted a fraudulent transfer under § 548 of the Code. Petitioner alleged that the home was actually worth over $725,000 at the time of the sale to Osborne. Acting on separate motions, the Bankruptcy Court dismissed the complaint as to the private respondents and granted summary judgment in favor of Imperial. The Bankruptcy Court found, *inter alia,* that the foreclosure sale had been conducted in compliance with California law and was neither collusive nor fraudulent. In an unpublished opinion, the District Court affirmed the Bankruptcy Court's granting of the private respondents' motion to dismiss. A divided bankruptcy appellate panel affirmed the Bankruptcy Court's entry of summary judgment for Imperial. 132 B.R. 748 (1991). Applying the analysis set forth in *In re Madrid*, 21 B.R. 424 (Bkrtcy.App.Pan. CA9 1982), affirmed on other grounds, 725 F.2d 1197 (CA9), (1984), the panel majority held that a "non-collusive and regularly conducted nonjudicial foreclosure sale. . . cannot be challenged as a fraudulent conveyance because the consideration received in such a sale establishes 'reasonably equivalent value' as a matter of law." 132 B.R., at 750.

Petitioner sought review of both decisions in the Court of Appeals for the Ninth Circuit, which consolidated the appeals. The Court of Appeals affirmed. *In re BFP*, 974 F.2d 1144 (1992). BFP filed a petition for certiorari, which we granted.

## II

Section 548 of the Bankruptcy Code sets forth the powers of a trustee in bankruptcy (or, in a Chapter 11 case, a debtor in possession) to avoid fraudulent transfers. It permits to be set aside not only transfers infected by actual fraud but certain other transfers as well—so-called constructively fraudulent transfers. The constructive fraud provision at issue in this case applies to transfers by insolvent debtors. It permits avoidance if the trustee can establish (1) that the debtor had an interest in property; (2) that a transfer of that interest occurred within one year of the filing of the bankruptcy petition; (3) that the debtor was insolvent at the time of the transfer or became insolvent as a result thereof; and (4) that the debtor received "less than a reasonably equivalent value in exchange for such transfer." § 548(a)(2)(A). It is the last of these four elements that presents the issue in the case before us.

Section 548 applies to any "transfer," which includes "foreclosure of the debtor's equity of redemption." § 101(54). Of the three critical terms "reasonably equivalent value," only the last is defined: "value" means, for purposes of § 548, "property, or satisfaction or securing of a. . . debt of the debtor," § 548(d)(2)(A). The question presented here, therefore, is whether the amount of debt (to the first and second lienholders) satisfied at the foreclosure sale (viz., a total of $433,000) is "reasonably equivalent" to the worth of the real estate conveyed. The Courts of Appeals have divided on the meaning of those undefined terms. In *Durrett v. Washington Nat. Ins. Co.,* 621 F.2d 201 (1980), the Fifth Circuit, interpreting a provision of the old Bankruptcy Act analogous to § 548(a)(2), held that a foreclosure sale that yielded 57% of the property's fair market value could be set aside, and indicated in dicta that any such sale for less than 70% of fair market value should be invalidated. *Id.,* at 203-204. This "*Durrett* rule" has continued to be applied by some courts under § 548 of the new Bankruptcy Code. * * * In *In re Bundles,* 856 F.2d 815, 820 (1988), the Seventh Circuit rejected the *Durrett* rule in favor of a case-by-case, "all facts and circumstances" approach to the question of reasonably equivalent value, with a *rebuttable* presumption that the foreclosure sale price is sufficient to withstand attack under § 548(a)(2). In this case the Ninth Circuit, agreeing with the Sixth Circuit, see *In re Winshall Settlor's Trust,* 758 F.2d 1136, 1139 (CA6 1985), adopted the position first put forward in *In re Madrid,* 21 B.R. 424 (Bkrtcy.App.Pan. CA9 1982), affirmed on other grounds, 725 F.2d 1197 (CA9 1984), that the consideration received at a noncollusive, regularly conducted real estate foreclosure sale constitutes a reasonably equivalent value under § 548(a)(2)(A). The Court of Appeals acknowledged that it "necessarily part[ed] from the positions taken by the Fifth Circuit in *Durrett.* . . and the Seventh Circuit in *Bundles.*" 974 F.2d, at 1148.

In contrast to the approach adopted by the Ninth Circuit in the present case, both *Durrett* and *Bundles* refer to fair market value as the benchmark against which determination of reasonably equivalent value is to be measured. In the context of an otherwise lawful mortgage foreclosure sale of real estate,[3] such reference is in our opinion not consistent with the text of the Bankruptcy Code. The term "fair market value," though it is a well-established concept, does not appear in § 548. In contrast, § 522, dealing with a debtor's exemptions, specifically provides that, for purposes of that section, "'value' means fair market value as of the date of the filing of the petition." § 522(a)(2). "Fair market value" also appears in the Code provi-

---

[3] We emphasize that our opinion today covers only mortgage foreclosures of real estate. The considerations bearing upon other foreclosures and forced sales (to satisfy tax liens, for example) may be different.

sion that defines the extent to which indebtedness with respect to an equity security is not forgiven for the purpose of determining whether the debtor's estate has realized taxable income. § 346(j)(7)(B). Section 548, on the other hand, seemingly goes out of its way to avoid that standard term. It might readily have said "received less than fair market value in exchange for such transfer or obligation," or perhaps "less than a reasonable equivalent of fair market value." Instead, it used the (as far as we are aware) entirely novel phrase "reasonably equivalent value." "[I]t is generally presumed that Congress acts intentionally and purposely when it includes particular language in one section of a statute but omits it in another," *Chicago v. Environmental Defense Fund*, 511 U.S. 328, 338 (1994), and that presumption is even stronger when the omission entails the replacement of standard legal terminology with a neologism. One must suspect the language means that fair market value cannot—or at least cannot *always*—be the benchmark.

That suspicion becomes a certitude when one considers that market value, as it is commonly understood, has no applicability in the forced-sale context; indeed, it is the very *antithesis* of forced-sale value. "The market value of. . . a piece of property is the price which it might be expected to bring if offered for sale in a fair market; not the price which might be obtained on a sale at public auction or a sale forced by the necessities of the owner, but such a price as would be fixed by negotiation and mutual agreement, after ample time to find a purchaser, as between a vendor who is willing (but not compelled) to sell and a purchaser who desires to buy but is not compelled to take the particular. . . piece of property." Black's Law Dictionary 971 (6th ed. 1990). In short, "fair market value" presumes market conditions that, by definition, simply do not obtain in the context of a forced sale.* * *

Neither petitioner, petitioner's *amici,* nor any federal court adopting the *Durrett* or the *Bundles* analysis has come to grips with this glaring discrepancy between the factors relevant to an appraisal of a property's market value, on the one hand, and the strictures of the foreclosure process on the other. Market value cannot be the criterion of equivalence in the foreclosure-sale context. The language of § 548(a)(2)(A) ( "received less than a reasonably equivalent value in exchange") requires judicial inquiry into whether the foreclosed property was sold for a price that approximated its worth at the time of sale. An appraiser's reconstruction of "fair market value" could show what similar property would be worth if it did not have to be sold within the time and manner strictures of state-prescribed foreclosure. But property that *must* be sold within those strictures is simply *worth less.* No one would pay as much to own such property as he would pay to own real estate that could be sold at leisure and pursuant to normal marketing techniques. And it is no more realistic to ignore that characteristic of the property (the fact that state foreclosure law permits the mortgagee to sell it at forced sale) than it is to ignore other price-affecting characteristics (such as the fact that state zoning law permits the owner of the neighboring lot to open a gas station). Absent a clear statutory requirement to the contrary, we must assume the validity of this state-law regulatory background and take due account of its effect. "The existence and force and function of established institutions of local government are always in the consciousness of lawmakers and, while their weight may vary, they may never be completely overlooked in the task of interpretation." *Davies Warehouse Co. v. Bowles*, 321 U.S. 144, 154 (1944).

There is another artificially constructed criterion we might look to instead of "fair market price." One might judge there to be such a thing as a "reasonable" or "fair" forced-sale price. Such a conviction must lie behind the *Bundles* inquiry into whether the state foreclosure proceedings "were calculated. . . to return to the debtor-mortgagor his equity in the property." 856 F.2d, at 824. And perhaps that is what the courts that follow the *Durrett* rule have in mind when they select 70% of fair market value as the outer limit of "reasonably equivalent value" for forecloseable property (we have no idea where else such an arbitrary percentage could have come from). The problem is that such judgments represent policy determinations that the Bankruptcy Code gives us no apparent authority to make. How closely the price received in a forced sale is likely to approximate fair market value depends upon the terms of the forced sale—how quickly it may be made, what sort of public notice must be given, etc. But the terms for foreclosure sale are not *standard.* They vary considerably from State to State, depending upon, among other things, how the particular State values the divergent interests of debtor and creditor. To specify a federal "reasonable" foreclosure-sale price is to extend federal bankruptcy law well beyond the traditional field of fraudulent transfers, into realms of policy where it has not ventured before. Some sense of history is needed to appreciate this.

The modern law of fraudulent transfers had its origin in the Statute of 13 Elizabeth, which invalidated "covinous and fraudulent" transfers designed "to delay, hinder or defraud creditors and others." 13 Eliz., ch. 5 (1570). English courts soon developed the doctrine of "badges of fraud": proof by a creditor of certain objective facts (for example, a transfer to a close relative, a secret transfer, a transfer of title without transfer of possession, or grossly inadequate consideration) would raise a rebuttable presumption of actual fraudulent intent. See *Twyne's Case,* 3 Coke Rep. 80b, 76 Eng.Rep. 809 (K.B. 1601); O. Bump, Fraudulent Conveyances: A Treatise upon Conveyances Made by Debtors to Defraud Creditors 31-60 (3d ed. 1882). Every American bankruptcy law has incorporated a fraudulent transfer provision; the 1898 Act specifically adopted the language of the Statute of 13 Elizabeth. Bankruptcy Act of July 1, 1898, ch. 541, § 67(e), 30 Stat. 564-565.

The history of foreclosure law also begins in England, where courts of chancery developed the "equity of redemption"—the equitable right of a borrower to buy back, or redeem, property conveyed as security by paying the secured debt on a later date than "law day," the original due date. The courts' continued expansion of the period of redemption left lenders in a quandary, since title to forfeited property could remain clouded for years after law day. To meet this problem, courts created the equitable remedy of foreclosure: after a certain date the borrower would be forever foreclosed from exercising his equity of redemption. This remedy was called strict foreclosure because the borrower's entire interest in the property was forfeited, regardless of any accumulated equity. See G. Glenn, 1 Mortgages 3- 18, 358-362, 395-406 (1943); G. Osborne, Mortgages 144 (2d ed. 1970). The next major change took place in 19th-century America, with the development of foreclosure by sale (with the surplus over the debt refunded to the debtor) as a means of avoiding the draconian consequences of strict foreclosure. *Id.*, at 661-663; Glenn, *supra*, at 460-462, 622. Since then, the States have created diverse networks of judicially and legislatively crafted rules governing the foreclosure process, to achieve what each of them considers the proper balance between the needs of lenders and borrowers. All States permit judicial foreclosure, conducted under direct judicial oversight; about half of the States also permit foreclosure by exercising a private power of sale provided in the mortgage documents.* * * Foreclosure laws typically require notice to the defaulting borrower, a substantial lead time before the commencement of foreclosure proceedings, publication of a notice of sale, and strict adherence to prescribed bidding rules and auction procedures. Many States require that the auction be conducted by a government official, and some forbid the property to be sold for less than a specified fraction of a mandatory presale fair-market-value appraisal. * * * When these procedures have been followed, however, it is "black letter" law that mere inadequacy of the foreclosure sale price is no basis for setting the sale aside, though it may be set aside (*under state foreclosure law,* rather than fraudulent transfer law) if the price is so low as to "shock the conscience or raise a presumption of fraud or unfairness." *Gelfert v. National City Bank of N.Y.*, 313 U.S. 221, 232 (1941).

Fraudulent transfer law and foreclosure law enjoyed over 400 years of peaceful coexistence in Anglo-American jurisprudence until the Fifth Circuit's unprecedented 1980 decision in *Durrett.* To our knowledge no prior decision had ever applied the "grossly inadequate price" badge of fraud under fraudulent transfer law to set aside a foreclosure sale. To say that the "reasonably equivalent value" language in the fraudulent transfer provision of the Bankruptcy Code requires a foreclosure sale to yield a certain minimum price beyond what state foreclosure law requires, is to say, in essence, that the Code has adopted *Durrett* or *Bundles.* Surely Congress has the power pursuant to its constitutional grant of authority over bankruptcy, U.S. Const., Art. I, § 8, cl. 4, to disrupt the ancient harmony that foreclosure law and fraudulent conveyance law, those two pillars of debtor-creditor jurisprudence, have heretofore enjoyed. But absent clearer textual guidance than the phrase "reasonably equivalent value"—a phrase entirely compatible with pre-existing practice—we will not presume such a radical departure. [7]

Federal statutes impinging upon important state interests "cannot. . . be construed without regard to the implications of our dual system of government. . .. [W]hen the Federal Government takes over. . . local radiations in the vast network of our national economic enterprise and thereby radically readjusts the balance of state and national authority, those charged with the duty of legislating [must be] reasonably explicit." Frankfurter, Some Reflections on the Reading of Statutes, 47 Colum.L.Rev. 527, 539-540 (1947). It is beyond question that an essential state interest is at issue here: We have said that "the general welfare of society is involved in the security of the titles to real estate" and the power to ensure that security "inheres in the very nature of [state] government." *American Land Co. v. Zeiss,* 219 U.S. 47, 60 (1911). Nor is there any doubt that the interpretation urged by petitioner would have a profound effect upon that interest: The title of every piece of realty purchased at foreclosure would be under a federally created cloud. (Already, title insurers have reacted to the *Durrett* rule by including specially crafted exceptions from coverage in many policies issued for properties purchased at foreclosure sales. * * * To displace traditional state regulation in such a manner, the federal statutory purpose must be "clear and manifest," *English v. General Elec. Co.,* 496 U.S. 72, 79 (1990). * * * Otherwise, the Bankruptcy Code will be construed to adopt, rather than to displace, pre-existing state law. * * *

For the reasons described, we decline to read the phrase "reasonably equivalent value" in § 548(a)(2) to mean, in its application to mortgage

---

[7] We are unpersuaded by petitioner's argument that the 1984 amendments to the Bankruptcy Code codified the *Durrett* rule. Those amendments expanded the definition of "transfer" to include "foreclosure of the debtor's equity of redemption," 11 U.S.C. § 101(54) (1988 ed., Supp. IV), and added the words "voluntarily or involuntarily" as modifiers of the term "transfer" in § 548(a). The first of these provisions establishes that foreclosure sales fall within the general definition of "transfers" that may be avoided under several statutory provisions, including (but not limited to) § 548. See § 522(h) (transfers of exempt property), § 544 (transfers voidable under state law), § 547 (preferential transfers), § 549 (postpetition transfers). The second of them establishes that a transfer may be avoided as fraudulent even if it was against the debtor's will. See *In re Madrid,* 725 F.2d 1197, 1199 (CA9 1984) (preamendment decision holding that a foreclosure sale is not a "transfer" under § 548). Neither of these consequences has any bearing upon the meaning of "reasonably equivalent value" in the context of a foreclosure sale.

Nor does our reading render these amendments "superfluous," as the dissent contends, *post,* at 1770. Prior to 1984, it was at least open to question whether § 548 could be used to invalidate even a *collusive* foreclosure sale, see *Madrid, supra,* at 1204 (Farris, J., concurring). It is no superfluity for Congress to clarify what had been at best unclear, which is what it did here by making the provision apply to involuntary as well as voluntary transfers and by including foreclosures within the definition of "transfer." See *infra,* at 1765-1766.

foreclosure sales, either "fair market value" or "fair foreclosure price" (whether calculated as a percentage of fair market value or otherwise). We deem, as the law has always deemed, that a fair and proper price, or a "reasonably equivalent value," for foreclosed property, is the price in fact received at the foreclosure sale, so long as all the requirements of the State's foreclosure law have been complied with.

This conclusion does not render § 548(a)(2) superfluous, since the "reasonably equivalent value" criterion will continue to have independent meaning (ordinarily a meaning similar to fair market value) outside the foreclosure context. Indeed, § 548(a)(2) will even continue to be an exclusive means of invalidating some foreclosure sales. Although *collusive* foreclosure sales are likely subject to attack under § 548(a)(1), which authorizes the trustee to avoid transfers "made. . . with actual intent to hinder, delay, or defraud" creditors, that provision may not reach foreclosure sales that, while not intentionally fraudulent, nevertheless fail to comply with all governing state laws. * * * Any irregularity in the conduct of the sale that would permit judicial invalidation of the sale under applicable state law deprives the sale price of its conclusive force under § 548(a)(2)(A), and the transfer may be avoided if the price received was not reasonably equivalent to the property's actual value at the time of the sale (which we think would be the price that would have been received if the foreclosure sale had proceeded according to law).

* * *

For the foregoing reasons, the judgment of the Court of Appeals for the Ninth Circuit is

*Affirmed.*

Justice SOUTER, with whom Justice BLACKMUN, Justice STEVENS, and Justice GINSBURG join, dissenting. [Opinion omitted.]


## NOTES

**1.** In dissent, Justice Souter gleefully noted that Justice Scalia, the prince of the plain meaning rule, had taken liberties with the meaning of a statute clear to any "ordinary speaker of English." Ouch! He pointed out the absurdity that under the majority's test a peppercorn paid at a noncollusive and procedurally regular foreclosure sale must be treated as the reasonably equivalent value of a California beachfront estate (the property involved in *BFP*). And, indeed, in *In re T.F. Stone Co., Inc.*, 72 F.3d 466 (5th Cir.1995), the court relied on *BFP* to hold that a regularly conducted, noncollusive tax sale for $325 was a sale "for present fair equivalent value" under § 549(c) even though the buyer resold the property a few months later for $39,500! *See also In re Grandote Country Club Co.*, 252 F.3d 1146 (10th Cir.2001) (refusing to upset tax sale under Colorado fraudulent transfer law).

**2.** The scope of *BFP* is in dispute in the lower courts. *See, e.g., In re Ford*, 296 B.R. 537 (Bankr. N.D. Ga.2003) (rejecting *T.F.Stone's* holding that *BFP* applies to § 549(c)); *In re D'Alfonso*, 211 B.R. 508 (Bankr. E.D. Pa. 1997) (refusing to extend *BFP* to tax sales). The Court emphasized that its opinion covers only mortgage foreclosures of real estate, but its forced-sale rationale would seem to apply as well to foreclosures of personal property collateral under the UCC and, as noted above, *T.F. Stone* applied it to local government tax sales. 511 U.S. at 537 n.3. Uniform Fraudulent Transfer Act § 3(b) adopts the irrebuttable presumption rule that was later accepted by the Court in *BFP* with respect to § 548, and the UFTA applies both to real and personal property foreclosures. Courts have generally limited *BFP* to situations where the transfer involved forced sale at public auction pursuant to statutes requiring an opportunity for competitive bidding. *In re Sherman*, 223 B.R. 555 (B.A.P. 10th Cir.1998) (finding tax sale in which competitive bidding was not permitted to be a constructively fraudulent transfer).

## 4. CORPORATE DISTRIBUTIONS AS FRAUDULENT TRANSFERS

We have seen that a gratuitous transfer by an insolvent debtor is a fraudulent transfer even if there is no fraudulent intent by the debtor. An insolvent person who gives away property that is subject to levy by creditors is disposing of the property unfairly. The debtor is transferring economic value to the transferee that in equity belongs to creditors. The protection of this interest of creditors is recognized in other areas of the law as well. Corporation law protects creditors of corporations by limiting the extent to which dividends and other distributions can be made to stockholders. A dividend, although not a gift, is gratuitous in the sense that it is a transfer of property for which no value is received in exchange. Limitations on dividends and other distributions to stockholders are analogous to limitations found in fraudulent transfer law on transfers by debtors, and they cover distributions made by both solvent and insolvent corporations.

A distribution by a corporation to its stockholders might violate both the corporation law and the fraudulent transfer law. Or, it might not be prohibited by the corporation law, but it may fall within the fraudulent transfer law. If the distribution violates both laws, the remedy provided by one law may differ from the remedy provided by the other. The relationship between the corporation law and the law of fraudulent transfers was noted by Judge Learned Hand in *Wood v. National City Bank*, 24 F.2d 661, 662–663 (2d Cir.1928) as follows:

> [Plaintiff] depends upon the fact that the directors have paid, and the defendants received, dividends when the corporation was insolvent. Merely because this impairs the capital stock, it is commonly regarded as a wrong to creditors on the directors' part, and it is often made such by statute. We may, without discussion, assume that it would be a wrong in the case at bar. Even so, it is primarily only the wrong of

those who commit it, like any other tort, and innocent participants are not accomplices to its commission. Hence it has been settled, at least for us, that when the liability is based merely on the depletion of the capital, a stockholder must be charged with notice of that fact. * * *

* * *

However, there is quite another theory, and quite another liability, if the payments not only impair the capital, but are taken out of assets already too small to pay the existing debts. The situation then strictly is not peculiar to corporation law, but merely an instance of a payment from an insolvent estate. Since, as we have said, a stockholder is a donee, he receives such payments charged with whatever trust they were subject to in the hands of the corporation. In that situation it can indeed be said with some truth that the corporate assets have become a "trust fund." * * * Hence it has never been doubted, so far as we can find, at least in any federal court, that if the dividends are paid in fraud of creditors the stockholder is so liable.

Judge Hand distinguished between dividends paid by an insolvent corporation and dividends paid by a solvent corporation that merely impair capital, stating that the former case is governed by fraudulent transfer law. But even the second case may be covered by the UFTA.

If payment of a dividend violates UFTA § 4(a)(2)(i), can the dividend be recovered from a stockholder who received it in good faith and without knowledge that it was unlawfully paid? California Corporations Code § 506(a), for example, limits liability to a stockholder who receives any distribution prohibited by the Corporations Code "with knowledge of facts indicating the impropriety thereof." Similar provisions are found in some other corporation statutes. Provisions of this kind reflect the fact that in many cases stockholders are passive investors who would not normally have any basis for determining whether a distribution was lawful or not. Quite apart from the practical difficulty of recovering relatively small amounts from large numbers of stockholders, it may be unfair to force disgorgement of payments innocently received and already spent. But UFTA § 8 does not recognize innocent receipt of a gratuitous fraudulent transfer as a defense. Thus, there may be a conflict between corporation law and fraudulent transfer law with respect to available remedies. California Corporations Code § 506(d) resolves the conflict in favor of the UFTA. It states that "nothing contained in this section affects any liability which any shareholder may have under [the UFTA]." The question of the relationship between corporation law and fraudulent transfer law is addressed by Robert C. Clark, *Corporate Law* 88–89 (1986) (arguing fraudulent transfer law should preempt dividend rules of corporation laws).

## PROBLEM

Debtor Corporation, while insolvent, issued stock to Defendant in order to raise capital. Defendant paid $100,000 for the shares and shortly thereafter sold them for more than that amount. When Debtor filed in Chapter 7 bankruptcy, its Trustee filed a complaint in bankruptcy court to avoid the issuance of the stock as a fraudulent transfer because Debtor did not receive reasonably equivalent value. On similar facts, the Ninth Circuit affirmed the bankruptcy court's dismissal of Trustee's claim on the ground that "unissued stock is not an interest of the debtor corporation in property; it is merely equity in the corporation itself." *Decker v. Advantage Fund Ltd.*, 362 F.3d 593, 596 (9th Cir. 2004). An earlier decision had explained: "Since an action directed at recovery of corporate stock could only effect equitable ownership of the corporation and would not restore property to the estate or avoid an estate obligation, then it is not a transfer subject to question under Section 548." *In re Curry and Sorensen, Inc.*, 57 B.R. 824, 829 (B.A.P. 9th Cir. 1986). Do you agree with this analysis?

## Robinson v. Wangemann

United States Court of Appeals, Fifth Circuit, 1935.
75 F.2d 756.

■ FOSTER, Circuit Judge.

This is an appeal from a judgment affirming an order of the referee allowing a claim against the estate of Reichardt–Abbott Company, Inc., bankrupt, based on a note given by the corporation in payment for shares of its own stock purchased by it.

The facts are not in dispute. In October, 1922, Arthur Wangemann, who was its president and a large stockholder in Wangemann–Reichardt Company, Inc., sold 500 shares of its own stock owned by him to the corporation at $110 per share, a total of $55,000, to be paid for on or before January 1, 1923. The purchase was authorized by a meeting of stockholders and the company's note, due January 1, 1923, bearing 7 per cent interest from October 1, 1922, was delivered to him in payment. At that time the corporation was solvent and its surplus in cash, over and above its liabilities, was more than $55,000. The note, due January 1, 1923, was not paid. From time to time, renewal notes were issued and the debt was reduced to $35,000. The name of the corporation was changed to Reichardt–Abbott Company, Inc., and under that name it was adjudicated bankrupt. Its assets are not sufficient to pay creditors in full. The claim of appellee is based on one of the renewal notes for $30,000, due January 1, 1933, and four notes each for $500, given in payment of interest on said note, together with interest on all the said notes. Appellee holds said notes as executrix under his will and sole legatee of Arthur Wangemann.

The referee held that the corporation had the right to purchase its own stock, * * * that the transaction was in good faith, and, as the corporation had sufficient surplus out of which the stock could have been paid for at the time it was purchased, without prejudice to creditors, appellee was entitled to prove her claim and participate equally with the other creditors in the distribution of the assets.

It may be conceded that if Arthur Wangemann had received cash for his stock at the time he relinquished it the transaction would have been valid, but that is not the case here presented.

* * * Arthur Wangemann loaned no money to the corporation. The note he accepted for his stock did not change the character of the transaction nor did the renewals have that effect. A transaction by which a corporation acquires its own stock from a stockholder for a sum of money is not really a sale. The corporation does not acquire anything of value equivalent to the depletion of its assets, if the stock is held in the treasury, as in this case. It is simply a method of distributing a proportion of the assets to the stockholders. The assets of a corporation are the common pledge of its creditors, and stockholders are not entitled to receive any part of them unless creditors are paid in full. When such a transaction is had, regardless of the good faith of the parties, it is essential to its validity that there be sufficient surplus to retire the stock, without prejudice to creditors, at the time payment is made out of assets. In principle, the contract between Wangemann and the corporation was executory until the stock should be paid for in cash. It is immaterial that the corporation was solvent and had sufficient surplus to make payment when the agreement was entered into. It is necessary to a recovery that the corporation should be solvent and have sufficient surplus to prevent injury to creditors when the payment is actually made. This was an implied condition in the original note and the renewals accepted by Arthur Wangemann.

As the assets of the bankrupt are not sufficient to pay the creditors in full and there is no surplus out of which the note could be paid, appellee, who is in no better position than the original holder of the notes, cannot be permitted to share with the other unsecured creditors in the distribution of the assets of the bankrupt estate. She may be permitted to file her claim, but it is subordinate to the claims of the other creditors. * * *

Reversed and remanded for further proceedings not inconsistent with this opinion.

## NOTES

**1.** In *In re SPM Manufacturing Corp.*, 163 B.R. 411 (Bankr.D. Mass.1994), the court said: "*Robinson v. Wangemann* is a policy statement that redemption debt must come behind general creditors in bankruptcy because of the priority creditors enjoy in bankruptcy over stockholders." 163 B.R. at 415.

**2.** As the court in *Robinson* recognized, the purchase by a corporation of its own shares is simply a distribution of assets of the corporation to the stockholder selling the shares. It is economically indistinguishable from the payment of a dividend, except that a dividend is a general distribution paid pro rata to all holders of the same class of stock while in a purchase of shares the distribution is limited to the selling stockholder. Repurchased stock, sometimes known as "treasury stock" because it is held in the corporation's treasury, may retain the status of issued stock until it is cancelled. Since it can be resold it might resemble an asset, but corporations can usually issue additional shares without first repurchasing those already issued; hence, repurchased shares are no more an asset than authorized but unissued shares. Indeed, both California, Cal.Corp.Code § 510(a), and the Revised Model Business Corporation Act § 6.31(a), eliminate the concept of treasury stock by providing that repurchased stock reverts to the status of authorized but unissued stock. William L. Cary & Melvin A. Eisenberg, *Cases and Materials on Corporations* 1388 (7th ed.1995). Dean Clark admonishes:

> Remember that there is never "fair consideration," in the sense meant by the [Uniform Fraudulent Conveyance Act] when a corporation makes a distribution to shareholders, because the corporation receives nothing the creditors could levy on or, if they did levy on it (as in the case of repurchased stock) nothing that would have value in their hands equivalent to the assets transferred to the shareholders. That is, from the creditor's perspective, distributions clearly reduce or deplete the "estate of the debtor."

Robert C. Clark, *Corporate Law* 638, n.9 (1986). In *Buncher Co. v. Official Committee of Unsecured Creditors*, 229 F.3d 245 (3d Cir.2000), the court likened the purchase by a limited partnership of the shares of some of its limited partners to a stock redemption by a corporation and held that the limited partnership received no value.

The similarity between the payment of a dividend and the purchase of the corporation's shares is reflected in corporation statutes that impose similar restrictions on the ability of the corporation to make either kind of distribution. For example we have seen that Model Business Corporation Act § 1.40(6) defines "distribution" to include "a purchase, redemption, or other acquisition of shares."

**3.** In *Robinson* the corporation had sufficient assets to allow it to lawfully pay cash for the shares at the date of purchase. If the parties choose to have the then solvent corporation pay for the shares by giving its promissory note instead of cash, why should the enforceability of the note depend upon the financial condition of the corporation at the time the note is paid? The statutory response to this issue varies among the states.

Section 166 of the California Corporations Code follows the rationale of *Robinson* by stating that "the time of any distribution by purchase or redemption of shares shall be the date cash or property is transferred by the corporation, whether or not pursuant to a contract of an earlier date * * *." An exception to this rule is provided for the case in which the corporation purchases its shares by issuing to the seller a debt obligation that is an investment security of a type commonly traded in the securities markets. In that case the distribution occurs when the corporation acquires the purchased shares. What is the rationale for applying one rule to the case in which the corporation pays with a simple promissory note and a different rule when the corporation pays with a debenture that is an investment security?

The Model Act is contrary to the California statute and to most prior case law. It provides that the validity of a distribution by purchase, redemption or other acquisition of a corporation's shares shall be measured "as of the earlier of (i) the date money or other property is transferred or debt incurred by the corporation or (ii) the date the shareholder ceases to be a shareholder with respect to the acquired shares." § 6.40(e)(1). Section 6.40(f) goes further by stating: "A corporation's indebtedness to a shareholder incurred by reason of a distribution made in accordance with this section is at parity with the corporation's indebtedness to its general, unsecured creditors except to the extent subordinated by agreement."

## 5.  REASONABLY EQUIVALENT VALUE IN CORPORATE TRANSACTIONS

### a.  Transactions For Benefit of Stockholders

## PROBLEM

Corporation's obligation to Bank was secured by stock of Subsidiary, whose stock was wholly owned by Corporation. When Corporation defaulted on its loan to Bank, Corporation and Bank negotiated a transaction whereby Subsidiary's stock was released from Bank's security interest, Bank loaned Subsidiary $2 million, and Bank was granted a security interest in Subsidiary's assets. On the same day as the new loan was made, Subsidiary paid Corporation as a dividend $2 million, and Corporation paid $2 million to Bank in partial payment of Corporation's prior debt to bank. Subsidiary was solvent when the deal was made but, owing to the large amount of debt it incurred, began to experience cash flow problems thereafter and sank into insolvency. Subsidiary filed in Chapter 7 within one year of the $2 million loan transaction.

**(a)** Can Subsidiary's trustee avoid Bank's security interest in Subsidiary's assets? Avoid Subsidiary's obligation to repay the debt? *See Wells Fargo Bank v. Desert View Bldg. Supplies, Inc.*, 475 F.Supp. 693 (D.Nev. 1978), *aff'd*, 633 F.2d 221 (9th Cir. 1980). *See* § 548(a)(1)(B).

**(b)** Can Subsidiary's trustee proceed against Corporation on the ground that the dividend was a fraudulent conveyance? A violation of the state corporation laws?

# In re Northern Merchandise, Inc.

United States Court of Appeals, Ninth Circuit (2004).
371 F.3d 1056.

■ WARDLAW, Circuit Judge:

Frontier Bank ("Frontier") appeals a decision of the Bankruptcy Appellate Panel ("BAP") affirming in part the bankruptcy court's summary judgment in favor of Ronald G. Brown, Chapter 7 Trustee ("Trustee"), in the Trustee's action alleging that Frontier received a fraudulent transfer from Chapter 7 Debtor Northern Merchandise, Inc. ("Debtor"). Specifically, Frontier challenges the BAP's ruling that Debtor did not receive reasonably equivalent value under 11 U.S.C. § 548(a)(1)(B) in exchange for a security interest it granted to Frontier and, thus, Frontier was not protected under 11 U.S.C. § 548(c). * * * Reviewing the bankruptcy court's decision to grant summary judgment de novo * * * we reverse.

## I. Background

In 1997, Debtor, a company that sold general merchandise to grocery stores, was incorporated by Paul Weingartner, Gary David, and Paul Benjamin. In February 1998, Frontier loaned $60,000 to the newly formed company. The loan was evidenced by a promissory note in the amount of $60,000, secured by a commercial financing agreement granting Frontier a security interest in Debtor's inventory, chattel paper, accounts, equipment, and general intangibles. The security interest was later perfected by the filing of a Uniform Commercial Code financing statement on February 24, 1998.

In October 1998, Debtor sought a second loan of $150,000 from Frontier to provide Debtor with working capital. Frontier refused to give such a loan to Debtor after determining that Debtor's financial performance did not support an additional direct loan to the company. However, Frontier agreed to loan $150,000 (the "October Loan") to Paul Weingartner, Paul Benjamin, and Stephen Comer, Debtor's shareholders (collectively, "Shareholders"), whose credit warranted such a loan.[1] Frontier understood that the Shareholders would, in turn, allow Debtor to utilize the money to fund its business operations. In fact, the loan transaction was structured so that Frontier deposited the proceeds of the October Loan directly into Debtor's checking account. However, while the funds themselves were transferred directly from Frontier to Debtor, the transaction was documented as a loan to Shareholders, who then turned the funds over to Debtor. The October Loan was evidenced by a promissory note in favor of Frontier executed by Shareholders. However, on the same day that Shareholders entered into the October Loan with Frontier, Debtor executed a commercial security agreement granting Frontier a security interest in its inventory, chattel paper, accounts, equipment, and general intangibles.

---

[1] Shareholders were also officers and/or directors of Debtor.

On March 5, 1999, Debtor ceased doing business, leaving approximately $875,000 in unsecured debt. At the time, Debtor had approximately $400,000 worth of inventory. Debtor transferred the $400,000 worth of inventory to Benjamin News Group, a company owned by shareholder Paul Benjamin, for $125,000.[2] On March 19, 1999, Benjamin News Group paid Frontier, not Debtor, the $125,000, which amount was credited to the October Loan. The remaining $25,000 due on the October Loan was paid to Frontier by the Safeway Corporation from the proceeds of prior sales of inventory to the Safeway Corporation.

On March 22, 1999, creditors filed an involuntary Chapter 7 petition against Debtor, and a trustee was appointed. Debtor scheduled assets of $4,116.17 and debts of $875,847.32. On February 9, 2001, Trustee filed a complaint against Frontier, and thereafter a motion for partial summary judgment, arguing that the grant of the security interest and the $125,000 transfer were fraudulent conveyances under 11 U.S.C. § 548(a). The bankruptcy court granted the motion for summary judgment, holding that a fraudulent conveyance had occurred. On appeal before the BAP, Frontier argued, *inter* alia, that the bankruptcy court erred in finding a fraudulent conveyance because (1) Debtor received reasonably equivalent value for the security interest * * * The BAP ruled in favor of Trustee * * * .

## II. Reasonably Equivalent Value

11 U.S.C. § 548(a)(1) provides:

> The trustee may avoid any transfer of an interest of the debtor in property, or any obligation incurred by the debtor, that was made or incurred on or within one year before the date of the filing of the petition, if the debtor voluntarily or involuntarily. . . received less than a reasonably equivalent value in exchange for such transfer or obligation.

It is well settled that "reasonably equivalent value can come from one other than the recipient of the payments, a rule which has become known as the indirect benefit rule." *Harman v. First Am. Bank (In re Jeffrey Bigelow Design Group, Inc.),* 956 F.2d 479, 485 (4th Cir.1992). For example, in *Rubin v. Manufacturers Hanover Trust Co.,* the court explained:

> a debtor may sometimes receive "fair" consideration even though the consideration given for his property or obligation goes initially to a third person. . . although transfers solely for the benefit of third parties do not furnish fair consideration. . . the transaction's benefit to the debtor need not be direct; it may come indirectly through benefit to a third person. . . .. If the consideration given to the third person has ultimately landed in the debtor's hands, or if the giving of the considera-

---

[2] Trustee filed a fraudulent conveyance action against Benjamin News Group and ultimately recovered $45,000.

tion to the third person otherwise confers an economic benefit upon the debtor, then the debtor's net worth has been preserved, and [the statute] has been satisfied—provided, of course, that the value of the benefit received by the debtor approximates the value of the property or obligation he has given up.

661 F.2d 979, 991-92 (2d Cir.1981) (internal quotation marks and citations omitted).

*Jeffrey Bigelow* is such an example. In Jeffrey Bigelow, shareholders of a debtor entered into a line of credit agreement with First American Bank for $1,000,000. 956 F.2d at 481. Although the shareholders were the makers of the line of credit, "only the debtor received the draws and all payments were made directly from the debtor to First American." *Id.* Subsequently, "the debtor executed a note for $1,000,000 to [the shareholders] with substantially the same terms as the line of credit between First American and [the shareholders]." *Id.* As the debtor directly repaid First American, its liability on the note to the shareholders likewise decreased. *Id.* Holding that the payments made by the debtor on the shareholders' line of credit did not constitute fraudulent conveyances, the Fourth Circuit reasoned:

> [T]he proper focus is on the net effect of the transfers on the debtor's estate, the funds available to the unsecured creditors. As long as the unsecured creditors are no worse off because the debtor, and consequently the estate, has received an amount reasonably equivalent to what it paid, no fraudulent transfer has occurred.

*Id.* at 484. Because it was "apparent that the transfers [had] not resulted in the depletion of the bankruptcy estate," but rather "served simply as repayment for money received," the Fourth Circuit held that "no fraudulent transfer occurred." *Id.* at 485.

As *Jeffrey Bigelow* illustrates, the primary focus of Section 548 is on the net effect of the transaction on the debtor's estate and the funds available to the unsecured creditors. *See id.* ("the focus is whether the net effect of the transaction has depleted the bankruptcy estate"); *see also Nordberg v. Republic Nat'l Bank (In re Chase & Sanborn Corp.),* 51 B.R. 739, 740 (Bankr.S.D.Fla.1985) ("the indirect benefit cases are bottomed upon the ultimate impact to the debtor's creditors"); *Rubin,* 661 F.2d at 992 ("decisions in [indirect benefit cases] turn on the statutory purpose of conserving the debtor's estate for the benefit of creditors."). Trustee contends that Debtor's grant of the security interest to Frontier resulted in a $150,000 loss to Debtor's estate and thus the funds available to the unsecured creditors. Trustee reasons that because the transfer of $150,000 from Shareholders to Debtor was technically a capital contribution, rather than a loan, Debtor was under no legal obligation to grant a security interest to Frontier. Therefore, Trustee argues, Debtor would have been justified to not grant the security interest to Frontier, which would have resulted in an additional $150,000 in Debtor's estate.

We reject this formalistic view. Although Debtor was not a party to the October loan, it clearly received a benefit from that loan. In fact, Frontier deposited the $150,000 proceeds of the October Loan directly into Debtor's checking account. Because Debtor benefited from the October Loan in the amount of $150,000, its grant of a security interest to Frontier to secure Shareholder's indebtedness on that loan, which totaled $150,000, resulted in no net loss to Debtor's estate nor the funds available to the unsecured creditors. To hold otherwise would result in an unintended $150,000 windfall to Debtor's estate. Accordingly, Debtor received reasonably equivalent value in exchange for the security interest it granted to Frontier. * * *

### IV. Conclusion

For the foregoing reasons, the BAP erred in holding that Debtor did not receive reasonably equivalent value under § 548(a)(1)(B) in exchange for the security interest it granted to Frontier and that Frontier was not protected under § 548(c).

REVERSED.


## PROBLEM

Holding, Inc. acquired all the stock of Galaxy Pictures, a old line film studio that produced and distributed films for theatrical release as well as television. Its earnings came from distribution fees from its new films and licensing fees from its large library of classic motion pictures and TV films. In January 2005, Holding initiated discussions with Bank for a loan.

**a.** Holding offered Bank a security interest in the stock of Galaxy Pictures as security for the loan. Bank rejected this proposal and declared that it would not make the loan to Holding unless Galaxy Pictures guaranteed the loan and secured its guarantee with a security interest in all Galaxy's assets. Why does Bank prefer a security interest in Galaxy's assets instead of its stock?

**b.** Bank would advance the money to Holding only if Galaxy guaranteed Holding's obligation to repay Bank and granted a security interest to Bank in its assets to secure its guarantee. Galaxy complied and Bank advanced the funds to Holding in January; Holding used the funds to pay some debts that had nothing to do with Galaxy. Unfortunately, 2005 was a disastrous year for both Holding and Galaxy, which produced several over-budget box office bombs, and word went out that Galaxy might have to sell its film library piecemeal to survive. On this news, Galaxy's creditors forced it into involuntary bankruptcy in early December. Holding defaulted on its loan to Bank. Galaxy's trustee sought to avoid both Galaxy's obligation to Bank under the guarantee and Bank's security interest in Galaxy's assets on the ground that Galaxy did not receive reasonably equivalent value from Bank for either the obligation or the security interest. You may assume that Galaxy was insolvent at all times during 2005. Should Trustee prevail?

**c.** Would your answer change if Galaxy had been solvent during the first six months of 2005? *See* § 548(a)(1)(B)(ii).

**d.** Would your answer change if Holding had used the proceeds of the loan to purchase the stock of Globe Theaters, Inc., which owned a chain of theaters where Galaxy's films would be shown? See *Telefest, Inc. v. VU-TV, Inc.*, 591 F.Supp. 1368 (D.N.J. 1984); *Mellon Bank v. Metro Communications, Inc.*, 945 F.2d 635 (3d Cir.1991), discussed below.

---

The court in *Rubin v. Manufacturers Hanover Trust Co.*, 661 F.2d 979 (2d Cir. 1981), recognized that subsidiaries of a debtor may receive reasonably equivalent value for their guaranties even if the benefit derived from the guaranties was indirect. The court, however, went on to hold that the benefit had to be quantified and compared to the amount of the obligations incurred or the property transferred under the guaranty. In *Telefest* the court did not require quantification of the benefit received for the guaranty. The debtor, VU-TV, was engaged in the business of distributing TV programming to TV stations and cable companies. VU-TV was a wholly-owned subsidiary of CATV. MHT, a bank, loaned money to CATV to enable CATV to acquire the capital stock of San Antonio, a cable television company. As security for this loan and other loans made by MHT to any of the three affiliated corporations, CATV, VU-TV and San Antonio executed cross-corporate guaranties under which each corporation guaranteed the obligation of each other corporation and each corporation granted to MHT a security interest in the assets of the corporation to secure payment of its obligations and the obligations of each other corporation. In the bankruptcy of VU-TV a security interest in assets of VU-TV to secure VU-TV's guaranty of the loan obligation of CATV to MHT was challenged as a fraudulent transfer on the ground that VU-TV did not receive fair consideration under UFCA § 4. The court stated:

> I am satisfied that it was intended that a benefit would flow to VU-TV through the loans to CATV and San Antonio ultimately guaranteed by VU-TV. In April, 1982, when MHT was considering whether or not to extend a $300,000 loan to CATV for the purchase of San Antonio, MHT certainly regarded CATV and VU-TV as having an identity of interest. An internal memo * * * evidences what MHT has consistently argued, i.e. that it always regarded VU-TV and its parent in tandem in its dealing with these companies. Such an outlook is relevant in considering whether the transferee of a conveyance acted in good faith. * * *
>
> Even more important than good faith in considering whether fair consideration passed is the nature of the transferor's business and its relationship with its parent. It is clear * * * that VU-TV was devoted to providing programming for cable television companies * * *. Monies loaned to VU-TV's parent to purchase a cable television system or for other moves directed toward expansion would most probably pro-

vide an additional and obviously secure market for VU–TV. The consideration for VU–TV's guarantee of the loans of its parent and sister companies may not have been a direct benefit, but it was a specific enough benefit for a reasonable trier of fact to conclude that fair consideration inhered in the conveyance.

In any event, the notion that a benefit accrues to a subsidiary only when there is a direct flow of capital to that entity the result of its guarantee of a loan to its parent is inhibitory of contemporary financing practices, which recognize that cross-guarantees are often needed because of the unequal abilities of interrelated corporate entities to collateralize loans.

591 F.Supp. at 1378–1379.

The analysis in *Telefest* is supported by *Mellon Bank v. Metro Communications, Inc.*, 945 F.2d 635 (3d Cir.1991), a case involving facts somewhat similar to those in *Telefest*. The court stated that a synergistic business relationship between the parent, which received the loan, and the subsidiary, which guaranteed the loan debt, was a substantial indirect benefit to the subsidiary. That benefit, along with the subsidiary's enhanced ability to borrow working capital resulting from the relationship, could amount to reasonably equivalent value for the guaranty. Another case taking the view that an indirect benefit may constitute reasonably equivalent value is *Butler Aviation International, Inc. v. Whyte*, 6 F.3d 1119 (5th Cir.1993). In that case, debtor, an airplane manufacturer, wished to keep an affiliate, a small airline, in business so that it would eventually buy airplanes from the debtor, which expected to make a profit of $800,000 for each airplane sold. In pursuance of this objective, the debtor agreed with a gasoline supplier to pay for gasoline that supplier delivered to the affiliate in order to keep its planes flying. The airline failed before buying any of the debtor's aircraft, although it did lease three. Nonetheless, the court, citing *Rubin* and *Mellon Bank*, held that the debtor had received reasonably equivalent value for its payments (amounting to $432,381) to the supplier that enabled the airline to stay in business. The economic benefit must, according to the court, be determined at the time the investment is made, not later when the deal turns sour.

## 6. Leveraged Buyouts

A person may want to buy a corporation but lacks the money or collateral necessary to finance the purchase. If the corporation has unencumbered assets, it may be possible to use those assets to provide most of the capital necessary to make the purchase. Doing so, however, may violate fraudulent transfer law with serious consequences if the acquired firm subsequently files in bankruptcy. Corporate acquisitions in which assets of the acquired firm are encumbered require careful attention to the fraudulent transfer issues raised by the transaction.

## PROBLEM

**Case #1.** Shareholder agrees to sell the stock of Target Corporation to Acquirer who is unable to pay for the stock out of its own assets. Acquirer offers Shareholder a security interest in the stock of Target to secure the unpaid amount of the purchase price. Shareholder isn't interested in this because under the absolute priority rule debt must be paid before equity and creditors of Target would come ahead of Shareholder in any liquidation. Shareholder will sell on credit only if it can have a security interest in Target's assets. Acquirer agrees, and Target grants Shareholder a security interest in Target's assets to secure Acquirer's debt to Shareholder. This rudimentary transaction is what used to be called "bootstrap financing" and is potentially a constructively fraudulent transfer under § 548(a)(1)(B)(i) because Target does not receive "reasonably equivalent value" for its transfer of the security interest; in fact it receives no value, all the benefit flows to Acquirer and Shareholder. Thus, if the transfer rendered Target insolvent or left it with unreasonably small capital to engage in business and Target filed in bankruptcy, the trustee of Target may avoid the security interest under § 548.

**Case #2.** Same facts, except that instead of Shareholder financing the deal Acquirer borrows the money to buy the stock from Bank and causes Target to grant Bank a security interest in its assets to secure the loan. Bank advances the loan proceeds to Acquirer who pays the money to Shareholder for the stock. Again, this is a potentially fraudulent transaction because Target granted Bank a security interest in its assets and got nothing that its creditors could reach in return. The value went to Acquirer and Shareholder. If the insolvency test of § 548(a)(1)(B)(ii)(I) is met, Target's trustee may avoid the security interest under § 548.

**Case #3.** Same facts. But Bank is wise to the problem posed by Case #2 transaction, and loan officers are taught to be sure that the loan proceeds go to the entity that grants Bank the security interest. The transaction is structured so that the loan goes to Target which grants Bank a security interest in its assets. Target then reloans the money to Acquirer, an acquisition entity without significant assets, and Acquirer uses the money to pay Shareholder for the stock in Target. Now Bank believes that it is safe; it received a security interest in Target's assets and gave hard cash in exchange. What Target does with the loan proceeds is its own business. Surely this meets the requirements of "reasonably equivalent value" under § 548(a)(1)(B)(i).

When *United States v. Tabor Court Realty Corp.*, 803 F.2d 1288 (3d Cir.1986) (often referred to by its district court title, *"Gleneagles"*), held that under the facts of Case #3 Bank was the recipient of a fraudulent transfer, the ancient law of fraudulent transfers became required reading for mergers and acquisitions lawyers throughout the land. The court invalidated Bank's security interest as a fraudulent transfer on the ground that although Bank had given value to Target at the time it received the security interest, the money "merely passed through" Target to Acquirer and ultimately to the shareholders of Target. Acquirer's note to Target was worthless because Acquirer had virtually no assets other than the stock of now insolvent Target; hence, Target's loan to Acquirer was a gratuitous transfer. Bank countered by insisting that there were two separate transactions, first, its loan to Target and, second, Target's loan to Acquirer. Bank gave good value to Target and what Target chose to do with the proceeds of the loan was a decision that should not affect the legitimacy of Bank's security interest. The court rejected this argument; since Bank knew the purpose of the loan, the two transactions were in fact "part of one integrated transaction."

---

*Gleneagles* was a case that concerned the liability of the lender in a leveraged buyout situation. The following opinion considers the liability of the old stockholders whose interest was bought out under the LBO. Judge Bufford is a well known law teacher and scholar.

# Bay Plastics, Inc. v. BT Commercial Corp.

United States Bankruptcy Court, C.D. California, 1995.
187 B.R. 315.

■   SAMUEL L. BUFFORD, Bankruptcy Judge.

### I. Introduction

The debtor has brought this adversary proceeding against the selling shareholders of a leveraged buyout ("LBO") to recover the funds that they received in the buyout transaction. While the action was also brought against the bank that financed the transaction, the bank has settled. The Court grants summary judgment to the debtor on the undisputed facts.

The Court holds that the transaction may be avoided as a constructive fraudulent transfer under the California version of the Uniform Fraudulent Transfer Act ("UFTA"), on which the debtor relies pursuant to Bankruptcy Code § 544(b), and that in consequence the debtor is entitled to recover against the selling shareholders. The Court finds that the transaction rendered the debtor insolvent, and that the sellers did not act in good faith.

## II. Facts

The Court finds that the following facts are undisputed. Defendants Bob Younger, Abner Smith and Paul Dodson ("the selling shareholders") formed debtor Bay Plastics, Inc. ("Bay Plastics") in 1979 to manufacture polyvinyl chloride ("PVC") plastic pipe for water well casings and turf irrigation. Bay Plastics filed this bankruptcy case on January 25, 1990.

### A. The Buyout

Because they were nearing retirement, on October 31, 1988 (fifteen months before this bankruptcy filing) the selling shareholders sold their Bay Plastics stock to Milhous Corporation ("Milhous") for $3.5 million in cash plus $1.8 million in deferred payments.[2] Milhous did not acquire the Bay Plastics stock directly. Instead, it caused its subsidiary Nicole Plastics to form its own subsidiary, BPI Acquisition Corp. ("BPI"), to take ownership of the Bay Plastics stock. Formally, the parties to the stock sale transaction were ultimately BPI and the selling shareholders.

The sale was unexceptional. The difficulty lay in the financing of the purchase. Milhous put no money of its own, or even any money that it borrowed, into this transaction. Instead, it caused Bay Plastics to borrow approximately $3.95 million from defendant BT Commercial Corp. ("BT") (a subsidiary of Bankers Trust), and then caused Bay Plastics to direct that $3.5 million of the loan be disbursed to BPI. BPI in turn directed that the $3.5 million be paid directly to the selling shareholders in substantial payment for their stock. Thus, at the closing, $3.5 million of the funds paid into escrow by BT went directly to the selling shareholders.

As security for its $3.95 million loan, BT received a first priority security interest in essentially all of the assets of Bay Plastics. In consequence, BT has received all of the proceeds of debtor's assets in this bankruptcy case, and nothing is left for unsecured or even for administrative creditors.

The financing also provided a revolving credit facility for working capital, in addition to the payment for the LBO, up to a total loan of $7 million.[4] A total of just over $4 million was owing to BT at the time of the bankruptcy filing, according to the debtor's schedules. Thus most of the debt (all but approximately $500,000) owing to BT at the time of the filing resulted from the LBO.

The selling shareholders were not in the dark about the financing. On October 25, 1988 they and their attorney met with Milhous representatives in Los Angeles to finalize the deal. While the Milhous representatives pro-

---

[2] Apparently the deferred payments have not been made. All but $100,000 of the deferred payments were designated as compensation for a non-competition agreement.

[4] While working capital advances were authorized up to $3.35 million, the Court has received no evidence on whether such advances were actually made.

vided rather little information about the Milhous finances, they did disclose the details of the BT secured loan to Bay Plastics to finance the stock purchase. In addition, the selling shareholders received a projected post-transaction balance sheet, which showed a balance of $250,000 in equity only because of the addition to the asset side of the ledger the sum of $2,259,270 in goodwill. Both the selling shareholders and their attorney were experienced in LBOs, and the selling shareholders discussed this feature of the transaction, and their exposure on a fraudulent transfer claim, with their attorney on that date. With this information in hand, Younger, Smith and Dodson approved the terms of the sale.

In contrast to the selling shareholders, the industry did not know about the LBO character of the transaction until a number of months later. Shintech Corp., a creditor at the time of the transaction (and continuously thereafter), did not learn of it until ten months later, in August, 1989.

### B. The Shintech Debt

Some three months before the LBO, on July 22, 1988, Bay Plastics entered into a requirements contract with Shintech to supply PVC resin. Shintech agreed under the contract to supply up to 2.6 million pounds of PVC resin per month on payment terms of 30 days after shipment. To induce Shintech to enter into this contract, Bay Plastics granted Shintech a security interest in all its assets, and the shareholders gave personal guaranties. This arrangement stood in the way of the BT transaction.

In consequence, the selling shareholders, their attorney, and Milhous representatives met with Shintech in late October, 1988 (after Milhous had disclosed to the selling shareholders the terms of the LBO), to arrange a new deal with Shintech. The parties to the LBO persuaded Shintech of Milhous' good credit, and induced Shintech to release both its security interest and the guaranties.[5] However, they did not disclose the LBO character of the transaction, and Shintech did not learn of this until ten months later.

The impact of this transaction on the balance sheet of Bay Plastics was dramatic. Immediately after the transaction, its balance sheet showed tangible assets of approximately $7 million, and liabilities of approximately $9 million. Only the addition of almost $2.26 million in goodwill, which had not appeared on prior balance sheets, and for which no explanation has been provided, permitted the balance sheet to show a modest shareholder equity of $250,000. But for the newly discovered goodwill, there would have been a net deficiency of some $2 million. In contrast, immediately before the transaction Bay Plastics had assets of $6.7 million and liabilities of $5.6 million, and a net equity of $1.1 million.

---

[5] In consequence of giving up its security and its guaranties, Shintech now holds more than 99% of the unsecured debt in this case.

Bay Plastics was unable to service this overload of debt, and filed its bankruptcy petition fifteen months later. According to the debtor's schedules, at the time of filing its two principal creditors were BT and Shintech: it owed approximately $4 million in secured debt to BT, and $3.5 million in unsecured debt to Shintech. No other creditor was owed more than $20,000.

### III. Discussion

The Bankruptcy Code gives a trustee the power to avoid a variety of kinds of prepetition transactions. Such transactions include preferential payments to creditors (§ 547), fraudulent transfers (§ 548), the fixing of statutory liens (§ 545), and setoffs (§ 553). A debtor in possession in a chapter 11 case has all of the rights (except the right to compensation) and the powers of a trustee under chapter 11. This includes the right to exercise the avoiding powers. Bankruptcy Code § 1107(a).

However, the debtor is unable to use the fraudulent transfer provision of the Bankruptcy Code (§ 548) in this case, because it is only applicable to transfers made or obligations incurred on or within one year before the date of the filing of the petition. § 548(a). Where state law provides a similar avoiding power to a creditor, on the other hand, Bankruptcy Code § 544(b)[7] permits a trustee (or a debtor in possession) to stand in the shoes of the creditor and to assert the same cause of action. *Kupetz v. Wolf,* 845 F.2d 842, 845 (9th Cir.1988). Trustees and debtors in possession routinely utilize this provision to make fraudulent transfer claims under applicable state law, which typically provides a statute of limitations of four to seven years. *See, e.g.,* Cal.Civ.Code § 3439.09 (West Supp.1995). Thus the debtor has brought this adversary proceeding under § 544(b) and the UFTA as adopted in California.

#### A. Fraudulent Transfer Law

The purpose of fraudulent transfer law is to prevent a debtor from transferring away valuable assets in exchange for less than adequate value, if the transfer leaves insufficient assets to compensate honest creditors. * * *

Modern fraudulent transfer law traces its origins to a statute of Elizabeth enacted in 1570. This statute provided that a conveyance made "to the End, Purpose and Intent to delay, hinder or defraud creditors" is voidable. Courts often relied on circumstantial "badges of fraud" to presume fraudulent intent. *See, e.g.,* Twyne's Case, 76 Eng.Rep. 809, 810–14 (1601). The English law of fraudulent conveyance passed into the common law in the United States. This law was revised and codified by the

---

[7] Section 544(b) provides:

The trustee may avoid any transfer of an interest of the debtor in property or any obligation incurred by the debtor that is voidable under applicable law by a creditor holding an unsecured claim. . . .

National Conference of Commissioners on Uniform State Laws ("NCCUSL") in 1918, when it promulgated the Uniform Fraudulent Conveyance Act ("UFCA"). The UFCA was adopted by California in 1939, and by a number of other states on various dates.

The NCCUSL rewrote the UFCA and promulgated it as the UFTA in 1984. California adopted its version of the UFTA, which is applicable in this case, in 1986. Bankruptcy Code § 548 contains a similar fraudulent transfer provision.[9]

### 1. The Species of Fraudulent Transfer

A transfer or conveyance is fraudulent if it is (1) an intentional fraudulent transfer, i.e., a transfer made with the intent to defeat, hinder or delay creditors; or (2) a transfer that is constructively fraudulent because the debtor is in financial distress. There are three kinds of financial distress that make a transaction a fraudulent transfer: (a) a transfer while a debtor is insolvent or that renders a debtor insolvent; (b) a transfer that leaves a debtor undercapitalized or nearly insolvent (i.e., with insufficient assets to carry on its business); (c) a transfer when the debtor intends to incur debts beyond its ability to pay. See UFTA §§ 4, 5; UFCA § 4; Bankruptcy Code § 548(a). Constructive fraudulent transfer law applies without regard to intent (except the intent to incur debts in the last alternative). * * *

In this adversary proceeding the debtor relies on the first two varieties of constructive fraudulent transfer, and is entitled to prevail if either cause of action is upheld. The Court addresses only the first (a transfer that renders the debtor insolvent), because it finds that the debtor is entitled to prevail on this cause of action.

### 2. Fraudulent Transfer Resulting in Insolvency

The UFTA [§ 5(a)], adopted in California effective for transactions after January 1, 1987, provides in relevant part:

> A transfer made or obligation incurred by a debtor is fraudulent as to a creditor whose claim arose before the transfer was made or the obligation was incurred if the debtor made the transfer or incurred the obligation without receiving a reasonably equivalent value in exchange for the transfer or obligation and the debtor was insolvent at the time or the debtor became insolvent as a result of the transfer or obligation.

Cal.Civ.Code § 3439.05 (West Supp.1995).

---

[9] The Bankruptcy Code and its predecessor the Bankruptcy Act of 1898 have traditionally included their own fraudulent transfer provisions, because a number of states did not adopt the UFCA, and some have not yet adopted the UFTA.

### 3. Application of Fraudulent Transfer Law to LBOs
#### a. General

The basic structure of an LBO involves a transfer of corporate owner-ship financed primarily by the assets of the corporation itself.[11] Typically the corporation borrows the funds, secured by the assets of the corpora-tion, and advances them to the purchasers, who use the funds to pay the purchase price to the selling shareholders. Kathryn V. Smyser, *Going Pri-vate and Going Under: Leveraged Buyouts and the Fraudulent Convey-ance Problem*, 63 Ind.L.J. 781, 784–85 (1988). LBOs have two essential features:

> First, the purchaser acquires the funds necessary for the acquisition through borrowings secured directly or indirectly by the assets of the company being acquired. Second, the lender who provides such funds is looking primarily to the future operating earnings of the acquired company and/or to the proceeds from future sales of assets of the com-pany, rather than to any other assets of the purchasers, to repay the borrowings used to effect the acquisition.

Id., at 785. LBO investors thus generally consider cash flow, the money available for working capital and debt service, as the most important fac-tor in assessing a potential buyout candidate.

The application of fraudulent transfer law to LBOs has generated con-siderable debate among courts and commentators. LBOs were a popular form of consensual corporate takeover in the 1980's. They fell into disuse at the end of that decade for economic reasons. However, the use of the LBO as an acquisition device has recently become popular again. See Laura Jereski, *'Recaps' Are Secret Fuel for Leveraged Buyouts*, Wall St.J., July 25, 1995, at C1.

The LBO dates back long before the 1980's. In earlier years, it was known as a "bootstrap acquisition." Some of these transactions were in-validated as fraudulent conveyances. * * *

* * *

#### B. Trustee's Prima Facie Case

After having explored the applicable statutes and governing case law, the Court is now in position to apply this law to the facts of the instant case.

The Court notes at the outset that this case is not determined by the Ninth Circuit case law as set forth in *Lippi v. City Bank*, 955 F.2d 599 (9th Cir.1992), and *Kupetz v. Wolf*, 845 F.2d 842 (9th Cir.1988). Those cases both involved a fraudulent transfer attack on behalf of subsequent credi-

---

[11] While LBOs have frequently been used by management to buy out existing sharehold-ers and take over the ownership of a business, management is not an essential party to an LBO. Indeed, in this case the purchaser was an outside third party.

tors. This case, in contrast, is brought for the principal benefit of a creditor existing at the time of the transaction, which holds more than 99% of the outstanding unsecured debt.

We begin with the elements of the cause of action under the UFTA § 5, as adopted in California, for a constructive fraudulent transfer rendering the debtor insolvent. The elements of a cause of action under this statute are as follows: the debtor (1) made a transfer or incurred an obligation, (2) without receiving a reasonably equivalent value in exchange, (3) which rendered the debtor insolvent (or the debtor was already insolvent),[22] and (4) which is attacked by a pre-transaction creditor.

### 1. Transfer or Obligation

The selling shareholders do not dispute that, in making the BT loan, the debtor made a transfer or incurred an obligation. In fact, the debtor did both. The debtor undertook the $3.95 million obligation to BT, it transferred a security interest in essentially all of its assets to BT, and it transferred $3.5 million ultimately to the selling shareholders. Thus the first element of the cause of action is satisfied.

### 2. Lack of Reasonably Equivalent Value

The selling shareholders likewise do not contest whether the debtor received reasonably equivalent value for the BT loan. However, this element is not apparent on its face.

Nominally, BT's transaction was only with Bay Plastics. It lent the $3.95 million *to the debtor*, the debtor promised to repay the loan, and the debtor gave a first priority security interest in essentially all of its assets to secure the repayment. If this were the transaction, creditors likely would have no grounds for complaint, and it would not be vulnerable to fraudulent transfer attack.

However, the foregoing structure obscures the reality of the transaction. The selling shareholders' transaction was formally with Milhous, and eventually with BPI, the new owner of Bay Plastics. BPI purchased their stock, and arranged for their payment with funds that Bay Plastics borrowed from BT. Before Bay Plastics received the funds, it directed that $3.5 million be transferred to its incoming parent, BPI, and BPI in turn directed that the funds be paid out for the stock purchase. Thus in sub-

---

[22] The definitions of insolvency under the various fraudulent transfer statutes differ. The UFCA adopts the "equity" or "cash flow" test of insolvency, under which a debtor is insolvent if the present fair salable value of the debtor's assets is less than the amount required to pay existing debts as they become due. UFCA § 2(a). The Bankruptcy Code § 101(32)(A) adopts the balance sheet definition of insolvency, under which a debtor is insolvent if the debtor's liabilities exceed the debtor's assets. § 101(32)(A). Under the UFTA, a debtor is insolvent if the debtor's liabilities exceed the debtor's assets (the balance sheet definition), and the debtor is presumed to be insolvent if the debtor is generally not paying his or her debts as they become due (the equity or cash flow test). UFTA § 2(a), (c).

stance $3.5 million of the funds that Bay Plastics borrowed from BT went to pay for the stock of the selling shareholders, rather than to Bay Plastics.

This raises the question whether the Court should collapse the various transactions in this case into one integrated transaction. Under *Lippi* this turns on whether, from the perspective of the selling shareholders, the transaction appeared to be a straight sale without an LBO. *Lippi*, 955 F.2d at 612. If, in contrast, there is evidence that the parties knew or should have known that the transaction would deplete the assets of the company, the Court should look beyond the formal structure. *Id.* In *Kupetz* the Ninth Circuit found it improper to collapse the transactions where the selling shareholders had no knowledge of the LBO character of the transaction, and there were no pre-transaction creditors.

In this case, in contrast, the selling shareholders had full knowledge that this was an LBO. The Milhous representatives informed them of this at the October 25 meeting before the transaction was finalized, and it was disclosed in the financial projections provided at that time. In addition, the selling shareholders discussed this feature with their legal counsel on October 25, and specifically discussed their exposure to a fraudulent transfer claim. Both the selling shareholders and their legal counsel were familiar with leveraged buyouts, because they had done others previously, and they knew the fraudulent transfer risks.

This knowledge of the selling shareholders distinguishes this case from both *Kupetz* (where the selling shareholders did not know or have reason to know of the LBO) and from *Lippi* (where the evidence was disputed). Instead, this case is like *In re Richmond Produce Co.*, 151 B.R. 1012 (Bankr.N.D.Cal.1993), *United States v. Tabor Court Realty Corp.*, 803 F.2d 1288 (3d Cir.1986), and *Wieboldt Stores, Inc. v. Schottenstein*, 94 B.R. 488 (N.D.Ill.1988), where the transaction was collapsed because of the knowledge of the selling shareholders.

In addition, because Shintech qualifies as a pre-transaction creditor, the Court does not need to reach the issue of the knowledge of the LBO feature of the transaction by the selling shareholders: this is material to whether the transaction's various parts should be collapsed only when challenged by post-transaction creditors.

Thus, in this case the Court finds it appropriate to collapse the various pieces of this transaction into one integral transaction, in which the funds went to the selling shareholders, not to Bay Plastics or to its new parent BPI. The loan obligation, in contrast, was undertaken by Bay Plastics, which also provided the security for the loan.

Bay Plastics received no reasonably equivalent value for the security interest in all of its assets that it gave to BT in exchange for BT's funding of the stock sale. Under California law, reasonable equivalence must be determined from the standpoint of creditors. *Hansen v. Cramer*, 39 Cal.2d 321 (1952) (applying rule to "fair consideration" under predecessor statute) * * *. The Ninth Circuit has adopted the same view in interpreting the California version of the UFTA. * * * Payment of funds to a parent corporation prevents a transaction from satisfying the "reasonably equivalent value" requirement. A financially healthy entity may give away its assets as it pleases so long as there remains enough to pay its debts. A financially distressed donor, however, may not be so generous.

From the debtor's perspective, it is apparent that the $450,000 that Bay Plastics presumably received (the $3.95 million loan less the $3.5 million paid to the selling shareholders) is not reasonably equivalent to the $3.95 million obligation that it undertook. *Cf. Shape, Inc. v. Midwest Engineering (In re Shape, Inc.)*, 176 B.R. 1, 3 (Bankr.D.Me.1994) (payment of $70,000 for stock worth more than $1.5 million lacks reasonably equivalent value). Thus Bay Plastics did not receive reasonably equivalent value for the loan obligation and security interest that it granted to BT.

### 3. Insolvency of the Debtor

The third element of the fraudulent transfer cause of action at issue in this litigation is that the transaction rendered the debtor insolvent, if it was not so already. In this case the Court finds the evidence undisputed that the LBO rendered the debtor insolvent.

Insolvency is defined in California Civil Code § 3439.02(a) (West Supp.1995): "A debtor is insolvent if, at fair valuations, the sum of the debtor's debts is greater than all of the debtor's assets." UFTA § 2(a) is essentially the same. These statutes adopt the balance sheet test for insolvency: a debtor is insolvent if the liabilities exceed the assets.

The usual starting point for determining the sufficiency of assets is the balance sheet, particularly if the balance sheet is prepared according to generally accepted accounting principles consistently applied. * * * However, these principles do not control a court's decision regarding the solvency of an entity. * * *

The valuation of assets for insolvency purposes is based on "a fair valuation." This differs from a balance sheet, where most assets apart from publicly traded stocks and bonds are carried at historic cost, rather than current market value. The values of assets must be updated in light of subsequent use and market conditions: in accounting parlance, they must be "marked to market."

In addition, a balance sheet may include intangible assets such as goodwill[24] that may have no liquidation or going concern value, and

---

[24] Goodwill is generally understood to represent the value of intangible factors that are expected to translate into greater than normal earning power. In addition to the advantageous relationship that a business enjoys with its customers, goodwill also includes advantageous relationships with employees, suppliers, lenders and others. * * *

Because goodwill has no independent market or liquidation value, generally accepted accounting principles require that goodwill be written off over a period of time. In acquisition accounting, going concern value in excess of asset value is treated as goodwill. Dictionary of Finance & Investment Terms 157 (2d ed. 1987).

which thus must be deleted in evaluating the solvency of an entity. Goodwill cannot be sold to satisfy a creditor's claim. Thus, in a liquidation bankruptcy case it must be disregarded in determining solvency of the debtor at the time of an LBO.

Nominally, Bay Plastic's corporate balance sheet showed the debtor to be solvent after the LBO. But this resulted only from the addition of $2.26 million of goodwill to the asset side of the balance sheet. Bay Plastics had not previously carried any goodwill on its balance sheets.

The parties to this litigation have accepted the debtor's balance sheet immediately after the LBO as a fair presentation of the debtor's financial status, with the exception of goodwill. Thus the Court is relieved of the burden of marking to market the debtor's assets. However, the trustee contends that the goodwill of $2.26 million that first appeared at that time must be deleted in determining the debtor's solvency.

The Court finds that the balance sheet must be adjusted by deleting the unamortized goodwill of $2.26 million. It was not carried on the balance sheet before the LBO, and in any case it could not be sold to satisfy a creditor's claim. * * * This is a liquidation case, where goodwill has no other value. This downward adjustment left Bay Plastics with a negative net worth of approximately $2 million immediately after the LBO. For fraudulent transfer purposes, it was rendered insolvent by the transaction.

> Indeed, this is exactly the type of transaction that poses the extreme risk of an LBO. No Milhous entity put any funds or assets at risk in the investment at all. In consequence of the structure of the transaction, all of the risks of the enterprise were placed on its creditors. Milhous retained only the right to reap the benefits if the business was sufficiently profitable to avoid bankruptcy.[25]

### 4. Attack by a Pre–Transaction Creditor

The final element of the cause of action for fraudulent transfer rendering a debtor insolvent is that the transaction must be attacked by a pre-transaction creditor. This element is satisfied in this case.

Shintech, the principal unsecured creditor in this case, which holds more than 99% of the unsecured debt, is the pre-existing creditor. It was secured until this transaction, and in addition it held guaranties from each

---

Goodwill frequently appears on a balance sheet after the sale of a business, where it represents the excess of the purchase price over the net value of the other assets purchased. * * * It appears that this may be the explanation for the appearance of goodwill on the debtor's balance sheet in this case.

[25] In such a transaction there is a danger that the selling shareholders will be paid more than their stock is worth. With nothing at risk if the business is not sufficiently profitable, the purchaser has less incentive to make sure that the price is not excessive. Absent fraudulent transfer law, there is nothing to deter the buyers, sellers and bank from imposing all of the risks of loss on the creditors, as they did in this case.

of the selling shareholders. In this transaction the selling shareholders and Milhous induced it to relinquish its security and guaranties to permit the transaction to be consummated. Although knowing the LBO character of the transaction, both the selling shareholders and Milhous failed to disclose this feature to Shintech.

\* \* \*

### C. Application of Fraudulent Transfer Law to LBOs

The Court finds it appropriate to apply fraudulent transfer law to an LBO. An LBO is different, not just in degree, but in character from the ordinary business and investment transactions engaged in by a corporation's management. An LBO is not a routine business transaction that should normally be given deference by the courts. It is not a corporate investment in a new venture, new equipment or property. Indeed, an LBO normally does not affect the business of the corporation at all: it only changes the ownership and adds a large layer of secured debt. Rather, an LBO is an investment of corporate assets, by borrowing against them, for the *personal* benefit of both old and new equity owners. Thus, the application of fraudulent transfer law to LBOs does not limit corporate entrepreneurial decisions.

Since an LBO reduces the availability of unencumbered assets, the buyout depletes estate assets available to pay creditors' claims. As the Ninth Circuit has stated:

> Existing unsecured creditors are vulnerable in [an LBO]. From their perspective, a pledge of the company's assets as collateral to finance the purchase of the company reduces the assets to which they can look for repayment.

*Kupetz*, 845 F.2d at 846; *accord, Moody v. Security Pacific Business Credit, Inc.*, 971 F.2d 1056, 1073 (3d Cir.1992). An LBO is attractive to the sellers, the buyers and the lender because it shifts most of the risk of loss to other creditors of the corporation. *Mellon Bank v. Metro Communications, Inc.*, 945 F.2d 635 (3d Cir.1991). The acquired corporation receives little or nothing in exchange for the debt that it incurs.

From a creditor's point of view, an LBO is indistinguishable from a distribution or a gift to shareholders. The harm is quite like the harm imposed on creditors by donative transfers to third parties, which is one of the most traditional kinds of fraudulent transfers.[30] If the value of the security interest given by the corporation does not exceed the shareholders' equity as shown on the balance sheet (after suitable revisions to mark the assets to market and to eliminate intangible assets of dubious value), there is usually no substantial harm to creditors. Indeed, typical corporate distri-

---

[30] David Epstein and his co-authors state: "[The creditors] are harmed just as much as if the debtor had given away the equity in its assets as a gift." Epstein, [Bankruptcy], § 6–52 at 69.

bution statutes permit the payment of dividends in such circumstances, to the extent of the balance sheet equity. *See, e.g.,* Cal.Corp.Code § 166 (West Supp.1995). If the price paid to selling shareholders is higher, however, there may be insufficient assets remaining to satisfy creditors.

The vice of an LBO lies in the fact that the selling shareholders are paid indirectly with assets from the corporation itself, rather than by the purchasers. In effect, in an LBO the shareholders are paid with a corporate dividend or distribution. An LBO enables the selling shareholders to liquidate their equity interests, which are otherwise subordinate to general unsecured claims, without first paying creditors, which a normal liquidation would require. The selling shareholders in the transaction in effect disregard the status of the corporation as a separate entity for their benefit, but insist on respect of the corporation's separate status when it comes to creditors' claims (apart from those of the lender providing the funds for the transaction).

The possible detriment to creditors is exacerbated if the corporation's cash flow is not sufficient to service the loan. The bank eventually proceeds to foreclose on the corporation's assets and sells them at foreclosure prices, and leaves nothing for other creditors. Such foreclosure is frequently interrupted by the filing of a bankruptcy case. So it happened in this case.

Most courts that have considered the issue have decided that fraudulent transfer law should apply to LBOs. * * * In fact, despite the reservations expressed in *Kupetz, supra,* and, 629 F.Supp. 175 (C.D.Cal.1985), there appears to be no published opinion to *Credit Managers Ass'n of Southern California v. Federal Co.*the contrary.[31]

It does not follow, however, that the fraudulent transfer analysis of an LBO will result in a recovery for the benefit of the bankruptcy estate. In both *Moody* and *Mellon Bank* the Third Circuit upheld the transactions at issue against the fraudulent transfer attack. In *Lippi,* similarly, the Ninth Circuit ruled in favor of some of the defendants, and remanded for further consideration as to the remainder.

Should all LBO's be exposed to fraudulent transfer challenge? Certainly not. Under this Court's analysis, two kinds of LBO's ordinarily escape fraudulent transfer attack. This includes many, if not most, LBOs.[32]

---

[31] *But see Kaiser Steel Corp. v. Pearl Brewing Co. (In re Kaiser Steel Corp.),* 952 F.2d 1230 (10th Cir.1991), where the court held that the trustee could not recover from selling shareholders of a publicly traded corporation because their payments constituted non-avoidable "settlement payments" under Bankruptcy Code § 546(e).

[32] In *Credit Managers Association v. Federal Co.,* 629 F.Supp. 175, 179 (C.D.Cal.1985), a district judge in this district stated, "it is not at all clear that fraudulent conveyance law is broadly applicable to [LBOs]." That court relied substantially on Baird & Jackson, [38 Vand.L.Rev. 829 (1985)] Ten years of court decisions and scholarly commentary since that decision have helped to refine the application of fraudulent

First, in a legitimate LBO, in which the assets mortgaged by a corporation to support an LBO do not exceed the net equity of the business (after appropriate adjustments), the transaction will not make the corporation insolvent, at least according to the balance sheet test.[34] If in addition it has sufficient projected cash flow to pay its debts as they come due, the cash flow solvency test is met, also. This leaves an LBO exposed to fraudulent transfer attack only if the margin of equity is too thin to support the corporation's business.

A second kind of LBO also escapes fraudulent transfer attack, even though it leaves the subject corporation insolvent. If the cash flow is sufficient to make the debt payments, the transaction also is unassailable. This ordinarily turns on two factors: the degree of risk of default undertaken in the first instance, and the degree to which projected economic developments impacting the business are not overly optimistic. These LBOs escape fraudulent transfer attack either because of good financial projections or because of good luck: either factor is sufficient.

The Court's view of the proper application of fraudulent transfer law to LBO's does not make the selling shareholders the guarantors of the success of the LBO. A legitimate LBO, as described supra, shifts the risk of failure off their shoulders. As to subsequent creditors, they should not be required to shoulder the risk if the failure is caused by outside forces not reasonably foreseeable at the time of the transaction. *Moody v. Security Pacific Business Credit, Inc.*, 971 F.2d 1056, 1073 (3d Cir.1992) (failure caused by increased competition rather than lack of capital) * * *.

However, an LBO that is leveraged beyond the net worth of the business is a gamble. A highly leveraged business is much less able to weather temporary financial storms, because debt demands are less flexible than equity interest. The risks of this gamble should rest on the shoulders of the shareholders (old and new), not those of the creditors: the shareholders enjoy the benefits if the gamble is successful, and they should bear the burdens if it is not. This, after all, is the role of equity owners of a corporation. The application of fraudulent transfer law to LBOs shifts the risks of an LBO transaction from the creditors, who are not parties to the transaction, back to the old and new shareholders who bring about such transactions. As Sherwin states:

---

transfer law to LBOs. Even the *Credit Managers* court, however, apparently would permit pre-transaction creditors, such as exist in this case, to attack an LBO.

[34] It makes sense to limit legitimate LBOs to transactions that do not leave a corporation insolvent. In a perfect world (as typically assumed by economists), an LBO would never run afoul of this rule, because the price paid for the stock would be the net equity in the firm. Baird & Jackson, [38 Vand.L.Rev.] at 851. Such an LBO would place the corporation on the verge of insolvency, but not beyond. In the real world, some LBOs leave corporations insolvent, perhaps because of imperfect information about the value of the corporation's stock.

These parties, who are directly involved as the principal engineers and beneficiaries of the buyout, should bear the risk of negative consequences if the transaction does not in fact comply with the standards for creditor protection set out in the fraudulent conveyance statutes. ... They should be accountable to creditors for the benefits diverted from the corporation if they knew or should have known. . . of facts the court determines to establish a constructive fraud against creditors.

Sherwin, [72 Minn.L.Rev.] at 519.

How long should selling shareholders be exposed to the risk that an LBO will go bad? There is a traditional answer to this question: until the statute of limitations runs. Perhaps there should be a shorter statute of limitations for LBOs than the four to seven years that is common under the UFTA. This is a decision for the legislature to make.

The Court perceives no unfairness in imposing the risks of an overleveraged LBO on the old and new shareholders who undertake the risks, rather on the creditors who do not intend to do so. Indeed, it is the selling shareholders who are ordinarily least worthy of sympathy in an LBO. As Epstein states:

In the beginning of the transaction they are below existing creditors. In the end, they "cash out" and march off over the heads of the existing creditors. It is a neat trick of legal magic that allows the shareholders to subordinate, unilaterally, the creditors' claims.

2 Epstein, [Bankruptcy], at 74.

### D. Good Faith Defense

The selling shareholders claim that they acted in good faith, and that this is a defense to the fraudulent transfer claim. From the earliest fraudulent transfer statutes, a good faith transferee for value has enjoyed an affirmative defense to the cause of action. *See, e.g.*, 13 Stat.Eliz. ch. 5, § 6 (1570). However, this defense has been greatly restricted in recent statutes.

The UFTA, including California's version thereof, provides a complete defense to an intentional fraudulent transfer for a transferee who took "in good faith and for a reasonably equivalent value." UFTA § 8(a); * * *. This defense is not available for a constructive fraudulent conveyance, and thus is not applicable in this adversary proceeding.

A second good faith provision is contained in UFTA § 8(d) and the California Civil Code, which provide:

Notwithstanding voidability of a transfer or an obligation under this chapter, a good faith transferee or obligee is entitled, *to the extent of the value given the debtor* for the transfer or obligation, to the following:

**(1)** A lien on or a right to retain any interest in the asset transferred.

**(2)** Enforcement of any obligation incurred.

**(3)** A reduction in the amount of the liability on the judgment.

UFCA § 8(d) * * * (emphasis added).[36]

In this case the selling shareholders gave up their shares of stock in the debtor in exchange for their payment of $3.5 million. However, this provision is not applicable in this case, because the shareholders did not transfer their shares or give any other value *to the debtor*. The shares went to BPI, the new parent corporation of Bay Plastics, and from there to Milhous. The debtor itself received neither shares nor money. This did not constitute "value given the debtor", within the meaning of UFTA § 8(d) or California Civil Code § 3439.08(d). Thus the good faith defense fails.

### IV. Conclusion

Having found no triable issue of material fact, the Court concludes that the trustee is entitled to a summary judgment setting aside the constructive fraudulent transfer in this case to the selling shareholders. After having collapsed the series of transactions into a single transaction, the Court finds that in substance the selling shareholders received payment for their shares that was secured by the assets of debtor, and that this transaction defrauded an existing creditor. The payment to the selling shareholders is thus avoidable under UFTA § 5, as adopted in California in California Civil Code § 3439.05, which in turn is incorporated in Bankruptcy Code § 544(b).

### NOTE

Under the court's reasoning, would BT's security interest have been subject to avoidance had it not settled with the trustee? Would Bay Plastic's obligation be avoidable as well, leaving BT without even an unsecured claim in Bay Plastic's bankruptcy? If this case had been brought under § 548, would § 548(c) have been of any help to BT? Were Bay Plastic's $3.5 million obligation to BT avoided, the effect would be to increase Bay Plastic's equity by that amount, giving the stock acquirer, BPI, a huge windfall. Would a better result be to subordinate BT's claim to that of Shintech and the other creditors under the broad powers given courts under § 105(a) or the principles of equitable subordination pursuant to § 510(c) that we will discuss in the next chapter? *See In re Pajaro Dunes Rental Agency, Inc.*, 174 B.R. 557 (Bankr.N.D.Cal.1994). For a comprehensive treatment of the remedial issues raised by fraudulent transfer avoidance of leveraged buyouts see Robert J. White, *Leveraged Buyouts and Fraudulent Conveyance Laws Under the Bankruptcy Code—Like Oil and Water, They Just Don't Mix*, 1991 Ann.Surv.Am.L. 357. *See also*

---

[36] Bankruptcy Code § 548(c) provides a transferee with a similar defense to a fraudulent conveyance claim to the extent of the value given to the debtor if such transferee acted in good faith.

*Zahn v. Yucaipa Capital Fund*, 218 B.R. 656, 664 (D.R.I.1998) (permitting avoidance recovery to be shared between plan proponent and unsecured creditors).

### a.  Insolvency

However sophisticated the structure of the LBO transaction, one must assume that a bankruptcy court may look through the form of the transaction and conclude that the target corporation did not receive reasonably equivalent value. Given this possibility, lenders and selling stockholders are never really safe in an LBO transaction (until the statute of limitations has run) unless the target corporation can pass all the solvency tests prescribed by § 548(a)(1)(B)(ii) and any applicable under state law in bankruptcy through § 544(b). The "bankruptcy" test of insolvency is found in § 101 ("insolvent") ("the sum of such entity's debts is greater than all of such entity's property, at a fair valuation"). This test must be contrasted with the "equity" test, which finds insolvency when a debtor is unable to pay debts as they become due, that is often applicable under state fraudulent transfer laws. UFTA § 2. A functionally similar test is found in the "unreasonably small capital" requirement of § 548(a)(1)(B)(ii)(II) and UFTA § 5. Since, as *Bay Plastics* points out, the expectation in LBOs is usually that the acquisition debt is to be paid out of the earnings of the acquired company, it is fair to say that the key inquiry that courts make about the solvency of the acquired company is whether it is left with the ability to generate sufficient profits after paying its debts (including acquisition-related debt) to sustain operations. From this, courts reason that a business debtor is left with adequate capital only when its projected cash flow is sufficient to meet its reasonably foreseeable obligations, particularly those arising from the LBO transaction. Perhaps the best judicial discussion of the issue is found in *Moody v. Security Pacific Business Credit, Inc.*, 971 F.2d 1056 (3d Cir.1992). *See* Bruce A. Markell, *Toward True and Plain Dealing: A Theory of Fraudulent Transfers Involving Unreasonably Small Capital*, 21 Ind.L.Rev. 469 (1988).

As the court explains in *Moody*, the equity test of insolvency and the unreasonably small capital test are not identical. The latter test requires that after the transfer the debtor have a reasonable likelihood of continuing to meet its obligations. Immediately after an LBO, a debtor can be solvent under the equity test in that it is able to pay its debts then coming due but still can be left with unreasonably small capital because its projected cash flow in the future may be insufficient to meet its future obligations. If the target company fails because of unforeseen adverse changes in its business, a court may uphold the LBO if its cash flow projections were reasonable at the time made. Of course, cash flow projections cannot rely on historical data alone; they must contain some margin for error regarding economic trends, interest rate fluctuations, and the like.

### b. The Innocent Shareholder Defense

Section 548(c) extends protection against avoidance to transferees or obligees who take for value and in good faith. On the face of it, this provision should not protect selling stockholders from having to disgorge in cases like *Bay Plastics*, in which the court has "collapsed" the transaction, because the transfer is treated as a corporate distribution to the selling stockholders for which they gave no value to the debtor corporation. Nevertheless, some courts have conceived an "innocent shareholder" defense that absolves selling stockholders from having to disgorge if they can distance themselves from the LBO transaction. Michael L. Cook, et al., *The Judicially Created "Innocent Shareholder" Defense to Constructive Fraudulent Transfer Liability in Failed Leveraged Buyouts*, 43 S.C.L.Rev. 777 (1992).

A break-through case was *Wieboldt Stores, Inc. v. Schottenstein*, 94 B.R. 488 (N.D.Ill.1988), in which, in a rather smelly transaction, corporate insiders arranged for a tender of stock of a sinking retail chain to an acquisition entity, knowing that this entity intended to use none of its own funds to finance the acquisition. The court made the insider selling stockholders disgorge but allowed other selling stockholders to retain the money they received. In *Kupetz v. Wolf*, 845 F.2d 842 (9th Cir.1988), the innocent stockholder defense was extended to protect two sellers who owned all the debtor corporation's stock, on the dubious finding of fact that these two experienced businessmen were somehow unaware that the purchase of their stock was being financed through an LBO. Perhaps in reaction to *Kupetz, Lippi v. City Bank*, 955 F.2d 599 (9th Cir.1992), held that for a selling stockholder in a close corporation to take advantage of the innocent stockholder defense it had some duty to investigate the nature of the acquisition transaction.

The high-water mark of the innocent shareholder defense may have passed. In *Zahn v. Yucaipa Capital Fund*, 218 B.R. 656 (D.R.I.1998), the federal district court in Rhode Island, construing California law, rejected *Kupetz* and *Lippi* head-on:

> Applying these principles to [Cal. Civ. Code] § 3439, this Court is confident that the California Supreme Court would not follow the Ninth Circuit cases, but rather would apply the statute as written. Limiting the remedy of § 3439 to LBOs that are not "above-board" essentially limits fraudulent-transfer attacks on LBOs to those which are "actually" fraudulent, in effect writing the constructive fraudulent transfer provisions out of the statute when an LBO is involved.

218 B.R. at 669.

With respect to public corporations with widely held stock, it is usually infeasible to compel disgorgement from widely scattered public stockholders. Corporation laws commonly protect stockholders who receive illegal distributions without knowledge of the impropriety, e.g., Cal.Corp.Code § 506(a). Public shareholders, moreover, are more likely to benefit from the judge-made innocent shareholder defense discussed above than are shareholders in close corporations. In addition, *In re Kaiser Steel Corp.*, 952 F.2d 1230 (10th Cir.1991), adopted a controversial position that would insulate from liability former stockholders in LBO transactions involving publicly owned corporations in virtually all cases. The court based its holding on § 546(e), which exempts "settlement payments" made to or by stockbrokers, financial institutions and securities clearing institutions from liability under § 548(a)(2).

Most publicly issued corporate stock is held by financial intermediaries, like brokers, banks, and depositaries like Depositary Trust Company. When an LBO involves an illegal distribution to selling stockholders, the stock transfers will inevitably be cleared through these financial intermediaries, and § 546(e) makes clear that they are not liable as transferees of illegal distributions. The policy basis of § 546(e) is to safeguard the clearance and settlement system in the securities industry against the risks of upsetting otherwise final transactions between buyers and sellers of securities. *Kaiser Steel* went a step further and held that "settlement payments" included payments made by financial intermediaries to their customers, the beneficial owners of the stock, because these payments were made to settle a customer's account with its intermediary.

*In re Munford, Inc.*, 98 F.3d 604 (11th Cir.1996), took a different view and held that LBO payments received by the selling stockholders were not covered by § 546(e), even though they may have qualified as "settlements" of a customer's account, because in substance these payments were distributions from the debtor to the selling stockholders. "And, of course, section 546(e) offers no protection from the [trustee's] avoiding powers to shareholders; rather section 546(e) protects only * * * stockbrokers, financial institutions, and securities clearing agencies." 98 F.3d at 610. In *Munford,* there was no transfer to these entities because they never acquired a beneficial interest in the property transferred; they served merely as conduits. *In re Resorts International, Inc.*, 181 F.3d 505 (3d Cir.1999), rejected *Munford* as reading into § 546(e) a beneficial interest requirement that is not justified by the plain wording of the statute; the court endorsed *Kaiser Steel.*

## 7. INSIDER PREFERENCES

The common law allowed the debtor to freely prefer one creditor over another. *See, e.g. Shelley v. Boothe*, 73 Mo. 74 (1880). Still today non-bankruptcy law generally permits a debtor who cannot pay all creditors to discriminate in favor of some to the detriment of others, and favored creditors are entitled to the benefit of the discrimination as well as any advantages they can otherwise seize under applicable law on the eve of bankruptcy. *Wyzard v. Goller*, 28 Cal.Rptr.2d 608 (Cal.Ct. App.1994).

Preferences by an insolvent corporation present an independent issue. If the preference is made to a creditor who is an officer, director or affiliate of the corporation, the general rule is that the preference can be recovered for the benefit of the creditors of the corporation. *Pennsylvania Co. v. South Broad St. Theatre Co.*, 174 A. 112 (Del. Ch. 1934). The reason for the rule was stated by the court in the latter case as follows:

> The principle upon which the rule rests that forbids a director-creditor to enjoy a preference over others in the circumstance of the company's insolvency, is variously stated. By most of the authorities it is posited on the so-called 'trust fund theory' by which capital assets are said to constitute a trust fund for creditors. By others it is said to be based on the inequity of allowing a director to take advantage of the superior means of information which he enjoys over other creditors, conjoined as it is with a power or influence which enables the possessor to reap a personal advantage over others whose claims are equally meritorious.

*Id.* at 116.

The rule against insider preferences by an insolvent corporation was extended by some courts to cover a preference made to a creditor whose debt was guaranteed by an insider. In *Davis v. Woolf*, 147 F.2d 629 (4th Cir.1945), the corporation was obliged to construct a building. Its obligation was guaranteed by a completion bond on which Woolf was liable. The corporation got into financial difficulty, which prevented completion of the building. In order to facilitate completion of the building by the corporation and thus relieve himself of his obligation on the completion bond, Woolf loaned $18,000 to the corporation, and as security he was given a mortgage on the corporation's property which fully secured the debt. The building was completed and the corporation eventually went into bankruptcy. The trustee in bankruptcy attempted to avoid the mortgage. The trustee argued that because the mortgage was an illegal preference under state law, it could under that law have been avoided by creditors who had claims in bankruptcy. Under the Bankruptcy Act, the trustee succeeded to the rights of those creditors. The court stated that when a surety advances funds to an insolvent principal debtor to satisfy the guaranteed debt and the principal debtor transfers property to the surety to indemnify or reimburse the surety, a preference to the surety is made. The effect of the transaction is the same as though the principal debtor had paid the guaranteed debt with its funds in order to relieve the surety of its obligation. In both cases the surety has suffered no loss and the insolvent principal debtor has lost property equal to the obligation satisfied. The court stated that the trustee's action was meritorious if the trustee could prove that Woolf was a director of the corporation at the time the mortgage was granted and that the corporation was then insolvent.

Suppose an insolvent corporation at the behest of X, a director of the corporation, pays a debt owing to Y which had been guaranteed by X. Against whom can the payment be recovered? In *Arnold v. Knapp*, 84 S.E. 895 (W.Va.1915), the court treated the payment as an unlawful preference to X, the director, on the theory that the payment was made for X's benefit. Could the payment also be recovered from Y? That question was not addressed under the common law, but several cases involving this question have arisen under the Bankruptcy Code. They were not decided, however, on principles of corporation law or fraudulent transfer law. Rather, they involved § 547(b)(4)(B) and § 550 and they reached different results. The majority rule was established in the seminal decision, *Levit v. Ingersoll Rand Financial Corp.*, 874 F.2d 1186 (7th Cir. 1989), which held that the plain meaning of § 550 was that both insider and noninsider initial transferees had liability for insider preferences.

A firestorm ensued. One of the strongest forces in moving the Bankruptcy Reform Act of 1994 through Congress was creditor dislike of *Levit.*

The 1994 Reform Act added subsection § 550(c):

(c) If a transfer made between 90 days and one year before the filing of the petition—

(1) is avoided under section 547(b) of this title; and

(2) was made for the benefit of a creditor that at the time of such transfer was an insider;

the trustee may not recover under subsection (a) from a transferee that is not an insider.

Subsequent to the enactment of § 550(c), a division of authority developed over whether trustees could avoid security interests granted to noninsider transferees even if they could not recover payments since the avoidance of security interests (as opposed to the recovery of payments) was governed by § 547, not § 550(c). The 2005 Act closed the remaining loophole by adding § 547(i):

If the trustee avoids under subsection (b) a transfer made between 90 days and 1 year before the date of filing of the petition, by the debtor to an entity that is not an insider for the benefit of a creditor that is an insider, such transfer shall be considered to be avoided under this section only with respect to the creditor that is an insider.

## D.  THE STRONG ARM CLAUSE

### 1.  INTRODUCTION

For centuries a battle has raged between trustees in bankruptcy and creditors with secured claims in personal property of the debtor's estate. The stakes are high: since, as we have seen, under bankruptcy law secured claims are prior to unsecured claims, a creditor holding a security interest on all the debtor's property, now owned or thereafter acquired, can clean out the estate, leaving the unsecured creditors with nothing. For many years courts found ways to prevent this from happening. The story is definitively told in Grant Gilmore, *Security Interests in Personal Property* (1965). But enactment of Article 9 of the Uniform Commercial Code in the 1950s and 1960s gave secured creditors total victory: under the UCC, creditors can indeed take a security interest in all the personal property, tangible or intangible, that a debtor owns or will acquire in the future. The major weapon remaining that trustees can use to attack Article 9 security interests is the strong arm clause of § 544(a), which allows for invalidation of unperfected security interests in property.

Section 544(a) arms the trustee with the power of a hypothetical creditor under state law to avoid transfers in real and personal property. Under UCC § 9-317(a)(2)(A), an unperfected security interest in personal property, although enforceable against the debtor under UCC § 9-203(b), is subordinated to the rights of a person who acquires a judicial lien in the collateral. However, an exception to this rule in § 9-317(a)(2)(B) provides that a lien creditor is also subordinate to an unperfected security interest for which a filing has been made and the parties have entered into a security agreement. The most common situation in which the exception would apply is the case in which the secured party has done everything to perfect a security interest except give value. The court in *In re Bell*, 194 B.R. 192 (Bankr.S.D.Ill.1996), explains the application of § 544(a)(1):

> Section 544(a)(1) provides that a bankruptcy trustee acquires, as of the commencement of a case, the status of a hypothetical judicial lien creditor and "may avoid" any lien or encumbrance on property of the debtor that is voidable by such a creditor under state law. Under this provision, federal and state law work in tandem. First, the substance of the trustee's rights as judicial lien creditor—primarily the priority of his claim in relation to other interests in the property—is determined by reference to state law. If the trustee has priority over a third party's interest under state law, federal law prescribes the consequence. Under § 544(a)(1), the trustee may entirely avoid the inferior third-party interest in the property, and the third party is left with only an unsecured claim against the debtor's estate. * * * This result obtains even if state law provides that the competing interest is subordinate, rather than void, as to a judicial lienholder. State law generally ranks interests in priority so that a subordinate junior interest is not voided but survives and is paid from any surplus value that remains after senior claims are paid. Nevertheless, and notwithstanding the literal language of 544(a)(1), an interest that is merely subordinate to the claim of a judicial lienholder under state law is completely eliminated in bankruptcy as a matter of federal law.

194 B.R. at 195.

Sections 546(b) and 362(b)(3) allow perfection after bankruptcy to defeat the rights of the trustee under § 544(a) in cases in which the applicable nonbankruptcy law gives retroactive effect to the perfection. An example is UCC § 9-317(e). If a purchase money security interest is perfected by filing within 20 days of the debtor's taking of possession of the collateral, the security interest is good in bankruptcy even if the debtor goes into bankruptcy before the filing is made.

Mortgages on real property that are unrecorded at the time of bankruptcy can also be avoided under § 544(a), but a different technique is used. In most states an unrecorded mortgage on real property has priority over a subsequent judicial lien. But an unrecorded mortgage is normally not enforceable against a subsequent bona fide purchaser of the real property. By virtue of § 544(a)(3), unrecorded mortgages are invalidated in bankruptcy if under the nonbankruptcy law they are subject to the rights of a bona fide purchaser of the real property. "Purchaser" means any voluntary transferee including an encumbrancer (§ 101(43)). "Transfer" is defined in §101(54).

---

Although the strong arm clause is primarily directed at secret liens, its language also covers other obligations or transfers of the debtor that are voidable by bona fide purchasers of real property or judicial lienholders. The case that follows is illustrative.

## 2. KNOWLEDGE OF THE TRUSTEE IN BANKRUPTCY

## McCannon v. Marston
United States Court of Appeals, Third Circuit, 1982.
679 F.2d 13.

■ GIBBONS, Circuit Judge:

\* \* \*

On March 19, 1973, Miriam H. McCannon entered into an agreement with a partnership doing business as The Drake Hotel (the debtor) for the sale of a condominium apartment and of a certain percentage of the common areas in that hotel. \* \* \*

Pursuant to the agreement, McCannon paid a deposit of $500 toward the purchase price of $17,988. She began residence in the apartment in April of 1975 and resides there presently. The bankruptcy court found, however, that "[f]or a variety of reasons, settlement on the property has never taken place." *In re Hotel Associates, Inc.*, 10 B.R. 668, 669 (Bankr.E.D.Pa.1981). McCannon never recorded her agreement for sale.

In November of 1979, the debtor filed a petition under Chapter 11 of the Code. McCannon filed a complaint in February of 1981 seeking relief from the automatic stay imposed by Section 362 of the Code and requesting specific performance of the agreement to purchase the apartment. Holding that the trustee, as a bona fide purchaser without regard to any knowledge on his part, may avoid McCannon's interest in the property pursuant to Pennsylvania law and to Section 544(a)(3) of the Code, the bankruptcy court granted the trustee's motion for judgment at the close of the plaintiff's case. * * * The district court affirmed the bankruptcy court's judgment, employing the same interpretation of Section 544 * * *. This appeal followed.

* * * At issue in this case is the interrelationship of [§ 544(a)(3)] concerning the rights of transferees of real property and the prepositional phrase [in the introductory clause of § 544(a)], "without regard to any knowledge of the trustee or of any creditor," an interrelationship of state and federal law.

The law of Pennsylvania considers a purchaser under a written agreement for the sale of real property to be the equitable owner of that property. * * * After reviewing the contract, we find no fault with the conclusion of the bankruptcy court that McCannon acquired such an equitable interest * * *.

Pennsylvania law gives subsequent purchasers of real property priority over the rights of prior purchasers if the subsequent purchasers are bona fide purchasers for value without notice. Record notice defeats the claims of a subsequent purchaser. McCannon's equitable interest was unrecorded. However, in Pennsylvania, clear and open possession of real property generally constitutes constructive notice to subsequent purchasers of the rights of the party in possession. Such possession, even in the absence of recording, obliges any prospective subsequent purchaser to inquire into the possessor's claimed interests, equitable or legal, in that property. * * * Thus in Pennsylvania the rights of a subsequent purchaser do not take priority over those of one in clear and open possession of real property.

The bankruptcy and district courts, however, concluded that any notice which might be imputed to the trustee from possession is irrelevant because of the language of the above-quoted prepositional phrase in Section 544: "without regard to any knowledge of the trustee or of any creditor." Equating "knowledge" with "notice," both courts ruled that the trustee assumes the powers of a bona fide purchaser without notice, whether or not a transferee has given the rest of the world actual or constructive notice by possession.[2]

Although the word "knowledge" is not defined in the Code and the legislative history of its inclusion is scant, in our view Congress cannot have intended such an interpretation. Once a transferee of real property in Pennsylvania has given all potential subsequent purchasers actual or constructive notice of an interest in that property, nothing else need be done to protect against claims of future purchasers. According to the bankruptcy and district courts, however, nothing can be done to protect against the claims of a future trustee in bankruptcy who assumes the role of a hypothetical bona fide purchaser without actual knowledge. The trustee, under

---

[2] The reasoning of the bankruptcy and district courts would apparently allow a trustee to avoid even the interests of those who had given proper record notice.

that interpretation of Section 544, has been clothed not only with the rights of a bona fide purchaser, but has been granted as well a substantial additional mantle of power not available to any actual subsequent purchaser in Pennsylvania. Such a conclusion is not to be lightly inferred.

That the words "without regard to any knowledge" were not meant by Congress to nullify all state law protections of holders of equitable interests is suggested both by the history of its inclusion in the statutory language and by other language within Section 544(a)(3). The reference to the trustee's or creditors' knowledge appears to have originated out of a concern that actual knowledge might affect the trustee's status as a hypothetical judicial lien creditor. In a draft bankruptcy act prepared in 1973 by the Commission on Bankruptcy Laws of the United States, a note by the Commission explained that the trustee's status as hypothetical lien creditor should not be affected by any knowledge which he, personally, or any or all creditors may have. Report of the Commission on the Bankruptcy Laws of the United States, H.R.Doc. No. 93–137, Part II, 93rd Cong., 1st Sess. 160–61 & n. 3 (1973). The note referred to an article by Professor Vern Countryman criticizing cases construing both the "strong arm" provision of the former Bankruptcy Act, Section 70(c), and Article 9 of the Uniform Commercial Code, holding that a trustee with actual knowledge of unperfected security interests could not avoid those interests despite his status as hypothetical lien creditor. *See* Countryman, *The Use of State Law in Bankruptcy Cases,* 47 N.Y.U.L.Rev. 631, 652–55 (1972). In 1977 Congress first provided the trustee with the status of bona fide purchaser of real property. At that time it inserted the clarification regarding the trustee's actual knowledge. * * *

Viewed in the context of this history, congressional desire to disregard the trustee's knowledge of the debtor's previous transactions with various claimants is appropriately understood to respond to the Article 9 problems referred to by Professor Countryman, rather than to obliterate the rights of equitable owners in possession of real property. Further evidence that the latter result was not intended by Congress is found in the language of Section 544(a)(3). Congress was careful to modify the status of bona fide purchasers by inserting the words "against whom applicable law permits such transfer to be perfected." As explained in statements made by Representative Edwards of California and Senator DeConcini of Arizona, sponsors of the proposed Code:

> Section 544(a)(3) modifies similar provisions contained in the House bill and Senate amendment so as not to require a creditor to perform the impossible in order to perfect his interest. Both the lien creditor test in section 544(a)(1), and the bona fide purchaser test in section 544(a)(3) should not require a transferee to perfect a transfer against an entity with respect to which applicable law does not permit perfection.

124 Cong.Rec.H. 11097 (daily ed. Sept. 28, 1978); 124 Cong.Rec.S. 17413 (daily ed. October 6, 1978). Such solicitude for transferees subject

to laws not permitting perfection as to certain purchasers is not consistent with an interpretation of Section 544(a) that would ignore constructive notice under governing state law when a trustee was appointed.

One further point of dispute must be addressed. The trustee argues that the circumstances of McCannon's possession, as the occupant of one of many condominium apartments, a number of which were leased, are not constructive notice obliging a subsequent purchaser to inquire as to her interests. The only Pennsylvania cases cited, however, find no obligation to inquire in circumstances where the grantor was both record owner and in possession and where the one in possession was sharing possession with the record owner. * * * We believe that were the Pennsylvania Supreme Court asked to consider whether a subsequent purchaser *of a condominium building* had a duty to make inquiry as to the rights of persons in possession of apartments in that building, it would hold that such possession provides constructive notice, as a matter of law, no different than in the case of possession of a single family home.

* * *

## NOTES

**1.** The court in *McCannon* refers to an article by Professor Countryman in which he discussed a dispute under Bankruptcy Act § 70c with respect to the status of unperfected Article 9 security interests of which the trustee or all creditors of the debtor had knowledge before bankruptcy. Under the 1962 Official Text of the UCC, which was in effect at the time, an unperfected security interest was subordinated to the rights of a subsequent judicial lienholder only if the lienholder at the time the lien arose did not have knowledge of the security interest. One point of view, supported by a few judicial decisions, was that an unperfected Article 9 security interest could not be avoided under § 70c if either the person who eventually became trustee or all of the actual creditors in the bankruptcy had knowledge of the security interest before bankruptcy. The issue was resolved against this view in states adopting the 1972 Official Text of the UCC which gave a subsequent judicial lien creditor priority regardless of knowledge, but in states which retained the 1962 Official Text the issue remained open. The issue was finally resolved in favor of avoidance by the trustee in all states by the language in the introductory clause of § 544(a), "without regard to any knowledge of the trustee or of any creditor."

A trustee in bankruptcy in a Chapter 7 case would not normally have knowledge of an unrecorded real property mortgage at the time of bankruptcy because at that time the person who eventually becomes trustee would not normally be acquainted with the debtor's activities. But in Chapter 11 cases the opposite is true because the debtor normally takes the powers of the trustee in bankruptcy as debtor in possession. § 1107(a). The quoted language of the introductory clause of § 544(a) makes clear that a debtor in possession may avoid an unrecorded mortgage executed by that debtor before bankruptcy if a bona fide purchaser could take free of the unrecorded mortgage.

**2.**  An amendment in 1984 added the phrase "and has perfected such transfer," which now appears in § 544(a)(3). Under the laws of some states a bona fide purchaser of real property defeats the rights of a previous transferee of an interest in the property who has not recorded the interest only if the bona fide purchaser records before the prior transferee records. Before the amendment it was not entirely clear whether § 544(a)(3) would invalidate an unrecorded transfer of real property under statutes of this kind. For example, it could be argued that a postbankruptcy recording of the previously unrecorded transfer cut off the rights of the trustee if it was assumed that the hypothetical § 544(a)(3) bona fide purchaser did not record. §§ 546(b) and 362(b)(3). This argument was rejected in a number of cases. The amendment disposed of this ambiguity in § 544(a)(3) by adopting the view expressed by these cases.

### 3.  PROPERTY HELD BY DEBTOR AS NOMINEE OR TRUSTEE.

Section 541(a)(1) includes in property of the estate "all legal or equitable interests of the debtor in property." How does that section apply to property of which the debtor is the nominal or legal owner but with respect to which the debtor has no beneficial interest? Suppose, for example, that David, an experienced investor, from time to time has invested money of members of his family and some close personal friends who are not sophisticated about investments. For example, Aunt Minnie gave him $40,000 to invest, Cousin Harry gave him $25,000 and George, his next door neighbor, gave him $35,000. With that money David bought 100 shares of stock for $15,000, he bought Blackacre, a vacant lot, for $50,000, and he loaned $35,000 to Roe who gave him a promissory note to evidence the debt. The promissory note is secured by a second mortgage on Whiteacre, which is Roe's residence. For convenience the stock was registered in the name of David, the deed to Blackacre was in the name of David and the promissory note was made payable to David. The mortgage on Whiteacre states that it is given to secure the promissory note payable to David who is named as mortgagee. The deed to Blackacre and the mortgage on Whiteacre were duly recorded. David signed documents clearly indicating that the transactions were made for the benefit of Minnie, Harry and George and that they hold undivided interests in the stock, Blackacre and the promissory note proportionate to the investments made by them, i.e., 40%, 25% and 35% respectively.

Suppose David goes into bankruptcy. Does any of the property held by David as a result of the $100,000 investment become part of the estate? Section 541(a)(1) is somewhat ambiguous. David does not have any beneficial interest in the property; he acted solely as an agent. But he is the holder of the note and is the record owner of the stock and Blackacre. It should be clear that, without more, the nominal ownership of David is not sufficient to divest Minnie, Harry and George of their beneficial ownership. Bankruptcy Act § 70a, which is the predecessor of 541(a), gave to the trustee "the title of the bankrupt." Since David had only nominal title, under the Bankruptcy Act, the trustee got nothing more. The same result should follow under 541(a)(1). In any event, 541(d) clearly supports that conclusion.

Can Minnie, Harry and George be divested of their property by virtue of 541(a)(3) and 544(a)? Although 541(a)(1) gives David's legal title to the bankruptcy estate it does not affect the claims of beneficial ownership of Minnie, Harry and George. But how about 544(a)? That provision gives to the trustee in bankruptcy the rights and powers of a judicial lien creditor with respect to all the property held by David and of a bona fide purchaser of the real property. The trustee could argue that the equitable title of the beneficial owners can be avoided to the extent the holder of a judicial lien in personal property or a bona fide purchaser of real property could have taken the property free of the interests of those owners.

The stock is clearly personal property. The note is also personal property even though it is secured by a real property mortgage. The mortgage has no independent significance. It is an interest in real property, but that interest is a security interest that simply follows ownership of the note which is personal property. Thus, avoidance depends upon whether a judicial lien would defeat the interest of the owner of the note. In the absence of a statute specifically giving priority, a judicial lien is not effective against property not beneficially owned by the debtor. Thus, the normal result would be that the bankruptcy estate cannot keep the stock and the promissory note free of the claims of beneficial owners. But a bona fide purchaser of Blackacre from David would normally defeat the unrecorded equitable title of Minnie, Harry, and George. Could the trustee therefore avoid those interests under 544(a)(3)? Does 541(d) change that result?

Before amendment of 541(d) in 1984, the reference in 541(d) was to "subsection (a) of this section" rather than the present "subsection (a)(1) or (2) of this section."

The Senate Report on the Bankruptcy Code contained the following statement regarding the original version of 541(d).

> [541(d)] confirms the current status under the Bankruptcy Act of bona fide secondary mortgage market transactions as the purchase and sale of assets. Mortgages or interests in mortgages sold in the secondary market should not be considered as part of the debtor's estate. To permit the efficient servicing of mortgages or interests in mortgages the seller often retains the original mortgage notes and related documents, and the purchaser records under State recording statutes the purchaser's ownership of the mortgages or interests in mortgages purchased. [541(d)] makes clear that the seller's retention of the mortgage documents and the purchaser's decision not to record do not impair the asset sale character of secondary mortgage market transactions. The committee notes that in secondary mortgage market transactions the

parties may characterize their relationship as one of trust, agency, or independent contractor. The characterization adopted by the parties should not affect the [status] in bankruptcy of bona fide secondary mortgage market purchases and sales.

Sen.Rep. No. 95–989, 1978 U.S.C.C.A.N. 5869–5870.

The original version of 541(d) is discussed in the case that follows.

## Belisle v. Plunkett

United States Court of Appeals, Seventh Circuit, 1989.
877 F.2d 512.

■ EASTERBROOK, Circuit Judge.

May the trustee in a bankruptcy case bring into the estate property that the debtor holds in constructive trust for victims of fraud? Oliver Plunkett [the debtor] organized partnerships that provided funds to buy a 50–year leasehold interest in a shopping center, Pan–Am Pavilion in Christiansted, St. Croix, Virgin Islands. Plunkett treated the leasehold as his own—including making a collateral assignment to secure a loan of $100,000 that Plunkett put to personal use. Invoking the strong-arm powers of [Bankruptcy Code] § 544, the Trustee claimed the status of a bona fide purchaser for value. Both the bankruptcy court and the district court held that § 544(a)(3) allows the Trustee to claim the leasehold for the estate, leaving the partners to participate as creditors. The partners contend that § 541(d) keeps the leasehold out of the estate and that the Trustee may not employ § 544(a) to fetch into the estate something that § 541(d) excludes.

Stripped of irrelevant detail, the facts are that in March 1979 Plunkett (a real estate entrepreneur operating out of Milwaukee) signed a contract, in his own name, to buy the leasehold from W.O.F. Associates for $1.2 million. Through the spring and summer of 1979 Plunkett formed five partnerships to raise the money for the acquisition. After getting the cash, Plunkett closed the deal in October 1979—in his own name, despite using partnership funds. He recorded the assignment of the leasehold in the St. Croix real estate records, again in his own name. Although Plunkett recognized the partnerships for tax purposes—he reported a share between 5% and 7%—and informed the partners of the income and deductions they should report on their own returns, he dealt with tenants and creditors as if he owned the leasehold.

Plunkett and his wife filed petitions under the Bankruptcy Code in 1982. After the Trustee asserted that the leasehold is an asset of the estate, the partners filed an adversary proceeding, seeking to quiet title in the partnerships. Chief Judge Clevert of the bankruptcy court granted the Trustee's motion for summary judgment, and the district judge affirmed on appeal * * *.

\* \* \*

Plunkett bamboozled the partners and used for his own benefit the leasehold acquired with partnership funds. Virgin Islands law impresses a constructive trust on the leasehold and its fruits. A constructive trust ordinarily survives bankruptcy: the property may not be used to satisfy the debtor's obligations to other creditors, and the debts to the victims of the fraud may not be discharged. § 523(a)(2), (4). \* \* \* The Trustee acknowledges all of this but relies on § 544(a)(3):

The trustee shall have, as of the commencement of the case, and without regard to any knowledge of the trustee or of any creditor, the rights and powers of, or may avoid any transfer of property of the debtor or any obligation incurred by the debtor that is voidable by—\* \* \*

**(3)** a bona fide purchaser of real property from the debtor, against whom applicable law permits such transfer to be perfected, that obtains the status of a bona fide purchaser at the time of the commencement of the case, whether or not such a purchaser exists.

A bona fide purchaser of the leasehold interest, without notice of the earlier claim, would take ahead of a person who has not recorded his entitlement. Not only Virgin Islands real estate law, but also the Uniform Partnership Act, adopted in both the Virgin Islands and Wisconsin provides this. *See also In re Marino*, 813 F.2d 1562, 1565 (9th Cir.1987) (trustee may avoid undisclosed partnership claim against real property under similar California statute). So the Trustee submits that the Plunkett estate includes the Pan–Am leasehold, "as of the commencement of the case", without need for action on his part.

Not so fast!, the partners rejoin. The estate can't contain the leasehold "as of the commencement of the case" because § 541(d) says that it does not contain property in which the debtor holds bare legal title:

Property in which the debtor holds, as of the commencement of the case, only legal title and not an equitable interest, such as a mortgage secured by real property, or an interest in such a mortgage, sold by the debtor but as to which the debtor retains legal title to service or supervise the servicing of such mortgage or interest, becomes property of the estate under subsection (a) of this section only to the extent of the debtor's legal title to such property, but not to the extent of any equitable interest in such property that the debtor does not hold.

If this were not enough, the partners continue, § 544(a)(3) speaks of a "transfer," yet Plunkett did not transfer the Pan–Am leasehold, and there is therefore nothing for the Trustee to avoid. As the partners see things, §§ 541(d) and 544(a)(3) allow a trustee to recover property transferred out of the estate before the filing, but not to claim for the estate property held in a constructive trust. Several courts have perceived a "conflict" between § 541(d) and § 544(a)(3). *E.g., In re General Coffee Corp.*, 828 F.2d 699, 704–06 (11th Cir.1987); *In re Quality Holstein Leasing*, 752 F.2d 1009,

1013–14 (5th Cir.1985). The parties ask us to decide which statute prevails. We believe, however, that there is no conflict.

Section 544(a)(3) pulls into the debtor's estate property that ostensibly was there all along. Dealing with ostensible ownership is not, however, the statute's objective—at least not its only one—because the benefits are not limited to those who relied on the asset in extending credit. Section 544(a)(3) complements §§ 544(a)(1) and (2), which give the trustee the status of a judgment creditor vis-à-vis chattels in the debtor's possession. If one creditor had (or could get) a judgment effective against the chattels, the trustee secures the same advantage for all—which reduces any creditor's incentive to try to be first in line, a rush that may reduce the value of the debtor's assets. Thomas H. Jackson, *The Logic and Limits of Bankruptcy Law* 70–79 (1986); *cf.* Douglas H. Baird, *Notice Filing and the Problem of Ostensible Ownership*, 12 J. Legal Studies 53 (1983). Sections 544(a)(1) and (2), follow state law, however, in giving the trustee no *greater* rights than the judgment creditor would have. If the debtor possesses a stolen diamond ring, the real owner's rights would trump those of a judgment creditor, and under the Code therefore would defeat the claims of all the debtor's creditors. Whether or not we say that the debtor holds the ring in "constructive trust" for the owner is a detail. Under state law the owner's claims are paramount; the debtor could not defeat those rights by pledging or selling the ring, and the creditors in bankruptcy receive only what state law allows them. * * * Under most states' laws, however, the buyer in good faith of *real* property can obtain a position superior to that of the rightful owner, if the owner neglected to record his interest in the filing system. Section 544(a)(3) gives the trustee the same sort of position.

A bona fide purchaser from Plunkett would have taken ahead of the partners under local law. They neglected to record the partnerships' interest, though recording is easy. (The partners could, and in retrospect should, have refused to invest funds except through an escrow agent, who would have held the cash until good title had been recorded in the partnerships' names.) One of Plunkett's creditors, extending $100,000 against a collateral assignment of the leasehold, actually obtained a position superior to that of the partners. The Trustee claimed the same position for the estate (meaning the creditors collectively, including the partners).

Nothing in the text or function of § 544(a)(3) makes the force of this claim turn on whether Plunkett once owned the leasehold and then sold it to the partnerships (but failed to record their interest) or whether, instead, Plunkett acquired the leasehold through the partnerships. The sequence W.O.F. to Plunkett (perhaps with a bridge loan) to Pan–Am partnerships, with Plunkett retaining ostensible ownership, is identical in every respect to the sequence W.O.F. to Pan–Am partnerships to Plunkett, with Plunkett obtaining ostensible ownership. Identical from the perspective of Plunkett, of the partners, and of Plunkett's (other) creditors—and identical from the perspective of § 544(a)(3). Section 544(a)(3) allows the trustee to have a bona fide purchaser's rights *or* avoid a transfer, so a "transfer" by the debtor cannot be a necessary condition of the exercise of the strong-arm power. The statute mentions "transfer" only in the sense of the *hypothetical* transfer that measures the trustee's rights: if a hypothetical bona fide transferee from the debtor would come ahead of the "true" owner's rights, then the trustee takes ahead of the true owner.

Section 541(d) does not have anything to say about the effects of § 544(a)(3). It forbids including property in the debtor's estate "under subsection (a) of this section" and does not address whether property may be included under some other part of the Code. The courts that have perceived a conflict between §§ 541(d) and 544(a)(3) did not discuss this limitation on the domain of § 541(d). Moreover, even if we confine attention to the estate defined by § 541(a), § 541(d) carves out only "an equitable interest in such property that the debtor does not hold." This could mean, as the partners treat it, "an equitable *interest* * * * that the debtor does not hold" (here, because subject to constructive trust), but perhaps the statute addresses "*property* that the debtor does not hold", on which, therefore, lenders were unlikely to rely in extending credit. If read to exclude any "equitable interest * * * that the debtor does not hold", the statute would remove from the estate even the Plunketts' house, if it had been mortgaged to secure a loan. Estates commonly include such property.

Section 541(d) was designed, its text and history reveal, to deal with persons with title to property who had sold the equitable interests. *E.g.*, S.Rep. 95–989, 95th Cong., 2d Sess. 83–84 (1978). This is a common arrangement in secondary mortgage markets: a person with many titles sells certificates representing shares in the pool of income generated by the notes. Section 541(d) ensures that the creditors of the service corporation stand in line behind the owners of the income stream. The bankruptcy court thought that because the legislative history speaks only of secondary mortgage markets, § 541(d) is limited to such cases. Legislative history does not carry so much force. Mortgage markets may have been the impetus for § 541(d), but statutes often create rules that reach beyond the immediate concerns that spawned them. "It is not the law that a statute can have no effects which are not explicitly mentioned in its legislative history." *Pittston Coal Group v. Sebben*, 488 U.S. 105 (1988). Section 541(d)'s genesis helps us understand, however, that reading the law as limited to inclusions in the estate under § 541(a) makes legal as well as linguistic sense. * * *

Although our reading of § 541(d) and § 544(a)(3) does not conflict with the holding of any other court of appeals, there is some tension between the course we believe appropriate and statements in other opinions. The Fifth Circuit said in *Quality Holstein Leasing*, 752 F.2d at 1013 (note omitted) that "[a]s a general rule, it must be held that section 541(d) prevails over the trustee's strong-arm powers * * *. Congress did not mean to authorize a bankruptcy estate to benefit from property that the debtor did not own." With all respect to the Fifth Circuit, we believe that allowing the estate to "benefit from property that the debtor did not own" is exactly what the strong-arm powers are about: they give the trustee the status of a bona fide purchaser for value, so that the estate contains interests to which the debtor lacked good title. The estate gets what the debtor could *convey* under local law rather than only what the debtor *owned* under local law—a critical distinction that the Fifth Circuit did not mention. The discussion of § 541(d) in *Quality Holstein Leasing* is dictum, however, because the court held that state law did not impress a constructive trust on the property, and the trustee prevailed under § 544(a)(3).

The Eleventh Circuit took a course opposite to that of the Fifth. It said in *General Coffee,* 828 F.2d at 704, "that § 544(a) would bring the [constructive] trust property into the estate in spite of § 541(d)." But having proclaimed the supremacy of the strong-arm power, the court retreated to neutrality, and then held that a bona fide purchaser for value would not have defeated the interest in question under state law. So in *Quality Holstein Leasing,* which proclaimed the supremacy of § 541(d), the trustee won, and in *General Coffee,* which treated § 544(a) as the victor, the trustee lost. For the reasons already canvassed, we believe that both the Fifth and Eleventh Circuits got off on the wrong foot by finding a "conflict" in need of resolution.

Section 544(a)(3) gives the Trustee the status of a bona fide purchaser for value. The bankruptcy and district courts reached the same conclusion. The partners' remaining contentions were waived or are insubstantial, so the judgment is

Affirmed.


## NOTES

**1.** The 1984 amendment to § 541(d) appears to bolster the court's holding in *Belisle.* Under that amendment, the reference in § 541(d) is now limited to §541(a)(1) and (2). We are not aware of legislative history that explains what Congress intended by the 1984 amendment, but the effect of limiting § 541(d) to § 541(a)(1) or (2) is to allow § 544(a) to operate without any limitation by § 541(d). The result would seem to be that if under § 544(a)(3) the equitable title of another person in real property in which the debtor holds legal title is avoided, the estate gets the beneficial interest in the property as well as the legal title. The legal title passes to the estate under § 541(a)(1) and the beneficial interest passes to the estate under § 541(a)(3). If this conclusion is correct, § 541(d) does not protect a person whose equitable title is avoidable under § 544(a) or other avoiding power.

**2.** If the decision in *In re Omegas Group, Inc.,* 16 F.3d 1443 (6th Cir.1994), is followed, the complexities encountered in *Quality Holstein Leasing* and *Belisle* in attempting to reconcile § 541(d) with § 544(a) with respect to constructive trusts are avoided completely. In a sweeping holding the *Omegas* court decided that a constructive trust recognized in a bankruptcy case does not give the claimant an equitable interest in fraudulently obtained property "as of the commencement of the case" and, therefore, § 541(d) cannot apply to exclude the property from the debtor's estate. A constructive trust is merely a remedy for unjust enrichment. "Because a constructive trust, unlike an express trust, is a remedy, it does not exist until a plaintiff obtains a judicial decision finding him to be entitled to a judgment 'impressing' defendant's property or assets with a constructive trust. Therefore, a creditor's claim of entitlement to a constructive trust is not an 'equitable interest' in the debtor's estate existing prepetition, excluded from the estate under § 541(d)." 16 F.3d at 1451. But what if under state law a constructive trust is deemed to have come into existence at the time the property was fraudulently obtained? Although in *Omegas* the state law was not entirely clear on this subject, the court gave it short shrift: "The equities of bankruptcy are not the equities of the common law. Constructive trusts are anathema to the equities of bankruptcy since they take from the estate, and thus directly from competing creditors and not from the offending debtor." *Id.* at 1452. The court concluded that the defrauded creditor merely has a claim that it may be able to show is nondischargeable under § 523(a)(2)(A). It failed to point out that Debtor is a corporation in Chapter 7 that cannot be discharged and that the hapless claimant would be left with a nondischargeable claim against a corporate shell. In a world-weary mode, the court observed that in most bankruptcies there are creditors who, for good reason or bad, believe they have been defrauded, and the claimant in this case is just one of a crowd.

## CHAPTER 8

# EQUITABLE SUBORDINATION AND SUBSTANTIVE CONSOLIDATION

---

## A. EQUITABLE SUBORDINATION

### 1. CLAIMS OF INSIDERS

In accordance with equitable traditions, bankruptcy courts may "sift the circumstances surrounding any claim" in order to avoid unfairness in distributing the assets of the estate among claimants. *Pepper v. Litton*, 308 U.S. 295, 308 (1939). Thus, bankruptcy courts may depart from the basic rule of equality of distribution to subordinate particular claims and interests to others in the exercise of their equitable powers. The great bulk of equitable subordination cases in bankruptcy concern the activities of fiduciaries or "insiders" (§ 101), usually the officers, directors, or controlling stockholders of corporations.

#### a. Inequitable Conduct

The Bankruptcy Act made no specific reference to equitable subordination. Bankruptcy Code § 510(c) merely authorizes the court to subordinate claims and interests "under principles of equitable subordination." In giving meaning to this undefined phrase, the post-Code case law has heavily relied on a set of principles announced by the court in *In re Mobile Steel Co.*, 563 F.2d 692 (5th Cir.1977), a Bankruptcy Act case. Under this case equitable subordination is appropriate if the creditor (i) has engaged in inequitable conduct, (ii) the misconduct has resulted in injury to the creditors of the bankrupt or conferred an unfair advantage on the claimant, and (iii) the subordination is not inconsistent with the provisions of the Bankruptcy Act. Although the term "inequitable conduct" cannot be precisely delineated, the court in *In re Clark Pipe & Supply Co.*, 893 F.2d 693 (5th Cir.1990), reprinted *infra*, states that it encompasses (i) fraud, illegality and breach of fiduciary duties, (ii) undercapitalization, and (iii) the claimant's use of the debtor corporation as a mere instrumentality or alter ego.

Thus, under *Mobile Steel* there can be no equitable subordination of a claim without some degree of inequitable conduct on the part of the claim holder. During the 1990s a line of cases rejected this requirement with respect to the priority of tax penalties, which are awarded a first priority in bankruptcy as an administrative expense, §§ 503(b)(1)(C), 507(a)(1). In *Matter of Virtual Network Services Corp.*, 902 F.2d 1246 (7th Cir.1990), the leading case on the subject, the court subordinated a tax penalty claim not because of any inequitable conduct by the government but because it would be unfair to punish innocent creditors by reducing funds available to pay unsecured claims for the acts of the debtor that gave rise to the penalty. Section 726(a)(4), which automatically subordinates noncompensatory penalties, is based on that principle but it applies only to Chapter 7 cases. The court in *Virtual Network* declared expansively: "It is clear that in principle, equitable subordination no longer requires, in all circumstances, some inequitable conduct on the part of the creditor." 902 F.2d at 1250.

In *United States v. Noland*, 517 U.S. 535 (1996), the Supreme Court rejected *Virtual Network* on the ground that subordination in such a case "runs directly counter to Congress's policy judgment that a postpetition tax penalty should receive the priority of an administrative expense, §§ 503(b)(1)(C), 507(a)(1)." 517 U.S. at 541. The Court concluded: "In this instance, Congress could have, but did not, deny noncompensatory, postpetition tax penalties the first priority given to other administrative expenses, and bankruptcy courts may not take it upon themselves to make that categorical determination under the guise of equitable subordination." 517 U.S. at 543. This decision is a rare illustration of the third prong of the *Mobile Steel* test: the subordination may not be inconsistent with the provisions of the Bankruptcy Code. Having decided the case on this ground, the Court left undecided the question whether a bankruptcy court must always find creditor misconduct before a claim may be equitably subordinated. The court in *In Matter of Lifschultz Fast Freight*, 132 F.3d 339, 344 (7th Cir.1997), held that the general rule after *Noland* is that inequitable conduct is required for equitable subordination in all but extraordinary circumstances.

A seminal case on inequitable conduct is *Pepper v. Litton*. This case involved a claim of about $30,000 for accumulated salary, dating back at least five years, by Litton, who was the dominant stockholder of Dixie Splint Coal Company. The court held that the claim could be disallowed or subordinated in the bankruptcy of Dixie Splint because of fraudulent conduct by Litton. The salary claim was asserted in an action by Litton against Dixie Splint for the first time after Pepper had brought action against Dixie Splint for an accounting of royalties due to Pepper. While the Pepper action was pending, Litton caused Dixie Splint to confess judgment on Litton's action. "Execution was issued on this judgment the same day but no return was made thereon, Litton waiting 'quietly until the outcome of the Pepper suit was definitely known.'" When Pepper obtained judgment, Dixie Splint obtained suspension of execution by Pepper for 90 days to permit an appeal although no appeal was ever made. During the 90–day period Litton levied on his judgment. "Litton 'had no intention of trying to satisfy his confessed judgment' against his corporation "unless and until it became necessary to do so'; he was using it 'only as a shield against the Pepper debt.' Thus, when execution and levy were made * * * no steps were taken for over two months towards a sale of the property on which levy had been made." When Pepper levied on her judgment Litton caused the sheriff "who seems to have been cooperating with Litton" to sell the property on which Litton had levied. Litton purchased the property at the execution sale for $3,200. "The next step in the "planned and fraudulent' scheme was the formation by Litton of "another of his one-man corporations' * * * to which Litton transferred the property he had acquired at the execution sale at a valuation [fixed by the board of directors at over $20,000] to be paid for in stock of the new company." As the "third step in Litton's scheme" Dixie Splint filed in bankruptcy two days after Litton's execution sale. "This step, according to the findings below, was 'plainly for the sole purpose of avoiding payment of the Pepper debt.'" 308 U.S. at 297–298. The Court concluded:

> * * * Litton allowed his salary claims to lie dormant for years and sought to enforce them only when his debtor corporation was in financial difficulty. Then he used them so that the rights of another creditor were impaired. Litton as an insider utilized his strategic position for his own preferment to the damage of Pepper. Litton as the dominant influence over Dixie Splint Coal Company used his power not to deal fairly with the creditors of that company but to manipulate its affairs in such a manner that when one of its creditors came to collect her just debt the bulk of the assets had disappeared into another Litton company. Litton, though a fiduciary, was enabled by astute legal maneuvering to acquire most of the assets of the bankrupt not for cash or other consideration of value to creditors but for bookkeeping entries representing at best merely Litton's appraisal of the worth of Litton's services over the years.

308 U.S. at 311–312.

An interesting contemporary application of the principles of *Pepper v. Litton* is found in *Citicorp Venture Capital, Ltd. v. Committee of Creditors Holding Unsecured Claims*, 160 F.3d 982 (3d Cir.1998). In that case Citicorp Venture Capital (CVC) owned 28% of the common stock of the debtor, Papercraft Corporation, and designated a member of Papercraft's board of directors. After bankruptcy, without notice to Papercraft's board or creditors' committee, CVC purchased approximately $60 million face amount of Papercraft's publicly traded bonds at an average price of fifteen cents on the dollar. CVC then formulated a plan of reorganization pursuant to which it proposed to acquire control of Papercraft and threatened to block the debtor's own plan (which incidentally CVC had also participated in formulating) by voting its newly acquired bonds against the debtor's plan. The bankruptcy court nevertheless confirmed the debtor's plan over CVC's objections and limited CVC's allowed claim to approximately $10 million, the discounted amount CVC paid for the bonds. The Court of Appeals agreed that CVC breached its fiduciary duties by purchasing the bonds at a discount, without notice to the selling bondholders, board of directors and creditors' committee, while having access to confidential material inside information, with the intention of influencing the debtor's reorganization in a manner favoring CVC's self-interest. But it rejected the bankruptcy court's remedy of limiting the CVC claim to $10 million, the aggregate purchase price of the bonds, and instructed the bankruptcy court to equitably subordinate CVC's claim only to the extent necessary to compensate the Papercraft estate and prevent CVC from retaining any profit from its purchase of the bonds. On remand, following the instructions of the Court of Appeals, the bankruptcy court equitably subordinated a portion of CVC's claim sufficient to prevent CVC from realizing any profit and further reduced CVC's distributions by an amount sufficient to compensate the Papercraft estate for damages caused by CVC's machinations. The net result was that CVC received only $5 million in distributions from the Papercraft estate, far less than the $10 million it had paid for the bonds. Note that this use of equitable subordination fails to compensate bondholders who sold out to CVC at a discount and creates a windfall for other creditors whose claims would have otherwise had to share with the holders of the $60 million face amount of purchased bonds.

### b.  Undercapitalization

The court in *Mobile Steel* defined undercapitalization as follows:

(1)  Capitalization is inadequate if, in the opinion of a skilled financial analyst, it would definitely be insufficient to support a business of the size and nature of the bankrupt in light of the circumstances existing at the time the bankrupt was capitalized;

(2)  Capitalization is inadequate if, at the time when the advances were made, the bankrupt could not have borrowed a similar amount of money from an informed outside source.

## Matter of Herby's Foods, Inc.

United States Court of Appeals, Fifth Circuit, 1993.
2 F.3d 128.

■  POLITZ, Chief Judge:

We review the propriety of a bankruptcy court's equitable subordination of certain creditors' claims to a level equivalent to that of equity stockholders. Finding no infirmity in the bankruptcy court's rulings or in the upholding thereof by the district court, we affirm.

Herby's Foods, Inc. produced and distributed fast foods to convenience stores. The Summit Coffee Company, Inc., Dunnam–Snyder Company, and The Snyder Company, Inc. (collectively, the Insiders) are interrelated companies that advanced funds to Herby's and possess claims as unsecured creditors in the Herby's bankruptcy.

The corporate "food chain" was as follows: (1) Herby's was a wholly owned subsidiary of Summit; (2) all of the voting securities of Summit were owned by Dunnam; (3) Dunnam is a partnership composed of seven trusts for the benefit of William Snyder's ex-wife and children; and (4) the managing agent for Dunnam at the time of Summit's acquisition of Herby's was Snyder Co., owned by William Snyder's ex-wife and children. In addition to the commonality of ownership interests, these companies enjoyed a commonality of management. At various times, William Snyder personally held several management positions, including president of Snyder Co., managing agent of Dunnam, an officer of Summit, and president of Herby's. The Insiders stipulated that they are "insiders" of Herby's as defined in the Bankruptcy Code.

Summit purchased Herby's on October 26, 1987 pursuant to a Stock Purchase Agreement.[2] The purchase price was $5,500,000, $2,800,000 of which was actually a loan to Herby's to pay off an intercompany debt to its previous owner. Herby's executed a note and security agreement in favor of Summit for $2,800,000. Like the Stock Purchase Agreement, these documents were dated October 26, 1987; the security interest, however, was not perfected at that time.

In addition, Dunnam provided a working capital line of credit to Herby's in the amount of $4,000,000. The parties have stipulated that no third-party lender would make a working capital loan to Herby's on any terms. The line of credit was evidenced by Herby's promissory note and security agreement, both dated October 26, 1987. Once again, the security interest was not timely perfected. Through a series of draws, Herby's eventually borrowed the maximum amount available under this line of credit.

Summit did not file a UCC–1 to perfect its security interest under the purchase money loan until November 10, 1988, 13 months after the note and security agreement had been executed. Similarly, Dunnam did not file a UCC–1 to perfect its security interest under the working capital loan until June 9, 1989, 20 months after the date of the underlying note and security agreement. According to Snyder, both of these security agreements covered "basically everything" owned by Herby's. Snyder also admitted that, "[w]e delayed putting in the UCC's because we were hoping to get a secured lender."

Between Summit's acquisition of Herby's and the filing of its petition in bankruptcy on September 7, 1989, the amount that Herby's owed to its unsecured creditors (other than the Insiders) increased fivefold, from $929,550.23 to $4,635,675. Further, between January 6, 1989 and September 1, 1989, Snyder Co. made unsecured advances to Herby's exceeding $579,000, advances which were not evidenced by loan agreements or any other documentation and which apparently bore no interest.

---

[2] As no bank would finance Summit's acquisition of Herby's on terms that were acceptable to the Insiders, Summit borrowed the funds from Dunnam.

After Herby's filed its voluntary Chapter 11 bankruptcy petition, the Insiders, as unsecured creditors, submitted these proofs of claims:

| | |
|---|---|
| Summit | $ 3,086,394.52 |
| Dunnam | $ 4,054,696.12 |
| Snyder Co. | $ 579,276.47 |

The Official Unsecured Creditors Committee (the Committee) responded with a Complaint to Subordinate Claims, Avoid Liens and Object to Claims. In its complaint the Committee sought to subordinate and object to the claims of the Insiders and to avoid the liens of Summit and Dunnam. Neither Summit nor Dunnam asserted liens, nor did they oppose their avoidance, apparently in recognition of their avoidability under § 547. The Insiders opposed the avoidance of their claims and, alternatively their subordination to a level below that of general unsecured creditors.

The bankruptcy court applied the test for equitable subordination which we detailed in *In re Mobile Steel Co.* Under that test, equitable subordination is justified only if: (1) the claimant engaged in inequitable conduct; (2) the misconduct resulted in injury to the creditors or conferred an unfair advantage on the claimant; and (3) equitable subordination of the claim would not be inconsistent with the provisions of the Bankruptcy Act (now Bankruptcy Code). The bankruptcy court found in the affirmative on each of the three *Mobile Steel* inquiries and subordinated the claims of the Insiders to the level of equity holders, finding that this ranking was necessary to offset the harm that the debtor and its non-insider creditors had suffered as a result of the inequitable conduct of the Insiders.

Timely appealing the affirmance by the district court, the Insiders assert five points of error: (1) the finding that Herby's was undercapitalized on the date of Summit's acquisition; (2) the finding that the late perfection by Summit and Dunnam of their security interests constituted inequitable conduct; (3) the characterization of the sums advanced to Herby's by Summit, Dunnam, and Snyder Co. as equity contributions rather than loans; (4) the finding that the Insiders' actions harmed the other creditors sufficiently to warrant subordination; and (5) the affirmance of the extent of the equitable subordination ordered by the bankruptcy court.

\* \* \*

## B. Principles of Equitable Subordination

The Bankruptcy Code provides that the bankruptcy court may "under principles of equitable subordination, subordinate for purposes of distribution all or part of an allowed claim to all or part of another allowed claim or all of part of an allowed interest to all or part of another allowed interest."[8] The legislative history of this provision reflects that Congress "in-

---

[8] § 510(c)(1).

tended that the term 'principles of equitable subordination' follow existing case law and leave to the courts development of this principle."[9] The equitable powers of a bankruptcy court, including the power to subordinate, may be "invoked to the end that fraud will not prevail, that substance will not give way to form, that technical considerations will not prevent substantial justice from being done."[10]

In *Mobile Steel* we established the test to determine when equitable subordination is appropriate. In addition to the tripartite test noted above, we further held in *Mobile Steel* that three additional principles must be considered in determining whether the three prongs of the subordination test have been satisfied. First, the inequitable conduct by the claimant may be sufficient to warrant subordination whether or not the misconduct related to the acquisition or assertion of the claim. Second, a claim should be subordinated only to the extent necessary to offset the harm that the bankrupt and its creditors suffered as a result of the inequitable conduct. Third, the claims arising from the dealings between the debtor and its fiduciaries must be subjected to rigorous scrutiny, and, if sufficiently challenged, the burden shifts to the fiduciary to prove both the good faith of the transaction and its inherent fairness.

Subsequent to *Mobile Steel*, we expanded the class of claims that are subject to rigorous scrutiny to include insider claims. Additionally, if the claimant is an insider, less egregious conduct may support equitable subordination. The determination of insider status is a question of fact subject to the clearly erroneous standard of review.

Although the exact parameters of inequitable conduct have not been comprehensively or precisely delineated, such conduct does encompass: (1) fraud, illegality, breach of fiduciary duties; (2) undercapitalization; and (3) the claimant's use of the debtor corporation as a mere instrumentality or alter ego.

Undercapitalization generally refers to the insufficiency of capital contributions made to the debtor corporation. Inadequate capitalization may be established by the testimony of a skilled financial analyst that the capitalization "would definitely be insufficient to support a business of the size and nature of the bankrupt in light of the circumstances existing at the time the bankrupt was capitalized."[16] Capitalization is also inadequate "if, at the time when the advances were made, the bankrupt could not have borrowed a similar amount of money from an informed outside source."[17]

Even though undercapitalization alone generally does not justify equitable subordination, evidence of additional inequitable conduct may do so.

---

[9] 124 Cong.Rec.H 11095, H 11113 (Sept. 28, 1978).

[10] Pepper v. Litton, 308 U.S. 295, 305 (1939).

[16] Mobile Steel, 563 F.2d at 703.

[17] Id.

For example, if an insider makes a loan to an undercapitalized corporation, the combination of undercapitalization and the insider loan may allow the bankruptcy court to recharacterize the loan as a capital contribution, or to equitably subordinate the loan to the claims of other creditors.

### C. Equitable Subordination of Appellants' Claims

#### 1. Undercapitalization

The record contains evidence to support the finding that Herby's was undercapitalized on the date of Summit's purchase. An expert financial witness tendered by the Committee testified that as of the date of its acquisition by Summit, Herby's capital was not sufficient to support its operations. The testimony of a former financial officer of Herby's corroborated the fact that on the date of its acquisition, Herby's was incapable of paying its debts as they became due and therefore was insolvent. William Snyder conceded that Herby's was insolvent on the date of acquisition.

We need not rely solely on the first prong of the *Mobile Steel* test for inadequate capitalization, however. The Insiders stipulated before trial that:

> Prior to the closing, Snyder [Co.] on behalf of Dunnam, solicited certain financial institutions seeking a loan to complete the acquisition. No independent third-party lender, after reviewing the financial position of the Debtor and Summit, would lend Dunnam or the Debtor money secured by the assets of the debtor on terms acceptable to the Insider Claimants. Indeed, only one lender offered financing but it required personal guarantees. . . . The Debtor was not able to obtain working capital from a third-party lender after the Acquisition.

As evidenced by this stipulation, Herby's could not have borrowed a similar amount from an informed outside source on acceptable terms, either to complete the acquisition or to obtain working capital. We find no error in the bankruptcy court's determination that Herby's was undercapitalized on the date of acquisition. The finding is fully supported by the evidence.

#### 2. Delayed Perfection as Inequitable Conduct

As stated, undercapitalization alone generally is insufficient to justify equitable subordination. The Insiders contend that the bankruptcy court erroneously treated the untimely perfection of their security interests as sufficient additional inequitable conduct to warrant subordination. We need not decide, however, whether the combination of undercapitalization plus merely the late perfection of security for the avowed purpose of "hoping to get a secured lender" constitutes sufficient inequitable conduct to support subordination; the Insiders herein did more.

The Insiders never injected any equity capital into Herby's, electing instead to advance funds through tardily perfected secured loans made at times when no bona fide third-party lender would have done so. With full knowledge that Herby's was undercapitalized and insolvent, the Insiders persisted with their practice of advancing funds only in the form of loans.

Further, the loan from Summit was not initially reflected on Herby's books. When finally booked, it was listed as an unsecured loan. Similarly, the Dunnam debt was never definitively identified on Herby's books. Finally, the purported working capital loans from Snyder Co., totaling over one-half million dollars, were never evidenced by any form of loan agreement.

Summit received only minimal interest payments and no principal payments on its note. It perfected its security position only after Herby's stopped making the interest payments. Likewise, Dunnam received only five interest payments and did not perfect its security interest until seven months after Herby's stopped payments. The working capital advances from Snyder Co. apparently never purported to bear any interest. We find more than adequate evidence of inequitable conduct on the part of the Insiders to support the court's equitable subordination of their claims.

### 3. Recharacterization

The Insiders also charge that the bankruptcy court erred in recharacterizing as equity contributions the sums advanced by the Insiders as loans, citing as support *Tomlinson v. 1661 Corporation.*[20] They also complain that the Committee did not seek recharacterization, but only equitable subordination.

This point of error need not long detain us. We affirm the bankruptcy court's decision to subordinate the Insiders' claims to the level of equity, not any decision it might have made to recharacterize these advances from loan to equity. The Insiders concede in their brief that a court is authorized to recharacterize a loan as an equity contribution even when circumstances do not warrant equitable subordination. They further concede that in the instant case the practical effects of recharacterization on the one hand and equitable subordination to the level of equity on the other would be the same.

The judgment of the bankruptcy court declares that the claims of the Insiders "are hereby fully subordinated to those of the other unsecured creditors in this case." Even though that ranks the Insiders below the level of all other unsecured creditors, thereby putting the claims of the Insiders on the same level as equity holders, no mention of recharacterizing the Insiders' loans is made in the bankruptcy court's judgment. We recognize that language in the Memorandum Opinion and Order could be read to support the suggestion that the court recharacterized the claims at issue;[21]

---

[20] 377 F.2d 291 (5th Cir.1967).

[21] Although the Insider claimants' brief is unclear on the matter, this claim appears to be based on a single sentence in the bankruptcy Court's Memorandum Opinion and Order: "The claimants' attempt to characterize as loans what were, in fact, equity capital contributions to the debtor constitutes an aggravating circumstance." Although the Insider claimants' brief is unclear on the matter, this claim appears to be based on a single sentence in the bankruptcy Court's Memorandum Opinion and Order: "The

however, such an implicit recharacterization was not essential to the bankruptcy court's judgment. Consequently, we need not decide whether the bankruptcy court in fact recharacterized the loans as equity and, if so, whether such recharacterization was proper. The court a quo expressly subordinated the Insiders' claims to a position below the level of unsecured creditors and we find that such subordination was fully justified in this case.

### 4. Harm to Other Creditors

The Insiders next maintain that their conduct did not harm the creditors of Herby's sufficiently to warrant subordination. They acknowledge, however, that the aggregate size of Herby's unsecured debt to its trade creditors increased from approximately $900,000 to over $4,600,000, and that the average number of days outstanding for trade payables increased almost eleven-fold, from approximately seven to approximately seventy-five, between the date of Summit's acquisition of Herby's and its filing for relief in bankruptcy. Nevertheless, they insist that no evidence was presented to the bankruptcy court that any specific creditor was deceived or lured into extending additional unsecured credit by the actions as required by *Fabricators*. The Insiders' reliance on this argument is misplaced.

The *Fabricators* court found that inducing other creditors to extend additional credit through misrepresentations to be one form of inequitable conduct. In this point of error, the Insiders are not contesting the existence of inequitable conduct but, rather, whether such misconduct either produced injury to the arms-length creditors of the bankrupt or secured an unfair advantage for the miscreant claimants. Both injury and unfair advantage may be established by proving that a specific creditor was deceived or lured into extending additional credit to the bankrupt. "It is well established that actual fraud need not be shown for equitable subordination."[22] Mere good faith on the part of the Insiders would not negate the harm sustained by Herby's creditors; neither would it lessen the advantage gained by the Insiders.

The bankruptcy court found that the Insiders' conduct harmed Herby's outside creditors by significantly increasing their trade credit exposure and by reducing their ultimate dividend in the liquidation. Most importantly, the court found that the Insiders had secured an unfair advantage by structuring their cash contributions to Herby's as loans, rather than as equity capital. If the Insiders were allowed to retain their ranking as unsecured creditors, they would have gained an advantage in the priority scheme by encouraging outside creditors to increase their credit exposure to Herby's.

---

claimants' attempt to characterize as loans what were, in fact, equity capital contributions to the debtor constitutes an aggravating circumstance."

[22] Machinery Rental, Inc. v. Herpel (In re Multiponics, Inc.), 622 F.2d 709, 720 (5th Cir.1980).

Their efforts were successful; those trade creditors substantially increased their credit to Herby's during the period in question. We are persuaded that the inequitable conduct of the Insiders produced sufficient injury to the unsecured trade creditors and secured a sufficiently unfair advantage for the Insiders to warrant equitable subordination.

### 5. Cure by Nonassertion

The Insiders argue that they cured any prior inequitable conduct by not trying to enforce their liens in bankruptcy and by seeking only the status of general unsecured creditors. They previously admitted, however, in their answer to the Complaint to Subordinate Claims, that Summit's and Dunnam's liens were avoidable, that they could only assert unsecured claims against the estate, and that they had no security interest in the proceeds of the sale of Herby's assets. They also admitted that Snyder never had a security interest to perfect. We cannot accept the proposition that the nonassertion of invalid claims results in the legal legerdemain suggested by the Insiders.

Even assuming that the Insiders had arguably valid claims as secured parties, their failure to file secured claims would not have cured what appears to be a previously obtained advantage. One might suggest that if the trade creditors had known that the Insiders early on had made secured loans to Herby's (thereby signaling that security was essential), the larger trade creditors would have declined to extend credit or would have sought secured status for themselves. The facts of the instant case support the proposition that the Insiders were able to lull the trade creditors into extending more unsecured credit to Herby's than they would have had they understood the Insiders' own assessment of Herby's financial health. The fact that the Insiders now seek only to be treated as unsecured creditors would not cure the effect of such deception of the trade creditors.

### 6. Degree of Subordination

The Insiders finally contend that their claims should have been subordinated only to the level of general unsecured creditors. "The prerogative to relegate claims to inferior status on equitable grounds, though broad, is not unlimited."[25] As noted earlier, a claim should be subordinated only to the extent necessary to correct the harm or unfair advantage caused by the inequitable conduct.

The harm or unfair advantage that resulted from the Insiders' inequitable conduct is not limited to whatever may have resulted from their late perfection of Summit's and Dunnam's security interests. Both the harm and the unfair advantage are much more pervasive. Herby's was undercapitalized from the date of Summit's acquisition, and the Insiders did nothing to rectify that situation. Further, the advances from Summit and Dunnam were neither accurately nor timely reflected on Herby's financial

---

[25] Mobile Steel, 563 F.2d at 699.

records and the purported loans from Snyder Co. were never evidenced on the records or by any form of a loan agreement.

While these deceptive practices were being perpetrated, the aggregate sums owed by Herby's to its trade creditors increased by 3.7 million dollars. According to the record before us, the total amount distributable from Herby's estate will approximate 2.1 million dollars. If the claims of the Insiders are allowed a ranking equal to that of the unsecured trade creditors, the Insiders would receive approximately 75% of Herby's estate. This cannot be permitted. Even with subordination, the harm to the trade creditors will not be completely rectified. Anything less than full subordination would lend judicial approval to the unfair advantage secured by the Insiders. This we will not do.

AFFIRMED.

## NOTES

**1.** The Commission on the Bankruptcy Laws of the United States, appointed by Congress in 1970 to study revision of the bankruptcy laws, recommended adoption of a new bankruptcy statute. Section 4–406(a)(2) of the Commission's proposed statute subordinated "any claim, whether secured or unsecured, of any principal officer, director or affiliate of a debtor, or of any member of the immediate family of such officer, director, or affiliate." This proposal was not included in the Bankruptcy Code of 1978. Section 510(c) reflects the rejection by Congress of automatic subordination of insider claims. The rationale is that insiders may deal honestly and fairly with their firms and should not be discouraged by the automatic subordination doctrine from lending money to them. *See* Robert C. Clark, *The Duties of the Corporate Debtor to its Creditors*, 90 Harv.L.Rev. 505, 538 (1977). Does *Herby's Foods* adopt a rule of automatic subordination of insider claims if no third party lender would extend credit on comparable terms? Why would insiders of a financially distressed firm ever loan money to the firm if it can obtain credit on comparable terms from a bank or other third party? Jonathan M. Landers, in *A Unified Approach to Parent, Subsidiary and Affiliate Questions in Bankruptcy*, 42 U. Chi.L.Rev. 589, 604 (1975), suggests that adoption of a rule such as that stated by the court in *Mobile Steel* is merely an indirect method of achieving the result of mandatory subordination of insider claims proposed by the Bankruptcy Commission.

**2.** What reaction do you have to the following observation of the court in *Matter of Lifschultz Fast Freight*, 132 F.3d 339, 346 (7th Cir.1997)?

So what is wrong with undercapitalization in itself? The trustee argues that "insufficient capital leads to financing the operation with secured debt, and that exposes unsecured commercial creditors to a greater risk of loss." Quite so. But again, where is the wrong? Creditors extend credit voluntarily to a debtor. The debtor owes no duties to the creditor beyond those it promises in its contract (and beyond whatever common and statutory law may apply). A debtor decidedly does not owe a fiduciary duty to a creditor. * * * And a debtor is just as surely not obliged to be the lender's insurer. A lender will not offer a loan to a borrower unless the rate of return justifies the risk of default or underpayment. The same is true for the sub-class of lenders called trade creditors, for prudent business people assess the risk of default before allowing customers to pay for goods or services on credit. The higher that risk, the more interest (or collateral) the lender will demand. If a firm is poorly capitalized, and thus less likely to repay than a better capitalized firm in the same line of business, the lender may require more security or more interest. But that a highly leveraged company exposes its creditors to serious risks is no new fact of commerce. Creditors are free to lend elsewhere. If they choose to lend to a company that then loses their investment, they cannot go to the bankruptcy court and cry misconduct.

**3.** In *In re Autostyle Plastics, Inc.*, 269 F.3d 726 (6th Cir.2001), the court distinguished between equitable subordination and recharacterization of debt as equity: In equitable subordination, the remedy is subordination of a creditor's claim to that of another creditor only to the extent necessary to offset the injury suffered by the other creditor. In recharacterization, the purported creditor has no legitimate claim; it has only an ownership interest and is subordinate to all claims under the rule that debt has priority over equity. The court concedes that some courts intermix the two doctrines in that similar factors are relied on to show each status. For determining whether a debt should be recharacterized as equity, the court cited a number of factors set out in *Roth Steel Tube Co. v. Comm'r of Internal Revenue,* 800 F.2d 625 (6th Cir.1986). Among these are: (1) the absence of notes or other instruments of indebtedness with stated payment schedules and interest rates is evidence that no loan was intended; (2) if expectation of payment depends solely on the success of the borrower's business, the transaction is likely a capital contribution; (3) inadequacy of capitalization is evidence that the advances are capital contributions; (4) if stockholders make advances in proportion to their respective stock ownership, an equity contribution is indicated; (5) absence of security is evidence of capital contributions; (6) debtor's inability to obtain outside financing tends to show a capital contribution; and (7) use of advances as working capital to meet daily operating needs of debtor is evidence of bona fide indebtedness.

## 2. CLAIMS OF NONINSIDERS

When a business debtor files in bankruptcy, a relationship between the debtor and its dominant creditor, usually a secured lender, that allows the lender to exert control over the business decisions of the debtor, may form the basis for an attempt by the trustee to convince the bankruptcy court that the claim of the lender should be subordinated to the claims of other creditors. The following quotation from *In re Teltronics Services*, 29 B.R. 139, 170–171 (Bankr.E.D.N.Y.1983), raises some of the difficulties facing creditors who exert control over their debtors:

> The general rule that a creditor is not a fiduciary of his debtor is not without exception. In the rare circumstance where a creditor exercises such control over the decision-making processes of the debtor as amounts to a domination of its will, he may be held accountable for his actions under a fiduciary standard. * * * Accordingly, several commentators have admonished creditors to avoid becoming overly involved in the debtor's management:
>
> > Where the creditor controls the corporate debtor by voting control of its stock, dominant influence in its management or ability otherwise to control its business affairs, the creditor may have a fiduciary duty to its corporate debtor.
> >
> > * * *
> >
> > * * * [W]henever a creditor interferes in the business affairs of a financially troubled corporate debtor, it risks the possibility that such interference may provide a basis for the equitable adjustment of its claims against the debtor, the imposition of statutory liability or the imposition of liabilities at common law.
>
> Douglas–Hamilton, Creditor Liabilities Resulting from Improper Interference with the Management of a Financially Troubled Debtor, 31 Bus.Law. 343, 352, 365 (1975).
>
> > * * * [O]nce the creditor is not satisfied with simply insulating himself from the risk of loss of capital and interest, and instead insists upon affirmative participation in the entrepreneurial effort being financed * * * he has entered into a relationship whose expected extraordinary economic benefit justifies the requirement of special obligations.
> >
> > * * *
> >
> > With affirmative conduct thus has come voluntary assumption of duty, and the fact that the creditor's motives are not altruistic will strengthen arguments for the imposition of liability.
>
> Bartlett & Lapatin, *The Status of a Creditor as a Controlling Person*, 28 Mercer L.Rev. 639, 655–57 (1977).
>
> While it is possible for a creditor to be cast in the role of fiduciary, several cases illustrate the difficulty in demonstrating that the claimant so dominated the will of the debtor to the detriment of the other creditors that his claim should be relegated to inferior status. In affirming the subordination of a claim asserted by a creditor bank, the district court in *In re American Lumber*, 5 B.R. 470, 478 (D.Minn.1980) [dis-

cussed below in *Clark Pipe*] found "overwhelming" evidence that the bank purposefully manipulated the bankrupt's operations in a manner detrimental to the debtor's unsecured creditors. Among the indicia of control deemed sufficient to manifest a complete domination of will were the following: (1) the bank had the right to a controlling interest in debtor's stock pledged as collateral in the event of default in certain loan obligations; (2) the bank, which was the debtor's sole source of credit, placed the debtor within its coercive powers by refusing to honor the debtor's payroll checks, and by foreclosing on its security interests in the debtor's only source of ready cash, to wit, its accounts receivable and contract rights; and (3) the bank forced compliance with its wishes by imposing such harsh measures on the debtor as: forcing termination of most employees, requiring drastic reduction of officers' salaries, coercing execution of security agreements on the debtor's only remaining assets, and determining which creditors were to be paid by the debtor.

* * *

In the *W.T. Grant* case, 4 B.R. 53 (Bankr.S.D.N.Y.1980), the objectants sought to have the claims of creditor banks subordinated where it was alleged that the banks influenced several of the debtor's key financial decisions. Judge Galgay, in recognizing that the courts have denied the application of equitable subordination even where a creditor exercises a significant degree of daily monitoring of its debtor, rejected objectants' argument on the theory that the actions taken by the debtor "reflected independent policy decisions and not rigid submission to the dictates of the Bank claimants." 4 B.R. at 77. In affirming Judge Galgay's decision, the Second Circuit found nothing improper about the banks' "careful watch" of the bankrupt's activities, and suggested that the banks indeed would have been derelict in their duty to their own creditors and equityholders if they had not done so:

> The cases cited above strongly suggest that a non-insider creditor will be held to a fiduciary standard only where his ability to command the debtor's obedience to his policy directives is so overwhelming that there has been, to some extent, a merger of identity. Unless the debtor has become, in effect, the alter ego of the creditor, he will not be held to an ethical duty in excess of the morals of the marketplace.

In *In re Beverages International, Ltd.*, 50 B.R. 273 (Bankr.D.Mass.1985), the court subordinated the claim of a dominant creditor after finding that the creditor exercised control over the debtor. Evidence showed that the creditor required the debtor to change attorneys and accountants, participated in board meetings and engineered the sales of inferior inventory. The creditor also delayed in obtaining and recording a blanket security interest in all of the debtor's assets in order to encourage third parties to extend credit to the debtor that they would not have given had they known of the security interest.

In the following case the decision by a bankruptcy court to subordinate the claim of a dominant creditor was initially affirmed by the Fifth Circuit which subsequently reconsidered the case, confessed error, and reversed itself in the opinion reproduced below.

## Matter of Clark Pipe & Supply Co.
United States Court of Appeals, Fifth Circuit, 1990.
893 F.2d 693.

■ E. GRADY JOLLY, Circuit Judge:

Treating the suggestion for rehearing en banc filed in this case by Associates Commercial Corporation ("Associates"), as a petition for panel rehearing, we hereby grant the petition for rehearing. After re-examining the evidence in this case and the applicable law, we conclude that our prior opinion was in error. We therefore withdraw our prior opinion and substitute the following:

\* \* \*

Clark Pipe and Supply Company, Inc., ("Clark") was in the business of buying and selling steel pipe used in the fabrication of offshore drilling platforms. In September 1980, Associates and Clark executed various agreements under which Associates would make revolving loans secured by an assignment of accounts receivable and an inventory mortgage. Under the agreements, Clark was required to deposit all collections from the accounts receivable in a bank account belonging to Associates. The amount that Associates would lend was determined by a formula, i.e., a certain percentage of the amount of eligible accounts receivable plus a certain percentage of the cost of inventory. The agreements provided that Associates could reduce the percentage advance rates at any time at its discretion.

When bad times hit the oil fields in late 1981, Clark's business slumped. In February 1982 Associates began reducing the percentage advance rates so that Clark would have just enough cash to pay its direct operating expenses. Clark used the advances to keep its doors open and to sell inventory, the proceeds of which were used to pay off the past advances from Associates. Associates did not expressly dictate to Clark which bills to pay. Neither did it direct Clark not to pay vendors or threaten Clark with a cutoff of advances if it did pay vendors. But Clark had no funds left over from the advances to pay vendors or other creditors whose services were not essential to keeping its doors open.

One of Clark's vendors, going unpaid, initiated foreclosure proceedings in February and seized the pipe it had sold Clark. Another attempted to do so in March. \* \* \* When a third unpaid creditor initiated foreclosure proceedings in May, Clark sought protection from creditors by filing for reorganization under Chapter 11 of the Bankruptcy Code.

The case was converted to a Chapter 7 liquidation on August 31, 1982, and a trustee was appointed. In 1983, the trustee brought this adversary proceeding against Clark's lender, Associates. The trustee sought * * * equitable subordination of Associates' claims. * * * The court * * * subordinated Associates' claims. The district court affirmed on May 24, 1988.

* * * This court has enunciated a three-pronged test to determine whether and to what extent a claim should be equitably subordinated: (1) the claimant must have engaged in some type of inequitable conduct, (2) the misconduct must have resulted in injury to the creditors of the bankrupt or conferred an unfair advantage on the claimant, and (3) equitable subordination of the claim must not be inconsistent with the provisions of the Bankruptcy Code. * * * Three general categories of conduct have been recognized as sufficient to satisfy the first prong of the three-part test: (1) fraud, illegality or breach of fiduciary duties; (2) undercapitalization; and (3) a claimant's use of the debtor as a mere instrumentality or alter ego.

In essence, the bankruptcy court found that once Associates realized Clark's desperate financial condition, Associates asserted total control and used Clark as a mere instrumentality to liquidate Associates' unpaid loans. Moreover, it did so, the trustee argues, to the detriment of the rights of Clark's other creditors.

Associates contends that its control over Clark was far from total. Associates says that it did no more than determine the percentage of advances as expressly permitted in the loan agreement; it never made or dictated decisions as to which creditors were paid. Thus, argues Associates, it never had the "actual, participatory, total control of the debtor" required to make Clark its instrumentality under Krivo Industrial Supply Co. v. National Distillers & Chemical Corp., 483 F.2d 1098, 1105 (5th Cir.1973) * * *. If it did not use Clark as an instrumentality or engage in any other type of inequitable conduct * * * argues Associates, then it cannot be equitably subordinated.

We first consider whether Associates asserted such control over the activities of Clark that we should consider that it was using Clark as its mere instrumentality. In our prior opinion, we agreed with the district court and the bankruptcy court that, as a practical matter, Associates asserted total control over Clark's liquidation, and that it used its control in a manner detrimental to the unsecured creditors. Upon reconsideration, we have concluded that we cannot say that the sort of control Associates asserted over Clark's financial affairs rises to the level of unconscionable conduct necessary to justify the application of the doctrine of equitable subordination. We have reached our revised conclusion primarily because we cannot escape the salient fact that, pursuant to its loan agreement with Clark, Associates had the right to reduce funding, just as it did, as Clark's sales slowed. We now conclude that there is no evidence that Associates exceeded its authority under the loan agreement, or that Associates acted inequitably in exercising its rights under that agreement.

We think it is important to note at the outset that the loan and security agreements between Associates and Clark, which are at issue here, were executed in 1980, at the inception of their relationship. There is no evidence that Clark was insolvent at the time the agreements were entered into. Clark was represented by counsel during the negotiations, and there is no evidence that the loan documents were negotiated at anything other than arm's length or that they are atypical of loan documents used in similar asset-based financings.

The loan agreement between Associates and Clark established a line of credit varying from $2.2 million to approximately $2.7 million over the life of the loan. The amount that Associates would lend was determined by a formula: 85% of the amount of eligible accounts receivables plus 60% of the cost of inventory. Under the agreement, Clark was required to deposit all collections from the accounts receivable in a bank account belonging to Associates. Associates would, in turn, readvance the agreed-upon portion of those funds to Clark on a revolving basis. The agreement provided that Associates could reduce the percentage advance rates at any time in its discretion.

When Clark's business began to decline, along with that of the oil patch generally, Associates advised Clark that it would reduce the advance ratio for the inventory loan by 5% per month beginning in January 1982. After that time, the company stopped buying new inventory and, according to the Trustee's expert witness, Clark's monthly sales revenues amounted to less than one-fifth of the company's outstanding accounts payable. Clark prepared a budget at Associates' request that indicated the disbursements necessary to keep the company operating. The budget did not include payment to vendors for previously shipped goods. Associates' former loan officer, Fred Slice, testified as to what he had in mind:

> If he [the comptroller of Clark] had had the availability [of funds to pay a vendor or other trade creditor] that particular day, I would have said, "Are you sure you've got that much availability, Jim," because he shouldn't have that much. The way I had structured it, he wouldn't have any money to pay his suppliers.
>
> * * *
>
> But you know, the possibility that—this is all hypothetical. I had it structured so that there was no—there was barely enough money— there was enough money, if I did it right, enough money to keep the doors open. Clark could continue to operate, sell the inventory, turn it into receivables, collect the cash, transfer that cash to me, and reduce my loans.
>
> And, if he had ever had availability for other things, that meant I had done something wrong, and I would have been surprised. To ask

me what I would have done is purely hypothetical[;] I don't think it would happen. I think it's so unrealistic, I don't know.

Despite Associates' motive, which was, according to Slice, "to get in the best position I can prior to the bankruptcy, i.e., I want to get the absolute amount of dollars as low as I can by hook or crook," the evidence shows that the amount of its advances continued to be based on the applicable funding formulas. Slice testified that the lender did not appreciably alter its original credit procedures when Clark fell into financial difficulty.

In our original opinion, we failed to focus sufficiently on the loan agreement, which gave Associates the right to conduct its affairs with Clark in the manner in which it did. In addition, we think that in our previous opinion we were overly influenced by the negative and inculpatory tone of Slice's testimony. Given the agreement he was working under, his testimony was hardly more than fanfaronading about the power that the agreement afforded him over the financial affairs of Clark. Although his talk was crass (e.g., "I want to get the absolute dollars as low as I can, by hook or crook"), our careful examination of the record does not reveal any conduct on his part that was inconsistent with the loan agreement, irrespective of what his personal motive may have been.

Through its loan agreement, every lender effectively exercises "control" over its borrower to some degree. A lender in Associates' position will usually possess "control" in the sense that it can foreclose or drastically reduce the debtor's financing. The purpose of equitable subordination is to distinguish between the unilateral remedies that a creditor may properly enforce pursuant to its agreements with the debtor and other inequitable conduct such as fraud, misrepresentation, or the exercise of such total control over the debtor as to have essentially replaced its decision-making capacity with that of the lender. The crucial distinction between what is inequitable and what a lender can reasonably and legitimately do to protect its interests is the distinction between the existence of "control" and the exercise of that "control" to direct the activities of the debtor. As the Supreme Court stated in *Comstock v. Group of Institutional Investors*, 335 U.S. 211, 229 (1948): "It is not mere existence of an opportunity to do wrong that brings the rule into play; it is the unconscionable use of the opportunity afforded by the domination to advantage itself at the injury of the subsidiary that deprives the wrongdoer of the fruits of his wrong."

In our prior opinion, we drew support from *In re American Lumber Co.* to reach our conclusion that Associates' claims should be equitably subordinated. Upon reconsideration, however, we find that the facts of that case are significantly more egregious than we have here. In that case, the court equitably subordinated the claims of a bank because the bank "controlled" the debtor through its right to a controlling interest in the debtor's stock. The bank forced the debtor to convey security interests in its remaining unencumbered assets to the bank after the borrower defaulted on an existing debt. Immediately thereafter, the bank foreclosed on the borrower's accounts receivable, terminated the borrower's employees, hired its own skeleton crew to conduct a liquidation, and selectively honored the debtor's payables to improve its own position. The bank began receiving and opening all incoming mail at the borrower's office, and it established a bank account into which all amounts received by the borrower were deposited and over which the bank had sole control. The bankruptcy court found that the bank exercised control over all aspects of the debtor's finances and operation including: payments of payables and wages, collection and use of accounts receivable and contract rights, purchase and use of supplies and materials, inventory sales, a lumber yard, the salaries of the principals, the employment of employees, and the receipt of payments for sales and accounts receivable.

Despite its decision to prohibit further advances to the debtor, its declaration that the debtor was in default of its loans, and its decisions to use all available funds of the company to offset the company's obligations to it, the bank in *American Lumber* made two specific representations to the American Lumbermen's Credit Association that the debtor was not in a bankruptcy situation and that current contracts would be fulfilled. Two days after this second reassurance, the bank gave notice of foreclosure of its security interests in the company's inventory and equipment. Approximately two weeks later the bank sold equipment and inventory of the debtor amounting to roughly $450,000, applying all of the proceeds to the debtor's indebtedness to the bank.

Associates exercised significantly less "control" over the activities of Clark than did the lender in *American Lumber*. Associates did not own any stock of Clark, much less a controlling block. Nor did Associates interfere with the operations of the borrower to an extent even roughly commensurate with the degree of interference exercised by the bank in *American Lumber*. Associates made no management decisions for Clark, such as deciding which creditors to prefer with the diminishing amount of funds available. At no time did Associates place any of its employees as either a director or officer of Clark. Associates never influenced the removal from office of any Clark personnel, nor did Associates ever request Clark to take any particular action at a shareholders meeting. Associates did not expressly dictate to Clark which bills to pay, nor did it direct Clark not to pay vendors or threaten a cut-off of advances if it did pay vendors. Clark handled its own daily operations. The same basic procedures with respect to the reporting of collateral, the calculation of availability of funds, and the procedures for the advancement of funds were followed throughout the relationship between Clark and Associates. Unlike the lender in *American Lumber*, Associates did not mislead creditors to continue supplying Clark. Perhaps the most important fact that distinguishes this case from *American Lumber* is that Associates did not coerce Clark into executing the security agreements after Clark became insolvent. Instead, the loan and security agreements between Clark and Associates were entered into at arm's length prior to Clark's insolvency, and all of Associates' activities were conducted pursuant to those agreements.

Associates' control over Clark's finances, admittedly powerful and ultimately severe, was based solely on the exercise of powers found in the loan agreement. Associates' close watch over Clark's affairs does not, by itself, however, amount to such control as would justify equitable subordination. "There is nothing inherently wrong with a creditor carefully monitoring his debtor's financial situation or with suggesting what course of action the debtor ought to follow." In re Teltronics Services, Inc., 29 B.R. 139, 172 (Bankr.E.D.N.Y.1983) (citations omitted). Although the terms of the agreement did give Associates potent leverage over Clark, that agreement did not give Associates total control over Clark's activities. At all material times Clark had the power to act autonomously and, if it chose, to disregard the advice of Associates; for example, Clark was free to shut its doors at any time it chose to do so and to file for bankruptcy.

Finally, on reconsideration, we are persuaded that the rationale of *In re W.T. Grant Co.* should control the case before us. In that case, the Second Circuit recognized that

> a creditor is under no fiduciary obligation to its debtor or to other creditors of the debtor in the collection of its claim. [citations omitted] The permissible parameters of a creditor's efforts to seek collection from a debtor are generally those with respect to voidable preferences and fraudulent conveyances proscribed by the Bankruptcy Act; apart from these there is generally no objection to a creditor's using his bargaining position, including his ability to refuse to make further loans needed by the debtor, to improve the status of his existing claims.

699 F.2d at 609–10. Associates was not a fiduciary of Clark, it did not exert improper control over Clark's financial affairs, and it did not act inequitably in exercising its rights under its loan agreement with Clark.

Finally, we should note that in our earlier opinion, we found that, in exercising such control over Clark, Associates engaged in other inequitable conduct that justified equitable subordination. Our re-examination of the record indicates, however, that there is not really any evidence that Associates engaged in such conduct. Our earlier opinion assumed that Associates knew that Clark was selling pipe to which the suppliers had a first lien, but the issue of whether the vendors had a first lien on the pipe was not decided by our court until a significantly later time. In addition, although the trustee made much of the point on appeal, after our re-study of the record, we conclude that it does not support the finding that Associates encouraged Clark to remove decals from pipe in its inventory.

We also note that the record is devoid of any evidence that Associates misled other Clark creditors to their detriment. See, e.g., Matter of CTS Truss, Inc., 868 F.2d 146, 149 (5th Cir.1989) (lender did not represent to third parties that additional financing was in place or that debtor was solvent, when the opposite was true).

When the foregoing factors are considered, there is no basis for finding inequitable conduct upon which equitable subordination can be based.

We therefore conclude that the district court erred in affirming the bank-ruptcy court's decision to subordinate Associates' claims.

\* \* \*

## NOTES

**1.** In *Kham & Nate's Shoes No. 2, Inc. v. First Bank of Whiting*, 908 F.2d 1351 (7th Cir.1990), Bank opened a $300,000 line of credit for Debtor that permitted Bank to cancel at its discretion. After advancing $75,000, of which Debtor repaid $10,000, Bank refused to make further advances. The lower court equitably subordinated Bank's $65,000 claim on the ground that Bank's refusal to extend further credit was inequitable conduct. In overruling the lower court, Judge Easterbrook, speaking for the court, stated:

> "Inequitable conduct" in commercial life means breach *plus* some advantage-taking, such as the star who agrees to act in a motion picture and then, after $20 million has been spent, sulks in his dressing room until the contract has been renegotiated.

\* \* \*

> Bank did not break a promise at a time Debtor was especially vulnerable, then use the costs and delay of obtaining legal enforcement of the contract as levers to a better deal. Debtor and Bank signed a contract expressly allowing the Bank to cease making further advances. The $300,000 was the maximum loan, not a guarantee. The Bank exercised its contractual privilege after loaning Debtor $75,000; it made a clean break and did not demand improved terms. It had the right to do this for any reason satisfactory to itself.

\* \* \*

> Although Bank's decision left Debtor scratching for other sources of credit, Bank did not create Debtor's need for funds, and it was not contractually obliged to satisfy its customer's desires. The Bank was entitled to advance its own interest, and it did not need to put the interests of Debtor and Debtor's other creditors first. To the extent *K.M.C. Co., Inc. v. Irving Trust Co.*, 757 F.2d 752, 759–63 (6th Cir.1985), holds that a bank must loan more money or give more advance notice of termination than its contract requires, we respectfully disagree. First Bank of Whiting is not an eleemosynary institution. It need not throw good money after bad, even if other persons would catch the lucre.

\* \* \*

> Debtor stresses, and the bankruptcy judge found, that Bank would have been secure in making additional advances. Perhaps so, but the contract did not oblige Bank to make all advances for which it could be assured of payment. *Ex post* assessments of a lender's security are

no basis on which to deny it the negotiated place in the queue. Risk must be assessed *ex ante* by lenders, rather than *ex post* by judges. If a loan seems secure at the time, lenders will put up the money; their own interests are served by making loans bound to be repaid. What is more, the bankruptcy judge's finding that Bank would have been secure in making additional advances is highly questionable. The judgment of the market vindicates Bank. If more credit would have enabled Debtor to flourish, then other lenders should have been willing to supply it. Yet no one else, not even the SBA, would advance additional money to Debtor.

908 F.2d at 1357–1358.

**2.** Even if the claimant has not controlled the conduct of the debtor in the degree required by *Clark Pipe,* a noninsider claim may be subordinated in case of gross misconduct by the claimant. The court in *In re 604 Columbus Ave. Realty Trust,* 968 F.2d 1332, 1360 (1st Cir.1992), observed: "Claims arising from dealings between a debtor and an insider are rigorously scrutinized by the court. * * * On the other hand, if the claimant is not an insider, "then evidence of more egregious misconduct such as fraud, spoliation or overreaching is necessary.' "

In *In re Osborne,* 42 B.R. 988 (W.D.Wis.1984), Debtor was indebted to its principal lender, the Production Creditor Association (PCA), as well as to a bank and several trade creditors. When Debtor filed in bankruptcy, a dispute very familiar in agricultural financing arose: the other creditors asserted that the PCA, which was trying to keep Debtor afloat, had misled them about their prospect of being paid after it knew that Debtor was in serious financial trouble. At least with respect to one of the trade creditors, the court found PCA's remarks about the prospect of payment to be a knowingly false misrepresentation that amounted to gross misconduct. The court held that PCA's claim would be subordinated only with respect to the particular creditor who was injured by PCA's misconduct and only to the extent of that injury.

## B. SUBSTANTIVE CONSOLIDATION

The priority and treatment of claims can be dramatically affected by the bankruptcy doctrine of substantive consolidation. Under this doctrine, the assets of several debtors, usually affiliated corporations in a family of corporations operated as a unit, are pooled in bankruptcy and the claims of creditors of any member of the corporate family are treated as claims against the consolidated assets of all members of the family. In a substantive consolidation, creditors of a debtor whose asset-to-liability ratio is higher than that of affiliated debtors will lose to the extent the asset-to-liability ratio of the pooled estates is lower. Hence, substantive consolidation is sparingly invoked. On the other hand procedural consolidation, which is authorized by Bankruptcy Rule 1015, is quite common. In procedural consolidation two or more bankruptcy estates are administered together, but the assets are not pooled and each creditor has a claim only against the assets of its debtor. The usual examples are husband and wife, debtor and affiliate, and two or more partners.

No Code provision specifically authorizes substantive consolidation. The general powers of a bankruptcy court under § 105(a) to issue orders "necessary or appropriate to carry out the provisions" of the Code constitute the authority to act in this area.

The following opinion is important not only for its apparently restricted view of substantive consolidation but also because it binds courts in Delaware where many large companies and their affiliates file for Chapter 11 protection.

## In re Owens Corning, Inc.

United States Court of Appeals, Third Circuit, 2005.
419 F.3d 195.

■ AMBRO, Circuit Judge.

We consider under what circumstances a court exercising bankruptcy powers may substantively consolidate affiliated entities. Appellant Credit Suisse First Boston ("CSFB") is the agent for a syndicate of banks (collectively, the "Banks")[1] that extended in 1997 a $2 billion unsecured loan to Owens Corning, a Delaware corporation ("OCD"), and certain of its subsidiaries. This credit was enhanced in part by guarantees made by other OCD subsidiaries. The District Court granted a motion to consolidate the assets and liabilities of the OCD borrowers and guarantors in anticipation of a plan of reorganization.

The Banks appeal and argue that the Court erred by granting the motion, as it misunderstood the reasons for, and standards for considering, the extraordinary remedy of substantive consolidation, and in any event did not make factual determinations necessary even to consider its use. Though we reverse the ruling of the District Court, we do so aware that it acted on an issue with no opinion on point by our Court and differing rationales by other courts.

While this area of law is difficult and this case important, its outcome is easy with the facts before us. Among other problems, the consolidation sought is "deemed." Should we approve this non-consensual arrangement, the plan process would proceed as though assets and liabilities of separate entities were merged, but in fact they remain separate with the twist that the guarantees to the Banks are eliminated. From this we conclude that the proponents of substantive consolidation request it not to rectify the seldom-seen situations that call for this last-resort remedy but rather as a ploy

---

[1] Though CSFB is the named appellant, the real parties in interest are the Banks (which include CSFB). Thus, unless the context requires otherwise, CSFB and the Banks are referred to interchangeably in this opinion.

to deprive one group of creditors of their rights while providing a windfall to other creditors.

## I. Factual Background and Procedural History

### A. Owens Corning Group of Companies

OCD and its subsidiaries (which include corporations and limited liability companies) comprise a multinational corporate group. Different entities within the group have different purposes. Some, for example, exist to limit liability concerns (such as those related to asbestos), others to gain tax benefits, and others have regulatory reasons for their formation.

Each subsidiary was a separate legal entity that observed governance formalities. Each had a specific reason to exist separately, each maintained its own business records, and intercompany transactions were regularly documented. Although there may have been some "sloppy" bookkeeping, two of OCD's own officers testified that the financial statements of all the subsidiaries were accurate in all material respects. Further, through an examination of the subsidiaries' books, OCD's postpetition auditors (Ernst & Young) have eliminated most financial discrepancies, particularly with respect to the larger guarantor subsidiaries.

### B. The 1997 Credit Agreement

In 1997 OCD sought a loan to acquire Fibreboard Corporation. At this time OCD faced growing asbestos liability and a poor credit rating that hindered its ability to obtain financing. When CSFB was invited to submit a bid, it included subsidiary guarantees in the terms of its proposal. The guarantees gave the Banks direct claims against the guarantors for payment defaults. They were a "credit enhancement" without which the Banks would not have made the loan to OCD. All draft loan term sheets included subsidiary guarantees.

A $2 billion loan from the Banks to OCD closed in June 1997. The loan terms were set out primarily in a Credit Agreement. Among those terms were the guarantee provisions and requirements for guarantors, who were defined as "present or future Domestic Subsidiar[ies]. . . having assets with an aggregate book value in excess of $30,000,000." Section 10.07 of the Agreement provided that the guarantees were "absolute and unconditional" and each "constitute[d] a guarant[ee] of payment and not a guarant[ee] of collection."[4] A "No Release of Guarantor" provision in § 10.8 stated that "the obligations of each guarantor. . . shall not be reduced, limited or terminated, nor shall such guarantor be discharged from any such obligations, for any reason whatsoever," except payment and performance in full or through waiver or amendment of the Credit Agree-

---

[4] This standard guarantee term means simply that, once the primary obligor (here OCD) defaults, the Banks can proceed against the guarantors directly and immediately without first obtaining a judgment against OCD and collecting against that judgment to determine if a shortfall from OCD exists.

ment. Under § 13.05 of the Credit Agreement, a guarantor could be released only through (i) the unanimous consent of the Banks for the guarantees of Fibreboard subsidiaries or through the consent of Banks holding 51% of the debt for other subsidiaries, or (ii) a fair value sale of the guarantor if its cumulative assets totaled less than 10% of the book value of the aggregate OCD group of entities.

CSFB negotiated the Credit Agreement expressly to limit the ways in which OCD could deal with its subsidiaries. For example, it could not enter into transactions with a subsidiary that would result in losses to that subsidiary. Importantly, the Credit Agreement contained provisions designed to protect the separateness of OCD and its subsidiaries. The subsidiaries agreed explicitly to maintain themselves as separate entities. To further this agreement, they agreed to keep separate books and financial records in order to prepare separate financial statements. The Banks were given the right to visit each subsidiary and discuss business matters directly with that subsidiary's management. The subsidiaries also were prohibited from merging into OCD because both entities were required to survive a transaction under § 8.09(a)(ii)(A) of the Credit Agreement. This provision also prohibited guarantor subsidiaries from merging with other subsidiaries unless there would be no effect on the guarantees' value.

### C. Procedural History

On October 5, 2000, facing mounting asbestos litigation, OCD and seventeen of its subsidiaries (collectively, the "Debtors") filed for reorganization under Chapter 11 of the Bankruptcy Code, § 1101 *et seq* Twenty-seven months later, the Debtors and certain unsecured creditor groups (collectively, the "Plan Proponents") proposed a reorganization plan (as amended, the "Plan") predicated on obtaining "substantive consolidation" of the Debtors along with three non-Debtor OCD subsidiaries. Typically this arrangement pools all assets and liabilities of the subsidiaries into their parent and treats all claims against the subsidiaries as transferred to the parent. In fact, however, the Plan Proponents sought a form of what is known as a "deemed consolidation," under which a consolidation is deemed to exist[7] for purposes of valuing and satisfying creditor claims, voting for or against the Plan, and making distributions for allowed claims under it. Plan § 6.1. Yet "the Plan would not result in the merger of or the transfer or commingling of any assets of any of the Debtors or Non-Debtor Subsidiaries,. . . [which] will continue to be owned by the respective Debtors or Non-Debtors." Plan § 6.1(a). Despite this, on the Plan's effective date "all guarantees of the Debtors of the obligations of any other Debtor will be deemed eliminated, so that any claim against any such Debtor and any guarantee thereof. . . will be deemed to be one obli-

---

[7] "[A]ll assets and liabilities of each Subsidiary Debtor. . . *will be treated as though they were merged into and with the assets and liabilities of OCD. . . .*" Plan § 6.1(b) (emphasis added).

gation of the Debtors with respect to the consolidated estate." Plan § 6.1(b). Put another way, "the Plan eliminates the separate obligations of the Subsidiary Debtors arising from the guarant [e]es of the 1997 Credit Agreement." Plan Disclosure Statement at A-9897.

The Banks objected to the proposed consolidation. Judge John Fullam * * * granted the consolidation motion in an order accompanied by a short opinion. *In re Owens Corning,* 316 B.R. 168 (Bankr.D.Del.2004).

Judge Fullam concluded that there existed "substantial identity between. . . OCD and its wholly-owned subsidiaries." *Id.* at 171. He further determined that "there [was] simply no basis for a finding that, in extending credit, the Banks relied upon the separate credit of any of the subsidiary guarantors." *Id.* at 172. In Judge Fullam's view, it was "also clear that substantive consolidation would greatly simplify and expedite the successful completion of this entire bankruptcy proceeding. More importantly, it would be exceedingly difficult to untangle the financial affairs of the various entities." *Id.* at 171. As such, he held substantive consolidation should be permitted, as not only did it allow "obvious advantages. . . [, but was] a virtual necessity." *Id.* at 172. In any event, Judge Fullam wrote, "[t]he real issue is whether the Banks are entitled to participate, *pari passu,* with other unsecured creditors, or whether the Banks' claim is entitled to priority, in whole or in part, over the claims of other unsecured creditors." *Id.* But this issue, he stated, "cannot now be determined." *Id.*

CSFB appeals on the Banks' behalf. * * *

### III. Substantive Consolidation

Substantive consolidation, a construct of federal common law, emanates from equity. It "treats separate legal entities as if they were merged into a single survivor left with all the cumulative assets and liabilities (save for inter-entity liabilities, which are erased). The result is that claims of creditors against separate debtors morph to claims against the consolidated survivor." *Genesis Health Ventures, Inc. v. Stapleton (In re Genesis Health Ventures, Inc.),* 402 F.3d 416, 423 (3d Cir.2005). Consolidation restructures (and thus revalues) rights of creditors and for certain creditors this may result in significantly less recovery.

While we have not fully considered the character and scope of substantive consolidation, we discussed the concept in *Nesbit,* 347 F.3d at 86-88 (surveying substantive consolidation case law for application by analogy to the Title VII inquiry of when to consolidate employers for the purpose of assessing a discrimination claim), and *In re Genesis Health Ventures,* 402 F.3d at 423-24 (examining, *inter alia,* whether a "deemed" consolidation for voting in connection with, and distribution under, a proposed plan of reorganization is a substantive consolidation for purposes of calculating U.S. Trustee quarterly fees under 28 U.S.C. § 1930(a)(6)). Other courts, including the Supreme Court itself in an opinion that spawned the concept of consolidation, have holdings more on point than heretofore have we. We begin with a survey of key cases, drawing from them when substantive consolidation may apply consistent with the principles we perceive as cabining its use, and apply those principles to this case.

### A. History of Substantive Consolidation

The concept of substantively consolidating separate estates begins with a commonsense deduction. Corporate disregard[10] as a fault may lead to corporate disregard as a remedy.

Prior to substantive consolidation, other remedies for corporate disregard were (and remain) in place. For example, where a subsidiary is so dominated by its corporate parent as to be the parent's "alter ego," the "corporate veil" of the subsidiary can be ignored (or "pierced") under state law. Kors, *supra,* at 386-90 (citing as far back as I. Maurice Wormser, *Piercing the Veil of Corporate Entity,* 12 Colum. L.Rev. 496 (1912)). Or a court might mandate that the assets transferred to a corporate subsidiary be turned over to its parent's trustee in bankruptcy for wrongs such as fraudulent transfers, Kors, *supra,* at 391, in effect bringing back to the bankruptcy estate assets wrongfully conveyed to an affiliate. If a corporate parent is both a creditor of a subsidiary and so dominates the affairs of that entity as to prejudice unfairly its other creditors, a court may place payment priority to the parent below that of the other creditors, a remedy known as equitable subordination, which is now codified in § 510(c) of the Bankruptcy Code. *See generally id.* at 394-95.

Adding to these remedies, the Supreme Court, little more than six decades ago, approved (at least indirectly and perhaps inadvertently) what became known as substantive consolidation. *Sampsell v. Imperial Paper & Color Corp.,* 313 U.S. 215 (1941). In *Sampsell* an individual in bankruptcy had transferred assets prepetition to a corporation he controlled. (Apparently these became the corporation's sole assets.) When the bankruptcy referee ordered that the transferred assets be turned over by the corporation to the individual debtor's trustee, a creditor of the non-debtor corporation sought distribution priority with respect to that entity's assets. In deciding that the creditor should not be accorded priority (thus affirming the bankruptcy referee), the Supreme Court turned a typical turnover/fraudulent transfer case into the forebear of today's substantive consolidation by terming the bankruptcy referee's order (marshaling the corporation's assets for the benefit of the debtor's estate) as "consolidating the estates." *Id.* at 219.

Each of these remedies has subtle differences. "Piercing the corporate veil" makes shareholders liable for corporate wrongs. Equitable subordination places bad-acting creditors behind other creditors when distributions are made. Turnover and fraudulent transfer bring back to the transferor debtor assets improperly transferred to another (often an affiliate).

---

[10] A term used by Mary Elisabeth Kors in her comprehensive and well-organized article entitled *Altered Egos: Deciphering Substantive Consolidation,* 59 U. Pitt. L.Rev. 381, 383 (1998) (hereinafter "Kors").

Substantive consolidation goes in a direction different (and in most cases further) than any of these remedies; it is not limited to shareholders, it affects distribution to innocent creditors, and it mandates more than the return of specific assets to the predecessor owner. It brings all the assets of a group of entities into a single survivor. Indeed, it merges liabilities as well. "The result," to repeat, "is that claims of creditors against separate debtors morph to claims against the consolidated survivor." *In re Genesis Health Ventures,* 402 F.3d at 423. The bad news for certain creditors is that, instead of looking to assets of the subsidiary with whom they dealt, they now must share those assets with all creditors of all consolidated entities, raising the specter for some of a significant distribution diminution.

Though the concept of consolidating estates had Supreme Court approval, Courts of Appeal (with one exception) were slow to follow suit. * * * Little occurred thereafter for more than two decades, until the Second Circuit issued several decisions * * * that brought substantive consolidation as a remedy back into play and premise its modern-day understanding.

Other Circuit Courts fell in line in acknowledging substantive consolidation as a possible remedy. * * *

The reasons of these courts for allowing substantive consolidation as a possible remedy span the spectrum and often overlap. * * *

Ultimately most courts slipstreamed behind two rationales-those of the Second Circuit in *In re Augie/Restivo Baking Co., Ltd.,* 860 F.2d 515 (2d Cir. 1988) and the D.C. Circuit in *In re Auto-Train Corp.,* 810 F.2d 270 (D.C.Cir. 1987). The former found that the competing "considerations are merely variants on two critical factors: (i) whether creditors dealt with the entities as a single economic unit and did not rely on their separate identity in extending credit,. . . or (ii) whether the affairs of the debtors are so entangled that consolidation will benefit all creditors. . . ." *In re Augie/Restivo,* 860 F.2d at 518 (internal quotation marks and citations omitted). *Auto-Train* touched many of the same analytical bases as the prior Second Circuit cases, but in the end chose as its overarching test the "substantial identity" of the entities and made allowance for consolidation in spite of creditor reliance on separateness when "the demonstrated benefits of consolidation 'heavily' outweigh the harm." *In re Auto-Train,* 810 F.2d at 276 (citation omitted).

Whatever the rationale, courts have permitted substantive consolidation as an equitable remedy in certain circumstances. No court has held that substantive consolidation is not authorized, though there appears nearly unanimous consensus that it is a remedy to be used "sparingly." *In re Augie/Restivo,* 860 F.2d at 518.

### B. Our View of Substantive Consolidation

Substantive consolidation exists as an equitable remedy. But when should it be available and by what test should its use be measured? As already noted, we have commented on substantive consolidation only generally in *Nesbit,* 347 F.3d at 86-88, and *In re Genesis Health Ventures,*

402 F.3d at 423-24. The latter nonetheless left little doubt that, if presented with a choice of analytical avenues, we favor essentially that of *Augie/Restivo. Id.* at 423. The *Auto-Train* approach (requiring "substantial identity" of entities to be consolidated, plus that consolidation is "necessary to avoid some harm or realize some benefit," 810 F.2d at 276) adopts, we presume, one of the *Augie/Restivo* touchstones for substantive consolidation while adding the low bar of avoiding some harm or discerning some benefit by consolidation. To us this fails to capture completely the few times substantive consolidation may be considered and then, when it does hit one chord, it allows a threshold not sufficiently egregious and too imprecise for easy measure. For example, we disagree that "[i]f a creditor makes [a showing of reliance on separateness], the court may order consolidation... if it determines that the demonstrated benefits of consolidation 'heavily' outweigh the harm." *Id.* at 276 (citation omitted); *see also Eastgroup,* 935 F.2d at 249. If an objecting creditor relied on the separateness of the entities, consolidation cannot be justified *vis-à-vis* the claims of that creditor.

In assessing whether to order substantive consolidation, courts consider many factors * * * . Too often the factors in a check list fail to separate the unimportant from the important, or even to set out a standard to make the attempt. * * * This often results in rote following of a form containing factors where courts tally up and spit out a score without an eye on the principles that give the rationale for substantive consolidation (and why, as a result, it should so seldom be in play). *Id.* ("[D]iffering tests with... agreed... factors run the risk that courts will miss the forest for the trees. Running down factors as a check list can lead a court to lose sight of why we have substantive consolidation in the first instance... and often [to] fail [to] identify a metric by which [it] can... [assess] the relative importance among the factors. The... [result is] resort to ad hoc balancing without a steady eye on the... [principles] to be advanced. ...").

What, then, are those principles? We perceive them to be as follows.

(1) Limiting the cross-creep of liability by respecting entity separateness is a "fundamental ground rule[ ]." Kors, *supra,* at 410. As a result, the general expectation of state law and of the Bankruptcy Code, and thus of commercial markets, is that courts respect entity separateness absent compelling circumstances calling equity (and even then only possibly substantive consolidation) into play.

(2) The harms substantive consolidation addresses are nearly always those caused by *debtors* (and entities they control) who disregard separateness. Harms caused by creditors typically are remedied by provisions found in the Bankruptcy Code (*e.g.,* fraudulent transfers, § § 548 and 544(b)(1) , and equitable subordination, § 510(c)).

(3) Mere benefit to the administration of the case (for example, allowing a court to simplify a case by avoiding other issues or to

make postpetition accounting more convenient) is hardly a harm calling substantive consolidation into play.

**(4)** Indeed, because substantive consolidation is extreme (it may affect profoundly creditors' rights and recoveries) and imprecise, this "rough justice" remedy should be rare and, in any event, one of last resort after considering and rejecting other remedies (for example, the possibility of more precise remedies conferred by the Bankruptcy Code).

**(5)** While substantive consolidation may be used defensively to remedy the identifiable harms caused by entangled affairs, it may not be used offensively (for example, having a primary purpose to disadvantage tactically a group of creditors in the plan process or to alter creditor rights).

The upshot is this. In our Court what must be proven (absent consent) concerning the entities for whom substantive consolidation is sought is that (i) prepetition they disregarded separateness so significantly their creditors relied on the breakdown of entity borders and treated them as one legal entity,[19] or (ii) postpetition their assets and liabilities are so scrambled that separating them is prohibitive and hurts all creditors.[20]

Proponents of substantive consolidation have the burden of showing one or the other rationale for consolidation. The second rationale needs no explanation. The first, however, is more nuanced. A *prima facie* case for it typically exists when, based on the parties' prepetition dealings, a proponent proves corporate disregard creating contractual expectations of creditors that they were dealing with debtors as one indistinguishable entity. Kors, *supra,* at 417-18 * * * . Proponents who are creditors must also show that, in their prepetition course of dealing, they actually and reasonably relied on debtors' supposed unity. Kors, *supra,* at 418-19. Creditor opponents of consolidation can nonetheless defeat a *prima facie* show-

---

[19] This rationale is meant to protect in bankruptcy the prepetition expectations of those creditors. *Accord* Kors, *supra,* at 419. The usual scenario is that creditors have been misled by debtors' actions (regardless whether those actions were intentional or inadvertent) and thus perceived incorrectly (and relied on this perception) that multiple entities were one.

[20] This rationale is at bottom one of practicality when the entities' assets and liabilities have been "hopelessly commingled." *In re Gulfco Inv.,* 593 F.2d at 929; *In re Vecco,* 4 B.R. at 410. Without substantive consolidation all creditors will be worse off (as Humpty Dumpty cannot be reassembled or, even if so, the effort will threaten to reprise *Jarndyce v. Jarndyce,* the fictional suit in Dickens' *Bleak House* where only the professionals profited). With substantive consolidation the lot of all creditors will be improved, as consolidation "advance[s] one of the primary goals of bankruptcy-enhancing the value of the assets available to creditors. . .-often in a very material respect." Kors, *supra,* at 417 (citation omitted).

ing under the first rationale if they can prove they are adversely affected and actually relied on debtors' separate existence.

### C. Application of Substantive Consolidation to Our Case

With the principles we perceive underlie use of substantive consolidation, the outcome of this appeal is apparent at the outset. Substantive consolidation fails to fit the facts of our case and, in any event, a "deemed" consolidation cuts against the grain of all the principles.

To begin, the Banks did the "deal world" equivalent of "Lending 101." They loaned $2 billion to OCD and enhanced the credit of that unsecured loan indirectly by subsidiary guarantees covering less than half the initial debt. What the Banks got in lending lingo was "structural seniority"-a direct claim against the guarantors (and thus against their assets levied on once a judgment is obtained) that other creditors of OCD did not have. This kind of lending occurs every business day. To undo this bargain is a demanding task.

### 1. No Prepetition Disregard of Corporate Separateness

Despite the Plan Proponents' pleas to the contrary, there is no evidence of the prepetition disregard of the OCD entities' separateness. To the contrary, OCD (no less than CSFB) negotiated the 1997 lending transaction premised on the separateness of all OCD affiliates. Even today no allegation exists of bad faith by anyone concerning the loan. In this context, OCD and the other Plan Proponents cannot now ignore, or have us ignore, the very ground rules OCD put in place. Playing by these rules means that obtaining the guarantees of separate entities, made separate by OCD's choice of how to structure the affairs of its affiliate group of companies, entitles a lender, in bankruptcy or out, to look to any (or all) guarantor(s) for payment when the time comes. As such, the District Court's conclusions of "substantial identity" of OCD and its subsidiaries, and the Banks' reliance thereon, are incorrect. For example, testimony presented by both the Banks and the Debtors makes plain the parties' intention to treat the entities separately. CSFB presented testimony from attorneys and bankers involved in negotiating the Credit Agreement that reflected their assessment of the value of the guarantees as partially derived from the separateness of the entities. As OCD concedes, these representatives "testified that the guarant[e]es were. . . intended to provide 'structural seniority' to the banks," and were thus fundamentally premised on an assumption of separateness. Debtors Ans. Br. at 26.

In the face of this testimony, Plan Proponents nonetheless argue that the Banks intended to ignore the separateness of the entities. In support of this contention, they assert, *inter alia,* that because the Banks did not receive independent financial statements for each of the entities during the negotiating process, they must have intended to deal with them as a unified whole. Because the Banks were unaware of the separate financial makeup of the subsidiaries, the argument goes, they could not have relied on their separateness.

This argument is overly simplistic. Assuming the Banks did not obtain separate financial statements for each subsidiary, they nonetheless obtained detailed information about each subsidiary guarantor from OCD, including information about that subsidiary's assets and debt. Moreover, the Banks knew a great deal about these subsidiaries. For example, they knew that each subsidiary guarantor had assets with a book value of at least $30 million as per the terms of the Credit Agreement, that the aggregate value of the guarantor subsidiaries was over $900 million and that those subsidiaries had little or no debt. Additionally, the Banks knew that Fibreboard's subsidiaries (including the entities that became part of ESI) had no asbestos liability, would be debt-free post-acquisition and had assets of approximately $700 million.

Even assuming the Plan Proponents could prove prepetition disregard of Debtors' corporate forms, we cannot conceive of a justification for imposing the rule that a creditor must obtain financial statements from a debtor in order to rely reasonably on the separateness of that debtor. Creditors are free to employ whatever metrics they believe appropriate in deciding whether to extend credit free of court oversight. We agree with the Banks that "the reliance inquiry is not an inquiry into lenders' internal credit metrics. Rather, it is about the *fact* that the credit decision was made in reliance on the existence of separate entities. . .." CSFB Opening Br. at 31 (emphasis in original). Here there is no serious dispute as to that fact.

**2.** No Hopeless Commingling Exists Postpetition

There also is no meaningful evidence postpetition of hopeless commingling of Debtors' assets and liabilities. Indeed, there is no question which entity owns which principal assets and has which material liabilities. Likely for this reason little time is spent by the parties on this alternative test for substantive consolidation. It is similarly likely that the District Court followed suit.

The Court nonetheless erred in concluding that the commingling of assets will justify consolidation when "the affairs of the two companies are so entangled that consolidation *will be beneficial.*" *In re Owens Corning*, 316 B.R. at 171 (emphasis added). As we have explained, commingling justifies consolidation only when separately accounting for the assets and liabilities of the distinct entities will reduce the recovery of *every* creditor-that is, when every creditor will benefit from the consolidation. Moreover, the benefit to creditors should be from cost savings that make assets available rather than from the shifting of assets to benefit one group of creditors at the expense of another. Mere benefit to some creditors, or administrative benefit to the Court, falls far short. The District Court's test not only fails to adhere to the theoretical justification for "hopeless commingling" consolidation-that no creditor's rights will be impaired-but also suffers from the infirmity that it will almost always be met. That is, substantive consolidation will nearly always produce some benefit to some in the form of simplification and/or avoidance of costs. Among other things, following such a path misapprehends the degree of harm required to order substantive consolidation.

But no matter the legal test, a case for hopeless commingling cannot be made. Arguing nonetheless to the contrary, Debtors assert that "it would be practically impossible and prohibitively expensive in time and resources" to account for the voluntary bankruptcies of the separate entities OCD has created and maintained. Debtors Ans. Br. at 63. In support of this contention, Debtors rely almost exclusively on the District Court's findings that

> it would be exceedingly difficult to untangle the financial affairs of the various entities. . . [and] there are. . . many reasons for challenging the accuracy of the results achieved [in accounting efforts thus far]. For example, transfers of cash between subsidiaries and parent did not include any payment of interest; and calculations of royalties are subject to question.

*In re Owens Corning,* 316 B.R. at 171. Assuming *arguendo* that these findings are correct, they are simply not enough to establish that substantive consolidation is warranted.

Neither the impossibility of perfection in untangling the affairs of the entities nor the likelihood of some inaccuracies in efforts to do so is sufficient to justify consolidation. We find *R 2 Investments, LDC v. World Access, Inc. (In re World Access, Inc.),* 301 B.R. 217 (Bankr.N.D.Ill.2003), instructive on this point. In *World Access* the Court noted that the controlling entity "had no uniform guidelines for the recording of intercompany interest charges" and that the debtors failed to "allocate overhead charges amongst themselves." *Id.* at 234. The Court held, however, that those accounting shortcomings were "merely imperfections in a sophisticated system of accounting records that were conscientiously maintained." *Id.* at 279. It ultimately concluded that "all the relevant accounting data. . . still exist [ed]," that only a "reasonable review to make any necessary adjustments [was] required," and, thus, that substantive consolidation was not warranted. *Id.*

The record in our case compels the same conclusion. At its core, Debtors' argument amounts to the contention that because intercompany interest and royalty payments were not perfectly accounted for, untangling the finances of those entities is a hopeless endeavor. Yet imperfection in intercompany accounting is assuredly not atypical in large, complex company structures. For obvious reasons, we are loathe to entertain the argument that complex corporate families should have an expanded substantive consolidation option in bankruptcy. And we find no reason to doubt that "perfection is not the standard in the substantive consolidation context." *Id.* We are confident that a court could properly order and oversee an accounting process that would sufficiently account for the interest and royalty payments owed among the OCD group of companies for purposes of evaluating intercompany claims-dealing with inaccuracies and difficulties as they arise and not in hypothetical abstractions.

On the basis of the record before us, the Plan Proponents cannot fulfill their burden of demonstrating that Debtors' affairs are even tangled, let alone that the cost of untangling them is so high relative to their assets that the Banks, among other creditors, will benefit from a consolidation.

**3.   Other Considerations Doom Consolidation as Well**

Other considerations drawn from the principles we set out also counsel strongly against consolidation. First of all, holding out the possibility of later giving priority to the Banks on their claims does not cure an improvident grant of substantive consolidation. Among other things, the prerequisites for this last-resort remedy must still be met no matter the priority of the Banks' claims.

Secondly, substantive consolidation should be used defensively to remedy identifiable harms, not offensively to achieve advantage over one group in the plan negotiation process (for example, by deeming assets redistributed to negate plan voting rights), nor a "free pass" to spare Debtors or any other group from proving challenges, like fraudulent transfer claims, that are liberally brandished to scare yet are hard to show. If the Banks are so vulnerable to the fraudulent transfer challenges Debtors have teed up (but have not swung at for so long), then the game should be played to the finish in that arena.

But perhaps the flaw most fatal to the Plan Proponents' proposal is that the consolidation sought was "deemed" (*i.e.,* a pretend consolidation for all but the Banks). If Debtors' corporate and financial structure was such a sham before the filing of the motion to consolidate, then how is it that post the Plan's effective date this structure stays largely undisturbed, with the Debtors reaping all the liability-limiting, tax and regulatory benefits achieved by forming subsidiaries in the first place? In effect, the Plan Proponents seek to remake substantive consolidation not as a remedy, but rather a stratagem to "deem" separate resources reallocated to OCD to strip the Banks of rights under the Bankruptcy Code, favor other creditors, and yet trump possible Plan objections by the Banks. Such "deemed" schemes we deem not Hoyle.

### IV. Conclusion

Substantive consolidation at its core is equity. Its exercise must lead to an equitable result. "Communizing" assets of affiliated companies to one survivor to feed all creditors of all companies may to some be equal (and hence equitable). But it is hardly so for those creditors who have lawfully bargained prepetition for unequal treatment by obtaining guarantees of separate entities. *Accord Chemical Bank New York Trust Co. v. Kheel,* 369 F.2d 845, 848 (Friendly, J., concurring) ("Equality among creditors who have lawfully bargained for different treatment is not equity but its opposite. . . ."). No principled, or even plausible, reason exists to undo OCD's and the Banks' arms-length negotiation and lending arrangement, especially when to do so punishes the very parties that conferred the prepetition benefit-a $2 billion loan unsecured by OCD and guaranteed by others only in part. To overturn this bargain, set in place by OCD's own pre-loan choices of organizational form, would cause chaos in the marketplace, as it would make this case the Banquo's ghost of bankruptcy.

With no meaningful evidence supporting either test to apply substantive consolidation, there is simply not the nearly "perfect storm" needed to invoke it. Even if there were, a "deemed" consolidation-"several zip (if not area) codes away from anything resembling substantive consolidation," *In re Genesis Health Ventures,* 402 F.3d at 424-fails even to qualify for consideration. Moreover, it is here a tactic used as a sword and not a shield.

We thus reverse and remand this case to the District Court.


## NOTES

**1.** The most common use of substantive consolidation is in consensual cases in which the parties agree on the distribution of value in a reorganization plan approved by the court. It is in these cases that "deemed consolidation" may be sought in which a consolidation is deemed to exist for purposes of valuing creditor claims and voting on the plan. But the plan does not result in the merger of affiliates or commingling of assets of the different entities.

**2.** The question left by *Owens Corning* is what remains of nonconsensual substantive consolidation in the Third Circuit. Senior District Court Judge Fullam, sitting in bankruptcy, stated:

> I have no difficulty in concluding that there is indeed substantial identity between the parent debtor OCD and its wholly-owned subsidiaries. All of the subsidiaries were controlled by a single committee, from central headquarters, without regard to the subsidiary structure. Control was exercised on a product-line basis. For example, the president of the insulating systems business managed all aspects of the production, marketing, and distribution of insulation products, regardless of whether those products were manufactured in a factory owned by OCD or by a foreign subsidiary. The officers and directors of the subsidiaries did not establish business plans or budgets, and did not appoint senior management except at the direction of the central committee * * * Subsidiaries were established for the convenience of the parent company, primarily for tax reasons. All the subsidiaries were dependent upon the parent company for funding and capital. The financial management of the entire enterprise was conducted in an integrated manner. No subsidiary exercised control over its own finances.

> It is also clear that substantive consolidation would greatly simplify and expedite the successful completion of this entire bankruptcy proceeding. More importantly, it would be exceedingly difficult to untangle the financial affairs of the various entities. * * *

There can be no doubt that the Banks relied upon the overall credit of the entire Owens Corning enterprise. The decision as to whether funds would be borrowed by the parent company, or by one or more of the subsidiaries, was made by the borrowers, not by the lenders. All of Owens Corning's financial reporting was done on a consolidated basis, and only that consolidated information was provided to the Banks.

In short, there is simply no basis for a finding that, in extending credit, the Banks relied upon the separate credit of any of the subsidiary guarantors. This is not to say that the guarantees were not important to the Banks. * * *

*In re Owens Corning*, 316 B.R. 168, 171-172 (Bankr. D. Del. 2004).

In view of these findings, why did the Third Circuit, in reversing, consider this an easy case for rejecting substantive consolidation?

**3.** After *Owens Corning*, is it fair to conclude that, assuming formal corporate governance boundaries are observed, nonconsensual substantive consolidation in the Third Circuit is effectively limited to cases in which no objecting creditor is prejudiced by the consolidation? For an analysis favoring a restrictive view of substantive consolidation, see the amicus brief of seven law professors in support of the Appellant. The authors are Barry Adler, Susan Block-Lieb, G. Marcus Cole, Marcel Kahan, Ronald J. Mann, Robert K. Rasmussen and David A. Skeel, Jr.

**4.** Although Courts of Appeals frequently repeat that use of substantive consolidation should be "sparing," hundreds of reported decisions approve Chapter 11 plans providing for substantive consolidation on a bewildering set of fact patterns. The authorities are collected and analyzed in Mary Elisabeth Kors, *Altered Egos: Deciphering Substantive Consolidation*, 59 U.Pitt.L.Rev. 381 (1998), which is cited in *Owens Corning*.

**5.** In *Grupo Mexicano de Desarrollo, S.A. v. Alliance Bond Fund, Inc.*, 527 U.S. 308 (1999), the Supreme Court found that the so-called *Mareva* injunction developed in the courts of the United Kingdom beginning in 1975 was not within the general equitable power of the federal district courts. The *Mareva* injunction is a pre-judgment asset freeze order that reaches property outside the jurisdiction of the court but under the control of the defendant. It is a way of preventing the defendant from disposing of property not subject to a prejudgment writ of attachment because of its physical location. But (at least based on the Supreme Court majority's reading of the historical materials) prejudgment asset freeze injunctions like *Mareva* injunctions were not generally available in courts of equity in the 18th century when the federal Constitution and Judiciary Act of 1789 were adopted and conferred jurisdiction over suits in equity upon the federal courts. The Court reasoned:

We do not question the proposition that equity is flexible; but in the federal system, at least, that flexibility is confined within the broad boundaries of traditional equitable relief. To accord a type of relief that has never been available before—and especially (as here) a type of relief that has been specifically disclaimed by longstanding judicial precedent—is to invoke a "default rule" not of flexibility but of omnipotence. When there are indeed new condition that might call for a wrenching departure from past practice, Congress is in a much better position than we both to perceive them and to design the appropriate remedy.

527 U.S. at 322.

Consider the following argument that *Grupo Mexicano* effectively undermines the bankruptcy courts' jurisdiction to substantively consolidate separate estates:

> In the absence of 18th Century English law precedent for an order of substantive consolidation, such equitable remedy is not available. * * * [T]he federal law remedy of substantive consolidation can be traced back to a series of legal opinions rendered in the1940's and 1960's. It is not plausible that a similar remedy existed in 18th Century practice before the Chancellor. Under the *Grupo Mexicano* case, the federal courts are not authorized to predict what the Chancellor might have done if presented with the corporate structures routinely used in the 20th Century. *Grupo Mexicano* requires an 18th Century precedent before a federal court may fashion equitable remedies not authorized by statute.

* * *

> Resort to equitable remedies may appear to be a reasonable approach to the difficult problem of collecting debts. Frequently, it may appear reasonable to enjoin an alleged debtor from conveying assets where the creditor faces the risk of irreparable injury. Likewise, it may seem reasonable under certain facts and circumstances to permit a creditor of one entity to have recourse to the assets of an affiliated entity under the doctrine of substantive consolidation. The law of many states recognizes similar remedies, such as pre-judgment injunctive and "alter-ego" relief. Prior to *Grupo Mexicano*, it was plausible that the federal equity power was available to create such remedies in the absence of state law. However, in light of *Grupo Mexicano*, the development of new federal equitable remedies has been curtailed. As a result of *Grupo Mexicano*, the merits of new remedies for creditors should be a matter of debate and decision in legislatures and Congress.

J. Maxwell Tucker, *Grupo Mexicano and the Death of Substantive Consolidation*, 8 Am. Bankr. Inst. L.Rev. 427 (2000).

6. The doctrine of substantive consolidation appears to be debtors' lawyers' last best remaining hope for attacking the increasingly common practice of segregating accounts receivable and other payment rights into "bankruptcy remote vehicles" through the process of "asset securitization." The history and nature of "asset securitization" or "structured finance" is described in two Reports of the Association of the Bar of the

City of New York, *New Developments in Structured Finance*, 56 Bus. Law. 95 (2000), and *Structured Financing Techniques*, 50 Bus. Law. 527 (1995), which identifies the "one central, core principle" of asset securitization: "a defined group of assets can be structurally isolated and thus serve as the basis of a financing that is independent from the bankruptcy risks of the originator of the assets." The proponents of asset securitization argue that by transferring assets to a trust or limited liability company that engages in no business activity other than the ownership and management of the segregated assets, the transferred assets are removed from the estate of the transferor. Credit rating agencies like Moody's and Standard and Poor's have agreed to rate securities issued by these trusts or limited liability companies based on the quality and value of the assets transferred rather than the general credit of the transferor. This enables a transferor with, say, a single A credit rating to obtain financing at AAA rates by segregating assets into "bankruptcy remote vehicles." Bankruptcy lawyers have long been skeptical of this stratagem, at least when the transferor remains heavily involved in the management of the assets after the transfer through ownership of the trust, or issued guarantees or similar "credit enhancement" activities or owned a residual interest in the entity holding the transferred assets. In the *LTV Steel Co.* case, reported at 37 Bankr.Ct.Dec. 232 (2001), to the apparent horror of "the structured finance community," Bankruptcy Judge William T. Bodoh of the Northern District of Ohio, refused to consider the segregation of LTV's accounts receivables and inventory into bankruptcy remote vehicles a "true sale" and authorized the bankruptcy debtor to treat these assets as property of the estate, authorizing their use subject to an adequate protection order on an interim basis. The cash collateral litigation in *LTV Steel Co.* thereafter settled before a final order was entered on the question of the "true sale" nature of the securitization.

But attacking a securitization transaction as not a true sale is not the only possibility. If debtors could substantively consolidate the bankruptcy remote vehicle with the estate of the transferor, then presumably they could obtain use of the cash collateral and the protection of the automatic stay. This avenue of attack becomes more feasible the more intertwined the bankruptcy remote vehicle and the transferred assets are with the affairs of the bankruptcy debtor.

A third possibility is that the bankruptcy remote vehicle could itself initiate bankruptcy proceedings or suffer the filing of an involuntary bankruptcy. The structured finance community has developed elaborate forms to avoid this possibility, but it cannot be entirely eliminated. See *In re Kingston Square Associates*, 214 B.R. 713 (Bankr.S.D.N.Y.1997), which upheld an involuntary filing against a bankruptcy remote vehicle orchestrated by an insider of the debtor.

# CHAPTER 9

# THE CONSUMER DEBTOR IN CHAPTERS 7 AND 13

---

## A. INTRODUCTION

The American consumer enjoys the highest standard of living in the world. The eagerness of consumers to borrow and buy has been matched by the willingness of the consumer finance industry to supply plentiful credit on increasingly lower standards of creditworthiness. And, in ever-growing numbers—over 1.5 million in recent years—consumers who can't pay their bills have turned to bankruptcy for relief. The terms on which this relief should be granted or denied has long perplexed Congress and the courts and has become a significant social as well as legal issue. As the volume of consumer credit grew rapidly in the second half of the past century, Congress twice appointed commissions to study the issue. The Bankruptcy Law Revision Commission of the 1970s, on which the 1978 Bankruptcy Code was based, concluded that existing bankruptcy laws gave inadequate attention to consumer debtor problems and proposed major reforms. The principal consumer reform in the 1978 Act was the strengthening of Chapter 13. H.R.Rep. 95- 595, 95th Cong., 1st Sess. (1977). The National Bankruptcy Review Commission (NBRC) of the 1990s concluded that the 1978 Code had also proved inadequate to meet consumer debtor problems and proposed major changes, but no legislation resulted. In the late 1990s the consumer finance industry—banks, credit card issuers, finance companies, credit unions and retailers—took matters in its own hands and presented to Congress a "Bankruptcy Reform Act," which almost entirely ignored the recommendations of the NBRC. This measure, the "Bankruptcy Abuse Prevention and Consumer Protection Act of 2005," became law after eight years of legislative wrangling and lobbying. We will discuss in detail the provisions of this statute. Throughout this chapter we make several references to the *Report of the National Bankruptcy Review Commission* (1997) (*NBRC Rep.*), which fully discusses a number of the issues dealt with by the 2005 Act.

Efforts have been made to draw a profile of the kinds of individuals who are filing in bankruptcy today. Perhaps the best advice on this issue is that if you seek the modern consumer debtor in bankruptcy, look about you. Bankruptcy is no longer exclusively for poor people; it has become a middle class phenomenon. Filers come from mid-level as well as from lower-level income groups, though on the whole their incomes fall in the lower half. They own as well as rent their residences. They are as well educated as those who do not file. In short, they are a cross-section of society. What all these people have in common is that they are in financial trouble, usually big trouble. *See, e.g.,* Teresa A. Sullivan, Elizabeth Warren & Jay Lawrence Westbrook, *The Fragile Middle Class* 27 (2000); Kenneth N. Klee, *Restructuring Individual Debts*, 71 Am.Bankr.L.J. 431, 445-446 (1997).

## 1. PRIVATE SECTOR DEBT RELIEF

Despite the importance of consumer spending to the economy, consumers in default on their debts find little institutional assistance from the private sector. Creditors are usually willing to work with defaulting debtors on an informal basis so long as there is promise of repayment. Extensions and other workout agreements may be reached, but consumers who find themselves out of work or otherwise generally unable to pay their monthly bills have few alternatives to bankruptcy. For debtors with income, personal finance companies offer debtors in default on multiple debts consolidation loans in which existing debts are paid off by a finance company loan and the debtors, closely monitored by the lender, make a single monthly payment on the consolidated debt. If a payment is late, their telephone—still the most effective collection device—begins to ring. In more recent years home equity lenders have moved into the debt-consolidation business by offering to consolidate loans at lower interest rates by taking second mortgages against the debtors' homes. *NBRC Rep.* at 93–94. Some of the more aggressive lenders will lend as much as 125% of the value of the residence (less outstanding senior liens).

Various "credit repair" businesses have been spawned in recent years that charge substantial fees to rehabilitate a debtor's credit reputation. They advertise on television, radio and the Internet, falsely promising to repair a debtor's credit rating or, somehow, to erase a debtor's debts, but dispensing little advice. These groups have been targets for numerous suits by the Federal Trade Commission and state attorneys general. Of course, if all defensive tactics fail, the debtor is left under state law to the tender mercies of judgment creditors and collection agencies. They can garnish her pay, seize her nonexempt assets and stain her credit report. Another option is to seek credit counseling, an issue discussed later in this chapter.

## 2. BANKRUPTCY RELIEF

The traditional remedy available to individual debtors in financial difficulty is discharge of their debts in bankruptcy at the cost of liquidation of their nonexempt assets for the benefit of their creditors. The public policy implemented by the discharge/liquidation bargain is that individual debtors should not be burdened perpetually by their debts; they should be given a "fresh start" and encouraged to resume their lives as productive members of society. An even older principle is that creditors should share equitably in their bankrupt debtors' assets. Bankruptcy law replaces the race-to-the-courthouse, winner-take-all nature of state collection law with more efficient and fair collective action procedures. The modern process that offers a fresh-start discharge for debtors and equitable distribution of nonexempt assets of the debtor's estate for creditors is Chapter 7 of the Bankruptcy Code.

## B. THE CONSUMER DEBTOR IN CHAPTER 7

We have dealt extensively with some of the basic substantive issues that arise in Chapter 7 in the previous chapters of this book. In Chapter 3 (Claims), we found that the Code sets out elaborate provisions on how the liquidated value of a debtor's assets is distributed among claimants in Chapter 7: secured claims, priority claims, and unsecured claims. In Chapter 4 (Discharge), we visited the complex set of rules for determining when individual debtors in Chapter 7 may be discharged. But it turns out that in over 95% of the cases, Chapter 7 consumer debtors have no equity in nonexempt assets to liquidate, and, therefore, the provisions of the Code assuring equitable distribution of assets are almost wholly irrelevant. This means that in the vast majority of consumer cases Chapter 7 offers nothing to unsecured creditors but much to debtors: an automatic stay against creditor collection action and a discharge of prepetition debts, leaving the debtor's postpetition earnings free of prepetition claims.

In the remainder of the material on the consumer debtor in Chapter 7, we emphasize three hotly contested issues on which the 2005 Act has had a major impact on consumer debtors: limitation of access to Chapter 7 under the means test, reaffirmation and "ride-through."

### 1. ACCESS TO CHAPTER 7 UNDER 1978 CODE

The most contentious policy issue concerning consumer debtors has been the extent to which debtors should be allowed free access to Chapter 7 and its promise of a rapid discharge of unsecured claims. The 2005 Act radically changed the direction of the Code on this issue. The 1978 Bankruptcy Code offered two alternatives for consumer relief, Chapter 7 liquidation and Chapter 13 rehabilitation. In Chapter 7 the debtor surrendered all nonexempt assets to a trustee in bankruptcy who liquidated the assets for distribution to creditors; in turn, the debtor received a discharge of most of her unsecured debts. In Chapter 13 the debtor was allowed to retain her assets by undertaking a repayment plan under which she devoted a portion of her income over a three-year period to the payment of her debts. Upon completion of the plan, the debtor received a broad discharge, sometimes referred to as a super-discharge.

Under the 1978 Code, a debtor had a virtually unfettered right to opt for Chapter 7 liquidation with its fresh start discharge in preference to rehabilitation under Chapter 13. With respect to the choice between liquidation under Chapter 7, or repayment under Chapter 13, debtors were in complete control and they chose Chapter 7 in the great majority of cases. In the year ending in September 2004, there were 1,153,865 Chapter 7 filings and 454,412 Chapter 13 filings. *Annual Report of Director, Adminis-*

*trative Office of U.S. Courts* (2004). This can be described as a regime of "debtor's choice." David A. Skeel, Jr., *Debt's Dominion: A History of Bankruptcy Law in America* 2 (2001), observes that no other country was as generous to debtors in bankruptcy. Even England, whose economy and legal culture resembles our own, has an administrative official determine the debtor's treatment in bankruptcy who may require further payments to creditors before discharge is granted.

### 2.  THE 1984 SUBSTANTIAL ABUSE TEST

In the years immediately following enactment of the 1978 Code, the number of consumer bankruptcies rose substantially, and creditor groups began to contend that debtors were abusing the open access policy of Chapter 7, which allowed discharge of unsecured prepetition debts without regard to debtors' ability to pay these debts. Creditors believed that this was unfair and put forth an argument designed to resonate with the large majority of the public that pay their bills more or less on time, and, more importantly, with their representatives in Congress: debtors with enough postpetition income to pay a significant part of their prepetition debts over a period of a few years should not be entitled to an immediate fresh start discharge in Chapter 7. Rather they should be granted a discharge only through Chapter 13 in which they would have to make periodic payments on their prepetition debts over a period of years. Accordingly, creditors in the 70s and 80s urged Congress to allow bankruptcy judges to convert, *sua sponte*, Chapter 7 cases filed by debtors with enough income to pay a substantial portion of their prepetition debts to Chapter 13. This would have introduced a regime of "judge's choice." In support of such an amendment, creditors complained that open access to Chapter 7 had altered the public perception of bankruptcy from a humiliating last resort for hard pressed debtors to a routine financial planning tool, increasingly free of moral stigma, which the public accepted as a normal alternative for financial woes that allowed debtors to move on with their lives at the expense of their creditors.

When Congress considered a series of amendments to the Bankruptcy Code in 1984, the consumer finance industry clamored for a "means" test, barring access to Chapter 7 for debtors who had sufficient excess income to pay a significant portion of their debts under a Chapter 13 plan. But in 1984 Congress flatly rejected a means test and renewed its traditional commitment to keep the door open to Chapter 7 for "honest debtors" seeking a "fresh start." However, as part of the legislative end game, Congress threw the credit industry a bone by enacting former § 707(b) that allowed dismissal of a Chapter 7 case for "substantial abuse." Consumer advocates believed this to be an innocuous concession that finally put to rest any future means test. The quoted phrase, undefined by the legislation,  was thought to be so vague as to be almost meaningless. As originally drafted, this provision seemed to offer creditors very little: only the court could move for dismissal for substantial abuse, and it was thought unlikely that overworked bankruptcy judges would expend additional time poring over a debtor's schedules to decide *sua sponte* that Chapter 7 should be denied the petitioner. Moreover, Congress showed its support for free access to Chapter 7 by adding to § 707(b): "There shall be a presumption in favor of granting the relief requested by the debtor." Nevertheless, in the years following 1984, creditors were able to snatch partial victory from the jaws of almost total defeat by persuading a number of courts to view the substantial abuse test as a proxy for a means test and by obtaining amendment of § 707(b) to allow U.S. Trustees, as well as courts, to move for dismissal for substantial abuse.

We include the following pre-2005 decision, *In re Green*, for its discussion of different judicial views of debtor abuse in interpreting the former version of § 707(b), the first legislative response to the financial community's push for limiting access to Chapter 7. Its relevance to the 2005 statute becomes apparent when we see that the new law uses the term "totality of circumstances" in § 707(b)(3)(B) as a residual test for abuse.

## In re Green

United States Court of Appeals, Fourth Circuit, 1991.
934 F.2d 568.

■ ERVIN, Chief Judge:

\* \* \*

On March 17, 1989, Walter Green filed a voluntary petition in the Bankruptcy Court for the District of Maryland for relief under Chapter 7 of the Bankruptcy Code. The United States Trustee, upon reviewing Green's case, dismiss Green's Chapter 7 case on the ground that granting a discharge under determined that Green had income of $638 a month in excess of the income required to pay his necessary expenses. Accordingly, the Trustee filed a motion to Chapter 7 would be a substantial abuse of the Chapter pursuant to § 707(b).

The Bankruptcy Court conducted a hearing at which Green testified that he had $40,000 in unsecured debt, had monthly income of at least $638 in excess of his necessary expenses, and was currently employed as a bus driver with Mass Transit, the same job he had held for the past 13 years. Nevertheless, Green claimed that, because of a leg injury which had caused him to be out of work for six months, he had fallen far behind in his debt payments. His 1988 income was $46,000, much of which Green attributed to substantial overtime pay. Green stated that he would not be able to work overtime in the future if his leg continued to "stiffen up." Without overtime, Green estimated that his annual pay in 1989 would be only $26,000.

It was also adduced at the hearing that Green had no dependents and that he had filed for bankruptcy once previously, in 1973. His largest current debt, to a credit union for $21,900, had been accumulating for 10 years. The court noted that the schedule of unsecured claims that Green submitted lacked detail, but that many creditors were department stores, including elegant ones like Saks Fifth Avenue and Miller Brothers, jewelers, and consumer loan companies.

On August 17, 1989, the Bankruptcy Court issued an opinion granting the Trustee's motion, with leave to Green to convert his Chapter 7 case into a Chapter 13 filing within 30 days of the date of the Order. The basis for the court's dismissal of Green's Chapter 7 petition was that Green's possession of income in excess of his necessary expenses was sufficient, standing alone, to constitute substantial abuse of the provisions of Chapter 7 under § 707(b). On appeal, the United States District Court for the District of Maryland affirmed the Bankruptcy Court's dismissal of Green's petition. The district court held that the Bankruptcy Court acted properly in finding substantial abuse on the sole ground of Green's excess monthly income. Green appeals.

Green's appeal requires us to interpret a provision of the Bankruptcy Code and to review the Bankruptcy Court's findings of fact. The question of what constitutes "substantial abuse" for purposes of § 707(b) is a matter of law, to be reviewed de novo.

\* \* \*

Section 707(b) is one of several consumer credit amendments Congress added to the Code in response to pressure from retailers and consumer lenders who complained of an increasing number of Chapter 7 bankruptcies being filed by non-needy debtors. Prior to 1984, debtors enjoyed a virtually unfettered right to a "fresh start" under Chapter 7, in exchange for liquidating their nonexempt assets for the benefit of their creditors. Section 707(b) introduced an additional restraint upon a debtor's ability to gain Chapter 7 relief, by allowing a bankruptcy court to deal equitably with the situation in which an unscrupulous debtor seeks to gain the court's assistance in a scheme to take unfair advantage of his creditors. Unfortunately, Congress did not define the term "substantial abuse" in the text of the 1984 amendments to the Code. Moreover, no committee reports exist on the final version of the amending Act. The lone piece of legislative history which may give some insight into Congressional intent in enacting Section 707(b) is the Senate report on S. 445, an earlier draft of the 1984 amendments. This report states that "if a debtor can meet his debts without difficulty as they come due, use of Chapter 7 would represent a substantial abuse." S.Rep. No. 98-65, 98th Cong., 1st Sess. 54 (1983). This definition is not especially helpful, however, since it neither explains what constitutes meeting one's debts without difficulty nor attempts to reconcile itself to the previous legislative history on Section 707(a), which states in pertinent part:

> This section does not contemplate. . . that the ability of the debtor to repay his debts in whole or in part constitutes adequate cause for dismissal.

S.Rep. No. 95-989, 95th Cong., 2d Sess. 94.

It is not surprising that Congress was not anxious to explicitly define the permissible grounds for substantial abuse dismissal. Section 707(b) reflects the tension between the fundamental policy concern of the Bankruptcy Code, granting the debtor an opportunity for a fresh start, and the interest of creditors in stemming abuse of consumer credit. The ambiguity of the statutory language is no doubt a reflection of Congress's inability to agree on a definition of substantial abuse which would encompass these countervailing considerations in all situations. Nevertheless, in unsuccessfully attempting to carve out such a definition, Congress considered and rejected the use of a threshold future income or ability to repay test (known as "mandatory Chapter 13") as a qualification for Chapter 7 relief for consumer debtors. * * *

Appellee Staples, the United States Trustee (the Trustee) argues that we should adopt the *per se* rule embraced by the Bankruptcy Court below and affirmed by the district court, to the effect that a debtor's possession of income in excess of his necessary expenses, standing alone, constitutes substantial abuse of Chapter 7 justifying dismissal. The primary source of this rule, for both of the lower courts, was a recent Ninth Circuit decision, *In re Kelly*, 841 F.2d 908 (9th Cir.1988). A few bankruptcy courts in other jurisdictions appear to have adopted this *per se* rule. * * *

We are not persuaded by the *Kelly* court's reasoning. The court, citing a string of cases standing for the proposition that the debtor's ability to repay is a *principal* factor to be considered in determining substantial abuse, announced that proposition as a holding. In the next sentence, the court characterized this proposition as a rule, adopted by "the overwhelming majority of the courts considering the issue," that "a debtor's ability to pay his debts will, *standing alone,* justify a section 707(b) dismissal." *Id.* [at 914] (emphasis added). This logical leap is unsupported, for to say that a conclusion may be justified by a certain factor as the principal one of several does not imply that the conclusion may also be drawn from that factor alone.

*Kelly* is correct, however, insofar as it indicates that the majority of the cases hold that the debtor's ability to repay is the *primary* factor to be considered. The consensus among these courts is that the substantial abuse determination must be made on a case-by-case basis, in light of the totality of the circumstances. * * * The "totality of the circumstances" approach involves an evaluation of factors such as the following:

(1) Whether the bankruptcy petition was filed because of sudden illness, calamity, disability, or unemployment;

(2) Whether the debtor incurred cash advances and made consumer purchases far in excess of his ability to repay;

(3) Whether the debtor's proposed family budget is excessive or unreasonable;

**(4)** Whether the debtor's schedules and statement of current income and expenses reasonably and accurately reflect the true financial condition; and

**(5)** Whether the petition was filed in good faith.

\* \* \*

Exploring these factors, as well as the relation of the debtor's future income to his future necessary expenses, allows the court to determine more accurately whether the particular debtor's case exemplifies the real concern behind Section 707(b): abuse of the bankruptcy process by a debtor seeking to take unfair advantage of his creditors. The debtor's relative solvency may raise an inference that such a situation exists. Nevertheless, in light of the statutory presumption that a debtor's Chapter 7 petition should be granted, solvency alone is not a sufficient basis for a finding that the debtor has in fact substantially abused the provisions of Chapter 7.

\* \* \* Section 109, which the 1984 Amendments left unchanged, allows any person to be a debtor under Chapter 7 unless he comes within one of several limited exceptions, none of which apply to consumer debtors and none of which are predicated upon anticipated income. \* \* \* Section 109, taken together with the Senate report on Section 707(a) cited infra, provides a strong indication that Section 707(b) was intended to explicitly recognize the court's ability to dismiss a Chapter 7 petition for lack of good faith—when "the total picture is abusive." *Waites v. Braley*, 110 B.R. 211, 215 (E.D.Va.1990) \* \* \*.

We think that a totality of the circumstances analysis is much to be preferred to the application of a *per se* rule, not only because it better accords with what is known of Congressional thinking surrounding the adoption of Section 707(b), but also because it is consistent with the statutory presumption in favor of granting the relief requested by the debtor. The establishment of a future income threshold of eligibility for Chapter 7 by means of the *per se* rule we are urged to adopt would render this presumption toothless. A debtor who has filed a Chapter 7 petition has elected to discharge his debts by liquidating his non-exempt assets. If the debtor, acting in good faith, preferred to effect the discharge by making extended payment to his creditors over time, presumably he would have filed under Chapter 13. The court may advise the latter, but the election remains with the debtor, a point underscored by Congress's explicit refusal to adopt a mandatory Chapter 13 provision.

We therefore adopt the totality of the circumstances test as the appropriate analysis to be followed in determining whether substantial abuse exists. We remand this case to the district court with instructions to return it to the bankruptcy court, which should apply the five factors we have enumerated. The bankruptcy court's analysis should reflect consideration of the Section 707(b) presumption in favor of granting the requested relief. In making a judgment on the question of substantial abuse, the court may find it helpful to consult the following cases: In re Grant, 51 B.R. 385, 396

(Bankr.N.D.Ohio 1985) (citing debtor's "freewheeling spending," which included monthly entertainment expenses of $450 and Christmas expenditures of $900); In re Peluso, 72 B.R. 732, 738 (Bankr.N.D.N.Y.1987) (debtor with substantial income altered his monthly obligations in statements to the court at least three times; filing of petition was not precipitated by any injury, illness, or loss of employment); In re Shands, 63 B.R. 121, 123 (Bankr.E.D.Mich.1985) (debtor's choice of Chapter 7 over Chapter 13 was not motivated by inability to afford repayment but by some personal motive, where debtor was voluntarily paying favored creditors a weekly amount greater than her claimed excess income).

The district court's decision in this case is

REVERSED AND REMANDED.

## NOTE

Professor Carl Felsenfeld, in *Denial of Discharge for Substantial Abuse: Refining—Not Changing—Bankruptcy Law*, 67 Fordham L. Rev. 1369, 1396 (1999), contends that a close comparison of the *Kelly* line of cases with the *Green* decisions embracing the "totality of circumstances" test reveals that most decisions are actually based on the existence of surplus income. He asserts that this is even true of *Green* itself. Do you agree? He concludes that if surplus income is effectively the test used by most courts under § 707(b), standardization by use of a mechanical formula featured in the bankruptcy reform legislation discussed below, is justified.

## C. THE 2005 ACT

In the later 1980s bankruptcy filings doubled, and in the 1990s filing rates exploded. Over a period of 20 years, consumer bankruptcy filings grew by 500%. Under these conditions creditors greatly increased their efforts to impose a means test and Congress began to listen: preliminary versions of the 2005 Act were drafted in the late 1990s in response. The 2005 Act, containing a means test designed to make it more difficult for higher income debtors to file in Chapter 7, was met by a fusillade of criticism by the consumer and academic communities, and the ensuing debate has probed the economic and social bases of a policy of access to bankruptcy. After eight years of debate, the bill became the Bankruptcy Abuse Prevention and Consumer Protection Act of 2005, enacted by large majorities in each house (74-25 in the Senate and 302-126 in the House).

In this debate, opponents of a means test maintained that consumer bankruptcies are caused by adverse changes in household financial conditions and that bankruptcy is a much needed safety net. This view is documented by detailed empirical studies in Teresa A. Sullivan, Elizabeth Warren and Jay L. Westbrook in *The Fragile Middle Class* (2000). The authors see the rapid increase in the debt burden shouldered by consumers as making debtors increasingly vulnerable to unforeseen changes in family income caused by problems related to illness, employment, divorce, housing and the like. Thus, increased bankruptcy filings track the massive increase in consumer debt. Household debt doubled to more than $10 trillion between 1992 and 2004, after accounting for inflation. Bob Davis, *Lagging Behind the Wealthy, Many Use Debt to Catch Up*, Wall St.J., May 17, 2005, at A1. Much of this growth was owing to the impact of credit cards and lower standards in housing financing, featuring interest-only loans. The authors' recommendation with respect to the great rise in consumer bankruptcies is to leave access to bankruptcy open and to allow the credit market to solve the problem. If there are too many bankruptcies, creditors can deal with the problem by tightening their credit standards and monitoring their debtors more effectively.

A recent addition to the literature in this area is an empirical study, David Himmelstein, Elizabeth Warren, Deborah Thorn & Steffi Woolhandler, *Illness and Injury as Contributors to Bankruptcy*, Vol. 24, No. 2, of *Health Affairs*, W5-63 (2005). The study concludes that in 2001 medical problems contributed to about half of all bankruptcies in this country. Illness contributes both to high medical bills and lost income. Health insurance coverage tied to employment often lapses when employment terminates, and lapsed insurance coverage was ruinous for many families. From 1981 to 2001, the number of "medical bankruptcies" increased twenty-threefold.

Moreover, opponents of the means test note that while bankruptcies have soared, creditors have managed to flourish. This is particularly true in the credit card industry: bankruptcy filings increased from 0.9 million in 1995 to over 1.6 million in 2004, while credit card profits increased from $12.9 billion to $31.6 billion in this period. Peter G. Gosselin, *Credit Card Firms Won As Users Lost*, L.A.Times, Mar. 4, 2005, at A1. How did this happen? In the 1960s and 70s credit cards were issued to middle-class users with annual fees and fixed interest rates. By the 1990s that market was saturated, and the user base was broadened to include lower income ("sub-prime") customers, who were a more risky group. Credit issuers remade their operations to accommodate additional risk. Fees became a major source of income. The cardholder agreements began to contain provisions saying that if the cardholder failed to make two minimum payments on a timely basis within a year or twice exceeded the cardholder's credit limit, the debtor's 13% or 14% interest rate would skyrocket to a penalty rate of 29.25%. But the cardholder could stay out of default in the future by making a small minimum payment on the balance each month, a course of action that could dig the cardholder more deeply in debt because the portion of the payment allocated to interest charges and fees was so large that it left little to be applied to the balance of the principal. A "company store" effect was created in which the cardholder could never get out of debt. Chapter 7 bankruptcy was often the debtor's only way out. Concerns about minimum payments bondage led bank regulators in 2003 to issue guidelines requiring that payments be large enough to cover fees, interest and enough of the principal to pay the balance over "a reasonable period of time." Jane J. Kim, *Minimums Due on Credit Cards Are On the Increase*, Wall St.J., March 24, 2005, at D2.

Proponents of a means test maintain that the findings of Sullivan, et al., cannot explain the great rise in bankruptcy filings during the 1990s on the ground of increased debtor distress because the decade was a period of great prosperity, very low unemployment, lower divorce rates, and health costs that fell during the introduction of managed care in the mid-90s. *See* Todd J. Zywicki, *Why So Many Bankruptcies and What to Do About It: An Economic Analysis of Consumer Bankruptcy Law and Bankruptcy Reform* (2004 paper in possession of editors). *See also* Edith H. Jones & Todd J. Zywicki, *It's Time for Means-Testing*, 1999 B. Y. U. L. Rev. 177. Professor Zywicki, who participated in drafting the 2005 Act, contends that since consumer financial distress has not significantly increased during the period of rapid growth of bankruptcies, this growth is more likely owing to the increasing tendency of more debtors to choose bankruptcy as a first response to financial distress rather than toughing it out, reducing spending or using savings to avoid bankruptcy. Zywicki attributes this tendency to social changes (the decrease in shame and social stigma relating to bankruptcy), financial changes (the shift of consumer credit from person-to-person transactions to impersonal credit card transactions has eroded the reputational constraints on extensions of consumer credit), and changes in the economic costs and benefits of filing (retirement funds are largely exempt as are valuable homesteads; reduction in search costs of learning about bankruptcy as more and more debtors share experiences and more lawyers advertise their services; and the greater availability of post-bankruptcy credit). He further suggests that the research underpinning the open-access position is flawed because it finds only that individuals in bankruptcy are there because of financial distress, but it does not deal with the possibility that there may be others with comparable financial distress who do not chose bankruptcy. His remedy is (1) imposition of a means test to keep out of Chapter 7 the 7 to 10% of filers with higher incomes who could pay a substantial portion of debt out of disposable income under Chapter 13, and (2) to place limits on bankruptcy exemptions regarding homesteads and deal with opportunistic behavior on the part of debtors in moving to more generous jurisdictions on the eve of bankruptcy. In short, by making bankruptcy more expensive for those who find bankruptcy most advantageous.

## 1. INTRODUCTION

In the wake of the 2004 elections, which increased the Republican majorities in both the Senate and the House, Congress enacted the "Bankruptcy Abuse Prevention and Consumer Protection Act of 2005." In this extensive revision of bankruptcy law, the tables are decisively turned: an individual debtor seeking a discharge in Chapter 7 faces formidable barriers. The traditional goal of bankruptcy law offering a "fresh start for the honest debtor" is less attainable; in some cases it is not obtainable at all.

In the following sections, we examine the complex series of barriers that an individual debtor encounters in filing for Chapter 7 bankruptcy.

*A summary of these barriers follows*: (1) In order to be eligible for Chapter 7, individual debtors must obtain a briefing from an approved credit counseling agency outlining opportunities for available credit counseling and assisting the individual in performing a budget analysis within 180 days before filing. § 109(h)(1). (2) At the time of filing, individuals must provide detailed information about current income and expenses in order to allow the U.S. Trustee to screen the filer for application of the means test. § 707(b)(2)(C). (3) The court may dismiss, or with the consent of the debtor, convert to Chapter 11 or 13, a case filed by an individual debtor whose debts are primarily consumer debts if it finds that granting relief in Chapter 7 would be an "abuse." § 707(b)(1). (4) Under the means test, if the individual will have enough projected postpetition income after payment of certain allowable expenses to pay a prescribed amount of nonpriority, unsecured prepetition debts over a five-year period, a rebuttable presumption of abuse arises. § 707(b)(2)(A)(i). (5) The individual may rebut the presumption only by showing "special circumstances." (6) If the individual's current monthly income is below the state median family income, the individual is exempt from having its petition dismissed on the basis of the means test. § 707(b)(7). Hence, the means test would pose no barrier to filing in Chapter 7 for the great majority of persons seeking relief under earlier law. (7) Before receiving a discharge in Chapter 7 all individuals must complete a course in financial management. § 727(a)(11).

One barrier immediately encountered is the traditional view that debtors should not receive discharges in bankruptcy too often; we don't want to create a class of habitual bankrupts, so the argument goes. The waiting period between Chapter 7 discharges was six years under the 1978 Code. Under the 2005 Act the waiting period is increased to eight years. Thus, a debtor may not be discharged in Chapter 7 if she files her petition within eight years after having received a discharge in a previous Chapter 7 or Chapter 11 case. § 727(a)(8). As we will see later in this chapter, waiting periods for Chapter 13 discharges are also imposed in § 1328(f).

## 2. THE MEANS TEST

The centerpiece of the 2005 Act with respect to consumer bankruptcy reform is the use of a means test to identify those debtors who are allegedly abusing credit and to deny them access to Chapter 7. The means test is found in a complex series of amendments to § 707(b).

### a. General Power To Dismiss

The organization of § 707(b) is confusing. Paragraph (1) states a broad general power: the bankruptcy court on its own motion or on that of the U.S. Trustee, the panel trustee or a party in interest (*e.g.* a creditor), may dismiss or, with the consent of the debtor, convert to Chapter 11 or 13, a case filed by an individual debtor whose debts are primarily consumer debts if it finds that granting relief "would be an abuse of the provisions of this chapter." Consumer debts are those incurred by an individual primarily for a personal, family or household purpose. § 101(8). There is no definition of "abuse," and even the modifier "substantial" that appeared in the 1984 version is dropped. Also omitted is the sentence: "There shall be a presumption in favor of granting the relief requested by the debtor." The only limitation stated in paragraph (1) on the power of the court to limit access to Chapter 7 on the basis of abuse deals with charitable contributions.

### b.  Presumption of Abuse

After 20 years of experience with the "substantial abuse" test, Congress moved decisively to deprive courts of discretion in the determination of credit abuse. In the search for automatic rules, arbitrary rules were often the result. Every individual debtor filing in Chapter 7 whose debts are consumer debts must be screened by the means test. Section 707(b)(2) sets out the circumstances under which a rebuttable presumption of abuse arises under the means test. If the debtor has enough projected postpetition income after payment of certain allowable expenses to pay a prescribed amount of nonpriority, unsecured prepetition debts over a five-year period, a presumption of credit abuse arises.

Section 707(b)(2)(A)(i) provides the following formula:

> In considering under paragraph [b](1) whether the granting of relief would be an abuse of the provisions of this chapter, the court shall presume abuse exists if the debtor's current monthly income reduced by the amounts determined under clauses (ii), (iii), and (iv), and multiplied by 60 is not less than the lesser of
>
> (I)  25 percent of the debtor's nonpriority unsecured claims in the case, or $6,000, whichever is greater; or
>
> (II)  $10,000.

This formula compares the amount of the debtor's projected income over the next five years with the debtor's projected expenses during this period. As explained in the following section, the income projection is based on the debtor's average monthly income over the six months before filing. This is the debtor's presumed "current monthly income" under § 101(10A), which is multiplied by 60, the length of a typical Chapter 13 repayment plan under the 2005 Act. For debtors with more than $40,000 in debt, a presumption of abuse arises if their presumed net income exceeds $10,000 (or $167/month) over the next 60 months no matter how small a percentage this may be of their total debt. Debtors with net presumed income of less than $6,000 (or $100/month) over the next 60 months are not subject to the presumption of abuse no matter how great a percentage of their debts they may have been capable of repaying. For debtors with between $24,000 and $40,000 in debt, the presumption of abuse will arise if their presumed net income over the next 60 months exceeds 25% of their total nonpriority unsecured debt.

It is not easy for debtors to rebut the presumption of abuse based on the formula. Section 707(b)(2)(B)(i) provides: "In any proceeding brought under this subsection, the presumption of abuse may only be rebutted by demonstrating special circumstances, such as a serious medical condition or a call or order to active duty in the Armed Forces, to the extent such special circumstances that justify additional expenses or adjustments of current monthly income for which there is *no reasonable alternative*" (emphasis added). The remainder of subparagraph (B) makes clear that the "special circumstances" provision was not intended to grant courts general equity powers to remedy injustices under the statute; rather, the debtor must be able to document each additional expense or adjustment to income allowed and the total must be great enough to exclude the case under the "objective" means test. After hurricanes Katrina and Rita in 2005, the U.S. Trustee announced enforcement guidelines providing that it will consider the adverse effects of natural disasters to constitute "special circumstances." The natural disaster provision may portend that the U.S. Trustee will heed political pressure in determining the scope of special circumstances.

It is noteworthy that an individual whose debts are primarily business debts is not subject to the means test. § 707(b)(1). Such a person may file in Chapter 7 whatever her income. Apparently business debtors may abuse credit with impunity; no five-year penance in Chapter 13 for them.

### c. Current Monthly Income

The formula set out in § 707(b)(2)(A)(i) for determining abuse calls for an estimate of the debtor's likely income and expenses over a future five-year period, the length of a typical Chapter 13 repayment plan. The income estimate is based on the debtor's "current monthly income" (CMI), defined in § 101(10A) as the debtor's average monthly income for the six months before filing. The debtor's CMI includes all the income the debtor receives from all sources, excluding Social Security benefits, and, in a joint case, the income of the debtor and the debtor's spouse. A crude five-year projection is made by multiplying the average monthly income by 60. As we will see in the Problems below, this method of estimating the debtor's postpetition income is highly arbitrary. The debtor may have been unemployed during all or part of the six-month period prepetition period, or may have received a bonus during that period. Some opportunistic behavior on the part of debtors in the choice of the date of filing is to be expected. Moreover, the assumption that a few months of prepetition income will be an adequate basis for predicting the debtor's income over the next five years might have made sense in an earlier age in which it was not unusual for a debtor to hold the same job for five years, but employees today are likely to hold several jobs, with intermittent times of unemployment, during any five-year period.

### d.  Debtor's Monthly Expenses

#### (i)  Introduction

In its search for uniform standards, Congress turned to Internal Revenue Service for the categories of expenses that are used for determining payment plans for overdue taxes. But, as we will see, the Bankruptcy Code provisions vary from the IRS standards in some important instances. The expenses designated in § 707(b)(2)(A)(ii) (living expenses), (iii) (secured debts) and (iv)(priority claims) are deducted from the debtor's estimated postpetition income in order to determine how much prepetition debt the debtor would be able to pay over a five-year period. Living expenses under (2)(A)(ii) are, for the most part, not determined by the debtor's actual living expenses, rather by monthly living expenses as calculated under the IRS categories of expenses for delinquent taxpayers. Since these standards were conceived to deal with lawbreakers, they are quite stingy. (A)(ii) refers to three different IRS categories of expenses. Uniform national food, cleaning, clothing and miscellaneous allowances (the "National Standards") are set annually by income level and family size. In 2005, these allowances ranged from $403 per month for one person earning less than $833 per month, to $1564 per month for a family of four with a monthly household income over $5,834. Housing, utility and transportation costs vary widely across the United States and the IRS uses "Local Standards" derived from Census and Bureau of Labor Statistics data on a county by county basis to determine allowances for these types of expenses for households of varying sizes. As an example, in California, for a family of four in 2005, the Local Standards for Housing and Utilities ranged from a low of $987 per month (Modoc County) to a high of $3,136 per month (Marin County). If the debtor can demonstrate that it is reasonable and necessary, the debtor's monthly expenses may include an additional allowance for food and clothing of up to 5 percent of the food and clothing categories under the National Standards issued by the IRS. § 707(b)(2)(A)(ii)(I).

Finally, debtors may deduct their actual monthly expenses under the IRS category of "Other Necessary Expenses." These expenses are determined on an individual basis and include health and disability insurance, certain charitable contributions, child or dependent care (if there are no reasonable alternatives), court-ordered payments including alimony and child support, health care costs, education expenses that are a condition of employment or for children who cannot attend public schools, all state, local and federal taxes, and life insurance costs.

#### (ii)  Repayment of Debts

*Secured Debts.* Under § 707(b)(2)(A)(iii) debtors may deduct "average monthly payments" on secured debts calculated by taking the total of all amounts scheduled to be due in each month for 60 months following the date of the bankruptcy. Obligations secured by home mortgages and security interests in automobiles are usually the consumer's largest debts, and monthly mortgage and car payments are usually a consumer's largest payments. Given the heavily leveraged basis of much lending in real estate and motor vehicle financing, monthly deductions of many thousand dollars would be common, leading many debtors to avoid exclusion from Chapter 7 under the means test. Home mortgage debtors can also deduct housing and utilities expenses under Local Standards (§ 707(b)(2)(A)(ii)), including insurance, maintenance expenses, property taxes. Debtors who have financed their cars can also deduct operating costs such as maintenance and registration.

*Priority Debts.* Section 707(b)(2)(A)(iv) allows debtors to treat as monthly expenses payments of priority claims in an amount of 1/60th of the total amount of debts entitled to priority. Common priority debts in consumer bankruptcies are domestic support obligations and taxes. If the debtor is paying alimony or child support, this provision may allow the debtor to deduct a substantial amount each month as expenses.

*Unsecured, Nonpriority Debts.* Although the IRS treats both secured and unsecured debts as "Other Necessary Expenses," § 707(b)(2)(A)(ii)(I) contains this sentence: "Notwithstanding any other provisions *of this clause*, the monthly expenses of the debtor shall not include any payments for debts." The following clauses, (II) through (V), allow deduction of a series of unsecured debts: support of the elderly, administrative expenses of Chapter 13 plans, certain educational expenses, and additional actual expenses for housing and utilities. And, as indicated above, subparagraphs (iii) and (iv) deal with secured and priority claims. The implication is that payments for other unsecured, nonpriority debts cannot be deducted as ordinary expenses. This would mean that home renters and automobile lessees could not deduct their monthly payments as expenses. This is contrary to the IRS Local Standards under which debtors can deduct both rental or lease payments in addition to related costs. But under the Bankruptcy Code, home renters could deduct only allowances for housing costs, and car lessees could deduct only transportation expenses. It is difficult to believe that Congress intended such a result. A consumer debtor's home rentals and car lease payments will usually be among her largest monthly payments. If the purpose of the means test formula is to determine whether a debtor will have enough income after payment of her living expenses to pay off a portion of her prepetition debts, excluding home rentals and car lease payments from deductible expenses is indefensible. Whether bankruptcy courts can find a way around this injustice in the labyrinthine provisions of § 707 remains to be seen.

### e.   Residual Power of Court to Dismiss

*Section 707(b)(3).* As we have seen, § 707(b)(1) gives the court the power to dismiss a case filed in Chapter 7 by a consumer debtor on the basis of abuse but fails to define the term. The absence of such definition raises no difficulty in cases falling within the means test. The question arises about the scope of the court's power to dismiss for abuse in cases falling outside the means test. Section 707(b)(3) offers some guidance:

> (3) In considering under paragraph (1) whether the granting of relief would be an abuse of the provisions of this chapter in a case in which the presumption in subparagraph (A)(i) of such paragraph does not apply or has been rebutted, the court shall consider—
>
> **(A)** whether the debtor filed the petition in bad faith; or
>
> **(B)** the totality of circumstances (including whether the debtor seeks to reject a personal services contract and the financial need for such rejection as sought by the debtor) of the debtor's financial situation demonstrates abuse.

A difficulty we have in construing paragraph (3) is that paragraph (1) of § 707(b) has no subparagraph (A)(i). Congress must have been referring to § 707(b)(2)(A)(i). So read, paragraph (3) means that if no presumption arises under paragraph (2), the court "shall consider" whether the debtor filed in bad faith or the totality of circumstances shows abuse, and dismiss or convert if it finds such conduct. Thus, the large body of case law on these issues, of which *In re Green, supra,* is an example, still lives. The usual reason the presumption does not apply is that, under the formula, the debtor does not have enough excess postpetition income to pay the relatively small amount of prepetition debt required by the statute. Paragraph (3) directs bankruptcy courts to examine the circumstances of these cases to detect possible bad faith or other facts that point to abuse before granting a discharge. The general power of paragraph (b)(1) allows courts to examine for any abuse under § 707 but it does not compel them to do so.

*Charitable contributions.* The only limitation we find on the court's general power to dismiss under paragraph (1) follows:

> In making a determination whether to dismiss a case under this section, the court may not take into consideration whether a debtor has made, or continues to make, charitable contributions (that meet the definition of "charitable contribution" under section 548(d)(3)) to any qualified religious or charitable entity or organization (as that term is defined in section 548(d)(4)).

Questions arise about the purpose of this statement. Allowable charitable expenses are covered in the IRS Manual as "Other Necessary Expenses" but are not mentioned in the § 707(b)(2)(A)(ii)(I) category as "Other Necessary Expenses." A possible explanation for the § 707(b)(1) provision is that it was intended to make clear that making charitable contributions cannot constitute an abuse for purpose of dismissal under § 707(b). Thus, charitable contributions, meeting the requirements set out, may not be relied on to show bad faith and should not be a factor in applying the "totality of circumstances" test under § 707(b)(3). Presumably, if in assessing good faith the court may not take into account the debtor's lack of any history of charitable giving, any debtor on a going forward basis would be well advised to budget for substantial charitable giving in order to avoid dismissal based on a presumption of abuse. There does not appear to be any mechanism to compel a debtor who has received a Chapter 7 discharge from following through on this projected charitable giving.

### f.  Safe Harbor

*Paragraph 707(b)(7).* This provision creates a safe harbor that exempts debtors whose CMI, multiplied by 12, is below the state median family income from having their Chapter 7 filings dismissed on the basis of the means test. Paragraph (b)(7) accomplishes this end by providing that no "judge, United States Trustee (or bankruptcy administrator, if any), trustee, or other party in interest" (creditors) can file a motion to dismiss under paragraph (2) if the debtor's CMI, when multiplied by 12, is equal to or less than the median family income in the State. Thus, debtors whose income is less than the state's median income cannot be denied access to Chapter 7 on the basis of the means test. For purposes of this provision, a debtor's income is augmented by the income of a spouse even in nonjoint cases unless the debtor certifies that the parties live apart. Since historically most debtors who file in Chapter 7 are under the state median income standard, this important provision promises to exempt the great bulk of cases filed in Chapter 7 from the presumption of abuse. But these debtors are not exempt from being screened under the means test, which requires filing the burdensome disclosure forms that we discuss in the next section.

Median family income is reported from time to time for each of the states by the Census Bureau. § 101(39A). If no figures are reported for the current year, the figures last reported by the Census Bureau must be adjusted annually to reflect the change in the Consumer Price Index for All Urban Consumers during the period of years after the last report. Subparagraph 707(b)(7)(A) contemplates that the Census Bureau will report median incomes for 1 earner households, and families of 2, 3, and 4 individuals. For families exceeding 4 individuals, $525 per person per month (subject to adjustment under § 104(b)) is added to the median income amounts for a family of 4. In 2005 the Census Bureau published tables meeting these requirements.

*Paragraph § 707(b)(6).* This provision operates to differentiate the parties who can file motions for dismissal for abuse under § 707(b). Paragraph (6) provides that motions to dismiss for abuse under § 707(b) can be filed only by judges and U.S. Trustees (including bankruptcy administrators) if the debtor's annualized CMI is at or below the state median family income. The effect of this is that creditors and panel trustees can file motions to dismiss under § 707(b) only in cases in which the debtor's annualized CMI exceeds the state's median income. For instance, a motion to dismiss a case under paragraph (3) on the basis of bad faith or one in which the totality of circumstances shows credit abuse can be filed by judges and U.S. Trustees whatever the income level of the debtor. But such a motion can be filed by creditors or panel trustees only if the debtor's CMI is greater than the state median. In this provision a debtor's income includes the income of a spouse only in joint cases.

As we have seen above, paragraph (7) bars, in effect, everyone from bringing a motion to dismiss on the basis of the means test in paragraph (2) if the debtor's annualized CMI is less than the state median. But paragraph (6) broadly allows judges and U.S. Trustees to bring motions to dismiss for any form of abuse under § 707(b). Reconciling the two, paragraph (6) should control with respect to grounds for dismissal under § 707(b) other than the means test under paragraph (2); means test cases are governed exclusively by paragraph (7).

A further safe harbor is found in § 707(b)(2)(D), which provides that the court may not dismiss or convert a case based on any form of means testing if the debtor is a disabled veteran and the debt arose primarily during a period when the debtor was either on active duty or performing a homeland defense activity. Query whether any such person (an above median income bankrupt disabled vet who somehow ran up his consumer debt primarily while on active duty) exists.

Predictions vary on the percentage of consumer debtors that will actually be excluded by the means test from filing in Chapter 7; some predict that less than 5 % of those who would otherwise seek relief under Chapter 7 will be excluded. National Bankruptcy Conference, Analysis of Bankruptcy Legislation 2 (2001). The state-wide median income data are troublingly anomalous because they are based on surveys between censuses of rather small numbers of families. The standard error in these surveys tends to be about $2,000 so there can be large but statistically insignificant fluctuations in the figures of up to $10,000 or so especially within and between smaller states from year to year. State median incomes vary greatly: according to the Census Bureau, in 2003 the median income for a family of four in West Virginia was $51,534, but in New Jersey it was $83,482. Moreover, residents of small urbanized States like New Jersey and Connecticut ($79,599) will benefit from much higher state-wide medians than residents of large States with both urban and rural populations like New York ($66,206) and California ($62,916), even though incomes and costs of living in the urban centers of these large States are surely among the very highest in the country. And residents of adjoining States within the same metropolitan area may have very different access to bankruptcy even though they are otherwise similarly situated. For example, in 2003, the state-wide median income applicable to a four person household in St. Louis, Missouri was $60,528, while the comparable median applicable to residents in (much poorer) East St. Louis, Illinois was $69,141.

The four rather elementary Problems below will demonstrate the complexities of administering the means test in § 707(b)(2) and suggest the kinds of cases in which the formula does a better or worse job in selecting the parties who should be denied Chapter 7 access.

## PROBLEMS

**1.** Paul is an unmarried 26-year old computer programmer who earns $57,000 annually, pays $15,000 per year in taxes, lives in a $1,500 a month apartment in Los Angeles, pays $584 a month in lease payments on his 2004 BMW, owns negligible household furnishings (principally discarded milk cartons and a used waterbed), wears fashionable clothes, and impresses dates by taking them to expensive restaurants. He owes $60,000 in unsecured debts to various retailers and credit card issuers. He helps his impoverished, widowed mother with her living expenses by paying her rent of $150 each month. He is contemplating marriage and wants to clear up his debts before the wedding by filing in Chapter 7. Assume that under § 707(b)(2)(A)(ii), his "applicable monthly expense amounts" under the National Standards are $691 per month (this includes costs of food, housekeeping supplies, apparel and services, personal care products and services, and miscellaneous) and under the Local Standards for housing and utilities in Los Angeles County are $1,563. For transportation costs, Local Standards for Los Angeles for one car are $353 for operating costs and $475 for the ownership costs. Assume the $150 per month for Paul's mother's rent is deductible as a dependent care expense under § 707(b)(2)(A)(ii)(II), as are the taxes ($1,250 per month) as an "other necessary expense" under § 707(b)(2)(A)(ii)(I). Thus, the total amount to be deducted from Paul's current monthly income of $4,750 is $4,482. The state median income for a one-earner household in California is $40,167. If Paul files in Chapter 7 on May 1, 2006, is there a presumption of abuse under § 707(b)(2)(A)? Is Paul's Chapter 7 petition subject to dismissal or conversion under § 707(b)(7)? See § 101(10A), the definition of "current monthly income."

**2.** Bridget is a third-year law student at Old Brigham Law School in Salt Lake City set to graduate in May, 2006. Last summer she worked for eight weeks at Cravath, Kirkland & Myers earning $2,500 weekly and receiving an offer of permanent employment at an annual salary of $140,000 beginning in September 2006. Since returning to law school in September 2005, she has earned no income. Her student loans total $100,000 (payable $1,500 per month commencing six months after graduation) and she has ten credit cards all of which are maxed out with an aggregate outstanding balance of $75,000 on account of BAR-BRI tuition and materials, long afternoons at the mall, numerous ski trips to Park City, Christmas vacation in Las Vegas and a mid-February trip to Maui purchased with a credit card at a Public Interest Law Foundation fundraiser. She lives in a guest house rented from her generous parents for only $150 monthly; her utilities run $102 monthly. She has no automobile (though she is thinking of buying or leasing an expensive one before she starts at the firm) and uses public transportation to get around, if she can't beg a ride. Bridget wants a "fresh start" as she enters the legal profession and files in Chapter 7 on May 15, 2006. Assume that under § 707(b)(2)(A)(ii), her "applicable monthly expense amounts" under the National Standards are $577. The Local Standards for Salt Lake City for housing and utilities allow $1,195. For transportation costs, the Local Standards for the West Region for a person without a car are $246. Thus, the total amount to be deducted from Bridget's current monthly income under § 707(b)(2)(A)(i) is $2,018. The Bureau of the Census median income for a one-earner household in Utah (based on the 2000 census) is $39,371.

a.  Is there a presumption of abuse in this case? § 707(b)(2)(A). If so, does the safe harbor provision of § 707(b)(7) apply?

b.  Would a bankruptcy court have a general power under § 707(b)(1) to dismiss because it finds that Bridget could easily repay a substantial part of her debts over five years? See § 707(b)(3) and *Green*.

c.  What part does Bridget's obligation to repay student loans play in calculations for application of the means test? *See* § 707(b)(2)(A)(ii)(I).

**3.** Her deadbeat ex-husband left Marta with $100,000 in debts, on which she is jointly liable, and $30,000 in unpaid legal bills from the divorce and related disputes. He has departed the state and failed to honor his child support obligation of $1,200 per month to assist her in raising their three-year old daughter. After her divorce, Marta moved to San Diego with her daughter to find employment in the burgeoning telecommunications industry. She began working in January 2004 with Xpert, a placement agency for experienced personnel with unique high-tech skills, at $12,000 per month, which was at the time a market salary given her experience in this highly specialized high demand area. On May 1, 2006, Xpert closed its doors and summarily discharged all its employees, leaving Marta with some worthless stock options. Marta's energetic, nationwide job search has been fruitless; at that time no one was hiring in the telecommunications industry, least of all in placement agencies serving that depressed industry. During May and June of 2006, she supported herself and her daughter by borrowing on her credit cards and by loans from her sister to pay for food, shelter, clothing, child care and travel expenses while she vainly sought employment. She cancelled her automobile lease and turned in her car. Beset by collection agencies, she became despondent when she realized that she now had $200,000 in unsecured debts and no prospect of employment for other than low or minimum wage jobs. The income she earned in the six months from January 1, 2006 until July 1, 2006, the date she filed in Chapter 7, was $48,000. Assume that under § 707(b)((2)(A)(ii), her "applicable monthly expense amounts" under the National Standards for two people are $1,280. The amounts under the Local Standards for housing and utilities in San Diego are $1,633. For transportation costs, the Local Standards for San Diego for a person without a car are $311. The median family income for a two-person household in California is $52,280.

  **a.**    Does the safe harbor provision of § 707(b)(7) apply? Is there a presumption of abuse in this case? § 707(b)(2)(A). If so, is her Chapter 7 petition subject to dismissal or conversion? § 707((b)(7).

  **b.**    Does the bankruptcy court have discretion to allow her to file in Chapter 7 on equitable grounds to avoid hardship? Does the "special circumstances" exception under § 707(b)(2)(B) apply here? Later in this chapter, we will inquire whether Marta can obtain relief in Chapter 13 if she is denied access to Chapter 7.

**4.**    Mark and Luke work for the same employer for the same annual salary of $48,000. Each receives a holiday bonus of 10% each December. After the first of the year, they both encountered serious financial problems. Mark files in Chapter 7 in May, but Luke, with better legal advice, waits until July. If the median income for one-earner households for the state in which they live is $50,000, does either of these debtors fall within the safe harbor provision of § 707(b)(7)?

## g.  Critique

As we see in these Problems, Congress has not been successful in drawing means-testing rules that offer a coherent and reliable method of separating true credit abusers from honest debtors who need relief. As critics have noted, "[T]he rule focuses exclusively on the ability of the debtor to repay and not the circumstances that led to the debtor's present condition. The rule treats an abandoned spouse the same way it treats an MBA or lawyer who overspent on many vacations and fancy restaurants." National Bankruptcy Conference, Analysis of Bankruptcy Legislation 3 (2001). The probably unavoidable shortcomings of novel legislation of this sort could have been somewhat lessened by granting bankruptcy judges some discretion in applying the rules to avoid unjust results, and perhaps it is not too much to expect that courts will assume some responsibility for doing justice by stretching the reach of the "special circumstances" provision of § 707(b)(2)(B). Creditors, Congress and, probably, the general public, agree that debtors who can afford to pay a significant amount of prepetition debt with postpetiton income should be allowed to obtain a discharge in bankruptcy only through performance of a Chapter 13 plan. However, in their quest to reach this goal, the drafters crafted a complex means test, often yielding anomalous results, that appears to offer very modest benefits compared to the considerable costs that implementation of the test imposes on debtors and their attorneys, U.S. Trustees and the bankruptcy courts. The Congressional Budget Office estimates that the 2005 Act will add $400 million to the federal budget deficit because more bankruptcy judges and U.S. Trustees and staff will have to be hired. James Flanigan, *Bankruptcy Bill Needs Reforming*, L.A. Times, April 10, 2005, at C1. No one has a clue on the effect of the Act on the behavior of consumers and creditors: will creditors offer more credit on better terms because they are more sure of getting their money back? Will consumers become more prudent in taking on credit?

*A Chapter 11 solution?* Some individual debtors who fall within the means test and therefore cannot use Chapter 7 are not eligible for Chapter 13 either because their debt levels are too high. Other individual debtors desiring to preserve their assets and future income who fall within the means test may be eligible for Chapter 13 relief but find highly undesirable the prospect of living for five years on an IRS expense diet under a Chapter 13 plan that demands all their disposable income. But neither group wishes to confront their unpaid creditors under unforgiving state collection laws allowing seizure of assets and garnishment of future income. It is possible that these groups will be looking seriously at Chapter 11 for bankruptcy relief. Normally thought of as the means of reorganizing business entities, Chapter 11 is fully available to individual debtors who are not in business. *Toibb v. Radloff*, 501 U.S. 157 (1991).

As we will see in the next chapter, there usually is no trustee in Chapter 11; the debtor negotiates its own plan with its creditors, with no statutorily prescribed payment period. Debtors retain much more control and flexibility than they enjoy in Chapter 13. With creditor consent, debtors can make their own deals, and the automatic stay holds off creditors while this is being done. *See* Colleen DeBaise, *Bankruptcy Bill May Spur More Chapter 11 Filings*, Wall St.J., Mar. 15, 2005, at D2. However, under the usual Chapter 11 plan the debtor still has to devote her future income to the plan, and individual debtors cannot be discharged from debts excepted from discharge by § 523. § 1141(d)(2). A liquidation under Chapter 11 might be considered, but individual debtors not engaged in business cannot be discharged in Chapter 11 if the debtor would be denied discharge under § 727(a). § 1141(d)(3).

But consumer debtor cases are not a good fit with Chapter 11 procedures. It is inconceivable that consumer finance companies would be willing to make up creditors' committees. How creditor voting could be carried out is not at all clear. And these creditors would surely be uncomfortable with a consumer as a debtor in possession, wheeling and dealing with the assets of the estate without close supervision of a creditors' group. A trustee would surely have to be appointed, and if consumer cases came into Chapter 11 in volume, something resembling a Chapter 13 trustee would have to established.

Whether consumer Chapter 11 filings will be tolerated is, at least in the first instance, up to the bankruptcy judges. In the year ending in September 2004, only 932 nonbusiness Chapter 11 cases were filed. *Annual Report of Director, Administrative Office of U.S. Courts* (2004). The judges may frown on a debtor who is eligible to file in Chapter 13 opting for Chapter 11. Possibly they would be more accepting of consumer cases in which the debtor is not eligible for Chapter 13. They might be inhospitable toward liquidating Chapter 11s, perhaps viewing them as bad faith filings. It will take a long time for the courts to create a workable body of law on this by-product of the 2005 Act.

### 3. DEBTOR'S DISCLOSURES

In order for the court, the U.S. Trustee and the panel trustee to administer the means test, detailed disclosure by the debtor is required under the 2005 Act. Under § 707(b)(2)(C), at the time of filing the debtor must include as part of the schedule of current income and expenditures required by § 521(a)(1)(B)(ii), a statement of "current monthly income" (defined in § 101(10A)) and the calculations that determine whether the presumption of abuse arises. As we have seen, these calculations require reference to the IRS National Standards and Local Standards (§ 707(b)(2)(A)(ii)(I)), rules laid down for tax delinquents. Presumably, software will be developed, similar to that used by tax practitioners, that will allow the calculations and disclosures to be made. This is imperative because *all cases* filed by individual debtors under Chapter 7 whose debts are primarily consumer debts fall within the scope of § 707(b)(1), and, under § 707(b)(2)(C) all these debtors must furnish their lawyers with enough information to make this disclosure even though their incomes are obviously under the state median income standards, below which their status as a presumed abuser is wholly irrelevant for means test purposes. Additional disclosures include copies of paychecks received within the 60-day period before filing, a statement of monthly net income, itemized to show how the amount is calculated, all deductible expenses, and a statement disclosing any reasonably anticipated increase in income or expenditures over the 12-month period following the date of filing, 521(a)(1)(B). Subjecting every consumer filing in Chapter 7—even low-income individuals who could not remotely be affected by the means test—to a detailed screening for means test purposes imposes on the attorney's staff a task that may consume hours for each client and needlessly increase the costs of bankruptcies.

In even the simplest income disclosure, the most useful substantiation of the debtor's representations is a federal tax return, and § 521(e)(2)(A) requires that the debtor provide a copy (or a transcript) of the most recent federal tax return to the trustee and to any creditor who requests a copy. However, privacy concerns arise. Section 521(g)(2) provides that these tax returns "shall be available to the United States trustee * * * any trustee, and any party in interest for inspection and copying. . ." What is to stop a creditor from making tax returns available to the public on the Internet? The issue is tentatively addressed by making the rights of the parties to inspect and copy tax returns under § 521(g)(2) subject to § 315(c) of the 2005 Act, which provides (1) that within 180 days after enactment the Director of the Administrative Office of the United States Courts "shall establish procedures for safeguarding the confidentiality of any tax information required to be provided by this section [§ 521]"; (2) that these "procedures shall include restrictions on creditor access to tax information that is required to be provided under this section"; and (3) no later than 540 days after enactment, the Director shall submit to Congress a report assessing the effectiveness of the procedures adopted and, if appropriate, any proposals for legislative reform. Finding a foolproof means of safeguarding the confidentiality of debtors' tax information is problematic.

## 4. DUTIES OF DEBTOR'S ATTORNEY AND U.S. TRUSTEE

*Attorneys.* The provisions of § 707(b)(4) may well reduce the availability of attorneys willing to represent debtors seeking relief in Chapter 7 and will surely significantly increase the cost of their services. If an attorney files a debtor's case in Chapter 7 and the trustee's motion to convert or dismiss is granted on the ground that the case is an abuse under § 707(b), the attorney may be subject to sanctions. The court may order the attorney to reimburse the trustee for the reasonable costs of prosecuting the motion or may assess a civil penalty. § 707(b)(4). We have seen that the determination of whether the means test applies is often difficult, and prudent counsel will not be likely to test the outer boundaries of § 707(b) until the law becomes settled on what those boundaries are. Reliable software must be developed to incorporate the IRS and state median income standards so that debtors' counsel can accurately and efficiently deal with the means test. In developing the software, the vagaries of the IRS and Census Bureau data may pose a challenge. Fortunately, imposition of sanctions is discretionary on the part of the court; in earlier drafts they were mandatory.

Moreover, § 707(b)(4)(D) makes the debtor's attorney's signature on the petition a certification that the attorney has no knowledge, after an inquiry, that the information on the schedules filed with the petition is incorrect.

Holding attorneys as, in effect, guarantors of the accuracy of the information supplied by the debtor will force them to devote more time and resources to verification of schedules, leading to higher costs that debtors must inevitably bear. Before the 2005 Act, legal fees for a Chapter 7 filing usually ran between $500 and $1,000. Those days are over.

The 2005 Act introduces the terms "debt relief agency" (§ 101(12A)), "bankruptcy assistance" (§ 101(4A)), "assisted person" (§ 101(3)), and redefines "bankruptcy petition preparer" (§ 110(a)(1)). An "assisted person" is a one whose debts consist primarily of consumer debts and whose nonexempt assets are valued at less that $150,000; this definition presumably includes most of the individual debtors filing in Chapter 7. A person renders "bankruptcy assistance" if it counsels an assisted person on bankruptcy law or provides legal representation with respect to a case or proceeding. Since these services constitute the practice of law, presumably one must be a licensed attorney under nonbankruptcy law to render bankruptcy assistance and must be admitted to practice before a bankruptcy court to appear for a debtor. Bankr. Rule 9010(a). A "bankruptcy petition preparer" is a person other than an attorney or an attorney's employee (paralegal) who prepares for a fee documents for filing. A "debt relief agency" is a person who either provides bankruptcy assistance for payment (an attorney) or is a bankruptcy petition preparer.

Section 526 regulates the activities of debt relief agencies in their dealings with assisted persons in the most detailed manner with respect to: failing to perform promised duties, making untrue or misleading statements in documents filed in a case, misrepresenting services promised or benefits or risks that may result, advising assisted persons to incur more debt to pay attorneys or bankruptcy petition preparers, and failure to comply with the disclosure provisions of § 527 and § 528. Section 527 requires debt relief agencies providing bankruptcy assistance services (attorneys) to give a large volume of disclosure to an assisted person, including what amounts to a short course in bankruptcy law. Section 528 calls for written contracts between debt relief agencies and assisted persons and regulates advertising by these agencies. In § 526(c), liabilities are set out and remedies are prescribed. Section 110 regulates in great detail the activities of bankruptcy petition preparers.

It is difficult to think of another area of commercial activity in which attorneys are so heavily regulated with respect to their dealings with their clients. Each case file will have to contain a detailed compliance checklist with respect to meeting the numerous requirements of §§ 526, 517, and 528. Whether the consumer protection benefits of these provisions will outweigh their effect in discouraging counsel from dealing with consumer debtors remains to be seen.

*U.S. Trustees.* Under the 2005 Act, the U.S. Trustee is the enforcer of the means test and, as such, becomes the gatekeeper to Chapter 7. Section 704(b)(1) provides that within 10 days after the first meeting of creditors, which must be held no less than 20 days and no more than 40 days after the order for relief (Bankr. Rule 2003(a)), the U.S. Trustee must file a statement with the court as to whether the debtor's case would be presumed to be an abuse under § 707(b). Within 30 days after filing this statement, § 704(b)(2) requires the U.S. Trustee to file either a motion to dismiss or convert or a statement setting out the reasons why such a motion is not appropriate if the presumption of abuse applies and the debtor's income is greater than the state median income standard. Thus, the U.S. Trustee's staff must go over in detail the hundreds of thousands of Chapter 7 filings by individual debtors and make the decision whether to move to dismiss or convert in less than three months. U.S. Trustees must have expanded funding and staffing to do the job.

In short, the means test has raised the price of bankruptcy to debtors, courts, and the U.S. Trustee's office. While means testing probably excludes no more than five to ten percent of the individual debtors who might have filed in Chapter 7 under the old rules, all individual debtors desiring bankruptcy relief from consumer debts, including the great majority who are not abusers, must file petitions accompanied by detailed disclosures including complex means testing calculations.

*Audits.* Section 603 of the 2005 Act addresses concerns about the potential for cheating by debtors in their bankruptcy case submissions. Debtors' attorneys, U.S. Trustees and bankruptcy courts must rely on information given them by debtors in order to apply the means test and for other purposes under the Code, but heretofore there has been no systematic audit of this information for veracity. Section 603(a) requires the Attorney General to establish procedures for auditing the accuracy, veracity and completeness of petitions, schedules and other information that the debtor is required submit in a bankruptcy case. These procedures must call for random audits in not less than one out of every 250 cases, as well audits of schedules that reflect certain variances in the statistical norms of income and expenses in the district. Section 603(b) adds 28 U.S.C. § 586(f), which authorizes the U.S. Trustee to contract with auditors to perform audits in cases designated by the Trustee and to report the results to the Trustee. If material misstatement of income or expenditures or of assets is reported, the Trustee must report the misstatement to the United States Attorney and take appropriate action, which includes but is not restricted to revocation of the debtor's discharge under § 727(d)(4). Just as the possibility of being audited gives taxpayers incentive to file honest returns, bankruptcy audits should have a similar effect in bankruptcy submissions. For an early proposal calling for audits, *see* Kenneth N. Klee, *Restructuring Individual Debts,* in *Reforming Consumer Bankruptcy Law: Four Proposals,* 71 Am. Bankr. L.J. 431, 437, 442 (1997).

## 5. MANDATORY CREDIT COUNSELING

An assumption of the 2005 Act is that is not unreasonable to deny debtors of all income levels access to bankruptcy, except in emergency cases, until they have received instruction from an independent source on alternatives to bankruptcy and budget analysis. In pursuit of this goal, the 2005 Act provides that an individual is not eligible for bankruptcy unless she has during the 180-day period before filing received from "an approved nonprofit budget and credit counseling agency described in section 111(a) an individual or group briefing (including a briefing conducted by telephone or on the Internet) that outlined the opportunities for available credit counseling and assisted that individual in performing a related budget analysis." § 109(h)(1). The debtor must prove compliance by filing with the court a certificate stating that an approved agency provided the debtor with the services described under § 109(h) and a copy of the repayment plan, if any, developed thereunder. A debtor need not complete an instructional course concerning personal financial management described in § 111 in order to be eligible for filing, but completion of such a course is a prerequisite for discharge in both Chapter 7, § 727(a)(11), and Chapter 13, § 1328(g).

A prospective debtor may avoid compliance with the credit counseling requirement of § 109(h) for eligibility to file bankruptcy by obtaining a waiver from the court by proving the existence of "exigent circumstances that merit a waiver" and showing that the credit counseling agency could not provide the required services within five days after request was made. § 109(h)(3)(A). U.S. Trustees may also exempt debtors who live in districts that do not have approved agencies able to provide the needed services. § 109(h)(2). The U.S. Trustee granted a temporary waiver of the credit counseling requirement for Louisiana and the Southern District of Mississippi owing to the effects of hurricane Katrina. The Act says nothing about who pays for the mandated instruction; we must assume it is the usually insolvent, sometimes indigent, debtor who must foot the bill.

In justifying mandatory credit counseling, Todd Zywicki contends that bankruptcy lawyers have no financial incentive to encourage debtors to work their problems out with creditors informally or to seek formal credit counseling. This leads them to "stampede their clients into bankruptcy without fully explaining the full consequences of filing or the alternatives to bankruptcy a debtor may have. . ... Mandatory credit counseling will ensure that debtors receive advice from a party other than an attorney, creating an important gate-keeping function that will reduce at least some filings." *Why So Many Bankruptcies?* (*supra*) at 108. He concedes that mandatory credit counseling will increase the cost of filing bankruptcy but believes that this cost would be outweighed by the effects of such a provision in keeping more debtors out of bankruptcy.

What mandatory credit counseling and financial management instruction will become under the 2005 Act will be shaped largely by the U.S. Trustees. They must approve the agencies as satisfying the broad standards prescribed by the statute. To be approved, a credit counseling agency must be nonprofit and provide adequate counseling with respect to client credit problems that includes an analysis of their current situation, what brought them to that financial status, and how they can develop a plan to handle the problem without incurring negative amortization of their debts. § 111(c)(2)(A) and (E). These agencies may charge reasonable fees but must "provide services *without regard to ability to pay the fee*." § 111(c)(2)(B). U.S. Trustees may approve financial management instructional courses only if the course provides "trained personnel with adequate experience and training in providing effective instruction and services." § 111(d)(1)(A). Courses may be offered by telephone or through the Internet. § 111(d)(1)(C). Agencies offering financial management courses must maintain records permitting auditors to evaluate whether the courses are effective. § 111(d)(1)(D).

At the time the 2005 Act became effective, the credit counseling field was teeming with debt counselors hoping to be selected by the U.S. Trustee's Office as approved agencies. The IRS has been besieged by credit counseling businesses seeking nonprofit status so that they may qualify. The quality of these enterprises varies widely from established agencies affiliated with the National Foundation for Consumer Credit, which limits the fees that its members may charge clients, to scandalous operators who advertise on radio, TV and the Internet miraculous cures erasing debts and repairing credit records. The FTC and the state attorneys general are actively pursuing these scammers. Christopher Conkey, *Deterrent to Bankruptcy: Counseling*, Wall St.J., Apr. 6, 2005, at D2. The U.S. Trustees will have their hands full in making the investigations necessary to make appropriate choices.

Will the credit counseling prerequisite as set out in the 2005 Act in fact encourage debtors and creditors to reach extra-bankruptcy workout agreements or will § 109(h) in operation amount to little more than an expensive obstruction that discourages debtors from filing in bankruptcy? Congress would like to know the answer, and it has taken steps to find out. The Director of the Executive Office of the U. S. Trustees is required by § 105 of the 2005 Act to develop financial management training curricula and materials after consulting with a wide range of experts in debtor education, including Chapter 13 trustees and operators of financial management education programs. The curricula and materials will be tested in six selected judicial districts over an 18-month period beginning within 270 days of enactment of the Act. They will then be evaluated by Chapter 13 trustees and consumer counseling groups. These experts will also examine representative consumer education programs carried out by the credit industry. Not later than three months after the evaluation, the Director must submit a report to Congress containing the Director's findings regarding the effectiveness and costs of the curricula, materials and programs. Thus, it may be some time before all districts have agencies using materials that have proved effective. Since U. S. Trustees may exempt debtors from meeting the credit counseling requirement if they live in districts that do not have approved agencies, nationwide credit counseling under the 2005 Act may be awhile in coming.

## D. REAFFIRMATION OF DISCHARGED DEBTS

### 1. INTRODUCTION

Although the primary reason most individuals file bankruptcy is to discharge debts, creditors frequently induce debtors to "reaffirm" (agree to repay) otherwise dischargeable debts. Contract law enforces the agreement to pay the discharged debt. Restatement (Second) of Contracts § 83 (1981). "The rule of law is well-nigh universal that such a promise made has an obligating and validating consideration in the moral obligation of the debtor to pay. The debt is not paid by the discharge in bankruptcy. It is due in conscience, although discharged in law, and this moral obligation, uniting with the subsequent promise to pay, creates a right of action." *Herrington v. Davitt*, 115 N.E. 476, 477 (N.Y.1917).

Nothing in bankruptcy policy disfavors voluntary repayment by the debtor out of debtor's postpetition earnings, and § 524(f) specifically allows voluntary repayment. It is a different matter, however, for the debtor to become obligated to repay. Since reaffirmation negates discharge, there is a prima facie conflict between reaffirmation and the bankruptcy policy of giving a fresh start to the debtor. The consequences of reaffirming a discharged debt are often more serious than incurring the original debt: the reaffirmed obligation cannot be discharged in a later Chapter 7 case for another eight years. § 727(a)(8).

In some cases reaffirmation is clearly against the debtor's self interest, but in others there may be a compelling reason to reaffirm. The compulsion can take various forms. The debtor may wish to reaffirm in order to protect the guarantor of the debt who is a relative or close friend, or stay in the good graces of a creditor on whom the debtor is dependent. For example, the creditor may be the debtor's employer or a supplier of vital services. But the most common reason for reaffirming is to protect property such as the debtor's home, household goods or automobile that is collateral for the debt and that the secured creditor will seize absent reaffirmation. Discharge frees the debtor of personal liability on a secured debt, but it does not affect the secured creditor's right to collateral that secures the debt. Debtors often reaffirm to prevent seizure of household goods and automobiles subject to indefeasible liens. Section 522(f), which we have already examined, lessens the need for reaffirmation by avoiding nonpurchase-money security interests in the household goods cases. The automobile and purchase-money lien cases are covered by § 722, which, under pre-2005 law, allowed the debtor to redeem the collateral by paying the value of the secured claim, *i.e.*, the value of the collateral. Since in many cases the amount of the discharged debt is substantially more than the value of the collateral, redemption may be a less onerous alternative to reaffirmation as a means of saving the collateral. But redemption under § 722 requires a lump-sum cash payment by the debtor. The creditor is not required to accept payment in installments. The 2005 Act erased any doubt about this issue by adding at the end of § 722: "in full at the time of redemption."

## 2. THE 2005 ACT

At the time Congress first addressed the subject in the eight-year long legislative process that led to the 2005 Act, reaffirmation was a hot potato. The National Bankruptcy Review Commission devoted a great deal of time and effort to its treatment of reaffirmation agreements. *NBRC Rep.* at 145 *et seq.* It found scandalous conditions existing. Some of the most reputable creditors in the country (*e.g.* Sears, May Company, GE Capital, Federated Department Stores, and AT&T) conceded in the mid-1990s that they had not been in compliance with the law in a significant percentage of their reaffirmation agreements. *NBRC Rep.* at 163-164. The most common violation was the failure of creditors to file agreements with the bankruptcy courts as required by § 524(c)(2). Research cited by the Commission suggests that as many as half of all reaffirmation agreements were unenforceable because they did not meet even this threshold test of validity. *NBRC Rep.* at 162. Debtors continued to pay under these agreements, unaware of their invalidity. Moreover, a significant percentage of reaffirmations were for totally unsecured debt in which debtors reaffirmed their debts but retained no property in exchange. *NBRC Rep.* at 153. It is questionable whether many of these reaffirmations were in the best interests of debtors.

Consumer representatives demanded that reaffirmations be banned; creditors strongly disagreed. In the face of a series of media exposes of creditor abuse, Congress apparently thought that it had to take some action to protect gullible consumers from giving away their bankruptcy discharges under pressure by creditors, but their response was modest. Section 524(k) of the 2005 Act requires that the debtor be given a great deal of additional disclosure, including detailed Truth-in-Lending type disclosures concerning the reaffirmation transaction the debtor is entering into and information about how to enter into a reaffirmation agreement, the enforceability of the agreement, the consequences of reaffirmation, and the debtor's right to rescind.

The principal substantive change that the 2005 Act made toward reducing abuses in reaffirmation cases is the requirement that the bankruptcy court intervene to invalidate reaffirmations that constitute undue hardship on the debtor, even in cases in which the debtor is represented by counsel. Section 524(k)(6)(A) requires that the debtor submit a "Statement in Support of Reaffirmation Agreement," which expresses the debtor's belief that the agreement will not impose an undue hardship and confirms the reasonableness of this belief by showing that the amount of income the debtor has left over after payment of expenses is adequate to meet the required payments on the reaffirmed debt. Section 524(m)(1) provides that for 60 days after a reaffirmation agreement is filed with the court there is a presumption that the reaffirmation agreement is an undue hardship on the debtor if the debtor's statement in support of reaffirmation shows that the debtor's income available to fund the reaffirmation agreement is less than the scheduled payments on the reaffirmed debt. "This presumption *shall* be reviewed by the court." § 524 (m)(1) (emphasis added). The presumption may be rebutted in writing by the debtor if the statement identifies additional sources of funds to make the agreed payments. If the presumption is not rebutted to the satisfaction of the court, it may disapprove the agreement after notice and hearing. The U.S. Attorney and the FBI are brought in to address abusive reaffirmations. 18 U.S.C. § 158. In the 2005 Act, Congress mandated a General Accounting Office study of the overall treatment of consumers in the reaffirmation process, with a report to Congress within one and one-half years after enactment making recommendations addressing any abusive or coercive tactics found.

A cynical view of the 2005 Act's reaffirmation provisions might be that Congress has marshaled all the "usual suspects" of consumer protection: more disclosure, a GAO study, enforcement duties imposed on federal agencies that have better things to do, and more participation by judges who are so busy that they flatly ignored previous attempts to get them involved in reaffirmation matters. So long as creditors are allowed to talk debtors into reaffirmation agreements, we doubt that the new Act's regulatory provisions will have much effect, given the vast number of consumer credit transactions that have to be policed. Modern consumer financers could probably get along without reaffirmations. In secured transactions, debtors who need the collateral can usually hold onto it by making voluntary payments: debtors have incentive to continue payments in order to keep the property; creditors have incentive to avoid being stuck with the repossessed goods. Informal arrangements of this sort are common. The remedy suggested by the National Bankruptcy Reform Commission (and ignored by Congress) was to bar reaffirmations for certain debts thought to be usually imprudent for debtors to reaffirm. *NBRC Rep.* at 148.

## E. REDEMPTION, REAFFIRMATION OR RIDE-THROUGH?

There has been a long-running battle between debtors and secured creditors over whether a debtor who is not in default in payments on an installment contract can retain possession of the property (often called a "ride-through") in Chapter 7 bankruptcy without reaffirming or redeeming. The courts have divided on the subject in a number of cases involving the repossession of motor vehicles; the prevailing view at the time of enactment of the 2005 Act favored allowing debtors a ride through, *e.g.*, *In re Boodrow*, 126 F.3d 43 (2d Cir. 1997). The new Act emphatically takes the creditors' viewpoint in providing that the automatic stay against repossession by the creditor is terminated if the debtor fails either to redeem (§ 722) or reaffirm (§ 524(c)) within 45 days after the § 341(a) meeting of the creditors. § 521(a)(6). If the debtor fails to file within a 30-day period after the § 341(a) meeting the required statement of intention either to surrender or retain the property, or, once the intention to retain is stated, the debtor fails to redeem or reaffirm within the prescribed period, the stay is terminated. § 362(h)(1).

However, terminating the stay merely allows the creditor to proceed under nonbankruptcy law to enforce its security interest, and the debtor may contend that the creditor has no right to repossess the property under state law because the debtor is not in default on the security agreement. This won't work if the creditor has included a clause in the security agreement declaring the debtor to be in default at the time of filing in bankruptcy. Resolving divided authority on the validity of such default-on-filing or "ipso facto" clauses in bankruptcy, § 521(d) provides that nothing in the Code "shall prevent or limit the operation of" such provisions. We suspect that in many cases secured creditors are happy to allow debtors to continue to drive their cars after they have filed in bankruptcy so long as they keep up their payments. What do creditors have to lose by doing so?

## F.  CHAPTER 13 AS AN ALTERNATIVE FOR THE CONSUMER DEBTOR

### 1.  AN OVERVIEW OF CHAPTER 13

Chapter 13 of the 1978 Code was drafted to offer an appealing alternative to debtors to induce them to repay part or all of their debts rather than to opt for Chapter 7, in which unsecured creditors usually recover nothing. But only approximately 30% of all debtors chose Chapter 13 over Chapter 7. On the eve of enactment of the 2005 Act, Chapter 13 offered the following: The debtor was not required to surrender any of her property. In lieu thereof, she was required to submit a plan in which she pledged to devote all her "disposable income" to debt repayment for three to five years. Disposable income is defined as all income projected by the debtor during the period of the plan that was not reasonably necessary for the maintenance and support of the debtor and her dependents. § 1325(b)(2). This plan had to be approved by the court; creditor approval was not required. There were two critical additional limitations on this plan. The plan must return to each unsecured creditor at least what that creditor would have received in a Chapter 7 liquidation of debtor's nonexempt property, sometimes called the "best interests" test. § 1325(a)(4). And the plan must provide that each secured creditor receive deferred cash payments with sufficient interest to give that creditor present value equal to the allowed amount of that claim. § 1325(a)(5).

These provisions, by requiring the debtor to devote future earnings to debt repayment, should work to enhance the rights of both unsecured and secured creditors in comparison to what they would be in a Chapter 7 liquidation. And to some degree they do: Chapter 13 payments to creditors are substantially larger than those under Chapter 7. According to the Office of U.S. Trustees, in 2003 creditors received only $1.5 billion in Chapter 7 cases and $4.2 billion in Chapter 13 cases. Michael Schroeder & Suein Hwang, *Sweeping New Bankruptcy Law to Make Life Harder for Debtors*, Wall St.J., Apr. 6, 2005, at A1. But the American Bankers Association estimates that in a recent year personal bankruptcies discharged debts totaling about $60 billion, and creditors want a greater percentage of this repaid than they were getting before 2005. Constance Mitchell Ford, *Creditor-Friendly South Offers Preview of Bankruptcy Changes*, Wall St.J., March 10, 2005, at A1. There are a number of reasons why Chapter 13 payments are not higher: (i) the limited definition of "disposable income," (ii) the reality that many debtors would pay no or only tiny dividends to unsecured creditors in applying the best interests test in a hypothetical Chapter 7, (iii) the ability to "strip down" secured claims other than home mortgages to the value of the collateral, leaving the deficiency classified as an unsecured claim, and (iv) Chapter 13's "super-discharge" provisions.

Requiring the debtor to devote all disposable income to debt repayment for at least three years was usually not meaningful to unsecured creditors since debtors commonly projected little income in excess of their living costs and secured debt obligations. Although some bankruptcy courts have asserted the power to reject plans that do not call for reductions in living costs, there is no statutory requirement that a debtor reduce living expenses, and most courts were loathe to find expenses associated with an ordinary middle class standard of living unreasonable. Accordingly, many Chapter 13 plans provided for no or only very small payments to unsecured creditors. These plans could nevertheless be confirmed if the debtor could show that unsecured creditors would have received nothing in Chapter 7. In many cases, it was quite possible for the debtor to make this showing, and when this was so unsecured creditors did no better in Chapter 13 than in Chapter 7.

With respect to secured claims, each secured creditor must receive only the value of its interest in its collateral, usually not the full amount it was owed, in the form of deferred cash payments with interest. With important exceptions noted below, this provision allows the debtor to "strip-down" the amount of her payment obligation to the value of the over-encumbered property she wished to retain. In effect, the debtor could "redeem" overencumbered property by paying to the creditor its value (as determined by the bankruptcy court) over time with interest. No comparable provision existed in Chapter 7. In that chapter, the debtor had to obtain the creditor's consent to any rescheduling of payments if she wished to remain in possession of encumbered property, while in Chapter 13 the debtor could impose a rescheduling based on judicial valuation of the collateral. Home mortgages were specially excepted from this power to modify the amount owed, although the debtor was permitted to pay out arrearages over the life of the plan with interest even in the case of home mortgages. § 1322(b).

Finally, former Chapter 13 permitted the discharge of some debts that could not be discharged in Chapter 7 cases. The only debts excepted from the super-discharge in Chapter 13 cases were claims for alimony and child support, criminal restitution orders, most educational loans, claims arising out of drunk driving accidents and long-term debts. § 1328(a). Moreover, some courts permitted debtors to separately classify and give preferred treatment to the holders of claims that were nondischargeable in Chapter 13. Allowing this discrimination in treatment was extremely favorable to debtors because it permitted them to devote all disposable income to the repayment of claims that in any event would survive the Chapter 13 plan while leaving nothing for the claims that would be discharged upon completion of the plan.

Unlike Chapter 7, which, pre-2005, had a six-year bar rule, nothing in Chapter 13 prevented repeated filings. This omission was deliberate, the assumption being that if a debtor was willing to subject all her disposable income to debt repayment for at least three years there was no harm in allowing her to re-enter Chapter 13. But filing under Chapter 13 (like all bankruptcy filings) has the effect of automatically staying all nonbankruptcy debt collection proceedings, including foreclosures. A particular form of abuse of the bankruptcy process that frustrated mortgage lenders was repeated Chapter 13 filings intended to forestall foreclosure rather than confirm a debt repayment plan.

Experience showed that Chapter 13 plans are likely to fail. If the debtor's income fails to meet projections or her expenses exceed projections, she may be unable to make the payments called for under the plan. In these circumstances, it was common for the Chapter 13 case to be converted to Chapter 7 if no feasible plan remained possible. In these cases, the debtor generally forfeited whatever payments she had made under the plan to unsecured creditors and had to give up her nonexempt property in exchange for the more limited Chapter 7 discharge. There were provisions for a hardship discharge in Chapter 13 if the debtor had made enough payments under the plan to satisfy the best interests test and the plan nevertheless could not be completed on account of circumstances beyond her control. § 1328(b). In other cases, Chapter 13 plans could be modified in order to take into account changed circumstances. § 1329.

Some debtors have both large unsecured and large secured debts and seek to take advantage of the most favorable aspects of both Chapters 7 and 13. By first invoking Chapter 7, the debtor could discharge her unsecured claims. The debtor could then file in Chapter 13 in order to deal with recalcitrant secured creditors or the holders of certain nondischargeable claims. The Supreme Court has found that these "Chapter 20" cases (that is, *seriatim* Chapters 7 and 13 cases) are generally permitted. *Johnson v. Home State Bank*, 501 U.S. 78 (1991).

Based on the above description of the differences between Chapter 7 and Chapter 13, one might predict that those debtors with relatively large unsecured debts, few secured debts, and little nonexempt property would disproportionately choose Chapter 7, while those with substantial nonexempt assets and secured debts would prefer Chapter 13. Teresa A. Sullivan, Elizabeth Warren & Jay Lawrence Westbrook have made available a chapter, entitled *Who Uses Chapter 13?*, which they contributed to a book entitled *Consumer Bankruptcy in Global Perspective*, edited by Ian Ramsey, published abroad. This chapter brings forward the work the authors commenced in their 1981 study (*As We Forgive Our Debtors: Bankruptcy and Consumer Credit in America* 236-238 (1989)) and continued in their 1991 work. Their findings, based on 1999 data, revealed that: (1) The proportion of consumer cases filed in Chapter 13 has remained stable since 1981 at approximately 30%. (2) The strongest predictor of Chapter 13 filing was ownership; homes are assets debtors want to hold on to. (3) The second strongest predictor was local legal culture. (4) The total amount of debt was mildly negative correlated with filing in Chapter 13. And (5) demographic variables, such as sex, age, and ethnicity, were not significant.

In some jurisdictions, particularly in the Southeastern United States where the predecessor to Chapter 13 was developed in the Depression, bankruptcy courts and the local bar prefer Chapter 13, reasoning that debtors who can pay pre-bankruptcy debts out of future income ought to, and such cases are disproportionately filed in those districts. An Alabama attorney says: "People here want to pay back their debts." Constance Mitchell Ford, *Creditor-Friendly South Offers Preview of Bankruptcy Changes*, Wall St.J., Mar. 10, 2005, at A1. In other districts, judges will dismiss Chapter 7 filings if the debtor appears to have sufficient income to fund a Chapter 13 plan, making Chapter 13 virtually mandatory for those debtors. Still other jurisdictions, with judges who are either indifferent or hostile to Chapter 13 plans, tend to see disproportionately more Chapter 7 filings.

As we have seen earlier in this chapter, the principal thrust of the 2005 Act with respect to consumer debtors is to employ a means test in order to restrict access to Chapter 7. What is the excluded debtor's alternative to Chapter 7? Under the 2005 Act, a court may convert debtors who are excluded from Chapter 7 by the means test to Chapter 13 only if the debtor consents (§ 707(b)(1)) and, of course, meets the eligibility requirements discussed in the following section. Even under the rather attractive regime offered debtors by pre-2005 Chapter 13 described above, only 30% of debtors opted for Chapter 13 in preference to Chapter 7, and in some regions significant numbers of those debtors were pushed into Chapter 13 filings in accordance with the preferences of local judges and lawyers. Of these, only about a third actually completed their plan. If, as is commonly assumed, a goal of the 2005 Act is to reduce the number of consumer debtors availing themselves of Chapter 7 discharges, one might think that a step in this direction would be making Chapter 13 even more appealing to consumer debtors, but as we see in the following sections Congress has most emphatically made Chapter 13 less friendly to consumer debtors than it was before. The noble experiment of the 1978 Act to make Chapter 13 attractive to debtors has been abandoned.

A summary of the major changes made in Chapter 13 by the 2005 Act follows:

**(1)**   The debtor is not eligible for Chapter 13 unless she has met the credit counseling requirements discussed with respect to Chapter 7. She must also file detailed information about finances.

**(2)**   A debtor can no longer take the "Chapter 20" route of obtaining a Chapter 7 discharge to cut off unsecured claims and an immediate Chapter 13 filing to take advantage of its "super-discharge."

**(3)**   Repeated and abusive filings in Chapter 13 are aggressively addressed.

**(4)**   The debtor must directly pay lessors and secured creditors the amounts of their rentals and periodic payments.

(5) Domestic Support Obligations ("DSO") are given special priorities and a debtor cannot receive a discharge in Chapter 13 unless current on DSO payments.

(6) The duration of a Chapter 13 plan is lengthened to five years for debtors whose incomes are not less than the state median family income.

(7) In determining disposable income, debtors with income not less than the state median must commit all their income to their Chapter 13 plan that is in excess of IRS standards for expenses (whatever the amount of their actual expenses) unless they can show special circumstances.

(8) Section 506(a) no longer applies to purchase money transactions in motor vehicles acquired within approximately two-and-one-half years before filing and other collateral purchased within one year before filing. Hence, the entire purchase obligation is considered secured whatever the value of the collateral, and lien-stripping is barred.

(9) If a Chapter 13 plan is dismissed or converted, a secured party retains a lien in its collateral for the entire unpaid balance of the secured obligation.

(10) New exceptions are made to the super-discharge.

## 2. ELIGIBILITY FOR CHAPTER 13

Chapter 13 has always been voluntary and under the 2005 Act it still is. If the debtor files in Chapter 7 but passes the means test, the court may convert the debtor to Chapter 13 only with the debtor's consent. § 707(b)(1). But, when the severity of the changes made in Chapter 13 by the 2005 Act is fully grasped, one wonders why any debtor in financial difficulty would volunteer for Chapter 13.

Most individual debtors can file in Chapter 13; the requirements for eligibility are set forth in § 109(e). The debtor must be a natural person. Even a one-stockholder corporation or family partnership is barred and may seek rehabilitation only in Chapter 11. The debtor must be an "individual with regular income," defined in § 101(30) as one with income "sufficiently stable and regular to enable such individual to make payments under a plan under chapter 13." The source of the income is not material. An objective of the drafters of the Code was to allow the small individual proprietorship to reorganize under Chapter 13 rather than under the more costly and burdensome procedures of Chapter 11. Hence, debtors may be self-employed as well as employees. Even unemployed or retired individuals are eligible so long as they receive regular income, which might be from investments, social security, private pensions, or other welfare or retirement programs. Spouses of debtors with regular income are eligible for Chapter 13 even though they have no income. The debtor must have noncontingent and liquidated debts of less than $307,675 of unsecured claims and $922,975 of secured claims. Pursuant to § 104(b), these amounts are adjusted every three years by the Judicial Conference to reflect changes in the Consumer Price Index; the levels were last adjusted in 2004. They were chosen to make Chapter 13 available to most consumer debtors and many small business debtors, leaving to Chapter 11 cases involving larger amounts of debt. In the year ending in September 2004, out of 454,412 Chapter 13 filings, 4,799 were business filings. *Annual Report of Director, Administrative Office of U.S. Courts* (2004). The value of the debtor's assets is not relevant to her eligibility for Chapter 13.

Under § 109(h), added in 2005, debtors are not eligible for Chapter 13 unless they have met the credit counseling requirements discussed above with respect to access to Chapter 7. Like Chapter 7 debtors, Chapter 13 debtors must file a certificate from the nonprofit budget and credit counseling agency that provided the debtor with the services required by § 109(h), together with any debt repayment plan developed through that agency, § 521(b). Since a debtor doesn't have to meet the means test to file in Chapter 13, she doesn't have to file schedules containing the means test calculations that are required of a Chapter 7 filer, but, under § 521(e)(2) and (f)(1) through (3), she must file the same information about her financial situation, including tax returns, that is required of Chapter 7 debtors. In addition, a Chapter 13 debtor must annually file a statement of the income and expenditures of the debtor that shows how income, expenditures and monthly income are calculated. § 521(f)(4) and (g)(1). The tax returns and statement of income and expenditures shall be available to the U.S. Trustee, the Chapter 13 trustee, and "any party of interest" for inspection and copying, subject to the requirements of § 315(c) of the 2005 Act, discussed previously with respect to Chapter 7. § 521(g)(2).

## PROBLEMS

**1.** In Problem 3 on p. 527, will Marta be able to fund a repayment plan in Chapter 13? Is she even eligible for Chapter 13 given her current lack of regular income? Is it possible for a consumer debtor to be denied access both to Chapters 7 and 13?

**2.** Debtor mortgaged the family home to Bank to secure a debt of $600,000. Debtor has unsecured debts amounting to $50,000. Owing to a recession, Debtor suffered a reduction in income, and fell into default on the mortgage and other debts. Real estate values also plunged and the home is now valued at no more than $300,000. Debtor wishes to file in Chapter 13. Is Debtor eligible for Chapter 13 under § 109(e)? On the question of whether the deficiency portion of an undersecured claim can count as an unsecured debt for Chapter 13 eligibility purposes, *see In re Scovis*, 249 F. 3d 975 (9th Cir. 2001).

### 3. REPEATED DISCHARGES AND FILINGS

#### a. Repeated Discharges

Should a debtor be able to have the best of both worlds by first getting rid of ordinary debts in Chapter 7 and then filing in Chapter 13 to deal with nondischargeable debts and security interests? In *Johnson v. Home State Bank*, 501 U.S. 78 (1991), the Court answered in the affirmative, noting that Congress had expressly limited various forms of serial filings, *e.g.*, § 109(g), but did not categorically foreclose the power of a debtor to file in Chapter 13 subsequent to a Chapter 7 discharge. Lower courts imposed a good faith test to limit somewhat debtors' use of "Chapter 20." See, *e.g.*, *In re Rasmussen*, 888 F.2d 703 (10th Cir. 1989) (nondischargeable debts); *In re Cushman*, 217 B.R. 470 (Bankr. E.D. Va. 1998) (lien stripping).

The effect of § 1328(f)(1) is to overrule *Johnson v. Home State Bank* and to bar a debtor who has received a discharge in Chapter 7 from receiving a Chapter 13 discharge in a case in which the Chapter 13 petition is filed within four years after the Chapter 7 discharge. This amendment ends the "Chapter 20" stratagem, but § 1328(f)(2) imposes a new limit on successive Chapter 13 filings that has no relation to the "Chapter 20" problem and is a clear break from the view that debtors should be able to propose good faith Chapter 13 repayment plans as often as they were needed. Section 1328(f)(2) bars a court from granting a discharge in Chapter 13 in Case #2 if the debtor had been discharged in Chapter 13 in Case #1 within two years before the date on which Case #2 was filed.

### PROBLEM

Herman believes in paying his debts. When he found himself in financial difficulties, he filed in Chapter 13 in January 2002. His plan was confirmed and he completed it by paying all his creditors in full. He was discharged in January 2005. In June 2006 he was laid off from his job and was living on unemployment compensation while he searched for a new job. His mortgagee was threatening foreclosure on his residence, and he sought protection in Chapter 13 again so that he could retain his home and pay his creditors in an orderly manner.

**(a)** What are Herman's rights to a discharge in Chapter 13? *See* § 1328(f)(2).

**(b)** Herman wants a discharge. What if he files in Chapter 7 and, under the means test, the court converts his case to Chapter 13, with his consent. Does this mean that because of § 1328(f)(2) he can't be discharged in the second Chapter 13 case?

### b.   Repetitive Filings Under 2005 Act

Some debtors have relied on repeated Chapter 13 filings to take advantage of the automatic stay to stave off foreclosure or eviction. After the creditor requests relief from the automatic stay under § 362(d) in order to foreclose or evict, the debtor dismisses under § 1307(b), only to file again when the mortgagee or landlord initiates another foreclosure or eviction. The bankruptcy court clerk is required to accept the bankruptcy petition of a debtor who files the correct papers and pays the fee. This process can go on indefinitely. Seeing the potential for abuse in this situation, Congress enacted § 109(g)(2) in 1984, which provides that an individual who has been a debtor at any time within the preceding 180-day period is ineligible to file in Chapter 13 if that individual had obtained voluntary dismissal of the prior case following the filing of a request for relief from the automatic stay by the creditor.

The 2005 Act aggressively addresses the repeated filings issue in an elaborate set of provisions that should keep bankruptcy courts busy for years in reaching consensus on the prescribed standards for compliance. The amendments adding § 362(c)(3) and (4) approach the problem of bad faith repeated filings by limiting the debtor's protection under the automatic stay against creditor collection actions. Under paragraph (3), a debtor who files a Chapter 13 petition within a year after dismissal of a previous case loses protection of the stay 30 days after filing the later case unless the debtor affirmatively demonstrates to the court, at a hearing completed within the 30-day period, that the filing of the later case was in good faith as to the creditors to be stayed. It seems unlikely under these provisions that a debtor will be able to stay creditor collection actions for more than 30 days by filing a second Chapter 13 within a year of dismissal of an earlier case. No stay at all arises upon a third filing within a year absent an affirmative showing of good faith.

The 2005 Act also added § 362(d)(4) aimed at curbing abusive filings calculated to forestall foreclosure. Mortgagees found the practice of debtors (often acting on the advice of unscrupulous "foreclosure consultants") of transferring title (or fractional interests in title) to other entities in order to frustrate foreclosure to be particularly troublesome. Section 362(d)(4) authorizes courts to grant a powerful new form of *in rem* relief from the stay "if the court finds that the bankruptcy petition was part of a scheme to delay, hinder and defraud creditors" that involved either transfer of the real property without the mortgagee's consent or multiple bankruptcy filings. The order lifting the stay may be recorded in the real property records and is binding for two years on any new bankruptcy cases affecting the real property. The provision is triggered only if the mortgagee can show that the mortgagor's activities were part of a fraudulent scheme.

Another species of bad faith filings relates to tenants who seek to delay eviction proceedings by filing in bankruptcy. Section 362(b)(22) excepts from the stay the continuation of eviction proceedings involving residential property if the lessor has obtained a judgment for possession before the tenant filed bankruptcy. The debtor can postpone the application of § 362(b)(22) until 30 days after her petition is filed by filing with her petition a certification that she has the right to cure her default and has deposited with the clerk any rent that would become due during the 30-day delay. If the lessor objects, a hearing must be held within 10 days after its objection is filed. § 362(*l*)(3).

## 4. COMMENCING A CHAPTER 13 CASE

Chapter 13 debtors keep their property and pay their debts out of future earnings pursuant to a plan confirmed by the court. At the time of filing, the debtor must file schedules with the petition in bankruptcy giving information about the debtor's employment, income, expenses, debts and property as well as estimates of future monthly income and expenses. § 521(a)(1). The debtor must file a plan with the petition or within 15 days thereafter unless an extension is granted for cause. Bankr. Rule 3015(b). Debtors are not allowed to delay in commencing their payments under the plan. Under § 1326(a), the debtor "shall" commence payments proposed under the plan within 30 days after the plan is filed or the order for relief, whichever is earlier, even though the plan is not yet confirmed. Furthering the goal of the 2005 Act to shore up the Chapter 13 position of lessors and secured creditors, § 1326(a) provides that the debtor must pay the trustee the amount "proposed by the plan" but, in addition, pay directly to any personal property lessor the amount of the rentals coming due after the case was filed and to any personal property secured party the amount of adequate protection payments coming due after filing. The trustee must be provided with evidence of these payments. The debtor may reduce the amount of payments made to the trustee under the proposed plan by the amount of any payments made to lessors and secured parties. Upon notice and hearing, the court may modify the amount of payments required by subsection (a) pending confirmation of the plan. Within 60 days after filing the plan, the debtor in possession of personal property subject to a lease or security interest must provide the lessor or secured creditor with evidence of insurance coverage on the property. Any payment received by the trustee before confirmation is to be held by the trustee until the plan is either confirmed or not confirmed. If the plan is confirmed, the trustee must distribute the money under the plan. If confirmation is denied, the trustee must give the money collected back to the debtor. Section 1302 requires the trustee to ensure that the debtor commences making timely payments under § 1302(b)(5). If the debtor fails to commence payments on time, the court may convert the case to Chapter 7 or dismiss it. § 1307(c)(4). The debtor in *In re McDonald*, 118 F.3d 568 (7th Cir.1997), was late on her *first* payment and the bankruptcy court dismissed her case. In an eat-your-carrots opinion, the appellate court held that the bankruptcy judge did not abuse his discretion.

Within 20 to 50 days after the petition, the U.S. Trustee must call a meeting of creditors pursuant to § 341(a). Bankr. Rule 2003(a). Proofs of claim are to be filed within 90 days after the first date set for the meeting of creditors. Bankr. Rule 3002(c). The notice of confirmation hearing must include either the plan or a summary of it so that creditors will know whether they wish to object to it at the confirmation hearing. Bankr. Rule 3015(d). Although the U.S. Trustee or a designee presides at the meeting of creditors (Bankr. Rule 2003(b)), and the court ultimately decides whether to confirm the debtor's plan, the gatekeeper in the Chapter 13 confirmation process is the standing trustee. The trustee's staff examines the debtor's plan before the creditors' meeting and the trustee may use that meeting to raise with the debtor's counsel any deficiencies in the plan. Further information may be sought from the debtor who must be present at the meeting. § 343. If these problems can be worked out at the meeting, the trustee may place the debtor's case on what amounts to a consent calendar and allow the hearing on the confirmation of the plan to take place immediately. The 2005 Act validates this accelerated hearing practice in § 1324(b), which provides that the confirmation hearing may be held not earlier than 20 days and not later than 45 days after the § 341 meeting "unless the court determines that it would be in the best interests of the creditors and the estate to hold such hearing at an earlier date and there is no objection to such earlier date." Time and money are saved and the creditors receive distributions more promptly. Money to fund the plan may be paid to the trustee directly by the debtor or, pursuant to court order, by the debtor's employer or other source of income. § 1325(c). When all payments under the plan have been completed, the debtor is discharged. § 1328(a).

## 5. PROPERTY OF THE ESTATE AND THE AUTOMATIC STAY

### a.  Role of Property of the Estate

Upon the filing of a Chapter 13 petition, § 362(a) automatically stays creditor proceedings, judicial or extrajudicial, to collect prepetition claims. The stay continues until the plan is completed and the debtor is discharged, usually about three to five years after the petition. § 362(c)(2). During the period of the plan the debtor may acquire new property and incur new debts. In order to understand the effect of the stay on postpetition property and debts, we must examine the concept of property of the estate in Chapter 13. Section 1306(a) provides that property of the estate includes not only that property owned by the debtor at the date of the petition but also property, including earnings, that the debtor acquires after commencement of the case.

Property of the estate is an artificial concept in Chapter 13. Although all of the debtor's property is technically property of the estate until confirmation of the plan, the debtor can and does use that property as before bankruptcy. Section 1322(b)(8) provides that the plan may provide for payments from property of the estate or of the debtor. In some cases it may be advantageous for a debtor to propose liquidation of some property so that a smaller portion of future earnings will be paid to creditors. But such plans are unusual. In most cases only future earnings are used to make payments under the plan, and we assume for the purposes of this discussion that this usual pattern is followed.

In Chapter 7, property of the estate must be identified because it is the property the trustee liquidates and distributes to creditors. But in Chapter 13 the debtor usually retains the property and pays creditors out of future earnings. Nevertheless, identification of property of the estate is necessary in Chapter 13 because a plan may be confirmed only if each unsecured claim receives not less than it would in liquidation under Chapter 7. § 1325(a)(4). Thus, until a court knows the extent of the property of the estate, it cannot confirm a plan.

### b.  Automatic Stay

The concept of property of the estate in Chapter 13 also determines the scope of the automatic stay. Before confirmation of the plan, the automatic stay operates in Chapter 13 much the same as it does in Chapter 7. After confirmation, the automatic stay, insofar as it protects property of the estate, operates primarily to prevent creditors with postpetition claims from disrupting execution of the plan by seizing postpetition income of the debtor to be distributed by the trustee. How is this accomplished? Normally a Chapter 13 debtor will fund the plan from future earnings that, under § 1306(a)(2), are property of the estate protected by the automatic stay from all creditors of the debtor. But § 1327(b) provides that confirmation of the plan, which may occur soon after the petition is filed, revests the property of the estate in the debtor. Since under § 362(c)(1) the stay of an act against property of the estate continues only "until such property is no longer property of the estate," the effect of § 1327(b) is to terminate the stay, at the time the plan is confirmed, to the extent it protects property of the estate. But § 1327(b) is limited by the phrase "except as otherwise provided in the plan or the order confirming the plan." Cases are divided on what, if anything, must be stated in the plan or order to prevent future earnings from revesting in the debtor after confirmation. The court in *In re Heath*, 115 F.3d 521 (7th Cir. 1997), read §§ 1306(a)(2) and 1327(b) to mean that the debtor's filing vests all property of the debtor in the estate, but confirmation of the plan revests in the debtor as much of that property as is not necessary to the fulfillment of the plan. Although the court did not rely on it in deciding the case, the order of the court confirming the plan in *Heath* stated that the debtor's income and other assets remain property of the estate to the extent necessary to fulfill the plan. *Telfair v. First Union Mortgage Corporation*, 216 F.3d 1333 (11th Cir. 2000), agreed with *Heath*. Other cases require the plan or order of confirmation to clearly identify the property that is to remain property of the estate. *In re Petruccelli*, 113 B.R. 5 (Bankr. S.D. Cal. 1990). Charles Jordan Tabb, *The Law of Bankruptcy* 946 (1997), approves of *Petruccelli*.

All property that is not covered by the plan is free of the stay. A post-petition creditor can subject that property to judicial process. A prepetition creditor, other than the holder of a valid lien, cannot reach any property of the debtor because the stay prevents any act to collect a prepetition debt. § 362(a)(6). The stay continues until the plan is completed at which point the debtor is discharged. Prepetition creditors are therefore limited to recovering under the plan and may not otherwise collect their debts unless the debtor fails to complete the plan.

A series of amendments added by the 2005 Act provide increased protection for the rights of claimants under "domestic support obligations" (DSO), defined in § 101(14A) to include alimony and support payments to spouses or children. One of these establishes that DSO claimants may withhold the postpetition earnings of debtors pursuant to judicial or administrative order or statute whether these earnings are property of the estate or of the debtor. § 362(b)(2)(C). This amendment allows a spouse or child to take a debtor's earnings even if those earnings are needed to fund the plan.

### c.   Conversion to Chapter 7

A large body of highly contradictory case law centers around what is property of the estate in the common case in which a Chapter 13 debtor converts to Chapter 7. As we have seen, under § 1306(a) property of the estate in Chapter 13 may include earnings and other property acquired by the debtor after filing the petition. Under § 541(a)(1), property of the estate in Chapter 7 consists of property owned by the debtor at the time of filing. When the debtor converts from Chapter 13 to Chapter 7, does the debtor's estate now include the property that the debtor acquired after the Chapter 13 filing? Section 348(a) states that in a conversion case the date of commencement of the case is the time of the original filing and not the time of the conversion. Thus, the debtor's Chapter 7 case is deemed to have been filed at the time of the Chapter 13 filing. This leads to the conclusion that only property owned by the debtor at the time of the Chapter 13 filing can be property of the estate after the conversion. But § 541(a)(7) points the other way by defining property of the estate in Chapter 7 as including "property that the estate acquires after the commencement of the case." The welter of conflicting cases on the subject are collected in 3 Keith Lundin, *Chapter 13 Bankruptcy* § 8.17 (2d ed.1994, Cum. Supp. 1997).

The much needed statutory clarification came in 1994 with the addition of § 348(f), which provides that, with respect to a conversion from Chapter 13 to Chapter 7, the property of the estate in the Chapter 7 case is only the property that the debtor had at the time of filing the Chapter 13 petition that is still in the possession of or under the control of the debtor on the date of the conversion. Thus, property acquired by the debtor after filing the Chapter 13 petition but before conversion to Chapter 7 is property of the debtor and not of the converted estate. The Section-by-Section

Description § 311, 140 Cong.Rec. H10770 (1994), justifies this resolution on the ground that a contrary view would create disincentive for debtors to file in Chapter 13 by depriving them of their postpetition property in case they later had to convert to Chapter 7. The amendment rejects the concern of Judge Posner in *In re Lybrook*, 951 F.2d 136 (7th Cir.1991), that to allow a Chapter 13 debtor to convert to Chapter 7 and keep all postpetition property encourages strategic conversions in cases in which the debtor, as in *Lybrook*, acquires substantial property after filing in Chapter 13.

## 6. THE PLAN

The requirements that the debtor must meet to confirm a Chapter 13 plan are, for the most part, found in § 1322 (contents of plan) and § 1325 (confirmation of plan). Before the 2005 Act, § 1322(a) prescribed only three mandatory requirements: (1) the plan must provide for payment to the trustee of all or part of the debtor's future earnings or income "as is necessary for the execution of the plan;" (2) the plan must provide for full payment of priority claims in deferred payments unless the claimant agrees to different treatment; and (3) if the plan classifies claims, the plan must provide the same treatment for each claim within a class. The 2005 Act added a fourth requirement regarding the duration of a plan involving DSO claims that is discussed below. § 1322(a)(4).

### a. Domestic Support Obligations

As we saw in Chapter 3 on Claims, women's and children's advocates urged Congress to shore up the position of children and spouses with respect to alimony, maintenance and support in the 2005 Act. As the rights of credit card issuers, retailers, motor vehicle financers and other consumer creditors improved under early drafts of the 2005 Act, less of the debtor's postpetition income remained to support children and ex-spouses. What these advocates wanted was, in substance, that bankruptcy not interfere with rights to collect support payments from debtors, that within the bankruptcy estate support obligations be given first dibs on the debtor's assets, and that a debtor not come out of Chapter 13 with a discharge unless current on support payments. Congress delivered.

Although some of these provisions are discussed further in this and other chapters, it is useful to summarize the amendments having relevance in Chapter 13 cases. Since a number of provisions throughout the 2005 Act are concerned with support provisions, the drafting approach was to define "domestic support obligations" ("DSO") in § 101(14A) as including alimony, maintenance or support payments owing to spouses, children and governmental units, as assignees for Social Security Act purposes, and to refer to the defined term in the substantive provisions of the Act.

DSO balances owing at the time of filing are accorded a first priority under § 507(a)(1), even ahead of administrative expenses (including lawyers fees!). A Chapter 13 plan must provide for full payment in deferred cash payments of all priority claims, unless the holder of the claim agrees to a different treatment. § 1322(a)(2). DSO payments coming due after the filing must be paid in full before the plan can be confirmed (§ 1325(a)(8)), and failure to keep payments current on DSOs before or after confirmation is grounds for dismissal. § 1307(c)(11). In calculating the debtor's "disposable income," DSO claims are included as "reasonably necessary" expenses, thus reducing the amount payable to other creditors. § 1325(b)(2). DSO claimants may garnish the pay of debtors without violating the automatic stay. § 362(b)(2)(C). DSO claims are nondischargeable, § 523(a)(5), § 1328(a)(2), and a discharge cannot be given in Chapter 13 unless the debtor certifies that all amounts payable under a DSO "that are due on or before the date of the certification (including amounts due before the petition was filed, but only to the extent provided for in the plan) have been paid." § 1328(a) (preamble). Debtors who are unable or unwilling to handle their DSOs will not find relief in Chapter 13.

### b.   Duration

A major change under the 2005 Act is lengthening the duration of Chapter 13 plans to five years for debtors whose annual incomes are not less than the state median family income for the relevant family size. For families with incomes under the median, the duration of a plan may not exceed three years unless the court, for cause, approves a longer period not in excess of five years. §§ 1322(d), 1325(b)(4). Plan duration may be less than three or five years, whichever is applicable, only if the plan provides full payment for all allowed unsecured claims over a shorter period. § 1325(b)(4)(B). Thus, debtors whose Chapter 7 cases are dismissed because of application of the means test and have annual income greater than or equal to the state median family income will find that Chapter 13 relief is available to them only under a five-year plan. In one instance, a five-year duration is mandated without respect to the amount of the debtor's income: a plan may provide for less than full payment of a DSO priority claim owing to a governmental unit (§ 507(a)(1)(B)) only if all the debtor's projected disposable income for a five-year period is applied to payment of this claim. § 1322(a)(4). Given that only one-third of the plans were sustainable for the three-year duration under pre-2005 law, there is no basis for optimism for the success of five-year plans under the 2005 Act.

### c.   Disposable Income

#### (i)   Before the 2005 Act

The legislative history quoted below indicates that Congress, in exchange for allowing debtors to keep their property and enjoy a super-discharge, contemplated in the 1978 Code that Chapter 13 plans would result in some payment to unsecured creditors:

> The purpose of chapter 13 is to enable an individual, under court supervision and protection, to develop and perform under a plan for

the repayment of his debts over an extended period. *In some cases, the plan will call for full repayment. In others, it may offer creditors a percentage of their claims in full settlement.* * * *

The benefit to the debtor of developing a plan of repayment under chapter 13, rather than opting for liquidation under chapter 7, is that it permits the debtor to protect his assets. In a liquidation case, the debtor must surrender his nonexempt assets for liquidation and sale by the trustee. *Under chapter 13, the debtor may retain his property by agreeing to repay his creditors.* Chapter 13 also protects a debtor's credit standing far better than a straight bankruptcy, because he is viewed by the credit industry as a better risk. In addition, it satisfies many debtors' desire to avoid the stigma attached to straight bankruptcy and to retain the pride attendant on being able to meet one's obligation. The benefit to creditors is self-evident: their losses will be significantly less than if their debtors opt for straight bankruptcy.

H.R.Rep. 95-595, 95th Cong., 1st Sess., reprinted in 1978 U.S.C.C.A.N. 6079 (emphasis added).

Years of controversy have centered around how much that payment must be. The only guidance in the original Code was the "best interests" test of § 1325(a)(4), which requires that unsecured creditors must receive as much in Chapter 13 as they would have received in a Chapter 7 liquidation, taking into account the fact that payment in Chapter 13 is on a deferred basis. However, in many cases, debtors, even those with substantial incomes, have no nonexempt assets, and in such cases, the best interests test, literally read, is satisfied by a "zero payment" plan that pays off secured creditors and gives unsecured creditors nothing, even though the debtor could afford to pay more. In these cases, debtors seemed to be getting a free super-discharge: they pay their secured creditors over time based on the current value of their encumbered property, and pay their unsecured creditors nothing. Judicial tolerance for zero payment plans has been low, and some courts rejected them as not being proposed in good faith under § 1325(a)(3). But judicial reaction has been uneven and unpredictable.

Clearly, the best interests test failed to assure unsecured creditors that they would receive payment under Chapter 13. Discontent from the creditor community led in 1984 to the requirement, imposed by former § 1325(b)(1)(B), that the plan include "all of the debtor's projected disposable income to be received in the three-year period" of the plan. "Disposable income" was defined as "income which is * * * not reasonably necessary to be expended for the maintenance or support of the debtor or a dependent of the debtor." Former § 1325(b)(2). Far from resolving the "how-much" problem, this language dragged bankruptcy courts into a fact-intensive morass. Judges not only had to become prognosticators (how can income be reliably predicted three years ahead?) but, much worse, life-style arbiters (what expenses are reasonably necessary for the debtor's family?). The National Bankruptcy Review Commission viewed the test as so indeterminate that it recommended dropping it altogether.

> [I]t is all too clear that after thirteen years' experience with the disposable income requirement, courts seem no closer to sharing a collective view of what constitutes "reasonably necessary expenses" than they were at the inception. Some courts believe that private schools are necessary, while others do not. Orthodontia, piano lessons, college tuition, home repairs, dry cleaning, newspapers, tithing, utility payments, and food allocations are just a few of the expenses that are scrutinized in this context. Personal views of what is and what is not necessary for the family inescapably factor into the equation. The amount that debtors must pay to their unsecured creditors will differ from courtroom to courtroom not because of different circumstances, but because of divergent views on the expenses perceived to be reasonably necessary. Because the inquiry is so fact-specific and non-legal, published opinions have little precedential value. Any party can threaten to litigate, knowing that there is some case law to support any position. The confusion over standards increases the leverage of any party with the resources and the stamina to fight about disposable income.

*NBRC Rep.* at 263-265.

The "Religious Liberty and Charitable Donation Protection Act of 1998" (Donation Protection Act) introduced further complications by adding charitable contributions, up to 15% of the debtor's gross income for the year in which the contributions are made, to the amounts for maintenance and support that are considered reasonably necessary to be expended by the debtor. Former § 1325(b)(2)(A). The Act says nothing about limiting the number of 15% gifts the debtor can make each year, nor is there a requirement that the debtor have a consistent practice of making charitable contributions, as would be true with debtors who tithe. Apparently, on the face of this provision, any debtor in Chapter 13 can make any number of annual gifts, each within the 15% ceiling, to a qualified charity at the expense of her creditors. This measure safeguards the right of Chapter 13 debtors to continue to tithe but, if pushed to its limits, might substantially reduce the amount that will be paid to creditors. Since the 15% ceiling is based on the debtor's gross income, the disposable income test could leave unsecured creditors with little or nothing. Kenneth N. Klee, *Tithing and Bankruptcy*, 75 Am. Bankr. L.J. 157, 186 (2001), suggests that abuse of the Donation Protection Act could bring back the zero payment plans that were approved by some judges before Congress imposed the disposable income test in 1984. The Donation Protection Act is also discussed in chapter 7 of the Casebook, *supra.*

### (ii)   The 2005 Act

Under the pre-2005 disposable income test, the higher debtors lived the less their unsecured creditors were likely to be paid, and they had no incentive to lower their living standards because the money saved would go to their creditors. Experience showed that debtors with good legal advice had little disposable income. *NBRC Rep.* at 266. The National Bankruptcy Review Commission recommended that payments on unsecured debts be determined by guidelines based on a graduated percentage of the debtors' income. *NBRC Rep.* at 262-273. In a limited way, the 2005 Act moves toward a more objective test for determining disposable income. Section § 1325(b) bifurcates debtors into those with annual incomes greater than the state median family income (§ 1325(b)(3)) and those with lesser incomes (§ 1325(b)(2)). For the lower income group, doubtless the much larger group in bankruptcy, the law remains much as it was: disposable income is determined by deducting "amounts reasonably necessary to be expended for the maintenance or support of the debtor or a dependent of the debtor" plus contributions to "qualified religious or charitable entit[ies] or organization[s]" (§ 548(d)(4)) in an amount not to exceed 15 % of the debtor's gross income. § 1325(b)(2). These debtors may deduct the amount of domestic support obligations. For the higher income group, the 2005 Act standardizes the amounts necessary to be expended by adopting the IRS standards that are incorporated into § 707(b)(2)(A) and (B) for calculating the means test. Now higher income debtors will have to commit all their income to Chapter 13 plans that is in excess of the IRS standards whatever the amount of their actual expenses unless they can show special circumstances that justify additional expenses. § 707(b)(2)(B). This could result in these debtors having to lower their standard of living.

Before the 2005 Act, debtors were ingenious in creating enough "reasonably necessary" expenses to limit the payout of "disposable income" to their creditors. On the face of it, § 1325(b)(3) will make this more difficult for debtors with above median income. That provision, unlike the paragraph that precedes it, makes no direct reference to including domestic support obligations and charitable or religious gifts in calculating disposable income. However, by incorporating the expenses set out for the means test in § 707(b)(2)(A) and (B), § 1325(b)(3) brings in both deductions for debtors with above median income. DSOs are priority claims covered by § 707(b)(2)(A)(iv), and any charitable or religious gifts that may fall under Other Necessary Expenses in § 707(b)(2)(A)(ii). *See* IRS, Handbook 105.1 p. 17 (2001). As indicated above, a debtor can reduce her disposable income by adding charitable donations to her Chapter 13 plan. The dark side of this is that it is difficult for standing trustees to monitor whether the debtor is really making these gifts over the term of the plan.

Thus, the 2005 Act resolves the contentious issues regarding the duration of Chapter 13 repayment plans and the amounts unsecured creditors must receive by adopting a bifurcated approach, differentiating between lower income and higher income debtors. Since the lower income groups have incomes lower than the state median for their family group and location, they are not excluded from Chapter 7 by the means test and have a choice between Chapters 7 and 13. With respect to the three-year duration of plans and the amounts debtors must pay to fund these plans, the law remains largely unchanged. Members of the higher income group may find themselves excluded from Chapter 7 by the means test and left with only the alternatives of filing in Chapters 13 or 11 or facing their creditors under state collection law. The 2005 Act has made Chapter 13 less attractive for this group by requiring them to submit to five-year plans and to devote all their income to funding the plan above the IRS levels for reasonable expenses, whatever their actual expenditures are. As we said above, under pre-2005 law opportunistic behavior in manipulating "reasonable expenses" could unfairly limit the amount of repayment available to creditors, but use of the low IRS standards for family expenses under the 2005 Act may endanger the viability of the plan by leaving the debtor with insufficient funds to meet the demands of the plan over a five-year stretch. Given other barriers to completion of a Chapter 13 plan, discussed below, the harried higher income debtor may conclude that no feasible bankruptcy relief is available.

Nor, as we will see below, does much else in the 2005 Act make Chapter 13 any more attractive to debtors. Changes in the treatment of secured creditors make it more difficult for Chapter 13 debtors to retain property subject to security interests, such as automobiles. The super-discharge is no longer very super, and in most cases is no more broad than the discharge available in Chapter 7.  The avowed thrust of the 2005 Act is to induce debtors to pay more of their debts to earn a discharge, and Chapter 13 offers a process for debtors to pay their debts, while  Chapter 7 is viewed as a method for avoiding such payment. But new Chapter 13 offers reduced benefits and increased burdens to debtors, and we are left with a paradox: debtors who might have preferred old Chapter 13 may be more likely to file in Chapter 7 under the new Act if they are eligible to do so.  Although Chapter 13 never attained the popularity the drafters of the 1978 Code had hoped for, debtor payments under Chapter 13, as indicated earlier in the chapter, had risen to over $4 billion annually. Bankruptcy judges are concerned that the 2005 changes in Chapter 13 will undermine the very provision of the law in which debtors are repaying significant amounts to their creditors. The leading authority on Chapter 13, Judge Keith Lundin, cautions: "The folks who brought you 'those who can pay, should pay' are pulling the stuffing out of the very part of the bankruptcy law where debtors do pay." Peter G. Gosselin, *Judges Say Overhaul Would Weaken Bankruptcy System*, L.A. Times, Mar. 29, 2005, at A1. Although before the 2005 Act estimates were that a Chapter 13 filer could usually expect to pay between $1,500 and $2,000 for legal fees, after fees will surely be higher.

## PROBLEM

The court confirmed Debtor's Chapter 13 plan that proposed to pay 50% of the claims of unsecured creditors out of all her disposable income over a three-year period. Shortly after confirmation, Debtor sold real property that she owned at the time of her petition, and, after payment of all encumbrances, received $20,000 for the property. Trustee moved to modify Debtor's plan to include the proceeds of the sale as disposable income. Section 1325(b)(2) defines disposable income as meaning "income received by the debtor." Should the Trustee's motion be granted? *See In re Burgie*, 239 B.R. 406 (9th Cir. B.A.P. 1999).

### d. Payments "Outside the Plan"

Once a Chapter 13 plan is confirmed, the court may issue a payroll deduction order under which the debtor's employer must pay the required amount to the standing trustee for distribution to creditors entitled to payment under the plan. Or, the plan may provide for the debtor to pay the required amounts to the trustee. The advantage in having the trustee as the disbursing agent is that if the debtor were allowed to pay creditors directly without notifying the trustee, the trustee might not learn whether payments were being made unless creditors complained; the situation could become chaotic and difficult to administer.

In the case of a residential mortgage, however, the debtor is commonly allowed to make payments directly to the creditor. This is referred to as making payments "outside the plan." A justification for allowing a debtor to do this in the case of a residential mortgage is that the debtor usually owes the same payments on the mortgage after confirmation as before, and these payments will continue after the plan is completed because debtors are not discharged from long-term debts. § 1328(a)(1). The clear implication from § 1326(c) is that the court may approve a plan allowing the debtor to act as disbursing agent, and the residential mortgage case is an appropriate one for so designating the debtor. *In re Aberegg*, 961 F.2d 1307 (7th Cir.1992).

The 2005 Act expressly requires direct payments in certain cases. In its vigilance to safeguard the interests of lessors and secured creditors in Chapter 13 cases, the Act requires that, within 30 days after filing, with respect to amounts coming due after filing, debtors must make direct payments of rentals to personal property lessors and of adequate protection payments to creditors having security interests in personal property. § 1326(a)(1)(B) and (C). The payments required under the proposed plan to the trustee under § 1326(a)(1)(A) are reduced by the amounts of these payments, and, in order to keep the trustee informed, the debtor must provide the trustee with evidence of these direct payments. After confirmation of the plan the terms of the plan determine whether the payments are made directly to the creditors or to the trustee. § 1326(c).

Is the trustee entitled to claim a fee with respect to payments disbursed by the debtor in such cases? 28 U.S.C. § 586(e)(2) gives the trustee fees only on "payments received by [the trustee] under plans * * *." *Aberegg* concluded that under this provision the trustee is not entitled to a commission on funds disbursed by the debtor directly to a creditor. In deciding whether direct payments from the debtors to the creditor were appropriate, the court in *In re Slaughter*, 188 B.R. 29 (Bankr.D.N.D.1995), took into consideration the fact that if the debtors were required to pay the trustee's 10% fee, amounting to $1,700 annually, on payments made through the trustee, the plan would be infeasible for the debtors to carry out.

### e.   Modification of Plan

Some debtors who file in Chapter 13 have had a troubled financial past and face an unstable future. During the three- to five-year period of the plan, their income may be affected by employment disruptions and illnesses; moreover, the expenses necessary for the maintenance and support of their families may change. Accordingly, § 1329(a) allows for postconfirmation modification of a plan upon request of the debtors, the unsecured creditors or the trustee, which may increase or reduce the amounts of payments and, under § 1329(c), extend or reduce the term of the plan within the term limits stated in §§ 1322(d) and 1325(b)(4). Section 1329(a) states no threshold requirement that there be a change in the debtor's circumstances for when a court should approve a proposed modification. Section 1329(b) merely provides that the plan as modified must meet the same requirements as the original plan with respect to the contents of the plan (§ 1322(a) and (b)) and the provisions of § 1325(a), such as the value to be distributed to creditors and the good faith of the proponents. Must a court approve any modification meeting these basic standards? As chronicled in 2 Keith M. Lundin, *Chapter 13 Bankruptcy* § 6.42 *et seq.* (2d ed.1994, Cum. Supp. 1997), many bankruptcy court opinions have dealt with aspects of this question, and it is not surprising, given the lack of guidance found in the statute, that their views have differed. As in so many other areas of Chapter 13, appeals are rare, authoritative appellate opinions are few, and the unpublished and varying practices of the local bankruptcy courts effectively govern.

The most common reason for seeking modification of a plan is a change in circumstances with respect to the debtor's income. In such a case, if the court believes that the modification is proposed in good faith (§ 1325(a)(3)), and the debtor will be able to make the payments under the modified plan (§ 1325(a)(6)), the modification is likely to be approved, often without opposition from creditors who would receive even less in Chapter 7. We should assume that the modified plan must meet the disposable income test under § 1325(b), although the omission of any reference to § 1325(b) in § 1329(b) is baffling. In *In re Hoggle*, 12 F.3d 1008 (11th Cir.1994), the debtors were allowed to modify their plans in order to cure postconfirmation defaults in payments on their mobile home mortgages. The court construed § 1322(b)(5) to mean that a debtor may cure a default on a secured claim even though the default is postpetition. Accord, *In re Mendoza*, 111 F.3d 1264 (5th Cir.1997).

In *In re Witkowski*, 16 F.3d 739 (7th Cir.1994), the plan called for unsecured creditors to receive a fixed percentage of their claims, in this case 10%, over a period of 47 months. Fewer creditors than expected filed claims and the trustee moved to modify the plan to require a 19% payment. The bankruptcy court's approval of the modification was affirmed. The case is notable for its rejection of the view adopted by a number of cases that the proponent of a modification must meet a threshold requirement of showing an unanticipated, substantial change in the debtor's financial circumstances. The court found no such requirement in § 1329 and declined to imply one. The differing views on the threshold requirements for modification are discussed in *Barbosa v. Soloman*, 235 F. 3d 31 (1st Cir. 2000). In that case the debtors' confirmed plan called for payment with interest of a mortgage on real property retained by debtors and payment of a dividend of 10% of the unsecured claims. After confirmation the property was sold and brought 215% of the valuation stipulated by the parties at the time of confirmation. The court allowed the trustee to modify the plan to require payment of 100% of the unsecured claims. In rejecting the debtors' contention that modification was inappropriate because the sale was not unanticipated, the court adopted the *Witkowski* view, but noted that as a practical matter parties seeking modification must have a legitimate reason for doing so and must strictly conform to the limited circumstances set forth in § 1329. Even though there is no requirement of changed circumstances in the statute, the existence of changed circumstances bears on the debtor's good faith in proposing the modification. 2 Keith M. Lundin, *Chapter 13 Bankruptcy* § 6.47 (2d ed. 1994, Cum. Supp. 1997).

### f.    Classification of Unsecured Claims

Section 1322(b)(1) allows for classification of unsecured claims so long as all claims within each class are substantially similar (as required in § 1122(a)) and are treated the same (§ 1322(a)(3)), but the debtor's plan may not unfairly discriminate between the classes. We will find in the next chapter that creditors vote on a debtor's Chapter 11 plan by classes; hence, classification may play an important role in the debtor's strategy for gaining acceptance of the plan. In Chapter 13 debtors do not have to obtain the approval of creditors for the plan; the court confirms the plan if it meets the requirements of § 1325. Thus, the reason for a debtor to have separate classes of nonpriority unsecured claims in Chapter 13 is the desire to prefer one class over another in terms of how much the members of each class are paid. The only guidance offered by the Code to govern the degree of discrimination permitted is that it must not be unfair. There are innumerable bankruptcy court cases on the meaning of "discriminate unfairly" (§ 1322(b)(1)), and they differ widely in their interpretation of the term. Relatively few court of appeals decisions shed any light on the issue. The problem is treated extensively in 1 Keith M. Lundin, *Chapter 13 Bankruptcy* § 4.60 *et seq.* (2d ed.1994, Cum. Supp. 1997).

Among the first cases on unfair discrimination in classification were those in which the debtor classified a debt separately on which there was a cosigner and proposed to pay the holder of the claim a greater percentage than that allocated to holders of other unsecured claims. In *Barnes v. Whe-*

*lan*, 689 F.2d 193 (D.C.Cir.1982), the debtor's plan called for 100% payment on a cosigned debt and only 1% on the other unsecured claims. The motive of debtors in these cosigner cases was to safeguard the cosigner, usually a family member or friend, from having to pay the debt, an obligation that the debtor would feel morally obligated to pay later. *Barnes* took the position that although there was a rational basis for classifying co-signed debts separately, still a 99% differential was unfair. Other cases disagreed, and Congress undertook to clarify the issue by the addition of the "however" clause to § 1322(b)(1). The question left open by the amendment is how "differently" can Chapter 13 plans treat cosigned debts. May it pay them in full even though other classes of claims receive nothing, or may courts continue to examine the classification of cosigned claims on fairness grounds? In *In re Ramirez*, 204 F.3d 595 (5th Cir. 2000), the court denied confirmation of a plan that paid the cosigner debt in full plus 12% interest, prior to any payments to other unsecured claims. The court found no justification for "such a high and preferential interest rate." 204 F.3d at 596. Under § 502(b)(2), unsecured debts do not accrue interest after filing. The difficulty in determining when unfair discrimination is present is addressed in the following case.

## In re Crawford

United States Court of Appeals, Seventh Circuit, 2003.
324 F.3d 539.

■   POSNER, Circuit Judge:

Wayne Crawford appeals from the district court's affirmance of the bankruptcy court's refusal to confirm his Chapter 13 plan. Chapter 13 is a counterpart to Chapter 11 (reorganization) but designed for individuals of modest means. *In re Heath,* 115 F.3d 521, 522 (7th Cir.1997). It enables an individual, as an alternative to the liquidation of his assets, to submit for approval by the bankruptcy court a plan for paying his creditors as much as possible over a period of years, upon completion of which he is given a discharge of his remaining dischargeable debts. Crawford's appeal requires us to consider the circumstances in which and the degree to which a Chapter 13 debtor may shift the burden of a nondischargeable debt from his shoulders to those of his unsecured creditors by invocation of § 1322(b)(1), which provides that a Chapter 13 plan may "designate a class or class of unsecured claims. . . but may not discriminate unfairly against any class so designated." Classification is not unique to Chapter 13; it is available under other chapters of the Bankruptcy Code as well. *See* §§§ 901(a), 1122(a), 1222(b)(1).

Crawford's nonpriority unsecured debts consist of some $19,000 owed the IRS; $18,000 owed the county as a result of Crawford's having been delinquent for a period in his child support payments (he is now current) and the county's having paid welfare to the mother and taken in exchange an assignment of her entitlement to child support; and $500 owed to a pair of trade creditors. The debt that Crawford owes the county is nondischargeable. § 523(a)(5)(A).

The plan proposed to divide Crawford's debts into two classes, one consisting of the debt to the county and the other of the other debts. The county debt would be paid first and only after it was paid in full would he begin to pay the debts of the second class. Originally the plan envisaged that over the course of its three years the county debt would be paid in full with enough left over to pay the other unsecured creditors between 3 and 6 percent of what they were owed. But this was contingent on Crawford's prevailing in a dispute he had with the IRS. He did not prevail and as a result the plan had to be amended. Under the amended plan, the county debt will not be paid in full but two-thirds of it will be paid, while the other unsecured creditors will get nothing at all, whereas without the preferred treatment of the county debt but with the same aggregate level of periodic payment as under the amended plan each unsecured creditor would receive roughly 32 cents on the dollar.

Section 1322(b) of the Bankruptcy Code, while forbidding as we have said classifications that discriminate unfairly against creditors, does not explain what "unfairly" means in this context. The courts have striven to formulate a more precise standard for determining the legitimacy of classifications proposed by Chapter 13 debtors, but without success.

A number of cases use a four-factor test: "1) whether the discrimination has a reasonable basis; 2) whether the debtor can carry out a plan without the discrimination; 3) whether the discrimination is proposed in good faith; and 4) whether the degree of discrimination is directly related to the basis or rationale for the discrimination." *In re Leser,* 939 F.2d 669, 672 (8th Cir.1991) * * * . With respect, this test is empty except for point 2, which does identify an important factor bearing on the reasonableness of a classification, as we shall illustrate shortly.

Another test one finds in some cases is whether the debtor has a "legitimate" basis for the classification. *In re Brown,* 152 B.R. 232, 237-40 (Bankr.N.D.Ill.), reversed under the name *McCullough v. Brown,* 162 B.R. 506 (N.D.Ill.1993) * * * . This, if it means anything, leans too far in favor of the debtor (as Judge Shadur explained in his opinion reversing the bankruptcy judge's decision in the *Brown* case), as it gives no consideration to the interest of creditors. The first test, the four-factor one, also fails to mention the creditors' interests, at least explicitly.

A third test insists that the classification presumptively give the disfavored creditors at least 80 percent of what they would get without the classification, *In re Sullivan,* 195 B.R. 649, 656 (Bankr.W.D.Tex.1996), and a fourth test adds a similar consideration as a fifth factor to the four-factor *Leser* test. * * * The third test is arbitrary, and the fourth test makes the first collapse of its own weight.

We haven't been able to think of a good test ourselves. We conclude, at least provisionally, that this is one of those areas of the law in which it is not possible to do better than to instruct the first-line decision maker, the bankruptcy judge, to seek a result that is reasonable in light of the purposes of the relevant law, which in this case is Chapter 13 of the Bankruptcy Code; and to uphold his determination unless it is unreasonable (an abuse of discretion). This approach has support in *In re Bentley,* 266 B.R. 229, 239-40 (1st Cir. B.A.P. 2001), and 8 *Collier on Bankruptcy* ¶ 1322.05 (15th ed.2002), as well as in the statutory language of "unfair" discrimination against creditors. It is true that the use of "fair" in a statute or a legal doctrine need not preclude judicial development of a particularized standard; the "fair use" doctrine of copyright law and the "duty of fair representation" in labor law have considerable structure, and other examples could be given. But success has not attended efforts to give comparable structure to the classification provision of Chapter 13.

Mention of the statute's language should at least serve to remind bankruptcy judges that Chapter 13 is designed for the protection of creditors as well as debtors. * * * It is true that only the debtor can invoke Chapter 13. But he may not use it to deny consideration of the legitimate interest of creditors in repayment. * * * This point implies, however, that if without classification the debtor is unlikely to be able to fulfill a Chapter 13 plan and the result will be to make his creditors as a whole worse off than they would be with classification, then classification will be a win-win outcome. Suppose the debtor is a truck driver and one of his creditors is the state driver's license bureau which unless paid in full will yank his license, with the consequence that he won't have earnings out of which to make the payments called for in his plan. Or suppose the creditor is a supplier of the tools of the debtor's trade, and unless paid in full will cut him off and thereby prevent him from plying his trade, again with the result of depriving him of the earnings he needs to fund his plan. The creditor might be the supplier of the bottled gas that the debtor uses to heat his home, and if not paid in full will refuse to sell him more gas. (We use this example rather than that of natural gas or electricity because a public utility is not permitted to refuse to restore service because of nonpayment of fees incurred before the filing of a bankruptcy petition, § 366(a) (2003) * * * .) All these are substantial cases for a classification that will permit one creditor or class of creditors to be paid disproportionately to the rest because the creditors as a whole will be better off and so will the debtor. * * *

At the other extreme is a nondischargeable debt consisting of a fine imposed, or restitution ordered, in respect of a criminal fraud that the Chapter 13 debtor committed, together with other unsecured debts, and he proposes a classification under which the nondischargeable debt will be paid in full and the other creditors will receive nothing at all. Approval of such a plan would be unreasonable. * * * The effect of the plan if approved in such a case would be to make the debtor's other unsecured creditors pay his fine or restitution!

Crawford's rejected plan lies in between our examples, but it is closer to the second and close enough to require us to affirm its rejection. The nonpayment of child support is a serious matter and in fact a nationwide problem, which is why Congress has determined that child-support debts, of which the debt owed the county is a version, are nondischargeable. The retributive and deterrent interests are weaker than in the case of a deliberate criminal act, since nonpayment can be involuntary as well as voluntary; but no reason has been shown for allowing Crawford to shift two-thirds of this debt to his other unsecured creditors. Had he proposed to carve-down his nondischargeable debt to the principal owed on it (roughly $12,000), and had he shown that without such a carve-down he would be staggering under such a crushing load of undischarged debt as to make it inevitable or nearly so that he would soon be back in bankruptcy court, this time under Chapter 7, the bankruptcy court might deem such a plan reasonable and we presumably would affirm—especially if the unsecured creditors would do worse in Chapter 7 than they would do under Crawford's revised Chapter 13 plan. It is true that he has a previous Chapter 7 discharge and so must wait six years from the filing of his previous Chapter 7 petition before seeking another such discharge. 11 U.S.C. § 727(a). But although we don't know the exact date of his previous filing, we do know that he received his discharge in September 1997 and this means that he'll be eligible to file another Chapter 7 petition no later than September of this year—for all we know, he can do so right now.

We do not hold that child-support debts, or, as in this case, a debt arising from the assignment of the right to child support, cannot be classified. Nor do we hold that Crawford cannot formulate an acceptable plan that would involve an element of classification. We hold only that the bankruptcy court did not abuse its discretion in rejecting, as an unfair discrimination against his other creditors, the plan he proposed, which would if approved have shifted two-thirds of his nondischargeable debt to his other creditors, leaving them with nothing.

AFFIRMED.

## NOTES

**1.** Judge Posner is recognized as a leading business law jurist and his opinions are frequently cited. What should this case be cited for? Although he forswears setting forth comprehensive standards for determining unfair discrimination, he does offer some baseline principles. How would you state those principles?

**2.** An area of controversy has been the extent to which student loan debts can be preferentially classified. In 1990, § 1328(a) was amended to make such debts nondischargeable in Chapter 13, and debtors began to propose plans paying off their student loans in full with only nominal allocations for other unsecured claims. Assume the following facts: Debtors financed part of their college education through student loans. They live in an apartment; their possessions, including an automobile, are entirely exempt under state law. They owe $25,000 in student loans and, owing to their excessive use of credit cards in the early years of their marriage, $50,000 to a variety of other creditors. They are behind in some of their payments and are being pressed by their creditors. They have consulted a financial counselor and have decided to turn over a new leaf and clear up their financial problems so that in the future they can consider buying a house and having a family. They do not wish to have a Chapter 7 discharge on their credit record because they believe that it would inhibit their ability to obtain a home loan later on. They file in Chapter 13 and propose a five-year plan classifying their student loans separately from their other unsecured debts. The portion of their annual income that qualifies as "disposable" is $6,000. The plan calls for $5,000 per year to be devoted to paying their student loans and $1,000 per year to be paid on the debts owed to their "other creditors." By the end of the plan, Debtors will have paid off all of their student loans but only 10% of the debts owing to their other creditors. Should the court deny confirmation on the ground that the plan unfairly discriminates against the other creditors under § 1322(b)(1)?

The bankruptcy court in the *Brown* case, cited by Judge Posner for its support of the "legitimate basis" for classification, upheld such a plan on the following reasoning: In order to be fair under § 1322(b)(1), the classification must rationally further an articulated, legitimate interest of the debtor. The interest of the debtor must be controlling because the right to preferentially classify is one of the incentives placed in Chapter 13 by Congress to induce debtors to choose Chapter 13 over Chapter 7 under which creditors must be paid pro rata. The legitimate interest of the debtor is to gain a fresh start and preferential classification may be utilized to achieve this goal. So long as the other creditors are paid as much as they would have received in Chapter 7 (§ 1325(a)(4)), they are not prejudiced by preferential classification; creditors have no right to pro rata payment in Chapter 13. If debtors were to exercise their right to convert to Chapter 7, the other creditors would get nothing and debtors would have their postpetition income to pay off their nondischargeable student loans. The right of a debtor to preferentially classify nondischargeable debts should be limited only by the requirement that the plan be filed in good faith. § 1325(a)(3). Debtors have not engaged in misconduct or abuse of the bankruptcy system; preferential classification of a nondischargeable debt does not in itself constitute bad faith. The district court promptly reversed. *See In re Brown*, 152 B.R. 232 (Bankr.N.D.Ill.1993), *rev'd, McCullough v. Brown*, 162 B.R. 506 (N.D.Ill.1993),

The contrary view is found in *In re Chapman*, 146 B.R. 411 (Bankr. N.D.Ill.1992), which rejected a similar plan on the following reasoning: Section 1322(b)(1)'s prohibition against unfair discrimination is a creditor protection device. Conceding that § 1322(b) allows debtors to discriminate in a reasonable manner in classifying claims and that debtors are in good faith in this case, still the plan unfairly imposes on the other creditors the burden of paying the debtors' student loans. The benefits run entirely to debtors who have an education at the expense of the other creditors.

When Congress made student loans nondischargeable in Chapter 13 in 1990, it could have provided a special classification for student loans, as it did for cosigned consumer debts in 1984 (§ 1322(b)(1)), or could have made payments of student loans a priority in Chapter 13. It did neither, hence, there is no reason to believe that Congress intended to favor student loans in Chapter 13 by, in effect, subordinating the claims of other creditors. Bankruptcy is not merely for the relief of impecunious debtors; Chapter 13 requires a balancing of the debtors' need for a fresh financial start against the creditors' right to fair treatment. Debtors' plan does not fairly balance these interests and should not be confirmed.

### g.   Secured Claims in Personal Property

#### (i)   In Chapter 7

The treatment of secured claims in Chapter 13 is best understood by viewing it first in the context of the Chapter 7 alternative. Take as an example the most common, and usually the most valuable, piece of personal property owned by consumer debtors: an automobile. Suppose Debtor owns a car, subject to a perfected purchase money security interest held by Seller that secures an unpaid loan balance of $18,000. Assume the value of this hard-driven vehicle is now only $15,000. Debtor's financial condition is such that bankruptcy relief is imperative, but she wishes to retain the car, which she needs to drive to work because of the absence of public transportation. Since she has no equity in the car, a Chapter 7 trustee would likely abandon the vehicle to her (§ 554(a)), subject to Seller's security interest. Although she is behind on her large credit card debts, she has never missed a car payment and would like to work out a deal with Seller under which she could retain possession of the car after filing. What do Chapters 7 and 13 offer her?

If she files in Chapter 7, her alternatives are not inviting: she can either redeem the car pursuant to § 722 or reaffirm her obligation to Seller under § 524(c). In order to redeem she would have to pay Seller the amount of its allowed secured claim, which under § 506(a)(1) is $15,000, the value of the car. On its face, this is not a bad deal: she pays $15,000, gets to keep her car, and the $3,000 deficiency is discharged as an unsecured claim. But § 722 requires that the $15,000 must be paid in cash at the time of the redemption, and she doesn't have the money. Reaffirmation is also unappealing, for the Seller may insist that she be allowed to keep her car only by, in effect, waiving her discharge and assuming liability for the full $18,000 owed under the original obligation. If she later faltered on her car payments, Seller could repossess and get a judgment against her for the deficiency remaining after foreclosure sale. Debtor could not obtain discharge of this judgment in a subsequent Chapter 7 for another eight years. § 727(a)(8).

Before 2005, some courts allowed debtors to retain possession of their automobiles, without the consent of their secured creditors, without either redeeming or reaffirming merely by keeping their payments current after filing. This practice is referred to as "ride-through." See, *e.g.*, *In re Boodrow*, 126 F.3d 43 (2d Cir. 1997). The 2005 Act ended that practice.  The automatic stay is terminated and the car is no longer property of the estate, unless she, within 45 days, both files a statement of intention indicating that Debtor either surrenders the property or, if retaining it, will either redeem or reaffirm, and follows the statement with timely action consistent with it. §§ 362(h)(1), 521(a)(6). However, terminating the stay merely allows Seller to proceed under nonbankruptcy law to enforce its security interest. Debtor may contend that Seller cannot repossess the car because she is not in default under the security agreement. Seller will point out to Debtor the clause in the security agreement that declares Debtor to be in default if she files in bankruptcy. Before the 2005 Act some courts refused to enforce default-on-filing clauses, also known as bankruptcy or ipso facto clauses, even though no specific provision of the Code invalidated them in repossession cases. Under the 2005 Act, § 521(d) specifically validates use of such clauses in cases in which a debtor fails to redeem or reaffirm within the statutory period.

## PROBLEM

Assume that Debtor in the case described above files in Chapter 7 and fails to redeem the car or reaffirm the car loan within the statutory period. In negotiations with Seller, she informally indicates that she will continue to make the regular payments under the contract if Seller allows her to retain possession of the collateral. She tells Seller that it has nothing to lose: if she makes all her payments, Seller wins, and if she later defaults, Seller can repossess the automobile. If Debtor receives a discharge in Chapter 7, what does Seller have to lose by allowing her to keep the car?

### (ii)  In Chapter 13

Under the fact situation stated at the beginning of the section, the 1978 version of Chapter 13 offered Debtor a favorable option. Her plan could, without Seller's consent, strip down Seller's lien to the amount of the allowed secured claim, which under § 506(a) is $15,000, and permit Debtor to pay off this amount in installments with interest. This "cramdown" was authorized by former § 1325(a)(5)(B), which stated that a plan modifying the rights of secured creditors could be confirmed if it provided that the secured party retains the lien and the plan provides for deferred payments over the life of the plan with a present value equal to the secured claim. The $3,000 unsecured deficiency claim could be classified with the other unsecured claims and paid off pro rata over the life of the plan, usually at a pennies on the dollar. One of the principal incentives for debtors to opt for Chapter 13 was this power to engage in lien-stripping to retain possession of automobiles and other items of personal property while shifting the costs of prepetition depreciation to the holders of security interests. It allowed debtors to do in Chapter 13 what they could not do under § 722 in

Chapter 7: retain their property by paying in installments the present value of the property over the life of the plan.

The 2005 Act limits lien-stripping with respect to purchase money security interests in motor vehicles, as well as in certain other collateral. This is done by making inapplicable the bifurcation effect of § 506, in which an undersecured claim is divided into a secured claim for the value of the collateral and an unsecured claim for the remainder of the debt. The following language is added at the end of § 1325(a):

> For the purposes of paragraph (5), section 506 shall not apply to a claim described in that paragraph if the creditor has a purchase money security interest securing the debt that is the subject of the claim, the debt was incurred within the 910-day period preceding the filing of the petition, and the collateral for that debt consists of a motor vehicle * * * acquired for the personal use of the debtor, or if collateral for that debt consists of any other thing of value, if the debt was incurred during the 1-year period preceding that filing.

After this amendment, if Debtor wishes to retain her car by making installment payments to Seller under her Chapter 13 plan, the balance she must pay (with interest) over the life of the plan is $18,000 rather than $15,000, the value of the secured claim under § 506(a). Treating undersecured purchase money automobile loans as fully secured reduces the amount of a debtor's disposable income payable to unsecured creditors to the great advantage of secured auto lenders. The effect is similar to reaffirmation of such debts. There is little incentive for the buyer to retain the car under such circumstances. Since paying off auto loans at the depreciated value of the vehicles allowed distressed debtors a reduction in their car payments, it was a major attraction for debtors to file in Chapter 13; abrogation of this practice in the 2005 Act removes a major incentive for debtors to opt for that chapter.

The purpose of the language in the amendment quoted above that does not relate to motor vehicles is obscure. It abrogates lien-stripping with respect to purchase money security interests in "any other thing of value" if the debt secured was incurred within one year of filing. What Congress had in mind for this provision has yet to be revealed, but its very breadth assures the inevitability of unintended consequences. Since the largest unsecured debt most consumer debtors have is their credit card balances, the death of lien-stripping in automobile financing under the provision quoted above, which allocates more of a debtor's income to secured auto financiers and less to unsecured creditors, would seem to be a blow to credit card issuers. But, in recent years, there has been a trend toward requiring credit card holders to grant security interests in the goods purchased by use of the card. This amendment would give retailers taking security interests in goods bought with credit cards an advantage over other unsecured creditors with respect to goods still unpaid for at the time of bankruptcy that had been purchased within one year of the bankruptcy. However, there are difficult operational problems in calculating the purchase money status of goods purchased under the open-end revolving charge accounts commonly used in credit card sales, and it may be that the amendment will be of little use to credit card issuers.

A complementary provision is § 1325(a)(5)(B)(i), which requires as a condition of confirmation that the plan provide that the secured party retain a lien on the collateral until payment of the underlying debt determined under nonbankruptcy law or until discharge of the debtor under § 1328, whichever is earlier. Under nonbankruptcy law a creditor has a lien on collateral for the full unpaid balance of the obligation secured, whatever the value of the collateral. Most Chapter 13 plans are not completed, and under § 1325(a)(5)(B)(i)(II) the plan must provide that if the case is dismissed or converted before the plan is completed, Seller retains a lien to the extent recognized by nonbankruptcy law. Assume that the original balance that Debtor owed Seller to finance the car was $18,000, but that at the time Debtor's case was dismissed Debtor had paid enough to reduce the balance owed to $15,000; owing to depreciation, the value of the car at that time was only $14,000. The creditor's lien on the car is for the amount of the full balance owed, $15,000. Thus, Debtor has paid $3,000 on a car now worth only $14,000, but the car is still subject to a lien for the full $15,000 amount of the unpaid balance. The effect is that all the payments made during the bankruptcy before dismissal are allocated first to the unsecured portion of the debt, here $4,000.

Section 1325(a)(5)(B)(iii) is added to require that periodic payments to secured creditors called for by the plan "shall be in equal monthly amounts" and "not be less than an amount sufficient to provide to the holder of such claim adequate protection during the period of the plan." Thus, balloon payments and other irregular payments are barred, and the payments must be adequate to protect the creditor against decline in value of the collateral. Uncertainties over the measure of adequate protection, together with the requirement of regular payments, may push debtors that wish to retain their cars toward plans that pay secured creditors the amounts called for in the loan agreement.

All told, the provisions on the treatment of secured claims constitute a major disincentive to debtors to file in Chapter 13. With respect to purchase money security interests in motor vehicles acquired within 910 days before the debtor's filing, debtors must treat the secured creditor's claim as fully secured, whatever the value of the collateral, and pay it off accordingly. § 1325(a)(final paragraph). Moreover, unless the debtor completes her plan (something that happens in only about one-third of the cases), the secured creditor retains a lien for the remaining unpaid amount. § 1325(a)(5)(B)(i)(II).

## PROBLEM

Secured Party (SP) sold Debtor for family use a unit consisting of a computer, monitor and printer ("the unit") and retained a perfected security interest in the unit to secure $10,000, the unpaid portion of the purchase price. Two years later Debtor filed in Chapter 13. She wished to retain possession of these goods so that her children could continue to use them for school work. The value of the goods at the time of Debtor's filing was $6,000 as fixed by the bankruptcy court, and her remaining obligation to SP was $8,000. Debtor's plan proposed that: she pay SP $6,000 plus interest over the life of the plan, and the $2,000 unpaid balance be classified as an unsecured claim and paid off pro rata with other unsecured claims at 5% on the dollar. Debtor's disposable income was adequate to make the required payments over the three-year duration of the plan. The plan complied with § 1325(a)(5)(B)(i) in providing that SP retains a lien on the unit until the earlier of Debtor's discharge under § 1328 or payment of the underlying debt determined under nonbankruptcy law, and that if the case is dismissed or converted before completion, SP's lien shall be retained until the underlying debt is paid.

(a) Should the court confirm Debtor's plan under § 1325(a)(5)?

(b) Debtor was unable to complete her plan and her case was dismissed after she had paid SP $3,000 on the secured claim and $150 on the unsecured claim. SP claimed a lien on the unit in the amount of the remaining $5,850 unpaid on the original contract. Is SP correct? § 1325(a)(5)(B)(i)(II).

*(iii) Valuation of Collateral*

If a Chapter 13 debtor wishes to retain collateral and the secured creditor will not consent, the debtor may "cramdown" the secured creditor's security interest under § 1325(a)(5). The debtor may retain the collateral only if the plan provides that the secured party receives the present value of the secured claim. In order to determine this amount, the court must value the collateral and set an interest rate that will assure the creditor this value in deferred payments over the term of the plan. In giving directions for how to value the secured creditor's claim, § 506(a)(1) paints with a broad brush: "Such value shall be determined in the light of the purpose of the valuation and of the proposed disposition or use of such property * * *." The two most common cases in which the amount of the creditor's secured claim had to be determined in consumer debtor cases under the 1978 Code were with respect to redemption in Chapter 7 under § 722 and cramdown in Chapter 13 under § 1325(a)(5)(B). Litigation on the valuation issue has centered on whether a retail or wholesale value is appropriate. Creditors, favoring a high valuation, contend that a retail valuation is appropriate because the debtor will continue to use the automobile and should have to pay its replacement cost–the retail price. Debtors, seeking a low valuation, assert that the value of the creditor's interest is what the creditor would receive for the automobile at a foreclosure sale of a repossessed automobile, often an auction sale to dealers. In *Associates Commercial Corp. v. Rash*, reprinted *supra* in chapter 3, the Supreme Court undertook to resolve the contentious cramdown issue, holding the previously unknown concept of "replacement value" (which it defined as retail value less costs of resale, warranties and accessions not subject to the lien) was the appropriate metric for valuing collateral to be retained under a Chapter 13 plan.

Under § 1325(a), Chapter 13 cramdown is no longer based on the value of the collateral in the case of certain purchase money loans secured by motor vehicles and other property. In these cases, *Rash* has only limited applicability. Moreover, *Rash*'s replacement value interpretation of § 506(a) insofar as it still applies to individual debtors under Chapters 7 and 13 was further modified by the 2005 Act by the addition of § 506(a)(2) as follows:

> **(2)** In the case of an individual debtor under chapters 7 and 13, such value with respect to personal property securing an allowed claim shall be determined based on the replacement value of such property as of the date of filing the petition without deduction for costs of sale or marketing. With respect to property acquired for personal, family, or household purpose, replacement value shall mean the price a retail merchant would charge for property of that kind considering the age and condition of the property at the time value is determined.

Even after *Rash* the view of the bankruptcy courts had consistently been that the § 722 redemption price was fixed by liquidation, not replacement value. *In re Weathington*, 254 B.R. 895 (6th Cir. B.A.P. 2000). But § 506(a)(2) changes Chapter 7 law by requiring a modified "replacement value" standard for determining the value of a secured claim for redemption under § 722.

### (iv) Interest Rate

The Code requires that a secured creditor receive under the plan property with a present value equal to the allowed amount of its secured claim, § 1325(a)(5)(B)(ii), but offers no specific guidance on the interest rate to be used in discounting future payments to arrive at the present value of a secured claim. 2 Keith M. Lundin, *Chapter 13 Bankruptcy* § 5.51 (2d ed. 1994, Cum. Supp. 1997). Chapter 13 cases were widely divided on the issue until *Till v. SCS Credit Corporation*, 541 U.S. 465 (2004), addressed the issue in an opinion included in the following chapter. The *Till* plurality adopts a rule that appears to require the bankruptcy court to use a market based rate (such as the "prime rate") that is current as of the time confirmation to compensate the secured creditor for delay in payment and adjust that rate upward to compensate the secured creditor for the risk of nonpayment. Dicta in *Till* appear to suggest that in most circumstances a risk adjustment in the range of 1-3% above the prime rate is appropriate, at least in the Chapter 13 car loan context.

### h.   Secured Claims in Debtor's Residence

*(i)   Modification of Home Mortgages*

In the Congressional debate on the 1978 Code, the provision allowing a Chapter 13 plan to modify the rights of holders of secured claims ran into stiff opposition from real estate mortgage lenders. Industry lobbyists predicted that the specter of mortgages being subject to modification in bankruptcy by changing the amount or number of installment payments or by stripping down the mortgage debt to the value of the real property, would result in a drying up of home loans. Congress reacted to these predictions by amending the proposed § 1322(b)(2) to provide that the power of the debtor's plan to "modify the rights of holders of secured claims" was limited to claims "other than a claim secured only by a security interest in real property that is the debtor's principal residence." This language was intended to preclude debtors from using § 1325(a)(5)(B) to rewrite home mortgages in Chapter 13 plans. The plan might provide for cure of defaults, but the debtor could not otherwise modify debts secured by home mortgages.

These expectations of the real estate finance industry were undermined by a series of court decisions that applied the concept of "bifurcation" to the quoted language of § 1322(b)(2). Bifurcation is based on § 506(a) that relates to claims "secured by a lien on property." As we have seen, if the value of the property is less than the amount of the debt, § 506(a) bifurcates the claim into a secured claim to the extent of the value of the property and an unsecured claim for the remaining part of the debt. Hence, if the debt secured by a mortgage on the debtor's residence is $100,000 but the value of the residence has shrunk to $60,000, the mortgagee has a secured claim for $60,000 and an unsecured claim for $40,000. Four courts of appeals held that that under the literal wording of § 1322(b)(2) the phrase "other than a claim secured only by a security interest in real property that is the debtor's principal residence" immediately follows the part of § 1322(b)(2) that states that the plan may modify the rights of holders of "secured claims." Thus, the quoted phrase modifies the immediately preceding words "secured claims" and not the entire claim that is secured by the residence. Under this reading of § 1322(b)(2), only the $60,000 secured claim was immune from modification. To the extent the debt owed to the mortgagee was greater than the value of the residence, the mortgagee had only an unsecured claim that could be dealt with by the debtor's plan in the same way as other unsecured claims. In the following opinion, the Supreme Court rejected this interpretation.

## Nobelman v. American Savings Bank

Supreme Court of the United States, 1993.
508 U.S. 324.

■ Justice THOMAS delivered the opinion of the Court.

This case focuses on the interplay between two provisions of the Bankruptcy Code. The question is whether § 1322(b)(2) prohibits a Chapter 13 debtor from relying on § 506(a) to reduce an undersecured homestead mortgage to the fair market value of the mortgaged residence. We conclude that it does and therefore affirm the judgment of the Court of Appeals.

### I

In 1984, respondent American Savings Bank loaned petitioners Leonard and Harriet Nobelman $68,250 for the purchase of their principal residence, a condominium in Dallas, Texas. In exchange, petitioners executed an adjustable rate note payable to the bank and secured by a deed of trust on the residence. In 1990, after falling behind in their mortgage payments, petitioners sought relief under Chapter 13 of the Bankruptcy Code. The bank filed a proof of claim with the Bankruptcy Court for $71,335 in principal, interest, and fees owed on the note. Petitioners' modified Chapter 13 plan valued the residence at a mere $23,500—an uncontroverted valuation—and proposed to make payments pursuant to the mortgage contract only up to that amount (plus prepetition arrearages). Relying on § 506(a) of the Bankruptcy Code, petitioners proposed to treat the remainder of the bank's claim as unsecured. Under the plan, unsecured creditors would receive nothing.

The bank and the Chapter 13 trustee, also a respondent here, objected to petitioners' plan. They argued that the proposed bifurcation of the bank's claim into a secured claim for $23,500 and an effectively worthless unsecured claim modified the bank's rights as a homestead mortgagee, in violation of § 1322(b)(2). The Bankruptcy Court agreed with respondents and denied confirmation of the plan. The District Court affirmed, as did the Court of Appeals. We granted certiorari to resolve a conflict among the Courts of Appeals. * * *

### II

Under Chapter 13 of the Bankruptcy Code, individual debtors may obtain adjustment of their indebtedness through a flexible repayment plan approved by a bankruptcy court. Section 1322 sets forth the elements of a confirmable Chapter 13 plan. * * * Section 1322 (b)(2), the provision at issue here, allows modification of the rights of both secured and unsecured creditors, subject to special protection for creditors whose claims are secured only by a lien on the debtor's home. It provides that the plan may

"modify the rights of holders of secured claims, *other than a claim secured only by a security interest in real property that is the debtor's principal residence*, or of holders of unsecured claims, or leave unaffected the rights of holders of any class of claims." § 1322(b)(2) (emphasis added).

The parties agree that the "other than" exception in § 1322 (b)(2) proscribes modification of the rights of a homestead mortgagee. Petitioners maintain, however, that their Chapter 13 plan proposes no such modification. They argue that the protection of § 1322(b)(2) applies only to the extent the mortgagee holds a "secured claim" in the debtor's residence and that we must look first to § 506(a) to determine the value of the mortgagee's "secured claim." Section 506(a) provides that an allowed claim secured by a lien on the debtor's property "is a secured claim to the extent of the value of [the] property"; to the extent the claim exceeds the value of the property, it "is an unsecured claim." Petitioners contend that the valuation provided for in § 506(a) operates automatically to adjust downward the amount of a lender's undersecured home mortgage before any disposition proposed in the debtor's Chapter 13 plan. Under this view, the bank is the holder of a "secured claim" only in the amount of $23,500—the value of the collateral property. Because the plan proposes to make $23,500 worth of payments pursuant to the monthly payment terms of the mortgage contract, petitioners argue, the plan effects no alteration of the bank's rights as the holder of that claim. Section 1322(b)(2), they assert, allows unconditional modification of the bank's leftover "unsecured claim."

This interpretation fails to take adequate account of § 1322(b)(2)'s focus on "rights." That provision does not state that a plan may modify "claims" or that the plan may not modify "a claim secured only by" a home mortgage. Rather, it focuses on the modification of the *"rights of holders"* of such claims. By virtue of its mortgage contract with petitioners, the bank is indisputably the holder of a claim secured by a lien on petitioners' home. Petitioners were correct in looking to § 506(a) for a judicial valuation of the collateral to determine the status of the bank's secured claim. It was permissible for petitioners to seek a valuation in proposing their Chapter 13 plan, since § 506(a) states that "[s]uch value shall be determined. . . in conjunction with any hearing. . . on a plan affecting such creditor's interest." But even if we accept petitioners' valuation, the bank is still the "holder" of a "secured claim," because petitioners' home retains $23,500 of value as collateral. The portion of the bank's claim that exceeds $23,500 is an "unsecured claim componen[t]" under § 506(a), *United States v. Ron Pair Enterprises, Inc.*, 489 U.S. 235, 239, n. 3 (1989); however, that determination does not necessarily mean that the "rights" the bank enjoys as a mortgagee, which are protected by § 1322(b)(2), are limited by the valuation of its secured claim.

The term "rights" is nowhere defined in the Bankruptcy Code. In the absence of a controlling federal rule, we generally assume that Congress has "left the determination of property rights in the assets of a bankrupt's estate to state law," since such "[p]roperty interests are created and defined by state law." *Butner v. United States*, 440 U.S. 48, 54–55 (1979). * * * Moreover, we have specifically recognized that "[t]he justifications for application of state law are not limited to ownership interests," but "apply with equal force to security interests, including the interest of a mortgagee." *Butner*, *supra*, at 55. The bank's "rights," therefore, are reflected in the relevant mortgage instruments, which are enforceable under Texas law. They include the right to repayment of the principal in monthly installments over a fixed term at specified adjustable rates of interest, the right to retain the lien until the debt is paid off, the right to accelerate the loan upon default and to proceed against petitioners' residence by foreclosure and public sale, and the right to bring an action to recover any deficiency remaining after foreclosure. * * * These are the rights that were "bargained for by the mortgagor and the mortgagee," *Dewsnup v. Timm*, 502 U.S. 410, 417 (1992), and are rights protected from modification by § 1322(b)(2).

This is not to say, of course, that the contractual rights of a home mortgage lender are unaffected by the mortgagor's Chapter 13 bankruptcy. The lender's power to enforce its rights—and, in particular, its right to foreclose on the property in the event of default—is checked by the Bankruptcy Code's automatic stay provision. § 362. * * * In addition, § 1322(b)(5) permits the debtor to cure prepetition defaults on a home mortgage by paying off arrearages over the life of the plan "notwithstanding" the exception in § 1322(b)(2). These statutory limitations on the lender's rights, however, are independent of the debtor's plan or otherwise outside § 1322(b)(2)'s prohibition.

Petitioners urge us to apply the so-called "rule of the last antecedent," which has been relied upon by some Courts of Appeals to interpret § 1322(b)(2) the way petitioners favor. * * * According to this argument, the operative clause "other than a claim secured only by a security interest in. . . the debtor's principal residence" must be read to refer to and modify its immediate antecedent, "secured claims." Thus, § 1322(b)(2)'s protection would then apply only to that subset of allowed "secured claims," determined by application of § 506(a), that are secured by a lien on the debtor's home—including, with respect to the mortgage involved here, the bank's secured claim for $23,500. We acknowledge that this reading of the clause is quite sensible as a matter of grammar. But it is not compelled. Congress chose to use the phrase "claim secured. . . by" in § 1322(b)(2)'s exception, rather than repeating the term of art "secured claim." The unqualified word "claim" is broadly defined under the Code to encompass any "right to payment, whether. . . secure[d] or unsecured" or any "right to an equitable remedy for breach of performance if such breach gives rise to a right to payment, whether. . . secure[d] or unsecured." § 101(5). It is also plausible, therefore, to read "a claim secured only by a [homestead lien]" as referring to the lienholder's entire claim, including both the secured and the unsecured components of the claim. Indeed, § 506(a) itself uses the phrase "claim. . . secured by a lien" to encompass both portions of an undersecured claim.

This latter interpretation is the more reasonable one, since we cannot discern how § 1322(b)(2) could be administered under petitioners' interpretation. Petitioners propose to reduce the outstanding mortgage principal to the fair market value of the collateral, and, at the same time, they insist that they can do so without modifying the bank's rights "as to interest rates, payment amounts, and [other] contract terms." * * * That appears to be impossible. The bank's contractual rights are contained in a unitary note that applies at once to the bank's overall claim, including both the secured and unsecured components. Petitioners cannot modify the payment and interest terms for the unsecured component, as they propose to do, without also modifying the terms of the secured component. Thus, to preserve the interest rate and the amount of each monthly payment specified in the note after having reduced the principal to $23,500, the plan would also have to reduce the term of the note dramatically. That would be a significant modification of a contractual right. Furthermore, the bank holds an adjustable rate mortgage, and the principal and interest payments on the loan must be recalculated with each adjustment in the interest rate. There is nothing in the mortgage contract or the Code that suggests any basis for recalculating the amortization schedule whether by reference to the face value of the remaining principal or by reference to the unamortized value of the collateral. This conundrum alone indicates that § 1322(b)(2) cannot operate in combination with § 506(a) in the manner theorized by petitioners.

In other words, to give effect to § 506(a)'s valuation and bifurcation of secured claims through a Chapter 13 plan in the manner petitioners propose would require a modification of the rights of the holder of the security interest. Section 1322(b)(2) prohibits such a modification where, as here, the lender's claim is secured only by a lien on the debtor's principal residence.

The judgment of the Court of Appeals is therefore

Affirmed.

Justice STEVENS, concurring.

At first blush it seems somewhat strange that the Bankruptcy Code should provide less protection to an individual's interest in retaining possession of his or her home than of other assets. The anomaly is, however, explained by the legislative history indicating that favorable treatment of residential mortgagees was intended to encourage the flow of capital into the home lending market. *See Grubbs v. Houston First American Savings Assn.*, 730 F.2d 236, 245-246 (C.A.5 1984) (canvassing legislative history of Chapter 13 home mortgage provisions). It therefore seems quite clear that the Court's literal reading of the text of the statute is faithful to the intent of Congress. Accordingly, I join its opinion and judgment.

NOTE

Section 1322(b)(2) bars modification of claims secured "only by a security interest in real property that is the debtor's principal residence." Hence, mortgages secured by vacation homes or covering other collateral in addition to the debtor's residence can be modified. In *Wilson v. Commonwealth Mortgage Corp.*, 895 F.2d 123, 124 (3d Cir.1990), the mortgage included not only debtor's residence but also "any and all appliances, machinery, furniture and equipment (whether fixtures or not) of any nature whatsoever now or hereafter installed in or upon said premises." This was an easy case for allowing modification because a lien on both personal property and real property is not common in residential mortgages. But typical residential mortgages often contain boilerplate clauses that may cause unanticipated difficulty. For example, residential mortgages often grant the mortgagee a security interest in "rents, royalties, profits, and fixtures," even though there is no expectation that the property will ever be rented. This kind of clause has usually not been held to involve additional collateral because these benefits are merely incidental to an interest in real property. *In re Davis*, 989 F.2d 208 (6th Cir.1993).

Another clause discussed in *Davis* is the common provision requiring the mortgagor to maintain fire insurance on improvements with the proceeds payable to the mortgagee. This clause has not usually been held to give rise to additional collateral. Since this provision is present in virtually all home mortgages, a contrary holding would allow nearly all home mortgages to be modified. Mortgagors sometimes buy optional credit life and disability insurance at the time of the loan, the proceeds of which are used to pay the balance of the loan if the mortgagor dies or is disabled. Although the cases are divided on the issue of whether such insurance allows the mortgagee's claim to be modified under § 1322(b)(2), the court in *In re Washington*, 967 F.2d 173 (5th Cir.1992), views the trend of authority as holding that such clauses do not allow modification of the claim. Another boilerplate provision that raises problems for creditors is that granting mortgagees a security interest in funds held in an escrow account into which the mortgagor is required to pay sums each month to cover annual tax and insurance obligations. *In re Dent*, 130 B.R. 623 (Bankr. Ga.1991), held that the money in the escrow was separate from the real property and, therefore, the clause granted the mortgagee additional collateral. *Accord*, *In re Reed*, 247 B.R. 618 (E.D. Pa. 2000).

Courts have usually been reluctant to find additional collateral in cases involving the more common home mortgage boilerplate clauses, and the 2005 Act gives real estate lenders still more protection from modification. "Debtor's principal residence" is defined in § 101(13A) to include mobile homes, thereby resolving a dispute in the decisions. The new definition also provides that a residential structure includes "incidental property," which is defined in § 101(27B) to make clear that familiar boilerplate provisions on easements, fixtures, rents, mineral rights, escrow funds or insurance proceeds are merely incidental to the residence.

The following Problem shows the kinds of troublesome questions the home mortgage provision in § 1332(b)(2) continues to raise.

## PROBLEM

Debtors own a duplex; they live in one unit and rent the other. They borrowed $100,000 from Lender to buy the property and gave a 20-year mortgage to secure the loan. When they filed in Chapter 13, they still owed $90,000 on the mortgage, but by then the property was worth only $75,000. Their plan proposed to strip down Lender's secured claim to the value of the property and to pay it off over a 20-year period in accordance with the requirements of § 1325(a)(5)(B). The $15,000 unsecured deficiency claim was classified with other unsecured claims on which the plan proposed to pay 10% over a period of three years. Lender objected to the plan on the ground that it impermissibly modified the rights of the holder of a home mortgage under § 1322(b)(2). Is Lender correct in contending that this case involves a "claim secured only by a security interest in real property that is the debtor's principal residence"? *See Lomas Mortgage v. Louis,* 82 F.3d 1 (1st Cir.1996).

### (ii) *Modification of Wholly Unsecured Home Loans*

## In re Tanner

United States Court of Appeals, Eleventh Circuit, 2000.
217 F.3d 1357.

■ KRAVITCH, Circuit Judge.

In the wake of *Nobelman v. American Savings Bank,* in which the Supreme Court held that the rights of an undersecured homestead lender are protected from modification in Chapter 13 bankruptcy proceedings, we address whether this holding extends to wholly unsecured homestead lenders.[1] We conclude that it does not.

### I. BACKGROUND AND PROCEDURAL HISTORY

In the fall of 1995, Plaintiff-Appellant Pamela Tanner ("Debtor") purchased her primary residence for $62,000.00 which was financed entirely by a mortgage from Inland Mortgage Co. ("Inland Mortgage"). The following spring, Debtor obtained a debt consolidation and home improvement loan from Defendant-Appellee FirstPlus Financial, Inc. ("FirstPlus") in the amount of $23,000.00. Both mortgages were secured solely by

---

[1] In this context, an undersecured lender is one for whom the value of the underlying collateral has fallen below the amount of the loan, and an unsecured lender is one for whom no equity in the collateral supports its loan. Both types of lenders are therefore secured creditors only in the sense that a security interest in collateral has been given to them by the debtor in exchange for their loans.

Debtor's residence. When Debtor subsequently filed a voluntary petition under Chapter 13 of the Bankruptcy Code on September 17, 1997, her home was valued at $62,000.00. Inland Mortgage filed proof of its secured claim for the existing balance of $62,880.01 on the senior mortgage, and FirstPlus filed its secured claim of $22,968.65 for the junior mortgage. Debtor's proposed Chapter 13 plan contemplated paying Inland Mortgage in full and treating FirstPlus's claim as an unsecured claim entitled to a six-percent dividend. Pursuant to that end, Debtor filed an adversary complaint in which she requested that the bankruptcy court value FirstPlus's interest in the residence at $0 and then "strip off" the lien as unsecured.[4] In its motion to dismiss, FirstPlus argued that it was a secured creditor and that Debtor therefore could not "strip off" its claim. The bankruptcy court, agreeing with FirstPlus, granted the motion to dismiss and the district court affirmed. This appeal followed.

## II. DISCUSSION

\* \* \*

This appeal lies at the intersection of two provisions of the bankruptcy code: § 506(a) and § 1322(b)(2). Section 506(a) defines the secured and unsecured components of debts according to the value of the underlying collateral:

> An allowed claim of a creditor secured by a lien on property in which the estate has an interest. . . is a secured claim to the extent of the value of such creditor's interest in the estate's interest in such property,. . . and is an unsecured claim to the extent that the value of such creditor's interest or the amount so subject to setoff is less than the amount of such allowed claim.

§ 506(a).

Section 1322(b)(2) permits a Chapter 13 debtor's plan to "modify the rights of holders of secured claims, other than a claim secured only by a security interest in real property that is the debtor's principal residence." The Supreme Court considered the interplay of these two provisions in *Nobelman v. American Savings Bank* in which the debtor sought to "strip down" the homestead lender's secured claim of $71,335.00 to the home's reduced value of $23,500.00. The Court foreclosed this option by holding that " § 1322(b)(2) prohibits a Chapter 13 debtor from relying on § 506(a) to reduce an undersecured homestead mortgage to the fair market value of the mortgaged residence." 508 U.S. at 325-26. Acknowledging that section 506(a) allows bifurcation of claims into secured and unsecured components, the Court nevertheless concluded that the most sensible interpretation of section 1322(b)(2) was that it protected even the unsecured com-

---

[4] In bankruptcy parlance, a "strip down" of an undersecured lien reduces it to the amount of its extant collateral and a "strip off" removes an unsecured claim in its entirety.

ponents of a partially secured claim. The concurring opinion found this result also comported with Congress's intent. *See id.* at 332 (Stevens, J., concurring) (Section 1322(b)(2)'s "legislative history indicate[s] that favorable treatment of residential mortgagees was intended to encourage the flow of capital into the home lending market.").

The *Nobelman* Court left open the issue before us in this appeal, that is, whether its holding extends to wholly unsecured homestead mortgages. Subsequent consideration of this issue has sharply divided bankruptcy and district courts, see 5 Norton Bankruptcy Law and Practice 2d § 121:5, nn. 57 & 57.5 (2000) (citing cases), and bankruptcy scholars, compare 8 Collier on Bankruptcy § 1322.06 (Lawrence P. King ed., 15th ed.2000) with Keith M. Lundin, Chapter 13 Bankruptcy § 4.46 (2d ed.1994). This split is understandable in light of the seemingly contradictory language used in *Nobelman*, dividing the courts into two interpretive camps. The majority view has focused on the following language to support its conclusion that the antimodification provision protects only undersecured, and not wholly unsecured, homestead lenders: "even if we accept petitioners' valuation [under section 506(a)], the bank is still the 'holder' of a 'secured claim,' because petitioners' home retains $23,500 of value as collateral." *Nobelman*, 508 U.S. at 329. Under this view, the antimodification protection afforded by section 1322(b)(2) applies only when the creditor's claim is at least partially secured.

The burgeoning minority view has instead relied on the *Nobelman* Court's emphasis on the "rights" of the homestead lender rather the valuation of its claim. *See id.* ("[D]etermination [that a claim is undersecured] does not necessarily mean that the 'rights' the bank enjoys as a mortgagee, which are protected by § 1322(b)(2), are limited by the valuation of its secured claim."). According to this interpretation, it is the status of the homestead lender, rather than the value of the collateral underlying the lender's claim, that shields its claim from modification.

Since this appeal was filed, two other courts of appeals have confronted this issue and adopted the majority view. The Third Circuit resolved the apparent tension in the *Nobelman* decision as follows:

> Perhaps the clearest explanation of how the Court's discussion of the two sections can be reconciled is to point out that while the antimodification clause uses the term "claim" rather than "secured claim" and therefore applies to both the secured and unsecured part of a mortgage, the antimodification clause still states that the claim must be "secured only by a security interest in. . . the debtor's principal residence." If a mortgage holder's claim is wholly unsecured, then after the valuation that [the Court] said that debtors could seek under § 506(a), the bank is not in any respect a holder of a [secured claim]. . . and the antimodification clause does not apply. On the other hand, if any part of the bank's claim is secured, then, under [the Court]'s interpretation of the term "claim," the entire claim, both secured and unsecured parts, cannot be modified.

*McDonald v. Master Fin. Inc. (In re McDonald)*, 205 F.3d 606, 611-12 (3d Cir.2000). The Fifth Circuit agreed and drew further support from the legislative history of section 1322(b)(2) and public policy considerations favoring only those mortgage lenders involved with homestead purchases rather than home improvement or debt consolidation.

Although this is a close issue, we find the reasoning of the Third and Fifth Circuits persuasive and adopt the majority view. We agree with those courts that the only reading of both sections 506(a) and 1322(b)(2) that renders neither a nullity is one that first requires bankruptcy courts to determine the value of the homestead lender's secured claim under section 506(a) and then to protect from modification any claim that is secured by any amount of collateral in the residence. Any claim that is wholly unsecured, however, would not be protected from modification under section 1322(b)(2). To hold otherwise and extend the antimodification clause to even wholly unsecured claims would vitiate the *Nobelman* Court's pronouncement that "[debtors] were correct in looking to § 506(a) for a judicial valuation of the collateral to determine the status of the bank's secured claim." 508 U.S. at 328.

Contrary to FirstPlus's contention, this holding does not derogate the protected rights alluded to by the *Nobelman* Court, but rather recognizes that only the rights secured by some remaining equity will be protected from modification. Indeed,

> [a]n analysis of the state law "rights" afforded a holder of an unsecured "lien", if such a situation exists, indicates these rights are empty rights from a practical, if not a legal, standpoint. A forced sale of the property would not result in any financial return to the lienholder, even if a forced sale could be accomplished where the lien attaches to nothing.

*Lam v. Investors Thrift (In re Lam)*, 211 B.R. 36, 40 (9th Cir. BAP 1997), appeal dismissed, 192 F.3d 1309 (9th Cir.1999). Extending section 1322(b)(2)'s protection to wholly unsecured junior mortgages would enlarge the rights afforded to those lenders when the mortgagors are forced to file a Chapter 13 petition, inviting unwelcome, and certainly unintended, consequences. See *id.* at 41. The better reading of sections 506(a) and 1322(b)(2), therefore, protects only mortgages that are secured by some existing equity in the debtor's principal residence.

### III. CONCLUSION

We REVERSE the district court's judgment affirming the bankruptcy court's decision.

## NOTES

**1.** The Second, Third, Fifth, Ninth and Eleventh Circuits, as well as the First Circuit BAP, support the view that the anti-modification exception of § 1322(b)(2) does not apply to a mortgage loan that is wholly unsecured under § 506(a). *See In re Zimmer,* 313 F.3d 1220 (9th Cir. 2002).

**2.** In a case in which the land is not the debtor's principal residence and the rights of mortgagees can be modified, the debtor's Chapter 13 plan can strip-down the mortgage to the current value of the land and deal with the deficiency as an unsecured claim. Section 1325(a)(5)(B)(i), on retention of liens, should cause no difficulties: If the plan is completed, the debtor is discharged and  the mortgagee's lien expires. If the case is dismissed because the debtor failed to carry out the plan, the mortgagee retains a lien in the land to secure the unpaid amount of the mortgage obligation. If an underwater junior lien is involved, as in *Tanner*, the junior lien would also revive upon dismissal of the case, but the senior mortgagee could foreclose on the land under state law and cut off the rights of both the mortgagor and the junior lienholder. If the land appreciated to the extent of making the junior lien partially secured, foreclosure by the senior might produce a surplus, which under state law would be turned over to the junior creditor.

### (iii) Section 1322(c)(2)

Why did Congress enact § 1322(c)(2)? The court in *In re Bartee*, 212 F.3d 277 (5th Cir. 2000), posits that by enactment of § 1322(c)(2) Congress sought to withdraw anti-modification protection from certain classes of second mortgages, including short-term, high interest rate home equity loans that are disguised personal loans, some of which are made without regard to the value of the debtor's residence. An example of potential consumer abuse arises in cases in which creditors advertise loans of 125% of the value of the debtor's real estate in order to allow the debtor to pay off credit card debts. Jane Kaufman Winn, *Lien Stripping After* Nobelman, 27 Loy. L.A. L. Rev. 541 (1994), discusses the predatory lending practices aspects of the lien-stripping dispute.

However, the circuits are divided on the meaning of § 1322(c)(2). The court in *In re Witt*, 113 F.3d 508 (4th Cir.1997), held that the 1994 amendment did not state an exception to *Nobelman*. It viewed the amendment as merely permitting the plan to rewrite the payments schedule and not to strip down the secured claim and concluded that if Congress had intended to repeal *Nobelman*, decided only a few months before, with respect to mortgages whose terms expire during the plan, the legislative history would surely have mentioned *Nobelman*. The weight of authority is contra, *see, e.g., In re Paschen*, 296 F.3d 1203 (11th Cir. 2002), in which the court allowed Chapter 13 debtors to modify an undersecured short-term home loan by bifurcating it into secured and unsecured claims, with the only the secured claim to be paid off in monthly installments under § 1325(a)(5). The court discussed and rejected *Witt*. The importance of § 1322(c)(2) has grown in recent years because of the great increase in home-equity lending encouraged by the low interest rate climate of the early years of the century that has contributed to higher real estate values.

### (iv)  Cure of Defaults

The wish to protect their homes from mortgage foreclosure is a major reason for debtors opting for Chapter 13. Assume the common case in which Debtor is behind on her mortgage payments and the mortgage obligation on her home has 10 or 15 years left on the repayment schedule when Debtor files in Chapter 13. The mortgagee is threatening foreclosure. How can debtor to save her home? Under § 1322(b)(2), she cannot modify her obligation, but even if she could modify, she usually lacks the resources to pay off the entire obligation during the term of a three- to five-year plan. She finds her remedy in § 1322(b)(5), which allows her to maintain the current schedule of mortgage payments throughout the plan and cure her default by making up the arrearages in payments over the period of the plan. If she completes her plan, she is no longer in default and the mortgage is reinstated. Of course, the portion of the mortgage debt falling due in the years after her case is closed is not discharged, § 1328(a)(1), and the mortgagee retains a lien on the property until the remaining debt is paid. But if she cannot carry out the plan and converts to Chapter 7 before the default is cured, the 2005 Act § 348(f)(1)(C)(ii) provides that the mortgage is in default to the same extent it would be outside bankruptcy.

*Meaning of cure.* The use in Chapter 13 of broad undefined terms like "cure" or "modify" has led to some confusion about the scope of each term. For example, if a debtor has been in default for an extended period, the mortgagee will commonly declare an acceleration of the entire unpaid balance of the loan before commencing foreclosure. After acceleration, is a proposal to pay the amounts in default at the time of acceleration a permissible cure or an impermissible modification? In a resolution of the issue that has been widely followed, the court in *In re Taddeo*, 685 F.2d 24 (2d Cir.1982), held that it is a permissible cure:

> When Congress empowered Chapter 13 debtors to "cure defaults," we think Congress intended to allow mortgagors to "de-accelerate" their mortgage and reinstate its original payment schedule. We so hold for two reasons. First, we think that the power to cure must comprehend the power to "de-accelerate." This follows from the concept of "curing a default." A default is an event in the debtor-creditor relationship which triggers certain consequences—here, acceleration. Curing a default commonly means taking care of the triggering event and returning to pre-default conditions. The consequences are thus nullified. This is the concept of "cure" used throughout the Bankruptcy Code. * * *

> Secondly, we believe that the power to "cure any default" granted in § 1322(b)(3) and (b)(5) is not limited by the ban against "modifying" home mortgages in § 1322(b)(2) because we do not read "curing defaults" under (b)(3) or "curing defaults and maintaining payments" under (b)(5) to be *modifications* of claims.

> It is true that § 1322(b)(5)'s preface, "notwithstanding paragraph (2)," seems to treat the power to cure in (b)(5) as a subset of the power to modify set forth in (b)(2), but that superficial reading of the statute

must fall in the light of legislative history and legislative purpose. The "notwithstanding" clause was added to § 1322(b)(5) to emphasize that defaults in mortgages could be cured notwithstanding § 1322(b)(2).

685 F.2d at 26-27.

Case law after *Taddeo* has not been uniform on the reach of the cure remedy. Some cases denied debtors the right to cure after a judgment of foreclosure was entered, even though the property had not yet been sold under the judgment, e.g., *In re Roach*, 824 F.2d 1370 (3d Cir.1987). Others allowed cure up to the point of the foreclosure sale. Still others allowed cure even after a foreclosure sale so long as the debtor had a right of redemption under state law. These views are discussed in *In re Glenn*, 760 F.2d 1428 (6th Cir.1985), which adopted what is probably the majority view that cure is permissible under a Chapter 13 plan until the foreclosure sale but not after. The argument in favor of this view is that allowing cure to upset foreclosure sales during the post-sale redemption period would tend to chill bidding at the foreclosure sale, to the detriment of all involved. State post-sale redemption statutes require the debtor to pay the full unpaid balance before the end of the redemption period in order to redeem. If cure is permitted after the sale, the apparent effect would be to make the purchaser at the foreclosure sale an involuntary creditor who would have to accept repayment on the terms of the original mortgage. One court addressed this issue as follows: "A foreclosure sale * * * may introduce another party to the relationship—a good faith purchaser. We hesitate to further cloud the interests and expectations of a third party purchaser through an expansive right of bankruptcy cure." *In re Thompson*, 894 F.2d 1227, 1230 (10th Cir.1990).

In 1994, § 1322(c)(1) was added, which states that "a lien on the debtor's principal residence may be cured under paragraph (3) or (5) of subsection (b) until such residence is sold at a foreclosure sale that is conducted in accordance with applicable non-bankruptcy law." The Section-by-Section Description § 301, 140 Cong.Rec. H10769 (1994), indicates that the intent was to overrule the *Roach* line of cases "by allowing the debtor to cure home mortgage defaults at least through completion of a foreclosure sale under applicable nonbankruptcy law. However, if the State provides the debtor more extensive 'cure' rights (through, for example, some later redemption period), the debtor would continue to enjoy such rights in bankruptcy."

The court in *Colon v. Option One Mortgage Corp.*, 319 F.3d 912, 920 (7th Cir. 2003), held that the phrase "applicable non-bankruptcy law" in § 1322(c)(1) "requires deference to state mortgage law on the scope of any right to cure after the sale." But *Cain v. Wells Fargo Bank, N.A.*, 423 F.3d 617 (6th Cir. 2005), took the view that a mortgage may not be cured after a foreclosure sale regardless of whether a right of redemption survives the sale under state law.

*Interest on arrearage.* If a debtor who is delinquent on installments due on a mortgage debt may cure the default by spreading the amount of the arrearage over the period of the plan, is an oversecured mortgagee entitled to interest on the delayed payments on the arrearage? The language of § 1322 is not helpful in answering this question, and the courts of appeals were sharply divided on the issue until it was eventually resolved by the Supreme Court in *Rake v. Wade*, 508 U.S. 464 (1993), which held that § 506(b) applies to cure cases and allows oversecured creditors interest. After *Rake* was decided, § 1322 was amended in 1994 by adding a new subsection (e). According to the legislative history, Section-by-Section Description § 305, 140 Cong.Rec. H10770 (1994), this provision was intended to overturn *Rake*. But mortgagees can assure their right to interest on the arrearage by inserting a clause in the mortgage requiring the mortgagor to pay it.

### (v)   Three-to-Five Year Limitation

Chapter 13 debtors voluntarily submit to a plan in which they must pay all their disposable income not needed for family support to their creditors to earn a discharge in bankruptcy. Unless reasonable time limits are imposed on this burdensome obligation, few volunteers would come forth. The three-to-five year limits spelled out in the section quoted below serve this purpose. The issue these limits raise is how effective Chapter 13 plans can be in dealing with long-term obligations of debtors that extend beyond the three-to-five year duration of the plan.

Section 1322(d) provides: "The plan may not provide for payments over a period that is longer than three years, unless the court, for cause, approves a longer period, but the court may not approve a period that is longer than five years." How does this provision apply in the following cases in which the mortgage on Debtors' land securing a $400,000 loan has a term extending beyond the duration of Debtors' Chapter 13 plan?

**Case #1.**   Debtors are in default and Creditor is threatening foreclosure. Section 1322(b)(5) allows for a plan that proposes to cure a default in a mortgage that has a duration longer than three to five years, so long as the arrearage can be paid off within the period of the plan.

**Case # 2.**   The value of Debtors' land has declined to $300,000 and Debtors wish to modify the security interest by stripping off the $100,000 deficiency.

>   **(a)**   If the land is Debtors' principal residence, *Nobelman* held that § 1322(b)(2) prevents modification without respect to the term of the indebtedness.

>   **(b)**   If the land is not Debtors' principal residence, § 1322(b) provides no bar to modification of a mortgage. The question is whether the three-to-five year limitation of § 1322(d) does so. What Debtors might desire in a case in which their mortgage is in default and the debt exceeds the value of the land is a plan that allows them (1) to cure the default within a three-to-five year plan, (2) classify the

$100,000 deficiency as an unsecured claim, to be paid off at a few cents on the dollar, and (3) maintain their regular payments until the $300,000 balance, with interest, is paid off. *In re Enewally*, 368 F.3d 1165 (9th Cir. 2004), denied this relief. It held that a modified secured debt cannot be paid off over a period in excess of the term of the plan. Thus, long-term mortgages may be cured but they may not be modified in a manner that requires payments to be made beyond the three-to-five year limit of the plan. Debtor's recourse is to Chapter 11.

## 7. DISCHARGE

### a.  Complete Payment Discharge

Although we have discussed discharge issues throughout this chapter, we bring the discharge material together in this section in summary form. Under the 1978 Code, the super-discharge offered by § 1328(a) was viewed as an important incentive for debtors to choose Chapter 13. Under the original version, a debtor on completion of her plan was discharged from all debts provided for by the plan except obligations for alimony, maintenance or support of spouses and children and those long term debts that cannot practicably be dealt by a three-year plan because the term of the obligation exceeds that of the plan. § 1322(b)(5). We discussed the nondischargeability of domestic support obligations in Chapter 4 on Discharge, but § 1322(b)(5) is unique to Chapter 13. It precludes discharge of debts that do not mature within the term of the plan. Obviously, a debtor cannot be expected to pay off a 25-year mortgage in a three-to-five-year Chapter 13 plan if the debtor files in the third year of the mortgage. Section 1322(a)(5) allows the debtor to propose the cure of arrearages and the maintenance of regular payments throughout the period of the plan; the debtor remains liable on the mortgage obligation after the plan ends.

Hence, at its inception, Chapter 13 was an avenue for relief from a number of debts that were nondischargeable in Chapter 7 under § 523, such as claims arising from student loans, fraud, embezzlement, larceny, and willful and malicious injury, including, presumably, even intentional torts. In providing for the super-discharge, Congress offered debtors burdened by debts not dischargeable in Chapter 7 salvation in Chapter 13 so long as they were willing to pay their debts over the period of the plan.

Over the years, however, Congress has severely cut back on the expansive nature of the Chapter 13 discharge, and, culminating with the 2005 Act, the super-discharge is no longer so super. Nondischargeable debts added to § 1328(a) include those for fraud, fiduciary defalcation, embezzlement, larceny, domestic support obligations, educational loans, drunk driving liability, criminal fines, and, under the 2005 Act, obligations for liability in civil actions "as a result of willful or malicious injury by the debtor that caused personal injury to an individual or the death of an individual." § 1328(a)(4).

The latter provision was doubtless  a reaction to cases like *In re Le-Maire*, 898 F.2d 1346 *en banc* (8th Cir. 1990), in which the debtor fired nine rifle shots at another man, hitting him five times. The debtor admitted his intent to kill and served 27 months in prison. The victim obtained a civil judgment against the debtor, which created a debt that was nondischargeable in Chapter 7 under § 523 as arising from "willful and malicious injury." Since at that time § 1328(a) made no reference to willful and malicious injuries, the debtor filed in Chapter 13 and the bankruptcy court confirmed his plan. The Eighth Circuit, struggling to find a basis for denying discharge, held in an *en banc* 6-3 decision that the debtor's plan was not filed in good faith, even though it called for payment of 42% of his creditors' claims.

A § 1328(a) discharge applies to all debts provided for the plan or disallowed. Although the plan may call for unsecured claims to receive only nominal payment or no payment at all, the claims are treated as provided for by the plan and are discharged. Under most circumstances, postconfirmation debts cannot be paid under the plan and are not discharged upon completion of the plan. If, during the term of the plan, the debtor needs additional credit, two options may be open: First, modification of the plan under § 1329 may be available to the debtor. Under the modified plan, the new creditor may receive payment, and the debtor may  be discharged of all debts included in the modified plan. Second, in the case of a consumer debt "for property or services necessary for the debtor's performance under the plan," § 1305 allows the creditor to share in the payments under the plan if the trustee approves the transaction in advance and  the creditor manifests its consent to coming under the plan by filing a proof of claim. If prior approval by the trustee "was practicable and was not obtained," the postconfirmation debt is not discharged, § 1328(d). The creditor's incentive to come under the plan is to receive payments immediately; the downside is that it will usually receive only partial payment and have the remainder of its claim discharged. If the creditor declines to file a claim, it cannot share under the plan and its claim will not be discharged. 3 Keith M. Lundin, *Chapter 13 Bankruptcy* § 1.97 (2d ed. 1994, Cum. Supp. 1997).

### b.   Hardship Discharge

For several years, about two-thirds of all confirmed Chapter 13 plans have failed before the debtor completed payments; some debtors convert to Chapter 7, but others receive no bankruptcy relief at all. A minor amelioration of this lamentable situation may be found in the "hardship" discharge offered by § 1328(b) to debtors whose "failure to complete such payments is due to circumstances for which the debtor should not justly be held accountable," but only if modification of the plan is not practicable. A third requirement, usually posing no difficulties, is that the debtor has satisfied the best interests test. The usual circumstances under which debtors are not responsible for failure to complete a plan are illness or loss of employment, but these are also the circumstances under which courts allow debtors to modify plans. The most obvious case in which modification is not practicable is that in which the debtor's misfortune has left inadequate disposable income to complete a modified plan. In such a case, under § 1325(a)(6), the modified plan would not be feasible and thus not confirmable and, presumably, not practicable under § 1328(b).

Judge Lundin notes that courts have made hardship discharges difficult to obtain by insisting on proof of more permanent types of hardships than temporary job loss or illness. Catastrophe seems to be what they are looking for: permanent disability qualifies. Lundin, supra, § 9.20. The common case in which the debtor loses her job or falls ill within the early months of a Chapter 13 plan is not a likely candidate for a hardship discharge. Even if a debtor scales the high wall that the courts have erected to qualify for a hardship discharge, she receives no better discharge, in terms of nondischargeable debts, than she would have received had she filed in Chapter 7 and not paid her creditors a cent. Section 1328(c)(1) excepts from a hardship discharge all the nondischargeable debts provided in § 523(a).

# CHAPTER 10

# REORGANIZATION IN CHAPTER 11: OPERATING THE DEBTOR AND PROPOSING A PLAN

## A. INTRODUCTION

### 1. RATIONALE OF REORGANIZATION

The Supreme Court has described the purpose of Chapter 11 as follows:

> In proceedings under the reorganization provisions of the Bankruptcy Code, a troubled enterprise may be restructured to enable it to operate successfully in the future. * * * By permitting reorganization, Congress anticipated that the business would continue to provide jobs, to satisfy creditors' claims, and to produce a return for its owners. * * * Congress presumed that the assets of the debtor would be more valuable if used in a rehabilitated business than if "sold for scrap."

*United States v. Whiting Pools, Inc.*, 462 U.S. 198, 203 (1983).

Reorganized debtors use their future earnings to repay pre-petition creditors. Liquidated debtors' assets are sold to repay those claims. If the present value of a given firm's future earning power (the "going concern" value) is greater than the liquidation value of its assets, Chapter 11 reorganization is an attractive alternative to Chapter 7 liquidation. In this situation, creditors as a group are better off if the business continues to operate. And society is better off also when a firm that is worth more alive than dead is successfully rehabilitated.

In some cases, the debtor's prospects of generating additional value by continued operations are very remote. Consuming assets in continuing operations can, nevertheless, further the interests of managers, other employees, and postpetition suppliers at the expense of prepetition creditors. Accordingly, the interests of the debtor and those of creditors may conflict on the issue of whether continued operation is desirable. Section 1112(b)(1) mandates dismissal of a Chapter 11 case or its conversion to Chapter 7 upon a finding of "cause" which is defined to include among other things "substantial or continuing loss to or diminution of the estate." § 1112(b)(4). Historically, courts have allowed debtors in possession to continue to operate for some period even in cases in which the enterprise is not economically viable. The Eastern Airlines debacle in which the doomed debtor, over the heated objection of creditors, spent $400 million in a futile continuation of operations is a graphic example. Christie Harlan & Bridget O'Brian, *After Eastern, Debtors Face Bumpier Ride*, Wall St.J., Jan. 22, 1991, at B3. So long as postpetition debts are being paid, debtors have been given a substantial period of time to attempt reorganization.

Conflict between creditors and the debtor also occurs even when a business is clearly capable of successful reorganization under Chapter 11. Reorganizing an operating business in Chapter 11 usually requires cooperation from the debtor. The price of debtor cooperation is usually a division of the value that is anticipated in the reorganization between creditors and ownership interests. If the anticipated reorganization value is not sufficient to pay all prepetition debt, all of that value, as a theoretical matter, belongs to creditors. But if that value cannot be obtained without the efforts or cooperation of the debtor, compensation of the ownership interests of the debtor may be in the interests of creditors. A successful reorganization is usually the product of a deal that is struck between creditors and the debtor. Bankruptcy reorganization can usefully be viewed from the perspective of the tension between the debtor and its creditors over the allocation of the reorganization value of the enterprise. Confirmation of a reorganization plan reflects an accommodation of this tension if it gives the debtor enough of this value to induce it to reorganize while, at the same time, according fair treatment to the claims of creditors.

For many years, Chapter 11 has been under attack by commentators. Professor Douglas Baird began this debate by challenging the assumption that the going concern value of a distressed business may commonly exceed its liquidation value. *The Uneasy Case for Corporate Reorganizations*, 15 J.Legal Studies 127 (1985). Businesses are frequently sold as entities both inside and outside bankruptcy. Baird argued that if the best use of a company's assets lies in the continued operation of the business, buyers at a liquidation sale will buy the firm at a price—the discounted value of future earnings—that equals the going concern value. Subsequently, two commentators called for the outright repeal of Chapter 11, arguing that Chapter 11 reorganizations provide less value for both equity and debt holders than the prior law and benefit principally corporate management. Michael Bradley & Michael Rosenzweig, *The Untenable Case for Chapter 11*, 101 Yale L.J. 1043 (1992). Replies to Bradley & Rosenzweig are found in Lynn M. LoPucki, *Strange Visions in a Strange World: A Reply to Professors Bradley and Rosenzweig*, 91 Mich.L.Rev. 79 (1992), and Elizabeth Warren, *The Untenable Case for Repeal of Chapter 11*, 102 Yale L.J. 437 (1992). Recent empirical work suggests that the direct costs of Chapter 11 reorganization of large public firms are a relatively modest 3% of the debtor's assets. Stephen J. Lubben, *The Direct Costs of Corporate Reorganization*, 74 Am. Bankr. L.J. 509 (2000). But Chapter 11's indirect costs in lost business opportunities, delays and strategic behavior have so far eluded measurement, and while varying greatly, undoubtedly loom large in some cases.

## 2. REORGANIZATION UNDER PREVIOUS LAW

The rich history of corporate reorganization law as it evolved from federal equity receivership law, the Bankruptcy Act of 1898, the 1933 and 1934 Amendments to the 1898 Act (§§ 77 and 77B), the 1938 Chandler Act (Chapters X, XI and XII), and the Bankruptcy Reform Act of 1978 (Chapter 11) is summarized in many places. The description below is drawn from Daniel J. Bussel, *Coalition–Building Through Bankruptcy Creditors' Committees*, 43 UCLA L.Rev. 1547, 1552–58 (1996).

Reorganization law developed out of the federal courts' struggle to fashion an alternative to forced liquidation for large, financially distressed corporations in the late 19th and early 20th centuries. Statutory bankruptcy law provided no satisfactory alternative. Indeed from 1878 to 1898, the period of the birth and early development of United States corporate reorganization law, no federal bankruptcy statute existed. Even the Bankruptcy Act of 1898, the first comprehensive federal bankruptcy statute, was directed towards liquidation rather than reorganization of distressed firms.

The "equity receivership" arose first to deal with the problems of distressed railroads. The value of an operating railroad was almost always greater than that of an unwieldy liquidation of railroad property scattered across many jurisdictions. Moreover, there was a significant public interest in maintaining operating railroads throughout the country. The interests of the railroad's American managers, owners, employees, shippers (especially farmers) and passengers clearly favored reorganization. Liquidation might arguably have been in the interest of certain classes of debtholders, but American railroads in the 19th century were built primarily with European capital supplied through investment bankers in New York and London. It is perhaps reasonable to believe that forced liquidation of American railroads in favor of these moneyed foreign interests was unlikely to be viewed with favor on this side of the Atlantic. Professors Baird and Rasmussen in *Control Rights, Priority Rights and the Conceptual Foundations of Corporate Reorganizations*, 87 Va.L.Rev. 921 (2001), have nevertheless suggested that the investment bankers who dominated the equity receivership process and who sometimes held significant equity stakes in the railroads, depended on their long-term relationships with these foreign investors and thus had an incentives to balance these creditor interests against local interests. Arguably, the system's success in balancing creditor and debtor interests depended on these close interlocking relationships and thus equity receiverships did not benefit the relatively unsophisticated and unconnected public investors who had become common by the 1930's. Nevertheless Baird and Rasmussen point to evidence that even these later public investors, if they held diversified bond portfolios, in fact outperformed the market.

In the absence of a viable statutory procedure, federal courts and lawyers for distressed corporations and their creditors made up the rules as they played the game, which they called the "federal equity receivership." Eight key steps evolved:

First, subject to pre-arrangement with the debtor, a cooperative out-of-state creditor would initiate a lawsuit under the federal diversity of citizenship jurisdiction in a venue of the debtor's liking. The creditor would seek appointment of a receiver (also of the debtor's liking) on the grounds of the debtor's equitable insolvency. The debtor would consent to the appointment of the receiver.

Second, pre-receivership management would continue to manage the company under the general supervision of the federal court while a plan was worked out.

Third, all creditor collection activity would be enjoined by the federal court during the receivership proceeding.

Fourth, committees representing each class of public debt would form. Each of these "protective" committees would solicit irrevocable proxies or the actual deposit of the securities for the particular class of debt that the committee purported to represent. The proxies and deposit agreements would give the protective committee broad discretion to negotiate a plan that would modify the rights of the securityholders it represented.

Fifth, the various protective committees would negotiate with each other and the debtor management over a plan. The plan would call for the surrender of old securities in exchange for new securities that would be allocated among creditors and shareholders in accordance with the terms of the plan. When a plan was agreed to, the protective committees and debtor management would join together and form a new "reorganization" committee.

Sixth, the court would then set rules for a foreclosure sale of all the debtor's property. Inevitably, the reorganization committee would be the only bidder, because the reorganization committee had the full cooperation of management and could use the securities controlled by the protective committees to "credit bid" for the firm's assets. Knowing there was only one likely bidder, the court would set a floor on the bidding, the "upset price." The "upset price" would generally be a low-end estimate of the value of the debtor's property. The court order authorizing the foreclosure sale would require notice and subsequent "confirmation" of the sale by the court. The negotiated reorganization plan would be disclosed to the court and subjected to a variable and uncertain degree of court scrutiny at this confirmation hearing. The sale of the debtor's property to the reorganization committee at the "upset price" would then be "confirmed" by the court.

Seventh, those creditors who chose not to participate in the reorganization would receive their pro rata share of the upset price in cash in accordance with the priority of their legal rights. This pro rata distribution would generally be a fraction of the amount owed on senior claims and nothing for junior claims—in both cases substantially less than the anticipated value of new securities distributed under the plan. The property purchased at the sale would be immediately transferred to a newly formed corporation and securities in that corporation would be distributed to participating creditors in accordance with the negotiated plan. Incumbent management would continue to operate the business under substantially the same ownership but with scaled down debt. The expenses of the proceeding (including the necessary cash payments to dissenters) would generally be funded by pre-receivership shareholders who would retain an equity interest in the new corporation in exchange for their cash contribution and the cancellation of their pre-receivership shares.

Finally, the whole process was constrained by the rule of *Northern Pacific Railway Co. v. Boyd*, 228 U.S. 482 (1913). *Boyd* held that a dissenting creditor could continue to assert its claims against the reorganized company notwithstanding the foreclosure sale if pre-receivership shareholders continued to hold an interest in the reorganized company, *unless* the dissenting creditor had refused a "fair offer" to participate in the reorganization. The practice developed that the court would make a specific finding that the reorganization plan was "fair" at the confirmation hearing or in connection with authorizing the foreclosure sale. A "fair offer" generally came to mean cash or securities of the reorganized company deemed by the court supervising the reorganization to be of a value equal to the face amount of the creditor's claim. *See Case v. Los Angeles Lumber Prods. Co.*, 308 U.S. 106 (1939). The *Boyd* rule became known variously as the "absolute priority rule" and the "fair and equitable rule," and in modified form is now codified in § 1129(b). The *Boyd* rule, though a significant obstacle, proved to be somewhat less onerous in practice than it might first appear. Courts proved reluctant to overturn plans as "unfair" when faced with substantial majorities of consenting creditors from all affected classes and no alternative but forced liquidation.

This odd little dance, a negotiated restructuring masquerading as a receivership and foreclosure, lent itself to various sorts of abuse. The most obvious abuses involved the unfair treatment of *dissenters*. Dissenters, a notoriously complaining and litigious breed, brought their problems to the attention of the federal courts, and the courts gave substantial, if imperfect, redress through the mechanisms of the upset price (protecting dissenting senior creditors) and the *Boyd* rule (protecting dissenting junior creditors). But the courts did little to protect uninformed or unsophisticated or powerless *consenters* who might be taken advantage of in the informal, ad hoc and extrajudicial process by which consent was obtained.

The Great Depression generated enormous pressure for the reform of this jerry-built system. The first reformers, however, were not the quiescent consenters but the reorganizers themselves. Reorganizers sought to preserve the substance of the equity receivership system by codifying, regularizing, and simplifying it. In 1934 Congress passed § 77B, the first statutory reorganization process for non-railroad corporations. Section 77B dispensed with the charade of the foreclosure sale altogether. With two-thirds of the amount of each affected class assenting to the plan, dissenters could be compelled to scale down their debts so long as the court found the plan was "fair and equitable," did not "discriminate unfairly," and was "feasible." These refinements obviated the need for the traditional foreclosure sale and more importantly the need to make pro rata cash distributions to dissenting senior creditors based upon the "upset price" bid at the sale.

Section 77B was relatively poorly drafted. The reorganization bar through the National Bankruptcy Conference undertook to make technical corrections and drafting improvements in the statute. Meanwhile William O. Douglas at the Securities and Exchange Commission launched a frontal assault on the reorganization processes born of equity receivership practice.

The essence of Douglas's attack was that the reorganization process was largely controlled by debtor management and its allies. These "insiders" generally created the protective committees and solicited the proxies and deposits of securityholders. Most often the insiders could control the reorganization process from beginning to end, perpetuating their control over the debtor corporation and realizing the "spoils" of the reorganization process—substantial fees of all kinds for legal, management and financial services and new securities to be issued by the reorganized company at discounts from their anticipated fair market value. More than occasionally sophisticated, noninsider interests would organize their own "protective" committees and contest with the insiders for control of the reorganization process and the reorganized company. Although public securityholders might incidentally benefit from such a contest, more often than not, insider committees and non-insider committees controlled by sophisticated investors would manage to negotiate a mutually satisfactory resolution whereby the spoils of the reorganization need not be too widely distributed.

Ample ammunition for the reform forces came in the form of the Securities and Exchange Commission monumental five volume Report on the Study and Investigation of the Work, Activities, Personnel and Functions of Protective and Reorganization Committees. Douglas's SEC investigated the most prominent reorganizations of the day. The picture of the reorganization process that emerged from this somewhat politicized account is of pervasive insider exploitation of the reorganization process. Insiders, in the SEC's account, converted their control over protective committees, the solicitation of proxies and deposits, and information into profit at the expense of public investors. The forces of reform (Douglas's SEC) and reaction (the National Bankruptcy Conference) collided and the result was the Chandler Act.

The Chandler Act provided for two very different types of reorganization procedures. One procedure, Chapter X directly addressed the perceived abuses of equity receivership practice as perpetuated in § 77B. Insider control of the process was diluted by the mandatory appointment of a disinterested trustee, SEC review of reorganization plans, a mandatory judicial hearing on the plan (requiring judicial valuation of the debtor) for compliance with the *Boyd* rule *before* the solicitation of consents to the plan, regulation of the solicitation of proxies, deposits and votes, and court supervision over compensation and fees.

The alternative reorganization procedure under the Chandler Act was Chapter XI. Secured debt and equity interests could not be directly restructured under Chapter XI. The proceedings under Chapter XI were far less formal. The debtor remained in possession of the property of the estate and had the exclusive right to file a plan of arrangement. The SEC had no official monitoring function. An official creditors' committee elected at the first meeting of creditors served as the only counterweight to the debtor. But the responsibilities and powers of the creditors' committee were unclear. The absolute priority rule was not applicable in Chapter XI arrangements, out-voted dissenters' only protection being that the plan had to be in "the best interests of creditors," that is provide each creditor with more value than a forced liquidation of the firm.

Although the Chandler Act did not specifically guide the debtor in deciding whether to file under Chapter X or Chapter XI, Congress intended Chapter X to be the normal procedure for reorganizing corporations having publicly held securities while Chapter XI was intended for small business arrangements in which the claims of trade creditors and unsecured lenders were scaled down or extended. But by the eve of the adoption of the Bankruptcy Code in 1978, Chapter XI, despite all of its limitations, was being used to reorganize corporations that were among the nation's largest and Chapter X was virtually a dead letter. The perceived reasons for the failure of Chapter X and the popularity of Chapter XI became guiding principles in the drafting of Chapter 11 of the Bankruptcy Code.

## 3. CHAPTER 11 APPROACH

Although Chapter 11 can be used by individuals who are not engaged in business, *Toibb v. Radloff*, 501 U.S. 157 (1991), the statute is clearly designed as a business reorganization procedure. Typically a Chapter 11 debtor is a business operated in the form of a corporation. The great majority of Chapter 11 cases are initiated by the debtor firm voluntarily filing a bankruptcy petition.

Chapter 11 fuses the Chandler Act's Chapter X and Chapter XI into a unitary reorganization procedure. Secured debt, unsecured debt and equity interests are all subject to restructuring under Chapter 11 reorganization plans. For a period after the petition, the debtor has the exclusive right to propose a plan. The plan must divide creditors and interest-holders into classes. Different classes may be treated differently under the plan, but all claimants within a class are entitled to identical treatment. After due disclosure regarding the plan is given, creditors and stockholders vote by class on the plan. If all classes approve the plan, confirmation by the court usually follows without the necessity for the Chapter X-style judicial valuation hearing. Dissenting minorities within a class may be bound by a supermajority vote of the class. Even if all classes accept the plan, however, the court can not confirm a plan that does not meet certain minimum conditions that we will discuss later in this Chapter. If any class dissents the court can nevertheless confirm the plan if the minimum conditions and certain additional standards are met including a statutory version of the absolute priority rule. Confirmation over the objections of a dissenting class is usually referred to as "cramdown." Although it is important to understand each class's minimum legal entitlement in "cramdown," in fact almost all confirmed plans are "consensual" in the special bankruptcy sense that all impaired classes have accepted the plan by the requisite majorities. Most often the cramdown entitlements form a reference point in the bargaining that goes into formulating and confirming a consensual plan.

The actual process of formulating the consensus around a Chapter 11 plan remains mysterious, unregulated and irregular. Here Chapter 11 frankly rejects Douglas's reforms of mandatory trustees, SEC scrutiny of plans, and mandatory pre-solicitation judicial fairness hearings. Chapter 11 implicitly assumes that there is no one right plan for a particular case, or, if there is, courts and government agencies are not competent to discover it. Chapter 11 establishes a process and provides incentives to encourage the parties to negotiate a consensus around one of many plausible solutions, while seeking to control insider abuse. Except within broad limits, the Bankruptcy Code does not seek to determine the terms of the reorganization plan.

Debtors usually file Chapter 11 cases to deal with one of four types of business or legal problems:

1. To stop secured parties or judgment creditors from foreclosing or exercising other coercive debt collection measures authorized by state law.

2. To bind dissenting creditors or securityholders ("holdouts") to a generally consensual debt restructuring.

3. To gain access to special bankruptcy powers not available under state law—for example to estimate and discharge contingent claims or to avoid prebankruptcy transfers or to appeal an adverse judgment without posting a supersedeas bond or to assume and assign defaulted leases.

4. To alleviate a liquidity crisis that immediately threatens the survival of the firm because it can not meet its financial obligations as they are maturing.

Notice that the asserted purpose of Chapter 11—the preservation of going concern value—is at best incidentally implicated in all these situations, with the possible exception of the use of Chapter 11 to deal with holdouts. Firms facing foreclosure or liquidity crises or that otherwise see advantage in exercising the powers of a bankruptcy trustee may or may not have any going concern value to protect. Professor LoPucki has made an empirical study of Chapter 11 bankruptcies which concludes:

> Congress has asserted that "the purpose of a reorganization * * * case is to formulate and have confirmed a plan of reorganization. * * *' It is likely that only a few of the debtors studied came to Chapter 11 for this purpose. A large majority of them entered Chapter 11 with one or more of their creditors in hot pursuit, and filing was probably the only way they could remain in business or avoid liquidation. Their focus, quite naturally, was on short term survival, and only later, if at all, would a substantial number of them turn their attention to the long range prospects for their businesses.

Lynn M. LoPucki, *The Debtor in Full Control—Systems Failure Under Chapter 11 of the Bankruptcy Code?* 57 Am.Bankr.L.J. 99, 114 (1983).

Three distinctive types of firms make use of the unified Chapter 11 procedure: large operating businesses, small operating businesses, and "single asset real estate" debtors. Chapter 11 was designed with the large operating business principally in mind and it has proven to be best-suited for such cases. Procedures that are workable in such cases, prove much less suitable for small businesses and entities that do not operate businesses but simply own a particular piece of commercial real estate or raw land held for investment subject to a mortgage.

Accordingly, though Chapter 11 is frequently the bankruptcy proceeding of first resort for financially troubled firms of all sizes, small businesses are notoriously unlikely to successfully reorganize. In the year ending December 31, 2004, 10,132 companies filed in Chapter 11, down more than 50% from the 1991–92 peak. 2001 and 2002, recession years, were characterized by an increase in large company filings: 178 public companies with combined assets exceeding $615 billion filed during this period, including 61 with more than $1 billion assets each and several of the largest cases ever filed, Pacific Gas & Electric, Enron, Worldcom, Adelphia, and United Air Lines. *See* Lynn M. LoPucki, WebBRD, at http: // lopucki.law.ucla.edu (last visited Sept. 25, 2005). Data on the rate of successful reorganization are surprisingly scarce, confused and contradictory. But there is little doubt that the great majority of firms filing for Chapter 11 reorganization do not successfully reorganize, however, one defines success. Small firms in Chapter 11 are unlikely to attract the necessary capital to fund reorganization and can ill afford the large expense associated with Chapter 11. Large firms that file under Chapter 11, on the other hand, do generally successfully reorganize, at least if success is defined in the minimal way of confirming a reorganization plan. The *NBRC Report* at 308 cites estimates that upwards of 95% of the largest firms in Chapter 11 confirm plans. The overall confirmation rate appears to be closer to 20–30%, with perhaps a third of all confirmed plans providing for some form of orderly liquidation rather than reorganization of the debtor.

The expense and delay that make Chapter 11 so unsuitable for small businesses produced calls for reform. Some bankruptcy courts instituted "fast-track" Chapter 11 procedures for small business bankruptcies that allowed these debtors to go though Chapter 11 on an accelerated basis. Some critics of Chapter 11 advocated a Chapter 13 type procedure that would allow small business debtors to keep their assets and to pay their creditors' claims out of disposable income over the period of the plan. Reformers in 1994 proposed a separate "Chapter 10," devoted to small business bankruptcies, which would speed the reorganization procedure and abolish some basic Chapter 11 creditor protections, considered later in this chapter, such as the absolute priority rule, the § 1111(b) election, and the creditors' right to vote on confirmation of the plan.

Creditor opposition defeated the ambitious "Chapter 10" proposal. Instead the 1994 amendments included a rather modest set of provisions that dealt with small business debtors within the familiar confines of Chapter 11. The modest procedural advantages of these amendments came at the cost to debtors of agreeing to further limit their exclusive right to file reorganization plans. The *NBRC Report* at 635 states, unsurprisingly in light of these considerations, that these small business provisions were "largely ignored." Congress responded in the 2005 Act by making these specialized procedures mandatory for business debtors with less than $2 million in liquidated debts, and coupling them with seemingly onerous reporting obligations and expanded grounds for dismissal and conversion, that promise to make small business reorganization in Chapter 11 even more difficult.

The single-asset real estate debtor raises another set of concerns. In such cases, "reorganization" in essence amounts to a contest between the debtor and the mortgage holder over who will own heavily encumbered real estate once the debtor has defaulted on its mortgage payments. There are generally no other creditors, no operating business, and no employees whose interests are implicated. Some theorists, and indeed some courts, question whether the use of Chapter 11 in these cases to merely stave off foreclosure and involuntarily restructure mortgage debt is appropriate. Although Chapter 11 remains open to single asset real estate debtors, over time, courts have grown increasingly hostile to their unfettered use (or abuse, depending upon one's view) of Chapter 11. Be aware as you work through the materials in this chapter of the difference in judicial attitude toward these debtors when you assess the construction placed upon generally applicable Chapter 11 provisions in single asset real estate cases. In a few areas, Congress has amended the Bankruptcy Code to place special limitations upon single asset real estate debtors. The 2005 Act expanded these provisions and broadened their applicability to all single asset real estate debtors, by removing the $4 million statutory cap formerly limiting the definition of single asset real estate debtor.

## B. MANAGEMENT AND CONTROL

### 1. ROLE OF DEBTOR IN POSSESSION

In Chapter 11 usually no bankruptcy trustee is appointed. The debtor (now called the "debtor-in-possession") succeeds to the trustee's rights, powers, and duties, and may operate its business without prior court approval. § 1107(a) and § 1108. One difference between the role of a bankruptcy trustee and that of the debtor in possession is that the debtor in possession does not investigate its own past conduct. § 1106(a)(3) and (4). Because it has the avoiding powers of the trustee, the debtor in possession may avoid preferential or fraudulent transfers that it made as debtor before bankruptcy.

In performing the trustee's duties, the debtor in possession is, under § 323(a), the "representative of the estate." In *Commodity Futures Trading Commission v. Weintraub*, 471 U.S. 343, 355 (1985), the Court said " * * * the willingness of courts to leave debtors in possession "is premised upon an assurance that the officers and managing employees can be depended upon to carry out the fiduciary responsibilities of a trustee.'" Thus, the board of directors of a Chapter 11 debtor owes fiduciary obligations not only to its stockholders (as all corporate boards do) but also to creditors of the debtor. One must distinguish between situations in which the debtor's officers and directors act for the estate from those in which they act as the representative of the economic interests of stockholders. The Bankruptcy Code refers to "the debtor in possession" when the debtor acts as representative of the bankruptcy estate in continuing its business and otherwise exercising the powers of the trustee. In that role it has the responsibilities of a fiduciary. But § 1121, which deals with the issue of who can propose a plan of reorganization, uses the term "the debtor" to refer to the corporation being reorganized. Plans are negotiated between creditors and shareholders. To the extent creditors get more under the plan shareholders may get less. The use of "debtor" in § 1121 recognizes that in proposing and negotiating the plan of reorganization the corporation is not acting as a representative of the estate, but rather in the interests of itself and its stockholders.

Another dimension of the role of the debtor in possession is the fact that the debtor's management may have interests that differ from those of its stockholders. In closely held corporations management and stockholders will be the same people. But in large corporations the managers who operate the debtor in possession and negotiate its reorganization may be quite remote from its stockholders. If at the end of the day, the plan of reorganization is likely to extinguish the interests of prebankruptcy shareholders, it may well be to the self-interest of management to be accommodating to the interests of those creditors who are likely to end up with the stock of the reorganized corporation for it is they who will decide on the management for the reorganized business. If stockholders are dissatisfied with management's representation of their interests they can attempt to change the membership of the board of directors. However, courts have prevented stockholders from electing a new board in cases in which it appeared their intent was to block a viable plan. *Manville Corp. v. Equity Security Holders Committee*, 801 F.2d 60 (2d Cir.1986), discusses the authorities.

## 2.  Appointment of Trustee in Bankruptcy

The appointment of a trustee in bankruptcy in Chapter 11 occurs only in exceptional cases. The court may order the appointment of a trustee "for cause, including fraud, dishonesty, incompetence or gross mismanagement of the affairs of the debtor by current management * * * or similar cause." § 1104(a)(1). The court may also appoint a trustee or an examiner in lieu of dismissing or converting the case. See § 1104(a)(3). It is also possible, under § 1104(a)(2), for the court to order appointment of a trustee "in the interests of creditors, any equity security holders, and other interests of the estate." The meaning of § 1104(a)(2) is unclear. It is apparently meant to apply to cases in which there is no gross misconduct by management, but in which there is some reason why the interests of everyone concerned would be better served by appointment of a trustee.

In the wake of the Chapter 11 cases involving Enron and Worldcom, which involved allegations of massive fraud in connection with accounting and financial reporting, Congress added § 1104(e) to the Code in the 2005 Act. Section 1104(a) continues to mandate appointment of a trustee "for cause, including fraud. . . by current management" on request of any party in interest or the U.S. Trustee. New § 1104(e) now requires the U.S. Trustee to move for the appointment of a trustee if there are "reasonable grounds to suspect" personal participation in fraud by the debtor's incumbent CEO, CFO or directors in connection with the debtor's management or financial reporting. Presumably, the U.S. Trustee's motion will be denied, notwithstanding its reasonable suspicions, if it cannot prove fraud by at least a preponderance of the admissible evidence introduced at the hearing. What is the point of requiring the U.S. Trustee to move for a trustee based only on reasonable suspicion? Once having made the motion, is the U.S. Trustee required to prosecute it, rather than settle it?

If the court finds that exceptional circumstances do warrant appointment of a trustee, the appointing is done in the first instance by the U.S. Trustee unless a trustee is elected by creditors. To lawfully elect a trustee at least 20 percent of the creditors must vote and the trustee must receive the votes of creditors holding the majority in amount of claims who actually vote. § 702. Since Chapter 11 trustees are responsible for managing a distressed operating business, it is not uncommon to see the parties and the U.S. Trustee seek out specialized "turnaround" managers for this role rather than the lawyers and accountants who typically serve as Chapter 7 trustees.

If a trustee is appointed, the debtor's board of directors continues to exist after the appointment, but its powers are severely limited. In *Commodity Futures Trading Comm. v. Weintraub*, 471 U.S. 343, 352–53 (1985), the Court stated that upon appointment of a trustee: "[The board's] role is to turn over the corporation's property to the trustee and to provide certain information to the trustee and to the creditors. §§ 521, 343. Congress contemplated that when a trustee is appointed, he assumes control of the business, and the debtor's directors are 'completely ousted.'"

An important collateral consequence of the appointment of a Chapter 11 trustee is to terminate the debtor's exclusive right to file a reorganization plan, assuming that the statutory period has not otherwise expired.

### 3. Examiners

The Bankruptcy Code provides for a middle ground between ousting the debtor by appointment of a trustee and leaving the debtor in possession subject to only general supervision by the court and any creditors' committee or other interested parties. The middle ground is the appointment of an examiner "to conduct such an investigation of the debtor as is appropriate, including an investigation of any allegations of fraud, dishonesty, incompetence, misconduct, mismanagement, or irregularity. . . ." § 1104(c). Under § 1106(b) the examiner is given the investigatory powers of the trustee. In addition, the examiner is required to perform "any other duties of the trustee that the court orders the debtor in possession not to perform" unless the court orders otherwise. Thus, an examiner's functions can be limited to a particular investigatory role or can be expanded to include all of the functions of the trustee except those that the court allows the debtor in possession to perform.

Section 1104(c) states that on request of a party, the court "shall" appoint an examiner if (1) the appointment "is in the interests of creditors, any equity security holders, and other interests of the estate" or (2) the unsecured non-trade and non-insider claims exceed $5,000,000. § 1104(c). The language of § 1104(c) suggests that any party has the right to have an examiner appointed in any medium to large size case. But examiners are not routinely requested or appointed in such cases. Some courts refuse to read § 1104(c) literally and weigh the costs and benefits of appointing an examiner given the circumstances of the case or sharply limit the nature, extent, cost and duration of any investigation.

### 4. Creditors' Committees

Section 1102(a)(1) requires the U.S. Trustee to promptly appoint a committee of creditors holding unsecured claims. This committee "shall ordinarily consist of the persons, willing to serve, that hold the seven largest claims against the debtor * * * ". § 1102(b)(1). The "seven-largest" standard set out in the statute is merely precatory. H.R.Rep.No. 595, 95th Cong., 1st Sess. 401–02 (1977). Since the committees are intended to be the "primary negotiating bodies for the formulation of the plan of reorganization," the U.S. Trustee and bankruptcy courts have wide "latitude in appointing a committee that is manageable and representative in light of the circumstances of the case." Id. The debtor may have been negotiating a workout with a committee of its creditors before filing. If this committee is representative of the claims to be represented and was "fairly chosen," § 1102(b)(1) allows the U.S. Trustee to appoint its members as the creditors' committee.

What constitutes an adequately representative committee is unclear. One conception of the creditors' committee focuses on the need to control insider abuse and emphasizes committee members' undivided duty of loyalty to all unsecured creditors. A competing view focuses on the committee as an institutional device for building consensus around a plan and sees it as mediating and resolving conflicting interests among various constituencies of unsecured creditors. Daniel J. Bussel, *Coalition–Building Through Bankruptcy Creditors' Committees*, 43 UCLA L.Rev. 1547 (1996).

In complex cases either the U.S. Trustee or the court may cause additional committees of creditors or equity security holders to be appointed to ensure "adequate representation" of creditors or equity security holders. § 1102(a). "Equity security" is defined in § 101 to include a share in a corporation and the interest of a limited partner in a limited partnership. Committees of equity security holders are appropriate in cases in which the securities are publicly held and where they may arguably have rights to substantial reorganization value. A committee of equity security holders "shall ordinarily consist of the persons, willing to serve, that hold the seven largest amounts of equity securities of the debtor * * * ". § 1102(b)(2).

Creditors' committees are given broad powers by § 1103(c). But the most important role of creditors' committees is to negotiate with the debtor in possession or trustee about the terms of the reorganization plan. In complex cases these negotiations may take years. If no agreement can be reached and the debtor exhausts its statutory exclusivity period, the creditors' committee may submit a rival plan. Whether in connection with its own plan or the debtor's plan, the committee may solicit acceptances or rejections of plans.

In the usual case no trustee or examiner is appointed, and the creditors' committee is the only participant in the case that can carry out an investigation of the debtor's financial condition and of the debtor's chances for a successful reorganization. One of us has suggested that "the most sensible way to view these powers is as powers, not responsibilities. Their use, in the hands of a creditors' committee, is. . . the carrying on of plan negotiations by other means." Daniel J. Bussel, *Coalition–Building Through Bankruptcy Creditors' Committees*, 43 UCLA L.Rev. 1547, 1629 (1996). Committees on this view properly use their investigative powers strategically to advance their objectives in the plan formulation and confirmation processes.

Creditors' committees may intervene in adversary proceedings and initiate proceedings, such as the recovery of preferences or fraudulent transfers, if the debtor in possession declines to do so. *See Phar–Mor, Inc. v. Coopers & Lybrand*, 22 F.3d 1228 (3d Cir.1994).

Under the majority view, specific bankruptcy court authorization is required to permit committees to prosecute estate causes of action. Some authorities, in the light of the Supreme Court's decision in *Hartford Underwriters*, p. 631, have questioned the source of statutory authority to designate committees as estate representatives for these purposes in light of the statute's express designation of the trustee or debtor-in-possession. For a fuller discussion and analysis of these issues, see *Official Committee of Unsecured Creditors of Cybergenics Corp. v. Chinery*, 330 F.3d 548 *en banc* (3d Cir.2003) and Daniel J. Bussel, *Creditors' Committees as Estate Representatives in Bankruptcy Litigation*, 10 Stan. J.L. Bus. & Fin. 28 (2004).

It is difficult to appraise how well creditors' committees carry out the functions contemplated by Chapter 11. As a practical matter, the committee normally carries out its functions by employing professionals such as lawyers and accountants whose fees constitute expenses of administration under §§ 330(a) and 503(b). If a successful reorganization is a remote possibility or if the size of the debtor is not large enough to warrant the expense of lawyers and accountants there may be little that a creditors' committee can do to affect the outcome. Creditors' committees, however, have played prominent roles in Chapter 11 cases involving large debtors in which the financial stakes justified the expenditure of the time and money required to effectively investigate and negotiate on behalf of unsecured creditors. *See* Daniel J. Bussel, *Coalition–Building Through Bankruptcy Creditors' Committees*, 43 UCLA L.Rev. 1547 (1996) (studying 37 cases involving debtors with more than $50 million in assets filed in the Central District of California from 1986–1991 including 13 in which the creditors' committees played a major role in the case).

## C. ADEQUATE PROTECTION OF SECURITY INTERESTS OF UNDERSECURED CREDITORS

An example of conflict between the rights of a creditor and the interests of the debtor in reorganizing a troubled enterprise is provided by the following case. A Chapter 11 debtor owns an asset that is encumbered by a security interest. The debt owed to the secured creditor is in default. The value of the collateral is less than the amount of the debt. If the collateral is needed for continued operation of the debtor's business, repossession and foreclosure is inconsistent with reorganization. Thus, the creditor is barred by § 362(a) from seizing the collateral. But the creditor is entitled to relief from the stay under § 362(d)(1) if adequate protection of the creditor's security interest is not provided. The creditor suffers an economic loss by being denied the immediate right to seize and sell the collateral; a dollar received today is worth more than a dollar to be received in the future. The creditor is not entitled to interest on the debt after the filing of the petition in bankruptcy because the value of the collateral is less than the amount of the debt. §§ 502(b)(2), 506(b). If the creditor's collateral is being used for the benefit of the debtor and other creditors, does adequate protection require that the creditor be compensated for the loss resulting from the creditor's inability to seize and sell the collateral during the period from the filing of the petition until confirmation of the plan of reorganization? The House Report stated with respect to the meaning of adequate protection: "Secured creditors should not be deprived of the benefit of their bargain." 1978 U.S.C.C.A.N at 6295. The secured creditor's bargain is that upon default by the debtor the creditor may immediately take possession of the collateral, sell it, and reinvest the proceeds. If there are to be any successful reorganizations under Chapter 11, creditors must be denied the right to seize collateral upon the debtor's filing in bankruptcy. But, perhaps, secured creditors should be compensated for the economic loss caused by staying repossession and foreclosure during the bankruptcy.

Professor Thomas Jackson, in his book, *The Logic and Limits of Bankruptcy Law* 189–190 (1986), argued that the creditor should be entitled to compensation. Costs of reorganization should not be imposed on secured creditors who do not benefit from reorganization. Rather, they should be imposed on the debtor and unsecured creditors who may benefit from reorganization. An insolvent debtor gains by a successful reorganization and loses nothing if reorganization fails because its interest is, by definition, worthless in liquidation. Unsecured creditors may have something to gain from a successful reorganization and may have something to lose if it fails. An unsecured creditor who would have 35% of its claim satisfied in liquidation may lose it all if reorganization fails, or may receive 100% of the claim if the reorganization succeeds. But with respect to a secured claim, the creditor can receive no more than the amount of the claim if the reorganization succeeds and in this sense does not benefit from the reorganization. A rule requiring compensation for secured creditors for the interim loss of their collateral imposes costs; debtors may find it more difficult to reorganize and unsecured creditors may find their share of the estate reduced if liquidation ensues. But Professor Jackson contends that such a rule places the costs of reorganization on the parties who stand to benefit from it.

Professor Jackson's reasoning was accepted in *In re American Mariner Industries, Inc.*, 734 F.2d 426 (9th Cir.1984), but was rejected by the Fifth Circuit opinion in *Timbers*. In *Timbers* this conflict was resolved by the Supreme Court.

# United Savings Assoc. of Texas v. Timbers of Inwood Forest Assoc., Ltd.

Supreme Court of the United States, 1988.
484 U.S. 365.

■ Justice SCALIA delivered the opinion of the Court.

\* \* \*

## I

On June 29, 1982, respondent Timbers of Inwood Forest Associates, Inc. executed a note in the principal amount of $4,100,000. Petitioner is the holder of the note as well as of a security interest created the same day in an apartment project owned by respondent in Houston, Texas. The security interest included an assignment of rents from the project. On March 4, 1985, respondent filed a voluntary petition under Chapter 11 of the Bankruptcy Code \* \* \*.

On March 18, 1985, petitioner moved for relief from the automatic stay of enforcement of liens triggered by the petition, see § 362(a), on the ground that there was lack of "adequate protection" of its interest within the meaning of § 362(d)(1). At a hearing before the Bankruptcy Court, it was established that respondent owed petitioner $4,366,388.77, and evidence was presented that the value of the collateral was somewhere between $2,650,000 and $4,250,000. The collateral was appreciating in value, but only very slightly. It was therefore undisputed that petitioner was an undersecured creditor. Respondent had agreed to pay petitioner the postpetition rents from the apartment project (covered by the after-acquired property clause in the security agreement), minus operating expenses. Petitioner contended, however, that it was entitled to additional compensation. The Bankruptcy Court agreed and on April 19, 1985, it conditioned continuance of the stay on monthly payments by respondent, at the market rate of 12% per annum, on the estimated amount realizable on foreclosure, $4,250,000—commencing six months after the filing of the bankruptcy petition, to reflect the normal foreclosure delays. \* \* \* The court held that the postpetition rents could be applied to these payments. Respondent appealed to the District Court and petitioner cross–appealed on the amount of the adequate protection payments. The District Court affirmed but the Fifth Circuit en banc reversed.

We granted certiorari to determine whether undersecured creditors are entitled to compensation under § 362(d)(1) for the delay caused by the automatic stay in foreclosing on their collateral.

## II

When a bankruptcy petition is filed, § 362(a) of the Bankruptcy Code provides an automatic stay of, among other things, actions taken to realize the value of collateral given by the debtor. The provision of the Code central to the decision of this case is § 362(d), which reads as follows:

"On request of a party in interest and after notice and a hearing, the court shall grant relief from the stay provided under subsection (a) of this section, such as by terminating, annulling, modifying, or conditioning such stay—

"(1) for cause, including the lack of adequate protection of an interest in property of such party in interest; or

"(2) with respect to a stay of an act against property under subsection (a) of this section, if—

"(A) the debtor does not have an equity in such property; and

"(B) such property is not necessary to an effective reorganization."

The phrase "adequate protection" in paragraph (1) of the foregoing provision is given further content by § 361 of the Code * * *.

It is common ground that the "interest in property" referred to by § 362(d)(1) includes the right of a secured creditor to have the security applied in payment of the debt upon completion of the reorganization; and that that interest is not adequately protected if the security is depreciating during the term of the stay. Thus, it is agreed that if the apartment project in this case had been declining in value petitioner would have been entitled, under § 362(d)(1), to cash payments or additional security in the amount of the decline, as § 361 describes. The crux of the present dispute is that petitioner asserts, and respondent denies, that the phrase "interest in property" also includes the secured party's right (suspended by the stay) to take immediate possession of the defaulted security, and apply it in payment of the debt. If that right is embraced by the term, it is obviously not adequately protected unless the secured party is reimbursed for the use of the proceeds he is deprived of during the term of the stay.

The term "interest in property" certainly summons up such concepts as "fee ownership," "life estate," "co-ownership," and "security interest" more readily than it does the notion of "right to immediate foreclosure." Nonetheless, viewed in the isolated context of § 362(d)(1), the phrase could reasonably be given the meaning petitioner asserts. Statutory construction, however, is a holistic endeavor. A provision that may seem ambiguous in isolation is often clarified by the remainder of the statutory scheme—because the same terminology is used elsewhere in a context that makes its meaning clear, * * * or because only one of the permissible meanings produces a substantive effect that is compatible with the rest of the law * * *. That is the case here. Section 362(d)(1) is only one of a series of provisions in the Bankruptcy Code dealing with the rights of secured creditors. The language in those other provisions, and the substantive dispositions that they effect, persuade us that the "interest in property" protected by § 362(d)(1) does not include a secured party's right to immediate foreclosure.

Section 506 of the Code defines the amount of the secured creditor's allowed secured claim and the conditions of his receiving postpetition interest. In relevant part it reads as follows:

"(a) An allowed claim of a creditor secured by a lien on property in which the estate has an interest * * * is a secured claim to the extent of the value of such creditor's interest in the estate's interest in such property, * * * and is an unsecured claim to the extent that the value of such creditor's interest * * * is less than the amount of such allowed claim * * *.

"(b) To the extent that an allowed secured claim is secured by property the value of which * * * is greater than the amount of such claim, there shall be allowed to the holder of such claim, interest on such claim, and any reasonable fees, costs, or charges provided for under the agreement under which such claim arose."

In subsection (a) of this provision the creditor's "interest in property" obviously means his security interest without taking account of his right to immediate possession of the collateral on default. If the latter were included, the "value of such creditor's interest" would increase, and the proportions of the claim that are secured and unsecured would alter, as the stay continues—since the value of the entitlement to use the collateral from the date of bankruptcy would rise with the passage of time. No one suggests this was intended. The phrase "value of such creditor's interest" in § 506(a) means "the value of the collateral." H.R.Rep. No. 95–595, pp. 181, 356 (1977) * * * We think the phrase "value of such entity's interest" in § 361(1) and (2), when applied to secured creditors, means the same.

Even more important for our purposes than § 506's use of terminology is its substantive effect of denying undersecured creditors postpetition interest on their claims—just as it denies *over*-secured creditors postpetition interest to the extent that such interest, when added to the principal amount of the claim, will exceed the value of the collateral. Section 506(b) provides that "*[t]o the extent that* an allowed secured claim is secured by property the value of which * * * is greater than the amount of such claim, there shall be allowed to the holder of such claim, interest on such claim." (Emphasis added.) Since this provision permits postpetition interest to be paid only out of the "security cushion," the undersecured creditor, who has no such cushion, falls within the general rule disallowing postpetition interest. See § 502(b)(2). If the Code had meant to give the undersecured creditor, who is thus denied interest on his *claim,* interest on the value of his *collateral,* surely this is where that disposition would have been set forth, and not obscured within the "adequate protection" provision of § 362(d)(1). Instead of the intricate phraseology set forth above, § 506(b) would simply have said that the secured creditor is entitled to interest "on his allowed claim, or on the value of the property securing his allowed claim, whichever is lesser." Petitioner's interpretation of § 362(d)(1) must be regarded as contradicting the carefully drawn disposition of § 506(b).

Petitioner seeks to avoid this conclusion by characterizing § 506(b) as merely an alternative method for compensating oversecured creditors, which does not imply that no compensation is available to undersecured creditors. This theory of duplicate protection for oversecured creditors is implausible even in the abstract, but even more so in light of the historical principles of bankruptcy law. Section 506(b)'s denial of postpetition interest to undersecured creditors merely codified pre-Code bankruptcy law, in which that denial was part of the conscious allocation of reorganization benefits and losses between undersecured and unsecured creditors. "To allow a secured creditor interest where his security was worth less than the value of his debt was thought to be inequitable to unsecured creditors." Vanston Bondholders Protective Committee v. Green, 329 U.S. 156, 164 (1946). It was considered unfair to allow an undersecured creditor to recover interest from the estate's unencumbered assets before unsecured creditors had recovered any principal. * * * We think it unlikely that § 506(b) codified the pre-Code rule with the intent, not of achieving the principal purpose and function of that rule, but of providing over-secured creditors an alternative method of compensation. Moreover, it is incomprehensible why Congress would want to favor undersecured creditors with interest if they move for it under § 362(d)(1) at the inception of the reorganization process—thereby probably pushing the estate into liquidation—but not if they forbear and seek it only at the completion of the reorganization.

Second, petitioner's interpretation of § 362(d)(1) is structurally inconsistent with § 552. Section 552(a) states the general rule that a prepetition security interest does not reach property acquired by the estate or debtor postpetition. Section 552(b) sets forth an exception, allowing postpetition "proceeds, product, offspring, rents, or profits" of the collateral to be covered only if the security agreement expressly provides for an interest in such property, and the interest has been perfected under "applicable nonbankruptcy law." * * * Section 552(b) therefore makes possession of a perfected security interest in postpetition rents or profits from collateral a condition of having them applied to satisfying the claim of the secured creditor ahead of the claims of unsecured creditors. Under petitioner's interpretation, however, the undersecured creditor who lacks such a perfected security interest in effect achieves the same result by demanding the "use value" of his collateral under § 362. It is true that § 506(b) gives the *over*secured creditor, despite lack of compliance with the conditions of § 552, a similar priority over unsecured creditors; but that does not compromise the principle of § 552, since the interest payments come only out of the "cushion" in which the oversecured creditor *does have* a perfected security interest.

* * *

Section 362(d)(2) also belies petitioner's contention that undersecured creditors will face inordinate and extortionate delay if they are denied compensation for interest lost during the stay as part of "adequate protection" under § 362(d)(1). Once the movant under § 362(d)(2) establishes that he is an undersecured creditor, it is the burden of the *debtor* to establish that the collateral at issue is "necessary to an effective reorganization." See § 362(g). What this requires is not merely a showing that if there is conceivably to be an effective reorganization, this property will be needed for it; but that the property is essential for an effective reorganization *that is in prospect.* This means, as many lower courts, including the en banc court in this case, have properly said, that there must be "a reasonable possibility of a successful reorganization within a reasonable time." The cases are numerous in which § 362(d)(2) relief has been provided within less than a year from the filing of the bankruptcy petition. And while the bankruptcy courts demand less detailed showings during the four months in which the debtor is given the exclusive right to put together a plan, see § 1121(b), (c)(2), even within that period lack of any realistic prospect of effective reorganization will require § 362(d)(2) relief.

## III

### A

Petitioner contends that denying it compensation under § 362(d)(1) is inconsistent with sections of the Code other than those just discussed. Petitioner principally relies on the phrase "indubitable equivalent" in § 361(3), which also appears in § 1129(b)(2)(A)(iii). Petitioner contends that in the latter context, which sets forth the standards for confirming a reorganization plan, the phrase has developed a well-settled meaning connoting the right of a secured creditor to receive present value of his security—thus requiring interest if the claim is to be paid over time. It is true that under § 1129(b) a secured claimant has a right to receive under a plan the present value of his collateral. This entitlement arises, however, not from the phrase "indubitable equivalent" in § 1129(b)(2)(A)(iii), but from the provision of § 1129(b)(2)(A)(i)(II) that guarantees the secured creditor "deferred cash payments * * * of a value, *as of the effective date of the plan,* of at least the value of such [secured claimant's] interest in the estate's interest in such property." (Emphasis added.) Under this formulation, even though the undersecured creditor's "interest" is regarded (properly) as solely the value of the collateral, he must be rendered payments that assure him that value *as of the effective date of the plan.* In § 361(3), by contrast, the relief pending the stay need only be such "*as will result in the realization * * * of the indubitable equivalent*" of the collateral. (Emphasis added.) It is obvious (since §§ 361 and 362(d)(1) do not entitle the secured creditor to immediate payment of the principal of his collateral) that this "realization" is to "result" not at once, but only upon completion of the reorganization. It is *then* that he must be assured "realization * * * of the indubitable equivalent" of his collateral. To put the point differently: similarity of outcome between § 361(3) and § 1129 would be demanded only if the former read "such other relief * * * as will give such entity, *as of the date of the relief,* the indubitable equivalent of such entity's interest in such property."

Nor is there merit in petitioner's suggestion that "indubitable equivalent" in § 361(3) connotes reimbursement for the use value of collateral because the phrase is derived from In re Murel Holding Corp., 75 F.2d 941 (C.A.2 1935), where it bore that meaning. *Murel* involved a proposed reorganization plan that gave the secured creditor interest on his collateral for 10 years, with full payment of the secured principal due at the end of that term; the plan made no provision, however, for amortization of principal or maintenance of the collateral's value during the term. In rejecting the plan, *Murel* used the words "indubitable equivalence" with specific reference not to interest (which was assured), but to the jeopardized principal of the loan:

> "Interest is indeed the common measure of the difference [between payment now and payment 10 years hence], but a creditor who fears the safety of his principal will scarcely be content with that; he wishes to get his money or at least the property. We see no reason to suppose that the statute was intended to deprive him of that in the interest of junior holders, unless by a substitute of the most indubitable equivalence."

Of course *Murel,* like § 1129, proceeds from the premise that in the confirmation context the secured creditor is entitled to present value. But no more from *Murel* than from § 1129 can it be inferred that a similar requirement exists as of the time of the bankruptcy stay. The reorganized debtor is supposed to stand on his own two feet. The debtor in process of reorganization, by contrast, is given many temporary protections against the normal operation of the law.

\* \* \*

### B

Petitioner contends that its interpretation is supported by the legislative history of §§ 361 and 362(d)(1), relying almost entirely on statements that "[s]ecured creditors should not be deprived of the benefit of their bargain." H.R.Rep. No. 95–595, at 339; S.Rep. No. 95–989. Such generalizations are inadequate to overcome the plain textual indication in §§ 506 and 362(d)(2) of the Code that Congress did not wish the undersecured creditor to receive interest on his collateral during the term of the stay. If it is at all relevant, the legislative history tends to subvert rather than support petitioner's thesis, since it contains not a hint that § 362(d)(1) entitles the undersecured creditor to postpetition interest. Such a major change in the existing rules would not likely have been made without specific provision in the text of the statute \* \* \* ; it is most improbable that it would have been made without even any mention in the legislative history.

\* \* \*

The Fifth Circuit correctly held that the undersecured petitioner is not entitled to interest on its collateral during the stay to assure adequate protection under § 362(d)(1). Petitioner has never sought relief from the stay under § 362(d)(2) or on any ground other than lack of adequate protection. Accordingly, the judgment of the Fifth Circuit is

Affirmed.

## NOTES

**1.** In *Timbers* the Court refuted the contention that undersecured creditors would suffer "inordinate and extortionate delay" if they are denied compensation for interest lost during the stay as part of "adequate protection" under § 362(d)(1). In a famous dictum the Court answered that under § 362(d)(2), once the creditor establishes that the debtor has no equity in the collateral, the debtor has the burden of establishing that the collateral

is "necessary to an effective reorganization.' * * * What this requires is not merely a showing that if there is conceivably to be an effective reorganization, this property will be needed for it; but that the property is essential for an effective reorganization *that is in prospect.* This means, as many lower courts, including the en banc court in this case, have properly said, that there must be "a reasonable possibility of a successful reorganization within a reasonable time.'

484 U.S. at 375–376.

There had been a split of authority on the meaning of "necessary to an effective reorganization" in § 362(d)(2)(B). Under the majority view (the "feasibility test") the debtor had to show that the property was necessary for a reorganization and that a reorganization was reasonably likely. The opposing view, referred to as the "necessity test," did not require a showing of a reasonable likelihood of a successful reorganization. *See, e.g., In re Koopmans*, 22 B.R. 395 (Bankr.D.Utah 1982). The Court's dictum in *Timbers* quoted above is looked upon as its approval of the feasibility test and it has been followed in the cases. *See, e.g., Matter of Canal Place Limited Partnership*, 921 F.2d 569 (5th Cir.1991); *In re 8th Street Village Limited Partnership*, 94 B.R. 993, 996 (N.D.Ill.1988) ("even if the discussion of § 362(d)(2) [in *Timbers*] was *dictum,* that discussion of the Supreme Court should not be lightly ignored").

**2.** Section 361, stating ways in which adequate protection may be given, was influenced by three decisions of the Second Circuit. *In re Murel Holding Corp.*, 75 F.2d 941 (2d Cir.1935), which is discussed in *Timbers*, is the source of the term "indubitable equivalent" in § 361(3). *In re Yale Express*, 384 F.2d 990 (2d Cir.1967), involved the question of how to compensate a creditor, Fruehauf, for the use of trucks and trailers in which it had a security interest. Yale Express, a Chapter X debtor, needed the equipment for its reorganization. The court declined to grant periodic payments to Fruehauf because "to grant rental payments or their equivalent to all such creditors would nullify the reorganization as effectively as granting the petition for reclamation." 384 F.2d at 992. The court concluded: "But to such extent as Fruehauf has been damaged by the use of its property pending the reorganization, it is entitled to equitable consideration in the reorganization plan." 384 F.2d at 992. The court probably meant that, to the extent damaged, Fruehauf would have a right to payment of an administrative expense. The third case, *In re Bermec,* 445 F.2d 367 (2d Cir.1971), also concerned creditors with a security interest in the trucks of a Chapter X debtor that were necessary to the reorganization of the debtor's leasing business. The court stated that it was "conscious of the deep concern of the * * * secured creditors lest their security depreciate beyond adequate salvage, but we must balance that with the Congressional mandate to encourage attempts at corporate reorganization where there is a reasonable possibility of success." The court denied reclamation but the debtor was required to preserve the status quo by paying to the secured creditors amounts to cover the "economic depreciation" of the equipment it was using.

At a late stage in the legislative process, § 361 had four subsections illustrating forms of adequate protection: (1) periodic cash payments (*Bermec*); (2) additional or replacement liens; (3) administrative expense priority (*Yale Express*); and (4) other relief amounting to the indubitable equivalent of the entity's interest in the property (*Murel*). In the end the administrative priority illustration was deleted, and new subsection (3) provided that an administrative expense priority was not an acceptable means of adequate protection. Even though the administrative expense method of adequate protection espoused by *Yale Express* was rejected in § 361, Congress adopted the concept in § 507(b) by providing a super-priority administrative expense as back-up protection to a secured creditor who had been given an approved method of adequate protection that subsequently turned out not to be adequate in fact.

**3.** A question that courts have struggled with in trying to interpret § 507(b) (described by Judge Mabey in *In re Callister,* 15 B.R. 521, 526 (Bankr.D.Utah 1981), as "the proverbial prism in the fog") is the tension between § 507(b), which builds us up to expect that the creditor is going to be able to recover any loss it suffers on account of inadequate "adequate protection," and § 503(b) which lets us down by limiting recovery to the benefits conferred on the debtor's estate. Why should the creditor's loss owing to an error in setting the degree of protection the creditor is entitled to receive under § 361 be limited to the estate's gain from having the stay remain? What's the connection? As Judge Mabey opines in *Callister*: "The language of 507(b), specially in relation to 503(b), is difficult to plumb. Indeed, 503(b) and 507(b) may be at odds. One is keyed to preserving the estate, the other is designed to protect secured creditors. * * * If 507(b) is faithful to one of these purposes, it may be untrue to the other." 15 B.R. at 528–529. *In re Carpet Center Leasing Co.,* 991 F.3d 682, *amended on reh'g,* 4 F.3d 940 (11th Cir.1993), concludes: "Section 507(b) thus implies that an administrative expense claim under § 503(b) will be allowed where adequate protection payments prove insufficient to compensate a secured creditor for the diminution in the value of its collateral." But the court went on to show that the estate was in fact benefited in that case during the Debtor's failed attempt to reorganize. *Ford Motor Credit Company v. Dobbins*, 35 F.3d 860 (4th Cir.1994), adopting a seemingly contrary approach, holds that a creditor cannot receive a superpriority administrative expense under § 507(b) unless it shows that the debtor's estate actually benefited from the stay. The fact that in *Dobbins* the estate depreciated in value during the period of the stay while the debtor was permitted to seek out a buyer, which it never found, was not enough to entitle the creditor to relief under § 507(b) because it does not qualify under § 503(b)(1)(A) as a legitimate administrative expense. "[W]e interpret the terms "actual' and "necessary' [in § 503(b)] with care and we require an *actual use* by (and therefore an actual benefit to) the estate for a creditor to have a § 503(b) claim." 35 F.3d at 868 n. 7. (Emphasis in original.)

**4.** Does § 507(b) apply when there is no court order awarding adequate protection to the creditor? A secured creditor may withdraw its motion to lift the stay upon the debtor's undertaking to make periodic payments to compensate the creditor for the use of the collateral. If it turns out that these payments are inadequate to cover the depreciation in the value of the collateral, is the creditor entitled to invoke the super-priority of § 507(b) for the loss? Although prudent creditors can assure their recourse to § 507(b) by getting a court order for the protection to be provided by the debtor under § 361, the majority view appears to be that § 507(b) also applies to private adequate protection agreements for which no court approval has been obtained. Epstein, et al., *Bankruptcy* § 7–13 (1992). With respect to private agreements, some courts scrutinize the agreement to be sure that the creditor was not guilty of inequitable conduct in negotiating the agreement.

**5.** In the Eastern Airlines debacle discussed at p. 590, indenture trustees for secured bondholders failed to timely request adequate protection of their liens against certain airplanes. They defended in part on the theory that making such a motion would have accomplished nothing—it had no chance of being granted and if it were denied, the denial would not have amounted to the "provision" of adequate protection that is the predicate for a superpriority claim under § 507(b). The airplanes depreciated and the bondholders turned out to be undersecured. The district court judge found that the denial of the bondholders' adequate protection motion would not have been the "provision" of adequate protection and that accordingly no superpriority claim would have arisen under § 507(b). This decision could not be right, could it? *See LNC Investments, Inc. v. First Fidelity Bank*, 247 B.R. 38 (S.D.N.Y.2000), *aff'd sub nom. LNC Investments, Inc. v. National Westminister Bank*, 308 F.3d 169 (2d Cir. 2002).

## NOTE: SINGLE ASSET REAL ESTATE

*Timbers* has been effectively limited with respect to cases involving what § 101 defines as "single asset real estate." The commercial real estate depression of the 1980s filled the bankruptcy courts of the 1980s and 1990s with many cases in which single asset real estate enterprises struggled to reorganize. *Timbers* is such a case. Typically these are cases in which there is one large secured lender, whose claim is often undersecured, with a few small unsecured trade claims. Later in this chapter, we discuss some of the problems in classifying claims in debtors' plans in these cases. *Greystone*, p. 704. The debtor's objective is usually to hold on to the property for as long as possible in the forlorn hope that a market upturn will produce sufficient rents to enable the debtor to meet its mortgage payments. Understandably, secured creditors view this conduct as stalling, and, after *Timbers* denied them compensation for the economic loss occasioned by the stay, they sought relief from Congress. In 1994 § 362(d)(3) was added to provide that, with respect to single asset real estate cases, a court shall grant relief from the stay unless the debtor, within 90 days of entering Chapter 11, can either show that it has filed a plan of reorganization that has "a reasonable possibility of being confirmed within a reasonable time," or that it has commenced monthly payments equal to interest at "current fair market rate on the value of the creditor's interest in the real estate." The significance of the amendment was initially greatly reduced by the fact that the definition of single asset real estate in § 101 was limited to projects "having aggregate noncontingent, liquidated secured debts in an amount no more than $4,000,000." The dollar cap left a large number of the projects owned by single purpose entities unaffected by the amendment. Research by our colleague Kenneth Klee indicates that the likelihood of successful reorganization by single asset real estate cases varies directly with the debtor's value.

The 2005 Act eliminated the $4 million cap from the definition of "single asset real estate." The elimination of the cap means that for the first time the SARE rules will apply in large cases. Note however that the definition will still exclude real estate projects upon which the debtor operates a "real" business—hotels, farms, health care and so forth. Also there will be significant pressure on defining exactly what is a single "project" for purposes of application of the SARE rules as multiple project entities remain excluded.

The special rule in § 362(d)(3) governing SARE has also been amended as shown in <u>underline</u> below.

(d)   On request of a party in interest and after notice and a hearing, the court shall grant relief from the stay provided under subsection (a) of this section, such as by terminating, annulling, modifying, or conditioning such stay—

(3)   with respect to a stay of an act against single asset real estate under subsection (a), by a creditor whose claim is secured by

an interest in such real estate, unless, not later than the date that is 90 days after the entry of the order for relief (or such later date as the court may determine for cause by order entered within that 90-day period) or <u>30 days after the court determines that the debtor is subject to this paragraph, whichever is later</u>—

**(A)** the debtor has filed a plan of reorganization that has a reasonable possibility of being confirmed within a reasonable time; or

**(B)** <u>the debtor has commenced monthly payments that</u>—

    **(i)** may, in the debtor's sole discretion, notwithstanding section 363(c)(2), be made from rents or other income generated before or after the commencement of the case by or from the property to each creditor whose claim is secured by such real estate (other than a claim secured by a judgment lien or by an unmatured statutory lien); and

    **(ii)** <u>are in an amount equal to interest at the then applicable nondefault contract rate of interest on the value of the creditor's interest in the real estate;</u>

To date there has been little case law or experience with § 362(d)(3) because of the cap. It remains to be seen how significant the SARE rules will be in practice in light of this limited experience. But at least in theory, the debtor will have to pay to play, that is stay current on monthly payments to secured creditors. Application of those monthly payments will depend on whether the creditor is over or undersecured. If the creditor is undersecured, under *Timbers*, the payments should be applied to reduce principal. Alternatively, the debtor can avoid foreclosure by getting a confirmable plan on file within 90 days.

As under existing law, revised § 362(d)(3) will allow the debtor (or presumably any party resisting relief from stay) to move to extend the time period for commencement of payments within the 90 days for "cause." The 2005 Act further loosens up the time frame for the commencement of monthly payments by allowing the debtor to contest the applicability of the SARE rules and only requiring payments to commence within 30 days after a determination that SARE is applicable. Especially in the larger cases, debtors may well take advantage of these provisions to defer payment. There had been a split of authority under pre-2005 law on whether rents may be a source of required adequate protection payments. The 2005 Act's § 362(d)(3)(B), clarifies that it is possible for debtors to commence making payments to secured creditors from pledged rents. Since rents are the only likely source of cash payments in a SARE case, this is a major concession to debtors.

Finally, prior to the 2005 Act, a single asset real estate debtor had to commence making monthly payments "equal to interest at a *fair market value* of the creditor's interest in real estate." 11 U.S.C. § 362(d)(3)(B) (emphasis added). The 2005 Act changed the applicable rate of interest to "[a]n amount equal to interest at the then applicable *nondefault contract rate* of interest on the value of the creditor's interest in the real estate. . . ." This should simplify administration of the statute.

Note that the payments are measured in the amount of interest; they are not interest payments. Whether they will be attributable to interest or principal probably should depend on whether the property is over or undersecured.

## D. OPERATING THE BUSINESS FROM PETITION TO CONFIRMATION

### 1. INTRODUCTION

In order to operate its business the debtor must be able to use its plant, equipment, inventory, and deposit accounts. It must be able to sell its product, pay its employees, and buy necessary services and supplies. But these needs of the debtor collide with the rights of secured creditors in the collateral that the debtor must use, and frustrate the demands of unsecured creditors to be paid out of the unencumbered assets of the estate. In this conflict between the debtor's need to use and sell the property of the estate and the interests of creditors with respect to this property, § 363(c) comes down resoundingly on the side of the debtor. So long as it is acting in the ordinary course of business, a debtor may continue to use all property of the estate, except for cash collateral, and may sell or lease without prior notice and hearing. The debtor in possession, as well as any bankruptcy trustee, in operating the business must still obey otherwise applicable state laws and regulations. 28 U.S.C. § 959(b).

The interests of secured creditors are safeguarded by § 363(e) that allows the court to prohibit or condition use, sale, or lease of the property of the estate "as is necessary to provide adequate protection of" the secured creditors' interests in this property. The rights of unsecured creditors to share in unencumbered assets find protection, such as it is, in § 1112(b) which allows the court to convert the case to Chapter 7 if there are "substantial and continuing" losses that cannot be cured.

### 2. USE OF DEPOSIT ACCOUNTS AND OTHER CASH COLLATERAL

Whether a debtor in possession may continue to use property in which creditors have security interests is usually decided not under § 363 but under § 362 on the issue of lifting the automatic stay. As we have seen, the debtor's right to use property of the estate may be abridged by relief obtained pursuant to § 362(d) in lifting the automatic stay and allowing secured creditors to proceed to foreclose against the property outside bankruptcy. § 362(d). The ultimate issue in deciding to lift the stay under § 362(d) and in determining the debtor's right to use the property under § 363(c) may often be the same: has the debtor offered the secured creditor adequate protection? Compare § 362(d)(1) with § 363(e).

Section 363(c)(2) provides a special rule for "cash collateral," which, as defined in § 363(a), includes the cash or cash equivalent proceeds of pre-petition collateral including, for example, inventory and accounts. The debtor may use cash collateral only if the creditor having a security interest in the collateral consents or if the court, after notice and hearing, authorizes the use. The court may prohibit or condition the use of cash collateral on the debtor's providing adequate protection of the secured creditor's interest in its collateral.

A business can operate only a few days without cash. It must meet its payroll and buy vital services and supplies or close its doors. Given its often desperate need for cash, a debtor must have its cash collateral strategy worked out when it files. It must either have consents from creditors with security interests in its bank accounts or have a request to use cash collateral ready to present to the court. An accelerated hearing is possible under § 363(c)(3) and Bankruptcy Rule 4001(b).

## PROBLEM

Debtor Corporation manufactures widgets. Debtor finances its widget business with revolving loans from Bank. Over the past year, Debtor's sales have fallen and it has suffered $1 million in operating losses. Bank's loans are secured by a perfected first priority security interest in all Debtor's accounts, inventory, and general intangibles and their proceeds. Debtor has just filed a petition under Chapter 11. As of the petition date, Debtor's balance sheet reads:

**Assets**

| | |
|---|---|
| Cash | $ 400,000 |
| Accounts Receivable | 5,000,000 |
| Inventory (at cost) | 6,500,000 |
| Prepaid Expenses | 100,000 |
| Property & Plant (leasehold & improvements net of depreciation) | 1,500,000 |
| Equipment (net of depreciation) | 2,500,000 |
| Total Assets | 16,000,000 |

## Liabilities & Net Worth (Deficit)

| | |
|---|---:|
| Accounts Payable | $ 7,500,000 |
| Bank Debt | 10,000,000 |
| Capitalized Lease Obligations | 1,000,000 |
| (discounted rent for leasehold expiring 2004) | |
| | |
| Total Liabilities | 18,500,000 |
| Accumulated Capital Deficit | (2,500,000) |
| Total Liabilities and Deficit | 16,000,000 |

Bank has prepared the following liquidation analysis:

## Debtor Corporation—Liquidation Analysis

| | |
|---|---:|
| Cash | $ 400,000 |
| Accounts Receivable | 3,500,000 |
| (assumes collection costs and uncollectable accounts equal to 30% of receivables book value) | |
| Inventory | 2,600,000 |
| (assumes finished goods liquidated at 50% of cost and semifinished goods at 30% of cost) | |
| Prepaid Expenses | — |
| Property, Plant & Equipment | 1,250,000 |
| (assumes leasehold & improvements forfeited to landlord and equipment liquidated at 50% of book value) | |
| Total Assets Forced Liquidation Value | 7,750,000 |

Assume that all Debtor's existing cash, as well any cash that might be generated from collection of prepetition accounts and sales of prepetition inventory will be Bank's cash collateral under § 363(a) and subject to § 363(c)(2).

(a) Representing Bank what sort of conditions on the Debtor's use of cash collateral would you seek? § 363(c)(2)(A) & (e).

(b) Representing Debtor what alternatives do you have to acceding to the Bank's demands? § 363(c)(2)(B).

(c) Representing Debtor's general unsecured creditors what concerns might you have with an agreement between Bank and Debtor over the use of Bank's cash collateral? *See* Bankr.R. 4001(c).

(d) What are the critical legal and factual issues that will determine the provisions of any agreement between Bank and Debtor regarding postpetition use of Debtor's cash collateral? §§ 361, 363(e).

### 3. SALE OR LEASE OF PROPERTY IN ORDINARY COURSE

Under § 363(c)(1) a debtor in possession may sell or lease property of the estate without court approval if done in the ordinary course of the debtor's business. Ordinary course of business is not defined in the Bankruptcy Code. The court in *In re James A. Phillips, Inc.*, 29 B.R. 391, 394 (S.D.N.Y.1983), made the following comment on that term:

> The legislative history of § 363 provides no test or guideline concerning the scope of the "ordinary course of business" standard. * * * Nonetheless, the apparent purpose of requiring notice only where the use of property is extraordinary is to assure interested persons of an opportunity to be heard concerning transactions different from those that might be expected to take place so long as the debtor in possession is allowed to continue normal business operations under § 1107(a) & § 1108. The touchstone of "ordinariness" is thus the interested parties' reasonable expectations of what transactions the debtor in possession is likely to enter in the course of its business. So long as the transactions conducted are consistent with these expectations, creditors have no right to notice and hearing, because their objections to such transactions are likely to relate to the bankrupt's chapter 11 status, not the particular transactions themselves. Where the debtor in possession is merely exercising the privileges of its chapter 11 status, which include the right to operate the bankrupt business, there is no general right to notice and hearing concerning particular transactions. To preclude such transactions, interested parties must apply to the Bankruptcy Court for relief from the stay, § 362(d)(1), or for conversion or dismissal of the chapter 11 petition, § 1112(b).

Hence, a debtor in the business of selling goods or leasing equipment may continue to operate after filing with no notice to creditors or court authorization. The "ordinary course of business" language should allow the debtor to continue selling or leasing on the same terms it employed before filing or on terms generally followed in the business in which the debtor is engaged. Creditors or other parties in interest may request the court to place limits on the debtor's practices. § 363(c)(1).

### 4. OBTAINING CREDIT

#### a. Critical Vendors

Among the most important of the "first day motions" that debtors make on the date of filing are those related to obtaining credit to enable the debtor company to continue to do business. Generally speaking these motions seek authority to obtain "DIP financing" from institutional lenders under § 364, discussed in the following section, and to pay prepetition debts to "critical vendors" in the expectation that these vendors will continue to extend postpetition trade credit to the debtor. In the latter case, the debtor is asking the court to approve preferential postpetition payments to those prepetition creditors deemed critical to the continued operations of the debtor's enterprise outside of any plan of reorganization and inconsistently with the statutory priority scheme. In the following case, we see that the bankruptcy court treated the motion as routine even though it resulted in full payment of the prepetition debts of more than half of the debtor's vendors, leaving the other vendors only a 10% dividend on their claims mostly paid in reorganized Kmart stock. Judge Easterbrook examines both the legality of postpetition payments to prepetition critical vendors and, assuming payments to prepetition critical vendors are valid, how the determination is made that vendors are critical.

## Matter of Kmart Corporation

United States Court of Appeals, Seventh Circuit, 2004.
359 F.3d 866.

■ EASTERBROOK, Circuit Judge.

On the first day of its bankruptcy, Kmart sought permission to pay immediately, and in full, the pre-petition claims of all "critical vendors." (Technically there are 38 debtors: Kmart Corporation plus 37 of its affiliates and subsidiaries. We call them all Kmart.) The theory behind the request is that some suppliers may be unwilling to do business with a customer that is behind in payment, and, if it cannot obtain the merchandise that its own customers have come to expect, a firm such as Kmart may be unable to carry on, injuring all of its creditors. Full payment to critical vendors thus could in principle make even the disfavored creditors better off: they may not be paid in full, but they will receive a greater portion of their claims than they would if the critical vendors cut off supplies and the business shut down. Putting the proposition in this way implies, however, that the debtor must *prove,* and not just allege, two things: that, but for immediate full payment, vendors *would* cease dealing; and that the business will gain enough from continued transactions with the favored vendors to provide some residual benefit to the remaining, disfavored creditors, or at least leave them no worse off.

Bankruptcy Judge SONDERBY entered a critical-vendors order just as Kmart proposed it, without notifying any disfavored creditors, without receiving any pertinent evidence (the record contains only some sketchy representations by counsel plus unhelpful testimony by Kmart's CEO, who could not speak for the vendors), and without making any finding of fact that the disfavored creditors would gain or come out even. The bankruptcy court's order declared that the relief Kmart requested-open-ended permission to pay any debt to any vendor it deemed "critical" in the exercise of unilateral discretion, provided that the vendor agreed to furnish goods on "customary trade terms" for the next two years-was "in the best interests of the Debtors, their estates and their creditors". The order did not explain why, nor did it contain any legal analysis, though it did cite § 105(a).

Kmart used its authority to pay in full the pre-petition debts to 2,330 suppliers, which collectively received about $300 million. This came from the $2 billion in new credit (debtor-in-possession or DIP financing) that the bankruptcy judge authorized, granting the lenders super-priority in post-petition assets and revenues. * * * Another 2,000 or so vendors were not deemed "critical" and were not paid. They and 43,000 additional unsecured creditors eventually received about 10¢ on the dollar, mostly in stock of the reorganized Kmart. Capital Factors, Inc., appealed the critical-vendors order immediately after its entry on January 25, 2002. A little more than 14 months later, after all of the critical vendors had been paid and as Kmart's plan of reorganization was on the verge of approval, District Judge Grady reversed the order authorizing payment. 291 B.R. 818 (N.D.Ill.2003). He concluded that neither § 105(a) nor a "doctrine of necessity" supports the orders.

\* \* \*

Section 105(a) allows a bankruptcy court to "issue any order, process, or judgment that is necessary or appropriate to carry out the provisions of" the Code. This does not create discretion to set aside the Code's rules about priority and distribution; the power conferred by § 105(a) is one to implement rather than override. * * * Every circuit that has considered the question has held that this statute does not allow a bankruptcy judge to authorize full payment of any unsecured debt, unless all unsecured creditors in the class are paid in full. * * * We agree with this view of § 105. "The fact that a [bankruptcy] proceeding is equitable does not give the judge a free-floating discretion to redistribute rights in accordance with his personal views of justice and fairness, however enlightened those views may be." *In re Chicago, Milwaukee, St. Paul & Pacific R.R.,* 791 F.2d 524, 528 (7th Cir.1986).

A "doctrine of necessity" is just a fancy name for a power to depart from the Code. Although courts in the days before bankruptcy law was codified wielded power to reorder priorities and pay particular creditors in the name of "necessity"-see *Miltenberger v. Logansport Ry.,* 106 U.S. 286 (1882) ; *Fosdick v. Schall,* 99 U.S. 235 (1878)-today it is the Code rather than the norms of nineteenth century railroad reorganizations that must prevail. *Miltenberger* and *Fosdick* predate the first general effort at codification, the Bankruptcy Act of 1898. Today the Bankruptcy Code of 1978 supplies the rules. Congress did not in terms scuttle old common-law doctrines, because it did not need to; the Act curtailed, and then the Code replaced, the entire apparatus. Answers to contemporary issues must be found within the Code (or legislative halls). Older doctrines may survive as glosses on ambiguous language enacted in 1978 or later, but not as freestanding entitlements to trump the text.

So does the Code contain any grant of authority for debtors to prefer some vendors over others? Many sections require equal treatment or specify the details of priority when assets are insufficient to satisfy all claims. E.g., §§ 507 , 1122(a) , 1123(a)(4). Appellants rely on §§ 363(b) , 364(b) , and 503 as sources of authority for unequal treatment. Section 364(b) reads: "The court, after notice and a hearing, may authorize the trustee to obtain unsecured credit or to incur unsecured debt other than under subsection (a) of this section, allowable under section 503(b)(1) of this title as an administrative expense." This authorizes the debtor to obtain credit (as Kmart did) but has nothing to say about how the money will be disbursed or about priorities among creditors. * * * Section 503, which deals with administrative expenses, likewise is irrelevant. Pre-filing debts are not administrative expenses; they are the antithesis of administrative expenses. Filing a petition for bankruptcy effectively creates two firms: the debts of the pre-filing entity may be written down so that the post-filing entity may reorganize and continue in business if it has a positive cash flow. See *Boston & Maine Corp. v. Chicago Pacific Corp.,* 785 F.2d 562 (7th Cir.1986). Treating pre-filing debts as "administrative" claims against the post-filing entity would impair the ability of bankruptcy law to prevent old debts from sinking a viable firm.

That leaves § 363(b)(1): "The trustee [or debtor in possession], after notice and a hearing, may use, sell, or lease, other than in the ordinary course of business, property of the estate." This is more promising, for satisfaction of a pre-petition debt in order to keep "critical" supplies flowing is a use of property other than in the ordinary course of administering an estate in bankruptcy. Capital Factors insists that § 363(b)(1) should be limited to the commencement of capital projects, such as building a new plant, rather than payment of old debts-as paying vendors would be "in the ordinary course" but for the intervening bankruptcy petition. To read § 363(b)(1) broadly, Capital Factors observes, would be to allow a judge to rearrange priorities among creditors (which is what a critical-vendors order effectively does), even though the Supreme Court has cautioned against such a step. Yet what these decisions principally say is that priorities do not change unless a statute supports that step; and if § 363(b)(1) is such a statute, then there is no insuperable problem. If the language is too open-ended, that is a problem for the legislature. Nonetheless, it is prudent to read, and use, § 363(b)(1) to do the least damage possible to priorities established by contract and by other parts of the Bankruptcy Code. We need not decide whether § 363(b)(1) could support payment of some pre-petition debts, because *this* order was unsound no matter how one reads § 363(b)(1).

The foundation of a critical-vendors order is the belief that vendors not paid for prior deliveries will refuse to make new ones. Without merchandise to sell, a retailer such as Kmart will fold. If paying the critical vendors would enable a successful reorganization and make even the disfavored creditors better off, then all creditors favor payment whether or not they are designated as "critical." This suggests a use of § 363(b)(1) similar to the theory underlying a plan crammed down the throats of an impaired class of creditors: if the impaired class does at least as well as it would have under a Chapter 7 liquidation, then it has no legitimate objection and cannot block the reorganization. See generally *Bank of America v. 203 N. LaSalle St. Partners,* 526 U.S. 434 (1999). For the premise to hold true, however, it is necessary to show not only that the disfavored creditors *will* be as well off with reorganization as with liquidation-a demonstration never attempted in this proceeding-but also that the supposedly critical vendors would have ceased deliveries if old debts were left unpaid while the litigation continued. If vendors will deliver against a promise of current payment, then a reorganization can be achieved, and all unsecured creditors will obtain its benefit, without preferring any of the unsecured creditors.

Some supposedly critical vendors will continue to do business with the debtor because they must. They may, for example, have long term contracts, and the automatic stay prevents these vendors from walking away as long as the debtor pays for new deliveries. See § 362. Fleming Companies, which received the largest critical-vendors payment because it sold Kmart between $70 million and $100 million of groceries and related goods weekly, was one of these. No matter how much Fleming would have liked to dump Kmart, it had no right to do so. It was unnecessary to compensate Fleming for continuing to make deliveries that it was legally required to make. Nor was Fleming likely to walk away even if it had a legal right to do so. Each new delivery produced a profit; as long as Kmart continued to pay for new product, why would any vendor drop the account? That would be a self-inflicted wound. To abjure new profits because of old debts would be to commit the sunk-cost fallacy; well-managed businesses are unlikely to do this. Firms that disdain current profits because of old losses are unlikely to stay in business. They might as well burn money or drop it into the ocean. Again Fleming illustrates the point. When Kmart stopped buying its products after the contract expired, Fleming collapsed (Kmart had accounted for more than 50% of its business) and filed its own bankruptcy petition. Fleming was hardly likely to have quit selling of its own volition, only to expire the sooner.

Doubtless many suppliers fear the prospect of throwing good money after bad. It therefore may be vital to assure them that a debtor will pay for new deliveries on a current basis. Providing that assurance need not, however, entail payment for pre-petition transactions. Kmart could have paid cash or its equivalent. (Kmart's CEO told the bankruptcy judge that COD arrangements were not part of Kmart's business plan, as if a litigant's druthers could override the rights of third parties.) Cash on the barrelhead was not the most convenient way, however. Kmart secured a $2 billion line of credit when it entered bankruptcy. Some of that credit could have been used to assure vendors that payment would be forthcoming for all post-petition transactions. The easiest way to do that would have been to put some of the $2 billion behind a standby letter of credit on which the bankruptcy judge could authorize unpaid vendors to draw. That would not have changed the terms on which Kmart and any of its vendors did business; it just would have demonstrated the certainty of payment. If lenders are unwilling to issue such a letter of credit (or if they insist on a letter's short duration), that would be a compelling market signal that reorganization is a poor prospect and that the debtor should be liquidated post haste.

Yet the bankruptcy court did not explore the possibility of using a letter of credit to assure vendors of payment. The court did not find that any firm would have ceased doing business with Kmart if not paid for prepetition deliveries, and the scant record would not have supported such a finding had one been made. The court did not find that discrimination among unsecured creditors was the only way to facilitate a reorganization. It did not find that the disfavored creditors were at least as well off as they would have been had the critical-vendors order not been entered. For all the millions at stake, this proceeding looks much like the Chapter 13 reorganization that produced *In re Crawford,* 324 F.3d 539 (7th Cir.2003). Crawford had wanted to classify his creditors in a way that would enable him to pay off those debts that would not be discharged, while stiffing the creditors whose debts were dischargeable. We replied that even though classification (and thus unequal treatment) is possible for Chapter 13 proceedings, see § 1322(b), the step would be proper only when the record shows that the classification would produce some benefit for the disfavored creditors. Just so here. Even if § 362(b)(1) allows critical-vendors orders in principle, preferential payments to a class of creditors are proper only if the record shows the prospect of benefit to the other creditors. This record does not, so the critical-vendors order cannot stand.

Affirmed.

## NOTES

**1.** If Kmart had introduced sufficient evidence to support a factual finding that the vendors it sought to pay were critical to the success of the reorganization and would not ship to Kmart without receiving payment on their prepetition debts, is there a statutory basis to permit payment outside of a plan of reorganization?

**2.** Why would the court delegate to Kmart discretion to determine who was critical enough to receive early payment? Doesn't the Bankruptcy Court Order authorize Kmart to pay vendors who it likes or who cooperate with its reorganization effort in full while punishing troublemaking vendors by withholding payment? Would such orders ever be justifiable on grounds of "necessity"?

**3.** Note that the old caselaw "rule of necessity" justifying early priority payment of certain unsecured claims evolved in old railroad equity receiverships and was codified with respect to railroad reorganizations in 11 U.S.C. § 1171(b). Does the special rule of § 1171(b) suggest that Chapter 11 does not authorize such payment in nonrailroad cases?

## NOTE: RECLAMATION

The 2005 Act sharply bolstered the position of trade vendors generally, whether or not such vendors would otherwise qualify for "critical vendor" status.  Under state law, sellers of goods to insolvents may have the right to "reclaim" goods.  *See e.g.* U.C.C. § 2-702(2).  Before 2005 those "reclamation" rights were preserved only to a very limited extent in bankruptcy.  After a bankruptcy filing a vendor asserting such a right could preserve it only  with respect to goods shipped to the debtor within 10 days of bankruptcy by promptly serving a notice of reclamation under § 546(c).  The reclamation right could be extinguished by a prior lien in the debtor's inventory or by other disposition of the collateral prior to the serving of the notice under § 546(c) and the bankruptcy court would generally substitute an administrative claim for the value of any goods subject to reclamation for the reclamation right itself.  Under the 2005 Act a general administrative priority is created in favor of vendors for the value of all goods shipped to the debtor within 20 days of the bankruptcy filing whether or not there is any state law reclamation right with respect to such shipments or any notice served, § 503(b)(9) and reclamation rights are preserved with respect to goods shipped within 45 days of the bankruptcy filing.  At least arguably under the amended Code the court is no longer authorized to substitute an administrative priority claim for the reclamation right.  § 546(c).  This expansion of reclamation rights may well overwhelm any limitations on "critical vendor" orders in the wake of the *Kmart Corporation* decision.  If most prepetition vendor claims are entitled to administrative priority, critical vendor orders matter far less.  For a fuller discussion of the new rules relating to reclamation *see* Richard Levin & Alesia Ranney-Marinelli, *The Creeping Repeal of Chapter 11*, 79 Am. Bankr. L. J. 603, 604-608 (2005).

### b.   Rights of Administrative Claimants

In order to operate the business in the interim between petition and confirmation, the debtor in possession may have to borrow money or buy goods and services on unsecured credit. Section 364 gives the debtor this power. If the credit is obtained in the ordinary course of the debtor's business, no court approval is required. § 364(a). Otherwise, court approval must be obtained. § 364(b).

Under either § 364(a) or (b) the authorized credit is an administrative expense under § 503(b)(1) giving the creditor a first priority under § 507(a). The administrative expense priority is an incentive to deal with the debtor in possession in a Chapter 11 case. If a simple administrative expense priority will not induce a person to grant credit to the debtor in possession, § 364(c) allows the court to authorize (1) a priority over any or all of the other administrative expenses, (2) a lien on any unencumbered property of the estate, or (3) a junior lien on property already encumbered. If still no one is willing to grant credit, § 364(d) allows the court to authorize a lien senior or equal to an existing lien on property of the estate so long as adequate protection is given to the holder of the existing lien. Thus § 364 allows debtors to award priorities to postpetition lenders in an ascending order of attractiveness.

Suppose the bankruptcy court issues an order authorizing the debtor in possession to incur a debt on the basis of a priority or lien to the creditor under § 364. Other creditors appeal the order. While the appeal is pending, the debt is incurred. If the order is reversed or modified on appeal, what are the rights of the creditor that extended the credit in reliance on the order? Section 364(e) states that reversal or modification of the order does not affect the validity of the debt or the priority or lien granted to the creditor unless the incurring of the debt or the granting of the priority or lien was stayed pending the appeal. A creditor acting in good faith is protected even if the creditor had knowledge of the appeal. The apparent purpose is to stop other creditors from preventing an emergency extension of credit by simply filing an appeal. Without § 364(e), the creditor would have no assurance that the priority or lien would not be taken away by the appellate court after value was given to the debtor in possession. Under § 364(e) the creditor is usually safe if no stay has been issued at the time it gave value to the debtor in possession, but in *Saybrook*, p. 638, we will see that an exception to § 364(e) may apply in some cases.

Section 364 creates risks as well as opportunities for postpetition creditors. Any creditor who deals with a Chapter 11 debtor and receives anything less than a lien as security is taking a risk that it may not be paid even if the court has approved the grant of credit. But even a postpetition secured lender may find its position substantially changed. It may have to share its collateral with a new lender or may even be subordinated to the lien of the new lender. The prior secured party is entitled only to adequate protection of its lien under § 364(d)(1)(B).

The plight of priority creditors under § 364 is illustrated by the case that follows.

## General Electric Credit Corp. v. Levin & Weintraub

United States Court of Appeals, Second Circuit, 1984.
739 F.2d 73.

■ Van Graafeiland, Circuit Judge:

General Electric Credit Corporation (GECC) appeals from an order of the United States District Court for the Southern District of New York (Broderick, J.) which affirmed a bankruptcy court order awarding appellees interim compensation for professional services and disbursements and directing that payment thereof be made from assets of the debtors in possession in which GECC had a security interest. For reasons hereafter discussed, we reverse.

On July 21, 1981, Flagstaff Foodservice Corporation and its related companies (Flagstaff) filed petitions for reorganization under Chapter 11 of the Bankruptcy Reform Act of 1978 (the Code). As permitted by the Code, the companies continued to operate their businesses as debtors in possession.

GECC had been financing Flagstaff's operations since 1978 by making loans and advances on accounts receivable and inventory. As of July 21, 1981, Flagstaff owed GECC approximately $22 million, which was secured by assets worth $42 million. Shortly before commencement of the Chapter 11 proceedings, Flagstaff's attorneys met with representatives of GECC to obtain immediate short-term financing in order to maintain sufficient cash flow to support Flagstaff's operations. These negotiations resulted in an order which permitted Flagstaff to use up to $750,000 of GECC's collateral for the limited period of five days. Flagstaff's attorneys also prepared an application for a more permanent financing arrangement with GECC. An order (the "Financing Order") was issued by the bankruptcy court authorizing Flagstaff to borrow additional money from GECC, the loans to be secured by a super-priority interest in all present and future property of the estate. In pertinent part, the order provided that:

> any and all obligations and Liabilities of Borrowers and debtors in possession to GECC (as defined in the Loan Agreement and the Security Agreement) shall have priority in payment over any other debts or obligations now in existence or incurred hereafter of Borrowers and debtors in possession and over all administrative expenses of the kind specified in Sections 503(b) or 507(b) of the Bankruptcy Code, and said Liabilities and obligations of Borrowers and debtors in possession to GECC shall be secured by a first and prior lien on all property of whatever kind and nature of the Borrowers and debtors in possession, and proceeds thereof, until all such obligations and Liabilities of the Borrowers and debtors in possession to GECC shall have been paid in full.

By December 21, 1981, Flagstaff had generated enough income from its accounts receivable to pay all of GECC's pre-petition liabilities. However, during the chapter 11 proceedings, GECC advanced an additional $9 million to Flagstaff pursuant to the Financing Order. Despite this infusion of funds, the Flagstaff reorganization ultimately failed. No chapter 11 plan ever was proposed; no bulk purchaser appeared; and no buyer emerged to take over any of the debtor companies. Accordingly, although Flagstaff's indebtedness to GECC had been reduced substantially, the realizable value of the collateral which remained was insufficient to satisfy the unpaid balance.

The issue before us is whether, despite the super-priority lien given GECC in the Financing Order, the bankruptcy court subsequently might direct that interim fees and disbursements of attorneys and accountants be paid from the encumbered collateral. The bankruptcy court awarded [almost $250,000 to attorneys and accountants]. In each instance, the award was 70% of the amount claimed. These awards were affirmed by the district court. We hold this to be error.

Section 364(c)(1) of the Code authorizes the issuance of a financing order, such as the one secured by Flagstaff, which will have "priority over any or all administrative expenses of the kind specified in section 503(b) or 507(b) of [the Code]." Among the administrative expenses listed in section 503(b), and thus reduced in priority by the Flagstaff Financing Order, are "compensation and reimbursement awarded under section 330 of [the Code]." Section 330 is the section that authorizes the bankruptcy court to make awards for services and expenses to attorneys and professional persons representing debtors or creditors' committees, which awards may be made on an interim basis pursuant to section 331.

Looking to the plain language of these sections, as we are bound to do, * * * we conclude that GECC's security interest has priority over appellees' claims for professional services * * *. To the extent that *In re Callister* * * *, relied upon by appellees, is to the contrary, we decline to follow it. Where, as here, the statutory language clearly expresses the congressional intent, a court may not read another meaning into the statute in order to arrive at a result which the court deems preferable. * * * Attorneys may * * * secure a portion of their fee in advance. * * * If attorneys need more encouragement than this to participate in chapter 11 proceedings, Congress, not the courts, must provide it. Under the law as it presently exists, knowledgeable bankruptcy attorneys must be aware that the priority ordinarily given to administration expenses may "prove illusive in light of the various provisions in the Code for competing or super-priorities." 2 Collier on Bankruptcy ¶ 364.02, at 364–6 (15th ed.1984). Section 364(c)(1) is such a provision.

We conclude that the district court erred in holding that section 330 "empower[ed] the Bankruptcy Judge to make awards without reference to any schedule of priorities, without reference to any contractual agreement with respect to those priorities and on the basis of his assessment in the course of supervising the bankruptcy proceeding that if actual and necessary services have been rendered, they should be compensated for." We hold, instead, that any fees payable from GECC's collateral must be for services which were for the benefit of GECC rather than the debtor or other creditors. * * * Provision for such allowance is made in section 506(c), which provides: "The trustee [debtor in possession] may recover from property securing an allowed secured claim the reasonable, necessary costs and expenses of preserving, or disposing of, such property to the extent of any benefit to the holder of such claim." Congress's express intent in enacting section 506(c) was to ensure that, any time a debtor in possession "expends money to provide for the reasonable and necessary cost and expenses of preserving or disposing of a secured creditor's collateral, the * * * debtor in possession is entitled to recover such expenses from the secured party or from the property securing an allowed secured claim held by such party." 124 Cong.Rec. H11089 (daily ed. Sept. 28,

1978) (Statement of Rep. Edwards) * * * * That is not the situation disclosed in appellees' affidavits.

It is undisputed that the chapter proceedings were initiated with the hope of effectuating Flagstaff's rehabilitation and with optimism that this could be accomplished. Indeed, a less forthright purpose in seeking chapter 11 relief might preclude the awarding of any fees at all. * * * Such benefits as might be said to have accrued to GECC from the attempt to reorganize were incidental to the reorganization efforts and did not fall within the intended scope of section 506(c). * * *

As a matter of fact, it requires rather strained logic to conclude that GECC actually benefited from appellees' services. At the outset of the chapter 11 proceedings, GECC's $22 million claim against Flagstaff was secured by $42 million in collateral. When the chapter 11 proceedings aborted, the indebtedness had been reduced to $4 million, but this balance was substantially undercollateralized. In return for this "benefit", appellees now seek to reduce the remaining collateral another quarter of a million dollars to pay their interim fee allowances.

Although GECC requested a hearing in connection with the fee applications, none was held, appellees being content to rest on their written applications. We are as well equipped as the district court to evaluate these documents. * * * Having done so, we are satisfied that, conclusory allegations aside, they do not justify the allowances made herein. For example [one] application, which is not atypical, states that "[a]ll of the professional services for which an interim allowance is being sought were rendered solely on behalf of the Committee in connection with the Debtors' Chapter 11 proceedings, pursuant to the responsibility of Applicant as attorneys for the Committee, and in accordance with the instructions of the Committee, and not on behalf of any other person, as such term is defined in Section 101(30) of the Code." The application then outlines the steps which [the attorneys] took to carry out their duties to the Committee, including, among other things, an extensive court challenge to the "validity, extent and priority" of GECC's security interest. [The attorneys] contend that they "performed services which benefited all creditors of the estate including GECC." The district court, whose opinion contains no reference whatever to section 506(c), adopted this argument, holding that the "context" of the case "necessarily imports" that appellees' services benefited GECC "by preserving or enhancing the bankrupt estate."

Approval of the fee award on this basis was error. Payment of administration expenses traditionally has been the responsibility of the debtor's estate, not its secured creditors. * * * However, if expenses for the preservation or disposition of property are incurred primarily for the benefit of a creditor holding a security interest in the property, such expenses, properly identified, may be charged against the secured creditor. * * * Appellees had the burden of proving that the administration expenses for which they sought recovery were covered by section 506(c). They failed to sustain that burden.

We find no merit in appellees' alternative argument that GECC impliedly consented to bearing the costs of their professional services by employing the chapter 11 procedure to effect the disposition of its collateral. * * * Appellees assert that GECC's active involvement in devising a program aimed at reducing its secured claims justified resorting to the secured assets for payment of the interim fees. Although a secured creditor may consent to bearing the costs of professional fees incurred by a debtor in possession, "such consent is not to be lightly inferred." In re S & S Indus., Inc., 30 B.R. 395, 398 (Bankr.E.D.Mich.1983). "It is not to be inferred merely because a secured creditor cooperates with the debtor." Id. * * * We find no evidence of such consent in appellees' fee application. Moreover, the existence of consent is negatived by the provisions of the Financing Order.

Saddling unconsenting secured creditors with professional fees, such as are sought by appellees, would discourage those creditors from supporting debtors' reorganization efforts. "To hold that mere cooperation with the debtor exposes a secured creditor to payment of all expenses of administration would * * * make it difficult, if not impossible, to induce new lenders to finance a chapter 11 operation." In re S & S Indus., Inc., *supra.* The Financing Order granting GECC a super-priority position was intended to give GECC protection against the very awards made herein. The lack of sufficient unencumbered assets to pay appellees' fees is not an adequate basis for denying GECC its super-priority status. * * * Although it has been well said that "professionals should not be expected to finance the administration of liquidation or reorganization cases," 2 Collier on Bankruptcy ¶ 331.01, at 331–3 (15th ed.1984), "it does not follow that in the event the estate has no unencumbered funds from which to pay such expenses, the secured creditor becomes obligated to satisfy these obligations." In re S & S Indus., Inc., *supra.*

As stated above, GECC, alone, sought a hearing in connection with appellees' fee applications. Appellees have been content to rest on their written submissions. Because those documents do not warrant the allowances made herein, the order of the district court is reversed. The district court is instructed to direct the bankruptcy court to disallow payment of appellees' claims from the assets of the estate in which GECC has a security interest covered by the Financing Order.

## NOTES

**1.** How can Chapter 11 professionals ensure payment of their post-bankruptcy fees given the teaching of this case? Is it consistent with the debtor's attorney's professional obligations to insist that some property be left unencumbered to ensure payment of attorneys' fees if the debtor and the postpetition lender are otherwise prepared to agree to a postpetition secured loan needed to fund reorganization? Note that under current practice financing orders commonly approve negotiated "carve outs" that grant priority to a limited amount of professional fees for the debtors' and creditors' committee's professionals. The size and terms of the carve-outs can be one of the most contentious issues in negotiations between the debtor and its lenders.

**2.** The cases are in conflict over the proper standard for determining when expenses benefit the holder of a secured claim. In a proceeding subsequent to *General Electric Credit,* Flagstaff attempted to use proceeds of GECC's collateral to pay payroll taxes incurred during Flagstaff's reorganization. Again the court held that § 506(c) did not permit use of the proceeds for this purpose. *In re Flagstaff Foodservice Corp.,* 762 F.2d 10 (2d Cir.1985). In so holding the court rejected the assertion that payment of the taxes contributed to the reorganization and increased the going concern value of the assets and announced a narrow view of § 506(c): "The debtor in possession must show that its funds were expended primarily for the benefit of the creditor and that the creditor directly benefited from the expenditure." 762 F.2d at 12. A broader view of § 506(c) was embraced by *In re McKeesport Steel Castings Co.,* 799 F.2d 91 (3d Cir.1986), in which the court allowed payments to a utility for providing natural gas to the debtor during its attempted reorganization to be paid out of the proceeds of collateral of a secured creditor. The court held that preservation of the going concern value of a business can constitute a benefit to a secured creditor under § 506(c). More recently, the Supreme Court narrowed the scope of recovery under § 506(c) in the following case.

**3.** Note that confirmation of the plan requires payment in full of all administrative expenses. § 1129(a)(9). So long as the lender prefers to exit the case through a reorganization plan rather than a Chapter 7 liquidation, administrative claimants retain significant leverage even if they are otherwise "out-of-the-money."

## Hartford Underwriters Ins. Co. v. Union Planters Bank, N.A.

Supreme Court of the United States, 2000.
530 U.S. 1.

■ Justice SCALIA delivered the opinion of the Court.

In this case, we consider whether § 506(c) allows an administrative claimant of a bankruptcy estate to seek payment of its claim from property encumbered by a secured creditor's lien.

### I

This case arises out of the bankruptcy proceedings of Hen House Interstate, Inc., which at one time owned or operated several restaurants and service stations, as well as an outdoor-advertising firm. On September 5, 1991, Hen House filed a voluntary petition under Chapter 11 of the Bankruptcy Code in the United States Bankruptcy Court for the Eastern District of Missouri. As a Chapter 11 debtor-in-possession, Hen House retained possession of its assets and continued operating its business.

Respondent had been Hen House's primary lender. At the time the Chapter 11 petition was filed, it held a security interest in essentially all of Hen House's real and personal property, securing an indebtedness of over $4 million. After the Chapter 11 proceedings were commenced, it agreed to lend Hen House an additional $300,000 to help finance the reorganization. The Bankruptcy Court entered a financing order approving the loan agreement and authorizing Hen House to use loan proceeds and cash collateral to pay expenses, including workers' compensation expenses.

During the attempted reorganization, Hen House obtained workers' compensation insurance from petitioner Hartford Underwriters (which was unaware of the bankruptcy proceedings). Although the policy required monthly premium payments, Hen House repeatedly failed to make them; Hartford continued to provide insurance nonetheless. The reorganization ultimately failed, and on January 20, 1993, the Bankruptcy Court converted the case to a liquidation proceeding under Chapter 7 and appointed a trustee. At the time of the conversion, Hen House owed Hartford more than $50,000 in unpaid premiums. Hartford learned of Hen House's bankruptcy proceedings after the conversion, in March 1993.

Recognizing that the estate lacked unencumbered funds to pay the premiums, Hartford attempted to charge the premiums to respondent, the secured creditor, by filing with the Bankruptcy Court an "Application for Allowance of Administrative Expense, Pursuant to § 503 and Charge Against Collateral, Pursuant to § 506(c)." The Bankruptcy Court ruled in favor of Hartford, and the District Court and an Eighth Circuit panel affirmed. The Eighth Circuit subsequently granted en banc review, however, and reversed, concluding that § 506(c) could not be invoked by an administrative claimant.

\* \* \*

### III

Because we believe that by far the most natural reading of § 506(c) is that it extends only to the trustee, petitioner's burden of persuading us that the section must be read to allow its use by other parties is " "exceptionally heavy.' " To support its proffered reading, petitioner advances arguments based on pre-Code practice and policy considerations. We address these arguments in turn.

### A

Section 506(c)'s provision for the charge of certain administrative expenses against lienholders continues a practice that existed under the Bankruptcy Act of 1898. It was not to be found in the text of the Act, but traced its origin to early cases establishing an equitable principle that where a court has custody of property, costs of administering and preserving the property are a dominant charge. It was the norm that recovery of costs from a secured creditor would be sought by the trustee. Petitioner cites a number of lower court cases, however, in which–without meaning-ful discussion of the point–parties other than the trustee were permitted to pursue such charges under the Act, sometimes simultaneously with the trustee's pursuit of his own expenses, but sometimes independently. Peti-tioner also relies on early decisions of this Court allowing individual claimants to seek recovery from secured assets. *Wilson* and *Burnham* in-volved equity receiverships, and were not only pre-Code, but predate the Bankruptcy Act of 1898 that the Code replaced; while *New York Dock* was a case arising in admiralty.

It is questionable whether these precedents establish a bankruptcy practice sufficiently widespread and well recognized to justify the conclu-sion of implicit adoption by the Code. We have no confidence that the al-lowance of recovery from collateral by nontrustees is "the type of 'rule' that. . . Congress was aware of when enacting the Code." *United States v. Ron Pair Enterprises, Inc.* In any event, while pre-Code practice "informs our understanding of the language of the Code," *id.,* it cannot overcome that language. It is a tool of construction, not an extratextual supplement. We have applied it to the construction of provisions which were "subject to interpretation," *id.,* or contained "ambiguity in the text," *Dewsnup, su-pra.* "[W]here the meaning of the Bankruptcy Code's text is itself clear. . . its operation is unimpeded by contrary. . . prior practice," *BFP v. Resolu-tion Trust Corporation.*

In this case, we think the language of the Code leaves no room for clarification by pre-Code practice. If § 506(c) provided only that certain costs and expenses could be recovered from property securing a secured claim, without specifying any particular party by whom the recovery could be pursued, the case would be akin to those in which we used prior prac-tice to fill in the details of a pre-Code concept that the Code had adopted without elaboration. See, *e.g., United States v. Noland,* 517 U.S. 535, 539 (1996) (looking to pre-Code practice in interpreting Code's reference to "principles of equitable subordination"); *Midlantic Nat. Bank v. New Jer-sey Dept. of Environmental Protection,* 474 U.S. 494, 501 (1986) (codifi-cation of trustee's abandonment power held to incorporate established ex-ceptions). Here, however, it is not the unelaborated concept but only a specifically narrowed one that has been adopted: a rule allowing the charge of costs to secured assets *by the trustee.* Pre–Code practice cannot transform § 506(c)'s reference to "the trustee" to "the trustee and other parties in interest."

### B

Finally, petitioner argues that its reading is necessary as a matter of policy, since in some cases the trustee may lack an incentive to pursue payment. Section 506(c) must be open to nontrustees, petitioner asserts, lest secured creditors enjoy the benefit of services without paying for them. Moreover, ensuring that administrative claimants are compensated may also serve purposes beyond the avoidance of unjust enrichment. To the extent that there are circumstances in which the trustee will not use the section although an individual creditor would,[4] allowing suits by nontrustees could encourage the provision of postpetition services to debtors on more favorable terms, which would in turn further bankruptcy's goals.

Although these concerns may be valid, it is far from clear that the policy implications favor petitioner's position. The class of cases in which § 506(c) would lie dormant without nontrustee use is limited by the fact that the trustee is obliged to seek recovery under the section whenever his fiduciary duties so require. And limiting § 506(c) to the trustee does not leave those who provide goods or services that benefit secured interests without other means of protecting themselves as against other creditors: They may insist on cash payment, or contract directly with the secured creditor, and may be able to obtain superpriority under § 364(c)(1) or a security interest under §§ 364(c)(2), (3) or § 364(d). And of course postpetition creditors can avoid unnecessary losses simply by paying attention to the status of their accounts, a protection which, by all appearances, petitioner neglected here.

On the other side of the ledger, petitioner's reading would itself lead to results that seem undesirable as a matter of policy. In particular, expanding the number of parties who could use § 506(c) would create the possibility of multiple administrative claimants seeking recovery under the section. Each such claim would require inquiry into the necessity of the services at issue and the degree of benefit to the secured creditor. Allowing recovery to be sought at the behest of parties other than the trustee could therefore impair the ability of the bankruptcy court to coordinate proceedings, as well as the ability of the trustee to manage the estate. Indeed, if administrative claimants were free to seek recovery on their own, they could proceed even where the trustee himself planned to do so.[5] Fur-

---

[4] The frequency with which such circumstances arise may depend in part on who ultimately receives the recovery obtained by a trustee under § 506(c). Petitioner argues that it goes to the party who provided the services that benefited collateral (assuming that party has not already been compensated by the estate). Respondent argues that this reading, like a reading that allows creditors themselves to use § 506(c), upsets the Code's priority scheme by giving administrative claimants who benefit collateral an effective priority over others–allowing, for example, a Chapter 11 administrative creditor (like petitioner) to obtain payment via § 506(c) while Chapter 7 administrative creditors remain unpaid, despite § 726(b)'s provision that Chapter 7 administrative claims have priority over Chapter 11 administrative claims. Thus, respondent asserts that a trustee's recovery under § 506(c) simply goes into the estate to be distributed according to the Code's priority provisions. Since this case does not involve a trustee's recovery under § 506(c), we do not address this question, or the related question whether the trustee may use the provision prior to paying the expenses for which reimbursement is sought, see *In re K & L Lakeland, Inc.,* 128 F.3d 203, 207, 212 (C.A.4 1997).

[5] We do not address whether a bankruptcy court can allow other interested parties to act in the trustee's stead in pursuing recovery under § 506(c). *Amici* American Insurance Association and National Union Fire Insurance Co. draw our attention to the

ther, where unencumbered assets were scarce, creditors might attempt to use § 506(c) even though their claim to have benefited the secured creditor was quite weak. The possibility of being targeted for such claims by various administrative claimants could make secured creditors less willing to provide postpetition financing.

In any event, we do not sit to assess the relative merits of different approaches to various bankruptcy problems. It suffices that the natural reading of the text produces the result we announce. Achieving a better policy outcome–if what petitioner urges is that–is a task for Congress, not the courts.

* * *

We have considered the other points urged by petitioner and find them to be without merit. We conclude that 11 U.S.C. § 506(c) does not provide an administrative claimant an independent right to use the section to seek payment of its claim. The judgment of the Eighth Circuit is affirmed.

## NOTE

Following the Supreme Court's decision in *Hartford Underwriters*, parties began to challenge the bankruptcy courts' power to authorize creditors' committees to prosecute estate causes of action, the question specifically reserved in footnote 5 of the decision. In *Official Committee of Unsecured Creditors of Cybergenics Corp. v. Chinery*, 330 F.3d 548 *en banc* (3d Cir.2003), the Third Circuit, reversing an earlier panel decision, found that the Code did provide bankruptcy courts authority to designate official committees as estate representatives for the purpose of prosecuting lawsuits, relying upon §§ 105(a), 503(b) & 1103(c)(5) as well as pre-Code precedent and practice. The competing views on the question of court power to authorize committees to bring suit on behalf of the bankruptcy estate are set forth in Keith Sharfman, *Derivative Suits in Bankruptcy*, 10 Stan. J.L. Bus. & Fin. 1 (2004); Daniel J. Bussel, *Creditors' Committees as Estate Representatives in Bankruptcy Litigation*, 10 Stan. J.L. Bus. &

---

practice of some courts of allowing creditors or creditors' committees a derivative right to bring avoidance actions when the trustee refuses to do so, even though the applicable Code provisions, see 11 U.S.C. §§ 544, 545, 547(b), 548(a), 549(a), mention only the trustee. See, *e.g., In re Gibson Group, Inc.,* 66 F.3d 1436, 1438 (C.A.6 1995). Whatever the validity of that practice, it has no analogous application here, since petitioner did not ask the trustee to pursue payment under § 506(c) and did not seek permission from the Bankruptcy Court to take such action in the trustee's stead. Petitioner asserted an independent right to use § 506(c), which is what we reject today. Cf. *In re Xonics Photochemical, Inc.,* 841 F.2d 198, 202–203 (C.A.7 1988) (holding that creditor had no right to bring avoidance action independently, but noting that it might have been able to seek to bring derivative suit).

Fin. 28 (2004); and Keith Sharfman, *Creditor(s' Committee) Derivative Suits: A Reply to Professor Bussel*, 10 Stan. J.L. Bus. & Fin. 38 (2004) .

### c.    Rights of Prepetition Creditors

Citing Woody Allen, the court in *In re Omegas Group, Inc.*, 16 F.3d 1443, 1445 (6th Cir.1994), observed: "Understandably, creditors of bankrupt debtors often feel like restaurant patrons who not only hate the food, but think the portions are too small."

If the position of postpetition unsecured creditors under Chapter 11 is sometimes risky, that of prepetition unsecured creditors is always speculative and often bleak. The debtor's initial choice of Chapter 11—a choice prepetition creditors have virtually no power to influence—dictates that prepetition creditors will receive no payment on claims unless and until the debtor's reorganization plan is confirmed and becomes effective, months or years later. They will earn no interest on claims during this period. § 502(b)(2). Their right to share in a prompt Chapter 7 liquidation is taken away and in its stead they are given the hope, often unrealized, that the debtor will keep the business afloat and be able someday to pay part or all of the time-reduced claims. If the debtor fails in Chapter 11, liquidation in Chapter 7 usually follows, but the amount paid to prepetition creditors may be drastically less than the amount that would have been paid had the debtor originally filed in Chapter 7.

One of the principal reasons for a reduction in the liquidation value of a prepetition unsecured claim in Chapter 11 is the tendency of administrative expenses to balloon during the interim period during which the debtor is struggling to reorganize its business. Although prepetition creditors may eventually get to vote on the debtor's plan of reorganization, they have no effective voice in determining how much credit is approved as administrative expense having priority over their claims. They must sit back and wait while the court gives the debtor its run at a successful reorganization. Meanwhile prepetition creditors behold a growing number of postpetition creditors stepping ahead in line: lawyers, accountants, appraisers, examiners, trade creditors, tax collectors, and lenders.

Are there limits beyond which courts should not go in authorizing debtors to acquire postpetition credit? One restraint, is the fact that a plan cannot be confirmed unless all administrative expenses, which would include virtually all postpetition credit, can be paid in cash upon the effective date of the plan. § 1129(a)(9)(A). Before administrative expenses escalate to the point at which it is improbable that the debtor will be able to pay them in full and still carry out the plan, prepetition creditors should ask the court to restrict the operation of the business by the debtor. § 1108. The court should not allow further operation on credit unless there is a reasonable probability of a successful reorganization.

Prepetition secured lenders are of course in a better position. But remarkably even a properly perfected and nonavoidable lien may be subordinated to postpetition lending under § 364(d), subject to the provision of "adequate protection" to the prepetition secured lenders. In *In re Swedeland Development Group, Inc.*, 16 F.3d 552 (3d Cir.1994), the debtor was developing a residential community and adjacent golf course. By the time of the debtor's bankruptcy, it had borrowed $36 million from Carteret Federal Savings Bank, but its partly developed golf course and subdivision was worth only about $18 million. The debtor then sought to borrow an additional $4 million under § 364(d) to complete construction of 900 residences, to be secured by a first mortgage against the property senior to Carteret's prior perfected undersecured prepetition mortgage. The bankruptcy court approved the proposed § 364(d) credit on the ground that the likely increase in value in the property on account of the completion of the units meant that Carteret's subordinated lien would be adequately protected. As the completed residences were sold, Carteret would receive partial repayments from the proceeds, albeit at a lower rate than that contemplated by Carteret's original loan. The bankruptcy court found that, over time, if the debtor met its projections, that Carteret would eventually be repaid in full. The Third Circuit rejected the bankruptcy court's approval of this postpetitition financing arrangement:

> We cannot close this portion of our opinion without pointing out that what happened here is quite disturbing. There, of course, is no doubt that the policy underlying Chapter 11 is important. Nevertheless, Congress did not contemplate that a creditor could find its priority position eroded and, as compensation for the erosion, be offered an opportunity to recoup dependent upon the success of a business with inherently risky prospects. We trust that in the future bankruptcy judges in this circuit will require that adequate protection be demonstrated more tangibly than was done in this case.

16 F.3d at 567.

Nevertheless, the superpriority lien of the postpetition lender was held to be valid to the extent of monies that had already been advanced in reliance on the bankruptcy court's order approving the credit. § 364(e).

Section 364(d) embodies a paradox. It provides that "priming" liens that subordinate prepetition secured lenders are permitted only when two conditions are satisfied: first, that money necessary to fund reorganization is not otherwise available; and, second, that the subordinated prepetition lenders be "adequately protected." How can both conditions be simultaneously satisfied? If the protections being offered the prepetition lender are truly adequate, why aren't those same protections sufficient to induce a postpetition lender to provide credit without subordinating the prepetition lender?

### d.   Cross–Collateralization

Suppose a creditor with a prepetition claim is asked to grant postpetition credit. The creditor is willing so long as the creditor is given a lien on assets of the estate that secures not only payment of the postpetition credit but the prepetition claim as well. Is such a lien permissible? To the extent the lien secures payment of the prepetition claim, the granting of the lien amounts to a postpetition preference. The next case discusses the issue.

## Matter of Saybrook Manufacturing Co.

United States Court of Appeals, Eleventh Circuit, 1992.
963 F.2d 1490.

■ Cox, Circuit Judge:

Seymour and Jeffrey Shapiro, unsecured creditors, objected to the bankruptcy court's authorization for the Chapter 11 debtors to "cross-collateralize" their pre-petition debt with unencumbered property from the bankruptcy estate. The bankruptcy court overruled the objection and also refused to grant a stay of its order pending appeal. The Shapiros appealed to the district court, which dismissed the case as moot under section 364(e) of the Bankruptcy Code because the Shapiros had failed to obtain a stay. We conclude that this appeal is not moot and that cross-collateralization is not authorized under the Bankruptcy Code. Accordingly, we reverse and remand.

### I. Facts and Procedural History

Saybrook Manufacturing Co., Inc., and related companies (the "debtors"), initiated proceedings seeking relief under Chapter 11 of the Bankruptcy Code on December 22, 1988. On December 23, 1988, the debtors filed a motion for the use of cash collateral and for authorization to incur secured debt. The bankruptcy court entered an emergency financing order that same day. At the time the bankruptcy petition was filed, the debtors owed Manufacturers Hanover approximately $34 million. The value of the collateral for this debt, however, was less than $10 million. Pursuant to the order, Manufacturers Hanover agreed to lend the debtors an additional $3 million to facilitate their reorganization. In exchange, Manufacturers Hanover received a security interest in all of the debtors' property—both property owned prior to filing the bankruptcy petition and that which was acquired subsequently. This security interest not only protected the $3 million of post-petition credit but also secured Manufacturers Hanover's $34 million pre-petition debt.

This arrangement enhanced Manufacturers Hanover's position vis-a-vis other unsecured creditors, such as the Shapiros, in the event of liquidation. Because Manufacturers Hanover's pre-petition debt was undersecured by approximately $24 million, it originally would have shared in a pro rata distribution of the debtors' unencumbered assets along with the other unsecured creditors. Under the financing order, however, Manufacturers Hanover's pre-petition debt became fully secured by all of the debtors' assets. If the bankruptcy estate were liquidated, Manufacturers Hanover's entire debt—$34 million pre-petition and $3 million post-petition—would have to be paid in full before any funds could be distributed to the remaining unsecured creditors.

Securing pre-petition debt with pre-and post-petition collateral as part of a post-petition financing arrangement is known as cross-collateralization. The Second Circuit aptly defined cross-collateralization as follows:

[I]n return for making new loans to a debtor in possession under Chapter XI, a financing institution obtains a security interest on all assets of the debtor, both those existing at the date of the order and those created in the course of the Chapter XI proceeding, not only for the new loans, the propriety of which is not contested, but [also] for existing indebtedness to it.

In re Texlon Corp., 596 F.2d 1092, 1094 (2d Cir.1979).

Because the Second Circuit was the first appellate court to describe this practice in *Texlon,* it is sometimes referred to as *Texlon*-type cross-collateralization. Another form of cross-collateralization involves securing post-petition debt with pre-petition collateral. * * * This form of non-*Texlon*-type cross-collateralization is not at issue in this appeal. * * * The Shapiros challenge only the cross-collateralization of the lenders' pre-petition debt, not the propriety of collateralizing the post-petition debt.

The Shapiros filed a number of objections to the bankruptcy court's order on January 13, 1989. After a hearing, the bankruptcy court overruled the objections. The Shapiros then filed a notice of appeal and a request for the bankruptcy court to stay its financing order pending appeal. The bankruptcy court denied the request for a stay on February 23, 1989.

The Shapiros subsequently moved the district court to stay the bankruptcy court's financing order pending appeal; the court denied the motion on March 7, 1989. On May 20, 1989, the district court dismissed the Shapiros' appeal as moot under 11 U.S.C. § 364(e) because the Shapiros had failed to obtain a stay of the financing order pending appeal, rejecting the argument that cross-collateralization is contrary to the Code. The Shapiros then appealed to this court.

## II. Issues on Appeal
* * *

### A. Mootness

We begin by addressing the lenders' claim that this appeal is moot under section 364(e) of the Bankruptcy Code. Section 364(e) provides that:

The reversal or modification on appeal of an authorization under this section to obtain credit or incur debt, or of a grant under this section of a priority or a lien, does not affect the validity of any debt so incurred, or any priority or lien so granted, to an entity that extended such credit in good faith, whether or not such entity knew of the pendency of the appeal, unless such authorization and the incurring of such debt, or the granting of such priority or lien, were stayed pending appeal.

The purpose of this provision is to encourage the extension of credit to debtors in bankruptcy by eliminating the risk that any lien securing the loan will be modified on appeal.

The lenders suggest that we assume cross-collateralization is authorized under section 364 and then conclude the Shapiros' appeal is moot under section 364(e). This is similar to the approach adopted by the Ninth Circuit in In re Adams Apple, Inc., 829 F.2d 1484 (9th Cir.1987). That court held that cross-collateralization was "authorized" under section 364 for the purposes of section 364(e) mootness but declined to decide whether cross-collateralization was illegal per se under the Bankruptcy Code. * * * See also In re Ellingsen MacLean Oil Co., 834 F.2d 599 (6th Cir.1987) * * *.

We reject the reasoning of *Adams Apple* and *Ellingsen* because they "put the cart before the horse." By its own terms, section 364(e) is only applicable if the challenged lien or priority was authorized under section 364. See Charles J. Tabb, Lender Preference Clauses and the Destruction of Appealability and Finality: Resolving a Chapter 11 Dilemma, 50 Ohio St.L.J. 109, 116–35 (1989) (criticizing *Adams Apple, Ellingsen,* and the practice of shielding cross-collateralization from appellate review via mootness under section 364(e)); see also *Ellingsen,* 834 F.2d at 607 (Merritt, dissenting) (arguing that section 364(e) was not designed to prohibit creditors from challenging pre-petition matters and that "[l]enders should not be permitted to use their leverage in making emergency loans in order to insulate their prepetition claims from attack"). We cannot determine if this appeal is moot under section 364(e) until we decide the central issue in this appeal—whether cross-collateralization is authorized under section 364. Accordingly, we now turn to that question.

### B. Cross–Collateralization and Section 364

Cross-collateralization is an extremely controversial form of Chapter 11 financing. Nevertheless, the practice has been approved by several bankruptcy courts. See, e.g., In re Vanguard Diversified, Inc., 31 B.R. 364 (Bankr.E.D.N.Y.1983) * * *. Even the courts that have allowed cross-collateralization, however, were generally reluctant to do so. * * *

In *Vanguard,* for example, the bankruptcy court noted that cross-collateralization is "a disfavored means of financing" that should only be used as a last resort. *Vanguard,* 31 B.R. at 366. In order to obtain a financing order including cross-collateralization, the court required the debtor to demonstrate (1) that its business operations would fail absent the proposed financing, (2) that it is unable to obtain alternative financing on acceptable terms, (3) that the proposed lender will not accept less preferential terms, and (4) that the proposed financing is in the general creditor body's best interest. This four-part test has since been adopted by other bankruptcy courts which permit cross-collateralization. * * *

The issue of whether the Bankruptcy Code authorizes cross-collateralization is a question of first impression in this court. Indeed, it is essentially a question of first impression before any court of appeals. Neither the lenders' brief nor our own research has produced a single appellate decision which either authorizes or prohibits the practice.

\* \* \*

Cross-collateralization is not specifically mentioned in the Bankruptcy Code. \* \* \* We conclude that cross-collateralization is inconsistent with bankruptcy law for two reasons. First, cross-collateralization is not authorized as a method of post-petition financing under section 364. Second, cross-collateralization is beyond the scope of the bankruptcy court's inherent equitable power because it is directly contrary to the fundamental priority scheme of the Bankruptcy Code. See generally Charles J. Tabb, A Critical Reappraisal of Cross–Collateralization in Bankruptcy, 60 S.Cal.L.Rev. 109 (1986).

Section 364 authorizes Chapter 11 debtors to obtain secured credit and incur secured debt as part of their reorganization. \* \* \* By their express terms, sections 364(c) & (d) apply only to future—i.e., post-petition— extensions of credit. They do not authorize the granting of liens to secure pre-petition loans.

\* \* \*

Given that cross-collateralization is not authorized by section 364, we now turn to the lenders' argument that bankruptcy courts may permit the practice under their general equitable power. Bankruptcy courts are indeed courts of equity, \* \* \* § 105(a), and they have the power to adjust claims to avoid injustice or unfairness. \* \* \* This equitable power, however, is not unlimited.

> [T]he bankruptcy court has the ability to deviate from the rules of priority and distribution set forth in the Code in the interest of justice and equity. The Court cannot use this flexibility, however, merely to establish a ranking of priorities within priorities. Furthermore, absent the existence of some type of inequitable conduct on the part of the claimant, which results in injury to the creditors of the bankrupt or an unfair advantage to the claimant, the court cannot subordinate a claim to claims within the same class.

In re FCX, Inc., 60 B.R. 405, 409 (E.D.N.C.1986) (citations omitted).

Section 507 of the Bankruptcy Code fixes the priority order of claims and expenses against the bankruptcy estate. § 507. Creditors within a given class are to be treated equally, and bankruptcy courts may not create their own rules of superpriority within a single class. 3 Collier on Bankruptcy § 507.02[2] (15th ed.1992). Cross-collateralization, however, does exactly that. As a result of this practice, post-petition lenders' unsecured pre-petition claims are given priority over all other unsecured pre-petition claims. The Ninth Circuit recognized that "[t]here is no. . . applicable provision in the Bankruptcy Code authorizing the debtor to pay certain pre-petition unsecured claims in full while others remain unpaid. To do so would impermissibly violate the priority scheme of the Bankruptcy Code." In re Sun Runner, 945 F.2d 1089, 1094 (9th Cir.1991). \* \* \*

The Second Circuit has noted that, if cross-collateralization were initiated by the bankrupt while insolvent and shortly before filing a petition, the arrangement "would have constituted a voidable preference." *Texlon,* 596 F.2d at 1097. The fundamental nature of this practice is not changed by the fact that it is sanctioned by the bankruptcy court. We disagree with the district court's conclusion that, while cross-collateralization may violate some policies of bankruptcy law, it is consistent with the general purpose of Chapter 11 to help businesses reorganize and become profitable. Rehabilitation is certainly the primary purpose of Chapter 11. This end, however, does not justify the use of any means. Cross-collateralization is directly inconsistent with the priority scheme of the Bankruptcy Code. Accordingly, the practice may not be approved by the bankruptcy court under its equitable authority.

### VI. Conclusion

Cross-collateralization is not authorized by section 364. Section 364(e), therefore, is not applicable and this appeal is not moot. Because *Texlon*-type cross-collateralization is not explicitly authorized by the Bankruptcy Code and is contrary to the basic priority structure of the Code, we hold that it is an impermissible means of obtaining post-petition financing. The judgment of the district court is *Reversed* and the case is *Remanded* for proceedings not inconsistent with this opinion.

## PROBLEM

On the petition date, Bank had a security interest in Debtor's accounts receivable worth $120,000 securing a debt of $100,000. Debtor desperately needed a new advance. Debtor and Bank agreed Bank would advance an additional $100,000. The total prepetition and postpetition debt of $200,000 would be secured by Debtor's prepetition and postpetition accounts receivable. The agreement called for Debtor to deposit the proceeds of its prepetition and postpetition receivables in Bank. Debtor would be allowed to withdraw up to 90% of the deposits provided it had generated at least that amount of new receivables. Bank could retain the remaining 10% and apply it first to reduce Debtor's prepetition and then postpetition debts. In short, Debtor was "rolling over" its prepetition receivables into postpetition receivables. Is a cross-collateralization clause in which prepetition debt is secured by postpetition accounts receivable justified in this case? See *In re General Oil Distributors, Inc.,* 20 B.R. 873 (Bankr.E.D.N.Y.1982).

## 5. SALES NOT IN ORDINARY COURSE: PARTIAL LIQUIDATION

If a debtor in possession wants to sell or lease property of the estate "other than in the ordinary course of business" it can do so "after notice and a hearing." §§ 102(1)(b), 363(b)(1). Under this provision and § 363(c)(1) a distinction is made between ordinary dispositions of property that are part of normal day-to-day business transactions that the debtor in possession may engage in without court supervision and those that are so unusual that judicial oversight is justified to protect the interests of creditors whose interests might be adversely affected by the transaction.

Under § 1123(b)(4), a Chapter 11 plan may provide for liquidation of all or part of the estate, but the plan is subject to acceptance by holders of claims and interests and confirmation by the bankruptcy court. § 1126 and § 1129. Is there a conflict with the voting and confirmation provisions if a sale of a major part of the assets of the estate is permitted under § 363(b)(1)? That question is considered in *Lionel* which follows.

## In re Lionel Corp.

United States Court of Appeals, Second Circuit, 1983.
722 F.2d 1063.

■ CARDAMONE, Circuit Judge:

This expedited appeal is from an order of United States District Judge Dudley B. Bonsal dated September 7, 1983, approving an order entered earlier that day by the United States Bankruptcy Court for the Southern District of New York (Ryan, J.). The order authorized the sale by Lionel Corporation, a Chapter 11 debtor in possession, of its 82% common stock holding in Dale Electronics, Inc. to Peabody International Corporation for $50 million.

### I. FACTS

On February 19, 1982 the Lionel Corporation—toy train manufacturer of childhood memory—and two of its subsidiaries, Lionel Leisure, Inc. and Consolidated Toy Company, filed joint petitions for reorganization under Chapter 11 of the Bankruptcy Code. Resort to Chapter 11 was precipitated by losses totaling $22.5 million that Lionel incurred in its toy retailing operation during the two year period ending December 1982.

There are 7.1 million shares of common stock of Lionel held by 10,000 investors. Its consolidated assets and liabilities as of March 31, 1983 were $168.7 million and $191.5 million, respectively, reflecting a negative net worth of nearly $23 million. Total sales for 1981 and 1982 were $295.1 million and $338.6 million. Lionel's creditors hold approximately $135.6 million in pre-petition claims, and they are represented in the ongoing bankruptcy proceedings by an Official Creditors' Committee whose 13 members hold $80 million of those claims. The remaining $55 million is scattered among thousands of small creditors.

Lionel continues to operate its businesses and manage its properties pursuant to §§ 1107–1108, primarily through its wholly-owned subsidiary, Leisure. Leisure operates Lionel's presently owned 56 specialty retail stores, which include a number of stores formerly managed by Lionel's other subsidiary, Consolidated Toy. In addition to the stock of Leisure and

Consolidated Toy, Lionel has other assets such as the right to receive royalty payments relating to the manufacture of toy trains.

Lionel's most important asset and the subject of this proceeding is its ownership of 82% of the common stock of Dale, a corporation engaged in the manufacture of electronic components. Dale is not a party to the Lionel bankruptcy proceeding. Public investors own the remaining 18 percent of Dale's common stock, which is listed on the American Stock Exchange. Its balance sheet reflects assets and liabilities as of March 31, 1983 of $57.8 million and $29.8 million, respectively, resulting in shareholders equity of approximately $28.0 million. Lionel's stock investment in Dale represents approximately 34 percent of Lionel's consolidated assets, and its interest in Dale is Lionel's most valuable single asset. Unlike Lionel's toy retailing operation, Dale is profitable. For the same two-year period ending in December 1982 during which Lionel had incurred its substantial losses, Dale had an aggregate operating profit of $18.8 million.

On June 14, 1983 Lionel filed an application under section 363(b) seeking bankruptcy court authorization to sell its 82% interest in Dale to Acme–Cleveland Corporation for $43 million in cash. Four days later the debtor filed a plan of reorganization conditioned upon a sale of Dale with the proceeds to be distributed to creditors. Certain issues of the reorganization remain unresolved, and negotiations are continuing; however, a solicitation of votes on the plan has not yet begun. On September 7, 1983, following the Securities and Exchange Commission's July 15 filing of objections to the sale, Bankruptcy Judge RYAN held a hearing on Lionel's application. At the hearing, Peabody emerged as the successful of three bidders with an offer of $50 million for Lionel's interest in Dale.

The Chief Executive Officer of Lionel and a Vice–President of Salomon Brothers were the only witnesses produced and both testified in support of the application. Their testimony established that while the price paid for the stock was "fair," Dale is not an asset "that is wasting away in any sense." Lionel's Chief Executive Officer stated that there was no reason why the sale of Dale stock could not be accomplished as part of the reorganization plan, and that the sole reason for Lionel's application to sell was the Creditors' Committee's insistence upon it. The creditors wanted to turn this asset of Lionel into a "pot of cash," to provide the bulk of the $70 million required to repay creditors under the proposed plan of reorganization.

In confirming the sale, Judge Ryan made no formal findings of fact. He simply noted that cause to sell was sufficiently shown by the Creditors' Committee's insistence upon it. Judge Ryan further found cause— presumably from long experience—based upon his own opinion that a present failure to confirm would set the entire reorganization process back a year or longer while the parties attempted to restructure it.

The Committee of Equity Security Holders, statutory representatives of the 10,000 public shareholders of Lionel, appealed this order claiming that the sale, prior to approval of a reorganization plan, deprives the equity holders of the Bankruptcy Code's safeguards of disclosure, solicitation and acceptance and divests the debtor of a dominant and profitable asset which could serve as a cornerstone for a sound plan. The SEC also appeared and objected to the sale in the bankruptcy court and supports the Equity Committee's appeal, claiming that approval of the sale side-steps the Code's requirement for informed suffrage which is at the heart of Chapter 11.

The Creditors' Committee favors the sale because it believes it is in the best interests of Lionel and because the sale is expressly authorized by § 363(b) of the Code. Lionel tells us that its ownership of Dale, a non-operating asset, is held for investment purposes only and that its sale will provide the estate with the large block of the cash needed to fund its plan of reorganization.

From the oral arguments and briefs we gather that the Equity Committee believes that Chapter 11 has cleared the reorganization field of major pre-plan sales—somewhat like the way Minerva routed Mars—relegating § 363(b) to be used only in emergencies. The Creditors' Committee counters that a bankruptcy judge should have absolute freedom under § 363(b) to do as he thinks best. Neither of these arguments is wholly persuasive. Here, as in so many similar cases, we must avoid the extremes, for the policies underlying the Bankruptcy Reform Act of 1978 support a middle ground—one which gives the bankruptcy judge considerable discretion yet requires him to articulate sound business justifications for his decisions.

## II. DISCUSSION

The issue now before this Court is to what extent Chapter 11 permits a bankruptcy judge to authorize the sale of an important asset of the bankrupt's estate, out of the ordinary course of business and prior to acceptance and outside of any plan of reorganization. Section 363(b), the focal point of our analysis, provides that "[t]he trustee, after notice and a hearing, may use, sell, or lease, other than in the ordinary course of business, property of the estate."

On its face, section 363(b) appears to permit disposition of any property of the estate of a corporate debtor without resort to the statutory safeguards embodied in Chapter 11 of the Bankruptcy Code. Yet, analysis of the statute's history and over seven decades of case law convinces us that such a literal reading of section 363(b) would unnecessarily violate the congressional scheme for corporate reorganizations.

### A. Bankruptcy Act of 1867—The "Perishable" Standard

An early statutory reference providing for the sale of a debtor's property prior to final liquidation of the estate in limited circumstances was Section 25 of the Bankruptcy Act of 1867. Congress there stated:

> "*And be it further enacted,* That when it appears to the satisfaction of the court that the estate of the debtor, or any part thereof, is of a *perishable nature,* or *liable to deteriorate in value,* the court may order

the same to be sold, in such manner as may be deemed most expedient, under the direction of the messenger or assignee, as the case may be, who shall hold the funds received in place of the estate disposed of * * *." (emphasis added and in original).

The 1867 Act did not provide for reorganizations; nevertheless, the requirements that the property be of a perishable nature or liable to deteriorate in value and that there be loss if the same is not sold immediately were also found in General Bankruptcy Order No. XVIII(3), adopted by the Supreme Court in 1898. * * *

From 1898 through 1937, the Bankruptcy Act did not contain a specific provision permitting pre-adjudication sales of a debtor's property. But, pursuant to General Order XVIII, this Circuit over fifty years ago upheld an order that approved a private, pre-adjudication sale of a bankrupt's stock of handkerchiefs. Not only was merchandise sold at a price above its appraised value, but Christmas sales had commenced and the sale of handkerchiefs would decline greatly after the holidays. Our court held that the concept of "perishable" was not limited to its physical meaning, but also included property liable to deteriorate in price and value. * * *

### B. Chandler Act of 1938—The "Upon Cause Shown" Standard

Section 116(3) of the 1938 Act, which was the immediate predecessor of § 363(b), was originally enacted as section 77B(c) in 1937. Section 116(3) provided:

> "Upon the approval of a petition, the judge may, in addition to the jurisdiction, powers and duties hereinabove and elsewhere in this chapter conferred and imposed upon him and the court * * * (3) authorize a receiver or a trustee or a debtor in possession, upon such notice as the judge may prescribe and upon cause shown, to lease or sell any property of the debtor, whether real or personal, upon such terms and conditions as the judge may approve."

This section applied in Chapter X proceedings, and a similar provision, § 313(2), pertained to Chapter XI cases. Thus, when reorganization became part of the bankruptcy law, the long established administrative powers of the court to sell a debtor's property prior to adjudication were extended to cover reorganizations with a debtor in possession under Chapter XI pursuant to § 313(2), as well as a trustee in control under Chapter X pursuant to § 116(3). These sections, as their predecessors, were designed to handle leases or sales required during the time lag between the filing of a petition for reorganization and the date when the plan was approved.[2]

---

[2] A letter from a district judge in California addressed to the House Committee holding hearings on these sections illustrates one of the reasons for the addition in 1937 of rules permitting pre-confirmation sales. The letter recounted the difficulty the writer had in a reorganization involving a California land company whose business consisted of selling real property. Because of the lack of clear authority to sell, title companies

The Rules of Bankruptcy Procedure applicable in Chapters X and XI, the Act's reorganization procedures, provided for a sale of all or part of a bankrupt's property after application to the court and "upon cause shown." * * * Despite the provisions of this Rule, the "perishable" concept, expressed in the view that a pre-confirmation or pre-adjudication sale was the exception and not the rule, persisted. As one commentator stated, "[o]rdinarily, in the absence of perishable goods, or depreciation of assets, or actual jeopardy of the estate, a sale will not be ordered, particularly prior to adjudication." 1 Collier on Bankruptcy ¶ 2.28(3) (14th ed.1978) (footnotes omitted).

* * * [I]n *Frank v. Drinc–O–Matic, Inc.*, we upheld the sale of a debtor's 19 vending machines that were subject to a vendor's lien and in the possession of their manufacturer. We noted that the trustee had no funds with which to redeem the machines and that six months had passed from the filing of the petition without proposal of a reorganization plan. Finally, we stated that appellate review of the power exercised by a lower court in directing a sale pursuant to § 116(3) was limited to whether the district court had abused its discretion.

Citing § 116(3) of the Act, we next affirmed an order of a sale of vats, kettles and other brewing machinery which, with " "the approach of warm weather * * * will, because of lack of use and refrigeration, deteriorate rapidly and lose substantially all their value.' " *In re V. Loewer's Gambrinus Brewery Co.*, 141 F.2d 747, 748 (2d Cir.1944). While the court acknowledged the viability of the "perishable" property concept, it upheld the sale even though virtually all of the income producing assets of the debtor were involved. The same proceeding, then entitled *Patent Cereals v. Flynn*, 149 F.2d 711 (2d Cir.1945), came before us the following year. We said it made no difference whether sale of a debtor's property preceded or was made part of a plan of reorganization. Nothing, we continued, in former section 216 (providing for the sale of a reorganizing debtor's property pursuant to a plan) precluded approval of a plan after a sale of all or a substantial part of the debtor's property. Section 216 merely permitted a plan providing for such sale and did not forbid a plan after such a sale has already taken place.

Judge Ryan, in authorizing the sale of the Dale stock cited *Patent Cereals* as his authority. Appellees here cite *Patent Cereals* for the proposition that this court has abandoned the perishable property or emergency concept. We reject such a broad reading of *Patent Cereals* for several reasons. First, the decision involved an appeal from a denial of confirmation of a plan of reorganization, i.e., the sale in that case was a *fait accompli,* it

---

refused to certify title to the land during the time interval after a petition had been filed and prior to plan approval. The writer therefore recommended adoption of legislation that would grant the bankruptcy judge authority to issue orders during the time from filing to approval permitting the sale or lease of the debtor's property. * * *

was not as here an appeal from an authorization of sale. Second, the earlier decision in *Loewer's Gambrinus Brewery* indicates that the court did view the original sale as involving perishable property. Third, subsequent cases in this Circuit confirm the misapprehension in appellees' and Judge Ryan's broad interpretation. * * *

The Third Circuit took an even stricter view in *In re Solar Mfg. Corp.*, 176 F.2d 493 (3d Cir.1949). Acknowledging that a sale of corporate assets could occur outside and prior to a plan yet expressing concern that sales of that nature do not adequately "protect the interests of those whose money is tied up in the tottering enterprise," the court concluded that pre-confirmation sales should be "confined to emergencies where there is imminent danger that the assets of the ailing business will be lost if prompt action is not taken." This "emergency" approach was so appealing that our court cited *Solar Mfg. Corp.* with approval and held in *In re Pure Penn Petroleum Co.*, 188 F.2d 851 (2d Cir.1951), that the debtor must plead and prove "the existence of an emergency involving imminent danger of loss of the assets if they were not promptly sold."

Finally, in *In re Sire Plan, Inc.*, 332 F.2d 497 (2d Cir.1964), corporate owners of a seven-story skeletal building then under construction filed for reorganization under Chapter X of the Act. Because of the site's close proximity to the impending 1964 World's Fair, Holiday Inns felt it was a favorable location for a hotel and accordingly offered to purchase it. The sale to Holiday Inns was affirmed under the *Patent Cereals* rationale. The Court stated that there is no requirement that the sale be in aid of a reorganization; but we further noted, as in *Pure Penn*, that the evidence demonstrated that in its exposed state a "partially constructed building is a 'wasting asset' [that] can only deteriorate in value the longer it remains uncompleted."

More recently, other circuits have upheld sales prior to plan approval under the Bankruptcy Act where the bankruptcy court outlined the circumstances in its findings of fact indicating why the sale was in the best interest of the estate. * * * In essence, these cases evidence the continuing vitality under the old law of an "emergency" or "perishability" standard. As we shall see, the new Bankruptcy Code no longer requires such strict limitations on a bankruptcy judge's authority to order disposition of the estate's property; nevertheless, it does not go so far as to eliminate all constraints on that judge's discretion.

### C. The Bankruptcy Reform Act of 1978

Section 363(b) of the Code seems on its face to confer upon the bankruptcy judge virtually unfettered discretion to authorize the use, sale or lease, other than in the ordinary course of business, of property of the estate. Of course, the statute requires that notice be given and a hearing conducted, but no reference is made to an "emergency" or "perishability" requirement nor is there an indication that a debtor in possession or trustee contemplating sale must show "cause." Thus, the language of § 363(b) clearly is different from the terms of its statutory predecessors. And, while

Congress never expressly stated why it abandoned the "upon cause shown" terminology of § 116(3), arguably that omission permits easier access to § 363(b). * * * Various policy considerations lend some support to this view.

First and foremost is the notion that a bankruptcy judge must not be shackled with unnecessarily rigid rules when exercising the undoubtedly broad administrative power granted him under the Code. As Justice Holmes once said in a different context, "[s]ome play must be allowed for the joints of the machine * * *." To further the purposes of Chapter 11 reorganization, a bankruptcy judge must have substantial freedom to tailor his orders to meet differing circumstances. This is exactly the result a liberal reading of § 363(b) will achieve.

Support for this policy is found in the rationale underlying a number of earlier cases that had applied § 116(3) of the Act. In particular, this Court's decision in *Sire Plan* was not hinged on an "emergency" or "perishability" concept. Lip service was paid to the argument that a partially constructed building is a "wasting asset"; but the real justification for authorizing the sale was the belief that the property's value depended on whether a hotel could be built in time for the World's Fair and that an advantageous sale after the opening of the World's Fair seemed unlikely. Thus, the reason was not solely that a steel skeleton was deteriorating, but rather that a good business opportunity was presently available, so long as the parties could act quickly. In such cases therefore the bankruptcy machinery should not straightjacket the bankruptcy judge so as to prevent him from doing what is best for the estate.

Just as we reject the requirement that only an emergency permits the use of § 363(b), we also reject the view that § 363(b) grants the bankruptcy judge *carte blanche*. Several reasons lead us to this conclusion: the statute requires notice and a hearing, and these procedural safeguards would be meaningless absent a further requirement that reasons be given for whatever determination is made; similarly, appellate review would effectively be precluded by an irreversible order; and, finally, such construction of § 363(b) swallows up Chapter 11's safeguard. In fact, the legislative history surrounding the enactment of Chapter 11 makes evident Congress' concern with rights of equity interests as well as those of creditors.[3]

Chapter 5 of the House bill dealing with reorganizations states that the purpose of a business reorganization is to restructure a business' finances to enable it to operate productively, provide jobs for its employees, pay its creditors and produce a return for its stockholders. The automatic stay

---

[3] The Commission on the Bankruptcy Laws of the United States submitted a draft provision that would have permitted resort to section 363(b) in the absence of an emergency, even in the case of "all or substantially all the property of the estate." * * * Congress eventually deleted this provision without explanation, an action which we hardly consider dispositive of the issue before us here.

upon filing a petition prevents creditors from acting unilaterally or pressuring the debtor. * * * The plan of reorganization determines how much and in what form creditors will be paid, whether stockholders will continue to retain any interests, and in what form the business will continue. Requiring acceptance by a percentage of creditors and stockholders for confirmation forces negotiation among the debtor, its creditors and its stockholders. A fair analysis of the House bill reveals that reorganization under the 1938 Chandler Act, though designed to protect creditors had, over the years, often worked to their detriment and to the detriment of shareholders as well. The primary reason reorganization under the Act had not served well was that disclosure was minimal and reorganization under the Act was designed to deal with trade debt, not secured or public debt or equity. The present bill, it was believed, provides some form of investor protection to make it a "fairer reorganization vehicle." The key to the reorganization Chapter, therefore, is disclosure. To make disclosure effective, a provision was included that there be a disclosure statement and a hearing on the adequacy of the information it contains. The essential purpose served by disclosure is to ensure that public investors are not left entirely at the mercy of the debtor and its creditors. * * *

The Senate hearings similarly reflect a concern as to how losses are to be apportioned between creditors and stockholders in the reorganization of a public company. Noting that "the most vulnerable today are public investors," the Senate Judiciary Committee Report states that the bill is designed to counteract "the natural tendency of a debtor in distress to pacify large creditors with whom the debtor would expect to do business, at the expense of small and scattered public investors." * * *

### III. CONCLUSION

The history surrounding the enactment in 1978 of current Chapter 11 and the logic underlying it buttress our conclusion that there must be some articulated business justification, other than appeasement of major creditors, for using, selling or leasing property out of the ordinary course of business before the bankruptcy judge may order such disposition under section 363(b).

The case law under section 363's statutory predecessors used terms like "perishable," "deteriorating" and "emergency" as guides in deciding whether a debtor's property could be sold outside the ordinary course of business. The use of such words persisted long after their omission from newer statutes and rules. The administrative power to sell or lease property in a reorganization continued to be the exception, not the rule. In enacting the 1978 Code Congress was aware of existing case law and clearly indicated as one of its purposes that equity interests have a greater voice in reorganization plans—hence, the safeguards of disclosure, voting, acceptance and confirmation in present Chapter 11.

Resolving the apparent conflict between Chapter 11 and § 363(b) does not require an all or nothing approach. Every sale under § 363(b) does not automatically short-circuit or side-step Chapter 11; nor are these two statutory provisions to be read as mutually exclusive. Instead, if a bankruptcy judge is to administer a business reorganization successfully under the Code, then—like the related yet independent tasks performed in modern production techniques to ensure good results—some play for the operation of both § 363(b) and Chapter 11 must be allowed for.

The rule we adopt requires that a judge determining a § 363(b) application expressly find from the evidence presented before him at the hearing a good business reason to grant such an application. In this case the only reason advanced for granting the request to sell Lionel's 82 percent stock interest in Dale was the Creditors' Committee's insistence on it. Such is insufficient as a matter of fact because it is not a sound business reason and insufficient as a matter of law because it ignores the equity interests required to be weighed and considered under Chapter 11. The court also expressed its concern that a present failure to approve the sale would result in a long delay. As the Supreme Court has noted, it is easy to sympathize with the desire of a bankruptcy court to expedite bankruptcy reorganization proceedings for they are frequently protracted. "The need for expedition, however, is not a justification for abandoning proper standards." *Protective Committee for Independent Stockholders of TMT Trailer Ferry, Inc. v. Anderson*, 390 U.S. 414, 450 (1968). Thus, the approval of the sale of Lionel's 82 percent interest in Dale was an abuse of the trial court's discretion.

In fashioning its findings, a bankruptcy judge must not blindly follow the hue and cry of the most vocal special interest groups; rather, he should consider all salient factors pertaining to the proceeding and, accordingly, act to further the diverse interests of the debtor, creditors and equity holders, alike. He might, for example, look to such relevant factors as the proportionate value of the asset to the estate as a whole, the amount of elapsed time since the filing, the likelihood that a plan of reorganization will be proposed and confirmed in the near future, the effect of the proposed disposition on future plans of reorganization, the proceeds to be obtained from the disposition vis-a-vis any appraisals of the property, which of the alternatives of use, sale or lease the proposal envisions and, most importantly perhaps, whether the asset is increasing or decreasing in value. This list is not intended to be exclusive, but merely to provide guidance to the bankruptcy judge.

Finally, we must consider whether appellants opposing the sale produced evidence before the bankruptcy court that such sale was not justified. While a debtor applying under § 363(b) carries the burden of demonstrating that a use, sale or lease out of the ordinary course of business will aid the debtor's reorganization, an objectant, such as the Equity Committee here, is required to produce some evidence respecting its objections. Appellants made three objections below: First, the sale was premature because Dale is not a wasting asset and there is no emergency; second, there was no justifiable cause present since Dale, if anything, is improving; and third, the price was inadequate. No proof was required as to the first objection because it was stipulated as conceded. The second and third objections are interrelated. Following Judge Ryan's suggestion that objections could as a practical matter be developed on cross-examination, Equity's counsel elicited testimony from the financial expert produced by Lionel that Dale is less subject than other companies to wide market fluctuations. The same witness also conceded that he knew of no reason why those interested in Dale's stock at the September 7, 1983 hearing would not be just as interested six months from then.[4] The only other witness who testified was the Chief Executive Officer of Lionel, who stated that it was only at the insistence of the Creditors' Committee that Dale stock was being sold and that Lionel "would very much like to retain its interest in Dale." These uncontroverted statements of the two witnesses elicited by the Equity Committee on cross-examination were sufficient proof to support its objections to the present sale of Dale because this evidence demonstrated that there was no good business reason for the present sale. Hence, appellants satisfied their burden.

Accordingly, the order appealed from is reversed and the matter remanded to the district court with directions to remand to the bankruptcy court for further proceedings consistent with this opinion.

■  WINTER, Circuit Judge, dissenting:

In order to expedite the decision in this matter, I set forth my dissenting views in summary fashion.

The following facts are undisputed as the record presently stands: (i) Lionel sought a buyer for the Dale stock willing to condition its purchase upon confirmation of a reorganization plan. It was unsuccessful since, in the words of the bankruptcy judge, "the confirmation of any plan is usually somewhat iffy," and few purchasers are willing to commit upwards of $50 million for an extended period without a contract binding on the other party; (ii) every feasible reorganization plan contemplates the sale of the Dale stock for cash; (iii) a reorganization plan may be approved fairly soon if the Dale stock is sold now. If the sale is prohibited, renewed negotiations between the creditors and the equity holders will be necessary, and the submission of a plan, if any, will be put off well into the future; and (iv) the Dale stock can be sold now at or near the same price as it can be sold later.

The effect of the present decision is thus to leave the debtor in possession powerless as a legal matter to sell the Dale stock outside a reorganization plan and unable as an economic matter to sell it within one. This, of course, pleases the equity holders who, having introduced no evidence demonstrating a disadvantage to the bankrupt estate from the sale of the

---

[4] As noted, the bidding for Dale started with a $43 million offer from Acme–Cleveland and has since jumped to $50 million. There is no indication that this trend will reverse itself.

Dale stock, are now given a veto over it to be used as leverage in negotiating a better deal for themselves in a reorganization.

The likely results of today's decision are twofold: (i) The creditors will at some point during the renewed protracted negotiations refuse to extend more credit to Lionel, thus thwarting a reorganization entirely; and (ii) notwithstanding the majority decision, the Dale stock will be sold under Section 363(b) for exactly the same reasons offered in support of the present proposed sale. However, the ultimate reorganization plan will be more favorable to the equity holders, and they will not veto the sale.

It seems reasonably obvious that result (i) is something that the statutory provisions governing reorganizations, including Section 363(b), are designed to avoid. Result (ii) not only is contrary to the purpose of the reorganization provisions in causing delay and further economic risk but also suffers from the legal infirmity which led the majority to reject the proposed sale, the only difference between the two sales being the agreement of the equity holders.

The equity holders offered no evidence whatsoever that the sale of Dale now will harm Lionel or that Dale can in fact be sold at a reasonable price as part of a reorganization plan. The courts below were quite right in not treating their arguments seriously for they are the legal equivalent of the "Hail Mary pass" in football.[5]

## NOTES

**1.** Section 1123(b)(4) states that a plan may "provide for the sale of all or substantially all of the property of the estate, and the distribution of

---

[5] With due respect to my colleagues, the problem of statutory interpretation is entirely straightforward and not deserving of a lengthy exegesis into legal history. The language of Section 363(b) is about as plain as it could be and surely does not permit a judicial grafting of stringent conditions on the power of trustees. As for its legislative history, the words "upon cause shown" were dropped by the Congress from the predecessor to Section 363(b) in 1978, a signal clearly dictating that Congress meant what it said.

The equity holders argue that Chapter 11's provisions for disclosure, hearing and a vote before confirmation of a reorganization plan stringently limit the authority of trustees under § 363(b). However, a reorganization plan affects the rights of the parties as well as the disposition of assets, and there is no inconsistency in allowing the disposition of property outside the confirmation proceedings. Arguably, some transactions proposed under Section 363(b) would, if carried out, eliminate a number of options available for reorganization plans and thereby pre-ordain a particular kind of plan or preclude a reorganization entirely. In such a case, a colorable claim can be made for a limitation on a trustee's power under Section 363(b) narrowly tailored to prevent such a result in order to effectuate the core purposes of Chapter 11. However, it is not disputed that in the present case the final reorganization plan will include a sale of Dale stock. A sale now thus does not preclude any feasible reorganization plan.

the proceeds of such sale among holders of claims or interests." Why would a debtor prefer to liquidate under Chapter 11 than under Chapter 7? Would creditors have the same preference? Note that by liquidating under a plan, the equity interest holders of an insolvent debtor are likely to do better in retaining some property or interest than under § 363 sales. After the property is reduced to cash, distribution must generally follow the Chapter 7 priorities, see § 1129(a)(7), rather than a negotiated solution that provides for sharing with equity. *See* Lee R. Bogdanoff, *Purchase and Sale of Assets in Reorganization,* 47 Bus. Law. 1367, 1397–99 (1992).

**2.** In *In re Braniff Airways, Inc.,* 700 F.2d 935 (5th Cir.1983), the debtor Braniff, PSA, and certain secured and unsecured creditors agreed to a sale of a major part of Braniff's airline assets to PSA on certain conditions: (1) PSA would issue $7.5 million of scrip to Braniff entitling the holders to ride free on PSA's airline; (2) secured creditors were required to vote a portion of their deficiency claim in favor of any future reorganization plan approved by a majority of the unsecured creditors' committee; and (3) all claims against Braniff, its officers and directors, and its secured creditors would be released. The bankruptcy court approved the transaction under its authority to approve sales under § 363(b). The district court affirmed. The Fifth Circuit reversed:

> The courts below approved the PSA transaction pursuant to Section 363(b) of the Bankruptcy Code * * *
>
> The appellants contend that § 363(b) is not applicable to sales or other dispositions of all the assets of a debtor, and that such a transaction must be effected pursuant to the voting, disclosure and confirmation requirements of the Code. * * * Braniff responds that cases decided before and after promulgation of the Code authorize a § 363(b) sale of all of a debtor's assets. * * *
>
> We need not express an opinion on this controversy because we are convinced that the PSA transaction is much more than the "use, sale or lease" of Braniff's property authorized by § 363(b). Reduced to its barest bones, the PSA transaction would provide for Braniff's transfer of cash, airplanes and equipment, terminal leases and landing slots to PSA in return for travel scrip, unsecured notes, and a profit participation in PSA's proposed operation. The PSA transaction would also require significant restructuring of the rights of Braniff creditors. Appellants raise a blizzard of objections to each of these elements of the deal. It is not necessary, however, to decide whether each individual component of the PSA transaction is or is not authorized by § 363 because the entire transaction was treated by both courts below as an integrated whole. Since certain portions of the transaction are clearly outside the scope of § 363, the district court was without power under that section to approve it. Its order must be reversed.

Three examples will illustrate our rationale. The PSA Agreement provided that Braniff would pay $2.5 million to PSA in exchange for $7.5 million of scrip entitling the holder to travel on PSA. It further required that the scrip be used only in a future Braniff reorganization and that it be issued only to former Braniff employees or shareholders or, in a limited amount, to unsecured creditors. This provision not only changed the composition of Braniff's assets, the contemplated result under § 363(b), it also had the practical effect of dictating some of the terms of any future reorganization plan. The reorganization plan would have to allocate the scrip according to the terms of the PSA agreement or forfeit a valuable asset. The debtor and the Bankruptcy Court should not be able to short circuit the requirements of Chapter 11 for confirmation of a reorganization plan by establishing the terms of the plan *sub rosa* in connection with a sale of assets.

Second, under the agreement between Braniff and its creditors, the secured creditors were required to vote a portion of their deficiency claim in favor of any future reorganization plan approved by a majority of the unsecured creditors' committee. Again, such an action is not comprised by the term "use, sell, or lease," and it thwarts the Code's carefully crafted scheme for creditor enfranchisement where plans of reorganization are concerned. See § 1126.

Third, the PSA transaction also provided for the release of claims by all parties against Braniff, its secured creditors and its officers and directors. On its face, this requirement is not a "use, sale or lease" and is not authorized by § 363(b).

For these reasons, we hold that the district court was not authorized by § 363(b) to approve the PSA transaction and that its order is reversed. In any future attempts to specify the terms whereby a reorganization plan is to be adopted, the parties and the district court must scale the hurdles erected in Chapter 11. See e.g. § 1125 (disclosure requirements); § 1126 (voting); § 1129(a)(7) (best interest of creditors test); § 1129(b)(2)(B) (absolute priority rule). Were this transaction approved, and considering the properties proposed to be transferred, little would remain save fixed based equipment and little prospect or occasion for further reorganization. These considerations reinforce our view that this is in fact a reorganization.

700 F.2d at 939–940.


## NOTE: PERSONAL INDENTIFIABLE INFORMATION

In the *Toysmart.com* Chapter 11 case the question arose whether the debtor Toysmart.com could sell its customer list (containing approximately 250,000 names, addresses, billing information, shopping preferences and family profiles) free of its contractual obligation to maintain customer privacy. Toysmart.com, a retailer of educational toys, was 60% owned by Buena Vista Internet Group, a subsidiary of Walt Disney. Shortly after the commencement of its Chapter 11 liquidating case, Toysmart.com filed a motion pursuant to Bankruptcy Code section 363(b) seeking approval to motion pursuant to Bankruptcy Code section 363(b) seeking approval to sell substantially all of its assets, including its customer list. Several parties objected to the sale motion, including the Federal Trade Commission (the "FTC"), the attorneys general of 39 states and TRUSTe, an organization that certifies companies that adhere to online privacy guidelines. See *F.T.C. v. Toysmart.com, LLC*, 2000 WL 1523287 (D.Mass.). Just before the hearing on the sale motion, Toysmart.com and the FTC reached a settlement, which would have allowed Toysmart.com to sell its customer list to a buyer that was willing to purchase Toysmart.com's entire Web site. The bankruptcy court did not approve the FTC settlement. The matter was eventually settled when Buena Vista Internet Group offered Toysmart.com $50,000 to destroy its customer list. 13 Bankr. L. Rep. 58 (Jan. 18, 2001). The *Toysmart.com* case began the debate over the protection of consumer privacy in the context of Bankruptcy Code § 363 asset sales. The consumer privacy issue raised many questions about how consumer privacy could be protected during the age of Internet bankruptcies, in which customer lists often constitute a major portion of the debtor's assets.

The 2005 Act amended § 363(b) to prohibit a debtor from selling personally identifiable information in a manner that is inconsistent with its prepetition privacy policy (unless the court orders otherwise). In determining whether a debtor can sell personally identifiable information in a manner that is inconsistent with its prepetition privacy policy, the court is required to give due consideration to the facts and circumstances of the sale or lease. Ironically, these nominally privacy protective provisions appear to broaden the authority of the debtor to use, and the court to authorize the sale of, customer lists, in derogation of the debtor's prepetition contractual privacy obligations.

## 6. BREAK–UP FEES AND BIDDING PROCEDURES

Negotiated sales of going concern businesses commonly occur in stages over time. Prudent buyers engage in thorough due diligence investigation, and it takes time to arrange financing, negotiate the details of transferring the business to the new owner and prepare the necessary legal documentation. Moreover, when public companies are involved shareholder approval is generally necessary. These processes cost money and more than occasionally deals are not successfully closed. In light of these realities, it is a commonplace business practice for parties to insist on a binding letter of intent prior closing the transaction that provides for some sum as liquidated damages if the transaction fails to close. In recent years, transactions involving public companies have generally included termination or "break-up" fees that average 2.5–3.0% of the transaction price.

This represents a general increase in the frequency and amount of such fees. In the 1980s the average tended to be approximately 1%. John Coates IV & Guhan Subramian, *A Buy–Side Model of M & A Lockups: Theory and Evidence*, 53 Stan.L.Rev. 307 (2000).

Buyers demand break-up fees and other protections partly to compensate them for the substantial out-of-pocket and intangible costs associated with the failed transaction, but also to make it costly for the seller to back out of the deal. Buyers may also fear being used as a "stalking horse," that is incurring the costs of negotiating the transaction while the seller uses their bids to flush out other higher bids. Sellers commonly agree to such protections in order to induce buyers to enter into transactions. Strong initial bids are essential to starting the auction process for a going concern business and a strong initial bid may be unobtainable without some protections for the bidder. Such protections can be structured in a way that maximizes the efficiency of the auction process by setting orderly bid increments, screening out noncredible putative bidders and providing information and access to serious prospective bidders while protecting confidentiality. But in other situations, sellers may have special incentives to consummate the transaction without regard to higher competing bids. In these cases, the break-up fee and other protections may serve the function of chilling unwanted competing offers. This is particularly a problem when the persons negotiating the sale for the seller have interests in the transaction other than maximizing the sale's price. Management contracts, releases and other forms of consideration that are of no benefit to the estate are classic examples. See Coates & Subramian, *supra.*

Commonly, a letter of intent is agreed to between debtor and purchaser that contemplates a court supervised overbid procedure with agreed upon protections for the purchaser and rules for the auction. The buyer also has a strong incentive to lock-up the form of the bid, that is to preclude competing bids for some, but not all, of the assets or for additional assets or for different forms of consideration than those contemplated in the original bid. Presumably, buyer and debtor have configured buyer's bid, the assets being sold and the consideration being paid in a manner that is especially advantageous to this particular buyer. Forcing others to compete on those terms (rather than their own preferred terms) places those others at an immediate disadvantage. But buyers are infrequently content to rest on this advantage alone. Additional protections often demanded range from reimbursement of buyer's expenses in the event that the transaction does not close, to "break up fees" (payable if the transaction does not close for any reason), to "topping fees" (payable if the initial bidder does not end up being the high bidder), minimum overbid requirements, minimum bidding increments, bidders deposits, sealed or open bidding procedures, "no solicitation" clauses (barring the seller from soliciting competing bids) and even "no cooperation" clauses (barring the seller from cooperating with a competing bidder, except when necessary to avoid breach of fiduciary duty).

All of these devices have been used in ordinary out-of-court transactions. Even when public companies are involved, unless self-dealing by managers or directors is involved, the loose "business judgment" standard of judicial review, generally insulates them from legal attack except in cases where the protections are "draconian" or clearly and unreasonably chill competing offers. Courts have been loathe to strike such provisions as unlawful penalties in nonbankruptcy litigation. *See, e.g., St. Jude Medical, Inc. v. Medtronic, Inc.*, 536 N.W.2d 24 (Minn.App.1995). Beginning in the late 1980s and increasingly through the 1990s the bankruptcy sale practice has mimicked the out-of-court two-stage pattern. Bankruptcy courts are now accustomed to approving bidding procedures in advance of a final auction sale and parties frequently seek protections for the initial bidder at this stage. Although early cases seemed to passively accept the loose nonbankruptcy restrictions on bidder protections, bankruptcy courts have grown increasingly skeptical of substantial break fees and related protections in bankruptcy. An early and persuasive critic of this passive acceptance of the nonbankruptcy business judgment standard was Professor Markell. *See* Bruce A. Markell, *The Case Against Breakup Fees In Bankruptcy*, 66 Am.Bankr.L.J. 349 (1992) (recommending that bankruptcy courts disallow all break-up fees in excess of the reimbursement of out-of-pocket marginal expenditures of the initial bidder).

The trend in the recent cases is to decisively reject the nonbankruptcy business judgment rule. Most cases apply a free-form balance-all-the-factors approach to determine whether the proposed bidding arrangements are in the best interests of the bankruptcy estate. Key considerations include the amount of the fees that will be paid if the transaction is not consummated, whether the procedures are well adapted to maximizing the price for the business being sold, whether the procedures seem more likely to catalyze or chill competing bids, and whether there is any hint of self dealing or collusion with the bidder by debtor management. The only court of appeals decision on point, *In re O'Brien Environmental Energy, Inc.*, 181 F.3d 527 (3d Cir.1999), takes an even more restrictive view, finding that the disappointed buyer had to establish that the break-up fee was actually necessary to preserve the value of the estate. § 503(b). Since the disappointed buyer had continued to bid even though allowance of the break-up fee had been reserved by the bankruptcy court, the later award of the fee was not "necessary" to preserve the estate.

Skepticism increases as the protections proceed along a spectrum of increasingly onerous hurdles for competing bidders. Expense reimbursement is the most innocuous of the protections commonly offered to bidders and the most likely to be approved. Modest fees are more likely to win court approval than large ones. Topping fees (which seem more nearly aimed at chilling competition than compensating the disappointed bidder) are more suspect than modest break-up fees. No-solicitation clauses, and certainly non-cooperation clauses, on their face appear to be inconsistent with the fiduciary obligations of the debtor and are even less likely to win court approval.

## E. Proposing the Plan

### 1. Introduction

In this section, we consider the process under which a plan of reorganization is conceived by the debtor, accepted by holders of claims and interests, and confirmed by the bankruptcy court. Under § 1121, for 120 days after the filing of the petition in bankruptcy, only the debtor may file a plan. If the debtor files a plan within 120 days, the debtor is given an additional period ending 180 days after the filing of the petition in bankruptcy to obtain acceptance of the plan by holders of claims and equity interests. The court may reduce or increase these periods, and in complex cases debtors have been granted protracted extensions. The debtor's exclusive right to file a plan ends if a trustee in bankruptcy is appointed. § 1121(c)(1).

The plan is then presented to creditors and equity security holders whose rights are impaired by the plan. In drafting its plan the debtor may classify claims and interests and deal with the different classes in different ways. § 1122 and § 1123. The composition of the classes is important for they are the voting units for acceptance of the plan under § 1126. A class of creditors has accepted a plan if two-thirds in amount and more than one-half in number of those voting have accepted. § 1126(c).

If any class impaired by the plan rejects it, § 1129(a)(8) is not met and the court cannot confirm the plan under § 1129(a). On request of the proponent of the plan, the court may, nevertheless, confirm the plan under § 1129(b) if the plan is in compliance with all other requirements of § 1129(a) and meets the overall standard stated in § 1129(b)(1) that "the plan does not discriminate unfairly and is fair and equitable" with respect to each nonconsenting class that is impaired. Fair and equitable is defined in § 1129(b)(2). In the case of unsecured claims, confirmation without consent (cramdown) can be accomplished if the absolute priority rule is satisfied. § 1129(b)(2)(B). But confirmation cannot be accomplished unless at least one class of impaired claims has accepted the plan. § 1129(a)(10). In the case of priority claims full payment must be made. § 1129(a)(9). In the case of secured claims, the secured creditor must be given the economic equivalent of its secured claim. § 1129(b)(2)(A). If ownership interests of the debtor are eliminated those interests are impaired and are treated as a nonconsenting class. § 1126(g). Under § 1129(b)(2)(C) the plan can be confirmed only if those interests are found to have no value under the absolute priority rule. If the debtor is unable to effectuate a plan and no other proponent steps forth, the case may be converted to Chapter 7 or may be dismissed. § 1112(b)(2).

## 2. EXCLUSIVITY

The debtor's exclusive right under § 1121 to propose a plan for the first 120 days of the Chapter 11 case and to obtain acceptance of it within an additional 60 days, together with the court's discretionary authority to grant extensions of those periods under § 1121(d), is of great strategic importance to the debtor in its plan negotiations. So long as exclusivity remains intact, time is on the side of the debtor. Since unsecured and undersecured creditors receive no postpetition interest on their claims, delay is very costly to them. Creditors normally want prompt confirmation. If the exclusivity periods are extended over a substantial period of time, creditors may feel compelled to accept an unfavorable plan of the debtor when, absent exclusivity, they might have been able to propose their own plan—one more favorable to their interests. The case that follows, discusses the issue of when there is sufficient "cause" under § 1121(d) to extend the periods of exclusivity. We discuss the 18-month limitation on extensions imposed by the 2005 Act in Note 2 on p. 678.

## In re Public Service Company of New Hampshire
United States Bankruptcy Court, D. New Hampshire, 1988.
88 B.R. 521.

■ JAMES E. YACOS, Bankruptcy Judge.

This chapter 11 case was commenced by a voluntary petition filed by the debtor on January 28, 1988. Accordingly, the debtor's statutory 120–day exclusive period within which to file a plan of reorganization under 1121(b) of the Bankruptcy Code was scheduled to expire on May 27, 1988. On April 28, 1988 the debtor filed a motion for an eight-month extension of its exclusive period to file a plan, i.e., an extension to January 27, 1989. Section 1121(d) of the Code provides that the court may "for cause" reduce or increase the 120–day period after appropriate notice and hearing.* * *

In pleadings filed prior to and at the May 19th hearing, the debtor's request for extension was generally supported by the Official Committee Of Unsecured Creditors (hereinafter "Creditors Committee"), but with the suggestion that the extension be limited to six months. The Committee Of Equity Security Holders (hereinafter "Equity Committee") supported the full eight-month extension request, as did the United States Trustee. The extension request was also generally supported by certain of the joint owners of the Seabrook project.

The State of New Hampshire contended that an early termination of debtor plan exclusivity was essential to resolving the manifold issues presented by this reorganization and opposed any exclusivity extension beyond three months.

The Maryland National Bank as trustee under a "first mortgage indenture", and the Bank of New England, N.A. as indenture trustee for the "G

& R Mortgage Bonds" (hereinafter collectively referred to as "Senior Indenture Trustees") opposed the full eight-month extension and suggested a four-month extension instead. The Senior Indenture Trustees did indicate that the six-month extension recommended by the Creditors Committee would not be unreasonable. The Senior Indenture Trustees did not otherwise take an active part in the proceeding.

The most active opposition to the extension request at the May 19, 1988 hearing came from the First Fidelity Bank, National Association, New Jersey, and Amoskeag Bank, New Hampshire, as Indenture Trustees for the Third Mortgage Bond Holders under the "Third Mortgage Indenture", and from Consolidated Utilities & Communications, Inc. and Citicorp, holders of a large block of the third mortgage bonds (hereinafter referred to collectively as "The Third Mortgage Bond Holders"). On various grounds, the Third Mortgage Bond Holders opposed any exclusivity extension beyond a two-month extension, i.e., an extension to July 27, 1988.

\* \* \*

## NATURE OF DEBTOR AND CASE

This chapter 11 proceeding is unique in that it involves the reorganization of a regulated monopoly utility company owned by private investors. The case is also unique in the sense that it involves an otherwise financially sound utility company that but for the delay in getting a completed nuclear power plant on line would not have had any need for bankruptcy relief. The delay in getting Seabrook "on line" did not stem from economic factors in the ordinary sense, but rather from an assortment of historical events, including active opposition by certain citizen environmental and safety groups, which have lengthened the regulatory process considerably. For various historical, political and other reasons it apparently has been possible to put $5.5 billion into the ground at the Seabrook plant location *before* determining whether the location would permit safe evacuation of the public in the event of an accident. The delay itself has increased the cost of the completed plant to the point where the "economics" of putting the plant on line, i.e., the effect on rates, have now added substantial economic questions for the reorganization effort.

There in fact have been *no* reorganization cases in the federal courts dealing with privately-owned utility companies since the 1930's. Moreover, the reorganization cases from that prior period usually involve layers of public utility holding companies with convoluted financial dealings that are in no sense analogous to the present proceeding. In a real sense it may well be said that this case is unprecedented. In terms of assets and liabilities it apparently is the fourth largest bankruptcy case of any that are on record.

The size and scope of the debtor's operations are well summarized in the memorandum of the debtor in support of its extension request:

Public Service is the largest electrical utility in New Hampshire, providing electricity to nearly three-quarters of the State's population, by sales at retail to approximately 350,000 customers in over 200 cities and towns and at wholesale to five municipalities and utilities. It employs 2700 people. Its annual revenues exceed $500 million, its assets and liabilities exceed $2 billion. Public Service has tens of thousands of public and private creditors and equity holders, hundreds of executory contracts and leases. Its public debt consists of 24 series of bonds and debentures, its public equity of 14 separate series. Its debt issues differ in security, priority, interest rate, maturity, and other terms. Its equity issues differ in par value, dividend rights, voting rights, and priority. * * * Public Service is subject to extensive regulation of every aspect of its business by the New Hampshire Public Utilities Commission (NHPUC) and the Federal Energy Regulatory Commission (FERC). * * *

* * *

As for the effect of these reorganization proceedings upon the debtor and other parties in interest, and the effect of delay herein, it can be noted that professional fees and expenses unique to the reorganization may well exceed one million dollars per month.[8] It can also be noted as a *functional* "administrative cost of delay" that the unsecured creditors are losing perhaps in excess of ten million dollars per month in lost interest on their monies because they will not be paid interest under reorganization law.

A full picture of the nature of the debtor in this case also requires recognition that chapter 11 as presently enacted does not lend itself easily or clearly to the unique problems presented by the reorganization of a regulated, monopoly utility entity. * * *

Another unique facet of this case, as has become increasingly obvious at the various hearings held before the court, is that the reorganization of a regulated monopoly utility company under chapter 11 presents an extensive and perplexing array of "circular questions" of both fact and law that are not normally found in a chapter 11 proceeding.[10] This circularity stems primarily from the provisions of § 1129(a)(6) of the Bankruptcy Code requiring regulatory approval of any rate changes included in a reorganization plan. The circularity is not due to that Bankruptcy Code provision

---

[8] The three investment bankers appointed separately as financial advisors to the debtor and the two committees alone have been authorized flat fees totalling $375,000.00 per month.

[10] It has become abundantly clear to this court in the five months that have transpired in this proceeding that the deceptively simple and discrete words "rates" and "rate-base", and "tariffs" and "prudency" that govern the utility regulation world are clearly overlapping and conflicting with the words "valuation" and "claims determination" and "sales of assets" and "fair and equitable" that largely govern the bankruptcy reorganization world.

alone, however, since it is inherent in the very concepts of "rates" and "ratebase" necessarily involved in the operations of a debtor of this nature.

The general subject of possible reorganization proceedings for a regulated utility company has been the subject of a number of recent law review articles. * * * Alas, however, as the articles themselves recognize, they raise far more questions than they answer.

As will be developed later in this opinion, it would appear that the major task of achieving a consensual plan if possible in this proceeding will require creative lawyering and financial evaluation by all concerned to avoid a "World War III" jurisdictional conflict which could result if the parties involved ultimately have to resort to litigation to resolve the large gap left by Congress in chapter 11 in this context.

## DEBTOR'S SHOWING OF "CAUSE" FOR EXTENSION

The debtor's primary showing to justify an extension of its exclusivity period is based upon its assertion that this large and complex case simply requires more time for the debtor to grapple with the myriad of factors and uncertainties necessary for the negotiation of a consensual plan of reorganization. * * * [T]he court has already recognized that the unique complexity of this case has justified at least a 120–day extension beyond the May 27, 1988 statutory termination of the debtor's exclusivity period.

There is no question of course that this case is large and complex by anyone's definition. It will be useful, not only for present purposes but for future reference, to set forth at some length various aspects of that complexity. Fortunately for the court, the well-briefed positions of the various parties on the present motion set forth a number of the variables, uncertainties, and circular questions relating to a successful reorganization in this case. These assertions by the parties, I believe, are not seriously contested by any party for the purposes here employed.

It is not possible to understand the complexity of this case without some general understanding of the regulatory context within which the debtor must operate.

* * *

The debtor itself notes its own view of its place in the regulatory firmament, adding perhaps a few adversarial views as well, in its initial memorandum in support of its motion. The pertinent passage is as follows:

> Outside of chapter 11, the NHPUC has general supervisory power over all public utilities and the plants owned, operated, or controlled by utilities to the extent required to exercise its specific statutory authority. It has a duty to keep informed as to all aspects of the management and operation of utilities and their compliance with applicable laws and regulations. * * * Outside of chapter 11, a public utility must obtain NHPUC approval, based on whether the proposed action is in the public good, to transfer or lease any or all of this utility property or to contract with another entity for the operation of its system. * * * A

public utility must obtain NHPUC approval for the issuance of any debt or equity securities, for the mortgaging of any of its property, or for an increase in its capital stock or bonds beyond the amounts fixed by its articles of association, its charter, or any act of the General Court. * * * Approval extends not only to the kind of security or its amount but also to the purpose to which the issue proceeds will be applied, once again, based on the public good, and subject to reasonable terms and conditions as the NHPUC may find in the public interest. * * * Inside a chapter 11, the bankruptcy court has exclusive jurisdiction over the property of the debtor and over property of the estate. 28 U.S.C. § 1334(e). Any sale or other transfer of property of the estate is subject to the jurisdiction of the bankruptcy court, whether during the case, or under a plan. §§ 363, 1123(a)(5). Gain on a sale is for the benefit of the estate and creditors. Rejection of contracts for the purchase or sale of power or fuel is explicitly subject to bankruptcy court approval. § 365(a). The bankruptcy court has jurisdiction over the obtaining of credit and the issuance of debt, either secured or unsecured, during a chapter 11 case. § 364. Similarly, issuance of new secured or unsecured debt or equity securities under a plan in satisfaction of prepetition claims and equity interests is subject exclusively to bankruptcy court approval. §§ 1123(a), 1129, 1141, 1142.

Traditional ratemaking in New Hampshire is based on historical operating expenses (adjusted for known changes) plus the opportunity to earn a reasonable return on rate base. Return on rate base is calculated as a weighted average cost of capital, which includes the embedded cost of long term debt, the embedded cost of preferred stock, and the cost of common equity, applied to the historical, depreciated cost of assets included in the rate base. If the cost of capital decreases, the NHPUC might assert that rates should be reduced. Outside of chapter 11, the NHPUC has authority to force such a reduction on its own motion. Thus, if Public Service's plan results in lower interest rates on its debt without a write-up of rate base, then the NHPUC may try to lower rates even if the plan itself does not contemplate any changes in rates. Such an attempt, if successful, could jeopardize the feasibility of a plan.

This Court has already noted the potential circularity in valuation. Valuation is based on revenues, which are derived from rates set by the NHPUC. Rates are based in part on capital structure, which is fixed under a plan approved by this Court. Capital structure is based in part on valuation, for value determines distributions under a plan. The Bankruptcy Code, however, only requires that the appropriate regulatory agency approve any rate *change* proposed under a plan. § 1129(a)(6). Nevertheless, a new capital structure may tempt the NHPUC to commence a new rate case, as noted above. Accordingly, any plan proposing changes in capital cost, rate base, or any of the other matters described above, must necessarily include some provision for regulation of Public Service or its successor on a non-traditional basis until such time as more traditional rate-making can be used without undoing the effects of confirmation of a plan and reorganization of the debtor. Except in the context of an industry as heavily regulated as the utility industry, any suggestion that a state agency could nullify bankruptcy court approval of any of these transactions or interfere with the implementation of a plan would be ludicrous. * * * However, the NHPUC can be expected to assert here that a plan involving a sale of assets, a corporate restructuring, an issuance of new securities, or even the rejection of executory contracts for the purchase or sale of fuel or power presents a conflict between the jurisdictions of this Court and the NHPUC and that concurrent approval is required.

These issues are novel and complex, have no precedent, and must be fully analyzed from a financial, legal, practical, and strategic basis before meaningful negotiations toward a consensual plan can proceed. Public Service may be able to determine and argue successfully that this Court's jurisdiction is paramount in these circumstances or may be able to negotiate successfully with the NHPUC toward a consensual resolution of these difficult issues. Both require time. Public Service should be given that time in order to formulate a consensual plan.

* * *

The debtor in its reply memorandum adds some additional questions relating to contingencies primarily involved at the Seabrook plant:

[I]f Seabrook is to remain part of Public Service after a reorganization, from where will the funds come to support it? If it is to be spun off, who will fund its continued operation pending licensing? If the funding is at a fixed dollar amount, will that be a signal to its opponents as to how long they need persevere before they succeed by time and not on the merits? If Seabrook funding is not adequate, will the other joint owners assert claims against either Public Service or the new Seabrook company? If those claims are asserted in the chapter 11 case, how will it affect distribution to unsecured creditors? If the claims are to be asserted only against the new Seabrook company, what assurance of feasibility can a plan provide without the funding necessary to carry Seabrook? Can Public Service's interest in the Seabrook Joint Owners Agreement be assigned to a new company? What assurance of future performance can be provided?[13]

---

[13] It has been indicated at various hearings throughout this case that the other joint owners of the Seabrook nuclear plant might assert a claim of a magnitude in excess of

The debtor also made a showing that it has in fact engaged in analysis of various possible "plan scenarios" since the filing of the chapter 11 petition indicating diligent effort on the debtor's part to proceed toward plan formulation. As set forth in its initial memorandum these plan alternatives are four in number. The following extracts from the memorandum give a general reference to the alternatives being contemplated:

a.   *Sale of Assets.* Since the filing of the chapter 11 case, Public Service has received expressions of interest in the acquisition of its operating assets from two different New England utilities. Public Service believes that others may also be interested in acquiring Public Service or its operating assets. Accordingly, Public Service, with the assistance of its financial advisor, is preparing an orderly process for the possible sale of the company as a whole.

* * *

b.   *Internal Reorganization—Formation of a Holding Company.* One of the principal causes of Public Service's financial difficulties has been the effect of New Hampshire's "anti-CWIP" statute, which excludes investment in construction work in progress from retail rate base until the construction is completed and the plan is operating and prohibits recovery of investment in cancelled or abandoned plants. * * * Public Service has invested over $2 billion in Seabrook. This accounts for approximately 69% of the book value of the company's assets. Because most of Public Service's rates are subject to New Hampshire regulatory jurisdiction, the anti-CWIP statute effectively prevents Public Service from recovering on its investment in Seabrook until the plant is operational.

In contrast, the Federal Energy Regulatory Commission ("FERC"), which exclusively regulates the sale of electric power for resale, permits a utility to include in its rate base a portion of its investment in construction work in progress and in abandoned or cancelled construction. A restructuring of Public Service's operations to provide for the sale of electricity at wholesale under FERC regulation could thus significantly increase Public Service's revenues and value.

---

$5 billion dollars against the debtor in the event that the plant does not ultimately go on line and has to be abandoned. The particulars of this possible claim have never been made specific in the hearings before this court. The court is of the impression that no party wants to precipitate a definition of that hypothetical claim until and unless it becomes necessary in the proceedings.

* * *

Before Public Service's chapter 11 filing, a maze of obstacles stood in the way of accomplishing such a restructuring. These obstacles included franchise restrictions and merger requirements imposed under New Hampshire law, time consuming regulatory procedures and burdensome standards established by the NHPUC, and other state and federal regulations. In contrast, chapter 11 may provide an opportunity for Public Service to avoid such obstacles to achieve a transfer, merger or consolidation by means of a confirmed plan of reorganization. See, e.g., § 1123(a)(5)(B), (C).

* * *

c. *Internal Reorganization—NHPUC Regulation.* Public Service's underlying business of supplying electricity to nearly three-quarters of New Hampshire's population is sound. With its current corporate structure, NHPUC regulation, and current rates, Public Service can continue to operate and service some level of debt and equity securities, although it is unlikely that this would provide maximum value to existing creditors and equity holders. Thus, an internal reorganization without formation of a holding company is likely a feasible, though probably undesirable, option.

However, favorable resolution of either of two outstanding issues could enable Public Service to increase its rates under its current corporate structure and NHPUC rate-making to a level that would provide a substantial return to parties in interest while providing reliable electric service to the citizens of New Hampshire. The two issues played central roles in prompting this chapter 11 case: the pending litigation over the "anti-CWIP" statute and the licensing of the Seabrook Nuclear Power Plant.

* * *

d. Liquidation. * * *

Whether the foregoing showing made by the debtor constitutes the "cause" justifying the requested § 1121(d) exclusivity extension will be considered below. First, however, the relevant statutory provision and case law pertaining thereto needs to be discussed.

### THE STATUTORY STANDARD

* * *

The district court in Matter of Lake in the Woods, 10 B.R. 338, 340, 345 (E.D.Mich.1981), succinctly summarizes the statutory context and legislative intent underlying § 1121 of the Bankruptcy Code as follows:

The scope of a plan of reorganization may vary widely under Chapter 11, although certain provisions are mandatory. Among other requirements the plan must contain specific classifications for each claim or interest a debtor bears, a description of the treatment to be afforded the various classifications and the means by which the proponent intends to execute the plan. The terms of the plan itself are necessarily a product of negotiation between the debtor and those with outstanding claims or interests, and Chapter 11 is drafted to afford maximum flexibility to the parties in the structuring of a plan of reorganization. As the legislative history of Chapter 11 notes:

> The bill does not impose a rigid financial rule for the plan. The parties are left to their own to negotiate a fair settlement. The question of whether creditors are entitled to the going-concern or liquidation value of the business is impossible to answer. It is unrealistic to assume that the bill could or even should attempt to answer that question. Instead, negotiation among the parties after full disclosure will govern how the value of the reorganizing company will be distributed among creditors and stockholders.

> \* \* \*

> Section 1121 of the new Code, which allows both debtors and creditors to file plans of reorganization after an initial 120–period, represents the legislative solution to the problems created by Chapter XI's exclusive filing provision, and by Chapter X's inflexibility. Under Chapter 11 the debtor is not automatically required to turn its operation over to a trustee, nor is it permitted to retain control of the enterprise until an unwilling creditor agrees to accept a proposed plan of reorganization.

> \* \* \*

The legislative history behind the enactment of § 1121 of the Code, as part of the Bankruptcy Reform Act of 1978, is set forth in some detail in the report by the House of Representatives that eventually became the law:

> Chapters X and XI of current law permit different entities to propose plans of reorganization. Under chapter X, because an independent trustee has been appointed, the debtor has lost control of the business, and the financial standard rules restrict the possibilities for negotiation in the formulation of a plan, any party in interest, including the trustee, creditors, and the debtor, may propose a plan. This feature has been heavily disfavored by debtors when choosing a reorganization chapter, because they lose control over the future of the enterprise.

> By contrast, chapter XI gives the debtor the exclusive right to propose a plan. Creditors are excluded. The exclusive right gives the debtor undue bargaining leverage, because by delay he can force a settlement out of otherwise unwilling creditors, and they have little recourse except to move for conversion of the case to chapter X. That is contrary to their interests as it is to the debtor's, and thus is rarely

done. The debtor is in full control, often to the unfair disadvantage of creditors.

Proposed chapter 11 recognizes the need for the debtor to remain in control to some degree, or else debtors will avoid the reorganization provisions in the bill until it would be too late for them to be an effective remedy. At the same time, the bill recognizes the legitimate interests of creditors, whose money is in the enterprise as much as the debtor's, to have a say in the future of the company. The bill gives the debtor an exclusive right to propose a plan for 120 days. In most cases, 120 days will give the debtor adequate time to negotiate a settlement, without unduly delaying creditors. The court is given the power, though, to increase or reduce the 120–day period depending on the circumstances of the case. For example, if an unusually large company were to seek reorganization under chapter 11, the court would probably need to extend the time in order to allow the debtor to reach an agreement. If, on the other hand, a debtor delayed in arriving at an agreement, the court could shorten the period and permit creditors to formulate and propose a reorganization plan. Again, the bill allows the flexibility for individual cases that is unavailable today.

The report of the United States Senate on essentially the same legislative proposal added the following comment:

Subsection (d) permits the court, for cause, to increase or reduce the 120–day and 180–day periods specified. Since, the debtor has an exclusive privilege for 6 months [120 days in final bill] during which others may not file a plan, the granted extension should be based on a showing of some promise of probable success. An extension should not be employed as a tactical device to put pressure on parties in interest to yield to a plan they consider unsatisfactory.

The court in *In re Tony Downs Food Company*, made reference to the intended tension among the parties that lies at the heart of the § 1121 structure:

Congress has attempted through various provisions of the Bankruptcy Code to balance the rights and obligations of a Chapter 11 debtor in possession and its creditors, thus creating a tension among interested parties which will hopefully lead to appropriate administration of and a successful conclusion to the Chapter 11 case. Section 1121 is one of the important sections intended by Congress to create such tension. The debtor is given a 120–day breathing spell in which it exclusively can file a plan. However, at the expiration of the 120 days, any party in interest can file a plan. I think that Congress attempted to strike a careful balance in this section which was intended to put a certain amount of pressure on the debtor. While Congress has given the Bankruptcy Court the authority to extend or shorten the time, I see nothing special in this case to alter the Congressional policy nor any cause to increase the time as requested by the debtor. The debtor argued at the hearing that it needed more time in order to develop its plan. Section 1121 does not create a deadline for filing a plan; the debtor is free to take as much time to develop and file its plan as it feels appropriate. The risk is, of course, that while it is developing its plan, another party in interest will file a plan. However, that is as Congress intended.

The court in In re *Perkins*, noted that the debtor's exclusivity period, with regard to confirmation of plan, can be considered more leniently than extensions of exclusivity when a plan has not yet been filed:

> This court is of the opinion that an extension of the exclusive time in which to file a plan presents an enhanced potential for skewing the bargaining balance in favor of the debtor, contrary to the intent of the legislature. If no plan is filed, the creditor body has no information upon which to formulate either a positive or negative opinion. On the other hand, if the debtor has filed a plan; potential for upsetting the bargaining balance is more remote. No longer in the dark with respect to the debtor's intentions, the creditors have a basis for decision, and can either accept the plan or fight extensions to the exclusivity period, in order to file a competing plan. Therefore, extensions of the exclusivity period for gaining acceptances do not have the potential for detrimental impact upon the creditor's bargaining position occurring where no plan has been filed. Accordingly, cause may be measured by a more lenient standard in the determination to grant an enlargement of time in which to gain acceptances to a filed plan.

More recently the Court of Appeals for the Fifth Circuit, in In re Timbers of Inwood Forest Associates, Ltd., 808 F.2d 363 (5th Cir.1987), aff'd, 484 U.S. 365 (1988), expressed itself with regard to the proper construction of § 1121 of the Bankruptcy Code:

> Finally, we note that Congress, in 1978, expressly recognized the problems faced by creditors of a debtor who unreasonably delays in proposing a plan of reorganization. In § 1121 of the Bankruptcy Code, Congress gave the debtor a period of 120 days, after the commencement of the Chapter 11 case, during which the debtor has the exclusive right to file a plan of reorganization. Thereafter, if the debtor has not filed a plan, any party in interest, including any creditor, may file a plan. The 120-day period may be reduced or increased for cause, on request of a party in interest, after notice and a hearing.
>
> The limited exclusivity period which is a feature of Chapter 11 proceedings under the Bankruptcy Code contrasts with the procedure under Chapter XI of the Bankruptcy Act which gave the debtor the exclusive right, throughout the Chapter XI proceedings, to propose a plan. The House Report accompanying H.R. 8200 noted that "[t]he exclusive right [under old Chapter XI] gives the debtor undue bargaining leverage, because by delay he can force a settlement out of otherwise

unwilling creditors." * * * Additionally, § 1121 represents a congressional acknowledgement that creditors, whose money is invested in the enterprise no less than the debtor's, have a right to a say in the future of that enterprise. . . .. We think that any bankruptcy court involved in an assessment of whether "cause" exists should be mindful of the legislative goal behind § 1121. The bankruptcy court must avoid reinstituting the imbalance between the debtor and its creditors that characterized proceedings under the old Chapter XI. Section 1121 was designed, and should be faithfully interpreted, to limit the delay that makes creditors the hostages of Chapter 11 debtors.

* * *

The bankruptcy court, in In re Pine Run Trust, Inc., 67 B.R. 432, 434–35 (Bankr.E.D.Pa.1986), noted that a balance had to be struck between "the need for the debtor to remain in control to some degree" and "the legitimate interests of creditors, whose money is in the enterprise as much as the debtor's, to have a say in the future of the company." The court also noted as an element of cause for an exclusivity extension ". . .. Some promise of probable success in formulating a plan of reorganization. . . .."

Finally, it must be recognized in applying the statutory standard that some delay for senior classes in realizing their rights may be justified by the attempt in reorganization to realize the maximum value out of the entity in the reorganization. Reasonable delay to foster a successful reorganization in that sense, even at the temporary expense of senior classes, is an integral part of the reorganizational progress in the federal courts. * * *

It seems clear from a review of the relevant authorities that size and complexity alone cannot suffice as "cause" for a continuation of a debtor's plan exclusivity right in a chapter 11 reorganization. If that were so, a debtor in a case such as the present would automatically have a right to plan exclusivity throughout the proceedings—contrary to the "balancing" and "tension" rationale underlying § 1121 as detailed above. It does stand to reason that a debtor in a large and complex case may make a showing of cause on those facts for exclusivity extension in the initial stages of the reorganization by virtue of that factor. * * * The court in *Texaco* gave an initial 120–day extension and ultimately extended plan exclusivity for a total period of approximately nine months following the commencement of the case before the debtor's plan of reorganization was filed. If size and complexity *alone* were sufficient cause, that interpretation of the statutory standard would in effect eat up the rule.

The court concludes that an appropriate interpretation of the "for cause" language of § 1121(d) would provide that size and complexity must be accompanied by other factors pertinent to the particular debtor and its reorganization to justify extension of plan exclusivity, except perhaps in the very early, initial stages of the chapter 11 proceeding. Such factors include those developed in the cases, i.e., the likelihood of an imminent consensual plan if the debtor retains control, no alternate substantial plan being held off by debtor exclusivity, and the general balancing analysis to avoid allowing the debtor to hold the creditors and other parties in interest "hostage" so that the debtor can force its view of an appropriate plan upon the other parties.

## APPLICATION OF STATUTORY STANDARD TO PRESENT CASE

The Third Mortgage Bond Holders and the debtor come up with diametrically-opposed reactions to the showing of complexity and uncertainties relating to a plan of reorganization in this case. The Third Mortgage Bond Holders note the uncontroverted fact that all such uncertainties will clearly not be resolved by the expiration of the eight-month extension request. Therefore, the Third Mortgage Bond Holders contend that the court should open up the process of competing plans now rather than being forced to such an inevitable conclusion at the expiration of the requested plan exclusivity extension.

The debtor and its supporters argue to the contrary that, while all uncertainties will not be resolved by January of 1989, some matters will be determined and other uncertainties will have "boxed around them" a more definite and meaningful range of possible results and thereby foster a better understanding of the factors involved. On balance the court is left with the impression that the debtor does not realistically see itself filing a plan of reorganization by January of 1989, but rather will request a further extension until the various contingencies are further resolved.

I agree with the debtor to the extent that the Third Mortgage Bond Holders' position is essentially an implicit non sequitur, in that they are seeking to have the court rule that since the various contingencies will not be resolved within eight months the debtor should be directed to formulate and file a plan within two months. It seems to me that with the legions of sophisticated reorganization attorneys, accountants, and investment bankers already engaged in this reorganization effort it need not be concluded that it is beyond the pale of human achievement to negotiate an appropriate plan of reorganization within some limited extension of the exclusive period beyond that presently granted.

As noted above, the debtor and its financial advisor have accomplished the necessary computerized model to permit serious negotiations to go forward on various plan alternatives. The debtor has also assured the court that all qualified negotiating parties will have full access to that computerized information. In effect the base model computer program serves as the "talking piece" for plan negotiations that were employed in an earlier age. The characteristics and usefulness of the computer program were further detailed in a May 20, 1988 hearing, regarding the appointment of a financial advisor for the equity committee, at which all parties were also present.

The professionals, both legal and financial, engaged in this reorganization effort are all consummate professionals and should be able to devise a plan of reorganization which "works around" any remaining unresolved factors or uncertainties. The creative resolution of any uncertainties that cannot be finessed in that sense may require some innovative procedures suitable only to a case of this nature. However, there are indications that such thinking is in process as evidenced in this record. It should also be possible for experienced reorganization professionals to devise—for those variables or uncertainties that cannot be adequately quantified within a reasonable time—appropriate "after-shock mechanisms" in the plan itself, together with "expandable" financial devices, such as warrants or participation certificates, income bonds, zero-coupon bonds or preferred stock, that can appropriately take into account such variables. * * * Such flexible mechanisms and financial devices could be especially appropriate in the reorganization of a utility company.

Accordingly, I find and conclude that the debtor has shown cause within the meaning of § 1121(d) of the Code for some further extension of the plan exclusivity period. I do believe that it is not beyond reason to expect that an appropriate plan could be filed before the end of this year by the debtor and, accordingly, I reject the argument of the Third Mortgage Bond Holders that because an extension would be fruitless in producing a plan the exclusivity period should be cut off now.

## THE "CHAOS" OR "FREE FALL" CAVEAT

Since I have found cause for a further extension of plan exclusivity, it is perhaps unnecessary at this stage to deal with the debtor's *leitmotif* argument throughout its pleadings and oral argument to the effect that a dire fate awaits this court and the various parties in interest if a denial of further plan exclusivity results in the filing of multiple plans of reorganization in this proceeding. The debtor contends that multiple plans result in "chaos" or a "free fall" into chaos—on the basis of past experience in some chapter 11 cases.

This court believes that this danger is more of a myth than a demonstrated fact from specific cases—or, more accurately, it is a danger that can be adequately controlled by appropriate use of a bankruptcy court's powers with regard to a reorganization pending before it. The debtor's position in this regard again would eat up the rule if literally followed.[16]

There is no reason to assume that the reorganization court cannot control that process in a sensible manner * * *[17]

---

[16] If taken literally, the debtor's position would mean that the debtor must have the sole power to present a plan, because multiple plans will bring chaos; therefore, the debtor's exclusivity period must be continued indefinitely. * * *

[17] The bankruptcy judge in *United Press* commented as follows:

Thus, this Court adopted a middle approach, initially suggested by the parties themselves—opening up the right to file a plan on a limited basis to those two entities (besides the Debtor itself) that have the most at stake in this case and have shown themselves to be responsible parties, while refraining from opening the floodgates com-

This court, in the present case, queried the parties * * *:

> To the extent that refusal by the court to extend the statuto-
> rily-prescribed exclusivity period for the debtor might result
> in multiple plan filings, what discretion if any would this
> court have to hold back submission of multiple plans until
> they were merged into a consensual plan, or until it be deter-
> mined that each plan had been improved by competition to
> the maximum benefit of all constituencies involved? * * *
> Would not the asserted strong legislative policy fostering con-
> sensual plans in chapter 11 justify delaying submission of
> multiple plans until it becomes apparent that there is no rea-
> sonable likelihood of negotiating one, consolidated consen-
> sual plan?

In the court's judgment no substantial answer to that question was presented by the parties, in their pleadings or in oral argument, that negated
the implicit power of this court to employ reasonable means to facilitate a
consensual plan of reorganization if at all possible.

To deny that power would be in effect to "skew the balance" in favor
of the debtor under § 1121(d) in complex cases for the reasons indicated
above. The Creditors Committee did indicate that such activity by the
court might be considered as inappropriate "pre-selection" of a plan, contrary to the terms and spirit of the 1978 Code. That response misconstrues
the concept intended; there would be no selection whatsoever by the court
as to an ultimate plan, but simply the exercise of discretion in delaying
submission of one or more plans to the parties in interest for voting until
any reasonable prospect for merging those plans into one consensual plan
has expired. Analogous imaginative exercises of a reorganization court's
power with regard to exclusivity extensions appears in the history of prior
complex chapter 11 proceedings.

If in fact it is a "strong policy" underlying chapter 11 of the Bankruptcy Code to foster consensual plans, as the debtor and the committees
here argue, and as the cases hold, then it appears to this court at least that
that strong policy does not simply evaporate when it is determined in a
particular case that the period of debtor plan exclusivity should end.
Moreover, it perhaps needs to be remembered that ending plan exclusivity
does not by itself mean that multiple plans *will* be filed, or that the parties
may not *still* agree to a consensual debtor plan. It simply returns the parties to a level playing field after the period of debtor control intended by
Congress has expired.

---

pletely. The statute does not expressly prohibit this eminently sensible middle course,
and I can perceive no reason to find any such prohibition by implication. * * *

## CONCLUSION

A useful "battle of aphorisms" regarding the pending matter appears in the debtor's memorandum, i.e., "unresolved issues require extensions", and in the Third Mortgage Bond Holder's memorandum, i.e., "deadlines facilitate resolutions." Another factor that should be borne in mind—although not a pithy aphorism—is some reference to the extremely high administrative cost of these reorganization proceedings. On a conservative basis, based upon the figures noted above, the "per diem" cost of these proceedings in the total functional sense is somewhere in the vicinity of $350,000 per day. That number is "pithy" enough to suggest avoidance of all unnecessary delay in reaching a plan of reorganization.[19]

Delay is not only costly in terms of administrative expense but it could also be damaging to the prospects of realizing the intrinsic economic value of the Seabrook nuclear plant.[20] The problems presently besetting the Seabrook nuclear plant are basically related to safety and environmental concerns, which will ultimately be resolved by the appropriate federal and state agencies.

* * *

From the entire record before me it would appear that there is a "window of opportunity" of approximately six months in which a relatively painless reorganization plan might be negotiated on a consensual basis. While the questions are complex and many, the professionals approved by the court in this case should be able to do the job. As for the timing of the extension date I also take into account the quadrennial event scheduled to occur on November 8, 1988.

---

[19] I realize that an argument can be made, and has been made, that delay in the reorganization of a troubled utility company is not necessarily an evil in terms of realizing maximum value for the lower ranks of interests. * * * Of course the lowest interests in danger of being wiped out always have a "risk everything" motivation to realize top values. * * * That may mean however in a particular case that the lower ranks just want to "risk other people's money." The reorganization court always has to strike an appropriate balance between the risk of delay and the prospect of possible gain in these matters.

[20] The court takes no position as to whether economically a reorganization plan incorporating an operating Seabrook plant, as part of the reorganized company, is in fact the best choice in the ultimate plan to be negotiated by the parties. The answer to that question involves complex questions regarding rates, rate structure, and allocation of the cost of the plant. A net operating tax loss carry-forward of approximately $2.0 billion, in the event of abandonment of the plant, which could shield the reorganized company from taxes for a considerable period, must also be factored into the equation. * * * The allocation of the costs of an abandoned plant between shareholders and creditors—or the reverse allocation of gain in the sale of appreciated utility assets—present other complex questions to be resolved in the plan. * * * But regardless of the ultimate answer to all these questions in a negotiated plan, or in litigation, it behooves no constituency involved in this case to allow Seabrook to be prematurely lost by default.

While the court does not "follow the election returns" normally, it is somewhat relevant that the Governor of Massachusetts, who has opposed as unfeasible any evacuation plan for Seabrook, and the Vice–President of the United States, who has supported the completion and the licensing of the Seabrook plant, appear to be the likely nominees of their respective parties in the presidential election to be held on that date. To the extent that one or the other may be influential as President in speeding up or delaying the prospects for the Seabrook Plant coming on line, and thus producing or denying substantial new revenues for this debtor, it does appear appropriate as the Creditors Committee suggested that any extension of plan exclusivity be to a date after the results of that election are known.

After consideration of all of the foregoing factors impinging upon an exclusivity extension determination in this rather unusual chapter 11 proceeding, I conclude that a further extension of the debtor's plan exclusivity until December 27, 1988 is appropriate and justified under the "for cause" standard in this case, even though such a seven-month extension is rare in chapter 11 proceedings. I do so on the basis that a lengthy extension of that nature will give the debtor the necessary time free from distraction to get the job done.[22] * * *

I have written at unusual length in reaching this decision in order that the debtor and all other parties will have full advance notice as to my reading of the appropriate factors justifying extensions of plan exclusivity for a debtor in a chapter 11 proceeding. I do not now rule that a further extension of plan exclusivity will not be granted. I will have to react to the situation then presented if a further request is made. But the debtor is forewarned that it will have the full burden for showing cause for further extension beyond the self-evident size and complexity of the case.

It will not do to justify any further exclusivity extension request by providing generalized references to on-going "negotiations" which might result in a consensual plan. At a bare minimum any such request will have to address specifically the factors set forth in this opinion, and will have to be accompanied by a definitive "action plan" which details the debtor's realistic prospects for reaching a consensual plan within a definite period.[23]

---

[22] At the conclusion of the May 19th hearing I indicated some concern and anticipation as to issues that could be raised as to access to the necessary data by qualified negotiating parties. I then indicated that I would probably have an "interim hearing" during the period of any extension to review the access question. However, as the debtor points out, no party has claimed any denial of access and I recede from that position. If access problems should develop, it suffices that such parties have the mechanism of the regular Friday hearings to air their complaints.

[23] While a good bit of the court's commentary in this opinion deals with the duty of the debtor to move full speed forward and take full advantage of its exclusivity period, it should be observed that it also will not do for the State of New Hampshire to simply sit by passively waiting for the debtor to create such a plan out of thin air. The state

In sum, the court considers it important that the debtor, as well as all other parties in interest in this case, understand that "waiting around to see what happens to Seabrook" is not a sufficient explanation for non-results by professionals paid at the compensation levels authorized by this court's orders regarding said professionals. If the response is to be "we can't get there from here" we probably can find professionals at much lower rates who can also tell us that. Or, alternatively, opening up the plan process to competing plans may well be the way to break up such an impasse.

## NOTES

**1.** The further course of proceedings in *PSNH* is set out in Judge Yacos's opinion in connection with the professionals' final fee applications, 160 B.R. 404 (Bankr.D.N.H.1993). Judge Yacos proved overly optimistic in his assessment that a consensual plan was achievable within six months, but he wasn't bluffing about his willingness to terminate exclusivity. Unable to work out an accommodation with the New Hampshire regulatory authorities within the extended exclusivity period, the debtor filed its "FERC Plan" on December 27, 1988, the last day of the extension granted above. The FERC Plan adopted the approach of the debtor's "Internal Reorganization—Holding Company" alternative and sought to preempt the New Hampshire authorities' regulatory power by transferring PSNH's assets and operations to a new federally regulated entity. The FERC Plan, in the words of then Governor John Sununu, amounted to a "declaration of war" against New Hampshire, state regulation of electric power rates apparently being an uncodified exception to the libertarian faith of the citizenry of the "Live Free or Die" State. Judge Yacos, dismayed by the lack of progress in negotiations between the regulatory authorities and PSNH, refused to grant any further extension of exclusivity, 99 B.R. 155, and appointed an examiner to help mediate the issues holding up plan negotiations. 99 B.R. at 177. He also suspended consideration of the FERC Plan and any competing plans until September 15, 1989. 99 B.R. at 177. At that point, five competing plans were considered, including one proposed by Northeast Utilities that contemplated PSNH's merger with Northeast Utilities and continued operation as a New Hampshire

---

must realize that unresolved questions as to that portion of the cost of the Seabrook plant determined to be prudent and entitled to enter into the ratebase of the debtor, and the essential economic question as to the maximum "bearable" rates New Hampshire electric consumers can pay, are questions in which the state as well as the debtor must soon "bite the bullet" in pragmatic terms if this reorganization is not to go into a downward spiral of circular questions and litigation which will prevent a timely resolution "before the patient dies." This court stands ready, either directly or through appointment of an examiner or other expert under the Bankruptcy Code or the Federal Rules, to engage with the professionals in this estate and the appropriate state officials in whatever single, combined, or dual process that may be required to speedily determine those matters.

regulated private utility. By December, 1989, the Northeast Utilities plan had garnered the support of all the major constituents—including the New Hampshire regulatory authorities, creditors, equity holders and the debtor—and that plan was confirmed on April 20, 1990. 114 B.R. 820. On May 16, 1991 after final regulatory approvals were obtained the plan became effective and the final merger of PSNH into Northeast Utilities occurred on June 5, 1992. 160 B.R. at 411. Today Seabrook is a fully licensed and operating nuclear power plant successfully managed by Northeast Utilities. Judge Yacos's eventual decision to terminate exclusivity seems to have dramatically changed the bargaining dynamic in the case. He later wrote: "[N]one of the other major parties in interest took either the debtor's first stand-alone plan [the FERC Plan], or the second stand-alone plan filed in September of 1989, as a serious alternative once the debtor lost its exclusivity and the confidence of the two committees." 160 B.R. at 404. Judge Yacos's estimate that professional fees were accruing at $1 million per month was on the mark. The professionals ultimately requested fees in an aggregate amount of $62 million including "enhancements" based upon their contribution to the successful reorganization. Judge Yacos, denied most of the requested enhancements, and allowed fees in an aggregate amount of $50,506,448. 160 B.R. at 404. Many of the issues of federalism and state regulatory power implicated in *Public Service Company of New Hampshire* were reprised in *In re Pacific Gas & Electric.* The Ninth Circuit in that case sharply limited the Bankruptcy Court's authority to exempt a regulated utility from compliance with otherwise applicable regulatory restrictions. *In re Pacific Gas & Electric Co. v. California,* 350 F.3d 932 (9th Cir. 2003).

**2.** Although large Chapter 11 cases commonly endure for two to three years or more, creditors' plans or a lapse in exclusivity are rare. Courts repeatedly extend exclusivity if they are persuaded the debtor is making reasonable progress towards reorganization. Even if a court refuses to extend exclusivity, the most common consequence is simply to provoke the debtor into quickly filing a plan in order to retain control over the terms of reorganization. Alleged abuses by courts in extending the debtor's exclusivity period led to pressure on Congress to place an outside time limit beyond which the period of exclusivity could not be extended.

The 2005 Act prohibits any further extension of the exclusive filing period beyond 18 months from the order of relief or of the exclusive solicitation period beyond 20 months from the order of relief. In small cases a lapse in exclusivity might be unimportant. No party other than the debtor is likely to be able to formulate other than a liquidating plan, and 18 months is probably about as long as any small debtor can remain in Chapter 11 and still be capable of successful reorganization. In large cases, however, it is possible that a non-extendable deadline on exclusivity would actually slow down cases as creditors have an incentive perhaps to wait out the exclusive period before making the concessions that might lead to a consensual plan. Also the deadline would limit the power of the Judge Yacoses of the world to manipulate exclusivity extensions in order to encourage the parties to move plan negotiations along. Consider again footnote 17 in *PSNH* in which Judge Yacos quotes from *In re United Press International, Inc.*, 60 B.R. 265 (Bankr.D.C.1986), which asserts a power to fashion a limited or partial termination of exclusivity in order to facilitate case administration. The 18–month deadline would seem to seriously limit the possibilities of this approach. Would this make the prospect of "chaos" or "free–fall" dismissed by Judge Yacos more likely?

Can the court notwithstanding termination of the exclusive periods effectively prevent plans from proceeding to confirmation by deferring far into the future hearing dates on the proponent's plan and disclosure statement? Can the court choose to grant some plan proponents earlier hearing dates than others, effectively mooting disfavored competing plans?

3.  ACCEPTANCE OF THE PLAN

a.    Solicitation

Once a plan is filed with the court, impaired classes of claims or interests vote to accept or reject it. Before these votes can be solicited, a court-approved disclosure statement must be first given to the holders of the claims or interests. § 1125(b). The statement must contain "adequate information," defined in § 1125(a)(1), to allow the holder to make an informed judgment about the plan. The plan of reorganization is usually the product of negotiation between the debtor and creditors who may negotiate individually in some cases or may be represented by a creditors' committee. In cases in which the debtor has a large number of stockholders a committee representing stockholders may also participate in negotiations. In many cases, the negotiation process will result in a non-binding de facto acceptance of the plan before a disclosure statement is submitted to the court for its approval. That normally occurs if the debtor is a closely-held corporation with relatively few creditors. In those cases, the disclosure statement must be used to solicit binding acceptance, but it may amount to little more than a formality.

The disclosure statement is more than a formality in cases in which there are large numbers of creditors or stockholders whose rights will be impaired by the plan. If the plan involves the offering of securities by the reorganized debtor, the plan raises issues of disclosure and protection of investors that are normally dealt with by securities laws. By virtue of §§ 1125(d), 1145, the adequacy of disclosure in the disclosure statement is governed by the Bankruptcy Code rather than securities laws that otherwise would be applicable. A discussion of the relationship between the Bankruptcy Code and the securities laws can be found in Richard W. Jennings, Harold Marsh & John C. Coffee, *Securities Regulation* 440–448 (7th ed.1992). The proper relationship between the negotiation, disclosure, solicitation and voting processes within a Chapter 11 case is the central issue in the following case.

# Century Glove, Inc. v. First American Bank of New York
United States Court of Appeals, Third Circuit, 1988.
860 F.2d 94.

■   JAMES HUNTER, III, Circuit Judge:

Century Glove, Inc. ("Century Glove"), a debtor seeking reorganization under the federal bankruptcy laws, seeks review of a district court order dismissing sanctions imposed on its creditors. Century Glove claims that one of its creditors, First American Bank ("FAB"), unlawfully solicited the votes of other creditors, in violation of Bankruptcy Code § 1125. The bankruptcy court agreed, imposing sanctions against FAB and invalidating another creditor's rejection of Century Glove's plan. On appeal, the district court reversed, holding FAB's action lawful. Century Glove now appeals to this court. We will affirm the order of the district court.

## I.

Century Glove filed its petition seeking reorganization in bankruptcy on November 14, 1985. On August 1, 1986, Century Glove filed its reorganization plan, along with a draft of the disclosure statement to be presented along with the plan. Arguing that Century Glove's largest claimed assets are speculative lawsuits (including one against FAB), FAB presented a copy of an alternative plan to the unsecured creditors' committee. FAB advised that it would seek court approval to present its plan as soon as possible. The committee ultimately rejected the plan in favor of that of the debtor. On December 2, 1986, the bankruptcy court approved Century Glove's disclosure statement. A copy of the plan, the statement, and a sample ballot were then sent to Century Glove's creditors entitled to vote on the plan's acceptance.

Between December 12 and December 17, 1986, an attorney for FAB, John M. Bloxom, telephoned attorneys representing several of Century Glove's creditors. Among these creditors were Latham Four Partnerships ("Latham Four") and Bankers Trust New York Corporation ("BTNY"). Bloxom sought to find out what these creditors thought of the proposed reorganization, and to convince them to vote against the plan. He said that, while there was no other plan approved for presentation, and thus no other plan "on the table," FAB had drafted a plan and had tried to file it. The creditors' attorneys then asked for a copy of the plan, which FAB provided. The copies were marked "draft" and covering letters stated that they were submitted to the creditors for their comments. The draft did not contain certain information necessary for a proper disclosure statement, such as who would manage Century Glove after reorganization.

With a copy of its draft plan, FAB also sent to Latham Four a copy of a letter written to the unsecured creditors' committee by its counsel. In the letter, dated August 26, 1986, counsel questioned the committee's endorsement of the Century Glove plan, arguing that the lawsuits which Century Glove claims as assets are too speculative. As stated, the committee endorsed the plan anyway. Upset with this decision, one of its members sent a copy of the letter to a former officer of Century Glove. The officer then sent a copy, unsolicited, to FAB. Uncertain whether the letter was protected by an attorney-client privilege, FAB asked the committee member whether he had disclosed the letter voluntarily. He said that he had, and furnished a second copy directly to FAB. FAB attached this letter to a motion before the bankruptcy court seeking to have the committee replaced. The bankruptcy court later held the letter a privileged communication.

BTNY had made a preliminary decision on September 12, 1986, to reject Century Glove's plan. It reaffirmed this decision on December 15, when it received a copy of the plan and disclosure. Counsel for BTNY spoke with Bloxom the next day, December 16, 1986, and Bloxom mailed a letter confirming the call, but by mistake Bloxom did not send a draft of the alternate plan until December 17. On that day, counsel for BTNY prepared its ballot rejecting Century Glove's plan, and informed Bloxom of its vote.

After receiving the several rejections, Century Glove petitioned the bankruptcy court to designate, or invalidate, the votes of FAB, Latham Four and BTNY. Century Glove argued that FAB had acted in bad faith in procuring these rejections.

## II.

The bankruptcy court held that FAB had violated § 1125(b), which allows solicitation of acceptance or rejections only after an approved disclosure statement has been provided the creditor. Though a statement had been filed and provided, the bankruptcy court stated that:

> solicitations * * * must be limited by the contents of the plan, the disclosure statement, and any other court-approved solicitation material. The solicitee may not be given information outside of these approved documents.

The bankruptcy court found that FAB violated the section by providing additional materials such as copies of its draft plan.

The bankruptcy court also concluded that FAB had violated "the spirit of § 1121(b), since FAB was apparently seeking approval of a plan which was not yet filed and which it could not file * * *." This "impropriety" was "heightened" by the absence from the FAB plan of such information as "who will manage the debtor." The bankruptcy court also found "improper" the disclosure by FAB of the August 26, 1986 letter to the creditors' committee. The court found that FAB's "machinations" in procuring a second copy of the letter showed that it was "obviously wary" that the letter might be privileged.

The bankruptcy court held invalid Latham Four's vote. It allowed the vote of BTNY, however, finding that the creditor had proved it had not relied on FAB's statements in deciding to reject Century Glove's plan. The court declined to bar FAB from participating further in the reorganization, finding such a sanction "too harsh," but instead, ordered FAB to pay for "all costs incurred by [Century Glove] in prosecuting" its motions. The amount of these damages was not specified. Both parties appealed the decision to the district court.

In a decision dated January 5, 1988, the district court affirmed the bankruptcy court rulings allowing BTNY's vote, but reversed the designation of Latham Four and the imposition of money sanctions against FAB. The district court disagreed that § 1125(b) requires approval for all materials accompanying a solicitation, and found such a reading in conflict with the bankruptcy code's policy of fostering free negotiation among creditors. The district court held that merely supplying additional information does not constitute "bad faith" or a violation of the bankruptcy rules. Therefore, the court concluded, the bankruptcy court had erred in finding that FAB had improperly solicited rejections of the Century Glove plan.

The district court next considered whether FAB had improperly sought acceptance of its own plan. The court found that, in order to facilitate negotiations, communications between creditors should not easily be read as solicitations. Because Bloxom did not make a "specific request for an official vote," In re Snyder, 51 B.R. 432, 437 (Bankr.D.Utah 1985), FAB's action "may only be fairly characterized as part of FAB's negotiations." Because FAB did not unlawfully solicit rejections, and did not solicit acceptances, the designation and sanction orders of the bankruptcy court were reversed. Century Glove appeals to this court.

\* \* \*

## IV.

Century Glove argues that the district court erred in holding FAB did not improperly solicit rejections of Century Glove's reorganization plan. Since a district court sits in an appellate capacity over bankruptcy decisions, our review of the district court's decision is plenary. \* \* \* We should apply the same standard of review the district court should have applied. The bankruptcy court based its finding that FAB had violated § 1125(b) primarily on its determination that a solicitee may not be provided with materials not approved by the court. The district court disagreed with this reading of the law. As a question of the proper interpretation of the bankruptcy code, we have plenary review. However, we can reverse the factual findings of the bankruptcy court only if, applying the proper law, they are clearly erroneous. Bankruptcy Rule 8013.

Section 1125(b) states, in pertinent part, that:

An acceptance or rejection of a plan may not be solicited after the commencement of the case under this title from a holder of a claim or interest with respect to such claim or interest, unless, at the time of or before such solicitation, there is transmitted to such holder the plan or summary of the plan, and a written disclosure statement approved, after notice and a hearing, by the court as containing adequate information.

There is no question that, at the time of FAB's solicitations, the solicitees had received a summary of the plan and a court-approved statement disclosing adequate information. Also, the bankruptcy court's factual conclusion that FAB was seeking rejections of Century Glove's plan is not clearly erroneous, and so must be assumed. Century Glove argues that FAB also was required to get court approval before it could disclose additional materials in seeking rejections.

Century Glove's interpretation of the section cannot stand. Century Glove argues, and the bankruptcy court assumed, that only approved statements may be communicated to creditors. The statute, however, never limits the facts which a creditor may receive, but only the time when a creditor may be solicited. Congress was concerned not that creditors' votes were based on misinformation, but that they were based on no information at all. * * * Rather than limiting the information available to a creditor, § 1125 seeks to guarantee a minimum amount of information to the creditor asked for its vote. See S.R. 95–989, at pp. 121 ("A plan is necessarily predicated on knowledge of the assets and liabilities being dealt with and on factually supported expectations as to the future course of the business * * *.") (*Senate Report*). The provision sets a floor, not a ceiling. Thus, we find that § 1125 does not on its face empower the bankruptcy court to require that all communications between creditors be approved by the court.

As the district court pointed out, allowing a bankruptcy court to regulate communications between creditors conflicts with the language of the statute. A creditor may receive information from sources other than the disclosure statement. Section 1125 itself defines "typical investor" of a particular class in part, as one having "such ability to obtain such information from sources other than the disclosure required by this section * * *." § 1125(a)(2)(C). In enacting the bankruptcy code, Congress contemplated that the creditors would be in active negotiations with the debtor over the plan. The necessity of "adequate information" was intended to help creditors in their negotiations. * * * Allowing the bankruptcy court to regulate communications between creditors under the guise of "adequate information" undercuts the very purpose of the statutory requirement.

Lastly, Century Glove's reading of § 1125 creates procedural difficulties. Century Glove provides this court no means to distinguish predictably between mere interpretations of the approved information, and additional information requiring separate approvals. Therefore, to be safe, the creditor must seek prior court approval for every communication with another creditor (or refrain from communication), whether soliciting a rejection or an acceptance. Congress can hardly have intended such a result. It would multiply hearings, hence expense and delay, at a time when efficiency is greatly needed.[7] We also note that, as expressed in the House Report, Congress evidently contemplated a single hearing on the adequacy of the disclosure statement.[8]

Century Glove argues that two additional instances show that FAB violated § 1125(b). First, it claims that FAB's draft plan contained material misrepresentations, mostly omissions. Second, it claims that FAB improperly disclosed to Latham Four a letter the bankruptcy court later found privileged. The bankruptcy court found both "improper" in support of its finding under § 1125(b), and Century Glove argues that the bankruptcy court's decision can be affirmed on these grounds. The problem with the argument is that it rests on an erroneous interpretation of the law. Once adequate information has been provided a creditor, § 1125(b) does not limit communication between creditors. It is not an anti-fraud device. Thus, the bankruptcy court erred in holding that FAB had violated § 1125(b) by communicating with other materials. The district court therefore properly reversed the bankruptcy court on this issue.

## V.

Though FAB was not limited in its solicitation of rejections, § 1125 did prevent FAB from soliciting acceptances of its own plan. The bankruptcy court held that, "since FAB was apparently seeking approval of a plan which was not yet filed," FAB violated § 1125. The court also found that FAB's actions violated the spirit of § 1121, which provides the debtor with a limited, exclusive right to present a plan. Reversing, the district court held that solicitations barred by § 1125(b) include only the "specific request for an official vote," and not discussions of and negotiations over a plan leading up to its presentation. * * * Because Bloxom explained that he was sending the draft only for discussion purposes, the district court found that the transmittal "may only be fairly characterized as part of FAB's negotiations." We exercise plenary review over the proper interpretation of the legal term "solicitation."

We agree with the district court that "solicitation" must be read narrowly. A broad reading of § 1125 can seriously inhibit free creditor negotiations. All parties agree that FAB is not barred from honestly negotiating with other creditors about its unfiled plan. "Solicitations with respect to a

---

[7] Expense was a prime reason Congress suspended the applicability of the securities laws to reorganizations. * * * The costs of delay was a prime reason the debtor was given a limited "exclusivity period" to present its reorganization plan.
* * *

[8] Century Glove relies for its interpretation of § 1125 entirely on statements in a bankruptcy treatise. See 5 Collier on Bankruptcy § 1125.03, at 1125–39 (15th ed.1987). The author found the provision ambiguous, and states only that a creditor "should" seek approval. As argued above, strong policy and administrative reasons—not to mention the likely intent of Congress—argue that this court should not impose any additional requirements on communications between creditors.

plan do not involve mere requests for opinions." *Senate Report*, 1978 U.S.C.C.A.A.N. at 5907. The purpose of negotiations between creditors is to reach a compromise over the terms of a tentative plan. The purpose of compromise is to win acceptance for the plan. We find no principled, predictable difference between negotiation and solicitation of future acceptances. We therefore reject any definition of solicitation which might cause creditors to limit their negotiations.[9]

A narrow definition of "solicitation" does not offend the language or policy of § 1121(b). The section provides only that the debtor temporarily has the exclusive right to *file* a plan (and thus have it voted on). It does not state that the debtor has a right to have its plan *considered* exclusively.[10] A right of exclusive consideration is not warranted in the policy of the section. Congress believed that debtors often delay confirmation of a plan, while creditors want quick confirmation. Therefore, *unlimited* exclusivity gave a debtor "undue bargaining leverage," because it could use the threat of delay to force unfair concessions. House Report, 1978 U.S.C.C.A.A.N. at 6191. On the other hand, Congress evidently felt that creditors might not seek the plan fairest to the debtor. Therefore, Congress allowed a *limited* period of exclusivity, giving the debtor "adequate time to negotiate a settlement, without unduly delaying creditors." Id. Section 1121 allows a debtor the threat of limited delay to offset the creditors' voting power of approval. FAB did nothing to reduce Century's threat of limited delay, and so did not offend the balance of bargaining powers created by § 1121 or the "spirit" of the law.

On the contrary, Century Glove's reading of § 1121(b) would in fact give the debtor powers not contemplated by Congress. The ability of a creditor to compare the debtor's proposals against other possibilities is a powerful tool by which to judge the reasonableness of the proposals. A broad exclusivity provision, holding that only the debtor's plan may be "on the table," takes this tool from creditors. Other creditors will not have comparisons with which to judge the proposals of the debtor's plan, to the benefit of the debtor proposing a reorganization plan. The history of § 1121 gives no indication that Congress intended to benefit the debtor in this way. The legislative history counsels a narrow reading of the section, one which FAB's actions do not violate.

We recognize that § 1125(b) bars the untimely solicitation of an "acceptance or rejection," indicating that the same definition applies to both. A narrow definition might allow a debtor to send materials seeking to prepare support for the plan, "for the consideration of the creditors," without

---

[9] Barring negotiations also would provide an unwarranted boon for the debtor: creditors wholly unable to be sure that an alternative plan can be agreed [to] are more likely to vote for the debtor's proposal rather than risk unknown delay.

[10] The bankruptcy court, perhaps recognizing this, found only that FAB violated the section's "spirit."

adequate information approved by the court. Though such preparatory materials may undermine the purpose of adequate disclosure, the potential harm is limited in several ways. First, a creditor still must receive adequate information before casting a final vote, giving the creditor a chance to reconsider its preliminary decision. The harm is further limited by free and open negotiations between creditors. Last, because they are not "solicitations," pre-disclosure communications may still be subject to the stricter limitations of the securities laws. § 1125(e). Where, as here, the creditors are counseled and already have received disclosure about the debtor's business, there seems little need for additional procedural formalities. * * *

Therefore, we hold that a party does not solicit acceptances when it presents a draft plan for the consideration of another creditor, but does not request that creditor's vote. Applying this definition, FAB did not solicit acceptances of its plan. Century Glove does not dispute that FAB never asked for a vote, and clearly stated that the plan was not yet available for approval. Bloxom communicated with lawyers for the creditors, and there is no suggestion by Century that these lawyers did not understand the limitations. Also as Century argues, FAB never sent its plan to Hartford Insurance because Hartford firmly opposed Century's plan. Contrary to Century's conclusion, though, this fact argues that FAB sent copies of its plan because it was interested in obtaining rejections, not acceptances. (An opponent of Century's plan would be an ideal person to solicit for acceptances.) These undisputed facts require a finding that FAB did not "solicit" acceptances within the meaning of § 1125(b).

**VI.**

We hold that the district court correctly determined that Century Glove failed to show that FAB violated § 1125 by soliciting acceptances or improperly soliciting rejections. We therefore will affirm the district court's order reversing the imposition of costs against FAB. We do not decide, however, whether the circumstances merit designation of the votes of any creditors.

## NOTE

*Century Glove*'s narrow reading of solicitation has become the majority rule. However, in *In re Clamp–All Corp.*, 233 B.R. 198 (Bankr.D.Mass.1999), *Century Glove* was criticized for failing to "sufficiently recognize Congress' intention to allow the debtor a reasonable time to obtain confirmation of a plan without the threat of a competing plan." A § 1121(b) violation must be evaluated "not only in terms of its effect on the ability of a debtor to delay reorganization, but also in terms of its interference with the debtor's efforts to propose and confirm a plan of reorganization." The court then held that non-debtor parties are prohibited from circulating solicitation materials before a disclosure statement has been approved under § 1125(b). Therefore, two creditors, who had distributed their proposed competing plan of reorganization and unapproved disclosure statement to all other creditors during the exclusivity period and before the disclosure hearing, violated both §§ 1121(b) and 1125(b). Faced with the difficult task of finding a remedy for the creditors' irreversible acts, the court turned to § 510(c), subordinated their claims to all other non-insider claims, and required them to pay the debtor's attorney's fees.

## NOTE: PREPACKAGED BANKRUPTCIES

"Prepackaged bankruptcies" or "pre-packs" are Chapter 11 cases that are filed solely to implement an already fully negotiated restructuring that requires confirmation of a reorganization plan. In such cases, the debtor will solicit acceptances pre-bankruptcy using a prospectus that complies with applicable securities laws and regulations rather than a court-approved disclosure statement, and assuming sufficient acceptances are obtained will thereafter concurrently file a Chapter 11 petition, the preapproved plan and the pre-bankruptcy acceptances in order to finally implement the restructuring through confirmation of a Chapter 11 plan. Section 1126(b) specifically authorizes the court to rely upon pre-bankruptcy acceptances solicited in accordance with applicable nonbankruptcy law. What if the acceptances come in after the commencement of the prepackaged bankruptcy in light of the general rule that a debtor cannot solicit acceptances or rejections to a plan postpetition until the holders of each claim or interest have received a bankruptcy court-approved disclosure statement? Does the confirmation process need to be put on hold pending court approval of a disclosure statement and resolicitation? The 2005 Act added § 1125(g), making it clear that "an acceptance or rejection of the plan may be solicited from a holder of a claim or interest if such solicitation complies with applicable nonbankruptcy law and if such holder was solicited before the commencement of the case in a manner complying with applicable nonbankruptcy law."

## NOTE: SMALL BUSINESS CASES

Prior to 2005, small business debtors (of whom there were virtually none, since the prior small businesses provisions were both unattractive and elective) had the exclusive right to file a plan until 100 days after the date of the order for relief. The exclusivity deadline could be extended for cause under § 1121(e)(3)(B) if it were demonstrated that "[t]he need for an increase is caused by circumstances for which the debtor should not be held accountable."

Under the 2005 Act, the small business provisions are no longer optional. All business debtors with less than $2 million in debt (other than single asset real estate debtors who are treated separately) must comply with the special small business provision. Section 1121(e) extends the small business debtor's exclusivity period to 180 days and the absolute plan-filing deadline to 300 days after the date of the order for relief. The court will not be permitted to extend those periods unless: (1) it is demonstrated by a preponderance of the evidence that it is more likely than not that the court will confirm the plan within a reasonable period of time; (2) a new deadline is imposed at the time the extension is granted; and (3) an order is signed before the existing deadline expires.

The new law may make it more difficult for the small business debtor to successfully extend the exclusivity period. The preponderance of the evidence standard places the burden on the movant (usually the debtor in these instances) to show that it will propose a confirmable plan. The old standard only required the debtor to establish that it should not be held accountable for its failure to file a plan. Moreover, small business debtors will need to ensure that they move quickly to seek extensions before the expiration of the statutory periods.

The 2005 Act also added § 1129(e), which requires a small business debtor to confirm a plan no later than 45 days after it is filed with the court. Section 1121(e)(3) provides for an extension of that period if the debtor can demonstrate that it is more likely than not that the court will confirm a plan within a reasonable period of time. If the period is to be extended, a new deadline must be imposed at the time the period is extended and the order must be signed before the statutory period expires.

The 2005 Act directs the Advisory Committee on Bankruptcy Rules of the Judicial Conference of the United States to propose a standard form disclosure statement and plan of reorganization for small business debtors. These forms are supposed to strike a balance between the needs of the courts, creditors, and other parties in interest to receive complete information, and economy and simplicity for debtors.

Under pre-2005 law, a court could conditionally approve a disclosure statement in a small business case or combine the hearings on the disclosure statement and plan. The 2005 Act goes further by authorizing the court to determine that the plan itself provides adequate information, making it unnecessary to file a separate disclosure statement.

The 2005 Act imposes significant additional reporting and recordkeeping requirements on small business debtors, § 1116, and the U.S. Trustee will have increased monitoring responsibilities in small business cases. 28 U.S.C. § 586(a). This represents a potentially important shift toward involving the U.S. Trustee in business operations as well as case administration. It is difficult to determine how the U.S. Trustee's increased monitoring function in small business cases will affect a small business debtor's ability to conduct its normal business operations. However, many contend that requiring the U.S. Trustee to have that much involvement in a small business debtor's business affairs will only hinder the small business debtor's reorganization efforts.

Finally, under § 362(n), serial filing of small business cases is discouraged by limiting the application of the automatic stay in subsequent cases. It is unclear why Congress is discouraging subsequent orderly liquidation under Chapter 11 in the event a small business reorganization effort fails.

### b. Trading Claims

In *Century Glove*, the debtor and FAB are struggling over the solicitation of votes on the debtor's plan. FAB persuades other creditors to vote against the debtor's plan—in part by indicating a possible alternative—in order to defeat a plan it believes to be against its interests. The secured creditor in the following case follows a somewhat different strategy—buying the claims, rather than soliciting the votes of the holders. There is no requirement that a court-approved disclosure statement be delivered to the seller before a claim is purchased, but the effect of the transfer of the claim is to transfer the vote as well. Some of the issues raised by strategic claim-buying are discussed in the following case.

## In re Figter Limited

United States Court of Appeals, Ninth Circuit, 1997.
118 F.3d 635.

■ FERNANDEZ, Circuit Judge.

Figter Limited, a Chapter 11 debtor and owner of Skyline Terrace, an apartment complex, appeals from the district court's affirmance of the bankruptcy court's decision that Teachers Insurance and Annuity Association of America (Teachers), the holder of a $15,600,000 promissory note secured by a first deed of trust on Skyline Terrace, bought twenty-one unsecured claims in good faith and that it could vote each one separately. We affirm.

### BACKGROUND

Figter filed a voluntary petition under Chapter 11 of the Bankruptcy Code. It owns Skyline Terrace, a 198–unit residential apartment complex located in Los Angeles. Teachers is a creditor. It holds a $15,600,000 promissory note executed by Figter. The note is secured by a first deed of trust on Skyline Terrace and by $1,400,000 of cash on hand. In fact, Teachers is Figter's only secured creditor and is the only member of Class 2 in a reorganization plan proposed by Figter. The plan contemplates full payment of Teachers' secured claim, but at a disputed rate of interest. Thus, under Figter's plan, Teachers' claim is not impaired. The plan calls for the impairment of Class 3 unsecured claims by payment at only 80% of their face value.

Teachers has opposed Figter's reorganization plan from its inception because, among other things, that plan contemplates the conversion of Skyline Terrace Apartments into condominiums, with payment to and partial releases by Teachers as the units sell. That could easily result in a property that was part condominium and part rentals, if the plan ultimately fails in operation.

Teachers proposed a plan of its own, which provided for the transfer of Skyline Terrace and the cash collateral to Teachers in satisfaction of its secured claim, as well as a payment of Class 3 unsecured claims at 90%. Teachers' plan was premised on the assumption that its claim was partly unsecured. However, on May 31, 1994, before the purchases of other claims took place, the bankruptcy court determined that Skyline Terrace had a value of $19,300,000. Thus, Teachers' claim in the amount of $17,960,000 was fully secured. It did not thereafter pursue its plan. From October 27, 1994 until October 31, 1994, Teachers purchased twenty-one of the thirty-four unsecured claims in Class 3 at one hundred cents on the dollar, for a total purchase price of $14,588. Teachers had made the same offer to all of the Class 3 claim holders, but not all accepted it. The offer remained open. Teachers then filed notices of transfer of claims with the court, as is required under Bankruptcy Rule 3001(e)(2). Those notices were served on all affected parties, including Figter. No objections were filed by the unsecured creditors. The district court upheld the bankruptcy court's determination regarding Teachers' purchase of the unsecured claims. As a result, Figter's plan is unconfirmable because it is unable to meet the requirements of § 1129(a)(10); there will not be an impaired, consenting class of claims. That will preclude a "cram down" of Teachers' secured claim under § 1129(b). Figter has appealed in an attempt to avoid that result.

\* \* \*

## DISCUSSION

Figter asserts that Teachers should be precluded from voting its purchased Class 3 claims because it did not buy them in good faith. Figter also asserts that even if the claims were purchased in good faith, Teachers cannot vote them separately, but is limited to one total vote as a Class 3 creditor. If Figter were correct in either of its assertions, it could obtain Class 3 approval of its plan and enhance its chances of cramming down Teachers' Class 2 claims. But Figter is not correct.

### A. Good Faith.

The Bankruptcy Code provides that "[o]n request of a party in interest, and after notice and a hearing, the court may designate any entity whose acceptance or rejection of [a] plan was not in good faith, or was not solicited or procured in good faith or in accordance with the provisions of this title." 11 U.S.C. § 1126(e). In this context, designate means disqualify from voting. The Bankruptcy Code does not further define the rather murky term "good faith." That job has been left to the courts.

The Supreme Court brought some clarity to this area when it decided *Young v. Higbee Co.*, 324 U.S. 204 (1945). In *Young*, the Court was discussing the predecessor to § 1126(e) when it declared that if certain persons "had declined to accept [the] plan in bad faith, the court, under section 203 could have denied them the right to vote on the plan at all." Id. at

210–11. It went on to explain that the provision was intended to apply to those "whose selfish purpose was to obstruct a fair and feasible reorganization in the hope that someone would pay them more than the ratable equivalent of their proportionate part of the bankrupt assets." Id. at 211. In other words, the section was intended to apply to those who were not attempting to protect their own proper interests, but who were, instead, attempting to obtain some benefit to which they were not entitled. * * * While helpful, those reflections by the Court do not fully answer the question before us. Other courts have further illuminated the area.

If a person seeks to secure some untoward advantage over other creditors for some ulterior motive, that will indicate bad faith. * * * But that does not mean that creditors are expected to approach reorganization plan votes with a high degree of altruism and with the desire to help the debtor and their fellow creditors. Far from it.

> If a selfish motive were sufficient to condemn reorganization policies of interested parties, very few, if any, would pass muster. On the other hand, pure malice, "strikes" and blackmail, and the purpose to destroy an enterprise in order to advance the interests of a competing business, all plainly constituting bad faith, are motives which may be accurately described as ulterior.

In re Pine Hill Collieries Co., 46 F.Supp. 669, 671 (E.D.Pa.1942).

That is to say, we do not condemn mere enlightened self interest, even if it appears selfish to those who do not benefit from it. * * *

Thus, if Teachers acted out of enlightened self interest, it is not to be condemned simply because it frustrated Figter's desires. That is true, even if Teachers purchased Class 3 claims for the very purpose of blocking confirmation of Figter's proposed plan. * * * That self interest can extend even further without being an ulterior motive. It has been held that a creditor commits no wrong when he votes against a plan of a debtor who has a lawsuit pending against the creditor, for that will not, by itself, show bad faith. * * * It has also been held that no bad faith is shown when a creditor chooses to benefit his interest as a creditor as opposed to some unrelated interest. * * * And the mere fact that a creditor has purchased additional claims for the purpose of protecting his own existing claim does not demonstrate bad faith or an ulterior motive. "As long as a creditor acts to preserve what he reasonably perceives as his fair share of the debtor's estate, bad faith will not be attributed to his purchase of claims to control a class vote." In re Gilbert, 104 B.R. 206, 217 (Bankr.W.D.Mo.1989).

Courts, on the other hand, have been sensitive to situations where a company, which was not a preexisting creditor, has purchased a claim for the purpose of blocking an action against it. They have seen that as an indication of bad faith. * * * The same has been true where creditors were associated with a competing business and desired to destroy the debtor's business in order to further their own. * * * And when the debtor had claims against itself purchased by an insider or affiliate for the purpose of blocking a plan, or fostering one, that was seen as a badge of bad faith. * * * Figter would have us add that in a single asset bankruptcy, claim purchasing activities, like those of Teachers, are in bad faith. It cites no authority for that, and we see no basis for establishing *that* as a per se rule.

In short, the concept of good faith is a fluid one, and no single factor can be said to inexorably demand an ultimate result, nor must a single set of factors be considered. It is always necessary to keep in mind the difference between a creditor's self interest as a creditor and a motive which is ulterior to the purpose of protecting a creditor's interest. Prior cases can offer guidance, but, when all is said and done, the bankruptcy court must simply approach each good faith determination with a perspicacity derived from the data of its informed practical experience in dealing with bankrupts and their creditors.

Here, the bankruptcy court did exactly that. It decided that Teachers was not, for practical purposes, the proponent of an alternate plan when it sought to purchase the Class 3 claims. Nor, it found, did Teachers seek to purchase a small number of claims for the purpose of blocking Figter's plan, while injuring other creditors, even if it could do that in some circumstances. Rather, Teachers offered to purchase all Class 3 claims, and only some of those claimants' refusals to sell precluded it from doing so. Moreover, Teachers was a lender, not a competing apartment owner. It acted to protect its interests as Figter's major creditor. It reasonably feared that it could be left with a very complex lien situation, if Figter went forward with its plan. Instead of holding a lien covering the whole of the property, it could have wound up with separate fractured liens on various parts of the property, while other parts were owned by others. That could create a very undesirable mix of owners and renters and of debtors and nondebtors. Added to that was the actual use of cash, which was collateral for the debt owed to Teachers. It cannot be said that Teachers' concerns were irrational.

Based on all that was before it, the bankruptcy court decided that in this case Teachers was a creditor which acted in a good faith attempt to protect its interests and not with some ulterior motive. We cannot say that it erred in making that ultimate determination.

**B. Voting.**

Figter's fallback position is that even if Teachers did act in good faith, it must be limited to one vote for its twenty-one claims. That assertion is answered by the language of the Bankruptcy Code, which provides that:

> A class of claims has accepted a plan if such plan has been accepted by creditors. . . that hold at least two-thirds in amount and *more than one-half in number of the allowed claims* of such class held by creditors. . . that have accepted or rejected such plan.

§ 1126(c) (emphasis added). That language was interpreted in *Gilbert*, 104 B.R. at 211, where the court reasoned:

The formula contained in Section 1126(c) speaks in terms of the *number of claims*, not the number of creditors, that actually vote for or against the plan. . ... Each claim arose out of a separate transaction, evidencing separate obligations for which separate proofs of claim were filed. Votes of acceptance. . . are to be computed only on the basis of filed and allowed proofs of claim. . ... [The creditor] is entitled to one vote for each of his unsecured Class X claims.

That same view was iterated in *Concord Square Apartments of Wood Cty., Ltd. v. Ottawa Properties, Inc.*, 174 B.R. 71, 74 (Bankr.S.D.Ohio 1994), where the court held that a creditor with "multiple claims, has a voting right for each claim it holds." We agree. It would not make much sense to require a vote by creditors who held "more than one-half in number of the allowed claims" while at the same time limiting a creditor who held two or more of those claims to only one vote. If allowed claims are to be counted, they must be counted regardless of whose hands they happen to be in.

Figter seeks some succor from the Supreme Court's indication in *Dewsnup v. Timm* that ambiguous language in the Code should not be taken to effect a sea change in pre-Code practice. However, that does not help Figter's cause. In the first place, as we have indicated, the present language is not ambiguous. In the second place, the old law to which Figter refers relied upon a code section which required voting approval by a "majority in number of all creditors whose claims have been allowed." Bankruptcy Act of 1898, ch. 541, § 12 (repealed 1938). It is pellucid that "a majority in number of all creditors" is not at all like "more than one-half in number" of all claims. The former focuses on claimants; the latter on claims.

Nor is our conclusion affected by cases where other sections of the bankruptcy code, or other acts by creditors, were involved. For example, the predecessor to § 702 indicated that a creditor could vote for the trustee. In *In re Latham Lithographic Corp.*, 107 F.2d 749 (2d Cir.1939), there was an attempt to split a single claim into multiple claims for the purpose of creating multiple creditors who could vote in a trustee election. It is not surprising that the court did not permit that. * * * And in *In re Gilbert*, 115 B.R. 458, 461 (Bankr.S.D.N.Y.1990), the court held that an involuntary petition in bankruptcy must be filed by three creditors, and a single creditor with three separate claims is still one creditor. * * * In fact, the involuntary petition section actually requires that there be three or more *entities*. See § 303(b). Certainly, a creditor with three claims is still a single entity.

Of course, that is not to say that a creditor can get away with splitting one claim into many, but that is not what happened here. Teachers purchased a number of separately incurred and separately approved claims (each of which carried one vote) from different creditors. There simply is no reason to hold that those separate votes suddenly became one vote, a result which would be exactly the opposite of claim splitting.

Therefore, the bankruptcy court did not err.

## CONCLUSION

Figter hoped to obtain approval of a reorganization plan, which would require Teachers to thole what it saw as a diminution of its creditor's rights. Those hopes were dashed when Teachers bought up most of the Class 3 claims in an effort to protect its own Class 2 claim. Because the bankruptcy court determined that Teachers acted to protect its valid creditor's interest, rather than for ulterior motives, it held that Teachers had acted in good faith. That precluded designation of Teachers' purchased claims. The bankruptcy court also determined that Teachers could vote each of its twenty-one claims separately; it was not limited to a single vote. The district court affirmed those decisions. Because the bankruptcy court did not err in either its factual or its legal determinations, we agree with the district court and affirm the decision.

AFFIRMED.

## NOTES

**1.** Note that debtors and their insiders cannot use the *Figter* claim buying strategy to confirm their plans. Debtors ordinarily cannot use estate funds to purchase claims outside of a plan. And if insiders do so using their own funds, the one-consenting-class requirement of § 1129(a)(10) must be determined "without including any acceptance of the plan by any insider."

**2.** In *Figter*, Teachers was able to buy sufficient claims to cause the unsecured class to reject the debtor's plan. Although Teachers was not seeking to confirm a competing plan in *Figter*, the Ninth Circuit's discussion of the majority-in-number requirement in § 1126(c) suggests that a claim buyer may not only be able to block opposing plans, but also affirmatively cause creditor classes to accept its own plan. If Teachers had acquired two-thirds in amount of the unsecured claims in addition to a majority in number (as well as the $17 million secured claim it began with), it presumably would have had the votes not only to reject the debtor's plan, but also to confirm its own plan. Does the Ninth Circuit's plain meaning interpretation of the majority-in-number requirement accord with the purpose of the requirement? Why do we measure the number as well as the dollar amount of the accepting claims? If one creditor holds a majority of the number of claims and two-thirds of the dollar amount, should it be able to impose a reorganization plan on all the other members of its class?

**3.** In *In re Allegheny Int'l, Inc.*, 118 B.R. 282 (Bankr. W.D. Pa. 1990), after almost two years of extensive plan negotiations, the debtor filed an internal reorganization plan. After the debtor's disclosure statement had been approved, Japonica Partners, L.P. launched a hostile takeover bid by filing a competing reorganization plan calling for the distribution of the equity in Reorganized Allegheny to Japonica.

Thereafter Japonica began to aggressively purchase bank claims until it held slightly more than one-third of the bank claims. In addition, Japonica purchased slightly less than one-third of the senior unsecured debt. When Japonica's no votes on the debtor's plan caused both the bank class and the senior unsecured class to reject the debtor's plan, the debtor sought to designate Japonica's votes under § 1126. The bankruptcy court found that Japonica acted in bad faith:

> Under Chapter 11, creditors and interest holders vote for or against a plan of reorganization, after adequate disclosure, if such vote is in their best economic interests. If, as in the instant case, an outsider to the process can purchase a blocking position, those creditors and interest holders are disenfranchised. * * * Moreover, Japonica, who chose to become a creditor, should not have veto control over the reorganization process.

118 B.R. at 290.

As a footnote, although the *Allegheny* court confirmed the debtor's plan, when Japonica sought to appeal the confirmation order, the parties negotiated a settlement whereby Japonica acquired control of Allegheny. Is Teacher's strategic claim buying in *Figter* meaningfully distinguishable from Japonica's in *Allegheny*? The legal issues and risks associated with strategic claim-buying in Chapter 11 are discussed in a series of articles by Chaim J. Fortgang & Thomas Moers Mayer published at 12 Cardozo L.Rev. 1 (1990), 13 Cardozo L. Rev. 1 (1991), and 15 Cardozo L. Rev. 733 (1993).

### 4. IMPAIRMENT OF CLAIMS OR INTERESTS

Only impaired classes vote. §§ 1126, 1129(a)(8). Unimpaired classes are deemed to have accepted the plan. § 1126(f). "Impairment" is defined in § 1124.

Under the Bankruptcy Act of 1898 a class of creditors was "affected" by a plan only if "its interest shall be materially and adversely affected thereby." The Code shifted from the standard of "materially and adversely affected" to the standard of § 1124(1) which states that impairment is present unless the plan leaves "unaltered" the rights of the holder of the claim or interest. Thus if stockholders are given nothing in a reorganization of an insolvent corporation they may not have been materially and adversely affected because they have lost nothing that had any present value. Nevertheless, under § 1124(1), they have been impaired because their rights as stockholders are being taken away by the plan. This is an important distinction. As an impaired class, they can effectively demand a valuation of the reorganizing firm before their interests can be eliminated without their consent. § 1129(b). Section 1124(1) makes it clear that an eliminated class is impaired even if that class would not be entitled to share in the reorganization in the event of cramdown, and, therefore, is a player in the negotiation process.

Since the § 1124(1) test of impairment is so broad, virtually all claims and interests are impaired in a Chapter 11 reorganization unless there is cure under § 1124(2). Under § 1124(2), the plan may effectively reinstate prepetition obligations on the prepetition terms. One reason to do so is to avoid soliciting votes and valuation hearings. Another may be to preserve for the reorganized firm favorable terms in the prebankruptcy loans, especially a below-market interest rate.

In *In re Southeast Co.*, 868 F.2d 335 (9th Cir.1989), the issue raised was the scope of the cure necessary to effect reinstatement under § 1124(2) as an alternative to cramdown under § 1129(b). The note evidencing the mortgage loan in *Southeast* provided for current interest at 4% plus additional deferred interest, payable at maturity, of 2%. Upon default, the debtor obligated itself to pay current cash interest at 9%. The debtor defaulted prebankruptcy, and interest began to accrue at the default rate. The following year, the debtor filed in Chapter 11. Seeking to preserve the very favorable original loan terms on this secured claim, the debtor provided that the claim would be treated as unimpaired. The plan provided the debtor would bring the mortgage current by making the missed payments plus interest at 12% accruing from date due. The plan provided for future interest payments at the pre-default 6% rate, rather than the post-default 9% rate demanded by the mortgagee. The Ninth Circuit affirmed quoting *In re Entz–White Lumber and Supply, Inc.*, 850 F.2d 1338, 1342 (9th Cir.1988): "[§ 1124] authorizes a plan to nullify all consequences of default, including avoidance of default penalties such as higher interest."

The Fifth Circuit in *In re Southland Corp.*, 160 F.3d 1054 (1998), was sharply critical of *Southeast* in rejecting the debtor's efforts to avoid default interest payments in that case. The bank demanded default interest for the period between the prebankruptcy default and the effective date of the reorganization plan. The court agreed with the bank's position and held that the "reinstatement" of the credit agreement under the reorganization plan did not automatically imply a "cure;" instead, the reinstatement simply returned the parties to their pre-bankruptcy status, not their pre-default status. Therefore, the debtor remained responsible for paying the default interest rate.

In 1994 § 1123(d) was added, ostensibly to prevent holders of residential mortgages from receiving the windfall of unbargained for interest-on-interest under *Rake v. Wade,* 508 U.S. 464 (1993). Section 1123(d) provides "Notwithstanding subsection (a) of this section and sections 506(b), 1129(a)(7), and 1129(b) of this title, if it is proposed in a plan to cure a default the amount necessary to cure the default shall be determined in accordance with the underlying agreement and applicable nonbankruptcy law." Section 1123(d) can be read as requiring that the cure amount include default rate interest if "applicable nonbankruptcy law" would allow default rate interest. But see *In re Phoenix Business Park, Ltd. Part-*

*nership*, 257 B.R. 517 (Bankr.D.Ariz.2001), which reaffirmed *Southeast* notwithstanding the 1994 Amendment to § 1123(d).

Until 1994, § 1124 contained subsection (3), which provided that if the plan called for payment of a claim on the effective date of the plan by cash equal to "the allowed amount of such claim," the claim was not impaired. Thus, if the plan "cashed-out" a class of claims, under § 1126(f) the class, being unimpaired, was conclusively presumed to have accepted the plan. No solicitation of acceptances from that class was required because the class could not vote on confirmation of the plan. The most common application of the practice of cashing out classes under Chapter 11 plans is with respect to classes of small claims under § 1122(b) that are paid off to relieve the debtor of the burden of having to obtain the assent of what may be a host of small claims holders. According to the Section-by-Section Description § 213, 140 Cong.Rec. H10768 (1994), the reason for the deletion of § 1124(3) was to overrule *In re New Valley Corp.*, 168 B.R. 73 (Bankr.D.N.J.1994), which held that a claim cashed out under § 1124(3) was not entitled to postpetition interest even though the estate was solvent. This Section-by-Section Description contains a detailed explanation of how the deletion of § 1124(3) accomplishes the overruling of *New Valley*, but it gives no inkling that Congress grasped that the consequences of the amendment go far beyond the issue of postpetition interest. For example, it may no longer be possible to leave "convenience classes" of small claims, expressly authorized by § 1122(b), unimpaired. If so, there may be no administrative convenience in convenience classes since all impaired classes—convenience or not—must be solicited and vote in accordance with §§ 1125, 1126. Does the deletion of § 1124(3) de facto repeal § 1122(b) as well?

## 5. CLASSIFICATION OF CLAIMS

Since voting on acceptance or rejection of the plan is done by classes, the composition of the classes may have great strategic importance. If a class accepts the plan dissenting members of that class as well as accepting members may not assert rights under the absolute priority rule. The proponent of the plan normally knows in advance which creditors oppose the plan and are likely to vote against it. The proponent may tailor the plan so that these claims are not impaired, or may provide in the plan for a classification of claims which puts dissenting claims in a class in which it anticipates there will be sufficient favorable votes to assure approval by that class.

Two major questions arise with respect to classification. First, must the proponent place all similar claims and interests in the same class or may they be divided into more than one class? Section 1122(a) states that a claim or interest may be placed in a class "only if such claim or interest is substantially similar to other claims and interests of such class." Thus, claims that are not similar may not be classified together. But, except for a limited authorization of "convenience classes" of small claims, nothing in the Code either expressly authorizes or prohibits placing similar claims or interests in different classes.

Second, if the proponent can separate similar claims or interests into different classes, may the plan discriminate in the treatment accorded the different classes? Section 1123(a)(4) requires that the plan provide the same treatment for each claim or interest within the class. Thus, all claims classified together must be treated alike. There is no express requirement of equal treatment for similar claims in different classes, but § 1129(b)(1) mandates that the plan not "discriminate unfairly" against rejecting classes. Accepting classes waive their § 1129(b) objections, and so unfair discrimination is no more objectionable as to such classes than deviations from absolute priority. Moreover, as to dissenting classes, there is very little caselaw establishing the limits § 1129(b)(1) places on differential treatment of similar claims in different classes.

Bankruptcy Rule 3013 provides that on motion the court may determine classes of creditors and stockholders after notice and hearing. Hence, the proponent may obtain the court's approval of the makeup of the classes before acceptances of the plan are solicited.

Although § 1122(a) requires that claims and interests classified together be "substantially similar," the Code does not define "substantially similar." Claims or interests that are of unequal priority rank in liquidation are not similar. Thus, separate classification must be given to preferred stock and common stock, or to general unsecured debt and a debt that is subject to a clause subordinating it to all other debt of the debtor. Secured claims cannot be put into the same class if they are secured by different collateral. If there is more than one claim secured by the same collateral, separate classification is necessary if the claims have unequal priority, but a single class is appropriate if they have the same priority. For example, claims of bondholders secured by the same mortgage or deed of trust belong in the same class.

Unsecured debt of equal rank might be dissimilar because of the transaction out of which it grew or the identity of the creditor. Is it proper or necessary to separately classify debt owed to an insider and similar debt owed to other creditors? A 20-year debenture and a 30-day account payable are equal in priority if both are unsecured and there is no subordination clause in the debenture. Does the fact that the debenture represents a long-term investment and the account payable grew out of a nearly cash transaction justify separate classification and different treatment in the plan?

# In re U.S. Truck Co.

United States Court of Appeals, Sixth Circuit, 1986.
800 F.2d 581.

■ CORNELIA G. KENNEDY, Circuit Judge.

The Teamsters National Freight Industry Negotiating Committee (the Teamsters Committee), a creditor of U.S. Truck Company, Inc. (U.S. Truck)—the debtor-in-possession in this Chapter 11 bankruptcy proceeding—appeals the District Court's order confirming U.S. Truck's Fifth Amended Plan of Reorganization. The Teamsters Committee complains that the plan does not satisfy three of the requirements of § 1129. The District Court, which presided over the matter after the resignation of Bankruptcy Judge STANLEY B. BERNSTEIN, held that the requirements of section 1129 had been satisfied. We agree.

## I

Underlying this appeal is the Teamsters Committee's claim that U.S. Truck is liable to its employees for rejecting a collective bargaining agreement between the local union and U.S. Truck. After filing its petition for relief under Chapter 11 of the Bankruptcy Code on June 11, 1982, U.S. Truck, a trucking company primarily engaged in intrastate shipping of parts and supplies for the automotive industry, sought to reject the collective bargaining agreement. U.S. Truck rejected the agreement with the approval of then-Bankruptcy Judge WOODS, in December 1982. Judge Woods found that rejection of the agreement was "absolutely necessary to save the debtor from collapse." New agreements have been negotiated to the satisfaction of each participating local union. Such agreements have been implemented over the lone dissent of the Teamsters Joint Area Rider Committee. Under the most recently mentioned agreement in the record (due to have expired in March 1985), U.S. Truck was able to record monthly profits in the range of $125,000 to $250,000. These new agreements achieved such results by reducing wages and requiring employees to buy their own trucking equipment, which the employees then leased to the company.

The parties agreed to an estimate of the size of the Teamsters Committee claim against U.S. Truck so that the confirmation plan could be considered. The District Court held a hearing to consider the plan on January 23, 1985. The court considered three objections by the Teamsters Committee to the plan. Consideration of the objections, and the court's treatment of them, requires an understanding of the statutory scheme for approval of a chapter 11 reorganization plan.

## II

Section 1129 contains two means by which a reorganization plan can be confirmed. The first way is to meet all eleven of the requirements of subsection (a), including (a)(8) which requires all impaired classes of claims or interests to accept the plan. The other way is to meet the requirements of subsection (b), which, first, incorporates all of the requirements of subsection (a), except for that contained in subsection (a)(8), and, second, imposes two additional requirements. Confirmation under subsection (b) is commonly referred to as a "cram down" because it permits a reorganization plan to go into effect over the objections of one or more impaired classes of creditors. In this case, U.S. Truck sought approval of its plan under this "cram down" provision.

### III

The Teamsters Committee's first objection is that the plan does not meet the requirement that at least one class of impaired claims accept the plan, see § 1129(a)(10), because U.S. Truck impermissibly gerrymandered the classes in order to neutralize the Teamsters Committee's dissenting vote. The reorganization plan contains twelve classes. The plan purports to impair five of these classes—Class VI (the secured claim of Manufacturer's National Bank of Detroit based on a mortgage); Class VII (the secured claim of John Graham, Trustee of Transportation Services, Inc., based on a loan); Class IX (the Teamsters Committee's claim based on rejection of the collective bargaining agreement); Class XI (all unsecured claims in excess of $200.00 including those arising from the rejection of executory contracts); and Class XII (the equity interest of the stockholder of the debtor). As noted above, § 1129(a)(10), as incorporated into subsection (b)(1), requires at least one of these classes of impaired claims to approve the reorganization plan before it can be confirmed. The parties agree that approval by Class XII would not count because acceptance must be determined without including the acceptance of the plan by any insider. See § 1129(a)(10). The Code's definition of "insider" clearly includes McKinlay Transport, Inc. * * * Thus, compliance with subsection (a)(10) depends on whether either of the other three classes that approved the plan—Class VI, Class VII, or Class XI—was a properly constructed impaired class. The Teamsters Committee argues that Classes VI and VII were not truly impaired classes and that Class XI should have included Class IX, and hence was an improperly constructed class.[6] Because we find that Class XI was a properly constructed class of impaired claims, we hold that the plan complies with subsection (a)(10).[7]

The issue raised by the Teamsters Committee's challenge is under what circumstances does the Bankruptcy Code permit a debtor to keep a creditor out of a class of impaired claims which are of a similar legal nature and are against the same property as those of the "isolated" creditor. The District Court held that the Code permits such action here because of

---

[6] Had the debtor included the Teamsters Committee's claim in Class XI, the Committee's vote to reject the plan would have swung the results of the Class XI vote from an acceptance to a rejection. See § 1126(c) (setting forth the requirement that creditors holding at least two-thirds in amount of allowed claims of a class accept).

[7] For this reason, we need not decide the challenge to the status of Class VI and Class VII.

the following circumstances: (1) the employees represented by the Teamsters Committee have a unique continued interest in the ongoing business of the debtor; (2) the mechanics of the Teamsters Committee's claim differ substantially from those of the Class XI claims; and (3) the Teamsters Committee's claim is likely to become part of the agenda of future collective bargaining sessions between the union and the reorganized company. Thus, according to the court, the interests of the Teamsters Committee are substantially dissimilar from those of the creditors in Class XI. We must decide whether the Code permits separate classification under such circumstances.

Congress has sent mixed signals on the issue that we must decide. Our starting point is § 1122.

\* \* \*

The statute, by its express language, only addresses the problem of dissimilar claims being included in the same class. It does not address the correlative problem—the one we face here—of similar claims being put in different classes. Some courts have seized upon this omission, and have held that the Code does not require a debtor to put similar claims in the same class.

> We think the courts erred in holding that section 1122(a) prohibits classification based on the presence of a co-debtor. Section 1122(a) specifies that only claims which are "substantially similar" may be placed in the same class. It does not require that similar claims *must* be grouped together, but merely that any group created must be homogenous. \* \* \* \* Although some courts have held that section 1122(a) prohibits classification based on any criterion other than legal right to the debtor's assets, \* \* \* the plain language of the statute contradicts such a construction. Moreover, section 1122(a) so interpreted would conflict with section 1322(b)(1), which specifically authorizes designation of more than one class of unsecured creditor, each presumably with equal legal rights to the debtor's estate.

Barnes v. Whelan, 689 F.2d 193, 201 (D.C.Cir.1982) (emphasis in original) (holding that Chapter 13 debtor may group his unsecured creditors according to whether or not a co-debtor is present) \* \* \*.

Further evidence that Congress intentionally failed to impose a requirement that similar claims be classified together is found by examining the "classification" sections of the former Bankruptcy Act. The applicable former provisions were 11 U.S.C., sections 597 (from former Chapter X) and 751 (from former Chapter XI).

§ 597. Classification of creditors and stockholders

> For the purposes of the plan and its acceptance, the judge shall fix the division of creditors and stockholders into classes according to the nature of their respective claims and stock. For the purposes of such classification, the judge shall, if necessary, upon the application of the

trustee, the debtor, any creditor, or an indenture trustee, fix a hearing upon notice to the holders of secured claims, the debtor, the trustee, and such other persons as the judge may designate, to determine summarily the value of the security and classify as unsecured the amount in excess of such value.

§ 751. Classification of creditors

For the purposes of the arrangement and its acceptance, the court may fix the division of creditors into classes and, in the event of controversy, the court shall after hearing upon notice summarily determine such controversy.

Section 597 was interpreted to require all creditors of equal rank with claims against the same property to be placed in the same class. * * * Congress' switch to less restrictive language in section 1122 of the Code seems to warrant a conclusion that Congress no longer intended to impose the now-omitted requirement that similar claims be classified together. * * * However, the legislative history indicates that Congress may not have intended to change the prior rule. The Notes of the Senate Committee on the Judiciary state:

This section [1122] codifies current case law surrounding the classification of claims and equity securities. It requires classification based on the nature of the claims or interests classified, and permits inclusion of claims or interests in a particular class only if the claim or interest being included is substantially similar to the other claims or interests of the class.

* * *

In this case, U.S. Truck is using its classification powers to segregate dissenting (impaired) creditors from assenting (impaired) creditors (by putting the dissenters into a class or classes by themselves) and, thus, it is assured that at least one class of impaired creditors will vote for the plan and make it eligible for cram down consideration by the court. We agree with the Teamsters Committee that there must be some limit on a debtor's power to classify creditors in such a manner. The potential for abuse would be significant otherwise. Unless there is some requirement of keeping similar claims together, nothing would stand in the way of a debtor seeking out a few impaired creditors (or even one such creditor) who will vote for the plan and placing them in their own class.[8]

---

[8] We need not speculate in this case whether the purpose of separate classification was to line up the votes in favor of the plan. The debtor admitted that to the District Court. * * *

We are unaware of any cases that deal with this problem as it arises in this case.[9] As we noted above, the legislative history of the Code provides little assistance in determining what limits there are to segregating similar claims. Nevertheless, we do find one common theme in the prior case law that Congress incorporated into section 1122. In those pre-Code cases, the lower courts were given broad discretion to determine proper classification according to the factual circumstances of each individual case.

\* \* \*

The District Court noted three important ways in which the interests of the Teamsters Committee differ substantially from those of the other impaired creditors. Because of these differences, the Teamsters Committee has a different stake in the future viability of the reorganized company and has alternative means at its disposal for protecting its claim. The Teamsters Committee's claim is connected with the collective bargaining process. In the words of the Committee's counsel, the union employees have a "virtually unique interest." \* \* \* These differences put the Teamsters Committee's claim in a different posture than the Class XI claims. The Teamsters Committee may choose to reject the plan not because the plan is less than optimal to it as a creditor, but because the Teamsters Committee has a noncreditor interest—e.g., rejection will benefit its members in the ongoing employment relationship. Although the Teamsters Committee certainly is not intimately connected with the debtor, to allow the Committee to vote with the other impaired creditors would be to allow it to prevent a court from considering confirmation of a plan that a significant group of creditors with similar interests have accepted. Permitting separate classification of the Teamsters Committee's claim does not automatically result in adoption of the plan. The Teamsters Committee is still protected by the provisions of subsections (a) and (b), particularly the requirements of subsection (b) that the plan not discriminate unfairly and that it be fair and equitable with respect to the Teamsters Committee's claim. In fact, the Teamsters Committee invokes those requirements, but as we note in the following sections, the plan does not violate them.

---

[9] In those cases where the courts have held that, as a general rule, similar claims need not be classified together, the debtor had not created the separate classes for the purpose of assuring acceptance \* \* \* and the allegedly similar claims were treated differently under the plan \* \* \*. In those cases where the courts have held that similar claims must be classified together, they have often faced problems of discriminatory treatment \* \* \* and they have not had occasion to decide whether claims of the sort in this case are substantially similar \* \* \*.

* * *

## NOTE

Judge Kennedy states: "The Teamsters Committee claim is connected with the collective bargaining process." 800 F.2d at 587. The district court opinion elaborates on this point by noting that the primary goal of the union was to restore, through the collective bargaining process, the terms of the labor contract which the debtor had rejected. In order to attain this end the union was willing to give up the damage claim that it was asserting in the bankruptcy. Apparently, the union believed that its opposition to the plan gave it leverage in the collective bargaining process. In an omitted portion of Judge Kennedy's opinion, she discussed the concern of the Teamsters that if the plan were confirmed the person taking control of the reorganized entity would liquidate the debtor and cause the loss of their jobs.

## PROBLEM

Bank and various trade creditors held substantially all of the unsecured claims in Debtor's Chapter 11 bankruptcy. Bank held 60% in amount of the claims and opposed Debtor's plan. The trade creditors were willing to approve Debtor's plan. Debtor sought confirmation of its plan without approval of Bank by cramdown under § 1129(b). To that end Debtor placed Bank and the trade creditors in separate classes, anticipating that the trade creditor class would approve the plan and thus satisfy § 1129(a)(10). Debtor justified the classification on the ground that the trade creditors had advanced goods and services to Debtor in the past and would likely continue to do so in the future. Thus, their stake in the future viability of Debtor's business was different from that of Bank that wanted liquidation of Debtor's business. Would this classification meet the test of *U.S. Truck* for separate classes? *Hanson v. First Bank of South Dakota*, 828 F.2d 1310 (8th Cir.1987).

## Matter of Greystone III Joint Venture
United States Court of Appeals, Fifth Circuit, 1991.
995 F.2d 1274.

■ EDITH H. JONES, Circuit Judge:

This appeal pits a debtor whose only significant asset is an office building in the troubled Austin, Texas real estate market against a lender who possesses a multi-million dollar lien on the property. After obtaining bankruptcy relief under Chapter 11, Greystone III proposed a "cramdown" plan of reorganization, hoping to force a write-down of over $3,000,000 on the secured lender's note and to retain possession and full ownership of the property. Over the secured lender's strenuous objections, the bankruptcy court confirmed the debtor's plan. On appeal, the district court upheld the bankruptcy court's judgment.

\* \* \* [W]e must reverse. First, the Greystone plan impermissibly classified like creditors in different ways and manipulated classifications to obtain a favorable vote. Second, tenant security deposit holders were not properly deemed an "impaired" class under the circumstances of this plan. \* \* \*

## I.

Appellant Phoenix Mutual Life Insurance Corporation ("Phoenix") lent $8,800,000, evidenced by a non-recourse promissory note secured by a first lien, to Greystone to purchase the venture's office building. When Greystone defaulted on the loan, missing four payments, Phoenix posted the property for foreclosure. Greystone retaliated by filing a Chapter 11 bankruptcy reorganization petition.

At the date of bankruptcy Greystone owed Phoenix approximately $9,325,000, trade creditors approximately $10,000, and taxing authorities approximately $145,000. The bankruptcy court valued Phoenix's secured claim at $5,825,000, the appraised value of the office building, leaving Phoenix an unsecured deficiency of approximately $3,500,000—the difference between the aggregate owed Phoenix and its secured claim.

As filed, Greystone's Second Amended Plan of Reorganization (the "Plan"), the confirmation of which is challenged in this appeal, separately classified the Code-created unsecured deficiency claim of Phoenix Mutual, see § 1111(b), and the unsecured claims of the trade creditors. The Plan proposed to pay Phoenix and the trade creditors slightly less than four cents on the dollar for their unsecured claims, but it also provided that Greystone's general partner would satisfy the balance of the trade creditors' claims after confirmation of the Plan.

In a separate class, the Plan further provided for security deposit "claims" held by existing tenants of the office building. These claimants were promised, notwithstanding the debtor's eventual assumption of their leases \* \* \*, 25% of their deposits upon approval of the Plan and 50% of their deposits at the expiration of their respective leases. The Plan stipulated that the general partner would "retain its legal obligations and. . . pay the [tenant]. . . creditors the balance of their claims upon confirmation."

Finally, Greystone's Plan contemplated a $500,000 capital infusion by the debtor's partners, for which they would reacquire 100% of the equity interest in the reorganized Greystone.

Unsurprisingly, Phoenix rejected this Plan, while the trade creditors and the class of holders of tenant security deposits voted to accept it. On January 27, 1989, the bankruptcy court held a confirmation hearing at which the Debtor orally modified its Plan to delete the statements that the general partner would pay the balance of trade debt and tenant security deposit claims after confirmation. A Phoenix representative testified that the insurance company was willing to fund its own plan of reorganization by paying off all unsecured creditors in cash in full after confirmation. The bankruptcy court refused to consider this proposal and then confirmed Greystone's modified Plan. The district court upheld the confirmation.

Phoenix Mutual now appeals on several grounds: (a) the plan classified Phoenix's unsecured deficiency claim separately from that of other unsecured creditors for no valid reason; * * * and (c) unpaid tenant security deposits were not impaired claims that could vote on the plan.

II.

Phoenix first attacks Greystone's classification of its unsecured deficiency claim in a separate class from that of the other unsecured claims against the debtor. This issue benefits from some background explanation.

Chapter 11 requires classification of claims against a debtor for two reasons. Each class of creditors will be treated in the debtor's plan of reorganization based upon the similarity of its members' priority status and other legal rights against the debtor's assets. § 1122. Proper classification is essential to ensure that creditors with claims of similar priority against the debtor's assets are treated similarly. Second, the classes must separately vote whether to approve a debtor's plan of reorganization. § 1129(a)(8), (10). A plan may not be confirmed unless either (1) it is approved by two-thirds in amount and more than one-half in number of each "impaired" class, §§ 1126(c), 1129(a)(8); or (2) at least one impaired class approves the plan, § 1129(a)(10), and the debtor fulfills the cramdown requirements of § 1129(b) to enable confirmation notwithstanding the plan's rejection by one or more impaired classes. Classification of claims thus affects the integrity of the voting process, for, if claims could be arbitrarily placed in separate classes, it would almost always be possible for the debtor to manipulate "acceptance" by artful classification.

In this case, Greystone's plan classified the Phoenix claim in separate secured and unsecured classes, a dual status afforded by § 1111(b) despite the nonrecourse nature of Phoenix's debt. Because of Phoenix's opposition to a reorganization, Greystone knew that its only hope for confirmation lay in the Bankruptcy Code's cramdown provision. § 1129(b). The substantive impact of cramdown will be discussed later. Procedurally, Greystone faced a dilemma in deciding how to obtain the approval of its cramdown plan by *at least one* class of "impaired" claims, as the Code requires.[3] § 1129(a)(10). Greystone anticipated an adverse vote of Phoenix's secured claim. If the Phoenix $3.5 million unsecured deficiency claim shared the same class as Greystone's other unsecured trade claims, it would swamp their $10,000 value in voting against confirmation. The only other arguably impaired class consisted of tenant security deposit claims, which, the bankruptcy court found, were not impaired at all.

---

[3] An impaired claim is defined at § 1124. For present purposes, it suffices to say that Phoenix was impaired both as a secured and unsecured creditor.

Greystone surmounted the hurdle by classifying Phoenix's unsecured deficiency claim separately from the trade claims, although both classes were to be treated alike under the plan and would receive a cash payment equal to 3.42% of each creditor's claim. Greystone then achieved the required favorable vote of the trade claims class.

Phoenix contends that Greystone misapplied § 1122 by classifying its unsecured claim separately from those of trade creditors. The lower courts rejected Phoenix's argument in three steps. First, they held that § 1122 of the Code does not unambiguously prevent classification of like claims in separate classes. The only question is what types of class differentiations among like claims are acceptable. Second, Greystone's unsecured deficiency claim is "legally different" from that of the trade claims because it arises statutorily, pursuant to § 1111(b). Third, "good business reasons" justify the separate classification of these unsecured claims. We must address each of these arguments.

Section 1122 prescribes classification of claims for a reorganization as follows:

(a)  Except as provided in subsection (b) or this section, a plan may place a claim or an interest in a particular class only if such claim or interest is substantially similar to the other claims or interests of such claims.

(b)  A plan may designate a separate class of claims consisting only of every unsecured claim that is less than or reduced to an amount that the court approves as reasonable and necessary for administrative convenience.

We observe from this language that the lower courts' suggestion that § 1122 does not prevent classification of like claims in separate classes is oversimplified. It is true that § 1122(a) in terms only governs permissible *inclusions* of claims in a class rather requiring that all similar claims be grouped together. One cannot conclude categorically that § 1122(a) prohibits the formation of different classes from similar types of claims. But if § 1122(a) is wholly permissive regarding the creation of such classes, there would be no need for § 1122(b) specifically to authorize a class of smaller unsecured claims, a common feature of plans in reorganization cases past and present.[4] The broad interpretation of § 1122(a) adopted by the lower courts would render § 1122(b) superfluous, a result that is anathema to elementary principles of statutory construction.

---

[4] Greystone has never sought to justify its separate class of trade creditors under § 1122(b), nor did the lower courts employ that provision in their analysis. There is no suggestion in the Code, however, that a class may be created under § 1122(b) in order to manipulate the outcome of the vote on a plan, rather than simply to enhance administration of the plan.

Section 1122 consequently must contemplate some limits on classification of claims of similar priority. A fair reading of both subsections suggests that ordinarily "substantially similar claims," those which share common priority and rights against the debtor's estate, should be placed in the same class. Section 1122(b) expressly creates one exception to this rule by permitting small unsecured claims to be classified separately from their larger counterparts if the court so approves for administrative convenience. The lower courts acknowledged the force of this narrow rather than totally permissive construction of § 1122 by going on to justify Greystone's segregation of the Phoenix claim. Put otherwise, the lower courts essentially found that Phoenix's unsecured deficiency claim is not "substantially similar" to those of the trade creditors.

Those courts did not, however, adhere to the one clear rule that emerges from otherwise muddled caselaw on § 1122 claims classification: thou shalt not classify similar claims differently in order to gerrymander an affirmative vote on a reorganization plan. As the Sixth Circuit observed:

> [T]here must be some limit on a debtor's power to classify creditors in such a manner. . ... Unless there is some requirement of keeping similar claims together, nothing would stand in the way of a debtor seeking out a few impaired creditors (or even one such creditor) who will vote for the plan and placing them in their own class.

In re U.S. Truck Co., 800 F.2d 581, 586 (6th Cir.1986). * * * We agree with this rule, and if Greystone's proffered "reasons" for separately classifying the Phoenix deficiency claim simply mask the intent to gerrymander the voting process, that classification scheme should not have been approved.

Greystone's reliance on *Brite v. Sun Country Development, Inc.,* 764 F.2d 406 (5th Cir.1985), as an allegedly contrary rule is misplaced. That case allowed the debtor to impair a previously unimpaired class of creditors not for purposes of vote-getting but because the debtor belatedly discovered that it did not have sufficient funds to pay the creditors' claims in full. The court found that the debtor's decision to reclassify previously unimpaired creditors as impaired was necessary. * * * *Sun Country* does not support Greystone's argument that plan proponents possess unlimited discretion to classify unsecured claims separately. We conclude that if § 1122(a) permits classification of "substantially similar" claims in different classes, such classification may only be undertaken for reasons independent of the debtor's motivation to secure the vote of an impaired, assenting class of claims. To those proffered reasons we now turn.

Greystone contends that the "legal difference" between Phoenix's deficiency claim and the trade creditors' claims is sufficient to sustain its classification scheme. The alleged distinction between the legal attributes of the unsecured claims is that under state law Phoenix has no recourse against the debtor personally. However, state law is irrelevant where, as here, the Code has eliminated the legal distinction between non-recourse deficiency claims and other unsecured claims. See § 1111(b)(1)(A); * * *.[5]

The purpose of § 1111(b) is to provide an undersecured creditor an election with respect to the treatment of its deficiency claim. Generally, the creditor may elect recourse status and obtain the right to vote in the unsecured class, or it may elect to forego recourse to gain an allowed secured claim for the entire amount of the debt. If separate classification of unsecured deficiency claims arising from non-recourse debt were permitted solely on the ground that the claim is non-recourse under state law, the right to vote in the unsecured class would be meaningless. Plan proponents could effectively disenfranchise the holders of such claims by placing them in a separate class and confirming the plan over their objection by cramdown. With its unsecured voting rights effectively eliminated, the electing creditor's ability to negotiate a satisfactory settlement of either its secured or unsecured claims would be seriously undercut. It seems likely that the creditor would often have to "elect" to take an allowed secured claim under § 1111(b)(2) in the hope that the value of the collateral would increase after the case is closed.[6] Thus, the election under § 1111(b) would be essentially meaningless. We believe Congress did not intend this result.

As the bankruptcy court viewed this issue, the debtor's ability to achieve a cramdown plan should be preferred over the creditor's § 1111(b) election rights because of the Code's policy of facilitating reorganization. The bankruptcy court resorted to policy considerations because it believed Congress did not foresee the potential impact of an electing creditor's deficiency claim on the debtor's aspiration to cramdown a plan. We disagree with this approach for three reasons. First, it results here in

---

[5] Greystone argues that *Hanson* is not controlling because the issue there was whether it was clearly erroneous for the bankruptcy court to *deny* separate classification whereas the issue here is whether it was clearly erroneous for the court to *approve* the classification. The clearly erroneous rule has no application in this context. Whether a deficiency claim is legally similar to an unsecured trade claim turns not on fact findings but on their legal characteristics. This is an issue of law, freely reviewable on appeal. * * * Subsidiary fact findings however, may be entitled to the deference of the clearly erroneous test.

[6] In this case, for example, Greystone proposed to extinguish Phoenix's $3,500,000 deficiency claim by the promised payment of $140,000. Under the valuation process, it confined Phoenix's secured claim to $5.8 million. § 506(a). Phoenix obviously objects to this arrangement because, in the future, it might ultimately receive more than the written-down value of the office building in a liquidation following foreclosure. Yet, with its voting rights effectively eliminated by separate classification, Phoenix has no leverage to persuade the Debtor to consider a more reasonable settlement. Had this scenario triumphed, Phoenix's most realistic option might have been to take an allowed secured claim in the hope that eventually the market value of the office building will increase by more than $140,000 over the presently estimated value of the collateral.

violating § 1122, by gerrymandering the plan vote, for the sake of allegedly effectuating a § 1129(b) cramdown. "Policy" considerations do not justify preferring one section of the Code, much less elevating its implicit "policies" over other sections, where the statutory language draws no such distinctions. Second, as shown, it virtually eliminates the § 1111(b) election for secured creditors in this type of case. Third, the bankruptcy court's concern for the viability of cramdown plans is overstated. If Phoenix's unsecured claim were lower and the trade debt were higher, or if there were other impaired classes that favored the plan, a cramdown plan would be more realistic. That Greystone's cramdown plan may not succeed on the facts before us does not disprove the utility of the cramdown provision. The state law distinction between Code-created unsecured deficiency claims and other unsecured claims does not alone warrant separate classification.

Greystone next argues that separate classification was justified for "good business reasons." The bankruptcy court found that the debtor "need[s] trade to maintain good will for future operations." * * * The court further reasoned:

> [I]f the expectation of trade creditors is frustrated. . . [they] have little recourse but to refrain from doing business with the enterprise. The resulting negative reputation quickly spreads in the trade community, making it difficult to obtain services in the future on any but the most onerous terms.

* * * Greystone argues that the "realities of business" more than justify separate classification of the trade debt from Phoenix's deficiency claim. This argument is specious, for it fails to distinguish between the *classification* of claims and the *treatment* of claims. Greystone's justification for separate classification of the trade claims might be valid if the trade creditors were to receive different treatment from Phoenix. Indeed, Greystone initially created a separate class of unsecured creditors that could be wooed to vote for the plan by the promise to pay their remaining claims in full *outside the plan*. Greystone then changed course and eliminated its promise. Because there is no separate treatment of the trade creditors in this case, we reject Greystone's "realities of business" argument.

Even if Greystone's Plan had treated the trade creditors differently from Phoenix, the classification scheme here is still improper. At the confirmation hearing, none of the Debtor's witnesses offered any reason for classifying the trade debt separately from Phoenix's unsecured deficiency claim. There is no evidence in the record of a limited market in Austin for trade goods and services. Nor is there any evidence that Greystone would be unable to obtain any of the trade services if the trade creditors did not receive preferential treatment under the Plan. Thus, the bankruptcy court's finding that there were good business reasons for separate classification is without support in the record and must be set aside as clearly erroneous.[7]

Phoenix's unsecured deficiency claim approximates $3,500,000, while the claims of the unsecured trade creditors who voted to accept the Plan total less than $10,000. Greystone's classification scheme, which effectively disenfranchised Phoenix's Code-created deficiency claim, is sanctioned neither by the Code nor by caselaw. The lower courts erred in approving it.

### III.

As a fall-back position, Greystone argues that the office-building tenants constitute an impaired class whose votes for Greystone's Plan should have been considered for purposes of satisfying the pre-condition of cramdown that there be one assenting, impaired class. The bankruptcy court held that the tenants were not an impaired class and could not vote on the Plan because Greystone had assumed their leases. The district court disagreed and held that despite the Debtor's assumption of the leases, the tenants could be counted as an impaired accepting class. Phoenix argues this was error.

* * * Under the Code, only creditors are entitled to vote on a plan of reorganization. See § 1126(c). A party to a lease is considered a "creditor" who is allowed to vote, § 1126(c), only when the party has a claim against the estate that arises from *rejection* of a lease. * * * If, however, the debtor * * * assumes a lease, the lessee has no "claim" against the debtor under § 1126(a). See §§ 365(g), 502(g). The rights created by assumption of the lease constitute a post-petition administrative claim under § 503(b)(1)(A) of the Code. * * * The holder of such a claim is not entitled to vote on a plan of reorganization. § 1126(a); * * * *

Here, Greystone never rejected its leases with the tenants. There is thus no support for the assertion that the tenants' "claims" entitled them to vote on Greystone's Plan. The district court erred in alternatively permitting confirmation of the Plan based on the tenants' affirmative votes.

* * *

### V.

For the foregoing reasons, the judgment of the district court affirming the bankruptcy court's confirmation of Greystone's plan of reorganization is REVERSED. The case is REMANDED for proceedings consistent with this opinion.

---

[7] Two standards of appellate review apply to the debtor's classification of claims. Issues such as the similarity in priority and legal attributes and the ultimate question whether treatment in the same or separate classes is necessary, are legal issues reviewable by our court de novo. See n. 5 supra. Whether there were any good business reasons to support the debtor's separate classification of claims is a question of fact.

## NOTES

**1.** How can *Greystone* be reconciled with *U.S. Truck*? In *U.S. Truck* the debtor concedes its intent to gerrymander. In both cases the two classes of unsecured claims are treated identically by the plan. Are single asset real estate cases treated differently from "operating" cases with respect to classification of claims?

**2.** *Greystone* is one of the many Chapter 11 single asset real estate cases resulting from the real estate recession of the 1980s. We discuss on pp. 614-616 the impact on these cases of § 362(d)(3). *Greystone* is typical of these cases in that it involved an attempt to use § 1129(b)(2)(A) cramdown against an undersecured creditor with a mortgage on the debtor's real property. As *Greystone* demonstrates, one obstacle in the path to cramdown is the requirement of § 1129(a)(10) that there be at least one impaired class of creditors that will assent to the plan. Unsecured trade creditors to whom relatively small amounts are owed may be willing to agree to the debtor's plan, but the holding of *Greystone* prevents the debtor from creating a separate class of trade creditors. The court's opinion implies that if the mortgagee loses on the classification issue, cramdown will necessarily follow with highly undesirable consequences for the mortgagee. It speaks of the effect of allowing the debtor to classify the creditor's deficiency claim separately as *disenfranchising* the holder of the deficiency claim. But we will see later that for the mortgagee loss of the classification battle is not necessarily defeat in the cramdown war, for § 1111(b) and the "fair and equitable" requirement of § 1129(b) were crafted to protect creditors like Phoenix from unfair treatment in cramdown plans.

**3.** The *Greystone* rule has been widely followed in single asset real estate reorganization cases. E.g. *In re Boston Post Road Limited Partnership*, 21 F.3d 477 (2d Cir.1994); *John Hancock Mutual Life Insurance Co. v. Route 37 Business Park Assoc.*, 987 F.2d 154 (3d Cir.1993); *In re Bryson Properties, XVIII*, 961 F.2d 496 (4th Cir.1992); and *Matter of Lumber Exchange Building Ltd. Partnership*, 968 F.2d 647 (8th Cir.1992). The Seventh Circuit is the first to take a contrary view in *Matter of Woodbrook Associates*, 19 F.3d 312 (7th Cir.1994). In *Woodbrook* the undersecured mortgagee apparently made a loan to the debtor without recourse, i.e., the loan debt was secured by the real property but the debtor was not personally liable to pay the debt. But, in *Woodbrook* as in *Greystone* § 1111(b)(1)(A) accorded the undersecured mortgagee an unsecured claim for the amount of the deficiency which the debtor sought to classify in a separate class, leaving a class of trade creditors that would approve the debtor's plan. The mortgagee argued that separate classification violated the *Greystone* rule. The Seventh Circuit panel in *Woodbrook*, in refusing to follow *Greystone*, not only allowed separate classification but held that separate classification was required because § 1122(a) prohibits the inclusion of a claim in a class unless that claim "is substantially similar to the other claims" in the class. The *Woodbrook* court held that there were significant disparities between the legal rights of the holder of a claim arising under § 1111(b) and the holder of a general unsecured claim which precluded their classification in a single class. Judge Zagel stated:

> * * * These disparities in rights stem from the most obvious difference between the two claims: a general unsecured claim exists in all chapters of the Code, while a § 1111(b) claim exists only as long as the case remains in Chapter 11 and, once converted to a Chapter 7 case, recovery is limited to its collateral. * * * This difference is amplified when the debtor is a partnership (as in this case) and the creditors face possible failure of its Chapter 11 case. Under such circumstances, the general unsecured creditors can seek equitable relief to prevent dissipation of the assets of the general partners, who upon conversion to Chapter 7, are liable for the debts of the partnership. Such equitable relief is not likely to be available to a § 1111(b) claimant, whose recovery is confined to its collateral.
>
> This legal difference between the two claims also can lead to anomalous results when applying other sections of the Code to a class containing both § 1111(b) claimants and general unsecured claimants. First, § 1129(a)(7) requires that, for confirmation of a plan where a holder of a claim or interest in an impaired class rejects the plan, each claimant must "receive or retain. . . property of a value, as of the effective date of the plan, that is not less than the amount. . . receive[d] or retain[ed] if the debtor were liquidated under [C]hapter 7." A § 1111(b) claimant is not entitled to payment under Chapter 7. Yet, because the § 1111(b) claimant has been classified with other general unsecured creditors and because § 1123(a)(4) mandates the same treatment of all claims in the class, the § 1111(b) claimant can block confirmation unless it receives payment of an amount equal to that of the general unsecured creditors.

19 F.3d at 318–319.

The Ninth Circuit rejected the *Woodbrook* reasoning in *In re Barakat*, 99 F.3d 1520 (9th Cir.1996), in denying separate classification of the secured creditor's deficiency claim in circumstances similar to *Greystone III*.

**4.** What if the note in *Woodbrook* had been recourse so that the claim of the mortgagee had arisen under § 506(a) rather than under § 1111(b)(1)(A)? The disparities outlined in the quotation by Judge Zagel in *Woodbrook* would not apply. Nevertheless, is there sufficient disparity between the § 506(a) deficiency claim of an undersecured mortgagee and unsecured claims of trade creditors to preclude classification in a single class? In *Woodbrook*, Judge Zagel also discussed § 1111(b)(1)(A)(i). Under that provision, an undersecured mortgagee with a § 506(a) unsecured deficiency claim may elect under § 1111(b)(2) to have the entire mortgage debt treated as a secured claim notwithstanding § 506(a). The mortgagee has the option of waiving the unsecured deficiency claim and increasing the amount of the secured claim. That option is not available to holders of general unsecured claims. Thus, at the time of commencement of the Chapter 11 case, § 1122(a) would seem to prohibit putting the unsecured deficiency claim and general unsecured claims into one class because the various claims are not substantially similar. The § 1111(b) option is made by vote of the class of which the mortgagee's claim is a part. § 1111(b)(1)(A)(i). This provision clearly means that only "a claim secured by a lien on property of the estate" can be included in the class making the election. See Bankruptcy Rule 3014. In the usual case the mortgagee is the only member of the class. Thus, § 1111(b)(1)(A)(i) supports the conclusion in *Woodbrook* that a deficiency claim and general unsecured claims cannot be put into the same class. Courts following the *Greystone* rule seem to assume that the requirements of § 1122(a) are to be applied after it is determined whether the § 1111(b) election is or is not made. They then treat the unsecured deficiency claim and the general unsecured claims as similar for the purposes of § 1122(a). On the other hand, in support of the *Woodbrook* rule, it can be argued that the special election available to deficiency claims in § 1111(b) demonstrates that the interests of holders of general unsecured claims and those of mortgagees are so much at odds that they cannot be considered to be substantially similar under § 1122(a).

**5.** Single asset Chapter 11 cases usually deal with *undersecured* creditors. As we have seen, under the *Greystone* line of cases, such a creditor may be able to prevent cramdown by insisting that its deficiency claim be classified with the other unsecured claims. Since its deficiency claim will usually be much larger than the other unsecured claims, its vote will prevent that class from assenting to the plan and may make it impossible for the debtor to fashion a consenting impaired class required by § 1129(a)(10) for confirmation. But an *oversecured* creditor has no deficiency claim and therefore cannot control the vote of the class of unsecured claims. If the debtor can formulate a plan that both impairs that class of claims and is attractive enough to the class to win its approval, § 1129(a)(10) has been satisfied and cramdown can ensue over the opposition of the oversecured creditor.

In *In re Windsor on the River Associates, Ltd.*, 7 F.3d 127 (8th Cir.1993), the debtor, faced by a dissenting oversecured creditor whose claim amounted to $9.8 million, created a consenting impaired class of trade creditors by agreeing to pay them $13,000, the full amount of their claims, 60 days after the effective date of the plan. By postponing the date of payment by 60 days, the plan clearly impaired the rights of this class under the literal language of § 1124(1) which provides that impairment has occurred unless these rights have been left "unaltered." However, the court denied confirmation on the ground that the trade creditor class was only "artificially impaired." The court put a gloss on § 1124(1) as follows: if impairment of a class is discretionary on the part of the debtor and is done for the purpose of creating an impaired class that will provide the consenting class required by § 1129(a)(10), the impairment is artificial and that class will not be treated as impaired within the meaning of § 1124(1). In justifying its decision to ignore the words of § 1124(1), the court assimilates its views on artificial impairment to those of the courts that have rejected gerrymandering classes of claims to create a consenting class of impaired claims, e.g., the *Greystone* line of authority. One problem with this view is that while the statute is quite vague on what is proper classification of claims, it is crystal clear on what is impairment. The court goes on to say that allowing artificial impairment would result in undermining the policy of § 1129(a)(10) that there must be some showing of creditor support before a plan is crammed down. But the policy behind § 1129(a)(10) is very obscure. From a policy standpoint, why should the vote of $13,000 of trade claims be decisive with respect to the lawfulness of cramming down a plan on a separately classified and differently treated secured lender with a $9.8 million claim? *See* Gregory K. Jones, *The Classification and Cramdown Controversy in Single Asset Bankruptcy Cases: The Need For Repeal of § 1129(a)(10)*, 42 U.C.L.A. L. Rev. 623 (1994). Given the shaky premise of § 1129(a)(10) when applied to the facts of *Windsor on the River*, together with the clear wording of § 1124(1) on what constitutes impairment, the result in this case is questionable. As we shall see later, the oversecured creditor would still enjoy the protection of the absolute priority rule in the cramdown plan. The deletion of § 1124(3) in 1994 may have ended the unedifying debate over "artificial" impairment. If even claims paid in full on the effective date are impaired, and therefore may vote on the plan and constitute the required impaired accepting class, *Windsor on the River* may become irrelevant. *In re Atlanta–Stewart Partners*, 193 B.R. 79, 82 (Bankr.N.D.Ga.1996).

**6.** Although the requirement of one consenting impaired class may prevent cramdown of a debtor's plan, as in *Windsor on the River*, it is unlikely to bar cramdown of a plan proposed by a secured creditor if the view of *In re L & J Anaheim Associates*, 995 F.2d 940 (9th Cir.1993), is followed. In that case, Debtor failed to propose a plan within the 120–day exclusivity period of § 1121(b). Secured Creditor then proposed a plan allowing it to sell the assets of the estate (a hotel and a cause of action for mismanagement of the property) and to use the proceeds to pay the outstanding liens in order of priority. Although Secured Creditor was the only class to vote to approve the plan, the court confirmed the plan over Debtor's contention that Secured Creditor's rights were not truly impaired because they were, in fact, improved under the plan. The court held that under § 1124(1) the issue is not whether rights are enhanced or reduced under the plan, it is whether the plan leaves rights "unaltered." Since the plan changed somewhat the rights Secured Creditor would have had under state law, its rights were altered and thus impaired. Under this holding, any secured creditor who proposes a plan can nominally impair its rights in order to ensure that there will be at least one impaired class that will consent to the plan. If a creditor class proposing a plan can comply with § 1129(a)(10) by nominal impairment of its rights, why shouldn't a debtor be able to do so by proposing a plan nominally impairing the rights of a creditor class that will consent to the plan?

# REORGANIZATION IN CHAPTER 11: CONFIRMING THE PLAN

---

## A. FEASIBILITY

With respect to a plan of reorganization that does not provide for liquidation, § 1129(a)(11) requires the bankruptcy court to find that confirmation of the plan is not likely to be followed by liquidation or further financial reorganization of the debtor. This requirement is usually referred to as the "feasibility" requirement. The issue of whether a particular plan is or is not feasible is obviously a very fact-intensive inquiry and therefore general rules are not very helpful. *Orfa,* the case that follows, illustrates the standard for determining feasibility and the kind of factors that a bankruptcy judge must consider in evaluating feasibility.

*Orfa* involved three related corporations who filed in Chapter 11 in separate cases. A consolidated plan of reorganization, referred to in the case as "the Plan," was proposed for confirmation. The Plan was filed by two creditors, EAFC and Corsair, referred to in the case as the "Proponents." Debtors held valuable licenses to use a process for recycling solid waste. Confirmation of the Plan was opposed by two creditors, BEC and SPNB, and Licensors, the grantors of the licenses held by Debtors. The bankruptcy judge held that the Plan could not be confirmed for various reasons, but the court assumed that the defects in the Plan could be cured by amendment. In anticipation of the re-filing of the Plan, amended to cure the defects, the court addressed the issue of whether the Plan met the requirements of § 1129(a)(11). That part of the opinion follows.

## In re Orfa Corp. of Philadelphia
United States Bankruptcy Court, E.D. Pennsylvania, 1991.
129 B.R. 404.

■ DAVID A. SCHOLL, Bankruptcy Judge.

\* \* \*

The most important "fact" at issue requiring some description is the Plan. Although the Debtors have never been formally consolidated, the Plan, for the most part, treats the creditors of each of the Debtors as one body, i.e., as if their cases were consolidated. Nevertheless, in a paragraph addressing "revesting of assets," the Plan provides that the Debtors will operate as separate entities post-petition.

All secured and unsecured claims of SPNB are placed into a single class. SPNB is to receive full payment on the effective date if the Proponents obtain financing sought from Chase Manhattan Bank, N.A. ("Chase"). If the Chase loan is not consummated, as has not occurred to date, the Proponents, who are investment brokers and counsellors by profession, will undertake a private placement of preferred stock of the Debtors. From the proceeds of this placement, which, according to the Proponents, cannot be effected until the plan is confirmed, SPNB will be paid interest "at the prime rate" and will receive a final balloon payment after ten years of $8,225,000, which is about $150,000 greater than SPNB's $8,072,065.76 Proofs of Claim as of the bankruptcy filings * * *

BEC's claim * * * is placed into a class (Class H) including unsecured noteholders and all other unsecured claims of the Debtors. Payment of twenty (20%) percent of such claims is contemplated on the effective date, with the remaining eighty (80%) percent to be paid in quarterly payments extending over five years.

The Debtors' licenses with the Licensors are to be assumed, and the Licensors are to be paid their claims in full on the effective date.

The Debtors' report of plan voting, as supplemented, although not having been formally introduced into the record, indicates that all classes have accepted the Plan except the class including SPNB. SPNB, BEC, and the Licensors all filed Objections to confirmation of the Plan.

* * *

All three objecting parties—SPNB, BEC, and the Licensors—contend that the Plan fails to meet the "feasibility" requirement of § 1129(a)(11), that confirmation is "not likely to be followed by liquidation, or the need for future financial reorganization,. . ." Of the three, only SPNB levels an attack at the technological backbone of the Plan, i.e., that the Orfa process merits development. However, on February 28, 1988, SPNB agreed to advance as much as $13.55 million to build the Philadelphia plant and thereby promulgate the Orfa process. Its own expert, Thomas Vence, a financial consultant who was involved in the process which led to the approval of the earlier loan, admitted that he did not question the viability of the technology behind the Orfa process.

The principal thrust of the criticisms of the technological feasibility of the Plan by SPNB emphasizes skepticism not with the process itself but with the facts that the Debtors' business has had little earning capacity in the past and that the Debtors have no outstanding written contracts by which they can generate the tipping fees and revenue from sales of the recycled end products which the Proponents' witnesses project will make its technology profitable in the future. The Philadelphia plant, built with SPNB's loan funds as a demonstration of the workability of the Orfa process, is of limited effectiveness due to defects in construction. Unless this plant is put into a better condition, the Proponents are capable of demonstrating only the Debtors' failure to transfer the Orfa process into a workable reality.

However, SPNB's purported contemporary skepticism is contrary to its own past behavior. In 1988, at a time when the Debtors' incumbent management, with a track record that all parties agree was unenviable, was in control, SPNB was willing to advance considerable funds to the Debtors. The Proponents are prepared to install, as President and Chief Executive Officer, Joseph G. Munisteri, who has a distinguished record in the engineering construction industry. Munisteri previously served as Chief Executive Officer and Board member of several engineering firms. Having testified at length in several hearings, Munisteri has impressed the court as knowledgeable and realistic in his assessment of the Debtors' prospects. He identified Lorin B. Ellison, a certified public accountant and previously Vice President of Finance of Bausch & Lomb, as the reorganized Debtors' proposed Secretary, Treasurer and Chief Financial Officer. The Board of Directors of the Debtors presently includes William F. Ballhaus, former Chief Executive Officer of Beckman Instruments; John Dutton, Corsair's Director of Corporate Finance and Senior Vice President of a large healthcare company; and R. Eric Miller, former President for Fluor Constructors, Inc. and Vice President of Bechtel Corporation. Ballhaus testified in prior proceedings and Dutton testified in December proceedings. Both have been optimistic, yet are tempered with a sense of realism, about the Debtors' prospects. This constellation of individuals is a vast improvement over the group of "dreamers" who were the Debtors' principals when SPNB made its loan in 1988.

Munisteri, Dutton, and Alexander Capello, EAFC's principal, acknowledged the basically inoperable status of the Debtors' Philadelphia plant. Their plan was to hire Fluor Daniel, Inc. and Thyssen AG, European companies of impeccable reputation, to repair and provide guarantees of the operation of the Philadelphia plant, at a cost of $4.5 million.

We accept Cappello's testimony that the private placement cannot be finalized until plan confirmation occurs. Unless the Chase loan materializes, the funds to repair the Philadelphia plant will therefore not appear until after the private placement is solicited. It is only after the repairs are made to the plant that it is realistic to expect contracts yielding tipping fees and end-product purchases to appear. This proposed progression of development of the Debtors by the Proponents appears reasonable. We accept the Proponents' assertions that it is unrealistic to expect definite commitments from investors and prospective customers at this juncture.

BEC and the Licensors voice little concern about the technology of the Orfa process. Indeed, BEC attempted several means of obtaining the Orfa license to incorporate it into a proposal for trash disposal in the City of Toronto, reflecting BEC's confidence in the efficacy of the process. Although the October 1, 1990, deadline by which BEC was compelled to make a presentation to the City of Toronto has passed, BEC has remained an active party in this case, either due to a hope that it can still compete in the Toronto process or a desire to develop the process in other Canadian municipalities. The Licensors of the process could hardly be expected to challenge its technological feasibility.

The thrust of the objection to feasibility from these parties is focused upon the use of the private placement as a means for raising capital. The effective date of the Plan is triggered by the Proponents' raising at least $7 million within 150 days after confirmation. The total debt of the three Debtors is $19.35 million, according to Dutton. The cost to repair the plant will be at least $4.5 million. Operating costs will result in a need for millions more, unless and until operations of the Debtors are profitable. The objectors are troubled because the Debtors have no funds and the Proponents themselves have insufficient resources to fund the Plan. Moreover, the source of the funds is not a recognizable financial institution, but an unidentified, amorphous group of individuals who have not been identified and indeed could not be identified because they do not yet exist.

Cappello and Dutton are aware of these aspects (drawbacks, if you will) of the Plan. However, they point out that solicitation of investors is unrealistic and perhaps illegal unless it is first backed by a confirmation order. Cappello points to his Companies' past success in raising $22 million on the Debtors' behalf. These funds were raised at a time when the incumbent management was in control. They reason, not illogically, that investments will be more readily obtainable with their proposed competent management team in place.

The standards for determining plan feasibility are not rigorous. See, e.g., In re Temple Zion, 125 B.R. 910, 914–15 (Bankr.E.D.Pa.1991) * * *

> Caselaw has established that bankruptcy court[s] must consider several factors in making a feasibility determination: (1) the adequacy of the debtor's capital structure; (2) the earning power of its business; (3) economic conditions; (4) the ability of the debtor's management; (5) the probability of the continuation of the same management; and (6) any other related matters which determine the prospects of a sufficiently successful operation to enable performance of the provisions of the plan. * * *

*Temple Zion,* supra, 125 B.R. at 915.

The Proponents have made a very strong showing of the fourth factor referenced supra. Since the management team which has been proven unable to accomplish the end of making the Debtors profitable is now out of the picture, the absence of probability that the same management will continue constitutes a positive showing of the fifth factor referenced supra.

The second factor referenced above is another strong element in the Proponents' favor. The possible earning power of the Debtors' business is very high. The Debtors' technology is highly regarded. The issue of waste disposal is very important and the prospect of a recycling process is a very attractive prospect at this stage in the history of our planet. In an era when many Chapter 11 cases present real estate developments which often have no upward potential or businesses engaged in industries in which growth potential is neither present nor likely, these Debtors stand out as presenting a relatively high probability of increased future earning power.

The third factor noted supra is difficult to measure, but appears to be positive in light of the type of financial plan offered by the Proponents. Loans from recognizable lending institutions are presently very difficult to obtain. However, the climate for new investments is positive, especially since alternatives such as real estate trusts have become less attractive investments. A plan which proposes a sale of stock is one of the few means of raising capital which has at least the potential for success in the current financial environment. The fact that the Proponents are professionals in the investment field who have not been tainted by past transactions renders them capable candidates to put together a private placement which can succeed. We therefore would classify current economic conditions as conducive to the plan proposed.

The first factor * * * recited above is, of course, not in the Proponents' favor. The Debtors have no capital at all, and the focus of the Plan is to provide them with capital. However, we believe that the Proponents' prospect of achieving that end are relatively bright.

No other parties have materialized who have been willing to invest the time, energy, and financial resources into the development of the Debtors that the Proponents have. The Proponents appear to have two strong incentives for doing so: (1) to prevent a loss of their prior investments in this venture; and (2) to obtain placement fees and future financial advantages from being on the ground floor of the Debtors' new financial life. These incentives, though selfish, assure that their participation will be ongoing. They provide the sort of "other related matters" within the scope of the sixth factor cited supra which are properly to be considered in determining plan feasibility.

The Proponents cite *In re American Solar King Corp.*, 90 B.R. 808, 831–33 (Bankr.W.D.Texas 1988), as an example of a Chapter 11 case in which a plan based upon funding from new investments was deemed feasible and was confirmed. SPNB and BES are quick to point out the distinctions between the instant case and that case. In *American Solar King,* two large potential investors in the debtor's private placement were identified, whereas here we have only the investment brokers identified and the large body of investors are faceless. However, the overall picture presented by the Proponents compares favorably with that in *American Solar King.* The very Proponents of the Plan are investment brokers, who, as we noted, appear quite capable of accomplishing a successful placement.

We therefore conclude that the weight of the factors relevant to a feasibility analysis supports the conclusion that the Plan is feasible.

\* \* \*

## B. TREATMENT OF PRIORITY CLAIMS

Under § 1129(a)(9)(A) administrative expenses, having second priority under § 507(a), must be paid in full in cash on the effective date of the plan unless the claimant agrees to different treatment. Third priority "gap creditor" claims must also be fully paid in cash on the effective date of the plan. ("Gap creditors" arise only in involuntary cases on account of the delay between the filing of the petition and order for relief.) We saw earlier that administrative expenses can balloon as the debtor in possession borrows or buys on credit in an attempt to keep the business alive. If administrative expenses get too large the requirement that these expenses be paid in cash at the effective date of the plan may preclude confirmation of a plan.

A different rule applies to claims with first, fourth, fifth, sixth and seventh priority. The plan may provide for deferred payment of the amount of these claims with interest if the affected class accepts the plan. If the class does not accept, these claims must be fully paid in cash on the effective date of the plan. Any claimant can agree to different treatment. § 1129(a)(9)(B).

Prior to 2005, one of the requirements for confirmation of a plan is that the plan provide that the allowed unsecured claims of governmental units "[r]eceive on account of such claim deferred cash payments, over a period not exceeding six years after the date of assessment of such claim, of a value, as of the effective date of the plan, equal to the allowed amount of such claim." Former § 1129(a)(9)(C). This flexible provision allowed for a significant deferral of priority tax liabilities, even while lower priority claims received prompt payment. Secured tax claims could receive even less favorable treatment in a restructuring in accordance with § 1129(b)(2)(A). The 2005 Act significantly revised § 1129(a)(9)(C) to improve the treatment of priority and secured tax claims in the following ways.

First, governmental units holding allowed unsecured claims must receive on account of such claim, regular installment payments in cash "[o]f a total value, as of the effective date of the plan, equal to the allowed amount of such claim. . . ."

Second, payments to taxing authorities can no longer be stretched out for a period of six years from the date of the assessment. Under revised § 1129(a)(9)(C), those claims must be paid in full within five years after the date of the entry of the order for relief.

Third, and perhaps most significant, a taxing authority must not receive less favorable treatment than other non-priority unsecured claims provided for in the plan. Thus, if a class (other than a convenience class) is paid on the effective date of the plan, it is arguable that the taxing agency must be paid on the effective date as well.  On the other hand, if trade claims are paid at a discount on the effective date, perhaps the payment in full of the tax claim a few years later is not less favorable.

Finally, taxing authorities that hold secured claims which would otherwise meet the description of unsecured priority claims will be entitled to cash payments in the same manner and over the same period as described above.

## C. TREATMENT OF SECURED CLAIMS

### 1. § 1129(b)(2)(A) STANDARDS FOR CRAMDOWN

The proponent of a reorganization plan may deal with a class of secured claims in one of three ways: (1) Leave the class unimpaired under § 1124; (2) Obtain acceptance of the plan by the class and qualify for a § 1129(a) consensual confirmation; or (3) Seek cramdown pursuant to § 1129(b)(2)(A).

Suppose Lender has a security interest in Debtor's property having a resale value of $150,000. The debt owed to Lender is $100,000 and it is now due and owing. How can Debtor restructure this secured obligation without Lender's consent?

By hypothesis Lender has rejected the plan so confirmation is not possible under § 1129(a) because all impaired classes have not accepted the plan. § 1129(a)(8). Moreover, restructuring the loan implies altering Lender's present legal rights and so Lender's class is impaired. § 1124(1). Confirmation, however, can still occur under § 1129(b)(1) if the plan is fair and equitable. That standard requires compliance with one of the three subparagraphs of § 1129(b)(2)(A).

#### a.  Deferred Cash Payments

Under the first alternative (subparagraph (i)) the plan could provide that Lender both retain its lien in the collateral *and* receive deferred cash payments having a value at the effective date of the plan of at least the amount of its secured claim.

This is the most common method for non-consensually restructuring a secured claim under § 1129(b) and it is the debtor's approach to cramdown against SPNB in *Orfa*. The creditor's right to "retain[] the lien" under § 1129(b)(2)(A)(i)(I) is usually understood as being limited to the essential attributes of the property interest of the secured party under otherwise applicable law—not necessarily all the rights created by the prepetition security agreement and certainly not the rights to a particular payment schedule or interest rate or covenant protections under the prepetition note or credit agreement. The present value requirement of § 1129(b)(2)(A)(i)(II) necessarily implies that if there is deferral of the payments on account of the secured claim past the plan's effective date fully compensatory interest at the then market rate must be paid as well. The Code offers no guidance on how to choose the appropriate interest rate, how long the payments may be deferred or when interest must be paid. *Collier on Bankruptcy* ¶ 1129.06[1][c] (15th ed. rev. 2004) describes three competing views on the question of the applicable rate of interest:

> One group of courts look at the creditor's costs in bearing the treatment provided for in the plan. These courts focus on the characteristics of the creditor, and its ability to obtain capital to lend. This inquiry, however, leads to diverse results based on the peculiarities of the secured creditor. * * *

> Some courts, however, treat any deferred payment of an obligation under a plan as a coerced loan and the rate of return with respect to such loan must correspond to the rate which would be charged or obtained by the creditor making a loan to a third party with similar terms, duration, collateral and risk. * * * Thus in determining the discount rate, the court must consider the prevailing market rate for a loan of a term equal to the payout period, with due consideration of the quality of the security and the risk of subsequent default.

> * * *

> A third group of courts * * * start[] with a baseline of a 'riskless' loan, and then [take] evidence on the risk presented by the loan proposed in the plan. In short, they have developed a formula for the discount rate required * * *.

The Supreme Court appears to have adopted a version of this third approach in the following Chapter 13 case. It remains a matter of debate whether the same principles for present valuing the secured creditor's payments under a plan apply in Chapter 11.

## Till v. SCS Credit Corporation

Supreme Court of the United States, 2004.
541 U.S. 465.

■ Justice STEVENS announced the judgment of the Court and delivered an opinion, in which Justice SOUTER, Justice GINSBURG, and Justice BREYER join.

To qualify for court approval under Chapter 13 of the Bankruptcy Code, an individual debtor's proposed debt adjustment plan must accommodate each allowed, secured creditor in one of three ways: (1) by obtaining the creditor's acceptance of the plan; (2) by surrendering the property securing the claim; or (3) by providing the creditor both a lien securing the claim and a promise of future property distributions (such as deferred cash payments) whose total "value, as of the effective date of the plan,. . . is not less than the allowed amount of such claim." The third alternative is commonly known as the "cram down option" because it may be enforced over a claim holder's objection.[2]

Plans that invoke the cram down power often provide for installment payments over a period of years rather than a single payment. In such circumstances, the amount of each installment must be calibrated to ensure that, over time, the creditor receives disbursements whose total present value[4] equals or exceeds that of the allowed claim. The proceedings in this case that led to our grant of certiorari identified four different methods of determining the appropriate method with which to perform that calibration. Indeed, the Bankruptcy Judge, the District Court, the Court of Appeals majority, and the dissenting Judge each endorsed a different approach. We detail the underlying facts and describe each of those approaches before setting forth our judgment as to which approach best meets the purposes of the Bankruptcy Code.

## I

On October 2, 1998, petitioners Lee and Amy Till, residents of Kokomo, Indiana, purchased a used truck from Instant Auto Finance for $6,395 plus $330.75 in fees and taxes. They made a $300 down payment and financed the balance of the purchase price by entering into a retail installment contract that Instant Auto immediately assigned to respondent, SCS Credit Corporation. Petitioners' initial indebtedness amounted to $8,285.24—the $6,425.75 balance of the truck purchase plus a finance charge of 21% per year for 136 weeks, or $1,859.49. Under the contract, petitioners agreed to make 68 biweekly payments to cover this debt; Instant Auto—and subsequently respondent—retained a purchase money security interest that gave it the right to repossess the truck if petitioners defaulted under the contract.

On October 25, 1999, petitioners, by then in default on their payments to respondent, filed a joint petition for relief under Chapter 13 of the Bankruptcy Code. At the time of the filing, respondent's outstanding claim amounted to $4,894.89, but the parties agreed that the truck securing the claim was worth only $4,000. In accordance with the Bankruptcy Code, therefore, respondent's secured claim was limited to $4,000, and the $894.89 balance was unsecured. Petitioners' filing automatically stayed debt-collection activity by their various creditors, including the Internal Revenue Service (IRS), respondent, three other holders of secured claims, and unidentified unsecured creditors. In addition, the filing created a bankruptcy estate, administered by a trustee, which consisted of petitioners' property, including the truck.

---

[2] As we noted in *Associates Commercial Corp. v. Rash,* 520 U.S. 953, 962 (1997), a debtor may also avail himself of the second option (surrender of the collateral) despite the creditor's objection.

[4] In the remainder of the opinion, we use the term "present value" to refer to the value as of the effective date of the bankruptcy plan.

Petitioners' proposed debt adjustment plan called for them to submit their future earnings to the supervision and control of the Bankruptcy Court for three years, and to assign $740 of their wages to the trustee each month. The plan charged the trustee with distributing these monthly wage assignments to pay, in order of priority: (1) administrative costs; (2) the IRS's priority tax claim; (3) secured creditors' claims; and finally, (4) unsecured creditors' claims.

The proposed plan also provided that petitioners would pay interest on the secured portion of respondent's claim at a rate of 9.5% per year. Petitioners arrived at this "prime-plus" or "formula rate" by augmenting the national prime rate of approximately 8% (applied by banks when making low-risk loans) to account for the risk of nonpayment posed by borrowers in their financial position. Respondent objected to the proposed rate, contending that the company was "entitled to interest at the rate of 21%, which is the rate. . . it would obtain if it could foreclose on the vehicle and reinvest the proceeds in loans of equivalent duration and risk as the loan" originally made to petitioners.

At the hearing on its objection, respondent presented expert testimony establishing that it uniformly charges 21% interest on so-called "subprime" loans, or loans to borrowers with poor credit ratings, and that other lenders in the subprime market also charge that rate. Petitioners countered with the testimony of an Indiana University-Purdue University Indianapolis economics professor, who acknowledged that he had only limited familiarity with the subprime auto lending market, but described the 9.5% formula rate as "very reasonable" given that Chapter 13 plans are "supposed to be financially feasible."[8] Moreover, the professor noted that respondent's exposure was "fairly limited because [petitioners] are under the supervision of the court." The bankruptcy trustee also filed comments supporting the formula rate as, among other things, easily ascertainable, closely tied to the "condition of the financial market," and independent of the financial circumstances of any particular lender. Accepting petitioners' evidence, the Bankruptcy Court overruled respondent's objection and confirmed the proposed plan.

The District Court reversed. It understood Seventh Circuit precedent to require that bankruptcy courts set cram down interest rates at the level the creditor could have obtained if it had foreclosed on the loan, sold the collateral, and reinvested the proceeds in loans of equivalent duration and risk. Citing respondent's unrebutted testimony about the market for subprime loans, the court concluded that 21% was the appropriate rate.

On appeal, the Seventh Circuit endorsed a slightly modified version of the District Court's "coerced" or "forced loan" approach. Specifically, the

---

[8] The requirement of financial feasibility derives from 11 U.S.C. § 1325(a)(6), which provides that the bankruptcy court shall "confirm a plan if. . . the debtor will be able to make all payments under the plan and to comply with the plan."

majority agreed with the District Court that, in a cram down proceeding, the inquiry should focus on the interest rate "that the creditor in question would obtain in making a new loan in the same industry to a debtor who is similarly situated, although not in bankruptcy." To approximate that new loan rate, the majority looked to the parties' prebankruptcy contract rate (21%). The court recognized, however, that using the contract rate would not "duplicat[e] precisely. . . the present value of the collateral to the creditor" because loans to bankrupt, court-supervised debtors "involve some risks that would not be incurred in a new loan to a debtor not in default" and also produce "some economies." To correct for these inaccuracies, the majority held that the original contract rate should "serve as a presumptive [cram down] rate," which either the creditor or the debtor could challenge with evidence that a higher or lower rate should apply. Accordingly, the court remanded the case to the Bankruptcy Court to afford petitioners and respondent an opportunity to rebut the presumptive 21% rate.[9]

Dissenting, Judge Rovner argued that the majority's presumptive contract rate approach overcompensates secured creditors because it fails to account for costs a creditor would have to incur in issuing a new loan. Rather than focusing on the market for comparable loans, Judge Rovner advocated either the Bankruptcy Court's formula approach or a "straightforward. . . cost of funds" approach that would simply ask "what it would cost the creditor to obtain the cash equivalent of the collateral from an alternative source." Although Judge Rovner noted that the rates produced by either the formula or the cost of funds approach might be "piddling" relative to the coerced loan rate, she suggested courts should "consider the extent to which the creditor has already been compensated for. . . the risk that the debtor will be unable to discharge his obligations under the reorganization plan. . . in the rate of interest that it charged to the debtor in return for the original loan." We granted certiorari and now reverse.

## II

The Bankruptcy Code provides little guidance as to which of the rates of interest advocated by the four opinions in this case—the formula rate, the coerced loan rate, the presumptive contract rate, or the cost of funds rate—Congress had in mind when it adopted the cram down provision. That provision, 11 U.S.C. § 1325(a)(5)(B), does not mention the term "discount rate" or the word "interest." Rather, it simply requires bankruptcy courts to ensure that the property to be distributed to a particular secured creditor over the life of a bankruptcy plan has a total "value, as of the effective date of the plan," that equals or exceeds the value of the creditor's allowed secured claim—in this case, $4,000.

---

[9] As 21% is the maximum interest rate creditors may charge for consumer loans under Indiana's usury statute, the remand presumably could not have benefited respondent.

That command is easily satisfied when the plan provides for a lump-sum payment to the creditor. Matters are not so simple, however, when the debt is to be discharged by a series of payments over time. A debtor's promise of future payments is worth less than an immediate payment of the same total amount because the creditor cannot use the money right away, inflation may cause the value of the dollar to decline before the debtor pays, and there is always some risk of nonpayment. The challenge for bankruptcy courts reviewing such repayment schemes, therefore, is to choose an interest rate sufficient to compensate the creditor for these concerns.

Three important considerations govern that choice. First, the Bankruptcy Code includes numerous provisions that, like the cram down provision, require a court to "discoun[t] . . . [a] stream of deferred payments back to the[ir] present dollar value," *Rake v. Wade,* 508 U.S. 464, 472, n. 8 (1993), to ensure that a creditor receives at least the value of its claim.[10] We think it likely that Congress intended bankruptcy judges and trustees to follow essentially the same approach when choosing an appropriate interest rate under any of these provisions. Moreover, we think Congress would favor an approach that is familiar in the financial community and that minimizes the need for expensive evidentiary proceedings.

Second, Chapter 13 expressly authorizes a bankruptcy court to modify the rights of any creditor whose claim is secured by an interest in anything other than "real property that is the debtor's principal residence." 11 U.S.C. § 1322(b)(2). Thus, in cases like this involving secured interests in personal property, the court's authority to modify the number, timing, or amount of the installment payments from those set forth in the debtor's original contract is perfectly clear. Further, the potential need to modify the loan terms to account for intervening changes in circumstances is also clear: On the one hand, the fact of the bankruptcy establishes that the debtor is overextended and thus poses a significant risk of default; on the other hand, the postbankruptcy obligor is no longer the individual debtor but the court-supervised estate, and the risk of default is thus somewhat reduced.[12]

---

[10] See 11 U.S.C. § 1129(a)(7)(A)(ii) (requiring payment of property whose "value, as of the effective date of the plan" equals or exceeds the value of the creditor's claim); §§ 1129(a)(7)(B), 1129(a)(9)(B)(i), 1129(a)(9)(C), 1129(b)(2)(A)(ii), 1129(b)(2)(B)(i), 1129(b)(2)(C)(i), 1173(a)(2), 1225(a)(4), 1225(a)(5)(B)(ii), 1228(b)(2), 1325(a)(4), 1228(b)(2) (same).

[12] Several factors contribute to this reduction in risk. First, as noted below, a court may only approve a cram down loan (and the debt adjustment plan of which the loan is a part) if it believes the debtor will be able to make all of the required payments. § 1325(a)(6). Thus, such loans will only be approved for debtors that the court deems creditworthy. Second, Chapter 13 plans must "provide for the submission" to the trustee "of all or such portion of [the debtor's] future. . . income. . . as is necessary for the execution of the plan," § 1322(a)(1), so the possibility of nonpayment is greatly re-

Third, from the point of view of a creditor, the cram down provision mandates an objective rather than a subjective inquiry.[13] That is, although § 1325(a)(5)(B) entitles the creditor to property whose present value objectively equals or exceeds the value of the collateral, it does not require that the terms of the cram down loan match the terms to which the debtor and creditor agreed prebankruptcy, nor does it require that the cram down terms make the creditor subjectively indifferent between present foreclosure and future payment. Indeed, the very idea of a "cram down" loan *precludes* the latter result: By definition, a creditor forced to accept such a loan would prefer instead to foreclose.[14] Thus, a court choosing a cram down interest rate need not consider the creditor's individual circumstances, such as its prebankruptcy dealings with the debtor or the alternative loans it could make if permitted to foreclose.[15] Rather, the court should aim to treat similarly situated creditors similarly, and to ensure that an objective economic analysis would suggest the debtor's interest payments will adequately compensate all such creditors for the time value of their money and the risk of default.

### III

These considerations lead us to reject the coerced loan, presumptive contract rate, and cost of funds approaches. Each of these approaches is complicated, imposes significant evidentiary costs, and aims to make each

---

duced. Third, the Bankruptcy Code's extensive disclosure requirements reduce the risk that the debtor has significant undisclosed obligations. Fourth, as a practical matter, the public nature of the bankruptcy proceeding is likely to reduce the debtor's opportunities to take on additional debt.

[13] We reached a similar conclusion in *Associates Commercial Corp. v. Rash,* when we held that a creditor's secured interest should be valued from the debtor's, rather than the creditor's, perspective. *Id.,* at 963 ("[The debtor's] actual use, rather than a foreclosure sale that will not take place, is the proper guide. . .").

[14] This fact helps to explain why there is no readily apparent Chapter 13 "cram down market rate of interest": Because every cram down loan is imposed by a court over the objection of the secured creditor, there is no free market of willing cram down lenders. Interestingly, the same is *not* true in the Chapter 11 context, as numerous lenders advertise financing for Chapter 11 debtors in possession. See, *e.g.,* Balmoral Financial Corporation, http://www.balmoral.com/bdip.htm (all Internet materials as visited Mar. 4, 2004, and available in Clerk of Court's case file) (advertising debtor in possession lending); Debtor in Possession Financing: 1st National Assistance Finance Association DIP Division, http://www.loanmallusa.com/dip.htm (offering "to tailor a financing program. . . to your business' needs and. . . to work closely with your bankruptcy counsel"). Thus, when picking a cram down rate in a Chapter 11 case, it might make sense to ask what rate an efficient market would produce. In the Chapter 13 context, by contrast, the absence of any such market obligates courts to look to first principles and ask only what rate will fairly compensate a creditor for its exposure.

[15] See *supra* (noting that the District Court's coerced loan approach aims to set the cram down interest rate at the level the creditor could obtain from new loans of comparable duration and risk).

individual creditor whole rather than to ensure the debtor's payments have the required present value. For example, the coerced loan approach requires bankruptcy courts to consider evidence about the market for comparable loans to similar (though nonbankrupt) debtors—an inquiry far removed from such courts' usual task of evaluating debtors' financial circumstances and the feasibility of their debt adjustment plans. In addition, the approach overcompensates creditors because the market lending rate must be high enough to cover factors, like lenders' transaction costs and overall profits, that are no longer relevant in the context of court—administered and court—supervised cram down loans.

Like the coerced loan approach, the presumptive contract rate approach improperly focuses on the creditor's potential use of the proceeds of a foreclosure sale. In addition, although the approach permits a debtor to introduce some evidence about each creditor, thereby enabling the court to tailor the interest rate more closely to the creditor's financial circumstances and reducing the likelihood that the creditor will be substantially overcompensated, that right comes at a cost: The debtor must obtain information about the creditor's costs of overhead, financial circumstances, and lending practices to rebut the presumptive contract rate. Also, the approach produces absurd results, entitling "inefficient, poorly managed lenders" with lower profit margins to obtain higher cram down rates than "well managed, better capitalized lenders." 2 K. Lundin, Chapter 13 Bankruptcy § 112.1, p. 112-8 (3d ed.2000). Finally, because the approach relies heavily on a creditor's prior dealings with the debtor, similarly situated creditors may end up with vastly different cram down rates.[17]

The cost of funds approach, too, is improperly aimed. Although it rightly disregards the now-irrelevant terms of the parties' original contract, it mistakenly focuses on the creditworthiness of the *creditor* rather than the debtor. In addition, the approach has many of the other flaws of the coerced loan and presumptive contract rate approaches. For example, like the presumptive contract rate approach, the cost of funds approach imposes a significant evidentiary burden, as a debtor seeking to rebut a creditor's asserted cost of borrowing must introduce expert testimony about the creditor's financial condition. Also, under this approach, a creditworthy lender with a low cost of borrowing may obtain a lower cram down rate than a financially unsound, fly-by-night lender.

---

[17] For example, suppose a debtor purchases two identical used cars, buying the first at a low purchase price from a lender who charges high interest, and buying the second at a much higher purchase price from a lender who charges zero-percent or nominal interest. Prebankruptcy, these two loans might well produce identical income streams for the two lenders. Postbankruptcy, however, the presumptive contract rate approach would entitle the first lender to a considerably higher cram down interest rate, even though the two secured debts are objectively indistinguishable.

## IV

The formula approach has none of these defects. Taking its cue from ordinary lending practices, the approach begins by looking to the national prime rate, reported daily in the press, which reflects the financial market's estimate of the amount a commercial bank should charge a creditworthy commercial borrower to compensate for the opportunity costs of the loan, the risk of inflation, and the relatively slight risk of default.[18] Because bankrupt debtors typically pose a greater risk of nonpayment than solvent commercial borrowers, the approach then requires a bankruptcy court to adjust the prime rate accordingly. The appropriate size of that risk adjustment depends, of course, on such factors as the circumstances of the estate, the nature of the security, and the duration and feasibility of the reorganization plan. The court must therefore hold a hearing at which the debtor and any creditors may present evidence about the appropriate risk adjustment. Some of this evidence will be included in the debtor's bankruptcy filings, however, so the debtor and creditors may not incur significant additional expense. Moreover, starting from a concededly *low* estimate and adjusting *upward* places the evidentiary burden squarely on the creditors, who are likely to have readier access to any information absent from the debtor's filing (such as evidence about the "liquidity of the collateral market," *post* (SCALIA, J., dissenting). Finally, many of the factors relevant to the adjustment fall squarely within the bankruptcy court's area of expertise.

Thus, unlike the coerced loan, presumptive contract rate, and cost of funds approaches, the formula approach entails a straightforward, familiar, and objective inquiry, and minimizes the need for potentially costly additional evidentiary proceedings. Moreover, the resulting "prime-plus" rate of interest depends only on the state of financial markets, the circumstances of the bankruptcy estate, and the characteristics of the loan, not on the creditor's circumstances or its prior interactions with the debtor. For these reasons, the prime-plus or formula rate best comports with the purposes of the Bankruptcy Code.[19]

---

[18] We note that, if the court could somehow be certain a debtor would complete his plan, the prime rate would be adequate to compensate any secured creditors forced to accept cram down loans.

[19] The fact that Congress considered but rejected legislation that would endorse the Seventh Circuit's presumptive contract rate approach, H.R. 1085, 98th Cong., 1st Sess., § 19(2)(A) (1983); H.R. 1169, 98th Cong., 1st Sess., § 19(2)(A) (1983); H.R. 4786, 97th Cong., 1st Sess., § 19(2)(A) (1981), lends some support to our conclusion. It is perhaps also relevant that our conclusion is endorsed by the Executive Branch of the Government and by the National Association of Chapter Thirteen Trustees. Brief for United States as *Amicus Curiae;* Brief for National Association of Chapter Thirteen Trustees as *Amicus Curiae.* If we have misinterpreted Congress' intended meaning of "value, as of the date of the plan," we are confident it will enact appropriate remedial legislation.

We do not decide the proper scale for the risk adjustment, as the issue is not before us. The Bankruptcy Court in this case approved a risk adjustment of 1.5%, and other courts have generally approved adjustments of 1% to 3%. Respondent's core argument is that a risk adjustment in this range is entirely inadequate to compensate a creditor for the real risk that the plan will fail. There is some dispute about the true scale of that risk—respondent claims that more than 60% of Chapter 13 plans fail, Brief for Respondent 25, but petitioners argue that the failure rate for *approved* Chapter 13 plans is much lower, Tr. of Oral Arg. 9. We need not resolve that dispute. It is sufficient for our purposes to note that, under 11 U.S.C. § 1325(a)(6), a court may not approve a plan unless, after considering all creditors' objections and receiving the advice of the trustee, the judge is persuaded that "the debtor will be able to make all payments under the plan and to comply with the plan." Together with the cram down provision, this requirement obligates the court to select a rate high enough to compensate the creditor for its risk but not so high as to doom the plan. If the court determines that the likelihood of default is so high as to necessitate an "eye-popping" interest rate, the plan probably should not be confirmed.

V

The dissent's endorsement of the presumptive contract rate approach rests on two assumptions: (1) "subprime lending markets are competitive and therefore largely efficient"; and (2) the risk of default in Chapter 13 is normally no less than the risk of default at the time of the original loan. Although the Bankruptcy Code provides little guidance on the question, we think it highly unlikely that Congress would endorse either premise.

First, the dissent assumes that subprime loans are negotiated between fully informed buyers and sellers in a classic free market. But there is no basis for concluding that Congress relied on this assumption when it enacted Chapter 13. Moreover, several considerations suggest that the subprime market is not, in fact, perfectly competitive. To begin with, used vehicles are regularly sold by means of tie-in transactions, in which the price of the vehicle is the subject of negotiation, while the terms of the financing are dictated by the seller.[20] In addition, there is extensive fed-

---

[20] The dissent notes that "[t]ie-ins do not *alone* make financing markets noncompetitive; they only cause prices and interest rates to be considered *in tandem* rather than separately." This statement, while true, is nonresponsive. If a market prices the cost of goods and the cost of financing together, then even if that market is perfectly competitive, all we can know is that the *combined* price of the goods and the financing is competitive and efficient. We have no way of determining whether the allocation of that price between goods and financing would be the same if the two components were separately negotiated. But the only issue before us is the cram down interest rate (the cost of financing); the value of respondent's truck (the cost of the goods) is fixed. See *Rash,* 520 U.S. at 960 (setting the value of collateral in Chapter 13 proceedings at the "price a willing buyer in the debtor's trade, business, or situation would pay to obtain

eral[21] and state[22] regulation of subprime lending, which not only itself distorts the market, but also evinces regulators' belief that unregulated subprime lenders would exploit borrowers' ignorance and charge rates above what a competitive market would allow.[23] Indeed, Congress enacted the Truth in Lending Act in part because it believed "consumers would individually benefit not only from the more informed use of credit, but also from heightened competition which would result from more knowledgeable credit shopping." S.Rep. No. 96-368, p. 16 (1979).[24]

Second, the dissent apparently believes that the debtor's prebankruptcy default—on a loan made in a market in which creditors commonly charge the maximum rate of interest allowed by law, Brief for Respondent 16, and in which neither creditors nor debtors have the protections afforded by Chapter 13—translates into a high probability that the same debtor's confirmed Chapter 13 plan will fail. In our view, however, Congress intended to create a program under which plans that qualify for confirmation have a high probability of success. Perhaps bankruptcy judges currently confirm too many risky plans, but the solution is to confirm fewer such plans, not to set default cram down rates at absurdly high levels, thereby increasing the risk of default.

Indeed, as Justice THOMAS demonstrates, the text of § 1325(a)(5)(B)(ii) may be read to support the conclusion that Congress did not intend the cram down rate to include *any* compensation for the risk of default.[25] That reading is consistent with a view that Congress believed

---

like property from a willing seller"). The competitiveness of the market for cost-*cum*-financing is thus irrelevant to our analysis.

[21] For example, the Truth in Lending Act regulates credit transactions and credit advertising.

[22] Usury laws provide the most obvious examples of state regulation of the subprime market.

[23] Lending practices in Mississippi, "where there currently is no legal usury rate," support this conclusion: in that State, subprime lenders charge rates "as high as 30 to 40%"—well above the rates that apparently suffice to support the industry in States like Indiana. Norberg, Consumer Bankruptcy's New Clothes: An Empirical Study of Discharge and Debt Collection in Chapter 13, 7 Am. Bankr.Inst. L.Rev. 415, 438-439 (1999).

[24] See also H.R.Rep. No. 1040, 90th Cong., 1st Sess., 17 (1967) ("The basic premise of the application of disclosure standards to credit advertising rests in the belief that a substantial portion of consumer purchases are induced by such advertising and that if full disclosure is not made in such advertising, the consumer will be deprived of the opportunity to effectively comparison shop for credit").

[25] The United States, too, notes that "[t]he text of Section 1325 is consistent with the view that the appropriate discount rate should reflect only the time value of money and not any risk premium." Brief for United States as *Amicus Curiae* 11, n. 4. The remainder of the United States' brief, however, advocates the formula approach. See, *e.g., id.,* at 19-28.

Chapter 13's protections to be so effective as to make the risk of default negligible. Because our decision in *Rash* assumes that cram down interest rates are adjusted to "offset," to the extent possible, the risk of default, and because so many judges who have considered the issue (including the authors of the four earlier opinions in this case) have rejected the risk-free approach, we think it too late in the day to endorse that approach now. Of course, if the text of the statute required such an approach, that would be the end of the matter. We think, however, that § 1325(a)(5)(B)(ii)'s reference to "value, as of the effective date of the plan, of property to be distributed under the plan" is better read to incorporate all of the commonly understood components of "present value," including any risk of nonpayment. Justice THOMAS' reading does emphasize, though, that a presumption that bankruptcy plans will succeed is more consistent with Congress' statutory scheme than the dissent's more cynical focus on bankrupt debtors' "financial instability and. . . proclivity to seek legal protection."

Furthermore, the dissent's two assumptions do not necessarily favor the presumptive contract rate approach. For one thing, the cram down provision applies not only to subprime loans but also to prime loans negotiated prior to the change in circumstance (job loss, for example) that rendered the debtor insolvent. Relatedly, the provision also applies in instances in which national or local economic conditions drastically improved or declined after the original loan was issued but before the debtor filed for bankruptcy. In either case, there is every reason to think that a properly risk-adjusted prime rate will provide a better estimate of the creditor's current costs and exposure than a contract rate set in different times.

Even more important, if all relevant information about the debtor's circumstances, the creditor's circumstances, the nature of the collateral, and the market for comparable loans were equally available to both debtor and creditor, then in theory the formula and presumptive contract rate approaches would yield the same final interest rate. Thus, we principally differ with the dissent not over what final rate courts should adopt but over which party (creditor or debtor) should bear the burden of rebutting the presumptive rate (prime or contract, respectively).

Justice SCALIA identifies four "relevant factors bearing on risk premium[:] (1) the probability of plan failure; (2) the rate of collateral depreciation; (3) the liquidity of the collateral market; and (4) the administrative expenses of enforcement." In our view, any information debtors have about any of these factors is likely to be included in their bankruptcy filings, while the remaining information will be far more accessible to creditors (who must collect information about their lending markets to remain competitive) than to individual debtors (whose only experience with those markets might be the single loan at issue in the case). Thus, the formula approach, which begins with a concededly low estimate of the appropriate interest rate and requires the creditor to present evidence supporting a higher rate, places the evidentiary burden on the more knowledgeable party, thereby facilitating more accurate calculation of the appropriate interest rate.

If the rather sketchy data uncovered by the dissent support an argument that Chapter 13 of the Bankruptcy Code should mandate application of the presumptive contract rate approach (rather than merely an argument that bankruptcy judges should exercise greater caution before approving debt adjustment plans), those data should be forwarded to Congress. We are not persuaded, however, that the data undermine our interpretation of the statutory scheme Congress has enacted.

The judgment of the Court of Appeals is reversed, and the case is remanded with instructions to remand the case to the Bankruptcy Court for further proceedings consistent with this opinion.

*It is so ordered.*

■ Justice THOMAS, concurring in the judgment.

This case presents the issue of what the proper method is for discounting deferred payments to present value and what compensation the creditor is entitled to in calculating the appropriate discount rate of interest. Both the plurality and the dissent agree that "[a] debtor's promise of future payments is worth less than an immediate payment of the same total amount because the creditor cannot use the money right away, inflation may cause the value of the dollar to decline before the debtor pays, and there is always some risk of nonpayment." Thus, the plurality and the dissent agree that the proper method for discounting deferred payments to present value should take into account each of these factors, but disagree over the proper starting point for calculating the risk of nonpayment.

I agree that a "*promise* of future payments is worth less than an immediate payment" of the same amount, in part because of the risk of nonpayment. But this fact is irrelevant. The statute does not require that the value of the *promise* to distribute property under the plan be no less than the allowed amount of the secured creditor's claim. It requires only that "the value. . . of *property* to be distributed under the plan," at the time of the effective date of the plan, be no less than the amount of the secured creditor's claim. 11 U.S.C. § 1325(a)(5)(B)(ii) (emphasis added). Both the plurality and the dissent ignore the clear text of the statute in an apparent rush to ensure that secured creditors are not undercompensated in bankruptcy proceedings. But the statute that Congress enacted does not require a debtor-specific risk adjustment that would put secured creditors in the same position as if they had made another loan. It is for this reason that I write separately.

## I

"It is well established that 'when the statute's language is plain, the sole function of the courts—at least where the disposition required by the text is not absurd—is to enforce it according to its terms.'" [citation omitted]. Section 1325(a)(5)(B) provides that "with respect to each allowed secured claim provided for by the plan," "the value, as of the effective date of the plan, of property to be distributed under the plan on account of such claim [must] not [be] less than the allowed amount of such claim." Thus, the statute requires a bankruptcy court to make at least three separate determinations. First, a court must determine the allowed amount of the claim. Second, a court must determine what is the "property to be distributed under the plan." Third, a court must determine the "value, as of the effective date of the plan," of the property to be distributed.

The dispute in this case centers on the proper method to determine the "value, as of the effective date of the plan, of property to be distributed under the plan." The requirement that the "value" of the property to be distributed be determined "as of the effective date of the plan" incorporates the principle of the time value of money. To put it simply, $4,000 today is worth more than $4,000 to be received 17 months from today because if received today, the $4,000 can be invested to start earning interest immediately.[1] *See* Encyclopedia of Banking & Finance 1015 (9th ed. 1991). Thus, as we explained in *Rake v. Wade*, "[w]hen a claim is paid off pursuant to a stream of future payments, a creditor receives the 'present value' of its claim only if the total amount of the deferred payments includes the amount of the underlying claim plus an appropriate amount of interest to compensate the creditor for the decreased value of the claim caused by the delayed payments."

Respondent argues, and the plurality and the dissent agree, that the proper interest rate must also reflect the risk of nonpayment. But the statute contains no such requirement. The statute only requires the valuation of the "property to be distributed," not the valuation of the plan (*i.e.,* the promise to make the payments itself). Thus, in order for a plan to satisfy § 1325(a)(5)(B)(ii), the plan need only propose an interest rate that will compensate a creditor for the fact that if he had received the property immediately rather than at a future date, he could have immediately made use of the property. In most, if not all, cases, where the plan proposes simply a stream of cash payments, the appropriate risk-free rate should suffice.

Respondent here would certainly be acutely aware of any risk of default inherent in a Chapter 13 plan, but it is nonsensical to speak of a debtor's risk of default being inherent in the value of "property" unless that property is a promise or a debt. Suppose, for instance, that it is currently time A, the property to be distributed is a house, and it will be distributed at time B. Although market conditions might cause the value of the house to fluctuate between time A and time B, the fluctuating value of the house itself has nothing to do with the risk that the debtor will not de-

---

[1] For example, if the relevant interest rate is 10%, receiving $4,000 one year from now is the equivalent to receiving $3,636.36 today. In other words, an investor would be indifferent to receiving $3,636.36 today and receiving $4,000 one year from now because each will equal $4,000 one year from now.

liver the house at time B. The value of the house, then, can be and is determined entirely without any reference to any possibility that a promise to transfer the house would not be honored. So too, then, with cash: the value of the cash can be and is determined without any inclusion of any risk that the debtor will fail to transfer the cash at the appropriate time.

The dissent might be correct that the use of the prime rate,[2] even with a small risk adjustment, "will systematically undercompensate secured creditors for the true risks of default."[3] This systematic undercompensation might seem problematic as a matter of policy. But, it raises no problem as a matter of statutory interpretation. Thus, although there is always some risk of nonpayment when A promises to repay a debt to B through a stream of payments over time rather than through an immediate lump sum payment, § 1325(a)(5)(B)(ii) does not take this risk into account.

This is not to say that a debtor's risk of nonpayment can never be a factor in determining the value of the property to be distributed. Although "property" is not defined in the Bankruptcy Code, nothing in § 1325 suggests that "property" is limited to cash. Rather, "'property' can be cash, notes, stock, personal property or real property; in short, anything of value." 7 Collier on Bankruptcy ¶ 1129.03 [b][i], p. 1129-44 (15th ed.2003) (discussing Chapter 11's cram down provision). And if the "property to be distributed" under a Chapter 13 plan is a note (*i.e.,* a promise to pay), for instance, the value of that note necessarily includes the risk that the debtor will not make good on that promise. Still, accounting for the risk of nonpayment in that case is not equivalent to reading a risk adjustment requirement into the statute, as in the case of a note, the risk of nonpayment is part of the value of the note itself.

Respondent argues that "Congress crafted the requirements of section 1325(a)(5)(B)(ii) for the protection of *creditors,* not debtors," and thus that the relevant interest rate must account for the true risks and costs associated with a Chapter 13 debtor's promise of future payment. Brief for Respondent 24. In addition to ignoring the plain language of the statute, which requires no such risk adjustment, respondent overlooks the fact that secured creditors are already compensated in part for the risk of nonpayment through the valuation of the secured claim. In *Associates Commercial Corp. v. Rash,* we utilized a secured-creditor-friendly replacement-value standard rather than the lower foreclosure-value standard for valuing secured claims when a debtor has exercised Chapter 13's cram down option. We did so because the statute at issue in that case reflected Congress' recognition that "[i]f a debtor keeps the property and continues to use it, the creditor obtains at once neither the property nor its value and is ex-

---

[2] The prime rate is "[t]he interest rate most closely approximating the riskless or pure rate for money." Encyclopedia of Banking & Finance 830 (9th ed.1991).

[3] Of course, in an efficient market, this risk has been (or will be) built into the interest rate of the original loan.

posed to double risks: The debtor may again default and the property may deteriorate from extended use."

Further, the plain language of the statute is by no means specifically debtor protective. As the Court [has] pointed out, § 1325 contains a number of provisions to protect creditors: A bankruptcy court can only authorize a plan that "has been proposed in good faith," § 1325(a)(3); secured creditors must accept the plan, obtain the property securing the claim, or "retain the[ir] lien[s]" and receive under the plan distributions of property which equal "not less than the allowed amount of such claim," § 1325(a)(5); and a bankruptcy court must ensure that "the debtor will be able to make all payments under the plan and to comply with the plan," § 1325(a)(6). Given the presence of multiple creditor-specific protections, it is by no means irrational to assume that Congress opted not to provide further protection for creditors by requiring a debtor-specific risk adjustment under § 1325(a)(5). Although the dissent may feel that this is insufficient compensation for secured creditors, given the apparent rate at which debtors fail to complete their Chapter 13 plans, this is a matter that should be brought to the attention of Congress rather than resolved by this Court.

## II

The allowed amount of the secured claim is $4,000. The statute then requires a bankruptcy court to identify the "property to be distributed" under the plan. Petitioners' Amended Chapter 13 Plan (Plan) provided:

"The future earnings of DEBTOR(S) are submitted to the supervision and control of this Court, and DEBTOR(S) shall pay to the TRUSTEE a sum of $740 per month in weekly installments by voluntary wage assignment by separate ORDER of the Court in an estimated amount of $170.77 and continuing for a total plan term of 36 months unless this Court approves an extension of the term not beyond 60 months from the date of filing the Petition herein."

From the payments received, the trustee would then make disbursements to petitioners' creditors, pro rata among each class of creditors. The Plan listed one priority claim and four secured claims. For respondent's secured claim, petitioner proposed an interest rate of 9.5%. Thus, petitioners proposed to distribute to respondent a stream of cash payments equaling respondent's pro rata share of $740 per month for a period of up to 36 months.

Although the Plan does not specifically state that "the property to be distributed" under the Plan is cash payments, the cash payments are the only "property" specifically listed for distribution under the Plan. Thus, although the plurality and the dissent imply that the "property to be distributed" under the Plan is the mere *promise* to make cash payments, the plain language of the Plan indicates that the "property to be distributed" to respondent is up to 36 monthly cash payments, consisting of a pro rata share of $740 per month.

The final task, then, is to determine whether petitioners' proposed 9.5% interest rate will sufficiently compensate respondent for the fact that instead of receiving $4,000 today, it will receive $4,000 plus 9.5% interest over a period of up to 36 months. Because the 9.5% rate is higher than the risk-free rate, I conclude that it will. I would therefore reverse the judgment of the Court of Appeals.

■　Justice SCALIA, with whom the Chief Justice, Justice O'CONNOR, and Justice KENNEDY Join, Dissenting.

My areas of agreement with the plurality are substantial. We agree that, although all confirmed Chapter 13 plans have been deemed feasible by a bankruptcy judge, some nevertheless fail. We agree that any deferred payments to a secured creditor must fully compensate it for the risk that such a failure will occur. Finally, we agree that adequate compensation may sometimes require an "'eye-popping'" interest rate, and that, if the rate is too high for the plan to succeed, the appropriate course is not to reduce it to a more palatable level, but to refuse to confirm the plan.

Our only disagreement is over what procedure will more often produce accurate estimates of the appropriate interest rate. The plurality would use the prime lending rate—a rate we *know* is too low—and require the judge in every case to determine an amount by which to increase it. I believe that, in practice, this approach will systematically undercompensate secured creditors for the true risks of default. I would instead adopt the contract rate—*i.e.,* the rate at which the creditor actually loaned funds to the debtor—as a presumption that the bankruptcy judge could revise on motion of either party. Since that rate is generally a good indicator of actual risk, disputes should be infrequent, and it will provide a quick and reasonably accurate standard.

## I

The contract-rate approach makes two assumptions, both of which are reasonable. First, it assumes that subprime lending markets are competitive and therefore largely efficient. If so, the high interest rates lenders charge reflect not extortionate profits or excessive costs, but the actual risks of default that subprime borrowers present. Lenders with excessive rates would be undercut by their competitors, and inefficient ones would be priced out of the market. We have implicitly assumed market competitiveness in other bankruptcy contexts. *See Bank of America Nat. Trust and Sav. Assn. v. 203 North LaSalle Street Partnership,* 526 U.S. 434, 456-458 (1999). Here the assumption is borne out by empirical evidence: One study reports that subprime lenders are nearly twice as likely to be unprofitable as banks, suggesting a fiercely competitive environment. *See* J. Lane, Associate Director, Division of Supervision, Federal Deposit Insurance Corporation, A Regulator's View of Subprime Lending: Address at the National Automotive Finance Association Non-Prime Auto Lending Conference 6 (June 18-19, 2002) (available in Clerk of Court's case file). By relying on the prime rate, the plurality implicitly assumes that the *prime* lending market is efficient; I see no reason not to make a similar assumption about the *sub*prime lending market.

The second assumption is that the expected costs of default in Chapter 13 are normally no less than those at the time of lending. This assumption is also reasonable. Chapter 13 plans often fail. I agree with petitioners that the relevant statistic is the percentage of *confirmed* plans that fail, but even resolving that issue in their favor, the risk is still substantial. The failure rate they offer—which we may take to be a conservative estimate, as it is doubtless the lowest one they could find—is 37%. *See* Girth, *The Role of Empirical Data in Developing Bankruptcy Legislation for Individuals,* 65 Ind. L.J. 17, 40-42 (1989) (reporting a 63.1% success rate).[1] In every one of the failed plans making up that 37%, a bankruptcy judge had found that "the debtor will be able to make all payments under the plan," 11 U.S.C. § 1325(a)(6), and a trustee had supervised the debtor's compliance, § 1302. That so many nonetheless failed proves that bankruptcy judges are not oracles and that trustees cannot draw blood from a stone.

While court and trustee oversight may provide some marginal benefit to the creditor, it seems obviously outweighed by the fact that (1) an already-bankrupt borrower has demonstrated a financial instability and a proclivity to seek legal protection that other subprime borrowers have not, and (2) the costs of foreclosure are substantially higher in bankruptcy because the automatic stay bars repossession without judicial permission. It does not strike me as plausible that creditors would *prefer* to lend to individuals already in bankruptcy than to those for whom bankruptcy is merely a possibility—as if Chapter 13 were widely viewed by secured creditors as some sort of godsend. Certainly the record in this case contradicts that implausible proposition. *See* App. 48 (testimony of Craig Cook, sales manager of Instant Auto Finance) ("Q. Are you aware of how other lenders similar to Instant Auto Finance view credit applicants who appear to be candidates for Chapter 13 bankruptcy?" "A. Negative[ly] as well").

---

[1] The true rate of plan failure is almost certainly much higher. The Girth study that yielded the 37% figure was based on data for a single division (Buffalo, New York) from over 20 years ago (1980-1982). See 65 Ind. L. J., at 41. A later study concluded that "the Buffalo division ha [d] achieved extraordinary results, far from typical for the country as a whole." Whitford, The Ideal of Individualized Justice: Consumer Bankruptcy as Consumer Protection, and Consumer Protection in Consumer Bankruptcy, 68 Am. Bankr.L.J. 397, 411, n. 50 (1994). Although most of respondent's figures are based on studies that do not clearly exclude unconfirmed plans, one study includes enough detail to make the necessary correction: It finds 32% of filings successful, 18% dismissed without confirmation of a plan, and 49% dismissed after confirmation, for a postconfirmation failure rate of 60% (*i.e.,* 49%/(32% + 49%)). See Norberg, Consumer Bankruptcy's New Clothes: An Empirical Study of Discharge and Debt Collection in Chapter 13, 7 Am. Bankr.Inst. L.Rev. 415, 440-441 (1999). This 60% failure rate is far higher than the 37% reported by Girth.

The better assumption is that bankrupt debtors are riskier than other sub-prime debtors—or, at the very least, not systematically *less* risky.

The first of the two assumptions means that the contract rate reasonably reflects actual risk at the time of borrowing. The second means that this risk persists when the debtor files for Chapter 13. It follows that the contract rate is a decent estimate, or at least the lower bound, for the appropriate interest rate in cramdown.[2]

The plurality disputes these two assumptions. It argues that subprime lending markets are not competitive because "vehicles are regularly sold by means of tie-in transactions, in which the price of the vehicle is the subject of negotiation, while the terms of the financing are dictated by the seller." [3] Tie-ins do not *alone* make financing markets noncompetitive; they only cause prices and interest rates to be considered *in tandem* rather than separately. The force of the plurality's argument depends entirely on its claim that "the terms of the financing are dictated by the seller." *Ibid.* This unsubstantiated assertion is contrary to common experience. Car sellers routinely advertise their interest rates, offer promotions like "zero-percent financing," and engage in other behavior that plainly assumes customers are sensitive to interest rates and not just price.[4]

---

[2] The contract rate is only a presumption, however, and either party remains free to prove that a higher or lower rate is appropriate in a particular case. For example, if market interest rates generally have risen or fallen since the contract was executed, the contract rate could be adjusted by the same amount in cases where the difference was substantial enough that a party chose to make an issue of it.

[3] To the extent the plurality argues that subprime lending markets are not "*perfectly* competitive," (emphasis added), I agree. But there is no reason to doubt they are *reasonably* competitive, so that pricing in those markets is *reasonably* efficient.

[4] I confess that this is "nonresponsive" to the argument made in the plurality's footnote (that the contract interest rate may not accurately reflect risk when set jointly with a car's sale price), see *ante,* at n. 20; it is in response to the quite different argument made in the plurality's text (that joint pricing shows that the subprime lending market is not competitive). As to the *former* issue, the plurality's footnote makes a fair point. When the seller provides financing itself, there is a possibility that the contract interest rate might not reflect actual risk because a higher contract interest rate can be traded off for a lower sale price and vice versa. Nonetheless, this fact is not likely to bias the contract-rate approach in favor of creditors to any significant degree. If a creditor offers a promotional interest rate—such as "zero-percent financing"—in return for a higher sale price, the creditor bears the burden of showing that the true interest rate is higher than the contract rate. The opposite tactic—inflating the interest rate and decreasing the sale price—is constrained at some level by the buyer's option to finance through a third party, thus taking advantage of the lower price while avoiding the higher interest rate. (If a seller were to condition a price discount on providing the financing itself, the debtor should be entitled to rely on that condition to rebut the presumption that the contract rate reflects actual risk.) Finally, the debtor remains free to rebut the contract rate with any other probative evidence. While joint pricing may introduce some inaccuracy, the contract rate is still a far better initial estimate than the prime rate.

The plurality also points to state and federal regulation of lending markets. It claims that state usury laws evince a belief that subprime lending markets are noncompetitive. While that is one *conceivable* explanation for such laws, there are countless others. One statistical and historical study suggests that usury laws are a "primitive means of social insurance" meant to ensure "low interest rates" for those who suffer financial adversity. Glaeser & Scheinkman, Neither a Borrower Nor a Lender Be: An Economic Analysis of Interest Restrictions and Usury Laws, 41 J. Law & Econ. 1, 26 (1998). Such a rationale does not reflect a belief that lending markets are inefficient, any more than rent controls reflect a belief that real estate markets are inefficient. Other historical rationales likewise shed no light on the point at issue here. The mere existence of usury laws is therefore weak support for any position.

The federal Truth in Lending Act, 15 U.S.C. § 1601 *et seq.,* not only fails to support the plurality's position; it positively refutes it. The plurality claims the Act reflects a belief that full disclosure promotes competition; the Act itself says as much. But that belief obviously *presumes* markets are competitive (or, at least, that they were noncompetitive only because of the absence of the disclosures the Act now requires). If lending markets were not competitive—if the terms of financing were indeed "dictated by the seller,"—disclosure requirements would be pointless, since consumers would have no use for the information.[5]

As to the second assumption (that the expected costs of default in Chapter 13 are normally no less than those at the time of lending), the plurality responds, not that Chapter 13 *as currently administered* is less risky than subprime lending generally, but that it *would* be less risky, if only bankruptcy courts would confirm fewer risky plans. *Ante,* at 1963. Of course, it is often quite difficult to predict which plans will fail. *See* Norberg, Consumer Bankruptcy's New Clothes: An Empirical Study of Discharge and Debt Collection in Chapter 13, 7 Am. Bankr.Inst. L.Rev. 415, 462 (1999). But even assuming the high failure rate primarily reflects judicial dereliction rather than unavoidable uncertainty, the plurality's argument fails for want of any reason to believe the dereliction will abate. While full compensation can be attained either by low-risk plans and low interest rates, or by high-risk plans and high interest rates, it cannot be attained by *high*-risk plans and *low* interest rates, which, absent cause to anticipate a change in confirmation practices, is precisely what the formula approach would yield.

The plurality also claims that the contract rate overcompensates creditors because it includes "transaction costs and overall profits." But the

---

[5] The plurality also argues that regulatory context is relevant because it "distorts the market." Federal disclosure requirements do not distort the market in any meaningful sense. And while state usury laws do, that distortion works only to the benefit of debtors under the contract-rate approach, since it keeps contract rates artificially low.

same is true of the rate the plurality prescribes: The prime lending rate includes banks' overhead and profits. These are necessary components of *any* commercial lending rate, since creditors will not lend money if they cannot cover their costs and return a level of profit sufficient to prevent their investors from going elsewhere. *See Koopmans v. Farm Credit Services of Mid-America, ACA,* 102 F.3d 874, 876 (C.A.7 1996). The plurality's criticism might have force if there were reason to believe subprime lenders made exorbitant profits while banks did not—but, again, the data suggest otherwise. *See* Lane, Regulator's View of Subprime Lending, at 6.[6]

Finally, the plurality objects that similarly situated creditors might not be treated alike. But the contract rate is only a presumption. If a judge thinks it necessary to modify the rate to avoid unjustified disparity, he can do so. For example, if two creditors charged different rates solely because they lent to the debtor at different times, the judge could average the rates or use the more recent one. The plurality's argument might be valid against an approach that *irrebuttably* presumes the contract rate, but that is not what I propose.[7]

## II

The defects of the formula approach far outweigh those of the contract-rate approach. The formula approach starts with the prime lending rate—a number that, while objective and easily ascertainable, is indis-

---

[6] Some transaction costs are avoided by the creditor in bankruptcy—for example, loan-origination costs such as advertising. But these are likely only a minor component of the interest rate. According to the record in this case, for example, the average interest rate on new-car loans was roughly 8.5%—only about 0.5% higher than the prime rate and 2.5% higher than the risk-free treasury rate. App. 43 (testimony of Professor Steve Russell). And the 2% difference between prime and treasury rates represented "mostly. . . risk [and] to some extent transaction costs." *Id.,* at 42. These figures suggest that loan-origination costs included in the new-car loan and prime rates but not in the treasury rate are likely only a fraction of a percent. There is no reason to think they are substantially higher in the subprime auto lending market. Any transaction costs the creditor avoids in bankruptcy are thus far less than the additional ones he incurs.

[7] The plurality's other, miscellaneous criticisms do not survive scrutiny either. That the cramdown provision applies to prime as well as subprime loans, proves nothing. Nor is there any substance to the argument that the formula approach will perform better where "national or local economic conditions drastically improved or declined after the original loan was issued." To the extent such economic changes are reflected by changes in the prime rate, the contract rate can be adjusted by the same amount. See n. 2, *supra.* And to the extent they are not, they present the same problem under either approach: When a party disputes the presumption, the court must gauge the significance of the economic change and adjust accordingly. The difference, again, is that the contract-rate approach starts with a number that (but for the economic change) is reasonably accurate, while the formula approach starts with a number that (with or without the economic change) is not even close.

putably too low. It then adjusts by adding a risk premium that, unlike the prime rate, is neither objective nor easily ascertainable. If the risk premium is typically small relative to the prime rate—as the 1.5% premium added to the 8% prime rate by the court below would lead one to believe—then this subjective element of the computation might be forgiven. But in fact risk premiums, if properly computed, would typically be substantial. For example, if the 21% contract rate is an accurate reflection of risk in this case, the risk premium would be 13%—nearly two-thirds of the total interest rate. When the risk premium is the greater part of the overall rate, the formula approach no longer depends on objective and easily ascertainable numbers. The prime rate becomes the objective tail wagging a dog of unknown size.

As I explain below, the most relevant factors bearing on risk premium are (1) the probability of plan failure; (2) the rate of collateral depreciation; (3) the liquidity of the collateral market; and (4) the administrative expenses of enforcement. Under the formula approach, a risk premium must be computed in every case, so judges will invariably grapple with these imponderables. Under the contract-rate approach, by contrast, the task of assessing all these risk factors is entrusted to the entity most capable of undertaking it: the market. *See Bank of America*, 526 U.S., at 457 ("[T]he best way to determine value is exposure to a market"). All the risk factors are reflected (assuming market efficiency) in the debtor's contract rate—a number readily found in the loan document. If neither party disputes it, the bankruptcy judge's task is at an end. There are straightforward ways a debtor *could* dispute it—for example, by showing that the creditor is now substantially oversecured, or that some other lender is willing to extend credit at a lower rate. But unlike the formula approach, which requires difficult estimation in every case, the contract-rate approach requires it only when the parties choose to contest the issue.

The plurality defends the formula approach on the ground that creditors have better access to the relevant information. But this is not a case where we must choose between one initial estimate that is too low and another that is too high. Rather, the choice is between one that is far too low and another that is generally reasonably accurate (or, if anything, a bit too low). In these circumstances, consciously choosing the less accurate estimate merely because creditors have better information smacks more of policymaking than of faithful adherence to the statutory command that the secured creditor receive property worth "*not less than* the allowed amount" of its claim, 11 U.S.C. § 1325(a)(5)(B)(ii) (emphasis added). Moreover, the plurality's argument assumes it is plausible—and desirable—that the issue will be litigated in most cases. But the costs of conducting a detailed risk analysis and defending it in court are prohibitively high in relation to the amount at stake in most consumer loan cases. Whatever approach we prescribe, the norm should be—and undoubtedly will be—that the issue is not litigated because it is not worth litigating. Given this reality, it is far more important that the initial estimate be accurate than that the burden of proving inaccuracy fall on the better informed party.

There is no better demonstration of the inadequacies of the formula approach than the proceedings in this case. Petitioners' economics expert testified that the 1.5% risk premium was "very reasonable" because Chapter 13 plans are "supposed to be financially feasible" and "the borrowers are under the supervision of the court." Nothing in the record shows how these two platitudes were somehow manipulated to arrive at a figure of 1.5%. It bears repeating that feasibility determinations and trustee oversight do not prevent at least 37% of confirmed Chapter 13 plans from failing. On cross-examination, the expert admitted that he had only limited familiarity with the subprime auto lending market and that he was not familiar with the default rates or the costs of collection in that market. In light of these devastating concessions, it is impossible to view the 1.5% figure as anything other than a smallish number picked out of a hat.

Based on even a rudimentary financial analysis of the facts of this case, the 1.5% figure is obviously wrong—not just off by a couple percent, but probably by roughly an order of magnitude. For a risk premium to be adequate, a hypothetical, rational creditor must be indifferent between accepting (1) the proposed risky stream of payments over time and (2) immediate payment of its present value in a lump sum. Whether he is indifferent—*i.e.,* whether the risk premium added to the prime rate is adequate—can be gauged by comparing benefits and costs: on the one hand, the expected value of the extra interest, and on the other, the expected costs of default.

Respondent was offered a risk premium of 1.5% on top of the prime rate of 8%. If that premium were fully paid as the plan contemplated, it would yield about $60.[8] If the debtor defaulted, all or part of that interest would not be paid, so the expected value is only about $50.[9] The prime rate itself already includes some compensation for risk; as it turns out, about the same amount, yielding another $50.[10] Given the 1.5% risk pre-

---

[8] Given its priority, and in light of the amended plan's reduced debtor contributions, the $4,000 secured claim would be fully repaid by about the end of the second year of the plan. The average balance over that period would be about $2,000, *i.e.,* half the initial balance. The total interest premium would therefore be 1.5% x 2 x $2,000 = $60. In this and all following calculations, I do not adjust for time value, as timing effects have no substantial effect on the conclusion.

[9] Assuming a 37% rate of default that results on average in only half the interest's being paid, the expected value is $60 x (1—37%/2), or about $50.

[10] According to the record in this case, the prime rate at the time of filing was 2% higher than the risk-free treasury rate, and the difference represented "mostly. . . risk [and] to some extent transaction costs." App. 42 (testimony of Professor Steve Russell); see also Federal Reserve Board, Selected Interest Rates, http:// www.federalreserve.gov/releases/ h15/data.htm (as visited Apr. 19, 2004) (available in Clerk of Court's case file) (historical data showing prime rate typically exceeding

mium, then, the total expected benefit to respondent was about $100. Against this we must weigh the expected costs of default. While precise calculations are impossible, rough estimates convey a sense of their scale.

The first cost of default involves depreciation. If the debtor defaults, the creditor can eventually repossess and sell the collateral, but by then it may be substantially less valuable than the remaining balance due—and the debtor may stop paying long before the creditor receives permission to repossess. When petitioners purchased their truck in this case, its value was almost equal to the principal balance on the loan.[11] By the time the plan was confirmed, however, the truck was worth only $4,000, while the balance on the loan was $4,895. If petitioners were to default on their Chapter 13 payments and if respondent suffered the same relative loss from depreciation, it would amount to about $550.[12]

The second cost of default involves liquidation. The $4,000 to which respondent would be entitled if paid in a lump sum reflects the *replacement* value of the vehicle, *i.e.,* the amount it would cost the debtor to purchase a similar used truck. If the debtor defaults, the creditor cannot sell the truck for that amount; it receives only a lesser *foreclosure* value because collateral markets are not perfectly liquid and there is thus a spread between what a buyer will pay and what a seller will demand. The foreclosure value of petitioners' truck is not in the record, but, using the relative liquidity figures in *Rash* as a rough guide, respondent would suffer a further loss of about $450.[13]

The third cost of default consists of the administrative expenses of foreclosure. While a Chapter 13 plan is in effect, the automatic stay prevents secured creditors from repossessing their collateral, even if the debtor fails to pay. The creditor's attorney must move the bankruptcy court to lift the stay. In the District where this case arose, the filing fee for such motions is now $150. *See* United States Bankruptcy Court for the Southern District of Indiana, Schedule of Bankruptcy Fees (Nov. 1, 2003) (available in Clerk of Court's case file). And the standard attorney's fee

---

3-month constant-maturity treasury rate by 2%- 3.5%). If "mostly" means about three-quarters of 2%, then the risk compensation included in the prime rate is 1.5%. Because this figure happens to be the same as the risk premium over prime, the expected value is similarly $50. See nn. 8-9, *supra.*

[11] The truck was initially worth $6,395; the principal balance on the loan was about $6,426.

[12] On the original loan, depreciation ($6,395—$4,000, or $2,395) exceeded loan repayment ($6,426—$4,895, or $1,531) by $864, *i.e.,* 14% of the original truck value of $6,395. Applying the same percentage to the new $4,000 truck value yields approximately $550.

[13] The truck in *Rash* had a replacement value of $41,000 and a foreclosure value of $31,875, *i.e.,* 22% less. 520 U.S., at 957. If the market in this case had similar liquidity and the truck were repossessed after losing half its remaining value, the loss would be 22% of $2,000, or about $450.

for such motions, according to one survey, is $350 in Indiana and as high as $875 in other States. *See* J. Cossitt, Chapter 13 Attorney Fee Survey, American Bankruptcy Institute Annual Spring Meeting (Apr. 10-13, 2003) (available in Clerk of Court's case file). Moreover, bankruptcy judges will often excuse first offenses, so foreclosure may require multiple trips to court. The total expected administrative expenses in the event of default could reasonably be estimated at $600 or more.

I have omitted several other costs of default, but the point is already adequately made. The three figures above total $1,600. Even accepting petitioners' low estimate of the plan failure rate, a creditor choosing the stream of future payments instead of the immediate lump sum would be selecting an alternative with an expected cost of about $590 ($1,600 multiplied by 37%, the chance of failure) and an expected benefit of about $100 (as computed above). No rational creditor would make such a choice. The risk premium over prime necessary to make these costs and benefits equal is in the neighborhood of 16%, for a total interest rate of 24%.[14]

Of course, many of the estimates I have made can be disputed. Perhaps the truck will depreciate more slowly now than at first, perhaps the collateral market is more liquid than the one in *Rash,* perhaps respondent can economize on attorney's fees, and perhaps there is some reason (other than judicial optimism) to think the Tills were unlikely to default. I have made some liberal assumptions,[15] but also some conservative ones.[16] When a risk premium is off by an order of magnitude, one's estimates need not be very precise to show that it cannot possibly be correct.

In sum, the 1.5% premium adopted in this case is far below anything approaching fair compensation. That result is not unusual, see, *e.g., In re Valenti,* 105 F.3d 55, 64 (C.A.2 1997) (recommending a 1%-3% premium over the *treasury* rate—*i.e.,* approximately a 0% premium over prime); it is the entirely predictable consequence of a methodology that tells bankruptcy judges to set interest rates based on highly imponderable factors. Given the inherent uncertainty of the enterprise, what heartless bankruptcy judge can be expected to demand that the unfortunate debtor pay *triple* the prime rate as a condition of keeping his sole means of transportation? It challenges human nature.

---

[14] A 1.5% risk premium plus a 1.5% risk component in the prime rate yielded an expected benefit of about $100, so, to yield $590, the total risk compensation would have to be 5.9 times as high, *i.e.,* almost 18%, or a 16.5% risk premium over prime.

[15] For example, by ignoring the possibility that the creditor might recover some of its undersecurity as an unsecured claimant, that the plan might fail only after full repayment of secured claims, or that an oversecured creditor might recover some of its expenses under 11 U.S.C. § 506(b).

[16] For example, by assuming a failure rate of 37%, cf. n. 1, *supra,* and by ignoring all costs of default other than the three mentioned.

**III**

Justice THOMAS rejects both the formula approach and the contract-rate approach. He reads the statutory phrase "property to be distributed under the plan," 11 U.S.C. § 1325(a)(5)(B)(ii), to mean the proposed payments *if made as the plan contemplates,* so that the plan need only pay the risk-free rate of interest. I would instead read this phrase to mean the right to receive payments that the plan vests in the creditor upon confirmation. Because there is no guarantee that the promised payments will in fact be made, the value of this property right must account for the risk of non-payment.

Viewed in isolation, the phrase is susceptible of either meaning. Both the promise to make payments and the proposed payments themselves are property rights, the former "to be distributed under the plan" immediately upon confirmation, and the latter over the life of the plan. Context, however, supports my reading. The cramdown option which the debtors employed here is only one of three routes to confirmation. The other two—creditor acceptance and collateral surrender, § 1325(a)(5)(A), (C)—are both creditor protective, leaving the secured creditor roughly as well off as he would have been had the debtor not sought bankruptcy protection. Given this, it is unlikely the third option was meant to be substantially *under*protective; that would render it so much more favorable to debtors that few would ever choose one of the alternatives.

The risk-free approach also leads to anomalous results. Justice THOMAS admits that, if a plan distributes a note rather than cash, the value of the "property to be distributed" must reflect the risk of default on the note. But there is no practical difference between obligating the debtor to make deferred payments under a plan and obligating the debtor to sign a note that requires those same payments. There is no conceivable reason why Congress would give secured creditors risk compensation in one case but not the other.

Circuit authority uniformly rejects the risk-free approach. While Circuits addressing the issue are divided over *how* to calculate risk, to my knowledge all of them require some compensation for risk, either explicitly or implicitly. [citations omitted]. Justice THOMAS identifies no decision adopting his view.

Nor does our decision in *Rash* support the risk-free approach. There we considered whether a secured creditor's claim should be valued at what the debtor would pay to replace the collateral or at the lower price the creditor would receive from a foreclosure sale. Justice THOMAS contends that *Rash* selected the former in order to compensate creditors for the risk of plan failure, and that, having compensated them once in that context, we need not do so again here. I disagree with this reading of *Rash.* The Bankruptcy Code provides that "value shall be determined in light of the purpose of the valuation and of the proposed disposition or use of [the] property." 11 U.S.C. § 506(a). *Rash* held that the foreclosure-value approach failed to give effect to this language, because it assigned the same value whether the debtor surrendered the collateral or was allowed to retain it in exchange for promised payments. "From the creditor's perspective as well as the debtor's, surrender and retention are not equivalent acts." We did point out that retention entails risks for the creditor that surrender does not. But we made no effort to correlate that increased risk with the difference between replacement and foreclosure value. And we also pointed out that retention benefits the debtor by allowing him to continue to use the property—a factor we considered "[o]f prime significance." *Rash* stands for the proposition that surrender and retention are fundamentally different sorts of "disposition or use," calling for different valuations. Nothing in the opinion suggests that we thought the valuation difference reflected the degree of increased risk, or that we adopted the replacement-value standard *in order to compensate* for increased risk. To the contrary, we said that the debtor's "actual use . . . is the proper guide under a prescription hinged to the property's 'disposition or use.'"

If Congress wanted to compensate secured creditors for the risk of plan failure, it would not have done so by prescribing a particular method of valuing collateral. A plan may pose little risk even though the difference between foreclosure and replacement values is substantial, or great risk even though the valuation difference is small. For example, if a plan proposes immediate cash payment to the secured creditor, he is entitled to the higher replacement value under *Rash* even though he faces no risk at all. If the plan calls for deferred payments but the collateral consists of listed securities, the valuation difference may be trivial, but the creditor still faces substantial risks. And a creditor oversecured in even the slightest degree at the time of bankruptcy derives no benefit at all from *Rash*, but still faces some risk of collateral depreciation.[17]

There are very good reasons for Congress to prescribe full risk compensation for creditors. Every action in the free market has a reaction somewhere. If subprime lenders are systematically undercompensated in bankruptcy, they will charge higher rates or, if they already charge the legal maximum under state law, lend to fewer of the riskiest borrowers. As a result, some marginal but deserving borrowers will be denied vehicle loans in the first place. Congress evidently concluded that widespread access to credit is worth preserving, even if it means being ungenerous to sympathetic debtors.

---

[17] It is true that, if the debtor defaults, one of the costs the creditor suffers is the cost of liquidating the collateral. But it is illogical to "compensate" for this risk by requiring all plans to pay the full cost of liquidation (replacement value minus foreclosure value), rather than an amount that reflects the possibility that liquidation will actually be necessary and that full payments will not be made.

\* \* \*

Today's judgment is unlikely to burnish the Court's reputation for reasoned decisionmaking. Eight Justices are in agreement that the rate of interest set forth in the debtor's approved plan must include a premium for risk. Of those eight, four are of the view that beginning with the contract rate would most accurately reflect the actual risk, and four are of the view that beginning with the prime lending rate would do so. The ninth Justice takes no position on the latter point, since he disagrees with the eight on the former point; he would reverse because the rate proposed here, being above the risk-free rate, gave respondent no cause for complaint. Because I read the statute to require full risk compensation, and because I would adopt a valuation method that has a realistic prospect of enforcing that directive, I respectfully dissent.

## NOTES

**1.** The *Till* plurality opinion at n. 10 and accompanying text goes out of its way to note that nonconsensual deferred payment of secured claims under Chapter 11 and Chapter 12 reorganization plans ("cramdown") requires the bankruptcy court to fix a risk-adjusted interest rate based on statutory provisions that are parallel to § 1325(a)(5). But Justice Thomas in his separate concurrence and the four dissenting Justices make no direct reference to Chapter 11, and the plurality also notes at n. 14 that in Chapter 11 cases there may exist an efficient debtor-in-possession lending market that distinguishes corporate Chapter 11 cases from this case involving a treatment of a used car loan in Chapter 13. After *Till*, is the secured creditor cramdown standard the same in Chapter 11 as in Chapter 13? *See In re Prussia Associates*, 322 B.R. 572 (Bankr. E.D. Pa. 2005) (*Till* is persuasive not controlling authority in Chapter 11 cases) and *In re Cook*, 322 B.R. 336 (Bankr. W.D. Ohio 2005) (finding no opinion in *Till* whose reasoning commanded a majority of the Court or otherwise established controlling precedent).

**2.** Assuming arguendo that the *Till* plurality establishes a rule applicable in Chapter 11 cases what is the content of that rule? Is it that secured claims under feasible reorganization plans may be restructured at an interest rate equal to prime plus 1-3%, and that plans that would require higher (*i.e.* "eye-popping") rates should not be confirmed? Or is that the court should apply whatever risk-adjustment it believes is appropriate based on the evidence presented at trial? Or is it that the current market rate should be used so long as there is sufficient evidence of an "efficient market"?

**3.** Why does it matter that one establishes "present value" by starting with the contract rate and adjusting upward or downward based on changes in market interest rates, rather than by starting with the current "prime rate" and adjusting upward for risk? Shouldn't you end up in the same place—the current market rate for comparable loans?

**4.** Justice Thomas's view that the plain language of § 1325 does not authorize risk adjustment but rather only authorizes compensation for the time value of money (unless, apparently, the debtor's obligation is embodied in a "note" rather that a commitment to make the payments under a plan!), if applied to § 1129(b)(2), would be inconsistent with essentially all reorganization practice and caselaw developed under the absolute priority rule since *Northern Pacific Railway Co. v. Boyd*, 228 U.S. 482 (1913). Note that if Justice Thomas were to determine that risk adjustment is appropriate under § 1129(b) notwithstanding his construction of § 1325, and further that the *Till* dissenters' "presumptive contract rate" approach were the proper methodology, that position would command a majority of the current Justices.

## NOTE: CHAPTER 12—FAMILY FARMERS

The agricultural depression of the 1980s had roots in the inflation of the 1960s and 1970s when American farmers reacted to higher commodity prices by greatly increasing production. Production increases required additional capital and farm debt went from about $80 billion in 1960 to nearly $220 billion by the early 1980s. 1987 U.S.C.C.A.N. 2725. When commodity prices dropped in the 1980s, many farmers could not pay their debts and farm foreclosures were widespread. Congress reacted to the plight of over-extended farmers with the addition to the Bankruptcy Code of Chapter 12 on family farmer debt adjustment, effective November 26, 1986, and the enactment of the Agricultural Credit Act ("the ACA"), effective January 6, 1988, Public Law 100–233, 12 U.S.C. § 2001 et seq. One of the avowed objectives of the ACA is to keep farmers on the land. Among the ACA's debtor-protection provisions is one requiring federal farm credit system lenders to restructure loans of financially distressed farmers instead of foreclosing on collateral if the restructuring will produce more return to the creditor than will foreclosure. 12 U.S.C. § 2202(a). This provision requires these lenders, in appropriate cases, to meet with the debtor and attempt to effectuate a workout before foreclosing. *In re Hilton Land & Cattle Co.*, 101 B.R. 604 (D.Neb.1989), held that the restructuring requirement applies even if the debtor is in bankruptcy. In that case the debtor had filed a petition in Chapter 11 before the effective date of the ACA and the case was pending on the effective date. Courts of appeal have uniformly held that there is no private right of action under the ACA. E.g., *Wagner v. PennWest Farm Credit, ACA*, 109 F.3d 909 (3d Cir.1997). Some courts, nevertheless, permit farmers to block foreclosure by asserting that the creditor has failed to comply with the provisions of the ACA. See, e.g., *Western Farm Credit Bank v. Pratt*, 860 P.2d 376 (Utah App.1993); Grant Nelson & Dale Whitman, *Real Estate Finance Law* § 7.7 at 552 (4th ed. 2001).

According to the Administrative Office of the United States Courts, over 6,000 Chapter 12 cases were filed in 1987, but this number dropped to 2,034 in 1988, and has continued to decrease since. In 2004, only 108

Chapter 12 cases were filed throughout the United States. Clearly the decrease in filings reflects better economic times in the farm belt and decreasing importance of family farms in agricultural production, but the ACA's restructuring requirements, which became effective in 1988, may have been a factor as well.

Chapter 12 was thought necessary because neither Chapter 11 nor Chapter 13 met the needs of the financially distressed farmer. Farmers usually were not eligible for Chapter 13 because their secured debts exceeded $350,000, the ceiling under the version of § 109(e) in effect at that time. Application of the absolute priority rule of § 1129(b)(2) made Chapter 11 counterproductive for insolvent farmers in that it deprived them of any ownership interest in the farm unless all creditors consented. In *In re Ahlers*, 794 F.2d 388 (8th Cir.1986), the court attempted to alter the absolute priority rule by allowing farmers to count the promise of future services as value for the purpose of applying the *Los Angeles Lumber* exception to that rule. As we will see, p. 782, the Supreme Court squelched this attempt.

Chapter 12 is largely based on Chapter 13, but it incorporates some elements of Chapter 11. The debtor continues to operate the farm as a debtor in possession and can be removed only for cause. § 1203 and § 1204. Unlike Chapter 11, however, there is always a trustee in bankruptcy in Chapter 12. The trustee is usually a standing trustee appointed by the U.S. Trustee to serve in Chapter 12 cases. The duties of a Chapter 12 trustee are similar to those of a Chapter 13 trustee. The trustee's primary function is to disburse part or all of the payments required by the plan. In the unlikely event that the debtor is removed as debtor in possession, the trustee can operate the business. § 1202(b)(5). The plan must be filed not later than 90 days after the petition unless an extension is granted, and only the debtor can file a plan. § 1221. Normally the confirmation hearing must be concluded not later than 45 days after the plan if filed. § 1224. As is true in Chapter 13, creditors do not vote on the plan.

The plan may modify the rights of the holders of both secured and unsecured claims and may provide for curing prepetition defaults. § 1222(b). Chapter 12, like Chapter 13, allows secured claims to be written down to the value of the collateral and paid off with interest over a period of time. § 1225(a)(5). But there is a fundamental difference between the two chapters with respect to long-term secured debt. Long-term mortgage debt cannot be effectively dealt with in Chapter 13 except for curing of defaults. But a primary purpose of Chapter 12 is to allow the debtor to deal with long-term secured debt on the farm and farm equipment. This debt can be written down and restructured and paid off over a period of time that may exceed the normal three-year period for other payments under the plan. § 1222(b)(9). The period is not specifically limited by Chapter 12. There is no provision like § 1111(b) in Chapter 12. Unsecured claims are protected only by the best interests rule and discharged to the extent they are not paid from the debtor's disposable income over the three-year term of the plan. There is no absolute priority rule in Chapter 12—the debtor may retain ownership of the farm even if unsecured claims are not paid or receive property worth only a fraction of the claims.

A discharge comparable to that available in Chapter 13 is granted when the debtor completes the plan. § 1228(a). Hardship discharge is also provided for on terms similar to those stated in Chapter 13. § 1228(b) and (c). In recognition of the emergency nature of Chapter 12, Congress provided a seven-year sunset provision for the statute. Political interests serving the farm belt successfully ensured that the sun never set on Chapter 12 and the 2005 Act made the now rarely invoked Chapter 12 a permanent feature of the Code.

### b. Sale of Property

Suppose that rather than allow Lender to retain its lien and make deferred payments, Debtor's plan provided that the property be sold and Lender paid out of the proceeds. Under subparagraph (ii) of § 1129(b)(2)(A), the plan could provide for a sale of the collateral free of Lender's lien and for Lender to acquire a lien in the proceeds of sale. The sale, however, must be subject to § 363(k) which would allow Lender to protect its interest in its collateral by bidding the amount of its claim. If no one bids a higher amount, Lender could purchase the collateral by offsetting the purchase price against Lender's claim. If the collateral is purchased by someone else by bidding a higher amount, Lender obtains a lien in the cash proceeds that could be satisfied by payment in cash equal to Lender's secured claim, or that lien could be replaced by a substitute lien in other property to serve as security for deferred cash payments stated in subparagraph (i). The substitute lien would have to meet the requirement of indubitable equivalence in subparagraph (iii) discussed below.

### c. Indubitable Equivalence

Could Debtor's plan, in lieu of selling the property or making deferred payments with interest secured by Lender's pre-petition lien against all the property, surrender 2/3 of the property to Lender, judicially valued at $100,000 in full satisfaction of the secured claim? Under subparagraph (iii) the plan could provide "for the realization by [Lender] of the indubitable equivalent of [the secured claim]." The meaning of "indubitable equivalence" in a "dirt for debt" plan is discussed in the following case.

## In re Arnold & Baker Farms

United States Court of Appeals, Ninth Circuit, 1996.
85 F.3d 1415.

■ WILLIAM A. NORRIS, Circuit Judge:

Debtor Arnold and Baker Farms petitioned for relief under Chapter 11 and filed a plan of reorganization which proposed to satisfy the claims of the creditors by transferring real property to them—colloquially known as a "dirt for debt" plan. When Arnold and Baker's largest creditor, the Farmers Home Administration (FmHA), objected to the plan, Arnold and Baker invoked the "cram down" provision of the Bankruptcy Code, § 1129(b). The question presented is whether the plan's proposal to transfer to FmHA a portion of the collateral securing FmHA's claim will provide FmHA with the "indubitable equivalent" of its secured claim, as required by the "cram down" provision. See § 1129(b)(2)(A)(iii).

## I

We adopt and quote verbatim the statement of facts set forth by the Bankruptcy Appellate Panel:

> The debtor Arnold and Baker Farms is an Arizona general partnership. The partnership was formed. . . for the purpose of farming and the sale and lease of farmland. Arnold and Baker purchased 1120 acres from Philip and Dorothy Ladra in 1975 and an additional 320 acres in 1979. The Ladras were given a first deed of trust on the property. In 1977, the farm began to experience financial difficulties.

> [FmHA] and Western Cotton Services Corporation, a wholly owned subsidiary of Anderson Clayton Company, financed certain crops for the years 1978 through 1981. Additionally, FmHA lent Arnold and Baker sufficient funds to make the annual payments on the installments due to the Ladras in the years 1979, 1980, and 1983. In return, FmHA held a second deed of trust on Arnold and Baker's real property. . . . Western Cotton held a third deed of trust on Arnold and Baker's real property.

> The Ladras ultimately instituted a judicial foreclosure proceeding against Arnold and Baker's real property. Subsequently, in April 1984, the Bakers individually filed a voluntary petition for relief under Chapter 11 of the Bankruptcy Code. The Ladras obtained relief from the automatic stay and continued their judicial foreclosure proceedings. Arnold and Baker, the partnership, filed a voluntary petition for relief under Chapter 11 of the Bankruptcy Code in April 1986.

> In May 1986, the bankruptcy court approved the sale of two pieces of real property free and clear of liens: 360 acres of real property to Cardon Oil Company and 480 acres to the entity known as the Corks. From the net proceeds of the sale and the payment of annual installments, Arnold and Baker satisfied the secured claim of the Ladras in the amount of $1,650,000. FmHA thereafter held a first priority and Western Cotton held a second priority lien in the property.

> Arnold and Baker subsequently formulated two plans based on the income generated from the Cardon and Cork sales which proposed to pay in full the allowed claims of all creditors. The first plan was withdrawn when the Corks defaulted on their note and the other, a revised plan, was withdrawn when Cardon Oil defaulted on its note. With re-

spect to the Corks' default, Arnold and Baker negotiated a settlement pursuant to which the Corks tendered 360 acres to Arnold and Baker in lieu of foreclosure. With respect to the Cardon default, Arnold and Baker ultimately purchased the 320 acre parcel at a nonjudicial foreclosure.

In January 1991, Arnold and Baker filed a second amended plan and disclosure statement. The second amended plan proposed to pay FmHA's $3,837,618 note and Western Cotton's $565,044 note in full. The plan proposed to transfer a proportionate fee simple interest in the 635 acre parcel of real property to FmHA and Western Cotton. FmHA was earmarked to receive 515 acres of real property and Western Cotton was earmarked to receive 77 acres. Arnold and Baker was earmarked to retain ownership of 48 of the 640 acres scheduled for distribution. Arnold and Baker proposed to sell the adjoining 360 acre parcel of real property in order to pay the administrative claims, United States Trustee's fees, attorney fees, accountant fees, postpetition taxes, the real estate commission due and owing to Walter Arnold, and use the remainder to pay the unsecured creditors. Arnold and Baker retained an interest in the property remaining after distribution and sale.

Both FmHA and Western Cotton initially objected to confirmation of Arnold and Baker's second amended plan. However, during the course of the confirmation hearing, Western Cotton reached a settlement with Arnold and Baker pursuant to which Western Cotton agreed to accept 130 acres of real property in full satisfaction of its debt. Western subsequently withdrew its objection to confirmation and voted to accept the plan.

For purposes of the confirmation hearing, the parties stipulated that the second amended plan met all the requirements of § 1129(a)(1–13) with the exception of subsections (a)(3), (7), and (8). Additionally, FmHA objected to being crammed down pursuant to § 1129(b)(2). The principal factual issue concentrated on the fair market value of Arnold and Baker's 1320 acres of land. Arnold and Baker estimated the per acre value to be $7,322 for the 640 acre lot, $8,300 for the 360 acre lot, and $8,631 for the 320 acre lot. FmHA estimated the per acre value for the entire 1320 acres at $1,381.

On May 5, 1993, the bankruptcy court confirmed the plan finding that the property had an estimated value of $7,300 per acre. However, the bankruptcy court modified the transfer to FmHA in the plan by ordering an additional 10% transfer to FmHA in order to compensate it for the costs associated with a sale [resulting in a total of 566.5 acres].

FmHA appealed to the Bankruptcy Appellate Panel ("BAP"), which reversed the bankruptcy court's order confirming the plan. In consolidated appeals, Arnold and Baker and Western Cotton appeal the BAP's reversal.

* * *

### III

* * * Appellant Arnold and Baker argues that the BAP erred in reversing the confirmation of the plan on the ground that the proposed transfer of 566.5 acres to FmHA would not provide "for the realization by [FmHA] of the indubitable equivalent" of its secured claim, as required by § 1129(b)(2)(A)(iii).

Because FmHA objected to confirmation of the plan, Arnold and Baker invoked the "cram down" provision of Chapter 11, which provides that the court, on request of the proponent of the plan, shall confirm the plan notwithstanding the objection of an impaired creditor "if the plan does not discriminate unfairly, and is fair and equitable, with respect to each class of claims or interests that is impaired under, and has not accepted, the plan." § 1129(b)(1). To be "fair and equitable" the plan must satisfy, with respect to secured claims, one of the following three tests:

**(1)** The creditor is to retain the lien securing its claim and is to receive deferred cash payments with a present value at least equal to the claim;

**(2)** The property securing the claim is to be sold and the lien is to attach to the proceeds of the sale; the lien on the proceeds is then to be treated as described in test (1) or (3);

**(3)** The creditor is to realize the indubitable equivalent of its secured claim. * * *

The bankruptcy court confirmed the plan on the ground that the plan satisfied the third requirement. After an evidentiary hearing on the issue of valuation, the court found that the property was worth $7,300 per acre. It then concluded that the receipt of 566.5 acres at $7,300 per acre would provide for FmHA to realize the indubitable equivalent of its secured claim.

As an initial matter, we must address the appropriate standard of review of such a determination. Arnold and Baker argues that the question of indubitable equivalence is a question of fact to be reviewed under the clearly erroneous standard. We disagree. Although the value of the land is a finding of fact which we review for clear error, the ultimate conclusion of indubitable equivalence is a question of law which we review de novo because it requires analysis of the meaning of the statutory language in the context of the Bankruptcy Code's "cram down" scheme. See Woods v. Pine Mountain, Ltd. (In re Pine Mountain), 80 B.R. 171, 172 (9th Cir.BAP 1987) ("Whether a plan provides a secured creditor with the indubitable equivalent of its claim is. . . a mixed question of law and fact. Although the facts underlying such a determination are reviewed under the clearly erroneous standard, the question of whether the legal standard has been satisfied is reviewed de novo.") * * * But see Matter of James Wilson Assocs., 965 F.2d 160, 172 (7th Cir.1992) (holding that indubitable equivalence is a question of fact reviewed for clear error).

The BAP reviewed de novo the bankruptcy court's determination that the proposed transfer would provide FmHA with the indubitable equivalent of its secured claim, and reversed. Stressing that "[t]he determination of whether a partial dirt for debt distribution will provide the creditor with the indubitable equivalence of its secured claim must be made on a case-by-case basis," the BAP reasoned that the bankruptcy court's valuation of the property was an insufficient basis on which to conclude that the property was the indubitable equivalent of FmHA's secured claim. Again, we adopt and quote verbatim from the BAP's opinion:

> The finding of a trial court of a particular value of real property. . . will not necessarily determine whether the creditor will receive the indubitable equivalent of its secured claim. Experience has taught us that determining the value of real property at any given time is not an exact science. Because each parcel of real property is unique, the precise value of land is difficult, if not impossible, to determine until it is actually sold. Nevertheless, bankruptcy courts have traditionally been requested, out of necessity, to determine the value of various types of property, including real property, and yet courts have recognized the difficulty of being able to determine accurately the value of land. For instance, in In re Walat Farms, Inc., 70 B.R. 330 (Bankr.E.D.Mich.1987), the court stated:
>
> > Similarly, we concede to doubts about our ability to fix the "value" of the land in question. We need not make a pronouncement that no plan proposing the surrender of a portion of mortgaged land to a mortgagee in return for a compelled release of the lien on the remainder of the property will ever be confirmed. Suffice it to say, however, that no matter how hot the market for real estate may become in the future, the market for farm real estate here and now is not such which would permit us to hold that the value of the land being offered is the indubitable equivalent of [the mortgagee]'s claim. "Indubitable" means "too evident to be doubted." Webster's Ninth New Collegiate Dictionary (1985). We profess doubt on the facts of this case.
>
> [T]he determination of whether a dirt for debt distribution provides a secured creditor with the indubitable equivalent of its secured claim must be made on a case-by-case basis, and we must decide whether the bankruptcy court's finding with respect to the value of the real property for the purpose of determining the amount of the creditor's secured claim provided the secured creditor with the indubitable equivalent of its claim. In addition, we conclude that in order for a partial distribution to constitute the most "indubitable equivalence," the partial distribution must insure the safety of or prevent jeopardy to the principal.

Although we conclude that the bankruptcy court's valuation in this case is not clearly erroneous, we are not convinced that its finding regarding the value of the real property provided the indubitable equivalence of the particular secured claim in question, nor are we convinced that the partial distribution of 566.5 acres to FmHA will insure the safety of or prevent jeopardy to the principal.

The evidence at trial demonstrated that the value of the real property was far from certain. The Arnold and Baker appraisal admitted that due to unfavorable market conditions, including the fact that the [Resolution Trust Company had acquired 19,000 acres near Arnold and Baker's property and was considering bulk sale offers at no more than $2,105 per acre], the normal one year marketing period for the property would be extended by another two years [by which time the appraisal estimated that the Resolution Trust Company's activities would have ceased affecting the market]. The bankruptcy court agreed with Arnold and Baker's valuation of $7,300 per acre. FmHA, however, proffered a valuation of $1,381 per acre.[7] The large disparity in the parties' valuation of the same property illustrates the obvious uncertainty in attempting to forecast the price at which real property will sell at some uncertain future date.

The bankruptcy court found the value of each acre to be $7,300, and thus the value of the 566.5 acres to be transferred to FmHA to be $4,135,450 ($7,300 x 566.5). We must decide, therefore, whether a distribution of land with an estimated value of $4,135,450 constitutes the indubitable equivalent of a $3,837,618 claim secured by 1,320 acres. Under the circumstances of this case, we conclude that it does not.

The partial distribution of 566.5 acres to FmHA will not insure the safety of or prevent jeopardy to the principal. FmHA originally lent funds to Arnold and Baker secured by 1320 acres of land. If Arnold and Baker defaulted on the terms of the note, FmHA bargained for the right to foreclose on the entire 1320 acres of land in order to satisfy the outstanding obligation. In this situation, the principal is protected to the extent of the entire 1320 acres held as security. . ..

If FmHA subsequently sells the property for less than the value calculated by the bankruptcy court, FmHA has no recourse to the remaining collateral to satisfy the deficiency. As a result, the distribution to FmHA may not be "completely compensatory." See In re Murel

---

[7] The disparity was due in part to the parties' disagreement about the highest and best use of the property. Arnold and Baker argued that it was for land development, whereas FmHA maintained that it was for an irrigated farm.

Holding Corp., 75 F.2d 941, 942 (2d Cir.1935) (Learned Hand, J.).[8] FmHA is forced to assume the risk of receiving less on the sale without being able to look to the remaining undistributed collateral for security. "[T]o the extent a debtor seeks to alter the collateral securing a creditor's loan, providing the "indubitable equivalent' requires that the substitute collateral not increase the creditor's risk exposure." In re Keller, 157 B.R. 680, 683–84 (Bankr.E.D.Wash.1993); see also Aetna Realty Investors, Inc., v. Monarch Beach Venture, Ltd., 166 B.R. 428, 436 (C.D.Cal.1993) (fair and equitable prohibits a plan from unfairly shifting risk of plan failure to the creditor).

Arnold and Baker challenges the BAP's decision on the ground that it conflicts with Matter of Sandy Ridge Development Corp., 881 F.2d 1346 (5th Cir.1989),[9] in which the Fifth Circuit held that a "dirt for debt" plan satisfied the indubitable equivalence standard.[10] The BAP distinguished *Sandy Ridge* on the ground that the plan in that case provided for the transfer of all of the secured creditor's collateral, rather than only a portion of the collateral as in the present case. Arnold and Baker argues that even in the *Sandy Ridge* situation, the court's valuation of the collateral is critical to the creditor's substantive rights because the valuation directly impacts the creditor's rights regarding an unsecured deficiency claim, as was the case in *Sandy Ridge*.

However, this argument misapprehends the indubitable equivalence analysis. Section 1129(b)(2)(A)(iii) does not require that a creditor receive the indubitable equivalent of its entire claim, but only of its secured claim. *See Sandy Ridge*, 881 F.2d at 1350; 11 U.S.C. § 1129(b)(2)(A)(iii) ("With respect to a class of *secured claims*, the plan provides. . . (iii) for the realization by such holders of the indubitable equivalent of *such claims*.") (emphasis added). *Sandy Ridge* explained that, in the case of an undersecured creditor:

> [s]ection 506(a) of the Bankruptcy Code bifurcates. . . [the] total claim into secured and unsecured portions. . . . In situations involving only one creditor and one debtor, the value of the undersecured creditor's secured claim is simply the value of the underlying collateral.

---

[8] The legislative history of § 1129 indicates that *Murel Holding* was the source of the "indubitable equivalence" standard. * * *

[9] Arnold and Baker also cites a number of decisions from bankruptcy courts approving dirt for debt plans. * * * However, none of the plans in these cases required a secured creditor to accept part of its collateral in full satisfaction of its secured claim.

[10] A subsequent opinion denying the petition for rehearing clarifies that this was the holding of *Sandy Ridge*. See Matter of Sandy Ridge Development Corp., 889 F.2d 663, 663 (5th Cir.1989) (*Sandy Ridge II* ) ("In denying the petition for rehearing, we observe that we have held that. . . the plan in question meets the requirements of § 1129(b)(2)(A)(iii). . . .")

The difference between the collateral's value and the amount of the debt becomes an unsecured claim and is added to the existing pool of unsecured claims.

In other words, the value of the secured portion of an undersecured creditor's total claim is *by definition* equal to the value of the collateral securing it. Therefore, a creditor necessarily receives the indubitable equivalent of its secured claim when it receives the collateral securing that claim, regardless of how the court values the collateral. For this reason, the *Sandy Ridge* court did not need a judicial determination of value, explaining that "for the present analysis, the exact value of [the collateral] is unimportant." * * * The court's valuation of the collateral does, as Arnold and Baker observes, determine the amount of any remaining *unsecured* claim, but the Code requires only that the creditor receive the indubitable equivalent of its *secured* claim.

In this case, in contrast, the amount of collateral deemed to be the indubitable equivalent of FmHA's secured claim depends entirely on the court's valuation of the collateral. If the court had found that the land was worth more than $7,300 per acre, FmHA would receive correspondingly less land, and if the court had found that the land was worth less, FmHA would receive correspondingly more. Our holding that this plan does not satisfy the indubitable equivalent requirement is therefore entirely consistent with *Sandy Ridge*'s holding that the plan in that case did.

### CONCLUSION

In conclusion, while we do not hold that the indubitable equivalent standard can never as a matter of law be satisfied when a creditor receives less than the full amount of the collateral originally bargained for, we do hold, as did the BAP, that the Arnold and Baker plan does not provide FmHA with the indubitable equivalent of its secured claim as required by the Bankruptcy Code.

The judgment of the BAP reversing the bankruptcy court's order confirming the plan is AFFIRMED.

## NOTES

**1.** The meaning of indubitable equivalence is hardly clear, but that standard might be met if the plan provided for surrender of all the collateral to a secured party. As a practical matter, debtors do not surrender all the collateral if the collateral is worth more than secured claim—and secured creditors wouldn't object if they did. But what if the collateral is worth less than the secured creditor's claim? In that case, satisfying the secured claim through the surrender of the collateral is only the first step in determining the creditor's treatment. The court will have to fix the value of the collateral in order to determine the amount of the creditor's deficiency claim. Note that if the property is sold, the sale price (that is, the market) fixes the deficiency, but if it is surrendered to the secured creditor, the court does. Should debtors be permitted to use the power to cramdown under § 1129(b)(2)(A)(iii) to avoid market valuations of property they will not retain under the plan?

**2.** What if the plan proposes that Lender will lose its security interest and will be given in exchange common stock in the reorganized Debtor with an estimated value equal to the value of Lender's secured claim? Lender doesn't want the stock and rejects the plan. Does payment to Lender of the amount of its secured claim in common stock of the reorganized Debtor satisfy subparagraph (iii)? One could argue that if the stock was actually worth the amount of the secured claim it is the equivalent of a payment in cash. That argument, however, has no merit unless there was a ready market for the common stock that made it a cash equivalent. Ownership of an equity interest in Debtor that is not a cash equivalent is not the same as lien status in assets of Debtor. Senator DeConcini, the Senate manager of the Bankruptcy Reform Act of 1978, stated:

> Abandonment of the collateral to the creditor would clearly satisfy indubitable equivalence, as would a lien on similar collateral. * * * Unsecured notes as to the secured claim or equity securities of the debtor would not be the indubitable equivalent. * * *

1978 U.S.C.C.A.N. 6544.

## 2. § 1129(b)(1) "FAIRNESS" AND NEGATIVE AMORTIZATION

## Great Western Bank v. Sierra Woods Group
United States Court of Appeals, Ninth Circuit, 1992.
953 F.2d 1174.

■ FERNANDEZ, Circuit Judge:

Sierra Woods Group (Sierra Woods) appeals the district court's decision that Sierra Woods' proposed reorganization plan, which included negative amortization, was not "fair and equitable" under § 1129(b). The bankruptcy court did not make specific factual findings regarding the fairness of the proposed deferral of interest, but rather adopted a per se rule against negative amortization. The district court did not address the legal permissibility of negative amortization, but concluded based upon a review of the record that the proposed plan was not fair and equitable. We hold that the fairness of a reorganization plan that includes the deferral of interest must be determined on a case-by-case basis. Therefore we reverse the district court's decision and remand to the district court for further remand to the bankruptcy court so that the bankruptcy court may make factual findings concerning the fairness of the proposed plan.

### FACTUAL AND PROCEDURAL BACKGROUND

This dispute centers on the Chapter 11 reorganization plan proposed by Sierra Woods. Its only asset is a ten-year-old apartment complex located in Sparks, Nevada. Bank of America owns a note secured by a first deed of trust on the property. As of April 17, 1989, Bank of America was owed $4,098,000. Great Western Bank (Great Western) owns a note secured by a second deed of trust, and was owed $3,845,124.47 plus $103,124.47 in interest as of April 17, 1989. The terms of Great Western's note called for an adjustable interest rate 3% over the Federal Home Loan Bank of San Francisco Eleventh District Cost of Funds Rate. The note was fully amortized over 30 years and was to mature in the year 2015.

Originally Sierra Woods proposed a reorganization plan under which it would make interest-only payments of 8% to Great Western for the first three years, and would then make interest-only payments at the prevailing note rate for the remaining term. The deferred interest and principal payments would be capitalized and would incur interest at the existing note rate. Sierra Woods later modified this proposal to include interest-only payments for the first five years. For the first three years, Sierra Woods proposed to pay interest of 8% and allow interest in excess of that amount to accrue and be added to principal. After five years, the note would fully amortize over the balance of the term at the adjustable note rate. The result would be negative amortization for three years because during that time the debt would increase rather than decrease.

Sierra Woods presented its modified proposal at a bankruptcy court hearing. Great Western cited *In re McCombs Properties VIII, Ltd.,* 91 B.R. 907, 911 (Bankr.C.D.Cal.1988), for the proposition that the promise to make up lost interest payments is not the legal equivalent of having those interest payments today. Sierra Woods told the court that its accountants were prepared to testify that the stream of payments under its proposal was equivalent to the stream of payments under the original note. Great Western responded that the permissibility of negative amortization was a "legal issue," and argued that interest deferral was not appropriate "under any circumstances."

The bankruptcy judge ruled in favor of Great Western. He said:

> I read the Code, and it's very clear, and I've always applied it in this manner. . . . [§ 1129(b)(2)(A)(i)(II) requires that] Mr. Beesley's client receive, on account of his claim, deferred cash payments totaling at least the amount of this claim as of the debt on the effective date of the plan. And that means a payment today, the next deferred payment, and next deferred payment, and the next. That's all it's ever meant. And I'm interpreting it that way. And I don't think negative amortization even—it just doesn't comply with that. . . ..

Thereafter, the bankruptcy court confirmed a reorganization plan that required Sierra Woods to make timely interest payments at the market rate of interest. Sierra Woods appealed the bankruptcy court's ruling against deferral of interest to the district court. The district court examined the record and concluded that Sierra Woods had not honored its previous promises to pay Great Western, that the negative amortization proposal required a 100–percent value loan from Great Western to Sierra Woods, and that Great Western was in a secondary position to Bank of America on the loan. According to the district court, "the bankruptcy court properly determined that the deferral proposed in the plan. . . did not under the circumstances provide Great Western Bank with the equivalent of the present value of its claim. . ."

\* \* \*

## DISCUSSION

Under § 1129(b), the bankruptcy court can confirm a plan of reorganization without creditor approval if the plan "does not discriminate unfairly, and is fair and equitable. . .." § 1129(b)(1). The "fair and equitable" condition includes the requirement that the holder of a secured claim receive "deferred cash payments totaling at least the allowed amount of such claim, of a value, as of the effective date of the plan, of at least the value of such holder's interest in the estate's interest in such property." § 1129(b)(2)(A)(i)(II).

Sierra Woods argues that § 1129(b) permits the deferral of interest, or negative amortization. Negative amortization refers to "a provision wherein part or all of the interest on a secured claim is not paid currently but instead is deferred and allowed to accrue," with the accrued interest added to the principal and paid when income is higher. In re Club Associates, 107 B.R. 385, 398 (Bankr.N.D.Ga.1989). The extent of negative amortization depends upon the difference between the "accrual rate," or the overall rate of interest to be paid on a claim, and the "pay rate," or the rate of interest to be paid on a monthly basis. Even when a debtor defers payments of interest on its debt obligation, the deferred amount can be capitalized at a rate of interest which enables the deferred amount to equal the present value of the creditor's allowed secured claim. \* \* \* See also In re Memphis Partners, L.P., 99 B.R. 385, 388 (Bankr.M.D.Tenn.1989) (with an appropriate interest rate, a negative amortization plan can mathematically provide present value).

### A. The Bankruptcy Court Ruling and District Court Review

The bankruptcy court did not make specific findings regarding the fairness of the proposed deferral of interest under § 1129(b), but rather objected to negative amortization on legal grounds. The bankruptcy court rejected appellant's proposal for the deferred payment of interest because, in that court's view, deferral of interest does not comport with the statutory requirement that secured creditors receive the present value of their claims.

The district court did not address the legal argument against negative amortization, but rather found support in the record for the proposition that in the context of this particular case the deferral of interest would not be fair and equitable. We have held, however, that the district court may not make its own factual findings when reviewing a decision of the bankruptcy court. \* \* \* The question of whether a reorganization plan is fair and equitable involves questions of fact. \* \* \* Because the bankruptcy court did not make factual findings on this issue, the district court erred when it independently determined that appellant's proposed plan was not fair and equitable. The district court should have decided whether the bankruptcy judge erred in adopting a blanket prohibition of negative amortization. If so, the district court should have remanded the case to the bankruptcy court for the making of necessary findings regarding the fairness of the plan, rather than conducting its own review of the record. * * *

### B. The Fairness of Negative Amortization under § 1129(b)

We have not previously decided whether negative amortization is permissible under § 1129(b). See In re Fowler, 903 F.2d 694, 699 n. 6 (9th Cir.1990), where we noted the existence of the issue. One court has ruled that deferral of interest is not fair and equitable under section 1129(b) if the payment rate falls below the market rate of interest. In re McCombs, 91 B.R. at 911. In *McCombs*, the debtor sought to "cram down" a reorganization plan under which interest would accrue at the market rate of 10.5%, but the debtor would make payments of 9% and accrue the difference until sufficient funds were available. The court indicated a willingness to accept deferral of interest only if the debtor's payments at least equaled the market interest rate. * * * The court stated that even if it could adjust the interest rate to reflect "this accrual concept," it would only be guessing at the proper adjustment. * * *

As the *McCombs* court seemed to acknowledge, even when the payment rate falls below market rate, the accrual rate can be adjusted in order to give creditors the present value of their claims. * * * Assuming that such an adjustment is possible, the *McCombs* court offered no reason why negative amortization should be deemed impermissible under § 1129(b) whenever the payment rate on a secured claim falls below the market rate.

Our research has discovered no other court which has accepted the reasoning of the *McCombs* court. Rather, courts have decided on a case-by-case basis whether negative amortization under a given plan was fair and equitable, and have treated the market rate of interest as a necessary, but not sufficient, factor in that alchemy. * * *

In all of the above cases, save one, the court concluded that negative amortization was not fair and equitable under the circumstances, and the case approving of the deferral of interest concerned a contract that already provided for negative amortization. Thus while most courts have been reluctant to adopt a per se rule against negative amortization, there are commonly held reservations about the practice. That is not surprising because plans of that type tend to be fraught with pitfalls that unfairly endanger creditors. Even so, we see no reason to conclude that negative amortization is per se impermissible under § 1129(b). We hold that the fairness of a reorganization plan that includes negative amortization should be determined on a case-by-case basis. *In re Apple Tree Partners* contains a list of some of the factors that are relevant to this determination:

1.  Does the plan offer a market rate of interest and present value of the deferred payments;

2.  Is the amount and length of the proposed deferral reasonable;

3.  Is the ratio of debt to value satisfactory throughout the plan;

4.  Are the debtor's financial projections reasonable and sufficiently proven, or is the plan feasible;

5.  What is the nature of the collateral, and is the value of the collateral appreciating, depreciating, or stable;

6.  Are the risks unduly shifted to the creditor;

7.  Are the risks borne by one secured creditor or class of secured creditors;

8.  Does the plan preclude the secured creditor's foreclosure;

9.  Did the original loan terms provide for negative amortization; and

10. Are there adequate safeguards to protect the secured creditor against plan failure.

We agree with that listing, without intending to limit consideration to those factors alone, and without intending to require courts to expressly refer to each one of them when considering proposed plans.

## CONCLUSION

Because the bankruptcy court erroneously concluded that negative amortization is per se impermissible and failed to make findings concerning the fairness of the proposed reorganization plan, we REVERSE the decision of the district court and REMAND to the district court for further remand to the bankruptcy court for further proceedings.

■ POOLE, Circuit Judge, concurring in part and dissenting in part:

I agree with the majority that negative amortization is not always disallowed by the bankruptcy code, and I concur in that part of the opinion. I write separately, however, because I do not believe it is either necessary or appropriate to reverse and remand in this case.

* * * The district court had, and this Court has, sufficient factual findings by the bankruptcy court to draw the legal conclusion that the "negative amortization" plan, as proposed by the debtor, was not fair and equitable. The plan rejected by the bankruptcy court originally called for three years of interest-only payments at 8%, followed by two years of interest-only payments at the prevailing adjustable note rate of 3% over the Eleventh District Cost of Funds Rate, after which the claim would fully amortize over the balance of the term at the adjustable note rate. Following the bankruptcy court's denial of this plan because of its provision for negative amortization, Sierra Woods filed a First Amended Plan of Reorganization proposing payments to Great Western Bank over five years at interest-only payments based on the prevailing note rate (3% over Eleventh District Cost of Funds Rate), after which the claim would fully amortize over a period of time extending ten years beyond the present maturity date of the note. The bankruptcy court found, however, that even this plan would not give Great Western Bank value, and thus provided Great West-

ern with an interest rate of 4.5% over the 11th District Cost of Funds. The increased rate was necessary because the court found that:

> Great Western's second position is inherently at greater risk. The equity cushion ahead of it is approximately 10% and risk of default and failure to consummate the plan will bear the heaviest on it. Also to be considered is that the physical deterioration of the apartment complex has been significantly arrested and improved since the petition has been filed. However, the debtor's cash flow projection only covers current maintenance and no provision is made therein for deferred maintenance and repairs.

Thus the rejected plan, less favorable to Great Western than the First Amended Plan of Reorganization, would certainly have also been rejected by the court for failing to return present value.

Even had the interest rate in the original plan been set at market rate, that would only have aggravated the deferral and accrual of interest, resulting effectively in a full value loan to Sierra Woods, and have ultimately led to a deficiency which would have entirely consumed Great Western's equity cushion. Approval of a plan calling for negative amortization under such circumstances might itself constitute an abuse of discretion. Analyzed under the ten factors listed in the majority opinion, such a plan would (3) not have a satisfactory debt-to-value for a significant portion of the life of the loan, (4) not have reasonable financial projections in light of the inability to provide for deferred maintenance and repairs, (6) unduly shift the risks to Great Western, (7) cause Great Western to bear the risks, and (9) contravene the original loan terms which did not provide for negative amortization. Furthermore, the court could reasonably find that (2) the amount of the proposed deferral is not reasonable.

Based on the findings of fact made by the bankruptcy court, the district court was correct in concluding that the original plan calling for negative amortization would not have been fair and equitable. As a result, the failure of the bankruptcy court to conduct a hearing on the plan constituted harmless error. * * * Because reversing and remanding now would unnecessarily prolong the bankruptcy proceedings to the prejudice of the creditor, I respectfully dissent.

## 3. The § 1111(b) Election

Section 1111(b) is best understood by first considering the situation to which that provision was directed. At the time § 1111(b) was enacted, § 1124(3) provided that a claim was not impaired if the claimant was paid cash equal to the allowed amount of the claim on the effective date of the plan. In 1994 § 1124(3) was deleted from the Code for reasons having nothing to do with § 1111(b). First we shall examine § 1111(b) against the Code background that existed when it was enacted, as though § 1124(3) were still in effect; then, at the end of this discussion, we will comment on the effect of the deletion of § 1124(3).

Assume Debtor borrowed money from Lender to buy an apartment building. As is frequently the case in commercial real property financing, the loan was nonrecourse, i.e., the loan was secured by a mortgage against the real property but Debtor was not personally liable on the loan. If Debtor defaulted, Lender's rights were limited to foreclosing on the property. If the property were worth more than the outstanding debt at the time of foreclosure, Lender would either be paid in full from the proceeds of a sale to a third party, or, in the absence of a higher third party bid, Lender could buy the property for a price equal to the amount of the debt; Lender pays for the property by simply canceling the debt. If the property were worth less than the debt at the time of foreclosure, Lender, by taking over the property, gets whatever speculative value the property has.

Assume further that because of a large increase in interest rates that reduced demand for real property, Debtor was unable to sell the building for what it considered a reasonable price. Debtor defaulted on Lender's loan. When Lender commenced foreclosure proceedings, Debtor filed in Chapter 11. Lender is the only secured creditor and the real property is Debtor's principal asset. Assume that at the time of bankruptcy the debt owed to Lender was $1,000,000 and the value of the property, based on the net proceeds that would be received if the property were sold at that time, was $750,000.

Both Debtor and Lender believe the property will increase substantially in value within 18 months owing to a likely decline in interest rates. There are no other creditors except for a class of impaired unsecured claims of trade creditors totaling less than $50,000. Debtor's Chapter 11 plan calls for a cash payment to that class that complies with the best interests rule. That class will consent to the plan. Debtor's plan provides that Debtor keeps the property and pays Lender $750,000 on the effective date of the plan.

Can Lender prevent confirmation of the plan in the absence of § 1111(b)? Lender has a claim against Debtor (§ 102(2)) and, under § 506(a), it is a secured claim of $750,000. Lender does not have an allowable unsecured claim because Debtor was not personally liable on the $1,000,000 debt. To be allowable a claim must be enforceable either against the debtor or against property of the debtor. Lender's claim is enforceable against the property to the extent of the $750,000 value of the property. It is not enforceable with respect to the remaining $250,000. Lender is a separate class and that class is not impaired because the plan provides for a cash payment to Lender on the effective date of the plan equal to the amount of Debtor's claim. Former § 1124(3). Since the class is not impaired it is deemed to have accepted the plan. § 1126(f). Since the only impaired class, the trade creditors, will accept the plan, the plan can be confirmed under § 1129(a). There is compliance with both § 1129(a)(8) and (10). Thus, if these sections are the only sections that apply to the case, Lender is powerless to prevent Debtor from imposing a forced redemption of the property at the depressed $750,000 value if that value is used to determine the amount of Lender's secured claim. Outside of bankruptcy Lender would have been able to foreclose and to buy the property at the foreclosure sale by credit bidding the amount of the $1,000,000 debt. In that case Lender would own the property and get the benefit of any rise in value. In bankruptcy Lender loses this benefit under the provisions which we have just examined. But § 1111(b) changes this result.

The facts in the hypothetical case resemble those in *In re Pine Gate Associates, Ltd.,* 2 B.C.D. 1478 (Bankr.N.D.Ga.1976), decided under Chapter XII of the Bankruptcy Act. There the court allowed the debtor to keep the property by paying the nonrecourse creditor the depressed value of the property. Hence, the creditor lost its expectation either of being paid in full or of getting the property to hold in anticipation of an economic upturn. In the familiar metaphor, the debtor used bankruptcy as a sword and not a shield. Section 1111(b) was added in large part as a reaction to *Pine Gate.* Section 1111(b) changes the rights of Lender in the hypothetical case.

First, assume that Lender does not make the election provided by § 1111(b)(1)(A)(i) to have its rights determined under § 1111(b)(2). Under § 1111(b)(1)(A) Lender is treated as having a secured claim for $750,000 and an unsecured claim for $250,000. Under former § 1124(3) the plan does not impair Lender's secured claim because Lender is receiving cash equal to the allowed amount of that claim. But the plan impairs Lender's unsecured claim because that claim will not be paid in full. Lender's unsecured claim will either be separately classified or it will be classified with the unsecured trade creditor claims. In the latter case Lender would control the class because other claims in the class are less than $50,000. Lender can cause that class to reject the plan, thereby making confirmation impossible. Confirmation requires that at least one class of impaired claims accept the plan. § 1129(a)(10) and § 1129(b)(1).

If Lender's unsecured claim is separately classified, § 1129(a)(10) will be satisfied because the trade creditors will accept the plan. But the absolute priority rule applies under § 1129(b). If Lender is not paid the full amount of the $250,000 unsecured claim under the plan, the equity security holders of Debtor cannot receive or retain any property under the plan. § 1129(b)(2)(B). Thus, confirmation is infeasible because it can occur only if the equity security holders are not allowed to retain any interest in Debtor.

Second, assume that Lender makes the § 1111(b)(2) election. Under that provision, Lender is treated as having a secured claim in the amount of $1,000,000. The reference to "claim" in § 1111(b)(2) is to "claim secured by a lien on property of the estate" in § 1111(b)(1)(A). Lender has a claim of $1,000,000 against Debtor even though Debtor is not personally liable. § 101 ("claim"), § 101 ("creditor"), and § 102(2). We saw earlier that $250,000 of that claim is not allowable in the absence of § 1111(b), but it is allowable under § 1111(b)(1)(A). By electing application of § 1111(b)(2), Lender waives the unsecured claim that it has under

§ 1111(b)(1)(A) and receives instead a $1,000,000 secured claim. That claim is impaired. Former § 1124(3) is not satisfied because the plan gives Lender less than the full amount of the claim. The plan would have to be revised to meet the cramdown requirements of § 1129(b)(2)(A). The plan could allow Debtor to keep the property if Lender's lien is preserved and Lender is given deferred payments of at least $1,000,000 having a present value of at least "the value of [Lender's] interest in the estate's interest" in the property. Since that value can't be higher than the value of the property, it is $750,000 in this case. If the plan is so revised, it might not be favorable to Lender. Lender is assured of eventually receiving $1,000,000 but the amount over $750,000 may simply represent interest to reflect deferred payment. Lender has no assurance under § 1129(b)(2)(A) of receiving economic value beyond the present value of the property which in this case is $750,000.

But Lender obtains another benefit by electing § 1111(b)(2). The primary purpose of that section is to allow Lender to have a lien in the real property measured by the full value of Lender's claim rather than the value of the property. Debtor wants to be free to sell the property after confirmation of the plan in order to capture the anticipated appreciation in value of the property. This goal is denied to Debtor because the property is encumbered with Lender's lien and the lien secures the entire $1,000,000 claim of Lender. If Debtor sells the property it would have to satisfy that claim. Thus, Lender gets the economic benefit of a rise in value of the property if the property is sold.

As best we can tell, creditors rarely make the § 1111(b)(2) election. However, according to the court in *In re Cook*, 126 B.R. 575, 581–582 (Bankr.D.S.D.1991), before enactment of Chapter 12 the Farmers Home Administration (FmHA) routinely made the election in Chapter 11 cases involving farm land during the depression of the mid–1980s under plans allowing the farmer to retain the land. The FmHA anticipated that market value of the land was likely to increase during the payment period and, if the reorganization failed and the land was sold, the FmHA's lien would cover the appreciated value.

In Chapter 11 cases, the undersecured creditor may not elect to have its claim treated as fully secured in two instances. The first is when the creditor's interest "is of inconsequential value." § 1111(b)(1)(B)(i). An example is a case in which liens having priority over the lien of the creditor exhaust almost all of the collateral, leaving the creditor functionally unsecured. The second is when there is recourse against the debtor and the property is sold under § 363 or is to be sold under the plan. § 1111(b)(1)(B)(ii). If the property is sold pursuant to § 363(b), the creditor can protect itself by credit bidding the full amount of its claim. § 363(k). If there is a higher third party bid, the creditor will be paid in full; if not, the creditor will take the property. In either case the expectations of the undersecured creditor are realized and it has no need of the § 1111(b) protection.

Similarly, in Chapter 7 cases, the real property will be sold or foreclosed upon, the expectations of the undersecured party are realized and there is no need for § 1111(b) protection. Accordingly, § 1111(b) does not apply in Chapter 7 cases. § 103(f).

What are the consequences on the above analysis of § 1111(b) of the repeal in 1994 of § 1124(3)? After this amendment, secured claims are impaired even though they are cashed out under the plan on its effective date. In the hypothetical case discussed above, Lender's $750,000 secured claim is impaired and Lender can vote to reject the plan. If Lender does so, Debtor can achieve confirmation of the plan only through cramdown under § 1129(b). Debtor can comply with this provision only if it can create at least one consenting class under § 1129(a)(10), discussed earlier, and comply with the absolute priority rule, discussed later. Without § 1111(b), cashing out Lender for $750,000 while leaving Lender technically impaired appears to comply with § 1129(b)(2)(A)(i), making the plan confirmable, even though Lender votes to reject the plan. With § 1111(b), however, Debtor's plan must provide either for Lender's $250,000 deficiency claim or, if the § 1111(b)(2) election is made, for a full $1 million secured claim. Hence, after the 1994 amendment deleting § 1124(3), creditors in *Pine Gate* type cases may still need § 1111(b) as a shield against an unwanted cash-out.

## PROBLEM

Debtor filed in Chapter 11. Its sole asset was an apartment building worth $3.3 million. Creditor has a lien on the property securing nonrecourse debt of $6.6 million. Debtor's plan provided for the sale of the property to a new corporate entity in exchange for all its capital stock which would be distributed to the owners of Debtor. Creditor's secured claim would be paid by periodic cash payments having a present value equal to the value of the building as determined by the bankruptcy court. Creditor would be paid nothing for the portion of its debt that was not covered by the value of the building. Creditor argued that under § 1111(b)(1)(A) it had an unsecured claim to the extent the $6.6 million nonrecourse debt was not covered by the value of the building. Since the plan did not provide for the payment of this unsecured claim in full, it contended that the plan could not be crammed down because the old owners would receive value under the plan and, therefore, the absolute priority rule of § 1129(b)(2)(B)(ii) was not satisfied. Debtor answered that the normal rule of § 1111(b)(1)(A) did not apply in this case because the building would be "sold under the plan" and thus § 1111(b)(1)(A)(ii) applied and the nonrecourse debt could not be treated as recourse under § 1111(b)(1); therefore, Creditor had no unsecured claim in bankruptcy. Does Creditor have an unsecured claim in this case? What is the reason for the exception in § 1111(b)(1)(A)(ii)? Would this purpose be frustrated if Creditor were not awarded an unsecured claim in this case? *See In re Woodridge North Apts., Ltd.*, 71 B.R. 189 (Bankr.N.D.Cal.1987).

## D. Treatment of Unsecured Claims and Ownership Interests

### 1. Best Interests Rule

If a plan of reorganization is approved by all impaired classes of claims and interests as provided in § 1126(c) and (d), dissenting members of each class are bound so long as the best interests rule is met. Within each class dissenters must receive at least as much under the plan as they would have received under a Chapter 7 liquidation. § 1129(a)(7). With respect to § 1129(a)(7) Richard Broude, an experienced bankruptcy lawyer, has observed:

> Subsection 1129(a)(7) thus requires that the proponent of the plan present an appraisal demonstrating that, if the debtor were liquidated under Chapter 7, each of the creditors and holders of interest in each of the classes of claims or interests would receive no more than it will receive under the plan. Testimony about this hypothetical liquidation might be provided by auctioneers and other experts who could testify about the liquidation value of the receivables, inventory, equipment, and other assets of the debtor. It is important to include a valuation of off-balance sheet assets such as patents, trade secrets, and other like intangibles. In addition, the hypothetical Chapter 7 analysis will have to take into account the increase in unsecured claims which would inevitably occur in Chapter 7. For example, secured creditors generally would receive less from foreclosure than they would receive under the plan. Therefore, the liquidation analysis under section 1129(a)(7) would require that any estimated deficiency of the secured creditors be added to the class of unsecured claims. Similarly, where a lease is being assumed in the Chapter 11 plan, it might logically be concluded that the lease would be rejected in a Chapter 7 case, and the damages that would be allowed the landlord under the rejected lease would be added to the body of unsecured claims. Thus, the best interests test of section 1129(a)(7) requires an analysis not only of the value of the assets of the debtor upon liquidation but also of the unsecured claims among which the proceeds of the liquidation (after deducting the expenses of the Chapter 7 liquidation) would be distributed.

Richard F. Broude, *Cramdown and Chapter 11 of the Bankruptcy Code: The Settlement Imperative*, 39 Bus.Law. 441, 448–449 (1984).

## 2.  ABSOLUTE PRIORITY RULE

### PROBLEMS

The following problems illustrating application of the absolute priority rule are taken from Kenneth N. Klee, *All You Ever Wanted to Know About Cram Down Under the New Bankruptcy Code*, 53 Am.Bankr.L.J. 133, 146–150 (1979).

**1.**  Suppose an insolvent corporation has assets with a going concern value of $2 million, $1 million face amount in secured debt and $1.2 million face amount in unsecured debt. If the plan leaves the secured debt and shareholders unaffected and proposes to pay $1 million cash to unsecured creditors, can the plan be confirmed over the objection of the unsecured class?

**2.**  What if the debtor in Problem 1 proposes to distribute non-interest bearing notes payable in three years at a face amount of $1.5 million in lieu of cash and the unsecured class still rejects the plan?

**3.**  Suppose the shareholders reject the plan proposed by the corporation in Problem 1. What must the plan proponents establish at the confirmation hearing to confirm the plan?

**4.**  Suppose a solvent corporation with cash-flow problems, $2 million going concern value, $1.2 million in unsecured claims and no other liabilities. The plan proposes to issue notes with a present value of $1 million and 100,000 common shares to unsecured creditors pro rata. Old shareholders retain their 100,000 common shares. The unsecured class accepts the plan and the old shareholders reject it. Can the plan be confirmed?

**5.**  Formulate a different plan for the corporation in Problem 4 that (i) leaves old shareholders with their 100,000 shares, (ii) issues 100,000 new shares to the unsecured class and (iii) can be confirmed over the objection of the old shareholder class.

———

Chapter X of the Bankruptcy Act failed as a means of voluntary reorganization because it gave the management of the debtor too little incentive to use it. One disincentive was caused by the "fair and equitable" rule which prevailed in Chapter X. This rule, which is usually referred to as the absolute priority rule, required that each member of a senior class of claims or interests must receive full compensation before members of a junior class could receive anything. If there was a senior and junior class of unsecured creditors, the junior class could not share under a reorganization plan unless the senior class had been provided for to the full extent of its claims. Since creditor claims have priority over ownership interests, the most devastating impact of the absolute priority rule was to deprive stockholders of any interest in the reorganized entity unless the plan paid all creditors in full.

On its face the absolute priority rule appears to be one of elemental fairness. Seniors bargained for a priority position in any liquidation of the company. Juniors accepted the risk that the business might not prosper and that its assets might not cover both their claims and those of the seniors. Owners always understand that debt must come before equity. But in operation, the absolute priority rule, though seemingly "fair and equitable," often meant that an insolvent debtor had no incentive to reorganize under Chapter X because its shareholders could not gain a share in the reorganized business.

One problem with the absolute priority rule is that it is difficult to apply in some cases. Suppose the most junior class of unsecured claims will not receive full payment in cash under the plan of reorganization. Rather, that class will receive stock in the reorganized corporation. Suppose the plan provides that the reorganized corporation will be a new entity created to carry out the plan. The reorganized corporation will acquire all of the assets of the debtor corporation and all of the obligations to creditors under the plan. The debtor corporation becomes an empty shell when the plan goes into effect. The reorganized corporation will issue common stock and the junior class of unsecured claims will receive half of that stock. The other half of the common stock will be issued to the former stockholders of the debtor corporation. The absolute priority rule requires that the creditor class be compensated in full before the former stockholders of the debtor receive anything, but the issue of whether the creditor class is compensated in full depends upon the value of the reorganized corporation as a going concern. This valuation was done under the Bankruptcy Act by making estimates of the future earnings of the reorganized corporation and applying a multiple to them. The multiple was determined by considering the risk factors for the reorganized corporation and for the industry in which the corporation was competing. On the basis of expert testimony the court might decide that the appropriate multiple was five. Future annual earnings were then estimated. If the appropriate earnings figure was $1,000,000 the value of the reorganized corporation was $5,000,000. Professor Walter Blum and Professor Stanley Kaplan made the following comment on the valuation procedure in their article, *The Absolute Priority Doctrine in Corporate Reorganizations*, 41 U. of Chi.L.Rev. 651, 656–657 (1974):

> The valuation procedure always produces a dollars and cents figure. Although that figure looks mathematically exact, it actually reflects in a single number a whole series of highly conjectural and even speculative judgments concerning long-range business expectations and hazards as well as future social and general economic conditions. To exclude a class of creditors or investors from participation in a reorganization plan based upon so illusory a figure is criticized as capricious. The process is said to deceive by treating "soft" information as if it were "hard" and by cloaking predictions in the guise of mathe-

matical certainty, under circumstances where consequences are drastic and final.

Dependency of the valuation process upon the future outlook as of a particular moment adds to this dissatisfaction. The resultant value figure is inextricably related to the then accepted set of expectations and assumptions. If the situation improves shortly after the reorganization proceedings have been terminated (so that the risk factor used in determining valuation may appear to have been too high and the valuation too low), the elimination of certain investors from participation in the plan might be regarded as having been unwarranted and unduly harsh. Valuation is also considered somewhat arbitrary; values are always in flux because relevant conditions are always changing. A particular valuation figure, obtained at a given instant on the basis of the special circumstances of that moment, may well not be the same figure that would be obtained by the same process at a later date when circumstances have changed. Pushed to an extreme, the position suggests that no valuation should ever take place because any valuation is always subject to attack as evanescent—the valuation figure would always be different if it had been made either earlier or later. Thus, criticism of valuation on the basis of changing conditions can prove too much, undermining the entire concept.

The imprecision of the valuation process has also led to the argument that valuation is so malleable that the entire process is perverse—that, in actuality, it is the reverse of what it seems to be. On this view, valuation is not an objective process by which projected earnings are capitalized to reach an ultimate figure under a procedure that has admitted infirmities. Instead, these critics assert, the trustees or the courts first determine the classes of claimants that should participate in the reorganization plan—on the basis of rough judgment or visceral reactions or other unexpressed or even unexpressable criteria—and then select the projection of earnings or the capitalization ratio necessary to reach a valuation figure that will include the preselected groups. The valuation process is not viewed as unduly harsh or rigid, but rather as so flexible that it is subject to abuse.

Moreover, valuation hearings could be expensive, protracted and rancorous. To the extent they were resorted to for purposes of delay and to obtain a better bargaining position they frequently were wasteful and counterproductive to a successful reorganization.

A second and even greater objection to the absolute priority rule under Chapter X of the Bankruptcy Act was that the rule could not be altered by an agreement between the parties that could bind dissenters. Even if creditors, voting by large majorities, were willing to grant stockholders without equity a share of the reorganization value to induce them to reorganize, they often could not do so if there were dissenting creditor claims. Unless these claims were paid off, the plan could be confirmed only if claims and equity interests were treated in the plan according to what the absolute priority rule gave them; no more and no less. Bankruptcy Act § 221(2). This objection to Chapter X has been eliminated in the Bankruptcy Code. Dissenters in a class that accepts a Chapter 11 plan are protected only to the extent they have rights under the best interests rule of § 1129(a)(7). But the absolute priority rule continues to apply in Chapter 11 if a class of claims or interests rejects the plan.

If an impaired class of unsecured claims does not accept the plan, confirmation of the plan is possible only if cramdown under § 1129(b) is permitted. Under § 1129(b)(2)(B) the absolute priority rule applies. If a creditor class is not fully paid no junior class can receive anything under the plan. Since any class of stockholder interests is junior to any class of claims the effect is to bar participation by stockholders in the reorganized corporation unless the nonconsenting class of claims is paid in full. The absolute priority rule is a powerful incentive to the debtor to offer a plan that unsecured creditors will accept.

*Inter-Class "Give-Ups."* A line of authority stemming from *In re SPM Manufacturing Corp.*, 984 F. 2d 1305 (1st Cir. 1993), has emerged which suggests that a secured class may assign distributions to junior classes in ways that appear inconsistent with the traditional understanding of the absolute priority rule. The justification for this practice is said to be that a creditor may give its property to another as it chooses. But when that "gift" is implemented through or in connection with a reorganization plan, the absolute priority rule may be implicated. The following case is a good analysis of this emerging practice in confirmation strategy.

## In re Armstrong World Industries, Inc.
United States District Court, D. Delaware, 2005.
320 B.R. 523.

■ EDUARDO C. ROBRENO, District Judge.

This case involves the Chapter 11 bankruptcy of Armstrong World Industries, Inc. and two of its subsidiaries. The Court must determine whether the Fourth Amended Plan of Reorganization, which the Bankruptcy Court endorsed in its Proposed Findings of Fact and Conclusions of Law, should be confirmed.

As the Third Circuit recognized in *In re Combustion Engineering, Inc.*, 391 F.3d 190 (3d Cir.2004), "[f]or some time now, mounting asbestos liabilities have pushed otherwise viable companies into bankruptcy." *Id.* at 201. The instant case exemplifies this trend. Facing significant asbestos liabilities, Armstrong World Industries, Inc. and two of its wholly owned subsidiaries ("AWI") voluntarily commenced a Chapter 11 proceeding in the United States Bankruptcy Court for the District of Delaware. Upon filing the petition, AWI became a debtor-in-possession ("Debtor"). * * *

After extensive negotiations with the Committees and other interested parties, Debtor filed its Fourth Amended Plan of Reorganization (the "Fourth Amended Plan" or the "Plan") and Amended Disclosure Statement. Under the Plan, eleven classes of claims and one class of equity interests were created. The proposed distributions of Debtor's property to three of these classes-the Unsecured Creditors, the Asbestos PI Claimants, and the Equity Interest Holders-are particularly relevant to the issues before the Court. Debtor estimates that the Unsecured Creditors, Class 6, have claims amounting to approximately $1.651 billion. Under the Plan, the Unsecured Creditors would recover about 59.5% of their claims. The Asbestos PI Claimants, Class 7, have claims estimated at $3.146 billion and would recover approximately 20% of their claims under the Plan. The Equity Interest Holders, Class 12, would be issued New Warrants valued at approximately $35 million to $40 million.

A key to the Plan lies in the consent by the class of Asbestos PI Claimants to share a portion of its proposed distribution with the Equity Interest Holders. Under Articles 3.2(1) and 10.1(b) of the Plan, *in pari materia*, if the Unsecured Creditors reject the Plan, the Asbestos PI Claimants will receive the New Warrants, but then will automatically waive the distribution, causing the Equity Interest Holders to secure the New Warrants. The net result of the Asbestos PI Claimants' waiver is that the Equity Interest Holders (i.e., the old AWI shareholders) receive Debtor's property (i.e., the New Warrants) on account of their equity interests, although a senior class (i.e., the Unsecured Creditors) would not have full satisfaction of its allowed claims. It is the lawfulness of this arrangement that forms the central issue in the case.

The Court concludes that the distribution of New Warrants to the class of Equity Interest Holders over the objection of the class of Unsecured Creditors violates the "fair and equitable" requirement of § 1129(b)(2)(B)(ii), a codification of the absolute priority rule. Thus, the Court must deny confirmation of the Plan.

### I. PROCEDURAL HISTORY

* * *

On May 23, 2003, after extensive negotiations with the various creditors and several attempts at drafting an unobjectionable reorganization plan and disclosure statement, Debtor filed its Fourth Amended Plan of Reorganization and Amended Disclosure Statement, both of which were supported, at least initially, by the Unsecured Creditors and the other major players. Thereafter, the Bankruptcy Court approved the Amended Disclosure Statement and established notice, voting, and objections procedures for confirmation of the Plan.

On September 22, 2003, * * * the Unsecured Creditors filed timely objections (the "Conditional Objections") to the Plan. In their objections, the Unsecured Creditors argued that * * * Debtor could meet neither the "cramdown" requirements of Section 1129(b) nor the "best interests" test under Section 1129(a)(7).

By the October 31, 2003 voting deadline, all the impaired classes-the Convenience Claims (Class 3), the Unsecured Claims Other Than Convenience Claims (Class 6), the Asbestos PI Claims (Class 7), and the Equity Interests (Class 12) -voted on the Plan. Classes 3 and 7 accepted the Plan while Class 6, the Unsecured Creditors, rejected the Plan. Although Class 12, the Equity Interest Holders, voted to accept the Plan, a provision of the Plan rescinds Class 12's acceptance if Class 6 rejects the Plan. * * *

At the outset of the Confirmation Hearing, the Bankruptcy Court identified the issues before it: (1) whether the Plan unfairly discriminates against the Unsecured Creditors because of inflated present and future asbestos personal injury liabilities, resulting in a greater recovery for the Asbestos PI Claimants than for the Unsecured Creditors, and (2) whether the issuance of New Warrants to the Asbestos PI Claimants, who waive this distribution under the Plan, is a violation of Section 1145 and/or Section 1129(b)(2)(B)(ii) of the Bankruptcy Code. During the Confirmation Hearing, the parties offered evidence and argument on these, as well as other, issues.

On December 19, 2003, the Bankruptcy Court issued its Proposed Findings of Fact and Conclusions of Law, along with the Proposed Confirmation Order. In response, the Unsecured Creditors filed objections to the proposals with the District Court. Thereafter, Debtor, the Asbestos PI Claimants, and the Future Claimants' Representative filed a joint response to the Unsecured Creditors' objections. On December 15, 2004, this Court held a hearing on the objections.

Now, this Court must decide whether to affirm the Bankruptcy Court's Proposed Findings of Fact and Conclusions of Law.

* * *

### III. CONFIRMATION OF A REORGANIZATION PLAN UNDER § 1129

* * *

A plan may be confirmed under either of two scenarios. One is consensually, provided all classes have accepted the plan or are not impaired. § 1129(a). The other is non-consensually, over the non-acceptance of an impaired class if all the requirements of § 1129(a), except paragraph (8), have been met and the plan "does not discriminate unfairly" and is "fair and equitable." § 1129(b). This latter approach, typically referred to as a "cramdown," is sometimes necessary in order to allow the debtor to override certain objections under appropriate circumstances, which might otherwise allow a small minority to prevent confirmation of the plan. *See generally* Kenneth N. Klee, *All You Ever Wanted to Know About Cram Down Under the New Bankruptcy Code,* 53 Am. Bankr.L.J. 133 (1979).

In the present case, there is little doubt that the Plan satisfies all the requirements of Section 1129(a), except paragraph (8). Therefore, because there is at least one dissenting class and the Plan fails to meet the requirements of Section 1129(b)(2)(B)(ii), the Court must deny confirmation of the Plan.

## IV. SECTION 1129(b)(2)(B)(ii) IS ROOTED IN THE JUDICIALLY CRAFTED ABSOLUTE PRIORITY RULE

### A. Origins of the Absolute Priority Rule

The principles underpinning Section 1129(b)'s "fair and equitable" requirement are rooted in the judicially created absolute priority rule. * * * The Supreme Court first articulated and applied the absolute priority rule, originally referred to as the "fixed principle," in *Northern Pacific Railway Co. v. Boyd, 228 U.S. 482* (1913), which involved a corporate reorganization in an equity receivership. *Id.* at 507. In *Boyd,* a general unsecured creditor in a railway company's reorganization was not fully compensated, but the "old" stockholders received property in the reorganized entity. *Id.* at 501. The Supreme Court stated:

[I]f purposely or unintentionally a single creditor was not paid, or provided for in the reorganization, [that creditor] could assert [its] superior rights against the subordinate interests of the old stockholders in the property transferred to the new company. . . . Any device, whether by private contract or judicial sale under consent decree, whereby stockholders were preferred before the creditor, [is] invalid.*Id.* at 504.

In what would lead to the coining of the expression "fixed principle," the Supreme Court wrote: "[I]n cases like this, the question must be decided according to a *fixed principle,* not leaving the rights of the creditors to depend upon the balancing of evidence as to whether, on the day of sale, the property was insufficient to pay prior encumbrances." *Id.* at 507 (emphasis added). And with that, the "fixed principle"-now known as the absolute priority rule-was established. Through the early 1900s, the Supreme Court continued to apply this principle in equity receivership cases.* * * Moreover, the Supreme Court reinforced the importance of the "fixed principle," recognizing that this basic tenet should be strictly applied. *Kan. City Terminal Ry.,* 271 U.S. at 454 ("[T]he 'fixed principle'. . . declares [that] the character of reorganization agreements must be determined, and to it there should be rigid adherence.").

### B. Bankruptcy Act of 1898

In 1934, Congress enacted Section 77B of the Bankruptcy Act of 1898, which governed bankruptcy reorganizations. Section 77B(f) introduced the words "fair and equitable" to bankruptcy nomenclature. * * * In part, Section 77B(f) stated that "[a]fter hearing such objections as may be made to the [reorganization] plan, the judge shall confirm the plan if satisfied that (1) it is fair and equitable and does not discriminate unfairly in favor of any class of creditors or stockholders and is feasible." * * * "The reason for such a limitation was the danger inherent in any reorganization plan proposed by a debtor, then and now, that the plan will simply turn out to be too good a deal for the debtor's owners." *203 N. LaSalle St. P'ship,* 526 U.S. at 444.

The relationship between the judicially created "fixed principle" doctrine and Section 77B(f)'s "fair and equitable" standard was enunciated by the Supreme Court in *Case v. Los Angeles Lumber Products Co.,* 308 U.S. 106 (1939). There, the Supreme Court held that the "fixed principle" doctrine is "firmly imbedded in [Section] 77B," thereby determining that a "fair and equitable" reorganization plan must meet the requirements of the "fixed principle," i.e., the absolute priority rule. *Id.* at 118-19; *cf. 203 N. LaSalle St. P'ship,* 526 U.S. at 448 ("Any argument from drafting history has to account for the fact that the Code does not codify any authoritative pre-Code version of the absolute priority rule.").

### C. Bankruptcy Code of 1978

In an effort to modernize bankruptcy law, Congress enacted the Bankruptcy Code of 1978. * * * Under 11 U.S.C. § 1129(b)(2)(B)(ii), Congress codified a modified version of the absolute priority rule. Richard Maloy, *A Primer on Cramdown-How and Why It Works,* 16 St. Thomas L.Rev. 1, 34 (2003) ("Congress did not codify the Absolute Priority Rule in the form it had developed, which would prohibit any favoritism of claims and interests of higher priority, but rather an Absolute Priority Rule which would apply only if a prior, but impaired, class objected to the plan and a claim junior to that of the objecting party receives property under the plan. It would not be applied if all classes accepted it.") (footnotes omitted)* * * . For a reorganization plan to be considered "fair and equitable" to a class of dissenting unsecured creditors, "the holder of any claim or interest that is junior to the claims of such class will not receive or retain under the plan on account of such junior claim or interest any property." § 1129(b)(2)(B)(ii). Whether the Plan complies with this specific provision in the Bankruptcy Code is at issue in this case.

## V. THE FOURTH AMENDED PLAN OF REORGANIZATION VIOLATES THE PROVISIONS OF § 1129(b)(2)(B)(ii)

The Court must determine whether distribution to the Equity Interest Holders of New Warrants-a distribution that the Asbestos PI Claimants would allegedly receive under the Plan, but to which they have agreed to surrender to the Equity Interest Holders-violates § 1129(b)(2)(B)(ii) when the higher-priority class of Unsecured Creditors objects to the distribution and its allowed claims have not been paid in full under the Plan.

### A. The Plain Meaning Rule

"It is well settled that the first step in interpreting a statute is to determine whether the language at issue has a plain and unambiguous meaning with regard to the particular dispute in the case." *United States v. Cooper,* 396 F.3d 308, 310 (3d Cir.2005). * * *

In part, Section 1129(b) provides:

**(1)** [T]he court, on request of the proponent of the plan, shall confirm the plan notwithstanding the requirements of such paragraph if the plan does not discriminate unfairly, and is fair and equitable, with respect to each class of claims or interests that is impaired under, and has not accepted, the plan.

**(2)** For the purpose of this subsection, the condition that a plan be fair and equitable with respect to a class includes the following requirements:

\* \* \* \* \* \*

**(B)** With respect to a class of unsecured claims—

\* \* \* \* \* \*

**(ii)** the holder of any claim or interest that is junior to the claims of such class will not receive or retain under the plan on account of such junior claim or interest any property.

Therefore, a plan is not "fair and equitable" if a class of creditors that is junior to the class of unsecured creditors receives debtor's property because of its ownership interest in the debtor while the allowed claims of the class of unsecured creditors have not been paid in full. Applying these plain requirements to the instant case, it is clear that (1) the Equity Interest Holders hold a claim junior to the Unsecured Creditors; (2) under the Plan, the Equity Interest Holders will receive property of Debtor (by way of New Warrants) because of their ownership interest in Debtor; and (3) the Unsecured Creditors' allowed claims will not be satisfied in full. Under these circumstances, the Plan violates § 1129(b)(2)(B)(ii) and is not "fair and equitable" with respect to the Unsecured Creditors.

\* \* \*

### C. Cases That Do Not Strictly Apply Section 1129(b)(2)(B)(ii) Are Distinguishable or Wrongly Decided

[In a deleted portion of the opinion, the court distinguishes the holding in *In re SPM Manufacturing Corp.*, 984 F.2d 1305 (1st Cir. 1993), often cited as allowing "give-ups," and a series of cases apparently agreeing with that case, as limited to secured creditors agreeing to carve value out of their collateral in favor of junior creditors, while *Armstrong* involved an unsecured class passing value to equity over the objection of an intervening unsecured class.]

In any event, to the extent that [these cases] read *SPM* to stand for the unconditional proposition that "[c]reditors are generally free to do whatever they wish with the bankruptcy dividends they receive, including sharing them with other creditors, so long as recoveries received under the [p]lan by other creditors are not impacted," *In re WorldCom*, 2003 WL 23861928, at *61, without adherence to the strictures of § 1129(b)(2)(B)(ii), that contention is flatly rejected here. *See generally* Kenneth N. Klee, *Adjusting Chapter 11: Fine Tuning the Plan Process,* 69

Am. Bankr.L.J. 551, 570-71 (1995) ("[A] plan should not be permitted to be crammed down where a senior class gives up value to a junior class while skipping over an intermediate or co-equal class. Although the argument can be and has been made that senior creditors should be entitled to do what they want with their property, the lessons of history should suffice to impose a per se rule that precludes senior creditors from collaborating with junior creditors or equity owners at the expense of intervening classes.") (footnotes omitted). * * *

Bluntly put, no amount of legal creativity or counsel's incantation to general notions of equity or to any supposed policy favoring reorganizations over liquidation supports judicial rewriting of the Bankruptcy Code. Accordingly, the New Warrants distribution to the Equity Interest Holders under the Fourth Amended Reorganization Plan violates § 1129(b)(2)(B)(ii). The Plan, therefore, cannot be confirmed.

## NOTE

How do you square this case with *In re Figter Limited*, p. 689 in which the Ninth Circuit held that a debtor's mortgagee could purchase the claims of the debtor's unsecured creditors?

## 3. NEW VALUE RULE

If the debtor cannot offer creditors a plan that all classes will accept, the debtor must conceive a plan that will meet the absolute priority standard of § 1129(b)(2)(B)(ii). A familiar tactic is for the debtor to propose a plan that allows the debtor's stockholders to retain part or all of the ownership of the reorganized corporation based on their contributing new money equivalent to the value of the ownership interest they will retain under the plan. Judicial support for this procedure is found in *Case v. Los Angeles Lumber Products Co.*, 308 U.S. 106 (1939), an opinion of Justice Douglas discussed in *203 North LaSalle*, which follows. *Los Angeles Lumber* concerned the reorganization under § 77B of the Bankruptcy Act of a corporation whose assets were worth approximately $840,000 while its liabilities, mostly claims of first mortgage bondholders, totaled more than $3.8 million. Under § 77B a plan of reorganization could not be confirmed, even if all classes approved, unless the plan was "fair and equitable." Justice Douglas held that this requirement adopted the "full" or "absolute" priority rule. The plan provided for creation of a new corporation with new preferred stock issued to bondholders and new common stock issued to stockholders of the old corporation without any new contribution of money by those stockholders. The plan was approved by both bondholders and stockholders by majorities of over 90%. Confirmation of the plan was challenged by some dissenting bondholders on the ground that the plan did not satisfy the absolute priority rule. The stockholders attempted to justify their participation in the ownership of the new corporation by asserting that their commitment to continue as managers of the new corporation was a contribution of new value to the enterprise. They pointed to the fact that their experience and standing in the community would benefit the new corporation. The Court declared that it would be an evasion of the absolute priority rule to allow the owners of an insolvent business to take a share of the reorganized entity on the basis of intangibles like a promise to continue to provide management services that cannot be translated into money's worth reasonably equivalent to the value of the new stock. But Justice Douglas also said, in a much-discussed dictum, that the owners of an insolvent corporation can take ownership interests in a reorganized corporation to the extent they contribute money or money's worth.

In *Norwest Bank Worthington v. Ahlers*, 485 U.S. 197 (1988), the Supreme Court reaffirmed the principle that the equityholders' promise to provide future services to the reorganized debtor could not be used as a justification for passing value down to equity over the objections of dissenting classes of creditors. Such a plan violated the absolute priority rule as codified in § 1129(b)(2)(B). But in a startling footnote the Supreme Court went on to suggest that perhaps the codification of the rule in § 1129(b)(2)(B) was also inconsistent with Douglas's dictum in *Los Angeles Lumber* that the distribution of value to equity holders in exchange for "money or money's worth" might comply with the rule.

Though startling to bankruptcy specialists, the cloud the *Ahlers* court cast over the continued viability of the new value rule was supported by serious policy concerns with how the new value rule might be manipulated unfairly by the debtor. The kind of case that draws criticism of the new value rule is *In re Potter Material Service, Inc.*, 781 F.2d 99 (7th Cir.1986), in which the sole stockholder of Debtor proposed in a cramdown plan to retain the full ownership interest in the reorganized corporation by contributing $14,800 to fund a 3% payout to the class of unsecured creditors and $20,000 to pay debtor's attorneys. A previous version of the plan had proposed a 40% payout to the unsecured creditors. The stockholder also agreed to renew his personal guaranty of Debtor's $600,000 obligation to the bank on which, apparently, the stockholder was already liable. The court determined that Debtor's going concern value was between $10,000 and $15,000 and confirmed the plan. The court based its valuation on evidence of Debtor's past earnings record, the state of the economy, the highly competitive nature of Debtor's business, the current financial position of Debtor, and projections of Debtor's future earnings. There is no indication that the court allowed any third party to bid for the firm or considered any plan but Debtor's.

In the post-*Ahlers* dispute about whether the new value rule survived enactment of the Bankruptcy Code, three views emerged which, for convenience, we can discuss as the Reinhardt view in *Bonner Mall*, the Easterbrook view in *Kham & Nate's*, and the market approach. In *In re Bonner Mall Partnerships*, 2F3d 899 (9th Cir. 1993), Judge Reinhardt joined with some commentators and courts in rejecting the terminology "new value *exception*." He concludes that there is no exception in the Code to the absolute priority rule of § 1129(b)(2)(B)(ii). All classes of creditors must be fully paid before the old equity can retain any "property" under the reorganization plan "on account of such junior claim or interest." For the answer to the question whether old owners are in fact retaining property in a reorganized entity on account of their prior interest in the old entity, Judge Reinhardt turns to the traditional formulation of the new value rule which he describes as "an established pre-Code Bankruptcy practice." Under this principle an old owner was allowed to retain an interest in the new entity if it makes a capital contribution to the new entity that is (1) new, (2) substantial, (3) money or money's worth, (4) necessary for a successful reorganization and (5) reasonably equivalent to the value or interest received. Moreover, the debtor's plan may designate the old owners as having the exclusive right to purchase the ownership interest in the new entity so long as the new contribution is "necessary for a successful reorganization and in the best interest of all concerned." All this can be done in a cramdown plan over the opposition of classes of creditors holding impaired claims who believe the old equity is not making a contribution commensurate with the participation it is taking in the new entity.

The Easterbrook view was expressed in *Kham & Nate's Shoes No. 2, Inc. v. First Bank of Whiting*, 908 F.2d 1351 (7th Cir.1990), in which the court declined to confirm a cramdown plan under which the debtor's two stockholders proposed to retain ownership in exchange for their personal guaranties of a $435,000 loan to be made to the debtor corporation under the plan. Without deciding whether the new value rule was still in effect, the court held that the guaranties were not new value. Judge Easterbrook questioned the wisdom of the new value rule in the following paragraph:

> In principle, then, the exchange of stock for new value may make sense. When it does, the creditors should be willing to go along. Creditors effectively own bankrupt firms. They may find it worthwhile, as owners, to sell equity claims to the managers; they may even find it worthwhile to give the equity away in order to induce managers to stay on and work hard. Because the Code allows creditors to consent to a plan that impairs their interests, voluntary transactions of this kind are possible. Only collective action problems could frustrate beneficial arrangements. If there are many creditors, one may hold out, seeking to engross a greater share of the gains. But the Code deals with holdups by allowing half of a class by number (two-thirds by value) to consent to a lower class's retention of an interest. § 1126(c). Creditors not acting in good faith do not count toward the one-third required to block approval, § 1126(e). When there is value to be gained by allowing a lower class to kick in new value and keep its interest, the creditors should be willing to go along. A "new value exception" means a power in the *judge* to "sell" stock to the managers even when the creditors believe that this transaction will *not* augment the value of the firm.

908 F.2d at 1360. In stating that "creditors effectively own bankrupt firms," Judge Easterbrook means that if the value of the bankrupt business is not sufficient to pay in full the claims of the creditors, all of the value of the business equitably belongs to the creditors. If there is one dissenting class of claims, the class may argue that to the extent their claims are not paid in full any residual value of the business belongs to that class. That is the effect of the absolute priority rule. The ownership interest in the business represents the residual value. Presumably, Judge Easterbrook would not find it to be fair and equitable to allow the ownership interest to be sold to somebody else without the consent of the dissenting class of claims. If somebody is willing to pay for the ownership interest, that interest must have some value. To the extent the dissenting class is not paid in full, it follows that the payment for that interest should be for the benefit of the dissenting class and that class should have the right to decide whether the amount offered for the ownership interest is adequate.

Fundamental to the difference of opinion between Judge Easterbrook and Judge Reinhardt is *who* decides whether the new value contribution is, in fact, equal to the ownership interest retained in the new entity. Judge Easterbrook would have the creditors make that determination. If they believe the contribution is worth the interest taken, they will consent to the plan and confirmation can go forward under § 1129(a). Judge Reinhardt would have the court value the ownership interest in deciding whether to confirm the plan.

In terms of the pre-Code background of the new value rule, Judge Easterbrook seems to have the better of this argument. Judge Reinhardt resolves the contemporary problem of the terms on which old ownership interests can participate in a new entity by reference to a pre-Code common law rule that he holds was not abolished by enactment of the Code. What he does not disclose is that the legal regime in which the new value rule operated before the Code was quite different from that after the Code. Although Chapter X of the Act allowed two-thirds of a creditor class to accept a plan and bind dissenters, still the court could not confirm the plan over the objection of a single creditor unless it was "fair and equitable." *Case v. Los Angeles Lumber Products Co.*, 308 U.S. 106 (1939), held that the quoted phrase meant that the plan had to meet the absolute priority rule: old equity could retain nothing in the plan unless all creditors were fully paid or all of the value in the entity had passed to them. Thus, before the Code, creditors—even by a two-thirds vote—could not waive the absolute priority rule and allow old equity to participate. This rigidity could lead to extreme situations in which the reorganization plan of a company that had to have new capital to survive could not award the old owners an equity interest in the new entity even though the old owners were the only source of new capital and all creditor classes consented to the plan. In such a case the *Los Angeles Lumber* dictum offered a sensible safety valve by recognizing an "exception" to the absolute priority rule which permitted the old owners to participate in the reorganized entity if they gave new value reasonably equivalent to the participation they received in the new entity.

The common law rule that Judge Reinhardt brings into post-Code law was one that was carefully tailored to meet the extraordinary situation spelled out above: the contribution must not only be commensurate with the interest taken but it must also be "necessary for a successful reorganization." Moreover, before the Code, all classes of creditors had to agree to the plan before it could be confirmed, an act that indicated their satisfaction with the equivalence of the old owners' new capital infusion. Hence, the court's view that the new value rule was an established common law rule that Congress must have intended to continue under the Code seems undercut by the difference in function performed by the rule in the pre-Code era, when the new value rule operated as a means of saving a debtor under a plan approved by the creditors, as contrasted with the use the courts have made of it in cases like *Bonner Mall* and *Potter* in which a plan rejected by creditors is used to squeeze out the claims of those creditors. What is more, since § 1129(a) now allows creditor classes to waive the absolute priority rule by a vote of two-thirds in amount and one-half in number (§ 1126(c)) and to permit the old owners to retain their interests on almost any terms on which agreement can be reached, the emergency situation that the *Los Angeles Lumber* formulation of the new value rule was designed to address is now easily dealt with in a § 1129(a) consensual plan. Bruce A. Markell, *Owners, Auctions, and Absolute Priority in Bankruptcy Reorganizations*, 44 Stan.L.Rev. 69, 75–90 (1991), discusses the pre-Code legal regime under which the new value rule was developed.

A third view of the new value rule taken by some courts and commentators essentially denies the existence of or need for a new value rule in its classic pre-Code formulation under the Code. They agree with Judge Reinhardt that, without violating the absolute priority rule, a cramdown plan can be confirmed under which old owners take an ownership interest in the reorganized entity so long as they contribute new capital of value equal to the interest taken. But they disagree with his decision to permit a plan to give the old equity the exclusive right to buy the new equity. A technical argument against the Reinhardt view is that an exclusive right to buy the stock in a new company amounts to a warrant given to the old owners and is, within § 1129(b)(2)(B)(ii), "property" having some value (why else would they want it?) given them "on account of" their previous ownership interest. A more basic criticism of exclusivity relates to the question of who is to value the ownership interest in the reorganized entity which the old owners wish to buy.

Searching for a solution to the valuation problem in a case in which the owners of shares in a business trust proposed retention of their interest in exchange for a capital contribution, the court in *In re Bjolmes Realty Trust*, 134 B.R. 1000 (Bankr.D.Mass.1991), held that a "fresh contribution" of capital did not "dilute" § 1129(b)(2)(B)(ii) but that market forces should be allowed to determine the value of the residual interest by having the court hold an auction sale of that interest at which the shareholders and creditors of the debtor could bid. The court said "The decisions are particularly troubling in their handling of valuation of the retained stock interest. * * * And they do nothing to allay the suspicion that a court, intent on promoting reorganization, will gear the valuation to equal the contribution." 134 B.R. at 1008. The *Bjolmes* court saw the temptation for self-dealing on the part of the debtor in proposing a new value plan, in which only the old owners may participate, that places a low valuation on the new stock, as not adequately redressed by having the valuation decision made by a busy court "intent on promoting reorganization." Judge Easterbrook acidly comments that this, in effect, gives the *judge* the right to sell the stock to the insiders. The reaction to these concerns by critics is to urge that if stock in a new entity is to be sold for a new infusion of capital, market forces, rather than courts, should be relied on to fix the value of the stock to be sold. The *Bjolmes* holding ordered that the stock be sold on an auction basis at which the creditors could bid.

Our colleague, Kenneth Klee, observes:

> The vice of the new value exception is that it enables the debtor's owners to purchase an ownership interest based on a court-approved valuation without validation of the price in the market place. Valuation by the court is, of course the norm for distribution of reorganization securities under the fair and equitable test. But when a reorganization security is to be sold, in effect, for a new contribution, rather than distributed in satisfaction of claims or interests to a class of creditors or owners under a plan, perhaps a market test should be applied as would be done with the sale of any other asset of the estate. At the very least, to maintain the balance of relative right, chapter 11 creditors who argue that the proposed capital contribution is too low should have the opportunity to match or exceed the pending offer.

Kenneth N. Klee, *Cram Down II*, 64 Am.Bankr.L.J. 229, 244 (1990).

What these views have in common is the simple tenet that the old owners should have no better or worse rights to buy into the reorganized entity than other investors. Elizabeth Warren, *A Theory of Absolute Priority*, 1991 Annual Survey of American Law 9. If this principle is sound, then the classic formulation of the new value rule resurrected in *Bonner Mall* is an anachronism. Whether the contribution the old owners make is "substantial" or "necessary for a successful reorganization" should be irrelevant so long as they pay what the ownership interest in the new entity is worth in the market.

After doubt was cast on the new value rule in *Ahlers*, the continued viability of the new value exception became the most controversial and important unsettled issue of reorganization law. The Supreme Court seemed finally poised to resolve the issue in *In re Bonner Mall Partnership*, 2 F.3d 899 (9th Cir.1993), *cert. granted*, 510 U.S. 1039 (1994), but later dismissed *Bonner Mall* on procedural grounds. Finally, in 1999, the Supreme Court reached the new value issue in the following case.

## Bank of America N.T. & S.A. v. 203 North LaSalle Street Partnership

Supreme Court of the United States, 1999.
526 U.S. 434.

■ Justice SOUTER delivered the opinion of the Court.

The issue in this Chapter 11 reorganization case is whether a debtor's prebankruptcy equity holders may, over the objection of a senior class of impaired creditors, contribute new capital and receive ownership interests in the reorganized entity, when that opportunity is given exclusively to the old equity holders under a plan adopted without consideration of alternatives. We hold that old equity holders are disqualified from participating in such a "new value" transaction by the terms of 11 U.S.C. § 1129(b)(2)(B)(ii), which in such circumstances bars a junior interest holder's receipt of any property on account of his prior interest.

### I

Petitioner, Bank of America National Trust and Savings Association (Bank), is the major creditor of respondent, 203 North LaSalle Street Partnership (Debtor or Partnership), an Illinois real estate limited partnership. The Bank lent the Debtor some $93 million, secured by a nonrecourse first mortgage[3] on the Debtor's principal asset, 15 floors of an office building in downtown Chicago. In January 1995, the Debtor defaulted, and the Bank began foreclosure in a state court.

In March, the Debtor responded with a voluntary petition for relief under Chapter 11 of the Bankruptcy Code which automatically stayed the foreclosure proceedings, see § 362(a). The Debtor's principal objective was to ensure that its partners retained title to the property so as to avoid roughly $20 million in personal tax liabilities, which would fall due if the Bank foreclosed. The Debtor proceeded to propose a reorganization plan during the 120–day period when it alone had the right to do so, see 11 U.S.C. § 1121(b); see also § 1121(c) (exclusivity period extends to 180 days if the debtor files plan within the initial 120 days).[4] The Bankruptcy Court rejected the Bank's motion to terminate the period of exclusivity to

---

[3] A nonrecourse loan requires the Bank to look only to the Debtor's collateral for payment. But see n. 6, *infra*.

[4] The Debtor filed an initial plan on April 13, 1995, and amended it on May 12, 1995. The Bank objected, and the Bankruptcy Court rejected the plan on the ground that it was not feasible. See § 1129(a)(11). The Debtor submitted a new plan on September 11, 1995.

make way for a plan of its own to liquidate the property, and instead extended the exclusivity period for cause shown, under § 1121(d).

The value of the mortgaged property was less than the balance due the Bank, which elected to divide its undersecured claim into secured and unsecured deficiency claims under § 506(a) and § 1111(b).[6] Under the plan, the Debtor separately classified the Bank's secured claim, its unsecured deficiency claim, and unsecured trade debt owed to other creditors. See § 1122(a).[7] The Bankruptcy Court found that the Debtor's available assets were prepetition rents in a cash account of $3.1 million and the 15 floors of rental property worth $54.5 million. The secured claim was valued at the latter figure, leaving the Bank with an unsecured deficiency of $38.5 million.

So far as we need be concerned here, the Debtor's plan had these further features:

(1) The Bank's $54.5 million secured claim would be paid in full between 7 and 10 years after the original 1995 repayment date.[8]

(2) The Bank's $38.5 million unsecured deficiency claim would be discharged for an estimated 16% of its present value.[9]

(3) The remaining unsecured claims of $90,000, held by the outside trade creditors, would be paid in full, without interest, on the effective date of the plan.[10]

(4) Certain former partners of the Debtor would contribute $6.125 million in new capital over the course of five years (the contribu-

---

[6] Having agreed to waive recourse against any property of the Debtor other than the real estate, the Bank had no unsecured claim outside of Chapter 11. Section 1111(b), however, provides that nonrecourse secured creditors who are undersecured must be treated in Chapter 11 as if they had recourse.

[7] Indeed, the Seventh Circuit apparently requires separate classification of the deficiency claim of an undersecured creditor from other general unsecured claims. Nonetheless, the Bank argued that if its deficiency claim had been included in the class of general unsecured creditors, its vote against confirmation would have resulted in the plan's rejection by that class. The Bankruptcy Court and the District Court rejected the contention that the classifications were gerrymandered to obtain requisite approval by a single class and the Court of Appeals agreed. The Bank sought no review of that issue, which is thus not before us.

[8] Payment consisted of a prompt cash payment of $1,149,500 and a secured, 7–year note, extendable at the Debtor's option.

[9] This expected yield was based upon the Bankruptcy Court's projection that a sale or refinancing of the property on the 10th anniversary of the plan confirmation would produce a $19–million distribution to the Bank.

[10] The Debtor originally owed $160,000 in unsecured trade debt. After filing for bankruptcy, the general partners purchased some of the trade claims. Upon confirmation, the insiders would waive all general unsecured claims they held.

tion being worth some $4.1 million in present value), in exchange for the Partnership's entire ownership of the reorganized debtor.

The last condition was an exclusive eligibility provision: the old equity holders were the only ones who could contribute new capital.[11]

The Bank objected and, being the sole member of an impaired class of creditors, thereby blocked confirmation of the plan on a consensual basis. See § 1129(a)(8).[12] The Debtor, however, took the alternate route to confirmation of a reorganization plan, forthrightly known as the judicial "cramdown" process for imposing a plan on a dissenting class. § 1129(b). See generally Klee, All You Ever Wanted to Know About Cram Down Under the New Bankruptcy Code, 53 Am. Bankr.L.J. 133 (1979).

There are two conditions for a cramdown. First, all requirements of § 1129(a) must be met (save for the plan's acceptance by each impaired class of claims or interests, see § 1129(a)(8)). Critical among them are the conditions that the plan be accepted by at least one class of impaired creditors, and satisfy the "best-interest-of-creditors" test.[13] Here, the class of trade creditors with impaired unsecured claims voted for the plan,[14] and there was no issue of best interest. Second, the objection of an impaired creditor class may be overridden only if "the plan does not discriminate unfairly, and is fair and equitable, with respect to each class of claims or interests that is impaired under, and has not accepted, the plan." § 1129(b)(1). As to a dissenting class of impaired unsecured creditors, such a plan may be found to be "fair and equitable" only if the allowed value of the claim is to be paid in full, § 1129(b)(2)(B)(i), or, in the alternative, if "the holder of any claim or interest that is junior to the claims of such [impaired unsecured] class will not receive or retain under the plan on account of such junior claim or interest any property," § 1129(b)(2)(B)(ii). That latter condition is the core of what is known as the "absolute priority rule."

---

[11] The plan eliminated the interests of noncontributing partners. More than 60% of the Partnership interests would change hands on confirmation of the plan. The new Partnership, however, would consist solely of former partners, a feature critical to the preservation of the Partnership's tax shelter.

[12] A class of creditors accepts if a majority of the creditors and those holding two-thirds of the total dollar amount of the claims within that class vote to approve the plan. § 1126(c).

[13] Section 1129(a)(7) provides that if the holder of a claim impaired under a plan of reorganization has not accepted the plan, then such holder must "receive. . . on account of such claim. . . property of a value, as of the effective date of the plan, that is not less than the amount that such holder would so receive. . . if the debtor were liquidated under chapter 7. . . on such date." The "best interests" test applies to individual creditors holding impaired claims, even if the class as a whole votes to accept the plan.

[14] Claims are unimpaired if they retain all of their prepetition legal, equitable, and contractual rights against the debtor. § 1124.

The absolute priority rule was the basis for the Bank's position that the plan could not be confirmed as a cramdown. As the Bank read the rule, the plan was open to objection simply because certain old equity holders in the Debtor Partnership would receive property even though the Bank's unsecured deficiency claim would not be paid in full. The Bankruptcy Court approved the plan nonetheless, and accordingly denied the Bank's pending motion to convert the case to Chapter 7 liquidation, or to dismiss the case. The District Court affirmed, as did the Court of Appeals.

The majority of the Seventh Circuit's divided panel found ambiguity in the language of the statutory absolute priority rule, and looked beyond the text to interpret the phrase "on account of "as permitting recognition of a "new value corollary" to the rule. According to the panel, the corollary, as stated by this Court in *Case v. Los Angeles Lumber Products Co.,* provides that the objection of an impaired senior class does not bar junior claim holders from receiving or retaining property interests in the debtor after reorganization, if they contribute new capital in money or money's worth, reasonably equivalent to the property's value, and necessary for successful reorganization of the restructured enterprise. The panel majority held that

> "when an old equity holder retains an equity interest in the reorganized debtor by meeting the requirements of the new value corollary, he is not receiving or retaining that interest "on account of "his prior equitable ownership of the debtor. Rather, he is allowed to participate in the reorganized entity "on account of "a new, substantial, necessary and fair infusion of capital."

In the dissent's contrary view, there is nothing ambiguous about the text: the "plain language of the absolute priority rule. . . does not include a new value exception." Since "[t]he Plan in this case gives [the Debtor's] partners the exclusive right to retain their ownership interest in the indebted property *because of* their status as. . . prior interest holder[s]," the dissent would have reversed confirmation of the plan.

We granted certiorari to resolve a Circuit split on the issue. The Seventh Circuit in this case joined the Ninth in relying on a new value corollary to the absolute priority rule to support confirmation of such plans. The Second and Fourth Circuits, by contrast, without explicitly rejecting the corollary, have disapproved plans similar to this one.[15] We do not decide whether the statute includes a new value corollary or exception, but hold that on any reading respondent's proposed plan fails to satisfy the statute, and accordingly reverse.

---

[15] All four of these cases arose in the single-asset real estate context, the typical one in which new value plans are proposed. * * *

## II

The terms "absolute priority rule" and "new value corollary" (or "exception") are creatures of law antedating the current Bankruptcy Code, and to understand both those terms and the related but inexact language of the Code some history is helpful. The Bankruptcy Act preceding the Code contained no such provision as subsection (b)(2)(B)(ii), its subject having been addressed by two interpretive rules. The first was a specific gloss on the requirement of § 77B (and its successor, Chapter X) of the old Act, that any reorganization plan be "fair and equitable." The reason for such a limitation was the danger inherent in any reorganization plan proposed by a debtor, then and now, that the plan will simply turn out to be too good a deal for the debtor's owners. See H.R. Doc. No. 93–137, pt. I, p. 255 (1973) (discussing concern with "the ability of a few insiders, whether representatives of management or major creditors, to use the reorganization process to gain an unfair advantage"); *ibid.* ("[I]t was believed that creditors, because of management's position of dominance, were not able to bargain effectively without a clear standard of fairness and judicial control"); Ayer, Rethinking Absolute Priority After *Ahlers,* 87 Mich. L.Rev. 963, 969–973 (1989). Hence the pre-Code judicial response known as the absolute priority rule, that fairness and equity required that "the creditors. . . be paid before the stockholders could retain [equity interests] for any purpose whatever." *Northern Pacific R. Co. v. Boyd,* 228 U.S. 482, 508 (1913).

The second interpretive rule addressed the first. Its classic formulation occurred in *Case v. Los Angeles Lumber Products Co.,* in which the Court spoke through Justice DOUGLAS in this dictum:

> "It is, of course, clear that there are circumstances under which stockholders may participate in a plan of reorganization of an insolvent debtor. . .. Where th[e] necessity [for new capital] exists and the old stockholders make a fresh contribution and receive in return a participation reasonably equivalent to their contribution, no objection can be made. . ..
>
> "[W]e believe that to accord 'the creditor his full right of priority against the corporate assets' where the debtor is insolvent, the stockholder's participation must be based on a contribution in money or in money's worth, reasonably equivalent in view of all the circumstances to the participation of the stockholder." 308 U.S., at 121–122.

Although counsel for one of the parties here has described the *Case* observation as "'black-letter' principle," it never rose above the technical level of dictum in any opinion of this Court, which last addressed it in *Norwest Bank Worthington v. Ahlers,* holding that a contribution of "'labor, experience, and expertise'" by a junior interest holder was not in the "'money's worth'" that the *Case* observation required. Nor, prior to the enactment of the current Bankruptcy Code, did any court rely on the *Case* dictum to approve a plan that gave old equity a property right after reorganization. Hence the controversy over how weighty the *Case* dictum had become, as reflected in the alternative labels for the new value notion: some writers and courts (including this one, see *Ahlers, supra*) have spoken of it as an exception to the absolute priority rule, while others have characterized it as a simple corollary to the rule, see, *e.g., In re Bonner Mall Partnership.*

Enactment of the Bankruptcy Code in place of the prior Act might have resolved the status of new value by a provision bearing its name or at least unmistakably couched in its terms, but the Congress chose not to avail itself of that opportunity. In 1973, Congress had considered proposals by the Bankruptcy Commission that included a recommendation to make the absolute priority rule more supple by allowing nonmonetary new value contributions. Although Congress took no action on any of the ensuing bills containing language that would have enacted such an expanded new value concept, each of them was reintroduced in the next congressional session. See H.R. 31, 94th Cong., 1st Sess., §§ 7–303(4),[17] 7–310(d)(2)(B) (1975),[18] * * * After extensive hearings, a substantially revised House bill emerged, but without any provision for nonmonetary new value contributions. See H.R. 6, 95th Cong., 1st Sess., §§ 1123, 1129(b) (1977).[19] After a lengthy mark-up session, the House produced [the bill] which would eventually become the law. It had no explicit new value language, expansive or otherwise, but did codify the absolute priority rule in nearly its present form. See H.R. 8200, *supra,* § 1129(b)(2)(B)(iv) ("[T]he holders of claims or interests of any class of claims or interests, as the case

---

[17] Section 7–303(4) read: "[W]hen the equity security holders retain an interest under the plan, the individual debtor, certain partners or equity security holders will make a contribution which is important to the operation of the reorganized debtor or the successor under the plan, for participation by the individual debtor, such partners, or such holders under the plan on a basis which reasonably approximates the value, if any, of their interests, and the additional estimated value of such contribution."

[18] Section 7–310(d)(2)(B) read: "Subject to the provisions of section 7–303(3) and (4) and the court's making any findings required thereby, there is a reasonable basis for the valuation on which the plan is based and the plan is fair and equitable in that there is a reasonable probability that the securities issued and other consideration distributed under the plan will fully compensate the respective classes of creditors and equity security holders of the debtor for their respective interests in the debtor or his property."

[19] Section 1129(b) of H.R. 6 read, in relevant part: "[T]he court, on request of the proponent of such plan, shall confirm such plan. . . if such plan is fair and equitable with respect to all classes except any class that has accepted the plan and that is comprised of claims or interests on account of which the holders of such claims or interests will receive or retain under the plan not more than would be so received or retained under a plan that is fair and equitable with respect to all classes."

may be, that is junior to such class will not receive or retain under the plan on account of such junior claims or interests any property").[20]

For the purpose of plumbing the meaning of subsection (b)(2)(B)(ii) in search of a possible statutory new value exception, the lesson of this drafting history is equivocal. Although hornbook law has it that " "Congress does not intend *sub silentio* to enact statutory language that it has earlier discarded,' " *INS v. Cardoza—Fonseca,* 480 U.S. 421, 442–443, the phrase "on account of "is not *silentium,* and the language passed by in this instance had never been in the bill finally enacted, but only in predecessors that died on the vine. None of these contained an explicit codification of the absolute priority rule,[21] and even in these earlier bills the language in question stated an expansive new value concept, not the rule as limited in the *Case* dictum.[22]

The equivocal note of this drafting history is amplified by another feature of the legislative advance toward the current law. Any argument from drafting history has to account for the fact that the Code does not codify any authoritative pre-Code version of the absolute priority rule. Compare § 1129(b)(2)(B)(ii) ("[T]he holder of any claim or interest that is junior to the claims of such [impaired unsecured] class will not receive or retain under the plan on account of such junior claim or interest any property") with *Boyd,* 228 U.S., at 508, 33 S.Ct. 554 ("[T]he creditors were entitled to be paid before the stockholders could retain [a right of property] for any purpose whatever"), and *Case,* 308 U.S., at 116, 60 S.Ct. 1 (" "[C]reditors are entitled to priority over stockholders against all the property of an insolvent corporation.' " See H.R.Rep. No. 95–595, *supra,* at 414, U.S.Code Cong. & Admin. News 1978, p. 6370. (characterizing § 1129(b)(2)(B)(ii) as a "partial codification of the absolute priority rule"); *ibid.* ("The elements of the [fair and equitable] test are new[,] departing from both the absolute priority rule and the best interests of creditors tests found under the Bankruptcy Act").

The upshot is that this history does nothing to disparage the possibility apparent in the statutory text, that the absolute priority rule now on the books as subsection (b)(2)(B)(ii) may carry a new value corollary. Although there is no literal reference to "new value" in the phrase "on account of such junior claim," the phrase could arguably carry such an implication in modifying the prohibition against receipt by junior claimants of any interest under a plan while a senior class of unconsenting creditors goes less than fully paid.

---

[20] While the earlier proposed bills contained provisions requiring as a condition of confirmation that a plan be "fair and equitable," none of them contained language explicitly codifying the absolute priority rule. See, *e.g.,* nn. 17–19, *supra.*

[21] See n. 20, *supra.*

[22] See nn. 17–18, *supra.*

# III

Three basic interpretations have been suggested for the "on account of" modifier. The first reading is proposed by the Partnership, that "on account of" harks back to accounting practice and means something like "in exchange for," or "in satisfaction of." On this view, a plan would not violate the absolute priority rule unless the old equity holders received or retained property in exchange for the prior interest, without any significant new contribution; if substantial money passed from them as part of the deal, the prohibition of subsection (b)(2)(B)(ii) would not stand in the way, and whatever issues of fairness and equity there might otherwise be would not implicate the "on account of" modifier.

This position is beset with troubles, the first one being textual. Subsection (b)(2)(B)(ii) forbids not only receipt of property on account of the prior interest but its retention as well. A common instance of the latter would be a debtor's retention of an interest in the insolvent business reorganized under the plan. Yet it would be exceedingly odd to speak of "retain[ing]" property in exchange for the same property interest, and the eccentricity of such a reading is underscored by the fact that elsewhere in the Code the drafters chose to use the very phrase "in exchange for," § 1123(a)(5)(J) (a plan shall provide adequate means for implementation, including "issuance of securities of the debtor. . . for cash, for property, for existing securities, or in exchange for claims or interests"). It is unlikely that the drafters of legislation so long and minutely contemplated as the 1978 Bankruptcy Code would have used two distinctly different forms of words for the same purpose.

The second difficulty is practical: the unlikelihood that Congress meant to impose a condition as manipulable as subsection (b)(2)(B)(ii) would be if "on account of "meant to prohibit merely an exchange unaccompanied by a substantial infusion of new funds but permit one whenever substantial funds changed hands. "Substantial" or "significant" or "considerable" or like characterizations of a monetary contribution would measure it by the Lord Chancellor's foot, and an absolute priority rule so variable would not be much of an absolute. Of course it is true (as already noted) that, even if old equity holders could displace the rule by adding some significant amount of cash to the deal, it would not follow that their plan would be entitled to adoption; a contested plan would still need to satisfy the overriding condition of fairness and equity. But that general fairness and equity criterion would apply in any event, and one comes back to the question why Congress would have bothered to add a separate priority rule without a sharper edge.

Since the "in exchange for" reading merits rejection, the way is open to recognize the more common understanding of "on account of" to mean "because of." This is certainly the usage meant for the phrase at other places in the statute, see § 1111(b)(1)(A) (treating certain claims as if the holder of the claim "had recourse against the debtor on account of such claim"); § 522(d)(10)(E) (permitting debtors to exempt payments under certain benefit plans and contracts "on account of illness, disability, death, age, or length of service"); § 547(b)(2) (authorizing trustee to avoid a transfer of an interest of the debtor in property "for or on account of an antecedent debt owed by the debtor"); § 547(c)(4)(B) (barring trustee from avoiding a transfer when a creditor gives new value to the debtor "on account of which new value the debtor did not make an otherwise unavoidable transfer to. . . such creditor"). So, under the commonsense rule that a given phrase is meant to carry a given concept in a single statute the better reading of subsection (b)(2)(B)(ii) recognizes that a causal relationship between holding the prior claim or interest and receiving or retaining property is what activates the absolute priority rule.

The degree of causation is the final bone of contention. We understand the Government, as *amicus curiae,* to take the starchy position not only that any degree of causation between earlier interests and retained property will activate the bar to a plan providing for later property but also that whenever the holders of equity in the Debtor end up with some property there will be some causation; when old equity, and not someone on the street, gets property the reason is *res ipsa loquitur.* An old equity holder simply cannot take property under a plan if creditors are not paid in full.[23]

There are, however, reasons counting against such a reading. If, as is likely, the drafters were treating junior claimants or interest holders as a class at this point (see *Ahlers,* 485 U.S., at 202),[24] then the simple way to have prohibited the old interest holders from receiving anything over objection would have been to omit the "on account of" phrase entirely from subsection (b)(2)(B)(ii). On this assumption, reading the provision as a blanket prohibition would leave "on account of" as a redundancy, contrary to the interpretive obligation to try to give meaning to all the statutory lan-

---

[23] Our interpretation of the Government's position in this respect is informed by its view as *amicus curiae* in the *Bonner Mall* case: "the language and structure of the Code prohibit in all circumstances confirmation of a plan that grants the prior owners an equity interest in the reorganized debtor over the objection of a class of unpaid unsecured claims."

The Government conceded that, in the case before us, it had no need to press this more stringent view, since "whatever [the] definition of 'on account of,' a 100 percent certainty that junior equit[y] obtains property because they're junior equity will satisfy that."

[24] It is possible, on the contrary, to argue on the basis of the immediate text that the prohibition against receipt of an interest "on account of "a prior unsecured claim or interest was meant to indicate only that there is no *per se* bar to such receipt by a creditor holding both a senior secured claim and a junior unsecured one, when the senior secured claim accounts for the subsequent interest. This reading would of course eliminate the phrase "on account of "as an express source of a new value exception, but would leave open the possibility of interpreting the absolute priority rule itself as stopping short of prohibiting a new value transaction.

guage.[25] One would also have to ask why Congress would have desired to exclude prior equity categorically from the class of potential owners following a cramdown. Although we have some doubt about the Court of Appeals's assumption that prior equity is often the only source of significant capital for reorganizations, see, *e.g.,* Blum & Kaplan, The Absolute Priority Doctrine in Corporate Reorganizations, 41 U. Chi. L.Rev. 651, 672 (1974); Mann, Strategy and Force in the Liquidation of Secured Debt, 96 Mich. L.Rev. 159, 182–183, 192–194, 208–209 (1997), old equity may well be in the best position to make a go of the reorganized enterprise and so may be the party most likely to work out an equity-for-value reorganization.

A less absolute statutory prohibition would follow from reading the "on account of" language as intended to reconcile the two recognized policies underlying Chapter 11, of preserving going concerns and maximizing property available to satisfy creditors. Causation between the old equity's holdings and subsequent property substantial enough to disqualify a plan would presumably occur on this view of things whenever old equity's later property would come at a price that failed to provide the greatest possible addition to the bankruptcy estate, and it would always come at a price too low when the equity holders obtained or preserved an ownership interest for less than someone else would have paid.[26] A truly full value transaction, on the other hand, would pose no threat to the bankruptcy estate not posed by any reorganization, provided of course that the contribution be in

---

[25] Given our obligation to give meaning to the "on account of "modifier, we likewise do not rely on various statements in the House Report or by the bill's floor leaders, which, when read out of context, imply that Congress intended an emphatic, unconditional absolute priority rule. See, *e.g.,* H.R.Rep. No. 95–595, p. 224 (1977), U.S.Code Cong. & Admin. News pp. 5963, 6183. ("[T]he bill requires that the plan pay any dissenting class in full before any class junior to the dissenter may be paid at all"); *id.,* at 413 ("[I]f [an impaired class is] paid less than in full, then no class junior may receive anything under the plan"); 124 Cong. Rec. 32408 (1978) (statement of Rep. Edwards) (cramdown plan confirmable only "as long as no class junior to the dissenting class receives anything at all"); *id.,* at 34007 (statement of Sen. DeConcini) (same).

[26] Even when old equity would pay its top dollar and that figure was as high as anyone else would pay, the price might still be too low unless the old equity holders paid more than anyone else would pay, on the theory that the "necessity" required to justify old equity's participation in a new value plan is a necessity for the participation of old equity as such. On this interpretation, disproof of a bargain would not satisfy old equity's burden; it would need to show that no one else would pay as much. See, *e.g., In re Coltex Loop Central Three Partners, L. P.,* 138 F.3d 39, 45 (C.A.2 1998) ("[O]ld equity must be willing to contribute more money than any other source"); Strub, 111 Banking L. J., at 243 (old equity must show that the reorganized entity "needs funds *from the prior owner-managers* because no other source of capital is available"). No such issue is before us, and we emphasize that our holding here does not suggest an exhaustive list of the requirements of a proposed new value plan.

cash or be realizable money's worth, just as *Ahlers* required for application of *Case* 's new value rule.

## IV

Which of these positions is ultimately entitled to prevail is not to be decided here, however, for even on the latter view the Bank's objection would require rejection of the plan at issue in this case. It is doomed, we can say without necessarily exhausting its flaws, by its provision for vesting equity in the reorganized business in the Debtor's partners without extending an opportunity to anyone else either to compete for that equity or to propose a competing reorganization plan. Although the Debtor's exclusive opportunity to propose a plan under § 1121(b) is not itself "property" within the meaning of subsection (b)(2)(B)(ii), the respondent partnership in this case has taken advantage of this opportunity by proposing a plan under which the benefit of equity ownership may be obtained by no one but old equity partners. Upon the court's approval of that plan, the partners were in the same position that they would have enjoyed had they exercised an exclusive option under the plan to buy the equity in the reorganized entity, or contracted to purchase it from a seller who had first agreed to deal with no one else. It is quite true that the escrow of the partners' proposed investment eliminated any formal need to set out an express option or exclusive dealing provision in the plan itself, since the court's approval that created the opportunity and the partners' action to obtain its advantage were simultaneous. But before the Debtor's plan was accepted no one else could propose an alternative one, and after its acceptance no one else could obtain equity in the reorganized entity. At the moment of the plan's approval the Debtor's partners necessarily enjoyed an exclusive opportunity that was in no economic sense distinguishable from the advantage of the exclusively entitled offeror or option holder. This opportunity should, first of all, be treated as an item of property in its own right. Cf. * * * D. Baird, The Elements of Bankruptcy 261 (rev. ed. 1993) ("The right to get an equity interest for its fair market value is "property' as the word is ordinarily used. Options to acquire an interest in a firm, even at its market value, trade for a positive price"). While it may be argued that the opportunity has no market value, being significant only to old equity holders owing to their potential tax liability, such an argument avails the Debtor nothing, for several reasons. It is to avoid just such arguments that the law is settled that any otherwise cognizable property interest must be treated as sufficiently valuable to be recognized under the Bankruptcy Code. Even aside from that rule, the assumption that no one but the Debtor's partners might pay for such an opportunity would obviously support no inference that it is valueless, let alone that it should not be treated as property. And, finally, the source in the tax law of the opportunity's value to the partners implies in no way that it lacks value to others. It might, indeed, be valuable to another precisely as a way to keep the Debtor from implementing a plan that would avoid a Chapter 7 liquidation.

Given that the opportunity is property of some value, the question arises why old equity alone should obtain it, not to mention at no cost whatever. The closest thing to an answer favorable to the Debtor is that the old equity partners would be given the opportunity in the expectation that in taking advantage of it they would add the stated purchase price to the estate. But this just begs the question why the opportunity should be exclusive to the old equity holders. If the price to be paid for the equity interest is the best obtainable, old equity does not need the protection of exclusiveness (unless to trump an equal offer from someone else); if it is not the best, there is no apparent reason for giving old equity a bargain. There is no reason, that is, unless the very purpose of the whole transaction is, at least in part, to do old equity a favor. And that, of course, is to say that old equity would obtain its opportunity, and the resulting benefit, because of old equity's prior interest within the meaning of subsection (b)(2)(B)(ii). Hence it is that the exclusiveness of the opportunity, with its protection against the market's scrutiny of the purchase price by means of competing bids or even competing plan proposals, renders the partners' right a property interest extended "on account of" the old equity position and therefore subject to an unpaid senior creditor class's objection.

It is no answer to this to say that the exclusive opportunity should be treated merely as a detail of the broader transaction that would follow its exercise, and that in this wider perspective no favoritism may be inferred, since the old equity partners would pay something, whereas no one else would pay anything. If this argument were to carry the day, of course, old equity could obtain a new property interest for a dime without being seen to receive anything on account of its old position. But even if we assume that old equity's plan would not be confirmed without satisfying the judge that the purchase price was top dollar, there is a further reason here not to treat property consisting of an exclusive opportunity as subsumed within the total transaction proposed. On the interpretation assumed here, it would, of course, be a fatal flaw if old equity acquired or retained the property interest without paying full value. It would thus be necessary for old equity to demonstrate its payment of top dollar, but this it could not satisfactorily do when it would receive or retain its property under a plan giving it exclusive rights and in the absence of a competing plan of any sort.[27] Under a plan granting an exclusive right, making no provision for competing bids or competing plans, any determination that the price was top dollar would necessarily be made by a judge in bankruptcy court, whereas the best way to determine value is exposure to a market. See

---

[27] The dissent emphasizes the care taken by the Bankruptcy Judge in examining the valuation evidence here, in arguing that there is no occasion for us to consider the relationship between valuation process and top-dollar requirement. While we agree with the dissent as to the judge's conscientious handling of the matter, the ensuing text of this opinion sets out our reasons for thinking the Act calls for testing valuation by a required process that was not followed here.

Baird, Elements of Bankruptcy at 262; Bowers, Rehabilitation, Redistribution or Dissipation: The Evidence for Choosing Among Bankruptcy Hypotheses, 72 Wash. U.L.Q. 955, 959, 963 n. 34, 975 (1994); Markell, 44 Stan. L.Rev., at 73 ("Reorganization practice illustrates that the presence of competing bidders for a debtor, whether they are owners or not, tends to increase creditor dividends"). This is a point of some significance, since it was, after all, one of the Code's innovations to narrow the occasions for courts to make valuation judgments, as shown by its preference for the supramajoritarian class creditor voting scheme in § 1126(c), see *Ahlers, supra,* at 207 ("[T]he Code provides that it is up to the creditors–and not the courts–to accept or reject a reorganization plan which fails to provide them adequate protection or fails to honor the absolute priority rule").[28] In the interest of statutory coherence, a like disfavor for decisions untested by competitive choice ought to extend to valuations in administering subsection (b)(2)(B)(ii) when some form of market valuation may be available to test the adequacy of an old equity holder's proposed contribution.

Whether a market test would require an opportunity to offer competing plans or would be satisfied by a right to bid for the same interest sought by old equity, is a question we do not decide here. It is enough to say, assuming a new value corollary, that plans providing junior interest holders with exclusive opportunities free from competition and without benefit of market valuation fall within the prohibition of § 1129(b)(2)(B)(ii).

The judgment of the Court of Appeals is accordingly reversed, and the case is remanded for further proceedings consistent with this opinion.

*It is so ordered.*

■ Justice THOMAS with whom Justice SCALIA joins, concurring in the judgment.

[Omitted.]

---

[28] In *Ahlers,* we explained: "The Court of Appeals may well have believed that petitioners or other unsecured creditors would be better off if respondents' reorganization plan was confirmed. But that determination is for the creditors to make in the manner specified by the Code. 11 U.S.C. § 1126(c). Here, the principal creditors entitled to vote in the class of unsecured creditors (*i.e.,* petitioners) objected to the proposed reorganization. This was their prerogative under the Code, and courts applying the Code must effectuate their decision." 485 U.S., at 207, 108 S.Ct. 963. The voting rules of Chapter 11 represent a stark departure from the requirements under the old Act. "Congress adopted the view that creditors and equity security holders are very often better judges of the debtor's economic viability and their own economic self-interest than courts, trustees, or the SEC. . .. Consistent with this new approach, the Chapter 11 process relies on creditors and equity holders to engage in negotiations toward resolution of their interests." Brunstad, Sigal, & Schorling, Review of the Proposals of the National Bankruptcy Review Commission Pertaining to Business Bankruptcies: Part One, 53 Bus. Law. 1381, 1406, n. 136 (1998).

■ Justice STEVENS, dissenting.

Prior to the enactment of the Bankruptcy Reform Act of 1978, this Court unequivocally stated that there are circumstances under which stockholders may participate in a plan of reorganization of an insolvent debtor if their participation is based on a contribution in money, or in money's worth, reasonably equivalent in view of all the circumstances to their participation.[1] As we have on two prior occasions, we granted certiorari in this case to decide whether § 1129(b)(2)(B)(ii) of the 1978 Act preserved or repealed this "new value" component of the absolute priority rule. I believe the Court should now definitively resolve the question and state that a holder of a junior claim or interest does not receive property "on account of" such a claim when its participation in the plan is based on adequate new value.

The Court today wisely rejects the Government's "starchy" position that an old equity holder can never receive an interest in a reorganized venture as a result of a cramdown unless the creditors are first paid in full.[3] Nevertheless, I find the Court's objections to the plan before us unsupported by either the text of 11 U.S.C. § 1129(b)(2)(B)(ii) or the record in this case. I would, therefore, affirm the judgment of the Court of Appeals.

---

[1] As Justice Douglas explained in *Case v. Los Angeles Lumber Products Co.*: "It is, of course, clear that there are circumstances under which stockholders may participate in a plan of reorganization of an insolvent debtor. This Court, as we have seen, indicated as much in *Northern Pacific Ry. Co.* v. *Boyd* and *Kansas City Terminal Ry. Co. v. Central Union Trust Co.* Especially in the latter case did this Court stress the necessity, at times, of seeking new money 'essential to the success of the undertaking' from the old stockholders. Where that necessity exists and the old stockholders make a fresh contribution and receive in return a participation reasonably equivalent to their contribution, no objection can be made. . ..

"In view of these considerations we believe that to accord 'the creditor his full right of priority against the corporate assets' where the debtor is insolvent, the stockholder's participation must be based on a contribution in money or in money's worth, reasonably equivalent in view of all the circumstances to the participation of the stockholder."

[3] As I noted earlier, Justice Douglas made this proposition clear in *Case v. Los Angeles, supra.* Justice Douglas was a preeminent bankruptcy scholar, well known for his views on the dangers posed by management-controlled corporate reorganizations. Both his work on the Protective Committee Study for the Securities and Exchange Commission and on Chapter X of the Bankruptcy Act sought to "restore the integrity of the reorganization process" which "too often [was] masterminded from behind the scenes by reorganization managers allied with the corporation's management or its bankers." Jennings, Mr. Justice Douglas: His Influence on Corporate and Securities Regulation, 73 Yale L.J. 920, 935–937 (1964). To this end, Douglas placed special emphasis on the protection of creditors' rights in reorganizations. I find it implausible that Congress, in enacting the Bankruptcy Code, intended to be even more strict than Justice Douglas in limiting the ability of debtors to participate in reorganizations.

## I

Section 1129 of Chapter 11 sets forth in detail the substantive requirements that a reorganization plan must satisfy in order to qualify for confirmation.[4] In the case of dissenting creditor classes, a plan must conform to the dictates of § 1129(b). With only one exception, the requirements of §§ 1129(a) and 1129(b) are identical for plans submitted by stockholders or junior creditors and plans submitted by other parties. That exception is the requirement in § 1129(b)(2)(B)(ii) that no holder of a junior claim or interest may receive or retain any property "on account of such junior claim or interest."

When read in the light of Justice DOUGLAS' opinion in *Case v. Los Angeles Lumber Products Co.*, the meaning of this provision is perfectly clear. Whenever a junior claimant receives or retains an interest for a bargain price, it does so "on account of" its prior claim. On the other hand, if the new capital that it invests has an equivalent or greater value than its interest in the reorganized venture, it should be equally clear that its participation is based on the fair price being paid and that it is not "on account of" its old claim or equity.

Of course, the fact that the proponents of a plan offer to pay a fair price for the interest they seek to acquire or retain does not necessarily mean that the bankruptcy judge should approve their plan. Any proposed cramdown must satisfy all of the requirements of § 1129 including, most notably, the requirement that the plan be "fair and equitable" to all creditors whose claims are impaired. Moreover, even if the old stockholders propose to buy the debtor for a fair price, presumably their plan should not be approved if a third party, perhaps motivated by unique tax or competitive considerations, is willing to pay an even higher price.

In every reorganization case, serious questions concerning the value of the debtor's assets must be resolved.[5] Nevertheless, for the purpose of answering the legal question presented by the parties to this case, I believe that we should assume that all valuation questions have been correctly answered. If, for example, there had been a widely advertised auction in which numerous bidders participated, and if the plan proposed by respondents had been more favorable by a wide margin than any competing proposal, would § 1129(b)(2)(B)(ii) require rejection of their plan simply because it provides that they shall retain 100% of the equity?

Petitioner and the Government would reply "yes" because they think § 1129(b)(2)(B)(ii) imposes an absolute ban on participation by junior

---

[4] "Confirmation of a plan of reorganization is the statutory goal of every chapter 11 case. Section 1129 provides the requirements for such confirmation, containing Congress' minimum requirements for allowing an entity to discharge its unpaid debts and continue its operations." 7 Collier on Bankruptcy ¶ 1129.01 (rev. 15th ed.1998).

[5] See Warren, A Theory of Absolute Priority, 1991 Ann. Survey Am. L. 9, 13 ("In practice, no problem in bankruptcy is more vexing than the problem of valuation").

claimants without the consent of all senior creditors. The Court correctly rejects this extreme position because it would make the words "on account of" superfluous, and because there is no plausible reason why Congress would have desired such a categorical exclusion, given that in some cases old equity may be the most likely source of new capital. Indeed, the dissenting judge in the Court of Appeals thought "such a result would border on the absurd."[6] Thus, neither the dissenting judge in the Court of Appeals nor the Court appears to be in doubt about the proper answer to my hypothetical question. Instead, the decision is apparently driven by doubts concerning the procedures followed by the Bankruptcy Judge in making his value determinations, implicitly suggesting that the statute should be construed to require some form of competitive bidding in cases like this.[7]

Perhaps such a procedural requirement would be a wise addition to the statute, but it is surely not contained in the present text of § 1129(b)(2)(B)(ii). Indeed, that subsection is not a procedural provision at all. Section 1129 defines the substantive elements that must be met to render plans eligible for confirmation by the bankruptcy judge after all required statutory procedures have been completed. Cf. § 1121 (Who may file a plan); § 1122 (Classification of claims or interests); § 1125 (Post-petition disclosure and solicitation); § 1126 (Acceptance of plan); § 1127 (Modification of plan). Because, as I discuss below, petitioner does not now challenge either the procedures followed by the Bankruptcy Judge or any of his value determinations, neither the record nor the text of § 1129(b)(2)(B)(ii) provides any support for the Court's disposition of this case.

--------

[6] Judge KANNE wrote in dissent: "Perhaps the majority's reasoning is driven by the fear that a 'but for' interpretation would prevent old equity from ever participating in a reorganized entity-something Congress could never have intended. Indeed, such a result would border on the absurd, but a simpler, 'but for' causation requirement would not preclude junior interests from participating in a reorganized entity. If prior equity holders earn their shares in an open auction, for example, their received interests would not be 'on account of 'their junior interests but 'on account of 'their capital contributions." It would seem logical for adherents of this view also to find participation by junior interests in the new entity not "on account of "their prior interest, if it were stipulated that old equity's capital contributions exceeded the amount attainable in an auction, or if findings to that effect were not challenged.

[7] This doubt is unwarranted in this case. The bank does not challenge the Bankruptcy Court's finding that the 15 floors of office space had a market value of $55.8 million. The bank's original expert testimony on the value of the property differed from the Bankruptcy Judge's finding by only 2.8%. Therefore, although the bank argues that the policy implications of the "new value debate" revolve around judicial determinations of the valuation of the relevant collateral this concern was neither squarely presented in this case nor preserved for our review.

## II

As I understand the Court's opinion, it relies on two reasons for refusing to approve the plan at this stage of the proceedings: one based on the plan itself and the other on the confirmation procedures followed before the plan was adopted. In the Court's view, the fatal flaw in the plan proposed by respondent was that it vested complete ownership in the former partners immediately upon confirmation, and the defect in the process was that no other party had an opportunity to propose a competing plan.

These requirements are neither explicitly nor implicitly dictated by the text of the statute. As for the first objection, if we assume that the partners paid a fair price for what the Court characterizes as their "exclusive opportunity," I do not understand why the retention of a 100% interest in assets is any more "on account of" their prior position than retaining a lesser percentage might have been. Surely there is no legal significance to the fact that immediately after the confirmation of the plan "the partners were in the same position that they would have enjoyed had they exercised an exclusive option under the plan to buy the equity in the reorganized entity, or contracted to purchase it from a seller who had first agreed to deal with no one else."

As to the second objection, petitioner does not challenge the Bankruptcy Judge's valuation of the property or any of his other findings under § 1129 (other than the plan's compliance with § 1129(b)(2)(B)(ii)). Since there is no remaining question as to value, both the former partners (and the creditors, for that matter) are in the same position that they would have enjoyed if the Bankruptcy Court had held an auction in which this plan had been determined to be the best available. That the court did not hold such an auction should not doom this plan, because no such auction was requested by any of the parties, and the statute does not require that an auction be held. As with all the provisions of § 1129, the question of compliance with § 1129(b)(2)(B)(ii) turns on the substantive content of the plan, not on speculation about the procedures that might have preceded its confirmation.

In this case, the partners had the exclusive right to propose a reorganization plan during the first 120 days after filing for bankruptcy. See § 1121(b). No one contends that that exclusive right is a form of property that is retained by the debtor "on account of" its prior status.[8] The partners did indeed propose a plan which provided for an infusion of $6.125 million in new capital in exchange for ownership of the reorganized debtor. Since the tax value of the partnership depended on their exclusive participation, it is unsurprising that the partners' plan did not propose that unidentified outsiders should also be able to own an unspecified portion of the reorganized partnership. It seems both practically and economically

---

[8] Indeed, as the Court acknowledges it is not "property" within the meaning of the Act.

puzzling to assume that Congress would have expected old equity to provide for the participation of unknown third parties, who would have interests different (and perhaps incompatible) with the partners', in order to comply with § 1129(b)(2)(B)(ii).[9]

Nevertheless, even after proposing their plan, the partners had no vested right to purchase an equity interest in the post-reorganization enterprise until the Bankruptcy Judge confirmed the plan. They also had no assurance that the court would refuse to truncate the exclusivity period and allow other interested parties to file competing plans. As it turned out, the Bankruptcy Judge did not allow respondent to file its proposed plan, but the bank did not appeal that issue, and the question is not before us.[10]

The moment the judge did confirm the partners' plan, the old equity holders were required by law to implement the terms of the plan.[11] It was then, and only then, that what the Court characterizes as the critical "exclusive opportunity" came into existence. What the Court refuses to recognize, however, is that this "exclusive opportunity" is the function of the procedural features of this case: the statutory exclusivity period, the Bankruptcy Judge's refusal to allow the bank to file a competing plan, and the inescapable fact that the judge could confirm only one plan.

---

[9] It goes without saying that Congress could not have expected the partners' plan to include a provision that would allow for the Bankruptcy Judge to entertain competing plans, since that is a discretionary decision exclusively within the province of the court. See § 1121(d).

[10] Apparently, the bank's plan called for liquidation of the property. In order to flesh out all facts bearing on value, perhaps the Bankruptcy Judge should have terminated the exclusivity period and allowed the bank to file its plan. That the bank's plan called for liquidation of the property in a single-asset context does not necessarily contravene the purposes of Chapter 11.

[11] Section 1141(a) states: "Except as provided in subsections (d)(2) and (d)(3) of this section, the provisions of a confirmed plan bind the debtor, any entity issuing securities under the plan, any entity acquiring property under the plan, and any creditor, equity security holder, or general partner in the debtor, whether or not the claim or interest of such creditor, equity security holder, or general partner is impaired under the plan and whether or not such creditor, equity security holder, or general partner has accepted the plan." See 8 Collier on Bankruptcy ¶ 1141.02. ("Section 1141(a) of the Code provides that a plan is binding upon all parties once it is confirmed. Under this provision, subject to compliance with the requirements of due process under the Fifth Amendment, a confirmed plan is binding upon every entity that holds a claim or interest. . .."); see also § 1142(a).

In this case, the plan provided: "The general partners and limited partners of the Reorganized Debtor shall contribute or cause to be contributed $6.125 million of new capital (the "New Capital") to the Reorganized Debtor as follows: $3.0 million in cash ("Initial Capital") on the first business banking day after the Effective Date, and $625,000 on each of the next five anniversaries of the Effective Date." The "Effective Date" of the plan was defined as "[t]he first business day after the Confirmation Order is entered on the docket sheet maintained for the Case."

The Court's repeated references to the partners' "opportunity," is potentially misleading because it ignores the fact that a plan is binding upon all parties once it is confirmed. One can, of course, refer to contractual rights and duties as "opportunities," but they are not separate property interests comparable to an option which gives its holder a legal right either to enter into a contract or not to do so. They are simply a part of the bundle of contractual terms that have legal significance when a plan is confirmed.

When the court approved the plan, it accepted an offer by old equity. If the value of the debtor's assets has been accurately determined, the fairness of such an offer should be judged by the same standard as offers made by newcomers. Of course, its offer should not receive more favorable consideration "on account of "their prior ownership. But if the debtor's plan would be entitled to approval if it had been submitted by a third party, it should not be disqualified simply because it did not include a unique provision that would not be required in an offer made by any other party, including the creditors.

Since the Court of Appeals correctly interpreted § 1129(b)(2)(B)(ii), its judgment should be affirmed.

Accordingly, I respectfully dissent.

## NOTES

**1.** Among the proposals made to amend the Code to prevent debtors from taking unfair advantage of the new value exception in squeezing out creditors, perhaps the simplest is to terminate the debtor's exclusive right to propose a plan if the debtor proposes to cramdown a plan in which ownership interests are retained upon a contribution of new value. In *Owners, Auctions and Absolute Priority in Bankruptcy Reorganizations*, 44 Stan.L.Rev. 69 (1991), Professor Markell has proposed this reform. This would allow creditors the option either to consent to the debtor's plan or to propose their own plans which might terminate the interests of the old owners.

**2.** After more than ten years of suspense, the Supreme Court finally reached the question of whether bankruptcy debtors can impose new value reorganization plans on creditors in Chapter 11 cramdowns without distributing reorganization value to creditors that equal their claims in *203 North LaSalle Street Partnership*. Unfortunately, on first reading of the Supreme Court's *LaSalle* opinions, it is still not apparent what the answer is, although the Supreme Court majority appears to fall generally in the camp of the "market test" view.

The Supreme Court majority does decisively reject the "traditional" new value exception to the absolute priority rule that had previously been the law of the Seventh and Ninth Circuits. *Bonner Mall* and cases like it, had authorized courts to consider and confirm debtor proposed cramdown plans within the exclusivity period that permitted pre-bankruptcy equity holders to retain ownership in the reorganized firm if the retained interest was judicially determined to be equivalent in value to a fresh contribution of capital from the equity holders that was substantial, new, in the form of money or money's worth, and necessary for successful reorganization. This "traditional" new value exception did not, we now learn twenty years later, survive the enactment of the 1978 Bankruptcy Code.

The *LaSalle* court, however, also refused to absolutely forbid old equity from retaining an interest in the reorganized firm in violation of the absolute priority rule absent acceptance from all impaired classes of creditors. The prohibitionist position, advocated by the Solicitor General, was dismissed as "starchy" by the majority, and "almost absurd" by Justice Stevens, the lone dissenter.

The majority goes on to discuss why on historical, structural, precedent and policy bases, it was troubled by the confluence of judicial valuation, debtor exclusivity in determining the extent of the retained interest and the amount of the new value contribution, and the possibility of nonconsensual confirmation of the new value plan. It suggests that "some form" of market valuation was required before confirming a nonconsensual new value plan. But after alluding to the alternatives of competitive bidding and competing plans it expressly refuses to state whether either or both was required and what form the competition was supposed to take. Even this meager degree of guidance was considered injudicious and excessive by Justice Thomas and Justice Scalia in their omitted concurrence who, after looking up the phrase "on account of" in the Random House and Webster's Third New International dictionaries and finding that the dictionary definitions sufficed to establish that the *LaSalle* plan was unconfirmable, declared "speculations about the desirability of a market test. . . are dicta binding neither this Court nor the lower federal courts." (Talk about starchy!)

"Some form of market valuation" has an Alice-in-Wonderland quality in cases like *LaSalle*. There are exactly two bidders for the equity interest in real estate subject to a restructured secured claim measured by the present value of the real estate–the bank holding the mortgage and the old equity holders who for tax and speculative reasons wish to retain their ownership interest. A negotiation between these two parties, not an auction or competing "reorganization" plans is the answer. In many cases there will be some price at which the rational bank and debtor will agree to restructure the defaulted loan with continuing participation by old equity. If those parties cannot agree on a price for equity's continuing participation, then the holder of a defaulted mortgage of overencumbered real estate ought to be able to conduct a foreclosure sale.

In the context of the single asset real estate case like *LaSalle* there is nothing at all "starchy" much less "absurd" about this result. Indeed *any genuine* "form of market valuation" collapses into this result. If the bank can freely bid, the bank always has the capacity to overbid the old equity holders for the equity in real estate subject to its unsecured senior claim.

Up until the point at which its bid exceeds both its secured claim and its unsecured deficiency claim, none of the proceeds of the winning bid will be distributable to old equity. And so the money the bank invests if its bid prevails will either go into real estate it will thereafter own or will be returned to it as distributions on account of its claims. A bank bidding on overencumbered real estate subject to its own mortgage is playing a shell game. The old equity can only win if the bank likes the price the old equity is bidding. In which case there should be a consensual new value plan, not an auction or a cramdown. The result of requiring true competitive bidding is that no new value plan can be confirmed unless the bank consents.

Terminating exclusivity or requiring auctions of the reorganized firm's equity as a condition of debtor proposed new value plans would have real bite in a case involving an operating firm with significant third party unsecured claims and a genuine need for working capital–if there were such cases. In fact, as the Supreme Court noted in footnote 15, the new value plans are almost always proposed in single-asset real estate cases. In large operating cases with widely dispersed public shareholders, new value plans are generally impractical and public shareholders have no incentive to propose them anyway. In smaller cases with concentrated ownership, new value plans tend to be unnecessary–old equity participates on a negotiated basis without making new capital contributions, notwithstanding insolvency and absolute priority:

> [I]n the reorganization cases of small businesses in which managers are also the principal shareholders, equity frequently dominates the bargain to such an extent that the absolute priority rule is stood on its head. In such cases, the claims of creditors are compromised, but shareholder-managers usually retain their shares without dilution. The dependence of the business upon the continuing services of the shareholder-manager is the primary bargaining leverage used to accomplish this feat.

LoPucki & Whitford, *Bargaining Over Equity's Share in the Bankruptcy Reorganization of Large Publicly Held Companies*, 139 U.Pa.L.Rev. 125, 149 (1990).

Real estate is different, of course, precisely because the old owner-managers are ordinarily not essential to the continued economic viability of a commercial real estate project. In the single-asset real estate case, the underwater mortgagee, as senior claim holder, is effectively the seller as well as a potential bidder for the property. It is also the only potential bidder for the interest other than the prebankruptcy equityholders. Only when the mortgagee consents to a plan transferring that equity to another has some form of market valuation taken place. Practically and theoretically, no market transaction to which the mortgagee is not a willing party can occur. If the old equity retains an interest over the mortgagee's objection, the bankruptcy judge, not any market transaction, is fixing the price. *LaSalle*'s rejection of the noncompetitive debtor-exclusive new value plan effectively prohibits *any* nonconsensual new value plan. *La-Salle*, starchily or not, on this reading, precludes involuntary restructuring of defaulted mortgage debt on overencumbered real estate and significantly shifts the balance of power in such cases towards the mortgagee. In this light, the dearth of published decisions over the past three years confirming cramdown plans in single-asset real estate is unsurprising. *See Wilkow v. Forbes, Inc.*, 241 F.3d 552, 554 (7th Cir. 2001), characterizing *LaSalle* as having "hog-tied the [new value] doctrine."

## E. AN EMPIRICAL OVERVIEW: LOPUCKI–WHITFORD STUDY

We have seen the legal background against which bargaining between the debtor and its creditors is carried on in the adoption of a consensual plan. But other factors are involved in the bargaining process that are not easily discernible from the Code or the cases. Professors Lynn LoPucki and William Whitford in their article, *Bargaining Over Equity's Share in the Bankruptcy Reorganization of Large, Publicly Held Companies*, 139 U.Pa.L.Rev. 125 (1990), made a survey of Chapter 11 reorganizations and reviewed 43 cases of debtors with declared assets exceeding $100 million in which consensual plans were confirmed. Their objective was to determine the frequency with which the parties were able to settle large bankruptcy reorganization cases, the degree to which the settlements deviated from the absolute priority rule, and the causes of the deviations. Among their conclusions are the following:

**a.** A § 1129(b) contested cramdown was a rare event. If a plan was confirmed it was usually the result of bargaining and settlement.

**b.** The size of the case was a major factor in the extent to which the plan varied from the absolute priority rule. They observed:

> As has been reported in other studies, in the reorganization cases of small businesses in which managers are also the principal shareholders, equity frequently dominates the bargain to such an extent that the absolute priority rule is virtually stood on its head. In such cases, the claims of creditors are compromised, but shareholder-managers usually retain their shares without dilution. The dependence of the business upon the continuing services of the shareholder-manager is the primary bargaining leverage used to accomplish this feat. The dependence may result from the need to maintain personal relations with suppliers, customers, and key employees, the need for unique services that only the shareholder-manager can provide, or from the shareholder-manager's willingness to work for less than the economy generally pays for such effort. Unsecured creditors are willing to waive their right to priority in order to create a incentive for the shareholder-manager to continue her participation in the business. They realize that without such participation, the business will fail, and the assets will be liquidated for the benefit of the secured creditors, leaving nothing for the unsecured creditors.

139 U.Pa.L.Rev. at 149.

**c.** In large cases, their study showed that equity nearly always shared in distribution under the plan even though application of the absolute priority rule would have precluded their participation, but their share was almost invariably small when measured as a percentage of the total distributed. However, with one exception, equity took nothing in cases in which the company was so insolvent that its creditors received less than 14 cents on the dollar.

**d.** Perhaps their most controversial conclusion was that:

> Within the category of large cases, the relative size of equity's recovery appeared to be not so much a product of the financial conditions of the company as it was a product of the quality and aggressiveness of equity's representation.

> * * * [T]he observed deviations from absolute priority were not to any significant degree the product of difficulties in valuation. In nearly every case, the negotiators knew the company was insolvent and that equity would be entitled to nothing in an adjudication. Equity was allowed to share in the distribution for a wide variety of reasons. Central among them was a generalized desire to have a consensual plan—one supported by the debtor, the official committees, and major creditors. Part of the reason for seeking such a plan was a concern that equity might make trouble if there was an attempt to exclude it. Yielding to such a fear was easier for creditors because the cost of a distribution to equity was spread among so many creditors that the portion borne by each one was too small to justify resistance. To a large degree, however, the preference for a consensual plan rather than an adjudication was a matter of legal culture. Although these cases were spread throughout the United States, most of the lawyers who played key roles in them were members of the same legal community. They could expect to be involved in future cases with their current adversaries and were to various degrees dependent on those adversaries for professional respect and advancement. They were not entirely free to ignore the conventional wisdom that consensual plans were the responsible, appropriate means for accomplishing reorganization and that despite the absolute priority rule, everyone at the bargaining table was entitled to a share.

139 U.Pa.L.Rev. at 194–195.

## F. EFFECT OF CONFIRMATION OF PLAN

Upon confirmation of a Chapter 11 plan the property of the estate vests in the reorganized debtor unless the plan provides for sale or transfer to another entity. After confirmation the debtor may deal with that property in any manner consistent with the plan. § 1141(b) and § 1142. Confirmation of a plan results in discharge of the debtor from preconfirmation debts in most cases (§ 1141(d)) and in termination of the automatic stay. § 362(c). The bankruptcy court retains jurisdiction to aid in the implementation of the plan, the resolution of disputes regarding interpretation of the plan, modification of the plan, and for various other purposes. § 1142 and 28 U.S.C. § 1334(b). The jurisdiction of the bankruptcy court is not exclusive, however, and the debtor may be sued in other courts for breach of its obligations under the plan as well as for breach of obligations incurred after confirmation. *In re Paradise Valley Country Club*, 31 B.R. 613 (D.Colo.1983). Some of the jurisdictional puzzles that may arise post confirmation are discussed at length in Frank Kennedy & Gerald Smith, *Post Confirmation Issues: The Effect of Confirmation and Post Confirmation Proceedings*, 44 S.C.L. Rev. 621 (1993).

Confirmation of a Chapter 11 plan not only discharges individuals, as in Chapter 7, but corporations and partnerships as well. § 1141(d). Discharge for a liquidating corporation under Chapter 7 is of no importance because of the ability of the entity to dissolve after liquidation. But discharge of preconfirmation debts is essential to the Chapter 11 process. If creditors can assert claims against the reorganized debtor other than as provided in the plan, then, in effect, those creditors are not bound by the plan, and the plan is not a full and final settlement of claims. Moreover, allowing creditors to assert claims outside the plan threatens both plan feasibility and the value of securities distributed to creditors and interest holders pursuant to the plan. Congressman Edwards made this point in rejecting a limitation on the scope of the § 1141 discharge in favor of tax claims:

> It is necessary for a corporation or partnership undergoing reorganization to be able to present its creditors with a fixed list of liabilities upon which the creditors or third parties can make intelligent decisions. Retaining an exception for discharge with respect to nondischargeable taxes would leave an undesirable uncertainty surrounding reorganizations that is unacceptable.

Cong.Rec. (Sept. 28, 1978) reprinted in *Collier on Bankruptcy*, Vol. D App.Pt. 4–2474 (Rev.15th ed.2000).

The 2005 Act added a new paragraph (6) to section 1141(d) to circumscribe the scope of the corporate debtor's Chapter 11 discharge:

> **(6)** Notwithstanding paragraph (1), the confirmation of a plan does not discharge a debtor that is a corporation from any debt described in subparagraph (A) or (B) of section 523(a)(2) that is owed to a domestic governmental unit or owed to a person as the result of an action filed under subchapter III of chapter 37 of title 31, United States Code, or any similar statute, or for a tax or customs duty with respect to which the debtor –
>
> **(A)** made a fraudulent return; or

**(B)** willfully attempted in any manner to evade or defeat that tax or duty.

While seemingly limited to government claims for fraud, the reference to Subchapter III of chapter 37 to title 31 is to so-called *qui tam* actions or "whistleblower" suits brought under the federal False Claims Act. These actions may be brought by private persons, subject to the right of the Department of Justice to intervene and control the litigation. By opening the door to limitations on the scope of the Chapter 11 discharge, new paragraph (6) sets a troubling precedent. If tax fraud, government fraud and *qui tam* actions are now excepted from the corporate Chapter 11 discharge, why not the claims of other defrauded parties? Given the large number of bankruptcies where credible allegations of fraud are made, § 1141(d)(6) may represent the beginning of an erosion of the Chapter 11 discharge that may be difficult to contain.

Debtors may not use Chapter 11 with its broad discharge provisions to evade the limitations on discharge set out in § 727. A corporation or partnership cannot be discharged in a Chapter 7 liquidation (§ 727(a)(1)), and they cannot subvert this rule by a liquidation plan in Chapter 11. § 1141(d)(3). By the same token, an individual debtor who is barred from discharge in Chapter 7 by the provisions of § 727 cannot obtain a discharge in Chapter 11 by a liquidation plan. Nor may an individual debtor evade the limitations on discharge in § 523 by filing under Chapter 11.

The scope of the Chapter 11 discharge raises critical constitutional due process issues. It is common ground that parties who are given actual notice of the Chapter 11 case are bound by § 1141 discharge. But the discharge is deliberately cast in terms broader than this and persistent questions arise about the binding effect of the Chapter 11 plan with respect to those who either did not have or could not be given notice. The seminal decision is *Mullane v. Central Hanover Bank & Trust Co.*, 339 U.S. 306 (1950), where the Supreme Court held that constitutional due process was satisfied by giving known claimants actual notice of the proceeding and an opportunity to be heard and by giving unknown claimants notice by publication in a manner reasonably calculated to apprise them of the pending action.

In *Reliable Electric Co. v. Olson*, 726 F.2d 620 (10th Cir.1984), relying on *Mullane*, the court found that a known creditor who had knowledge of the pending Chapter 11 case but did not receive actual notice of the confirmation hearing was not bound by the discharge. Accord *In re Maya Constr. Co.*, 78 F.3d 1395 (9th Cir.1996). How would the *Reliable* doctrine apply to a case in which Creditor's claim is postpetition, Debtor knows that Creditor is a potential creditor, and Creditor knows that Debtor has filed in Chapter 11? The court in *In re Unioil*, 948 F.2d 678 (10th Cir.1991), held that Debtor had the burden of providing formal notice of its bankruptcy to Creditor; failure to do so meant that Creditor's claim was not discharged. *In re Christopher*, 28 F.3d 512 (5th Cir.1994), takes a different view. The court believed that nothing in the Code or Rules requires

a debtor to serve notice of a Chapter 11 proceeding on postpetition creditors. Under § 101 ("creditor"), a claimant is not a creditor unless its claim
arose prepetition. In absence of a statutory requirement to give notice, the
issue is whether Creditor's receipt of actual notice about the existence of
Debtor's filing was sufficient to satisfy the due process requirements of
*Mullane*. The court concluded that it was:

> Thus, given the actual notice of [Debtor's] bankruptcy proceeding pos-
> sessed by [Creditors], we conclude that due process is not offended in
> this case by requiring postpetition claimants in [Creditors'] position to
> come forward and protect their enhanced rights [the court is referring
> to the likelihood that they can assert that their claims are administra-
> tive expenses] under the Code or else lose their rights through the
> sweeping discharge of Chapter 11.

28 F.3d at 519.

*Chemetron Corp. v. Jones*, 72 F.3d 341 (3d Cir.1995), dealt with the
critical question of how "unknown" a creditor must be in order to be
bound to the Chapter 11 discharge by publication notice. The debtor had
been the owner of environmentally contaminated property and the claims
were based on occupancy and visitation to homes adjacent to the contaminated site. The claimants argued that had Chemetron conducted a reasonable investigation it could have ascertained their identities and given them
actual notice. The bankruptcy court agreed holding that the debtor could
have reasonably foreseen that individuals living near the dumpsite might
have toxic tort claims. The Third Circuit rejected this reasoning:

> A review of the facts in this case at bar reveals why the bankruptcy
> court's standard should not be followed. None of the claimants in-
> volved currently resides near either site. The claimants instead are
> scattered across Ohio and as far away as Texas. We are hard-pressed
> to conceive of any way the debtor could identify, locate, and provide
> actual notice to these claimants.
>
> It has been suggested that Chemetron could have conducted a title
> search on all properties surrounding the sites to determine all persons
> who might have lived in the area during the twenty years between
> Chemetron's operation of the sites and the Chapter 11 proceeding. We
> decline to chart a jurisprudential course through a Scylla of causational
> difficulties and a Charybdis of practical concerns.
>
> *       *       *
>
> *   *   * Debtors cannot be required to provide actual notice to anyone
> who potentially could have been affected by their actions; such a re-
> quirement would completely vitiate the important goal of prompt and
> effectual administration and settlement of debtors' estates.

72 F.3d at 347–348.

## G. MODIFICATION OF PLAN

A debtor that is unable to carry out a confirmed plan may propose a modification of the plan. § 1127(b). But modification must occur before "substantial consummation" of the plan, a term defined in § 1101(2). Each of the three subparagraphs of § 1101(2) must be satisfied before the plan is substantially consummated. A Chapter 11 plan will always provide for payments to claimants and, under subparagraph (C), the plan is substantially consummated when those payments commence if the requirements of subparagraphs (A) and (B) are also satisfied. Subparagraph (A) refers to "transfer of all or substantially all of the property proposed by the plan to be transferred." Since any payment to a claimant is a transfer of property, subparagraph (A) can be read to refer to distributions under the plan. That reading, however, is not reasonable because it nullifies subparagraph (C). The latter provision specifically refers to distribution under the plan and the relevant time for determining substantial consummation of the plan is when distribution is commenced, not when it is substantially completed.

Subparagraph (A) is intended to refer to a plan providing for a liquidation of assets of the estate. The typical case is a plan calling for a partial liquidation by sale of some assets and a continuation of the business with the remaining assets. In such a case the plan is not substantially consummated until sale of substantially all of the assets to be liquidated is completed. Section 1101(2)(A) is based on Bankruptcy Act § 229(a)(1). The latter provision more clearly referred to assets to be sold under the plan by its reference to "transfer, sale or other disposition of all or substantially all of the property dealt with by the plan." There is no evidence that Congress intended to change the law by adoption of the slightly different language of § 1101(2)(A). Thus, if the plan does not call for liquidation of assets or if any required liquidation is completed, modification cannot occur once distribution to creditors under the plan is commenced.

In some instances the plan may provide for subsequent alterations in the operation of the plan. In the *Manville* asbestos case the plan called for a property damage trust fund and a personal injury fund. Since it was contemplated that changes might have to be made in the system for paying claims, the trustees were given the power to make changes in the property damage trust fund. The trustees eventually agreed to suspend payments from the property damage trust fund because of exhaustion of funding and to reinstitute payments at a later date when additional funding was contemplated. This action was challenged as an impermissible modification of the plan under § 1127(b). The court upheld the action of the trustees even though the plan had been substantially consummated. *In re Johns–Manville Corp.*, 920 F.2d 121 (2d Cir.1990). The court viewed the alterations as procedural in nature and not as changes in substantive rights. It relied on the authority given the trustees in the plan to adjust the procedural aspects of payment of claims and noted the need for flexibility in dealing with the largely unexplored area of mass tort claims resolution. However, in a subsequent *Manville* case, *Findley v. Blinken*, 982 F.2d 721

(2d Cir.1992), the court held a substantive change in the personal injury trust fund, not authorized by the plan or the trust, to be an impermissible modification.

If a modification is permissible under § 1127, § 1127(c) requires that disclosure with respect to the plan as modified must be given as required by § 1125. But Rule 3019 ameliorates this requirement by providing that if the court finds that a proposed pre-confirmation modification does not "adversely change" the rights of creditors or equity owners who have not accepted the modification, the modified plan will be deemed accepted by all creditors and equity owners who have previously accepted the plan. In *In re American Solar King Corp.*, 90 B.R. 808 (Bankr.W.D.Tex.1988), the modification brought into the plan a creditor previously excluded. Since the result of the modification was to dilute the equity shares distributed under the plan by less than one percent the court held that the change, though adverse to other recipients of equity shares, was not sufficiently material to call for further disclosure. A modification is material only if it would likely lead those who voted for the plan to reconsider their vote.

If a modification is not possible and the debtor cannot carry out the plan, the debtor can convert to Chapter 7 and liquidate. But the effect of a postconfirmation conversion is at best unclear given revesting of property of the estate in the debtor under § 1141. Some courts have held the revested property does not revert to the estate upon conversion but remains property of the debtor. *In re K & M Printing, Inc.*, 210 B.R. 583 (Bankr.D.Ariz.1997). Others disagree. *In re Smith*, 201 B.R. 267 (D.Nev.1996), aff'd mem., 141 F.3d 1179 (9th Cir.1998). One commentator suggests amending the Code to make clear that the bankruptcy trustee may liquidate revested property after postconfirmation conversion. See Sean P. Gates, *Conversion of the Post–Confirmation Chapter 11 Case: Selected Problems, Needed Reforms and Proposed Amendments*, 6 Bankr.L. & Prac. 3 (1997). Does such a debtor have the option of filing a new Chapter 11 to alter its obligations instead of converting to Chapter 7? In *In re Northampton Corp.*, 39 B.R. 955 (Bankr.E.D.Pa.1984), Debtor defaulted in its obligation under the substantially consummated plan to pay the amount of a secured claim to Bank. Debtor filed a second Chapter 11 plan which, by reason of the automatic stay, halted Bank's foreclosure. The court converted Debtor's case to Chapter 7 for cause under § 1112(b), stating: "The filing of a chapter 11 petition, with an eye toward curing defaults arising under a previously confirmed chapter 11 plan, is so akin to modifying the previous plan within the meaning of § 1127(b) that we deemed the filing of a new chapter 11 petition an attempted modification under that section." 39 B.R. at 956. But is a second Chapter 11 filing precluded in a case in which new debts incurred after confirmation of the earlier plan are dealt with as well as debts arising from the earlier plan? Or in which circumstances have changed since confirmation of the first plan?

Nothing in the Code prohibits the serial filing of Chapter 11 cases concerning corporate debtors; compare § 109(g)'s restrictions on serial filing under Chapters 12 and 13. The view gaining acceptance is that the serial filing of Chapter 11 cases is not per se grounds for dismissal. In *In re Jartran, Inc.*, 886 F.2d 859 (7th Cir.1989), the court upheld a liquidating Chapter 11 following a failed reorganization Chapter 11 plan and stated, rather broadly: "Once a bankruptcy plan is effectuated, all indications from the Code would incline us to treat the reorganized entity as we would any other company." 886 F.2d at 870. The only limitation the court recognizes is a requirement that the subsequent plan be filed in good faith. The court in *In re Casa Loma Associates*, 122 B.R. 814 (Bankr.N.D.Ga.1991), found the requisite good faith to uphold the second Chapter 11, which in substance modified the plan confirmed and substantially consummated under the first Chapter 11, because unanticipated changes in circumstances made it impossible to carry out the earlier plan. The court cautioned that mere change in market conditions would not be enough to justify the new Chapter 11 but found additional unanticipated changed circumstances in enactment of a new federal regulatory law and in discovery of fire damage and structural defects in Debtor's apartment units.

# CHAPTER 12

# THE BANKRUPTCY COURTS

## A. ORIGINAL JURISDICTION

### 1. INTRODUCTION

History, politics and Article III of the federal constitution have combined to create a bankruptcy jurisdiction framework of staggering complexity. This Chapter describes how the existing system functions under the constraints imposed by Congress and the Supreme Court. It does not attempt to fully explore the history, rationale and soundness of those constraints. That subject is better suited for an advanced course in Federal Jurisdiction than an introductory course in Bankruptcy. A good starting place for most of these very complex issues is *Collier on Bankruptcy* ¶¶ 2.01–5.11 (15th ed. rev. 2004).

As an initial matter, original federal bankruptcy jurisdiction is vested in the federal district courts. 28 U.S.C. § 1334(a). With respect to bankruptcy *cases* that jurisdiction is exclusive. In addition to exclusive jurisdiction over bankruptcy *cases*, the federal district courts have original but non-exclusive jurisdiction over *proceedings* that arise in or are related to bankruptcy cases. 28 U.S.C. § 1334(b).

The federal district courts do not exercise this extensive grant of jurisdiction directly. While the jurisdiction is formally vested in the district courts, cases arising under the grant are automatically referred to the United States Bankruptcy Court for that district. The bankruptcy court is staffed by bankruptcy judges appointed to fourteen year terms by the United States Court of Appeals for the circuit. 28 U.S.C. § 152(a)(1). Depending on the volume of bankruptcy litigation in the particular district there may be from one to twenty-five bankruptcy judges sitting in the district. Each bankruptcy judge sits as a single-judge trial court.

Bankruptcy judges are clearly not appointed in accordance with the requirements of Article III of the Constitution: the President does not appoint bankruptcy judges, the Senate does not confirm the appointments and the bankruptcy judges do not hold lifetime appointments. Because bankruptcy judges are not appointed in accordance with Article III requirements, the Supreme Court has held that they may not exercise the full judicial power of the United States. *Northern Pipeline Constr. Co. v. Marathon Pipe Line Co.*, 458 U.S. 50, 71 (1982). *Marathon* stunned the world of bankruptcy judges, lawyers and litigants: in a set of complex and confusing opinions none of which commanded a majority, the Supreme

Court declared that the then existing jurisdictional statutes vesting the full breadth of the bankruptcy jurisdiction created by 28 U.S.C. § 1334 in non-Article III judges were unconstitutional. The case has not been well received by scholars. *E.g.,* Erwin Chemerinsky, *Ending the Marathon: It Is Time to Overrule Northern Pipeline,* 65 Am.Bankr.L.J. 311 (1991) ("It is time for the Supreme Court to recognize that *Northern Pipeline* was a mistake and to allow bankruptcy courts the authority accorded them under the 1978 Act.").

The most logical response to *Marathon* would have been to create a free-standing Article III bankruptcy court. Such a court would be able to exercise the full breadth of the federal judicial power and would avoid the great jurisdictional complexity and uncertainty implicit in maintaining an Article I bankruptcy court. Expert panels and commentators continue to recommend this simple solution. *See* NBRC Rep. at 718 (Recommendation 3.1.1 is "[t]he bankruptcy court should be established under Article III. . ..").

Congress, however, while unable to ignore *Marathon,* has been unwilling to create Article III bankruptcy judgeships or limit the bankruptcy jurisdiction in part owing to strong pressure from the Article III judiciary. Lawrence P. King, *The Unmaking of a Bankruptcy Court: Aftermath of Northern Pipeline v. Marathon,* 40 Wash. & Lee L.Rev. 99, 108–111 (1983). NBRC Recommendation 3.1.1 was no more appealing to Congress than the numerous similar prior expert recommendations.

Rather than reconstitute the bankruptcy court under Article III, the current jurisdictional statutes deal with the constitutional limitations on the Article I bankruptcy courts by dividing the full bankruptcy jurisdiction created by 28 U.S.C. § 1334 into "core" and "non-core" components and restricting the role of the bankruptcy courts in "non-core" matters. 28 U.S.C. § 157(b).

Although the Supreme Court has never decided whether the revised system meets constitutional requirements, the lower federal courts have unanimously found that it does and more recent Supreme Court cases seem to support a narrow reading of *Marathon. See Thomas v. Union Carbide Agricultural Products Co.,* 473 U.S. 568 (1985); *Commodity Futures Trading Commission v. Schor,* 478 U.S. 833 (1986). For a discussion of the impact of these two cases on *Marathon,* see George D. Brown, *Article III as a Fundamental Value—The Demise of Northern Pipeline and its Implications for Congressional Power,* 49 Ohio St. L.J. 55 (1988).

Assuming the existing system is constitutional, bankruptcy lawyers and litigants still face daunting problems in determining which court system (the state courts, the bankruptcy court or the federal district court) has original jurisdiction to determine their disputes.

Four sets of questions emerge from the complex existing framework governing the original jurisdiction of the bankruptcy court:

**(1)** What are the limits of the "related-to" jurisdiction under 28 U.S.C. § 1334? That is, which matters are excluded from the bankruptcy jurisdiction altogether without regard to whether that jurisdiction is exercised by the bankruptcy court or the federal district court?

**(2)** What are the limits of the "core" jurisdiction under 28 U.S.C. § 157? That is, which matters may be finally determined by the bankruptcy court and which must be subject to *de novo* review by the federal district court?

**(3)** What matters within the federal bankruptcy jurisdiction can not be adjudicated in the bankruptcy court on account of withdrawal of the reference, mandatory or permissive abstention, the policy favoring arbitration of certain matters, sovereign immunity, and comity with foreign courts?

**(4)** What are the scope of Seventh Amendment jury trial rights in both core and non-core matters? May the bankruptcy court conduct jury trials consistent with Article III?

We will explore each of these questions in this chapter and briefly touch on questions of venue and the bankruptcy appellate process as well. The first two sets of questions—the scope of related-to, core and non-core jurisdiction—are dealt with in the following section. Further limits on original jurisdiction and jury trial issues are discussed later in this Chapter. Comity with foreign courts is the subject of the final section on Transnational Bankruptcy.

## 2. "RELATED-TO," "CORE" AND "NON-CORE" JURISDICTION

28 U.S.C. § 157(b)(1) provides that for "core" cases, bankruptcy judges may "hear and determine" the matter and enter final judgment subject only to appeal under 28 U.S.C. § 158. However, for matters that are not core proceedings but are "otherwise related" to bankruptcy cases, 28 U.S.C. § 157(c)(1) provides that the bankruptcy judge acts, in effect, as a master. In that role the bankruptcy judge submits proposed findings of fact and conclusions of law to the district court which reviews *de novo* any "matters to which any party has timely and specifically objected." Furthermore, if the parties consent, the bankruptcy judge can enter a final order in an "otherwise related case" as well. 28 U.S.C. § 157(c).

The nonexclusive enumeration of core proceedings in 28 U.S.C. § 157(b)(2) includes administering the estate and adjudicating the debtor's rights and liabilities vis-a-vis creditors in such matters as the allowance of claims, counterclaims against persons filing claims, motions affecting stays, confirmation of plans, and the like. It also extends to some proceedings that involve recovery of money damages or property from third parties such as preference or fraudulent conveyance suits. Expressly excluded from the core proceedings category are claims against the estate for personal injury tort or wrongful death. 28 U.S.C. § 157(b)(2)(B). These claims must be tried in the district court. 28 U.S.C. § 157(b)(5). A jury may be demanded in such a case. 28 U.S.C. § 1411.

The following case deals with the questions of the limits of the "related-to" jurisdiction under § 1334 and the line between core and non-core matters.

## In re Toledo

United States Court of Appeals, Eleventh Circuit, 1999.
170 F.3d 1340.

■ ANDERSON, Circuit Judge:

Carmen Sanchez filed the instant adversary proceeding against the trustee of the bankruptcy estate ("Estate") of Orlando and Maria Toledo, the debtors themselves, and the Continental National Bank of Miami ("Bank"). The bankruptcy court invalidated the Bank's mortgage on real estate owned by a partnership of which the debtors and Sanchez were the partners. The district court affirmed the bankruptcy court, applying the deferential standards of review applicable to "core" proceedings under the Bankruptcy Code. The Bank appeals. The issues presented for review are (i) whether the bankruptcy court had jurisdiction to hear this adversary proceeding, and (ii) if so, whether the district court was correct in treating it as a core proceeding rather than as a non-core proceeding requiring de novo, plenary review. For the reasons stated below, we hold that the bankruptcy court had jurisdiction, but that this was a non-core matter necessitating plenary review by the district court.

### I. FACTS

In 1988, Orlando and Maria Toledo, debtors in the underlying bankruptcy case, formed a partnership with Tomas and Carmen Sanchez called the Latin Quarter Center Partnership ("Partnership"). Each of the four partners held an equal one-fourth share. The purpose of the partnership was to hold, develop, and deal in certain contiguous parcels of real estate in downtown Miami ("Partnership Property"). No formal partnership agreement was ever entered into, but Orlando Toledo, acting alone, generally managed and acted on behalf of the partnership. Shortly after the Partnership came into being, Tomas Sanchez died, and his wife Carmen Sanchez (plaintiff in the instant adversary proceeding) succeeded to his 25% share, so that she then owned a total 50% interest in the Partnership. Orlando Toledo continued to act as managing partner and Carmen Sanchez was uninvolved in Partnership affairs.

In April of 1989, Orlando Toledo encountered personal financial difficulties. In order to assuage the Bank's concern about its position as one of his creditors and to induce it not to foreclose on a mortgage it held on his Key Biscayne personal residence, Toledo purported to convey a mortgage on the Partnership Property to the Bank to secure Toledo's personal indebtedness to the Bank in the approximate amount of $1,100,000. This was done without Sanchez' consent or knowledge. In taking this action, Toledo claimed to be acting in the capacity of a general partner as an agent for the Partnership. If the mortgage was valid, the Partnership Property thereby became a guarantee for Toledo's personal debt. Toledo also convinced McDonald's Corp., which had a $275,000 pre-existing purchase money mortgage on the Partnership Property, to subordinate its mortgage to the one newly granted to the Bank.

Orlando Toledo's financial outlook did not improve, and the Bank eventually obtained a judgment of foreclosure on both the Partnership Property and Toledo's Key Biscayne personal residence (which secured the same indebtedness) in Dade County circuit court in November 1992. Despite her status as 50% partner, Sanchez was not served with the notice of foreclosure and therefore was not a party to these Florida state court proceedings; the Bank apparently relied on Florida law allowing service on a partnership to be effected by serving a single general partner. The circuit court rendering the foreclosure judgment held that Toledo's residence would be sold first, and if the debt to the Bank (now, including interest, real estate taxes, and subsequent advances, at some $1.8 million) was still unsatisfied thereafter, it would schedule sale of the Partnership Property. On January 11, 1993, the day before the scheduled foreclosure sale of the Key Biscayne residence, Orlando and Maria Toledo filed for Chapter 11 and thereby averted the sale.

Soon after the commencement of the bankruptcy case, a private sale of the Partnership Property to McDonald's Corp. was negotiated by Toledo, the Estate, and the Bank under supervision of the bankruptcy court. The terms of this sale, which the record indicates were favorable to the sellers, were that McDonald's Corp. would purchase the Partnership Property for an agreed sale price of $825,000. Of that $825,000, approximately $474,000 would go to satisfy amounts due under McDonald's Corp.'s purchase money mortgage (plus past real estate taxes paid by McDonald's and other costs), and about $351,000 would go to the Bank and/or the Partnership.[2] The parties, apparently assuming that the bankruptcy court's stamp of approval was necessary in order to consummate the sale, applied to the court for approval even though the Partnership Property was not property of the Estate. Acting under purported authority of 11 U.S.C. § 363(f), Judge Weaver approved the sale in an order dated April 12, 1993 (and modified in respects not material on June 4, 1993).[3] In that same sale

---

[2] For reasons not clear on this record, the Bank apparently was satisfied to receive $200,000 of the proceeds of the sale, even though its mortgage on the Partnership Property secured Toledo's personal debts in excess of $1.8 million.

[3] Section 363(f) of the Bankruptcy Code provides that "the trustee may sell property under subsections (b) and (c) of this section free and clear of any interest in such property of an entity other than the state" upon certain conditions. It is questionable

order, Judge Weaver directed that of the proceeds of the sale of the Partnership Property, $200,000 be disbursed to the Bank in satisfaction of its mortgage.[4] The sale was carried out and the Bank was so paid. Sanchez, as a 50% partner, consented to the terms of sale but asked that the proceeds be placed in escrow rather than being distributed immediately; Judge Weaver refused to consider the escrow proposal because Sanchez' counsel filed a pleading by facsimile transmission rather than appearing personally in court. Later, Sanchez signed a closing statement reflecting that the proceeds would be distributed in accordance with the sale order.

Meanwhile, Sanchez filed the instant adversary complaint in the bankruptcy court against the trustee of the Estate, the debtors themselves, and the Bank (i) to determine entitlement to the proceeds of the sale of the Partnership Property to McDonald's Corp., and (ii) to contest the validity of the Bank's lien (formerly on the Partnership Property, and now on $200,000 of the proceeds therefrom). The action was styled as a "Complaint to Determine Validity, Priority, and Extent of Lien and Ownership Interest." After four evidentiary hearings in which extensive testimony was taken from Orlando Toledo, employees of the Bank, and others, Judge Cristol of the bankruptcy court accepted Sanchez' argument and ordered that (i) the Bank had had no valid lien on the Partnership Property because it knew Toledo was conveying the mortgage for improper, non-partnership purposes, and (ii) the Bank must pay to Sanchez the $200,000 it had previously received from the sale of the Partnership Property. The bankruptcy court noted that it had jurisdiction under 28 U.S.C. § 1334, but never specifically confronted the question whether the adversary proceeding was core or non-core under 28 U.S.C. § 157. By issuing an order that purported to be final and binding, rather than submitting proposed findings of fact and conclusions of law to the district court, the bankruptcy court indicated that it viewed the proceeding as a core one of which it had full, plenary authority to dispose.

---

whether § 363(f) gives a bankruptcy court power to order or approve a sale of property that belongs only to an entity in which the estate holds an interest, and not to the estate itself. However, the validity of the sale order is not presently before this Court, and at any rate, it appears that the sale of the Partnership Property was a voluntary transaction, on favorable terms to the seller, to which all of the parties consented. Thus, we do not consider any issues relating to Judge Weaver's sale order.

[4] The sale price to McDonald's Corp. was $825,000. These proceeds were distributed as follows: (i) $200,000 to the Bank pursuant to its mortgage securing Toledo's personal indebtedness, (ii) $450,000 to McDonald's Corp. pursuant to its purchase money mortgage which had been contractually subordinated to the Bank's mortgage (since McDonald's was the purchaser, this amount was simply set off against the purchase price), and (iii) the remaining $175,000, less real estate taxes that had been paid by McDonald's Corp. as mortgagee over the course of the Partnership's ownership, to the Partnership (i.e., ultimately to Sanchez and/or the Toledos and the Estate).

Appealing to the district court, the Bank argued that (i) the bankruptcy court lacked subject matter jurisdiction to hear the adversary proceeding filed by Sanchez; (ii) the bankruptcy court erred in finding that the Bank knew Toledo lacked authority to mortgage the Partnership Property for personal purposes; and (iii) the doctrines of waiver or estoppel should have precluded the bankruptcy court from granting Sanchez relief. The district court held that the bankruptcy court had subject matter jurisdiction and that the matter was a core matter. It then found, applying the "clearly erroneous" standard of review to the bankruptcy court's fact findings (the appropriate standard of review for bankruptcy court orders regarding core matters), that Toledo lacked authority to mortgage the Partnership Property for his personal purposes, and that the Bank was aware thereof. The district court also held that the bankruptcy court did not abuse its discretion by not applying the doctrines of waiver or estoppel to bar relief invalidating the Bank's mortgage. Consequently, the district court affirmed the bankruptcy court's judgment.

On appeal to this court, the Bank argues first that the bankruptcy court lacked jurisdiction to entertain the adversary proceeding under 28 U.S.C. § 1334. Second, it argues that, even if the bankruptcy court had jurisdiction, such jurisdiction was in the nature of a non-core proceeding limiting the bankruptcy court's adjudicative powers. Third, the Bank reiterates its various substantive arguments as to why the bankruptcy court erred in its determination of the merits under Florida law; however, in light of our conclusion that this was a non-core proceeding, it is unnecessary for us to reach those issues.

## II. DISCUSSION

### A. Jurisdiction under 28 U.S.C. § 1334

The first question is whether the bankruptcy court had jurisdiction to entertain the instant adversary proceeding under 28 U.S.C. § 1334. Section 1334(b) provides that "the district courts shall have original but not exclusive jurisdiction of all civil proceedings arising under title 11, or arising in or related to cases under title 11." This provision creates jurisdiction in three categories of proceedings: those that "arise under title 11," those that "arise in cases under title 11," and those "related to cases under title 11." The bankruptcy court's jurisdiction is derivative of and dependent upon these three bases. *Celotex Corp. v. Edwards*, 514 U.S. 300 (1995); 1 Lawrence P. King, *Collier on Bankruptcy* ¶ 3.01[4] (15th ed.1998) [hereinafter *Collier on Bankruptcy* ]. The instant adversary proceeding did not "arise under" or "arise in" a case under the Bankruptcy Code. "Arising under" proceedings are matters invoking a substantive right created by the Bankruptcy Code. *In re Wood*, 825 F.2d 90, 97 (5th Cir.1987); 1 *Collier on Bankruptcy* ¶ 3.01[4][c][i]. The "arising in a case under" category is generally thought to involve administrative-type matters, 1 *Collier on Bankruptcy* ¶ 3.01[4][c][iv], or as the *Wood* court put it, "matters that could arise only in bankruptcy." Hence, the only one of the three categories of proceedings over which the district court is granted jurisdiction in

§ 1334(b) that is potentially relevant to the instant case is proceedings "related to cases under title 11." The "related to" connection has been described as "the minimum for bankruptcy jurisdiction." E. Scott Fruehwald, *The Related to Subject Matter Jurisdiction of Bankruptcy Courts*, 44 Drake L.Rev. 1, 7 (1995).

The Bank claims that the dispute between Sanchez and the Bank over entitlement to the proceeds of the Partnership Property was not related to Toledo's underlying bankruptcy case and had no effect on Toledo or the Estate, and therefore the bankruptcy court had no jurisdiction to adjudicate that dispute. Blending the concepts of jurisdiction and the core versus non-core dichotomy, the district court held that the bankruptcy court had jurisdiction because the dispute was a "core proceeding" under 28 U.S.C. § 157(b)(2)(K).[6]

As both parties acknowledge, *In re Lemco Gypsum, Inc.*, 910 F.2d 784 (11th Cir.1990), is the seminal case in this Circuit on the scope of the bankruptcy court's "related to" jurisdiction. In *Lemco Gypsum*, this Court adopted the following liberal test from *Pacor, Inc. v. Higgins*, 743 F.2d 984 (3d Cir.1984), for determining jurisdiction over an adversary proceeding:

> The usual articulation of the test for determining whether a civil proceeding is related to bankruptcy is whether the outcome of the proceeding could conceivably have an effect on the estate being administered in bankruptcy. The proceeding need not necessarily be against the debtor or the debtor's property. An action is related to bankruptcy if the outcome could alter the debtor's rights, liabilities, options, or freedom of action (either positively or negatively) and which in any way impacts upon the handling and administration of the bankrupt estate.

*Lemco Gypsum*, 910 F.2d at 788 (quoting *Pacor*); *see also Celotex Corp.*, 115 S. Ct. at 1499 & n. 6 (expressing approval of the *Pacor* test). The key word in the *Lemco Gypsum/Pacor* test is "conceivable," which makes the jurisdictional grant extremely broad.

In the instant case, Sanchez was seeking a judicial determination of the extent and priority of liens and other interests in the Partnership Property so that the proceeds of the sale earlier approved by Judge Weaver's order could be distributed appropriately. The nexus with the bankruptcy estate contemplated by the *Lemco Gypsum/Pacor* test was present in two ways. First, if the Bank's mortgage were adjudged valid, its $1.8 million

---

[6] Although whether something is a core proceeding is analytically separate from whether there is jurisdiction, by definition all core proceedings are within the bankruptcy court's jurisdiction. Core proceedings are defined in 28 U.S.C. § 157(b)(1) as "proceedings arising under title 11, or arising in a case under title 11," which is a subset of the cases over which jurisdiction is granted in § 1334(b).

claim against the Estate (partially secured by the Key Biscayne residence) would be reduced by the $200,000 due and paid to the Bank out of the proceeds of the sale of the Partnership Property. Thus, the payment of these $200,000 to the Bank from non-Estate property would ultimately free up an additional $200,000 for distribution to unsecured creditors.[7] In contrast, if the Bank's mortgage was held invalid, as actually occurred, the Bank would have to look entirely to the Key Biscayne residence (or, more precisely, to what remained from the proceeds of the residence after satisfaction of BankAtlantic's first mortgage thereon) for satisfaction of its $1.8 million indebtedness. To the extent the value to which it was entitled from the residence was insufficient to satisfy this debt, the Bank would become an unsecured creditor causing the funds available for unsecured claims to be spread more thinly. A conceivable effect on the Estate thus exists in the possible partial satisfaction and consequent downward adjustment of the claim filed against the Estate by the Bank.

The second connection to the Estate stems from the fact that if the mortgage were adjudged invalid, there would be more equity in the Partnership Property and an additional $200,000 would be freed up to go to the Partnership. Whatever interest the Toledos had in the Partnership at the time the petition was filed became part of the Estate. Under the terms of the sale order, approximately $151,000 already was available for distribution to the Partnership. It was originally contemplated that these proceeds would be split 50/50 between Sanchez and the Estate, according to Sanchez' and the Toledos' respective 50% interests in the Partnership. Under this arrangement, if the Bank's mortgage were held invalid, the Estate might have been enriched by $100,000 (one-half of $200,000)–clearly

---

[7] Because additional collateral (the Toledos' Key Biscayne residence) and an additional creditor (BankAtlantic) on that collateral were involved, the logical chain is fairly complicated and deserves some explanation. The Toledos owed the Bank about $1.8 million. Their residence was encumbered first by a BankAtlantic mortgage, then by the Bank's mortgage securing the $1.8 million indebtedness, then by a third mortgage also belonging to BankAtlantic. If $200,000 of the Toledos' indebtedness to the Bank were satisfied out of the proceeds of the sale of the Partnership Property, the Bank's "intermediate" mortgage on the Key Biscayne residence would secure only $1.6 million, i.e., $200,000 less than it would otherwise have secured. Put differently, the value of the residence would be exhausted more slowly and either the Bank or BankAtlantic (pursuant to its third mortgage) would be undersecured to a lesser extent than before. Consequently, depending on the value of the residence, more funds would be available either to satisfy BankAtlantic's third mortgage, or to go into the Estate to pay off unsecured creditors. General creditors of the Estate would ultimately benefit, either because (i) their claims were not diluted or were less diluted by the presence of the Bank as a competing unsecured creditor, (ii) their claims were not diluted or were less diluted by the presence of BankAtlantic (to the extent of its debt secured by the third mortgage on the Key Biscayne residence) as a competing unsecured creditor, or (iii) if the value of the residence was sufficient to satisfy both mortgages, the excess value that constituted equity in the property would go into the Estate.

a "conceivable effect" on the Estate that would support "related to" jurisdiction. *Cf. Wood*, 825 F.2d at 93–94 (holding that relatedness existed
where an action against the debtor personally for post-petition misappro-
priation of corporate assets would "resolve the disputed allocation of interest in the [corporation]" and where the debtor's stock holdings in the
corporation were property of the estate so that their value would affect the
estate).[8]

The instant case is distinguishable from a recent case in which we determined that the essential "related to" nexus under § 1334(b) was not present. In *In re Boone* this Court determined that the bankruptcy court
lacked jurisdiction over a lawsuit by Chapter 7 debtors against a creditor
for tortious interference with contract. The rationale was that the conduct
giving rise to the claim occurred after the date of the bankruptcy petition;
the cause of action therefore belonged to the debtors themselves rather
than to the estate, and consequently any recovery in the lawsuit would not
inure to the benefit of the estate. In the instant adversary proceeding, the
property interest whose value would be affected by the outcome of the
proceeding (the Toledos' interest in the Partnership) was a pre-petition
property interest and therefore belonged to the Estate. Unlike in *Boone*,
the value and extent of the Estate's indirect interest in the Partnership
Property would necessarily be affected by the outcome of the adversary
proceeding. Also, unlike in *Boone*, we have an additional connection with
the estate inasmuch that resolution of the dispute over the validity of the
mortgage ultimately affects whether the creditor whose mortgage is invalidated must look to other collateral or compete with general unsecured
creditors to satisfy the debt it is owed.

### B. Core Versus Non–Core

Having found that the district court had jurisdiction over the adversary
proceeding, we turn next to the question whether the district court correctly referred to it as a core proceeding under 28 U.S.C. § 157(b). If it
was a core proceeding, the district court correctly applied normal, deferential standards of appellate review to the bankruptcy court's disposition of
it. See 28 U.S.C. § 158(a); Fed. R. Bankr.P. 8013. If it was a noncore proceeding, the bankruptcy court could only submit proposed findings of fact

---

[8] * * * [T]he bankruptcy court ultimately determined that the Estate's and the debtors'
interests in the Partnership were worthless. Thus, the additional $200,000 flowing to
the Partnership by virtue of the invalidity of the Bank's mortgage did not ultimately
benefit the Estate. However, it is clear that the issue of the validity of the Bank's mortgage could conceivably have had an effect on the Estate, thus satisfying the test. *See
Wood*, 825 F.2d at 94 ("Although we acknowledge the possibility that this suit may
ultimately have no effect on the bankruptcy, we cannot conclude, on the facts before
us, that it will have no *conceivable* effect.") (emphasis in original). The presence or
absence of jurisdiction must be evaluated based on the state of affairs existing at the
time the adversary complaint was filed not at some later time when, for example, it
was ultimately determined here that the Estate had no interest in the sale proceeds.

and conclusions of law, not a final order or judgment, and the district court was obligated to conduct a de novo review of those matters to which the Bank objected. See 28 U.S.C. § 157(c)(1) ("In [a non-core] proceeding, the bankruptcy judge shall submit proposed findings of fact and conclusions of law to the district court, and any final order or judgment shall be entered by the district judge after considering the bankruptcy judge's proposed findings and conclusions and after reviewing de novo those matters to which any party has timely and specifically objected."); Fed. R. Bankr.P. 9033 (specifying the exact procedures to be followed by the district court in such cases).

Congress created the distinction between core and non-core proceedings in. . . 1984 in order to avoid the constitutional problems, identified in *Northern Pipeline Constr. Co. v. Marathon Pipe Line Co.*, associated with the expansive bankruptcy court jurisdiction permitted under prior law. 28 U.S.C. § 157(b)(2) lists fourteen specific types of actions that are considered core proceedings, id. § 157(b)(2)(A)-(N), and provides a fifteenth, catch-all category for "other proceedings affecting the liquidation[**21] of the assets of the estate or the adjustment of the debtor-creditor or the equity security holder relationship," 28 U.S.C. § 157(b)(2)(O). The statutory list provides that it is not intended to be exhaustive of the entire universe of core proceedings.

The district court held that the instant case was a core proceeding under 28 U.S.C. § 157(b)(2)(K), which applies to "determinations of the validity, extent, or priority of liens." This reliance on § 157(b)(2)(K) was misplaced. The district court apparently reasoned that since the purpose of the instant adversary proceeding was to obtain a judicial determination of the validity of the Bank's mortgage, which is a lien on real estate, it fit the language of subsection (b)(2)(K). However, the case law on (b)(2)(K) indicates that it encompasses only proceedings to determine the validity, extent, or priority of liens on the estate's or the debtor's property. "Otherwise, [bankruptcy courts] would be asserting a form of jurisdiction ferae naturae, capable of the adjudication of property rights wherever found and by whomever owned." *In re Dr. C. Huff Co.*, 44 B.R. 129, 134 (Bankr.W.D.Ky.1984). Here, the real property on which the disputed mortgage existed belonged to the non-debtor Partnership, not to the Toledos or the Estate. The Estate owned a 50% interest in the Partnership, but no direct interest in the Partnership Property. Thus, § 157(b)(2)(K) is no basis for calling the instant proceeding a "core proceeding." *Cf. In re Guild & Gallery Plus, Inc.*, 72 F.3d 1171, 1179 (3d Cir.1996) (holding that the § 157(b)(2)(A) core proceeding category for "matters concerning the administration of the estate" did not apply to an action concerning goods with respect to which the debtor was bailee but not owner).

The distinction between property belonging to a partnership of which the debtor was partner, and property belonging to the debtor-partner, is well-established in bankruptcy law. * * * *In re Palumbo*, 154 B.R. 357, 358 (Bankr.S.D.Fla.1992) (noting, with regard to a partner who had a 97%

interest in a partnership and claimed that foreclosure on the partnership property violated the automatic stay, that "it is firmly established that the assets of a partnership are not to be administered in a partner's bankruptcy proceeding since a partnership is a separate entity from its partners under bankruptcy law"); *In re Funneman*, 155 B.R. 197, 199 (Bankr.S.D.Ill.1993) ("It is well settled that assets owned by a partnership are not included in the bankruptcy estate of the individual partner. The only partnership property before the court during an individual's bankruptcy is the partner's personal property interest in the partnership, which consists of the individual's interest, if any, in the partnership assets after an accounting and payment of partnership debts out of the property belonging to the partnership."). The Partnership Property never entered the Estate in the instant case.

Nor do any of the other types of core proceedings appearing in § 157(b)'s list fit the instant adversary proceeding, especially in light of the fact that they are to be construed in light of the constitutional limitations that prompted their enactment. To the extent that the literal wording of some of the types of proceedings might conceivably seem to apply,[10] it should be remembered that engrafted upon all of them is an overarching requirement that property of the estate under § 541 be involved. *In re Gallucci*, 931 F.2d 738, 742 (11th Cir.1991) (noting that § 157(b)(2)(E) category for turnover actions applies only to orders to turn over property of the estate). Here, of course, the property in question was owned by the Partnership, not by Toledo himself.

Because the list in the statute is non-exhaustive, it is not the end of our inquiry whether the adversary proceeding was core. The most helpful explanation of what is a core proceeding, accepted almost universally by the courts, is found in the Fifth Circuit's decision in *Wood*:

> If the proceeding involves a right created by the federal bankruptcy law, it is a core proceeding; for example, an action by the trustee to avoid a preference. If the proceeding is one that would arise only in bankruptcy, it is also a core proceeding; for example, the filing of a proof of claim or an objection to the discharge of a particular debt. If the proceeding does not invoke a substantive right created by the federal bankruptcy law and is one that could exist outside of bankruptcy it is not a core proceeding; it may be *related to* the bankruptcy because of its potential effect, but under section 157(c)(1) it is an "otherwise related" or non-core proceeding.

825 F.2d at 97 (emphasis in original). In *Wood*, the adversary proceeding in question was an action by a shareholder of a corporation of which the bankruptcy debtor was the only other shareholder, to obtain redress for allegedly improper stock issued to and dividends received by the

---

[10] For example, "matters concerning the administration of the estate," § 157(b)(2)(A).

debtor-shareholder or the estate. The Fifth Circuit held that under the above test this adversary proceeding was not a core proceeding because it was "simply a state contract action that, had there been no bankruptcy, could have proceeded in state court." *Id.* Although the court had subject matter jurisdiction pursuant to the "related to" prong of § 1334(b), it was not a core proceeding.

*Wood*'s interpretation of § 157 rested heavily on the ostensible purpose of the 1984 Act, i.e., "to conform the bankruptcy statutes to the dictates of *Marathon.*" The Fifth Circuit's test breathes life into the terms "core" and "non-core" by construing them in light of the constitutional concerns that prompted the enactment of the statute. In fact, it appears that the use of the word "core" was itself borrowed from Justice Brennan's reference in the plurality opinion to "the core of the federal bankruptcy power." What the Supreme Court, and by extension Congress, was concerned about was the plenary adjudication by bankruptcy courts of proceedings "related only peripherally to an adjudication of bankruptcy." *Northern Pipeline*, 458 U.S. at 92 (Burger, C.J., dissenting). Hence, the issue before us ultimately depends on whether the instant case was of the type with respect to which the *Northern Pipeline* Court rejected giving bankruptcy courts full adjudicative power.

We are mindful that the dependence of the merits of an action on state law (as the instant case turns on various partnership law and real estate finance law issues) does not, in and of itself, mean that the action is non-core. 28 U.S.C. § 157(b)(3); see also *Wood*, 825 F.2d at 96, 97 n. 4; *Northern Pipeline*, 458 U.S. at 96–97, 102 S. Ct. 2858 (White, J., dissenting) ("The distinction between claims based on state law and those based on federal law disregards the real character of bankruptcy proceedings. . .. The bankruptcy judge is constantly enmeshed in state-law issues."). Nevertheless, based on the *Wood* test as well as the constitutional concerns expressed in *Northern Pipeline*, we conclude that the instant case was not a core proceeding. Sanchez' action to determine the validity, priority, and extent of liens on the Partnership Property did not invoke a substantive right created by bankruptcy law, and could clearly occur outside of bankruptcy.[11] Indeed, actions similar to the instant case are filed in state court all the time.

---

[11] *Wood* is especially instructive because its facts are roughly analogous to those in the instant case. In *Wood*, the complaint filed in the bankruptcy court concerned the debtors' post-petition wrongful issuance of stock and payment of dividends (the debtors were controlling shareholders and directors of the corporation) to themselves, which violated the plaintiff's right as an equal shareholder. By comparison, the instant case concerns a debtor-partner's alleged manipulation of a partnership to exploit its property to secure personal debts, to the detriment of the other partner. In both cases, the right that the plaintiffs sought to vindicate involved a wrongful manipulation of the property of an entity other than the debtor (i.e., a corporation or partnership), and was essentially a state-law right based on principles of contract and/or fiduciary duty. Nei-

The linguistic structure of § 157 lends further support to this conclusion. Subsection (b)(1) equates core proceedings with those "arising under title 11, or arising in a case under title 11," whereas subsection (c)(1) makes "non-core" proceedings synonymous with "otherwise related to" proceedings. "The phrases 'arising under' and 'arising in' are helpful indicators of the meaning of core proceedings." *Wood*, 825 F.2d at 97; *see also* 1 *Collier on Bankruptcy*, ¶ 3.01[4][c]. "Arising under" means that a proceeding invokes a cause of action, or substantive right, created by a specific section of the Bankruptcy Code. *Celotex Corp. v. Edwards*, 115 S. Ct. at 1506 & n. 13 (Stevens, J., dissenting); 1 *Collier on Bankruptcy* ¶ 3.01[4][c][I] . "Arising in" describes administrative matters unique to the management of a bankruptcy estate. 1 *Collier on Bankruptcy* ¶ 3.01[4][c][iv]. For example, as the *Wood* court explained, the filing of a claim against a bankruptcy estate triggers a core proceeding under § 157(b)(2)(B), but only because it "invokes the peculiar powers of the bankruptcy court." However, the administrative act of filing such a claim must be distinguished from the state-law right underlying the claim, which "could be enforced in a state court proceeding absent the bankruptcy" and is non-core. In the instant case, the adversary proceeding sought to vindicate state-created common-law rights but did not utilize any process specially established by the Bankruptcy Code. Clearly, Sanchez' adversary proceeding neither "arose under" nor "arose in" the Bankruptcy Code as those terms of art have been understood, and therefore it must necessarily fall within the residual category of "otherwise related," i.e., non-core matters.

### III. CONCLUSION

In conclusion, we hold that there was "related to" jurisdiction over the adversary proceeding under 28 U.S.C. § 1334, but that it was a non-core proceeding under 28 U.S.C. § 157. Because the district court mistook it for a core proceeding, it exercised only "clearly erroneous" review of the bankruptcy court's findings of fact and "abuse of discretion" review of the bankruptcy court's application of waiver and estoppel, despite the Bank's specific objections to those findings and applications.[12] We remand with instructions to the district court to treat the bankruptcy court's findings of fact and conclusions of law and "judgments" granting Sanchez relief, as merely proposed findings of fact and conclusions of law, and to conduct

---

ther case is one involving a right created by bankruptcy law, or one which would arise only in bankruptcy. Rather, both cases invoke purely state-law rights and could exist outside bankruptcy.

[12] It is evident from the tone of the district court's opinion that its review of certain issues was highly deferential to the bankruptcy court. For example, it stated that "there is a valid basis for the relief granted by the bankruptcy court to avoid an injustice to override the application of res judicata and collateral estoppel." On remand, the district court should undertake a fresh, independent analysis of these issues.

the *de novo* review contemplated by § 157(c)(1) and Bankruptcy Rule 9033. The judgment of the district court is

VACATED AND REMANDED.

## NOTES

**1.** The *Pacor* test for "related to" jurisdiction (whether the proceeding could have any conceivable effect on the estate), adopted in *Toledo*, has been widely followed. Judge Posner comments on the scope of "related to" jurisdiction in *Zerand-Bernal Group, Inc. v. Cox*, 23 F.3d 159 (7th Cir.1994). There Zerand bought the debtor's assets at a bankruptcy sale free and clear of liens. All property of the estate was subsequently distributed and the debtor went out of business. Four and a half years after the sale to Zerand, Cox, who was injured by a machine that debtor had sold to Cox's employer before the asset sale to Zerand, brought a products liability suit in federal district court against Zerand on the theory of successor liability. Zerand sought to reopen the bankruptcy case and asked that Cox be enjoined from proceeding with his products liability suit. The bankruptcy court held that it lacked jurisdiction over the proceeding brought by Cox because it was not related to the bankruptcy case within the meaning of 28 U.S.C. § 1334(b). In affirming the decision, Posner conceded that the "related to" language was probably broad enough to encompass Zerand's proceeding because it related to the bankruptcy sale at which Zerand acquired the debtor's assets and thereby exposed itself to Cox's suit.

> But the language should not be read so broadly. The reference to cases related to bankruptcy cases is primarily intended to encompass tort, contract, and other legal claims by and against the debtor, claims that, were it not for bankruptcy, would be ordinary stand-alone lawsuits between the debtor and others but that section 1334(b) allows to be forced into bankruptcy court so that all claims by and against the debtor can be determined in the same forum. * * * A secondary purpose is to force into the bankruptcy court suits to which the debtor need not be a party but which may affect the amount of property in the bankrupt estate.

23 F.3d at 161–162. Cox's suit was not covered by either test. The debtor company no longer exists and all its assets have been distributed to creditors; Cox's suit could not affect the amount of property available to creditors.

**2.** In 28 U.S.C. § 157(b)(2)(A) and (O), Congress has included two catch-all categories that give bankruptcy courts flexibility in identifying matters as core proceedings. The wording of § 157(b)(2)(O) is so broad that it could be interpreted to make the matter in *Marathon* a core proceeding. In adopting the view that a court should avoid characterizing a proceeding as core if to do so would raise constitutional problems, *In re*

*Castlerock Properties,* 781 F.2d 159 (9th Cir.1986), held that state law contract claims that do not specifically fall within § 157(b)(2)(B)-(N) are noncore proceedings under § 157(c) even if they fall within the literal wording of § 157(b)(2)(A) or (O).

**3.** The prevailing view is that a claim by a trustee or debtor in possession arising from a postpetition contract is a core matter. The court in *In re Arnold Print Works, Inc.,* 815 F.2d 165 (1st Cir.1987) (Breyer, J.), held that such a suit falls within 28 U.S.C. § 157(b)(2)(A) because it concerns the administration of the estate and within § 157(b)(2)(O) because the claim arose out of the debtor's efforts to liquidate estate assets. Can this case be reconciled with *Castlerock Properties* in Note 2? In *Arnold Print Works* the court asserts that its interpretation of § 157(b) is constitutional under *Marathon* because under the Bankruptcy Act bankruptcy courts had jurisdiction over postpetition contract claims on the fiction that a contract with a trustee is a contract with the court. The court said, "Quite apart from the force of the fiction, the history of bankruptcy court jurisdiction means that a post-petition contract made with a debtor-in-possession cannot be called a 'traditional' state contract action." 815 F.2d at 170. Several courts of appeal have also held that professional malpractice claims by trustees or debtors against court-appointed professionals are core proceedings. *See Southmark v. Coopers & Lybrand,* 163 F.3d 925 (5th Cir.1999) (accountants); *Billing v. Ravin, Greenberg, & Zackin, P.A.,* 22 F.3d 1242 (3d Cir.1994) (lawyers).

**4.** More surprising than the *Arnold Print Works* holding with respect to claims under postpetition contracts is that, despite *Marathon,* bankruptcy courts have split over whether the right of the trustee or debtor in possession to collect a prepetition debt is a core proceeding. One view reads Bankruptcy Code § 542(b) as authorizing a turnover order in cases in which a defendant owes the debtor a matured debt and sees 28 U.S.C. § 157(b)(2)(E) as making a proceeding under § 542(b) a core proceeding. For example, *In re Leco Enterprises, Inc.,* 125 B.R. 385 (S.D.N.Y.1991), holds that an action to collect a disputed account receivable is a core proceeding under § 157(b)(A), (E) and (O) because it sought an order to turn over property that would inure to the benefit of the estate and was, therefore, inextricably linked to the administration of the estate. Another line of cases rejects the *Leco* approach as creating an exception to *Marathon* that would swallow the rule of the case. *See, e.g., In re Orion Pictures Corp.,* 4 F.3d 1095, 1102 (2d Cir.1993).

It seems most unlikely that expansively interpreting 28 U.S.C. § 157(b)(2)(E) to encompass proceedings to collect prepetition contract claims like accounts receivable complies with *Marathon.* Under the Bankruptcy Act turnover orders were summary jurisdiction proceedings to establish ownership of property in the possession of others and not to enforce choses in action against obligors of the bankrupt. *In re Lehigh & Hudson River Ry. Co.,* 468 F.2d 430 (2d Cir.1972). That case is discussed in *Matter of Century Brass Products, Inc.,* 58 B.R. 838

(Bankr.D.Conn.1986), which denies core status to an action to collect accounts receivable. 28 U.S.C. § 157(b)(2)(E) includes as core proceedings "orders to turn over property of the estate." But property of the estate with respect to a prepetition account receivable is the right to payment or chose in action against the obligor. No further order is needed to establish the estate's ownership of this chose in action. Further proceedings would be needed only to enforce the chose in action, and such a proceeding closely resembles that in *Marathon*. The issue is discussed in *Beard v. Braunstein*, 914 F.2d 434 (3d Cir.1990), in which the court held that an action by a Chapter 7 trustee to recover prepetition and postpetition rents from a tenant under a prepetition lease was a noncore proceeding.

**5.** As *Toledo* indicates, 28 U.S.C. § 157(c)(1) requires that in a non-core proceeding the bankruptcy judge must submit proposed findings of fact and conclusions of law to the district court. The district court will enter a final order after reviewing *de novo* those matters to which any party has objected. Under Rule 9033(d) the district judge may accept, reject, or modify the proposed findings of fact or conclusions of law, receive further evidence or recommit the matter to the bankruptcy judge with instructions. In *In re Castro*, 919 F.2d 107 (9th Cir.1990), the circuit court remanded to the district court a case in which the district court had entered its order before it had a transcript of the testimony given in the bankruptcy court. The circuit court observed that for *de novo* review the district court need not hold new hearings but must review the record.

### 3. FURTHER LIMITS ON ORIGINAL JURISDICTION

The problems inherent in defining the scope of § 157(b) and § 1334(b) do not exhaust the legal limits on the original federal bankruptcy jurisdiction. Bankruptcy courts may also be precluded from adjudicating claims otherwise within the original federal bankruptcy jurisdiction under § 1334(b) for the following reasons:

**(a)** withdrawal of the reference under 28 U.S.C. § 157(d);

**(b)** abstention under 28 U.S.C. § 1334(c);

**(c)** enforcement of arbitration clauses; and

**(d)** state sovereign immunity under the Eleventh Amendment.

### a. Withdrawal of Case From Bankruptcy Court

Under 28 U.S.C. § 157(d) a district court may withdraw a case or proceeding from a bankruptcy court "for cause." The district court must withdraw a matter "if the court determines that resolution of the proceeding requires consideration of both title 11 and other laws of the United States regulating organizations or activities affecting interstate commerce." There is no indication that *Marathon* required mandatory withdrawal in this situation; the provision shows Congressional distaste for having bankruptcy courts deal with nonbankruptcy federal laws. Case law provides for mandatory withdrawal when "substantial and material consideration" of federal statutes, in addition to the Bankruptcy Code, is required. *See, e.g., Pension Benefit Guaranty Corporation v. Official Parent Creditors' Committee*, 108 B.R. 27 (S.D.N.Y.1989). Even though withdrawal is mandatory in these cases, the actual hearing may still be in the bankruptcy court. In *Official Parent,* the district court referred the proceedings to the bankruptcy court for findings of fact and conclusions of law under § 157(c)(1).

### b.  Abstention

In 1978, Senate conservatives wanted to require abstention by bankruptcy courts whenever a state law cause of action was present, whether the debtor was plaintiff or defendant. The compromise result was 28 U.S.C. § 1334(c)(2). This provision is only an attenuated version of what these Senators sought. Section 1334(c)(2) requires district courts to abstain from hearing a state cause of action over which they have jurisdiction solely because the claim is "related to a case under title 11" when the action on the claim "is commenced, and can be timely adjudicated, in a State forum of appropriate jurisdiction." Although this language is ambiguous, the majority view is that a state court proceeding must be pending at the time the order to abstain is entered. *In re West Coast Video Enterprises, Inc.*, 145 B.R. 484, 486 (Bankr.E.D.Pa.1992). This interpretation would usually restrict § 1334(c)(2) mandatory abstention to suits brought by debtors against third parties before bankruptcy. 28 U.S.C. § 1334(c)(2) does not apply to a case in which the "related to" action could have been commenced in a federal court under diversity jurisdiction or under any other nonbankruptcy federal jurisdiction.

In 1994, § 1334(d) was added to provide that decisions either to abstain or not to abstain under (c)(1) (discretionary abstention) and decisions *to* abstain under (c)(2) (mandatory abstention) are not reviewable by the court of appeals or Supreme Court; decisions *not* to abstain under (c)(2) are reviewable by these courts. Under Rule 5011(b) the motion to abstain is heard by the bankruptcy court. See Committee Note to Rule 5011. The bankruptcy court order determining the abstention motion remains appealable to the district court or BAP by leave of court, but further appeals are barred by § 1334(d) as are any appeals of district court abstention orders in withdrawn matters.

State court actions pending against the debtor at the time of bankruptcy are normally claims in the bankruptcy. The action would be automatically stayed by § 362 and, if the stay is not lifted, the claimant would have to file a proof of claim in the bankruptcy court which would then allow or disallow it. The proceeding to collect the claim in bankruptcy is one "arising in a case under title 11" rather than one "related to a case under title 11" and is a core proceeding. 28 U.S.C. § 157(b)(2)(B). Thus § 1334(c)(2) doesn't apply. Although § 1334(c)(2) refers to "the district court," that reference must also apply to the bankruptcy court which is treated as a unit of the district court. 28 U.S.C. § 151.

### c. Arbitration

Many commercial and consumer contracts provide that disputes arising under the agreement shall be arbitrated or subject to other forms of alternative dispute resolution. At common law agreements to arbitrate future disputes were generally unenforceable. Sections 3 and 4 of the Federal Arbitration Act of 1925, 9 U.S.C. §§ 3 & 4 reverse this common law rule and instruct federal courts to stay their own proceedings and order parties to proceed to arbitration if they have agreed in writing to arbitrate a matter otherwise within the federal court's jurisdiction. Over 50 years later, Congress passed the Bankruptcy Code which on its face stays arbitration proceedings, § 362(a)(1), and, subject to relief from stay "for cause," § 362(d)(1) and discretionary abstention, 28 U.S.C. § 1334(d), centralizes all dispute resolution in the federal bankruptcy court, particularly with respect to "core matters" as defined in 28 U.S.C. § 157(b).

Until the mid–1980s, it appears to have been accepted that bankruptcy courts had broad discretion with respect to whether or not to stay proceedings in the bankruptcy case properly falling within their jurisdiction and otherwise enforce contractual arbitration clauses. *Zimmerman v. Continental Airlines, Inc.*, 712 F.2d 55 (3d Cir.1983).

Thereafter, in two Securities Act cases, *Shearson/American Express, Inc. v. McMahon*, 482 U.S. 220 (1987) and *Rodriguez de Quijas v. Shearson/American Express, Inc.*, 490 U.S. 477 (1989), the Supreme Court strongly endorsed the general policy in favor of arbitration indicating that even in matters involving statutory schemes providing for judicial enforcement, written arbitration agreements should be enforced unless the party opposing arbitration could show that "Congress did intend to limit or prohibit waiver of a judicial forum for a particular claim. . . [as] 'deducible from [the statute's] text or legislative history' or from an inherent conflict between arbitration and the statute's underlying purposes." *McMahon*, 482 U.S. at 227.

In the wake of these securities law cases and the 1984 amendments to the bankruptcy jurisdictional statutes, there has been considerable confusion with respect to the scope of bankruptcy courts' discretion to refuse to enforce arbitration clauses. In *Hays & Co. v. Merrill, Lynch, Pierce, Fenner & Smith, Inc.*, 885 F.2d 1149 (3d Cir.1989), the Third Circuit overruled its own earlier decision in *Zimmerman* and held that the bankruptcy court had no discretion to refuse to enforce an arbitration clause in a non-core proceeding brought by the trustee under a prepetition agreement. *Hays* distinguished a related avoiding powers action brought under § 544(b), finding that although the claim of the estate based on the prepetition agreement had to be arbitrated, the avoiding power claim could be brought in the bankruptcy court.

Courts generally agree with *Hays* with respect to non-core claims based on prepetition agreements brought by trustees or debtors against third parties. The trustee or debtor is bound to arbitrate such claims if the agreement so provides. There is little agreement beyond this, however.

Some later courts interpret *Hays* to adopt a crucial distinction between core and non-core matters. These courts hold that *Hays* rule of no discretion applies only to non-core matters. As to core matters bankruptcy courts retain discretion to hear matters which would be otherwise subject to arbitration. *Selcke v. New England Ins. Co.*, 995 F.2d 688 (7th Cir.1993); *In re American Freight Sys., Inc.*, 164 B.R. 341 (D.Kan.1994); *In re Spectrum Info. Techs., Inc.*, 183 B.R. 360 (Bankr.E.D.N.Y.1995). Other courts have found that arbitration clauses must be enforced—even in core matters—unless the legal right at issue arises from the Bankruptcy Code itself rather than the agreement. In *Matter of National Gypsum Co.*, 118 F.3d 1056 (5th Cir.1997), the court adopted this narrower of view of the bankruptcy court's discretion, nevertheless holding that the arbitration agreement in that case would not be enforced because the legal questions at issue arose out of the effect of the debtor's confirmed plan of reorganization and the discharge provisions of the Code rather than from the pre-petition agreement assumed in the plan. *National Gypsum* appears to draw the line between bankruptcy and arbitration at the nature of the rights asserted—that is whether "bankruptcy rights" or "contract rights" are at issue, not whether the matter is "core" or "non-core." Until the Supreme Court directly resolves the conflict between the Bankruptcy Code and the Federal Arbitration Act, continuing confusion in the lower federal courts and bankruptcy courts concerning bankruptcy court jurisdiction over matters that would be otherwise subject to arbitration seems likely.

### d.   Sovereign Immunity

Yet a further limitation on the federal bankruptcy jurisdiction is the Eleventh Amendment which embodies a principle of state sovereign immunity.

The threat posed by the Eleventh Amendment to important bankruptcy policies is well summarized in the NBRC Rep. at 898–902 (footnotes omitted):

> Bankruptcy is a collective proceeding, providing a single forum for the resolution of claims against the debtor's property "wherever located."... By providing a single forum governed by a single set of procedural rules, the bankruptcy process ensures uniform procedural treatment for every type of claimant.... A single bankruptcy forum also advances a variety of fundamental policy goals, including, equal distribution and treatment for similarly situated creditors, promotion of a cost-effective and speedy process to minimize the cost to creditors, and the rehabilitation of individuals as well as business entities. Determining creditors' rights in the debtor's estate is a fundamental role

of the bankruptcy court. A single forum for the resolution of claims against a bankruptcy estate is a critical component of the court's responsibility for a number of reasons.

First, multiple proceedings in different courts may result in conflicting determinations. . . .. Moreover, separate treatment in multiple courts may also result in unequal treatment of similarly-situated creditors. A creditor that is able to enforce its rights in a separate forum without consideration of other possible claims in the property will benefit to the detriment of other creditors.

Second, the ability of a bankruptcy court to quickly restructure a debtor's obligations enhances the likelihood of saving a business or giving a family a fresh start and increasing the distribution to creditors. The bankruptcy court has the ability to give notice to all parties with an interest in the debtor's property and to bring those persons or entities into the bankruptcy court for a final binding determination of the rights in the property. . . .

Third, a single forum reduces the cost of collection for creditors. . . .

Fourth, Chapter 11 of the Bankruptcy Code favors the reorganization of debtors in an effort to preserve going-concern value, retain jobs, and promote the efficient use of capital. A bankruptcy court that does not control all critical aspects of a debtor's business will be unable to achieve a reorganization. . . .

Because the Eleventh Amendment protects *only* the states, the ability to bring actions against federal and municipal agencies remains unaffected [by the Eleventh Amendment]. . . .. As a result, states must be treated differently from all other creditors and parties in interest (including the federal government) in the bankruptcy process.

States play an important role in the bankruptcy process, appearing in many bankruptcy cases in a myriad of roles—as priority tax creditor, secured creditor, unsecured creditor, police and regulatory authority, environmental creditor, landlord, guarantor, bondholder, leaseholder, and equity interest holder. Similarly, a debtor may have a number of potential actions against a state, including a stay violation, preferences, turnover of property, and lien avoidance. . . . Different treatment of state entities will alter the statutory equilibrium struck in the Bankruptcy Code that balances the rights of creditors against each other as well as against the rights of the debtor.

Section 106 of the Bankruptcy Code dealt with this threat posed by the States' sovereign immunity by purporting to generally abrogate the sovereign immunity of any "governmental unit," which includes agencies of the United States, state governments, local governments and foreign governments. § 101(27). The unmistakable intent was to subject governmental units to the general provisions of the Bankruptcy Code, including for example the claims adjudication process, automatic stay, avoiding powers of the trustee and the discharge provisions, to the same extent as private parties.

Section 106 of the Bankruptcy Code was deliberately designed to meet the "clear statement" requirement that the Supreme Court has imposed on statutory abrogation of sovereign immunity. Earlier versions of § 106 had failed to meet the clear statement requirement with respect to those provisions of the Bankruptcy Code that authorized affirmative recovery of money damages from governmental units in excess of any claim filed by that governmental unit unless the claim for affirmative recovery arose out of the same transaction as a claim asserted by the governmental unit. *Hoffman v. Connecticut Dept. of Income Maintenance*, 492 U.S. 96 (1989) (state governments immune from affirmative recovery); *United States v. Nordic Village, Inc.*, 503 U.S. 30 (1992) (federal government immune from affirmative recovery). The premise of the amendments giving rise to the current version of § 106 is that Congress could accomplish the abrogation of sovereign immunity by a clear statement in the text of the statute. Though there is no ambiguity left in § 106's explicit statement that sovereign immunity is abrogated with respect to a long list of specifically enumerated Bankruptcy Code sections, it turns out the premise was mistaken.

In *Seminole Tribe of Florida v. Florida*, 517 U.S. 44 (1996), a closely divided Supreme Court overruled *Pennsylvania v. Union Gas Co.*, 491 U.S. 1 (1989), and found that the Eleventh Amendment precluded Congress from abrogating state sovereign immunity through the exercise of its powers under Article I of the Constitution, no matter how clear its intention to do so. Though *Seminole Tribe* did not involve the bankruptcy power, there is no apparent basis for distinguishing the bankruptcy power from the other Article I powers at issue in that case. Both majority and dissenting opinions recognized the implications of the majority holding for § 106. Accordingly, as to state governments, § 106 appears to unconstitutionally attempt to abrogate state sovereign immunity.

After *Seminole Tribe*, state sovereign immunity precludes federal courts (including both bankruptcy courts and the regular Article III courts) from exercising jurisdiction over non-consenting state governments. The reach of *Seminole Tribe* on its face exceeds the earlier limitation against affirmative money recovery in excess of, or unrelated to, claims asserted by non-consenting states. In *Seminole Tribe*, the civil action from which the State of Florida successfully argued it was immune involved orders to engage in federally supervised mediation and other non-monetary relief. Already, states appear to be raising the Eleventh Amendment defense to actions brought against them in bankruptcy court as a matter of course. In the years since it was decided, *Seminole Tribe* has been cited in a host of published bankruptcy decisions.

The historical and constitutional soundness of the *Seminole Tribe* decision limiting Congressional power to abrogate state sovereign immunity is beyond the scope of a course in Bankruptcy. The tangled history of the Eleventh Amendment and the jurisprudence thereunder is set out at great length in the *Seminole Tribe* opinions (especially Justice Souter's dissent) and the wealth of scholarly commentary on the Eleventh Amendment. The Supreme Court's latest statement on the application of sovereign immunity jurisprudence to bankruptcy cases follows.

# Tennessee Student Assistance Corp. v. Hood

Supreme Court of the United States, 2004.
541 U.S. 440.

■ Chief Justice REHNQUIST delivered the opinion of the Court.

Article I, § 8, cl. 4, of the Constitution provides that Congress shall have the power "[t]o establish. . . uniform Laws on the subject of Bankruptcies throughout the United States." We granted certiorari to determine whether this Clause grants Congress the authority to abrogate state sovereign immunity from private suits. Because we conclude that a proceeding initiated by a debtor to determine the dischargeability of a student loan debt is not a suit against the State for purposes of the Eleventh Amendment, we affirm the Court of Appeals' judgment, and we do not reach the question on which certiorari was granted.

## I

Petitioner, Tennessee Student Assistance Corporation (TSAC), is a governmental corporation created by the Tennessee Legislature to administer student assistance programs. TSAC guarantees student loans made to residents of Tennessee and to nonresidents who are either enrolled in an eligible school in Tennessee or make loans through an approved Tennessee lender.

Between July 1988 and February 1990, respondent, Pamela Hood, a resident of Tennessee, signed promissory notes for educational loans guaranteed by TSAC. In February 1999, Hood filed a "no asset" Chapter 7 bankruptcy petition in the United States Bankruptcy Court for the Western District of Tennessee; at the time of the filing, her student loans had an outstanding balance of $4,169.31. TSAC did not participate in the proceeding, but Sallie Mae Service, Inc. (Sallie Mae), submitted a proof of claim to the Bankruptcy Court, which it subsequently assigned to TSAC.[1] The Bankruptcy Court granted Hood a general discharge in June 1999.

---

[1] Sallie Mae was the original holder of Hood's student loan debt. On November 15, 1999, Sallie Mae signed an assignment of proof of claim, transferring the debt to TSAC. The actual proof of claim was filed by Sallie Mae in the Bankruptcy Court on November 29, and one month later, on December 29, the assignment of the proof of claim was filed.

Hood did not list her student loans in the bankruptcy proceeding, and the general discharge did not cover them. *See* § 727(b) (providing that a discharge under § 727(a) discharges the debtor from all prepetition debts except as listed in § 523(a)); § 523(a)(8) (providing that student loans guaranteed by governmental units are not included in a general discharge order unless the bankruptcy court determines that excepting the debt from the order would impose an "undue hardship" on the debtor). In September 1999, Hood reopened her bankruptcy petition for the limited purpose of seeking a determination by the Bankruptcy Court that her student loans were dischargeable as an "undue hardship" pursuant to § 523(a)(8). As prescribed by the Federal Rules of Bankruptcy Procedure, Hood filed a complaint against the United States of America, the Department of Education, and Sallie Mae, *see* Fed. Rules Bkrtcy. Proc. 7001(6) and 7003, and later filed an amended complaint in which she included TSAC and University Account Services as additional defendants and deleted Sallie Mae. The complaint and the amended complaint were served along with a summons on each of the named parties.

In response, TSAC filed a motion to dismiss the complaint for lack of jurisdiction, asserting Eleventh Amendment sovereign immunity.[2] The Bankruptcy Court denied the motion, holding that 11 U.S.C. § 106(a) was a valid abrogation of TSAC's sovereign immunity. TSAC took an interlocutory appeal, and a unanimous Bankruptcy Appellate Panel of the Sixth Circuit affirmed. TSAC appealed the Panel's decision to the United States Court of Appeals for the Sixth Circuit. That court affirmed, holding that the States ceded their immunity from private suits in bankruptcy in the Constitutional Convention, and therefore, the Bankruptcy Clause, U.S. Const., Art. 1, § 8, cl. 4, provided Congress with the necessary authority to abrogate state sovereign immunity in 11 U.S.C. § 106(a). One judge concurred in the judgment, concluding that TSAC waived its sovereign immunity when it accepted Sallie Mae's proof of claim.[3] We granted certiorari, and now affirm the judgment of the Court of Appeals. Because we hold that a bankruptcy court's discharge of a student loan debt does not implicate a State's Eleventh Amendment immunity, we do not reach the broader question addressed by the Court of Appeals.

## II

By its terms, the Eleventh Amendment precludes suits "in law or equity, commenced or prosecuted against one of the United States by Citizens of another State, or by Citizens or Subjects of any Foreign State." For over a century, however, we have recognized that the States' sovereign immunity is not limited to the literal terms of the Eleventh Amendment.

---

[2] Hood does not dispute that TSAC is considered a "State" for purposes of the Eleventh Amendment.

[3] Hood does not argue in this Court that TSAC waived its sovereign immunity, and we pass no judgment on the question.

Although the text of the Amendment refers only to suits against a State by citizens of another State, we have repeatedly held that an unconsenting State also is immune from suits by its own citizens.

States, nonetheless, may still be bound by some judicial actions without their consent. In *California v. Deep Sea Research, Inc.,* 523 U.S. 491 (1998), we held that the Eleventh Amendment does not bar federal jurisdiction over *in rem* admiralty actions when the State is not in possession of the property. In that case, a private corporation located a historic shipwreck, the S.S. *Brother Jonathan,* in California's territorial waters. The corporation filed an *in rem* action in federal court seeking rights to the wreck and its cargo. The State of California intervened, arguing that it possessed title to the wreck and that its sovereign immunity precluded the court from adjudicating its rights. While acknowledging that the Eleventh Amendment might constrain federal courts' admiralty jurisdiction in some instances, we held that the States' sovereign immunity did not prohibit *in rem* admiralty actions in which the State did not possess the res.

The discharge of a debt by a bankruptcy court is similarly an *in rem* proceeding. Bankruptcy courts have exclusive jurisdiction over a debtor's property, wherever located, and over the estate. In a typical voluntary bankruptcy proceeding under Chapter 7, the debtor files a petition for bankruptcy in which he lists his debts or his creditors; the petition constitutes an order for relief. The court clerk notifies the debtor's creditors of the order for relief, and if a creditor wishes to participate in the debtor's assets, he files a proof of claim. If a creditor chooses not to submit a proof of claim, once the debts are discharged, the creditor will be unable to collect on his unsecured loans. The discharge order releases a debtor from personal liability with respect to any discharged debt by voiding any past or future judgments on the debt and by operating as an injunction to prohibit creditors from attempting to collect or to recover the debt. §§§ 524(a)(1), (2).

A bankruptcy court is able to provide the debtor a fresh start in this manner, despite the lack of participation of all of his creditors, because the court's jurisdiction is premised on the debtor and his estate, and not on the creditors. *In re Collins,* 173 F.3d 924, 929 (C.A.4 1999) ("A federal court's jurisdiction over the dischargeability of debt. . . derives not from jurisdiction over the state or other creditors, but rather from jurisdiction over debtors and their estates" (internal quotation marks and citation omitted)). A bankruptcy court's *in rem* jurisdiction permits it to "determin[e] all claims that anyone, whether named in the action or not, has to the property or thing in question. The proceeding is 'one against the world.'" 16 J. Moore, et al., Moore's Federal Practice § 108.70, p. 108-106 (3d ed.2004). Because the court's jurisdiction is premised on the res, however, a nonparticipating creditor cannot be subjected to personal liability.

Under our longstanding precedent, States, whether or not they choose to participate in the proceeding, are bound by a bankruptcy court's discharge order no less than other creditors. In *New York v. Irving Trust Co.,*

288 U.S. 329 (1933), we sustained an order of the Bankruptcy Court which barred the State of New York's tax claim because it was not filed within the time fixed for the filing of claims. We held that "[i]f a state desires to participate in the assets of a bankrupt, she must submit to the appropriate requirements." *Id.,* at 333; *see also Gardner, supra,* [329 U.S.] at 574 (holding that a State waives its sovereign immunity by filing a proof of claim). And in *Van Huffel v. Harkelrode,* 284 U.S. 225, 228-229 (1931), we held that the Bankruptcy Court had the authority to sell a debtor's property "free and clear" of a State's tax lien. At least when the bankruptcy court's jurisdiction over the res is unquestioned, cf. *United States v. Nordic Village, Inc.,* 503 U.S. 30 (1992), our cases indicate that the exercise of its *in rem* jurisdiction to discharge a debt does not infringe state sovereignty.[4] Cf. *Hoffman v. Connecticut Dept. of Income Maintenance,* 492 U.S. 96, 102 (1989) (plurality opinion) (applying Eleventh Amendment analysis where a Bankruptcy Court sought to issue a money judgment against a nonconsenting State).

TSAC concedes that States are generally bound by a bankruptcy court's discharge order, *see* Tr. of Oral Arg. 17, but argues that the particular process by which student loan debts are discharged unconstitutionally infringes its sovereignty. Student loans used to be presumptively discharged in a general discharge. But in 1976, Congress provided a significant benefit to the States by making it more difficult for debtors to discharge student loan debts guaranteed by States. That benefit is currently governed by 11 U.S.C. § 523(a)(8), which provides that student loan debts guaranteed by governmental units are not included in a general discharge order unless excepting the debt from the order would impose an "undue hardship" on the debtor. *See also* § 727(b) (providing that a discharge under § 727(a) discharges the debtor from all prepetition debts except as listed in § 523(a)).

---

[4] *Missouri v. Fiske,* 290 U.S. 18 (1933), is not to the contrary. In that case, private individuals sought to enjoin the State of Missouri from prosecuting probate proceedings in state court, contending that the Federal District Court had made a final determination of the ownership of the contested stock. We held the Eleventh Amendment prevented federal courts from entertaining such a suit because a "[federal] court has no authority to issue process against the State to compel it to subject itself to the court's judgment." *Id.,* at 28. Although a discharge order under the Bankruptcy Code "operates as an injunction" against creditors who commence or continue an action against a debtor *in personam* to recover or to collect a discharged debt, 11 U.S.C. § 524(a)(2), the enforcement of such an injunction against the State by a federal court is not before us. To the extent that *Fiske* is relevant in the present context, it supports our conclusion that a discharge order is binding on the State. There, we noted the State might still be bound by the federal court's adjudication even if an injunction could not issue. 290 U.S., at 29. It is unlikely that the Court *sub silentio* overruled the holdings in *Irving Trust* and *Van Huffel* in *Fiske* as Justice THOMAS implies, see *post* (dissenting opinion), as *Fiske* was decided the same year as *Irving Trust.*

Section 523(a)(8) is "self-executing." Unless the debtor affirmatively secures a hardship determination, the discharge order will not include a student loan debt. Thus, the major difference between the discharge of a student loan debt and the discharge of most other debts is that governmental creditors, including States, that choose not to submit themselves to the court's jurisdiction might still receive some benefit: The debtor's personal liability on the loan may survive the discharge.

It is this change that TSAC contends infringes state sovereignty. Tr. of Oral Arg. 15-16. By making a student loan debt presumptively nondischargeable and singling it out for an "individualized adjudication," *ibid.,* TSAC argues that Congress has authorized a suit against a State. But TSAC misunderstands the fundamental nature of the proceeding.

No matter how difficult Congress has decided to make the discharge of student loan debt, the bankruptcy court's jurisdiction is premised on the res, not on the persona; that States were granted the presumptive benefit of nondischargeability does not alter the court's underlying authority. A debtor does not seek monetary damages or any affirmative relief from a State by seeking to discharge a debt; nor does he subject an unwilling State to a coercive judicial process. He seeks only a discharge of his debts.

Indeed, we have previously endorsed individualized determinations of States' interests within the federal courts' *in rem* jurisdiction. In *Van Huffel,* we affirmed the bankruptcy courts' power to sell property free from incumbrances, including States' liens, and approvingly noted that some courts had chosen specifically to discharge States' liens for taxes. [C]f. *Gardner,* 329 U.S., at 572-574 (noting "that the reorganization court had jurisdiction over the proof and allowance of the tax claims and that the exercise of that power was not a suit against the State"). Our decision in *California v. Deep Sea Research, Inc.,* also involved an individualized *in rem* adjudication in which a State claimed an interest, as have other *in rem* admiralty cases involving sovereigns. Although both bankruptcy and admiralty are specialized areas of the law, we see no reason why the exercise of the federal courts' *in rem* bankruptcy jurisdiction is more threatening to state sovereignty than the exercise of their *in rem* admiralty jurisdiction.

We find no authority, *in fine,* that suggests a bankruptcy court's exercise of its *in rem* jurisdiction to discharge a student loan debt would infringe state sovereignty in the manner suggested by TSAC. We thus hold that the undue hardship determination sought by Hood in this case is not a suit against a State for purposes of the Eleventh Amendment.[5]

---

[5] This is not to say, "a bankruptcy court's *in rem* jurisdiction overrides sovereign immunity," *United States v. Nordic Village, Inc.,* 503 U.S. 30, 38 (1992), as Justice THOMAS characterizes our opinion, but rather that the court's exercise of its *in rem* jurisdiction to discharge a student loan debt is not an affront to the sovereignty of the State. Nor do we hold that every exercise of a bankruptcy court's *in rem* jurisdiction

## III

Lastly, we deal with the procedure that was used in this case. Creditors generally are not entitled to personal service before a bankruptcy court may discharge a debt. *Hanover Nat. Bank,* 186 U.S., at 192. Because student loan debts are not automatically dischargeable, however, the Federal Rules of Bankruptcy Procedure provide creditors greater procedural protection. *See* Fed. Rules Bkrtcy. Proc. 7001(6), 7003, and 7004. The current Bankruptcy Rules require the debtor to file an "adversary proceeding" against the State in order to discharge his student loan debt. The proceeding is considered part of the original bankruptcy case, and still within the bankruptcy court's *in rem* jurisdiction as discussed above. But, as prescribed by the Rules, an "adversary proceeding" requires the service of a summons and a complaint. Rules 7001(6), 7003, and 7004.

Because this "adversary proceeding" has some similarities to a traditional civil trial, Justice THOMAS contends that the Bankruptcy Court cannot make an undue hardship determination without infringing TSAC's sovereignty under *Federal Maritime Comm'n v. South Carolina Ports Authority,* 535 U.S. 743 (2002). In *Federal Maritime Comm'n,* we held that the Eleventh Amendment precluded a private party from haling an unconsenting State into a proceeding before the Federal Maritime Commission (FMC). We noted that we have applied a presumption since *Hans v. Louisiana,* 134 U.S. 1 (1890), "that the Constitution was not intended to 'rais[e] up' any proceedings against the States that were 'anomalous and unheard of when the Constitution was adopted.'" 535 U.S., at 755. Because agency adjudications were unheard of at the time of the founding, we had to determine whether the FMC proceeding was "the type of proceedin[g] from which the Framers would have thought the States possessed immunity when they agreed to enter the Union." *Id.,* at 756. Noting the substantial similarities between a proceeding before the FMC and one before an Article III court, we concluded that the *Hans* presumption applied, and that the Eleventh Amendment therefore precluded private suits in such a forum.

In this case, however, there is no need to engage in a comparative analysis to determine whether the adjudication would be an affront to States' sovereignty. As noted above, we have long held that the bankruptcy courts' exercise of *in rem* jurisdiction is not such an offense. Nor is there any dispute that, if the Bankruptcy Court had to exercise personal jurisdiction over TSAC, such an adjudication would implicate the Eleventh Amendment. Our precedent has drawn a distinction between *in rem* and *in personam* jurisdiction, even when the underlying proceedings are, for the most part, identical. Thus, whether an *in rem* adjudication in a bankruptcy court is similar to civil litigation in a district court is irrele-

---

will not offend the sovereignty of the State. No such concerns are present here, and we do not address them.

vant. If Justice THOMAS' interpretation of *Federal Maritime Comm'n* were adopted, *Deep Sea Research, Van Huffel,* and *Irving Trust,* all of which involved proceedings resembling traditional civil adjudications, would likely have to be overruled. We are not willing to take such a step.

The issuance of process, nonetheless, is normally an indignity to the sovereignty of a State because its purpose is to establish personal jurisdiction over the State. We noted in *Seminole Tribe,* "The Eleventh Amendment does not exist solely in order to prevent federal-court judgments that must be paid out of a State's treasury; it also serves to avoid the indignity of subjecting a State to the coercive process of judicial tribunals at the instance of private parties." 517 U.S., at 58 (citations and internal quotation marks omitted).

Here, however, the Bankruptcy Court's *in rem* jurisdiction allows it to adjudicate the debtor's discharge claim without *in personam* jurisdiction over the State. *See* 4A C. Wright & A. Miller, Federal Practice and Procedure § 1070, pp. 280-281 (3d ed.2002) (noting jurisdiction over the person is irrelevant if the court has jurisdiction over the property). Hood does not argue that the court should exercise personal jurisdiction; all she wants is a determination of the dischargeability of her debt. The text of § 523(a)(8) does not require a summons, and absent Rule 7001(6) a debtor could proceed by motion, *see* Rule 9014 ("[I]n a contested matter. . . not otherwise governed by these rules, relief shall be requested by motion"), which would raise no constitutional concern. Hood concedes that even if TSAC ignores the summons and chooses not to participate in the proceeding the Bankruptcy Court cannot discharge her debt without making an undue hardship determination. Tr. of Oral Arg. 33-34.

We see no reason why the service of a summons, which in this case is indistinguishable in practical effect from a motion, should be given dispositive weight. As we said in *Idaho v. Coeur d'Alene Tribe of Idaho,* 521 U.S. 261, 270 (1997), "[t]he real interests served by the Eleventh Amendment are not to be sacrificed to elementary mechanics of captions and pleading." *See New York I,* 256 U.S., at 500 (a suit against a State "is to be determined not by the mere names of the titular parties but by the essential nature and effect of the proceeding, as it appears from the entire record"). To conclude that the issuance of a summons, which is required only by the Rules, precludes Hood from exercising her statutory right to an undue hardship determination would give the Rules an impermissible effect. 28 U.S.C. § 2075 ("[The Bankruptcy Rules] shall not abridge, enlarge, or modify any substantive right"). And there is no reason to take such a step. TSAC sought only to dismiss the complaint for lack of jurisdiction in the Bankruptcy Court. Clearly dismissal of the complaint is not appropriate as the court has *in rem* jurisdiction over the matter, and the court here has not attempted to adjudicate any claims outside of that jurisdiction. The case before us is thus unlike an adversary proceeding by the bankruptcy trustee seeking to recover property in the hands of the State on the grounds that the transfer was a voidable preference. Even if we were to hold that Congress lacked the ability to abrogate state sovereign immunity under the Bankruptcy Clause, as TSAC urges us to do, the Bankruptcy Court would still have the authority to make the undue hardship determination sought by Hood.

We therefore decline to decide whether a bankruptcy court's exercise of personal jurisdiction over a State would be valid under the Eleventh Amendment. If the Bankruptcy Court on remand exceeds its *in rem* jurisdiction, TSAC, of course, would be free to challenge the court's authority. At this point, however, any such constitutional concern is merely hypothetical. The judgment of the United States Court of Appeals for the Sixth Circuit is affirmed, and the case is remanded for further proceedings consistent with this opinion.

Justice SOUTER, with whom Justice GINSBURG Joins, Concurring.

[Omitted].

Justice THOMAS, with whom Justice SCALIA Joins, Dissenting.

[Omitted].

## NOTE

As *Hood* makes clear, notwithstanding *Seminole Tribe*, the States' sovereign immunity defense has meaningful limitations and it remains uncertain the extent to which States will be able to evade their obligations under bankruptcy law on the basis of the Eleventh Amendment.

First, § 106 remains an effective waiver of federal sovereign immunity and foreign sovereign immunity. The Eleventh Amendment does not affect the power of Congress to abrogate the sovereign immunity of the United States or that of foreign states. Moreover, local governments such as municipalities—even though they may be state actors for other constitutional purposes—cannot assert the Eleventh Amendment as a defense to federal jurisdiction. *Monell v. Department of Social Services*, 436 U.S. 658, 690 n. 54 (1978).

Second, only non-consenting state governmental units are immune. As with any affirmative defense, States may waive their sovereign immunity. Indeed the waiver may be implied from such conduct as filing or asserting a claim in the bankruptcy proceeding, at least to the extent of counterclaims arising out of the same transaction or set-offs that reduce the estate's liability on the claim, and perhaps to a greater extent. The latest and fullest statement of the scope of waiver occasioned by the State's filing of a proof of claim is *Arecibo Community Health Care, Inc. v. Puerto Rico*, 270 F.3d 17 (1st Cir.2001) (on rehearing). In *Arecibo*, the First Circuit found that Puerto Rico's (which enjoys 11th Amendment immunity as if it were a State) decision to assert a claim for breach of contract in the amount of $1.65 million exposed it to the debtor in bankruptcy's compulsory counterclaim in excess of $8.2 million arising out of the same contract. As to reducing the debtor's liability on account of Puerto Rico's claim, the result upholding waiver was foreordained by pre-*Seminole Tribe* precedent at both the Supreme Court and Court of Appeals level. *See Gardner v. New Jersey*, 329 U.S. 565 (1947). More difficult was the question whether the filing of the claim exposed the State to net affirmative liability. The First Circuit acknowledged that the issue was unsettled in most of the circuits, but wrote:

> Where a state avails itself of the federal courts to protect a claim, we think it reasonable to consider that action to waive the state's immunity *in toto* and, therefore, to construe that waiver to encompass compulsory counterclaims, even though they could require affirmative recovery from the state. The alternative approach would have the unfortunate effect of preventing the complete adjudication of the claims in a single forum, undermining the principles that led the framers of the Federal Rules to compel the litigation of certain counterclaims as a part of a single lawsuit.

270 F.3d at 28.

Some commentators have proposed using waiver as a means of escaping application of *Seminole Tribe* altogether—by recasting § 106 to require States to generally waive sovereign immunity to the extent set out in § 106 in all cases as a condition of participating as a creditor in any bankruptcy proceeding. *See, e.g.,* Laura B. Bartell, *Getting To Waiver–A Legislative Solution To State Sovereign Immunity in Bankruptcy After Seminole Tribe*, 17 Bank. Dev. J. 17 (2000). Would the First Circuit's rationale extend to upholding a waiver of this scope?

Whether the Supreme Court would uphold a general waiver of sovereign immunity extracted from the States in this way is doubtful in light of *College Savings Bank v. Florida Prepaid Postsecondary Education Expense Board,* 527 U.S. 666 (1999), in which the Court rejected a theory of "constructive waiver" of sovereign immunity based on Florida's interstate marketing and other federally-regulated activities. Under the Trademark Remedy Clarification Act, an amendment to the Lanham Act, Congress had provided that state agencies engaging in false representations in commerce "shall not be immune, under the Eleventh Amendment. . . or any other doctrine of sovereign immunity * * * *"

In passing upon the validity of this provision the Court stated:

> There is a fundamental difference between a State's expressing unequivocally that it waives its immunity, and Congress's expressing unequivocally its intention that if the State takes certain action it shall be deemed to have waived that immunity. In the latter situation, the most that can be said with certainty is that the State has been put on notice that Congress intends to subject it to suits brought by individuals. That is very far from concluding that the State has made an "altogether voluntary" decision to waive its immunity.

527 U.S. at 680–681.

The Court found that "recognizing a congressional power to exact constructive waivers of sovereign immunity through the exercise of Article I powers would. . . permit Congress to circumvent the antiabrogation holding of *Seminole Tribe*." Id. At 683

Third, the Eleventh Amendment only limits the jurisdiction of the federal courts. States may be sued in state court without implicating the Eleventh Amendment, though of course there may be other limitations on such suits under state law that might be enforceable in state courts. Legal scholars sharply debate the crucial question of whether the Eleventh Amendment is simply a "forum allocation" device or whether it may have the effect of precluding private party enforcement of federal law against non-consenting states altogether. The "forum allocation" view holds that States refusing to waive Eleventh Amendment immunity in federal courts must ensure that their own courts would hear and determine on the merits suits against State agencies that arise under the federal bankruptcy laws, subject to final certiorari review in the Supreme Court of the United States. *See* Henry Paul Monaghan, *The Sovereign Immunity "Exception,"* 110 Harv.L.Rev. 102 (1996); Vicki C. Jackson, *The Supreme Court, the Eleventh Amendment, and State Sovereign Immunity*, 98 Yale L.J. 1 (1988); but compare Carlos Manuel Vazquez, *What Is Eleventh Amendment Immunity?*, 106 Yale L.J. 1683 (1997). While it seems odd that core bankruptcy proceedings such as claims based on violation of the automatic stay or to recover preferences could be heard in state court even though they could not be heard in bankruptcy court, and though state court enforcement of these rights would undoubtedly be less convenient for trustees and other parties to the bankruptcy in many cases, state court enforcement of federal bankruptcy rights would under the "forum allocation" view of the Eleventh Amendment be a possibility. Unfortunately, for proponents of this approach to holding State agencies to their obligations under federal bankruptcy law, the Supreme Court has recently made clear that the Constitution does not require States to afford access to State courts to vindicate federal claims from which they are immune from federal process. *Alden v. Maine*, 527 U.S. 706 (1999).

Fourth, to the extent that the debtor or bankruptcy trustee may be in a position to assert a federal statutory right grounded on Congressional power under § 5 of the Fourteenth Amendment, the Eleventh Amendment would not apply. *Seminole Tribe* reaffirmed that the Eleventh Amendment does not limit Congressional power under the later-enacted Fourteenth Amendment, which as an outgrowth of the Civil War explicitly limited state power and expanded the role of the national government in the federal system. A few courts have attempted to defend the constitutionality of § 106 generally on the basis of § 5 of the Fourteenth Amendment. They suggest that § 106 is intended to prohibit state action (assertion of sovereign immunity) that would have the effect of denying private bankruptcy litigants "due process" or "privileges and immunities." *In re Straight*, 209 B.R. 540 (D.Wyo.1997). This argument, however, has been rejected by two courts of appeals and moreover appears to assume Congressional power to define the scope of Fourteenth Amendment rights to include statutory bankruptcy rights. In *City of Boerne v. Flores*, 521 U.S. 507 (1997), a case involving the First Amendment right of free exercise of religion, the Supreme Court held that Congress may not redefine the meaning of rights protected by the Fourteenth Amendment through the exercise of its § 5 powers. This principle has been recently applied to limit Congressional power to redress various forms of discrimination by State agencies that are not directly forbidden by the Court's Fourteenth Amendment jurisprudence. *Kimel v. Florida Board of Regents*, 528 U.S. 62 (2000) (States immune from federal age discrimination damage claims); *Board of Trustees of the University of Alabama v. Garrett*, 531 U.S. 356 (2001) (States immune from federal Americans with Disabilities Act damage claims). These holdings suggest that the prospects are not promising for the constitutionality of Congressional guarantees of the federal enforcement of bankruptcy rights against State agencies under § 5 of the Fourteenth Amendment.

Fifth, there may be situations where the debtor or bankruptcy trustee can invoke the equitable jurisdiction of the bankruptcy court to enjoin continuing violations of federal law by individual state officers. Under the doctrine of *Ex parte Young*, 209 U.S. 123 (1908), suits to prospectively enjoin state officials against violating federal law are not considered suits against the state for purposes of the Eleventh Amendment. Presumably, for example, the bankruptcy court could invoke *Ex parte Young* to enjoin state officials to desist from conduct that amounted to a continuing violation of the automatic stay notwithstanding the Eleventh Amendment, even though the state would be immune from suit for damages for the stay violation unless it had waived the Eleventh Amendment defense. But *Ex parte Young* has been arguably limited by *Idaho v. Coeur d'Alene Tribe of Idaho*, 521 U.S. 261 (1997). In *Coeur d'Alene Tribe*, the Supreme Court refused to permit the federal district court to enjoin Idaho officials from prospectively interfering with the Tribe's rights in a certain lakebed within the confines of the Tribe's reservation. Two Justices found that the availability of *Ex parte Young* injunctions to remedy prospective violations of federal law was subject to a wide-ranging balancing test and the balance in that case tipped against jurisdiction. Three more Justices concurred on the ground that though *Ex parte Young* injunctions are generally available to remedy prospective violations of federal law, the particular litigation against Idaho officials in *Coeur d'Alene Tribe* nevertheless fell within the Eleventh Amendment. There is a suggestion in the concurring opinion that the effect of the federal court injunction in permanently removing the lakebed from the State's police and regulatory jurisdiction took the case outside *Ex parte Young*. The upshot is that as of this writing it remains uncertain the extent to which the Supreme Court will allow bankruptcy courts to prospectively enforce bankruptcy law against non-consenting States through *Ex parte Young* injunctions.

Finally, as recognized in *Hood*, there is an "in rem" exception to the Eleventh Amendment. Like *Ex parte Young* this exception depends upon a legal fiction. The fiction is that if the federal court has jurisdiction over certain property, then it may issue orders that relate to that property, orders with which state officers must comply. A particular application of this in rem jurisdiction theory of great practical importance is the binding effect of orders of confirmation in Chapter 11, 12 and 13 cases and discharge orders in Chapter 7 cases. In *Maryland v. Antonelli Creditors' Liquidating Trust*, 123 F.3d 777 (4th Cir.1997), the Fourth Circuit found that the Eleventh Amendment did not insulate a non-consenting State seeking collection of postconfirmation taxes from the binding effect of a prior Chapter 11 discharge entered by the bankruptcy court properly vested with in rem jurisdiction over the property subject to the plan. If *Antonelli Creditors' Liquidating Trust* becomes the general view, debtors may be able to achieve through plan confirmation and discharge that which they might not be able to achieve through adversary proceedings against the State.

A crucial bankruptcy question for the 21st century will be: Given the potential for prospective equitable relief under *Ex parte Young*, the bankruptcy court's in rem jurisdiction, and the possibility of waiver, as a practical matter what will be the impact of the Eleventh Amendment defense in bankruptcy litigation?

## B. VENUE

### 1. COMMENCEMENT OF THE CASE

The Bankruptcy Code's venue provisions are found at 28 U.S.C. §§ 1408–1412. Under 28 U.S.C. § 1408(1), for a non-business individual the petition may be filed in the district in which the debtor has resided or was domiciled for the 180 days preceding the filing. An alternative basis for venue for such an individual would be the location of the debtor's principal assets, but in the typical case these would be in the same district as the residence.

For business debtors a petition may be filed under 28 U.S.C. § 1408 in any district where (1) the debtor resides or is domiciled (for a corporation this is usually the state of incorporation); (2) the debtor's principal place of business (usually the company's headquarters); (3) the debtor's principal assets are located; (4) an affiliate's bankruptcy is pending; or (5) wherever the case has been filed if no one moves to transfer or dismiss the case as one filed in an improper venue under Rule 1014(a)(2).

In their study of large Chapter 11 cases, Professors Lynn LoPucki and William Whitford found forum-shopping in a significant percentage of cases. *Venue Choice and Forum Shopping in The Bankruptcy Reorganization of Large, Publicly Held Companies*, 1991 Wis.L.Rev. 11. They found that some companies changed their corporate headquarters before filing. In a number of cases in which debtors filed in the district where their headquarters was located, the debtors had no significant assets or other operations in the district. Since it is common for large corporations to have affiliates headquartered in a number of districts, several corporations filed in the affiliate's district after the affiliate had filed. In some cases they did so only minutes after the affiliate had filed. One may speculate on the reasons for forum-shopping. Debtors may prefer to file in jurisdictions thought to be more pro-debtor or at least avoid pro-creditor courts. New York may attract filings because of its large and high quality bankruptcy bar. In some cases debtors apparently choose a venue for their convenience or that of their attorneys. In recent years Delaware, the state of incorporation for many large corporations, as well as New York, has become a venue of choice in large Chapter 11 reorganizations.

The large number of New York and Delaware filings that are clear examples of forum shopping by debtors has caused some to question the propriety of the liberal bankruptcy venue statutes. The National Bankruptcy Review Commission has recommended eliminating state of incorporation filing completely and affiliate filing unless debtor's corporate parent is a debtor in that forum. NBRC Rep. at 770–771 (Recommendation 3.1.5). There have been complaints that New York and Delaware bankruptcy judges have allowed their eagerness to maintain the flow of large Chapter 11 cases into their jurisdictions to cloud their judgment in confirming reorganization plans and perhaps in other matters affecting administration of debtors' estates. Lynn LoPucki and Sara Kalin have shown that the refiling rate for New York and Delaware Chapter 11 debtors is six to seven times as high as it is elsewhere for large public companies. Their controversial conclusion is: "Competing courts attract filings by applying lax standards for plan confirmation that lead to excessive refiling rates." Lynn M. LoPucki & Sara D. Kalin, *The Failure of Public Company Bankruptcies in Delaware and New York: Empirical Evidence of a "Race to the Bottom,"* 54 Vand.L.Rev. 231, 237 (2001). Professor LoPucki has expanded his analysis of the subject in his book, *Courting Failure* (2005). Defenders of the status quo respond by suggesting that New York and Delaware courts are tackling more difficult reorganization cases, that bankruptcy courts generally are not well situated to scrutinize plan feasibility, that the virtues of having certain jurisdictions with wide experience in large Chapter 11 cases outweigh its problems, and that to the extent there are problems the Delaware bankruptcy courts can be expected to promptly correct them. David A. Skeel, *What's So Bad About Delaware?*, 54 Vand.L.Rev. 309 (2001). As a political matter, the New York reorganization bar and Delaware's small but tenacious Congressional delegation have been strongly committed to, and thus far entirely successful in, preserving liberal venue provisions against all objections.

28 U.S.C. § 1412 states: "A district court may transfer a case or proceeding under title 11 to a district court for another district, in the interest of justice or for the convenience of the parties." The factors courts consider in deciding whether to transfer a case were stated in *In re Commonwealth Oil Refining Co.*, 596 F.2d 1239 (5th Cir.1979), to be: (1) proximity of creditors; (2) proximity of debtor; (3) proximity of witnesses; (4) location of assets; and (5) promotion of the economic and efficien. Critics

complain, however, that the venue chosen by the debtor are rarely, if ever, successfully challenged in any of the large Chapter 11 cases.

## PROBLEM

Debtor filed a petition for voluntary bankruptcy in New Jersey where Debtor resides. Without knowledge of this petition, Debtor's creditors then filed an involuntary petition in New York where Debtor's principal place of business is located. How is the conflict resolved? Bankruptcy Rule 1014(b).

### 2.  PROCEEDINGS IN THE CASE

Venue with respect to proceedings "arising under title 11 or arising in or related to a case under title 11" is governed by 28 U.S.C. § 1409. Subsection (a) states the general rule that these proceedings may be brought in the court where the case is pending, sometimes called the "home court." Subsection (b) carves out an exception for small claims. Trustees must sue in the defendant's district if the claim is less than $1000, or for a consumer debt of less than $5000. In small transactions the inconvenience to nonresident defendants of appearing in the home court is often greater than the value of the claim. If the claim were allowed to proceed in the trustee's home court he would generally prevail by default whatever the merits. These venue rules shift the burden of litigation to the trustee and make it impractical for trustees to collect small claims against nonresident defendants through litigation whatever the merits.

Subsection (c) offers an alternative to the home court rule of subsection (a) if the trustee is suing as a statutory successor to the debtor under § 541 or to a creditor under § 544(b). Under § 541 the bankruptcy estate may include causes of action and the trustee may be suing as the debtor's statutory successor. Section 544(b) allows the trustee to avoid transfers or obligations that are voidable by creditors having allowable unsecured claims. Taking 28 U.S.C. § 1409(a) and (c) together, the trustee has the alternative of suing either in the home court or in the district court of the district that would have had venue had the debtor or creditor brought suit under nonbankruptcy law. Subsection (c) is expressly made subject to subsection (b).

With respect to a postpetition claim by the trustee against others arising out of the operation of the debtor's business, subsection (d) provides that the trustee may sue only in the district court of the district in which the suit could have been brought under nonbankruptcy law. With respect to a postpetition cause of action against the bankruptcy estate arising out of the operation of the debtor's business, subsection (e) states that the suit may be brought either in the court in which the bankruptcy case is pending or in the district court of the district in which the suit could have been brought under nonbankruptcy law.

## C. APPELLATE JURISDICTION

Perhaps the only set of jurisdictional statutes more complex and confusing than those vesting original bankruptcy jurisdiction are those vesting the appellate bankruptcy jurisdiction.

After the 1994 amendments to 28 U.S.C. § 158(b), in most, but not all, federal circuits both bankruptcy appellate panels (BAPs) and federal district courts may hear appeals from both interlocutory orders and final decisions of bankruptcy judges. The bankruptcy appellate panels do not have regular full-time appellate judges. Rather they consist of three ordinary bankruptcy judges drawn on a rotating basis from districts within the circuit other than the district from which the appeal being heard arises. Appeals to the district courts are assigned to a single district judge on a rotating basis in accordance with local rules or practice.

The appellate jurisdiction statutes provide that in districts where a BAP is functioning and the local district court by majority vote of the local district judges has specifically authorized that appeals from that district may be heard by that BAP, unless one of the parties specifically demands that the appeal be routed to the local district court (or "opts-out"), the regional BAP hears the initial appeal. If there is no BAP for the circuit, or if a particular district within the circuit has not authorized appeals to BAP then, the local federal district court hears the initial appeal. If the matter is "non-core" and the parties have not consented to entry of a final judgement by the bankruptcy judge, then in lieu of an initial appeal to the district court or BAP, there is a right of de novo review in the district court. De novo review may involve rehearing evidence or may be limited to review of the record created in the bankruptcy court in the discretion of the reviewing district judge.

In the Ninth Circuit, where BAPs have operated since 1979, the quality of work done by BAPs is well regarded, but controversy has surrounded the precedential weight to be accorded their decisions.

Since the 1994 amendment, BAPs have become common throughout the nation, and the experience of the courts in the Ninth Circuit in dealing with BAP issues becomes important. Historically, approximately 60% of all bankruptcy appeals in the Ninth Circuit have been heard by the BAPs. The National Bankruptcy Review Commission found that "[t]he problems that arise from a lack of effective stare decisis in a two-tier appellate system can not be overestimated." NBRC Rep. at 754.

Daniel J. Bussel, *Power, Authority, and Precedent in Interpreting the Bankruptcy Code*, 41 UCLA L.Rev. 1063, 1071–75, 1094 (1994), discusses the precedential questions that have arisen with regard to both BAPs and district court decisions (footnotes omitted):

> Recently, bankruptcy courts in several jurisdictions have expressly refused to follow both district court and Bankruptcy Appellate Panel (BAP) precedents.

* * *

Bankruptcy courts rejecting district court precedents offer two distinct sets of arguments: one formal and one policy-based. The formal argument, typified by *In re Rheuban* [128 B.R. 551 (Bankr.C.D.Cal.1991)], suggests that a bankruptcy court, as a "unit" of the district court, is not "inferior" to a single district judge in a multi-judge district. *Rheuban* and similar cases assume that the principle of stare decisis binds only "inferior" courts, and conclude that bankruptcy courts are therefore not bound by district court decisions. * * *

* * *

Other bankruptcy courts supplement the formal *Rheuban* argument with a more policy oriented one. For example, in *In re Gaylor* [123 B.R. 236 (Bankr.E.D.Mich.1991)], the court recognized that one benefit of stare decisis is limiting the number of appeals. Appeals are costly to litigants and society, and lower court departures from established reviewing court precedent would surely multiply appeals. Stare decisis discourages appeals, but this function is served only when litigants have reason to believe that the reviewing court will adhere to its prior decisions. District judges, *Gaylor* notes, have no obligation to follow prior decisions of other judges even within the same district.

With respect to the non-binding effect of BAP decisions, bankruptcy courts [e.g., *In re Standard Brands Paint Co.*, 154 B.R. 563, 568 n. 3 (Bankr.C.D.Cal.1993)] and commentators make an essentially derivative argument: The BAP sits "in lieu of" the district court, and its precedent-setting power is limited to that of the district court in lieu of which it sits. Early versions of this "in lieu" argument suggested that BAP opinions had stare decisis effect only within the district from whence appeal was taken, rather than circuit-wide. Later versions of the argument suggest that since district court opinions do not bind bankruptcy courts for the reasons described above, then neither can BAP opinions. Of course, if one adopts the view that district court opinions *do* have stare decisis effect, this technical argument falls on its own terms.

At least one bankruptcy court in the Central District of California has advanced a formal argument suggesting BAP precedents are binding [*In re Globe Illumination Co.*, 149 B.R. 614 (Bankr.C.D.Cal.1993)]. According to this court, the jurisdictional statutes and Ninth Circuit rules make the BAP an "adjunct" of the United States Court of Appeals, which all apparently concede has the power to bind the bankruptcy courts (and for that matter the federal district courts) within the geographic area of the Ninth Circuit. As an "adjunct" of the Court of Appeals, the BAP shares the Ninth Circuit's power to create binding precedents circuit-wide, presumably on district as well as bankruptcy courts.

These formal arguments for and against the BAPs' authoritativeness, regardless of their technical merit, all share the premises of the *Rheuban* and *Gaylor* courts: that the rule of stare decisis is a deduction from the hierarchical nature of the judicial system and a related interest in judicial economy.

\* \* \*

\* \* \* [S]tripping the BAP of its ability to make precedents leads one to question the BAP's institutional role as an expert appellate panel. If the BAP cannot assist in the orderly and coherent development of bankruptcy law, it serves no function beyond case-by-case error-correction, a function the federal district court can serve at less cost. Deploying three expert Article I bankruptcy judges with all the appellate formalities solely to correct errors in individual cases and not to clarify the law seems an oddly wasteful experiment to impute to the Congress. I am unaware of any evidence or plausible rationale suggesting that Congress in fact intended to so limit the Bankruptcy Appellate Panels.

\* \* \*

Given the existing structure of the bankruptcy appellate system, if interstitial law is going to be made by appellate courts, the lion's share of the burden must fall on the first-tier court. Both the district court (acting in an appellate capacity) and the BAP are institutionally competent to assume the law-making function \* \* \*. Allocating law-making authority to these appellate courts results in a reasonable division of authority and labor between the appellate and trial courts and appropriately dilutes and constrains the otherwise relatively uncabined power of the bankruptcy court. \* \* \*

Although the bankruptcy jurisdictional statutes provide for district court and BAP jurisdiction over interlocutory appeals from bankruptcy court decisions, further appeals up the system to the Courts of Appeals lie only from final orders from either the BAPs or the district court or from those limited types of interlocutory orders reviewable under the general jurisdictional statutes of the Courts of Appeals—the grant or denial of injunctions, certified appeals and a special bankruptcy exception for interlocutory orders modifying the statutory period during which the debtor has the exclusive right to file a reorganization plan in Chapter 11 cases.

Because (i) the jurisdiction of the Courts of Appeals is limited to final orders, (ii) the bankruptcy case serves as an umbrella proceeding in which many discrete proceedings are litigated, (iii) initial appeals of interlocutory orders to BAP and district court are available and (iv) final orders entered at the bankruptcy court may be subject to further proceedings after the initial appeal to the BAP or district court, it becomes necessary to make difficult judgments about the meaning of finality in the context of a bankruptcy case at the Court of Appeals level. Most Courts of Appeals have tended to adopt a relatively loose "pragmatic" view of finality in bankruptcy cases in order to allow meaningful appellate review to occur on important questions. 16 Charles A. Wright, et al., *Federal Practice and Procedure: Jurisdiction* 2d § 3926.2 (2d ed.1996). But the "pragmatic" approach has led to substantial confusion and inconsistency in the caselaw and seems to turn primarily on the appellate court's perception of the importance of the issue and the effect of the lower court ruling on the parties. One of the most important unresolved questions is the appealability of district court's remand order from an appeal of an otherwise final bankruptcy court order. There is great disarray in the cases over the question of whether the fact that the remand requires substantial new proceedings in the bankruptcy court converts what was initially a final order into an interlocutory one.

In addition to the issue of finality, mootness is frequently a problem at the Court of Appeals level. Mootness commonly results when parties rely on unstayed orders of the bankruptcy court in a way that makes it impossible for an appellate court to fashion meaningful relief without creating injustice. The Courts of Appeals, of course, have no jurisdiction over moot cases and must dismiss appeals in these circumstances. 13A Charles A. Wright et al., *Federal Practice and Procedure: Jurisdiction* 2d § 3533 (2d ed.1996). In addition, the Bankruptcy Code itself precludes appellate review of post-petition financing orders and bankruptcy sales absent a stay. §§ 363(m) & 364(e). *But see Matter of Saybrook Mfg. Co.*, 963 F.2d 1490 (11th Cir.1992). Traditional statements of the bankruptcy mootness doctrine can be found in *In re Continental Airlines*, 91 F.3d 553, 565 *en banc* (3d Cir.1996). Perhaps in the last few years appellate courts have begun to exhibit more willingness to review appeals from unstayed confirmation orders. *See, e.g., In re 203 North LaSalle Street Partnership*, 126 F.3d 955, 961 (7th Cir.1997), *rev'd on other grounds*, 526 U.S. 434 (1999).

Given the intervening level of appellate review and the mootness and finality barriers to review, relatively few bankruptcy appeals reach the Courts of Appeals. Appeals from the Courts of Appeals are available as a matter of discretion in the Supreme Court on writ of certiorari under the Supreme Court's general jurisdictional statutes. But the Supreme Court usually reviews only a few bankruptcy cases each year.

Under 28 U.S. § 158(d)(1), the courts of appeal have jurisdiction over appeals from all final decisions, judgments, orders, and decrees entered under § 158(a) and (b). The 2005 Act added § 158(d)(2), which allows direct appeal to the courts of appeal under certain circumstances, making it possible to bypass district court or BAP review and appeal orders and decrees of the bankruptcy court directly to the courts of appeal. A court of appeals may authorize an immediate appeal of an order or decree, if the bankruptcy court, the district court, the BAP or the parties acting jointly certify that:

**(I)** the judgment, order or decree involves a question of law as to which there is no controlling decision of the court of appeals for the circuit or of the Supreme Court or involves a matter of public importance;

**(II)** the judgment, order or decree involves a question of law requiring resolution of conflicting decisions; or

**(III)** an immediate appeal from the judgment, order or decree may materially advance the progress of the case or the proceeding in which the appeal is taken.

An unusual innovation in new § 158(d)(2)(B) requires the court from whence the appeal originates to certify the appeal for direct review if "a majority of the appellants" and a "majority of the appellees" request such certification. The requirement of specific authorization from the court of appeals remains notwithstanding certification by the bankruptcy court, BAP or district court whether upon such court's own motion or the request of a majority of both appellants and appellees.

The certification standard is analogous to that authorizing certification of interlocutory appeals under the general jurisdictional statutes of the United States Courts of Appeals—28 U.S.C. § 1292(b). Section 1292(b) provides:

**(b)** When a district judge, in making in a civil action an order not otherwise appealable under this section, shall be of the opinion that such order involves a controlling question of law as to which there is substantial ground for difference of opinion and that an immediate appeal from the order may materially advance the ultimate termination of the litigation, he so shall state in writing in such order. The Court of Appeals. . . may thereupon, in its discretion, permit an appeal to by taken from such order. . . .

In general, courts have imposed a very high standard for certification of appeals under § 1292(b) and certification is rarely granted. Some courts adopt the § 1292(b) standard for determining when leave of court is appropriate in hearing an interlocutory appeal from the bankruptcy court, *see* 5 *Collier On Bankruptcy* ¶ 5.07[4] (15th ed. rev. 2004), but most courts appear to apply a less rigorous standard. The ability of the parties or the bankruptcy court (in lieu of the district court) to certify a direct appeal and the absence of § 1292(b)'s controlling question language in § 158(d) may allow a looser standard than that of § 1292(b) and more analogous to the leave of court standard to develop.

## D. RIGHT TO JURY TRIAL

Congress has not been notably successful in providing guidance on the issue of when parties are entitled to a jury trial in bankruptcy matters. The Bankruptcy Reform Act of 1978 contained 28 U.S.C. § 1480:

**(a)** Except as provided in subsection (b) of this section, this chapter and title 11 do not affect any right to trial by jury, in a case under title 11 or in a proceeding arising under title 11 or arising in or related to a case under title 11, that is provided by any statute in effect on September 30, 1979.

**(b)** The bankruptcy court may order issues arising under section 303 of title 11 to be tried without a jury.

Since September 30, 1979 was the last day on which the Bankruptcy Act was in force, 28 U.S.C. § 1480 was clearly intended to preserve the status quo, as the legislative history shows:

> Proposed section 1480 requires that the right of jury trial be preserved as it is under present law. Bankruptcy courts will be required to hold jury trials to adjudicate what are under present law called "plenary suits,' that is, suits that are brought in State or Federal Courts other than bankruptcy courts.

House Report, No. 95–595, 1978 U.S. Code Cong. & Admin.News 5973.

Under § 19(a) of the Bankruptcy Act, the debtor in an involuntary bankruptcy proceeding was entitled to a jury trial on the issues of insolvency and the existence of the acts of bankruptcy. 28 U.S.C. § 1480(b) changed that result with respect to issues arising under § 303(h).

As part of the 1984 post-*Marathon* amendments, 28 U.S.C. § 1480 was apparently repealed and replaced by 28 U.S.C. § 1411. If § 1480, when adopted in 1978, did nothing to clarify when a jury is appropriate in bankruptcy proceedings, at least it directed that the current state of the law on right to jury trial—whatever it was—should be continued. However § 1411 is one of Congress' more Delphic contributions to bankruptcy law:

**(a)** Except as provided in subsection (b) of this section, this chapter and title 11 do not affect any right to trial by jury that an individual has under applicable nonbankruptcy law with regard to a personal injury or wrongful death tort claim.

**(b)** The district court may order the issues arising under section 303 of title 11 to be tried without a jury.

We have seen that 28 U.S.C. § 157(b)(5) requires that district courts rather than bankruptcy judges hear personal injury tort and wrongful death claims against the estate. Section 1411(a) requires that in cases in which these kinds of claims are asserted, the parties have a right of jury trial if they would have had this right in a trial of such claims outside bankruptcy. Having said that, where does § 1411(a) leave the law of trial by jury on all the other issues that might arise in bankruptcy? In footnote 3 of *Granfi-*

*nanciera,* the case that follows, the Supreme Court describes 28 U.S.C. § 1411 as "notoriously ambiguous." If § 1411(a) excludes jury trials in all cases except those involving personal injuries or wrongful death claims, § 1411(b) is unneeded. Adding to the confusion is the disturbing fact that Congress may not have successfully repealed 28 U.S.C. § 1480 in 1984. In mistakenly enacting both §§ 113 and 121(a) of the Bankruptcy Amendments and Federal Judgeship Act of 1984, Congress might have kept § 1480 alive. When asked about the matter Senator Dole replied: "We goofed." In view of the contradictory guidance Congress has provided on the right to a jury trial in bankruptcy, it is not surprising that the cases are in disarray. Some take the position that 28 U.S.C. § 1480 was repealed and that jury trials are limited by 28 U.S.C. § 1411 to personal injury and wrongful death actions. Others hold that § 1480 still lives, and the courts must decide whether a jury trial is available under either § 1480 or § 1411. (*See generally In re Tripplett,* 115 B.R. 955, 959–961 n. 5 (Bankr.N.D.Ill.1990).)

In *Granfinanciera* the Supreme Court, in its first case concerning the right to jury trial in bankruptcy under the Code, prescribed a role for juries in bankruptcy proceedings grounded on the Seventh Amendment, thereby transcending the ambiguities of 28 U.S.C. § 1411 and plunging bankruptcy courts into a most difficult task of arcane historically-based line-drawing.

## Granfinanciera, S.A. v. Nordberg

Supreme Court of the United States, 1989.
492 U.S. 33.

■ BRENNAN, J., delivered the opinion of the Court, in which REHNQUIST, C.J., and MARSHALL, STEVENS, and KENNEDY, JJ., joined, and in Parts I, II, III, and V, of which SCALIA, J., joined. SCALIA, J., filed an opinion concurring in part and concurring in the judgment. White, J., filed a dissenting opinion. BLACKMUN, J., filed a dissenting opinion, in which O'CONNOR, J., joined.

The question presented is whether a person who has not submitted a claim against a bankruptcy estate has a right to a jury trial when sued by the trustee in bankruptcy to recover an allegedly fraudulent monetary transfer. We hold that the Seventh Amendment entitles such a person to a trial by jury, notwithstanding Congress' designation of fraudulent conveyance actions as "core proceedings" in 28 U.S.C. § 157(b)(2)(H).

### I

The Chase & Sanborn Corporation filed a petition for reorganization under Chapter 11 in 1983. A Plan of Reorganization approved by the United States Bankruptcy Court for the Southern District of Florida vested in respondent Nordberg, the trustee in bankruptcy, causes of action for fraudulent conveyances. In 1985, respondent filed suit against petitioners Granfinanciera, S.A. and Medex, Ltda. in the United States District Court for the Southern District of Florida. The complaint alleged that petitioners had received $1.7 million from Chase & Sanborn's corporate predecessor within one year of the date its bankruptcy petition was filed, without receiving consideration or reasonably equivalent value in return. Respondent sought to avoid what it alleged were constructively and actually fraudulent transfers and to recover damages, costs, expenses, and interest under §§ 548(a)(1) and (a)(2), 550(a)(1).

The District Court referred the proceedings to the Bankruptcy Court. Over five months later, and shortly before the Colombian Government nationalized Granfinanciera, respondent served a summons on petitioners in Bogota, Colombia. In their answer to the complaint following Granfinanciera's nationalization, both petitioners requested a "trial by jury on all issues so triable." The Bankruptcy Judge denied petitioners' request for a jury trial, deeming a suit to recover a fraudulent transfer "a core action that originally, under the English common law, as I understand it, was a non-jury issue." Following a bench trial, the court dismissed with prejudice respondent's actual fraud claim but entered judgment for respondent on the constructive fraud claim in the amount of $1,500,000 against Granfinanciera and $180,000 against Medex. The District Court affirmed, without discussing petitioners' claim that they were entitled to a jury trial.

The Court of Appeals for the Eleventh Circuit also affirmed. The court found that petitioners lacked a statutory right to a jury trial, because the constructive fraud provision under which suit was brought—§ 548(a)(2)—contains no mention of a right to a jury trial and 28 U.S.C. § 1411 "affords jury trials only in personal injury or wrongful death suits." The Court of Appeals further ruled that the Seventh Amendment supplied no right to a jury trial, because actions to recover fraudulent conveyances are equitable in nature, even when a plaintiff seeks only monetary relief, and because "bankruptcy itself is equitable in nature and thus bankruptcy proceedings are inherently equitable." The court read our opinion in *Katchen v. Landy*, 382 U.S. 323 (1966), to say that "Congress may convert a creditor's legal right into an equitable claim and displace any seventh amendment right to trial by jury," and held that Congress had done so by designating fraudulent conveyance actions "core proceedings" triable by bankruptcy judges sitting without juries.

We granted certiorari to decide whether petitioners were entitled to a jury trial * * * and now reverse.

\* \* \*

### III

Petitioners rest their claim to a jury trial on the Seventh Amendment alone.[3] The Seventh Amendment provides: "In Suits at common law,

---

[3] The current statutory provision for jury trials in bankruptcy proceedings—28 U.S.C. § 1411 enacted as part of the Bankruptcy Amendments and Federal Judgeship Act of

where the value in controversy shall exceed twenty dollars, the right of trial by jury shall be preserved * * *." We have consistently interpreted the phrase "Suits at common law" to refer to "suits in which *legal* rights were to be ascertained and determined, in contradistinction to those where equitable rights alone were recognized, and equitable remedies were administered." *Parsons v. Bedford,* 3 Pet. 433, 447 (1830). Although "the thrust of the Amendment was to preserve the right to jury trial as it existed in 1791," the Seventh Amendment also applies to actions brought to enforce statutory rights that are analogous to common-law causes of action ordinarily decided in English law courts in the late 18th century, as opposed to those customarily heard by courts of equity or admiralty. * * *

The form of our analysis is familiar. "First, we compare the statutory action to 18th-century actions brought in the courts of England prior to the merger of the courts of law and equity. Second, we examine the remedy sought and determine whether it is legal or equitable in nature." *Tull v. United States,* 481 U.S. 412, 417–418 (1987) (citations omitted). The second stage of this analysis is more important than the first. If, on balance, these two factors indicate that a party is entitled to a jury trial under the Seventh Amendment, we must decide whether Congress may assign and

---

1984 (1984 Amendments)—is notoriously ambiguous. Section 1411(a) provides: "[T]his chapter and title 11 do not affect any right to trial by jury that an individual has under applicable non-bankruptcy law with regard to a personal injury or wrongful death tort claim." Although this section might suggest that jury trials are available only in personal injury and wrongful death actions, that conclusion is debatable. Section 1411(b) provides that "[t]he district court may order the issues arising [in connection with involuntary bankruptcy petitions] to be tried without a jury," suggesting that the court lacks similar discretion to deny jury trials on at least some issues presented in connection with voluntary petitions. The confused legislative history of these provisions has further puzzled commentators. See, *e.g.,* Gibson, Jury Trials in Bankruptcy: Obeying the Commands of Article III and the Seventh Amendment, 72 Minn.L.Rev. 967, 989–996 (1988) (hereinafter Gibson); * * * Whatever the proper construction of § 1411, petitioners concede that this section does not entitle them to a jury trial. Section 122(b) of the 1984 Amendments, 98 Stat. 346, bars application of § 1411 to "cases under title 11 of the United States Code that are pending on the date of enactment of this Act or to proceedings arising in or related to such cases," and Chase & Sanborn's petition for reorganization was pending on that date. Nor does § 1411's predecessor—28 U.S.C. § 1480(a), which stated that "this chapter and title 11 do not affect any right to trial by jury, in a case under title 11 or in a proceeding arising under title 11 or arising in or related to a case under title 11, that is provided by any statute in effect on September 30, 1979"—seem to afford petitioners a statutory basis for their claim. As they recognize, § 1480 was apparently repealed by the 1984 Amendments. Petitioners therefore appear correct in concluding that "absent any specific legislation in force providing jury trials for cases filed before July 10, 1984, but tried afterwards, [their] right to jury trial in this proceeding must necessarily be predicated entirely on the Seventh Amendment."

has assigned resolution of the relevant claim to a non-Article III adjudica-tive body that does not use a jury as factfinder.[4]

### A

There is no dispute that actions to recover preferential or fraudulent transfers were often brought at law in late 18th-century England. As we noted in *Schoenthal v. Irving Trust Co.*, 287 U.S. 92, 94 (1932), "[I]n Eng-land, long prior to the enactment of our first Judiciary Act, common law actions of trover and money had and received were resorted to for the re-covery of preferential payments by bankrupts." * * * These actions, like all suits at law, were conducted before juries.

Respondent does not challenge this proposition or even contend that actions to recover fraudulent conveyances or preferential transfers were more than occasionally tried in courts of equity. He asserts only that courts of equity had concurrent jurisdiction with courts of law over fraudulent conveyance actions. While respondent's assertion that courts of equity sometimes provided relief in fraudulent conveyance actions is true, how-ever, it hardly suffices to undermine petitioners' submission that the pre-sent action for *monetary* relief would not have sounded in equity two hun-dred years ago in England. In *Parsons v. Bedford,* 3 Pet., at 447 (emphasis added), we contrasted suits at law with "those where equitable rights *alone* were recognized" in holding that the Seventh Amendment right to a jury trial applies to all but the latter actions. Respondent adduces no authority to buttress the claim that suits to recover an allegedly fraudulent transfer of money, of the sort that he has brought, were typically or indeed ever entertained by English courts of equity when the Seventh Amendment was adopted. * * *

We therefore conclude that respondent would have had to bring his action to recover an alleged fraudulent conveyance of a determinate sum of money at law in 18th-century England, and that a court of equity would not have adjudicated it.

### B

The nature of the relief respondent seeks strongly supports our pre-liminary finding that the right he invokes should be denominated legal rather than equitable. Our decisions establish beyond peradventure that "[i]n cases of fraud or mistake, as under any other head of chancery juris-diction, a court of the United States will not sustain a bill in equity to ob-

---

[4] * * * We consider this issue in Part IV, *infra*. Contrary to Justice White's conten-tion, * * * we do not declare that the Seventh Amendment provides a right to a jury trial on all legal rather than equitable claims. If a claim that is legal in nature asserts a "public right," as we define that term in Part IV, then the Seventh Amendment does not entitle the parties to a jury trial if Congress assigns its adjudication to an adminis-trative agency or specialized court of equity. * * * The Seventh Amendment protects a litigant's right to a jury trial only if a cause of action is legal in nature and it involves a matter of "private right."

tain only a decree for the payment of money by way of damages, when the like amount can be recovered at law in an action sounding in tort or for money had and received." *Buzard v. Houston*, 119 U.S., at 352 * * *.

Indeed, in our view *Schoenthal v. Irving Trust Co.* removes all doubt that respondent's cause of action should be characterized as legal rather than as equitable. In *Schoenthal,* the trustee in bankruptcy sued in equity to recover alleged preferential payments, claiming that it had no adequate remedy at law. As in this case, the recipients of the payments apparently did not file claims against the bankruptcy estate. The Court held that the suit had to proceed at law instead, because the long-settled rule that suits in equity will not be sustained where a complete remedy exists at law, then codified at 28 U.S.C. § 384, "serves to guard the right of trial by jury preserved by the Seventh Amendment and to that end it should be liberally construed." 287 U.S. at 94. The Court found that the trustee's suit—indistinguishable from respondent's suit in all relevant respects—could not go forward in equity because an adequate remedy was available at law. There, as here, "[t]he preferences sued for were money payments of ascertained and definite amounts," and "[t]he bill discloses no facts that call for an accounting or other equitable relief." *Id.*, at 95. Respondent's fraudulent conveyance action plainly seeks relief traditionally provided by law courts or on the law side of courts having both legal and equitable dockets. Unless Congress may and has permissibly withdrawn jurisdiction over that action by courts of law and assigned it exclusively to non-Article III tribunals sitting without juries, the Seventh Amendment guarantees petitioners a jury trial upon request.

## IV

Prior to passage of the Bankruptcy Reform Act of 1978 * * * "[s]uits to recover preferences constitute[d] no part of the proceedings in bankruptcy." *Schoenthal v. Irving Trust Co., supra,* at 94–95. Although related to bankruptcy proceedings, fraudulent conveyance and preference actions brought by a trustee in bankruptcy were deemed separate, plenary suits to which the Seventh Amendment applied. While the 1978 Act brought those actions within the jurisdiction of the bankruptcy courts, it preserved parties' rights to trial by jury as they existed prior to the effective date of the 1978 Act. 28 U.S.C. § 1480(a) (repealed). The 1984 Amendments, however, designated fraudulent conveyance actions "core proceedings," 28 U.S.C. § 157(b)(2)(H), which bankruptcy judges may adjudicate and in which they may issue final judgments, § 157(b)(1), if a district court has referred the matter to them. § 157(a). We are not obliged to decide today whether bankruptcy courts may conduct jury trials in fraudulent conveyance suits brought by a trustee against a person who has not entered a claim against the estate, either in the rare procedural posture of this case * * * or under the current statutory scheme. * * * Nor need we decide whether, if Congress has authorized bankruptcy courts to hold jury trials in such actions, that authorization comports with Article III when non-Article III judges preside over them subject to review in, or withdrawal by, the district courts. We also need not consider whether jury trials conducted by a bankruptcy court would satisfy the Seventh Amendment's command that "no fact tried by a jury, shall be otherwise re-examined in any Court of the United States, than according to the rules of the common law," given that district courts may presently set aside clearly erroneous factual findings by bankruptcy courts. Bankr. Rule 8013. The sole issue before us is whether the Seventh Amendment confers on petitioners a right to a jury trial in the face of Congress' decision to allow a non-Article III tribunal to adjudicate the claims against them.

### A

In *Atlas Roofing*, we noted that "when Congress creates new statutory "public rights,' it may assign their adjudication to an administrative agency with which a jury trial would be incompatible, without violating the Seventh Amendment's injunction that jury trial is to be "preserved' in "suits at common law.' " 430 U.S., at 455. We emphasized, however, that Congress' power to block application of the Seventh Amendment to a cause of action has limits. Congress may only deny trials by jury in actions at law, we said, in cases where "public rights" are litigated: "Our prior cases support administrative factfinding in only those situations involving "public rights,' *e.g.*, where the Government is involved in its sovereign capacity under an otherwise valid statute creating enforceable public rights. Wholly private tort, contract, and property cases, as well as a vast range of other cases, are not at all implicated." *Id.*, at 458.[8]

We adhere to that general teaching. As we said in *Atlas Roofing:* " "On the common law side of the federal courts, the aid of juries is not only deemed appropriate but is required by the Constitution itself.' " *Id.*, at 450, n. 7, quoting *Crowell v. Benson*, 285 U.S. 22, 51 (1932). Congress may devise novel causes of action involving public rights free from the strictures of the Seventh Amendment if it assigns their adjudication to tribunals without statutory authority to employ juries as factfinders. But it lacks the power to strip parties contesting matters of private right of their constitutional right to a trial by jury. As we recognized in *Atlas Roofing*, to hold otherwise would be to permit Congress to eviscerate the Seventh Amendment's guarantee by assigning to administrative agencies or courts of equity all causes of action not grounded in state law, whether they originate in a newly fashioned regulatory scheme or possess a long line of common-law forebears. The Constitution nowhere grants Congress such puissant authority. "[L]egal claims are not magically converted into equitable

---

[8] Although we left the term "public rights" undefined in *Atlas Roofing*, we cited *Crowell v. Benson*, approvingly. In *Crowell*, 285 U.S. 22 (1932), we defined "private right" as "the liability of one individual to another under the law as defined," *id.*, at 51, in contrast to cases that "arise between the Government and persons subject to its authority in connection with the performance of the constitutional functions of the executive or legislative departments." *Id.*, at 50.

issues by their presentation to a court of equity," *Ross v. Bernhard*, 396 U.S. 531, 538 (1970), nor can Congress conjure away the Seventh Amendment by mandating that traditional legal claims be brought there or taken to an administrative tribunal.

In certain situations, of course, Congress may fashion causes of action that are closely *analogous* to common-law claims and place them beyond the ambit of the Seventh Amendment by assigning their resolution to a forum in which jury trials are unavailable. *See, e.g., Atlas Roofing, supra,* at 450–461 (workplace safety regulations); *Block v. Hirsh,* 256 U.S. 135, 158 (1921) (temporary emergency regulation of rental real estate). * * * Congress' power to do so is limited, however, just as its power to place adjudicative authority in non-Article III tribunals is circumscribed. * * * Unless a legal cause of action involves "public rights," Congress may not deprive parties litigating over that right of the Seventh Amendment's guarantee to a jury trial.

In *Atlas Roofing,* we noted that Congress may effectively supplant a common-law cause of action carrying with it a right to a jury trial with a statutory cause of action shorn of a jury trial right if that statutory cause of action inheres in or lies against the Federal Government in its sovereign capacity. Our case law makes plain, however, that the class of "public rights" whose adjudication Congress may assign to administrative agencies or courts of equity sitting without juries is more expansive than *Atlas Roofing*'s discussion suggests. Indeed, our decisions point to the conclusion that, if a statutory cause of action is legal in nature, the question whether the Seventh Amendment permits Congress to assign its adjudication to a tribunal that does not employ juries as factfinders requires the same answer as the question whether Article III allows Congress to assign adjudication of that cause of action to a non-Article III tribunal. For if a statutory cause of action, such as respondent's right to recover a fraudulent conveyance under § 548(a)(2), is not a "public right" for Article III purposes, then Congress may not assign its adjudication to a specialized non-Article III court lacking "the essential attributes of the judicial power." *Crowell v. Benson, supra,* at 51. And if the action must be tried under the auspices of an Article III court, then the Seventh Amendment affords the parties a right to a jury trial whenever the cause of action is legal in nature. Conversely, if Congress may assign the adjudication of a statutory cause of action to a non-Article III tribunal, then the Seventh Amendment poses no independent bar to the adjudication of that action by a nonjury factfinder. * * * In addition to our Seventh Amendment precedents, we therefore rely as well on our decisions exploring the restrictions Article III places on Congress' choice of adjudicative bodies to resolve disputes over statutory rights to determine whether petitioners are entitled to a jury trial.

In our most recent discussion of the "public rights" doctrine as it bears on Congress' power to commit adjudication of a statutory cause of action to a non-Article III tribunal, we rejected the view that "a matter of public rights must at a minimum arise "between the government and others.' " *Northern Pipeline Construction Co.*, [458 U.S.] at 69 (opinion of Brennan, J.), quoting *Ex parte* Bakelite Corp., 279 U.S. 438, 451 (1929). We held, instead, that the Federal Government need not be a party for a case to revolve around "public rights." The crucial question, in cases not involving the Federal Government, is whether "Congress, acting for a valid legislative purpose pursuant to its constitutional powers under Article I, [has] create[d] a seemingly "private' right that is so closely integrated into a public regulatory scheme as to be a matter appropriate for agency resolution with limited involvement by the Article III judiciary." [*Thomas*, 473 U.S.], at 593–594. *See id.*, at 600 (BRENNAN, J., concurring in judgment) (challenged provision involves public rights because "the dispute arises in the context of a federal regulatory scheme that virtually occupies the field"). If a statutory right is not closely intertwined with a federal regulatory program Congress has power to enact, and if that right neither belongs to nor exists against the Federal Government, then it must be adjudicated by an Article III court. If the right is legal in nature, then it carries with it the Seventh Amendment's guarantee of a jury trial.

**B**

Although the issue admits of some debate, a bankruptcy trustee's right to recover a fraudulent conveyance under § 548(a)(2) seems to us more accurately characterized as a private rather than a public right as we have used those terms in our Article III decisions. In *Northern Pipeline Construction Co.*, the plurality noted that the restructuring of debtor-creditor relations in bankruptcy "may well be a "public right.' " But the plurality also emphasized that state-law causes of action for breach of contract or warranty are paradigmatic private rights, even when asserted by an insolvent corporation in the midst of Chapter 11 reorganization proceedings. The plurality further said that "matters from their nature subject to "a suit at common law or in equity or admiralty' lie at the "protected core" of Article III judicial power—a point we reaffirmed in *Thomas*. There can be little doubt that fraudulent conveyance actions by bankruptcy trustees— suits which, we said in *Schoenthal v. Irving Trust Co.*, 287 U.S., at 94–95, "constitute no part of the proceedings in bankruptcy but concern controversies arising out of it"—are quintessentially suits at common law that more nearly resemble state-law contract claims brought by a bankrupt corporation to augment the bankruptcy estate than they do creditors' hierarchically ordered claims to a pro rata share of the bankruptcy *res*. They therefore appear matters of private rather than public right.

Our decision in *Katchen v. Landy*, 382 U.S. 323 (1966), under the Seventh Amendment rather than Article III, confirms this analysis. Petitioner, an officer of a bankrupt corporation, made payments from corporate funds within four months of bankruptcy on corporate notes on which he was an accommodation maker. When petitioner later filed claims against the bankruptcy estate, the trustee counterclaimed, arguing that the payments petitioner made constituted voidable preferences because they reduced his potential personal liability on the notes. We held that the bankruptcy court had jurisdiction to order petitioner to surrender the preferences and that it could rule on the trustee's claim without according petitioner a jury trial. * * *

We read *Schoenthal* and *Katchen* as holding that, under the Seventh Amendment, a creditor's right to a jury trial on a bankruptcy trustee's preference claim depends upon whether the creditor has submitted a claim against the estate, not upon Congress' precise definition of the "bankruptcy estate" or upon whether Congress chanced to deny jury trials to creditors who have not filed claims and who are sued by a trustee to recover an alleged preference. Because petitioners here, like the petitioner in *Schoenthal,* have not filed claims against the estate, respondent's fraudulent conveyance action does not arise "as part of the process of allowance and disallowance of claims." Nor is that action integral to the restructuring of debtor-creditor relations. Congress therefore cannot divest petitioners of their Seventh Amendment right to a trial by jury. *Katchen* thus supports the result we reach today; it certainly does not compel its opposite.

The 1978 Act abolished the statutory distinction between plenary and summary bankruptcy proceedings, on which the Court relied in *Schoenthal* and *Katchen.* Although the 1978 Act preserved parties' rights to jury trials as they existed prior to the day it took effect, 28 U.S.C. § 1480(a) (repealed), in the 1984 Amendments Congress drew a new distinction between "core" and "non-core" proceedings and classified fraudulent conveyance actions as core proceedings triable by bankruptcy judges. 28 U.S.C. § 157(b)(2)(H). Whether 28 U.S.C. § 1411 purports to abolish jury trial rights in what were formerly plenary actions is unclear, and at any rate is not a question we need decide here. * * * The decisive point is that in neither the 1978 Act nor the 1984 Amendments did Congress "creat[e] a new cause of action, and remedies therefor, unknown to the common law," because traditional rights and remedies were inadequate to cope with a manifest public problem. *Atlas Roofing,* 430 U.S., at 461. Rather, Congress simply reclassified a pre-existing common-law cause of action that was not integrally related to the reformation of debtor-creditor relations and that apparently did not suffer from any grave deficiencies. This purely taxonomic change cannot alter our Seventh Amendment analysis. Congress cannot eliminate a party's Seventh Amendment right to a jury trial merely by relabeling the cause of action to which it attaches and placing exclusive jurisdiction in an administrative agency or a specialized court of equity. * * *

Nor can Congress' assignment be justified on the ground that jury trials of fraudulent conveyance actions would "go far to dismantle the statutory scheme," *Atlas Roofing,* 430 U.S., at 454 n.11, or that bankruptcy proceedings have been placed in "an administrative forum with which the jury would be incompatible." *Id.,* at 450. To be sure, we owe some deference to Congress' judgment after it has given careful consideration to the constitutionality of a legislative provision. But respondent has adduced no evidence that Congress considered the constitutional implications of its designation of all fraudulent conveyance actions as core proceedings. Nor can it seriously be argued that permitting jury trials in fraudulent conveyance actions brought by a trustee against a person who has not entered a claim against the estate would "go far to dismantle the statutory scheme," as we used that phrase in *Atlas Roofing,* when our opinion in that case, following *Schoenthal,* plainly assumed that such claims carried with them a right to a jury trial. In addition, one cannot easily say that "the jury would be incompatible" with bankruptcy proceedings, in view of Congress' express provision for jury trials in certain actions arising out of bankruptcy litigation. See 28 U.S.C. § 1411 * * * And Justice WHITE'S claim that juries may serve usefully as checks only on the decisions of judges who enjoy life tenure overlooks the extent to which judges who are appointed for fixed terms may be beholden to Congress or executive officials, and thus ignores the potential for juries to exercise beneficial restraint on their decisions.

It may be that providing jury trials in some fraudulent conveyance actions—if not in this particular case, because respondent's suit was commenced after the bankruptcy court approved the debtor's plan of reorganization—would impede swift resolution of bankruptcy proceedings and increase the expense of Chapter 11 reorganizations. But "these considerations are insufficient to overcome the clear command of the Seventh Amendment." *Curtis v. Loether*, 415 U.S., at 198. *See also Bowsher v. Synar*, 478 U.S. 714, 736 (1986) (" "[T]he fact that a given law or procedure is efficient, convenient, and useful in facilitating functions of government, standing alone, will not save it if it is contrary to the Constitution' "), quoting *INS v. Chadha*, 462 U.S. 919, 944 (1983); *Pernell v. Southall Realty*, 416 U.S., at 383–384 (discounting arguments that jury trials would be unduly burdensome and rejecting "the notion that there is some necessary inconsistency between the desire for speedy justice and the right to jury trial").

## V

We do not decide today whether the current jury trial provision—28 U.S.C. § 1411—permits bankruptcy courts to conduct jury trials in fraudulent conveyance actions like the one respondent initiated. Nor do we express any view as to whether the Seventh Amendment or Article III allows jury trials in such actions to be held before non-Article III bankruptcy judges subject to the oversight provided by the district courts pursuant to the 1984 Amendments. We leave those issues for future decisions. We do hold, however, that whatever the answers to these questions, the Seventh Amendment entitles petitioners to the jury trial they requested. Accordingly, the judgment of the Court of Appeals is reversed, and the case is remanded for further proceedings consistent with this opinion.

*It is so ordered.*

[The opinions of Justices BLACKMUN, SCALIA, and WHITE are omitted.]

## NOTES

**1.** In *Langenkamp v. Culp*, 498 U.S. 42 (1990), the Court held that if a creditor who files a claim is sued by the trustee to recover a voidable preference, the creditor is not entitled to a jury trial on the preference question under the Seventh Amendment. "In *Granfinanciera* we recognized that by filing a claim against a bankruptcy estate the creditor triggers the process of 'allowance and disallowance of claims,' thereby subjecting himself to the court's equitable power. * * * If the creditor is met, in turn, with a preference action from the trustee, that action becomes part of the claims-allowance process which is triable only in equity. * * * In other words, the creditor's claim and the ensuing preference action by the trustee become integral to the restructuring of the debtor-creditor relationship through the bankruptcy court's *equity jurisdiction.* * * * As such, there is no Seventh Amendment right to a jury trial. If the party does *not* submit a claim against the bankruptcy estate, however, the trustee can recover allegedly preferential transfers only by filing what amounts to a legal action to recover a monetary transfer. In those circumstances the preference defendant is entitled to a jury trial." 498 U.S. at 44–45. (Emphasis in original.)

**2.** An issue on which the circuits are divided is whether a debtor, who has a cause of action on which it would be entitled to a jury trial under the *Granfinanciera* test, is deprived of that right if the person against whom the action is brought files a claim in the debtor's bankruptcy. In *In re Hallahan*, 936 F.2d 1496 (7th Cir.1991), a creditor filed a claim for willful violation of a contract and tortious interference with business expectations and filed a complaint requesting a nondischargeability hearing under § 523(a)(6). The debtor requested a jury trial on the nondischargeability issue, arguing that the creditor's underlying breach of contract action was a suit at common law even though it was being tried as a part of an equitable bankruptcy proceeding. The court rejected the debtor's demand for a jury trial. Even assuming that a nondischargeability hearing is a legal matter (which the court thought it was not), by voluntarily filing its petition in bankruptcy, the debtor submitted to the equitable jurisdiction of the bankruptcy court and, in effect, waived its right to a jury trial. If the creditor lost its right to a jury trial by filing a claim, the debtor "cannot be endowed with any stronger right." 936 F.2d at 1505. *In re McLaren*, 3 F.3d 958, 960–61 (6th Cir.1993), is in accord.

Several courts hold that *Hallahan* went too far with its theory that a debtor's act in filing a petition in bankruptcy waives its right to a jury trial. In *In re Jensen*, 946 F.2d 369 (5th Cir.1991), the debtors filed suit against several third parties for prepetition breach of fiduciary duty, fraud and tortious interference with business relations and conspiracy having to do with the development and marketing of an invention of the debtors. The third parties were not creditors and did not file a claim in the debtors' bankruptcy. The court granted the debtors a jury trial on their claims over the objection that under *Hallahan* the debtors had waived their right to a jury trial by filing a petition in bankruptcy. "As we see it, the debtor was not entitled to a jury trial in *Hallahan*, not because the debtor had filed a petition in bankruptcy, but because the plaintiff had submitted his claim against the debtor to the equitable jurisdiction of the bankruptcy court. Filing a proof of claim denied both the plaintiff and the defendant, debtor, any right to a jury trial that they otherwise might have had on that claim." 946 F.2d at 374.

In *Germain v. Connecticut National Bank*, 988 F.2d 1323 (2d Cir.1993), the court thoroughly analyzed the issue and rejected both *Hallahan* and *Jensen*. In that case Bank filed a claim in the debtor's bankruptcy; later the trustee brought suit for money damages against Bank on an array of lender liability claims, all arising out of Bank's alleged postpetition misconduct. The court found that the trustee's suit was on a legal claim and granted the trustee a trial by jury. The trustee's postpetition lender liability claims against Bank had no relation to Bank's claim against the debtor. The court saw *Hallahan*'s waiver theory as unjustified and viewed *Jensen* as going too far in stating that *any* dispute between a debtor and a creditor who has filed a claim is equitable in nature. The question should be whether the trustee's claim has become a part of the equitable process of allowing claims. In *Germain* the trustee's claims may enhance the *amount* of the debtor's estate but they have nothing to do with the *allowance* of Bank's claim; thus the trustee's claims have not become a part of the equitable claims allowance process. *Billing v. Ravin, Greenberg & Zackin, P.A.*, 22 F.3d 1242 (3d Cir.1994), presents an extremely close case on that point. In *Billing* the law firm which advised the debtor filed a claim for postpetition legal fees. The debtor filed an objection to the fees and brought a separate action for malpractice. The majority opinion held that the debtor was not entitled to a jury trial on its malpractice claim because it was so closely related to the fee objection that the malpractice claim became part of the equitable process of allowance of claims. A strong dissenting opinion characterized the malpractice action as a separate proceeding to recover damages which was not closely related to the objection to the fee application; hence, the malpractice action had not been converted to an equitable dispute as part of the process of allowance of claims.

Contrast this approach with *In re Weinstein*, 237 B.R. 567 (Bankr.E.D.N.Y.1999), where the court bifurcated a dischargeability determination under § 523(a)(2)(A) from the question of the debtor's underlying liability for fraud, distinguishing between the "foundational" determination of liability and damages for fraud and the ultimate exercise of the bankruptcy court's "equitable jurisdiction" in establishing whether the claim should be excepted from the scope of the discharge. As a result, the creditor-plaintiff was entitled to receive a jury trial for the foundational determination only. The court refused to find a waiver of jury trial by the creditor by seeking a bankruptcy court determination of nondischargeability, arguing that there was no other court from which the creditor could have sought this relief. Acknowledging that demands for jury trials were usually "asserted for strategic leverage," the court nevertheless recognized that "many creditors perceive, rightly or wrongly, that bankruptcy judges tend to be more personally and institutionally sympathetic to debtors. . . .. In this respect, the demand for a jury trial is intended to protect the creditor against the adverse impact of that perceived bias." 237 B.R. at 574.

**3.** Assume the debtor in possession in a Chapter 11 case sues Bank to recover property as a preference or a fraudulent transfer. Under *Granfinanciera* and *Langenkamp,* Bank would have been entitled to a jury trial unless it filed a proof of claim. Since Bank had a large claim against Debtor, it wished both to file a claim and to preserve its right to jury trial. When Debtor filed a request that an order be entered barring all claims filed thereafter, Bank sought a modification of the order that would allow Bank to postpone the filing of its claim until after the adversary proceedings had been concluded. The court in *In re Hooker Investments, Inc.,* 937 F.2d 833 (2d Cir.1991), denied Bank's modification and stated that it would set a dangerous precedent to have to draft a bar order to preserve rights for anybody who believed that they would be prejudiced by filing a proof of claim. In *Travellers International AG v. Robinson,* 982 F.2d 96, 97 (3d Cir.1992), a creditor submitted a proof of claim stating: "claimant does not, by filing this claim, waive its demand for a jury trial * * *." It didn't work.

**4.** In *Granfinanciera* the Court expressly declined to decide whether bankruptcy judges can conduct jury trials. If they cannot, district courts must do so in those instances in which the parties in bankruptcy are entitled to a jury trial. The first circuit court opinion decided after *Granfinanciera* held that bankruptcy judges may conduct jury trials in core proceedings under their 28 U.S.C. § 157(b) authority to hear and determine these proceedings. *In re Ben Cooper, Inc.,* 896 F.2d 1394 (2d Cir.1990). Since then six circuits have disagreed. These courts rely on the fact that there is no express statutory grant to bankruptcy judges of the power to conduct jury trials and there are constitutional problems with implying such a power. The Supreme Court granted certiorari in *Ben Cooper,* but before oral argument the Court vacated the Second Circuit decision and remanded the case to the Second Circuit to determine whether it had jurisdiction. The Second Circuit held that it had jurisdiction and reinstated its prior decision. Inexplicably, the Supreme Court subsequently denied certiorari. 500 U.S. 928 (1991).

In 1994 Congress added 28 U.S.C. § 157(e) which provides: "If the right to a jury trial applies in a proceeding that may be heard under this section by a bankruptcy judge, the bankruptcy judge may conduct the jury trial if specially designated to exercise such jurisdiction by the district court and with the express consent of all the parties." District courts may be willing to designate bankruptcy judges to conduct jury trials, but it is unlikely that the parties will always consent. If one party wishes to delay the proceeding or to have a different judge, this party can achieve these ends by withholding consent. Forum shopping is, therefore, permitted.

Of course, this statute cannot solve the constitutional problems inherent in delegating one of the essential attributes of the judicial power of the United States—the authority to conduct a jury trial—to an Article I judge. Several of the courts, enumerated above, which deny bankruptcy judges the power to conduct jury trials, harbor grave concerns about the constitutionality of allowing them to do so. But in patterning § 157(e) after 28 U.S.C. § 636(c)(1), which authorizes U.S. magistrates to conduct jury trials when the parties consent and the district court specially designates, Congress has made its strongest case for the constitutionality of the statute. The court in *In re Clay*, 35 F.3d 190, 196 (5th Cir.1994) stated: " * * * consent matters. Because one function of Article III is to protect litigants, courts have accorded significant if not dispositive weight to consent and waiver. * * * Consent is a key factor empowering magistrates to conduct jury proceedings." A number of court of appeals decisions have upheld the constitutionality of § 636(c), e.g., *Pacemaker Diagnostic Clinic of America, Inc. v. Instromedix, Inc.*, 725 F.2d 537 (9th Cir.1984) (Kennedy, J.). A question that arises with respect to § 157(e) is whether Congress can constitutionally authorize bankruptcy judges to conduct jury trials in noncore cases. The Second Circuit, which allows bankruptcy judges to conduct jury trials under *Ben Cooper*, has barred them from doing so with respect to noncore matters because the Seventh Amendment permits only appellate review of facts tried by juries; the de novo review provided in § 157(c) for noncore matters does not meet this requirement. *In re Orion Pictures Corp.*, 4 F.3d 1095, 1101 (2d Cir.1993).

## E. TRANSNATIONAL BANKRUPTCY

In theory, bankruptcy laws provide a single collective proceeding to consistently and comprehensively solve the problems arising out of a given debtor's insolvency. But in an age in which economic activity to an ever increasing extent is not limited by national borders, one inherent limitation of the United States Bankruptcy Code presses itself upon us— the Bankruptcy Code is domestic United States law. Moreover, in many respects—for example, its intricate reorganization provisions and the broad avoiding powers—it is startlingly idiosyncratic when compared to the laws of other nations. The general problem of international coordination of laws governing international commercial activity has proven especially difficult in the bankruptcy field.

Historically, in bankruptcy matters, nations have insisted on the "territorial principle"—an idea that hardly seems principled: each nation uses its insolvency laws to grab assets within that jurisdiction and administer them locally according to the procedures and priorities of that nation's laws. The territorial principle leads to multiple inconsistent proceedings, dissipation of assets, inequality of distribution, debtor abuse, and de facto discrimination against foreign debtors and creditors. It also has an obvious adverse impact on the prospect of successful reorganization.

Unfortunately, achieving consensus on a more acceptable principle allowing for unified or coordinated proceedings has proved exceedingly difficult. One possibility would be harmonization of different nations' insolvency laws. Thus in the United States we have a uniform federal bankruptcy law and one could imagine a treaty imposing a uniform international bankruptcy law among the various signatory nations. Given the complexity and idiosyncratic nature of existing national laws—embedded as they are in distinct legal and economic systems—and the disagreement over bankruptcy policy even among the economically developed nations—this approach has proved infeasible. A second best approach would be a comprehensive principle governing conflict of laws. If nations could simply agree that the insolvency law of the jurisdiction where the debtor's principal place of business was located would govern all the property and all the creditors and interest holders wherever located, then at least there might be harmony within a particular bankruptcy case. This too has proved largely beyond the reach of diplomats. The most modest approach is to allow for greater *ad hoc* coordination of proceedings that are concurrently administered in various jurisdictions. Here, finally the international community has begun to make some significant progress.

## In re Maxwell Communication Corporation
United States Court of Appeals, Second Circuit, 1996.
93 F.3d 1036.

■ CARDAMONE, Circuit Judge:

The demise of the late British media magnate Robert Maxwell and that of the corporation bearing his name, the Maxwell Communication Corporation plc, followed a similar and scandalous path, spawning civil and criminal litigation in England and around the world. This case illustrates that some positive consequences have resulted from these parallel demises. From Maxwell's mysterious death, which forced his international corporation into bankruptcy, was born a unique judicial administration of the debtor corporation by parallel and cooperative proceedings in the courts of the United States and England aimed at harmonizing the laws of both countries and also aimed at maximizing the benefits to creditors and the prospects of rehabilitation.

We have before us a small but significant piece of the swirling legal controversy that followed the collapse of Robert Maxwell's media empire. The question to be addressed is whether Maxwell Communication, as a debtor estate in Chapter 11, may recover under American law millions of dollars it transferred to three foreign banks shortly before declaring bankruptcy. It has sought such relief in adversary proceedings in the bankruptcy court under those sections of the United States Bankruptcy Code,

11 U.S.C. §§ 101–1330 (1994) (Bankruptcy Code or Code), providing for what is known as "avoidance" of pre-petition transactions. Because, in our view, the doctrine of international comity supports deferring to the courts and laws of England, we affirm the dismissal of the Chapter 11 debtor's complaints.

## BACKGROUND

* * *

### A. Events Preceding the Dual Filings

The debtor was originally incorporated in England over 60 years ago as a limited company. Robert Maxwell acquired control of this limited company 15 years ago. The following year, the company was re-registered under English law as a public limited company and, in 1987, it became Maxwell Communication Corporation plc (hereafter Maxwell or the debtor). Before filing for bankruptcy protection, Maxwell functioned as a holding company for Robert Maxwell's "public side" holdings—as distinguished from Maxwell's private holdings, which at one time included the *New York Daily News*—and controlled a variety of media-related companies. Although Maxwell was headquartered and managed in England and incurred most of its debt there, approximately 80 percent of its assets were located in the United States, most notably its subsidiaries Macmillan, Inc. and Official Airlines Guide, Inc.

Maxwell alleges that in the fall of 1991, less than 90 days before its Chapter 11 filing, it made several transfers—transfers it now seeks to avoid—to three European banks (collectively, the banks) with whom it had credit arrangements. Two of these banks are Barclays Bank plc (Barclays) and National Westminster Bank plc (National Westminster), both of which have their headquarters in London and maintain an international presence, with branches in New York and elsewhere. The other bank is Société Générale, a French Bank headquartered in Paris with offices, among other places, in London and New York.

From 1985 until 1991 Maxwell obtained credit from Barclays under the terms of a credit arrangement known in England as an "overdraft facility." This written agreement, negotiated in London, stated that any disputes arising under it would be governed by English law. Maxwell drew $30 million under the overdraft facility, none of which had been repaid on November 24, 1991, the agreed-upon maturity date. Two days later, under pressure from Barclays' banking director in London, Maxwell repaid the $30 million from the proceeds of the sale of Que Computer Books, Inc. (Que), a subsidiary of Macmillan in New York. The Que proceeds had originally been deposited in a Maxwell account at the New York branch of National Westminster and subsequently credited to Maxwell's U.S. dollar account with National Westminster in London. On November 26, 1991 repayment was effected by transferring $30 million from Maxwell's dollar account in London to Barclays' New York branch, which was then credited the following day against the balance in the appropriate Maxwell overdraft account at Barclays in London. In addition to this transfer from the Que proceeds, Maxwell alleged in its amended complaint that 11 other transfers of funds were made to Barclays during the 90 days preceding Maxwell's bankruptcy filing, amounting to a total of £2,110,970 (net of various payments by Barclays to or on behalf of Maxwell during the same period). No connection between these other transfers and the United States was alleged in the complaint.

National Westminster's relationship with the debtor began in the 1930s and continued through the bankruptcy filing. As of late 1991 Maxwell maintained several accounts with National Westminster, with overdraft facilities to help it meet its cash needs. These arrangements were similar to those it had with Barclays in that they were negotiated in England and provided for the governance of English law. In October 1991 Maxwell received $145 million from the sale of Macmillan Directories, Inc. (another Macmillan subsidiary in the United States) and used the proceeds—which had been paid into a Maxwell account at Citibank in New York and thereafter credited to an account at Citibank in London—to purchase British pounds. Maxwell then paid £15 million from these proceeds to an account it maintained at National Westminster's London branch. Maxwell then applied the £15 million to satisfy an overdraft balance with National Westminster.

In November 1991 Maxwell converted a portion of the $157.5 million of Que proceeds (originally deposited in National Westminster's New York branch but then transferred to its London branch) into £27.5 million. It used this sum to cover its overdraft balances in National Westminster's London branch. The purchase of pounds sterling and subsequent credits to the National Westminster overdraft accounts occurred in London. Maxwell also alleges it made eight other transfers to National Westminster from accounts at Midland Bank in London shortly before Maxwell's bankruptcy filing, payments which amounted to £29,046,738 (net of payments by National Westminster to Maxwell during the same period).

Société Générale also extended credit to Maxwell under an agreement negotiated and administered in England. On October 7, 1991, in satisfaction of principal and interest on a $10 million loan extended under that credit arrangement, Maxwell made a payment of roughly £5.765 million to Société Générale. The funds were transferred from an account Maxwell maintained at Marine Midland Bank in London to Société Générale's London branch. Although the debtor did not allege that the transfer was connected to the United States, the district court assumed for purposes of its decision that the funds came from the sale of Macmillan Directories because that sale also occurred on October 7, 1991.

### B. The Dual Insolvency Proceedings

On December 16, 1991 Maxwell filed a petition for reorganization under Chapter 11 of the United States Bankruptcy Code in the Bankruptcy Court for the Southern District of New York. The next day, it petitioned the High Court of Justice in London for an administration order. Administration, introduced by the Insolvency Act 1986, is the closest equivalent in British law to Chapter 11 relief. Acting under the terms of the Insolvency Act, Justice HOFFMAN, then of the High Court (now a member of the House of Lords), appointed members of the London office of the accounting firm of Price Waterhouse as administrators to manage the affairs and property of the corporation.

Simultaneous proceedings in different countries, especially in multi-party cases like bankruptcies, can naturally lead to inconsistencies and conflicts. To minimize such problems, Judge Brozman appointed Richard A. Gitlin, Esq. as examiner, pursuant to 11 U.S.C. § 1104(c), in the Chapter 11 proceedings. The order of appointment required the examiner, inter alia, to investigate the debtor's financial condition, to function as a mediator among the various parties, and to "act to harmonize, for the benefit of all of [Maxwell's] creditors and stockholders and other parties in interest, [Maxwell's] United States chapter 11 case and [Maxwell's] United Kingdom administration case so as to maximize [the] prospects for rehabilitation and reorganization."

Judge Brozman and Justice HOFFMAN subsequently authorized the examiner and the administrators to coordinate their efforts pursuant to a so-called Protocol, an agreement between the examiner and the administrators. In approving the Protocol, Judge Brozman recognized the English administrators as the corporate governance of the debtor-in-possession. As the bankruptcy judge later explained, this recognition was motivated not only by the need for coordination but also because Maxwell was "incorporated in England and run... by [Maxwell] executives out of Maxwell House in London subject to the direction of an English board of directors." [Maxwell Communication Corp. v. Barclays Bank plc, 170 B.R. 800, 817 (Bankr.S.D.N.Y.1994) (Maxwell I)] * * * Justice HOFFMAN reciprocated, granting the examiner leave to appear before the High Court in England.

These joint efforts resulted in what has been described as a "remarkable sequence of events leading to perhaps the first world-wide plan of orderly liquidation ever achieved." Jay Lawrence Westbrook, The Lessons of Maxwell Communication, 64 Fordham L.Rev. 2531, 2535 (1996). The administrators, the examiner, and other interested parties worked together to produce a common system for reorganizing Maxwell by disposing of assets as going concerns and distributing the proceeds to creditors. The mechanism for accomplishing this is embodied in a plan of reorganization and a scheme of arrangement, which are interdependent documents and were filed by the administrators in the United States and English courts respectively.

The reorganization plan incorporates the scheme and makes it binding on Maxwell and its creditors. The plan and scheme thus constitute a single and integrated system for realizing the value of Maxwell's assets and paying its creditors. As was set forth in a letter from the administrators to Maxwell's creditors, the proposal was to pay in full all holders of secured claims and of claims enjoying preferential status under United States or English law. The plan and scheme treat all of Maxwell's assets as a single pool and leave them under Maxwell's control for distribution to claimants. They allow any creditor to submit a claim in either jurisdiction. And, in addition to overcoming many of the substantive differences in the insolvency laws of the two jurisdictions, the plan and scheme resolve many procedural differences, such as the time limits for submitting claims.

Following the requisite creditor voting in the United States and England, the plan was approved in the United States and the scheme was approved in England. Judge Brozman entered an order confirming the plan—and, by implication, the scheme incorporated therein—on July 14, 1993. Justice HOFFMAN thereafter entered an order sanctioning the scheme under § 425 of the Companies Act 1985 on July 21, 1993. Barclays, National Westminster, and Société Générale each filed a notice of claim with the administrators, seeking pro rata distributions on various unsecured claims against Maxwell.

Despite the unusual degree of cooperation and reconciliation of the laws of the two forums, the plan and scheme predictably did not resolve all the problems that might arise from the concurrent proceedings. For example, these documents did not specify which substantive law would govern the resolution of disputed claims by creditors. More importantly, they did not address the instant dispute regarding the debtor's ability to set aside pre-petition transfers to certain creditors.

### C. British Denial of Anti–Suit Injunction

In July 1992 Barclays faced the possibility that the administrators would institute litigation in the bankruptcy court to recover the $30 million it had received from Maxwell on November 26, 1991. Barclays therefore obtained an ex parte order in the High Court (not from Justice HOFFMAN) barring the commencement of such an action. In seeking to prevent litigation in the bankruptcy court, Barclays was apparently motivated by a difference in the American and British "avoidance" rules. Rules governing avoidance generally allow the estate to recover certain pre-petition transfers of property to creditors occurring within a defined period of time. Such rules are sometimes referred to as the law of preferences because such transfers, left unchecked, may put transferees in a better position than other creditors if the debtor becomes insolvent.

Thus, under § 547(b), a trustee may avoid certain transfers to outside creditors made within 90 days before the filing of the petition. The corresponding provision in English law is § 239 of the Insolvency Act 1986. That section is in many respects similar to the American law, but the British law imposes an additional condition—it limits avoidance to those situations where placing the transferee in a better position was something the debtor intended. See Insolvency Act 1986 § 239(5). This seemingly innocuous subjective intent requirement in English law apparently would be a significant or insurmountable obstacle for the administrators were they to litigate the preferences question in London under English law. For obvious reasons, they opposed the anti-suit injunction sought by Barclays, that is, they wanted this issue litigated in the Southern District bankruptcy court.

Following a hearing, Justice HOFFMAN vacated the ex parte order Barclays had obtained. The British judge declined to interfere with the American court's determination of the reach of our avoidance law. He cited the British presumption that in such a situation the foreign judge is normally in the best position to decide whether proceedings are to go forward in the foreign court, and the rule that anti-suit injunctions will issue only where an assertion of jurisdiction in the foreign court would be "unconscionable."

In so doing, Justice HOFFMAN noted the cooperative course of the parallel insolvency proceedings. He distinguished recent cases involving the extraterritorial application of American antitrust law, reasoning that injunctive relief is available only if it appears that a foreign court is likely to assert jurisdiction in a manner "contrary to accepted principles of international law." The High Court's decision did not pass judgment on the merits of whether the application of American law would violate such norms. It did assume, however, that the bankruptcy court would dismiss the anticipated suit if it found that there was an insufficient connection with the United States. This ruling was affirmed by the Court of Appeal, and leave for further review by the House of Lords was denied.

### D. The Adversary Complaints and the Bankruptcy and District Court Decisions

Freed from the constraints of an anti-suit injunction, the administrators commenced adversary proceedings in the bankruptcy court against Barclays, National Westminster, and Société Générale. The complaints sought the recovery of the above-described transfers to the banks on the theory that they were avoidable preferences under § 547(b) and therefore recoverable under § 550(a)(1). In addition, each complaint sought the disallowance under § 502(d) of any claims made by the defendant, unless the defendant first returns to the debtor the transferred funds, with interest. This subject is discussed and resolved in Part IV, *infra*. The examiner joined the administrators in instituting these adversary proceedings against National Westminster and intervened in the proceeding against Barclays; he is not a party in Maxwell's suit against Société Générale.

Defendants filed motions for dismissal under Fed.R.Civ.P. 12(b)(6) (made applicable in adversary bankruptcy proceedings by Bankr.R. 7012(b)) asserting, inter alia, that applying § 547 of the Bankruptcy Code to these transactions would violate the "presumption against extraterritoriality" and that dismissal was also warranted on grounds of international comity. The bankruptcy court granted the motions, holding that the transfers were extraterritorial and that the Bankruptcy Code does not apply to these transfers, whose "center of gravity" lies outside the United States and, in the alternative, that international comity precluded the application of the Code in this instance.

Treating comity as a "canon of statutory construction," the bankruptcy court emphasized choice-of-law principles and asked "which jurisdiction's laws and policies are implicated to the greatest extent." The answer, the court found, was England. It also noted Maxwell's insolvency did not jeopardize United States interests because its holdings were sold as going businesses, because most of its creditors were not residents of the United States, and because the two countries' preference laws in any event serve similar ends, and that England had a greater interest in applying its own laws.

The district court affirmed on both the extraterritoriality and comity grounds. On the latter question, it held that the "bankruptcy court did not abuse its discretion in finding that traditional choice of law principles "point decidedly towards the application of U.K. law.' " Maxwell II, 186 B.R. at 822. The district court's analysis of the relative interests was substantially similar to that of the bankruptcy court, but it also underscored the cooperation between the courts of the two countries and found that deference would comport with the previous efforts by both courts to harmonize the dual proceedings. Judge Scheindlin believed this to be "the unique aspect and the most important feature of this case." Id., at 813.

Maxwell and the examiner appealed. We consolidated the three cases on January 15, 1996 and now address the merits.

DISCUSSION

* * *

### III. Propriety of Dismissal by the Bankruptcy Court

#### A. Standard of Review

Having established that the doctrine of comity applies, we now explain why we think dismissal was warranted, that is to say, why the statute was properly construed not to reach the pre-petition fund transfers to the defendant banks. * * *

* * *

#### B. Primacy of English Law

England has a much closer connection to these disputes than does the United States. The debtor and most of its creditors—not only the beneficiaries of the pre-petition transfers—are British. Maxwell was incorporated under the laws of England, largely controlled by British nationals, governed by a British board of directors, and managed in London by British executives. These connecting factors indicated what the bankruptcy judge called the "Englishness" of the debtor, which was one reason for recognizing the administrators—who are officers of the High Court—as Maxwell's corporate governance. These same factors, particularly the fact that most of Maxwell's debt was incurred in England, show that England has the strongest connection to the present litigation.

Although an avoidance action concededly affects creditors other than the transferee, because scrutiny of the transfer is at the heart of such a suit it is assuredly most relevant that the transfers in this case related primarily to England. The $30 million received by Barclays came from an account at National Westminster in London and, while it was routed through Barclays' New York branch like all payments received in U.S. dollars, it was immediately credited to an overdraft account maintained in England. Plaintiffs claim no particular United States connection to the other alleged transfers to Barclays, all of which were denominated in the amended complaint in pounds sterling. Similarly, the transfers to National Westminster and Société Générale were made to and from accounts maintained in Great Britain.

Further, the overdraft facilities and other credit transactions between the transferee banks and the debtor resulted from negotiations that took place in England and were administered primarily there. English law applied to the resolution of disputes arising under such agreements. We recognize that some of the money transferred to the banks came from the proceeds of the sale of Maxwell subsidiaries in the United States, which is a subject we discuss in a moment. In almost all other respects, however, the credit transactions were centered in London and the fund transfers occurred there.

### C. Relative Interests of Forum and Foreign States

Given the considerably lesser American connection to the dispute, the bankruptcy court believed its forum's interests were "not very compelling." Maxwell I, 170 B.R. at 814. Virtually the only factor linking the transfers to the United States—that the sale of certain Maxwell subsidiaries in the United States provided the source of some of the funds—is not particularly weighty because those companies were sold as going concerns. Hence, the potential effect that such sales might have had on local economies is not here implicated.

The examiner warns that dire consequences would result from a failure to enforce the Code's avoidance provision. The first one he mentions is that such a course ignores § 103(a) of the Code. This contention is one we have already addressed and rejected. The examiner next urges that the purposes underlying § 547 and § 502(d) would be thwarted unless both of these provisions were applied in all Chapter 11 proceedings. Although the non-application of these or other Bankruptcy Code provisions certainly might detract from the Code's policies in other cases, here the negative effects are insubstantial. The principal policies underlying the Code's avoidance provisions are equal distribution to creditors and preserving the value of the estate through the discouragement of aggressive pre-petition tactics causing dismemberment of the debtor. Wolas, 502 U.S. at 161. These policies are effectuated, although in a somewhat different way, by the provisions' British counterpart.

In the present case, in which there is a parallel insolvency proceeding taking place in another country, failure to apply § 547 and § 502(d) does not free creditors from the constraints of avoidance law, nor does it severely undercut the policy of equal distribution. All avoidance laws are necessarily limited in scope because time limits and other conditions are imposed on the voidability of transactions. Although a different result might be warranted were there no parallel proceeding in England—and, hence, no alternative mechanism for voiding preferences—we cannot say the United States has a significant interest in applying its avoidance law. Moreover, as noted, international comity is a policy that Congress expressly made part of the Bankruptcy Code, and a decision consistent with comity therefore furthers the Code's policy.

Because of the strong British connection to the present dispute, it follows that England has a stronger interest than the United States in applying its own avoidance law to these actions. Its law implicates that country's interest in promoting what Parliament apparently viewed as the appropriate compromise between equality of distribution and other important commercial interests, for instance, ensuring potentially insolvent debtors' ability to secure essential ongoing financing. In addition, although complexity in the conduct of transnational insolvencies makes choice-of-law prognostication imprecise, we agree with the lower courts that English law could have been expected to apply. [S]ee also Canada S. Ry. v. Gebhard, 109 U.S. 527, 537–38 (1883) (domestic creditors of foreign bankrupts "presumed to have contracted with a view to. . . laws of th[e] [foreign] government").

The administrators further declare that the English court's decision vacating the ex parte anti-avoidance suit order established that the application of our preference law by the Southern District courts would not violate the law of nations, and that American courts should not use comity as a reason to decline to assert jurisdiction under section § 547. The decision in the English court implied nothing of the kind. Instead, that court ruled that Barclays could not obtain an injunction because an expression of the principle of comity that relied on the good sense of the bankruptcy court outweighed the risk that it would assume jurisdiction in violation of international law.

Rather than take a confrontational posture by enjoining this litigation and prejudice the cooperation which has thus far prevailed between the Chapter 11 and the English administration, the High Court left the merits of the question for the American courts to decide. Thus, the English court's decision affords no basis for concluding that England's interests are insubstantial.

### D. Cooperation and Harmonization: Systemic Interest

In addition to the relative strength of the respective jurisdictional interests of England and the United States, there is a compelling systemic interest pointing in this instance against the application of the Bankruptcy Code. These parallel proceedings in the English and American courts have resulted in a high level of international cooperation and a significant degree of harmonization of the laws of the two countries. The affected parties agreed to the plan and scheme despite differences in the two nations' bankruptcy laws. The distribution mechanism established by them— beyond addressing some of the most obvious substantive and procedural incongruities—allowed Maxwell's assets to be pooled together and sold as going concerns, maximizing the return to creditors. And, by not requiring a creditor to file its claim in both forums, the arrangement eliminated many of the inefficiencies usually attendant in multi-jurisdiction proceedings.

Taken together, these accomplishments—which, we think, are attributable in large measure to the cooperation between the two courts overseeing the dual proceedings—are well worth preserving and advancing. This collaborative effort exemplifies the "spirit of cooperation" with which tribunals, guided by comity, should approach cases touching the laws and interests of more than one country. Where a dispute involving conflicting avoidance laws arises in the context of parallel bankruptcy proceedings that have already achieved substantial reconciliation between the two sets of laws, comity argues decidedly against the risk of derailing that cooperation by the selfish application of our law to circumstances touching more directly upon the interests of another forum.

It should be remembered that the interest of the system as a whole—that of promoting "a friendly intercourse between the sovereignties," *Hilton*, 159 U.S. at 165—also furthers American self-interest, especially where the workings of international trade and commerce are concerned. * * *

We recognize that forbearance and goodwill in the conduct of international bankruptcies is an ideal not easily achieved in the near-term. Many commentators advocate centralized administration of each insolvency under one country's laws, which could require a multi-lateral treaty or, even, a greater degree of harmonization of the commercial laws throughout the world. See, e.g., Douglass G. Boshkoff, Some Gloomy Thoughts Concerning Cross–Border Insolvencies, 72 Wash.U.L.Q. 931, 931–36 (1994). In the meanwhile, bankruptcy courts may best be able to effectuate the purposes of the bankruptcy law by cooperating with foreign courts on a case-by-case basis. Congress contemplated this approach when it provided for "ancillary" proceedings under § 304. Although comity analysis admittedly does not yield the commercial predictability that might eventually be achieved through uniform rules, it permits the courts to reach workable solutions and to overcome some of the problems of a disordered international system. Given that the scheme and plan in this case did not clearly address the choice-of-law and choice-of-forum questions that have generated this litigation, resort to comity and choice-of-law principles should naturally have been foreseen. Consequently, the interests of the affected forums and the mutual interest of all nations in smoothly functioning international law counsel against the application of United States law in the present case.

### IV. Denial of Distributions Under § 502

The final issue to be resolved is the plaintiffs' contention that even if the pre-petition transfers to the banks may not be recovered under § 547 for comity reasons or otherwise, the administrators are nevertheless entitled under § 502(d) to deny distributions to the banks as unsecured creditors. Section 502(d) provides in relevant part that "the court shall disallow any claim of any entity. . . that is a transferee of a transfer avoidable under section. . . 547 of this title."

The district court turned this challenge aside on two separate grounds. It held that § 502 is inapplicable because § 547 does not govern the avoidance action by the administrators and the transfers are therefore not "avoidable" under § 547. Further, it stated that the banks have not filed "claims" under § 502(d) because they have never submitted themselves to the bankruptcy court's jurisdiction. Defendants declare that this argument was waived because it was not submitted to the bankruptcy court. We nonetheless exercise our appellate discretion to entertain the issue because it is one of law, it was clearly presented in the adversary complaints, it was argued before and decided by the district court, and the transcript of hearing on the Rule 12(b)(6) motions indicates the bankruptcy court was quite aware of the relevant statute.

We hold that § 502(d) does not apply, but for reasons slightly different than those expressed by the district court. The plaintiffs strongly urge that the district court conflated § 547 and § 502(d) by reading the words "transfer avoidable" in the latter to mean any transfer that actually could be recovered by the estate under the former. They rely on cases holding that disallowance is required under § 502(d) even where a transfer may not affirmatively be recovered because the limitations period for such recovery has expired. * * *

The rule that § 502(d) disallowance is not precluded by the expiration of the limitations period governing recovery under § 547, however sound it may be, does not control in this case. Where a transfer could be avoided under § 547 but for the running of the statute of limitations, disallowance may be warranted because the substantive provisions of § 547, as opposed to the time-limit set forth in § 546(a), still apply to the transfer at issue. See *McLean*, 184 B.R. at 15 (§ 502(d) refers to § 547, not § 546). But in the present case, the doctrine of comity leads to the conclusion that § 547 does not apply to the pre-petition transfers at all. Consequently, the transfers cannot in any way be included among the "transfers avoidable" listed in § 502(d). In addition, because § 502(d) and § 547 apply to the same types of transfers and serve similar purposes, the former is inapplicable to the present case for the reasons discussed in Part III of this opinion.

With respect to the district court's alternative ground for denying relief under § 502(d), we must agree with the administrators that the banks' decision to lodge notices of claim in England, rather than filing proofs of claim with the bankruptcy court, cannot be construed to mean that they have not submitted "claims" for purposes of the Bankruptcy Code. To be eligible for distributions under the plan, the banks had to submit "claims," which must be "allowed." See § 726(a).

* * * [B]y requiring the administrators to pass along to the bankruptcy court notices of claim filed in England, the plan and scheme comply with

the Code's requirement that a proof of claim be filed with the bankruptcy court. Such claims are "allowed" under the Code, see § 502(a), if they are accepted without objection by the administrators or liability is established by adjudication in the appropriate court, which may be the bankruptcy court or the English court depending upon the circumstances. We are therefore unable to agree with the district court's conclusion that § 502(d) is inapplicable because the banks have not submitted "claims."

## CONCLUSION

In sum, we hold that the binding effect of the confirmation order does not preclude the banks from challenging the applicability of the Bankruptcy Code's avoidance rules to these actions brought by the administrators. Further, in this unique case involving cooperative parallel bankruptcy proceedings seeking to harmonize two nations' insolvency laws for the common benefit of creditors, the doctrine of international comity precludes application of the American avoidance law to transfers in which England's interest has primacy. We decline to decide whether, setting aside considerations of comity, the "presumption against extraterritoriality" would compel a conclusion that the Bankruptcy Code does not reach the pre-petition transfers at issue. Thus, we express no view regarding the banks' contention that the Bankruptcy Code never applies to non-domestic conduct or conditions. Finally, we reject plaintiffs' argument that the defendant banks' claims against the estate must be disallowed under § 502(d) notwithstanding the non-applicability of § 547.

Accordingly, for the reasons stated, the order appealed from is affirmed.

## NOTES

**1.** The history and significance of the *Maxwell Communications* case is discussed in Jay L. Westbrook, *The Lessons of Maxwell Communications*, 64 Fordham L.Rev. 2531 (1996). *In re Treco*, 240 F.3d 148 (2d Cir.2001), suggests some of the limits to comity and international cooperation. In *Treco*, the Bank of New York asserted that certain funds sought by the Bahamian liquidators of the Meridien International Bank Ltd. (MIBL) were subject to set-off under United States law and accordingly refused to turnover the funds. The Second Circuit refused to require turnover because Bahamian insolvency law might subordinate the Bank of New York's secured claim to administrative expenses that threatened to consume the MIBL estate. It wrote:

> The principle of comity has never meant categorical deference to foreign proceedings. It is implicit in the concept that deference should be withheld where appropriate to avoid the violation of the laws, public policies or rights of citizens of the United States.

240 F.3d at 157.

**2.** The seeds for greater international cooperation in insolvency matters were first planted in the Bankruptcy Reform Act of 1978. Section 304 of that Act, now repealed, represented a tentative unilateral attempt by the Congress to open up United States bankruptcy courts to assist in coordinating and facilitating foreign proceedings involving American assets or parties. Under § 304, a "foreign representative" (an authorized trustee or other representative of a bankruptcy estate filed in a foreign country) could invoke the jurisdiction of a United States bankruptcy court to institute "ancillary" proceedings. Section 304 supplemented § 109, the general debtor eligibility provision. Thus, an entity that could not be a debtor under § 109 might nevertheless initiate proceedings in a foreign country and the representative of that foreign estate might initiate an ancillary bankruptcy case in the United States under § 304. *In re Brierley*, 145 B.R. 151 (Bankr.S.D.N.Y.1992). Venue for ancillary cases is prescribed by 28 U.S.C. § 1410, which directs filing to the district in the United States where the debtor maintains its principal place of business or principal assets. If the debtor has no such domestic location or assets, then the district in which the debtor is defending lawsuits is proper. Otherwise, the case may be filed anywhere consistent with the interests of justice. The bankruptcy court in ancillary proceedings has discretion to issue stays, enforce judgments and order turnover of property to the foreign representative and issue other relief in its discretion.

While § 304 amounted to an open invitation to other nations to reciprocate by recognizing proceedings ancillary to United States bankruptcy cases in their courts, other major commercial nations did not rush to accept the invitation. Until the early 1990s there was little movement from other countries to grant similar recognition to United States bankruptcy proceedings. In the 1990s some nations, see *Barclays Bank PLC v. Homan*, BCLC 680 (1993) (UK law), and the Australia Corporations Law §§ 580–581 (1997), made significant steps towards greater formal recognition of foreign bankruptcy cases in their domestic insolvency law. The European Union, after more than 20 years of failed diplomatic negotiations, has made modest progress towards greater coordination of proceedings within the EU with the much anticipated ratification of the European Union Convention on Insolvency Proceedings (Nov. 23, 1995). Unfortunately, the Convention allows states to continue to insist on enforcing local laws that give different treatment to creditors or other parties than they would be entitled to in the foreign proceeding recognized under the Convention. The scope and limitations of the Convention are discussed in Manfred Balz, *The European Convention on Insolvency Proceedings*, 70 Am.Bankr.L.J. 485 (1996). The full text of the Convention is set out in Nick Segal, *The Choice of Law Provisions in the European Union Convention on Insolvency Proceedings*, 23 Brook.J.Int'l L. 57 (1997). The American Law Institute has initiated a similar project to bring about greater coordination among the insolvency laws of Canada, Mexico and the United States. *See* Jay L. Westbrook, *Creating International Insolvency Law*, 70 Am.Bankr.L.J. 563 (1996).

**3.** The broadest international coordination effort is embodied in the United Nations Commission on International Trade Law (UNCITRAL) Model Law on Cross-Border Insolvency, adopted by the Commission in May 1997. The Model Law's key provisions grant recognition and standing to foreign representatives of insolvency estates (including, importantly from the American perspective, debtors in possession) in the adopting nation's own courts, and incorporate § 508(a)'s hotch-pot rule discussed in Note 4 below. Under the Model Law, recognition of the foreign representative of a foreign "main proceeding" results in a stay more or less comparable to the automatic stay available under § 362. The Model Law also provides for certain limited anti-discrimination and notice rules to protect foreign creditors.

The United States enacted the UNCITRAL Model Law in the form of new Chapter 15 in the 2005 Act. Both ancillary proceedings and transnational plenary proceedings are now governed by the Chapter 15/UNCITRAL procedure. Fundamentally, Chapter 15 seeks to ensure that foreign representatives of insolvent estates and foreign insolvency proceedings receive recognition in United States Courts, §§ 1509-1524 and that formal and informal mechanisms of cooperation and comity (like the *Maxwell Communications* protocol) receive official sanction and encouragement. §§ 1525-1532. The seeds of a broader conflict of laws principle, that all courts defer to the "main proceeding" taking place in "the center of the debtor's main interests," § 1502(4), are planted, but not implemented in the new Chapter 15, which presumes that existing United States bankruptcy law, subject to already recognized principles of conflicts of laws and comity, will continue to govern all United States bankruptcy proceedings. Moreover, even the limited provisions of new Chapter 15 remain subject to an overall public policy exception, § 1506, and the mandate for international cooperation is conditioned on the United States courts finding that "the interests of creditors in the United States are sufficiently protected." § 1521(b).

**4.** Section 304 deals with the situation in which the principal bankruptcy proceeding is foreign and the United States bankruptcy case ancillary thereto.

What if the principal case is in the United States, but there are foreign assets or parties and a concurrently pending foreign insolvency proceeding? The Bankruptcy Code seems to assert extraterritorial reach over all the debtor's "property wherever located and by whomever held. . ." § 541(a). One issue in *Maxwell Communications* not reached by the Second Circuit was the extraterritorial reach of § 547 in connection with the preferential transfers between foreign parties that was deemed to have occurred in London. In a controversial holding, the bankruptcy court and district court found that § 547 did not reach these transfers. *Maxwell Communication Corp. plc v. Societe Generale plc*, 186 B.R. 807 (S.D.N.Y.1995). Even assuming the extraterritorial reach of the Code, however, as a practical matter, some creditors may be able to achieve more favorable treatment in a foreign proceeding where the local court asserts control over property within the foreign jurisdiction. Section 508(a), the "hotch-pot rule," provides some relief in this situation by reducing a creditor's distributions under the Bankruptcy Code by the amount the creditor receives in any foreign proceeding. The hotch-pot rule seeks to put all claimants in the United States bankruptcy case on as equal a footing as possible in light of the reality that some creditors may be able to gain special advantages in foreign bankruptcy proceedings.

**5.** A person who may be a debtor under § 109 and is also the subject of a plenary foreign insolvency proceeding may choose to initiate a regular bankruptcy case under Chapter 7 or Chapter 11 rather than an ancillary proceeding. This is what happened in *Maxwell Communications*. Unfortunately, neither the Bankruptcy Code nor foreign bankruptcy statutes give any specific guidance with respect to coordination and management of cross-border insolvency cases involving plenary proceedings in both the United States and a foreign country. One prominent academic argues that game-theory suggests it is implausible to expect any greater degree of harmony than an ad hoc cooperative territoriality worked out on a case-by-case basis. Frederick Tung, *Skepticism about Universalism: International Bankruptcy and International Relations*, U.C. Berkeley Law and Economics Working Paper 2001–7 (2001). This "cooperative territoriality" solution may be the only realistic way of dealing with transnational bankruptcy. *See* Samuel L. Bufford, et al., *Federal Judicial Center, International Insolvency* (2001); Lynn M. LoPucki, *Cooperation in International Bankruptcy: A Post–Universalist Approach,* 84 Cornell L. Rev. 696 (1999).

As we begin the 21st century, the nations of the world apparently are not ready to accept the principle that one uniform law should govern the rights and liabilities of parties to an insolvent estate. In contrast, the 200 year-old American Constitution's Art. I, § 8 provision that Congress may establish "uniform laws on the subject of Bankruptcies throughout the United States" seems remarkably farsighted and non-parochial.

# INDEX